ADMINISTRATIVE LAW

ASPEN CASEBOOK SERIES

ADMINISTRATIVE LAW

A LIFECYCLE APPROACH

Jamelle C. Sharpe

Professor of Law
University of Illinois College of Law

Wolters Kluwer

Published by Wolters Kluwer in New York.

Wolters Kluwer Legal & Regulatory U.S. serves customers worldwide with CCH, Aspen Publishers, and Kluwer Law International products. (www.WKLegaledu.com)

To contact Customer Service, e-mail customer.service@wolterskluwer.com, call 1-800-234-1660, fax 1-800-901-9075, or mail correspondence to:

Wolters Kluwer
Attn: Order Department
PO Box 990
Frederick, MD 21705

Printed in the United States of America.

1 2 3 4 5 6 7 8 9 0

ISBN 978-1-4548-9111-6

Library of Congress Cataloging-in-Publication Data

Names: Sharpe, Jamelle C., author.
Title: Administrative law : a lifecycle approach / Jamelle C. Sharpe,
    Professor of Law, University of Illinois College of Law.
Description: New York : Wolters Kluwer, [2021] | Series: Aspen casebook
    series | Includes bibliographical references and index. | Summary:
    "Casebook for courses on Administrative Law"-- Provided by publisher.
Identifiers: LCCN 2020044649 | ISBN 9781454891116 (hardcover) | ISBN
    9781543823363 (ebook)
Subjects: LCSH: Administrative law--United States. | LCGFT: Casebooks (Law)
Classification: LCC KF5402 .S53 2021 | DDC 342.73/06--dc23
LC record available at https://lccn.loc.gov/2020044649

About Wolters Kluwer Legal & Regulatory U.S.

Wolters Kluwer Legal & Regulatory U.S. delivers expert content and solutions in the areas of law, corporate compliance, health compliance, reimbursement, and legal education. Its practical solutions help customers successfully navigate the demands of a changing environment to drive their daily activities, enhance decision quality and inspire confident outcomes.

Serving customers worldwide, its legal and regulatory portfolio includes products under the Aspen Publishers, CCH Incorporated, Kluwer Law International, ftwilliam.com and MediRegs names. They are regarded as exceptional and trusted resources for general legal and practice-specific knowledge, compliance and risk management, dynamic workflow solutions, and expert commentary.

For Nicola, Nate, Bella, Alex, and Selena

SUMMARY OF CONTENTS

CONTENTS

PREFACE

Administrative Law is a fascinating course both to teach and to learn. In surveying the modern regulatory landscape, one finds that administrative decision-making touches almost every conceivable aspect of modern social and economic life in the United States. Administrative agencies address issues of immediate and profound importance to everyday life, such as whether an applicant for public assistance is eligible to receive it, whether a small business will receive a federally subsidized loan, or whether a healthcare professional whose practice receives federal funds can discuss the full range of care options with her patients. In this respect, agencies often serve as the face of the federal government when interacting with the People. They also regulate subjects both technical and esoteric, such as the level of air pollutants that may be emitted from smelters and power plants or the safest methods for disposal of waste generated by nuclear reactors. In this regard, agencies routinely operate at the frontiers of epistemic uncertainty, far removed from the People's day-to-day concerns.

Such regulatory diversity provides innumerable opportunities for legal, political, social, and economic inquiry, certainly a boon to the intellectually curious. Unfortunately, this diversity also poses several significant and enduring challenges for both students and teachers of administrative law. First and foremost is that the sheer vastness of the subject matter is an impediment to its coherent organization and accessibility. The course focuses on the procedural constraints under which Executive Branch agencies exercise the limited executive, legislative, and judicial powers granted to them by Congress. While judicial opinions are the primary vehicle through which most casebooks (including this one) guide students through the course, a proper survey requires far more than reading cases and critiquing traditional modes of legal reasoning. Rather, the course necessitates exploration of public law and policy more generally. Students must engage with a host of tangentially related topics, including structural constitutionalism, political and economic theory, legislative and civil litigation processes, and judicial jurisdiction, just to name a few. Accordingly, the legal doctrines constituting the administrative law course can be conceptually complex.

In addition to this conceptual complexity, regulatory decision-making often involves legal and factual complexities. Administrative law is *transsubstantive* — it applies to all federal agency decision-making without regard to the social or economic activities on which particular agencies happen to focus. It consequently presents a smorgasbord of statutory and regulatory schemes with which students must familiarize themselves: environmental, employment, occupational safety, transportation, agricultural, financial, natural resources, along with a host of others. Additionally, these regulatory realms are typically ruled by subject matter experts both within the government and outside of it. Their terminology, methods of regulation, and modes of interaction can be unfamiliar and seemingly impenetrable, even when translated for a general audience by skilled judges.

This casebook addresses these challenges in a few ways. Its materials are arranged around three core stages of the federal administrative decision-making lifecycle: (1) the laws governing agency creation and assignment of powers; (2) the laws governing agency decision-making, with particular emphasis on policymaking and adjudication; and (3) those governing supervision of agency decision-making. This organizational approach distinguishes the book from others that sort their materials based on abstract legal themes. To be sure, such groupings can help students see connections between related doctrinal subjects. Unfortunately, it can also promote an understanding of the administrative decision-making process that divorces legal issues from important practical considerations, such as the chronological order and procedural contexts in which they typically arise. Perhaps more importantly, such theme-based compilations ask students to learn and apply legal concepts—particularly standards of judicial review—before they can properly learn about the activities to which those legal concepts apply. Some of this is certainly unavoidable; the case method necessarily requires students to know *something* about how courts review administrative conduct even when asked to focus on agencies' underlying activities. Nevertheless, it is hard for a student to fully understand when or why a particular judicial review standard applies if he or she knows little about the administrative decision-making process that is its object.

This "order of battle" problem is addressed by organizing the book's materials around the administrative decision-making lifecycle. Doing so familiarizes students with agencies' core functions before asking them to understand how courts and others (Congress, the President, the public, and civil servants) supervise the performance of those functions. Developing this sense of familiarity and concreteness helps students with both the positive aspect of learning (understanding "what is happening here"), and the normative aspect of learning (identifying the other paths decision-makers could or should have taken). For similar reasons, the book's first chapter provides students with foundational knowledge of the administrative state's historical development, its current organizational structure, and the separation-of-powers principles that govern its place in the constituitonal scheme. Each of these subjects—history, current structure, separation-of-powers—resurfaces implicitly and explicitly throughout the book, and so Chapter 1 acquaints students with them before delving into any doctrinal substance. Relatedly, opportunities for students to familiarize themselves with agency work product are sprinkled throughout. Considering that nonjudicial production of law and policy is a hallmark of administrative decision-making, a grounding in them helps students understand what generalist judges grapple with when reviewing agency actions. While this is very much a book about administrative *law*—it does not focus on related topics like regulatory design and analysis—students should have some direct exposure to administrative publications rather than relying solely on how judges describe them in legal opinions. This allows students to see, first-hand, the materials lawyers and judges encounter when applying salient legal concepts and doctrines. By highlighting critical steps in the administrative decision-making processes, and by giving students guided opportunities to place themselves in the position of administrative lawyers, this casebook advances students' understanding of both law and practice. Additionally, my hope is that this approach facilitates more engaged discussion of the theoretical puzzles created by the administrative state.

The book addresses complexity concerns in several other ways. First and foremost, discussion of almost every topic proceeds in the following order: explanation, example, review, and application. The explanations discuss relevant legal principles, historical developments, and questions to guide students' reading. Additionally, they often introduce students to "prototypical" fact patterns within given topics. Developing a sense of typicality is important for students; without it, they may have a difficult time appreciating the unusual features of the cases they read. Providing more guidance in this regard helps them to see what distinguishes hard cases from easy ones.

With respect to case selection, the governing criteria were precedential importance and ease of analytical access. I have excerpted or described the cases most experienced administrative law teachers would expect to find in a casebook. After all, such cases provide an effective and familiar vehicle for introducing students to critical turning points in administrative law development. Apart from inclusion of seminal opinions where factual or doctrinal complexity was unavoidable, I tried to exclude cases that needlessly erect barriers to student comprehension. For instance, cases with intricate fact patterns or statutory schemes too often invite students to differentiate among trees when their efforts are far better spent seeing forests. Where simpler cases offered similar instructional value, I selected them over their more convoluted peers.

Cases and similar materials are followed by "Question Sets," most of which are divided into two sections. The first section, called "Review & Synthesis," leads students back to the preceding explanations and examples. Drawing on Bloom's Taxonomy of Educational Objectives, these questions ask them to identify, understand, and synthesize the most salient aspects of the materials they read. The second section, called "Application & Analysis," likewise draws on Bloom's Taxonomy by directing students to use the legal concepts and doctrines presented in the materials. Students are accustomed to casebook questions that, while conceptually challenging, rarely ask them to actually conduct the type of analysis expected of administrative lawyers. Moreover, court opinions are predigested; judges have already chosen the materials in the administrative record they deem legally relevant. As standalone teaching materials, they deprive students of the opportunity to conduct that analysis themselves. For instance, students typically become acquainted with the Administrative Procedure Act's arbitrary and capricious review standard by studying how courts have previously applied it. Such a method of learning might be fine if students were subsequently asked to simply describe how the analysis was conducted. As we know, however, this is not how student learning is assessed in law school. Students are instead expected to competently conduct that analysis themselves on a final examination or similar form of assessment. Nevertheless, opportunities for assessments that are matched to the skills students are expected to demonstrate are too few and far between. It is somewhat like describing how to drive a car to a teenager and then expecting him or her to pass a road test after getting behind the wheel for the very first time. The Application & Analysis questions — largely based on federal judicial opinions and statutes — address this mismatch by providing students with some "hands-on" experience. My belief is that frequent opportunities for formative assessment — as provided by the Application & Analysis Questions — will effectively facilitate development of students' analytical skills.

In sum, it is my hope that the editorial choices made in this casebook — organization driven by the administrative decision-making lifecycle, case selection that balances seminality with accessibility, materials that expose students to agency work product, and questions that prioritize concept application and formative student learning — will minimize the challenges endemic to studying administrative law. As importantly, I hope that this book generates the enthusiastic discussion and debate that the subject matter so richly deserves.

Finally, a few words about the editorial decisions reflected in the materials that follow. I have used ellipses to indicate omissions from quoted text, and I have generally omitted footnotes and internal citations from edited cases and other quoted material without indication. Quoted footnotes are numbered as they appeared in the source material, to the extent I have retained them. Editor's footnotes (there are only a few) are set off with brackets and clearly attributed. For the most part, I have retained the original headings within excerpted cases and other materials but, in a handful of instances, I have omitted them without indication. I have also italicized full and abbreviated case names for emphasis, though doing so does not necessarily follow prevailing tenets of legal citation.

Jamelle C. Sharpe

December 2020

ACKNOWLEDGMENTS

I would like to express my heartfelt gratitude to all those whose generous support and encouragement made completion of this casebook possible: Steven Bieszczat, Jack Casey, Shalyn Caulley, Stephanie Davidson, Omar Andino Figueroa, Nicholas Fregeau, Mark Goldich, Christina Haleas, Pia Hunter, Faye Jones, Aldina Kahari, Christos Kapsalis, Jeff Lambert, Patrick McGlasson, Nicholas O'Donnell, Colin Nardone, Daniel Raymond, Sana Rizvi, Anne Robbins, and the staff of the University of Illinois College of Law Albert E. Jenner, Jr. Memorial Law Library for their invaluable proofreading and research assistance; Sarah Hains of The Froebe Group for managing the editorial production; and Nicola Sharpe for her consistently insightful commentary, criticism, and advice.

PART I

Introduction

Administrative law—derived from the Constitution, federal statutes, regulations, customs, and judicial opinions—strives to regularize how the federal bureaucracy regulates the nation's social and economic activities. To do so, it sets transsubstantive default procedures for agency decision-making. Unless overridden by targeted provisions, the doctrines and principles studied in this course apply to *all* federal agencies regardless of the particular regulatory policies they are tasked with implementing. Despite their generality, understanding these doctrines and principles requires some acquaintance with the workings of administrative agencies and their peculiar position in the governmental scheme. Today's administrative state is vast, varied, and seemingly involved in every conceivable aspect of American life. A comprehensive analysis of its idiosyncrasies and complexities would take up several volumes, and is accordingly well beyond the scope of this book. Fortunately, adequate preparation for the study of administrative law requires only an overview of the federal bureaucracy's historical development, its current organizational structure, and the basic constitutional principles that shape its authority. The materials that follow provide such a foundational survey. In doing so, they touch on several themes and tensions—e.g., law vs. executive discretion, private ordering vs. government regulation, competition among methods of bureaucratic control—that you will encounter repeatedly throughout the course.

Chapter 1 begins by tracing the administrative state's historical development from its pre-Founding Era origins to the present, highlighting key developments and challenges in each period. It then describes the organization of the modern federal bureaucracy, with a focus on two agencies—the Environmental Protection Agency and the National Labor Relations Board—both of which appear in numerous administrative law cases and illustrate the organizational diversity of federal agencies. Finally, Chapter 1 surveys the basic separation-of-powers principles around which the Constitution's Framers organized the three Branches of the federal government. Again, how the Constitution conceptualizes, distributes, and limits legislative, executive, and judicial authority figures prominently in many of the Supreme Court's most important administrative law decisions.

History, Structure, and Principles

The modern administrative state reaches an astonishing assortment of social and economic activities: it issues operating permits and licenses, promulgates rules, distributes benefits payments to those in financial need, advises private parties on their legal obligations, imposes legal consequences on those who fail to meet them, and employs millions of people. It is, for all practical purposes, ubiquitous. Nevertheless, the administrative state did not arrive on American shores fully formed. Quite the contrary, its history is one of perpetual adaptation to shifting political, social, and economic realities. Moreover, its development has been shaped by passionate philosophical disagreements about its place within a governmental system of separated powers and checks and balances. Can entities that simultaneously wield legislative, executive, and judicial powers be trusted to respect the People's freedoms and liberties? A robust understanding of the laws—constitutional, statutory, common, and regulatory—governing regulatory decision-making accordingly depends on some appreciation of the administrative state's developmental and philosophical features.

Accordingly, the discussion that follows proceeds in three parts. It first sketches a historical overview of the federal administrative state, beginning with its English precursors and ending with current concerns and challenges. It then provides snapshots of two agencies—the Environmental Protection Agency and the National Labor Relations Board—which figure prominently in many of the cases discussed in this book. Their differences illustrate the administrative state's diversity of regulatory purposes and organizational structures. Finally, it discusses the Constitution's reliance on the concepts of separation of powers and checks and balances. These readings provide a sound basis on which to assess the legal, philosophical, and practical arguments over administrative power that recur throughout this casebook.

A. A HISTORICAL OVERVIEW OF ADMINISTRATIVE LAW IN THE UNITED STATES

It is often remarked that administrative law in the United States has no distinct, readily identifiable founding "moment." This is largely true; it has developed in fits and starts across continents and over the course of centuries. The same can be said of American history more generally. It does not fit neatly into discrete periods easily identifiable by dates on a calendar. Trends first observed in one "era" bleed into the next, while the significance of particular events is not realized until many years after their occurrence. With these caveats in mind, what follows is a historical survey of administrative law roughly divided by familiar periods in American history. Each of the three branches of the federal government plays a prominent role in this account, driving the federal bureaucracy's development in some eras while deferring to its sister branches, to the states, or to the private sphere in others. Congress is perhaps the most consistent cast member in this drama, as administrative authority often is conferred by exercise of the legislative power. Though they played a secondary role for most of the history recounted below, presidents moved much closer to center stage beginning in the early twentieth century. In particular, the purposes of, the methods and instrumentalities for implementing, and the legal principles governing federal regulation seem to take more coherent shape during the presidencies of Theodore Roosevelt, Franklin D. Roosevelt, Lyndon B. Johnson, and Ronald Reagan. Additionally, presidents have become more active in managing the bureaucracies organized within the Executive Branch. The Supreme Court, for its part, also stepped to the forefront at various points, particularly during the New Deal and Modern Eras. Among other things, its decisions have set the constitutional boundaries within which the administrative state now operates.

Be sure to note a few recurring themes as you read this historical survey. The first is the tension between "law" and "discretion." In almost every era, government officials, judges, and scholars have asserted in some form that broad-ranging executive discretion invariably erodes individual freedoms. The corollary to this proposition is that laws—generally applicable rights and responsibilities that are prospective in effect and enforced by unbiased judges—afford the best protection from the arbitrariness and abuse that too often results from executive discretion. Others have responded that regulation through judicially enforced legal rules proves too slow, too harsh, and too inexpert to properly serve society's most pressing economic and social needs. Executive discretion—when lawfully exercised, transparent, politically accountable, and grounded in substantive expertise—is an indispensable component of any government that claims to serve its people.

Another recurring historical theme involves various models of bureaucratic control. For our purposes, we can identify three such models:

managerial, political, and judicial. The managerial model refers to formal and informal control of bureaucrats by bureaucrats. It includes an agency's tools for hiring, reviewing, promoting, disciplining, and firing its officers, as well as the development of an intra-agency culture of professionalism and colleagueship. The political model refers to the ways elected officials — Members of Congress and the President — select, oversee, supervise, and remove political appointees and civil servants in administrative agencies. The judicial model deals primarily with the circumstances under which courts review, direct, and overturn administrative decision-making. As you will see, the availability and scope of judicial review have ebbed and flowed throughout the nation's history.

A third recurring theme involves the respective roles of government regulation and private ordering. In the realm of economic regulation, politicians, judges, and scholars have long debated whether the federal government should leave the free market to sort itself out or whether the federal government should actively prevent or redress failures inevitably produced by the business cycle. Even those who agree that the latter is an abiding governmental obligation have disagreed on the means by which to fulfill it. Similar questions have been raised in the realm of social regulation. To what extent should the administrative state be tasked with protecting the people's health, safety, and welfare? For instance, should the federal government (through the administrative state) provide the means by which Americans financially sustain themselves? Would doing so foster dependence on government in a way that erodes individual initiatives or freedoms? Would failing to do so allow societal inequalities to fester, ultimately eroding the nation's social fabric?

Each of these big-picture issues has shaped the development of administrative law and practice in the United States. Each continues to do so today.

1. English Origins Through the Founding Era

The origins of American administrative law typically are traced to the common law courts of England in the form of lawsuits brought against individual agents of the Crown. Plaintiffs could bring common law damages actions — trespass, false imprisonment, assault, etc. — against government officials. The court in such a case would have to find that the official's actions could not be justified as a lawful exercise of governmental authority. Stated differently, the question in these suits was whether the official was acting as a private person, and not in the name of the Crown, when causing the plaintiff's injury.

The inadequacy of this method of accountability became increasingly clear over time. Created to chasten private rather than official behavior, these common law causes of action often failed to cover much abusive governmental conduct. Additionally, and to preserve the discretionary decision-making they viewed as critical to proper law administration, courts developed immunity doctrines to further shield the Crown's agents from common law liability. Even assuming a defendant official had the funds to pay an adverse personal judgment (often a dubious assumption), these court-created immunities voided otherwise meritorious claims of injury.

During the seventeenth century, King's Bench (the highest common law court in England, called Queen's Bench when a Queen held the throne) repurposed the prerogative writs—primarily mandamus, certiorari, and prohibition—to facilitate control over local administrative and judicial conduct. Stated differently, they were employed in suits involving some allegation of governmental wrongdoing by individual agents of the Crown (escheators, sheriffs, bailiffs, etc.), rather than in disputes involving purely private persons. They accordingly reflected the King's sovereign interest in ensuring the proper management of governmental functions, while incidentally providing redress or relief to his subjects. Certiorari was a royal demand for information from lower level government officials. It was used, among other things, to supervise the proceedings of inferior courts and to obtain information for supervisory purposes. Prohibition was an order directed to government officials (particularly ecclesiastical courts) to cease some action falling outside of the jurisdiction granted them by, and thus undertaken against the will of, the Crown. Mandamus was issued against officials who unlawfully withheld the performance of some public duty or to order officials to restore an unlawfully withheld entitlement (e.g., a person's right to a hold a particular public office or to vote). *See generally,* S.A. de Smith, *The Prerogative Writs,* 11 CAMBRIDGE L.J. 40 (1951). Aside from its focus on controlling the administrative and judicial functions of government, this writ system vested the courts with control over the conduct of the Crown's agents, rather than assigning that oversight function to legislative or executive officials. King's Bench thus became "a supreme court of administration, supervising much of the business of local government by keeping subordinate bodies within their legal limitations by writs of *certiorari* and prohibition, and ordering them to perform their duties by writs of *mandamus.*" *Id.* at 48.

Even after these adjustments, many regarded the common law methods of controlling governmental conduct as rigid, deliberate, and too often unfair. The most significant response to these perceived failings was the rise of equity, administered not by the courts, but by administrative tribunals led by the Crown's ministers. Chief among these was the Court of Chancery led by the Chancellor, the King's chief clerk and one of his most important advisors. Guided by equitable discretion rather than by judge-developed common law rules, the Chancellor used injunctions to stop unlawful official conduct where the petitioner could demonstrate likelihood of irreparable harm. Often the Chancellor would issue such injunctions against litigants in common law courts, thereby forbidding them from pursuing suits or enforcing judgments at law. Common law judges bristled at this indirect assertion of supervisory authority by one of the King's closest advisors, particularly if exercised after they had issued final judgments. They strongly believed that their decisional independence from political interference of this sort was essential to preserving the rule of law to which everyone, including the King and his ministers, ultimately were subject. Administrative discretion unmoored from courtlike constraints—adherence to common law rules, regularized procedures, and precedential decisions—could result only in corruption of government and abuse of the people. Chancellors, by contrast, believed that the discretionary power of injunction was indispensable to assuring fairness in governmental decision-making. More conceptually, the Chancellor's supporters argued that it was ultimately the King's duty, rather than the judges', to ensure that the government acted lawfully. Under this view, the common law courts lacked the agility or the remedial powers needed to do justice in some cases, and the vexatious conduct of common law litigants dictated the outcomes of lawsuits in others.

This schism between law and equity narrowed considerably by the close of the eighteenth century. English common law courts eventually made their decision-making more flexible by adopting injunctions and other tools of equity, while the Court of Chancery and similar administrative tribunals cabined their discretion through adoption of more regularized procedures and greater adherence to precedent. *See generally* THEODORE F.T. PLUCKNETT, A CONCISE HISTORY OF THE COMMON LAW (1929); David W. Raack, *A History of Injunctions in England Before 1700*, 61 IND. L.J. 539 (1985); Bernard Schwartz, *The Administrative Agency in Historical Perspective*, 36 IND. L.J. 263 (1961).

According to the traditional account of administration's history in America, first the colonies and then the states adopted England's general approach to regulation: market rather than governmental control over private social and economic activity, coupled with legal and equitable judicial remedies against individual government officials. To be sure, the new federal government almost immediately established executive departments directly answerable to and controlled by the President—the Departments of State, Treasury, and War were all created in 1789. Nevertheless, the size of the federal government in the Founding Era through much of the nineteenth century was small and its regulation of private conduct light as compared to subsequent periods in American history. To the extent such regulation was undertaken, it came primarily from the several states rather than the federal government and, in particular, from state common law courts. "[R]esponsibility for the allocation of resources in the economy and the distribution of wages, rents, and profits was shifted to a large degree from administrative officials to the marketplace and to the judges who formulated the rules of tort, property, and contract that defined the grounds and terms of market exchange." STEPHEN G. BREYER, ET AL., ADMINISTRATIVE LAW AND REGULATORY POLICY 17 (7th ed. 2011). Accordingly, the federal government did little in its first several decades to develop a centralized, territory-spanning administrative apparatus to direct the nation's social or economic activities.

Federal administrative activity in this early period largely was dedicated to providing "promotional and support services for the state governments . . . [leaving] the substantive tasks of governing to these regional units." STEPHEN SKOWRONEK, BUILDING A NEW AMERICAN STATE: THE EXPANSION OF NATIONAL ADMINISTRATIVE CAPACITIES, 1877-1920, at 23 (1982). This is not to say, however, that the federal government was solely focused on such interstitial concerns. It assumed regulation of several nationally oriented areas: naturalization of new citizens, customs and tax collection, coastal navigation, mail delivery, war and foreign trade relations, grants of public lands to war veterans, etc. It added administrative capacity prior to the Civil War—patent offices, land offices, post offices, customshouses—to manage these responsibilities. What's more, early understandings of the separation of powers permitted more fluidity of function within the federal bureaucracy than some might otherwise expect. "Early Congresses delegated broad policymaking powers to the President and to others, combined policymaking, enforcement, and adjudication in the same administrative hands, created administrative bodies outside of executive departments, provided for the direct responsibility of some administrators to Congress itself, and assigned 'nonjudicial' business to the courts." Jerry L. Mashaw, *Recovering American Administrative Law: Federalist Foundations, 1787-1801*, 115 YALE L.J. 1256, 1268 (2006). Examples abound. Congress created its first federal agency with the Act of July 31, 1789, which required "estimate[ing] the duties payable" on imports and related duties. The second agency was also created in 1789, but by President Washington rather than by Congress. He gave it the authority to make rules and adjudicate disputes relating to military pensions for "invalids who were wounded and disabled during the [Revolutionary War]." *Id.* at 1296. The Act of September 29, 1789, directed the President to make rules governing the payment of military pensions to veterans wounded in the Revolutionary War. Some months later, and as part of Alexander Hamilton's plan to bolster the government's creditworthiness, Congress directed "the President of the Senate, the Chief Justice, the Secretary of State, the Secretary of the Treasury, and the Attorney General," alone or in combination, to manage the federal government's purchase of the states' Revolutionary War debts. Apart from first securing the President's approval, the statute gave little direction on how these officials from each Branch of the federal government should undertake what today would be considered an exclusively Executive function. It simply instructed them "to cause said purchases to be made in such manner, and under such regulations as shall appear to them best calculated to fulfill the intent of this act." An Act Making Provision for the Reduction of Debt, ch. 47, § 2, 2 Stat. 186, 186 (1790).

Of course, the federal government also had to manage the conduct of its administrative agents. Notably, the development of federal administrative capacity in the Founding Era and even through the nineteenth century did not result in the adoption of a transsubstantive body of administrative law dedicated to this purpose. Congress enacted no comprehensive statutory mandates instructing administrative bodies on the conduct of their enforcement, rulemaking, or adjudicative activities. Nor did it enact provisions broadly subjecting administrative decision-making to direct judicial review. Instead, much of the control over federal agencies during this period was exercised through a host of nonjudicial measures — direct legislative action, political oversight, intra-agency managerial hierarchies, economic incentives, etc. For example, "Congress gave relief by private bills to petitioners who had been damaged by 'incompetent' administration," Mashaw, *supra,* at 1312, and "[m]ost field agents of the federal government were paid by fees . . . rather than regular salaries." Ann Woolhandler, *Judicial Deference to Administrative Action — A Revisionist History,* 43 ADMIN. L. REV. 197, 207 (1991). Thus, anyone looking solely to federal judicial opinions or comprehensive legislation for the rules governing administrative conduct would miss much of early American "administrative law." *See* Mashaw, *supra,* at 1260-66.

To the extent courts were involved in canalizing administrative decision-making, they did so through lawsuits brought against individual officials. The federal government itself relied heavily on lawsuits to chasten bureaucratic abuses. "Instead of providing disciplinary machinery within bureaus for the hierarchical control of wayward administrators, Congress peppered the early federal statutes with fines, penalties, and forfeitures." Mashaw, *supra,* at 1316. Thus, a customs or internal revenue agent suspected of pocketing monies collected on behalf of the government could be made to answer for such indiscretions in federal court. Private parties also relied heavily on state and federal courts and juries to check allegedly abusive or unlawful bureaucratic decision-making. Individual officials could thus be forced to defend themselves against lawsuits for damages, trespass, replevin, assumpsit, etc. Apart from a few specific protections afforded by statute, official immunities as we understand them today did not exist. Public officials would therefore be left to argue that they acted within the jurisdictional bounds set for them by Congress. This reflected the eighteenth- and nineteenth-century view that public officials who engaged in unlawful conduct stood before the law as private tortfeasors, or other such wrongdoers, and were personally liable even when pursuing their duties in demonstrably good faith. The nature of the review afforded by these suits was collateral rather than direct, and the standard applied was *de novo* and hence the opposite of deferential. Courts assessed the legality of an official's actions under federal law because doing so was necessary to determine his liability under the common law. Such assessment afforded the defendant official no deference with respect to his interpretation of the law or his understanding of the facts at the time he took the allegedly injurious action. Moreover, the state juries before whom most of these cases were tried were not eager to promote the enforcement of federal laws over the private interests of their neighbors. To make matters worse, Congress routinely refused to reimburse federal officials made liable for damages by state courts. Given the threat of financially ruinous personal judgments and the unlikelihood of indemnification, it is little wonder that public officials were often deterred from aggressive and creative implementation of federal law.

By contrast, judges seemed to believe that they had limited authority to conduct direct, appellate-style review of administrative conduct. *See* Ann Woolhandler, *Patterns of Official Immunity and Accountability*, 37 CASE W. RES. L. REV. 396, 417-19 (1987); *see generally* Frederick P. Lee, *The Origins of Judicial Control of Executive Action*, 36 GEO. L.J. 287 (1948). A federal plaintiff could seek a writ of mandamus or an injunction, but courts would not entertain such petitions unless they related to the performance of ministerial tasks (i.e., nondiscretionary tasks required of the official by law). *See Kendall v. United States ex rel. Stokes*, 37 U.S. 524, 610 (1838). Courts subsequently defined "discretion" broadly to include most decisions that involved even an element of agency judgment. *See, e.g., Decatur v. Paulding*, 39 U.S. (14 Pet.) 497 (1840). The overall effect was to shield from judicial review most administrative decision-making through the nineteenth century. This stands in stark contrast to modern administrative practice, wherein private persons adversely affected or aggrieved by agency decision-making have the statutory right to trigger comparatively searching judicial review.

2. The Antebellum Period

The nation continued to advance technologically, economically, and territorially in the years preceding the Civil War. Antebellum America shifted from a collection of dispersed agrarian communities with few large population centers to a nation characterized more and more by urbanization, industrialization, and immigration. Its population doubled between 1830 and 1860 and, perhaps unsurprisingly, the overall size of government increased along with it. Most of this growth was generated at the state and local level; to the extent government asserted itself into private life, state legislatures and state courts continued to be the nation's primary sources of social and economic regulation. Nevertheless, the federal government also expanded dramatically after Andrew Jackson assumed the presidency in 1829. Although Jacksonian Democrats generally resisted federalization of American social and economic life, countervailing interests—forced or negotiated relocation of Native American tribes, aggressive westward expansion, etc.—necessitated some federal institutional development to keep pace. By one measure, federal expenditures quadrupled in the years leading up to the Civil War, and growth of the federal government's corps of civilian employees outstripped the growth rate of the population as a whole. *See* Jerry L. Mashaw, *Administration and "The Democracy": Administrative Law from Jackson to Lincoln, 1829-1861*, 117 YALE L.J. 1568, 1576-77 (2008), citing LEONARD D. WHITE, THE JACKSONIANS: A STUDY IN ADMINISTRATIVE HISTORY 1829-1861 (1954).

3. The Civil War, Reconstruction, and the Gilded Age

The federal government built up a robust bureaucratic apparatus in response to the Civil War (1861-1865) and the period of Reconstruction that followed it (1865-1877). As one prominent scholar described it, "[t]he war had brought national military conscription, a military occupation of the South, a national welfare agency for former slaves, a national income tax, national monetary controls, and national citizenship." SKOWRONEK, *supra,* at 30. The Civil War Amendments—the Thirteenth, Fourteenth, and Fifteenth Amendments—promised not only hard-fought freedoms for African Americans and others, but a seismic power shift from the states to the federal government. The North's victory seemed to portend a consolidation and expansion of federal regulation of American social and economic life with concomitant bureaucratic development. In some sense, this was realized. Congress established new executive departments in the latter half of the nineteenth century, including the Department of Justice (1870), and reorganized others, like the Post Office Department (1872). Agencies also adopted practices to better organize and publicize their decisions, like publishing decisions and developing operating manuals. Administrative "courts" processed tens of thousands of claims across multiple agencies relating to a variety of governmental activities, including tax calculation and collection, patent awards, payment of veterans' pensions, and public land sales.

On balance, however, the reality of mid-nineteenth-century bureaucratic development deviated materially from the promise. Attempts to capitalize on the gains made during the war were hindered by a host of troubles, including corruption scandals under President Ulysses S. Grant, Northern weariness with the continued military occupation of the South, and Reconstruction's disastrous abandonment by President Rutherford B. Hayes. Instead, the Gilded Age (roughly the late 1870s to 1900) was "characterized by massive growth in the size, and a revolution in the organization, of industrial enterprises." Jerry L. Mashaw, *Federal Administration and Administrative Law in the Gilded Age*, 119 YALE L.J. 1362, 1370 (2010). The Supreme Court of this period approached the Civil War Amendments—particularly the Fourteenth Amendment—less as a bulwark against civil rights abuses than as the means by which to constrain governmental regulation of private markets and contracts, establish corporate personhood, and shield the employer-employee relationship from judicial scrutiny.

Judicial review of governmental decision-making remained limited until the 1880s; collateral *de novo* review through suits at common law against individual officers persisted, with limited opportunities for direct review through mandamus or injunctive actions. Similarly, the federal bureaucracy did little to regulate the economy. Nevertheless, the administrative state developed in several significant ways. The first relates to the competition for control over Executive Branch decision-making between Congress and the

President. Congress clearly had the upper hand in this contest in the mid-nineteenth century; by today's standards, the President exercised only weak control over those who, organizationally, appeared to report to him. No single event illustrates this point more than the impeachment of President Andrew Johnson. Johnson, a southern Democrat, assumed the presidency after President Abraham Lincoln's assassination on April 15, 1865. Johnson favored a much more moderate approach to reconstructing and reincorporating the former Confederate states than did Lincoln, most members of his cabinet, or the Radical Republicans who controlled both chambers of Congress. Congressional Republicans adopted a number of measures specifically calculated to restrict Johnson's control over the federal bureaucracy, the most notable of which was the Tenure of Office Act of 1867. Passed over his veto, the Act required Johnson to secure the Senate's approval before he could remove an officer appointed with that body's advice and consent. Additionally, the Act permitted Johnson to remove or suspend such an officer only for the causes it specified. Senate rejection of Johnson's removal or suspension decisions allowed the targeted official to return to his duties. Johnson fired Secretary of War Edwin Stanton, a holdover from the Lincoln Administration, after the Act's passage. The Senate rejected Johnson's proffered reasons for this removal and instructed Stanton to resume his responsibilities. Believing the Act to be an unconstitutional infringement on his constitutional authority, Johnson again removed Stanton and named an Acting Secretary of War to replace him. The House of Representatives responded by impeaching Johnson for violating the Act, and he survived removal from office by a single Senate vote. The Supreme Court would consider and reject the Tenure of Office Act's constitutionality about six decades later, even though it had by that time been repealed during Grover Cleveland's presidency. *See Myers v. United States,* 272 U.S. 52 (1926).

A second important development in this period was adoption of the Pendleton Civil Service Reform Act of 1883. Positions in the Executive Branch after the Civil War typically were doled out through the so-called "spoils system," a form of patronage by which elected officials granted their supporters government positions in exchange for their political loyalty and support. For years these patronage hires and their political benefactors successfully blocked attempts at reorienting the federal civil service toward competence, experience, and expertise. This changed when President James A. Garfield was assassinated in 1881 by a political supporter who expected but was refused a patronage job. Chester A. Arthur assumed the presidency and signed the Pendleton Act into law. Among its significant reforms, the Act based eligibility for certain federal positions on competitive examination performance, based demotion and removal decisions on inefficiency rather than political connections, and barred the solicitation of campaign contributions on federal government property. The Act also restored funding to the United States Civil Service Commission, an independent agency originally created under President Grant to oversee the civil service system.

As scholars have noted, this merit-driven hiring and promotion system did not drive instant systemic change. Initially, its provisions applied only to a small percentage of clerical and technical positions in Washington, D.C. Agency leadership was still selected through the political appointments process, and other high-level positions with policy discretion fell outside of the Act's protections. Moreover, the Act did not require the hiring of those office seekers with the highest examination scores. This allowed local political parties to fill open positions outside of Washington, D.C., as long as their preferred candidates' scores did not disqualify them outright. *See, e.g.,* Daniel P. Carpenter, The Forging of Bureaucratic Autonomy: Reputations, Networks, and Policy Innovation in Executive Agencies, 1862-1928, at 10-11, 45-46 (2001). Many of these issues would not be resolved until the New Deal Era.

The third and most significant development marked what many scholars consider the dawn of the modern administrative state: the passage of the Interstate Commerce Act ("ICA"), 24 Stat. 379 (1887) and its creation of America's first independent regulatory agency, the Interstate Commerce Commission ("ICC"). As made clear by the discussion above, the ICC was by no means the first bureaucratic institution the federal government had created. By the 1880s numerous executive departments—Agriculture and Interior, the Postal Office, the Patent Office, the General Land Office, the Pension Office, etc.—were already in operation and making numerous decisions directly affecting everyday life. Unlike the ICC, however, these executive agencies were led by a single individual; the ICC was led by a chairman and six other commissioners. Additionally, the executive agencies were charged with monitoring or managing those parts of American life connected to interstate commerce. Prior to the latter half of the nineteenth century, there was perhaps little need to do so as the volume and value of that commerce was small; economic activity was highly localized and regulated by the states. When interstate commerce was conducted, waterway transportation was the primary means by which distant parts of the nation could connect in trade. Due to a host of topographical challenges, the transport of goods over land was slow and often prohibitively expensive as compared to its water-based counterparts.

Advances in transportation and communication technologies—primarily the railroad but also the telegraph and eventually the telephone—substantially increased economic exchange between formerly disconnected regions of the country. Prior to this proliferation, landlocked farmers raised their crops and livestock primarily for subsistence as the costs and logistical challenges of transporting them to other markets proved too difficult to overcome. Railways connected their products to Chicago and other burgeoning commodities centers that were in turn connected to buyers around the country. Additionally, this new interconnectedness made possible by railroads promised to make the nation's continent-spanning size more governable. Travel between distant corners of the country could be accomplished in days or weeks rather than in months, "annihilating space and time" as the railroad was said to do. Land prices increased, populations boomed, and commerce often flourished almost anywhere railroads travelled. Moreover, communication by wire was becoming far faster and more reliable than sending written correspondence by post.

These advances came with a cost, however, as the number of accidents related to railroad construction and operations mounted. As importantly, the industry rapidly moved from a diverse collection of local lines toward accumulation by national corporate behemoths. The public—particularly farmers and small business owners—increasingly decried what they viewed as the railroads' reckless financial dealings, corruption of politicians and the political process, monopolistic ambitions, and inequitable rate discrimination among customers. For their part, railroad managers and sympathetic economists asserted that railroads were natural monopolies; the pooling of control over routes and rates was inevitable in an industry requiring large upfront investments in land, materials, and machinery. Far from increasing operational efficiency and decreasing rates, they argued that *competition* was inefficient, expensive, and ultimately wasteful.

Railroad regulations initially developed at the state level. Even before the Civil War, Rhode Island, New York, and other eastern states created commissions to collect operational information from and enforce reasonable service and rate requirements against the railroads. Midwestern states such as Illinois established commissions somewhat later, coincident with the later development of their commercial rail systems. As a practical matter, the sheer size, wealth, and political influence of the railroads swamped these decentralized regulatory efforts. As an eminent legal historian succinctly explained:

> [A]s railroads more and more were gathered up in huge national nets, town and county authorities were basically useless as controllers. Even statewide control was futile. The states could not deal with *national* businesses, either in law or in fact. The only remedy, then, was *federal* control.

Lawrence M. Friedman, A History of American Law 419 (4th ed. 2019) (emphasis in original). In any event, these state-based regulatory efforts—and the prior judicial opinions supporting them—were largely swept away by the Supreme Court's decision in *Wabash, St. Louis & Pacific Railway Co. v. Illinois*, 118 U.S. 557, 558 (1886): "Notwithstanding what is there said, [in previous judgments], this court holds now, and has never consciously held otherwise, that a statute of the State intended to regulate or to tax or to impose any other restriction upon the transmission of persons or property or telegraph messages from one State to another, is not within that class of legislation which the States may enact in the absence of legislation by Congress; and that such statutes are void even as to that part of such transmission which may be within the State." Largely in response to continued public disapprobation of the railroads and the regulatory void left by *Wabash*, Congress established the ICC.

The ICC was structured to insulate its decision-making from political influence that could be exercised by either Congress or the President. The apparent intent was for experience and technical expertise, rather than patronage or politics, to govern its decision-making. Its organization thus differed considerably from the executive departments led by lone members of the President's cabinet. While the President appointed its five commissioners to six-year terms with the advice and consent of the Senate, these terms were staggered to prevent the President from appointing all of the commissioners in a single term of office. Further, the President could not remove commissioners at will, but only for "inefficiency, neglect of duty, or malfeasance in office." The President could appoint no more than three commissioners from the same political party, ensuring that he had to choose some from outside of his own base of support. Finally, and to facilitate separation between the regulators and the regulated, no commissioner could work for or hold a financial interest in any common carrier subject to the ICA's provisions.

As for the manner and strength of its powers, the ICC had the potential to spearhead a new era of economic regulation: regulations limiting who could enter an industry and what prices industry entrants could charge. This new regime of economic regulation was national in scope, centralized in the federal government, and driven by industry expertise. The ICA granted the agency broad investigative and enforcement authority. It could demand financial, managerial, and operational information from common carriers and issue subpoenas for witnesses and documents. It could also impose on common carriers a uniform system for tracking this information and require them to submit annual reports detailing it. Where it suspected ICA violations, the ICC could issue cease and desist orders to alleged offenders or order the payment of reparations. If a carrier refused to comply with one of its orders or demands for information, the agency or other interested parties could petition the federal circuit courts for enforcement. The ICC also gave expansive reading to the ICA's more ambiguous provisions. Whereas the agency clearly was authorized to punish violations of the Act after they had already occurred, the ICC found statutory authority to address potential violations prophylactically. Most importantly, the Act adopted standards for limiting the rates common carriers could charge, requiring that such rates be "reasonable and just." It gave the ICC no express authority to prescribe such rates itself, but the agency claimed that power anyway in an attempt to become a more proactive regulator.

However formidable these administrative powers seemed in the abstract, they soon proved far less imposing in practice. The primary reason was a Supreme Court committed to a privately ordered and judicially protected economy largely free from legislative or administrative interference. This view framed bureaucratic decision-making based on technical expertise and informed discretion as a threat to the rule of law embodied by judicial decision-making. In a series of decisions toward the end of the nineteenth century, the Court stripped regulatory authority away from the ICC. Rather than deferring to ICC's investigative findings or its interpretations of the statute it was created to implement, the Court insisted on reviewing the agency's determinations of law and fact *de novo*. In doing so, it repeatedly rejected the agency's implied authority, narrowly construed its explicit authority, and otherwise adopted a restrictive approach to interpreting the ICA's provisions. *See, e.g., ICC v. Alabama Midland Railway Co.*, 168 U.S. 144 (1897); *ICC v. Cincinnati, N.O. & T.P. Ry. Co.*, 167 U.S. 479 (1897). The net effect was to substantially dilute the ICC's effectiveness.

4. The Progressive Era to the Great Depression

Despite the Supreme Court's antipathy toward the ICC, the federal government continued to take substantial steps toward bureaucratized economic regulation during the Progressive Era (1890-1920). President Theodore Roosevelt—an energetic enemy of the patronage system when he was a Civil Service Commissioner—drove much of the bureaucratic expansion and reforms of the early Progressive Era. Although his antebellum predecessors ceded management of the federal bureaucracy to standing and select committees in Congress, Roosevelt established himself as an aggressive defender of presidential prerogatives. "In his neo-Hamiltonian scheme, the position of the President as a nationally elected officer was to be coupled with the professional discipline of the bureaucrat to ensure that special interests would be kept at arm's length and that national interest would be raised above private power." SKOWRONEK, *supra*, at 172. This would necessarily require greater executive control over the duties, resources, and organization of administrative agencies with minimal congressional micromanagement. He accordingly took several steps to strengthen the Civil Service Commission and to prohibit ties between merit-based employment and politicians. Moreover, the federal government of the Progressive Era committed itself to rational and cost-conscious operations. "The list of official bodies formed in the early twentieth century to deal with questions of efficiency in civil administration lends credence to this characterization: The [Committee] on Department Methods, the Commission on Economy and Efficiency, the Bureau of Efficiency, the Central Bureau of Planning and Statistics, the Bureau of the Budget, the General Accounting Office, the Personnel Classification Board." *Id.* at 177. Of course, professionalization of the federal civil service corps during the Progressive Era was not forward-thinking in every respect. Though President Woodrow Wilson (1913-1921) built on some of the reforms undertaken by his immediate predecessors, he also infused federal hiring and promotion practices with segregation and racism, particularly against African Americans. *See* FRIEDMAN, *supra*, at 678. As one scholar explained, "Wilson's administration combined institutionalized racism with progressive reform in a way that devastated not only careers but also the very foundation of full citizenship for African Americans." ERIC S. YELLIN, RACISM IN THE NATION'S SERVICE: GOVERNMENT WORKERS AND THE COLOR LINE IN WOODROW WILSON'S AMERICA 2 (2013).

On the regulatory front, reigning in the railroads continued to be a regulatory preoccupation. In response to the Supreme Court's hostility to the ICC, Congress passed the Hepburn Act in 1906, which expanded the agency's regulatory authority. It authorized the ICC to set "just and reasonable" maximum rates through an early precursor of today's formal rulemaking procedure. *See* Ch. 1, § 15, 34 Stat. 589. It also made the agency's orders self-executing (directly enforceable without a court order). Public health and safety emerged as another prominent area of concern, particularly as it related to the nation's food supply. Newspapers revealed that the American military fed its soldiers rotten canned meat while they were fighting the Spanish-American War in 1898. European countries banned importation of U.S. meat due to concerns over its quality and cleanliness. Publication of Upton Sinclair's *The Jungle* in 1906 brought nationwide scorn to the unsanitary practices of the meat-packing industry. Federal legislation to regulate the industry initially failed, leading to passage of a comprehensive regulatory approach in the Pure Food and Drug Act in 1906. Substantively, the Act prohibited foreign and interstate sales of adulterated or mislabeled food and drugs. Its implementation was assigned to the Bureau of Chemistry—an agency led by a Chief Chemist appointed by the Secretary of Agriculture—indicating a science-driven rather than political approach to the problem of food and drug adulteration.

In addition to addressing specific issues like food and drug safety, Congress took measures to regulate more generalized economic activity. In 1913, the Sixty-third Congress passed the Federal Reserve Act, 38 Stat. 251, and established the Federal Reserve System (the "Fed"). A central bank organized into 12 regions, the Fed was charged with managing the nation's monetary policy and regulating certain private banking activities. Like the ICC, the Fed employed an independent agency structure to focus its decision-making on expertise and long-term planning as opposed to politics. Its Board of Governors was staffed by five members appointed by the President with the advice and consent of the Senate, along with two *ex officio* members (the Secretary of the Treasury and the Comptroller of the Currency). The appointed Governors served staggered ten-year terms, and at least two of them had to have prior experience in banking or finance. To further facilitate their decision-making neutrality, governors were prohibited from accepting employment from the banks they regulated for at least two years after leaving the Fed. A year later, Congress passed the Federal Trade Commission Act and created the Federal Trade Commission ("FTC"). A successor to the Bureau of Corporations within the Department of Commerce and Labor, the FTC was formed as another multimember independent agency. Its mission was to enforce federal civil antitrust laws and to protect consumers from unfair methods of competition in commerce.

Overall, the number of federal agencies doubled in the first three decades of the twentieth century. *See* George B. Shephard, *Fierce Compromise: The Administrative Procedure Act Emerges from New Deal Politics*, 90 Nw. U. L. Rev. 1557, 1561-62 (1996).

Among the more vexing puzzles of this period was the Judiciary's authority to review and set aside decisions by these new agencies. Availability of judicial review was sometimes determined by federal statute (e.g., the Hepburn Act of 1906). Where Congress did not make its intentions in this regard clear, or where the methods provided by Congress proved inadequate, litigants resorted either to the limited relief afforded by the common law writs or to various forms of collateral attack (e.g., bills for injunctions, petitions for declaratory judgments, damages actions against administrative officials).

With respect to the scope of judicial review, courts more readily deferred to agency actions when they did not interfere with private business affairs or otherwise implicate individual legal rights. At that time, a host of administrative activities — granting operating licenses, providing benefits payments like veterans pensions, or use of public lands — were regarded as mere privileges the government could grant or revoke in its sole discretion. As private individuals were thought to have no legal entitlement to such benefits (at least until the early 1970s), courts viewed their dispensation as discretionary and hence reviewable only for unreasonableness or arbitrariness. The same was true of other decisions where administrative officials acted within the discretion granted to them by Congress. Courts would not interfere with their decisions as long as they were not arbitrary or capricious. *See, e.g., United States ex rel. Knight v. Lane*, 228 U.S. 6, 13 (1913); *Garfield v. United States ex rel. Goldsby*, 211 U.S. 249, 262 (1908); *Commercial Solvents Corp. v. Mellon*, 277 F. 548, 550 (D.C. Cir. 1922). With respect to ICC rate orders, for instance, the Supreme Court stated that it had no power to "usurp merely administrative functions by setting aside a lawful administrative order upon [its] conception as to whether the administrative power has been wisely exercised." *ICC v. Illinois Central Railroad Co.*, 215 U.S. 452, 470 (1910). Where the orders were supported by substantial evidence in the record, the Court declined to "consider [their] expediency or wisdom . . . or whether, on like testimony, it would have made a similar ruling." *ICC v. Union Pacific Railroad Co.*, 222 U.S. 541, 547 (1912).

That being said, there were limits to how much discretion Congress could grant to agencies. Supreme Court jurisprudence dating back to the nineteenth century made clear that "legislative" decisions — the originating policy choices animating legally enforceable rules — had to be made by Congress. Congress could delegate to agencies the power to make lesser, subsidiary policy choices based on the originating ones. Such discretion was often vital to filling the gaps Congress routinely left in its statutory schemes. However, the Constitution did not allow Congress to delegate its exclusive power under Article I to make originating policy choices. Courts would invalidate such statutes along with the agency actions based on them. *See, e.g., Cargo of the Brig Aurora v. United States*, 11 U.S. (7 Cranch) 382 (1813); *J.W. Hampton, Jr. & Co. v. United States*, 276 U.S. 394 (1928).

Significantly, the Supreme Court was far less deferential to agency decision-making in cases involving jurisdictional questions or impositions on legal rights. The Court decided several such cases through the 1920s and into the early 1930s, undertaking review even in the absence of a federal statute otherwise permitting it. Particularly common were due process claims by railroads and utilities that states or the federal government had confiscated their property by placing low caps on the rates they could charge their customers. Rather than deferring to these rate determinations — prospective in scope and made after formal hearings — the Supreme Court might independently determine whether the caps were unconstitutionally confiscatory. Although Congress had statutorily vested administrative hearing officers with adjudicative authority to find facts and make determinations of law in individual cases, Article III courts afforded no deference to their conclusions unless compelled by statute to do so. *See, e.g., Prendergast v. New York Telephone Co.*, 262 U.S. 43, 50 (1923) (whether FCC rate order was confiscatory was "to be determined by the court upon the evidence submitted to it"); *cf. Ohio Valley Water Co. v. Borough of Ben Avon*, 253 U.S. 287, 289 (1920) (courts exercise independent judgment on both law and fact when determining whether a government rate-setting scheme is confiscatory). Indeed, the Court insisted that such independent determination of both factual and legal questions was a requirement of Article III when constitutional rights were at issue. *See Crowell v. Benson*, 285 U.S. 22, 46 (1932) (Congress can assign fact-finding to an administrative hearing officer, but district court can build and rely on additional evidence when determining constitutionality of that officer's determinations).

Whatever the limitations placed on agency decision-making by the Supreme Court, political sensibilities favored a more modest role for the federal bureaucracy after World War I than during it. Federal expenditures declined substantially in the years immediately following the war (though they remained higher than those in the years immediately preceding it). *See* Randall G. Holcombe, *The Growth of the Federal Government in the 1920s*, 16 Cato J. 175, 182 (1996). Under the Republican presidents who succeeded Wilson — Warren G. Harding, Calvin Coolidge, and Herbert C. Hoover — the Executive Branch assumed a secondary role to Congress in the formation of federal policy. Additionally, regulatory activity was again left largely to the courts and to the states.

Triggered by the stock market crash of October 24, 1929, the Great Depression began mere months after Hoover took office. Banks across the country failed, consumer spending and financial investment dried up, businesses shuttered, farmers went bankrupt, and unemployment skyrocketed. Although he took several steps to stimulate the economy, Hoover believed that states and private industry, not the federal government, should lead efforts to halt the country's economic implosion. His policies proved largely ineffective; he and the Republican Party were routed by Franklin D. Roosevelt ("FDR") and the Democrats in the 1932 election.

5. The New Deal Era

Spurred by his landslide Electoral College victory and majorities in both houses of Congress, Roosevelt launched a thoroughgoing reconceptualization of the federal government's role in American social and economic life. It directly asserted itself in markets and other areas of private life previously regulated (when regulated at all) by the courts or the state governments. "Banking, securities markets, agriculture, energy, industrial labor relations, and much more would fall under the authority of federal officers." Barry Cushman, *The Great Depression and the New Deal, in* CAMBRIDGE HISTORY OF LAW IN AMERICA 269 (M. Grossberg & C. Tomlins eds., 2008). A slew of so-called "alphabet" agencies sprung into being—some created by Congress and others by the President—to implement the New Deal: the Agricultural Adjustment Administration ("AAA"), the Federal Communications Commission ("FCC"), the Federal Deposit Insurance Corporation ("FDIC"), the Federal Power Commission ("FPC"), the National Labor Relations Board ("NLRB"), the National Recovery Administration ("NRA"), the Securities and Exchange Commission ("SEC"), the Social Security Administration ("SSA"), the Works Progress Administration ("WPA"), and more. Federal expenditures were almost 77 percent higher in 1936 than in 1932. Moreover, the locus of federal policymaking shifted decidedly to the Executive Branch, as Congress delegated an unprecedented amount of regulatory discretion to President Roosevelt and his expanding federal bureaucracy. Although some agencies such as the FCC, SEC, and ICC occasionally regulated through issuance of substantive rules, for the most part the federal bureaucracy regulated through enforcement actions and adjudication. It would not be until the 1960s that federal agencies would adopt rulemaking as the dominant method of policy formulation.

These sea changes in the scope of and control over federal regulatory policy did not sit well with everyone, economic catastrophe notwithstanding. Hoover, for one, became a frequent and vociferous critic of FDR's policies in his post-presidency. More impactful was the Supreme Court's resistance to the New Deal. The so-called "Four Horsemen"—Justices Butler, McReynolds, Sutherland, and Van Devanter—were not persuaded that the Constitution countenanced expansive bureaucratic policymaking and when joined by Chief Justice Hughes or Justice Owen Roberts, they formed an anti-delegation majority. They struck down key provisions in the New Deal keystone—The National Industrial Recovery Act of 1933 ("NIRA")—for unconstitutionally delegating legislative authority to the President. *A.L.A. Schechter Poultry Corp. v. United States*, 295 U.S. 495 (1935); *Panama Refining Co. v. Ryan*, 293 U.S. 388 (1935). The Court also rejected Congress' experiments with alternative forms of bureaucratic policymaking. Prior to attaining the presidency, Roosevelt believed that private market participants understood better than government regulators the economics and practices of their respective industries. Accordingly, he thought that trade associations and similar private organizations should be empowered to develop rules of conduct governing their respective industries. The NIRA provisions at issue in *Schechter Poultry* included a form of such private self-regulation, though the Court's analysis did not focus on it. The Bituminous Coal Conservation Act of 1935 did as well; as a practical matter, it gave rulemaking authority over maximum working hours in the coal industry to unions representing a majority of the nation's coal miners and companies producing more than two-thirds of the nation's coal. A closely divided Court struck it down. "The power conferred upon the majority is, in effect, the power to regulate the affairs of an unwilling minority. This is legislative delegation in its most obnoxious form; for it is not even delegation to an official or an official body, presumptively disinterested, but to private persons whose interests may be and often are adverse to the interests of others in the same business." *Carter v. Carter Coal Co.*, 298 U.S. 238, 311 (1936). These cases proved to be the highwater mark of conflict between the Court and the New Deal. Justice Van Devanter retired in 1937, and President Roosevelt replaced him with former Alabama Senator Hugo Black, whose views were much more sympathetic to the New Deal. By the mid-1940s, the Court signaled that it had lost interest in blocking broad delegations to the Executive Branch. *See Yakus v. United States*, 321 U.S. 414 (1944). Opponents of the New Deal, recognizing that the Court would no longer serve as their vanguard against expanding bureaucratic encroachments on individual liberties and the free market, eventually turned to Congress instead.

The federal government grew somewhat haphazardly during the New Deal Era, raising concerns that the powers of the presidency were inadequate to meet its size, complexity, scope of responsibility, and unwieldiness. In 1936, Roosevelt convened the Brownlow Committee to suggest ways the government might be made more susceptible to presidential control. Staffed by political science and public administration experts, the Committee stated flatly that "[t]he President needs help." Broadly speaking, it concluded that the President should be given power over the government similar to a CEO's power over a corporation. Among other things, the Committee advised that the independent departments (which it said had evolved into a fourth branch) be incorporated into the executive departments, the President be given funding for a larger staff that would help him oversee and direct the work of the agencies, and that the President be given continuing authority to reorganize the Executive Branch. Congress ultimately rejected the Committee's recommendations. Fears persisted that concentrating governmental power in the hands of the President would erode individual

> **Cross-Reference**
>
> Chapter 3 considers the topic of presidential reorganization of the federal government in greater depth.

liberties and undermine the proper operation of the free market. The rising tide of authoritarianism in Europe did little to allay such concerns. Congress nevertheless enacted a separate suite of less aggressive reforms not long thereafter. The Reorganization Act of 1939 formed the basis of the modern managerial presidency. Pursuant to the Act, Roosevelt issued three plans to create new offices and agencies to assist him, and to consolidate, eliminate, and reorganize several others. Notably, he created the Executive Office of the President including the Bureau of the Budget (later renamed the Office of Management and Budget). *See, e.g.,* Reorganization Plan No. 1 of 1939, 4 Fed. Reg. 2,727 (July 1, 1939). In exchange, Congress received its first legislative veto power (the authority for one chamber to invalidate agency actions by resolution), and a slew of independent agencies were exempted from the President's newfound reorganization authority.

The Reorganization Act addressed some of the managerial problems caused by the federal bureaucracy's rapid expansion during the 1930s, but it did not address other weighty concerns. Even those who accepted the benefits of bureaucratic expertise and specialization lamented the absence of uniform national standards and procedures to control federal administrative decision-making. Moreover, the American Bar Association and other New Deal critics decried agencies' mixture of prosecutorial, quasi-judicial, and quasi-legislative functions, which, in their view, upended constitutional principles of separation of powers and due process, infringed on individual property rights, and largely immunized agency determinations of law and fact from judicial correction. In response to these and other concerns, the House and Senate passed the Walter-Logan bill in 1939. Among other things, Walter-Logan would have created a cause of action, and uniform procedures and standards, for judicial review of agency actions. Although President Roosevelt vetoed the bill, he and his allies recognized the need for some type of reform. He accordingly instructed his Attorney General, Homer Cummings, to conduct a thorough study of the federal bureaucracy. In 1941, the Attorney General's Committee on Administrative Procedure produced a lengthy report that would form the basis for subsequent legislative efforts. Continued focus on the issue of administrative reform would have to wait, however, until after World War II.

6. The Administrative Procedure Act

President Harry S. Truman signed the Administrative Procedure Act ("APA") into law on June 11, 1946. Currently codified at 5 U.S.C. § 551 *et seq.*, it is frequently described as the constitution of the federal administrative state. As explained by the U.S. Department of Justice's highly influential report describing its provisions, Congress intended that the APA serve four basic purposes:

1. To require agencies to keep the public currently informed of their organization, procedures, and rules (sec. 3).
2. To provide for public participation in the rule making process (sec. 4).
3. To prescribe uniform standards for the conduct of formal rule making (Sec. 4(b)) and adjudicatory proceedings (sec. 5). . . .
4. To restate the law of judicial review (sec. 10).

U.S. DEP'T OF JUSTICE, ATTORNEY GENERAL'S MANUAL ON THE ADMINISTRATIVE PROCEDURE ACT 9 (1947) [hereinafter, the ATTORNEY GENERAL'S MANUAL]. Unless a non-APA statute says otherwise, the APA sets uniform default procedures for federal administrative decision-making. Although the Act's reach is broad, it is far from unlimited. Section 2 (5 U.S.C. § 551) excludes several governmental units from the Act's definition of "agency," including Congress, the federal judiciary, territorial governments, and specified military bodies. Other provisions exempt particular governmental functions.

Congress organized the APA around two core agency functions: rulemaking and adjudication. "Rulemaking," roughly speaking, is the process by which agencies formulate and publish general rules that regulate the future conduct of private persons and entities. It is the administrative version of legislating. "Adjudication"—the process by which agencies interpret pre-existing rules and apply them to particular circumstances and conduct—can take many forms. For instance, it can mimic the dispute resolution function performed by courts, involve an agency decision to fund a particular governmental initiative or project, or describe how an agency official determines an applicant's eligibility for governmentally conferred benefits.

Section 3 (5 U.S.C. § 552) facilitates greater transparency by directing agencies to make their rules, orders, organizational and decision-making structures, and other records publicly available (subject to confidentiality protections). In response to growing concerns about government secrecy during the early years of the Cold War, Congress substantially augmented the section in 1966. A begrudging President Lyndon B. Johnson signed the bill into law under a new (and now well-known) name: The Freedom of Information Act ("FOIA").

APA Sections 4 through 8 (5 U.S.C. §§ 553-558) set out default formal and informal procedures for conducting rulemaking and adjudication. Informal rulemaking and adjudication constitute the lion's share of the work undertaken by agencies. Due in large measure to their variation in forms and uses, Congress declined to adopt procedural defaults for informal adjudications. Section 4 (5 U.S.C. § 553) does, however, adopt several default procedures for informal rulemaking that guarantee the public notice and a chance to express its views on new regulations being considered by agencies. These provisions do not extend to all rulemaking, however. Military and foreign affairs functions as well as decisions relating to agency management and personnel, property, loans, grants, benefits, or government contracts are excluded (5 U.S.C. § 553(a)).

Agencies must use formal procedures when a statute other than the APA clearly requires agency decisions be made "on the record after opportunity for an agency hearing." Congress expected that agencies would rarely use these procedures, whether for rulemaking or for adjudications. It is for this reason that Section 5 (5 U.S.C. § 554(c)) guarantees parties an opportunity to informally resolve disputes through settlement offers and other means developed by agencies. When formal adjudications are required, they feature trial-like public hearings, oral presentation of evidence by interested parties, cross-examination of witnesses, and creation of an official evidentiary record. Section 5 adopts several additional measures to ensure that agencies conduct their formal adjudications with actual and apparent impartially. It separates the functions of hearing and deciding disputes from the function of investigating and prosecuting them on behalf of the agency. It also forbids *ex parte* contacts—off-the-record communications between a party and an administrative law judge—without giving all parties a chance to participate (5 U.S.C. § 557(d)). Additionally, it provides for administrative appeals within agencies of initial decisions rendered by its administrative law judges (5 U.S.C. § 557(b)).

Section 10 (5 U.S.C. §§ 701-706) directs courts to review the legality of agency actions unless they are committed to the agency's discretion by law or some non-APA statute precludes their review. To bolster protections of individual rights that might be affected by agency actions, Section 10 effects a partial waiver of the United States' sovereign immunity from lawsuits. It entitles "[a]ny person suffering legal wrong because of any action, or adversely affected or aggrieved by such action within the meaning of any relevant statute" to sue the allegedly offending agency. As explained in Chapter 10, the modern version of APA Section 10 directs courts to apply any of several review standards depending on the nature of the agency decision challenged by the plaintiff (5 U.S.C. § 706(2)).

Of the APA's provisions, those relating to judicial review generated the most controversy. Conservative members of the House and Senate argued that Section 10 realized a goal they and their allies had pursued since the New Deal's inception: it restricted agencies' discretion by greatly expanding judicial review of their actions. The Truman Administration, by contrast, asserted that Section 10 merely preserved the status quo and thus did nothing to expand the judiciary's power over the federal bureaucracy. This position was most clearly expressed in the ATTORNEY GENERAL'S MANUAL, which asserted that "[t]he provisions of section 10 constitute a general restatement of the principles of judicial review embodied in many statutes and judicial decisions." *See* ATTORNEY GENERAL'S MANUAL at 93. As the materials in this book will show, courts and scholars continue to wrestle with this issue today. In the end, the APA reflects a compromise between those who wanted to rein in administrative discretion and those who wanted to preserve administrative flexibility, apolitical expertise, and the development of bureaucratic capabilities nurtured during the New Deal. *See generally* McNollgast, *The*

Political Origins of the Administrative Procedure Act, 15 J.L. ECON. & ORG. 180 (1999).

7. The Great Society and the Emergence of Social Regulation

The decades following passage of the APA saw several significant changes in regulatory policy, agency decision-making practices, and judicial review. The federal regulatory agenda turned from issues of economic regulation to social regulation, highlighting issues of health, safety, poverty, and civil rights. After World War II and the Korean War, many Americans came to realize that clean air, water, and lands were finite resources that humankind could neither waste nor poison with impunity. Publication of Rachel Carson's SILENT SPRING in 1962 spotlighted the devastating environmental effects of chemical pesticide use. In 1969, *Time Magazine* published photos of the Cuyahoga River near Cleveland, Ohio, which was so saturated with industrial waste that it (not for the first time) spontaneously burst into flames. Innumerable species of wildlife were being driven toward extinction by unrelenting habitat destruction. These and other widely covered stories of environmental degradation increased pressure to balance economic prosperity with preservation of the natural world and the species living within it. Congress passed a raft of statutes between the 1950s and 1970s in response. It enacted the Air Pollution Control Act of 1955, the Clean Air Act of 1963, the Water Quality Act of 1965, the Air Quality Control Act of 1967, the National Environmental Policy Act of 1969, the Clean Air Act of 1970, the Clean Water Act in 1972, and the Safe Drinking Water Act in 1974, among others. In Reorganization Plan No. 3 dated July 9, 1970, President Richard M. Nixon announced his plan to consolidate the federal government's disparate environmental research, standard-setting, and enforcement efforts into a single Environmental Protection Agency.

Similar efforts were made to address safety in the workplace, on the roads, and in consumer products. For instance, Congress passed the Federal Coal Mine Health and Safety Act of 1969 and the Consumer Product Safety Act of 1972. It also created a bevy of new federal agencies in the 1960s and 1970s focused on these issues: the Department of Transportation (1966), the National Transportation Safety Board (1966), the National Highway Traffic Safety Administration (1970), the Occupational Safety and Health Administration (1971), the Consumer Product Safety Commission (1972), and the Mine Safety and Health Administration (1977). At the same time, Congress expanded the jurisdiction of several preexisting agencies like the FDA to better protect the public from harm.

The 1960s also witnessed the burgeoning of what Professor Charles A. Reich famously dubbed "the new property." According to Reich's account, a cornucopia of government-conferred entitlements sprung up alongside the privately generated wealth recognized and protected by the common law. "For a large number of people, government is a direct source of income although they hold no public job. Their eligibility arises from legal status. Examples are Social Security benefits, unemployment compensation, aid to dependent children, veterans benefits, and the whole scheme of state and local welfare." *See* Charles A. Reich, *The New Property*, 73 YALE L.J. 733, 734 (1964). Providing people with the financial means to sustain themselves marked a clear shift from the traditional ambit of administrative activity, which focused on regulating private conduct through investigations, enforcement actions, sanctions, and other similarly coercive activities.

President Lyndon B. Johnson's ambitious "Great Society" initiative, announced in 1964, expanded both the scope and variety of public entitlements. To execute what Johnson called a "war on poverty," the Great Society included expansions to Social Security and disability insurance while adding new programs such as Medicare and Medicaid. Its cornerstone was the Economic Opportunity Act of 1964, which created the Office of Economic Opportunity to administer several anti-poverty initiatives. In addition to waging a war on poverty, the Johnson Administration waged legislative battles to combat social inequality. Several pieces of Great Society legislation—the Civil Rights Acts of 1964 and 1968, the Voting Rights Act of 1965, the Immigration and Nationality Act of 1965, the Elementary and Secondary Education Act of 1965—advanced civil rights by targeting various forms of noneconomic hardship and discrimination. Taken together, these efforts pointed to a broader and enduring role for the federal government in Americans' daily lives.

With regard to administrative practice, the methods by which agencies formulated regulatory policy also shifted dramatically during this period. Rulemaking, while not exactly rare, was still uncommon in the years immediately following passage of the APA. Several agencies to whom Congress had granted rulemaking authority—including the NLRB and the FTC—declined to use it, opting instead to develop general regulatory policy through case-by-case adjudication. Administrative theorists met such persistent refusals to employ rulemaking with bemusement. *See, e.g.*, Cornelius J. Peck, *The Atrophied Rule-Making Powers of the National Labor Relations Board*, 70 YALE L.J. 729 (1961).

This indifference toward rulemaking reversed itself during the 1960s and 1970s. Many of the statutes Congress passed during this period expanded the regulatory responsibilities of existing agencies, while other statutes required newly created agencies to utilize informal rulemaking. Case-by-case rule promulgation was thought to be too slow to keep pace with the expected increase in regulatory activity, and rulemaking emerged as a preferred method for agencies to manage their swelling policymaking workloads. The shift toward rulemaking also was driven by numerous concerns about adjudication's shortcomings. A recurring criticism was that agencies undermined basic fairness when they created and enforced new rules in the same adjudication. Even if agencies solicited public comment (through amicus briefs and other means), critics believed that such common law rulemaking robbed private parties of the chance to know the legal consequences of their actions before taking them. Moreover, critics asserted that adjudication produced inconsistent standards and disparate results in factually similar cases. Unlike courts engaged in common law rulemaking, agencies could avoid these problems because Congress granted them the authority to promulgate prospective and comprehensive rules. *See, e.g., NLRB v. Majestic Weaving Co.*, 355 F.2d 854, 860-61 (2d. Cir. 1966). Separately, critics expressed fears that too many federal agencies were "captured." Rather than working in the public interest or to advance the broad policy goals set by Congress, agency decision-making evolved to protect the interests of the private entities whose conduct they were supposed to police. *See generally* RALPH NADER, UNSAFE AT ANY SPEED: THE DESIGNED-IN DANGERS OF THE AMERICAN AUTOMOBILE (1965); HENRY J. FRIENDLY, THE FEDERAL ADMINISTRATIVE AGENCIES: THE NEED FOR BETTER DEFINITION OF STANDARDS (1962); *cf.* George J. Stigler, *The Theory of Economic Regulation*, 2 BELL J. ECON. & MGMT. SCI. 3 (1971).

Proponents of expanded rulemaking argued that it could effectively address many of these concerns. It required broad solicitation of public input and disclosure of a rulemaking record, procedural features thought to improve the information on which an agency based their policy choices, increased awareness of agency activities, and reduced industry influence. It also required publication of proposed rules and final rules, providing regulated parties with ample notice of what the law may eventually require of them. The rate of agency rulemaking increased accordingly during the 1960s and 1970s. *See* Reuel E. Schiller, *Rulemaking's Promise: Administrative Law and Legal Culture in the 1960s and 1970s*, 53 ADMIN. L. REV. 1139, 1147 (2001) (reporting that the number of rulemaking notices published in the Federal Register increased from 41 per month in 1960 to 190 per month by the end of the 1970s). The Supreme Court signaled its approval of this shift to rulemaking, largely leaving the choice between it and adjudication to administrative discretion. *See, e.g., NLRB v. Bell Aerospace Co.*, 416 U.S. 267 (1974); *cf. SEC v. Chenery Corp.*, 332 U.S. 194, 202 (1947) (since agencies have "the ability to make new law prospectively through the exercise of [their] rule-making powers, [they] have less reason [than courts] to rely upon *ad hoc* adjudication to formulate new standards of conduct").

Even while the courts broadly supported more widespread adoption of the agency rulemaking process, they significantly stepped up their efforts to review the decisions produced by it. Whatever the benefits of rulemaking, it did not eliminate all concerns about agency rationality, capture, or protection of individual rights. Even if they could, agencies did not completely abandon their use of adjudication as a policymaking tool. This left an accountability gap that courts filled by recognizing additional legal challenges to agency actions. For example, the Supreme Court allowed challenges to agency rules before agencies could enforce them. *See Abbott Laboratories v. Gardner*, 387 U.S. 136 (1967). It also generously interpreted the APA as granting standing to persons "adversely affected or aggrieved" by agency actions as long as their interests fell within the zone of those Congress considered in a relevant statute. *See Association of Data Processing Serv. Organizations, Inc. v. Camp*, 397 U.S. 150 (1970).

The Supreme Court and the D.C. Circuit also adopted a more searching approach to review of agency policymaking during this period. They developed the so-called "hard look" review standard for testing whether agencies policy judgments made in informal rulemakings were arbitrary or capricious under APA § 706(2)(A). Prior to the 1970s, courts applied a minimum rationality test to agency findings of fact and policy judgments that was similar to the "rational basis" test applied to federal legislation. *See, e.g., Pacific States Box & Basket Co. v. White*, 296 U.S. 176, 186 (1935) ("[W]here the regulation is within the scope of authority legally delegated, the presumption of the existence of facts justifying its specific exercise attaches alike to statutes, to municipal ordinances, and to orders of administrative bodies."); Merrick B. Garland, *Deregulation and Judicial Review*, 98 Harv. L. Rev. 505, 532 n. 146 (1985). Courts would check whether agencies followed the proper procedures in making their factual findings and policy choices, upholding them unless they were wholly irrational. As initially conceived, the new "hard look" standard required more: agencies had to consider salient issues, consider alternative approaches to addressing them, and explain their final decisions. Courts would ensure these steps were followed. *See Citizens to Preserve Overton Park, Inc. v. Volpe*, 401 U.S. 402, 416 (1971) ("[T]he [reviewing] court must consider whether the decision was based on a consideration of the relevant factors and whether there has been a clear error of judgment. Although this inquiry into the facts is to be searching and careful, the ultimate standard of review is a narrow one.") (internal citations omitted).

This reflected the view that the Judiciary had an obligation "to do more than simply check that agencies had followed the procedural requirements of the APA and ensure that they were acting within the powers that Congress had delegated to them." Schiller, *supra,* at 1156. According to Judge Harold Leventhal of the D.C. Circuit, the APA required courts to scrutinize the substance of agency actions to ensure rationality and to protect the public interest. A court's "supervisory function calls on [it] to intervene . . . if the court becomes aware . . . that the agency has not really taken a 'hard look' at the salient problems, and has not genuinely engaged in reasoned decision-making." *Greater Boston Television Corp. v. FCC*, 444 F.2d 841, 851 (D.C. Cir. 1970). Eventually, however, "hard look" evolved to be even more demanding, leading courts to scrutinize the *quality* of agencies' factual findings and policy judgments. Not only did agencies have to consider salient facts and alternatives, courts required them to *adequately consider* the evidence in the rulemaking record and to provide *reasoned explanations* for their final actions based on that evidence. *See* Garland, *supra,* at 533.

In addition to engaging in more substantive scrutiny of agency policy-making, courts during the 1970s formulated and imposed additional procedural requirements on rulemaking not otherwise required by the Constitution, by Congress, or by the agencies themselves. For instance, the D.C. Circuit imposed limitations on agencies' *ex parte* (off-the-record) contacts with private parties outside of the informal rulemaking notice-and-comment period, even when the APA or some other statute imposed no such requirement. *See, e.g., Home Box Office, Inc. v. FCC*, 567 F.2d 9 (D.C. Cir. 1977). This and other judicially imposed procedural requirements led some to fear that courts were improperly increasing the costs of agency policymaking while decreasing the flexibility Congress intended to grant them. By the end of the decade, the Supreme Court put a stop to this particular method of controlling agency decision-making. *See Vermont Yankee Nuclear Power Corp. v. NRDC*, 435 U.S. 519 (1978). Courts nevertheless continue to review the substance of agency policy choices to ensure reasonableness and fidelity to the public interest.

Finally, the Supreme Court extended judicial protections to the government-provided entitlements Professor Reich labeled "the new property." The Fifth and Fourteenth Amendments prohibit federal and state governments, respectively, from depriving persons of "life, liberty, or property without due process of law." Historically, courts narrowly defined the property protected by due process as those interests recognized at common law (e.g., rights to control real property and physical property, or to be secure in one's physical person). Due process required the government to afford some predeprivation procedures—notice, an opportunity to be heard, and a neutral decision-maker—before harming those interests. By contrast, courts considered legislatively conferred entitlements—public assistance, government employment, licenses or permissions, etc.—to be mere "privileges" unprotected by due process and revocable at will by the government. Courts started to extend some due process protections to government entitlements starting in the early 1960s, and fully recognized them as "property" for due process purposes by the early 1970s. *See Goldberg v. Kelly*, 397 U.S. 254 (1970) (holding that eligible recipients hold a property interest in welfare payments protected by due process); *Perry v. Sindermann*, 408 U.S. 593 (1972) (holding that employment at state university can constitute property for due process purposes). Not only did this expanded view of property enhance judicial oversight of administrative decision-making (particularly in the context of informal adjudication), it helped to entrench the aims of the Great Society by increasing the difficulty with which government could scale back legislature-provided subsistence (in whatever form).

8. The Modern Era and Deregulation

The 1960s and 1970s witnessed the greatest expansion of federal administrative power since the New Deal. Perhaps because of this, deep dissatisfaction with the size, power, and priorities of the administrative state started brewing well before Ronald Reagan took the presidential oath of office on January 20, 1981. More so than social regulation, economic regulation was targeted for attack throughout the 1970s. Its defenders often pointed to the harms it prevented. For instance, unregulated markets would produce monopolistic consolidations of economic power. This, in turn, would result in consumer abuses such as supracompetitive pricing. To prevent these problems, federal agencies often relied on command-and-control regulations — permissions, prohibitions, performance standards, and enforcement actions — rather than financial incentives. These measures, it was argued, would ultimately protect the interests of the public as a whole.

A line of criticism from political scientists, economists, legal scholars, and others argued that such public goods justifications for economic regulation did not line up with how federal agencies actually operated. Rather than advancing the public interest, they argued that agencies instead *increased* social harm by protecting regulated industries from competition and introducing a host of inefficiencies into the marketplace. In a particularly influential article published in 1971, George Stigler offered an economic explanation for this alleged behavior: regulation is a product like any other in the market, and it is "sold" by administrative agencies. Like any seller of a product, agencies will supply it to those who provide the most in exchange for its receipt. Typically, businesses (particularly large ones) are the highest bidders. They can reward politicians with campaign contributions, lucrative employment for political allies, and a host of other financial benefits. All of this led to Stigler's succinct theory of economic regulation: "regulation is acquired by the industry and is designed and operated primarily for its benefit." In this deeply pessimistic narrative, anticompetitive biases and bureaucratic self-interest are embedded within the very structures and processes of the administrative state. The public, by contrast, is outmatched; it suffers from numerous collective action problems that make it much less effective at rewarding or punishing regulators or politicians. *See* Stigler, *supra,* at 3. The solution would be to dismantle the protectionist policies that inevitably resulted from even well-intentioned regulatory policies.

A separate line of criticism that emerged during this time attacked the basic rationality of agency decision-making. More and more, courts were willing to scrutinize the factual and analytical underpinnings of agency policymaking to ensure its basic "reasonableness." *See, e.g., Citizens to Preserve Overton Park, Inc. v. Volpe,* 401 U.S. 402 (1971); *Rodway v. United States Dep't of Agriculture,* 514 F.2d 809, 817 (D.C. Cir. 1975). Additionally, critics argued that agencies paid too little attention to the costs of the policies they adopted. They routinely adopted regulations without first assessing whether their benefits outweighed their costs to governments, industries, or individuals. This concern was frequently expressed in the environmental context. The Clean Air Act of 1970 prohibited cost consideration in designing national air quality standards. The alleged result was a needless decrease in the productivity and competitiveness of American businesses.

Beginning in the mid-1970s, Presidents, Congress, and federal agencies heeded calls to scale back economic regulation. President Gerald Ford wrote (somewhat dramatically) that "[r]ules and regulations churned out by federal agencies were having a damaging effect on almost every aspect of American life." Martha Derthick & Paul J. Quick, The Politics of Deregulation 29-30 (1985) (quoting Gerald R. Ford, A Time to Heal: The Autobiography of Gerald R. Ford 271 (1979)). Congress passed several pieces of legislation to decrease government control over industry in the hopes of increasing market competition, including the Securities Acts Amendments of 1975, the Airline Deregulation Act of 1978, and the Depositary Institutions Deregulation and Monetary Control Act of 1980. The Interstate Commerce Commission, the Civil Aeronautics Board, and the Federal Communications Commission all assumed deregulatory postures toward the transportation, airline, and telecommunications industries, respectively. The Civil Aeronautics Board would be abolished in 1985. The Interstate Commerce Commission, the first federal regulatory agency, would be abolished ten years later.

The movement toward deregulation did not end with Congress rewriting statutes or abolishing federal agencies. Echoing calls from Teddy Roosevelt during the Progressive Era and Franklin D. Roosevelt during the New Deal Era, presidents in the 1970s and 1980s pushed for more analytical rigor in agency decision-making and for more direct oversight of the federal bureaucracy as a general matter. In 1971, President Nixon established a "Quality of Life Review" process through a memorandum to the heads of executive departments and agencies. It required that drafts of "significant" proposed and final rules be submitted to the Office of Management and Budget ("OMB"), which would distribute them to other agencies for comments. President Ford issued Executive Order 11821, in 1974, a tentative step toward presidential control and adoption of cost-benefit analysis in agency policymaking. It required "all major legislative proposals, regulations, and rules emanating from the executive branch of the Government include a statement certifying that the inflationary impact of such actions on the Nation has been carefully considered." Exec. Order No. 11821, 39 Fed. Reg. 41501 (Nov. 27, 1974). Based on these statements, OMB would compare a rule's expected benefits with its overall costs to consumers, business, and the government. President Carter followed this in 1978 with Executive Order 12044. Limited to Executive Agencies, the order directed them to make rules "as simple and clear as possible," to "achieve legislative goals effectively and efficiently," and to avoid "unnecessary burdens on the economy, on individuals, on public or private organizations, or on State and local governments." Exec. Order No, 12044, 43 Fed. Reg. 12661 (Mar. 23, 1978). It imposed procedures to improve oversight of agency rulemaking by agency heads and was the first to direct agencies to review their existing regulations for retention, modification, or repeal.

During his run for the presidency, Ronald Reagan promised to go much further than his predecessors in scaling back the number and scope of federal regulations. This pledge was encapsulated in one of the more familiar lines from his inaugural address: "Government is not the solution to our problem, government is the problem." He issued Executive Order 12291, the blueprint for his deregulatory agenda, shortly thereafter. Unlike similar executive orders issued by Reagan's predecessors, E.O. 12291 explicitly required executive agencies (but not independent agencies) to apply cost-benefit analysis to major rules (as measured by their economic and competitive impact) and to develop regulatory impact analyses ("RIAs") for each. This was a controversial decision. From Reagan's perspective, development of sound public policy required assurance that regulatory benefits exceeded their costs. He also believed that prior administrations' failure to do this had forced the country to spend billions of dollars on regulations that provided no or negative returns on investment.

Rather than using the tool to make regulation more effective and efficient, critics argued that the administration would use cost-benefit analysis to undermine social and economic regulation (particularly environmental, health, and safety protections) substantively disfavored by the President and commercial interests. *See* Philip Shabecoff, *Reagan Order on Cost-Benefit Analysis Stirs Economic and Political Debate*, N.Y. TIMES, Nov. 7, 1981, § 2, at 28. E.O. 12291 also situated OMB — and hence the Executive Office of the President — squarely in the middle of the rulemaking process by mandating that agencies submit their past and expected major rules and RIAs to OMB. The OMB Director could return proposed rules to the agency with requests for additional information or with suggested changes, and final rules could not be published in the Federal Register until OMB completed its review. As (roughly) measured by the number of pages in the Federal Register each year, the overall level of federal rulemaking declined over the course of Reagan's presidency. *See Federal Register Pages Published 1936-2019*, FED. REGISTER, https://s3.amazonaws.com/production.uploads.wordpress.federalregister.gov/uploads/2020/04/01123259/pagesPublished2019.pdf.

Reagan's successors adopted and expanded upon the model of OMB-managed rulemaking, cost-benefit analysis, and close scrutiny of regulatory burdens established by E.O. 12291. *See* Exec. Order No. 12866, *Regulatory Planning and Review*, 58 Fed. Reg. 51735 (Oct. 4, 1993) (Bill Clinton); Exec. Order No. 13422, *Further Amendment to Executive Order 12866 on Regulatory Planning and Review*, 72 Fed. Reg. 2763 (Jan. 23, 2007) (George W. Bush); Exec. Order No. 13563, *Improving Regulation and Regulatory Review*, 76 Fed. Reg. 3821 (Jan. 21, 2011) (Barack Obama); Exec. Order No. 13777, *Enforcing the Regulatory Reform Agenda*, 82 Fed. Reg. 12285

(Mar. 1, 2017) (Donald J. Trump). Notably, these executive orders apply only to executive agencies and not to independent agencies, which, as their name indicates, are somewhat insulated from the President's control. Nevertheless, President Obama attempted to influence them more than did his predecessors. In E.O. 13579, titled "Regulation and Independent Regulatory Agencies," he exhorted them to comply with the directives he issued in E.O. 13563.

Presidents were not alone in trying to cabin agencies' power. In several decisions, the Supreme Court split on whether the administrative state violated the Constitution's commitment to separate powers. "Formalists" asserted that each Branch should exercise only the power vested in it by the Constitution. This position had the overall practical effect of limiting rather than expanding administrative authority. The Court's "functionalists," by contrast, took a more flexible view of separated powers. Rather than forbidding a Branch from even minor exercises of authority primarily held by the others, functionalists examined each instance of administrative action for whether it usurped or unduly interfered with the prerogatives of a coordinate Branch.

In a closely related vein, the late twentieth century also saw a relaunch of the nondelegation wars. As discussed above, the Supreme Court repeatedly invalidated New Deal legislation that, in its view, delegated too much legislative authority to the federal bureaucracy. The Court had not invalidated a single piece of federal legislation on nondelegation grounds since the 1930s, and Congress routinely passed legislation granting broad policymaking powers to agencies in the decades that followed. Sometimes these delegations were explicit; the statutory language directed agencies to make policies consistent with the statutory scheme established by Congress. Others, however, were less obvious; Congress passed regulatory statutes that were silent or ambiguous on key issues. Over time, the Court had adopted differing approaches to such statutes. At times it indicated that resolving statutory silence or ambiguity was principally the job of Article III courts, though they would consider persuasive constructions offered by expert agencies. At other times, the Court seemed to indicate that Congress intended that courts defer to how expert agencies interpreted such statutes. The seminal case of *Chevron U.S.A., Inc. v. NRDC*, 467 U.S. 837 (1984) opted for the latter course, and in doing so, became one of the most cited Supreme Court cases of all time. In a unanimous (6-0) opinion, it construed a statute's silence or ambiguity as an implicit delegation of policymaking authority from Congress to the agency charged with administering it. In the face of such a delegation, courts must accept — must defer to — the agency's interpretation as long as it is "reasonable." Though invoking *Chevron* deference less often than it probably could, the Court has expanded its reach to other contexts. *See, e.g., Auer v. Robbins*, 519 U.S. 452 (1997) (federal courts must defer to agencies' interpretations of their own ambiguous regulations unless plainly erroneous or inconsistent with the regulation or underlying statute). This trend has been criticized as exacerbating significant separation-of-powers problems already posed by the modern administrative state, and as being one of the single greatest impediments to continued federal deregulation. Numerous bills have been introduced to overturn *Chevron* and *Auer*. Supreme Court Justices, most notably Neil Gorsuch, have also been vocal in their criticism of these deference doctrines. *See, e.g.* Jamelle C. Sharpe, *Delegation and its Discontents*, 64 WAYNE ST. L. REV. 185 (2018) (discussing recent judicial criticisms of and legislative efforts to abolish the administrative deference doctrines).

As of this writing, two other significant trends in administrative law and regulatory policy bear mentioning. The first involves innovations in information technology. To many, "the most important current developments are not legal in nature; they are technological." BREYER ET AL., *supra,* at 29. Agencies have now moved many rulemaking functions online, allowing members of the public to have their say on proposed regulatory policies simply by accessing the Internet. Almost all agencies now have websites through which they engage with the public and from which the public can access a seemingly limitless amount of information on agencies' activities.

The second involves congressional oversight of the Executive Branch. Congress possesses a host of investigative, monitoring, and supervisory tools for ensuring that administrative officials execute federal laws, programs, and policies consistent with legislative intent. Though the Constitution nowhere mentions Congress' oversight authority, the Supreme Court has inferred it from Congress' array of enumerated legislative powers. *See Watkins v. United States*, 354 U.S. 178 (1957); *McGrain v. Daugherty*, 273 U.S. 135 (1927). Congress could not adequately fulfill its legislative responsibilities without keeping tabs on the Executive's activities. Typically, administrative officials voluntarily comply with Congress' investigative requests, understanding the importance of maintaining good relations with those who set their budgets. Even when there has been substantial disagreement between the Branches on the propriety of some requests, they have worked out compromises that dislodge at least some information. Recently, however, friction between the House of Representatives and the Trump Administration has thrown the viability of congressional oversight into question. The Administration has repeatedly refused to comply with requests for documents and testimony from government officials, including but not limited to White House personnel. House-issued contempt orders and federal lawsuits to force compliance with subpoenas have met with very mixed results. *See, e.g.*, Andrew Desiderio, *House Holds William Barr, Wilbur Ross in Criminal Contempt of Congress*, POLITICO (July 17, 2019, 6:48 PM), https://www.politico.com/story/2019/07/17/house-votes-to-hold-william-barr-wilbur-ross-in-criminal-contempt-of-congress-1418900. In a recent opinion, a split panel of the D.C. Circuit held that the House lacked standing to sue for the testimony of former White House Counsel Donald McGahn. The majority reasoned that federal courts have no authority to engage in "amorphous general supervision" of the government or to "resolve disputes between the Legislative and Executive Branches until their actions harm an entity beyond the federal government." *Committee on the Judiciary of the U.S. House of Representatives v. McGahn*, 951 F.3d 510, 516 (D.C. Cir. 2020) (internal quotations omitted). The full D.C. Circuit vacated the panel's decision, granted rehearing *en banc*, and heard arguments (telephonically) on April 28, 2020.

QUESTION SET 1.1

Review & Synthesis

1. According to the historical narrative above, what are three recurring themes in the development of American administrative law? Can you identify any others?

2. How is the tension between "law" and "discretion" evident in the conflicts between King's Bench and the Court of Chancery in seventeenth-century England? How is it evident in the conflicts between the Roosevelt Administration and the Supreme Court during the early New Deal Era?

3. What was the primary method by which private persons could secure judicial review of administrative decision-making prior to passage of the APA?

4. Has the availability of judicial review of administrative decision-making (the number of ways a private person can challenge agency decision-making in a federal court) expanded or contracted since the Founding Era? Provide some specific examples of that expansion or contraction.

5. What regulatory challenges resulted in Congress establishing the Interstate Commerce Commission in 1887? What features, functions, and/or powers distinguished the ICC from the executive departments established before it?

6. What were the primary bureaucratic reforms undertaken by the Theodore Roosevelt Administration, and why did President Roosevelt advocate for them? How do these reforms parallel the move toward cost-benefit analysis in the 1970s and 1980s?

7. What basic problems of agency decision-making did Congress design the Administrative Procedure Act to address, and around which core agency functions is it organized?

8. How has the President's role in supervising administrative agencies changed over time? Have executive departments and independent agencies been equally affected by these changes?

9. What was the primary method by which agencies developed and adopted new regulatory policies before the 1960s? What alternative policymaking tool came into prominence during the 1960s, and what factors accounted for its increased use?

10. As evidenced by the slew of statutes passed during and after the Great Society initiative, Congress and Presidents Johnson and Nixon clearly concluded that the federal government needed to focus (albeit with different points of emphasis) on issues of inequality, health, and safety. Is that so? Private industry was already developing more effective safety technologies for use in the workplace and on the roads. State and local governments, as well as charities and other private organizations, were already implementing subsistence programs to assist the poor. In light of these efforts, what justifications can you identify for a uniquely *federal* response to these concerns?

11. What is agency "capture," and how did concerns regarding it affect administrative law in the 1970s and 1980s?

12. Congress has often incorporated "command-and-control" provisions into its economic and social regulation statutes. These provisions empower administrative agencies to grant permissions to, enforce prohibitions against, and set minimum behavioral standards for private parties engaged in regulated activities. For example, the now-defunct Interstate Commerce Commission determined the reasonableness of rates charged by common carriers. The Environmental Protection Agency sets and enforces minimum standards for ambient air quality. The Occupational Safety and Health Administration does the same for workplace health and safety. Must the federal government employ such coercive methods to achieve its policy goals? Can you think of other ways Congress might do so?

B. OVERVIEW OF THE MODERN ADMINISTRATIVE STATE

1. Organization

As you will recall from your course on Constitutional Law, the first three articles of the Constitution establish the three core powers of the federal government: the legislative, executive, and judicial powers. The first three articles also vest those powers in three governmental repositories: Congress, the presidency, and the courts. No constitutional provision expressly authorizes or expressly forbids establishment of the administrative state in its present form. As the history recounted in the previous subsection shows, its existence is better attributed to ambiguous constitutional text, social and economic exigencies, political expediency, and popular demand. As Justice Robert H. Jackson famously wrote several years after passage of the Administrative Procedure Act:

> The rise of administrative bodies probably has been the most significant legal trend of the last century and perhaps more values today are affected by their decisions than by those of all the courts, review of administrative decisions apart. They also have begun to have important consequences on personal rights. They have become a veritable fourth branch of the Government, which has deranged our three-branch legal theories much as the concept of a fourth dimension unsettles our three-dimensional thinking.

Federal Trade Commission v. Ruberoid Co., 343 U.S. 470, 487 (1952) (Jackson, J., dissenting) (internal citations omitted).

Although Justice Jackson's "fourth branch" referred to administrative bodies located within the Executive Branch, federal agencies can be found within the Legislative and Judicial Branches as well. For example, and as shown in Figure 1.1 below, Congress has created several agencies to support its legislative, oversight, and investigative functions. For instance, the Congressional Budget Office produces economic analysis of and budgetary projections for statutes currently in force, cost estimates of bills approved by congressional committees, and analysis of federal spending and tax programs. The Library of Congress, including the Congressional Research Service, provide research support to congressional committees, Members, and their staffers. Likewise, the Judicial Branch is comprised of more than courthouses; it houses a number of administrative subunits that assist Article III judges in their duties. For instance, the Federal Judicial Center conducts research on the work of the Judiciary, recommends policies and practices to improve its operations, and provides educational and training programs for Judiciary personnel. The United States Sentencing Commission promulgates the

Figure 1.1

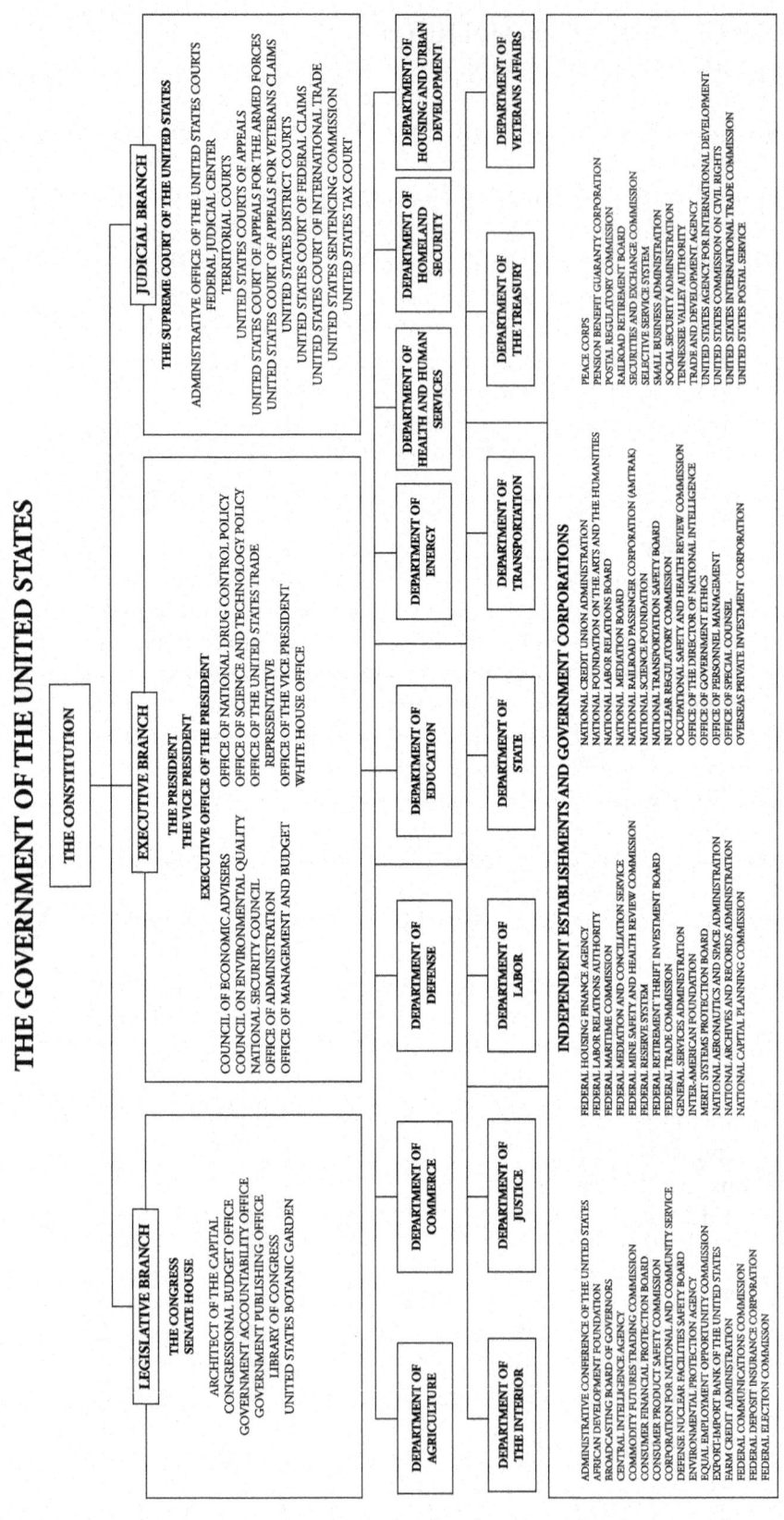

THE GOVERNMENT OF THE UNITED STATES

Source: The U.S. Government Manual.

Federal Sentencing Guidelines, nonbinding parameters for determining the sentences that attach to federal criminal convictions.

Though these legislative and judicial agencies perform important functions within their respective Branches, their responsibilities are largely limited to research, record-keeping, education, and/or advising. They are therefore distinguishable from the administrative bodies assigned to the Executive Branch, the focus of this casebook.

As indicated by Figure 1.1, agencies within the Executive Branch fall into two broad categories: executive departments and independent agencies. Each category has organizational features that distinguish it from the other. Each of the 15 executive departments—Agriculture, Defense, Homeland Security, State, etc.—is headed by a single official who holds the title "Secretary" (with the exception of the Department of Justice, the head of which is the Attorney General). Along with several other government officials,[1] these Secretaries comprise the President's cabinet (his or her primary advisory body). Their terms are coextensive with the President's (i.e., they do not serve past the President's term in office unless invited to do so by his or her successor) and are removable by the President at will (i.e., for any reason or for no reason at all). The Executive Office of the President ("EOP"), created by President Roosevelt's Reorganization Plan No. 1 of 1939 and overseen by the White House Chief of Staff, consists of several councils and offices—such as the National Security Council and the Council of Economic Advisors. They are tasked with assisting the President's execution of his or her duties. The largest unit within the EOP is the Office of Management and Budget ("OMB"), which, as discussed in the historical survey above, spearheads the President's supervision of the executive departments.

> **Cross-Reference**
>
> Congress uses the independent agency structure to insulate regulatory work from political influence, including that of the President. The extent to which Congress can statutorily insulate agency officials from the President—in particular, by limiting the President's power to remove independent agency leadership—is discussed in Chapter 8.

The second organizational category comprises so-called "independent" agencies that are insulated from the President's direct control. "There is no general, widely accepted definition of an independent agency across all government officials, practitioners, and scholarly disciplines...." JENNIFER L. SELIN & DAVID E. LEWIS, ADMINISTRATIVE CONFERENCE OF THE UNITED STATES, SOURCEBOOK OF UNITED STATES EXECUTIVE AGENCIES 42 (2d ed. 2018). Given this lack of consensus, the number of such agencies is the subject to debate. The Federal Register—the official daily publication for federal agency rules and notices—indicates that there are 450 agencies in the federal government. This figure includes executive departments and

---

[1] There are seven such "cabinet-level" officials: the White House Chief of Staff, the U.S. Trade Representative, the Director of National Intelligence, the OMB Director, the Director of the Central Intelligence Agency, the Administrator of the Environmental Protection Agency, and the Administrator of the Small Business Administration.

independent agencies, as well as dozens of other entities like government corporations (e.g., the U.S. Postal Service, the Federal Deposit Insurance Corporation, and the Tennessee Valley Authority). Figure 1.1, taken from the U.S. GOVERNMENT MANUAL identifies 58 independent agents. The U.S. SOURCEBOOK identifies 68. U.S. SOURCEBOOK, *supra* at 45-48.

The label "independent" can be applied both to agencies led by a single person and to agencies led by groups of five to seven members. The former, also referred to as independent executive agencies, are led by a single political appointee holding the title of director (e.g., the CIA Director and the Consumer Financial Protection Bureau Director) or administrator (e.g., the EPA Administrator and the SBA Administrator). The "independent" status of these agencies stems from their establishment outside of any executive departments. Their directors and administrators are thus independent from the cabinet secretaries. This distinguishes them from other agencies led by directors or administrators, like the Federal Bureau of Investigation (housed within the Department of Justice) or OSHA (housed within the Department of Labor). Importantly, however, they are not independent from the President. *See* Angel Manuel Moreno, *Presidential Coordination of the Independent Regulatory Process*, 8 ADMIN. L.J. AM. U. 461, 471-472 (1994); Geoffrey P. Miller, *Independent Agencies*, 1986 SUP. CT. REV. 41, 50. Moreover, and like cabinet secretaries, they are typically removable by the President at will.

The second variety of independent agency is led by a multimember commission or board (e.g., the Federal Trade Commission, the National Labor Relations Board, and the Federal Communications Commission). Like the leaders of executive departments and independent executive agencies, commissioners and board members are nominated by the President and confirmed by the Senate. The conditions of their appointments, however, are quite different. They serve fixed terms that are not tied to, and are often longer than, the President's four-year term of office. These terms are staggered, such that the President would normally be unable to fill a majority of a board's or commission's seats in a single term. They cannot be removed by the President except "for cause," typically defined as incapacity, inefficiency, neglect of duty, or malfeasance. Finally, most boards and commissions require bipartisan membership; the President is statutorily barred from making appointments solely from his or her own political party. Together, these innovations are intended to insulate these agencies from political influence, the President's included. In that respect, these agencies are more "independent" than executive independent agencies. As a practical matter, one can question the extent to which these structural features facilitate true political independence. For instance, a high turnover rate in an agency's leadership might allow the President to appoint a majority of its members. A President's reelection to a second four-year term (the rule rather than the exception over the past 40 years) presents him or her with similar opportunities. As a legal matter, and as discussed in Chapter 8, the courts have placed constitutional significance on the independent agency form. It has been the subject of several Supreme Court decisions interpreting the President's power under the Appointments Clause (Art. II, § 2, cl. 2) to appoint and remove government officials.

2. Functions and Powers

The modern administrative state wields tremendous governmental power over a seemingly endless variety of social and economic activities. As already described, administrative bodies in all three Branches can be tasked with research, record-keeping, educational, and/or advisory responsibilities. Such activities typically do not create, alter, enforce, or apply legal rules affecting anyone outside of the federal government. Accordingly, administrative law seldom focuses on the performance of such tasks. By contrast, Congress frequently vests executive departments and independent agencies with powers closely resembling those vested in the federal government's three Branches. Agencies can wield quasi-legislative authority to promulgate rules that are prospective, generally applicable, and legally binding on private persons and entities. Like the Executive, they can initiate and pursue enforcement actions against private persons and entities alleged to have violated agency rules or the statutes underlying them. Finally, and bearing verisimilitude to the Judiciary, agencies can adjudicate and render judgment in disputes involving private parties and entities. The extent and circumstances under which federal agencies employ such significant governmental authority is one of administrative law's central concerns.

While this casebook references dozens of federal agencies, its materials spotlight the activities of some more than others. The primary reason is that some agencies' actions have been challenged in court more frequently than the actions of others, producing seminal judicial decisions that advance our understanding of administrative law. Two of the most scrutinized agencies in this regard—one an independent executive agency, the other a multimember independent agency—are the Environmental Protection Agency ("EPA") and the National Labor Relations Board ("NLRB"). Established by President Richard M. Nixon's Reorganization Plan No. 3 of 1970, the EPA was tasked with consolidating and coordinating the federal government's various antipollution programs. Congress has since vested it with broad-ranging governmental power to carry out its regulatory mandates. The NLRB was created during the New Deal to implement the collective bargaining provisions of the National Labor Relations Act of 1935.

The following organizational charts and excerpts from the U.S. GOVERNMENT MANUAL describe the EPA's and NLRB's powers and missions. They provide concrete examples of the powers and structures of two important—and very different—federal agencies. The excerpts also provide helpful overviews of two agencies you will encounter several times throughout the casebook.

Figure 1.2

ENVIRONMENTAL PROTECTION AGENCY

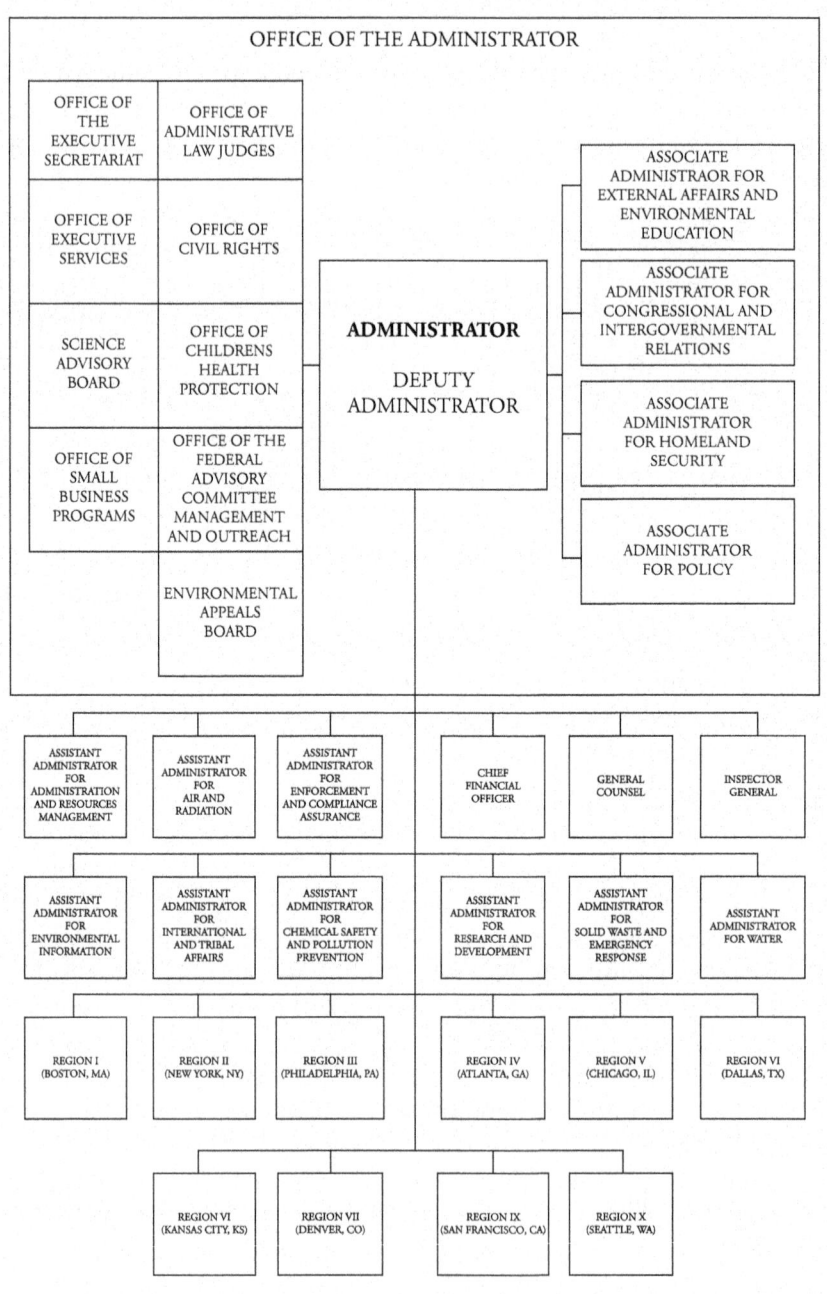

Source: THE U.S. GOVERNMENT MANUAL.

Environmental Protection Agency[2]

1200 Pennsylvania Avenue NW, Washington D.C. 20460
Phone, 202-272-0167, Internet, http://www.epa.gov

The Environmental Protection Agency (EPA) was established in the executive branch as an independent agency pursuant to Reorganization Plan No. 3 of 1970 (5 U.S.C. app.), effective December 2, 1970. The Agency facilitates coordinated and effective governmental action to protect the environment. It also serves as the public's advocate for a livable environment.

CORE FUNCTIONS

Air and Radiation. The Office of Air and Radiation develops air quality policies, programs, regulations, and standards, including emission standards for stationary sources, for mobile sources, and for hazardous air pollutants. It also conducts research and disseminates information on indoor air pollutants. This Office provides technical direction, support, and evaluation of regional air activities; offers training in the field of air pollution control; gives technical assistance to States and agencies operating radiation protection programs; and provides technical support and policy direction to international efforts to reduce global and transboundary air pollution and its effects.

Water. The Office of Water provides agencywide policy, guidance and direction for EPA's water quality, drinking water, groundwater, wetlands protection, marine and estuarine protection, and other related programs. The Office's responsibilities include: program policy development and evaluation; environmental and pollution source standards development; program policy guidance and overview, technical support, and evaluation of regional activities as they relate to drinking water and water programs; development and implementation of programs for education, technical assistance and technology transfer; development of selected demonstration programs; long-term strategic planning and special studies; economic and long-term environmental analysis; and development and implementation of pollution prevention strategies.

Solid Waste and Emergency Response. The Office of Solid Waste and Emergency Response provides agencywide policy, guidance, and direction for EPA's solid waste and emergency response programs. The Office's responsibilities include: development of guidelines and standards for the land disposal of hazardous wastes and for underground storage tanks; technical

---

[2] U.S. Government Manual 340-345 (2014).

assistance in the development, management, and operation of solid waste management activities; analyses on the recovery of useful energy from solid waste; and development and implementation of a program to respond to hazardous waste sites and spills.

Chemical Safety and Pollution Prevention. The Office of Chemical Safety and Pollution Prevention is responsible for EPA's strategies for implementation and integration of the pollution prevention, pesticides, and toxic substances programs and developing and operating Agency programs and policies for assessment and control of pesticides and toxic substances as well as recommending policies and developing operating programs for implementing the Pollution Prevention Act. The Office develops recommendations for EPA's priorities for research, monitoring regulatory and information gathering activities relating to implementing the Pollution Prevention Act, pesticides, and toxic substances; and monitoring and assessing pollution prevention, pesticides and toxic substances program operations in EPA headquarters and regional offices.

Research and Development. The Office of Research and Development conducts leading-edge research and fosters the sound use of science and technology to fulfill EPA's mission to protect human health and safeguard the natural environment. The Office of Research and Development is responsible for the research and development needs of EPA's operating programs and the conduct of an integrated research and development program for the Agency. The Assistant Administrator serves as the Agency's principal science adviser and is responsible for the development, direction, and conduct of a national environmental research, development, and demonstration program in health risk assessment, health effects, engineering and technology, processes and effects, acid rain deposition, monitoring systems, and quality assurance. The Office participates in the development of EPA's policy, standards, and regulations; provides for dissemination of scientific and technical knowledge, including analytical methods, monitoring techniques, and modeling methodologies; and provides technical and scientific advice on agency-wide technical program issues.

Enforcement and Compliance Assurance. The Office of Enforcement and Compliance Assurance serves as the primary adviser to the Administrator in matters concerning enforcement, compliance assurance, and environmental-equity efforts. It also provides the direction and review of all administrative, civil and criminal enforcement, and compliance monitoring and assurance activities. The Office manages the national criminal enforcement program as well as regulatory, site remediation, and Federal facilities enforcement and compliance assurance programs. The Office manages both administrative and judicial activities in the enforcement and compliance programs and provides case preparation and investigative expertise for enforcement activities through the National Enforcement Investigations Center.

Regional Offices. EPA's 10 regional offices are committed to the development of strong local programs for pollution abatement. The regional administrators are responsible for accomplishing, within their regions, the Agency's national program objectives. They develop, propose, and implement an approved regional program for comprehensive and integrated environmental protection activities.

Figure 1.3

NATIONAL LABOR RELATIONS BOARD

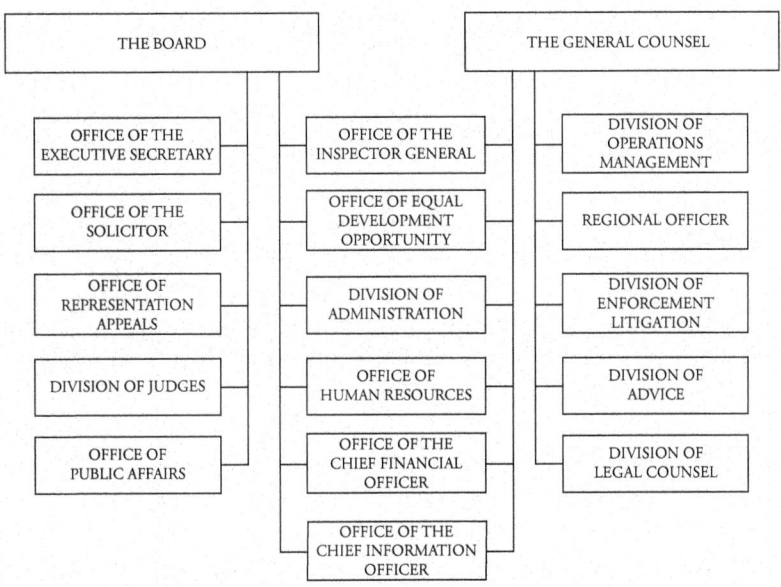

Source: The U.S. Government Manual.

National Labor Relations Board[3]

1099 Fourteenth Street NW., Washington, DC 20570
Phone, 202–273–1000. TDD, 202–273–4300.
Internet, http://www.nlrb.gov.

The National Labor Relations Board (NLRB) is an independent agency created by Congress to administer the National Labor Relations Act of 1935 (Wagner Act; 29 U.S.C. § 167). The Board is authorized to

---

[3] U.S. Government Manual 419-421 (2014).

designate appropriate units for collective bargaining and to conduct secret ballot elections to determine whether employees desire representation by a labor organization.

ACTIVITIES

In addition to preventing and remedying unfair labor practices, the NLRB conducts secret ballot elections among employees in appropriate collective-bargaining units to determine whether or not they desire to be represented by a labor organization in bargaining with employers over wages, hours, and working conditions. It also conducts secret ballot elections among employees who have been covered by a union-security agreement to determine whether or not they wish to revoke their union's authority to make such agreements. In jurisdictional disputes between two or more unions, the Board determines which competing group of workers is entitled to perform the work involved. The regional directors and their staffs process representation, unfair labor practice, and jurisdictional dispute cases. They issue complaints in unfair labor practice cases, seek settlement of unfair labor practice charges, obtain compliance with Board orders and court judgments, and petition district courts for injunctions to prevent or remedy unfair labor practices. The regional directors conduct hearings in representation cases, hold elections pursuant to the agreement of the parties or the decisionmaking authority delegated to them by the Board or pursuant to Board directions, and issue certifications of representatives when unions win or certify the results when they lose employee elections. The regional directors process petitions for bargaining unit clarification, for amendment of certification, and for rescission of a labor organization's authority to make a union-shop agreement. They also conduct national emergency employee referendums. Administrative law judges conduct hearings in unfair labor practice cases, make findings of fact and conclusions of law, and recommend remedies for violations found. Their decisions can be appealed to the Board for a final agency determination. The Board's decisions are subject to review in the U.S. courts of appeals.

QUESTION SET 1.2

Review & Synthesis

1. What are the two types of independent agencies, and how do their structures differ from executive departments and from each other? What do these structural differences seem to assume about the working relationship between agency leadership and the President?

2. Based on the U.S. GOVERNMENT MANUAL entries excerpted above, what types of significant authority—legislative, executive, or judicial—do the EPA and NLRB exercise? On which of these powers does each agency seem to rely most heavily in fulfilling its institutional mission? Which less significant, secondary powers do the EPA and NLRB exercise?

3. Notice that the NLRB General Counsel occupies a position that is coordinate to, rather than subordinate to, the Board in the NLRB organizational chart. The General Counsel is an independent officer within the NLRB, appointed by the President and confirmed by the Senate to a four-year term. He or she is responsible for supervising all NLRB attorneys (other than the Board's legal advisors) and for investigating and prosecuting unfair labor practice cases. What agency functions does that leave the Board to perform, and how do you think the Board and the General Counsel work together to achieve the agency's mission? *See* Further Amendment to Memorandum Describing Authority and Assigned Responsibilities of the General Counsel, Fed. 45,696 (Aug. 1, 2012). Also notice that the EPA General Counsel is subordinate to, rather than coordinate with, the EPA Administrator. What does this say about their organizational relationship and division of functions?

4. Based on the EPA and NLRB organization charts and their entries in the U.S. GOVERNMENT MANUAL, what can you infer about the scope of economic and social activity they regulate? Do they confine themselves to environmental and labor issues, respectively, or do they seem to broaden their reach to adjacent subjects as well?

Application & Analysis

1. As previously mentioned, a few agencies in addition to the EPA and the NLRB will make repeat appearances throughout this casebook. They include the Department of the Interior, the Food and Drug Administration, the Occupational Safety and Health Administration, the Social Security Administration, and the Federal Trade Commission. Read their entries in the most recent edition of the U.S. GOVERNMENT MANUAL (https://www.usgovernmentmanual.gov/). For each of them:
   a. Identify its institutional mission.
   b. Determine whether it is an executive department or an independent agency.
   c. If it is an independent agency, determine whether it is an independent executive agency or a multimember independent agency.
   d. Identify its enabling statute (the statute that created it) and the statutes it is charged with administering.

e. Determine whether Congress has delegated it legislative, executive, and/or judicial power.

Visit the agency's website if the U.S. Government Manual does not provide the information you need.

C. THE ADMINISTRATIVE STATE AND THE SEPARATION OF POWERS

Among the most long-standing and contentious debates in administrative law is whether combining significant governmental authority—legislative, executive, and judicial—under one bureaucratic umbrella violates the Constitution's commitment to the separation of powers. Some have passionately decried this administrative accretion of authority, arguing that it is both illegal and deeply threatening to individual liberty. *See, e.g.,* Philip Hamburger, Is Administrative Law Unlawful? (2014). Others have, just as passionately, rejected this view. *See, e.g.,* Adrian Vermeule, *No*, 93 Texas L. Rev. 1547 (2015) (reviewing Is Administrative Law Unlawful? and rejecting its core arguments).

Legal, philosophical, and practical arguments for and against granting federal agencies legislative, executive, and judicial powers will surface repeatedly throughout this casebook. They all trace back to two more fundamental questions: What does it mean to "separate" powers, and why is their separation relevant to the administrative state? A different but closely related question is what the concept of checks and balances adds to the separation of powers. To critically assess the answers offered to these questions, you must understand the basic precepts governing the inquiry. Accordingly, the following materials address the topic in broad strokes. The first, by British political scientist M. J. C. Vile, provides a theoretical framework for understanding separation-of-powers issues by identifying its key conceptual elements. This is followed by excerpts from *The Federalist Nos.* 47, 48, and 51, which argued that the Constitution translated separation-of-powers and checks-and-balances concepts into a workable blueprint for the proposed national government.

These materials will not answer all separation-of-powers or checks-and-balances questions raised by Congress' delegations of authority to administrative agencies. Indeed, when these questions arise in administrative law cases, they tend to be particularized and context-driven rather than generalized and abstract. Nevertheless, the materials below will provide you with an analytical baseline from which to formulate your own thoughts on these critical issues. They may prove particularly helpful in understanding the materials presented in Part II (agency creation and assignment of powers) and Part IV (control of administrative decision-making), where the Supreme Court repeatedly discusses separation-of-powers principles.

M.J.C. Vile, The Doctrine of the Separation of Powers and Institutional Theory[4]

A "pure doctrine" of the separation of powers might be formulated in the following way: It is essential for the establishment and maintenance of political liberty that the government be divided into three branches or departments, the legislature, the executive, and the judiciary. To each of these three branches there is a corresponding identifiable function of government, legislative, executive, or judicial. Each branch of the government must be confined to the exercise of its own function and not allowed to encroach upon the functions of the other branches. Furthermore, the persons who compose these three agencies of government must be kept separate and distinct, no individual being allowed to be at the same time a member of more than one branch. In this way each of the branches will be a check to the others and no single group of people will be able to control the machinery of the State.

This stark, extreme doctrine we shall then label the "pure doctrine," and other aspects of the thought of individual writers will be seen as modifications of, or deviations from, it. It is true, of course, that the doctrine has rarely been held in this extreme form, and even more rarely been put into practice, but it does represent a "bench-mark," or an "ideal-type," which will enable us to observe the changing development of the historical doctrine, with all its ramifications and modifications, by referring to this constant "pure doctrine." . . .

The first problem presented by the theory outlined above is its commitment to "political liberty," or the exclusion of "arbitrary power." Clearly the viability of the whole approach may turn upon the definition of liberty chosen. Thus perhaps one of the most persuasive general criticisms of the doctrine is that it has been associated with an essentially negative view of political liberty, one too concerned with the view of freedom as absence of restraint, rather than with a more positive approach to freedom. The concern to prevent the government from encroaching upon individual liberty leads to measures which weaken it to the point where it is unable to act in order to provide those prerequisites of social and economic life which are essential if an individual is to be able to make proper use of his faculties. The decline in the popularity of the doctrine in the twentieth century, both in the United States and in Britain, is closely related to the recognition of the

---

[4] M. J. C. Vile, Constitutionalism and the Separation of Powers 14-20 (1998).

need for "collectivist" activities on the part of government, which require a coordinated programme of action by all parts of the government machine. The doctrine of the separation of powers is clearly committed to a view of political liberty an essential part of which is the restraint of governmental power, and that this can best be achieved by setting up divisions within the government to prevent the concentration of such power in the hands of a single group of men [and women]. Restraints upon government are an essential part of the view of political liberty enshrined in this approach, but we shall have to consider the extent to which the proponents of the doctrine also recognized that a minimum degree of "strong government" was also necessary to political liberty, and the possible ways in which the tenets of the doctrine are compatible with the minimum needs of government action in the twentieth century. Indeed it will be assumed that the recognition of the need for government action to provide the necessary environment for individual growth and development is complementary to, not incompatible with, the view that restraints upon government are an essential part of a theory of political liberty.

The first element of the doctrine is the assertion of a division of the agencies of government into three categories: the legislature, the executive, and the judiciary. The earliest versions of the doctrine were, in fact, based upon a twofold division of government, or at any rate upon a twofold division of government functions, but since the mid-eighteenth century the threefold division has been generally accepted as the basic necessity for constitutional government. . . . This aspect of the doctrine, although usually assumed by political theorists rather than explicitly developed, is clearly central to the whole pattern of Western constitutionalism. The diffusion of authority among different centres of decision-making is the antithesis of totalitarianism or absolutism. Thus in the totalitarian State every aspect of the State machine is seen merely as an extension of the party apparatus, and subordinate to it. A continuous effort has been made to prevent any division of the machine from developing its own interest, or from creating a degree of autonomy in the taking of decisions. In practice the pressures which operate against this attempt to maintain a single monolithic structure are too strong, for the price in inefficiency which has to be paid is too high, and of necessity rival centres emerge in the bureaucracy and in industry or elsewhere. But the "ideal" of the totalitarian state is that of a single all-embracing agency of government.

The "separation of agencies," therefore, is an essential element in a theory which assumes that the government must be checked internally by the creation of autonomous centres of power that will develop an institutional interest. Without the other elements of the doctrine of the separation of powers being present we might still expect some limitation on the ability of a single group to dominate the government if separate agencies are established. Even if the personnel of the agencies overlap, powerful influences may arise to create divergences of interest within the government. Differing procedures introduce differing values and different restraints; the emergence of an "institutional interest," the development of professionalism, the influence of colleagues and traditions, all provide the possibility, at least, of internal checks. Separate agencies, composed of distinct bodies of men [and women] even where functions are shared can be made representative of different groups in the community, and so, as with bicameral legislatures, provide the basis of a check upon the activities of each of them.

The second element in the doctrine is the assertion that there are three specific "functions" of government. Unlike the first element, which recommends that there should be three branches of government, this second part of the doctrine asserts a sociological truth or "law," that there are in all governmental situations three necessary functions to be performed, whether or not they are in fact all performed by one person or group, or whether there is a division of these functions among two or more agencies of government. All government acts, it is claimed, can be classified as an exercise of the legislative, executive, or judicial functions. The recommendation then follows that each of these functions should be entrusted solely to the appropriate, or "proper," branch of the government. This view of the "functions" of government is extremely abstract, and some of the attempts to justify this threefold division have reached a very high degree of abstraction indeed. It must be distinguished from the very different view of the functions of government which enumerates them as, for example, the duty of keeping the peace, of building roads, or of providing for defence. These we might label the "tasks" of government in order to distinguish them from the more abstract notion of function. . . .

The third element in the doctrine, and the one which sets the separation of powers theorists apart from those who subscribe to the general themes set out above but are not themselves advocates of the separation of powers, is what, for want of a better phrase, we shall describe as the "separation of persons." This is the recommendation that the three branches of government shall be composed of quite separate and distinct groups of people with no overlapping membership. It is perfectly possible to envisage distinct agencies of government exercising separate functions, but manned by the same persons; the pure doctrine here argues, however, that separation of agencies and functions is not enough. These functions must be separated in distinct hands if freedom is to be assured. This is the most dramatic characteristic of the pure doctrine, and is often in a loose way equated with the separation of powers. The final element in the doctrine is the idea that if the recommendations with regard to agencies, functions, and persons are followed then each branch of the government will act as a check to the exercise of arbitrary power by the others, and that each branch, because it is restricted to the exercise of its own function will be unable to exercise an undue control or influence over the others.

Thus there will be a check to the exercise of the power of government over "the people" because attempts by one branch to exercise an undue degree of power will be bound to fail. This is, of course, the whole aim and purpose of the doctrine, but it is just here that the greatest theoretical difficulty is to be found; and as a result what we have termed the pure doctrine has therefore been modified by combining it with some rather different doctrine to produce a complex amalgam of ideas about the limitations to be placed upon government authorities. The pure doctrine as we have described it embodies what might be called a "negative" approach to the checking of the power of the agencies of government. The mere existence of several autonomous decision-taking bodies with specific functions is considered to be a sufficient brake upon the concentration of power. Nothing more is needed. They do not actively exercise checks upon each other, for to do so would be to "interfere" in the functions of another branch. However, the theory does not indicate how an agency, or the group of persons who wields its authority, are to be restrained if they do attempt to exercise power improperly by encroaching upon the functions of another branch. The inadequacy of the controls which this negative approach to the checking of arbitrary rule provides, leads on to the adaptation of other ideas to complement the doctrine of the separation of powers and so to modify it.

The most important of these modifications lies in the amalgamation of the doctrine with the theory of mixed government, or with its later form, the theory of checks and balances. . . . [F]rom an analytical point of view the main consideration is that these theories were used to import the idea of a set of positive checks to the exercise of power into the doctrine of the separation of powers. That is to say that each branch was given the power to exercise a degree of direct control over the others by authorizing it to play a part, although only a limited part, in the exercise of the other's functions. Thus the executive branch was given a veto power over legislation, or the legislative branch was given the power of impeachment. The important point is that this power to "interfere" was only a limited one, so that the basic idea of a division of functions remained, modified by the view that each of the branches could exercise some authority in the field of all three functions. This is the amalgam of the doctrine of the separation of powers with the theory of checks and balances which formed the basis of the United States Constitution. . . . These modifications of the doctrine have of course been much more influential than the doctrine in its pure form.

* * *

In *The Federalist No. 47*, James Madison defended the proposed Constitution against charges that it had *rejected* separation-of-powers principles. On what basis did the critics make this claim? What, according to the Constitution's critics, was the danger of permitting any combination of governmental powers? What was the crux of Madison's response?

The Federalist Papers: No. 47
The Particular Structure of the New Government
and the Distribution of Power Among Its Different Parts
February 1, 1788

To the People of the State of New York:

HAVING reviewed the general form of the proposed government and the general mass of power allotted to it, I proceed to examine the particular structure of this government, and the distribution of this mass of power among its constituent parts. One of the principal objections inculcated by the more respectable adversaries to the Constitution, is its supposed violation of the political maxim, that the legislative, executive, and judiciary departments ought to be separate and distinct. In the structure of the federal government, no regard, it is said, seems to have been paid to this essential precaution in favor of liberty. The several departments of power are distributed and blended in such a manner as at once to destroy all symmetry and beauty of form, and to expose some of the essential parts of the edifice to the danger of being crushed by the disproportionate weight of other parts. No political truth is certainly of greater intrinsic value, or is stamped with the authority of more enlightened patrons of liberty, than that on which the objection is founded.

The accumulation of all powers, legislative, executive, and judiciary, in the same hands, whether of one, a few, or many, and whether hereditary, self-appointed, or elective, may justly be pronounced the very definition of tyranny. Were the federal Constitution, therefore, really chargeable with the accumulation of power, or with a mixture of powers, having a dangerous tendency to such an accumulation, no further arguments would be necessary to inspire a universal reprobation of the system. I persuade myself, however, that it will be made apparent to everyone, that the charge cannot be supported, and that the maxim on which it relies has been totally misconceived and misapplied. In order to form correct ideas on this important subject, it will be proper to investigate the sense in which the preservation of liberty requires that the three great departments of power should be separate and distinct. The oracle who is always consulted and cited on this subject is the celebrated Montesquieu. If he be not the author of this invaluable precept in the

> **In Context**
>
> Charles de Secondat, Baron de Montesquieu, a French Judge and political philosopher, published *The Spirit of the Laws* in 1748. This work, based in part on John Locke's *Second Treatise of Government*, heavily influenced the Framers' conception of separated governmental powers.

science of politics, he has the merit at least of displaying and recommending it most effectually to the attention of mankind. Let us endeavor, in the first place, to ascertain his meaning on this point. The British Constitution was to Montesquieu what Homer has been to the didactic writers on epic poetry. As the latter have considered the work of the immortal bard as the perfect model from which the principles and rules of the epic art were to be drawn, and by which all similar works were to be judged, so this great political critic appears to have viewed the Constitution of England as the standard, or to use his own expression, as the mirror of political liberty; and to have delivered, in the form of elementary truths, the several characteristic principles of that particular system. That we may be sure, then, not to mistake his meaning in this case, let us recur to the source from which the maxim was drawn.

On the slightest view of the British Constitution, we must perceive that the legislative, executive, and judiciary departments are by no means totally separate and distinct from each other. The executive magistrate forms an integral part of the legislative authority. He alone has the prerogative of making treaties with foreign sovereigns, which, when made, have, under certain limitations, the force of legislative acts. All the members of the judiciary department are appointed by him, can be removed by him on the address of the two Houses of Parliament, and form, when he pleases to consult them, one of his constitutional councils. One branch of the legislative department forms also a great constitutional council to the executive chief, as, on another hand, it is the sole depositary of judicial power in cases of impeachment, and is invested with the supreme appellate jurisdiction in all other cases. The judges, again, are so far connected with the legislative department as often to attend and participate in its deliberations, though not admitted to a legislative vote. From these facts, by which Montesquieu was guided, it may clearly be inferred that, in saying "There can be no liberty where the legislative and executive powers are united in the same person, or body of magistrates," or, "if the power of judging be not separated from the legislative and executive powers," he did not mean that these departments ought to have no PARTIAL AGENCY in, or no CONTROL over, the acts of each other. His meaning, as his own words import, and still more conclusively as illustrated by the example in his eye, can amount to no more than this, that where the WHOLE power of one department is exercised by the same hands which possess the WHOLE power of another department, the fundamental principles of a free constitution are subverted. This would have been the case in the constitution examined by him, if the king, who is the sole executive magistrate, had possessed also the complete legislative power, or the supreme administration of justice; or if the entire legislative body had possessed the supreme judiciary, or the supreme executive authority.

This, however, is not among the vices of that constitution. The magistrate in whom the whole executive power resides cannot of himself make a law, though he can put a negative on every law; nor administer justice in person, though he has the appointment of those who do administer it.

The judges can exercise no executive prerogative, though they are shoots from the executive stock; nor any legislative function, though they may be advised with by the legislative councils. The entire legislature can perform no judiciary act, though by the joint act of two of its branches the judges may be removed from their offices, and though one of its branches is possessed of the judicial power in the last resort. The entire legislature, again, can exercise no executive prerogative, though one of its branches constitutes the supreme executive magistracy, and another, on the impeachment of a third, can try and condemn all the subordinate officers in the executive department. The reasons on which Montesquieu grounds his maxim are a further demonstration of his meaning. "When the legislative and executive powers are united in the same person or body," says he, "there can be no liberty, because apprehensions may arise lest THE SAME monarch or senate should ENACT tyrannical laws to EXECUTE them in a tyrannical manner." Again: "Were the power of judging joined with the legislative, the life and liberty of the subject would be exposed to arbitrary control, for THE JUDGE would then be THE LEGISLATOR. Were it joined to the executive power, THE JUDGE might behave with all the violence of AN OPPRESSOR." Some of these reasons are more fully explained in other passages; but briefly stated as they are here, they sufficiently establish the meaning which we have put on this celebrated maxim of this celebrated author.

If we look into the constitutions of the several States, we find that, notwithstanding the emphatical and, in some instances, the unqualified terms in which this axiom has been laid down, there is not a single instance in which the several departments of power have been kept absolutely separate and distinct. [Madison then describes the provisions of each state's constitution in support of this assertion.]

. . . In citing these cases, in which the legislative, executive, and judiciary departments have not been kept totally separate and distinct, I wish not to be regarded as an advocate for the particular organizations of the several State governments. I am fully aware that among the many excellent principles which they exemplify, they carry strong marks of the haste, and still stronger of the inexperience, under which they were framed. It is but too obvious that in some instances the fundamental principle under consideration has been violated by too great a mixture, and even an actual consolidation, of the different powers; and that in no instance has a competent provision been made for maintaining in practice the separation delineated on paper. What I have wished to evince is, that the charge brought against the proposed Constitution, of violating the sacred maxim of free government, is warranted neither by the real meaning annexed to that maxim by its author, nor by the sense in which it has hitherto been understood in America. . . .

PUBLIUS [James Madison].

* * *

In *The Federalist No.* 48, Madison explained that the prime difficulty in designing the new federal government was ensuring that each Branch had the means to protect itself from the others. Why, in his view, was simply delineating the powers each Branch would wield an insufficient safeguard against encroachment? Which the Branches did he consider most likely to usurp the powers of the others? Which was in most need of protection?

The Federalist Papers: No. 48
These Departments Should Not Be So Far Separated as to
Have No Constitutional Control Over Each Other
February 1, 1788.

It Was shown in the last paper that the political apothegm there examined does not require that the legislative, executive, and judiciary departments should be wholly unconnected with each other. I shall undertake, in the next place, to show that unless these departments be so far connected and blended as to give to each a constitutional control over the others, the degree of separation which the maxim requires, as essential to a free government, can never in practice be duly maintained. It is agreed on all sides, that the powers properly belonging to one of the departments ought not to be directly and completely administered by either of the other departments. It is equally evident, that none of them ought to possess, directly or indirectly, an overruling influence over the others, in the administration of their respective powers. It will not be denied, that power is of an encroaching nature, and that it ought to be effectually restrained from passing the limits assigned to it. After discriminating, therefore, in theory, the several classes of power, as they may in their nature be legislative, executive, or judiciary, the next and most difficult task is to provide some practical security for each, against the invasion of the others.

What this security ought to be, is the great problem to be solved. Will it be sufficient to mark, with precision, the boundaries of these departments, in the constitution of the government, and to trust to these parchment barriers against the encroaching spirit of power? This is the security which appears to have been principally relied on by the compilers of most of the American constitutions. But experience assures us, that the efficacy of the provision has been greatly overrated; and that some more adequate defense is indispensably necessary for the more feeble, against the more powerful, members of the government. The legislative department is everywhere extending the sphere of its activity, and drawing all power into its impetuous vortex. The founders of our republics have so much merit for the wisdom which they have displayed, that no task can be less pleasing than that of pointing out the errors into which they have fallen. A respect for truth, however, obliges us to remark, that they seem never for a moment to have turned their eyes from the danger to liberty from the overgrown and all-grasping prerogative of an hereditary magistrate, supported and fortified by an hereditary branch of the legislative authority. They seem never to have recollected the danger from legislative usurpations, which, by assembling all power in the same hands, must lead to the same tyranny as is threatened by executive usurpations. . . . In a democracy, where a multitude of people exercise in person the legislative functions, and are continually exposed, by their incapacity for regular deliberation and concerted measures, to the ambitious intrigues of their executive magistrates, tyranny may well be apprehended, on some favorable emergency, to start up in the same quarter. But in a representative republic, where the executive magistracy is carefully limited; both in the extent and the duration of its power; and where the legislative power is exercised by an assembly, which is inspired, by a supposed influence over the people, with an intrepid confidence in its own strength; which is sufficiently numerous to feel all the passions which actuate a multitude, yet not so numerous as to be incapable of pursuing the objects of its passions, by means which reason prescribes; it is against the enterprising ambition of this department that the people ought to indulge all their jealousy and exhaust all their precautions. The legislative department derives a superiority in our governments from other circumstances. Its constitutional powers being at once more extensive, and less susceptible of precise limits, it can, with the greater facility, mask, under complicated and indirect measures, the encroachments which it makes on the co-ordinate departments. It is not unfrequently a question of real nicety in legislative bodies, whether the operation of a particular measure will, or will not, extend beyond the legislative sphere.

On the other side, the executive power being restrained within a narrower compass, and being more simple in its nature, and the judiciary being described by landmarks still less uncertain, projects of usurpation by either of these departments would immediately betray and defeat themselves. Nor is this all: as the legislative department alone has access to the pockets of the people, and has in some constitutions full discretion, and in all a prevailing influence, over the pecuniary rewards of those who fill the other departments, a dependence is thus created in the latter, which gives still greater facility to encroachments of the former. . . .

PUBLIUS [James Madison].

* * *

In *The Federalist No.* 51, Madison outlined how the structure of the proposed federal government ensured that each Branch could protect itself from encroachment by the others. On what assumption about human nature did he base his analysis? Also, Madison again expressed his concerns about the power of legislatures. In his view, what constitutional safeguards reduced Congress' capacity to assume executive and legislative power for itself?

The Federalist Papers: No. 51
The Structure of the Government Must Furnish the Proper Checks and Balances Between the Different Departments
February 8, 1788

To the People of the State of New York:

To WHAT expedient, then, shall we finally resort, for maintaining in practice the necessary partition of power among the several departments, as laid down in the Constitution? The only answer that can be given is, that as all these exterior provisions are found to be inadequate, the defect must be supplied, by so contriving the interior structure of the government as that its several constituent parts may, by their mutual relations, be the means of keeping each other in their proper places. Without presuming to undertake a full development of this important idea, I will hazard a few general observations, which may perhaps place it in a clearer light, and enable us to form a more correct judgment of the principles and structure of the government planned by the convention.

In order to lay a due foundation for that separate and distinct exercise of the different powers of government, which to a certain extent is admitted on all hands to be essential to the preservation of liberty, it is evident that each department should have a will of its own; and consequently should be so constituted that the members of each should have as little agency as possible in the appointment of the members of the others. Were this principle rigorously adhered to, it would require that all the appointments for the supreme executive, legislative, and judiciary magistracies should be drawn from the same fountain of authority, the people, through channels having no communication whatever with one another. Perhaps such a plan of constructing the several departments would be less difficult in practice than it may in contemplation appear. Some difficulties, however, and some additional expense would attend the execution of it. Some deviations, therefore, from the principle must be admitted. In the constitution of the judiciary department in particular, it might be inexpedient to insist rigorously on the principle: first, because peculiar qualifications being essential in the members, the primary consideration ought to be to select that mode of choice which best secures these qualifications; secondly, because the permanent tenure by which the appointments are held in that department, must soon destroy all sense of dependence on the authority conferring them.

It is equally evident, that the members of each department should be as little dependent as possible on those of the others, for the emoluments annexed to their offices. Were the executive magistrate, or the judges, not independent of the legislature in this particular, their independence in every other would be merely nominal. But the great security against a gradual concentration of the several powers in the same department, consists in giving to those who administer each department the necessary constitutional means and personal motives to resist encroachments of the others. The provision for defense must in this, as in all other cases, be made commensurate to the danger of attack. Ambition must be made to counteract ambition. The interest of the man must be connected with the constitutional rights of the place. It may be a reflection on human nature, that such devices should be necessary to control the abuses of government. But what is government itself, but the greatest of all reflections on human nature? If men were angels, no government would be necessary. If angels were to govern men, neither external nor internal controls on government would be necessary. In framing a government which is to be administered by men over men, the great difficulty lies in this: you must first enable the government to control the governed; and in the next place oblige it to control itself.

A dependence on the people is, no doubt, the primary control on the government; but experience has taught mankind the necessity of auxiliary precautions. This policy of supplying, by opposite and rival interests, the defect of better motives, might be traced through the whole system of human affairs, private as well as public. We see it particularly displayed in all the subordinate distributions of power, where the constant aim is to divide and arrange the several offices in such a manner as that each may be a check on the other that the private interest of every individual may be a sentinel over the public rights. These inventions of prudence cannot be less requisite in the distribution of the supreme powers of the State. But it is not possible to give to each department an equal power of self-defense. In republican government, the legislative authority necessarily predominates. The remedy for this inconveniency is to divide the legislature into different branches; and to render them, by different modes of election and different principles of action, as little connected with each other as the nature of their common functions and their common dependence on the society will admit. It may even be necessary to guard against dangerous encroachments by still further precautions. As the weight of the legislative authority requires that it should be thus divided, the weakness of the executive may require, on the other hand, that it should be fortified.

An absolute negative on the legislature appears, at first view, to be the natural defense with which the executive magistrate should be armed. But perhaps it would be neither altogether safe nor alone sufficient. On ordinary occasions it might not be exerted with the requisite firmness, and on extraordinary occasions it might be perfidiously abused. May not this defect of an absolute negative be supplied by some qualified connection between this weaker department and the weaker branch of the stronger department, by which the latter may be led to support the constitutional rights of the former, without being too much detached from the rights of its own department? If the principles on which these observations are founded be just, as I persuade myself they are, and they be applied as a criterion to the several State constitutions, and to the federal Constitution it will be found that if the latter does not perfectly correspond with them, the former are infinitely less able to bear such a test. . . .

PUBLIUS [James Madison].

QUESTION SET 1.3

Review & Synthesis

1. According to Professor Vile, "pure" separation-of-powers doctrine has three constitutive elements: separation of "persons," separation of "agencies," and separation of "functions." Describe what each of these separations entails and how each contributes to the protection of individual liberty. Vile also drew a distinction between "positive" and "negative" liberty. What did he view as the difference between the two, and which does "pure" separation-of-powers doctrine protect?

2. According to Vile, does "pure" separation-of-powers doctrine effectively balance a government's need to serve its people against the dangers of concentrating government powers in the same sets of hands? How did he think the concept of checks and balances helps governments reach equilibrium in this respect?

3. In his analysis of separation-of-powers doctrine, Vile seemed to assume that any combination of legislative, executive, or judicial power would equally threaten individual liberty. Based on *The Federalist Nos.* 47, 48, and 51, do you think Madison would have agreed? In your view, are some powers, either in isolation or in combination, more inherently threatening to individual liberty than others?

4. Given that agencies are subunits of the executive branch rather than Branches of the federal government themselves, should their internal structures and combination of powers conform to the separation-of-powers principles described by Madison and Vile? Does the fact that agencies focus on narrow slices of private activity — labor, financial instruments, the environment, etc. — rather than on general economic and social life, lessen the urgency of the liberty concerns addressed by separation-of-powers doctrine? Citing the Federal Trade Commission as an example, one commentator emphatically answered this question in the negative:

The Commission promulgates substantive rules of conduct. The Commission then considers whether to authorize investigations into whether the Commission's rules have been violated. If the Commission authorizes an investigation, the investigation is conducted by the Commission, which reports its findings to the Commission. If the Commission thinks that the Commission's findings warrant an enforcement action, the Commission issues a complaint. The Commission's complaint that a Commission rule has been violated is then prosecuted by the Commission and adjudicated by the Commission. This Commission adjudication can either take place before the full Commission or before a semi-autonomous Commission administrative law judge. If the Commission chooses to adjudicate before an administrative law judge rather than before the Commission and the decision is adverse to the Commission, the Commission can appeal to the Commission. If the Commission ultimately finds a violation, then, and only then, the affected private party can appeal to an Article III court. But the agency decision, even before the bona fide Article III tribunal, possesses a very strong presumption of correctness on matters both of fact and of law.

This is probably the most jarring way in which the administrative state departs from the Constitution, and it typically does not even raise eyebrows. The post-New Deal Supreme Court has never seriously questioned the constitutionality of this combination of functions in agencies.

Gary Lawson, *The Rise and Rise of the Administrative State*, 107 HARV. L. REV. 1231, 1248-49 (1994). Are you persuaded by Professor Lawson's argument? Consider that the FTC separates its administrative law judges from its investigators and prosecutors. *See* 16 C.F.R. § 3.42(f). Do these structural safeguards matter if all agency personnel ultimately report to the Commissioners?

5. Note the scope of the design problem on which Madison and Vile focused. In their view, separation-of-powers addresses the distribution of legislative, executive, and judicial power *within* government. It concerns itself with government's internal operations and assumes that mismanagement will inevitably lead to diminutions of individual liberty. As such, the doctrine is concerned with problems that are at least one step removed from private daily life. But neither Madison nor Vile asserted that these intra-governmental concerns were the *only* threats government could pose to individual liberty. The manner in, and degree to which, government regulates private social and economic activities (i.e., nongovernmental conduct) can also threaten liberty. Madison mentioned this concern in *The Federalist No.* 51, wryly observing, "you must first enable the government to control the governed; and in the next place oblige it to control itself." Vile tangentially addressed issues of substantive regulation when he distinguished between the "tasks" and the "functions" of government, but

he made clear that the former fall outside separation-of-powers concerns. Their analyses do not imply, however, that separating powers completely eliminates the government's capacity for abusive regulation of private conduct. As you go through this casebook, you will encounter numerous other legal and political constraints on the exercise of administrative authority (e.g., due process protections).

6. The excerpts above alluded to but did not attempt to resolve a difficult problem for the application of separation-of-powers theory to administrative action: how do we confidently classify a particular action as "legislative," "executive," or "judicial"? Logically and practically, doing so is a prerequisite to separation by function, agency, or persons. In a portion of his analysis not excerpted above, Vile made the following observations when assessing the Supreme Court's efforts in this regard:

> [P]roblems met by the Supreme Court in attempting to define the "powers" or functions of government reflect very closely the chaotic discussion of this subject by the Committee on Ministers' Powers in Britain in the 1930's. It was clear may years ago that attempts to allocate particular functions precisely to particular branches of government must fail. It is possible to define four *abstract* functions — rule-making, a discretionary function, rule-application, and rule-adjudication — but quite impossible to allocate them exclusively to different branches of government, because all human behaviour involves all four functions to some degree.

VILE, *supra*, at 402. Did Madison agree with this observation? Do you? As you read the cases that follow, note how the Supreme Court deals with this problem.

7. Do you share Madison's concerns, expressed in *The Federalist No.* 48, that the Legislative Branch is more capable of exceeding the proper bounds of its powers than are the other Branches, and therefore is the Branch most in need of careful supervision? Does that description of Congress' power match what you currently understand about the modern administrative state? As detailed in the materials that follow, Congress routinely delegates quasi-legislative authority to administrative agencies located in the Executive Branch. These agencies are not subject to the structural or procedural restrictions the Constitution placed on Congress. If the legislative power is as difficult to control as Madison believed, should administrative agencies be permitted to wield it?

Agency Creation by Congress

In addition to surveying the administrative state's history and describing several agencies that appear in the cases discussed throughout this book, Part I introduced the basic separation-of-powers and checks-and-balances principles that inform the structure, limitations, and functions of the federal government. In Part II, we turn to how those principles, as well as legal doctrine and pragmatic considerations of effective governance, shape the creation of agencies and the assignment of their powers.

The path toward federal agency creation often begins with a problem. With that in mind, consider the following hypothetical. The 1995 National Highway System Designation Act, among other things, repealed all federal speed limit controls. As part of that legislation, Congress gave states primary responsibility for setting speed limits on the nation's interstate highways. Assume that the number of serious injuries and fatalities on these roadways has significantly increased over the past several years. Congress clearly has the constitutional authority to address this problem, but it is by no means compelled to do so. Pursuant to the legislative authority vested in it by Article I, it has the discretion to intervene now, to intervene later, or to leave the issue for someone else to figure out. If it does choose to act, Congress has wide discretion to identify the private conduct to which new or different legal consequences will attach.

Suppose it passes legislation imposing a *uniform* national speed limit of 50 miles per hour. Of course, Congress need not resort to speed limits to address increases in the number and severity of interstate highway accidents. It would be free to select some other means of increasing speed-linked road safety, such as travel advisories and other driver education initiatives. If it does adopt a 50-mph speed limit, this would turn conduct that is currently legal in almost every state—driving faster than 50 mph—into conduct that is illegal under federal law regardless of state borders. In addition to adopting a uniform speed limit, Congress would have the discretion to choose the speed at which that limit is set. It would largely be up to Congress whether that limit is 50 mph, 5 mph, or 500 mph; the choice would be limited by the laws of physics, but not by any prior statutory law adopted by humans. Similarly, Congress would not be constrained in the factors or the information it considers in choosing that speed limit. It would be free to consider traffic patterns and accident rates, road curvatures and their impact on driver visibility, road maintenance costs, resident complaints about the noise produced by cars travelling at high speeds, the costs of enforcing the new limits, the economic impact of slowed travel speeds, etc. Congress would also have wide latitude in choosing the penalties that would attend violations of its uniform speed limit — fines, imprisonment, vehicle impoundment. It would have considerable choice over its preferred enforcement mechanism: partnering with state or local law enforcement or creating a federal force of highway patrol officers, providing bounties to citizens who report verified incidents of speeding, installing closed-circuit cameras that record the speed and plate numbers of cars as they pass by, etc. Finally, Congress would have to decide how disputes arising from enforcement of its new speed limit would be adjudicated. Should they be decided by Article III courts, by state courts, or by administrative law judges employed by an agency? What would the appeals process look like?

In sum, Congress can decide that the problem of increased accidents on the nation's interstate highways is best addressed by others (states, local governments, the private market), and thus do nothing. If it does act, it has broad discretion in choosing the private conduct that will be regulated and in designating how disputes over the legal consequences of that conduct will be adjudicated.

As you can see, even something as seemingly simple as choosing a speed limit can involve decisions that are numerous, varied, and complex. They are made even more so when one realizes that social, economic, and technological changes may take place that Congress could not have foreseen or, even it if could have foreseen them, would not be able to address in a timely way. Its Members can be forgiven for concluding that they lack the time, the substantive expertise, and the foresight required for detailed and responsive policymaking. They may accordingly choose to create a new federal agency to carry some of that policymaking load or to assign some policymaking responsibility to a preexisting agency.

If Congress chooses to implement its interstate safety policy through an administrative agency, it must make another highly consequential decision: what powers will that agency be granted to fulfill its regulatory mandate? Should it be delegated the authority to make binding legal rules, to enforce those rules, and/or to adjudicate the cases to which those new rules would apply? If Congress decides as a policy matter that the agency should be given legislative and/or adjudicative powers, the question remains whether the agency can legally receive them.

When Congress' delegation of legislative or adjudicative powers to federal agencies comes under legal attack, courts have turned to the Constitution for rules of decision. Its text, however, provides few definitive answers. If the Framers prohibited the mixing and matching of powers that is the hallmark of the modern administrative state, they declined to do so explicitly. Denied clearer guidance on delegation questions, courts have tried to derive limiting principles from the Constitution's provisions, including the Vesting Clauses' open-ended references to "legislative," "executive," and "judicial" powers. They have likewise tried to translate the separation-of-powers and checks-and-balances principles discussed in Chapter 1 into legal doctrines susceptible to judicial application.

> **Cross-Reference**
>
> Congress' power to create and assign powers to federal agencies is related to, but separate from, the means by which it controls bureaucratic behavior. Both topics address the scope of Congress' legislative power under the Constitution. However, the former focuses on how legislation shapes agencies at the moment of their creation. The latter focuses on how legislation shapes Congress' relationship with agencies *after* they have been created and assigned their powers. Accordingly, its consideration is reserved for Part IV.

Given its legislative power, Congress is responsible for the lion's share of agency creation and powers assignment. Nevertheless, it does not occupy the whole field. As the historical overview in Chapter 1 shows, the President has limited authority to establish, reorganize, and empower federal agencies. Although the President lacks Congress' authority to create agencies with so broad an array of governmental powers, he or she nevertheless can establish or rearrange administrative resources to better advance his or her policy priorities.

Agency Creation and Delegation of Powers by Congress

The materials that follow ask two questions. First, how much of its *legislative* power—essentially, the power to turn discretionary policy choices into legal rights and obligations—does the Constitution permit Congress to bestow on federal agencies? Take the interstate highway safety example above. Can Congress delegate to an agency its policymaking discretion to choose private conduct that will be subject to new or different regulation (e.g., high-speed driving on interstate highways)? Apart from that, can Congress give the agency the discretion to choose how much that private conduct will be regulated (a 50-mph speed limit as opposed to a 60-mph or a 40-mph limit)? Can Congress allow agencies to determine the consequences for failing to meet that obligation (penalties)? Broadly speaking, how much discretion can Congress grant an agency to regulate private social or economic activity? Does the Constitution require that Congress make some or all of the pertinent regulatory choices itself, leaving only residual or subordinate decisions to agencies?

Second, how much *adjudicative* power—essentially, the authority to resolve disputes through application of law to facts—does the Constitution permit Congress to bestow on administrative agencies? Can Congress grant agencies the authority to empower government officials (state, local, or federal law enforcement) and/or private individuals to enforce compliance with a nationwide 50-mph speed limit? Can it designate an adjudicator (federal courts, state courts, administrative courts) to resolve any disputes arising from the obligation's enforcement? Given that the Constitution vests the federal judicial power in "one supreme Court, and in such inferior Courts as the Congress may from time to time ordain and establish," what types of disputes can administrative courts (also called Article I courts) hear and decide? Can they resolve legal disputes between private parties? Can they constitutionally resolve disputes under federal law and state law? Common law and positive law?

Allegedly injurious Executive Branch conduct—by the President, executive departments, executive independent agencies, multimember agencies—gave rise to all but one of the disputes considered in the subsections that follow. However, it is important to understand that the legal claims in these cases were not directed at that Executive Branch conduct. In fact, the complaining parties could have maintained their lawsuits while conceding that federal statutes fully authorized what the government allegedly did. This is because the real targets were the federal statutes themselves. The complaining parties argued that Congress had no constitutional authority to permit the government conduct that allegedly caused their injuries. Accordingly, pay close attention to how the Supreme Court uses evidence of constitutional and legislative intent (text, structure, drafting history, etc.) to resolve those disputes.

A. DELEGATIONS OF LEGISLATIVE POWER: THE NONDELEGATION DOCTRINE

How much of its policymaking discretion does the Constitution permit Congress to give to federal agencies? As already noted, Congress derives its legislative authority—the power to turn discretionary policy choices into legal rights and obligations—from the Article I Vesting Clause, which provides that "[a]ll legislative power herein granted shall be vested in a Congress...." The Supreme Court has often interpreted this to be an exclusive assignment of legislative power to Congress. "That Congress cannot delegate legislative power to the President is a principle universally recognized as vital to the integrity and maintenance of the system of government ordained by the Constitution." *Marshall Field & Co. v. Clark,* 143 U.S. 649, 692 (1892). To ensure that Congress and no one else wields that power, the Court has developed what is now known as the "nondelegation doctrine."

Despite the nondelegation doctrine's apparent simplicity, the Court vacillated between more permissive and more restrictive applications of it through the mid-twentieth century. The cases summarized below—which are divided into the Court's Early Cases and its New Deal Cases—chronicle this. As you read the case descriptions, try to sketch out the Court's framework for analyzing nondelegation issues. To help your analysis, ask yourself the following questions:

- Can you identify the initial policy choice Congress made in each statute analyzed by the Court?
- Does Congress detail what the Executive Branch must do or find before exercising regulatory authority granted by the statute at issue?

- On what kinds of statutory details or other factors does the Supreme Court focus when deciding whether Congress has cleared the constitutional threshold for "legislating"? For instance, is the President left to determine the consequences of statutory violations, or does Congress prescribe those punishments itself? Does Congress instruct the President to create rules, or does Congress provide the rules and leave it to the President to fill in any details needed to implement them?
- Does the Supreme Court test the sufficiency of Congress' enactments against a specific provision or provisions of the Constitution? Against other principles not explicitly stated in the Constitution?

1. The Early Cases

***Cargo of the Brig Aurora v. United States,* 11 U.S. (7 Cranch) 382 (1813).** During the Napoleonic Wars (1803-1815), France and Great Britain waged commercial warfare by maintaining naval blockades of each other's ports. The United States had declared its neutrality in the conflict and sought to continue trading with both sides. Nevertheless, the French and the British routinely seized and otherwise interfered with American trading vessels bound for their respective enemy's ports. The United States economy suffered severely, and, in response, President Thomas Jefferson signed the Non-Intercourse Act into law on March 1, 1809, a few days before leaving office. Under Sections 4 and 5 of the Act, any cargo imported into the United States from France or Great Britain was to be seized by the government. When the Act expired on May 1, 1810, another act signed into law the same day (Macon's Bill No. 2) required the President to issue a proclamation if either Great Britain or France stopped interfering with American trading vessels. The legal effect of this proclamation would be two-fold. First, it would immediately lift the embargo against the country that ended its interference with American trading vessels. Second, and more importantly for present purposes, it would trigger a three-month waiting period,

Peter Pencil. *Intercourse or Impartial Dealings Political Cartoon, 1809.*

immediately after which the Non-Intercourse Act would be fully revived against the country that did not cease its interference with American trading vessels. On November 2, 1810, President James Madison issued a proclamation declaring that France would no longer obstruct American trade efforts in Europe. This proclamation triggered the three-month waiting period, with the expectation that the Non-Intercourse Act would be revived against Great Britain on February 2, 1811, if it failed to follow France's example.

The Brig Aurora left Liverpool in December 1810, and the government seized its cargo upon its arrival in New Orleans on February 20, 1811. Burnside, who had tried to claim the cargo, challenged its seizure all the way to the Supreme Court. There he argued that the Non-Intercourse Act was inoperative when the Aurora arrived in New Orleans because President Madison's proclamation could not have revived it. "Congress could not transfer the legislative power to the President. To make the revival of a law depend upon the President's proclamation, is to give to that proclamation the force of a law." 11 U.S. at 386. Accordingly, he argued that the government's seizure of his property was illegal. The government countered that "[t]he legislature did not transfer any power of legislation to the President. They only prescribed the evidence which should be admitted of a fact, upon which the law should go into effect." *Id.*

Writing for the Court, Justice William Johnson decided in favor of the government. His opinion never used the term "delegation," made no direct reference to the Constitution, and did not directly address Burnside's assertion that Congress is forbidden from transferring legislative power to the President. Instead, it simply observed that the Court "can see no sufficient reason, why the legislature should not exercise its discretion in reviving the act of March 1st, 1809, either expressly or conditionally, as their judgment should direct." *Id.* at 388. Whether one would characterize the power given to the President in the Non-Intercourse Act as legislative or as executive, the Court did not view the President's exercise of it as problematic.

Wayman v. Southard, 23 U.S. (10 Wheat.) 1 (1825). During the early nineteenth century, the Commonwealth of Kentucky passed aggressive debtor protection laws that significantly impaired creditors' ability to collect on the debts owed to them. By contrast, and pursuant to the Federal Process Act of 1792, federal judges in Kentucky adopted judgment execution and other procedural rules that afforded debtors far fewer protections than they would receive in the state court system. As one would expect, out-of-state creditors took advantage of the federal courts' diversity-of-citizenship jurisdiction to avoid litigating their claims in Kentucky's courts. This undermined the protections the Kentucky legislature sought to give its citizen-debtors and led Kentuckians and their representatives in Congress to viciously condemn the federal courts as usurpers of the Commonwealth's sovereignty. It was in this acrimonious political climate that the John Marshall Court heard and decided this case.

The case involved out-of-state creditors' attempts to execute a federal judgment against their Kentucky debtors. When the time came to enforce the plaintiffs' judgment, the federal marshal followed Kentucky's stay-law rather than the judgment execution rules adopted by the federal Circuit Court under the Federal Process Act. This law, which was one of Kentucky's debtor protection measures mentioned above, presented creditors with two unpalatable choices. If the debtor provided the creditor with a bond with security (also known as a replevin bond), the creditor would either have to accept Kentucky bank notes (which were widely considered all but worthless) in satisfaction of the judgment, or she would have to wait two years before she could seize and sell the debtor's property to satisfy the judgment. In other words, the stay-law forced creditors to choose between accepting far less than they were owed or being significantly delayed in collecting their judgments. The rules of the federal Circuit Court, by contrast, required that judgments be paid in gold or silver and afforded debtors no mandatory "stays" of judgment execution. For obvious reasons, the plaintiffs argued in the Supreme Court that the marshal should have followed the Circuit Court's rules. The defendants asserted, among other things, that the Circuit Court's rules were void because giving such rulemaking power to the courts was an unconstitutional delegation of Congress' legislative authority. In support of this argument, the defendants made oblique reference to the Article I Vesting Clause and the Necessary & Proper Clause, and colored them with a restrictive application of the separation of powers:

> All the legislative power is vested exclusively in Congress. Supposing Congress to have power, under the clause, for making all laws necessary and proper, &c. to make laws for executing the judicial power of the Union, it cannot delegate such power to the judiciary. The rules by which the citizen shall be deprived of his liberty or property, to enforce a judicial sentence, ought to be prescribed and known: and the power to prescribe such rules belongs exclusively to the legislative department. Congress could not delegate this power to the judiciary, or to any other department of the government.

Wayman, 23 U.S. (10 Wheat.) 13. Put another way, the defendants argued that the power to make rules—including a court's procedural rules governing the execution of its judgments—is a legislative power and, as such, the Constitution forbids anyone besides Congress from wielding it. Accordingly, the defendants claimed that the Federal Process Act's delegation of rulemaking authority to the federal courts was unconstitutional, and the federal marshal properly followed Kentucky law instead.

Writing for the Court, Chief Justice Marshall rejected this all-or-nothing argument. He did freely acknowledge, however, the conceptual difficulties posed by delegations like the one provided in the Federal Process Act. In several passages, he endorsed the defendants' restrictive view of separation of powers, under which Congress is constitutionally barred from delegating its legislative authority: "It will not be contended that Congress can delegate to the Courts, or to any other tribunals, powers which are strictly and exclusively legislative." *Id.* at 42. At the same time, he recognized that "the maker of the law may commit something to the discretion of the other departments, and the precise boundary of this power is a subject of delicate and difficult inquiry, into which a Court will not enter unnecessarily." *Id.* at 46. It seems, then, that Marshall did not regard the rules adopted under the Federal Process Act as "legislative" in the same sense the Federal Process Act itself was "legislative." He elaborated on the difference as follows:

> But Congress may certainly delegate to others, powers which the legislature may rightfully exercise itself. Without going farther for examples, we will take that, the legality of which the counsel for the defendants admit. The 17th section of the Judiciary Act, and the 7th section of the additional act, empower the Courts respectively to regulate their practice. It certainly will not be contended, that this might not be done by Congress. The Courts, for example, may make rules, directing the returning of writs and processes, the filing of declarations and other pleadings, and other things of the same description. It will not be contended, that these things might not be done by the legislature, without the intervention of the Courts: yet it is not alleged that the power may not be conferred on the judicial department.

Id. at 43. According to Marshall, Congress is well within its constitutional right to delegate powers that are not "strictly and exclusively legislative." *Id.* at 42. The analytical challenge for constitutional purposes, then, is to distinguish these "strictly and exclusively legislative" powers from all of the others. To do this, Marshall said the Court must look into the "character of the power given to the Courts by the Process Act." *Id.* at 43. But here, Marshall admitted, "[t]he line has not been exactly drawn which separates those important subjects, which must be entirely regulated by the legislature itself, from those of less interest, in which a general provision may be made, and power given to those who are to act under such general provisions to fill up the details." *Id.*

Marshall did not sketch out a clear analytical framework for drawing this line. Instead, he considered several factors during the course of his analysis, including Congress' probable intent in adopting the Process Act, the discretion courts commonly enjoy in fashioning judgment execution rules and directing the activities of court officers, and the range of discretion typically given to court officers in enforcing court orders. Weighing these factors, he concluded that the discretionary procedural decisions a federal marshal made in the course of executing a judgment—such as whether to seize and sell the debtor's property immediately or leave it in the debtor's possession—was subordinate to other more important procedural decisions, such as whether payment of a judgment must be made with cash or on credit. In other words, such subordinate decisions were made within and in service of the general framework provided by the more important decisions; they merely "fill[ed] up the details." *Id.* Congress was certainly within its right to leave the courts and their officers no discretion by providing detailed instructions on both primary and subordinate procedural issues. However, courts routinely handled subordinate procedural details themselves without complaint or controversy, and without any specific instructions from their legislatures. He thus concluded that the act of supplying these details was not a strictly or exclusively legislative one, and so delegating it to the federal courts did not result in the constitutional violation claimed by the defendants.

***Marshall Field & Co. v. Clark*, 143 U.S. 649 (1892).** On October 1, 1890, President Benjamin Harrison signed the Tariff Act of 1890 into law. Also known as the McKinley Tariff Act—named after Representative (later President) William McKinley, its chief supporter in Congress—the Act was an exemplar of protectionist trade policy. As a general matter, its intended effect was to protect domestic industries from foreign competition. The primary mechanism by which it accomplished this goal was increasing to nearly 50 percent the average tariff on a slew of imported goods. Even those goods not subject to such categorical tariff increases—sugar, coffee, tea, molasses, and hides—were nevertheless used to serve the ends of protectionism. Normally these goods were allowed to enter the United States tariff-free. However, Section 3 of the Act required the President to suspend their tariff-free status if he found that the countries exporting them imposed "reciprocally unequal and unreasonable" tariffs "upon the agricultural or other products of the United States." While Section 3 instructed the President to use his suspension power to "secure reciprocal trade" with those countries, it did not identify any specific facts for him to consider, nor did it provide any guidance on how long those suspensions were to last. Rather, it instructed him to use his suspension power "whenever and so often as [he] shall be satisfied" that the targeted exporting countries were imposing unreasonable tariffs on American goods.

Several American importers, including Marshall Field & Co., were assessed duties under the Act on goods they imported from abroad. Though their goods were not covered by Section 3, they argued that the tariff suspension power given to the President in Section 3 was an unconstitutional delegation of legislative and treaty-making authority that voided the entire Act. Justice John Marshall Harlan, writing for the Supreme Court, rejected their argument.

Like Chief Justice Marshall in *Wayman v. Southard*, Justice Harlan did not provide a list of elements that together constituted a formalized non-delegation analysis. Instead, we have to infer the salient factors by characterizing the information on which his analysis relied. He first compared the case to *The Brig Aurora*, observing that "it was competent for congress to make the revival of an act depend upon the proclamation of the president" in the latter, and so it was within Congress' authority to permit "the suspension of an act upon a contingency to be ascertained by the president" in the former. *Marshall Field*, 143 U.S. at 683. He then turned to a lengthy review of how federal political actors—Congress and the President—had shown their understanding of the nondelegation issue through legislation passed since the Founding Era. Here he found numerous statutes, beginning with President Washington's Administration, that depended for their operation on "the action of the president based upon an occurrence of subsequent events, or the ascertainment by him of certain facts, to be made known by his proclamation." *Id.* While not necessarily dispositive of the nondelegation question (a constitutional one ultimately answerable by the courts), Justice Harlan asserted that Congress's frequent resort to these delegations since the country's founding "is entitled to great weight in determining the question before us." *Id.*

Finally, and perhaps most critically, Justice Harlan felt it necessary to situate the President's Section 3 suspension power within one of the three categories of core governmental power—legislative, executive, or judicial. He began with the restrictive view of separation of powers: "That congress cannot delegate legislative power to the president is a principle universally recognized as vital to the integrity and maintenance of the system of government ordained by the constitution." *Id.* at 692. Contrary to the petitioner Marshall Field's position, Harlan did not regard the President's Section 3 suspension power as "legislative:"

> The act of October 1, 1890 ... does not, in any real sense, invest the president with the power of legislation. For the purpose of securing reciprocal trade with countries producing and exporting sugar, molasses, coffee, tea, and hides, congress itself determined that the provisions of the act of October 1, 1890, permitting the free introduction of such articles, should be suspended as to any country producing and exporting them that imposed exactions and duties on the agricultural and other products of the United States, which the president deemed, that is, which he found to be, reciprocally unequal and unreasonable. Congress itself prescribed, in advance, the duties to be levied, collected, and paid on sugar, molasses, coffee, tea, or hides, produced by or exported from such designated country while the suspension lasted. Nothing involving the expediency or the just operation of such legislation was left to the determination of the president.... [W]hen he ascertained the fact that duties and exactions reciprocally unequal and unreasonable were imposed upon the agricultural or other products of the United States by

a country producing and exporting sugar, molasses, coffee, tea, or hides, it became his duty to issue a proclamation declaring the suspension, as to that country, which congress had determined should occur. He had no discretion in the premises except in respect to the duration of the suspension so ordered. But that related only to the enforcement of the policy established by congress.... Legislative power was exercised when congress declared that the suspension should take effect upon a named contingency. What the president was required to do was simply in execution of the act of congress. It was not the making of law. He was the mere agent of the law-making department to ascertain and declare the event upon which its expressed will was to take effect.

Marshall Field, 143 U.S. at 692-93. Needless to say, there are a host of subsidiary considerations that could inform the President's decision to issue a suspension proclamation, none of which are addressed in the language of the Act. For instance, the President could consider how long a trade imbalance with a trading partner has lasted, the extent of the imbalance with that trade partner, or more fundamentally, what evidence best indicates the existence of an imbalance. Presumably, Justice Harlan did not consider these subsidiary considerations to be sufficiently "legislative" to pose a constitutional problem.

J. W. Hampton & Co. v. United States, 276 U.S. 394 (1928). From 1920 to 1921, the American economy suffered through a severe contraction due, in part, to a massive surplus of agricultural products that could not be absorbed domestically and for which demand collapsed in the reinvigorated markets of post–World War I Europe. In response, President Warren G. Harding signed the Fordney-McCumber Tariff Act into law on May 21, 1922. In essence, the Act tied tariff levels on imported goods to the difference between their relative costs of production in the exporting country and in the United States. Where the production costs of a product in the United States were higher than the production costs in an exporting country, the tariff imposed on the exporting country's goods would be increased to reduce or eliminate the difference. The increased tariff would be paid when the foreign goods were imported into the United States. As one might guess, the purpose of the Act was to produce revenue for the federal government and to enable domestic producers to better compete with foreign producers in American markets.

Section 315 of the Act tasked the President with identifying and quantifying production cost differences between American and competing foreign goods and, through proclamation, to equalize those costs by adjusting applicable tariff rates. Prior to making the necessary tariff adjustments, Section 315 required the President to consider several factors, including any differences in wages and costs of materials, differences in wholesale selling prices, and any market or production advantages the exporter received from its home government. Moreover, the Act required the United States Tariff Commission to assist the President in his production cost investigations, and also required him to wait for the results of the Commission's investigation before issuing a tariff adjustment proclamation.

A shipment of barium dioxide imported into New York by J.W. Hampton, Jr. & Co. was assessed a tariff rate of 6¢ per pound, which was 2¢ per pound more than provided by federal statute. The increase was mandated by President Calvin Coolidge's May 19, 1924, barium dioxide proclamation, which he issued pursuant to Section 315 of the Act. The company challenged the tariff increase by arguing that Section 315 delegated legislative power to the President in violation of the Article I Vesting Clause.

Writing for a unanimous Court, Chief Justice William Howard Taft began his analysis with the now familiar restrictive view of the separation of powers. "[I]t is a breach of the national fundamental law if Congress gives up its legislative power and transfers it to the President, or to the judicial branch, or if by law it attempts to invest itself or its members with either executive power or judicial power." 276 U.S. at 406. Despite this clear and inviolable separation, he recognized that the Branches must still work together to conduct the government's business. Accordingly, each Branch "in the field of its duties may ... invoke the action of the other two branches in so far as the action invoked shall not be an assumption of the constitutional field of action of another branch." *Id.* As to where we draw the line between permissible invocation of power and impermissible assumption of power, Chief Justice Taft was as noncommittal as his predecessors. In lieu of a bright-line rule or clear analytical framework, he offered the following observation: "In determining what it may do in seeking assistance from another branch, the extent and character of that assistance must be fixed according to common sense and the inherent necessities of the governmental co-ordination." *Id.* at 406.

He then observed that Congress had been known to include delegations like the one in Section 315 out of necessity, as it "may feel itself unable conveniently to determine exactly when its exercise of the legislative power should become effective, because dependent on future conditions." *Id.* at 407. In such circumstances, "it may leave the determination of such time to the decision of an executive." *Id.* Practically speaking, Taft felt that Congress would be unable to wield any legislative power at all if it were required to provide all such details itself. Relying on several federal and state judicial opinions, Taft further assured that leaving the timing of a law's applicability to an executive official was not the same as transferring legislative power to that official. Although both actions may seem "legislative" in some general sense—they both seem to choose conduct that will subsequently be controlled by law—the key distinctions were the order in which the legislature and the executive acted, and how those acts related to each other operationally. If the legislature's action preceded the executive's, and if the executive's actions depended on what the legislature had already done, then it was the legislature and not the executive that had exercised legislative power. In the best-known passage of the opinion, Chief Justice Taft penned the modern test for the nondelegation doctrine:

> If Congress shall lay down by legislative act *an intelligible principle* to which the person or body authorized to fix [tariff] rates is directed to conform, such legislative action is not a forbidden delegation of legislative power.

Id. at 409 (emphasis added). Taft concluded his opinion by analogizing Section 315 to Section 3 of the McKinley Tariff Act, which the Court upheld in *Marshall Field & Co. v. Clark*. While the *Marshall Field* Court made clear that Congress cannot delegate its legislative power to the President, it also decided that Section 3 did not have that effect. Section 3 "did not in any real sense invest the President with the power of legislation, because nothing involving the expediency or just operation of such legislation was left to the determination of the President." *Id.* at 410. Rather, "the legislative power was exercised when Congress declared that the suspension [of the McKinley Tariff Act's tariff-free provisions] should take effect upon a named contingency. What the President was required to do was merely in execution of the act of Congress. It was not the making of law." *Id.* at 410-11. Taft concluded that the same was true for Section 315 of the Fordney-McCumber Tariff Act and so rejected Marshall Field's claim that it effected an unconstitutional delegation of legislative power to the President.

So stood the Court's views on the delegation of legislative authority to the Executive Branch on the eve of the Great Depression.

QUESTION SET 2.1

Review & Synthesis

1. Practically speaking, what is the basic purpose of the nondelegation doctrine? What harm(s) is it calculated to prevent?

2. Did the Supreme Court in any of the Early Cases find that Congress' delegates (the President, the federal courts) were wielding legislative power? If not, how did the Court characterize the powers given to those delegates in each case? Do you agree with those characterizations?

3. Did the Court adopt an expansive or a restrictive understanding of delegation in the Early Cases? In other words, did it require Congress to

provide its delegates with heavily detailed instructions before those delegates could act, or did it allow Congress to give its delegates free reign to identify factual and other details that would trigger enforcement of the law or determine the consequences for violating it?

4. With the exception of *Wayman v. Southard*, which dealt with judicial procedures, each of the Early Cases involved tariff or trade policies carried out by the President. Like other areas touching on foreign affairs, the Court historically has afforded Congress and the President a greater measure of policymaking latitude in these areas than in others.
   a. Do you think application of the nondelegation doctrine should differ depending on the subject of regulation? Stated differently, should "intelligible principle" mean something different when it comes to trade policy or foreign affairs than, say, in the transportation or workplace safety contexts?
   b. Do you think the nondelegation standard should differ depending on who Congress chooses as its delegate? In other words, should the Court enforce restrictions on delegations of legislative authority more forcefully when the delegate is the Secretary of State rather than the President? What if the delegate is the Supreme Court?

5. The Court in the Early Cases declined to adopt a definitive list of factors that must be considered when assessing the constitutionality of legislative delegations. Nevertheless, having some understanding of the factors the Court did consider will assist you in duplicating that analysis yourself.
   With that in mind, list the factors or types of evidence the Court used in testing the delegations at issue in each case. Can you find any consistencies in this evidence? Did it seem to weigh some factors more heavily than others? Are there factors that you believe to be relevant to the nondelegation inquiry that the Court did not consider?

---

2. The New Deal Cases

To provide fuller context for the New Deal Cases considered below, we should pause to emphasize a few points from the Early Cases summarized above. First, the Early Cases repeatedly endorsed a restrictive view of Congress' legislative power: the Article I Vesting Clause, general separation-of-powers principles, or both, reserved exercise of the federal government's legislative power to Congress alone. Second, the Court went to great lengths to explain that Congress, despite this delegation restriction, may still leave its delegates some discretion when tasking them with enforcing its statutes. Third, the Court did not clearly distinguish between executive and judicial decisions that were "legislative" for constitutional purposes and Executive and Judicial decisions that were not. "Legislation" seemed to include an initial, originating selection of some conduct to which legal consequences would subsequently attach. Though Congress alone could make that selection, it did not need to do so with the specificity of an all-encompassing code. Rather, it could leave its delegates to "fill up the details" necessary to enforce its statutes so long as it provided "intelligible principles" to guide how they did so. Stated differently, Executive Branch officials could extend or clarify, but not create, legal obligations in the course of enforcing them. Fourth, the Court did not adopt a definitive list of factors for its nondelegation testing. Rather, it considered different types and sources of evidence in different cases. Moreover, the Court appeared to weigh those sources differently from case to case.

Importantly, the Court never once struck down a federal statute due to the nondelegation doctrine prior to the New Deal Era. This informed a general sense that the doctrine was toothless, doing little if anything to discipline Congress in delegating policymaking authority to the other Branches. *See, e.g.*, Milton Handler, *The National Industrial Recovery Act*, 19 ABA J. 440, 445-446 (1933).

Like *The Brig Aurora*, *Marshall Field*, and *J.W. Hampton*, the New Deal Cases considered below involved delegations of policymaking authority from Congress to the Executive Branch. Nevertheless, they differ in at least two material respects. First, the statutes at issue in the New Deal Cases provided comparatively less guidance — i.e., they specified fewer facts or circumstances for agencies to find before acting under them — than those considered by the Court in the Early Cases. Second, the Early Cases featured foreign-affairs-adjacent concerns (international tariffs and trade policy), whereas the New Deal Cases focused on domestic economic regulation.

These differences lead to an important question: Are the Early Cases properly read as setting nondelegation floors or nondelegation ceilings? In other words, did the Court in those cases identify the *minimum* level of instruction the Constitution requires Congress to provide (the floor), or did the Court identify the *maximum* level of instruction the Constitution requires Congress to give (the ceiling)? If the former, statutes providing less instruction to Congress' delegates would be in danger of judicial invalidation. If the latter, those federal statutes would likely survive a nondelegation challenge. In large part, the New Deal Cases wrestle with this very question.

Panama Refining Co. v. Ryan, **293 U.S. 388 (1935) (The "Hot Oil" Case).** Like many of the federal statutes passed during the first few months of President Franklin D. Roosevelt's Administration, the goal of the National Industrial Recovery Act ("NIRA") was to jolt the American economy out of the Great Depression. A primary target in doing so was the deflationary spiral in which the country found itself, as prices had collapsed in multiple industries. To compete for declining sales opportunities, businesses too often responded by reducing their prices even further or by trying to boost their revenues by producing even more goods at rapidly falling prices. These responses only contributed to continuing price collapses.

Section 9(c) of the NIRA was directed at one area of urgent deflationary concern: the oil market. It delegated to the President the power to outlaw the interstate and foreign sale of so-called "hot oil" — oil that was produced in excess of (and hence in violation of) state-established production quotas. Congress and the Roosevelt Administration believed that federal enforcement of state-based oil-production quotas would reverse the commodity price collapse that resulted from an oversupply of oil in the market, facilitate a more even distribution of oil production profits, and help oil producers and businesses in related industries operate more profitably.

Section 9(c) stated, in total:

> The President is authorized to prohibit the transportation in interstate and foreign commerce of petroleum and the products thereof produced or withdrawn from storage in excess of the amount permitted to be produced or withdrawn from storage by any State law or valid regulation or order prescribed thereunder, by any board, commission, officer, or other duly authorized agency of a State. Any violation of any order of the President issued under the provisions of this subsection shall be punishable by fine of not to exceed $1,000, or imprisonment for not to exceed six months, or both.

Further, NIRA Section 10(a) authorized the President to "prescribe such rules and regulations as may be necessary to carry out the purposes" of NIRA Title I (including Section 9(c)), and stated that "any violation of any such rule or regulation shall be punishable by fine of not to exceed $500, or imprisonment for not to exceed six months, or both."

In a pair of executive orders issued on July 11 and 14, 1933, President Roosevelt banned the interstate sale of hot oil and authorized his Interior Secretary to exercise all of his powers to enforce Section 9(c) and the July 11 executive order. Among other actions, the Secretary issued regulations imposing a variety of reporting requirements on petroleum producers. These reports, which producers had to file under oath, required disclosure of a producer's residence and post office address, the location of its producing properties and wells, the maximum amount of petroleum production allowed under its state's law, the producer's actual daily petroleum production, a list of all petroleum deliveries made by the producer, and a declaration that none of the petroleum or petroleum products produced or shipped by the producer were taken out of storage in excess of the caps set by state law. Other regulations issued by the Secretary placed similar reporting obligations on petroleum shippers and refiners and required anyone covered by NIRA Section 9(c) and its related executive orders to keep production and transportation records available for inspection by the Interior Department's Division of Investigation.

Several companies owning oil production and refining facilities in Texas, including the Panama Refining Company, filed federal lawsuits to enjoin enforcement of the Interior Department's reporting regulations. In addition to raising objections under the Fifth and Fourteenth Amendments and the Commerce Clause, the plaintiffs asserted that Section 9(c) was an unconstitutional delegation of legislative authority to the President. Writing for the Court, Chief Justice Charles Evans Hughes framed the Court's analytical task as follows:

> [W]e look to the statute to see whether the Congress has declared a policy with respect to [the interstate and foreign transport of hot oil]; whether the Congress has set up a standard for the President's action; whether the Congress has required any finding by the President in the exercise of the authority to enact the prohibition [adopted by the President's July 11, 1933, executive order].

293 U.S. at 415. Next observing that Section 9(c) "is brief and unambiguous," Chief Justice Hughes enumerated all of the policy choices the provision did *not* make:

> It does not attempt to control the production of petroleum and petroleum products within a state. It does not seek to lay down rules for the guidance of state Legislatures or state officers. It leaves to the states and to their constituted authorities the determination of what production shall be permitted. It does not qualify the President's authority by reference to the basis or extent of the state's limitation of production. Section 9(c) does not state whether or in what circumstances or under what conditions the President is to prohibit the transportation of the amount of petroleum or petroleum products produced in excess of the state's permission. It establishes no criterion to govern the President's course. It does not require any finding by the President as a condition of his action.

Id. Based on this list of "does nots" and "noes," the Chief Justice concluded that Section 9(c) "declares no policy" on the transportation of hot oil, and instead "gives to the President an unlimited authority to determine the policy and to lay down the prohibition, or not lay it down, as he may see fit." *Id.* Nor did he find any congressional policymaking on the issue of transporting hot oil in any of the NIRA's other provisions, including the general declaration of the Act's policy provided in Section 1. Nowhere in the NIRA, in his view, did Congress "declare in what circumstances that transportation [of hot oil] should be forbidden, or require the President to make any determinations as to any facts or circumstances. . . . The President was not required to ascertain and proclaim the conditions prevailing in the industry which made the prohibition necessary." *Id.* at 418. Thus, and for the first time, the Court struck down a federal statutory provision as a violation of the nondelegation doctrine.

Apparently aware of the nondelegation doctrine's "rubber stamp" reputation, and perhaps anticipating the surprise (even outrage) the Court's decision would soon engender, Chief Justice Hughes went to great lengths to demonstrate its consistency with prior precedent. Returning to a prominent feature of the Early Cases he insisted that, under the Article I Vesting Clause, "Congress manifestly is not permitted to abdicate or to transfer to others the essential legislative functions with which it is thus vested." *Id.* at 421. He observed that the Constitution leaves Congress ample policy-making flexibility despite this restriction, as Congress is still able to "leav[e] to selected instrumentalities the making of subordinate rules within prescribed limits and the determination of facts to which the policy as declared by the Legislature is to apply." *Id.* In distinguishing impermissible non-congressional legislating from permissible subordinate rulemaking, Hughes drew a contrast between Section 9(c) and the comparatively more specific instructions in other statutes the Court had previously upheld. The Non-Intercourse Act considered in *The Brig Aurora*, Section 3 of the McKinley Tariff Act considered in *Marshall Field v. Clark*, and the flexible tariff provision considered in *J.W. Hampton*, among others, specified guiding policy goals (i.e., intelligible principles) setting the law's parameters and direction, the conditions that needed to be found before those policy goals could be pursued, and limitations on the actions that could be taken in pursuit of those policy goals. Whatever discretion these statutes left to Congress' delegates was necessarily interstitial and secondary in nature; the big, direction-defining questions having already been answered by Congress, all that was left was to flesh out some details. Section 9(c), by contrast, exhibited few if any of these features, and thus could not pass constitutional muster under the nondelegation doctrine.

***A.L.A. Schechter Poultry Corp. v. United States*, 295 U.S. 495 (1935) (The "Sick Chickens" Case).** From an early point in his political career, Franklin D. Roosevelt advocated collaborative self-regulation within private industries. He believed that industry self-regulation through trade associations or membership-driven industry groups was preferable in many ways to purely governmental regulation, as business leaders understood their markets far better than could politicians or bureaucrats. He also believed that building collaborative (critics would say anticompetitive) relationships among businesses within industries could prevent the negative market effects that sometimes result from bare-knuckle competition.

These sensibilities were readily apparent in NIRA Section 3. Under specified conditions, it authorized the President to approve and give legal effect to "codes of fair competition" drafted by private trade associations, if the President found (1) that those associations "impose[d] no inequitable restrictions on admission to membership therein and [were] truly representative of such trades or industries or subdivisions thereof, and (2) that such code or codes [were] not designed to promote monopolies or to eliminate or oppress small enterprises and [would] not operate to discriminate against them, and [would] tend to effectuate the policy of [NIRA Title I]." Title I, for its part, listed a variety of goals, including the removal of "obstructions to the free flow of interstate and foreign commerce which tend to diminish the amount thereof," to "eliminate unfair competitive practices," "to promote the fullest possible utilization of present productive capacity of industries," and "to avoid undue restriction of production (except as may be temporarily required)." As a condition of his approval, Section 3 gave the President the discretion to "impose such conditions (including requirements for the making of reports and the keeping of accounts) for the protection of consumers, competitors, employees, and others, in furtherance of the public interest," and to allow "such exceptions to and exemptions from the provisions of such code as the President in his discretion deems necessary to effectuate" the NIRA's policy. Section 3 also gave the President, "after such public notice and hearing as he shall specify," the authority to adopt his own codes of fair competition if he found "that abuses inimical to the public interest and contrary to the policy herein declared [were] prevalent in any trade or industry or subdivision . . . and if no code of fair competition" had yet been approved by the President for that trade or industry. Finally, Section 3 made it a misdemeanor to violate any code approved under it by the President, punishable by fine of "not more than $500 for each offense," with each day the violations continued being deemed a separate offense.

Petitioners in this case were New York City slaughterhouse operators. The U.S. Attorney for the Eastern District of New York charged them with violating the so-called "Live Poultry Code," a code of fair competition covering New York City's live poultry industry and adopted under NIRA Section 3 by executive order. The Federal District Court for the Eastern District of New York convicted the petitioners on 18 counts, including violation of the Code's prohibitions against allowing purchasers to select individual chickens rather than selling chickens by the "coop," selling unfit chickens, failing to make required reports or filing false reports regarding sales prices and number of sales, and selling chickens to purchasers not licensed under the Code. The petitioners appealed to the Second Circuit, which upheld the convictions on a majority of the counts. In the Supreme Court, the petitioners argued, among other things, that Section 3 effected an unconstitutional delegation of legislative power to the President.

Writing for a unanimous Court, Chief Justice Hughes (the author of *Panama Refining Co.*) once again found that Congress had delegated too much of its legislative authority to the President. He first rejected the government's argument that the delegation should be viewed in light of the ongoing economic emergency. While acknowledging that "[e]xtraordinary conditions may call for extraordinary remedies," he pointedly observed that "[e]xtraordinary conditions do not create or enlarge constitutional powers." 295 U.S. at 528. Whatever crisis the nation was facing, the federal government's capacity to address it was still limited by the Constitution. The Chief Justice similarly rejected the government's contention that Section 3 merely facilitated voluntary cooperation among the members of industrial and trade groups. Rather, he found that Section 3 constituted "the coercive exercise of the lawmaking power." *Id.* at 529. The codes were mandatory and thus "binding equally on those who assent and those who do not assent," and violations of them were "punishable as crimes." *Id.*

Turning more directly to the petitioners' nondelegation argument, and referring back to his opinion in *Panama Refining Co.*, Hughes underscored yet again Congress' unshakable responsibility under the Article I Vesting Clause:

> The Constitution provides that "All legislative powers herein granted shall be vested in a Congress of the United States, which shall consist of a Senate and House of Representatives." Article I, § I. And the Congress is authorized "To make all Law which shall be necessary and proper for carrying into Execution" its general powers. Article I, § 8, para. 18. The Congress is not permitted to abdicate or to transfer to others the essential legislative functions with which it is thus vested. We have repeatedly recognized the necessity of adapting legislation to complex conditions involving a host of details with which the national Legislature cannot deal directly. We pointed out in the *Panama Refining Company Case* that the Constitution has never been regarded as denying to Congress the necessary resources of flexibility and practicality, which will enable it to perform its function in laying down policies and establishing standards, while leaving to selected instrumentalities the making of subordinate rules within prescribed limits and the determination of facts to which the policy as declared by the Legislature is to apply. But we said that the constant recognition of the necessity and validity of such provisions, and the wide range of administrative authority which has been developed by means of them, cannot be allowed to obscure the limitations of the authority to delegate, if our constitutional system is to be maintained.

Id. at 529-30. Hughes then looked to Section 3 to determine whether Congress had "itself established the standards of legal obligation thus performing its essential legislative function." *Id.* at 530. First, Hughes addressed the scope of the section's subject matter. He framed the core issue in

Panama Refining Co. as whether NIRA Section 9(c) gave the President too much discretion in policing the sale of "hot oil" across state lines. The regulatory subject matter to which that discretion would be applied (the sale of "hot oil") was clearly provided in the statute and therefore never in question. He observed that, by contrast, Section 3 did not specify the conduct or activities that Congress wanted regulated. The section's operative term, "codes of fair competition," without more, could refer to almost any activity within the national economy. Moreover, Hughes felt that the various goals set forth in NIRA Section 1—e.g., to "eliminate unfair competitive practices"—did nothing to narrow the Act's potential scope. Second, he addressed the involvement of private industry in drafting the codes. That the substance of the codes would largely be drafted by industry representatives, and not by Congress, served only to further convince the Court of Section 3's unconstitutionality. Finally, he assessed whether Section 3 placed sufficient limits on the President's discretion, and he concluded that it did not. The conditions upon which the President could exercise his authority to approve a code—e.g., finding that the drafting associations imposed no undue restrictions on membership—did nothing to limit the range of potential activities upon which a code could operate. Rather, "these restrictions [left] virtually untouched the field of policy envisaged by [NIRA Section I], and, in that wide field of legislative possibilities, the proponents of a code ... may roam at will, and the President may approve or disapprove their proposals has he may see fit." *Id.* at 538. Moreover, Section 3 left the President equally free to impose any additional conditions on codes submitted for his approval or, if none were submitted for a particular trade or industry, to make up codes himself.

In sum, Chief Justice Hughes could see in Section 3 no policy choices made by Congress. It created no legal obligations itself, providing instead for President Roosevelt to create those obligations himself. It identified no facts or conditions that the President had to find before creating those legal obligations, providing only general statements of purpose that had little if any limiting effect on the President's discretion. Based on these defects, the Court concluded that Section 3 was "without precedent," and that "the code-making authority [it] conferred [was] an unconstitutional delegation of legislative power." *Id.* at 542.

QUESTION SET 2.2

Review & Synthesis

1. Summarize the Supreme Court's reasons for invalidating Section 3 of the National Industrial Recovery Act in *A.L.A Schechter*, and Section 9(c) in *Panama Refining Co.* Do you think the NIRA sections invalidated by the

Court in *Panama Refining Co.* and *A.L.A. Schechter* provided more, less, or just as much instruction to the Executive Branch as those the Court upheld in its Early Cases?

2. Chief Justice Hughes grounds the Court's decision in the Article I Vesting Clause, which grants all of the federal government's legislative power to Congress. Presumably relying on the term "all," he read the Vesting Clause as establishing a bright-line rule: "Congress is not permitted to abdicate or to transfer to others the essential legislative functions with which it is thus vested."

   a. Chief Justice Hughes did not define "legislative powers," the operative term in the Vesting Clause. Can you construct a partial definition of it from how he applied the Clause to NIRA Section 3 in *A.L.A. Schechter*? Identify the activities and decisions it included.

   b. Do you think the Article I Vesting Clause supports Chief Justice Hughes' narrow view of permissible delegation? Identify ways of reading it that would allow for more generous delegation.

   c. Apart from A.L.A. Schechter Poultry Co. having to comply with competition codes it believed would injure its business, precisely what injury would result from allowing the President to adopt codes of fair competition drafted by trade organizations?

3. In part of the *A.L.A. Schechter* opinion not summarized above, Chief Justice Hughes compared the authority granted to the President under NIRA Section 3 with the authority granted to the Federal Trade Commission ("FTC") by the Federal Trade Commission Act ("FTCA"). The FTCA prohibited "unfair methods of competition," which, he said, "does not admit of precise definition." Nevertheless, Hughes concluded that this phrase provided a sufficiently intelligible principle to satisfy the nondelegation doctrine, whereas NIRA Section 3's use of the phrase "fair competition" did not. Hughes also emphasized that the FTC was required to follow court-like procedures — complaints, notice, hearings, discovery, and judicial review — when determining whether a business has employed "unfair methods of competition." The NIRA imposed no such procedural restrictions on the President's adoption of fair competition codes.

   a. Do you find Hughes' distinction between "unfair methods of competition" in the FTCA and "fair competition" in NIRA Section 3 a meaningful one? Does the former clearly provide an "intelligible principle" that the latter does not?

   b. For purposes of nondelegation analysis, should the amount of legislative authority that Congress grants an agency be measured in part by the procedures Congress requires it to follow? Stated differently, can an open-ended delegation pass constitutional muster if the agency must follow demanding administrative procedures before acting under it?

    c. Suppose that President Roosevelt adopted rules placing substantive limits on the topics his fair competition codes would cover and on the industries to which any adopted codes would apply. In other words, he voluntarily gave up some of the policymaking discretion NIRA Section 3 otherwise granted him. Would that have cured the nondelegation defect identified by the Court?

4. NIRA Section 9(c) focused narrowly on the issue of unlawful petroleum sales, whereas Section 3 did not target a specific industry for development and adoption of codes of fair competition. Nevertheless, the Court found that both unconstitutionally delegated legislative power to the President. Should the breadth or depth of policymaking power a delegation confers factor into whether it provides an intelligible principle? Assume a federal statute instructed the Secretary of Agriculture to take all measures that are reasonable, in his or her discretion, to ensure safe operation of commercially operated grain elevators. Would such a delegation violate the nondelegation doctrine as applied in *Panama Refining Co.* and *A.L.A. Schechter?*

3. The Modern Cases

In its New Deal nondelegation cases, the Supreme Court staked out a clear position on Congress' delegations of legislative authority. Grounded in its understanding of the Article I Vesting Clause, the Court decided that Congress, and Congress alone, is constitutionally responsible for making the policy choices that animate federal legislation. The Court looked for evidence (primarily in statutory language) of whether Congress had in fact made those animating choices. That evidence could come in any of several forms: provisions defining the economic or social activities subject to regulation, language indicating the facts or conditions the Executive Branch had to find before initiating enforcement, specification of the penalties for noncompliance, etc.

    The Court heard nondelegation challenges in the years immediately following its decisions in *Panama Refining Co.* and *A.L.A. Schechter.* It did not sustain them, but then again the statutes scrutinized in those cases provided Executive Branch officials with more direction than did the invalidated provisions of the NIRA. *See, e.g., Opp Cotton Mills v. Administrator of Wage and Hour Division,* 312 U.S. 126, 144-46 (1941); *United States v. Rock Royal Co-op,* 307 U.S. 533, 574-77 (1939); *Mulford v. Smith,* 307 U.S. 38, 48-49 (1939). By 1944, the nation was in the thrall of World War II, and all but two members of the Court that decided *Panama Refining Co.* and *A.L.A. Schechter* had departed — including the author of both majority opinions, Chief Justice Charles Evans Hughes. The change in Court personnel, and perhaps a change in the nation's circumstances, resulted in an unmistakable retreat from the New Deal Court's stifling interpretation of the Article I Vesting Clause.

***Yakus v. United States*, 321 U.S. 414 (1944).** The outbreak of World War II in 1939 triggered a period of significant inflation in the United States. According to one study, wholesale prices more than doubled and the money supply had nearly tripled during the war and in the years immediately following it. *See* Milton Friedman & Anna Jacobson Schwartz, *World War II Inflation, September 1939-August 1948* in FROM NEW DEAL BANKING REFORM TO WORLD WAR II INFLATION (Milton Friedman & Anna Jacobson Schwartz eds., 1980). To combat this, Congress passed the Emergency Price Control Act of 1942, which sketched out a comprehensive regulatory scheme for stabilizing prices for goods and services, and for preventing profiteering that could hamper the nation's war efforts and injure consumers. To implement its price control scheme, the Act established the Office of Price Administration, led by a Price Administrator appointed by the President.

Albert Yakus and others were convicted in the Federal District Court for the District of Massachusetts for selling wholesale cuts of beef above the maximum price limits set by the Price Administrator. On appeal, they challenged the Emergency Price Control Act's constitutionality on nondelegation grounds. In upholding the Act's constitutionality, the Court found that it contained the requisite congressional policy choices that were absent in Sections 3 and 9(c) of the NIRA:

> Congress enacted the Emergency Price Control Act in pursuance of a defined policy and required that the prices fixed by the Administrator should further that policy and conform to standards prescribed by the Act. The boundaries of the field of the Administrator's permissible action are marked by the statute. It directs that the prices fixed shall effectuate the declared policy of the Act to stabilize commodity prices so as to prevent war-time inflation and its enumerated disruptive causes and effects. In addition the prices established must be fair and equitable, and in fixing them the Administrator is directed to give due consideration, so far as practicable, to prevailing prices during the designated base period, with prescribed administrative adjustments to compensate for enumerated disturbing factors affecting prices. In short the purpose of the Act specified in § 1 denote the objective to be sought by the Administrator in fixing prices—the prevention of inflation and its enumerated consequences.

Yakus, 321 U.S. at 423. The Court also concluded that the Act provided the Administrator with constitutionally sufficient guidance to implement it:

> The standards set out in § 2 define the boundaries within which prices ... must be fixed. It is enough to satisfy the statutory requirements

that the Administrator finds that the prices fixed will tend to achieve that objective and will conform to those standards, and that the courts in an appropriate proceeding can see that substantial basis for those findings is not wanting.

Id. In dissent, Justice Owen Roberts (one of two holdovers from the *Panama Refining Co.* and *A.L.A. Schechter* Court) regarded the Emergency Price Control Act as little different from those sections of the NIRA the Court had previously struck down on nondelegation grounds. In his view, the Act's several enumerated purposes—such as assuring "that defense appropriations [were] not dissipated by excessive prices," or "assist[ing] in securing adequate production of commodities and facilities," "set[] no limits upon the discretion or judgment of the Administrator." *Id.* at 420, 451. Despite the majority's silence on the matter, Justice Roberts surmised that its resolution of the nondelegation issues in the case left "no doubt that the decision [in *A.L.A. Schechter*] is now overruled." *Id.* at 452.

* * *

The Supreme Court's reluctance to invalidate federal legislation on nondelegation grounds became even clearer after *Yakus.* Although the Court would continue to insist that the Article I Vesting Clause placed firm limits on the amount of legislative power Congress could give away, it found not a single nondelegation violation in the decades following *A.L.A. Schechter.* This retreat from the doctrine did not go unnoticed and did not pass without criticism. In fact, one forceful critique came from within the Court itself.

In *Industrial Union Department, AFL-CIO v. American Petroleum Institute (The "Benzene Case")*, 448 U.S. 607 (1980), benzene producers challenged a health standard that strictly limited workplace exposure to the chemical. Section 3(8) of the Occupational Safety and Health Act of 1970 (the "OSH Act") defined an "occupational safety and health standard" as one that "requires conditions, or the adoption or use of one or more practices, means, methods, operations, or processes, reasonably necessary or appropriate to provide safe or healthful employment and places of employment." *Id.* at 612 (quoting 84 Stat. 1591, 29 U.S.C. § 652(8)). OSH Act § 6(b)(5) required the secretary of labor to "set the standard which most adequately assures, to the extent feasible, on the basis of the best available evidence, that no employee will suffer material impairment of health or functional capacity even if such employee has regular exposure to the hazard dealt with by such standard for the period of his working life." *Id.* at 612 (quoting 84 Stat. 1594, 29 U.S.C. § 655(b)(5)). Pursuant to § 6(b)(5), any exposure limit promulgated by the Secretary had to "be based upon research, demonstrations, experiments, and such other information as may be appropriate," and had to consider "the attainment of the highest degree of health and safety protection for the employee, . . . the latest available scientific data in the field, the feasibility of the standards, and experience gained under this and other

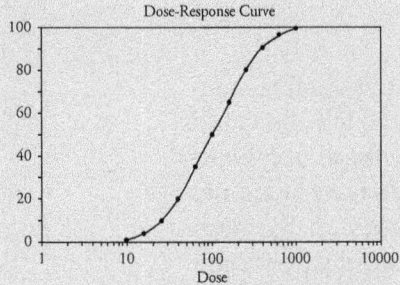
health and safety laws." *Id.* (quoting 84 Stat. 1594, 29 U.S.C. § 655(b)(5)). Benzene was widely recognized to cause blood disorders such as leukemia at high exposure levels. Accordingly, the Labor Secretary initially set the airborne exposure limit for benzene at 10 ppm (ten parts benzene per million parts of air) in 1971. The Labor Secretary significantly reduced the exposure limit to 1 ppm in 1977, concluding that the new level was "the lowest technologically feasible level that will not impair the viability of the industries regulated." *Id.* at 613. He also made employers responsible for implementing a host of monitoring and medical testing measures. A plurality of the Court invalidated the change from 10 ppm to 1 ppm, holding that the Secretary had failed to support it with the findings required by the OSH Act.

In a somewhat provocative concurrence, then-Justice William Rehnquist argued that OSH Act § 6(b)(5) constituted a clear violation of the nondelegation doctrine. After surveying the doctrine's theoretical underpinnings and its previous applications by the Court, Rehnquist arrived at the following conclusion:

> I believe that [OSH Act § 6(b)(5)] fails to pass muster. Read literally, the relevant portion of § 6(b)(5) is completely precatory, admonishing the Secretary to adopt the most protective standard if he can, but excusing him from that duty if he cannot. In the case of a hazardous substance for which a "safe" level is either unknown or impractical, the language of § 6(b)(5) gives the Secretary absolutely no indication where on the continuum of relative safety he should draw his line. Especially in light of the importance of the interests at stake, I have no doubt that the provision at issue, standing alone, would violate the doctrine against uncanalized delegations of legislative power. For me the remaining question, then, is whether additional standards are ascertainable from the legislative history or statutory context of § 6(b)(5) or, if not, whether such a standardless delegation was justifiable in light of the "inherent necessities" of the situation.

Id. at 675-76. Justice Rehnquist found no colleagues willing to join his invocation of the long-dormant nondelegation doctrine. Although nondelegation fears would occasionally convince members of the Court that federal legislation should be invalidated—*see, e.g., Am. Textile Mfrs. Inst. v. Donovan* (*The "Cotton Dust Case"*), 452 U.S. 490, 543-48 (1981) (Rehnquist, J., and Burger, C.J., dissenting); *Mistretta v. United States*, 488 U.S. 361, 415-22 (1989) (Scalia, J., dissenting)—the doctrine's dormancy continued through the late 1990s.

Then the D.C. Circuit issued a surprising opinion that afforded the Court an opportunity to reevaluate its position.

American Trucking Associations, Inc. v. Environmental Protection Agency
175 F.3d 1027 (D.C. Cir. 1999)

Before: WILLIAMS, GINSBURG and TATEL, Circuit Judges.
Per Curiam:

INTRODUCTION

The Clean Air Act requires EPA to promulgate and periodically revise national ambient air quality standards ("NAAQS") for each air pollutant identified by the agency as meeting certain statutory criteria.... For each pollutant, EPA sets a "primary standard"—a concentration level "requisite to protect the public health" with an "adequate margin of safety"—and a "secondary standard"—a level "requisite to protect the public welfare." 42 U.S.C. § 7409(b).

In July 1997 EPA issued final rules revising the primary and secondary NAAQS for particulate matter ("PM") and ozone [the PM Final Rule].... Numerous petitions for review have been filed for each rule....

I. DELEGATION

Certain "Small Business Petitioners" argue in each case that EPA has construed §§ 108 & 109 of the Clean Air Act so loosely as to render them unconstitutional delegations of legislative power. We agree. Although the factors EPA uses in determining the degree of public health concern associated with different levels of ozone and PM are reasonable, EPA appears to have articulated no "intelligible principle" to channel its application of these factors; nor is one apparent from the statute. The nondelegation doctrine requires such a principle. *See J.W. Hampton, Jr. & Co. v. United States*, 276 U.S. 394, 409 (1928). Here it is as though Congress commanded EPA to select "big guys," and EPA announced that it would evaluate candidates based on height and weight, but revealed no cut-off point. The announcement, though sensible in what it does say, is fatally incomplete. The reasonable person responds, "How tall? How heavy?"

EPA regards ozone definitely, and PM likely, as non-threshold pollutants, i.e., ones that have some possibility of some adverse health impact (however slight) at any exposure level above zero....

Thus the only concentration for ozone and PM that is utterly risk-free, in the sense of direct health impacts, is zero. Section 109(b)(1) says that EPA must set each standard at the level "requisite to protect the public health" with an "adequate margin of safety." 42 U.S.C. § 7409(b)(1). These are also the criteria by which EPA must determine whether a revision to existing NAAQS is appropriate.... For EPA to pick any non-zero level it must explain the degree of imperfection permitted. The factors that EPA has elected to examine for this purpose in themselves pose no inherent nondelegation problem. But what EPA lacks is any determinate criterion for drawing lines. It has failed to state intelligibly how much is too much.

We begin with the criteria EPA has announced for assessing health effects in setting the NAAQS for non-threshold pollutants. They are "the nature and severity of the health effects involved, the size of the sensitive population(s) at risk, the types of health information available, and the kind and degree of uncertainties that must be addressed." ... Although these criteria, so stated, are a bit vague, they do focus the inquiry on pollution's effects on public health. And most of the vagueness in the abstract formulation melts away as EPA applies the criteria: EPA basically considers severity of effect, certainty of effect, and size of population affected. These criteria, long ago approved by the judiciary, ... do not themselves speak to the issue of degree.

Read in light of these factors, EPA's explanations for its decisions amount to assertions that a less stringent standard would allow the relevant pollutant to inflict a greater quantum of harm on public health, and that a more stringent standard would result in less harm. Such arguments only support the intuitive proposition that more pollution will not benefit public health, not that keeping pollution at or below any particular level is "requisite" or not requisite to "protect the public health" with an "adequate margin of safety," the formula set out by § 109(b)(1).

Consider EPA's defense of the 0.08 ppm level of the ozone NAAQS. EPA explains that its choice is superior to retaining the existing level, 0.09 ppm, because more people are exposed to more serious effects at 0.09 than at 0.08.... In defending the decision not to go down to 0.07, EPA never contradicts the intuitive proposition, confirmed by [its data], that reducing the standard to that level would bring about comparable changes.... Instead, it [argues that]

> The most certain O3-related effects, while judged to be adverse, are transient and reversible (particularly at O3 exposures below 0.08 ppm), and the more serious effects with greater immediate and potential long-term impacts on health are less certain, both as to the percentage of individuals

exposed to various concentrations who are likely to experience such effects and as to the long-term medical significance of these effects.

Ozone Final Rule, 62 Fed. Reg. 38,868/2. In other words, effects are less certain and less severe at lower levels of exposure. This seems to be nothing more than a statement that lower exposure levels are associated with lower risk to public health....

In addition to the assertion quoted above, EPA cited the consensus of the Clean Air Scientific Advisory Committee ("CASAC") that the standard should not be set below 0.08. That body gave no specific reasons for its recommendations, so the appeal to its authority ... adds no enlightenment. [T]he question whether EPA acted pursuant to lawfully delegated authority is not a scientific one. Nothing in what CASAC says helps us discern an intelligible principle derived by EPA from the Clean Air Act.

Finally, EPA argued that a 0.07 standard would be "closer to peak background levels that infrequently occur in some areas due to nonanthropogenic sources of O_3 precursors, and thus more likely to be inappropriately targeted in some areas on such sources." But a 0.08 level, of course, is also closer to these peak levels than 0.09....

EPA frequently defends a decision not to set a standard at a lower level on the basis that there is greater uncertainty that health effects exist at lower levels than the level of the standard.... But the increasing-uncertainty argument is helpful only if some principle reveals how much uncertainty is too much. None does.

The arguments EPA offers here show only that EPA is applying the stated factors and that larger public health harms (including increased probability of such harms) are, as expected, associated with higher pollutant concentrations. The principle EPA invokes for each increment in stringency (such as for adopting the annual coarse particulate matter standard that it chose here)—that it is "possible, but not certain" that health effects exist at that level ... could as easily, for any nonthreshold pollutant, justify a standard of zero. The same indeterminacy prevails in EPA's decisions not to pick a still more stringent level. For example, EPA's reasons for not lowering the ozone standard from 0.08 to 0.07 ppm—that "the more serious effects ... are less certain" at the lower levels and that the lower levels are "closer to peak background levels," ... could also be employed to justify a refusal to reduce levels below those associated with London's "Killer Fog" of 1952. In that calamity, very high PM levels (up to 2,500 μg/m3) are believed to have led to 4,000 excess deaths in a week. Thus, the agency rightly recognizes that the question is one of degree, but offers no intelligible principle by which to identify a stopping point.

... Where (as here) statutory language and an existing agency interpretation involve an unconstitutional delegation of power, but an interpretation without the constitutional weakness is or may be available, our response is not to strike down the statute but to give the agency an opportunity to extract a determinate standard on its own.... Doing so serves at least two of three basic rationales for the nondelegation doctrine. If the agency develops determinate, binding standards for itself, it is less likely to exercise the delegated authority arbitrarily.... And such standards enhance the likelihood that meaningful judicial review will prove feasible.... A remand of this sort of course does not serve the third key function of non-delegation doctrine, to "ensure[] to the extent consistent with orderly governmental administration that important choices of social policy are made by Congress, the branch of our Government most responsive to the popular will" [*The Benzene Case,* at 685 (Rehnquist, J., concurring)]. The agency will make the fundamental policy choices. But the remand does ensure that the courts not hold unconstitutional a statute that an agency, with the application of its special expertise, could salvage. In any event, we do not read current Supreme Court cases as applying the strong form of the nondelegation doctrine voiced in Justice Rehnquist's concurrence. *See Mistretta,* 488 U.S. at 377-79.

[The court identified several possible "intelligible criteria" on which the EPA could have relied when identifying a constitutionally permissible standard. In doing so, it excluded cost-benefit analysis which the EPA was barred from considering under the D.C. Circuit's interpretation of the Clean Air Act. *See Natural Resources Defense Council, Inc. v. Administrator, U.S. EPA,* 902 F.2d 962 (D.C. Cir. 1990).]

. . . [A]n agency wielding the power over American life possessed by EPA should be capable of developing the rough equivalent of a generic unit of harm that takes into account population affected, severity and probability.... Alternatively, if EPA concludes that there is no principle available, it can so report to the Congress, along with such rationales as it has for the levels it chose, and seek legislation ratifying its choice.

[Parts II and III of the court's opinion are omitted.]

We remand the cases to EPA for further consideration of all standards at issue....

TATEL, Circuit Judge, dissenting from Part I:

The Clean Air Act has been on the books for decades, has been amended by Congress numerous times, and has been the subject of regular congressional oversight hearings. The Act has been parsed by this circuit no fewer than ten times in published opinions delineating EPA authority in the NAAQS setting process. Yet this court now threatens to strike down section 109 of the Act as an unconstitutional delegation of congressional authority unless EPA can articulate an intelligible principle cabining its discretion. In doing so, the court ignores the last half-century of Supreme Court nondelegation jurisprudence, apparently viewing these permissive precedents as mere exceptions to the rule laid down sixty-four years ago in *A.L.A. Schechter Poultry Corp. v. United States,* 295 U.S. 495 (1935)....

... The Clean Air Act does not delegate to EPA authority to do whatever is "reasonably necessary or appropriate" to protect public health. Instead, the statute directs the Agency to fashion standards that are "requisite" to protect the public health. In other words, EPA must set pollution standards at levels necessary to protect the public health, whether "reasonable" or not, whether "appropriate" or not.

Moreover, in setting standards "requisite to protect the public health," EPA discretion is not unlimited. The Clean Air Act directs EPA to base standards on "air quality criteria" that "accurately reflect the latest scientific knowledge useful in indicating the kind and extent of all identifiable effects on public health or welfare which may be expected from the presence of such pollutant in the ambient air, in varying quantities." 42 U.S.C. § 7408(a)(2); *see id.* § 7409(b)(1); *see also id.* § 7408(a)(2).... By directing EPA to set NAAQS at levels "requisite"—not reasonably requisite—to protect the public health with "an adequate margin of safety," the Clean Air Act tells EPA [to] ensure a high degree of protection....

EPA thus did not, as my colleagues charge, arbitrarily pick points on the ozone and particulate pollution continua indistinguishable from any other. Instead, acting pursuant to section 109's direction that it establish standards that, based on the "latest scientific knowledge," are "requisite" to protect the public health with "an adequate margin of safety," and operating within ranges approved by CASAC, the Agency set the ozone level just above peak background concentrations where the most certain health effects are not transient and reversible, and the fine particle level at the lowest long-term mean concentration observed in studies that showed a statistically significant relationship between fine particle pollution and adverse health effects. Whether EPA arbitrarily selected the studies it relied upon or drew mistaken conclusions from those studies (as petitioners argue), or whether EPA failed to live up to the principles it established for itself (as my colleagues believe ...), has nothing to do with our inquiry under the nondelegation doctrine. Those issues relate to whether the NAAQS are arbitrary and capricious. The Constitution requires that Congress articulate intelligible principles; Congress has done so here....

Whitman v. American Trucking Associations, Inc.
531 U.S. 457 (2001)

Justice SCALIA delivered the opinion of the Court.

These cases present the following questions: (1) Whether § 109(b)(1) of the Clean Air Act (CAA) delegates legislative power to the Administrator of the Environmental Protection Agency (EPA). (2) Whether the Administrator may consider the costs of implementation in setting national ambient air quality standards (NAAQS) under § 109(b)(1). (3) Whether the Court of Appeals had jurisdiction to review the EPA's interpretation of Part D of Title I of the CAA, 42 U.S.C. §§ 7501-7515, with respect to implementing the revised ozone NAAQS. (4) If so, whether the EPA's interpretation of that part was permissible.

[Part I of the opinion briefly describes the cases' procedural history and core facts. In Part II, the Court agrees with the D.C. Circuit that the Clean Air Act does not permit the EPA to consider implementation costs when setting NAAQS].

III

Section 109(b)(1) of the CAA instructs the EPA to set "ambient air quality standards the attainment and maintenance of which in the judgment of the Administrator, based on [the] criteria [documents of § 108] and allowing an adequate margin of safety, are requisite to protect the public health." 42 U.S.C. § 7409(b)(1). The Court of Appeals held that this section as interpreted by the Administrator did not provide an "intelligible principle" to guide the EPA's exercise of authority in setting NAAQS. "[The] EPA," it said, "lack[ed] any determinate criteria for drawing lines. It has failed to state intelligibly how much is too much." The court hence found that the EPA's interpretation (but not the statute itself) violated the nondelegation doctrine. We disagree.

In a delegation challenge, the constitutional question is whether the statute has delegated legislative power to the agency. Article I, § 1, of the Constitution vests "[a]ll legislative Powers herein granted ... in a Congress of the United States." This text permits no delegation of those powers, *Loving v. United States*, 517 U.S. 748, 771 (1996); *see id.* at 776-777 (Scalia, J., concurring in part and concurring in judgment), and so we repeatedly have said that when Congress confers decisionmaking authority upon agencies Congress must "lay down by legislative act an intelligible principle to which the person or body authorized to [act] is directed to conform." *J.W. Hampton, Jr., & Co. v. United States*, 276 U.S. 394, 409 (1928). We have never suggested that an agency can cure an unlawful delegation of legislative power by adopting in its discretion a limiting construction of the statute.... The idea that an agency can cure an unconstitutionally standardless delegation of power by declining to exercise some of that power seems to us internally contradictory. The very choice of which portion of the power to exercise—that is to say, the prescription of the standard that Congress had omitted—would itself be an exercise of the forbidden legislative authority. Whether the statute delegates legislative power is a question for the courts, and an agency's voluntary self-denial has no bearing upon the answer.

We agree with the Solicitor General that the text of § 109(b)(1) of the CAA at a minimum requires that "[f]or a discrete set of pollutants and based on published air quality criteria that reflect the latest scientific knowledge, [the] EPA must establish uniform national standards at a level that is requisite to protect public health from the adverse effects of the pollutant in the ambient air." Requisite, in turn, "mean[s] sufficient, but not more than necessary." These limits on the EPA's discretion are strikingly similar to the ones we approved in *Touby v. United States*, 500 U.S. 160 (1991), which permitted the Attorney General to designate a drug as a controlled substance for purposes of criminal drug enforcement if doing so was " 'necessary to avoid an imminent hazard to the public safety.' " *Id.* at 163. They also resemble the Occupational Safety and Health Act of 1970 provision requiring the agency to " 'set the standard which most adequately assures, to the extent feasible, on the basis of the best available evidence, that no employee will suffer any impairment of health' " — which the Court upheld in [*The Benzene Case*], 448 U.S. 607, 646 (1980), and which even then-Justice Rehnquist, who alone in that case thought the statute violated the nondelegation doctrine ... would have upheld if, like the statute here, it did not permit economic costs to be considered.

The scope of discretion § 109(b)(1) allows is in fact well within the outer limits of our nondelegation precedents. In the history of the Court we have found the requisite "intelligible principle" lacking in only two statutes, one of which provided literally no guidance for the exercise of discretion, and the other of which conferred authority to regulate the entire economy on the basis of no more precise a standard than stimulating the economy by assuring "fair competition." *See Panama Refining Co. v. Ryan*, 293 U.S. 388 (1935); *A.L.A. Schechter Poultry Corp. v. United States*, 295 U.S. 495 (1935). We have, on the other hand, upheld the validity of § 11(b)(2) of the Public Utility Holding Company Act of 1935, 49 Stat. 821, which gave the Securities and Exchange Commission authority to modify the structure of holding company systems so as to ensure that they are not "unduly or unnecessarily complicate[d]" and do not "unfairly or inequitably distribute voting power among security holders." *American Power & Light Co. v. SEC*, 329 U.S. 90, 104 (1946). We have approved the wartime conferral of agency power to fix the prices of commodities at a level that " 'will be generally fair and equitable and will effectuate the [in some respects conflicting] purposes of th[e] Act.' " *Yakus v. United States*, 321 U.S. 414, 420 (1944). And we have found an "intelligible principle" in various statutes authorizing regulation in the "public interest." *See, e.g., National Broadcasting Co. v. United States*, 319 U.S. 190, 225–226 (1943) (Federal Communications Commission's power to regulate airwaves); *New York Central Securities Corp. v. United States*, 287 U.S. 12, 24-25 (1932) (Interstate Commerce Commission's power to approve railroad consolidations). In short, we have "almost never felt qualified to second-guess Congress regarding the permissible degree of policy judgment that can be left to those executing or applying the law." *Mistretta v. United States*, 488 U.S. 361, 416 (1989) (Scalia, J., dissenting); *see id.* at 373 (majority opinion).

It is true enough that the degree of agency discretion that is acceptable varies according to the scope of the power congressionally conferred. *See Loving v. United States*, 517 U.S., at 772-773; *United States v. Mazurie*, 419 U.S. 544, 556-557 (1975). While Congress need not provide any direction to the EPA regarding the manner in which it is to define "country elevators," which are to be exempt from new-stationary-source regulations governing grain elevators, see 42 U.S.C. § 7411(i), it must provide substantial guidance on setting air standards that affect the entire national economy. But even in sweeping regulatory schemes we have never demanded, as the Court of Appeals did here, that statutes provide a "determinate criterion" for saying "how much [of the regulated harm] is too much." In *Touby*, for example, we did not require the statute to decree how "imminent" was too imminent, or how "necessary" was necessary enough, or even — most relevant here — how "hazardous" was too hazardous. 500 U.S., at 165-167.... It is therefore not conclusive for delegation purposes that, as respondents argue, ozone and particulate matter are "nonthreshold" pollutants that inflict a continuum of adverse health effects at any airborne concentration greater than zero, and hence require the EPA to make judgments of degree. "[A] certain degree of discretion, and thus of lawmaking, inheres in most executive or judicial action." *Mistretta v. United States*, at 417, (Scalia, J., dissenting); *see id* at 488 U.S., at 378-379 (majority opinion). Section 109(b)(1) of the CAA, which to repeat we interpret as requiring the EPA to set air quality standards at the level that is "requisite" that is, not lower or higher than is necessary — to protect the public health with an adequate margin of safety, fits comfortably within the scope of discretion permitted by our precedent.

We therefore reverse the judgment of the Court of Appeals remanding for reinterpretation that would avoid a supposed delegation of legislative power. It will remain for the Court of Appeals — on the remand that we direct for other reasons — to dispose of any other preserved challenge to the NAAQS under the judicial-review provisions contained in 42 U.S.C. § 7607(d)(9).

[In Part IV, the Court addressed the EPA's authority to implement the revised ozone NAAQS in so-called "nonattainment" areas; geographic locations in which ozone levels exceeded the maximum level permitted by the standard. First, the Court concluded that the D.C. Circuit had jurisdiction to review the implementation policy. Second, the Court deemed unreasonable the EPA's interpretation of the parts of the Clean Air Act dealing with implementation of the revised ozone NAAQS in nonattainment areas.]

The judgment of the Court of Appeals is affirmed in part and reversed in part, and the cases are remanded for proceedings consistent with this opinion.

It is so ordered.

Justice Thomas, concurring.

I agree with the majority that § 109's directive to the agency is no less an "intelligible principle" than a host of other directives that we have approved. I also agree that the Court of Appeals' remand to the agency to make its own corrective interpretation does not accord with our understanding of the delegation issue. I write separately, however, to express my concern that there may nevertheless be a genuine constitutional problem with § 109, a problem which the parties did not address.

The parties to these cases who briefed the constitutional issue wrangled over constitutional doctrine with barely a nod to the text of the Constitution. Although this Court since 1928 has treated the "intelligible principle" requirement as the only constitutional limit on congressional grants of power to administrative agencies, *see J. W. Hampton, Jr., & Co. v. United States*, 276 U.S. 394 (1928), the Constitution does not speak of "intelligible principles." Rather, it speaks in much simpler terms: "*All* legislative Powers herein granted shall be vested in a Congress." U.S. CONST., Art. 1, § 1 (emphasis added). I am not convinced that the intelligible principle doctrine serves to prevent all cessions of legislative power. I believe that there are cases in which the principle is intelligible and yet the significance of the delegated decision is simply too great for the decision to be called anything other than "legislative."

As it is, none of the parties to these cases has examined the text of the Constitution or asked us to reconsider our precedents on cessions of legislative power. On a future day, however, I would be willing to address the question whether our delegation jurisprudence has strayed too far from our Founders' understanding of separation of powers.

Justice STEVENS, with whom Justice SOUTER joins, concurring in part and concurring in the judgment.

Section 109(b)(1) delegates to the Administrator of the Environmental Protection Agency (EPA) the authority to promulgate national ambient air quality standards (NAAQS). In Part III of its opinion, the Court convincingly explains why the Court of Appeals erred when it concluded that § 109 effected "an unconstitutional delegation of legislative power." *American Trucking Assns., Inc. v. EPA*, 175 F.3d 1027, 1033 (D.C. Cir. 1999) (per curiam). I wholeheartedly endorse the Court's result and endorse its explanation of its reasons, albeit with the following caveat.

The Court has two choices. We could choose to articulate our ultimate disposition of this issue by frankly acknowledging that the power delegated to the EPA is "legislative" but nevertheless conclude that the delegation is constitutional because adequately limited by the terms of the authorizing statute. Alternatively, we could pretend, as the Court does, that the authority delegated to the EPA is somehow not "legislative power." Despite the fact that there is language in our opinions that supports the Court's articulation of our holding, I am persuaded that it would be both wiser and more faithful to what we have actually done in delegation cases to admit that agency rulemaking authority is "legislative power."

The proper characterization of governmental power should generally depend on the nature of the power, not on the identity of the person exercising it. *See* BLACK'S LAW DICTIONARY 899 (6th ed.1990) (defining "legislation" as, inter alia, "[f]ormulation of rule[s] for the future"); 1 K. DAVIS & R. PIERCE, ADMINISTRATIVE LAW TREATISE § 2.3, p. 37 (3d ed. 1994) ("If legislative power means the power to make rules of conduct that bind everyone based on resolution of major policy issues, scores of agencies exercise legislative power routinely by promulgating what are candidly called 'legislative rules'"). If the NAAQS that the EPA promulgated had been prescribed by Congress, everyone would agree that those rules would be the product of an exercise of "legislative power." The same characterization is appropriate when an agency exercises rulemaking authority pursuant to a permissible delegation from Congress.

My view is not only more faithful to normal English usage, but is also fully consistent with the text of the Constitution. In Article I, the Framers vested "All legislative Powers" in the Congress, Art. I, § 1, just as in Article II they vested the "executive Power" in the President, Art. II, § 1. Those provisions do not purport to limit the authority of either recipient of power to delegate authority to others. *See Bowsher v. Synar*, 478 U.S. 714, 752 (1986) (Stevens, J., concurring in judgment) ("Despite the statement in Article I of the Constitution that 'All legislative powers herein granted shall be vested in a Congress of the United States,' it is far from novel to acknowledge that independent agencies do indeed exercise legislative powers"); *INS v. Chadha*, 462 U.S. 919, 985-986 (1983) (White, J., dissenting) ("[L]egislative power can be exercised by independent agencies and Executive departments. . . ."); 1 DAVIS & PIERCE, ADMINISTRATIVE LAW TREATISE § 2.6, p. 66 ("The Court was probably mistaken from the outset in interpreting Article I's grant of power to Congress as an implicit limit on Congress' authority to delegate legislative power"). Surely the authority granted to members of the Cabinet and federal law enforcement agents is properly characterized as "Executive" even though not exercised by the President. *Cf. Morrison v. Olson*, 487 U.S. 654, 705-706 (1988) (Scalia, J., dissenting) (arguing that the independent counsel exercised "executive power" unconstrained by the President).

It seems clear that an executive agency's exercise of rulemaking authority pursuant to a valid delegation from Congress is "legislative." As long as the delegation provides a sufficiently intelligible principle, there is nothing inherently unconstitutional about it. Accordingly, while I join Parts I, II, and IV of the Court's opinion, and agree with almost everything said in Part III, I would hold that when Congress enacted § 109, it effected a constitutional delegation of legislative power to the EPA.

[Justice BREYER's opinion, concurring in part and concurring in the judgment, is omitted.]

QUESTION SET 2.3

Review & Synthesis

1. Is the "determinate criterion" test applied by the D.C. Circuit in *Whitman* more or less restrictive than the "intelligible principle" test established by the Supreme Court's nondelegation precedents? Stated differently, would the determinate criterion test find more or fewer delegations constitutional than the intelligible principle test?

2. In his *Whitman* concurrence, Justice Thomas accepted the majority's conclusion despite his disapproval of the nondelegation standard that produced it. From his perspective, the "intelligible principle" standard is judicial gloss that allows delegations the Article I Vesting Clause actually prohibits. Consider how a more restrictive nondelegation regime of the type favored by Justice Thomas might affect Congress' ability to legislate. Restrictive nondelegation could force Congress to resolve more policy issues in legislation, thereby making the content of legislation more specific. This would leave fewer policy issues to post-enactment resolution by agencies. Presumably, Congress would also want to make those policy choices more explicit. Otherwise, the courts might misunderstand its intentions and strike its legislation down in error. The need for greater specificity and explicitness would affect how Representatives and Senators bargain over legislative content. Such a need would likely make it harder for them to find mutually acceptable statutory language. This, in turn, would decrease legislative output by making it more difficult to secure the votes needed to pass bills or to overcome a presidential veto. Even when the requisite majority is achieved, the speed with which it coalesces may decrease. Do you think Justice Thomas would account for such effects when applying the nondelegation doctrine? If so, do you think he would consider them a "bug" or a "feature" (a problem to be avoided or a benefit to be secured)?

3. Justices Scalia and Stevens agreed that the D.C. Circuit misapplied the nondelegation doctrine in its *Whitman* decision. They disagreed, however, on whether the EPA was wielding "legislative" power when it promulgated the NAAQS challenged in the litigation. Discuss:
   a. Whether and why each of Justice Scalia and Justice Stevens believed that the EPA's NAAQS rulemaking was an exercise of legislative power or of executive power.
   b. Whether you find Justice Scalia's or Justice Stevens' position on the legislative-executive characterization more in line with the Constitution's text and general separation-of-powers principles.

c. Whether there are any practical consequences to characterizing agency rulemaking of the sort considered in *Whitman* as legislative or executive conduct, or whether their disagreement was purely an academic one. For instance, would choosing one framing over the other result in more or fewer nondelegation violations? If not, do the Justices disagree on a purely academic point?

4. Justice Thomas did not explicitly state whether, in his view, the EPA's rulemaking constituted legislative or executive action. Based on the analysis in his concurrence, do you think he believed it was the former or the latter?

5. Do you agree with the Court that nondelegation defects cannot be corrected by the agency voluntarily withholding part of the policymaking discretion Congress improperly granted it? Consider that the EPA did not exercise the policymaking discretion granted to it by the Clean Air Act Amendments in a vacuum. The statute's purpose, structure, and legislative history presumably cabined its decision-making freedom. Mandatory rulemaking procedures likewise would have limited how the EPA exercised its discretion to promulgate NAAQS. Should courts consider such facts when determining whether a delegation impermissibly grants agencies legislative power? *See, e.g.*, Kenneth Culp Davis, *A New Approach to Delegation*, 36 U. CHI. L. REV. 715 (1969) (arguing that the nondelegation analysis should account for the robustness of procedural safeguards against arbitrary agency decision-making).

Application & Analysis

1. The National Historic Preservation Act (the "NHPA") states, "it is a national policy to preserve for public use historic sites, buildings, and objects of national significance for the inspiration and benefit of the people of the United States." 54 U.S.C. § 320101. NPHA § 1 requires the Interior Secretary (the "Secretary"), to

> promote and regulate the use of the National Park System by means and measures that conform to the fundamental purpose of the System units, which purpose is to conserve the scenery, natural and historic objects, and wild life in the System units and to provide for the enjoyment of the scenery, natural and historic objects, and wild life in such manner and by such means as will leave them unimpaired for the enjoyment of future generations ...

54 U.S.C. § 100101. In promulgating regulations under the NHPA, the Secretary must "prescribe such regulations as the Secretary considers

necessary or proper for the use and management of System units," 54 U.S.C. § 100751(a), and any person who "violates any regulation authorized by section 100751(a) ... shall be imprisoned not more than 6 months, fined under this title, or both, and be adjudged to pay all cost of the proceedings." 18 U.S.C. § 1865.

Pursuant to this authority, the Secretary promulgated a rule prohibiting any person from operating or controlling a motor vehicle in any national park if that person is "[u]nder the influence of alcohol, or a drug, or drugs, or any combination thereof, to a degree that renders the operator incapable of safe operation." 36 C.F.R. § 4.23(a)(1). Further, the Secretary promulgated a rule providing that any person convicted of violating § 4.23(a)(1) "shall be subject to the criminal penalties provided under 18 U.S.C. 1865." 36 § 1.3. In promulgating these regulations, the Secretary explained that "[a]lthough visitors to the National Park System use a variety of access methods, the vast majority continue to rely on motor vehicles and roadways to reach park areas and to circulate within them. Consequently, the NPS has major program responsibilities in the areas of road construction and maintenance, traffic safety and traffic law enforcement." 52 Fed. Reg. at 10,670.

A park ranger stopped Gary Grey in Shenandoah National Park when she saw him driving erratically. Based on her observations and a field sobriety test, the park ranger arrested Grey for driving under the influence of alcohol. He was subsequently convicted in federal district court for violating § 4.23(a)(1).

On appeal, Grey argues that Congress' delegation of rulemaking authority to the Secretary failed to provide him with sufficient guidance. Assess the merits of his argument.

2. The Sex Offender Registration and Notification Act of 2006 ("SORNA") establishes a comprehensive national registration system "to protect the public from sex offenders and offenders against children." 34 U.S.C. § 20901. SORNA requires sex offenders to register and to update their names, addresses, employment, or student status with the jurisdictions in which they live. Failure to register or update this information can be met with criminal sanction. Sex offenders who have been convicted under federal law, or those who travel across state or international lines, and who knowingly fail to comply with SORNA can be fined or imprisoned for up to ten years. 18 U.S.C. § 2250(a).

SORNA does not state whether offenders convicted before its passage ("pre-enactment offenders") are subject to its registration requirements. Instead, Congress delegated to the Attorney General the authority to determine whether SORNA's registration requirements would apply retroactively to pre-enactment offenders. 34 U.S.C. § 20913(d). Section 20913(d) provides:

> The Attorney General shall have the authority to specify the applicability of the requirements of this subchapter to sex offenders convicted before the enactment of this chapter or its implementation in a particular jurisdiction, and to prescribe rules for the registration of any such sex offenders. . . .

In 2007, and pursuant to this authority, the Department of Justice promulgated a rule making SORNA's registration provisions applicable to pre-enactment offenders.

John Smith moved from Oklahoma to Delaware in 2011. Although SORNA required Mr. Smith to notify authorities of his change of residence, he did not tell either Oklahoma or Delaware that he had moved, and he did not register as a sex offender in Delaware after moving there. In 2012, Mr. Smith was arrested and charged with one count of failure to register as a sex offender, in violation of 18 U.S.C. § 2250(a). Mr. Smith moved to dismiss the indictment, arguing that SORNA's delegation of authority to the Attorney General to determine SORNA's retroactivity violated the nondelegation doctrine.

Analyze the merits of Mr. Smith's nondelegation argument.

3. Congress passed the Health Insurance Portability and Accountability Act of 1996 ("HIPAA") to better protect the privacy and facilitate efficient communication of patients' medical information. HIPAA's Administrative Simplification section (§ 264(a)) outlines a two-step process to adopt standards for safe electronic transmission of this information. First, § 264(a) directs the Department of Health and Human Services ("HHS") to recommend standards to Congress for protecting the privacy of individually identifiable health information. Second, § 264(a) requires HHS to promulgate final regulations based on its recommendations if Congress does not enact legislation based on them within three years. Section 264(a) also directs HHS to consider what rights individuals whose identifiable health information is transmitted should have, the procedures that should be established for the exercise of such rights, and the uses and disclosures of such information that should be authorized or required. Other HIPAA provisions specify who and what types of information the regulations would cover, and the types of penalties that would accrue for HIPAA violations.

Pursuant to the Administrative Simplification section, HHS submitted the required recommendations to Congress. However, Congress did not act on them. After the three-year statutory window closed, HHS engaged in notice-and-comment rulemaking and promulgated final regulations adopting the recommendations it had submitted to Congress. HHS gave covered entities a year to comply with them, and some smaller entities were granted additional time beyond that.

A private hospital has sued HHS to enjoin enforcement of the regulation, asserting that HIPAA violates the nondelegation doctrine for two reasons. First, it argues that § 264 lacks an "intelligible principle" that cabins the HHS Secretary's rulemaking discretion. Second, it argues that the two-step process for adopting the regulation grants HHS veto power over Congress' decision not to act on its recommendation. This veto power is legislative authority forbidden to HHS under the Article I Vesting Clause.

Assess the merits of the hospital's arguments.

4. Nondelegation Extensions and Developments

a. Delegation to Private Entities

Whitman dealt with delegation of rulemaking authority to the EPA, an independent executive agency. It accordingly did not address delegations of legislative power to entities outside of the federal government. How should courts approach nondelegation questions when the delegate is a private entity, or otherwise outside of the federal government?

Recall that in *A.L.A. Schechter*, the Roosevelt Administration asserted that a "broad and intensive co-operative effort by those engaged in trade and industry" was required to combat the Great Depression, and such cooperation should be facilitated by allowing private trade groups to formulate their own binding codes of fair competition. After a series of derisive rhetorical questions, the Court dismissed this argument out of hand:

> [W]ould it be seriously contended that Congress could delegate its legislative authority to trade or industrial associations or groups so as to empower them to enact the laws they deem to be wise and beneficent for the rehabilitation and expansion of their trade or industries? Could trade or industrial associations or groups be constituted legislative bodies for that purpose because such associations or groups are familiar with the problems of their enterprises? And could an effort of that sort be made valid by such a preface of generalities as to permissible aims as we find in [NIRA §1]? The answer is obvious. Such a delegation of legislative power is unknown to our law, and is utterly inconsistent with the constitutional prerogatives and duties of Congress.

295 U.S. at 537. The Court reiterated its distrust of private delegations the following year, in *Carter v. Carter Coal Co.*, 298 U.S. 238 (1936). Under the Bituminous Coal Conservation Act of 1935, local boards elected by coal producers had the collective power to set minimum prices for coal mines in their respective districts. Finding this arrangement unconstitutional, the Court flatly stated that "[t]he power conferred upon the majority is, in effect,

the power to regulate the affairs of an unwilling minority. This is legislative delegation in its most obnoxious form; for it is not even delegation to an official or an official body, presumptively disinterested, but to private persons whose interests may be and often are adverse to the interests of others in the same business." *Id.* at 311.

Department of Transportation v. Association of American Railroads, 575 U.S. 43 (2015).

In *A.L.A. Schechter* and *Carter Coal*, the private character of the entities delegated policymaking discretion was never in doubt. Much more recently, the Court was faced with a related and antecedent question: how do we know whether an entity delegated policymaking authority is public or private?

Amtrak does not own most of the track systems on which it operates. Rather, it uses track systems owned by freight railroad companies like Canadian National Railway, Union Pacific Railroad, and BNSF Railway. Although federal law grants Amtrak priority in using the track systems it shares with the freight railroad companies, Congress became increasingly concerned about Amtrak's mounting record of unreliability and poor on-time performance. It passed the Passenger Rail Investment and Improvement Act of 2008 ("PRIIA"), § 207(a) of which charged Amtrak and the Federal Railroad Administration ("FRA") with creating metrics and standards for assessing Amtrak's performance. The PRIIA also vested the Safety Transportation Board ("STB") with authority to investigate the causes of Amtrak's poor on-time performance as measured by those metrics and standards. Where Amtrak's performance shortcomings were attributable to freight train scheduling and congestion, the STB could order the responsible company to pay damages to Amtrak.

Amtrak and the FRA published notice in the Federal Register inviting comments on a draft of the metrics and standards and issued their final version in May 2010. Among other things, the metrics and standards required on-time performance at least 80 to 95 percent of the time for each of its routes, depending on the route and time of year. They also limited so-called host-responsible delays—delays attributable to freight railroad companies—to no more than "900 minutes per 10,000 Train-Miles," and assigned Amtrak train conductors the task of determining responsibility for particular delays. 575 U.S. at 49. The Association of American Railroads sued, alleging that its members would be injured if they had to modify their rail operations to accommodate the metrics and standards. Among other things, the Association argued that § 207 violated the nondelegation doctrine by "placing principal legislative and rulemaking authority in the hands of a private entity [Amtrak] that participates in the very industry it is supposed to regulate." *Id.* at 49-50 (internal quotations omitted).

In an exceedingly rare victory for advocates of aggressive nondelegation enforcement, the D.C. Circuit agreed. Relying heavily on 49 U.S.C. § 24301(a), which states that Amtrak "(2) shall be operated and managed as a for-profit corporation; and (3) is not a department, agency or instrumentality of the United States Government," the court concluded that Amtrak is a private entity. The court then found it "impermissible for Congress to delegate regulatory authority to a private entity." *Id.* at 51 (internal quotations omitted).

The Supreme Court reversed. Writing for the majority, Justice Anthony Kennedy took a functional approach to determining Amtrak's relationship to the federal government rather than relying solely on Congress' statutory description of it. He pointed out the numerous ways in which Amtrak's structure and governance thoroughly intertwine with congressional and executive branch decision-making. Most of Amtrak's stock is held by the Secretary of Transportation, who also sits on its board of directors; its seven appointed board members are selected by the President and are removable by him or her without cause; Board member salaries are subject to limits set by Congress; no more than five of the seven appointed Board members can be from the same political party; and the President must consult with House and Senate leaders before making Board appointments. *Id.* at 51-52. Justice Kennedy also pointed out that Congress and the President "exercise substantial, statutorily mandated supervision over Amtrak's priorities and operations." *Id.* at 52. For example, "Congress conducts frequent oversight hearings into Amtrak's budget, routes, and prices," and is required by Congress to meet several goals unrelated to "its own private economic interests." *Id.* The Court was led to conclude that Amtrak "is not an autonomous private enterprise." *Id.* at 53. In light of that conclusion, the Court remanded the case to the D.C. Circuit to reassess its prior holding.

> ### Cross-Reference
>
> Many of Amtrak's structural features mirror those used by Congress when creating so-called "independent" agencies. *See* Chapter 1. Rather than citing these features as evidence of independence from political influence, Justice Kennedy regarded them as evidence that Amtrak is actually controlled by the federal government. Are there enough structural differences between Amtrak and independent agencies like the Federal Trade Commission to persuade you that he was right?

b. Substance-Driven Nondelegation

Does application of the nondelegation doctrine depend on the regulatory context to which it is applied? On several occasions, and for a variety of reasons, the Supreme Court and lower federal courts have indicated that it might.

Foreign Affairs. In *Clinton v. New York*, 524 U.S. 417 (1998), the Court considered the constitutionality of the Line Item Veto Act of 1996, which permitted the President to cancel discrete spending provisions and tax benefits after he or she had already signed them into law. The government tried to cast the Act as an uncontroversial delegation of legislative authority to the President, materially similar to the delegation in the Tariff Act that the Court previously approved in *Marshall Field v. Clark*, 143 U.S. 649 (1892).

The Court found no such similarity, stating that it "has recognized that in the foreign affairs arena, the President has 'a degree of discretion and freedom from statutory restriction which would not be admissible were domestic affairs alone involved.'" *Clinton,* 524 U.S. at 445 (quoting *United States v. Curtiss–Wright Export Corp.,* 299 U.S. 304, 320 (1936)).

Criminal Law and Sentencing. The Supreme Court has addressed the nondelegation doctrine's applicability to the criminal context on several occasions. In *Mistretta v. United States,* 488 U.S. 361 (1989), federal prisoners challenged the United States Sentencing Commission's constitutionality. The Sentencing Reform Act of 1984 granted the Commission power to promulgate binding sentences for all federal criminal offenses, a power the plaintiffs argued was excessive and a violation of the nondelegation doctrine. In rejecting their claim, the Court did not focus on how the Commission's powers were to be applied in the criminal context. Rather than focusing on the legal context in which the Commission exercised its powers, the Court focused on whether the Act provided it with an "intelligible principle." *Mistretta,* 488 U.S. at 372. It ultimately found that the Act met and surpassed this standard: "The statute outlines the policies which prompted establishment of the Commission, explains what the Commission should do and how it should do it, and sets out specific directives to govern particular situations." *Id.* at 379 (internal quotations omitted).

Two years later, the Court again addressed a nondelegation challenge related to federal criminal law. In *Touby v. United States,* 500 U.S. 160 (1991), the Court considered the Attorney General's power under § 201(h) of the Controlled Substances Act of 1970 to temporarily schedule drugs as controlled substances. Petitioners, who were convicted of making a designer drug which the Attorney General had deemed a controlled substance, argued that § 201(h) was an unconstitutional delegation of legislative authority. Importantly, they did not argue that § 201(h) lacked an intelligible principle. In fact, they conceded that the Act contained one. The petitioners argued instead "that something more than an 'intelligible principle' is required when Congress authorizes another Branch to promulgate regulations that contemplate criminal sanctions," because such regulations "pose a heightened risk to individual liberty." *Touby,* 500 U.S. at 165-66. The Court conceded that its case law was unclear on whether this concern obligated Congress to provide its delegates with more specific instructions, but nevertheless rejected the petitioners' claim by concluding that

---

In Context

In his *Mistretta* dissent, Justice Scalia argued that the Sentencing Reform Act clearly violated the nondelegation doctrine. He first observed that "[t]he whole theory of *lawful* delegation is not that Congress is sometimes too busy or too divided and can therefore assign its responsibility of making law to someone else; but rather that a certain degree of discretion, and thus of lawmaking, *inheres* in most executive or judicial action." *Mistretta,* 488 U.S. at 417 (emphasis in original). Whatever lawmaking power the executive and judicial branches exercise merely supports the exercise of their primary powers of enforcement and adjudication, respectively. "Strictly speaking, there is *no* acceptable delegation of legislative power." *Id.* at 419. (emphasis in original). Accordingly, in Justice Scalia's view, the Commission was set up as an unconstitutional mini-Congress; it was impermissibly granted rulemaking authority while having no executive or judicial responsibilities. *Id.*

"§ 201(h) passes muster even if greater congressional specificity is required in the criminal context." *Id.* at 166.

In *Loving v. United States,* 517 U.S. 748 (1996), the Court more directly addressed the question it left unanswered in *Touby,* only this time it did so in a military setting. There the Court considered whether Congress properly delegated to the President the authority to choose the aggravating factors warranting the death penalty in murder cases tried in military courts. Loving had argued, among other things, that Congress could not delegate its authority to define criminal punishments. The Court observed that "[t]here is no absolute rule" against Congress doing so, as "long as [it] makes the violation of the regulations a criminal offense and fixes the punishment, and the regulations 'confin[e] themselves within the field covered by the statute.'" *Loving,* 517 U.S. at 768 (citing *United States v. Grimaud,* 220 U.S. 506, 518 (1911)). As to whether Congress must provide its delegates with more explicit instructions where the power to define criminal sanctions is involved, the Court did not rule it out "if [the] delegation were made to a newly created entity without independent authority in the area." *Id.* at 772 (citing *Mistretta,* 488 U.S. at 374-79). In the military context, however, the President as commander-in-chief possesses the kind of independent authority to manage military affairs that makes more explicit delegations inappropriate. *Id.*

Military Affairs and National Security. At least one federal court has ruled on the requisite specificity of legislative delegations in another context: the authority to go to war. On October 16, 2002, Congress issued a Joint Resolution authorizing President George W. Bush to initiate military action against Iraq "as he determines to be necessary and appropriate in order to — (1) defend the national security of the United States against the continuing threat posed by Iraq; and (2) enforce all relevant United Nations Security Council resolutions against Iraq." Authorization for Use of Military Force against Iraq Resolution of 2002, Pub. L. No. 107-243, 116 Stat. 1498 (2002). A group of plaintiffs, which included then-active members of the military, sought an injunction against the initiation of hostilities under the Joint Resolution. They argued that it unconstitutionally delegated Congress' power to declare war to the President. *Doe v. Bush,* 323 F.3d 133 (1st Cir. 2003). The court dismissed the case on justiciability grounds. As it was not clear at that point whether President Bush would declare war against Iraq, it found the plaintiffs' claims were not ripe for adjudication. *Id.* at 139. In dicta, the court went on to address the plaintiffs' nondelegation concerns. Citing several constitutional provisions, the court observed that the government's war powers are divided between Congress and the President. *Id.* at 142. Further, it observed that the Supreme Court had suggested that nondelegation is less of a concern in the related area of foreign affairs. *Id.* at 143-44. In such situations, the court argued that the nondelegation should be applied with less force than if Congress were delegating exclusively legislative power.

c. Recent Developments: The War over Delegation

On all but two occasions—*Panama Refining Co.* and *A.L.A. Schechter*—the Supreme Court has accepted Congress' right to delegate broad policymaking discretion to the Executive Branch. However, several of the Justices have accepted this state of affairs with begrudging resignation. As already discussed, Justice Thomas has long doubted that the "intelligible principles" test sufficiently limits Congress' ability to delegate its legislative power to the Executive Branch. Justice Samuel Alito has likewise expressed his doubts about the doctrine's fidelity to the Constitution.

Recent changes to the Court's personnel may trigger a shift in the status quo. Its two newest members, Justices Neil Gorsuch (who replaced Justice Scalia) and Brett Kavanaugh (who replaced Justice Anthony Kennedy) have vocally criticized broad delegations of legislative authority to the Executive Branch. Justice Gorsuch's dissent in *Gundy*, described below, is among the more recent examples. Although he did not participate in consideration of that case, Justice Kavanaugh later stated that the constitutional concerns raised by Gorsuch's *Gundy* dissent "may warrant further consideration in future cases." *Paul v. United States,* 140 S. Ct. 342 (2019) (Kavanaugh, J., statement respecting denial of *certiorari*).

***Gundy v. United States,* 139 S. Ct. 2116 (2019).** The Sex Offender Registration and Notification Act ("SORNA") imposes criminal penalties on sex offenders (including child sex offenders) who fail to satisfy its registration requirements. The Act delegated authority to the Attorney General to determine its applicability to sex offenders convicted prior to its enactment, and "to prescribe rules for [their] registration." 34 U.S.C. § 20913(d). Pursuant to that authority, the Attorney General issued a rule specifying that SORNA's registration requirements fully apply to pre-enactment offenders. Following his conviction for failing to register, Herman Gundy argued that § 20913(d) violated the nondelegation doctrine. A four-Justice plurality rejected Gundy's claim by finding the requisite intelligible principle to support the provision's constitutionality. Justice Alito concurred in the judgment, but only because most of the Justices seemed unwilling to revisit the nondelegation doctrine's "extraordinarily capacious standard." 139 S. Ct. at 2131(Alito, J., concurring). He made clear in the very next sentence that "[i]f a majority of this Court were willing to reconsider the [nondelegation] approach we have taken for the past 84 years, [he] would support that effort." *Id.*

In a dissent joined by Chief Justice Roberts and Justice Thomas, Justice Gorsuch read § 20913(d) as granting the Attorney General "free rein to write the rules for virtually the entire existing sex offender population in this country—a situation that promised to persist for years or decades until pre-[enactment] offenders passed away or fulfilled the terms of their registration obligations and post-[enactment] offenders came to predominate." *Id.* (Gorsuch, J., dissenting). Gorsuch argued that accepting such delegations has grave consequences for the liberty of all people, but particularly for members of politically disfavored groups like sex offenders. He also insisted that doing so ignores the Framers' rationale for making it so difficult to exercise the legislative power in the first place:

> If Congress could pass off its legislative power to the executive branch, the vesting clauses, and indeed the entire structure of the Constitution, would make no sense. Without the involvement of representatives from across the country or the demands of bicameralism and presentment, legislation would risk becoming nothing more than the will of the current President. And if laws could be simply declared by a single person, they would not be few in number, the product of widespread social consensus, likely to protect minority interests, or apt to provide stability and fair notice. Accountability would suffer too. Legislators might seek to take credit for addressing a pressing social problem by sending it to the executive for resolution, while at the same time blaming the executive for the problems that attend whatever measures he chooses to pursue. In turn, the executive might point to Congress as the source of the problem. These opportunities for finger-pointing might prove temptingly advantageous for the politicians involved, but they would also threaten to disguise responsibility for the decisions.

Id. at 2134-35 (Gorsuch, J., dissenting) (internal quotations and alterations omitted).

QUESTION SET 2.4

Review & Synthesis

1. With regard to *Association of American Railroads*:
   a. Justices Thomas and Alito, both of whom concurred in the Court's decision, repeatedly referred to a "private nondelegation doctrine." Justice Thomas described it thusly:

   > Although no provision of the Constitution expressly forbids the exercise of governmental power by a private entity, our so-called "private nondelegation doctrine" flows logically from the three Vesting Clauses. Because a private entity is neither Congress, nor the President or one of his agents, nor the Supreme Court or an inferior court established by Congress, the Vesting Clauses would categorically preclude it from exercising the legislative, executive, or judicial powers of the Federal Government. In short, the "private

nondelegation doctrine" is merely one application of the provisions of the Constitution that forbid Congress to allocate power to an ineligible entity, whether governmental or private.

575 U.S. at 87-88 (Thomas, J. concurring). Assuming the Court does apply a separate nondelegation standard for private entities, what is that standard, and is it more or less stringent than the "normal" nondelegation standard? Should it be?

b. The Court's decisions in *A.L.A. Schechter, Carter v. Carter Coal Co.*, and *Association of American Railroads* clearly indicate that constitutional concerns arise from Congress empowering private entities to wield governmental authority. Should those concerns be limited to delegations of *policymaking* authority? Section 702 of the Administrative Procedure Act (discussed in Chapter 9) allows any private person to sue in federal court if he or she has been adversely affected or aggrieved by an agency's actions. As long as the person can demonstrate factual injury (a constitutional requirement for Article III standing), they need not have a personal legal right to be protected from the agency's conduct. Is this a delegation of prosecutorial (i.e., executive) power to persons or entities outside of the government that raises "private nondelegation doctrine" concerns? *See* 575 U.S. at 68 (Thomas, J., concurring).

2. Can you think of other policy arenas apart from military affairs and national security to which a relaxed nondelegation standard might apply? What factors would you use to identify them? Given how toothless the nondelegation doctrine appears to be under normal circumstances, does it even matter if there are areas in which the courts will provide Congress greater latitude in its delegations?

3. What do you make of the Court's observation in *Loving v. United States* that Congress may have to provide more explicit instructions to "a newly created entity without independent authority" to select aggravating factors in criminal sentencing? Does the potential need for more instruction stem from the newness of the agency, from its independence, or from its role in criminal punishment? All three? What warrants a heightened concern about such delegations?

4. Most of the cases discussed above involved delegations of legislative authority to the President or to an administrative or private body subject to the President's direct supervision or control. Given the separation-of-powers concerns animating it, should the nondelegation doctrine apply with greater or lesser force if Congress delegates its policymaking powers to government entities that do not fall squarely under the President's control, like multimember boards and commissions?

5. In his *Gundy* concurrence, Justice Gorsuch asserted that broad delegations of policymaking power turn legislation into "nothing more than the will of the current President." If this degree of control over the federal government's legislative agenda is so pressing a concern, are we not there already? Consider that the President has the power to veto legislation presented to him or her by Congress, and Congress needs a supermajority (two-thirds in both the House and the Senate) to override it. According to a study published in 2004, Congress had overridden 7.1 percent of all President's vetoes in the nation's history. *See* Mitchel A. Sollenberger, Cong. Rsch. Serv., RS21750, The Presidential Veto and Congressional Procedure (2004).

B. DELEGATIONS OF JUDICIAL POWER: ARTICLE I COURTS

The Article III Vesting Clause states that the federal government's judicial power "shall be vested in one supreme Court, and in such inferior courts as the Congress may from time to time ordain and establish." It further provides that those government officials tasked with exercising this power "shall hold their Offices during good Behaviour, and shall, at stated Times, receive for their Services, a Compensation, which shall not be diminished during their Continuance in Office." Based on nothing other than this language, it would seem that any organ of the federal government performing a judicial function would have to fall within the Judiciary. It would also appear that any official tasked with performing a judicial function must have the protections of life tenure and an undiminishable salary. As the saying goes, however, the map is not the territory.

In fact, Congress has granted adjudicative authority to Executive Branch officials since the Founding Era. It also has created "legislative" or "Article I" courts whose judges receive none of the protections enumerated by the Article III Vesting Clause. All this has prompted the Supreme Court to issue numerous opinions addressing the constitutionality of non-Article III courts. It has also spurred the Court to explore what the Framers might have meant by "the judicial power." Are there disputes that do not fall within it, such that Congress may assign their resolution to other adjudicative bodies at its discretion? Even if a particular dispute does fall within "the judicial power," is the federal judiciary's authority over it exclusive? If Congress can assign initial resolution of disputes to non-Article III courts, does the Supreme Court retain appellate power over them? The following materials trace the Court's exploration of these issues.

1. Early Development: Public Rights and Private Rights

The practice of entrusting adjudication to non-Article III courts is far from new. The First Congress saw no issue in having Executive Branch officials resolve disputes regarding customs duties or Revolutionary War veterans' benefits payments. *See* Richard H. Fallon, Jr., *Of Legislative Courts, Administrative Agencies, and Article III*, 101 HARV. L. REV. 915, 919 (1988). The Supreme Court likewise gave early approval to the notion of non-Article III adjudication. In *American Insurance Co. v. Canter*, the Court, speaking through Chief Justice John Marshall, concluded that Congress' Article IV powers to govern U.S. territories included the authority to create adjudicative tribunals outside of the judicial branch. 26 U.S. (1 Pet.) 511 (1828).

Critically, Marshall distinguished such "legislative courts" from "constitutional courts." *Id.* at 546. While legislative and constitutional courts perform the same basic task — both apply preexisting rules to the facts of particular situations — the Chief Justice emphasized that the sources of their power and the conditions under which they exercise it are quite different. Constitutional courts derive their authority from Article III and the system of separated powers of which it is a part. Accordingly, Article III sets the basic rules for the operation of those courts, including ultimate supervision by the Supreme Court and judges who are insulated from political influences by life tenure and undiminishable salaries. By contrast, Article IV of the Constitution vests in Congress *complete and undivided* legislative, executive, and judicial power over U.S. territories. It is from *that* general power (not Article III) that the legislative courts at issue in *American Insurance Co.* derived their authority. Given that Congress' governance of the territories is not subject to the separation-of-powers principles organizing the federal Branches, the Constitution does not object if Congress supervises its legislative courts or affords their judges fewer protections than those owed to Article III judges. *See* 26 U.S. (1 Pet.) 511, 549 (1828).

A later case, *Murray's Lessee v. Hoboken Land & Improvement Co.*, extended non-Article III adjudication to administrative courts located in the Executive Branch (and thus subject to separation-of-powers principles). 59 U.S. 272 (1855). There, a customs agent left the country before turning over more than $1 million of customs he had collected on behalf of the Treasury Department. Pursuant to an 1820 statute, the solicitor of the treasury issued a distress warrant to seize the collector's personal property upon discovering the theft. This seizure also gave the government priority over the claims of the collector's other creditors. Those creditors sued the government, claiming that the 1820 statute gave the Solicitor judicial power in violation of Article III. *Id.* at 275.

The Court readily conceded "[t]hat the auditing of the accounts of a receiver of public moneys may be, in an enlarged sense, a judicial act" as are "all those administrative duties the performance of which involves an inquiry

into the existence of facts and the application to them of rules of law." *Id.* at
280. However, it also found that "it is not sufficient to bring such matters
under the judicial power, that they involve the exercise of judgment upon law
and fact." *Id.* (internal citation omitted). Such disputes over "public rights"
like the one at issue in the case—disputes between private parties and the
government—could be adjudicated by nonjudicial officials because they did
not automatically or exclusively fall within the Article III judicial power.
While they *could* be structured as cases or controversies that invoke the federal courts' original jurisdiction, it would be within Congress' discretion to
structure them that way. "[T]here are matters, involving public rights, which
may be presented in such form that the judicial power is capable of acting on
them, and which are susceptible of judicial determination but which congress
may or may not bring within the cognizance of the [federal] courts ... as it
may deem proper." *Id.* at 284. Congress did not enact such legislation here,
and the Court found no constitutional infirmity in the Treasury Solicitor's
power of seizure. In other words, an Executive Branch official could perform
adjudicative functions—at least those involving entitlement to government
benefits—outside the purview of the Judicial Branch without offending the
Constitution. Nevertheless, Marshall added that Congress could not "withdraw from judicial cognizance any matter which, from its nature, is the subject of a suit at the common law, or in equity, or admiralty." *Id.* at 284.

Much of the Supreme Court's early non-Article III adjudication case
law focused on this concept of "public rights" first mentioned in *Murray's
Lessee,* and its distinction from "private rights." Historically, public rights
disputes were not always regarded as a judicial matter. They were viewed
instead as essentially appropriations matters most appropriately handled
by legislatures rather than by courts. Under this view, the judicial power
established by Article III was limited to so-called "private rights" claims
(legal disputes between private parties that would have been resolved by the
courts at Westminster in 1789), disputes sounding in equity, and disputes
sounding in admiralty. Rather than sending public rights disputes to the
courts, Congress resolved them itself by passing so-called "private bills." It
also marshalled the Executive Branch's assistance by, for example, charging
the Treasury Department with adjudicating the merits of certain claims
against the government. Even here, however, Congress retained sole discretion whether to appropriate the funds required to pay Treasury's payment
recommendations.

Congress' dealing with the Judiciary had to be different. Pursuant to
the finality principle derived from Article III, federal courts must have
final authority to decide the cases it hears. In other words, the Judiciary's
decisions cannot be subject to revision or reversal by either the Legislative
or Executive Branches. *See Hayburn*'s Case, 2 U.S. 408, 409 (1792) (citing
opinions authored by Supreme Court Justices riding circuit that questioned
the constitutionality of the Invalid Pensions Act of 1792, which required that

circuit courts initially decide Revolutionary War veterans' disability pension claims subject to a stay by the Secretary of War and ultimate consideration by Congress). The price of judicial involvement in resolving public rights claims was Congress' relinquishment of its authority to finally decide them, and it was not until the late nineteenth century that Congress warmed to the idea of giving federal courts final say over how those cases were resolved.[1]

2. The Move Toward Agency Adjudication

Transferring final decision-making authority for public rights disputes to Article III courts meant that administrative agencies had to rely on judicial processes to sanction private parties or to compel their regulatory compliance. With cases like *Murray's Lessee* serving as legal predicates, this began to change near the turn of the twentieth century. It was during this period that Congress created independent agencies featuring greater autonomy from political considerations than the traditional executive department model. It vested independent commissions, like the Interstate Commerce Commission (created in 1887) and the Federal Trade Commission (created in 1914), with the power to regulate different aspects of interstate economic activity. As part of their broad portfolios, these agencies initially adjudicated disputes between private parties and the government that previously would have been heard in federal district courts. They received evidence, created factual records, and made initial judgments on the legal obligations of the parties appearing before them. Thus, the functions of adopting regulations, investigating and prosecuting their alleged violation, and judging the legal merits of those allegations came to be housed under one administrative roof. This development was followed by a similar expansion of executive department adjudicative responsibility before and during the New Deal. Overall, the trend toward more administrative adjudication shifted the judiciary's role away from case origination and toward review of decisions first made at the agency level.

As one might expect, this move toward more administrative adjudication did not sit well with everyone. As mentioned above, the Supreme Court had already sanctioned agency adjudication of public rights disputes in *Murray's Lessee*. Of recurring concern, however, was whether Congress could also delegate to agencies the power to adjudicate disputes based on *private* rights. For critics, Article III required that private rights disputes—even those based on federal statutes rather than on state common law—be decided by

---

[1] The foregoing historical account is largely drawn from three excellent sources. JAMES E. PFANDER, ONE SUPREME COURT: SUPREMACY, INFERIORITY, AND THE JUDICIAL POWER OF THE UNITED STATES 104-116, 117-119 (1st ed. 2009); Christine A. Desan, *The Constitutional Commitment to Legislative Adjudication in the Early American Tradition*, 111 HARV. L. REV. 1381 (1998); Floyd D. Shimomura, *The History of Claims Against the United States: The Evolution from Legislative Toward a Judicial Model of Payment*, 45 LA. L. REV. 625 (1985).

constitutional courts. They saw the shift of responsibility to administrative agencies as an unconstitutional dilution of the Judicial Branch's power and independence, regardless of whether federal courts retained the power of appellate review.

Shortly before the start of the New Deal, the Court addressed this issue in the landmark case of *Crowell v. Benson*, 285 U.S. 22 (1932). The Longshoremen's and Harbor Workers' Compensation Act of 1924 entitled maritime workers to compensation from their employers if, during the course of their employment, they suffered accidental injury or death on the navigable waters of the United States. Compensation claims were filed against employers with the Employee's Compensation Commission ("ECC"). The Act granted the ECC's deputy commissioners "full authority to hear and determine all questions" regarding compensation claims. *Id.* at 43. They could "issue subpoenas, administer oaths, compel the attendance and testimony of witnesses, the production of documents or other evidence or the taking of depositions, and ... do all things conformable to law which may be necessary to enable [them] effectively to discharge [their] duties." *Id.* Importantly, deputy commissioners' orders were not self-executing. Only a district court could compel compliance with them. Additionally, employers could seek review of those orders in federal district court. In those proceedings, courts reviewed deputy commissioners' conclusions of law *de novo.* The same was true of deputy commissioners' factual findings when constitutional violations were alleged. "[N]o express limitation [in the Act] attempt[ed] to preclude the court, in proceedings to set aside an order as not in accordance with law, from making its own examination and determination of facts whenever that is deemed to be necessary to enforce a constitutional right properly asserted." *Id.* at 46. The Act provided that deputy commissioners' factual determinations in all other circumstances were final when "supported by evidence and within the scope of [their] authority." *Id.*

An employer filed suit to challenge the Act's constitutionality. It argued, among other things, that permitting deputy commissioners to adjudicate private disputes usurped the judiciary's power in violation of Article III. The Court rejected this assertion. It first noted that the alleged Article III violation could not involve deputy commissioners' power over questions of law. Courts reviewed deputy commissioners' determinations of those questions *de novo.* Accordingly, the Court reasoned that the Act's alleged unconstitutionality must relate to deputy commissioners' fact-finding authority. Relying on *Murray's Lessee*, it observed that Congress may assign "public rights" cases—disputes between private persons and the government over how the latter performs its constitutional functions—to Article III courts, but it is not required to do so. Rather, "'the mode of determining matters of this class is completely within congressional control. Congress may reserve to itself the power to decide, may delegate that power to executive officers, or may commit it to judicial tribunals.'" *Id.* at 50 (citing *Ex parte Bakelite*

Corp., 279 U.S. 438, 451 (1929)). Put another way, public rights disputes do not automatically fall within the Article III judicial power. Congress could create "legislative" courts to adjudicate such public rights cases, and in fact had already done so for disputes relating to "interstate and foreign commerce, taxation, immigration, the public lands, public health, the facilities of the post office, pensions, and payments to veterans." *Id.* at 51 (citing cases).

Although the Court concluded that this particular dispute was private rather than public in nature, it still found that the narrow fact-finding authority granted to deputy commissioners did not violate Article III. Article III courts routinely used juries, special masters, commissioners, or assessors for similar purposes. *Id.* at 51, 54. Courts always retained the option of rejecting the facts found by such officials when they lacked a proper evidentiary basis, though they rarely did so. The Act placed deputy commissioners in a similar role regarding the basic facts of employers' liability to their employees. Moreover, the Act reserved "full authority to the court to deal with matters of law [and thus] provide[d] for the appropriate exercise of the judicial function in this class of cases." *Id.* at 54. Given these similarities to customary practice in Article III courts, the Court could find no constitutional infirmity in the Act.

The Court did, however, place an important limitation on administrative fact-finding. It held that so-called "jurisdictional facts" — those that are "a condition precedent to the operation of the statutory scheme" — must be independently decided by constitutional courts. *Id.* at 54-55. Jurisdictional facts establish Congress' constitutional authority to act and, as a result, determine the limits of Congress' authority vis-à-vis the rights of individuals. Administrative officers could make initial findings with respect to them, but those findings were in no way binding on the courts. With respect to the Act, those facts related to whether the injury complained of occurred on the navigable waters of the United States, and whether the person who suffered them was in fact an employee of the party from whom compensation was sought. Allowing administrative tribunals — or in this instance, a single deputy commissioner — to conclusively determine these facts would, in the Court's words, "sap the judicial power as it exists under the Federal Constitution, and ... establish a government of a bureaucratic character alien to our system." *Id.* at 57.

> **Cross-Reference**
>
> The Court returns, albeit in a different context, to whether agencies should determine the scope of their own jurisdiction in *City of Arlington, Texas v. Federal Communications Commission,* 569 U.S. 290 (2013). There, the Court considered whether the FCC's interpretation of an ambiguous jurisdictional provision in the Communications Act of 1934 was entitled to substantial deference under the *Chevron* doctrine. *See* Chapter 9, page 1078.

3. Agency Adjudication of "Private Disputes"

For several decades, courts relied on *Crowell's* holding that agencies could perform adjudicative functions in disputes between private parties as long as they did not finally decide jurisdictional facts or questions of law. The Court critically reassessed the matter after Congress passed the Bankruptcy Act of 1978.

In *Northern Pipeline Construction Co. v. Marathon Pipe Line Co.*, 458 U.S. 50 (1982), Northern filed a petition for Chapter 11 reorganization in federal bankruptcy court. As part of that proceeding, and pursuant to the jurisdiction over Chapter 11–related civil claims granted by the Bankruptcy Act of 1978, Northern also filed a state breach of contract claim against Marathon. Marathon countered that this grant of jurisdiction violated Article III. Bankruptcy courts are "legislative" courts staffed by judges whose salaries could be reduced, who received 14-year rather than lifetime appointments, and who could be removed for cause.

A plurality of the Court agreed. Writing for four Justices, William Brennan observed that "the judicial power of the United States must be vested in Art. III courts," *id.* at 63-64, administered by judges with the appointment and salary protections provided by Article III. *Id.* at 59. However, "the Court has [also] recognized certain exceptional powers bestowed upon Congress by the Constitution or by historical consensus" that allow it to delegate adjudicative power to legislative and administrative tribunals staffed by officials who are not protected by Article III. *Id.* at 70. These exceptional powers manifest in only three situations: disputes falling within the jurisdiction of territorial courts, courts-martial, and disputes adjudicating public rights. From the plurality's perspective, none of these situations described bankruptcy court jurisdiction over civil cases granted by the Bankruptcy Act.

Most importantly, the plurality did not believe that the substance of Northern's contract claim involved any public rights. While "[t]he distinction between public rights and private rights ha[d] not been definitively explained" by the Court in previous cases, *id.* at 69, Justice Brennan nevertheless concluded that "a matter of public rights must at a minimum arise 'between the government and others.'" *Id.* (citing *Ex parte Bakelite Corp.*, 279 U.S. 438, 451 (1929)). Speculating that a restructuring of the relationship between private debtors and creditors *might* involve a public right, Brennan emphasized that Northern's state law contract claim against Marathon "obviously" did not. *Id.* at 71. The final resolution of that claim "lie[s] at the core of the historically recognized judicial power," and therefore must be undertaken by an Article III court. *Id.* at 70.

The *Northern Pipeline* plurality distinguished rather than overturned *Crowell.* Justice Brennan pointed out that the rights at issue in the respective cases came from different sources of authority, even though both cases involved disputes between private parties. Whereas Northern's contract claim was based on state law, the compensation claim asserted in *Crowell* was based on a federal statute passed by Congress. "[W]hen Congress creates a substantive federal right, it possesses substantial discretion to prescribe the manner in which that right might be adjudicated — including the assignment to an adjunct of some functions historically performed by judges." *Id.* at 80.

The question, then, was whether the bankruptcy courts were independent of, or adjunct to, the federal district courts. Brennan noted that the Bankruptcy Act gave a substantial amount of federal district court authority to the bankruptcy courts, while the responsibilities given to the ECC deputy commissioners in *Crowell* were circumscribed so as not to infringe on "the essential attributes of judicial power" held by Article III courts. *Id.* at 81 (internal quotations omitted). Bankruptcy courts under the Bankruptcy Act were largely independent of the Article III courts: they held wide-ranging adjudicative powers to finally decide a host of private disputes with limited review by the federal courts, and their orders were binding and enforceable of their own accord. Contrast that with ECC deputy commissioners, who had limited fact-finding authority in a narrow area of law, had to rely on federal district courts to enforce their compensation orders, and whose decisions were subject to searching district court review. *Id.* at 84-85. Put another way, deputy commissioners' adjudicative powers supported, rather than operated outside of, the Article III decision-making framework. For the bankruptcy courts, it was the opposite.

Writing separately and joined by Justice O'Connor, Justice Rehnquist agreed that the bankruptcy courts could not be granted power to hear Northern's state law claims, but was unwilling to endorse Justice Brennan's reading of the Court's prior decisions. Observing that "[t]he cases dealing with the authority of Congress to create courts other than by use of its power under Art. III do not admit of easy synthesis," *id.* at 91-92 (Rehnquist, J., concurring), they were sufficiently satisfied that none of the Court's precedents supported the type of jurisdiction conferred by the Bankruptcy Act. They also found insufficient the level of appellate review to which the bankruptcy courts' decisions were subject (Justice Rehnquist dismissed it as "only traditional appellate review"). *Id.* at 91 (Rehnquist, J., concurring). Thus, in the end, six Justices agreed that the jurisdiction conferred on the bankruptcy courts by the Bankruptcy Act of 1978 violated Article III.

Perhaps dissatisfied with its fractured *Northern Pipeline* decision, the Court returned to the issue of non-Article III adjudication of private disputes only three years later. A 1978 amendment to the Federal Insecticide, Fungicide, and Rodenticide Act ("FIFRA") required companies to submit health, safety, and environmental data to the EPA in support of their pesticide registrations. That data could subsequently be used by other companies in support of their pesticide registrations, as long as they paid compensation to the original owners. If the parties could not reach agreement on the amount of payment, either had the option of invoking FIFRA's binding arbitration provision. The compensation would then be set by a civilian arbitrator, subject to limited judicial review.

In *Thomas v. Union Carbide Agricultural Products, Co.*, 473 U.S. 568 (1985), pesticide manufacturers claimed that this binding arbitration provision violated Article III by transferring traditional judicial functions to arbitrators and severely restricting judicial review. Writing for the Court, Justice

O'Connor upheld the provision's constitutionality. Unlike the state contract claim the Court considered in *Northern Pipeline*, she observed that compensation claims subject to FIFRA's arbitration requirement were creatures of federal law. Moreover, she rejected the manufacturers' reading of *Northern Pipeline* and *Crowell* that would have required that compensation disputes be resolved by Article III courts simply because the government was not a named party. She emphasized that "a bright-line test for determining the requirements of Article III did not command a majority of the Court in *Northern Pipeline*," nor did a majority "endorse the implication of the private right/public right dichotomy that Article III has no force simply because a dispute is between the Government and an individual." *Id.* at 586-87. In other words, whether an Article III court must adjudicate FIFRA compensation disputes did not turn on the identity of the parties. Rather, "[t]he enduring lesson of *Crowell* is that practical attention to substance rather than doctrinaire reliance on formal categories should inform application of Article III." *Id.* at 587.

Accordingly, Justice O'Connor cited several cases in which the Court treated disputes between private parties as essentially involving public rights and found that their adjudication by administrative agencies did not violate Article III. She then focused on several features of FIFRA's binding arbitration provision — each relating to judicial functions typically reserved to Article III courts — to reach the same conclusion. First, the right to compensation created by FIFRA bore many characteristics of public rights, as use of pesticide registrants' data supported Congress' regulatory goal of safeguarding public health. Congress' chosen mechanism for determining the amount of that compensation — binding arbitration between data providers and users — did not require the involvement of federal courts because it fell well within Congress' Article I power to have agencies allocate regulatory costs and benefits. *Id.* at 590–91. Second, she found that the arbitration scheme posed no threat to independent decision-making because the arbitrators were selected by the parties on a case-by-case basis. *Id.* at 591. Third, the fact that arbitrators' decisions did not depend on federal court enforcement against unwilling parties (invocation of the binding arbitration provision was optional) signaled that it fell outside of Article III's purview. *Id.* Finally, Justice O'Connor deemed appropriate the level of appellate review applied to arbitrators' findings and conclusions; courts could reverse for abuse, for arbitrators overstepping their statutorily granted authority, or for constitutional errors. *Id.* at 593. In sum, the Court concluded that "Congress, acting for a valid legislative purpose pursuant to its constitutional powers under Article I, may create a seemingly 'private' right that is so closely integrated into a public regulatory scheme as to be a matter appropriate for agency resolution with limited involvement by the Article III judiciary." *Id.* at 593-94.

Justice Brennan filed a concurrence opinion to quibble with how the majority characterized his plurality opinion in *Northern Pipeline*. He bristled at the suggestion that he based the necessity of federal court adjudication on a formalistic distinction between private and public rights, or on the simple fact that the federal government was or was not a party. Instead, he insisted that the *Northern Pipeline* plurality actually "concluded that public rights cases ... involved disputes arising from the Federal Government's administration of its laws or programs." *Id.* at 596 (Brennan, J., concurring). In other words, public rights disputes were not identified by the crude proxy of named parties, but by disagreements that result from the federal government's regulatory efforts. Although this seems like a *post hoc* expansion of *Northern Pipeline*'s analysis, Justice Brennan nevertheless agreed with the majority's context-driven approach, which focused on Congress' powers under Article I and the amount of adjudicative authority delegated to administrative courts.

The Court again tackled the issue of agency adjudication of private disputes a short three years later, this time in the important case of *Commodity Futures Trading Commission v. Schor*. As with *Thomas v. Union Carbide*, Justice O'Connor authored the majority's opinion with Justice Brennan expressing his differences (this time, in dissent).

Commodity Futures Trading Commission v. Schor
478 U.S. 833 (1986)

Justice O'Connor delivered the opinion of the Court.

The question presented is whether the Commodity Exchange Act (CEA or Act), 7 U.S.C. § 1 *et seq.*, empowers the Commodity Futures Trading Commission (CFTC or Commission) to entertain state law counterclaims in reparation proceedings and, if so, whether that grant of authority violates Article III of the Constitution.

I

The CEA broadly prohibits fraudulent and manipulative conduct in connection with commodity futures transactions. In 1974, Congress "overhaul[ed]" the Act in order to institute a more "comprehensive regulatory structure to oversee the volatile and esoteric futures trading complex." H.R. REP. No. 93-975, at 1 (1974). Congress also determined that the broad regulatory powers of the CEA were most appropriately vested in an agency which would be relatively immune from the "political winds that sweep Washington." H.R. REP. No. 93-975, at 44, 70. It therefore created an independent agency, the CFTC, and entrusted to it sweeping authority to implement the CEA.

Among the duties assigned to the CFTC was the administration of a reparations procedure through which disgruntled customers of professional commodity brokers could seek redress for the brokers' violations of the Act or CFTC regulations. Thus, § 14 of the CEA, 7 U.S.C. § 18 (1976 ed.), provides that any person injured by such violations may apply to the Commission for an order directing the offender to pay reparations to the complainant and may enforce that order in federal district court. Congress intended this administrative procedure to be an "inexpensive and expeditious" alternative to existing fora available to aggrieved customers, namely, the courts and arbitration. S. REP. No. 95-850, at 11 (1978).

In conformance with the congressional goal of promoting efficient dispute resolution, the CFTC promulgated a regulation in 1976 which allows it to adjudicate counterclaims "aris[ing] out of the transaction or occurrence or series of transactions or occurrences set forth in the complaint." (17 CFR § 12.23(b)(2) (1983)). This permissive counterclaim rule leaves the respondent in a reparations proceeding free to seek relief against the reparations complainant in other fora.

The instant dispute arose in February 1980, when respondents Schor and Mortgage Services of America, Inc., invoked the CFTC's reparations jurisdiction by filing complaints against petitioner ContiCommodity Services, Inc. (Conti), a commodity futures broker, and Richard L. Sandor, a Conti employee. Schor had an account with Conti which contained a debit balance because Schor's net futures trading losses and expenses, such as commissions, exceeded the funds deposited in the account. Schor alleged that this debit balance was the result of Conti's numerous violations of the CEA....

Before receiving notice that Schor had commenced the reparations proceeding, Conti had filed a diversity action in Federal District Court [alleging common law breach of contract] to recover the debit balance.... Schor counterclaimed in this action, reiterating his charges that the debit balance was due to Conti's violations of the CEA. Schor also moved on two separate occasions to dismiss or stay the District Court action, arguing that the continuation of the federal action would be a waste of judicial resources and an undue burden on the litigants in view of the fact that "[t]he reparations proceedings ... will fully ... resolve and adjudicate all the rights of the parties to this action with respect to the transactions which are the subject matter of this action." ...

Although the District Court declined to stay or dismiss the suit ..., Conti voluntarily dismissed the federal court action and presented its debit balance claim by way of a counterclaim in the CFTC reparations proceeding. Conti denied violating the CEA and instead insisted that the debit balance resulted from Schor's trading, and was therefore a simple debt owed by Schor....

After discovery, briefing, and a hearing, the Administrative Law Judge (ALJ) in Schor's reparations proceeding ruled in Conti's favor on both Schor's claims and Conti's counterclaims. After this ruling, Schor for the first time challenged the CFTC's statutory authority to adjudicate Conti's counterclaim. The ALJ rejected Schor's challenge, stating himself "bound by agency regulations and published agency policies." The Commission declined to review the decision and allowed it to become final, at which point Schor filed a petition for review with the Court of Appeals for the District of Columbia Circuit. Prior to oral argument, the Court of Appeals, *sua sponte*, raised the question whether CFTC could constitutionally adjudicate Conti's counterclaims in light of *Northern Pipeline Construction Co. v. Marathon Pipe Line Co.*, 458 U.S. 50 (1982), in which this Court held that "Congress may not vest in a non-Article III court the power to adjudicate, render final judgment, and issue binding orders in a traditional contract action arising under state law, without consent of the litigants, and subject only to ordinary appellate review." *Thomas v. Union Carbide Agricultural Products Co.*, 473 U.S. 568, 584 (1985) (*Thomas*).

After briefing and argument, the Court of Appeals upheld the CFTC's decision on Schor's claim in most respects, but ordered the dismissal of Conti's counterclaims on the ground that "the CFTC lacks authority (subject matter competence) to adjudicate" common law counterclaims. 740 F.2d, at 1264. In support of this latter ruling, the Court of Appeals reasoned that the CFTC's exercise of jurisdiction over Conti's common law counterclaim gave rise to "[s]erious constitutional problems" under *Northern Pipeline*. 740 F.2d, at 1277. The Court of Appeals therefore concluded that, under well-established principles of statutory construction, the relevant inquiry was whether the CEA was "'fairly susceptible' of [an alternative] construction," such that Article III objections, and thus unnecessary constitutional adjudication, could be avoided.

After examining the CEA and its legislative history, the court concluded that Congress had no "clearly expressed" or "explicit" intention to give the CFTC constitutionally questionable jurisdiction over state common law counterclaims. The Court of Appeals therefore ... [read] the CEA to authorize the CFTC to adjudicate only those counterclaims alleging violations of the Act or CFTC regulations. Because Conti's counterclaims did not allege such violations, the Court of Appeals held that the CFTC exceeded its authority in adjudicating those claims, and ordered that the ALJ's decision on the claims be reversed and the claims dismissed for lack of jurisdiction.

... This Court granted the CFTC's petition for certiorari, vacated the Court of Appeals' judgment, and remanded the case for further consideration....

On remand, the Court of Appeals reinstated its prior judgment....

We again granted certiorari ... and now reverse.

II

... Assuming that the Court of Appeals correctly discerned a "serious" constitutional problem in the CFTC's adjudication of Conti's counterclaim, we nevertheless believe that the court was mistaken in finding that the CEA could fairly be read to preclude the CFTC's exercise of jurisdiction over that counterclaim. Our examination of the CEA and its legislative history and purpose reveals that Congress plainly intended the CFTC to decide counterclaims asserted by respondents in reparations proceedings, and just as plainly delegated to the CFTC the authority to fashion its counterclaim jurisdiction in the manner the CFTC determined necessary to further the purposes of the reparations program....

In view of the abundant evidence that Congress both contemplated and authorized the CFTC's assertion of jurisdiction over Conti's common law counterclaim, we conclude that the Court of Appeals' analysis is untenable. The canon of construction that requires courts to avoid unnecessary constitutional adjudication did not empower the Court of Appeals to manufacture a restriction on the CFTC's jurisdiction that was nowhere contemplated by Congress and to reject plain evidence of congressional intent because that intent was not specifically embodied in a statutory mandate.... We therefore are squarely faced with the question whether the CFTC's assumption of jurisdiction over common law counterclaims violates Article III of the Constitution.

III

Article III, § 1, directs that the "judicial Power of the United States shall be vested in one supreme Court and in such inferior Courts as the Congress may from time to time ordain and establish," and provides that these federal courts shall be staffed by judges who hold office during good behavior, and whose compensation shall not be diminished during tenure in office. Schor claims that these provisions prohibit Congress from authorizing the initial adjudication of common law counterclaims by the CFTC, an administrative agency whose adjudicatory officers do not enjoy the tenure and salary protections embodied in Article III.

Although our precedents in this area do not admit of easy synthesis, they do establish that the resolution of claims such as Schor's cannot turn on conclusory reference to the language of Article III. Rather, the constitutionality of a given congressional delegation of adjudicative functions to a non-Article III body must be assessed by reference to the purposes underlying the requirements of Article III....

A

Article III, § 1, serves both to protect "the role of the independent judiciary within the constitutional scheme of tripartite government," *Thomas* at 583, and to safeguard litigants' "right to have claims decided before judges who are free from potential domination by other branches of government." *United States v. Will*, 449 U.S. 200, 218 (1980). Although our cases have provided us with little occasion to discuss the nature or significance of this latter safeguard, our prior discussions of Article III, § 1's guarantee of an independent and impartial adjudication by the federal judiciary of matters within the judicial power of the United States intimated that this guarantee serves to protect primarily personal, rather than structural, interests.

Our precedents also demonstrate, however, that Article III does not confer on litigants an absolute right to the plenary consideration of every nature of claim by an Article III court. Moreover, as a personal right, Article III's guarantee of an impartial and independent federal adjudication is subject to waiver, just as are other personal constitutional rights that dictate the procedures by which civil and criminal matters must be tried. Indeed, the relevance of concepts of waiver to Article III challenges is demonstrated by our decision in *Northern Pipeline*, in which the absence of consent to an initial adjudication before a non-Article III tribunal was relied on as a significant factor in determining that Article III forbade such adjudication.

In the instant cases, Schor indisputably waived any right he may have possessed to the full trial of Conti's counterclaim before an Article III court. Schor expressly demanded that Conti proceed on its counterclaim in the reparations proceeding rather than before the District Court, and was content to have the entire dispute settled in the forum he had selected until the ALJ ruled against him on all counts; it was only after the ALJ rendered a decision to which he objected that Schor raised any challenge to the CFTC's consideration of Conti's counterclaim.

Even were there no evidence of an express waiver here, Schor's election to forgo his right to proceed in state or federal court on his claim and his decision to seek relief instead in a CFTC reparations proceeding constituted an effective waiver. Three years before Schor instituted his reparations action, a private right of action under the CEA was explicitly recognized in the Circuit in which Schor and Conti filed suit in District Court. Moreover, at the time Schor decided to seek relief before the CFTC rather than in the federal courts, the CFTC's regulations made clear that it was empowered to adjudicate all counterclaims "aris[ing] out of the same transaction or occurrence or series of transactions or occurrences set forth in the complaint." 41 Fed. Reg. 3995 (1976). Thus, Schor had the option of having the common law counterclaim against him adjudicated in a federal Article III court, but, with full knowledge that the CFTC would exercise jurisdiction over that claim, chose to avail himself of the quicker and less expensive procedure Congress had provided him. In such circumstances, it is clear that Schor effectively agreed to an adjudication by the CFTC of the entire controversy by seeking relief in this alternative forum.

B

As noted above, our precedents establish that Article III, § 1, not only preserves to litigants their interest in an impartial and independent federal adjudication of claims within the judicial power of the United States, but also serves as "an inseparable element of the constitutional system of checks and balances." *Northern Pipeline*, 458 U.S., at 58. Article III, § 1 safeguards the role of the Judicial Branch in our tripartite system by barring congressional attempts "to transfer jurisdiction [to non-Article III tribunals] for the purpose of emasculating" constitutional courts, *National Insurance Co. v. Tidewater Co.*, 337 U.S. 582, 644 (1949) (Vinson, C.J., dissenting), and thereby preventing "the encroachment or aggrandizement of one branch at the expense of the other." *Buckley v. Valeo*, 424 U.S. 1, 122 (1976) (*per curiam*). To the extent that this structural principle is implicated in a given case, the parties cannot by consent cure the constitutional difficulty for the same reason that the parties by consent cannot confer on federal courts subject-matter jurisdiction beyond the limitations imposed by Article III, § 2. When these Article III limitations are at issue, notions of consent and waiver cannot be dispositive because the limitations serve institutional interests that the parties cannot be expected to protect.

In determining the extent to which a given congressional decision to authorize the adjudication of Article III business in a non-Article III tribunal impermissibly threatens the institutional integrity of the Judicial Branch, the Court has declined to adopt formalistic and unbending rules. Although such rules might lend a greater degree of coherence to this area of the law, they might also unduly constrict Congress' ability to take needed and innovative action pursuant to its Article I powers. Thus, in reviewing Article III challenges, we have weighed a number of factors, none of which has been deemed determinative, with an eye to the practical effect that the congressional action will have on the constitutionally assigned role of the federal judiciary. Among the factors upon which we have focused are the extent to which the "essential attributes of judicial power" are reserved to Article III courts, and, conversely, the extent to which the non-Article III forum exercises the range of jurisdiction and powers normally vested only in Article III courts, the origins and importance of the right to be adjudicated, and the concerns that drove Congress to depart from the requirements of Article III.

An examination of the relative allocation of powers between the CFTC and Article III courts in light of the considerations given prominence in our precedents demonstrates that the congressional scheme does not impermissibly intrude on the province of the judiciary. The CFTC's adjudicatory powers depart from the traditional agency model in just one respect: the CFTC's jurisdiction over common law counterclaims. While wholesale importation of concepts of pendent or ancillary jurisdiction into the agency context may create greater constitutional difficulties, we decline to endorse an absolute prohibition on such jurisdiction out of fear of where some hypothetical "slippery slope" may deposit us. . . .

In the instant cases, we are likewise persuaded that there is little practical reason to find that this single deviation from the agency model is fatal to the congressional scheme. Aside from its authorization of counterclaim jurisdiction, the CEA leaves far more of the "essential attributes of judicial power" to Article III courts than did that portion of the Bankruptcy Act found unconstitutional in *Northern Pipeline*. The CEA scheme in fact hews closely to the agency model approved by the Court in *Crowell v. Benson*, 285 U.S. 22 (1932).

The CFTC, like the agency in *Crowell*, deals only with a "particularized area of law," *Northern Pipeline*, 458 U.S., at 85, whereas the jurisdiction of the bankruptcy courts found unconstitutional in *Northern Pipeline* extended to broadly "all civil proceedings arising under title 11 or arising in or *related to* cases under title 11." 28 U.S.C. § 1471(b) (quoted in *Northern Pipeline*, 458 U.S., at 85) (emphasis added). CFTC orders, like those of the agency in *Crowell*, but unlike those of the bankruptcy courts under the 1978 Act, are enforceable only by order of the district court. CFTC orders are also reviewed under the same "weight of the evidence" standard sustained in *Crowell*, rather than the more deferential standard found lacking in *Northern Pipeline*. The legal rulings of the CFTC, like the legal determinations of the agency in *Crowell*, are subject to *de novo* review. Finally, the CFTC, unlike the bankruptcy courts under the 1978 Act, does not exercise "all ordinary powers of district courts," and thus may not, for instance, preside over jury trials or issue writs of habeas corpus.

Of course, the nature of the claim has significance in our Article III analysis quite apart from the method prescribed for its adjudication. The counterclaim asserted in this litigation is a "private" right for which state law provides the rule of decision. It is therefore a claim of the kind assumed to be at the "core" of matters normally reserved to Article III courts. Yet this conclusion does not end our inquiry; just as this Court has rejected any attempt to make determinative for Article III purposes the distinction between public rights and private rights . . . there is no reason inherent in separation of powers principles to accord the state law character of a claim talismanic power in Article III inquiries.

We have explained that "the public rights doctrine reflects simply a pragmatic understanding that when Congress selects a quasi-judicial method of resolving matters that 'could be conclusively determined by the Executive and Legislative Branches,' the danger of encroaching on the judicial powers" is less than when private rights, which are normally within the purview of the judiciary, are relegated as an initial matter to administrative adjudication. Similarly, the state law character of a claim is significant for purposes of determining the effect that an initial adjudication of those claims by a non-Article III tribunal will have on the separation of powers for the simple reason that private, common law rights were historically the types of matters subject to resolution by Article III courts. The risk that Congress may improperly have encroached on the federal judiciary is obviously magnified when Congress "withdraw[s] from judicial cognizance any matter which, from its nature, is the subject of a suit at the common law, or in equity, or admiralty" and which therefore has traditionally been tried in Article III courts, and allocates the decision of those matters to a non-Article III forum of its own creation. Accordingly, where private, common law rights are at stake, our examination of the congressional attempt to control the manner in which those rights are adjudicated has been searching. In this litigation, however, '[l]ooking beyond form to the substance of what" Congress has done, we are persuaded that the congressional authorization of limited CFTC jurisdiction over a narrow class of common law claims as an incident to the CFTC's primary, and unchallenged, adjudicative function does not create a substantial threat to the separation of powers. *Thomas*, 473 U.S., at 589.

It is clear that Congress has not attempted to "withdraw from judicial cognizance" the determination of Conti's right to the sum represented by the debit balance in Schor's account. Congress gave the CFTC the authority to adjudicate such matters, but the decision to invoke this forum is left entirely to the parties and the power of the federal judiciary to take jurisdiction of these matters is unaffected. In such circumstances, separation of powers concerns are diminished, for it seems self-evident that just as Congress may encourage parties to settle a dispute out of court or resort to arbitration without impermissible incursions on the separation of powers, Congress may make available a quasi-judicial mechanism through which willing parties may, at their option, elect to resolve their differences. This is not to say, of course, that if Congress created a phalanx of non-Article III tribunals equipped to handle the entire business of the Article III courts without any Article III supervision or control and without evidence of valid and specific legislative necessities, the fact that the parties had the election to proceed in their forum of choice would necessarily save the scheme from constitutional attack. But this case obviously bears no resemblance to such a scenario, given the degree of judicial control saved to the federal courts, ... as well as the congressional purpose behind the jurisdictional delegation, the demonstrated need for the delegation, and the limited nature of the delegation.

When Congress authorized the CFTC to adjudicate counterclaims, its primary focus was on making effective a specific and limited federal regulatory scheme, not on allocating jurisdiction among federal tribunals. Congress intended to create an inexpensive and expeditious alternative forum through which customers could enforce the provisions of the CEA against professional brokers. Its decision to endow the CFTC with jurisdiction over such reparations claims is readily understandable given the perception that the CFTC was relatively immune from political pressures, ... and the obvious expertise that the Commission possesses in applying the CEA and its own regulations. This reparations scheme itself is of unquestioned constitutional validity. It was only to ensure the effectiveness of this scheme that Congress authorized the CFTC to assert jurisdiction over common law counterclaims. Indeed, as was explained above, absent the CFTC's exercise of that authority, the purposes of the reparations procedure would have been confounded.

It also bears emphasis that the CFTC's assertion of counterclaim jurisdiction is limited to that which is necessary to make the reparations procedure workable. The CFTC adjudication of common law counterclaims is incidental to, and completely dependent upon, adjudication of reparations claims created by federal law, and in actual fact is limited to claims arising out of the same transaction or occurrence as the reparations claim.

In such circumstances, the magnitude of any intrusion on the Judicial Branch can only be termed *de minimis*. Conversely, were we to hold that the Legislative Branch may not permit such limited cognizance of common law counterclaims at the election of the parties, it is clear that we would "defeat the obvious purpose of the legislation to furnish a prompt, continuous, expert and inexpensive method for dealing with a class of questions of fact which are peculiarly suited to examination and determination by an administrative agency specially assigned to that task." *Crowell*, 285 U.S., at 46. We do not think Article III compels this degree of prophylaxis.

> **Cross-Reference**
>
> *Bowsher v. Synar* involved a challenge to the Gramm-Rudman-Hollings Act of 1985. The Act granted the Comptroller General, an official removable by Congress, the power to request cuts to the federal budget. Those cuts automatically took effect under conditions specified by the Act. The question in the case was whether the powers granted to the Comptroller General violated the constitutional separation of powers. *Bowsher* is more fully considered in Chapter 8.

Nor does our decision in *Bowsher v. Synar*, 478 U.S. 714 (1986), require a contrary result. Unlike *Bowsher*, this case raises no question of the aggrandizement of congressional power at the expense of a coordinate branch. Instead, the separation of powers question presented in this litigation is whether Congress impermissibly undermined, without appreciable expansion of its own power, the role of the Judicial Branch. In any case, we have, consistent with *Bowsher*, looked to a number of factors in evaluating the extent to which the congressional scheme endangers separation of powers principles under the circumstances presented, but have found no genuine threat to those principles to be present in this litigation.

C

... The judgment of the Court of Appeals for the District of Columbia Circuit is reversed, and the cases remanded for further proceedings consistent with this opinion.

It is so ordered.

Justice BRENNAN, with whom Justice MARSHALL joins, dissenting.

... On its face, Article III, § 1, seems to prohibit the vesting of any judicial functions in either the Legislative or the Executive Branch. The Court has, however, recognized three narrow exceptions to the otherwise absolute mandate of Article III: territorial courts; courts-martial; and courts that adjudicate certain disputes concerning public rights. Unlike the Court, I would limit the judicial authority of non-Article III federal tribunals to these few, long-established exceptions and would countenance no further erosion of Article III's mandate.

I

The Framers knew that "[t]he accumulation of all powers, Legislative, Executive, and Judiciary, in the same hands, whether of one, a few, or many, and whether hereditary, self-appointed, or elective, may justly be pronounced the very definition of tyranny." The Federalist No. [47], p. 334 (H. Dawson ed. 1876) (J. Madison). In order to prevent such tyranny, the Framers devised a governmental structure composed of three distinct branches—"a vigorous Legislative Branch," "a separate and wholly independent Executive Branch," and "a Judicial Branch equally independent." *Bowsher v. Synar*, 478 U.S. 714, 722 (1986). The separation of powers and the checks and balances that the Framers built into our tripartite form of government were intended to operate as a "self-executing safeguard against the encroachment or aggrandizement of one branch at the expense of the other." *Buckley v. Valeo*, 424 U.S. 1, 122 (1976) (*per curiam*). "'The fundamental necessity of maintaining each of the three general departments of government entirely free from the control or coercive influence, direct or indirect, of either of the others, has often been stressed and is hardly open to serious question.'" *Bowsher*, 478 U.S., at 725 (quoting *Humphrey's Executor v. United States*, 295 U.S. 602, 629 (1935)). The federal judicial power, then, must be exercised by judges who are independent of the Executive and the Legislature in order to maintain the checks and balances that are crucial to our constitutional structure.

The Framers also understood that a principal benefit of the separation of the judicial power from the legislative and executive powers would be the protection of individual litigants from decisionmakers susceptible to majoritarian pressures. Article III's salary and tenure provisions promote impartial adjudication by placing the judicial power of the United States "in a body of judges insulated from majoritarian pressures and thus able to enforce [federal law] without fear of reprisal or public rebuke." *United States v. Raddatz*, 447 U.S. 667, 704 (1980) (MARSHALL, J., dissenting). As Alexander Hamilton observed, "[t]hat inflexible and uniform adherence to the rights of the Constitution, and of individuals, which we perceive to be indispensable in the Courts of justice can certainly not be expected from Judges who hold their offices by a temporary commission." The Federalist No. 78, p. 546 (H. Dawson ed. 1876).

These important functions of Article III are too central to our constitutional scheme to risk their incremental erosion. The exceptions we have recognized for territorial courts, courts-martial, and administrative courts were each based on "certain exceptional powers bestowed upon Congress by the Constitution or by historical consensus." *Northern Pipeline*, 458 U.S., at 70 (opinion of BRENNAN, J.). Here, however, there is no equally forceful reason to extend further these exceptions to situations that are distinguishable from existing precedents....

II

... The Court requires that the legislative interest in convenience and efficiency be weighed against the competing interest in judicial independence. In doing so, the Court pits an interest the benefits of which are immediate, concrete, and easily understood against one, the benefits of which are almost entirely prophylactic, and thus often seem remote and not worth the cost in any single case. Thus, while this balancing creates the illusion of objectivity and ineluctability, in fact the result was foreordained, because the balance is weighted against judicial independence. The danger of the Court's balancing approach is, of course, that as individual cases accumulate in which the Court finds that the short-term benefits of efficiency outweigh the long-term benefits of judicial independence, the protections of Article III will be eviscerated....

[I]n *Bowsher v. Synar*, 478 U.S. 714 (1986), we rejected the appellants' argument that legislative convenience saved the constitutionality of the assignment by Congress to the Comptroller General of essentially executive functions, stating: " '[T]he fact that a given law or procedure is efficient, convenient, and useful in facilitating functions of government, standing alone, will not save it if it is contrary to the Constitution. Convenience and efficiency are not the primary objectives—or the hallmarks—of democratic government....' " *Id.* at 736....

It is impossible to reconcile the radically different approaches the Court takes to separation of powers in this litigation and in *Bowsher*. The Framers established three coequal branches of government and intended to preserve each from encroachment by either of the others. The Constitution did not grant Congress the general authority to bypass the Judiciary whenever Congress deems it advisable, any more than it granted Congress the authority to arrogate to itself executive functions.

III

According to the Court, the intrusion into the province of the Federal Judiciary caused by the CFTC's authority to adjudicate state-law counterclaims is insignificant, both because the CFTC shares in, rather than displaces, federal district court jurisdiction over these claims and because only a very narrow class of state-law issues are involved. The "sharing" justification fails under the reasoning used by the Court to support the CFTC's authority. If the administrative reparations proceeding is so much more convenient and efficient than litigation in federal district court that abrogation of Article III's commands is warranted, it seems to me that complainants would rarely, if ever, choose to go to district court in the first instance. Thus, any "sharing" of jurisdiction is more illusory than real.

More importantly, the Court, in emphasizing that this litigation will permit solely a narrow class of state-law claims to be decided by a non-Article III court, ignores the fact that it establishes a broad principle. The decision today may authorize the administrative adjudication only of state-law claims that stem from the same transaction or set of facts that allow the customer of a professional commodity broker to initiate reparations proceedings before the CFTC, but the reasoning of this decision strongly suggests that, given "legislative necessity" and party consent, any federal agency may decide state-law issues that are ancillary to federal issues within the agency's jurisdiction. Thus, while in this litigation "the magnitude of any intrusion on the Judicial Branch" may conceivably be characterized as "*de minimis*," the potential impact of the Court's decision on federal-court jurisdiction is substantial. The Court dismisses warnings about the dangers of its approach, asserting simply that it does not fear the slippery slope, and that this litigation does not involve the creation by Congress of a "phalanx of non-Article III tribunals equipped to handle the entire business of the Article III courts." A healthy respect for the precipice on which we stand is warranted, however, for this reason: Congress can seriously impair Article III's structural and individual protections without assigning away "the entire business of the Article III courts." It can do so by diluting the judicial power of the federal courts. And, contrary to the Court's intimations, dilution of judicial power operates to impair the protections of Article III regardless of whether Congress acted with the "good intention" of providing a more efficient dispute resolution system or with the "bad intention" of strengthening the Legislative Branch at the expense of the Judiciary....

* * *

Bankruptcy Redux: Stern v. Marshall, 564 U.S. 462 (2011). As of this writing, the Supreme Court has not revisited the issue of agency adjudication of private rights since its decision in *Schor*. It has, however, returned to the closely related issue of whether Congress can delegate that authority to other legislative courts (here, again, the bankruptcy courts). *Stern v. Marshall*, 564 U.S. 462 (2011) involved a protracted and acrimonious dispute between the widow (Vickie, also known as Anna Nicole Smith) and son (Pierce) of one of the richest men in Texas, J. Howard Marshall. Vickie filed for bankruptcy in federal court after Marshall's death, and Pierce filed a proof of claim in those proceedings alleging that Vickie had defamed him. Vickie responded by filing a state-based tortious interference counterclaim against Pierce as part of her bankruptcy proceeding, alleging that he impermissibly prevented Marshall from creating a trust for her benefit. The bankruptcy court found in Vickie's favor, and on appeal Pierce argued that the bankruptcy court lacked the authority to enter a final judgment on the counterclaim.

In a 5-4 opinion, Chief Justice John Roberts ruled in favor of Pierce's estate (both Vickie and Pierce predeceased the Court's decision). Under the Bankruptcy Amendments and Judgeship Act of 1984, which amended the act of 1978 after the Court's decision in *Northern Pipeline*, district courts could refer cases arising under, arising in, or related to Title 11 bankruptcies to the bankruptcy courts, or withdraw such cases from the bankruptcy courts for cause. Bankruptcy courts could enter final judgment in all "core" proceedings arising in or under Title 11, which included counterclaims by a debtor's estate against persons filing claims against that estate. These judgments were reviewable by the district court under traditional appellate standards.

Citing *Northern Pipeline*, Chief Justice Roberts emphasized that the Court's "public rights" exception to Article III adjudication did not extend to bankruptcy courts finally deciding state-based claims. Even though the Court had since rejected the notion that the exception was limited only to those cases in which the government was named as a party, it "continued ... to limit the exception to cases in which the claim at issue derives from a federal regulatory scheme, or in which resolution of the claim by an expert government agency is deemed essential to a limited regulatory objective within the agency's authority." To the Chief Justice, both *Thomas* and *Schor* satisfied this test, though neither named the government as a party. The compensatory rights at issue in *Thomas* were wholly created by federal statute and did not replace or depend on any state-based rights. In *Schor*, which invited more scrutiny because it involved agency adjudication of a state-based counterclaim, the counterclaim was part of the same transaction as the federal claim before the CFTC, the CFTC's assertion of authority over the counterclaim was narrow and a necessary part of the overall regulatory scheme, the area of law over which the CFTC asserted jurisdiction was limited, the parties had agreed to have their dispute resolved by the CFTC, and the agency's orders were enforceable only by order of a district court. *Id.* at 491. The Court summarized this analysis as follows: " '[i]f a statutory right is not closely intertwined with a federal regulatory program Congress has power to enact, and if that right neither belongs to nor exists against the Federal Government, then it must be adjudicated by an Article III court.' " *Id.* at 492 (citing *Granfinanciera, S.A. v. Nordberg,* 492 U.S. 33, 54-55 (1989)).

Applying these precedents, the Court found that Article III prevented the bankruptcy court from exercising jurisdiction over Vickie's tortious interference counterclaim. First, the Chief Justice explained that Congress lacked the Article I authority to grant jurisdiction over the counterclaim to the bankruptcy courts. He cited several reasons that the result here was different from the one reached in *Schor*: Vickie's counterclaim was not of the type that historically had been decided by the political branches; it did not derive from or depend on a federal statutory scheme or a right created by federal law, nor was its adjudication necessary to advancing federal regulatory goals; Pierce did not truly consent to suit in the bankruptcy court (there was no alternative forum in which he could seek recovery from Vickie's estate); and the jurisdiction granted to the bankruptcy courts by the 1984 Act could reach any area of law, and therefore exceeded the narrow adjudicative authority that could permissibly be delegated to a subject matter expect. *Id.* at 491-94. To the extent the federal government employs experts on state-based common law claims, they are Article III courts. *Id.* at 494. Second, Roberts concluded that bankruptcy courts under the 1984 Act could not be deemed "adjuncts" of the district courts, and thus were not constituted as district court helpers deriving their authority from Article III. The 1984 Act did not limit the bankruptcy courts to basic fact-finding. It instead allowed them to finally decide state-based claims that were subject only to traditional appellate review. What's more, their orders were binding and enforceable even in the absence of an appeal to an Article III court. With that amount of independent decision-making, "a bankruptcy court can no more be deemed a mere 'adjunct' of the district court than a district court can be deemed such an 'adjunct' of the court of appeals." *Id.* at 487-88.

Justice Breyer filed a dissent in which three of his colleagues joined, arguing that the majority had placed too much analytical emphasis on the *Northern Pipeline* plurality's formalistic analysis. The more "pragmatic" and hence proper approach, in his view, would have derived from *Crowell*, *Thomas*, and *Schor*. Those cases showed that the real question is whether "the challenged delegation of adjudicatory authority posed a genuine and serious threat that one branch of Government sought to aggrandize its own constitutionally delegated authority by encroaching upon a field of authority that the Constitution assigns exclusively to another branch." *Id.* at 510 (Breyer, J., dissenting). Justice Breyer divided this broader inquiry into a five-factor test, which ultimately favored the bankruptcy court's authority to resolve Vickie's counterclaim: the nature of the claim to be adjudicated (state or federal, the former indicating higher risk of encroachment); the nature of the non-Article III tribunal (whether its judges are adequately insulated from outside influence); the amount of control exercised by Article III judges over the bankruptcy proceedings; whether the parties have consented to the bankruptcy court's jurisdiction; and the nature and importance of the legislative purpose served by grant of adjudicative authority to the bankruptcy court. *Id.* at 519 (Breyer, J., dissenting).

Separate and apart from these disagreements with the dissent about how best to apply Article III to legislative adjudication, the majority took time to address the elephant in the room: what effect did its decision have on *administrative* adjudication of state-based claims? Chief Justice Roberts was resolutely noncommittal:

> We recognize that there may be instances in which the distinction between public and private rights—at least as framed by some of our recent cases—fails to provide concrete guidance as to whether, for example, a particular agency can adjudicate legal issues under a substantive regulatory scheme. Given the extent to which this case is so markedly distinct from agency cases discussing the public rights exception in the context of such a regime, however, we do not in this opinion express any view on how the doctrine might apply in that different context.

Id. at 494.

QUESTION SET 2.5

Review & Synthesis

1. Now that you have read *Schor,* state the current test for determining whether a delegation of judicial power to an administrative court violates Article III. Discuss how the current test is similar to or different from the Court's analyses in *Crowell, Northern Pipeline,* and *Thomas.*

2. By what constitutional authority can Congress grant adjudicative power to legislative or administrative courts outside of the Judicial Branch?

3. In *Schor,* Justice O'Connor eschewed "formalistic" tests for "determining the extent to which a given congressional decision to authorize the adjudication of Article III business in a non-Article III tribunal impermissibly threatens the institutional integrity of the Judicial Branch." Instead, she and the majority adopted a "pragmatic" approach that "weighed a number of factors, none of which has been deemed determinative, with an eye to the practical effect that the congressional action will have on the constitutionally assigned role of the federal judiciary." This is a classic multifactor balancing test.

   In his dissent, Justice Brennan argued that this balancing test is a *fait accompli.* The need in individual cases for convenience and efficiency will always seem more pressing a concern than preservation of judicial independence. Accordingly, its structure weighs too heavily in favor of diluting the jurisdiction of Article III courts. Do you agree? Recall that James Madison argued in *The Federalist No.* 51 that each Branch has built-in incentives to protect itself from encroachment by the others. In light of this, did Justice Brennan too heavily discount the fact that Article III judges would be responsible for weighing the *Schor* factors? Can you think of any alterations to the test that would have shifted consideration of the factors toward judicial independence?

4. What, precisely, makes adjudication of state common law breach of contract claims by the CFTC more convenient or efficient than adjudication by a federal district court? Is it consolidation of claims into a single proceeding, which avoids the costs that come with parallel litigation? Is it the CFTC's familiarity with the regulatory arena, including its experience with commodities transactions and the arrangements brokers typically make with their clients? It is also possible that the amount of cost-savings could be affected by the CFTC's substantive legal expertise. In this regard, is it reasonable to assume that the agency has the same or more experience with state contract law than a federal district court? If not, shouldn't the Court have acknowledged that the CFTC's error rate in construing that law might be higher than a federal district court's?

5. According to *Schor*, how does an individual's right to waive adjudication in an Article III court impact whether Article I courts can adjudicate private disputes?

Application & Analysis

1. You are a summer law clerk at a federal agency headquartered in Washington, D.C. Your supervising attorney is going to lead a continuing legal education session organized by members of a local bar association and has asked you to help her prepare. One of the topics she plans to cover is Congress' authority to delegate judicial power to federal administrative agencies. She has asked you to prepare two or three slides summarizing the topic, with a focus on the law as it currently stands. Prepare those slides.

2. The America Invents Act of 2012 grants the United States Patent and Trademark Office ("USPTO") limited authority to reconsider and cancel issued patents through a process called *inter partes* review. Any person seeking to challenge a patent's validity may file an *inter partes* review petition with the USPTO. The petition is referred to the Patent Trial and Appeal Board ("PTAB"), an adjudicatory body within the USPTO, if the USPTO Director determines that at least one of its claims is likely to prevail. The PTAB considers petitions in trial-like hearings that feature oral hearings, limited discovery and the filing of affidavits, declarations, and written memoranda. The PTAB can cancel the patent if it finds merit in the petition challenging it. Its final decisions are subject to review by the United States Court of Appeals for the Federal Circuit.

ABC Corp. obtained a patent on technology that significantly lengthens the useful life of lithium-ion batteries. It filed a lawsuit against XYZ Corp. in federal district court for infringement. In response, XYZ Corp. simultaneously challenged the patent's validity in the district court and in an *inter partes* review proceeding before the PTAB. The district court issued a claim-construction order favoring ABC Corp., while the PTAB concluded that ABC Corp.'s patent was invalid. ABC Corp. has appealed to the Federal Circuit. It argues that *inter partes* review is unconstitutional because patent challenges can only be heard by Article III courts.

You are a law clerk to one of the judges who will hear this case. Write a brief memorandum analyzing ABC Corp.'s argument.

3. Section 274A(b) of the Immigration and Nationality Act requires employers to verify that all of their employees are eligible to work in the United States. Pursuant to this requirement, all prospective employees must complete an Employment Eligibility Verification Form I-9 ("Form I-9") that documents their work eligibility.

Immigration and Customs Enforcement ("ICE"), an agency within the Department of Homeland Security, enforces compliance with this requirement through audits of employers' records. To enable these audits, employers must retain Form I-9s for all current employees. Employers must also retain Form I-9s for former employees for a period of at least three years from the date of hire or for one year after the employee is no longer employed, whichever is longer. ICE may issue a Notice of Intent to Fine ("NIF") if an employer has failed to maintain the required Form I-9s or has knowingly hired employees who are ineligible to work in the United States. The employer may then negotiate a settlement with ICE or request a hearing before the Office of the Chief Administrative Hearing Officer ("OCAHO"), an adjudicatory body within the Department of Justice. If a hearing is requested, the OCAHO will assign the case to an administrate law judge ("ALJ") who may impose fines of up to $23,000, issue cease and desist orders, and award attorneys' fees. These decisions are subject to review by the Chief Administrative Hearing Officer (or much more rarely by the Attorney General). Unsuccessful parties can then seek judicial review in the appropriate Federal Court of Appeals.

Several U.S. Senators plan to introduce a bill expanding the OCAHO's adjudicative powers. The bill would give OCAHO ALJs discretion to fine employers up to $100,000 per confirmed § 274A(b) violation. It would also allow them to sentence culpable employers' owners and managers to up to six months in federal prison. Judicial review would continue to be available in the appropriate Courts of Appeals.

You are the legal counsel to one of the Senators interested in sponsoring this bill. Provide your legal analysis of its constitutionality under Article III.

Agency Creation by the President

Recall the hypothetical from the beginning of Part II, in which a rise in interstate highway deaths prompted Congress to consider legislation addressing the problem. It would first have to choose a substantive policy for reducing injuries and fatalities. It would then have to select an implementation method to ensure those policies achieve the desired outcomes. Given the variety, numerosity, and complexity of these choices, Congress might then want to establish a federal agency to develop subsidiary policies and carry the initiative forward to full implementation. Just as likely, however, probably even more so, is that Congress will be unable to muster any response to the problem at all. Almost all bills introduced in Congress fail to become laws.

As political scientists and legal scholars have chronicled for decades, the legislative process is both labyrinthine and perilous. Much of this is by design. The Framers viewed the legislative power as the most dangerous of the three wielded by government and thus the one most in need of structural control. *See* THE FEDERALIST NO. 48 (James Madison) ("The legislative department is everywhere extending the sphere of its activity and drawing all power into its impetuous vortex. . . . [I]t is against the enterprising ambition of this department that the people ought to indulge all their jealousy and exhaust all their precautions."). The Constitution divides its exercise among the voting Members of Congress, and then further divides those Members into two separate chambers (currently 435 in the House and 100 in the Senate). Only through collective action—majorities within each chamber and agreement between the chambers—can Congress use the power assigned to it by the Article I Vesting Clause. Even when the requisite majorities are achieved for initial passage of a bill into law, a two-thirds majority is required to overcome a subsequent Presidential veto of it.

Some of Congress' difficulties in legislating come not through constitutional structure, but through custom. Bills not passed during the session in which they were introduced are "dead" and must be reintroduced during the next session (each "congress" consists of two one-year sessions). They must be voted out of the committees (and often subcommittees) to which they are assigned. Bills that survive the committee process are then sent to the floor for debate. In the House, the Rules Committee sets debate time limits and determines whether Members can offer amendments. By contrast, each Senator can talk about a bill—can "filibuster" it—for as long as he or she wants. Unless prevented from doing so by a cloture motion requiring 60 votes, a Senator can essentially talk a bill to death by delaying debate until a session expires. If the versions of a bill passed by both the House and the Senate differ, a conference committee will be convened in an attempt to reconcile them. Failure to reconcile means failure of the bill. If reconciliation is successful, the bill must then go back to both chambers for another majority vote. Only then can the bill be sent to the President for signature or veto.

In light of all this, many presidents have resorted to agency creation and assignment of powers that entail little or no congressional involvement. The materials that follow explore two categories of such activity. The first and more limited of these we shall term "unilateral" agency creation. It refers to presidential creation of agencies or assignments of administrative authority in the absence of Congress' express approval (and sometimes over its objections). The second category involved a now-defunct statutory authorization under the Reorganization Act. The Act granted presidents broad powers to rearrange administrative structures, which would become effective upon ratification by both the House and the Senate. As you read, think about how much independent discretion the President should enjoy in refashioning the administrative state. What are the legal constraints on that discretion? Do you think they are sufficient, or should Congress have more control over the structure and operations of administrative agencies?

A. UNILATERAL AGENCY CREATION

According to one study, "presidents have unilaterally created over half of all administrative agencies in the United States" since World War II, some 240 in total. William G. Howell & David E. Lewis, *Agencies by Presidential Design*, 64 J. OF POL. 1095, 1096 (2002). These agencies may differ in some significant respects to those created through legislation. They are generally smaller, far less likely to be led by boards or commissions that dilute presidential control of them, have longer lifespans, and tend to have smaller budgets. *See id.* at 1097-99. This is as one would expect. Though presidents influence the content of substantive and budgetary legislation, Congress has the ultimate authority to set legislative terms. Accordingly, presidents' efforts to reorganize the federal bureaucracy must be grounded in preexisting statutory authority. Moreover, they must operate within those confines when designing, empowering, and funding new agencies.

Many organic statutes and other provisions in the United States Code delegate broad responsibilities to the President or to implementing agencies without specifying particular officials or offices who must undertake them. This provides some freedom for presidents and agency leadership to delegate, redelegate, or subdelegate portions of their statutory powers to others within the government. Additionally, several statutes explicitly provide for some redelegation and subdelegation authority. The President has a general authority to rearrange parts of the federal bureaucracy by redelegating functions that Congress has vested in her or him. *See* 3 U.S.C. § 301. Many scattered provisions permit department or agency leadership to subdelegate their statutory powers. *See, e.g.,* 5 U.S.C. § 302 (general delegation to agency leadership to "take final action on matters pertaining to the employment, direction, and general administration of personnel under his [or her] agency); 18 U.S.C. § 4102(11) (Attorney General); 49 U.S.C. § 322(b) (Secretary of Transportation). *See generally,* JARED P. COLE, CONG. RSCH. SERV., LSB10158, ORGANIZING EXECUTIVE BRANCH AGENCIES: WHO MAKES THE CALL? (2018).

Perhaps the clearest example of presidents using existing delegated authority to reshape the federal bureaucracy comes when they act unilaterally and establish agencies that Congress either could not or would not create itself. The Peace Corps is an oft-cited example. Proposals for a national youth service program providing foreign aid to developing countries date back to at least late 1950s. Senator Hubert Humphrey of Minnesota introduced the first Peace Corps bill in 1957. By his own admission, "[m]any Senators, including liberal ones, thought it a silly and unworkable idea." HUBERT H. HUMPHREY, THE EDUCATION OF A PUBLIC MAN: MY LIFE IN POLITICS 185 (1991). The bill failed to garner significant support. He pushed for it again as part of his unsuccessful bid for the Democratic Party's presidential nomination in 1960. Framing it as "a program of national service in an international endeavor," *id.* at 168, he urged the federal government to "enlist[] young men and women in an overseas operation for education, health care, vocational training, and community development." *Id.* Others made similar proposals around that time. In 1960, Senator Richard L. Neuberger of Oregon and Representative Henry Reuss of Wisconsin introduced identical bills to study whether a federally funded program could link American volunteerism with the nation's foreign aid programs. *See* S. 2908, 86th Cong. (1960); H.R. 9638, 86th Cong (1960). Altruism provided some motivation for these proposals, but national interest was also important; they offered a way to improve America's image around the world. Congress approved $10,000 to the study as part of amendments to the Mutual Security Act of 1954. A few months later, Senator Humphrey returned to the issue by introducing Senate Bill 3675, which would have immediately established the Peace Corps. *See* S. 3675, 86th Cong. (1960). Again, his proposal received little support.

John F. Kennedy was nevertheless influenced by these efforts. In a speech at the University of Michigan in October 1960, he urged the gathered students to serve their nation by volunteering to serve those living outside of it. Although he continued to raise the point in subsequent speeches and press releases, some remained unpersuaded. For instance, Kennedy's electoral opponent, Richard M. Nixon, had criticized the idea as showing foreign policy naïveté. Others dismissed it as simply an opportunity for privileged youths to avoid the military draft. Although concerned about the political impact of these denunciations, candidate Kennedy continued to argue that the United States needed more direct and peaceful engagement with the developing world. President Kennedy established the Peace Corps by executive order a little over a month after taking the oath of office. *See* Exec. Order 10924, 26 Fed. Reg. 1789 (1961).

The Peace Corps' structure, powers, mission, and funding illustrate the limits of unilateral agency creation by the President. Kennedy based his authority to issue E.O. 10924 on "the authority vested in [him] by the Mutual Security Act of 1954," and thus he was constrained to act within the parameters set by that legislation. Structurally, he ordered that the Peace Corps be set up as an agency within the Department of State and headed by a Director who, presumably, reported directly to the Secretary of State. As the Secretary was a member of the President's cabinet and removable by him at will, the Director would also be subject to the President's influence and supervision. With regard to its powers and mission, E.O. 10924 did not grant the Peace Corps any "significant" authority; it received no rulemaking, adjudicative, or law-enforcement powers, conferral of which would have required a federal statute. Instead, the organization was tasked with "training and service abroad of men and women of the United States in new programs of assistance to nations and areas of the world, and in conjunction with or in support of existing economic assistance programs or the United States and of the United Nations and other international organizations." Finally, and with regard to funding, the Peace Corps received no congressional appropriation since Congress had not approved its creation. Accordingly, E.O. 10924 directed that it be supported by State Department funds already appropriated for implementation of the Mutual Security Act. Only after the agency started operations and had gained substantial public support did a bill for its establishment finally make into legislation. "[B]y the time Congress formally moved to grant a statutory basis for the Peace Corps, the Corps had 362 Washington employees and 600 volunteers at work in eight countries. Congress, then, had little choice but to continue funding, else fight the interest groups that had grown up around the fledgling organization." HOWELL & LEWIS, *supra*, at 1100 (citations omitted).

B. AGENCY REORGANIZATIONS

Reorganization, an alternative and once popular path to presidential agency creation, features much more congressional involvement than did creation of the Peace Corps. As with unilateral agency creation, executive reorganizations could only be undertaken within the statutory guardrails set by Congress. The Reorganization Act (5 U.S.C. § 901 *et seq.*) established a procedure by which the President could submit plans for wide-ranging government reorganizations to Congress, and Congress would approve or disapprove of them through procedures that could be completed much more quickly than the routine legislative process. The Congressional Research Service described the basic features of the reorganization authority as follows:

> Each of the elements of the reorganization authority are integral to its overall scope and effect, but several of these more strongly influence the relative authority of the President and Congress, and the resulting balance of power between the two branches. These elements are: the reorganization plan contents, the limitations on power, and the expedited parliamentary procedures. The provisions that define the potential scope of reorganization plan content, when combined with the provisions that further limit or prohibit certain reorganization plan content, set the boundaries of a reorganization that the President can propose under this special authority. The provisions that specify the parliamentary procedures to be used define the role of Congress in facilitating or impeding the enactment of a submitted plan. These procedures also define the requirements of the President during this process. Such requirements may be seen by the Administration as easing or making more difficult a plan's enactment and implementation.

HENRY HOGUE, CONG. RSCH. SERV., R42852, PRESIDENTIAL REORGANIZATION AUTHORITY: HISTORY, RECENT INITIATIVES, AND OPTIONS FOR CONGRESS 2-3 (2012). Establishment of the Environmental Protection Agency—an independent executive agency employing tens of thousands of people, supported by a multibillion-dollar budget, and wielding legislative, executive, and adjudicative powers—is perhaps the most notable modern example of how presidents used powers granted to them under the Reorganization Act.

The creation of the EPA is among the most significant events of the modern administrative state. Unlike many other regulatory agencies, the EPA was not created by statute and does not have a single statutory mandate. It was formed from a combination of different programs housed in different executive departments and was the result of President Nixon's efforts to address concerns raised by the strengthening environmental movement. The result was one of the most powerful administrative agencies in the federal government.

The American public grew increasingly concerned about the state of the natural environment in the years following World War II. Publication of

Rachel Carson's *Silent Spring* in 1962 was a major catalyst for an increase in the size and energy of the environmental movement. The book, originally serialized in the *New Yorker,* brought to the public's attention the use of pesticides in food and the impact of synthetic chemicals on the environment. Other disasters further increased the pressure for responsive regulation. A 1969 drilling accident befouled Santa Barbara's beaches and poured 210,000 gallons of oil into the surrounding environment each day. Apart from these flashpoints of degradation, the cumulative effects of poor environmental stewardship were coming into focus. By one account, at the time Nixon assumed the presidency in 1969, the United States annually produced 200 million tons of air pollutants and threw away 100 million automobile tires and 30 billion glass bottles. Meir Rinde, *Richard Nixon and the Rise of American Environmentalism*, Distillations (June 2, 2017), https://www.sciencehistory.org/distillations/richard-nixon-and-the-rise-of-american-environmentalism.

Cries for reform peaked in April 1970 with the first Earth Day, which precipitated the largest public demonstrations since the end of World War II. In all, an estimated 20 million Americans took part in Earth Day demonstrations. One commentator has described the energy surrounding the first Earth Day as a "republican moment": one in which traditional politics was replaced by "enhanced democratic participation and ideological struggle." Arthur McEvoy, *Environmental Law and the Collapse of New Deal Constitutionalism*, 46 Akron L. Rev. 881, 895 (2013) (discussing Daniel Farber, *Politics and Procedure in Environmental Law*, 8 J. L. Econ. & Org. 59 (1992)).

This public activism included calls for the federal government to take a more active role in environmental regulation. Prior to 1970, the field had been left almost entirely to the states. President Dwight D. Eisenhower's statement that air and water pollution were "uniquely local" problems is emblematic of the federal government's stance towards environmental protection in the first half of the twentieth century. *See* Richard N.L. Andrews, *The EPA at 40: An Historical Perspective*, 21 Duke Envtl. L. & Pol'y F. 223, 226 (2010). Some states, most notably California, had taken aggressive action to solve environmental problems. Most states did little, if anything. No state adopted air quality standards prior to 1960, and only ten states had done so by 1966. Arthur C. Stern, *History of Air Pollution Legislation in the United States*, 32 J. Air Pollution Control Ass'n 44, 47 (Jan. 1982).

The federal government previously had attempted to address these and other environmental problems, resulting in a decentralized regulatory patchwork. Congress passed the Air Pollution Control Act in 1955 and the Clean Air Act in 1963. The latter tasked the Secretary of Health, Education, and Welfare with addressing interstate and intrastate pollution. It also enabled the Secretary to initiate regulatory actions on his or her own or in response to a request by a state or local official. These allowances sparked little regulatory movement, however. By 1967, the Secretary had received no requests for intrastate pollution abatement and only three requests for interstate abatement. *Id.* at 52. The Secretary initiated only five interstate pollution abatement actions during the same period of time. *Id.* Apart from air pollution, Congress had tasked different departments with formulating environmental regulations in response to specific problems. The Department of Interior's Water Quality Administration was tasked with regulating issues relevant to water pollution; the Department of Interior, the Food and Drug Administration, and the Department of Agriculture each were directed to regulate different aspects of pesticides; the Atomic Energy Commission and the Federal Radiation Council set radiation criteria and standards. Jack Lewis, *The Birth of the EPA*, EPA JOURNAL (Nov. 1985); *see also EPA's Origins Duties Transferred to EPA from Other Federal Agencies*, ENVIRONMENTAL PROTECTION AGENCY (last updated Sept. 6, 2016), archived at https://archive.epa.gov/epa/aboutepa/epas-origins-duties-transferred-epa-other-federal-agencies.html (describing regulatory responsibilities later transferred to the EPA).

Thus, when Nixon entered the White House in 1969, he confronted a public demanding environmental reform and a regulatory apparatus ill-equipped to deliver it. Nixon was hardly an environmentalist by nature: other than a radio address during his 1968 campaign, he had given little public indication that he viewed it as a regulatory priority. *See* Andrews, *supra*, at 226. Whether his newfound commitment to reform was more political than substantive, Nixon took advantage of the public's growing support for environmentalism. Environmental issues figured prominently in his first State of the Union address, delivered on January 22, 1970. Earlier that month, in a live New Year's Day television broadcast, he signed the National Environmental Policy Act ("NEPA") into law. NEPA was the most comprehensive and ambitious federal environmental legislation in the nation's history. Its purpose was to establish "a national policy which will encourage productive and enjoyable harmony between man and his environment" as well as "promote efforts which will prevent or eliminate damage to the environment." National Environmental Policy Act of 1969, Pub. L. No. 91-190, 83 Stat. 852, 852 (1970) (codified at 42 U.S.C. 4321 § *et seq.*). Practically, NEPA required federal agencies to submit environmental impact statements before commencing projects that could significantly affect the environment, in addition to creating the White House Council on Environmental Quality to advise the President on environmental matters. The environmental impact statement provisions, in particular, greatly increased transparency and allowed the public to become aware of projects before they began. This, in turn, provided groups with the opportunity to organize in opposition to projects or otherwise act to influence them. *See* McEvoy, *supra*, at 892. The impact statement provisions of NEPA would become the basis for numerous lawsuits that delayed the licensing of nuclear power plants, oil drilling, and the Alaskan pipeline. Rinde, DISTILLATIONS, *supra*.

Most important for present purposes were President Nixon's maneuvers to centralize environmental policy development and implementation in the Executive Branch. In April of 1970, the President's Commission on Executive Reorganization, chaired by Roy Ash, submitted a report arguing for the creation of a new federal agency to coordinate and enforce the nation's environmental laws. This "Department of the Environment" would be legislatively created and would pull under a single bureaucratic umbrella all agencies with environmental responsibilities—including the Army Corp of Engineers, the Department of the Interior, and the Forest Service. *See* Richard J. Lazarus, *The Tragedy of Distrust in the Implementation of Federal Environmental Law*, 54 L. & CONTEMP. PROBS. 311, 315 (1991).

Although Nixon supported the concentration of environmental regulation within a single entity, he felt that the Commission's recommendation was politically untenable. A single Department of the Environment would have required Congress' approval and would have faced bureaucratic opposition from the Army Corps of Engineers, the Forest Service, and other interested agencies. Under the Reorganization Act, by contrast, Nixon could accomplish the same goal unilaterally, as long as Congress did not disapprove of his plan within 60 days of its submission.

Accordingly, Nixon submitted his plan to Congress in October 1970.

Reorganization Plan No. 3 of 1970

Prepared by the President and transmitted to the Senate and the House of Representatives in Congress assembled, July 9, 1970, pursuant to the provisions of chapter 9 of title 5 of the United States Code

ENVIRONMENTAL PROTECTION AGENCY

Section 1. Establishment of Agency

(a) There is hereby established the Environmental Protection Agency, hereinafter referred to as the "Agency."

(b) There shall be at the head of the Agency the Administrator of the Environmental Protection Agency, hereinafter referred to as the "Administrator." The Administrator shall be appointed by the President, by and with the advice and consent of the Senate. . . .

(c) There shall be in the Agency a Deputy Administrator of the Environmental Protection Agency who shall be appointed by the President, by and with the advice and consent of the Senate. . . . The Deputy Administrator shall perform such functions as the Administrator shall from time to time assign or delegate, and shall act as Administrator during the absence or disability of the Administrator or in the event of a vacancy in the office of Administrator.

(d) There shall be in the Agency not to exceed five Assistant Administrators of the Environmental Protection Agency who shall be appointed by the President, by and with the advice and consent of the Senate. . . . Each Assistant Administrator shall perform such functions as the Administrator shall from time to time assign or delegate.

Sec. 2. Transfers to Environmental Protection Agency

(a) There are hereby transferred to the Administrator:

(1) All functions vested by law in the Secretary of the Interior and the Department of the Interior which are administered through the Federal Water Quality Administration, all functions which were transferred to the Secretary of the Interior by Reorganization Plan No. 2 of 1966 (80 Stat. 1608), and all functions vested in the Secretary of the Interior or the Department of the Interior by the Federal Water Pollution Control Act or by provisions of law amendatory or supplementary thereof.

(2) (i) The functions vested in the Secretary of the Interior by the Act of August 1, 1958, 72 Stat. 479, 16 U.S.C. 742d-1 (being an Act relating to studies on the effects of insecticides, herbicides, fungicides, and pesticides upon the fish and wildlife resources of the United States), and (ii) the functions vested by law in the Secretary of the Interior and the Department of the Interior which are administered by the Gulf Breeze Biological Laboratory of the Bureau of Commercial Fisheries at Gulf Breeze, Florida.

(3) The functions vested by law in the Secretary of Health, Education, and Welfare or in the Department of Health, Education, and Welfare which are administered through the Environmental Health Service, including the functions exercised by the following components thereof:

(i) The National Air Pollution Control Administration,
(ii) The Environmental Control Administration:
(A) Bureau of Solid Waste Management,
(B) Bureau of Water Hygiene,
(C) Bureau of Radiological Health,

except that functions carried out by the following components of the Environmental Control Administration of the Environmental Health Service are not transferred: (i) Bureau of Community Environmental Management, (ii) Bureau of Occupational Safety and Health, and (iii) Bureau of Radiological Health, insofar as the functions carried out by the latter Bureau pertain to (A) regulation of radiation from consumer products, including electronic product radiation, (B) radiation as used in the healing arts, (C) occupational exposures to radiation, and (D) research, technical assistance, and training related to clauses (A), (B), and (C).

(4) The functions vested in the Secretary of Health, Education, and Welfare of establishing tolerances for pesticide chemicals under the Federal Food, Drug, and Cosmetic Act, as amended, 21 U.S.C. 346, 346a, and 348, together with authority, in connection with the functions transferred, (i) to monitor compliance with the tolerances and the effectiveness of surveillance and enforcement, and (ii) to provide technical assistance to the States and conduct research under the Federal Food, Drug, and Cosmetic Act, as amended, and the Public Health Service Act, as amended.

(5) So much of the functions of the Council on Environmental Quality under section 204(5) of the National Environmental Policy Act of 1969 (Public Law 91-190, approved January 1, 1970, 83 Stat. 855), as pertains to ecological systems.

(6) The functions of the Atomic Energy Commission under the Atomic Energy Act of 1954, as amended, administered through its Division of Radiation Protection Standards, to the extent that such functions of the Commission consist of establishing generally applicable environmental standards for the protection of the general environment from radioactive material. As used herein, standards mean limits on radiation exposures or levels, or concentrations or quantities of radioactive material, in the general environment outside the boundaries of locations under the control of persons possessing or using radioactive material.

(7) All functions of the Federal Radiation Council (42 U.S.C., 2021 (h)).

(8) (i) The functions of the Secretary of Agriculture and the Department of Agriculture under the Federal Insecticide, Fungicide, and Rodenticide Act, as amended (7 U.S.C.

135-135k), (ii) the functions of the Secretary of Agriculture and the Department of Agriculture under section 408(l) of the Federal Food, Drug, and Cosmetic Act, as amended (21 U.S.C. 346a(l)), and (iii) the functions vested by law in the Secretary of Agriculture and the Department of Agriculture which are administered through the Environmental Quality Branch of the Plant Protection Division of the Agricultural Research Service.

(9) So much of the functions of the transferor officers and agencies referred to in or affected by the foregoing provisions of this section as is incidental to or necessary for the performance by or under the Administrator of the functions transferred by those provisions or relates primarily to those functions. The transfers to the Administrator made by this section shall be deemed to include the transfer of (1) authority, provided by law, to prescribe regulations relating primarily to the transferred functions, and (2) the functions vested in the Secretary of the Interior and the Secretary of Health, Education, and Welfare by section 169 (d)(1) (B) and (3) of the Internal Revenue Code of 1954 (as enacted by section 704 of the Tax Reform Act of 1969, 83 Stat. 668); but shall be deemed to exclude the transfer of the functions of the Bureau of Reclamation under section 3(b)(1) of the Water Pollution Control Act (33 U.S.C. 466a(b)(1)).

(b) There are hereby transferred to the Agency:
(1) From the Department of the Interior, (i) the Water Pollution Control Advisory Board (33 U.S.C. 466f), together with its functions, and (ii) the hearing boards provided for in sections 10(c)(4) and 10(f) of the Federal Water Pollution Control Act, as amended (33 U.S.C. 466g (c)(4); 466g(f)). The functions of the Secretary of the Interior with respect to being or designating the Chairman of the Water Pollution Control Advisory Board are hereby transferred to the Administrator.

(2) From the Department of Health, Education, and Welfare, the Air Quality Advisory Board (42 U.S.C. 1857e), together with its functions. The functions of the Secretary of Health, Education, and Welfare with respect to being a member and the Chairman of that Board are hereby transferred to the Administrator.

Sec. 3. Performance of Transferred Functions

The Administrator may from time to time make such provisions as he shall deem appropriate authorizing the performance of any of the functions transferred to him by the provisions of this reorganization plan by any other officer, or by any organizational entity or employee, of the Agency.

Sec. 4. Incidental Transfers

(a) So much of the personnel, property, records, and unexpended balances of appropriations, allocations, and other funds employed, used, held available, or to be made available in connection with the functions transferred to the Administrator or the Agency by this reorganization plan as the Director of the Office of Management and Budget shall determine shall be transferred to the Agency at such time or times as the Director shall direct.

(b) Such further measures and dispositions as the Director of Office of Management and Budget shall deem to be necessary in order to effectuate the transfers referred to in subsection (a) of this section shall be carried out in such manner as he shall direct and by such agencies as he shall designate.

Sec. 5. Interim Officers

(a) The President may authorize any person who immediately prior to the effective date of this reorganization plan held a position in the executive branch of the Government to act as Administrator until the office of Administrator is for the first time filled pursuant to the provisions of this reorganization plan or by recess appointment, as the case may be.

(b) The President may similarly authorize any such person to act as Deputy Administrator, authorize any such person to act as Assistant Administrator, and authorize any such person to act as the head of any principal constituent organizational entity of the Administration.

(c) The President may authorize any person who serves in an acting capacity under the foregoing provisions of this section to receive the compensation attached to the office in respect of which he so serves. Such compensation, if authorized, shall be in lieu of, but not in addition to, other compensation from the United States to which such person may be entitled.

Sec. 6. Abolitions

(a) Subject to the provisions of this reorganization plan, the following, exclusive of any functions, are hereby abolished:

(1) The Federal Water Quality Administration in the Department of the Interior. . . .

(2) The Federal Radiation Council (73 Stat. 690; 42 U.S.C. 2021 (h)).

(b) Such provisions as may be necessary with respect to terminating any outstanding affairs shall be made by the Secretary of the Interior in the case of the Federal Water Quality Administration and by the Administrator of General Services in the case of the Federal Radiation Council.

Section 7. Effective Date

The provisions of this reorganization plan shall take effect sixty-days after the date they would take effect under 5 U.S.C. 906(a) in the absence of this section.

* * *

Under the Reorganization Act of 1949, Nixon's proposal went into effect when neither the House nor the Senate used its one-house veto (a resolution of disapproval from either chamber) to reject it. In the years following the EPA's creation, Congress enacted several statutes that drastically increased its power. This can be seen as a natural consequence of its structure: without a broad statutory mandate, Congress repeatedly had to expand its authority by passing new legislation it would be tasked with enforcing. The most important of these statutes to the new EPA was the Clean Air Act of 1970, which allowed the EPA to establish National Ambient Air Quality Standards (NAAQS). This legislation, in addition to the 1977 Clean Air Act Amendments, would be at issue in many Supreme Court cases in the following decades. Also significant to the development of the EPA's authority was the Federal Water Pollution Control Amendments of 1972 (more commonly known as the Clean Water Act) and the 1977 amendments to the Clean Water Act. Thus, by 1980, the EPA was possibly the most powerful environmental regulatory agency in the world.

C. THE PRESIDENT'S REORGANIZATION AUTHORITY TODAY

Presidents used their statutory reorganization authority to submit more than 100 plans to Congress between 1932 and 1984. These plans varied in both scope and purpose; they ranged "from relatively minor reorganizations within individual agencies to the creation of large new organizations" like the EPA. *See* HOGUE, PRESIDENTIAL REORGANIZATION, *supra*, at 2.

Apart from the EPA, Presidents used reorganization to establish a number of important agencies: examples include the Executive Office of the President, the Office of Science and Technology Policy in the Executive Office of the President, the National Oceanic and Atmospheric Administration in the Department of Commerce, the Drug Enforcement Administration in the Department of Justice, the Federal Emergency Management Agency, the Office of Personnel Management, and the Merit Systems Protection Board. *See* S. Rep. No. 115-381, at 5 (2018).

A key feature of the reorganization authority was the procedure by which Congress could approve or disapprove of the plans the President submitted to it. The Reorganization Act established expedited procedures that allowed a plan to go into effect unless either the House or the Senate passed a resolution rejecting it. This process, called a "legislative veto," set the decisional default at approval of reorganization; if both the House and the Senate took no action (i.e., remained silent), the plan would go into effect. "In contrast to the regular legislative process, the burden of action under these versions of presidential reorganization authority rested with opponents rather than supporters of the plan." HOGUE, PRESIDENTIAL REORGANIZATION, *supra*, at 2. The numbers bear this out: of the 126 reorganization plans Presidents sent to Congress between 1932 and 1984, only 33 were affirmatively rejected. *Id.* at 4.

In 1984, the default reorganization power abruptly shifted from the President back to Congress. The watershed Supreme Court decision *INS v. Chadha* ruled the one-house veto unconstitutional. 462 U.S. 919 (1983). In light of *Chadha*, Congress amended the Reorganization Act in several respects. It authorized the President to propose transferring agencies or their components to other executive agencies; abolishing all or part of the functions of an agency; combining part of an agency or its functions with another part of the same agency; authorizing agency officers to delegate any of their functions; and abolishing whole agencies or subparts if they would perform no functions after the reorganization plan became effective. Plans would be considered under procedures that moved them through Congress much more quickly than normal legislation. The plan would be disapproved if Congress voted against it or failed to hold a vote on it within the time allotted by the Act. This amended reorganization authority expired at the end of 1984, and Congress has never renewed it. It seems that the inability to use the one-house veto has dampened Congress' enthusiasm for the whole procedure.

Unsurprisingly, Presidents have periodically requested that Congress reauthorize the Reorganization Act since its expiration. Most recently, President Donald J. Trump instructed the Office of Management and Budget ("OMB") Director "to propose a plan to reorganize governmental functions and eliminate unnecessary agencies . . . , components of agencies, and agency programs." Exec. Order No. 13781, 82 Fed. Reg. 13959 (March 13, 2017). The OMB Director would develop a plan by soliciting public comments on how the government's operations might be improved and by receiving written plans from agency heads detailing improvements in "efficiency, effectiveness, and accountability" of their respective agencies. *Id.* In connection with the executive order and the OMB report issued pursuant to it, Senators Ron Johnson (R-WI) and James Lankford (R-OK) introduced S. 3137, which would have reauthorized the Reorganization Act for a period of two years. It stalled in the Senate and was not reintroduced the following session.

QUESTION SET 3.1

Review & Synthesis

1. Under what legal authority did President Kennedy establish the Peace Corps? What were the political conditions that led him to do so?

2. Prior to its expiration, how did presidential agency creation under the Reorganization Act differ from unilateral agency creation? How did the authority of the agencies created by the two mechanisms differ? Use the case studies on the Peace Corps and the EPA to formulate your answer.

3. As explained above, the Reorganization Act expired in 1984 when Congress could no longer condition its use on inclusion of a one-house veto provision. How did the Supreme Court's decision in *INS v. Chadha* change the distribution of reorganization power between Congress and the President?

4. To what extent should the President's power to reorganize the federal administrative apparatus be dependent on congressional approval? If Article II of the Constitution charges the President with faithfully executing the laws, why should his or her power to structure the agencies through which he or she does so depend on federal legislation? Based on the discussion of separation-of-powers principles in Chapter 1, would allowing the President broad agency creation or reorganization powers usurp powers granted to Congress or the Judiciary?

PART III

The Administrative Decision-Making Process

Part II explored the first stage of the agency lifecycle: how they are created and what governance responsibilities they are assigned. Legal analysis at this initial stage focuses on the actions of Congress and of the President. Through legislation and presidential directives (e.g., executive orders and reorganization plans), they bring federal agencies into being and assign them a variety of governmental functions. Specific constitutional provisions (e.g., the Article I and Article III Vesting Clauses) and general principles evident from the totality of the Constitution's provisions and structural arrangements (e.g., separation of powers and checks and balances) limit Congress's discretion to shape the federal bureaucracy. The President's powers in this regard are likewise cabined by both the Constitution and by the laws Congress chooses to enact. As responsibility for agency creation resides primarily in the Legislative Branch, presidents must work within preexisting statutory parameters if they want to advance their policy priorities through administration. Politics also plays a role, of course; Presidents may unilaterally attempt to rearrange the federal bureaucracy when engaging Congress seems too difficult or otherwise disadvantageous to them.

Part III turns to the next stage in the administrative lifecycle. Legal analysis at this second stage focuses on the actions of the agencies themselves; specifically, the procedural constraints under which they perform the functions assigned to them. Its materials are organized around three basic questions. First, in what types of activities do agencies engage? The answer is covered to some extent in the first two parts of this book, but it warrants elaboration here. Broadly speaking, agencies engage in two functions: policy formulation and policy application. Indeed, the Administrative Procedure Act ("APA") (5 U.S.C. §§ 551, *et seq.*)—often called the "constitution" of the federal administrative state—is itself organized around this distinction.

This should come as no surprise: the core functions of the federal Branches fit roughly within these categories, and it is from those core functions that the powers of federal agencies derive.

The rulemaking process is the primary vehicle for policy formation — for the formulation and adoption of rules. Here, agencies operate like "mini-legislatures." APA § 551(4) defines a "rule," in relevant part, as "the whole or a part of an agency statement of general or particular applicability and future effect designed to implement, interpret, or prescribe law or policy or describing the organization, procedure, or practice requirements of an agency." As explained by the ATTORNEY GENERAL'S MANUAL, "[t]he object of the rule making proceeding is the implementation or proscription of law or policy for the future, rather than the evaluation of a respondent's past conduct." U.S. DEP'T OF JUSTICE, ATTORNEY GENERAL'S MANUAL ON THE ADMINISTRATIVE PROCEDURE ACT 14 (1947) [hereinafter, ATTORNEY GENERAL'S MANUAL]. The APA further divides this rulemaking function by its formality or informality. A rulemaking is "formal" if a statute requires it to be conducted through on-the-record hearings. *See* APA §§ 556 & 557. Most rulemakings, however, are informal; they have robust public participation mechanisms and compile informational records, but do not obligate an agency to hold live, in-person hearings. *See* APA § 553.

Adjudication is the primary method for administrative policy application. Here, agencies interpret rules, apply them to discrete factual circumstances, and make final decisions. Seeking guidance again from the ATTORNEY GENERAL'S MANUAL, "adjudication is concerned with the determination of past and present rights and liabilities. Normally, there is involved a decision as to whether past conduct was unlawful. . . ." ATTORNEY GENERAL'S MANUAL 14. Adjudication is the broadest and most varied category of agency conduct, making it difficult to adopt a definition that is both comprehensive and descriptively accurate. To some extent, the APA declines to do so; it states that an "order" is "the whole or a part of a final disposition, whether affirmative, negative, injunctive, or declaratory in form, of an agency in a matter other than rule making but including licensing." APA § 551(6). While always involving the application of rules (or standards) to facts to reach some "final disposition," the forms that administrative adjudication takes are almost as varied as the areas of social and economic life that agencies are tasked with regulating. Additionally, and like rulemaking, adjudication can either be formal or informal, depending on whether they feature trial-like procedural protections for the private parties involved in them. On the more formal end of the spectrum, which is governed by APA §§ 556 and 557, agency adjudication can be almost indistinguishable from a trial conducted by the federal district courts; it features a presiding administrative law judge and a trial-like hearing. On the more informal end of the spectrum, it can involve a cabinet secretary's decision to fund a particular construction project based on factors established by statute, or a lone civil servant's determination that an applicant for government benefits is ineligible to receive them.

The second question, made immediately apparent by the first, is how do we know whether a given agency action is an instance of rulemaking or of adjudication? It's fine for Congress or the President to base procedural directives on this abstract distinction. The real world of administration is much messier. Agencies engage in a wide variety of conduct that does not clearly fit traditional models of legislative or judicial behavior. For instance, is an agency engaged in rulemaking or in adjudication when it issues a press release describing a change in its enforcement priorities? What about when a board or a commission adopts and then applies a new rule in the course of resolving a particular dispute involving a regulated party? Is it involved in rulemaking or adjudication when, at the end of a public hearing, it assigns exclusive ongoing use of public property—like a unique broadcast frequency—to one television station over others seeking the same privilege? Here, courts are often left to figure things out on their own, and so they search for coherence in the familiar. To pinpoint the procedures agencies are obliged to follow, judges compare their actions to those traditional legislative and judicial behavioral models. The more an agency's conduct resembles that of a legislature—consideration of generalizable and forward-looking information, absence of clear adversarial or individualized interests, etc.—the more likely it is that a court will determine that rulemaking procedures govern its conduct. The more an agency's conduct resembles a court's consideration of past and situation-specific information—clear adversarial interests raised by clearly identifiable parties, for example—the more likely its conduct will be governed by adjudicatory procedures.

The third organizing question for this part is what procedures must agencies follow as they perform their assigned functions? The sources of these procedures are easy enough to identify: they originate in the Constitution, the Administrative Procedure Act ("APA"), organic and other substantive statutes, and, in limited instances, executive orders issued by the President. Some are steadfast requirements (the Constitution), while others serve as defaults (the APA, executive orders) unless superseded by more specific provisions (organic statutes). Their provisions address a slew of operational issues: who is allowed or required to participate in agency adjudication, what form may that participation take, how much notice is provided prior to it, when must it be initiated and concluded, whether and to what extent agencies must explain the decisions produced by it, etc. The applicability of any given procedural requirement, and hence the resolution of these issues, typically depends on whether courts characterize them as rulemaking or as adjudication.

Part III proceeds as follows. Chapter 4 addresses how courts distinguish between rulemaking and adjudication and the discretion agencies have to choose between rulemaking and adjudication when formulating new policies. Chapter 5 explores APA and other procedures for formal and informal rulemaking. It also discusses the executive orders granting the Office of Management and Budget within the Executive Office of the President a role in the informal rulemaking process. Chapter 6 focuses on agency adjudication, both informal and formal. Chapter 7 analyzes the core constitutional limitation on administrative adjudications: The Due Process Clauses of the Fifth and Fourteenth Amendments.

CHAPTER 4

Choosing a Decision-Making Process

A. NAME THAT PROCESS: RULEMAKING OR ADJUDICATION?

As indicated above, courts determine which procedural rules administrative officials must follow by first characterizing their decisions as "quasi-legislative" or "quasi-adjudicative." Stated differently, the procedural requirements imposed on administrative decision-making can differ quite significantly depending on whether officials are formulating general policies or whether they are determining the legal significance of particular facts. Once courts have answered this initial question, they are positioned to assess the adequacy of the procedures the officials followed.

The plaintiffs in the two cases that follow—*Londoner v. City of Denver* and *Bi-Metallic Investment Co. v. State Board of Equalization*—claimed that local authorities denied them their right to participate in local taxing decisions. They situated this right in the Fourteenth Amendment Due Process Clause and its guarantee of "procedural due process." Procedural due process obligates the government—under the Fifth Amendment for the federal government, and under the Fourteenth Amendment for state or local governments—to provide certain procedural protections before depriving persons of their lives, their liberty, or their property. Critically, the Supreme Court has consistently held that procedural due protections generally do not extend to legislative action. *See* Minnesota Board for Community Colleges v. Knight, 465 U.S. 271, 283 (1984) ("The Constitution does not grant to members of the public generally a right to be heard by public bodies making decisions of policy."); Bernard W. Bell, *Marbury v. Madison and the Madisonian Vision*, 72 GEO.

> **Cross-Reference**
>
> The subject of procedural due process will be discussed in greater detail in Chapter 7.

WASH. L. REV. 197, 243 (2003). Rather, the personal right to procedural due process extends to the government's adjudicative decision-making.

Factually speaking, *Londoner* and *Bi-Metallic* seem far more similar than dissimilar. They both deal with a claim of property deprivation through government taxation; both assert a right to be heard prior to suffering that alleged deprivation; and both even deal with the City of Denver. Nevertheless, they have very different outcomes. To pinpoint why, keep two questions in mind as you read. First, on what types of facts does the Court focus in its analysis in each case? Second, what reasons does the Court provide for drawing legal significance from those facts? In other words, why are those facts important for determining whether the plaintiffs in each case had procedural due process rights?

Londoner v. City and County of Denver
210 U.S. 373 (1908)

Mr. Justice MOODY delivered the opinion of the court:

The plaintiffs in error began this proceeding in a state court of Colorado to relieve lands owned by them from an assessment of a tax for the cost of paving a street upon which the lands abutted. The relief sought was granted by the trial court, but its action was reversed by the supreme court of the state, which ordered judgment for the defendants. The case is here on writ of error. The supreme court held that the tax was assessed in conformity with the Constitution and laws of the state, and its decision of that question is conclusive. . . .

The tax complained of was assessed under the provisions of the charter of the city of Denver, which confers upon the city the power to make local improvements and to assess the cost upon property specially benefited. . . . The board of public works, upon the petition of a majority of the owners of the frontage to be assessed, may order the paving of a street. The board must, however, first adopt specifications, mark out a district of assessment, cause a map to be made and an estimate of the cost, with the approximate amount to be assessed upon each lot of land. Before action, notice by publication and an opportunity to be heard to any person interested must be given by the board. . . .

The fifth assignment [of error], though general, vague, and obscure, fairly raises, we think, the question whether the assessment was made without notice and opportunity for hearing to those affected by it, thereby denying to them due process of law [under the Fourteenth Amendment]. The trial court found as a fact that no opportunity for hearing was afforded, and the supreme court did not disturb this finding. The record discloses what was actually done, and there seems to be no dispute about it. After the improvement was completed, the board of public works . . . certified to the city clerk a statement of the cost, and an apportionment of it to the lots of land to be assessed. Thereupon the city clerk . . . published a notice, stating, *inter alia*, that the written complaints or objections of the owners, if filed within thirty days, would be "heard and determined by the city council before the passage of any ordinance assessing the cost." Those interested, therefore, were informed that if they reduced their complaints and objections to writing, and filed them within thirty days, those complaints and objections would be heard, and would be heard before any assessment was made. The notice given in this case, although following the words of the statute, did not fix the time for hearing, and apparently there were no stated sittings of the council acting as a board of equalization. But the notice purported only to fix the time for filing the complaints and objections, and to inform those who should file them that they would be heard before action. The statute expressly required no other notice. . . . Resting upon the assurance that they would be heard, the plaintiffs in error filed [their objections] within the thirty days. . . .

. . . Instead of affording the plaintiffs in error an opportunity to be heard upon [their] allegations, the city council, without notice to them, met as a board of equalization, not in a stated, but in a specially called, session, and, without any hearing, [approved the tax assessment apportionments made by the board of public works, and to which the plaintiffs now object].

Subsequently, without further notice or hearing, the city council enacted the ordinance of assessment whose validity is to be determined in this case. The facts out of which the question on this assignment arises may be compressed into small compass. The first step in the assessment proceedings was by the certificate of the board of public works of the cost of the improvement and a preliminary apportionment of it. The last step was the enactment of the assessment ordinance. From beginning to end of the proceedings the landowners, although allowed to formulate and file complaints and objections, were not afforded an opportunity to be heard upon them. Upon these facts, was there a denial by the state of the due process of law guaranteed by the 14th Amendment to the Constitution of the United States?

In the assessment, apportionment, and collection of taxes upon property within their jurisdiction, the Constitution of the United States imposes few restrictions upon the states. In the enforcement of such restrictions as the Constitution does impose, this court has regarded substance, and not form. But where the legislature of a state, instead of fixing the tax itself, commits to some subordinate body the duty of determining whether, in what amount, and upon whom it shall be levied, and of making its assessment and apportionment, due process of law requires that, at some stage of the proceedings, before the tax becomes irrevocably fixed, the taxpayer shall have an opportunity to be heard, of which he must have notice, either personal, by publication, or by a law fixing the time and place of the hearing. It must be remembered that the law of Colorado denies the landowner the right to object in the courts to the assessment, upon the ground that the objections are cognizable only by the board of equalization.

If it is enough that, under such circumstances, an opportunity is given to submit in writing all objections to and complaints of the tax to the board, then there was a hearing afforded in the case at bar. But we think that something more than that, even in proceedings for taxation, is required by due process of law. Many requirements essential in strictly judicial proceedings may be dispensed with in proceedings of this nature. But even here a hearing, in its very essence, demands that he who is entitled to it shall have the right to support his allegations by argument, however brief: and, if need be, by proof, however informal.

It is apparent that such a hearing was denied to the plaintiffs in error. The denial was by the city council, which, while acting as a board of equalization, represents the state. . . . The assessment was therefore void, and the plaintiffs in error were entitled to a decree discharging their lands from a lien on account of it. . . .

Judgment reversed.

The CHIEF JUSTICE [Melville W. Fuller] and Mr. Justice HOLMES dissent [without writing separate opinions].

Bi-Metallic Investment Co. v. State Board of Equalization
239 U.S. 441 (1915)

Mr. Justice HOLMES delivered the opinion of the court:

This is a suit to enjoin the State Board of Equalization and the Colorado Tax Commission from putting in force and the defendant Pitcher, as assessor of Denver, from obeying, an order of the boards, increasing the valuation of all taxable property in Denver 40 per cent. The order was sustained and the suit directed to be dismissed by the supreme court of the state. The plaintiff is the owner of real estate in Denver, and brings the case here on the ground that it was given no opportunity to be heard, and that therefore its property will be taken without due process of law, contrary to the 14th Amendment of the Constitution of the United States. That is the only question with which we have to deal. . . .

For the purposes of decision we assume that the constitutional question is presented in the baldest way,—that neither the plaintiff nor the assessor of Denver, who presents a brief on the plaintiff's side, nor any representative of the city and county, was given an opportunity to be heard, other than such as they may have had by reason of the fact that the time of meeting of the boards is fixed by law. On this assumption it is obvious that injustice may be suffered if some property in the county already has been valued at its full worth. But if certain property has been valued at a rate different from that generally prevailing in the county, the owner has had his opportunity to protest and appeal as usual in our system of taxation . . . so that it must be assumed that the property owners in the county all stand alike. The question, then, is whether all individuals have a constitutional right to be heard before a matter can be decided in which all are equally concerned,—here, for instance, before a superior board decides that the local taxing officers have adopted a system of undervaluation throughout a county, as notoriously often has been the case. . . .

Where a rule of conduct applies to more than a few people, it is impracticable that everyone should have a direct voice in its adoption. The Constitution does not require all public acts to be done in town meeting or an assembly of the whole. General statutes within the state power are passed that affect the person or property of individuals, sometimes to the point of ruin, without giving them a chance to be heard. Their rights are protected in the only way that they can be in a complex society, by their power, immediate or remote, over those who make the rule. If the result in this case had been reached, as it might have been by the state's doubling the rate of taxation, no one would suggest that the 14th Amendment was violated unless every person affected had been allowed an opportunity to raise his voice against it before the body intrusted [*sic*] by the state Constitution with the power. In considering this case in this court we must assume that the proper state machinery has been used, and the question is whether, if the state Constitution had declared that Denver had been undervalued as compared with the rest of the state, and had decreed that for the current year the valuation should be 40 per cent higher, the objection now urged could prevail. It appears to us that to put the question is to answer it. There must be a limit to individual argument in such matters if government is to go on. In [*Londoner v. Denver*], a local board had to determine "whether, in what amount, and upon whom" a tax for paving a street should be levied for special benefits. A relatively small number of persons was concerned, who were exceptionally affected, in each case upon individual grounds, and it was held that they had a right to a hearing. But that decision is far from reaching a general determination dealing only with the principle upon which all the assessments in a county had been laid.

Judgment affirmed.

QUESTION SET 4.1

Review & Synthesis

1. What is "procedural due process," to which category of governmental decision-making does it apply, and why does it apply only to that category of decision-making?

2. Several decades ago, Professor Kenneth Culp Davis argued that governments rely on different types of facts when making legislative and adjudicative decisions. "Adjudicative facts are facts about the parties and their activities, businesses, and properties" that "answer the question of who did what, where, when, how, why, and with what motive or intent: [they] are roughly the kind of facts that go to a jury in a jury case." By contrast, "[l]egislative facts do not usually concern the immediate parties but are general facts which help the tribunal decide questions of law and policy and discretion." *See* 1 KENNETH CULP DAVIS, ADMINISTRATIVE LAW TREATISE § 7.02 (1958). Identifying the facts on which government decision-makers rely enables courts to accurately categorize their decisions as legislative or adjudicative. This, in turn, helps courts to identify the procedures those decision-makers were required to follow.

    a. Applying Professor Davis' framework, would you categorize the facts on which the City of Denver relied in *Londoner* as "legislative" or as "adjudicative"? What about *Bi-Metallic*?

    b. Professor Davis' framework focuses on inputs rather than on outputs. Without more, it seems to assume that the legislative or adjudicative character of a decision is conclusively determined by the type information supporting it. Do you think that's right? Would an agency necessarily be precluded from basing a general rule on facts drawn from a particular adjudication or enforcement action?

    c. Should courts consider other factors—apart from the generality or specificity of the evidence—when characterizing an agency's actions as legislative or adjudicative? What about an agency's own characterization of its decision? Should courts consider an agency's claims that its decision is generally applicable or limited to identifiable parties when determining its legislative or adjudicative character? Should courts consider the temporal scope of a decision, given that most legislative acts are prospective in scope (deal with future conduct) whereas most adjudicatory acts are retrospective in scope (deal with past conduct)?

3. Writing for the Court in *Bi-Metallic*, Justice Holmes said that the property owners' rights to be spared from harmful legislative acts "are protected in the only way that they can be in a complex society, by their

power, immediate or remote, over those who make the rule." 239 U.S. at 445. Does this precept, which seems to be based on the notion of political accountability, make sense in the administrative context? The power of regulated persons and entities to remove those who regulate them is neither immediate nor remote. It is nonexistent. Given this reality (of which Holmes was almost certainly aware), should politicians require that administrative officials provide opportunities to hear the public's concerns before taking legislative actions?

Application & Analysis

1. The Endangered Species Act ("ESA") grants the U.S. Fish and Wildlife Service ("FWS") authority to promulgate regulations controlling the importation of sport-hunted African elephants. Pursuant to FWS's regulations, such importation is permitted if, among other things, FWS makes a "positive enhancement" finding that killing African elephants for sport actually enhances their chances of survival as a species. Twenty years ago, FWS made a positive enhancement finding for sport hunting of African elephants in Zimbabwe, which it published in the Federal Register. FWS based its finding on data it received from the Zimbabwean government showing that hunting revenues benefited rural communities, funded elephant conservation programs, and increased elephant population growth.

   This finding remained in place until last year, when FWS made a negative enhancement finding. FWS based its negative finding in part on publicly available survey information suggesting that Zimbabwe's elephant population had declined significantly over the past several years. FWS also emphasized that its inability to get complete and reliable information from the Zimbabwean government made issuing a positive enhancement finding impossible. The agency published a summary of the negative enhancement assessment and an announcement banning continued importation of sport-hunted elephants from Zimbabwe in the Federal Register. FWS subsequently received additional data from the Zimbabwean government as well as several hunting organizations based in the United States. After analyzing this new information, FWS concluded that it did not provide a sufficient basis for reversal of its negative enhancement finding.

   The hunting organizations that furnished FWS with additional information challenged the importation ban in federal district court. They argued that the ban was a rule that could only be promulgated under the Administrative Procedure Act's notice-and-comment rulemaking procedures (§ 553). FWS countered that the ban was an order that it could issue as part of an informal adjudication. Analyze the merits of these respective arguments.

B. CHOICE OF POLICYMAKING TOOLS

Taken together, *Londoner* and *Bi-Metallic* addressed the minimum constitutional procedures administrative bodies must provide when their decisions affect individual interests. More specifically, the Supreme Court in those cases first determined whether the state conduct in question was legislative or adjudicative in character. It in effect held that they are the former when government develops policies that affect all individuals in the same way and that they are the latter when government action affects only a handful of individuals in ways that differentiate them from the public as a whole. When engaged in adjudication, the Constitution's guarantee of due process constrains the government's ability to deprive individuals of their life, liberty, or property.

By contrast, the Fifth Amendment due process clause plays little to no role in how federal agencies undertake quasi-legislative decision-making, i.e., how they formulate and adopt generally applicable regulatory policies. As Justice Holmes put it in *Bi-Metallic*, individuals who may be harmed by such decisions "are protected in the only way that they can be in a complex society, by their power, immediate or remote, over those who make the rule." 239 U.S. at 445. Accordingly, we must look to federal statutes, rather than to the federal Constitution, for procedural controls on agency policymaking. Many organic statutes set the minimum procedures agencies must follow when engaging in rulemaking and adjudication. When organic statutes do not do so, the procedural minimums for rulemaking and (formal) adjudication are instead set by the Administrative Procedure Act ("APA").

Before exploring those procedural requirements in detail, we must answer a preliminary question: are agencies free to choose between rulemaking and adjudication when formulating and adopting new policies? Congress has granted policymaking authority to numerous agencies. Many of these agencies also have (or claim to have) the authority to regulate either through rulemaking or through adjudication. If their officials want to adopt new regulations, must they do so through the rulemaking process, or can they do so as part of adjudications resolving individual disputes? Congress sometimes answers this question for agencies by specifying that they must proceed by rulemaking. Most of the time, federal statutes are silent on the issue.

Such silence raises a number of critical questions. Is the choice of procedure simply left to agency discretion? Assuming the agency does have discretion, are there extra-statutory considerations—efficiency, flexibility, foreseeability, fairness, political accountability, prior procedural practices—that must or should inform its choice? What is the proper scope of new rules adopted through adjudication? Can they bind anyone other than the parties to the case that creates them? Can rules created through adjudication even bind parties in that originating case since they would be adopted *after* those parties have already acted? Stated differently, the parties would have no notice of what the law requires before deciding on a course of conduct.

The Supreme Court addressed some of these issues in the seminal pre-APA case of *Securities and Exchange Commission v. Chenery Corp.*, 332 U.S. 194 (1947). Often referred to as *Chenery II*, this case is the second part of a multiyear regulatory saga. In *Securities and Exchange Commission v. Chenery Corp.*, 318 U.S. 80 (1943) (*Chenery I*), respondents were controlling shareholders in Federal Water Services Corp., a holding company registered under the Public Utility Holding Company Act of 1935. Pursuant to §§ 7 and 11 of the Act, Federal's management filed four reorganization plans with the SEC, the first three of which the agency rejected. Under the fourth plan, Federal would convert its Class A and preferred stock into new shares of the reorganized company. The conversion would result in Federal's preferred stockholders holding almost all of the new shares. While the Commission was considering Federal's successive reorganization plans, Chenery and Federal's managers and controlling shareholders (together, "Chenery") purchased large amounts of Federal's preferred stock in the open market. They purchased the preferred stock on the same terms as any other market buyer, which was lower than the book value of the reorganized company's common stock. They also freely admitted that they made these purchases to retain a controlling interest in the reorganized company. The Commission did not find that Chenery had acquired Federal's preferred stock through fraud or deceit. To the contrary, it conceded that they had acquired it honestly and on terms no better than any other investor. Nevertheless, the Commission concluded that "in the process of formulation of a voluntary reorganization plan, the management of a corporation occupies a fiduciary position toward all of the security holders to be affected, and that it is subjected to the same standards as other fiduciaries with respect to dealing with the property which is the subject matter of the trust." *Chenery I,* 318 U.S. at 87 (internal quotations omitted). Accordingly, "the duty of fair dealing which the management owes to the stockholders is violated if those in control of the corporation purchase its stock, even at a fair price, openly and without fraud." *Id.* Applying this rule, which it based on Supreme Court case law, the Commission ordered that Chenery could not convert their preferred stock into shares of the reorganized company.

The Supreme Court reversed and remanded. It noted that neither Congress nor the Commission had promulgated a general rule forbidding the type of stock purchases at issue in the case. Instead, the SEC had based its order on the Supreme Court's prior decisions, which it read as establishing an equitable rule prohibiting the purchases. The Court then pointed to what have become two fundamental tenets of administrative law. First, reviewing courts can uphold an agency's decisions solely on the grounds the agency invoked at the time to justify them. Second, an agency's decisions must be set aside when they are based on misinterpretations of the law. *Id.* at 94-95. Applying these tenets, the Court found that SEC had based its order solely on the Court's prior decisions and that it had misinterpreted those decisions. Accordingly, the Court ordered the Commission to reconsider its order in light of a corrected understanding of the law.

The Commission on remand applied the same rule, reached the same conclusion, and issued the same order. The key difference this second go-round was the legal basis for the rule; the SEC recast its decision as based on its reading of the Public Utilities Holding Company Act, and not on its reading of the Court's equity jurisprudence. The case reached the Court a second time, whereupon it found that the Commission "definitely avoid[ed] the fatal error of relying on judicial precedents which do not sustain it." *Chenery II*, 332 U.S. at 199. Unlike the first time it barred Chenery's preferred stock conversion, the SEC conducted a "thorough reexamination of the problem in light of the purposes and standards of the Holding Company Act," had "drawn heavily upon its accumulated experience in dealing with utility reorganizations" and "expressed its reasons with a clarity and thoroughness that admit of no doubt as to the underlying basis of its order." *Id.*

More important for present purposes was Chenery's new argument before the Court. It asserted that the Public Utility Holding Company Act, on its own, did not prohibit Federal's managers from profiting from their preferred stock purchases. Accordingly, Chenery insisted that the SEC could impose such a prohibition only by adopting a new rule which, in turn, the SEC could only apply prospectively. In other words, Chenery objected to the idea that the SEC could both create *and* apply that new rule in the same case. The Court was unpersuaded, and instead concluded that the SEC could establish its new rule either by adjudication or by rulemaking:

> It is true that our prior decision explicitly recognized the possibility that the Commission might have promulgated a general rule dealing with this problem under its statutory rule-making powers, in which case the issue for our consideration would have been entirely different from that which did confront us. But we did not mean to imply thereby that the failure of the Commission to anticipate this problem and to promulgate a general rule withdrew all power from that agency to perform its statutory duty in this case. To hold that the Commission had no alternative in this proceeding but to approve the proposed transaction, while formulating any general rules it might desire for use in future cases of this nature, would be to stultify the administrative process. That we refuse to do.
>
> Since the Commission, unlike a court, does have the ability to make new law prospectively through the exercise of its rule-making powers, it has less reason to rely upon *ad hoc* adjudication to formulate new standards of conduct within the framework of the Holding Company Act. The function of filling in the interstices of the Act should be performed, as much as possible, through this quasi-legislative promulgation of rules to be applied

in the future. But any rigid requirement to that effect would make the administrative process inflexible and incapable of dealing with many of the specialized problems which arise. Not every principle essential to the effective administration of a statute can or should be cast immediately into the mold of a general rule. Some principles must await their own development, while others must be adjusted to meet particular, unforeseeable situations. In performing its important functions in these respects, therefore, an administrative agency must be equipped to act either by general rule or by individual order. To insist upon one form of action to the exclusion of the other is to exalt form over necessity.

In other words, problems may arise in a case which the administrative agency could not reasonably foresee, problems which must be solved despite the absence of a relevant general rule. Or the agency may not have had sufficient experience with a particular problem to warrant rigidifying its tentative judgment into a hard and fast rule. Or the problem may be so specialized and varying in nature as to be impossible of capture within the boundaries of a general rule. In those situations, the agency must retain power to deal with the problems on a case-to-case basis if the administrative process is to be effective. There is thus a very definite place for the case-by-case evolution of statutory standards. And the choice made between proceeding by general rule or by individual, *ad hoc* litigation is one that lies primarily in the informed discretion of the administrative agency.

... That such action might have a retroactive effect was not necessarily fatal to its validity. Every case of first impression has a retroactive effect, whether the new principle is announced by a court or by an administrative agency. But such retroactivity must be balanced against the mischief of producing a result which is contrary to a statutory design or to legal and equitable principles. If that mischief is greater than the ill effect of the retroactive application of a new standard, it is not the type of retroactivity which is condemned by law.

Id. at 202-03.

The APA was approved by President Harry S. Truman on June 11, 1946 and, pursuant to its Section 12, the earliest any of its provisions went into effect was three months thereafter. *Chenery I* was decided before the APA became binding on agencies (the Court published its opinion on June 23, 1947), and *Chenery II* simply reviewed the SEC's decisions it first considered in *Chenery I*. Accordingly, neither *Chenery I* nor *Chenery II* applied the APA's provisions to the SEC's orders.

The cases that follow address agencies' latitude to engage in policymaking by rules, by orders, and by internal agency documents after passage of the APA.

1. Policymaking by Rule

Congress has vested the Federal Trade Commission ("FTC") with one of the broadest regulatory missions in the entire federal government.

Constituted as a five-member independent agency, it is charged with anti-trust enforcement and consumer protection. It administers provisions of the Clayton Antitrust Act, a task it shares with the Antitrust Division of the Department of Justice. Its organic statute, the Federal Trade Commission Act ("FTC Act"), proscribes a host of problematic commercial practices. Section 5 prohibits "[u]nfair methods of competition in or affecting commerce, and unfair or deceptive acts or practices in or affecting commerce." 15 U.S.C. § 45(a). The first clause of this section refers to conduct directed at a business' competitors, whereas the second refers to conduct directed at consumers. Section 12 forbids false advertising in the sale of "food, drugs, devices, services, or cosmetics." 15 U.S.C. § 52. To enforce these provisions, Congress has granted the FTC regulatory power over most persons and businesses engaged in interstate commerce. It can conduct investigations (§ 6(a), 15 U.S.C. § 46(a)), require the filing of business activity reports (§ 6(b), 15 U.S.C. § 46(b)), and publicly disclose the information it gathers (§ 6(f), 15 U.S.C. § 46(f)). Most importantly for present purposes, the FTC Act directs the FTC to "classify corporations and ... to make rules and regulations for the purpose of carrying out the provisions of this subchapter." FTC Act § 6(g), 15 U.S.C. § 46(g).

For the first several decades of its existence, the FTC did not engage in substantive rulemaking to protect consumers and businesses from deceptive or unfair commercial practices. The Commission often pursued less formal means to encourage voluntary compliance with the FTC Act. For example, it would provide written opinions to businesses to advise them on the likely legality of conduct they were contemplating, and it would publish guides explaining how businesses could comply with various FTC Act provisions. When developing legally binding policies, the Commission heavily relied on formal adjudications. Under § 5(b), the Commission can serve a complaint on any person or business it believes is or has engaged in unfair or deceptive practices if doing so serves the public interest. These complaints state the charges and their factual basis, order the respondent to "show cause why an order should not be entered by the commission requiring [the respondent] to cease and desist from the violation so charged in said complaint," and set hearing dates. 15 U.S.C. § 45(b) (2018). An FTC administrative law judge ("ALJ") presides over the trial-like hearing under rules of evidence similar to those applied in federal district courts. Based on the factual record built at the hearing, the ALJ issues a decision that can be appealed to the full Commission. Cease-and-desist orders issued by the Commission can, in turn, be appealed to the appropriate United States Court of Appeals.

Over time, complaints mounted that the FTC's practice of developing regulatory policy through case-by-case adjudication was slow and ineffective. The FTC itself acknowledged as much, stating in its 1962 annual report that "it became all too apparent that the Commission's machinery needed to be redesigned to speed the prosecution of cases—to shorten the time between the initial investigation of a law violation and the issuance of an order stopping it." 1961 Ann. Rep. Fed. Trade Comm'n 1. Deceptive practices often were widespread in particular industries, yet an adjudication-based regulatory model limited the Commission to attacking them one violation at time. Its enforcement actions were also limited in substantive scope; they could remedy only the actions specifically described in a complaint. "By the time a complaint—or even application for a preliminary injunction—is entered, the firm has abandoned the questionable claims and has made many others." Alan Stone, Economic Regulation in the Public Interest: The Federal Trade Commission in Theory and Practice 202 (1977). That the Commission's cease-and-desist orders were not binding of their own force further impeded its regulatory efforts. If a party refused to comply, the Commission would be forced to file suit in federal court to enforce them. Even if litigation were successful, others who were not subject to it would engage in similar practices until the FTC targeted them directly. "Thus, it might take years to police an entire industry." William F. West, *The Politics of Administrative Rulemaking*, 42 Pub. Admin. Rev. 420, 421 (1982). The voluntary compliance measures the Commission adopted did not appear to compensate for these shortcomings.

In response, the Commission began promulgating Trade Regulation Rules ("TRRs") in 1962. The benefits of forming policy through rulemaking rather than adjudication seemed clear. The TRRs would serve as general statements of policy that applied to entire industries, and "which could be express in such a way as to preclude future inventiveness." *Id.* Stated differently, generally applicable rules could categorize conduct as unfair or deceptive for all future adjudications. Rather than having to show that the law proscribed particular conduct in each case, the Commission would only have to show that the respondent engaged in conduct that violated a TRR. This decision to regulate by rulemaking was controversial for a number of reasons. Historically, the Commission had never promulgated a rule, although some commentators and government officials had advocated that it do so for decades. Politically, industry opposed being subject to generalizable rules that would govern their conduct even when the FTC had not initiated cease-and-desist proceedings against them individually. Legally, some doubted that the FTC Act granted the Commission rulemaking authority, even though § 6(g) directed it "to make rules and regulations for the purpose of carrying out the provisions of this subchapter." 15 U.S.C. § 46(g). Administratively, assumption of rulemaking authority materially expanded the FTC's regulatory authority.

The issue came to a head in 1969, when the FTC proposed a rule requiring gas stations clearly to post gasoline octane ratings on their pumps. Octane numbers measure the resistance of gasoline to detonation ("engine knocking") in internal combustion engines. Typically, high-performance engines are more susceptible to detonation and thus require more expensive gasoline with higher octane numbers. Lower performance engines typically require less expensive lower octane gasoline. The FTC's notice of proposed rulemaking ("NPRM") indicated that purchasing gasoline with an inappropriate octane number could harm consumers. If the octane numbers were higher than appropriate, the consumer would spend more and would receive no performance benefit in return. If the octane number were lower than appropriate, the consumer's vehicle could be damaged from increased engine knocking. The NPRM asserted that the quality labels stations were placing on their pumps — "regular," "premium," etc. — misled consumers into purchasing gasoline that did not meet the needs of their vehicles' engines. The Commission received a large number of comments from industry and consumer advocates during the rulemaking's public comments period arguing for and against its adoption. In the end, the Commission moved forward and promulgated the final rule on December 16, 1971.

The following D.C. Circuit decision — *National Petroleum Refiners Association v. FTC* — involved a challenge to the FTC's statutory authority to adopt the octane posting rule through rulemaking.

National Petroleum Refiners Ass'n v. Federal Trade Commission
482 F.2d 672 (D.C. Cir. 1973)

Before BAZELON, Chief Judge, and WRIGHT and ROBINSON, Circuit Judges.

J. SKELLY WRIGHT, Circuit Judge.

This case presents an important question concerning the powers and procedures of the Federal Trade Commission. We are asked to determine whether the Commission, under its governing statute, the Trade Commission Act, 15 U.S.C. § 41 *et seq.* (1970), and specifically 15 U.S.C. § 46(g), is empowered to promulgate substantive rules of business conduct or, as it terms them, "Trade Regulation Rules." The effect of these rules would be to give greater specificity and clarity to the broad standard of illegality — "unfair methods of competition in commerce, and unfair or deceptive acts or practices in commerce" — which the agency is empowered to prevent. 15 U.S.C. § 45(a). Once promulgated, the rules would be used by the agency in adjudicatory proceedings aimed at producing cease and desist orders against violations of the statutory standard. . . .

Our duty here is not simply to make a policy judgment as to what mode of procedure — adjudication alone or a mixed system of rule-making and adjudication, as the Commission proposes — best accommodates the need for effective enforcement of the Commission's mandate with maximum solicitude for the interests of parties whose activities might be within the scope of the statutory standard of illegality. The Federal Trade Commission is a creation of Congress, not a creation of judges' contemporary notions of what is wise policy. The extent of its powers can be decided only by considering the powers Congress specifically granted it in the light of the statutory language and background. The question to be answered is "not what the [Commission] thinks it should do but what Congress has said it can do." CAB v. Delta Air Lines, 367 U.S. 316, 322 (1961).

As always, we must begin with the words of the statute creating the Commission and delineating its powers. Section 5 directs the Commission to "prevent persons, partnerships, or corporations ... from using unfair methods of competition in commerce and unfair or deceptive acts or practices in commerce." Section 5(b) of the Trade Commission Act specifies that the Commission is to accomplish this goal by means of issuance of a complaint, a hearing, findings as to the facts, and issuance of a cease and desist order. The Commission's assertion that it is empowered by Section 6(g) to issue substantive rules defining the statutory standard of illegality in advance of specific adjudications does not in any formal sense circumvent this method of enforcement. For after the rules are issued, their mode of enforcement remains what it has always been under Section 5: the sequence of complaint, hearing, findings, and issuance of a cease and desist order. What rulemaking does do, functionally, is to narrow the inquiry conducted in proceedings under Section 5(b). It is the legality of this practice which we must judge.

Appellees argue that since Section 5 mentions only adjudication as the means of enforcing the statutory standard, any supplemental means of putting flesh on that standard, such as rulemaking, is contrary to the overt legislative design. But Section 5(b) does not use limiting language suggesting that adjudication alone is the only proper means of elaborating the statutory standard. It merely makes clear that a Commission decision, after complaint and hearing, followed by a cease and desist order, is the way to force an offender to halt his illegal activities. Nor are we persuaded by appellees' argument that, despite the absence of limiting language in Section 5 regarding the role of adjudication in defining the meaning of the statutory standard, we should apply the maxim of statutory construction *expressio unius est exclusio alterius* and conclude that adjudication is the only means of defining the statutory standard. This maxim is increasingly considered unreliable, for it stands on the faulty premise that all possible alternative or supplemental provisions were necessarily considered and rejected by the legislative draftsmen. Here we have particularly good reason on the face of the statute to reject such arguments. For the Trade Commission Act includes a provision which specifically provides for rulemaking by the Commission to implement its adjudicatory functions under Section 5 of the Act. Section 6(g) of the Act, 15 U.S.C. § 46(g), states that the Commission may "[f]rom time to time ... classify corporations

and ... make rules and regulations for the purpose of carrying out the provisions of sections 41 to 46 and 47 to 58 of this title."

According to appellees, however, this rule-making power is limited to
specifying the details of the Commission's nonadjudicatory, investigative
and informative functions spelled out in the other provisions of Section 6
and should not be read to encompass substantive rulemaking in implementation of Section 5 adjudications. We disagree for the simple reason that
Section 6(g) clearly states that the Commission "may" make rules and regulations for the purpose of carrying out the provisions of Section 5 and it
has been so applied. For example, the Commission has issued rules specifying in greater detail than the statute the mode of Commission procedure
under Section 5 in matters involving service of process, requirements as to
the filing of answers, and other litigation details necessarily involved in the
Commission's work of prosecuting its complaints under Section 5. Such
rulemaking by the Commission has been upheld....

Of course, it is at least arguable that these cases go no farther than to
justify utilizing Section 6(g) to promulgate procedural, as opposed to substantive, rules for administration of the Section 5 adjudication and enforcement powers. But we see no reason to import such a restriction on the "rules
and regulations" permitted by Section 6(g). On the contrary, as we shall see,
judicial precedents concerning rule-making by other agencies and the background and purpose of the Federal Trade Commission Act lead us liberally to
construe the term "rules and regulations." The substantive rule here unquestionably implements the statutory plan. Section 5 adjudications — trial type
proceedings — will still be necessary to obtain cease and desist orders against
offenders, but Section 5 enforcement through adjudication will be expedited, simplified, and thus "carried out" by use of this substantive rule. And
the overt language of both Section 5 and Section 6, read together, supports
its use in Section 5 proceedings.

II

Our belief that "rules and regulations" in Section 6(g) should be construed to permit the Commission to promulgate binding substantive rules
as well as rules of procedure is reinforced by the construction courts have
given similar provisions in the authorizing statutes of other administrative
agencies. There is, of course, no doubt that the approved practices of agencies
with similar statutory provisions is a relevant factor in arriving at a sound
interpretation of the Federal Trade Commission's power here....

... [T]here is little question that the availability of substantive rule-making
gives any agency an invaluable resource-saving flexibility in carrying out its
task of regulating parties subject to its statutory mandate. More than merely
expediting the agency's job, use of substantive rule-making is increasingly
felt to yield significant benefits to those the agency regulates. Increasingly,

courts are recognizing that use of rule-making to make innovations in agency policy may actually be fairer to regulated parties than total reliance on case-by-case adjudication.

The Supreme Court made this suggestion initially in *SEC v. Chenery Corp.*, 332 U.S. 194 (1947) [(*Chenery II*)], where it dealt with an agency adjudication imposing novel restraints on the power of management of corporations to purchase stock during periods of reorganization under the Public Utility Holding Company Act of 1935. While the Court did not hold that the Securities and Exchange Commission was bound to follow rule-making procedures in making such a marked policy departure, it was clearly aware that exclusive reliance on adjudication could be criticized for unfairly focusing on a single defendant in a restricted proceeding when promulgating a new policy with industry-wide ramifications. The Court said:

> ... The function of filling in the interstices of the Act should be performed, as much as possible, through this quasi-legislative promulgation of rules to be applied in the future....

332 U.S. at 202.

Four years ago a majority of the Supreme Court hinted that there may be circumstances where agency policy innovations should be made only in rule-making proceedings. In *NLRB v. Wyman-Gordon Co.*, 394 U.S. 759 (1969), the Court upheld an adjudicatory order based on a prior decision where the Labor Board had decided that a new rule of management conduct during election campaigns should operate only prospectively. But the four-man plurality opinion by Mr. Justice Fortas sharply criticized the Board's initial promulgation in adjudicatory proceedings of a rule applicable in election campaigns generally.... Mr. Justice Douglas, dissenting from the majority's actual holding, argued similarly that where the Board imposed a new standard of conduct that is "not particularized to special facts ... [but] is a statement of far-reaching policy covering all future representation elections," *id.* at 777, it should be required to follow the APA's rule-making procedures....

This judicial trend favoring rule-making over adjudication for development of new agency policy does not, of course, directly dispose of the question before us. There was no question that the SEC in *Chenery [II]* had substantive rule-making powers. And *Wyman-Gordon* assumed that the NLRB also had substantive rule-making powers under 29 U.S.C. § 156 (1970). Here we must decide just that question, whether Congress has given the FTC the same alternate means of proceeding, not whether the FTC should be required to use rule-making in some circumstances. But *Chenery [II]* [and] *Wyman-Gordon* cannot be ignored, for they indisputably flesh out the contemporary legal framework in which both the FTC and

> **Cross-Reference**
>
> The more general trend toward formulating administrative policy through rulemaking during this period is discussed in the historical overview provided in Chapter 1.

this court operate and which we must recognize. To us, these cases suggest that contemporary considerations of practicality and fairness—specifically the advisability of utilizing the Administrative Procedure Act's rule-making procedures to provide an agency about to embark on legal innovation with all relevant arguments and information, 5 U.S.C. § 553—certainly support the Commission's position here. As *Wyman-Gordon* ... explicitly noted, utilizing rule-making procedures opens up the process of agency policy innovation to a broad range of criticism, advice and data that is ordinarily less likely to be forthcoming in adjudication. Moreover, the availability of notice before promulgation and wide public participation in rule-making avoids the problem of singling out a single defendant among a group of competitors for initial imposition of a new and inevitably costly legal obligation.

Such benefits are especially obvious in cases involving initiation of rules of the sort the FTC has promulgated here. The Commission's statement on basis and purpose indicated that the decision to impose the obligation of octane rating disclosure on gasoline dealers entailed careful consideration of automobile engine requirements, automobile dealers' practices in instructing purchasers how to care for their engines, consumer gasoline purchasing habits, and costs to gasoline dealers. In addition, the Commission had to choose exactly what kind of disclosure was the fairest. In short, a vast amount of data had to be compiled and analyzed, and the Commission, armed with these data, had to weigh the conflicting policies of increasingly knowledgeable consumer decision-making against alleged costs to gasoline dealers which might be passed on to the consumer. True, the decision to impose a bright-line standard of behavior might have been evolved by the Commission in a single or a succession of adjudicatory proceedings, much as the Supreme Court has imposed per se rules of business behavior in antitrust cases. But evolution of bright-line rules is often a slow process and may involve the distinct disadvantage of acting without the broad range of data and argument from all those potentially affected that may be flushed out through use of legislative-type rule-making procedures. And utilizing rule-making in advance of adjudication here minimizes the unfairness of using a purely case-by-case approach requiring "compliance by one manufacturer while his competitors [engaging in similar practices] remain free to violate the Act." In light of *Chenery* [*II*] [and] *Wyman-Gordon*, therefore, it is hard to escape noting that the policy innovation involved in this case underscores the need for increased reliance on rule-making rather than adjudication alone.

III

Appellees contend, however, that these cases and the general practice of agencies and courts in underwriting the broad use of rule-making are irrelevant to the FTC. They argue that the Trade Commission is somehow *sui generis*, that it is best characterized as a prosecuting rather than a regulatory agency, and that substantive rule-making power should be less readily implied from a general grant of rule-making authority where the agency does not stand astride an industry with pervasive license-granting, rate-setting, or clearance functions....

Given the expanse of the Commission's power to define proper business practices, we believe it is but a quibble to differentiate between the potential pervasiveness of the FTC's power and that of the other regulatory agencies merely on the basis of its prosecutorial and adjudicatory mode of proceeding. Like other agencies, wholly apart from the question of rule-making power it exerts a powerfully regulatory effect on those business practices subject to its supervision. Of course, its regulatory authority is not complete. But neither is the regulation exercised by other agencies. And the Commission has this regulatory effect irrespective of whether it chooses to elaborate the vague but comprehensive statutory standards through rule-making or through case-by-case adjudication. Businesses whose practices appear clearly covered by the Trade Commission's adjudicatory decisions against similarly situated parties presumably will comply with the Commission's holding rather than await a Commission action against them individually; we must presume that in many cases where a guideline is laid down in an individual case it is, like many common law rules, generally obeyed by those similarly situated. Moreover, there are ample indications in the Commission's legislative history that the agency, by gathering information on business practices, issuing periodic reports, and moving against those practices which appear "unfair," was meant to have just this sort of regulatory impact, despite the purely prosecutorial mode of proceeding provided in Section 5 of the Act. Not only is the Commission's regulatory power much broader than appellees would have us believe; there is simply no compelling evidence in the Act's legislative history or in the language of the statute itself which would limit the exercise of that power to the prosecutorial function or prevent the Commission from making that function more effective by rule-making.

IV

... There is little disagreement that the Commission will be able to proceed more expeditiously, give greater certainty to businesses subject to the Act, and deploy its internal resources more efficiently with a mixed system of rule-making and adjudication than with adjudication alone. With the issues in Section 5 proceedings reduced by the existence of a rule delineating what is a violation of the statute or what presumptions the Commission proposes to rely upon, proceedings will be speeded up. For example, in an adjudication proceeding based on a violation of the octane rating rule at issue here, the central question to be decided will be whether or not pumps owned by a given refiner are properly marked. Without the rule, the Commission might well be obliged to prove and argue that the absence of the rating markers in each particular case was likely to have injurious and unfair effects on consumers or competition. Since this laborious process might well have to be repeated every time the Commission chose to proceed subsequently against another defendant on the same ground, the difference in administrative efficiency between the two kinds of proceedings is obvious. Furthermore, rules, as contrasted with the holdings reached by case-by-case adjudication, are more specific as to their scope, and industry compliance is more likely simply because each company is on clearer notice whether or not specific rules apply to it.

Moreover, when delay in agency proceedings is minimized by using rules, those violating the statutory standard lose an opportunity to turn litigation into a profitable and lengthy game of postponing the effect of the rule on their current practice. As a result, substantive rules will protect the companies which willingly comply with the law against what amounts to the unfair competition of those who would profit from delayed enforcement as to them. This, too, will minimize useless litigation and is likely to assist the Commission in more effectively allocating its resources. In addition, whatever form rules take, whether bright-line standards or presumptions that are rebuttable, they are likely to decrease the current uncertainty many businesses are said to feel over the current scope and applicability of Section 5. But the important point here is not that rule-making is assuredly going to solve the Commission's problems. It is rather [that] recognition and use of rule-making by the Commission is convincingly linked to the goals of agency expedition, efficiency, and certainty of regulatory standards that loomed in the background of the 1914 passage of the Federal Trade Commission Act....

VI

Our conclusion as to the scope of Section 6(g) is not disturbed by the fact that the agency itself did not assert the power to promulgate substantive rules until 1962 and indeed indicated intermittently before that time that it lacked such power.... Here, the question is simply one of statutory interpretation concerning the procedures and setting in which the Commission may elaborate its statutory standard. Since this sort of question calls largely for the exercise of historical analysis and logical and analogical reasoning, it is the everyday staple of judges as well as agencies. Thus we feel confident in making our own judgment as to the proper construction of Section 6(g)....

... So far as we can tell, the earlier assertions of lack of rule-making power were based on an unduly crabbed and cautious analysis of the legislative background, an analysis that we have conducted independently and that has brought us to an opposite but, in our judgment, correct conclusion.

A more troubling obstacle to the Commission's position here is the argument that Congress was made fully aware of the formerly restrictive view of the Commission's power and passed a series of laws granting limited sub-stantive rule-making authority to the Commission in discrete areas allegedly on the premise that the 1914 debate withheld such authority. Where there has been evidence of congressional knowledge of and acquiescence in a long-standing agency construction of its own powers, courts have occasionally concluded that the agency construction had received a *de facto* ratification by Congress.

But *de facto* ratification through acquiescence in an administrative construction is not lightly attributed. The argument before us is not that Congress, by a combination of its knowledge of the agency construction and its inaction could be said to have accepted the construction. Even in these cases it can be argued quite plausibly that imputing ratification in this fashion fails to take into account significant practical aspects of the legis-lative process: those legislators actually aware of the construction in ques-tion may not have been so concerned as to raise it to the attention of most members, and even in the event some legislators were deeply troubled by the construction, the press of other business was such as to keep the ques-tion on the "back burner." Here the situation is different. The view that the Commission lacked substantive rule-making power has been clearly brought to the attention of Congress and, rather than simply failing to act on the question, Congress [has expanded] the agency's powers in several discrete areas of marketing regulation.... Thus it is argued that Congress would not have granted the agency such powers unless it had felt that otherwise the agency lacked rule-making authority.

Conceding the greater force of this argument than one premised on congressional inaction, we believe it must not be accepted blindly. In such circumstances, it is equally possible that Congress granted the power out of uncertainty, understand-able caution, and a desire to avoid litigation. While this argument, like any theory requiring us to draw inferences from congressional action or inaction, may be speculative, we believe it cannot be ignored here. For there is ample evidence that, while some of the limited rule-making legislation may well have been influenced by the belief that the 1914 Act did not grant the Commission substantive rule-making power, at least during the passage of the Packaging and Labeling Act of 1967, this assumption was not accepted and was thought by many congressmen to be an open question, despite the protestations of the Commission's chairman that the agency was power-less under the 1914 Act.... Where there is solid rea-son, as there plainly is here, to believe that Congress, in fact, has not wholeheartedly accepted the agency's

> ### In Context
>
> In the years following the D.C. Circuit's decision in *National Petroleum Refiners*, Congress repeatedly amended the FTC Act to place proce-dural and substantive limitations on the FTC's rulemaking authority over unfair and deceptive practices. The most significant of these amendments came in the Magnuson-Moss Warranty Act of 1975. Among other things, the Act imposes a number of procedural requirements — advanced notices, oral hearings, staff reports — that make rulemaking much slower and more costly than the APA § 553 notice-and-comment procedures the FTC used for the octane posting rule.

viewpoint and instead enacted legislation out of caution and to eliminate the kind of disputes that invariably attend statutory ambiguity, we believe that relying on the *de facto* ratification argument is unwise. In such circumstances, we must perform our customary task of coming to an independent judgment as to the statute's meaning, confident that if Congress believes that its creature, the Commission, thus exercises too much power, it will repeal the grant.

QUESTION SET 4.2

Review & Synthesis

1. What are the two main issues the D.C. Circuit addressed in *National Petroleum Refiners* regarding the FTC's statutory authority to engage in rulemaking?

2. Summarize the potential operational and regulatory benefits the D.C. Circuit believed the FTC would receive by making policy through rulemaking rather than through case-by-case adjudication.
   a. Will the benefits the court identified primarily accrue to the FTC, to regulated businesses, or to consumers?
   b. What are some of the potential costs that would come from the FTC adopting new policies by rule rather than by adjudication? Do you think the court gives those costs due consideration in its analysis?
   c. Assume that the benefits of rulemaking are as substantial as the D.C. Circuit claimed them to be. To what extent are they relevant to the question whether Congress intended to grant the FTC rulemaking authority? If you believe that they are of little to no relevance, what work did they do in the court's analysis?

3. Summarize the factors the D.C. Circuit considered in concluding that FTC Act § 6(g) granted the FTC rulemaking authority under the FTC Act.
   a. In your judgment, did the weight of the evidence support the court's conclusion? Consider that (1) the FTC had never promulgated a rule prior to 1962, based in part on its own interpretation of the FTC Act; and (2) the FTC Act specifically mentioned the FTC's authority to investigate, adjudicate, and publicize information but did not mention rulemaking (*expressio unius est exclusio alterius*).
   b. In a footnote not included in the above excerpt, the D.C. Circuit noted "that in both the just concluded 92nd Congress and the current 93rd Congress legislation granting the FTC limited substantive

rule-making power in the area of 'unfair and deceptive practices' has been under consideration." 482 F.2d at 697 n.40. This footnote also noted that several Senators during floor debate stated their belief that the FTC in fact did not have authority to make rules for unfair methods of competition or unfair or deceptive trade practices that could be applied in a cease-and-desist proceeding. Does this change your view about whether the court properly interpreted FTC Act § 6(g)?

c. Consider the court's statement that it "must presume that in many cases where a guideline is laid down in an individual case it is, like many common law rules, generally obeyed by those similarly situated." Does this presumption square with the court's own arguments regarding the benefits of rulemaking? Was the court making a narrow statement about the effect of administrative adjudication, or was it making a broader statement about the practical effects of common law adjudication?

Application & Analysis

1. By providing federal funding, the Urban Mass Transportation Act ("UMT Act") assists state and local governments in planning and financing municipal mass transit systems. 49 U.S.C. §§ 1601-21. The Act is administered by the Federal Transit Administration ("FTA") within the Department of Transportation. The FTA carries out its mandate by making grants or loans to state and local transportation agencies. Most grant distributions are based on a formula set by the UMTA, although the FTA is also authorized to make discretionary grants or loans to assist states and local agencies with projects that enhance the effectiveness of mass transportation. Consistent with federal procurement practices, the FTA has the authority to impose terms and conditions on its awards as necessary to ensure successful completion of the projects it funds. Under its discretionary grant authority, for example, the FTA must determine that the fund recipients have the "legal, financial, and technical capacity" to carry out the purposes of the grants, and that the applicant has or will have "satisfactory continuing control" over the use of the facilities and the equipment. Applicants must certify to the FTA that they meet these conditions. 49 U.S.C. §§ 1602(a)(2)(A)(i), (ii). In accordance with §§ 1602(a)(1) and 1641(f) of the Act, the FTA can also prescribe "terms and conditions" both for its formula-driven and its discretionary grants and loans programs. Additionally, Congress delegated to the Secretary of Transportation safety monitoring authority for the projects funded under the UMTA:

> The Secretary may investigate conditions in any facility, equipment, or manner of operation financed under this chapter which the Secretary

believes creates a serious hazard of death or injury. The investigation should determine the nature and extent of such conditions and the means which might best be employed to correct or eliminate them. If the Secretary determines that such conditions do create such a hazard, he shall require the local public body which has received funds under this chapter to submit a plan for correcting or eliminating such condition. The Secretary may withhold further financial assistance under this chapter from the local public body until he approves such plan and the local public body implements such plan.

49 U.S.C. § 1618. The Secretary subdelegated this authority to the FTA.

In a final rule published in the Federal Register, the FTA promulgated a regulation requiring all state and local transportation agencies to test their employees for drugs as a condition of receiving UMTA grants or loans. The final rule framed the drug-testing condition as a safety measure; "technical capacity" must include the ability to provide safe mass transportation services, and exercising "satisfactory continuing control" implies an ability to ensure the safe operation of FTA-assisted facilities and equipment. As the use of controlled substances has the potential to degrade safety performance, the regulation is designed to detect and deter drug use among mass transportation workers performing safety-sensitive functions. In addition to implementing mandatory testing, recipients have to develop policy statements and educational programs focused on drug use in the workplace. It based its authority to engage in rulemaking on § 1618.

A transit workers' union would like to challenge the rule in court and has engaged your law firm to represent it. The partner supervising the case has asked you to write a brief memorandum analyzing whether the UMTA grants the FTA authority to promulgate the rule.

---

2. Policymaking by Order

The D.C. Circuit in *National Petroleum Refiners* repeatedly referenced the Supreme Court's decision from four years prior, *National Labor Relations Board v. Wyman-Gordon*, in asserting that rulemaking boasts several advantages over adjudication when fashioning generally applicable policies. As the court noted, the issue in *Wyman-Gordon* was slightly different than the one raised in *National Petroleum Refiners*. The Court was not asked whether the NLRB had rulemaking authority under the National Labor Relations Act; the Court was content to assume that it did. Rather, the question was whether the NLRB could promulgate a rule by *not* using that authority. Stated differently, the *Wyman-Gordon* question was whether Congress granted the NLRB authority to promulgate legislative rules through its *adjudicative* proceedings rather than through notice-and-comment rulemaking.

In order to understand *Wyman-Gordon*, you must understand the actions taken by the NLRB in a separate labor dispute involving a company called Excelsior Underwear, Inc. Note that *Wyman-Gordon* is *not* part of the *Excelsior Underwear* litigation; the events and parties are completely unrelated. Rather, the cases are connected because of the *prospective rule* the NLRB promulgated in *Excelsior Underwear*, and the NLRB's *subsequent application* of that rule in the *Wyman-Gordon* litigation.

The four opinions in the Supreme Court's decision (there was no majority) provide a highly instructive back-and-forth about the differences between rulemaking and adjudication. Does the way the APA defines the two procedures constrain agencies' choices in making policy through one or the other? How do the procedural requirements imposed on each relate to their general applicability and prospective effect? How should the issue of notice—a party's opportunity to know the law governing its conduct before it acts—impact whether agencies are permitted to make policy by rulemaking or by adjudication?

Excelsior Underwear, Inc.
156 N.L.R.B. 1236 (1966)

Decisions and Certifications of Results of Elections

[The National Labor Relations Board ("NLRB" or "Board") consolidated two cases for consideration and decision, the primary one of which involved a claim by the Amalgamated Clothing Workers of America against Excelsior Underwear. Certain of Excelsior's workers voted by secret ballot on whether Amalgamated would be certified as their bargaining representative under the National Labor Relations Act ("NLRA"). Amalgamated lost the vote by an overwhelming margin (35 votes in favor, 206 against, 5 inconclusive). Amalgamated then challenged the result by filing objections with the NLRB. It asserted that Excelsior committed numerous violations of the NLRA, including mailing an eight-page letter to all of its employees containing "material misstatements regarding Union dues and initiation fees," and refusing to disclose its employees' names and addresses that would have allowed Amalgamated to address the misstatements made in the letter. *Id.* at 1236. An NLRB Regional Director investigated the claims and recommended that the election results be set aside and new election be conducted. The NLRB heard the consolidated cases, because they "presented a question of substantial importance in the administration of the National Labor Relations Act."]

[E]ach of these cases poses the question whether an employer's refusal to provide a union with the names and addresses of employees eligible to vote in a representation election should be grounds on which to set that election aside. The Board has not in the past set elections aside on this ground. For, while the Board has required that an employer, shortly before an election, make available for inspection by the parties and the Regional Director a list of employees claimed by him to be eligible to vote in that election, there has been no requirement that this list contain addresses in addition to names. The rules governing representation elections are not, however, fixed and immutable. They have been changed and refined, generally in the direction of higher standards.

We are persuaded ... that higher standards of disclosure than we have heretofore imposed are necessary, and that prompt disclosure of the information here sought by the Petitioners should be required in all representation elections. Accordingly, we now establish a requirement that will be applied in all election cases. That is, within 7 days after the Regional Director has approved a consent-election agreement entered into by the parties pursuant to Section 102.62 of the National Labor Relations Board Rules and Regulations, Series 8, as amended, or after the Regional Director or the Board has directed an election pursuant to Sections 102.67, 102.69, or 102.85 thereof, the employer must file with the Regional Director an election eligibility list, containing the names and addresses of all the eligible voters. The Regional Director, in turn, shall make this information available to all parties in the case. Failure to comply with this requirement shall be grounds for setting aside the election whenever proper objections are filed.[5]

The considerations that impel us to adopt the foregoing rule are these: The control of the election proceeding, and the determination of the steps necessary to conduct that election fairly [are] matters which Congress entrusted to the Board alone. In discharging that trust, we regard it as the Board's function to conduct elections in which employees have the opportunity to

---

[5] In the event that the payroll period for eligibility purposes is subsequent to the direction of election or consent-election agreement, the eligibility list shall be filed within 7 days after the close of the determinative payroll period for eligibility purposes. In order to be timely, the eligibility list must be received by the Regional Director within the period required. No extension of time shall be granted by the Regional Director except in extraordinary circumstances nor shall be filing of a request for review operate to stay the requirement here imposed.

However, the rule we have here announced is to be applied prospectively only. It will not apply in the instant cases but only in those elections that are directed, or consented to, subsequent to 30 days from the date of this Decision. We impose this brief period of delay to insure that all parties to forthcoming representation elections are fully aware of their rights and obligations as here stated.

cast their ballots for or against representation under circumstances that are free not only from interference, restraint, or coercion violative of the Act, but also from other elements that prevent or impede a free and reasoned choice. Among the factors that undoubtedly tend to impede such a choice is a lack of information with respect to one of the choices available. In other words, an employee who has had an effective opportunity to hear the arguments concerning representation is in a better position to make a more fully informed and reasonable choice. Accordingly, we think that it is appropriate for us to remove the impediment to communication to which our new rule is directed.

As a practical matter, an employer, through his possession of employee names and home addresses as well as his ability to communicate with employees on plant premises, is assured of the continuing opportunity to inform the entire electorate of his views with respect to union representation. On the other hand, without a list of employee names and addresses, a labor organization, whose organizers normally have no right of access to plant premises, has no method by which it can be certain of reaching all the employees with its arguments in favor of representation, and, as a result, employees are often completely unaware of that point of view. This is not, of course, to deny the existence of various means by which a party might be able to communicate with a substantial portion of the electorate even without possessing their names and addresses. It is rather to say what seems to us obvious—that the access of all employees to such communications can be insured only if all parties have the names and addresses of all the voters. In other words, by providing all parties with employees' names and addresses, we maximize the likelihood that all the voters will be exposed to the arguments for, as well as against, union representation. . . .

Inasmuch as the rule we have here announced is to be applied prospectively only (see footnote 5, *supra*) . . . we shall accept the Regional Director's recommendation and certify the results of that election.

National Labor Relations Board v. Wyman-Gordon Co.
394 U.S. 759 (1969)

Mr. Justice FORTAS announced the judgment of the Court and delivered an opinion in which the CHIEF JUSTICE [Earl WARREN], Mr. Justice STEWART, and Mr. Justice WHITE join.

On the petition of the International Brotherhood of Boilermakers and pursuant to its powers under § 9 of the National Labor Relations Act, 49 Stat. 453, 29 U.S.C. § 159, the National Labor Relations Board ordered an election among the production and maintenance employees of the respondent company. At the election, the employees were to select one of two labor unions as their exclusive bargaining representative, or to choose not to be represented by a union at all. In connection with the election, the Board ordered the respondent to furnish a list of the names and addresses of its employees who could vote in the election, so that the unions could use the list for election purposes. The respondent refused to comply with the order, and the election was held without the list. Both unions were defeated in the election.

The Board upheld the unions' objections to the election because the respondent had not furnished the list, and the Board ordered a new election. The respondent again refused to obey a Board order to supply a list of employees, and the Board issued a subpoena ordering the respondent to provide the list or else produce its personnel and payroll records showing the employees' names and addresses. The Board filed an action in the United States District Court for the District of Massachusetts seeking to have its subpoena enforced or to have a mandatory injunction issued to compel the respondent to comply with its order.

The District Court held the Board's order valid and directed the respondent to comply. The United States Court of Appeals for the First Circuit reversed. The Court of Appeals thought that the order in this case was invalid because it was based on a rule laid down in an earlier decision by the Board, *Excelsior Underwear Inc.*, 156 N.L.R.B. 1236 (1966), and the *Excelsior* rule had not been promulgated in accordance with the requirements that the Administrative Procedure Act prescribes for rule making, 5 U.S.C. § 553. We granted certiorari to resolve a conflict among the circuits concerning the validity and effect of the *Excelsior* rule.

I.

... Section 6 of the National Labor Relations Act empowers the Board "to make ..., in the manner prescribed by the Administrative Procedure Act, such rules and regulations as may be necessary to carry out the provisions of this Act." 29 U.S.C. § 156. The Administrative Procedure Act contains specific provisions governing agency rule making, which it defines as "an agency statement of general or particular applicability and future effect," 5 U.S.C. § 551(4).[2] The Act requires among other things, publication in the Federal Register of notice of proposed rule making and of hearing; opportunity to

---

[2] We agree with the opinion of Chief Judge Aldrich below that the *Excelsior* rule involves matters of substance and that it therefore does not fall within any of the Act's exceptions. *See* 5 U.S.C. § 553(b)(A).

be heard; a statement in the rule of its basis and purposes; and publication in the Federal Register of the rule as adopted. *See* 5 U.S.C. § 553. The Board asks us to hold that it has discretion to promulgate new rules in adjudicatory proceedings, without complying with the requirements of the Administrative Procedure Act.

The rule-making provisions of that Act, which the Board would avoid, were designed to assure fairness and mature consideration of rules of general application. *See* H.R. Rep. No. 79-1980, at 21-26 (1946); S. Rep. No. 79-752, at 13-16 (1945). They may not be avoided by the process of making rules in the course of adjudicatory proceedings. There is no warrant in law for the Board to replace the statutory scheme with a rule-making procedure of its own invention. Apart from the fact that the device fashioned by the Board does not comply with statutory command, it obviously falls short of the substance of the requirements of the Administrative Procedure Act. The "rule" created in *Excelsior* was not published in the Federal Register, which is the statutory and accepted means of giving notice of a rule as adopted; only selected organizations were given notice of the "hearing," whereas notice in the Federal Register would have been general in character; under the Administrative Procedure Act, the terms or substance of the rule would have to be stated in the notice of hearing, and all interested parties would have an opportunity to participate in the rule making.

The Solicitor General does not deny that the Board ignored the rule-making provisions of the Administrative Procedure Act.[3] But he appears to argue that *Excelsior*'s command is a valid substantive regulation, binding upon this respondent as such, because the Board promulgated it in the *Excelsior* proceeding, in which the requirements for valid adjudication had been met. This argument misses the point. There is no question that, in an adjudicatory hearing, the Board could validly decide the issue whether the employer must furnish a list of employees to the union. But that is not what the Board did in *Excelsior*. The Board did not even apply the rule it made to the parties in the adjudicatory proceeding, the only entities that could properly be subject to the order in that case. Instead, the Board purported to make a rule: i.e., to exercise its quasi-legislative power.

Adjudicated cases may and do, of course, serve as vehicles for the formulation of agency policies, which are applied and announced therein. *See* HENRY FRIENDLY, THE FEDERAL ADMINISTRATIVE AGENCIES 36-52 (1962). They generally provide a guide to action that the agency may be expected to take in future cases. Subject to the qualified role of *stare decisis* in the administrative process, they may serve as precedents. But this is far from saying, as the Solicitor General suggests, that commands, decisions, or policies

---

[3] The Board has never utilized the Act's rule-making procedures. It has been criticized for contravening the Act in this manner. *See, e.g.,* 1 KENNETH CULP DAVIS, ADMINISTRATIVE LAW TREATISE § 6.13 (Supp. 1965); Cornelius J. Peck, *The Atrophied Rule-Making Powers of the National Labor Relations Board,* 70 YALE L.J. 729 (1961).

announced in adjudication are "rules" in the sense that they must, without more, be obeyed by the affected public.

In the present case, however, the respondent itself was specifically directed by the Board to submit a list of the names and addresses of its employees for use by the unions in connection with the election. This direction, which was part of the order directing that an election be held, is unquestionably valid. Even though the direction to furnish the list was followed by citation to "*Excelsior Underwear Inc.*, 156 NLRB No. 111," it is an order in the present case that the respondent was required to obey. Absent this direction by the Board, the respondent was under no compulsion to furnish the list because no statute and no validly adopted rule required it to do so.

Because the Board in an adjudicatory proceeding directed the respondent itself to furnish the list, the decision of the Court of Appeals for the First Circuit must be reversed.[6]

[In Sections II and III, Justice Fortas addressed and rejected Wyman-Gordon's arguments that requiring employers to disclose their lists of employee names and addresses is substantively invalid under the NLRA, and that the NLRA does not give the NLRB the authority to subpoena those employee lists.]

The judgment of the Court of Appeals is reversed, and the case is remanded to that court with directions to enforce the Board's order against the respondent.

It is so ordered. . . .

Mr. Justice BLACK, with whom Mr. Justice BRENNAN and Mr. Justice MARSHALL join, concurring in the result.

I agree with Parts II and III of the prevailing opinion of Mr. Justice FORTAS, holding that the *Excelsior* requirement that an employer supply the union with the names and addresses of its employees prior to an election is valid on its merits and can be enforced by a subpoena. But I cannot subscribe to the criticism in that opinion of the procedure followed by the Board in adopting that requirement in the *Excelsior* case, 156 N.L.R.B. 1236 (1966). Nor can I accept the novel theory by which the opinion manages to uphold enforcement of the *Excelsior* practice in spite of what it considers to

---

[6] Mr. Justice HARLAN's dissent argues that because the Board improperly relied upon the *Excelsior* "rule" in issuing its order, we are obliged to remand. He relies on *SEC v. Chenery Corp.*, 318 U.S. 80 (1943) (*Chenery I*). To remand would be an idle and useless formality. *Chenery* does not require that we convert judicial review of agency action into a ping-pong game. In *Chenery*, the Commission had applied the wrong standards to the adjudication of a complex factual situation, and the Court held that it would not undertake to decide whether the Commission's result might have been justified on some other basis. Here, by contrast, the substance of the Board's command is not seriously contestable. There is not the slightest uncertainty as to the outcome of a proceeding before the Board, whether the Board acted through a rule or an order. It would be meaningless to remand.

be statutory violations present in the procedure by which the requirement was adopted. Although the opinion is apparently intended to rebuke the Board and encourage it to follow the plurality's conception of proper administrative practice, the result instead is to free the Board from all judicial control whatsoever regarding compliance with procedures specifically required by applicable federal statutes such as the National Labor Relations Act, 29 U.S.C. § 151 *et seq.*, and the Administrative Procedure Act, 5 U.S.C. § 551 *et seq.* Apparently, under the prevailing opinion, courts must enforce any requirement announced in a purported "adjudication" even if it clearly was not adopted as an incident to the decision of a case before the agency, and must enforce "rules" adopted in a purported "rule making" even if the agency materially violated the specific requirements that Congress has directed for such proceedings in the Administrative Procedure Act. I for one would not give judicial sanction to any such illegal agency action.

In the present case, however, I am convinced that the *Excelsior* practice was adopted by the Board as a legitimate incident to the adjudication of a specific case before it, and for that reason I would hold that the Board properly followed the procedures applicable to "adjudication" rather than "rule making." Since my reasons for joining in reversal of the Court of Appeals differ so substantially from those set forth in the prevailing opinion, I will spell them out at some length.

Most administrative agencies, like the Labor Board here, are granted two functions by the legislation creating them: (1) the power under certain conditions to make rules having the effect of laws, that is, generally speaking, quasi-legislative power; and (2) the power to hear and adjudicate particular controversies, that is quasi-judicial power. The line between these two functions is not always a clear one and in fact the two functions merge at many points. For example, in exercising its quasi-judicial function an agency must frequently decide controversies on the basis of new doctrines, not theretofore applied to a specific problem, though drawn to be sure from broader principles reflecting the purposes of the statutes involved and from the rules invoked in dealing with related problems. If the agency decision reached under the adjudicatory power becomes a precedent, it guides future conduct in much the same way as though it were a new rule promulgated under the rule-making power, and both an adjudicatory order and a formal "rule" are alike subject to judicial review. Congress gave the Labor Board both of these separate but almost inseparably related powers. No language in the National Labor Relations Act requires that the grant or the exercise of one power was intended to exclude the Board's use of the other.

Nor does any language in the Administrative Procedure Act require such a conclusion. The Act does specify the procedure by which the rule-making power is to be exercised, requiring publication of notice for the benefit of interested parties and provision of an opportunity for them to be heard, and, after establishment of a rule as provided in the Act, it is then to be published in the Federal Register. Congress had a laudable purpose in prescribing these requirements, and it was evidently contemplated that administrative agencies like the Labor Board would follow them when setting out to announce a new rule of law to govern parties in the future. In this same statute, however, Congress also conferred on the affected administrative agencies the power to proceed by adjudication, and Congress specified a distinct procedure by which this adjudicatory power is to be exercised. The Act defines "adjudication" as "agency process for the formulation of an order," and "order" is defined as "the whole or a part of a final disposition, whether affirmative, negative, injunctive, or declaratory in form, of an agency in a matter other than rule making but including licensing." 5 U.S.C. §§ 551(7), (6). Thus, although it is true that the adjudicatory approach frees an administrative agency from the procedural requirements specified for rule making, the Act permits this to be done whenever the action involved can satisfy the definition of "adjudication" and then imposes separate procedural requirements that must be met in adjudication. Under these circumstances, so long as the matter involved can be dealt with in a way satisfying the definition of either "rule making" or "adjudication" under the Administrative Procedure Act, that Act, along with the Labor Relations Act, should be read as conferring upon the Board the authority to decide, within its informed discretion, whether to proceed by rule making or adjudication.

In the present case there is no dispute that all the procedural safeguards required for "adjudication" were fully satisfied in connection with the Board's *Excelsior* decision, and it seems plain to me that that decision did constitute "adjudication" within the meaning of the Administrative Procedure Act, even though the requirement was to be prospectively applied.... The Board did not abstractly decide out of the blue to announce a brand new rule of law to govern labor activities in the future, but rather established the procedure as a direct consequence of the proper exercise of its adjudicatory powers....

The prevailing opinion seems to hold that the *Excelsior* requirement cannot be considered the result of adjudication because the Board did not apply it to the parties in the *Excelsior* case itself, but rather announced that it would be applied only to elections called 30 days after the date of the *Excelsior* decision. But the *Excelsior* order was nonetheless an inseparable part of the adjudicatory process. The principal issue before the Board in the *Excelsior* case was whether the election should be set aside on the ground, urged by the unions, that the employer had refused to make the employee lists available to them.... The Board decided that the election involved there should not be set aside and thus rejected the contention of the unions. In doing so, the Board chose to explain the reasons for its rejection of their claim, and it is this explanation, the Board's written opinion, which is the source of the *Excelsior* requirement. The Board's opinion should not be regarded as any less an appropriate part of the adjudicatory process merely because the reason it gave for rejecting the unions' position was not that the Board disagreed with them as to the merits of the disclosure procedure but rather, [*see Excelsior Underwear*, note 5], that while fully agreeing that disclosure should be required, the Board did not feel that it should upset the Excelsior Company's justified reliance on previous refusals to compel disclosure by setting aside this particular election.

Apart from the fact that the decisions whether to accept a "new" requirement urged by one party and, if so, whether to apply it retroactively to the other party are inherent parts of the adjudicatory process, I think the opposing theory accepted by the Court of Appeals and by the prevailing opinion today is a highly impractical one. In effect, it would require an agency like the Labor Board to proceed by adjudication only when it could decide, prior to adjudicating a particular case, that any new practice to be adopted would be applied retroactively. Obviously, this decision cannot properly be made until all the issues relevant to adoption of the practice are fully considered in connection with the final decision of that case. If the Board were to decide, after careful evaluation of all the arguments presented to it in the adjudicatory proceeding, that it might be fairer to apply the practice only prospectively, it would be faced with the unpleasant choice of either starting all over again to evaluate the merits of the question, this time in a "rule-making" proceeding, or overriding the considerations of fairness and applying its order retroactively anyway, in order to preserve the validity of the new practice and avoid duplication of effort. I see no good reason to impose any such inflexible requirement on the administrative agencies.

For all of the foregoing reasons I would hold that the Board acted well within its discretion in choosing to proceed as it did, and I would reverse the judgment of the Court of Appeals on this basis.

Mr. Justice DOUGLAS, dissenting.

The notice and hearing procedure prescribed by § 553(b) [of the Administrative Procedure Act] was not followed [by the Board in *Excelsior Underwear*]; and in this case, an election was directed seven months after the *Excelsior* decision, the Board applying the *Excelsior* rule.

I am willing to assume that, if the Board decided to treat each case on its special facts and perform its adjudicatory function in the conventional way, we should have no difficulty in affirming its action. The difficulty is that it chose a different course in the *Excelsior* case and, having done so, it should be bound to follow the procedures prescribed in the Act as my Brother HARLAN has outlined them. When we hold otherwise, we let the Board "have its cake and eat it too." ...

The Board apparently decided the *Excelsior* case with § 553(d) in mind, for it made the proposed new rule effective after 30 days. The House report states that § 553(d) (which was § 4(c) in its draft) "does not provide procedures alternative to notice and other public proceedings required by the prior sections." ... And that report added, "It will afford persons affected a reasonable time to prepare for the effective date of a rule or rules or to take any other action which the issuance of rules may prompt." ...

The "substantive" rules described by § 553(d) may possibly cover "adjudications," even though they represent performance of the "judicial" function. But it is no answer to say that the order under review was "adjudicatory." For as my Brother HARLAN says, an agency is not adjudicating when it is making a rule to fit future cases. A rule like the one in *Excelsior* is designed to fit all cases at all times. It is not particularized to special facts. It is a statement of far-reaching policy covering all future representation elections.

It should therefore have been put down for the public hearing prescribed by the [Administrative Procedure] Act....

Mr. Justice HARLAN, dissenting.

The language of the Administrative Procedure Act does not support the Government's claim that an agency is "adjudicating" when it announces a rule which it refuses to apply in the dispute before it. The Act makes it clear that an agency "adjudicates" only when its procedures result in the "formulation of an order." 5 U.S.C. § 551(7). (Emphasis supplied.) An "order" is defined to include "the whole or a part of a final disposition ... of an agency in a matter other than rule making...." 5 U.S.C. § 551(6). (Emphasis supplied.) This definition makes it apparent that an agency is not adjudicating when it is making a rule, which the Act defines as "an agency statement of general or particular applicability and future effect...." 5 U.S.C. § 551(4). (Emphasis supplied.) Since the Labor Board's *Excelsior* rule was to be effective only 30 days after its promulgation, it clearly falls within the rule-making requirements of the Act.

Nor can I agree that the natural interpretation of the statute should be rejected because it requires the agency to choose between giving its rules immediate effect or initiating a separate rule-making proceeding. An agency chooses to apply a rule prospectively only because it represents such a departure from preexisting understandings that it would be unfair to impose the rule upon the parties in pending matters. But it is precisely in these situations, in which established patterns of conduct are revolutionized, that rule-making procedures perform [their] vital functions....

Given the fact that the Labor Board has promulgated a rule in violation of the governing statute, I believe that there is no alternative but to affirm the judgment of the Court of Appeals in this case. If, as the plurality opinion suggests, the NLRB may properly enforce an invalid rule in subsequent adjudications, the rule-making provisions of the Administrative Procedure Act are completely trivialized. Under today's prevailing approach, the agency may evade the commands of the Act whenever it desires and yet coerce the regulated industry into compliance. It is no answer to say that "respondent was under no compulsion to furnish the list because no statute and no validly adopted rule required it to do so," ... when the Labor Board was threatening to issue a subpoena which the courts would enforce. In what other way would the administrative agency compel obedience to its invalid rule?

One cannot always have the best of both worlds. Either the rule-making provisions are to be enforced or they are not. Before the Board may be permitted to adopt a rule that so significantly alters pre-existing labor-management understandings, it must be required to conduct a satisfactory rule-making proceeding, so that it will have the benefit of wide-ranging argument before it enacts its proposed solution to an important problem....

I would affirm the judgment of the Court of Appeals.

QUESTION SET 4.3

Review & Synthesis

1. Given the number of competing opinions in *Wyman-Gordon*, one must count the votes of individual justices to identify whether any legal conclusions commanded a majority of the Court. Determine how many Justices concluded that:
   a. The *Excelsior* rule was invalid because it did not follow the APA § 553 notice-and-comment rulemaking procedures, and how many thought it was validly promulgated through adjudication.
   b. The NLRB's order in *Wyman-Gordon* was valid because it was based on the *Excelsior* rule, and how many thought it was valid as a separate and independent exercise of the NLRB's adjudicative authority.
   c. The order in *Wyman-Gordon* was invalid because it was based on the *Excelsior* rule.

2. Did the Court come to any definitive conclusion on whether the NLRB, or any other agency for that matter, was *required* to use rulemaking procedures when developing and adopting new rules? If not, did the opinions in the case point to any practical differences between rules adopted through adjudication and those adopted through rulemaking?

3. In his dissent, Justice Harlan argued that the order against Wyman-Gordon must be vacated because the NLRB based it on an illegal action, namely, the promulgation of a rule outside of the APA § 553 notice-and-comment rulemaking procedures. In doing so, he cited *Chenery I* for the proposition that a reviewing court can uphold an agency's decision only if that agency relied on a proper basis for it. Justice Fortas disagrees with this analysis (see footnote 6). Although Justice Fortas disagreed with Justice Harlan's application of *Chenery I*, he appeared to agree that it was applicable to the NLRB's order against Wyman-Gordon.
   a. Given that *Chenery I* was decided in 1943, was the principle of judicial review it asserted left undisturbed by passage of the APA?

b. Justice Fortas distinguished the SEC's order in *Chenery I* from the NLRB's order in *Wyman-Gordon* by pointing out the relative certainty of the agencies' decisions on remand. In *Chenery I*, because the SEC misinterpreted the Court's equity jurisprudence it was not clear whether it would reach the same legal conclusion on remand when applying a corrected understanding of the Court's precedents. In *Wyman-Gordon*, by contrast, the NLRB clearly was intent on requiring, and legally permitted to require, employers to share their employee name and address lists with prospective union representatives. Justice Harlan felt that such considerations were largely irrelevant; remand was required because the NLRB clearly disregarded the APA's rulemaking procedures. Whose position do you find more persuasive? Should *Chenery I* be understood as a bright-line rule requiring remand to agencies (as asserted by Justice Harlan), or should its application be tempered by practical considerations (as asserted by Justice Fortas)?

* * *

Several years after its fractured *Wyman-Gordon* decision, the Court returned to the issue of administrative policymaking through adjudication in *NLRB v. Bell Aerospace Co.* This dispute also involved allegations of unfair labor practices. This time, however, a majority of the Justices reached agreement on both a conclusion and a supporting rationale for approving the Board's authority to adopt new rules through case-by-case adjudication. Did the decision signal that the Court was getting out of the business of closely scrutinizing agencies' choice of policymaking procedures?

National Labor Relations Board v. Bell Aerospace Co.
416 U.S. 267 (1974)

Mr. Justice POWELL delivered the opinion of the Court.

This case presents two questions: first, whether the National Labor Relations Board properly determined that all "managerial employees," except those whose participation in a labor organization would create a conflict of interest with their job responsibilities, are covered by the National Labor Relations Act; and second, whether the Board must proceed by rulemaking rather than by adjudication in determining whether certain buyers are "managerial employees." We answer both questions in the negative.

[In Section I of its decision, the Court recounts the relevant facts of the case. Bell Aerospace Co. develops, designs, and manufactures aerospace products. Amalgamated Local No. 1286 of the United Automobile, Aerospace and Agricultural Implement Workers of America ("Amalgamated" or the "Union") petitioned the NLRB for an election to be the bargaining representative for buyers in the company's purchasing and procurement department. Bell Aerospace countered that these buyers were "managerial employees" and thus not covered by the National Labor Relations Act ("NLRA" or the "Act"). The Board sided with the buyers and ordered an election be held. The buyers elected the Union and the NLRB certified it. Bell Aerospace asked the Board to reconsider in light of a recent Eighth Circuit decision denying enforcement of a different NLRB order because "managerial employees" are not covered by the NLRA. The Board rejected the Eighth Circuit's interpretation and denied the motion. Bell Aerospace then refused to comply with the Board's order or to bargain with Amalgamated, and sought review in the Second Circuit. Finding that Congress had intended to exclude all managerial employees from the protections of the Act, the Second Circuit ruled in Bell Aerospace's favor. Although the Board had the statutory authority to classify the buyers as non-managerial employees, that Court found that doing so would require the Board to reject a long line of its own decisions to the contrary. So dramatic a change in policy, the court said, had to be adopted through notice-and-comment rulemaking rather than through adjudication. That section states that "[t]he Board shall have authority from time to time to make, amend, and rescind, in the manner prescribed by the Administrative Procedure Act, such rules and regulations as may be necessary to carry out the provisions of this Act."

In Section II of its decision, the Court concluded that the NLRA does not extend its protections to employees properly classified as "managerial."]

III

The Court of Appeals also held that, although the Board was not precluded from determining that buyers or some types of buyers were not "managerial employees," it could do so only by invoking its rulemaking procedures under § 6 of the Act, 29 U.S.C. § 156. We disagree.

[T]he present question is whether on remand the Board must invoke its rulemaking procedures if it determines, in light of our opinion, that these buyers are not "managerial employees" under the Act. The Court of Appeals thought that rulemaking was required because any Board finding that the company's buyers are not "managerial" would be contrary to its prior decisions and would presumably be in the nature of a general rule designed "to fit all cases at all times."

A similar issue was presented to this Court in its second decision in *SEC v. Chenery Corp.*, 332 U.S. 194 (1947) (*Chenery II*). There, the respondent corporation argued that in an adjudicative proceeding the Commission could not apply a general standard that it had formulated for the first time in that proceeding. Rather, the Commission was required to resort instead to its rulemaking procedures if it desired to promulgate a new standard that would govern future conduct. In rejecting this contention, the Court first noted that the Commission had a statutory duty to decide the issue at hand in light of the proper standards and that this duty remained "regardless of whether those standards previously had been spelled out in a general rule or regulation." *Id.*, at 201....

The Court concluded that "the choice made between proceeding by general rule or by individual, *ad hoc* litigation is one that lies primarily in the informed discretion of the administrative agency." *Id.* at 203.

And in *NLRB v. Wyman-Gordon Co.*, 394 U.S. 759 (1969), the Court upheld a Board order enforcing an election list requirement first promulgated in an earlier adjudicative proceeding in *Excelsior Underwear Inc.*, 156 N.L.R.B. 1236 (1966). The plurality opinion of Mr. Justice Fortas, joined by The Chief Justice, Mr. Justice Stewart, and Mr. Justice White, recognized that "[a]djudicated cases may and do ... serve as vehicles for the formulation of agency policies, which are applied and announced therein," and that such cases "generally provide a guide to action that the agency may be expected to take in future cases." The concurring opinion of Mr. Justice Black, joined by Mr. Justice Brennan and Mr. Justice Marshall, also noted that the Board had both adjudicative and rule-making powers and that the choice between the two was "within its informed discretion." *Id.* at 772.

The views expressed in *Chenery II* and *Wyman-Gordon* make plain that the Board is not precluded from announcing new principles in an adjudicative proceeding and that the choice between rulemaking and adjudication lies in the first instance within the Board's discretion. Although there may be situations where the Board's reliance on adjudication would amount to an abuse of discretion or a violation of the Act, nothing in the present case would justify such a conclusion. Indeed, there is ample indication that adjudication is especially appropriate in the instant context. As the Court of Appeals noted, "[t]here must be tens of thousands of manufacturing, wholesale and retail units which employ buyers, and hundreds of thousands of the latter." ... Moreover, duties of buyers vary widely depending on the company or industry. It is doubtful whether any generalized standard could be framed which would have more than marginal utility. The Board thus has reason to proceed with caution, developing its standards in a case-by-case manner with attention to the specific character of the buyers' authority and duties in each company. The Board's judgment that adjudication best serves this purpose is entitled to great weight.

The possible reliance of industry on the Board's past decisions with respect to buyers does not require a different result. It has not been shown that the adverse consequences ensuing from such reliance are so substantial that the Board should be precluded from reconsidering the issue in an adjudicative proceeding. Furthermore, this is not a case in which some new liability is sought to be imposed on individuals for past actions which were taken in good-faith reliance on Board pronouncements, Nor [*sic*] are fines or damages involved here. In any event, concern about such consequences is largely speculative, for the Board has not yet finally determined whether these buyers are "managerial."

It is true, of course, that rulemaking would provide the Board with a forum for soliciting the informed views of those affected in industry and labor before embarking on a new course. But surely the Board has discretion to decide that the adjudicative procedures in this case may also produce the relevant information necessary to mature and fair consideration of the issues. Those most immediately affected, the buyers and the company in the particular case, are accorded a full opportunity to be heard before the Board makes its determination.

The judgment of the Court of Appeals is therefore affirmed in part and reversed in part, and the cause remanded to that court with directions to remand to the Board for further proceedings in conformity with this opinion.

Judgment of the Court of Appeals affirmed in part and reversed in part, and cause remanded.

It is so ordered.

[The opinion of Justice White, dissenting in part and joined by Justices Brennan, Stewart, and Marshall, is omitted.]

QUESTION SET 4.4

Review & Synthesis

1. Did *Bell Aerospace* hold that agencies may adopt new policies in adjudications that (1) can be applied in the adjudication that creates them, (2) can be applied directly to regulated persons and entities who were not parties to the adjudication creating the rule, or (3) both? In this respect, is it consistent with *Wyman-Gordon*?

2. The Court points to the possibility that an agency's application of a new policy in an adjudication might constitute an abuse of discretion, but it finds that the facts of this case do not raise such concerns. What circumstances would? In addition to the Court's discussion of the topic here, consider its description of the presumption against statutory retroactivity:

> A statute does not operate "retrospectively" merely because it is applied in a case arising from conduct antedating the statute's enactment, or upsets expectations based in prior law. Rather, the court must ask whether the new provision attaches new legal consequences to events completed before its enactment. The conclusion that a particular rule operates "retroactively" comes at the end of a process of judgment

concerning the nature and extent of the change in the law and the degree of connection between the operation of the new rule and a relevant past event. Any test of retroactivity will leave room for disagreement in hard cases, and is unlikely to classify the enormous variety of legal changes with perfect philosophical clarity. However, retroactivity is a matter on which judges tend to have sound instincts, and familiar considerations of fair notice, reasonable reliance, and settled expectations offer sound guidance. Since the early days of this Court, we have declined to give retroactive effect to statutes burdening private rights unless Congress had made clear its intent.

Landgraf v. USI Film Products, 511 U.S. 244, 269-70 (1994) (internal citations and quotations omitted). Do you think that these principles should apply with equal force to policymaking by administrative adjudication? *See NLRB v. Majestic Weaving Co.,* 355 F.2d 854, 859-61 (2d Cir. 1966).

Application & Analysis

1. Smith Automotive sells more cars than any other dealership in Houston, Texas. Purchasers typically enter a financing contract with Smith that obligates them to pay for their cars in monthly installments. In the event a purchaser fails to pay, the contract also grants Smith a security interest in the car. Smith then sells this contract to a national bank that services the account and collects the payments. Each installment contract Smith assigns to the bank is on a "repurchase" basis that requires Smith to pay the loan's outstanding balance to the bank if the bank repossesses the car after the purchaser defaults. In exchange, the bank returns the car to Smith.

   Smith's transactional obligations are governed by the Uniform Commercial Code ("UCC"), which is incorporated into its repurchase contracts with the bank. Under the UCC, Smith has all of the rights and duties of a secured party. Accordingly, it must account to defaulting purchasers for any surpluses or deficiencies realized from its disposal of repossessed cars. Since Smith's practice is to refurbish and resell those cars, its obligation under the UCC is to seek the best possible resale price. If the resale results in a deficiency, the defaulting purchaser is obligated to pay it. If the resale results in a surplus, Smith is obligated to refund it to the defaulting purchaser. The UCC calculates deficiencies and surpluses by subtracting the outstanding loan amount plus expenses associated with refurbishing the car from the resale price.

   The Federal Trade Commission found that Smith's method for calculating surpluses and deficiencies was a deceptive practice in violation of Federal Trade Commission Act § 5. Smith's records showed that it always set a repossessed car's resale price at the amount of a defaulting purchaser's unpaid loan. This is because Smith believed that repurchasing a car from the bank for the unpaid loan amount constituted a "resale" under the UCC. As a result of this pricing practice, the "resale" price never exceeded the original loan amount, and the defaulting purchaser never received a surplus from the resale. The FTC rejected this understanding of the UCC, which it also found was standard for the car dealership industry nationwide. Accordingly, it held that the correct resale price under the UCC is the "best possible price," which is the amount for which a dealer sells a repossessed car to a new retail purchaser. In its order, it adopted a new rule requiring car dealers to use the "best possible price" calculation. Based on this new rule, it then ordered Smith to cease its current surplus calculation practices. Additionally, the FTC acknowledged in its order that no other federal or state case had adopted the "best possible price" interpretation of the UCC, nor had it previously sanctioned a car dealer for its surplus calculation practices.

You are an associate at the law firm Smith has hired to appeal the FTC's decision to the United States Court of Appeals. The partner supervising the case has asked you to analyze whether the FTC should have promulgated its "best possible price" calculation in a rulemaking, rather than adopting it in an adjudication.

3. Policymaking by Policy Statement

Agencies do not always act through rulemaking and adjudication. As we have already seen, they communicate with the public in a variety of less formal, less conspicuous, and less coordinated ways. They publish information describing current and past regulatory activities. They post to their websites general descriptions of their statutory authority and functions. Agency personnel—from the most junior civil servants to the most senior political appointees—answer phone calls, give speeches, testify at oversight hearings, write articles and letters, and engage in educational outreach to address questions and concerns raised by members of the public.

In many other instances, agency communications take on the appearance of formality, although they lack much of the procedural rigor that attends rulemaking and adjudication. Such communications are broadly referred to as "general statements of policy." They come in a variety of forms: guidance documents, guidelines, manuals, memoranda, staff instructions, advisory opinions or opinion letters, press releases, etc. They are considered "rules" under the APA; they constitute "the whole or a part of an agency statement of general or particular applicability and future effect designed to implement, interpret, or describe law or policy," 5 U.S.C. § 551(4). Unlike the "legislative" rules we have studied thus far, however, the APA classifies them as "nonlegislative" because they have no independent legal force. As the Attorney General's Manual explains, policy statements are "issued by an agency to advise the public prospectively of the manner in which the agency proposes to exercise a discretionary power." ATTORNEY GENERAL'S MANUAL at 30 n.3. They neither amend nor supplement statutory provisions or regulations. They are "designed to inform rather than control." *American Trucking Ass'n v. Interstate Commerce Comm'n*, 659 F.2d 452, 462 (5th Cir. 1981), *cert. denied* 460 U.S. 1022 (1983). Accordingly, they do not have to be promulgated through the rulemaking procedures set out in the APA or in other statutes. *See* 5 U.S.C. § 553(b)(A).

As you might guess, however, the use and effect of policy statements is not so easily circumscribed. For one thing, issuing policy documents is procedurally easier than promulgating rules, so agencies have an incentive to issue them instead of regulations. For another, members of the regulated public and even agencies themselves sometimes view guidance documents as legally binding even though they are not. "Agencies sometimes claim they are just trying to be 'customer friendly' and serve the regulated public when they issue advisory opinions and guidance documents. This may, in fact, be true in many cases. However, when the legal effect of such documents is unclear, regulated parties may well perceive this 'help' as coercive—an offer they dare not refuse." H.R. Rep. 106-1009, *Non-binding Effect of Agency Guidance Documents* (Oct. 26, 2000). The Administrative Conference of the United States ("ACUS"), itself an independent federal agency, raised similar concerns:

> Policy statements that inform agency staff and the public regarding agency policy are beneficial to both. While they do not have the force of law (as do legislative rules) and therefore can be challenged within the agency, they nonetheless are important tools for guiding administration and enforcement of agency statutes and for advising the public of agency policy....
>
> [But where] the policy statement is treated by the agency as binding, it operates effectively as a legislative rule but without the notice-and-comment protection of section 553. It may be difficult or impossible for affected persons to challenge the policy statement within the agency's own decisional process; they may be foreclosed from an opportunity to contend the policy statement is unlawful or unwise, or that an alternative policy should be adopted. Of course, affected persons could undergo the application of the policy to them, exhaust administrative remedies and then seek judicial review of agency denials or enforcement actions, at which time they may find the policy is given deference by the courts. The practical consequence is this process may be costly and protracted, and affected parties have neither the opportunity to participate in the process of policy development nor a realistic opportunity to challenge the policy when applied within the agency or on judicial review. The public is therefore denied the opportunity to comment and the agency is denied the educative value of any facts and arguments the party may have tendered.

ACUS Recommendations, 1 C.F.R. § 305.92-2 (1992). In addition to the vetting and accountability problems raised by the ACUS, agencies do not typically use regimented procedures to produce guidance documents. This can lead to statements that are not as carefully vetted as those issued through rulemaking or adjudication. Additionally, multiple employees at an agency may issue policy statements on the same subject, which promotes confusion as to the agency's official "policy." The government occasionally takes steps to address these problems. For example, the Office of Management and Budget issued the *Final Bulletin for Agency Good Practice* in 2007, which adopts standards for how Executive Branch departments and agencies develop, issue, and use "significant" guidance documents. 72 Fed. Reg. 3432 (Jan. 25, 2007). More recently, the Department of Justice issued the "Brand Memo," named for Associate Attorney General Rachel Brand. The Brand Memo states that the Justice Department will not use other agencies' guidance documents as the basis for civil enforcement actions for recovery of government funds lost to fraud or misconduct, or to penalize violations of federal health, civil rights, environmental, or safety laws. Memorandum from Assoc. Attorney Gen. Rachel Brand to Heads of Civil Litig. Components, U.S. Attorneys 2 (Jan. 25, 2018) (available at https://www.justice.gov/file/1028756/download).

Of course, these and similar measures are only as effective as one's ability to distinguish between an agency policy statement and a legally binding substantive rule. This is not always a straightforward exercise. As the ACUS observed, "[t]here are many facets that must be assessed in determining whether a policy statement is operationally a rule that binds affected persons.... Whether a statement is a matter of policy or interpretation, is issued in a permanent form, and is in fact binding (or to what extent it is binding) are often difficult questions that can only be decided in context." 1 C.F.R. § 305.92-2 n.1.

The following case, decided after *Wyman-Gordon* and shortly before *Bell Aerospace*, addressed two issues. The first was whether a Bureau of Indian Affairs ("BIA") rule was a legislative rule or a policy statement under the APA. The second was whether the BIA could promulgate the rule in an agency policy manual.

Morton v. Ruiz

415 U.S. 199 (1974)

Mr. Justice BLACKMUN delivered the opinion for a unanimous Court.

This case presents a narrow but important issue in the administration of the federal general assistance program for needy Indians:

> Are general assistance benefits available only to those Indians living on reservations in the United States (or in areas regulated by the Bureau of Indian

Affairs in Alaska and Oklahoma), and are they thus unavailable to Indians (outside Alaska and Oklahoma) living off, although near, a reservation?

The United States District Court for the District of Arizona answered this question favorably to petitioner, the Secretary of the Interior, when . . . it dismissed the respondents' complaint. The Court of Appeals, one judge dissenting, reversed. We granted certiorari because of the significance of the issue and because of the vigorous assertion that the judgment of the Court of Appeals was inconsistent with long-established policy of the Secretary and of the Bureau.

I

. . . The respondents, Ramon Ruiz and his wife, Anita, are Papago Indians and United States citizens. In 1940 they left the Papago Reservation in Arizona to seek employment 15 miles away at the Phelps-Dodge copper mines at Ajo. Mr. Ruiz found work there, and they settled in a community at Ajo called the "Indian Village" and populated almost entirely by Papagos. Practically all the land and most of the homes in the Village are owned or rented by Phelps-Dodge. The Ruizes have lived in Ajo continuously since 1940 and have been in their present residence since 1947. A minor daughter lives with them. They speak and understand the Papago language but only limited English. Apart from Mr. Ruiz' employment with Phelps-Dodge, they have not been assimilated into the dominant culture, and they appear to have maintained a close tie with the nearby reservation.

In July 1967, 27 years after the Ruizes moved to Ajo, the mine where he worked was shut down by a strike. It remained closed until the following March. . . .

On December 11, 1967, Mr. Ruiz applied for general assistance benefits from the Bureau of Indian Affairs (BIA). He was immediately notified by letter that he was ineligible for general assistance because of the provisions (in effect since 1952) in 66 Indian Affairs Manual 3.1.4 (1965) [the "BIA Manual" or the "Manual"] that eligibility is limited to Indians living "on reservations" and in jurisdictions under the BIA in Alaska and Oklahoma. An appeal to the Superintendent of the Papago Indian Agency was unsuccessful. A further appeal to the Phoenix Area Director of the BIA led to a hearing, but this, too, proved unsuccessful. The sole ground for the denial of general assistance benefits was that the Ruizes resided outside the boundaries of the Papago Reservation.

The respondents then instituted the present purported class action against the Secretary, claiming, as a matter of statutory interpretation, entitlement to the general assistance for which they had applied, and also challenging the eligibility provision as a violation of Fifth Amendment due process and of the Privileges and Immunities Clause of Art. IV, § 2, of the Constitution. . . .

[In Sections II through IV of its opinion, the Court analyzed the history, language, and purposes of the Snyder Act of 1921 (under the authority of which the Department of Interior established the general assistance program), and the subsequent appropriations passed by Congress to fund the general assistance program. It concluded that neither the Snyder Act nor the related appropriations acts contain language imposing geographical limitations on eligibility for the general assistance program. Although the BIA Manual limited program eligibility to those Native Americans living "on reservations," in practice the agency did not rigidly follow the limitation. The BIA provided Native Americans not living on reservations with benefits under the general assistance program, and the BIA had previously notified Congress that it had made such exceptions to the geographic limitation stated in the BIA Manual. Additionally, the BIA had used the terms "on reservations" and "on or near reservations" interchangeably for years when providing testimony about its assistance programs to congressional appropriations subcommittees. This indicated that the BIA considered Native Americans eligible for its programs regardless of whether they lived on or near a reservation, and the Court found no reason to conclude that the BIA had established a different eligibility policy for the general assistance program. Finally, the Court rejected the Secretary's argument that Congress legislatively ratified the BIA Manual's geographical limitation. The BIA Manual was an internal agency document circulated solely within the BIA; the geographic limitation contained in it had never been published in the Federal Register or in the Code of Federal Regulation. Accordingly, and although Congress passed appropriations acts after the limitation had been included in the Manual, there was no indication that the appropriations subcommittees were ever made aware of its existence.]

V

A.

Having found that the congressional appropriation was intended to cover welfare services at least to those Indians residing "on or near" the reservation, it does not necessarily follow that the Secretary is without power to create reasonable classifications and eligibility requirements in order to allocate the limited funds available to him for this purpose. Thus, if there were only enough funds appropriated to provide meaningfully for 10,000 needy Indian beneficiaries and the entire class of eligible beneficiaries numbered 20,000, it would be incumbent upon the BIA to develop an eligibility standard to deal with this problem, and the standard, if rational and proper, might leave some of the class otherwise encompassed by the appropriation without benefits. But in such a case the agency must, at a minimum, let the standard be generally known so as to assure that it is being applied consistently and so as to avoid both the reality and the appearance of arbitrary denial of benefits to potential beneficiaries.

Assuming, *arguendo*, that the Secretary rationally could limit the "on or near" appropriation to include only the smaller class of Indians who lived directly "on" the reservation plus those in Alaska and Oklahoma, the question that remains is whether this has been validly accomplished. The power of an administrative agency to administer a congressionally created and funded program necessarily requires the formulation of policy and the making of rules to fill any gap left, implicitly or explicitly, by Congress. In the area of Indian affairs, the Executive has long been empowered to promulgate rules and policies, and the power has been given explicitly to the Secretary and his delegates at the BIA. This agency power to make rules that affect substantial individual rights and obligations carries with it the responsibility not only to remain consistent with the governing legislation ... but also to employ procedures that conform to the law. *See NLRB v. Wyman-Gordon Co.*, 394 U.S. 759, 764 (1969) (plurality opinion). No matter how rational or consistent with congressional intent a particular decision might be, the determination of eligibility cannot be made on an *ad hoc* basis by the dispenser of the funds.

The Administrative Procedure Act was adopted to provide, *inter alia*, that administrative policies affecting individual rights and obligations be promulgated pursuant to certain stated procedures so as to avoid the inherently arbitrary nature of unpublished *ad hoc* determinations. That Act states in pertinent part:

> Each Agency shall separately state and currently publish in the Federal Register for the guidance of the public —
>
> (D) substantive rules of general applicability adopted as authorized by law, and statements of general policy or interpretations of general applicability formulated and adopted by the agency. 5 U.S.C. § 552(a)(1).

The sanction added in 1967 by Pub. L. 90-23, 81 Stat. 54, provides:

> Except to the extent that a person has actual and timely notice of the terms thereof, a person may not in any manner be required to resort to, or be adversely affected by, a matter required to be published in the Federal Register and not so published. *Ibid.*

In the instant case the BIA itself has recognized the necessity of formally publishing its substantive policies and has placed itself under the structure of the APA procedures. The 1968 introduction to the Manual reads:

> Code of Federal Regulations: Directives which relate to the public, including Indians, are published in the Federal Register and codified in 25 Code of Federal Regulations (25 CFR). These directives inform the public of privileges and benefits available; eligibility qualifications, requirements and procedures; and of appeal rights and procedures. They are published in accordance with rules and regulations issued by the Director of the Federal Register and the Administrative Procedure Act as amended....
>
> Bureau of Indian Affairs Manual: Policies, procedures, and instructions which do not relate to the public but are required to govern the

operations of the Bureau are published in the Bureau of Indian Affairs Manual. 0 BIAM 1.2.

Unlike numerous other programs authorized by the Snyder Act and funded by the annual appropriations, the BIA has chosen not to publish its eligibility requirements for general assistance in the Federal Register or in the CFR. This continues to the present time. The only official manifestation of this alleged policy of restricting general assistance to those directly on the reservations is the material in the Manual which is, by BIA's own admission, solely an internal-operations brochure intended to cover policies that "do not relate to the public." Indeed, at oral argument the Government conceded that for this to be a "real legislative rule," itself endowed with the force of law, it should be published in the Federal Register.

Where the rights of individuals are affected, it is incumbent upon agencies to follow their own procedures. This is so even where the internal procedures are possibly more rigorous than otherwise would be required. The BIA, by its Manual, has declared that all directives that "inform the public of privileges and benefits available" and of "eligibility requirements" are among those to be published. The requirement that, in order to receive general assistance, an Indian must reside directly "on" a reservation is clearly an important substantive policy that fits within this class of directives. Before the BIA may extinguish the entitlement of these otherwise eligible beneficiaries, it must comply, at a minimum, with its own internal procedures.

The Secretary has presented no reason why the requirements of the Administrative Procedure Act could not or should not have been met. *Cf. SEC v. Chenery Corp.*, 332 U.S. 194, 202 (1947) [*Chenery II*]. The BIA itself has not attempted to defend its rule as a valid exercise of its "legislative power," but rather depends on the argument that Congress itself has not appropriated funds for Indians not directly on the reservations. The conscious choice of the Secretary not to treat this extremely significant eligibility requirement, affecting rights of needy Indians, as a legislative-type rule, renders it ineffective so far as extinguishing rights of those otherwise within the class of beneficiaries contemplated by Congress is concerned....

B.

Even assuming the lack of binding effect of the BIA policy, the Secretary argues that the residential restriction in the Manual is a longstanding interpretation of the Snyder Act by the agency best suited to do this, and that deference is due its interpretation. *See Griggs v. Duke Power Co.*, 401 U.S. 424, 433-434 (1971). The thrust of this argument is not that the regulation itself has created the "on" and "near" distinction, but that Congress has intended to provide general assistance only to those directly on reservations, and that the Manual's provision is simply an interpretation of congressional intent. As we have already noted, however, the BIA, through its own practices and representations, has led Congress to believe that these appropriations

> ### Cross-Reference
>
> Here the Court is asking whether the geographic limitation in the general assistance program is a policy adopted by Congress, rather than one created by the BIA. According to the BIA, Congress intended to impose this eligibility requirement, and the only thing left to the BIA was to "find" Congress' intent through statutory interpretation. The Court disagrees, citing *Skidmore v. Swift & Co.*
>
> The broader issue of whether and to what extent courts must defer to an agency's interpretation of a federal statute is one of the most important in all of administrative law. It and the *Skidmore* case are discussed at length in Chapter 9.

covered Indians "on or near" the reservations, and it is too late now to argue that the words "on reservations" in the Manual mean something different from "on or near" when, in fact, the two have been continuously equated by the BIA to Congress.

We have recognized previously that the weight of an administrative interpretation will depend, among other things, upon "its consistency with earlier and later pronouncements" of an agency. *Skidmore v. Swift & Co.*, 323 U.S. 134, 140 (1944). In this instance the BIA's somewhat inconsistent posture belies its present assertion. In order for an agency interpretation to be granted deference, it must be consistent with the congressional purpose. It is evident to us that Congress did not itself intend to limit its authorization to only those Indians directly on, in contrast to those "near," the reservation, and that, therefore, the BIA's interpretation must fail.

The judgment of the Court of Appeals is affirmed and the case is remanded for further proceedings consistent with this opinion.

It is so ordered.

Affirmed and remanded.

QUESTION SET 4.5

Review & Synthesis

1. Why did the Court rule that the BIA's geographical eligibility criterion did not bar the Ruizes from receiving Snyder Act benefits? Was it because the BIA lacked substantive rulemaking authority under the Snyder Act to adopt the criterion? Because the BIA had, but did not use, the rulemaking authority Congress granted it to promulgate the criterion? For some other reason?

2. Did the Court's reasoning in *Morton* foreclose an agency's ability to issue legally binding rules through policy manuals or other documents that are not created through either the rulemaking process or an adjudication?

3. As *Chenery II*, *Wyman-Gordon*, and *Bell Aerospace* made clear, agencies have the authority to apply new policies in the adjudications that create them. The BIA denied the Ruizes' benefits claim in an informal adjudication. Why did the Court not sustain the BIA's denial of benefits to the Ruizes on this basis?

4. To what extent did lack of notice play a role in the Court's decision? In other words, do you think the Court would have accepted the BIA's geographic eligibility criterion if the BIA had simply published it in the Federal Register? If it had sought public comment before including the criterion in its policy manual?

Application & Analysis

1. The City Pollution Prevention Program ("CPPP") is designed to reduce the negative environmental effects of human activity in densely populated urban areas. Created and administered by the Office of Community Planning and Development ("CPD") in the Department of Housing and Urban Development ("HUD"), CPPP awards up to 20 grants each year for pilot field projects. The CPD published an announcement—complete with eligibility criteria and application procedures—in the Federal Register in early 2018. The public response was overwhelmingly positive; CPD received dozens of applications from all over the country.

CPD's procedures for evaluating applications are set out in an internal agency memorandum written by CPD staff members. The memorandum provides that CPD staff members will serve on the program's grant award committee. The first step in the selection process is a review to ensure that all applications are complete. Completed applications move on to the substantive evaluation stage and are scored by the committee. The top 30 become semifinalists. The committee then solicits external comments on the semifinalists' proposals, and committee members conduct site visits of the contending programs. After evaluating this additional information, the committee ranks all of the remaining applications and sends the top ten to the HUD Secretary for final selection.

Among the aspiring grant recipients was the Association for Civic Environmentalism ("ACE"). It sought funding for its Youth Sustainability Project, which its submission described as "a comprehensive program operated through 10 neighborhood organizations in Oklahoma City." The committee ranked its application ninth among the semifinalists. The HUD Secretary subsequently selected its application as one of five provisional award recipients, contingent upon successful resolution of some minor programmatic and financial issues raised by its submission. The Secretary instructed the committee to negotiate with all of the provisional award recipients and to finalize the formal award documents for her signature. The committee chair contacted all of the provisional award recipients, including ACE, to initiate final negotiations.

Despite this, several CPD staff members on the award committee continued to scrutinize ACE's application materials. They contacted Oklahoma City officials and asked a HUD attorney to conduct a separate review of ACE's application. Nearly three months after the HUD Secretary had selected the finalists, she again asked the committee to execute documents formalizing ACE's grant award. Instead, the staff members who continued to review ACE's application presented their additional findings to the Secretary. They did not provide this new information to the other staff members before doing so. Based on these findings, the Secretary rescinded her initial selection of ACE as an award recipient.

Per HUD regulations setting forth procedures to appeal adverse grant decisions, ACE would like to file an administrative protest with HUD's Office of Hearings and Appeals. Based on the foregoing facts, analyze whether ACE has a viable claim under *Morton v. Ruiz*.

2. The Harmonized Tariff Schedule of the United States,19 U.S.C. § 1202 (2011) ("HTSUS"), tasks the Customs Service ("Customs") with classifying and setting duty rates for goods imported into the United States, pursuant to rules issued by the Secretary of the Treasury. The Secretary's regulations authorize any of the nation's 46 port-of-entry Customs offices to issue "ruling letters" to importers looking to bring goods into the country. Additionally, the regulations provide detailed instructions on the issuance, effect, and publication of Customs' ruling letters. The letters set Customs' official tariff classifications and rates for those goods. They are binding on all Customs personnel until they are modified or revoked. Such modifications or revocations can occur without notice to anyone other than the original ruling letter recipient. Further, Customs warns that no one other than the recipient should rely on a ruling letter. Absent a change of practice or other modification of the principles on which a ruling letter is based, those principles may be cited as authority in the disposition of transactions involving the same transaction, issue, or goods. Similarly, ruling letters can be applied to other goods with identical descriptions. Since the letters are directed at particular goods, they are not subject to notice-and-comment rulemaking and are not routinely published. Customs officials issue thousands of these letters each year. *See* 19 C.F.R. § 177.8-177.10 (2019).

Mead Corp. imports "day planners," which are three-ring binders with pages for daily schedules, contact information, and calendars. For years, Customs classified them as tariff-free "diaries, other" under the HTSUS. In a recent ruling letter to Mead Corp., however, Customs reclassified its day planners as "diaries, bound," subjecting them to a 4 percent tariff. Customs explained that it had reinterpreted the terms "diary" and "bound" based on definitions in the Oxford English Dictionary. This reinterpretation led to the reclassification.

Mead Corp. paid the tariffs imposed by Customs, but it challenged the reclassification in the Court of International Trade. CIT ruled in

Customs' favor, and Mead Corp. has appealed to the Federal Circuit. It argues that ruling letters are policy statements under the APA that lack the force of law. Accordingly, it was under no legal obligation to pay tariffs based on Customs' reinterpretation of the terms "diary" and "bound." Customs counters that its ruling letters are not policy statements, but binding decisions produced by informal adjudications. You are a clerk for one of the judges on the Federal Circuit hearing the appeal. Write a brief memo assessing Mead Corp.'s claim.

CHAPTER 5

Rulemaking

As we have seen, the primary mechanisms by which agencies formulate and adopt legally binding policies are rulemaking and adjudication. We concentrate now on the former. While most of our attention will be dedicated to studying the rulemaking procedures contained in the Administrative Procedure Act, discussing them alone would provide a decidedly incomplete picture of both the history and development of modern federal rulemaking. Indeed, numerous political and legal developments have significantly altered the default approach to rulemaking established by the APA. Congress has passed a number of statutes creating "statutory hybrid" rulemaking procedures that augment or supersede the APA's defaults. *See, e.g.*, The Occupational Safety and Health Act, 29 U.S.C. § 655(b)(3) (requiring OSHA to hold public hearings at request of an interested person objecting to a proposed rule); The Clean Air Act, 42 U.S.C. § 7607(d) (replacing most of the APA's rulemaking procedures). Since the 1970s, Presidents have more aggressively inserted themselves into the rulemaking process, adding layers of analytical and political scrutiny enforced by the Office of Management and Budget and the Office for Information and Regulatory Affairs. For a time, lower federal courts were fond of creating "judicial hybrid" rulemaking procedures. Spurred by expanded pre-enforcement review of agency decisions (see *Abbott Laboratories v. Gardner, infra* at 833) and the Supreme Court's move toward a more searching review of informal agency decision-making (see *Citizens to Preserve Overton Park, Inc. v. Volpe, infra* at 898), they imposed additional procedures to guard against irrationality and unfairness in policymaking. Although they have since retreated from the more aggressive policing they undertook in the 1970s, the scope, depth, and availability of judicial review continues to shape whether and how agencies regulate through rules. Finally, agencies sometimes on their own initiative adopt procedures that restrict their capacity to engage in rulemaking. All of these extra checks—legislative, executive, judicial, and administrative—have fueled a robust "ossification" literature. Commentators have warned that these supra-APA burdens rob rulemaking of the speed and flexibility its Congressional architects envisioned for it. We will touch on several of these matters in the materials that follow. Again, however, our primary concern is understanding the core features of the rulemaking regime established by the APA.

As is the case with adjudication, rulemaking comes in two basic flavors: formal rulemaking and informal rulemaking. The default procedures for formal rulemaking, the rarer of the two, are set out in APA §§ 556 and 557. Agencies must employ them only, as APA § 553(c) states, "[w]hen rules are required by statute to be made on the record after opportunity for an agency hearing." Most rulemaking is conducted under the procedures set out in APA § 553, alternatively labeled "notice-and-comment," "APA," and "informal" rulemaking. At a minimum, it requires: (1) publication of a notice of proposed rulemaking; (2) an opportunity for interested members of the public to submit written comments regarding the proposed rule; and (3) publication of the final rule, at least 30 days before it becomes effective, that includes a statement of its basis and purposes.

Rules promulgated through formal and informal procedures are not the only ones adopted by federal agencies, and thus are not the only ones contemplated by the APA. APA § 551(4) defines a "rule" (in relevant part) as "the whole or a part of an agency statement of general or particular applicability and future effect designed to implement, interpret, or prescribe law or policy or describing the organization, procedure, or practice requirements of an agency." The first part of this definition refers to those rules that have the force of law; they alter the rights and obligations of private parties and so must be promulgated through formal or informal procedures. By contrast, the latter part of the definition—rules "describing the organization, procedure, or practice requirements of an agency"—do not have the force of law. They do not alter private parties' legal rights or obligations and, as a result, do not have to have to be adopted through formal or notice-and-comment rulemaking. The challenge comes in distinguishing between the two categories, a subject to which the APA dedicates several of its provisions.

As stories of its birth often recount, the APA is the offspring of vigorous debate and hard-fought compromise. Supporters of the New Deal agenda advocated for greater substantive discretion in, more procedural flexibility for, and increased Presidential control over administrative decision-making. Many who opposed the New Deal feared "administrative absolutism," abandonment of law for executive discretion, and usurpation of the Judiciary's traditional role in protecting private interests. *See* Chapter 1 at 21-22; Joseph Postell, Bureaucracy in America 231 (2017). Largely in response to this tension, the APA adopted flexible, minimal, default procedures that recognized the various ways agencies pursue their functions. It is important to keep this in mind when reading the APA's provisions. Its drafters did not aim to create an all-encompassing code, providing detailed prescriptions and proscriptions for every eventuality. Quite the contrary, many decisions are left to agency discretion, including to some extent when the notice-and-comment rulemaking provisions must be employed. The judicial challenge is reviewing exercises of that discretion to ensure it remains within its statutory bounds.

The materials that follow are organized into three broad categories. The first category addresses nonlegislative rules, which bypass most or all of the APA's rulemaking procedures. The second category addresses the basic formal and informal procedures by which agencies promulgate rules under the APA. Agencies utilize informal rulemaking far more frequently than formal rulemaking, and so discussion of the former comprises most of the materials in this chapter. The third category addresses three variations on or additions to the APA's basic (informal) rulemaking procedures: Presidential review of rulemaking, "judicial hybrid" rulemaking, and negotiated rulemaking.

A. RULES EXEMPT FROM THE APA'S REQUIREMENTS

We begin with rules that are exempt from some or all of the APA's procedural requirements applying to "legislative" or "substantive" rules. They fall into two categories. The first is populated by rules on military or foreign affairs functions, those governing internal agency management or personnel, and those relating to the government's proprietary interests (public loans, grants, benefits, or contracts). *See* § 553(a). Such rules are exempted from all of § 553's requirements. Several practical justifications have been offered in support of these fairly broad carveouts from public participation in rulemaking. Some have argued that, without these exemptions, agencies would be forced into lengthy rulemakings that increase workloads, costs, and decision-making delays. Agencies' ability to perform their regulatory tasks would be significantly undermined as a result. Others have argued that the exempted rules are of little public interest or touch on topics for which public input would be of little substantive value. Still others defend the exemptions because the increased public scrutiny and court challenges that would result from their absence would cause uncertainty in areas where clarity is especially prized (e.g., foreign relations and national security). Some have countered that all of these justifications, as well as others, apply with equal force to any rule promulgated under formal or informal adjudication. *See, e.g.*, Arthur E. Bonfield, *Public Participation in Federal Rulemaking Relating to Public Property, Loans, Grants, Benefits, or Contracts*, 118 U. PA. L. REV. 577-78 (1970) (discussing arguments for and against the exemptions). Additionally, bypassing the public undermines public participation in policy formation, an axiomatic value for democratic societies. In response to these concerns, Congress has sometimes required agencies whose rules otherwise fall within § 553(a) exemptions to allow for public participation. For example, the Social Security Act (which clearly deals with "benefits") requires the Social Security Administration to engage in § 553 notice-and-comment rulemaking when setting disability benefits eligibility standards. *See* 42 U.S.C. § 421(k)(2). Other agencies have voluntarily waived some or all of their exemptions. *See* Jeffrey S. Lubbers, A Guide to Federal Agency Rulemaking 54 n.68 (5th ed. 2012) (listing examples).

The second category is comprised of so-called "nonlegislative" rules and include interpretive rules, general statements of policy, and rules of agency organization, procedure, and practice. Under § 553(b)(A), these rules are subject to publication in the Federal Register but not to § 553's notice-and-comment requirements. Agencies exercise some measure of discretion in determining when the exemptions apply. The question for courts is whether agencies' judgments in this regard fit the terms and purposes of the exemptions. As one scholar succinctly framed it, "[t]he central inquiry in all nonlegislative rule cases is this: Is the agency document, properly conceived, a legislative rule that is invalid because it did not undergo notice and comment procedures, or a proper interpretive rule or general statement of policy exempt from such procedures?" John F. Manning, *Nonlegislative Rules*, 72 Geo. Wash. L. Rev. 893, 917 (2004). As the cases below illustrate, that question can prove difficult to answer.

1. Interpretive Rules

The APA's exemption for interpretive rules is intended to free agencies from "undertaking cumbersome proceedings" when simply "explain[ing] ambiguous terms in legislative enactments." *American Hospital Ass'n v. Bowen*, 834 F.2d 1037, 1045 (D.C. Cir. 1987). When appropriately utilized, the interpretive rule provision facilitates prompt dissemination of helpful regulatory guidance to the affected public and allows agencies to better manage the policy and practice coordination problems endemic to any bureaucracy. A problem arises, however, when agencies use (or are suspected of using) the exemption to adopt substantive regulations without the public participation and scrutiny mandated by Congress. Herein lies the challenge for those who oversee the federal bureaucracy: What distinguishes "substantive" rules that are subject to full notice-and-comment rulemaking from "interpretive" rules that are not?

We return once more to the Attorney General's Manual, which anticipated the problem and offered some guidance. Substantive rules are those, apart from organizational and procedural rules, "issued by an agency pursuant to statutory authority and which implement the statute." Attorney General's Manual at 30 n.3. Interpretive rules, by contrast, are "rules or statements issued by an agency to advise the public of the agency's construction of the statutes and rules which it administers." *Id.* These definitions may have some clarifying power. They indicate that an interpretive rule merely advises the public on substantive policy commitments that the interpretive rule itself did not create. Stated differently, the Manual implies that interpretive rules must "refer back" to some other pronouncement (statute or regulation) that has the force of law.

Unfortunately, the Manual's abstract distinctions quickly break down upon further inspection. For instance, an interpretive rule that restates, verbatim, the language of a statute or regulation clearly falls within the exemption. It merely rebroadcasts the original pronouncement and thus does nothing to supplement or alter it. But what if an interpretive rule translates statutory or regulatory provisions into a formula or a numerical value? What if an agency "interprets" statutory or regulatory provisions by relying on legislative history, dictionaries, or other extratextual sources to define their operative terms? Just how much linguistic distance must there be between a statute or regulation and an interpretive rule before the latter ceases to be "interpretive." By approaching the distinction between substantive and interpretive rules as binaries rather than as points on a spectrum, the Manual does little to answer this question.

The courts have filled the void by formulating a host of tests to detect substantive wolves masquerading as interpretive sheep. Two notable approaches are presented in the cases below, one offered by the D.C. Circuit, the other by the Seventh Circuit.

National Family Planning and Reproductive Health Association, Inc. v. Sullivan
979 F.2d 227 (D.C. Cir. 1992)

Before: MIKVA, Chief Judge, WALD and EDWARDS, Circuit Judges

WALD, Circuit Judge:

The central issue presented in this case is whether the Department of Health and Human Services ("HHS"), in announcing that a 1988 regulation which had theretofore been construed to strictly prohibit abortion counseling or referral of any kind in Title X programs, would thereafter be interpreted to permit doctors to counsel on abortion within the context of the doctor-patient relationship, erred in failing to first undertake the notice and comment rulemaking prescribed by the Administrative Procedure Act ("APA"), 5 U.S.C. § 553. The new "Directives" neither clarify nor explain the previous regulation, which was adopted by notice and comment rulemaking, but instead effectively amend the 1988 regulation to significantly alter its meaning, as previously interpreted and enforced by HHS and upheld by the

Supreme Court in *Rust v. Sullivan,* 500 U.S. 173 (1991). Accordingly, we conclude that the new Directives are not exempt from notice and comment rulemaking as an interpretative rule. We therefore affirm the judgment of the district court granting the National Family Planning and Reproductive Health Association, Inc. and the National Association of Nurse Practitioners in Reproductive Health (the "Associations") injunctive and declaratory relief enjoining the Secretary from proceeding with the enforcement of the new Directives without first adhering to the requirements of § 553 of the APA.

I. BACKGROUND

Title X of the Public Health Service Act, 42 U.S.C. §§ 300-300a-6, provides at section 1008 that: "None of the funds appropriated under this subchapter shall be used in programs where abortion is a method of family planning." 42 U.S.C. § 300a-6. In 1971, HHS issued regulations on this section, without notice and comment,[1] concluding that the statute simply required that a Title X "project will not provide abortions as a method of family planning." 36 Fed. Reg. 18,465, 18,466 (1971) (codified at 42 C.F.R. § 59.5(9) (1972)). During the mid-1970s, HHS General Counsel memoranda made a further distinction between directive ("encouraging or promoting" abortion) and nondirective ("neutral") counseling on abortion, prohibiting the former and permitting the latter. In 1980, through notice and comment rulemaking, HHS made a number of changes to the regulations governing Title X grants not relevant here and retained the 1971 language pertaining to the provision of abortion by Title X projects. 45 Fed. Reg. 37,433, 37,437 (1980) (codified at 42 C.F.R. § 59.5(5) (1980)). The following year, HHS issued "Program Guidelines," without notice or comment, "to assist current and prospective grantees in understanding and utilizing the Title X family planning services grants program." These guidelines mandated nondirective abortion counseling by Title X projects upon a patient's request.

In 1988, HHS promulgated by notice and comment rulemaking new regulations that established a much broader prohibition on abortion counseling or referrals including a "gag rule" applicable to all Title X project personnel against informing or discussing with clients the availability of abortion as an option for individual planning or treatment needs. 53 Fed. Reg. 2922 (1988) (codified at 42 C.F.R. pt. 59). The regulations provide that a "title X project may not provide counseling concerning the use of abortion as a method of family planning or provide referral for abortion as a method of family planning." 42 C.F.R. § 59.8(a)(1) (1991). A Title X project is permitted to refer pregnant clients "for appropriate prenatal and/or social services

---

[1] Notice and comment rulemaking was waived under the good cause exception of 5 U.S.C. § 553(b)(3)(B). 36 Fed. Reg. 18,465.

by furnishing a list of available providers that promote the welfare of mother and unborn child," *id.* at § 59.8(a)(2), but referrals may not be used

> as an indirect means of encouraging or promoting abortion as a method of family planning, such as by weighing the list of referrals in favor of health care providers which perform abortions, by including on the list of referral providers health care providers whose principal business is the provision of abortions, by excluding available providers who do not provide abortions, or by "steering" clients to providers who offer abortion as a method of family planning.

Id. at § 59.8(a)(3).

The Supreme Court upheld both the constitutional and statutory validity of these regulations in *Rust v. Sullivan*, 500 U.S. 173 (1991), against a specific challenge that they directly interfered with a doctor's professional right and duty to treat his patient as he thought best.

On November 5, 1991, responding to widespread concerns that § 59.8 would interfere with the doctor-patient relationship, President Bush issued a memorandum to the Secretary of HHS, urging that the "confidentiality" of the doctor-patient relationship be preserved and that operation of the Title X program be "compatible with free speech and the highest standards of medical care." To accomplish this result, the President directed that the implementation of the regulations adhere to four principles:

1. Nothing in these regulations is to prevent a woman from receiving complete medical information about her condition from a physician.
2. Title X projects are to provide necessary referrals to appropriate health care facilities where medically indicated.
3. If a woman is found to be pregnant and to have a medical problem, she should be referred for complete medical care, even if the ultimate result may be the termination of her pregnancy.
4. Referrals may be made by Title X programs to full-service health care providers that perform abortions, but not to providers whose principal activity is providing abortion services.

In a press conference, the President asserted: "[U]nder my directive, they can go ahead—patients and doctors can talk about absolutely anything they want, and they should be able to do that."

The Secretary therefore directed the Assistant Secretary to comply with the principles announced by the President in implementing the regulations. On March 20, 1992, Deputy Assistant Secretary for Population Affairs William Archer issued a memorandum to HHS Regional Health Administrators ("RHAs"). The Archer memorandum restated the President's first principle and explained that "[t]his statement is intended to apply to medical information provided only by a physician directly to his or her patient, in a clinic visit or a subsequent telephone conversation directly with the physician." Collectively, the memoranda from the President, the Secretary and Deputy Assistant Secretary Archer (the "Directives"), distinguished physicians from other health care professionals for purposes of providing medical information, including abortion counseling.

The appellees in this case, organizations composed primarily of Title X grantees and family planning nurse practitioners, filed suit on April 16, 1992, challenging the validity of these Directives, asserting that the process by which they were adopted did not comply with the notice and comment provisions of the APA, and that the new policy embodied in the Directives was arbitrary and capricious. They sought to enjoin the Secretary from implementing § 59.8 as allegedly modified by the Directives. On May 28, 1992, the district court held for the Associations, concluding that the Directives constituted legislative, as opposed to interpretative rulemaking, and thus required notice and comment prior to promulgation. The court also held that the modification of § 59.8's gag rule to allow doctors to freely communicate and advise their Title X patients regarding abortion, while continuing the prohibition for other health care professionals, lacked a rational basis in the record. Accordingly, the court enjoined implementation of the guidelines and remanded the case to the agency for compliance with the APA, denying the Secretary's motion to stay the injunction pending appeal. This court, however, stayed the injunction pending disposition of this appeal.

II. ANALYSIS

HHS is authorized to promulgate regulations governing the distribution of grants to Title X programs. 42 U.S.C. § 300a-4(a). An agency, in light of changing circumstances, is free to alter the interpretative and policy views reflected in regulations construing an underlying statute, so long as any changed construction of the statute is consistent with express congressional intent or embodies a "permissible" reading of the statute, *see Chevron U.S.A., Inc. v. Natural Resources Defense Council, Inc.*, 467 U.S. 837 (1984), and is otherwise "reasonable," *see Motor Vehicle Mfrs. Ass'n v. State Farm Mut. Auto. Ins. Co.*, 463 U.S. 29, 42 (1983). In this appeal, we do not ultimately decide whether the agency's revised interpretation of Title X, as announced in the Directives, is either permissible under *Chevron* or reasonable under *State Farm*. . . .[2] Instead, we confine our review to the more limited administrative law issue of whether HHS followed proper procedure in implementing the change.

---

[2] Because we find that the Directives should have been promulgated through notice and comment rulemaking, we do not pass on the Associations' claim that the Directives are arbitrary and capricious.

The APA provides in relevant part:

(b) General notice of proposed rule making shall be published in the Federal Register. . . . Except when notice or hearing is required by statute, this subsection does not apply—

(A) to interpretative rules, general statements of policy, or rules of agency organization, procedure, or practice. . . .

5 U.S.C. § 553(b). The Directives involved here seem clearly to constitute a "rule" under the APA, which defines that term as "the whole or a part of an agency statement of general or particular applicability and future effect designed to implement, interpret, or prescribe law or policy. . . ." 5 U.S.C. § 551(4). The Secretary's memorandum began by stating that, "the President expressed to me his decision that, in implementing the Title X regulations, the Department of Health and Human Services should adhere to [the principles identified by the President]." Similarly, the Deputy Assistant Secretary's memorandum explains that it "is for use by Regional Office staff in implementing the February 2, 1988, regulation. . . ." The only remaining question then is whether the statutory exception for interpretative rules is applicable so as to excuse notice and comment. The dividing line between legislative and interpretative rules has been deemed "fuzzy" in some cases, but in the unique circumstances of this case, we find it relatively easy to make the call that the Directives are legislative rules. Briefly summarized, our reasoning is as follows: When an agency promulgates a legislative regulation by notice and comment directly affecting the conduct of both agency personnel and members of the public, whose meaning the agency announces as clear and definitive to the public and, on challenge, to the Supreme Court, it may not subsequently repudiate that announced meaning and substitute for it a totally different meaning without proceeding through the notice and comment rulemaking normally required for amendments of a rule. To sanction any other course would render the requirements of § 553 basically superfluous in legislative rulemaking by permitting agencies to alter their requirements for affected public members at will through the ingenious device of "reinterpreting" their own rule.

A. *The 1988 Regulations Prohibited Physicians from Counseling on Abortion*

. . . In promulgating the [1988] regulations, HHS explained that its previous rules on abortion counseling had created "confusion about precisely which activities were proscribed by [§ 1008], and had resulted in variations in practice by grantees." 53 F.R. [2922,] 2924. . . .

. . . Further, HHS believed [the 1988 regulations made it clear] that "counseling and referral for abortion are prohibited by section 1008," and more specifically that "[c]ounseling in a Title X program, whether directive or nondirective, which results in abortion as a method of family planning simply cannot be squared with the language of section 1008. . . ." *Id.* at 2923. The absolute rule against abortion counseling or referral embodied in § 59.8 would, in HHS' words, "bring program practices into conformity with the language of the statute," and "establish far more specific and clearer standards for compliance with section 1008." *Id.* at 2923, 2925.

There was no hint in the agency's statement of basis and purpose accompanying the regulation, and certainly not in the regulation itself, to suggest that doctors would be exempt from the Title X abortion counseling ban. The [1988] rule was typically described in the broadest terms: "The rules . . . do not prevent a health professional or a provider organization from discussing, promoting, or otherwise encouraging a woman to have an abortion as a general matter; they simply do not permit them to do so within a Title X project." *Id.* at 2936. . . .

In arguing the validity of the regulations before the Supreme Court, HHS continued to stress that § 59.8 erected a complete prohibition on abortion counseling. Brief for Respondent, *Rust v. Sullivan*, 500 U.S. 173 (1991). The regulation was described as broadly applying to "health care professionals," "Title X project personnel," "staff," and "employees." *Id.* at 24-27. Responding to concerns that the regulations improperly manipulated the doctor-patient dialogue, the Secretary answered that "the health care professional's dialogue is restricted in only one limited sense. He is hired to provide only pre-pregnancy family planning and infertility services and must refer the client to *other* qualified health care professionals for post-pregnancy services." *Id.* at 25 note 25 (emphasis in original). The argument continued that the "regulations do not prevent a woman from obtaining abortion information; she simply must seek it from a source other than a Title X project," and that the rules "merely define the scope of the services that a federally subsidized Title X health care professional may provide in the context of a specific, limited program." *Id.* at 17.

Indeed, the Supreme Court, in upholding the regulations, underscored their application to all Title X personnel, including physicians. Chief Justice Rehnquist explained: "[The regulations] are designed to ensure that the limits of the federal program are observed. The Title X program is designed not for prenatal care, but to encourage family planning." *Id.* at [193]. The opinion asserted that "a doctor employed by the project may be prohibited in the course of his project duties from counseling abortion or referring for abortion." *Id.* [at 193-194]. . . .

In sum, the history unequivocally shows that HHS expressly based the 1988 regulations on a particular interpretation of the language and purpose of the statute as outlawing any counseling or referral services dealing with abortions, even by doctors. The record further demonstrates that these regulations were so understood by HHS personnel and by Title X grantees and applicants. It is also undisputed that the 1988 regulations, including § 59.8, were intended by HHS to be legislative rules, governing the conduct of Title X grantors and grantees. The agency was exercising its congressionally delegated authority to issue binding regulations to implement the statute, and in so doing necessarily followed the required process of notice and comment rulemaking. . . .

. . . [A]n agency issuing a legislative rule is itself bound by the rule until that rule is amended or revoked. HHS may not alter, without notice and comment, the 1988 regulations to permit doctors to give abortion counseling, unless such a change can be legitimately characterized as merely a permissible interpretation of the regulation, consistent with its language and original purpose. As we show in the next section, the Directives cannot meet such a test.

B. *The Directives Are Legislative Rules*

HHS counsel conceded at oral argument that the agency interpreted its own 1988 regulation prior to the Directives not to permit physicians to counsel patients on abortion. In 1991, the Directives changed that basic understanding. Section 59.8(a)(1) of the 1988 regulations states that a "Title X project may not provide counseling concerning the use of abortion as a method of family planning or provide referral for abortion as a method of family planning." 42 C.F.R. § 59.8(a)(1). The Directives say that Title X physicians may, pursuant to the same regulations, provide counseling and referrals for abortions when their medical judgment so dictates. According to HHS briefs, "[b]ecause of the 1988 regulations, nurses may not counsel about abortion; under the 1988 regulations, as construed by the [Directives], physicians are not so limited," and more pointedly, physicians are now "free to speak without any constraints about abortion" within the context of the doctor-patient relationship. . . .

It is a maxim of administrative law that: "If a second rule repudiates or is irreconcilable with [a prior legislative rule], the second rule must be an amendment of the first; and, of course, an amendment to a legislative rule must itself be legislative." Michael Asimow, *Nonlegislative Rulemaking and Regulatory Reform*, 1985 DUKE L.J. 381, 396. Judge Easterbrook has lucidly explained why in such circumstances notice and comment rulemaking must be followed:

> A *volte face* . . . may be an attempt to avoid the notice and opportunity for comment that the Administrative Procedure Act requires for the alteration of a rule. When an agency gets out the Dictionary of Newspeak and pronounces that for purposes of its regulation war is peace, it has made a substantive change for which the APA may require procedures. If in the air bags case, *Motor Vehicle Manufacturers Ass'n v. State Farm Mutual Automobile Insurance Co.*, 463 U.S. 29 (1983), instead of repealing the rule the agency had proclaimed that an ordinary seat belt is a "passive

restraint," the Court would have treated this the same as it treated revocation of the rule. Both require notice, an opportunity for comment, and an adequate record.

Homemakers North Shore, Inc. v. Bowen, 832 F.2d 408, 412 (7th Cir. 1987). In this case, while we do not accuse the Directives of Orwellian overtones, they do represent a nonobvious and unanticipated reading of the 1988 regulation, which has the effect of cutting back significantly on its scope and proscriptions. In reviewing the validity of agency interpretations, "a court should be guided by an administrative construction of a regulation only '*if the meaning of the words used is in doubt*.' Deference to agency interpretations is not in order if the rule's meaning is clear on its face." [*Pfizer, Inc. v. Heckler*, 735 F.2d 1502, 1509 (D.C. Cir. 1984) (emphasis in original)]. While an agency's construction of the statute need not always be correct for its rules to be considered interpretive . . . the fact that its subsequent interpretation runs 180 degrees counter to the plain meaning of the regulation gives us at least some cause to believe that the agency may be seeking to constructively amend the regulation. . . .

In this case we have the additional, and somewhat unique circumstance of a direct clash between a Supreme Court reading of the 1988 regulation and the Directives. The Supreme Court's clear understanding of the 1988 regulation was that it prohibited abortion counseling by doctors. Now we are asked to forget that and docilely accept the Secretary's new interpretation of the same regulation which is dramatically opposed to the one he argued to the Court. . . . The fact that the Supreme Court has read the 1988 regulation to prohibit abortion counseling by doctors, is persuasive evidence that HHS' current view that the regulation permits physicians to so counsel is a legislative rule. Obviously, HHS may for good cause, change the regulation and even its interpretation of the statute through notice and comment rulemaking, but it may not constructively rewrite the regulation, which was expressly based upon a specific interpretation of the statute, through internal memoranda or guidance directives that incorporate a totally different interpretation and effect a totally different result. . . .

An agency rule that reminds parties of existing statutory duties is also considered interpretative, not legislative. Similarly, a regulation that "merely tracked" the statutory requirements and thus "simply explained something the statute already required," has usually been deemed interpretative. [*Alcaraz v. Block*, 746 F.2d 593, 613 (9th Cir. 1984).] Sometimes courts also give weight on the interpretative side to the fact that an agency's rule is explicitly based upon an analysis of the meaning of the statute or regulation.

Conversely, a legislative or substantive rule is one that does more than simply clarify or explain a regulatory term, or confirm a regulatory requirement, or maintain a consistent agency policy. For instance, in *American Hospital Association*, this court shared the view of the district court that requirements in an HHS manual defining procedures governing review functions of Peer

Review Organizations were "not interpretations of any explicit statutory provisions," and did "not merely interpret or elucidate HHS' official position." *American Hosp. Ass'n v. Bowen*, 834 F.2d 1037, 1049-50 (D.C. Cir. 1987). . . . Thus, a rule is legislative if it attempts "to supplement [a statute], not simply to construe it." *Chamber of Commerce v. OSHA*, 636 F.2d 464, 469 (D.C. Cir. 1980). Other times, courts have explained that a rule which "effect[s] a change in existing law or policy" is legislative. *Powderly v. Schweiker*, 704 F.2d 1092, 1098 (9th Cir. 1983). . . .

. . . [T]he record does not support HHS' argument that the Directives do nothing more than make explicit something that was already implicit in the 1988 regulation. First, as previously mentioned, it is clear that there was never any confusion among HHS policymakers or the public over whether doctors were covered by the gag rule in § 59.8.

Second, the Directives themselves suggest that the amendment was motivated not by an interpretation of the regulation's terms, but instead by a previously unacknowledged concern for the special relationship between doctors and their patients. The President expressly premised his modification of the counseling ban as necessary to "ensure that the confidentiality of the doctor/patient relationship will be preserved," and the Secretary explained that he was "committed to preserving the confidentiality of the doctor/patient relationship." Nowhere in the Directives were interpretations of the regulatory terms "abortion" and "counseling" mentioned as the target of the new policy. . . .

Third, rather than simply interpreting the regulation, HHS clearly intends to "grant rights, impose obligations, or produce other significant effects on private interests," *Batterton* [*v. Marshall*], 648 F.2d [694,] 701-02 [(D.C. Cir. 1980)]. As part of the modification of the gag rule, the Directives require that Title X grantees sign an assurance within 30 days of notification by an RHA that the grantee will adhere to § 59.8 as altered by the Directives. . . . If a Title X program is found not to be in compliance with the Directives, "standard grants management procedures will be followed by the Department in seeking a remedy," which presumably means that the program could lose its grant. Moreover, doctors who were previously able to refuse to provide advice on abortion . . . now are expected to answer questions concerning abortion. Clearly, the agency intends the Directives to have present binding effect on Title X programs. HHS counsel explained to the district court that the Secretary's "officials have no latitude at all in this regard. They have to comply with these guidelines.". . .

In sum, the Directives do not simply explain or clarify the 1988 regulation or confirm requirements under that regulation. Instead, based on new concerns about the doctor-patient relationship, HHS is substantially amending and even repudiating part of its original regulation. We also find it revealing that this modification does not come at a point in time when the agency is first applying a possibly ambiguous and broad regulation but rather after the agency and the Supreme Court have very recently reaffirmed a clear and definitive meaning of the regulation as a prohibition on abortion coun-seling by all Title X personnel. Cumulatively, all of these factors impel us to the conclusion that the agency's current rule permitting physicians to coun-sel on abortion is legislative, and must proceed through notice and comment if the procedural mandate of § 553 of the APA is to be honored. . . .

Affirmed.

Hoctor v. United States Department of Agriculture
82 F.3d 165 (7th Cir. 1996)

Before POSNER, Chief Judge, and DIANE P. WOOD and EVANS, Circuit Judges.

POSNER, Chief Judge.

A rule promulgated by an agency that is subject to the Administrative Procedure Act is invalid unless the agency first issues a public notice of pro-posed rulemaking, describing the substance of the proposed rule, and gives the public an opportunity to submit written comments; and if after receiving the comments it decides to promulgate the rule it must set forth the basis and purpose of the rule in a public statement. 5 U.S.C. §§ 553(b), (c). These pro-cedural requirements do not apply, however, to "interpretative rules, general statements of policy, or rules of agency organization, procedure, or practice." 5 U.S.C. § 553(b)(A). Distinguishing between a "legislative" rule, to which the notice and comment provisions of the Act apply, and an interpretive rule, to which these provisions do not apply, is often very difficult — and often very important to regulated firms, the public, and the agency. Notice and comment rulemaking is time-consuming, facilitates the marshaling of opposition to a proposed rule, and may result in the creation of a very long record that may in turn provide a basis for a judicial challenge to the rule if the agency decides to promulgate it. There are no formalities attendant upon the promulgation of an interpretive rule, but this is tolerable because such a rule is "only" an interpretation. Every governmental agency that enforces a less than crystalline statute must interpret the statute, and it does the public a favor if it announces the interpretation in advance of enforcement, whether the announcement takes the form of a rule or of a policy statement, which the Administrative Procedure Act assimilates to an interpretive rule. It would be no favor to the public to discourage the announcement of agencies' interpre-tations by burdening the interpretive process with cumbersome formalities.

The question presented by this appeal from an order of the Department of Agriculture is whether a rule for the secure containment of animals, a rule promulgated by the Department under the Animal Welfare Act, 7 U.S.C. §§ 2131 *et seq.*, without compliance with the notice and comment require-ments of the Administrative Procedure Act, is nevertheless valid because it is merely an interpretive rule. Enacted in 1966, the Animal Welfare Act, as its title implies, is primarily designed to assure the humane treatment of animals. The Act requires the licensing of dealers (with obvious exceptions, for example retail pet stores) and exhibitors, and authorizes the Department to impose sanctions on licensees who violate either the statute itself or the rules promulgated by the Department under the authority of 7 U.S.C. § 2151, which authorizes the Secretary of Agriculture "to promulgate such rules, regulations, and orders as he may deem necessary in order to effectuate the purposes of [the Act]." The Act provides guidance to the exercise of this rulemaking authority by requiring the Department to formulate standards "to govern the humane handling, care, treatment, and transportation of animals by dealers," and these standards must include minimum requirements "for handling, housing, feeding, watering, sanitation," etc. 7 U.S.C. § 2143(a).

The Department has employed the notice and comment procedure to promulgate a regulation, the validity of which is not questioned, that is entitled "structural strength" and that provides that "the facility [housing the animals] must be constructed of such material and of such strength as appropriate for the animals involved. The indoor and outdoor housing facilities shall be structurally sound and shall be maintained in good repair to protect the animals from injury and to contain the animals." 9 C.F.R. § 3.125(a).

Enter the petitioner, Patrick Hoctor, who in 1982 began dealing in exotic animals on his farm outside of Terre Haute[, Indiana]. In a 25-acre compound he raised a variety of animals including "Big Cats"—a typical inventory included three lions, two tigers, seven ligers (a liger is a cross between a male lion and a female tiger, and is thus to be distinguished from a tigon), six cougars, and two snow leopards. The animals were in pens ("primary enclosures" in the jargon of the administration of the Animal Welfare Act). The area in which the pens were located was surrounded by a fence ("containment fence"). In addition, Hoctor erected a fence around the entire compound ("perimeter fence"). At the suggestion of a veterinarian employed by the Agriculture Department who was assigned to inspect the facility when Hoctor started his animal dealership in 1982, Hoctor made the perimeter fence six feet high.

The following year the Department issued an internal memorandum addressed to its force of inspectors in which it said that all "dangerous animals," defined as including, among members of the cat family, lions, tigers, and leopards, must be inside a perimeter fence at least eight feet high. This provision is the so-called interpretive rule, interpreting the housing regulation quoted above. An agency has, of course, the power, indeed the inescapable duty, to interpret its own legislative rules, such as the housing standard, just as it has the power and duty to interpret a statute that it enforces. . . .

On several occasions beginning in 1990, Hoctor was cited by a Department of Agriculture inspector for violating 9 C.F.R. § 3.125(a), the housing standard, by failing to have an eight-foot perimeter fence. Eventually the Department sanctioned Hoctor for this and other alleged violations, and he has sought judicial review limited, however, to the perimeter fence. He is a small dealer and it would cost him many thousands of dollars to replace his six-foot-high fence with an eight-foot-high fence. Indeed, we were told at argument that pending the resolution of his dispute over the fence he has discontinued dealing in Big Cats. The parties agree that unless the rule requiring a perimeter fence at least eight feet high is a valid interpretive rule, the sanction for violating it was improper.

We may assume, though we need not decide, that the Department of Agriculture has the statutory authority to require dealers in dangerous animals to enclose their compounds with eight-foot-high fences. The fence is a backup fail-safe device, since the animals are kept in pens, cages, or other enclosures within the compound, in an area that is itself fenced, rather than being free to roam throughout the compound. Since animals sometimes break out or are carelessly let out of their pens, a fail-safe device seems highly appropriate, to say the least. Two lions once got out of their pen on Hoctor's property, and he had to shoot them. Yet, when he did so, they were still within the containment fence. The Department's regulations do not require a containment fence, and it is unclear to us why, if that fence was adequate—and we are given no reason to suppose it was not—Hoctor should have had to put up an additional fence, let alone one eight-feet high. But we lay any doubts on this score to one side. And we may also assume that the containment of dangerous animals is a proper concern of the Department in the enforcement of the Animal Welfare Act, even though the purpose of the Act is to protect animals from people rather than people from animals. Even Big Cats are not safe outside their compounds, and with a lawyer's ingenuity the Department's able counsel reminded us at argument that if one of those Cats mauled or threatened a human being, the Cat might get into serious trouble and thus it is necessary to protect human beings from Big Cats in order to protect the Cats from human beings, which is the important thing under the Act. . . . The internal memorandum also justifies the eight-foot requirement as a means of protecting the animals from animal predators, though one might have supposed the Big Cats able to protect themselves against the native Indiana fauna.

Another issue that we need not resolve besides the issue of the statutory authority for the challenged rule is whether the Department might have cited Hoctor for having a perimeter fence that was *in fact*, considering the number and type of his animals, the topography of the compound, the design and structure of the protective enclosures and the containment fence, the proximity of highways or inhabited areas, and the design of the perimeter fence itself, too low to be safe, as distinct from merely being lower than eight feet. No regulation is targeted on the problem of containment other than 9 C.F.R. § 3.125, which seems to be concerned with the strength of enclosures rather than their height. But maybe there is some implicit statutory duty of containment that Hoctor might have been thought to have violated even if there were no rule requiring an eight-foot-high perimeter fence.

We need not decide. The only ground on which the Department defends sanctioning Hoctor for not having a high enough fence is that requiring an eight-foot-high perimeter fence for dangerous animals is an interpretation of the Department's own structural-strength regulation, and "provided an agency's interpretation of its own regulations does not violate the Constitution or a federal statute, it must be given 'controlling weight unless it is plainly erroneous or inconsistent with the regulation.'" [*Stinson v. United States*, 508 U.S. 36, 44-46 (1993)]. The "provided" clause does not announce a demanding standard of judicial review, although the absence of any reference in the housing regulation to fences or height must give us pause. The regulation appears only to require that pens and other animal housing be sturdy enough in design and construction, and suffi- ciently well maintained, to prevent the animals from breaking through the enclosure — not that any enclosure, whether a pen or a perimeter fence, be high enough to prevent the animals from escaping by jumping over the enclosure. The Department's counsel made the wonderful lawyer's argu- ment that the eight-foot rule is consistent with the regulation because a fence lower than eight feet has zero structural strength between its height (here six feet) and the eight-foot required minimum. The two feet by which Hoctor's fence fell short could not have contained a groundhog, let alone a liger, since it was empty space.

Our doubts about the scope of the regulation that the eight-foot rule is said to be "interpreting" might seem irrelevant, since even if a rule requiring an eight-foot perimeter fence could not be based on the regulation, it could be based on the statute itself, which in requiring the Department to establish minimum standards for the housing of animals presumably authorizes it to promulgate standards for secure containment. But if the eight-foot rule were deemed one of those minimum standards that the Department is required by statute to create, it could not possibly be thought an *interpretive* rule. For what would it be interpreting? When Congress authorizes an agency to create standards, it is delegating legislative authority, rather than itself setting forth a standard which the agency might then particularize through interpre- tation. Put differently, when a statute does not impose a duty on the persons subject to it but instead authorizes (or requires — it makes no difference) an agency to impose a duty, the formulation of that duty becomes a legislative task entrusted to the agency. Provided that a rule promulgated pursuant to such a delegation is intended to bind, and not merely to be a tentative state- ment of the agency's view, which would make it just a policy statement, and not a rule at all, the rule would be the clearest possible example of a legislative rule, as to which the notice and comment procedure not followed here is mandatory, as distinct from an interpretive rule; for there would be nothing to interpret. That is why the Department must argue that its eight-foot rule is an interpretation of the structural-strength regulation—itself a standard, and therefore interpretable, in order to avoid reversal.

Even if, despite the doubts that we expressed earlier, the eight-foot rule is consistent with, even in some sense authorized by, the structural-strength regulation, it would not necessarily follow that it is an interpretive rule. It is that only if it can be derived from the regulation by a process reasonably described as interpretation. Supposing that the regulation imposes a general duty of secure containment, the question is, then, Can a requirement that the duty be implemented by erecting an eight-foot-high perimeter fence be thought an interpretation of that general duty?

"Interpretation" in the narrow sense is the ascertainment of meaning. It is obvious that eight feet is not part of the meaning of secure containment. But "interpretation" is often used in a much broader sense. A process of "interpretation" has transformed the Constitution into a body of law undreamt of by the framers. To skeptics the *Miranda* rule is as remote from the text of the Fifth Amendment as the eight-foot rule is from the text of 9 C.F.R. § 3.125(a). But our task in this case is not to plumb the mysteries of legal theory; it is merely to give effect to a distinction that the Administrative Procedure Act makes, and we can do this by referring to the purpose of the distinction. The purpose is to separate the cases in which notice and comment rulemaking is required from the cases in which it is not required. As we noted at the outset, unless a statute or regulation is of crystalline transparency, the agency enforcing it cannot avoid interpreting it, and the agency would be stymied in its enforcement duties if every time it brought a case on a new theory it had to pause for a bout, possibly lasting several years, of notice and comment rulemaking. Besides being unavoidably continuous, statutory interpretation normally proceeds without the aid of elaborate factual inquiries. When it is an executive or administrative agency that is doing the interpreting it brings to the task a greater knowledge of the regulated activity than the judicial or legislative branches have, and this knowledge is to some extent a substitute for formal fact-gathering.

At the other extreme from what might be called normal or routine interpretation is the making of reasonable but arbitrary (not in the "arbitrary or capricious" sense) rules that are consistent with the statute or regulation under which the rules are promulgated but not derived from it, because they represent an arbitrary choice among methods of implementation. A rule that turns on a number is likely to be arbitrary in this sense. There is no way to reason to an eight-foot perimeter-fence rule as opposed to a seven-and-a-half foot fence or a nine-foot fence or a ten-foot fence. None of these candidates for a rule is uniquely appropriate to, and in that sense derivable from, the duty of secure containment. This point becomes even clearer if we note that the eight-foot rule actually has another component—the fence must be at least three feet from any animal's pen. Why three feet? Why not four? Or two?

The reason courts refuse to create statutes of limitations is precisely the difficulty of reasoning to a number by the methods of reasoning used by courts. One cannot extract from the concept of a tort that a tort suit should be barred unless brought within one, or two, or three, or five years. The choice is arbitrary and courts are uncomfortable with making arbitrary choices. They see this as a legislative function. Legislators have the democratic legitimacy to make choices among value judgments, choices based on hunch or guesswork or even the toss of a coin, and other arbitrary choices. When agencies base rules on arbitrary choices they are legislating, and so these rules are legislative or substantive and require notice and comment rulemaking, a procedure that is analogous to the procedure employed by legislatures in making statutes. The notice of proposed rulemaking corresponds to the bill and the reception of written comments to the hearing on the bill.

The common sense of requiring notice and comment rulemaking for legislative rules is well illustrated by the facts of this case. There is no process of cloistered, appellate-court type reasoning by which the Department of Agriculture could have excogitated the eight-foot rule from the structural-strength regulation. The rule is arbitrary in the sense that it could well be different without significant impairment of any regulatory purpose. But this does not make the rule a matter of indifference to the people subject to it. There are thousands of animal dealers, and some unknown fraction of these face the prospect of having to tear down their existing fences and build new, higher ones at great cost. The concerns of these dealers are legitimate and since, as we are stressing, the rule could well be otherwise, the agency was obliged to listen to them before settling on a final rule and to provide some justification for that rule, though not so tight or logical a justification as a court would be expected to offer for a new judge-made rule. Notice and comment is the procedure by which the persons affected by legislative rules are enabled to communicate their concerns in a comprehensive and systematic fashion to the legislating agency. The Department's lawyer speculated that if the notice and comment route had been followed in this case the Department would have received thousands of comments. The greater the public interest in a rule, the greater reason to allow the public to participate in its formation.

We are not saying that an interpretive rule can never have a numerical component. There is merely an empirical relation between interpretation and generality on the one hand, and legislation and specificity on the other. Especially in scientific and other technical areas, where quantitative criteria are common, a rule that translates a general norm into a number may be justifiable as interpretation. . . . Even in a nontechnical area the use of a number as a rule of thumb to guide the application of a general norm will often be legitimately interpretive. Had the Department of Agriculture said in the internal memorandum that it could not imagine a case in which a perimeter fence for dangerous animals that was lower than eight feet would provide secure containment, and would therefore presume, subject to rebuttal, that a lower fence was insecure, it would have been on stronger ground. For it would have been tying the rule to the animating standard, that of secure containment, rather than making it stand free of the standard, self-contained, unbending, arbitrary. To switch metaphors, the "flatter" a rule is, the harder it is to conceive of it as merely spelling out what is in some sense latent in a statute or regulation, and the eight-foot rule in its present form is as flat as they come. At argument the Department's lawyer tried to loosen up the rule, implying that the Department might have bent it if Hoctor proposed to dig a moat or to electrify his six-foot fence. But an agency's lawyer is not authorized to amend its rules in order to make them more palatable to the reviewing court.

The Department's position might seem further undermined by the fact that it has used the notice and comment procedure to promulgate rules prescribing perimeter fences for dogs and monkeys. 9 C.F.R. §§ 3.6(c)(2)(ii), 3.77(f). Why it proceeded differently for dangerous animals is unexplained. But we attach no weight to the Department's inconsistency, not only because it would be unwise to penalize the Department for having at least partially complied with the requirements of the Administrative Procedure Act, but also because there is nothing in the Act to forbid an agency to use the notice and comment procedure in cases in which it is not required to do so. We are mindful that the court in United States v. Picciotto, 875 F.2d 345, 348 (D.C. Cir. 1989), thought that the fact that an agency had used notice and comment rulemaking in a setting similar to the case before the court was evidence that the agency "intended" to promulgate a legislative rule in that case, only without bothering with notice and comment. The inference is strained, and in any event we think the agency's "intent," though a frequently cited factor, is rather a makeweight. What the agency intends is to promulgate a rule. It is for the courts to say whether it is the kind of rule that is valid only if promulgated after notice and comment. It is that kind of rule if, as in the present case, it cannot be derived by interpretation. The order under review, based as it was on a rule that is invalid because not promulgated in accordance with the required procedure, is therefore

Vacated.

QUESTION SET 5.1

Review & Synthesis

1. Now that you have read *Morton v. Ruiz* (from Chapter 4), *National Family Planning*, and *Hoctor*, describe the key differences between substantive rules (which require notice-and-comment rulemaking) and nonlegislative rules (which do not).

    How did the Bureau of Indian Affairs' defense of its "on reservation" requirement differ from the USDA's defense of its eight-foot-fence requirement in *Hoctor*? In formulating your answer, think about the source of authority on which the respective requirements depended for their legal force.

2. With respect to the D.C. Circuit's decision in *National Family Planning*:
   a. What was the court's test for differentiating substantive and interpretive rules? To what extent did the court rely on HHS's characterization of its rule as "interpretive"? How did HHS's prior interpretations of Title X's requirements factor into its analysis? How did the Supreme Court's prior decision in *Rust v. Sullivan* factor into the court's analysis?
   b. HHS's new interpretation permitted Title X grantees to engage in conduct that its prior interpretation prohibited. The court's conclusion that the new interpretation changed rather than clarified or echoed existing law therefore seems reasonable. But how much interpretive latitude does the court's standard permit? To some extent, all interpretations modify or supplement the rules on which they are based. Were that not the case, the rule itself would be sufficient to pronounce rights and obligations and its interpretation would be unnecessary. Since this is the case, did the court indicate how much modification or supplementation transforms an interpretive rule into a substantive rule?

3. With respect to the Seventh Circuit's decision in *Hoctor*:
   a. Describe the court's test for differentiating interpretive and legislative rules. How does it compare to the D.C. Circuit's test in *National Family Planning*? Did it consider similar or dissimilar factors? Did it give federal agencies more or less latitude to use the interpretive rule exemption?
   b. Why, exactly, was the USDA's fence height requirement in *Hoctor* not an interpretive rule exempted from notice-and-comment rulemaking? If the purpose of the USDA's structural strength regulation was to facilitate animal safety by ensuring their containment, and if animals can easily jump over fences below a certain height and thus thwart attempts at containment, wouldn't the height of the fence be directly relevant to the underlying purpose of the structural strength regulation? Why did Judge Posner observe that the USDA "would have been on stronger ground" had it tied "the rule to the animating standard"? Did the USDA err because the fence height requirement could not be persuasively derived from the structural strength regulation, or did it err by never *attempting* to derive it from the regulation?
   c. In what sense are numerical requirements "arbitrary" according to Judge Posner? Are they arbitrary because the USDA randomly chose the fence height requirement in the absence of any reasoned basis? Because the fence height requirement could not be inferred from any preexisting rules, and so was not based on policy choices previously made by Congress or by the USDA itself? Some other reason?

4. Lower courts over time have developed a few approaches to distinguishing interpretive rules from substantive rules. The first is called the "legal effect test." While formulations of it vary, in essence it tests whether an agency's rule creates new law (i.e., legal rights or obligations). "Rules

have been found to make 'new law,' and thus to be legislative, where they fill a statutory gap by imposing a standard of conduct, create an exemption from a general standard of conduct, establish a new regulatory structure, or otherwise complete an incomplete statutory design." *See* JEFFREY S. LUBBERS, A GUIDE TO FEDERAL AGENCY RULEMAKING 68 (5th ed. 2012) (citing Michael Asimow, *Nonlegislative Rulemaking and Regulatory Reform*, 1985 DUKE L.J. 381, 394 (1985)). Although the Supreme Court has done little to explain the difference between substantive and interpretive rules, it has applied the legal effect test (albeit without labelling it as such). *See, e.g., Shalala v. Guernsey Memorial Hospital*, 514 U.S. 87, 100 (1995) (observing, in dicta, that "APA rulemaking would still be required" had the HHS interpretive rule "adopted a new position inconsistent with any of the Secretary's existing rules"). An alternative test focuses on whether the interpretive rule has a "substantial" practical impact on the regulated public. "If the pronouncement in fact creates new rights or duties and is binding as a practical matter on those affected, then reviewing courts may well require compliance with notice-and-comment procedures." *Id.* at 72. Do either of these approaches fit the D.C. Circuit's analysis in *National Family Planning*? With the Seventh Circuit's approach in *Hoctor*?

Application & Analysis

1. The Internal Revenue Service ("IRS") was created to collect taxes and administer the Internal Revenue Code ("IRC"). The Secretary of the Treasury ("Secretary") is responsible for implementing the tax policy of the IRS. Under the Act of Congress establishing the Department of the Treasury (the "Act") the Secretary regulates the practice of representatives of persons before the Department of the Treasury (the "Department"). 31 U.S.C. § 330 *et seq.* The Act states that the Secretary may, "before admitting a representative to practice, require that the representative demonstrate" a series of characteristics such as: good character, good reputation, necessary qualifications to enable the representative to provide to persons valuable service, and competency to advise and assist persons in presenting their cases." § 330(a). Pursuant to that authority, the Secretary established a new program called the "Revenue Procedure in Protection of Consumers" ("Procedure"). The Procedure is designed to protect taxpayers who employ professionals to represent them before the IRS. The Program, prospectively, requires all tax preparers that have obtained a preparer tax identification number to heighten their level of competency and preparation by taking an annual "refresher course" and completing "a minimum of ten hours of continuing education." The Program also assures that all tax preparers who comply with the Program will be part of the online directory of professionals on the IRS website. The IRS

established the Program without complying with the APA's notice-and-comment requirements.

The National Association of Accountants ("NAA") challenged the procedure in federal district court, arguing that it was a substantive rule and thus not exempt from § 553's requirements. The IRS countered that the program was established by interpretive rule.

Assess the merits of the parties' arguments.

2. Medicaid is a cooperative federal-state health insurance program that enables states to provide medical assistance to eligible individuals "whose income and resources are insufficient to meet the costs of necessary medical services." 42 U.S.C. § 1396-1. It is funded by both the federal and state governments, but is operated by the states. Once a participating state establishes a state plan in compliance with the Medicaid Act (the "Act"), the federal government reimburses the state for certain patient care costs. *See* §§ 1396(a)-(b). The state, in turn, reimburses the hospitals that provided direct care. Unfortunately, these reimbursements do not always cover hospitals' full costs of treating Medicaid patients. To address this problem, Congress amended the Act in 1981 to provide payment adjustments to hospitals serving a disproportionate number of these patients ("DSHs"). It later learned, however, that some DSHs were receiving payment adjustments exceeding the total costs of care they provided. In 2003, Congress responded by capping the payment adjustment to the "costs incurred" in treating Medicaid-eligible individuals, minus Medicaid payments received (the "Cap"). 42 U.S.C. § 1396r-4(g)(1)(A). As required by the Medicaid Act, the Department of Health and Human Services ("HHS") then used APA notice-and-comment rulemaking to promulgate a rule requiring states to report their Caps on an annual basis.

Critically, neither the Medicaid Act nor the Cap regulation addresses whether "costs incurred" refers to the total costs of caring for patients or the net costs (i.e., the total costs *minus* reimbursements and payments from Medicare and private insurance). After receiving a number of questions regarding this aspect of the Cap calculation, HHS posted its answer in a "Frequently Asked Questions" document posted to www.medicaid.gov. It stated that the term "costs incurred" required a net costs calculation that deducts both Medicare and private insurance payments. It provided little in the way of explanation, simply stating that this interpretation "best effected Congress' objective of reducing DSH overpayments." The practical effect of this interpretation is a reduction of the Cap, which, in turn, reduces payment adjustments provided to DSHs through their states. HHS did not produce this interpretation through notice-and-comment rulemaking.

Several Maine hospitals and the Maine Hospital Association ("plaintiffs") challenged HHS's interpretation of "costs incurred" in federal district court. They argued that the interpretation has no legal force because

HHS was required to adopt it through APA notice-and-comment rulemaking. HHS countered that it was merely interpreting the term "costs incurred" as used in the Medicaid Act and its Cap regulation. HHS conceded, however, that both the statute and the regulation are silent on whether the Cap must be calculated on a total or net basis. The district ruled for the plaintiffs. HHS has filed an appeal with the United States Court of Appeals for the First Circuit.

You are a clerk for one of the First Circuit judges who will hear HHS's appeal. She has asked you to write a brief memorandum analyzing whether the Cap regulation is an interpretive rule.

2. Agency Reinterpretation of Interpretive Rules

As discussed above, agencies may bypass most of the APA's rulemaking requirements when they interpret rather than create or amend policies affecting individuals' legal rights and obligations. But does the APA allow them to use the same procedural shortcut when they *reinterpret or modify* a prior interpretive rule? For years the D.C. Circuit answered "no" under a doctrine derived from its decision in *Paralyzed Veterans of America v. D.C. Arena L.P.,* 117 F.3d 579 (D.C. Cir. 1997). In dictum, the D.C. Circuit asserted that "[o]nce an agency gives its regulation an interpretation, it can only change that interpretation as it would formally modify the regulation itself: through the process of notice and comment rulemaking." *Id.* at 586.

It extended this proposition to the interpretive rule context in *Alaska Professional Hunters Association, Inc. v. Federal Aviation Administration,* 177 F.3d 1030 (D.C. Cir. 1999). For decades, the Federal Aviation Administration ("FAA") maintained that guides flying clients to hunting and fishing expeditions were exempt from its commercial air operations rules as long as they did not charge separately for air travel. The agency pronounced that if "an agency has given its regulation a definitive interpretation, and later significantly revises that interpretation, the agency has in effect amended its rule, something it may not accomplish" under the APA "without notice and comment." *Id.* at 1034. The FAA then changed course, issuing a "notice" that it had changed its interpretation of the regulation. Alaska guides who would be affected by the change challenged it, arguing that the change constituted a substantive rule that had to be promulgated through notice-and-comment rulemaking. The D.C. Circuit agreed. Quoting *Paralyzed Veterans,* it stated that "[o]nce an agency gives its regulation an interpretation, it can only change that interpretation as it would formally modify the regulation itself: through the process of notice and comment rulemaking." *Id.* at 1033-34. The *Paralyzed Veterans* doctrine was adopted by several other circuits. As critics pointed out, however, it seemed to abandon the traditional view "an agency is free to change an interpretation that is not itself incorporated into a legislative rule." Mark Seidenfeld, *Rulemaking Chapter*, Developments in Administrative Law and Regulatory Practice 1998-1999, at 112 (Jeffrey S. Lubbers ed., 2000).

The Supreme Court assessed the validity of the *Paralyzed Veterans* doctrine in the case that follows.

Perez v. Mortgage Bankers Association
575 U.S. 92 (2015)

Justice Sotomayor delivered the opinion of the Court.

When a federal administrative agency first issues a rule interpreting one of its regulations, it is generally not required to follow the notice-and-comment rulemaking procedures of the Administrative Procedure Act (APA or Act). *See* 5 U.S.C. § 553(b)(A). The United States Court of Appeals for the District of Columbia Circuit has nevertheless held, in a line of cases beginning with *Paralyzed Veterans of Am. v. D.C. Arena L.P.*, 117 F.3d 579 ([D.C. Cir.] 1997), that an agency must use the APA's notice-and-comment procedures when it wishes to issue a new interpretation of a regulation that deviates significantly from one the agency has previously adopted. The question in these cases is whether the rule announced in *Paralyzed Veterans* is consistent with the APA. We hold that it is not.

I

A

The APA establishes the procedures federal administrative agencies use for "rule making," defined as the process of "formulating, amending, or repealing a rule." § 551(5). "Rule," in turn, is defined broadly to include "statement[s] of general or particular applicability and future effect" that are designed to "implement, interpret, or prescribe law or policy." § 551(4).

Section 4 of the APA, 5 U.S.C. § 553, prescribes a three-step procedure for so-called "notice-and-comment rulemaking." First, the agency must issue a "[g]eneral notice of proposed rule making," ordinarily by publication in the Federal Register. § 553(b). Second, if "notice [is] required," the agency must "give interested persons an opportunity to participate in the rule making through submission of written data, views, or arguments." § 553(c). An agency must consider and respond to significant comments received during the period for public comment. *See Citizens to Preserve Overton Park, Inc. v. Volpe*, 401 U.S. 402, 416 (1971). . . . Third, when the agency promulgates the final rule, it must include in the rule's text "a concise general statement of [its] basis and purpose." § 553(c). Rules issued through the notice-and-comment process are often referred to as "legislative rules" because they have the "force and effect of law." *Chrysler Corp. v. Brown*, 441 U.S. 281, 302-303 (1979) (internal quotation marks omitted).

Not all "rules" must be issued through the notice-and-comment process. Section 4(b)(A) of the APA provides that, unless another statute states otherwise, the notice-and-comment requirement "does not apply" to "interpretative rules, general statements of policy, or rules of agency organization, procedure, or practice." 5 U.S.C. § 553(b)(A). The term "interpretative rule," or "interpretive rule," is not further defined by the APA, and its precise meaning is the source of much scholarly and judicial debate. For our purposes, it suffices to say that the critical feature of interpretive rules is that they are "issued by an agency to advise the public of the agency's construction of the statutes and rules which it administers." *Shalala v. Guernsey Memorial Hospital*, 514 U.S. 87, 99 (1995) (internal quotation marks omitted). The absence of a notice-and-comment obligation makes the process of issuing interpretive rules comparatively easier for agencies than issuing legislative rules. But that convenience comes at a price: Interpretive rules "do not have the force and effect of law and are not accorded that weight in the adjudicatory process." *Ibid.*

B

These cases began as a dispute over efforts by the Department of Labor to determine whether mortgage-loan officers are covered by the Fair Labor Standards Act of 1938 (FLSA), 52 Stat. 1060, as amended, 29 U.S.C. § 201 *et seq.* The FLSA "establishe[s] a minimum wage and overtime compensation for each hour worked in excess of 40 hours in each workweek" for many employees. . . . Certain classes of employees, however, are exempt from these provisions. Among these exempt individuals are those "employed in a bona fide executive, administrative, or professional capacity . . . or in the capacity of outside salesman. . . ." § 213(a)(1). The exemption for such employees is known as the "administrative" exemption.

The FLSA grants the Secretary of Labor authority to "defin[e]" and "delimi[t]" the categories of exempt administrative employees. *Ibid.* The Secretary's current regulations regarding the administrative exemption were promulgated in 2004 through a notice-and-comment rulemaking. As relevant here, the 2004 regulations differed from the previous regulations in that they contained a new section providing several examples of exempt administrative employees. *See* 29 C.F.R. § 541.203. One of the examples is "[e]mployees in the financial services industry," who, depending on the nature of their day-to-day work, "generally meet the duties requirements for the administrative exception." § 541.203(b). The financial services example ends with a caveat, noting that "an employee whose primary duty is selling financial products does not qualify for the administrative exemption." *Ibid.*

In 1999 and again in 2001, the Department's Wage and Hour Division issued letters opining that mortgage-loan officers do not qualify for the administrative exemption. *See* Opinion Letter, Loan Officers/Exempt Status, 6A LRR, WAGES AND HOURS MANUAL 99:8351 (Feb. 16, 2001); Opinion Letter, Mortgage Loan Officers/Exempt Status, *id.* at 99:8249 (May 17, 1999). In other words, the Department concluded that the FLSA's minimum wage and maximum hour requirements applied to mortgage-loan officers. When the Department promulgated its current FLSA regulations in 2004, respondent Mortgage Bankers Association (MBA), a national trade association representing real estate finance companies, requested a new opinion interpreting the revised regulations. In 2006, the Department issued an opinion letter finding that mortgage-loan officers fell within the administrative exemption under the 2004 regulations. Four years later, however, the Wage and Hour Division again altered its interpretation of the FLSA's administrative exemption as it applied to mortgage-loan officers. Reviewing the provisions of the 2004 regulations and judicial decisions addressing the administrative exemption, the Department's 2010 Administrator's Interpretation concluded that mortgage-loan officers "have a primary duty of making sales for their employers, and, therefore, do not qualify" for the administrative exemption. The Department accordingly withdrew its 2006 opinion letter, which it now viewed as relying on "misleading assumption[s] and selective and narrow analysis" of the exemption example in § 541.203(b). Like the 1999, 2001, and 2006 opinion letters, the 2010 Administrator's Interpretation was issued without notice or an opportunity for comment.

C

MBA filed a complaint in Federal District Court . . . [arguing] that the Administrator's Interpretation was procedurally invalid in light of the D.C. Circuit's decision in *Paralyzed Veterans*, 117 F.3d 579. Under the *Paralyzed Veterans* doctrine, if "an agency has given its regulation a definitive interpretation, and later significantly revises that interpretation, the agency has in effect amended its rule, something it may not accomplish" under the APA "without notice and comment." *Alaska Professional Hunters Assn, Inc. v. FAA*, 177 F.3d 1030, 1034 (D.C. Cir. 1999).

The District Court granted summary judgment to the Department. *Mortgage Bankers Assn. v. Solis*, 864 F. Supp.2d 193 (D.D.C. 2012). Though it accepted the parties' characterization of the Administrator's Interpretation as an interpretive rule the District Court determined that the *Paralyzed Veterans* doctrine was inapplicable because MBA had failed to establish its reliance on the contrary interpretation expressed in the Department's 2006 opinion letter. The Administrator's Interpretation, the District Court further determined, was fully supported by the text of the 2004 FLSA regulations. The court accordingly held that the 2010 interpretation was not arbitrary or capricious.

The D.C. Circuit reversed. Bound to the rule of *Paralyzed Veterans* by precedent, the Court of Appeals rejected the Government's call to abandon the doctrine. In the court's view, "[t]he only question" properly before it was whether the District Court had erred in requiring MBA to prove that it relied on the Department's prior interpretation. Explaining that reliance was not a required element of the *Paralyzed Veterans* doctrine, and noting the Department's concession that a prior, conflicting interpretation of the 2004 regulations existed, the D.C. Circuit concluded that the 2010 Administrator's Interpretation had to be vacated.

We granted certiorari and now reverse.

II

The *Paralyzed Veterans* doctrine is contrary to the clear text of the APA's rulemaking provisions, and it improperly imposes on agencies an obligation beyond the "maximum procedural requirements" specified in the APA, *Vermont Yankee Nuclear Power Corp. v. Natural Resources Defense Council, Inc.*, 435 U.S. 519, 524 (1978).

A

The text of the APA answers the question presented. Section 4 of the APA provides that "notice of proposed rule making shall be published in the Federal Register." 5 U.S.C. § 553(b). When such notice is required by the APA, "the agency shall give interested persons an opportunity to participate in the rule making." § 553(c). But § 4 further states that unless "notice or hearing is required by statute," the Act's notice-and-comment requirement "does not apply . . . to interpretative rules." § 553(b)(A). This exemption of interpretive rules from the notice-and-comment process is categorical, and it is fatal to the rule announced in *Paralyzed Veterans*.

Rather than examining the exemption for interpretive rules contained in § 4(b)(A) of the APA, the D.C. Circuit in *Paralyzed Veterans* focused its attention on § 1 of the Act. That section defines "rule making" to include not only the initial issuance of new rules, but also "repeal[s]" or "amend[ments]" of existing rules. *See* § 551(5). Because notice-and-comment requirements may apply even to these later agency actions, the court reasoned, "allow[ing] an agency to make a fundamental change in its interpretation of a substantive regulation without notice and comment" would undermine the APA's procedural framework. 117 F.3d, at 586.

This reading of the APA conflates the differing purposes of §§ 1 and 4 of the Act. Section 1 defines what a rulemaking is. It does not, however, say what procedures an agency must use when it engages in rulemaking. That is the purpose of § 4. And § 4 specifically exempts interpretive rules from the notice-and-comment requirements that apply to legislative rules. So, the D.C. Circuit correctly read § 1 of the APA to mandate that agencies use the same procedures when they amend or repeal a rule as they used to issue the rule in the first instance. *See F.C.C. v. Fox Television Stations, Inc.*, 556 U.S. 502, 515 (2009) (the APA "make[s] no distinction . . . between initial agency action and subsequent agency action undoing or revising that action"). Where the court went wrong was in failing to apply that accurate understanding of § 1 to the exemption for interpretive rules contained in § 4: Because an agency is not required to use notice-and-comment procedures to issue an initial interpretive rule, it is also not required to use those procedures when it amends or repeals that interpretive rule.

B

The straightforward reading of the APA we now adopt harmonizes with longstanding principles of our administrative law jurisprudence. Time and again, we have reiterated that the APA "sets forth the full extent of judicial authority to review executive agency action for procedural correctness." *Fox Television Stations, Inc.*, 556 U.S., at 513. Beyond the APA's minimum requirements, courts lack authority "to impose upon [an] agency its own notion of which procedures are "best" or most likely to further some vague, undefined public good." *Vermont Yankee*, 435 U.S., at 549. To do otherwise would violate "the very basic tenet of administrative law that agencies should be free to fashion their own rules of procedure." *Id.* at 544.

These foundational principles apply with equal force to the APA's procedures for rulemaking. We explained in *Vermont Yankee* that § 4 of the Act "established the maximum procedural requirements which Congress was willing to have the courts impose upon agencies in conducting rulemaking procedures." *Id.* at 524. "Agencies are free to grant additional procedural rights in the exercise of their discretion, but reviewing courts are generally not free to impose them if the agencies have not chosen to grant them." *Ibid.*

The *Paralyzed Veterans* doctrine creates just such a judge-made procedural right: the right to notice and an opportunity to comment when an agency changes its interpretation of one of the regulations it enforces. That requirement may be wise policy. Or it may not. Regardless, imposing such an obligation is the responsibility of Congress or the administrative agencies, not the courts. We trust that Congress weighed the costs and benefits of placing more rigorous procedural restrictions on the issuance of interpretive rules. *See id.* at 523

> **Cross-Reference**
>
> The "arbitrary and capricious" standard of judicial review, codified in APA § 706(2)(A), is discussed in Chapter 9. The *Vermont Yankee* case and the courts' power to impose procedures on agencies apart from those required by statute or by the agencies themselves (so-called "judicial hybrids") are discussed in subsection E of this chapter.

(when Congress enacted the APA, it "settled long-continued and hard-fought contentions, and enact[ed] a formula upon which opposing social and political forces have come to rest" (internal quotation marks omitted)). In the end, Congress decided to adopt standards that permit agencies to promulgate freely such rules—whether or not they are consistent with earlier interpretations. That the D.C. Circuit would have struck the balance differently does not permit that court or this one to overturn Congress' contrary judgment.

III

MBA offers several reasons why the *Paralyzed Veterans* doctrine should be upheld. They are not persuasive. . . .

B

In the main, MBA attempts to justify the *Paralyzed Veterans* doctrine on practical and policy grounds. MBA contends that the doctrine reinforces the APA's goal of "procedural fairness" by preventing agencies from unilaterally and unexpectedly altering their interpretation of important regulations.

There may be times when an agency's decision to issue an interpretive rule, rather than a legislative rule, is driven primarily by a desire to skirt notice-and-comment provisions. But regulated entities are not without recourse in such situations. Quite the opposite. The APA contains a variety of constraints on agency decisionmaking—the arbitrary and capricious standard being among the most notable. As we held in *Fox Television Stations*, and underscore again today, the APA requires an agency to provide more substantial justification when "its new policy rests upon factual findings that contradict those which underlay its prior policy; or when its prior policy has engendered serious reliance interests that must be taken into account. It would be arbitrary and capricious to ignore such matters." 556 U.S., at 515 (citation omitted).

In addition, Congress is aware that agencies sometimes alter their views in ways that upset settled reliance interests. For that reason, Congress sometimes includes in the statutes it drafts safe-harbor provisions that shelter regulated entities from liability when they act in conformance with previous agency interpretations. The FLSA includes one such provision: As amended by the Portal-to-Portal Act of 1947, 29 U.S.C. § 251 *et seq.*, the FLSA provides that "no employer shall be subject to any liability" for failing "to pay minimum wages or overtime compensation" if it demonstrates that the "act or omission complained of was in good faith in conformity with and in reliance on any written administrative regulation, order, ruling, approval, or interpretation" of the Administrator of the Department's Wage and Hour Division, even when the guidance is later "modified or rescinded." §§ 259(a), (b)(1). These safe harbors will often protect parties from liability when an agency adopts an interpretation that conflicts with its previous position. . . .

For the foregoing reasons, the judgment of the United States Court of Appeals for the District of Columbia Circuit is reversed.

It is so ordered.

[The opinion of Justice A<small>LITO</small>, concurring in part and concurring in the judgment, is omitted.]

Justice S<small>CALIA</small>, concurring in the judgment. . . .

The APA exempts interpretive rules from [the Act's informal rulemaking requirements]. § 553(b)(A). But this concession to agencies was meant to be more modest in its effects than it is today. For despite exempting interpretive rules from notice and comment, the Act provides that "the *reviewing court* shall . . . interpret constitutional and statutory provisions, and determine the meaning or applicability of the terms of an agency action." § 706 (emphasis added). The Act thus contemplates that courts, not agencies, will authoritatively resolve ambiguities in statutes and regulations. In such a regime, the exemption for interpretive rules does not add much to agency power. An agency may use interpretive rules to advise the public by explaining its interpretation of the law. But an agency may not use interpretive rules to bind the public by making law, because it remains the responsibility of the court to decide whether the law means what the agency says it means. . . .

By supplementing the APA with judge-made doctrines of [judicial deference to agencies' interpretations of their regulations and the statutes on which they are based], we have revolutionized the import of interpretive rules' exemption from notice-and-comment rulemaking. Agencies may now use these rules not just to advise the public, but also to bind them. After all, if an interpretive rule gets deference, the people are bound to obey it on pain of sanction, no less surely than they are bound to obey substantive rules, which are accorded similar deference. Interpretive rules that command deference *do* have the force of law. . . .

[The opinion of Justice T<small>HOMAS</small>, concurring in the judgment, is omitted.]

QUESTION SET 5.2

Review & Synthesis

1. Even if the Court correctly analyzed APA §§ 1 (5 U.S.C. § 551) and 4 (5 U.S.C. § 553), did it ignore the reality that interpretive rules are often treated—both by the regulated public and by the agencies themselves—like substantive rules? Is it not the case that agencies issue interpretive rules to inform the public about the content of federal law, and is it not also the case that the public in turn relies on the information it issues?

2. In Section III.B. of its opinion, the Court implied that judicial review under the "arbitrary or capricious" standard (discussed in Chapter 9) will prevent agencies from abusing § 553(b)(A). In essence, the Court asserted that the APA permits *ex post* judicial review of interpretive rules, but not *ex ante* public review of those rules through notice-and-comment rulemaking. Given the different procedural protections these mechanisms afford, do you think this shift adequately protects the legal interests of the regulated public?

3. Does *Perez* incentivize agencies to promulgate ambiguous regulations? Such regulations are susceptible to more than one reasonable interpretation; they are consistent with any of several subsequent constructions of them. Can't agencies after *Perez* continually change their regulatory policies without notice-and-comment rulemaking by repeatedly "reinterpreting" their ambiguous regulations? Justice Scalia raised a different but related point in his concurrence. Under the *Chevron* doctrine (discussed at length in Chapter 9), courts must defer to agencies' reasonable interpretations of the ambiguous statutes they administer. That being the case, how availing is judicial review as a check on agency abuse of § 553(b)(A)?

Application & Analysis

1. Among many other responsibilities, the Social Security Administration ("SSA") issues social security numbers ("SSNs") to track the earnings of persons working in the United States. All U.S. citizens, as well as noncitizens authorized to work in the United States, are entitled to an SSN. *See* 42 U.S.C. § 405(c)(2)(B)(i) (2018). By regulation promulgated under APA § 553, the SSA extended the class of noncitizens eligible for SSNs to those "legally in the United States but not under authority of law permitting him or her to engage in employment, but only for a valid nonwork purpose." 20 C.F.R. § 422.104(a)(3) (2019). Twenty years ago, the SSA released an interpretative rule labeled "Valid Nonwork Clarification" (the "Clarification Rule"), which listed obtaining a state driver's license as a "valid nonwork reason" for the SSA to issue an SSN. The SSA continued to list obtaining a driver's license as a valid nonwork reason in subsequent versions of the Clarification Rule.

   Last year, the SSA promulgated another version of the Clarification Rule. This version listed obtaining a state driver's license as an "invalid nonwork purpose." The SSA stated publicly that the purpose in making this change was the prevention of fraud. It explained that imposing tighter requirements on the issuance of nonwork SSNs would reduce the number of fraudulent wage reports associated with those numbers. The SSA characterized the change as a reinterpretation of its Clarification Rule.

   Illinois requires all driver's license applicants, including noncitizens, to present valid SSNs. Two noncitizen Illinois residents ("plaintiffs") are not permitted to work due to their visa statuses, but would like to apply for driver's licenses. They challenged the Clarification Rule in the Federal District Court for Northern District of Illinois. They argued that the SSA's most recent Clarification Rule contradicts its previous versions, which would have allowed them to obtain SSNs. Accordingly, they argue that the SSA was required to promulgate the most recent Clarification Rule under the APA's notice-and-comment rulemaking procedures. The SSA has moved to dismiss the suit alleging, among other things, that the Clarification Rule was interpretative and thus exempt from the APA's notice-and-comment requirements.

You work as a summer clerk for the Northern District judge to whom the case has been assigned. She has asked you to draft a brief memorandum analyzing the plaintiffs' APA § 553(b)(A) claim.

3. Rules of Agency Organization, Procedure, or Practice

As with general statements of policy and interpretive rules, the Administrative Procedure Act relieves agencies of the burden of notice-and-comment rulemaking (though not the APA's publication or petition requirements) when they adopt "rules of agency organization, procedure, and practice." 5 U.S.C. § 553(b)(A). In essence, such rules are intended to be entirely procedural, in the sense that they establish the manner by which an agency will decide the substantive questions before it. The issue that most frequently arises when agencies seek this rulemaking exemption is a familiar one; the distinction between substantive and procedural rules. While many courts and scholars have long ago rejected the very idea that such a distinction could be drawn in any consistent or sensible way (we will see such arguments made in later chapters), the APA still insists that courts (and the lawyers appearing before them) make the attempt when this 553(b)(A) exemption is at issue.

Public Citizen v. Department of State
276 F.3d 634 (D.C. Cir. 2002)

Before: EDWARDS and TATEL, Circuit Judges, and SILBERMAN, Senior Circuit Judge.

TATEL, Circuit Judge:
When the State Department responds to Freedom of Information Act [("FOIA")] requests, it generally declines to search for documents produced after the date of the requester's letter. Challenging

> **Cross-Reference**
>
> The Freedom of Information Act is considered more fully in Chapter 10.

this "date-of-request cut-off" policy, appellant claims that the Department promulgated it without notice and opportunity to comment as required by the Administrative Procedure Act. . . . We reject [this] claim because the policy falls within the APA's exemption for "rules of agency organization, procedure or practice." . . .

I.

The State Department processes FOIA requests in four stages. During the first stage, it mails a letter to the requester acknowledging receipt and assigning an identification number. This initial letter also informs the requester that the "cut-off date . . . is the date of the requester's letter" and that "no documents . . . originat[ing] after the date of [the] letter will be retrieved." During the second stage, the Department's Statutory Compliance & Research Division determines "which offices, overseas posts, or other records systems within the Department may reasonably be expected to contain the information requested." The Department then "task[s]" these various components to search for responsive documents. The speed at which the tasked component completes a search depends largely on available personnel, the nature of the request and the number of outstanding requests. "By far" the most frequently tasked component is the Department's Central Foreign Policy File, a centralized automated records system containing the "most comprehensive authoritative compilation of documents," including documents "that establish, discuss or define foreign policy," as well as "official record copies of incoming and outgoing Department communications." Consequently, the Central File has the "longest queue" of any Department component. During the third phase of FOIA request processing, the Department reviews the retrieved documents to determine whether it should withhold any, or portions thereof, pursuant to one of FOIA's nine exemptions. During the final phase, the Department copies the documents, redacts classified material and releases them to the requester.

In April 1998, appellant Public Citizen, a non-profit, public interest organization "dedicated to the study and promotion of public health and . . . consumer welfare," sent a FOIA request to the Department asking for records describing its "current system for managing word processing files . . . and electronic mail messages," as well as "disposition schedule[s] submitted to the National Archives concerning the transfer or disposal" of these materials. Three months later, the Department released seven documents in full, as well as an eighth with portions redacted pursuant to FOIA's first exemption, the national security exemption, 5 U.S.C. § 552(b)(1). This final document was a thirty-five chapter "records disposition schedule," essentially a document index with each entry containing a brief description of a Department record and designating the record as "permanent" or "temporary." Although the Department initially withheld all 119 entries pertaining to the Bureau of Intelligence and Research, it eventually released all but portions of seventeen entries. . . . Significantly for this case, the letter accompanying the released documents stated that although the Department typically declines to retrieve documents produced after the date of the FOIA request, the Department had waived this "date-of-request cut-off" policy as a courtesy to Public Citizen.

Meanwhile, in response to the initial withholding, Public Citizen had filed suit in the United States District Court for the District of Columbia claiming that the Department promulgated the cut-off policy without the notice and comment required by the Administrative Procedure Act, 5 U.S.C. § 553(b). . . .

Before anything significant occurred in the district court, Public Citizen submitted [an] additional FOIA request[]. [M]ade in June, [it] sought documents relating to "international investment issues," including discussions or negotiations of the Multilateral Agreement on Investment. The Department acknowledged this request with its standard letter, which included a paragraph informing Public Citizen that it would apply its usual date-of-request cut-off policy. . . . Amending its complaint in the district court, Public Citizen challenged the application of the cut-off policy to the June request. . . .

In May 2000, the district court dismissed Public Citizen's challenge to the cut-off policy as applied to the April FOIA request because the Department had in fact not applied it. The court dismissed as unripe Public Citizen's challenge to the cut-off policy generally, finding it insufficiently "crystallized," as well as Public Citizen's challenge to the cut-off policy as applied to the June FOIA request, reasoning it was "not possible . . . to know" whether the cut-off policy would be applied to that request. Finding the policy a "rule[] of agency organization . . . or practice" exempt from notice and comment, the district court also granted summary judgment for the Department on Public Citizen's APA claim. . . .

II

We begin with Public Citizen's claim that the Department unlawfully promulgated the cut-off policy without the notice and opportunity to comment required by the APA. The Department responds that its cut-off policy is procedural and thus covered by the APA's exemption from notice and comment for "rules of agency organization, procedure, or practice," 5 U.S.C. § 553(b)(3)(A). According to Public Citizen, the cut-off policy cannot be considered procedural because it "substantially . . . affects rights" by "needlessly multipl[ying] the number of FOIA requests that must be submitted to obtain access to records." We have, however, characterized agency rules as procedural even where their effects were far harsher than the Department's date-of-request cut-off policy. For example, in *Ranger v. FCC*, we found an agency rule establishing a cut-off date for the filing of radio license applications to be procedural even though the failure to observe the rule cost appellants a radio broadcast license. 294 F.2d 240, 243-44 (D.C. Cir. 1961).

As we recognized in *American Hospital Ass'n v. Bowen*, "[o]ver time, our circuit in applying the § 553 exemption for procedural rules has gradually shifted focus from asking whether a given procedure has a 'substantial impact' on parties to . . . inquiring more broadly whether the agency action . . . encodes a substantive value judgment." 834 F.2d 1037, 1047 (D.C. Cir. 1987) (citation omitted). This "gradual move," we noted, "reflects a candid recognition that even unambiguously procedural measures affect parties to some degree." *Id.* More recently, in *JEM Broadcasting Co. v. FCC*, we found that FCC "hard look rules," which required the dismissal of flawed license applications without leave to amend, were procedural despite their sometimes harsh effects. 22 F.3d 320, 327-28 (D.C. Cir. 1994). In doing so, we rejected the argument that the rules encoded substantive value judgments because they valued applications without errors over those with minor errors. *Id.* Clarifying the *American Hospital* standard, we held that in referring to "value judgments" in that case, we had not intended to include "judgment[s] about what mechanics and processes are most efficient" because to do so would "threaten[] to swallow the procedural exception to notice and comment, for agency housekeeping rules often embody [such] judgment[s]." *Id.* at 328.

Because the Department's cut-off policy applies to all FOIA requests, making no distinction between requests on the basis of subject matter, it clearly encodes no "substantive value judgment," *Am. Hosp.*, 834 F.2d at 1047. To be sure, the policy does represent a "judgment" that a date-of-request cut-off promotes the efficient processing of FOIA requests, but a "judgment about procedural efficiency . . . cannot convert a procedural rule into a substantive one." *James V. Hurson Assocs., Inc. v. Glickman*, 229 F.3d 277, 282 (D.C. Cir. 2000) (internal quotation marks and citation omitted). Consequently, we agree with the district court that the Department's cut-off policy represents a prototypical procedural rule properly promulgated without notice and comment.

[In Section III of its opinion, the court rejected the State Department's argument that Public Citizen's claims are not ripe for adjudication. In Section IV, the court also rejected the State Department's attempted invocation of FIOA's national security exemption, under which agencies may withhold requested materials by demonstrating that they are classified. Section V of the opinion summarized the court's conclusions.]

So ordered.

QUESTION SET 5.3

Review & Synthesis

1. The D.C. Circuit acknowledged, albeit briefly, that procedural rules can have harsh substantive effects on individual rights. What test did it ultimately adopt for distinguishing substance from procedure, and how did that test differ from its previous methods for doing so?

2. Was the State Department's cut-off policy really procedural rather than substantive? One scholar expressed skepticism that it was the former: "[I]t is not so clear that this was a procedural rule; it directly affected what records had to be provided in response to a FOIA request. It was thus as 'substantive' as a regulation going to the scope of any of the FOIA exemptions, or a rule about whether old records have to be retrieved from an off-site location." Michael Herz, *Rulemaking Chapter*, DEVELOPMENTS IN ADMINISTRATIVE LAW AND REGULATORY PRACTICE 2001-2002, at 153 (Jeffrey S. Lubbers ed., 2003). Is that not the case with all procedural rules that result in denials of substantive claims and entitlements? Is the argument here one of degrees? For instance, a procedural rule can foreclose an argument or assertion, which then leads to a substantive denial. Did the State Department's cut-off policy operate differently here?

3. Even procedural rules, as the court acknowledges, reflect the values of those who adopt them. For example, a procedure can prioritize speed and efficiency in decision-making, while others eschew such considerations for an emphasis on decisional accuracy. Still others reflect the notion that procedures should demonstrate a government's respect for innate individual dignity or membership in a political community. *See generally* Lawrence B. Solum, *Procedural Justice*, 78 S. CAL. L. REV. 181 (2004). Whatever values may underly the State Department's cut-off policy, the D.C. Circuit deemed them irrelevant to judging their exemption eligibility under § 553(b)(A). What values or considerations might inform the State Department's adoption of the cut-off policy, and how does the court distinguish them from "substantive" considerations?

Application & Analysis

1. The Food Safety Inspection Service ("FSIS") of the Department of Agriculture ("USDA"), is charged with reviewing the labels affixed to certain commercial food products to guarantee that they are truthful, not

misleading, and otherwise comply with relevant regulations. In an APA § 553 rulemaking completed in 1998, the USDA adopted several ways for commercial food producers to seek approval of proposed food labels. They could do so by mailing an application to the FSIS, by personally visiting the agency, or by hiring an expediter firm whose employees would meet with agency representatives during office hours. This last method ("face-to-face") usually produced a decision by the agency in less time than the others.

In 2010, USDA announced it was eliminating "face-to-face" appointments with expediters. It issued a "Manual for Approval of Labels" ("Manual") in which it cited a number of reasons for eliminating face-to-face review. These reasons included the method's unfairness to food producers who submit by mail, and FSIS' need for more time to evaluate applications involving complex issues. The Manual further stated that it would not change the present system of labeling review, even though the new procedure would "eliminate routine, daily, time-set, face-to-face appointments with courier/expediting firms."

Jose Russe, who owns a small expediter firm in Puerto Rico, challenges the USDA's elimination of face-to-face review in the United States District Court for the District of Puerto Rico. He advances two arguments for why the USDA was required to engage in § 553 rulemaking. First, he argues that, even if elimination of the face-to-face option is procedural on its face, it has a profoundly negative substantive effect on his business interests and is therefore a substantive rule. Second, he argues that the USDA's action was based in a substantive value judgment that the new label-approval procedures would more readily promote the agency's goals of fairness and efficiency. The USDA has moved to dismiss the suit, arguing that its rule was procedural rather than substantive and thus exempt from § 553's notice-and-comment requirements.

You are a clerk for the judge hearing the case. Write a brief memorandum evaluating the parties' arguments.

---

4. Good Cause Exemptions

Administrative Procedure Act § 553(b)(B) allows agencies to forego notice-and-comment rulemaking procedures if agencies can demonstrate that those procedures are "impracticable, unnecessary, or contrary to the public interest." The ATTORNEY GENERAL's MANUAL provides the following explanation:

> It should be noted that the reasons for which an agency may dispense with notice under [APA] section 4(a) [§ 553(b)(B)] are written in the alternative so that if it is "impracticable" or "unnecessary" or "contrary to the public interest" the agency may dispense with notice. Should this be done, the

agency must incorporate in the rule issued its finding of "good cause" and "a brief statement of the reasons therefor." In general, it may be said that a situation is "impracticable" when an agency finds that due and timely execution of its functions would be impeded by the notice otherwise required in section 4(a). For example, the Civil Aeronautics Board may learn, from an accident investigation, that certain rules as to air safety should be issued or amended without delay; with the safety of the traveling public at stake, the Board could find that notice and public rule making procedures would be "impracticable" and issue its rules immediately. "Unnecessary" refers to the issuance of a minor rule or amendment in which the public is not particularly interested. . . . "Public interest" connotes a situation in which the interest of the public would be defeated by any requirement of advance notice. For example, an agency may contemplate the issuance of financial controls under such circumstances that advance notice of such rules would tend to defeat their purpose; in such circumstances, the "public interest" might well justify the omission of notice and public rule making proceedings.

ATTORNEY GENERAL'S MANUAL at 30-31.

Section 553 contains two "good cause" exemptions. The first applies to the notice and comment requirement itself (§ 553(c)), while the second applies to the 30-day waiting period before a rule becomes effective (§ 553(d)(3)). Although these procedural requirements have different underlying purposes—the former facilitates public participation in agency rulemaking whereas the latter provides regulated entities an opportunity to adjust to a new rule's requirements—courts tend to treat them the same when assessing an agency's use of the good cause exemption. *See* 1 CHARLES H. KOCH & RICHARD MURPHY, ADMINISTRATIVE LAW & PRACTICE § 4:13 (2017). Moreover, § 553(b)(B) requires agencies to make a specific finding of good cause if they wish to invoke the exemption and must incorporate that finding (along with the reasons supporting it) in the rules they publish. An agency's failure to include such a justification can lead a court to invalidate its rule.

While the subject matter of the following case may seem technical—the allowable amount of nitrogen oxide that may be emitted from diesel engines—the thrust of the petitioners' argument is quite straightforward. Without engaging in notice-and-comment rulemaking, the EPA promulgated a rule exempting one engine manufacturer from an emissions standard with which its competitors had to comply. The D.C. Circuit's opinion provides a good example of how courts understand and apply the "good cause" exception. As you read the case, note how the court understood and applied § 553(b)(B)'s procedural components (providing reasons for invoking the "good cause" exception and publicizing those reasons in an approved place), and operative terms (defining "impracticable," "unnecessary," and "contrary to the public interest"). These terms essentially function like standards; the subsection itself does not identify facts that would indicate whether they are satisfied. Accordingly, you should note the evidence on which the court relied to determine whether EPA has satisfied § 553(b)(B)'s requirements. The burden of justification rests on the agency (here the EPA), and so the court's decision largely turns on whether the EPA carried it.

Mack Trucks, Inc. v. Environmental Protection Agency
682 F.3d 87 (D.C. Cir. 2012)

Before: SENTELLE, Chief Judge, BROWN and GRIFFITH, Circuit Judges.

BROWN, Circuit Judge: . . .

I

In 2001, pursuant to Section 202 of the Clean Air Act ("the Act"), EPA enacted a rule requiring a 95 percent reduction in the emissions of nitrogen oxide from heavy-duty diesel engines. 66 Fed. Reg. 5,002 (Jan. 18, 2001). By delaying the effective date until 2010, EPA gave industry nine years to innovate the necessary new technologies. *Id.* at 5,010. (EPA and manufacturers refer to the rule as the "2010 NOx standard." 77 Fed. Reg. 4,678, 4,681 (Jan. 31, 2012).) During those nine years, most manufacturers of heavy-duty diesel engines, including Petitioners, invested hundreds of millions of dollars to develop a technology called "selective catalytic reduction." This technology converts nitrogen oxide into nitrogen and water by using a special after-treatment system and a diesel-based chemical agent. With selective catalytic reduction, manufacturers have managed to meet the 2010 NOx standard.

One manufacturer, Navistar, took a different approach. For its domestic sales, Navistar opted for a form of "exhaust gas recirculation," but this technology proved less successful; Navistar's engines do not meet the 2010 NOx standard. All else being equal, Navistar would therefore be unable to sell these engines in the United States—unless, of course, it adopted a different, compliant technology. But for the last few years, Navistar has been able to lawfully forestall that result and continue selling its noncompliant engines by using banked emission credits. Simply put, it bet on finding a way to make exhaust gas recirculation a feasible and compliant technology before its finite supply of credits ran out.

Navistar's day of reckoning is fast approaching: its supply of credits is dwindling and its engines remain noncompliant. In October 2011, Navistar informed EPA that it would run out of credits sometime in 2012. EPA, estimating that Navistar "might have as little as three to four months" of available credits before it "would be forced to stop introducing its engines into commerce," leapt into action. Without formal notice and comment, EPA hurriedly promulgated the IFR [interim final rule] on January 31, 2012, pursuant to its authority under 42 U.S.C. § 7525(g), to make NCPs available to Navistar.

To issue NCPs under its regulations, EPA must first find that a new emissions standard is "more stringent" or "more difficult to achieve" than a prior standard, that "substantial work will be required to meet the standard for which the NCP is offered," and that "there is likely to be a technological laggard." 40 C.F.R. § 86.1103-87 (2004). EPA found these criteria were met. The 2010 NOx standard permits a significantly smaller amount of emissions than the prior standard, so the first criterion is easily satisfied. As for the second, EPA simply said that, because compliant engines (like Petitioners') use new technologies to be compliant, "[i]t is therefore logical to conclude . . . that substantial work was required to meet the emission standard." 77 Fed. Reg. at 4,681. Finally, EPA determined that there was likely to be a technological laggard because "an engine manufac-

> ### In Context
>
> An "IFR" is an interim final rule. These are rules that become effective without prior public notice and before the public has an opportunity to comment. The adopting agency relies on an exemption from notice-and-comment rulemaking (as for "good cause") that allows it to bypass § 553. The adopting agency then states that it will solicit public comments after the IFR is already effective, will modify the rule in light of those comments, and will publish a final (final) rule. *See* Michael Asimow, *Interim-Final Rules: Making Haste Slowly*, 51 ADMIN. L. REV. 703 (1999).

turer [Navistar] . . . has not yet met the requirements for technological reasons" and because "it is a reasonable possibility that this manufacturer may not be able to comply for technological reasons." *Id.*

Having determined that NCPs are appropriate, EPA proceeded to set the amount of the penalty and establish the "upper limit" of emissions permitted even by a penalty-paying manufacturer. The IFR provides that manufacturers may sell heavy-duty diesel engines in model years 2012 and 2013 as long as they pay a penalty of $1,919 per engine and as long as the engines emit fewer than 0.50 grams of nitrogen oxide per horsepower-hour. *Id.* at 4,682-83. This "upper limit" thus permits emissions of up to two-and-a-half times the 0.20 grams permitted under the 2010 NOx standard with which Navistar is meant to comply and with which Petitioners do comply. *See id.* at 4,681.

EPA explained its decision to forego notice and comment procedures by invoking the "good cause" exception of the APA, which provides that an agency may dispense with formal notice and comment procedures if the agency "for good cause finds . . . that notice and public procedure thereon are impracticable, unnecessary, or contrary to the public interest," 5 U.S.C. § 553(b)(B). EPA cited four factors to show the existence of good cause: (1) notice and comment would mean "the possibility of an engine manufacturer [Navistar] . . . being unable to certify a complete product line of engines for model year 2012 and/or 2013," (2) EPA was only "amending limited provisions in existing NCP regulations," (3) the IFR's "duration is limited," and (4) "there is no risk to the public interest in allowing manufacturers to certify using NCPs before the point at which EPA could make them available through a full notice-and-comment rulemaking." 77 Fed. Reg. at 4,680.

Petitioners each requested administrative stays of the IFR, protesting that EPA lacked good cause within the meaning of the APA. . . .

[In Section II of its opinion, the court rejected Navistar's claim that the petitioners lacked standing to bring this suit.]

III

Petitioners argue first that Section 206 of the Act requires notice and comment; alternatively, they claim EPA lacked good cause in any event. The APA provides that, "[e]xcept when notice or hearing is required by statute," an agency is relieved of its obligation to provide notice and an opportunity to comment "when the agency for good cause finds (and incorporates the finding and a brief statement of reasons therefor in the rules issued) that notice and public procedure thereon are impracticable, unnecessary, or contrary to the public interest." 5 U.S.C. § 553(b)(B).

Is notice or hearing expressly required by statute? Section 206(g)(1) of the Act, 42 U.S.C. § 7525(g)(1), says that NCPs shall be provided "under regulations promulgated by the Administrator after notice and opportunity for public hearing." According to Petitioners, this is an express requirement of notice and comment that bars EPA from even invoking the good cause exception in this case. Read alone, this language seems to support their argument. But we cannot read one subsection in isolation. The rest of Section 206(g) clearly reveals, as EPA points out, that this requirement applies only to the very first NCP rule—which set out the regulatory criteria governing future NCPs—not for each and every NCP subsequently promulgated. Because EPA's position is clearly correct, we have no need to invoke any rule of deference. *Chevron, U.S.A., Inc. v. NRDC*, 467 U.S. 837, 843-44 (1984). . . .

Contrary to Petitioners' fears, the Act's lack of a notice and comment requirement does not mean that no procedures are statutorily required when NCPs are issued. The APA's general rule requiring notice and comment—absent identified exceptions—still obviously applies. Indeed, EPA has always argued that the IFR is justified under the good cause exception, not that it is justified because notice and comment is never required.

B

Because the Act does not contain any notice-and-comment requirement applicable to the IFR, EPA may invoke the APA's good cause exception. We must therefore determine whether notice and comment were "impracticable, unnecessary, or contrary to the public interest." 5 U.S.C. § 553(b)(B). On that question, it would appear we owe EPA's findings no particular deference. *See Jifry v. FAA*, 370 F.3d 1174, 1178-79 (D.C. Cir. 2004) (finding good cause without resorting to deference); *Util. Solid Waste Activities Grp.*

v. EPA, 236 F.3d 749, 754 (D.C. Cir. 2001) (finding no good cause without invoking deference). But we need not decide the standard of review since, even if we were to review EPA's assertion of "good cause" simply to determine if it is arbitrary or capricious, 5 U.S.C. § 706(2)(A), we would still find it lacking.

We have repeatedly made clear that the good cause exception "is to be narrowly construed and only reluctantly countenanced." *Util. Solid Waste Activities Grp.*, 236 F.3d at 754.

First, an agency may invoke the impracticability of notice and comment. 5 U.S.C. § 553(b)(B). Our inquiry into impracticability "is inevitably factor context-dependent," *Mid-Tex Electric Coop. v. FERC*, 822 F.2d 1123, 1132 (D.C. Cir. 1987). For the sake of comparison, we have suggested agency action could be sustained on this basis if, for example, air travel security agencies would be unable to address threats posing "a possible imminent hazard to aircraft, persons, and property within the United States," *Jifry*, 370 F.3d at 1179, or if "a safety investigation shows that a new safety rule must be put in place immediately," *Util. Solid Waste Activities Grp.*, 236 F.3d at 755 (ultimately finding that not to be the case and rejecting the agency's argument), or if a rule was of "life-saving importance" to mine workers in the event of a mine explosion, *Council of the S. Mountains, Inc. v. Donovan*, 653 F.2d 573, 581 (D.C. Cir. 1981) (describing that circumstance as "a special, possibly unique, case").

By contrast, the context of this case reveals that the only purpose of the IFR is, as Petitioners put it, "to rescue a lone manufacturer from the folly of its own choices." Pet. Br. at 29; *see* 77 Fed.Reg. at 4,680 (expressing EPA's concern that providing notice and comment would mean "the possibility of an engine manufacturer [Navistar] . . . being unable to certify a complete product line of engines for model year 2012 and/or 2013"). The IFR does not stave off any imminent threat to the environment or safety or national security. It does not remedy any real emergency at all, save the "emergency" facing Navistar's bottom line. Indeed, all EPA points to is the serious harm to Navistar and its employees and the ripple effect on its customers and suppliers, but the same could be said for any manufacturer facing a standard with which its product does not comply.

EPA claims the harm to Navistar and the resulting up- and down-stream impacts should still be enough under our precedents. The only case on which it relies, however, is one in which an entire industry and its customers were imperiled. *See Am. Fed. of Gov't Emps.*[*v. Block*, 655 F.2d 1153, 1157 (D.C. Cir. 1981)]. Navistar's plight is not even remotely close to such a weighty, systemic interest, especially since it is a consequence brought about by Navistar's own choice to continue to pursue a technology which, so far, is noncompliant. At bottom, EPA's approach would give agencies "good cause" under the APA every time a manufacturer in a regulated field felt a new regulation imposed some degree of economic hardship, even if the company could have avoided that hardship had it made different business choices. This is both nonsensical and in direct tension with our longstanding position that the exception should be "narrowly construed and only reluctantly countenanced." *Util. Solid Waste Activities Grp.*, 236 F.3d at 754.

Second, an agency may claim notice and comment were "unnecessary." 5 U.S.C. § 553(b)(B). This prong of the good cause inquiry is "confined to those situations in which the administrative rule is a routine determination, insignificant in nature and impact, and inconsequential to the industry and to the public." *Util. Solid Waste Activities Grp.*, 236 F.3d at 755. This case does not present such a situation. Just as in *Utility Solid Waste*, the IFR is a rule "about which these members of the public [the petitioners] were greatly interested," so notice and comment were not "unnecessary." *Id.* EPA argues that since the IFR is just an interim rule, good cause is satisfied because "the interim status of the challenged rule is a significant factor" in determining whether notice and comment are unnecessary. But we held, in the very case on which EPA relies, that "the limited nature of the rule cannot in itself justify a failure to follow notice and comment procedures." *Mid-Tex Electric Coop.*, 822 F.2d at 1132. And for good reason: if a rule's interim nature were enough to satisfy the element of good cause, then "agencies could issue interim rules of limited effect for any plausible reason, irrespective of the degree of urgency" and "the good cause exception would soon swallow the notice and comment rule." *Tenn. Gas Pipeline* [*Co. v. FERC*, 969 F.2d 1141, 1145 (D.C. Cir. 1992)].

EPA's remaining argument that notice and comment were "unnecessary" is that the IFR was essentially ministerial: EPA simply input numbers into an NCP-setting formula without substantially amending the NCP regime. But even if it were true that EPA arrived at the level of the penalty and the upper limit in this way (and Petitioners strenuously argue that EPA actually amended the NCP regime in order to arrive at the upper limit level in the IFR), that argument does not account for how EPA determined NCPs were warranted in this case in the first place—another finding to which Petitioners object. EPA's decision to implement an NCP, perhaps even more than the level of the penalty itself, is far from inconsequential or routine, and EPA does not even attempt to defend it as such.

Finally, an agency may invoke the good cause exception if providing notice and comment would be contrary to the public interest. 5 U.S.C. § 553(b)(B). In the IFR, EPA says it has good cause since "there is no risk to the public interest in allowing manufacturers to [use] NCPs before the point at which EPA could make them available through a full notice-and-comment rulemaking," 77 Fed. Reg. at 4,680, but this misstates the statutory criterion. The question is not whether dispensing with notice and comment would be contrary to the public interest, but whether providing notice and comment would be contrary to the public interest. By improperly framing the question in this way, the IFR inverts the presumption, apparently suggesting that notice and comment is usually unnecessary. We cannot permit this subtle malformation of the APA. The public interest prong of the good cause exception is met only in the rare circumstance when ordinary procedures—generally presumed to serve the public interest—would in fact harm that interest. It is appropriately invoked when the timing and disclosure requirements of the usual procedures would defeat the purpose of the proposal—if, for example, "announcement of a proposed rule would enable the sort of financial manipulation the rule sought to prevent." *Util. Solid Waste Activities Grp.*, 236 F.3d at 755. In such a circumstance, notice and comment could be dispensed with "in order to prevent the amended rule from being evaded." *Id.* In its brief, EPA belatedly frames the inquiry correctly, but goes on to offer nothing more than a recapitulation of the harm to Navistar and the associated "ripple effects." To the extent this is an argument not preserved by EPA in the IFR, we cannot consider it, *see SEC v. Chenery Corp.* [(*Chenery II*)], 332 U.S. 194, 196, (1947), but regardless, it is nothing more than a reincarnation of the impracticability argument we have already rejected.

IV

Because EPA lacked good cause to dispense with required notice and comment procedures, we conclude the IFR must be vacated without reaching Petitioners' alternative arguments. We are aware EPA is currently in the process of promulgating a final rule—with the benefit of notice and comment—on this precise issue. However, we strongly reject EPA's claim that the challenged errors are harmless simply because of the pendency of a properly-noticed final rule. Were that true, agencies would have no use for the APA when promulgating any interim rules. So long as the agency eventually opened a final rule for comment, every error in every interim rule—no matter how egregious—could be excused as a harmless error. . . .

QUESTION SET 5.4

Review & Synthesis

1. Restate the basic tests for whether promulgating a rule through the APA's notice-and-comment procedures would be "impracticable," "unnecessary," and "contrary to the public interest."
   a. Did the court's analysis of the impracticability exemption indicate that it is available to agencies absent imminent death and/or destruction? Had Navistar demonstrated that its business would be mortally wounded (rather than simply injured) by an inability to secure additional NPCs, would that have satisfied the standard? Does the standard apply differently to lives than to property, such that the imminence and degree of possible harm required is less for the former than it is for

the latter? For that matter, is imminence more important than harm in applying the standard? Vice versa?

b. The court measured whether it was "unnecessary" for the EPA to promulgate the IFR through pre-effectiveness notice-and-comment procedures in part by the level of interest shown by the public. Is that the right way to think about it? The court did not indicate which members of the "public" expressed interest in the IFR. Would the court's reasoning be as persuasive if we learned that most of the inquiries came from or were orchestrated by Navistar's competitors, the petitioners in this case? Relatedly, and in light of the difference between legislative and nonlegislative rules, shouldn't necessity be based on whether and how a rule will directly impact private interests, rather than how it is perceived?

Application & Analysis

1. Congress has delegated broad discretion to the Federal Aviation Administration ("FAA") to prescribe regulations and standards for safety in air commerce and national security. *See* 49 U.S.C. § 44701(a)(5). The FAA may "at any time" reexamine the issuance of an airman certificate—necessary for lawfully piloting aircrafts—and issue an order "modifying, suspending, or revoking" a certificate if doing so protects "safety in air commerce" and "the public interest." 49 U.S.C. §§ 44709(a)-(b). With regard to issuing airman certificates to qualified individuals, Congress distinguished between citizens and lawful permanent residents on the one hand, and nonimmigrants on the other. It granted the FAA broad discretion to issue airman certificates to nonimmigrant pilots. *See* § 44703(e). After the September 11, 2001, terrorist attacks, Congress established the Transportation Security Administration ("TSA") on November 19, 2001, and transferred much of the responsibility for making civil aviation security threat assessments from the FAA to the TSA. *See* 49 U.S.C. §§ 114(d), (f). In addition, Congress enacted 49 U.S.C. § 46111, which required the FAA to suspend, modify, or revoke a certificate if notified by the TSA that an individual holding an airman certificate poses a security risk.

Last year, the FAA published, without notice and comment, a new regulation governing the suspension and revocation of airman certificates for security reasons. This regulation provides for automatic suspension by the FAA of airman certificates upon written notification from the TSA that a pilot poses a security threat. The TSA simultaneously promulgated a regulation establishing the procedure by which it would notify the FAA and a nonimmigrant holding or applying for an airman certificate of its finding that the nonimmigrant poses a security threat. The TSA began serving Initial Notices of Threat Assessment on hundreds of nonimmigrant pilots, and in response the FAA began suspending and eventually revoking dozens of certificates.

Three pilots from Spain had their certificates revoked by the FAA because they "posed a security threat" to the United States. The pilots exhausted all administrative remedies at the FAA and appealed to the D.C. Circuit. They alleged that the FAA violated the APA by promulgating the new rule without notice and comment. The FAA countered that its action was covered by the APA's "good cause" exception.

You are a judge sitting on the United States Court of Appeals for the District of Columbia Circuit. Write a brief court opinion deciding whether the FAA contravened the APA.

B. FORMAL RULEMAKING

Unlike nonlegislative rules, and absent one of the exceptions discussed above, agencies must engage with the public before their substantive rules can bind members of the regulated public. Here, the Administrative Procedure Act sets out two methods by which they may do so. Most substantive rules are promulgated through the first, which is the § 553 notice-and-comment procedure. Pursuant to the second, far less frequently utilized method, Congress requires that substantive rules "be made on the record after opportunity for an agency hearing." 5 U.S.C. § 553(c). When that is the case, and barring other more specific statutory directives, agencies must follow the procedures specified in APA §§ 556 and 557. These provisions obligate the agency to hold a "hearing" to collect evidence, to appoint a hearing examiner to preside over that hearing, to permit parties to conduct cross-examination "as may be required for a full and true disclosure of the facts," prohibit *ex parte* contacts, and base its decisions on the whole record as supported by substantial evidence. These features—which trace back to early development of the modern administrative state[1]—have led commentators to analogize formal rulemaking to trial-like proceedings conducted in federal and state courts.

Formal rulemaking under the APA provides the public with more procedural protections than does its informal counterpart, and with obviously more opportunities for participation than the nonlegislative rulemaking process. Of course, these protections are far from costless. On-the-record procedures of any kind are generally more expensive and more time-consuming than off-the-record procedures, and the same is true of rulemaking. In a well-known article, Professor Robert Hamilton illustrated this point in his vivid (and rather scathing) depiction of formal rulemaking at the Food and Drug

---

[1] The Hepburn Act of 1906 required the Interstate Commerce Commission ("ICC") to hold "a full hearing" before it could set caps on railroad rates. This instruction apparently codified practices the ICC had already been following prior to the Act's passage. *See* Henry J. Friendly, *Some Kind of Hearing*, 123 U. PA. L. REV. 1267, 1271 (1975).

Administration ("FDA") during the 1960s. Robert W. Hamilton, *Procedures for the Adoption of Rules of General Applicability: The Need for Procedural Innovation in Administrative Rulemaking*, 60 CAL. L. REV. 1276 (1972):

> The sixteen formal hearings that were held during the last decade vary from unnecessarily drawn out proceedings to virtual disasters. In not one instance did the agency complete a rulemaking proceeding involving a hearing in less than two years, and in two instances more than ten years elapsed between the first proposal and the final order. The average time lapse was roughly four years. The hearings themselves tended to be drawn out, repetitious and unproductive. The Foods for Special Dietary Uses hearing consumed over 200 days of testimony and amassed a transcript of more than 32,000 pages. Most of the hearing was devoted to cross-examination of expert government witnesses. Another proceeding involving the standard of identity for peanut butter developed a transcript of over 7,700 pages, largely directed to the question whether the product peanut butter should consist of 90 percent peanuts or 87 1/2 percent peanuts. Both of these transcripts are largely monuments to free speech.

Id. at 1287-88.

Due in large part to such unremunerative debates and decisional delays, Congress rarely forces agencies to promulgate rules through formal proceedings. "Today, formal rulemaking is the Yeti of administrative law. There are isolated sightings of it in the ratemaking context, but elsewhere it proves elusive." *Perez v. Mortgage Bankers Association*, 575 U.S. 92, 128 n.5 (2015). One such example comes in 7 U.S.C. § 6c(e), which provides that the Commodity Futures Trading Commission "may adopt rules and regulations, after public notice and opportunity for a hearing on the record, prohibiting the granting, issuance, or sale of options . . . if the Commission determines that such options are contrary to the public interest." *See also* the Marine Mammal Protection Act, 16 U.S.C. § 1372(d) (2018) (requiring the Interior Secretary to use formal rulemaking when promulgating rules to protect marine mammals); Food, Drug and Cosmetic Act § 701(e)(3) (listing particular FDA decisions that have to be made through the formal rulemaking process); *Block v. Community Nutrition Institute*, 467 U.S. 340 (1984) (involving USDA rate orders for milk under the Agricultural Marketing Agreement Act of 1937, 7 U.S.C. § 608c(3)-(4)(1994)).

Congress, for the most part, does not speak nearly as clearly as it does in these examples when addressing the formality of many agencies' rulemaking procedures. This leaves courts to infer from ambiguous statutory provisions whether Congress intended for agencies to engage in on-the-record rulemaking. The seminal examples of this interpretive problem come from the early 1970s, and in the context of the Interstate Commerce Commission ("ICC"). The issue in *United States v. Allegheny-Ludlum Steel Corp.*, 406 U.S. 742 (1972), was whether § 1 of the Interstate Commerce Act (originally the Esch Car Service Act of 1917) required the ICC to adopt its "car service" rules through the APA's formal procedures. Section 1(14)(a) of the Act stated that the ICC "may, after hearing . . . establish reasonable rules, regulations, and practices. . . ." A unanimous Court concluded that it did not. Importantly for present purposes, the Court placed a very narrow construction on the provision's operative language:

[Section]1(14)(a), does not require that such rules "be made on the record." 5 U.S.C. § 553. "A good deal of significance lies in the fact that some statutes do expressly require determinations on the record." 2 K. Davis. Administrative Law Treatise § 13.08, p. 225 (1958). Sections 556 and 557 need be applied "only where the agency statute, in addition to providing a hearing, prescribes explicitly that it be 'on the record.'" *Siegel v. Atomic Energy Comm'n*, 400 F.2d 778, 785 (1968). We do not suggest that only the precise words "on the record" in the applicable statute will suffice to make §§ 556 and 557 applicable to rule-making proceedings, but we do hold that the language of the Esch Car Service Act is insufficient to invoke these sections.

406 U.S. at 757. The Court returned to this question a year later, again with respect to a rule promulgated by the ICC without formal proceedings. This time, the Court made a more definitive (and seminal) statement on just how clear statutory language must be to force agencies into APA §§ 556 and 557 rulemaking.

United States v. Florida East Coast Railway Company
410 U.S. 224 (1973)

Mr. Justice REHNQUIST delivered the opinion of the Court.

Appellees, two railroad companies, brought this action in the District Court for the Middle District of Florida to set aside the incentive *per diem* rates established by appellant Interstate Commerce Commission in a rule-making proceeding. . . . They challenged the order of the Commission on both substantive and procedural grounds. The District Court sustained appellees' position that the Commission had failed to comply with the applicable provisions of the Administrative Procedure Act, 5 U.S.C. § 551 *et seq.*, and therefore set aside the order without dealing with the railroads' other contentions. The District Court held that the language of § 1(14)(a)1 of the Interstate Commerce Act, 24 Stat. 379, as amended, 49 U.S.C. § 1(14)(a), required the Commission in a proceeding such as this to act in accordance with the Administrative Procedure Act, 5 U.S.C. § 556(d), and that the Commission's determination to receive submissions from the appellees only in written form was a violation of that section because the respondents were "prejudiced" by that determination within the meaning of that section. . . .

I. BACKGROUND OF CHRONIC FREIGHT CAR SHORTAGES

This case arises from the factual background of a chronic freight-car shortage on the Nation's railroads. . . . Congressional concern for the problem was manifested in the enactment in 1966 of an amendment to § 1(14)(a) of the Interstate Commerce Act, enlarging the Commission's authority to prescribe *per diem* charges for the use by one railroad of freight cars owned by another. . . .

In December 1967, the Commission initiated the rulemaking procedure giving rise to the order that appellees here challenge. It directed Class I and Class II line-haul railroads to compile and report detailed information with respect to freight-car demand and supply at numerous sample stations for selected days of the week during 12 four-week periods, beginning January 29, 1968.

Some of the affected railroads voiced questions about the proposed study or requested modification in the study procedures outlined by the Commission in its notice of proposed rulemaking. In response to petitions setting forth these carriers' views, the Commission staff held an informal conference in April 1968, at which the objections and proposed modifications were discussed. Twenty railroads, including appellee Seaboard, were represented at this conference, at which the Commission's staff sought to answer questions about reporting methods to accommodate individual circumstances of particular railroads. The conference adjourned on a note that undoubtedly left the impression that hearings would be held at some future date. A detailed report of the conference was sent to all parties to the proceeding before the Commission. . . .

The Commission . . . issued in December 1969 an interim report announcing its tentative decision to adopt incentive *per diem* charges on standard boxcars based on the information compiled by the railroads. The substantive decision reached by the Commission was that so-called "incentive" *per diem* charges should be paid by any railroad using on its lines a standard boxcar owned by another railroad. Before the enactment of the 1966 amendment to the Interstate Commerce Act, it was generally thought that the Commission's authority to fix *per diem* payments for freight car use was limited to setting an amount that reflected fair return on investment for the owning railroad, without any regard being had for the desirability of prompt return to the owning line or for the encouragement of additional purchases of freight cars by the railroads as a method of investing capital. The Commission concluded, however, that in view of the 1966 amendment it could impose additional "incentive" *per diem* charges to spur prompt return of existing cars and to make acquisition of new cars financially attractive to the railroads. It did so by means of a proposed schedule that established such charges on an across-the-board basis for all common carriers by railroads subject to the Interstate Commerce Act. Embodied in the report was a proposed rule adopting the Commission's tentative conclusions and a notice to the railroads to file statements of position within 60 days . . .

Both appellee railroads filed statements objecting to the Commission's proposal and requesting an oral hearing, as did numerous other railroads. In April 1970, the Commission, without having held further "hearings," issued a supplemental report making some modifications in the tentative conclusions earlier reached, but overruling *in toto* the requests of appellees.

The District Court held that in so doing the Commission violated § 556(d) of the Administrative Procedure Act, and it was on this basis that it set aside the order of the Commission.

II. APPLICABILITY OF ADMINISTRATIVE PROCEDURE ACT

In *United States v. Allegheny-Ludlum Steel Corp.* . . . we held that the language of § 1(14)(a) of the Interstate Commerce Act authorizing the Commission to act "after hearing" was not the equivalent of a requirement that a rule be made "on the record after opportunity for an agency hearing" as the latter term is used in § 553(c) of the Administrative Procedure Act. Since the 1966 amendment to § 1(14)(a), under which the Commission was here [proceeding], does not by its terms add to the hearing requirement contained in the earlier language, the same result should obtain here unless that amendment contains language that is tantamount to such a requirement. Appellees contend that such language is found in the provisions of that Act requiring that:

> (T)he Commission shall give consideration to the national level of ownership of such type of freight car and to other factors affecting the adequacy of the national freight car supply, and shall, on the basis of such consideration, determine whether compensation should be computed. . . .

While this language is undoubtedly a mandate to the Commission to consider the factors there set forth in reaching any conclusion as to imposition of *per diem* incentive charges, it adds to the hearing requirements of the section neither expressly nor by implication. We know of no reason to think that an administrative agency in reaching a decision cannot accord consideration to factors such as those set forth in the 1966 amendment by means other than a trial-type hearing or the presentation of oral argument by the affected parties. Congress by that amendment specified necessary components of the ultimate decision, but it did not specify the method by which the Commission should acquire information about those components.

Both of the district courts that reviewed this order of the Commission concluded that its proceedings were governed by the stricter requirements of §§ 556 and 557 of the Administrative Procedure Act, rather than by the provisions of § 553 alone.[6] The conclusion of the District Court for the Middle District of Florida, which we here review, was based on the assumption that the language in §1(14)(a) of the Interstate Commerce Act requiring rulemaking under that section to be done "after hearing" was the equivalent of a statutory requirement that the rule "be made on the record after opportunity for an agency hearing." Such an assumption is inconsistent with our decision in *Allegheny-Ludlum*.

The District Court for the Eastern District of New York reached the same conclusion by a somewhat different line of reasoning. That court felt that because § 1(14)(a) of the Interstate Commerce Act had required a "hearing," and because that section was originally enacted in 1917, Congress was probably thinking in terms of a "hearing" such as that described in the opinion of this Court in the roughly contemporaneous case of *ICC v. Louisville & Nashville R. Co.*, 227 U.S. 88, 93 (1913). The ingredients of the "hearing" were there said to be that "(a)ll parties must be fully apprised of the evidence submitted or to be considered, and must be given opportunity to cross-examine witnesses, to inspect documents and to offer evidence in explanation or rebuttal." Combining this view of congressional understanding of the term "hearing" with comments by the Chairman of the Commission at the time of the adoption of the 1966 legislation regarding the necessity for "hearings," that court concluded that Congress had, in effect, required that these proceedings be "on the record after opportunity for an agency hearing" within the meaning of § 553(c) of the Administrative Procedure Act.

Insofar as this conclusion is grounded on the belief that the language "after hearing" of § 1(14)(a), without more, would trigger the applicability of §§ 556 and 557, it, too, is contrary to our decision in *Allegheny-Ludlum*, *supra*. The District Court observed that it was "rather hard to believe that the last sentence of § 553(c) was directed only to the few legislative spots where the words 'on the record' or their equivalent had found their way into the statute book." . . . This is, however, the language which Congress used, and since there are statutes on the books that do use these very words, adherence to

---

[6] Both district court opinions were handed down before our decision in *United States v. Allegheny-Ludlum Steel Corp.*, 406 U.S. 742 (1972), and it appears from the record before us that the Government in those courts did not really contest the proposition that the Commission's proceedings were governed by the stricter standards of §§ 556 and 557. The dissenting opinion of Mr. Justice DOUGLAS relies in part on indications by the Commission that it proposed to apply the more stringent standards of §§ 556 and 557 of the Administrative Procedure Act to these proceedings. This Act is not legislation that the Interstate Commerce Commission, or any other single agency, has primary responsibility for administering. An agency interpretation involving, at least in part, the provisions of that Act does not carry the weight, in ascertaining the intent of Congress, that an interpretation by an agency "charged with the responsibility" of administering a particular statute does. Moreover, since any agency is free under the Act to accord litigants appearing before it more procedural rights than the Act requires, the fact that an agency may choose to proceed under §§ 556 and 557 does not carry the necessary implication that the agency felt it was required to do so.

that language cannot be said to render the provision nugatory or ineffectual. We recognized in *Allegheny-Ludlum* that the actual words "on the record" and "after . . . hearing" used in § 553 were not words of art, and that other statutory language having the same meaning could trigger the provisions of §§ 556 and 557 in rulemaking proceedings. But we adhere to our conclusion, expressed in that case, that the phrase "after hearing" in § 1(14)(a) of the Interstate Commerce Act does not have such an effect.

III. "HEARING" REQUIREMENT OF § 1(14)(a) OF THE INTERSTATE COMMERCE ACT

Inextricably intertwined with the hearing requirement of the Administrative Procedure Act in this case is the meaning to be given to the language "after hearing" in § 1(14)(a) of the Interstate Commerce Act. Appellees, both here and in the court below, contend that the Commission procedure here fell short of that mandated by the "hearing" requirement of § 1(14)(a), even though it may have satisfied § 553 of the Administrative Procedure Act. The Administrative Procedure Act states that none of its provisions "limit or repeal additional requirements imposed by statute or otherwise recognized by law." 5 U.S.C. § 559. Thus, even though the Commission was not required to comply with §§ 556 and 557 of that Act, it was required to accord the "hearing" specified in § 1(14)(a) of the Interstate Commerce Act. . . .

If we were to agree with the reasoning of the District Court for the Eastern District of New York with respect to the type of hearing required by the Interstate Commerce Act, the Commission's action might well violate those requirements, even though it was consistent with the requirements of the Administrative Procedure Act.

The term "hearing" in its legal context undoubtedly has a host of meanings. Its meaning undoubtedly will vary, depending on whether it is used in the context of a rulemaking-type proceeding or in the context of a proceeding devoted to the adjudication of particular disputed facts. It is by no means apparent what the drafters of the Esch Car Service Act of 1917, 40 Stat. 101, which became the first part of § 1(14)(a) of the Interstate Commerce Act, meant by the term. . . .

Under these circumstances, confronted with a grant of substantive authority [to the ICC by the ICA] after the Administrative Procedure Act was enacted, we think that reference to [the APA], in which Congress devoted itself exclusively to questions such as the nature and scope of hearings, is a satisfactory basis for determining what is meant by the term "hearing" used in another statute. Turning to that Act, we are convinced that the term "hearing" as used therein does not necessarily embrace either the right to present evidence orally and to cross-examine opposing witnesses, or the right to present oral argument to the agency's decisionmaker.

Section 553 excepts from its requirements rulemaking devoted to "interpretative rules, general statements of policy, or rules of agency organization, procedure, or practice," and rulemaking "when the agency for good cause finds . . . that notice and public procedure thereon are impracticable, unnecessary, or contrary to the public interest." This exception does not apply, however, "when notice or hearing is required by statute"; in those cases, even though interpretative rulemaking be involved, the requirements of § 553 apply. But since these requirements themselves do not mandate any oral presentation, it cannot be doubted that a statute that requires a "hearing" prior to rulemaking may in some circumstances be satisfied by procedures that meet only the standards of § 553. . . .

Similarly, even where the statute requires that the rulemaking procedure take place "on the record after opportunity for an agency hearing," thus triggering the applicability of § 556, subsection (d) provides that the agency may proceed by the submission of all or part of the evidence in written form if a party will not be "prejudiced thereby." Again, the Act makes it plain that a specific statutory mandate that the proceedings take place on the record after hearing may be satisfied in some circumstances by evidentiary submission in written form only.

We think this treatment of the term "hearing" in the Administrative Procedure Act affords sufficient basis for concluding that the requirement of a "hearing" contained in § 1(14)(a); in a situation where the Commission was acting under the 1966 statutory rulemaking authority that Congress had conferred upon it, did not by its own force require the Commission either to hear oral testimony, to permit cross-examination of Commission witnesses, or to hear oral argument. . . .

ICC v. Louisville & Nashville R. Co., 227 U.S. 88 (1913), involved what the Court there described as a "quasi-judicial" proceeding of a quite different nature from the one we review here. The provisions of the Interstate Commerce Act, 24 Stat. 379, as amended, and of the Hepburn Act, 34 Stat. 584, in effect at the time that case was decided, left to the railroad carriers the "primary right to make rates," 227 U.S., at 92, but granted to the Commission the authority to set them aside, if after hearing, they were shown to be unreasonable. . . . The type of proceeding there, in which the Commission adjudicated a complaint by a shipper that specified rates set by a carrier were unreasonable, was sufficiently different from the nationwide incentive payments ordered to be made by all railroads in this proceeding so as to make the *Louisville & Nashville* opinion inapplicable in the case presently before us.

The basic distinction between rulemaking and adjudication is illustrated by this Court's treatment of two related cases under the Due Process Clause of the Fourteenth Amendment. In *Londoner v. Denver*, cited in oral argument by appellees, 210 U.S. 373 (1908), the Court held that due process had not been accorded a landowner who objected to the amount assessed against his land as its share of the benefit resulting from the paving of a street.

Local procedure had accorded him the right to file a written complaint and objection, but not to be heard orally. This Court held that due process of law required that he "have the right to support his allegations by argument, however brief; and, if need be, by proof, however informal." *Id.*, at 386. But in the later case of *Bi-Metallic Investment Co. v. State Board of Equalization*, 239 U.S. 441 (1915), the Court held that no hearing at all was constitutionally required prior to a decision by state tax officers in Colorado to increase the valuation of all taxable property in Denver by a substantial percentage. The Court distinguished *Londoner* by stating that there a small number of persons "were exceptionally affected, in each case upon individual grounds." *Id.*, at 446, 36 S.Ct., at 142. . . .

Here, the incentive payments proposed by the Commission in its tentative order, and later adopted in its final order, were applicable across the board to all of the common carriers by railroad subject to the Interstate Commerce Act. No effort was made to single out any particular railroad for special consideration based on its own peculiar circumstances. Indeed, one of the objections of appellee Florida East Coast was that it and other terminating carriers should have been treated differently from the generality of the railroads. But the fact that the order may in its effects have been thought more disadvantageous by some railroads than by others does not change its generalized nature. Though the Commission obviously relied on factual inferences as a basis for its order, the source of these factual inferences was apparent to anyone who read the order of December 1969. The factual inferences were used in the formulation of a basically legislative-type judgment, for prospective application only, rather than in adjudicating a particular set of disputed facts.

The Commission's procedure satisfied both the provisions of § 1(14)(a) of the Interstate Commerce Act and of the Administrative Procedure Act, and were not inconsistent with prior decisions of this Court. We, therefore, reverse the judgment of the District Court, and remand the case so that it may consider those contentions of the parties that are not disposed of by this opinion.

It is so ordered.

Reversed and remanded.

Mr. Justice POWELL took no part in the consideration or decision of this case.

Mr. Justice DOUGLAS, with whom Mr. Justice STEWART concurs, dissenting.

The present decision makes a sharp break with traditional concepts of procedural due process. The Commission order under attack is tantamount to a rate order. Charges are fixed that non[-]owning railroads must pay owning railroads for boxcars of the latter that are on the tracks of the former. . . . This is the imposition on carriers by administrative fiat of a new financial liability. I do not believe it is within our traditional concepts of due process to allow an administrative agency to saddle anyone with a new rate, charge, or fee without a full hearing that includes the right to present oral testimony, cross-examine witnesses, and present oral argument. That is required by the Administrative Procedure Act, 5 U.S.C. § 556(d); § 556(a) states that § 556 applies to hearings required by § 553. Section 553(c) provides that § 556 applies "(w)hen rules are required by statute to be made on the record after opportunity for an agency hearing." A hearing under § 1(14)(a) of the Interstate Commerce Act fixing rates, charges, or fees is certainly adjudicatory, not legislative in the customary sense.

The question is whether the Interstate Commerce Commission procedures used in this rate case "for the submission of . . . evidence in written form" avoided prejudice to the appellees so as to comport with the requirements of the Administrative Procedure Act. . . .

Appellees . . . argue that the inadequacy of the supply of standard boxcars was not sufficiently established by the Commission's procedures. Seaboard contends that specialty freight cars have supplanted standard boxcars and Florida East Coast challenges the accuracy of the Commission's findings.

In its interim report, the Commission indicated that there would be an opportunity to present evidence and arguments. *See* 337 I.C.C. 183, 187. The appellees could reasonably have expected that the later hearings would give them the opportunity to substantiate and elaborate the criticisms they set forth in their initial objections to the interim report. That alone would not necessarily support the claim of "prejudice." But I believe that "prejudice" was shown when it was claimed that the very basis on which the Commission rested its finding was vulnerable because it lacked statistical validity or other reasoned basis. At least in that narrow group of cases, prejudice for lack of a proper hearing has been shown. . . .

The more exacting hearing provisions of the Administrative Procedure Act, 5 U.S.C. §§ 556-557, are only applicable, of course, if the "rules are required by statute to be made on the record after opportunity for an agency hearing." *Id.*, § 553(c).

United States v. Allegheny-Ludlum Steel Corp., 406 U.S. 742, was concerned strictly with a rulemaking proceeding of the Commission for the promulgation of "car service rules" that in general required freight cars, after being unloaded, to be returned "in the direction of the lines of the road owning the cars." *Id.*, at 743. We sustained the Commission's power with respect to these two rules on the narrow ground that they were wholly legislative. We held that § 1(14)(a) of the Interstate Commerce Act, requiring by its terms a "hearing," "does not require that such rules 'be made on the record'" within the meaning of § 553(c). We recognized, however, that the precise words "on the record" are not talismanic, but that the crucial question is whether the proceedings under review are "an exercise of legislative rulemaking" or "adjudicatory hearings." *Ibid.* The "hearing" requirement of

§ 1(14)(a) cannot be given a fixed and immutable meaning to be applied in each and every case without regard to the nature of the proceedings.

The rules in question here established "incentive" *per diem* charges to spur the prompt return of existing cars and to make the acquisition of new cars financially attractive to the railroads. Unlike those we considered in *Allegheny-Ludlum*, these rules involve the creation of a new financial liability. Although quasi-legislative, they are also adjudicatory in the sense that they determine the measure of the financial responsibility of one road for its use of the rolling stock of another road. The Commission's power to promulgate these rules pursuant to § 1(14)(a) is conditioned on the preliminary finding that the supply of freight cars to which the rules apply is inadequate. Moreover, in fixing incentive compensation once this threshold finding has been made, the Commission "shall give consideration to the national level of ownership of such type of freight car and to other factors affecting the adequacy of the national freight car supply. . . ."

The majority finds *ICC v. Louisville & Nashville R. Co.*, 227 U.S. 88, "sufficiently different" as to make the opinion in that case inapplicable to the case now before us. I would read the case differently, finding a clear mandate that where, as here, ratemaking must be based on evidential facts, § 1(14)(a) requires that full hearing which due process normally entails. . . . Congress was fully cognizant of our decision in *Louisville & Nashville R. Co.* when it first adopted the hearing requirement of § 1(14)(a) in 1917. And when Congress debated the 1966 amendment that empowered the Commission to adopt incentive *per diem* rates, it had not lost sight of the importance of hearings. . . . Nor should we overlook the Commission's own interpretation of the hearing requirement in § 1(14)(a) as it applies to this case. The Commission's order initiating the rulemaking proceeding notified the parties that it was acting "under authority of Part I of the Interstate Commerce Act (49 U.S.C. § 1 *et seq.*); more particularly, section 1(14)(a) and the Administrative Procedure Act (5 U.S.C. §§ 553, 556, and 557)." Clearly, the Commission believed that it was required to hold a hearing on the record. This interpretation, not of the Administrative Procedure Act, but of § 1(14)(a) of the Commission's own Act, is "entitled to great weight." *United States v. American Trucking Ass'ns*, 310 U.S. 534, 549. . . .

QUESTION SET 5.5

Review & Synthesis

1. What was the Court's holding with respect to usage of the terms "on the record" and "after hearing," as it related to whether Congress intended agencies to use the formal rulemaking procedures set out in 5 U.S.C. §§ 556 and 557? Did the Court hold that both were sufficient to trigger formal rulemaking? Only one of them?

2. The Court stated that Congress need not use the specific term "on the record" to direct agencies to engage in §§ 556 and 557 formal rulemaking. If that is the case, how should agencies determine when they are so directed? Assume, for instance, that Congress adopted a statutory provision requiring an agency to base its rules on "direct testimony from witnesses." Would that trigger §§ 556 and 557? Why or why not? *See* Gary Lawson, Federal Administrative Law 229 (5th ed. 2009) (finding that no court has found a statute lacking the term "on the record" as triggering §§ 556 and 557).

3. Justice Douglas was adamant that the railroads' "procedural due process rights" were violated by the ICC's decision to forego formal hearings. He pointed out that the *per diem* order was analogous to rate orders which, historically, had been set through formal proceedings. Moreover, he argued that the railroads had been "prejudiced" by the ICC's decision to forego formal hearings. Was he arguing that such hearings were required by the Fifth Amendment Due Process Clause, or something else? The majority dismissed these assertations in concluding that the ICC's *per diem* order was quasi-legislative. Which of these characterizations do you find the most apt, and why?

4. Justice Douglas pointed out that the ICC itself interpreted Interstate Commerce Act § 1(14)(a) as requiring formal rulemaking under §§ 556 and 557. The Court responded, in essence, that this did not matter. The APA was the statutory focal point for determining whether the ICC had to proceed formally, and neither it nor any other federal agency had any particular expertise to interpret its provisions that would warrant deference from the Court. Wouldn't the ICC's obligation to proceed formally under §§ 556 and 557 *depend on* what § 1(14)(a) — the statute it administers — directed it to do? Additionally, according some deference to agency interpretations of the statutes they administer was already a well-established practice when the Court decided *Florida East Coast* (about ten years before it decided *Chevron*). Assuming that Justice Douglas was correct that the Interstate Commerce Act's use of the term "hearing" controlled, shouldn't the Court have deferred to it?

C. INFORMAL (NOTICE-AND-COMMENT) RULEMAKING

In effect, *Florida East Coast* adopted a presumption against formal rulemaking. Courts will not assume that Congress has required agencies to use it unless statutory language unambiguously leads to that conclusion. Accordingly, the lion's share of administrative rule promulgation will be conducted through the APA's informal rulemaking procedures, which are set out in Section 4 (5 U.S.C § 553). "In general, the purpose of Section 4 is to guarantee to the public an opportunity to participate in the rule making process." Attorney General's Manual at 26. Absent more specific instructions to the contrary—like the exemptions discussed above or directives in particular organic statutes—agency rulemaking is governed by the informal rulemaking procedures set out in APA § 553. Its basic requirements include:

- Publication of a notice of proposed rulemaking ("NPRM") in the Federal Register. The NPRM must include a statement of the time, place, and nature of the public rulemaking proceedings; indication of the legal authority supporting the proposed rule; and either the language or a description of subjects and issues the proposed rule will address. (§ 553(b)).
- An opportunity for interested persons to submit written information—data, views, arguments—related to the proposed rule. Agencies need not provide such persons with an opportunity for oral presentations. (§ 553(c)).
- A "concise general statement" of the proposed rule's "basis and purpose" included with the final rule. (§ 553(d)).
- Publication of the final rule "not less than 30 days before its effective date," subject to certain exceptions (§ 553(d)).

As you likely surmised, the monikers "informal" and "notice-and-comment" derive from how § 553 facilitates participation from the public in rule formulation and development. Like formal rulemaking procedures, agencies typically must notify the public in advance when they consider adoption of legally binding regulatory policies. Unlike formal procedures, however, § 553 does not require that agencies facilitate public participation through trial-like hearings. Rather, it permits agencies to "informally" receive comments in written form and during the time periods they specify (often 30 days, maybe more for complex rules).

As Figure 5.1 illustrates, the informal rulemaking process is a massive multistep, multiparty, multi-institutional undertaking. At its genesis, and as previously discussed (see Part II), Congress identifies a problem that, in its judgment, warrants a regulatory response. It then passes a statute either requiring or authorizing promulgation of a regulation, thereby delegating responsibility to an administering federal agency. The agency's first step in the rulemaking process—one not mentioned in or governed by the APA—is to gather information about the issues that any potential rule will address. This due diligence helps the agency to settle on a rulemaking approach, avoid reliance on unfounded assumptions or poor information, and identify potential pushback from interested parties. The agency responds by drafting a proposed regulation, which it submits for review within the agency. If the agency is required

Figure 5.1

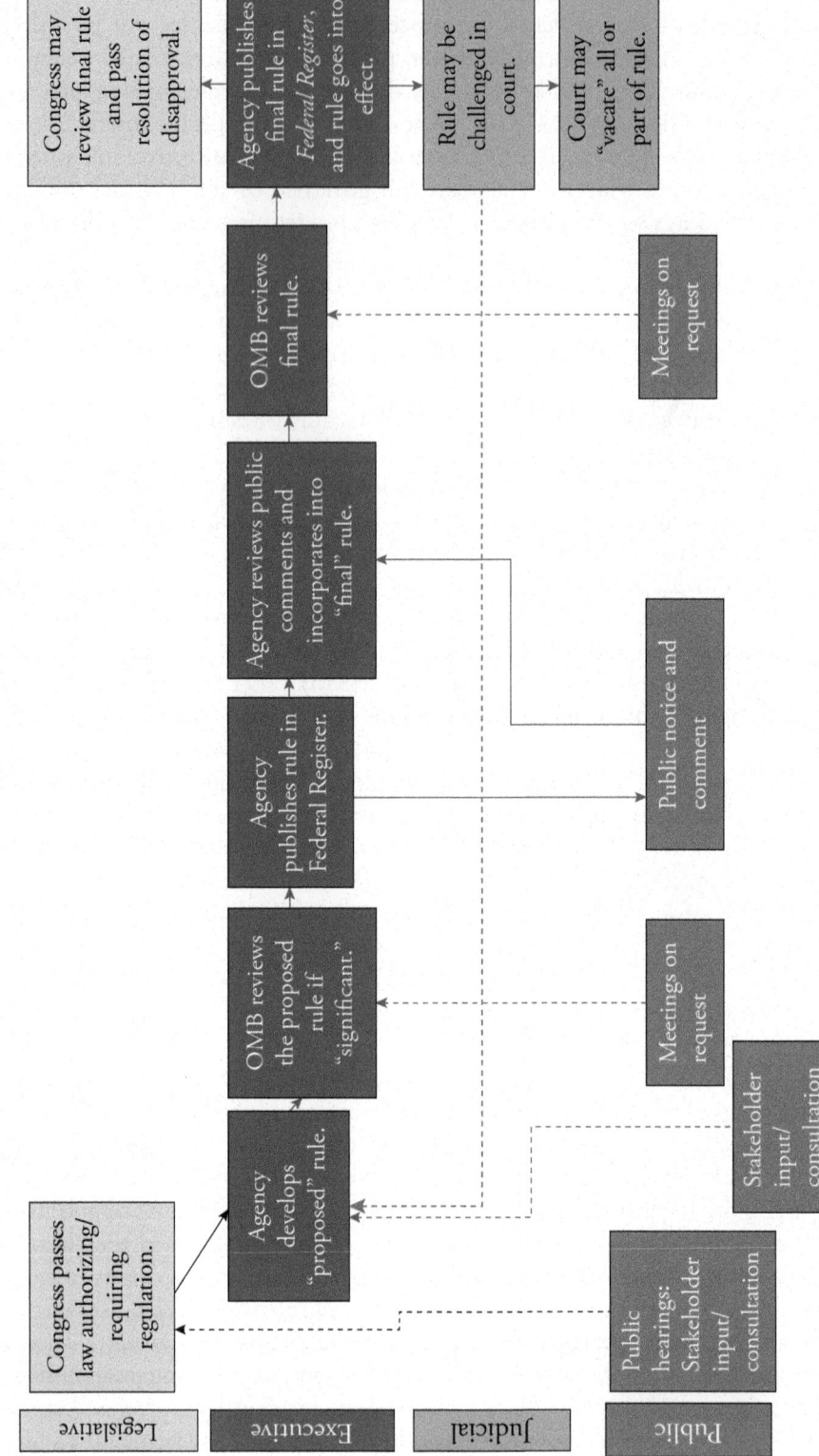

Source: Susan E. Dudley, "Opportunities for Stakeholder Participation in U.S. Rulemaking," GW Regulatory Studies Center.

to or has opted for negotiated rulemaking under the Negotiated Rulemaking Act, this is the point at which the negotiated rulemaking committee would do its work and make its recommendation. Once approved within the agency, the proposal receives White House scrutiny in the Office of Information and Regulatory Affairs ("OIRA," pronounced "oh-eye-ruh") review process. This review can involve several types of administrative analyses: cost-benefit, small business impact, paperwork burden, environmental impact, federalism, etc. Assuming that the agency gets sign-off, it publishes its NPRM in the Federal Register and furnishes the proposal to the public for comment. Depending on the public's response, the agency will analyze and respond to "significant" comments, extend the comments period, revise the rule, or abandon it altogether. If the agency decides (or is required) to press forward, it prepares the final rule for internal and another round of OIRA review. If all goes well, the agency publishes its final rule in the Federal Register, and it will generally become effective no fewer than 30 days thereafter. At this point, judicial and legislative scrutiny of the rule come into play (although lawsuits can be brought to challenge the rulemaking process well before this).

According to the Federal Register, "the number of final rules published each year is generally in the range of 3,000-4,500." MAEVE P. CAREY, CONG. RSCH. SERV., 43056, COUNTING REGULATIONS: AN OVERVIEW OF RULEMAKING, TYPES OF FEDERAL REGULATIONS, AND PAGES IN THE FEDERAL REGISTER 1 (2019). As Figure 5.2 shows, the number of rules promulgated by federal agencies, as measured by the number of final rule documents published in the Federal Register, declined significantly between 1976 and 2018.

Not all of the final rule documents tracked by Figure 5.2 are the product of notice-and-comment rulemaking; a relatively small portion are the result

Figure 5.2

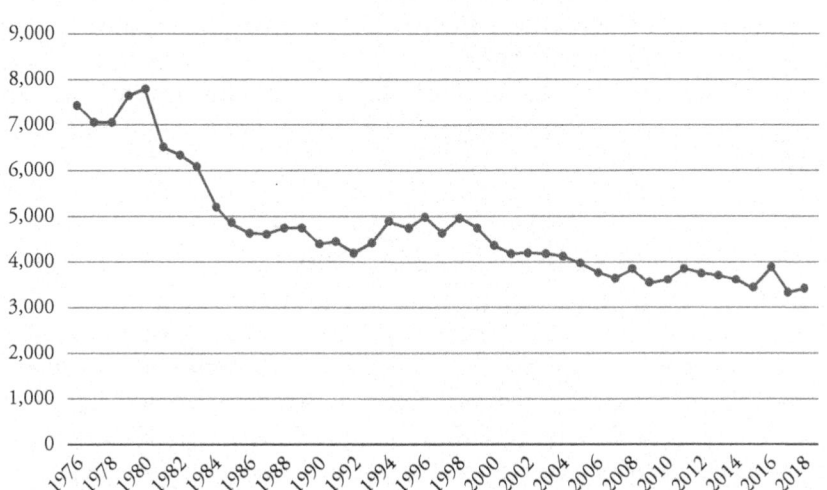

Source: Office of the Federal Register, Federal Register Documents Published 1976-2018. https://www.federalregister.gov/uploads/2019/04/stats2018Fedreg.pdf?page=4.

of the formal and negotiated rulemaking processes. Of those that were informally generated, not all have had (or were intended to have) a significant legal or practical impact. Many of these rules deal with routine agency matters, are temporary rather than permanent, or otherwise have a small regulatory footprint. *See id.* at 7. Nevertheless, informal rulemaking remains the dominant method for producing final rules, and so Figure 5.2 presents us with a rough sense of magnitude. With regard to trends, Figure 5.2 shows a precipitous decline in issuance of final rule documents throughout the 1980s, followed by slower but nevertheless steady decline thereafter. A significant factor in this decline is the deregulatory agenda adopted by President Reagan and to some extent continued by his successors. Upon taking office in 1981, Reagan vowed not only to repeal some regulations and reduce enforcement of others; he promised to reduce the issuance rate of new regulations. Review by OMB of "major rules" was a key to fulfilling that promise, and his successors have adopted and refined the tool of OMB review in one form or another. Congress has likewise contributed to this slowdown by adding procedures and layers of review to the basic rulemaking framework established by the APA.

The materials that follow focus on several critical phases in today's informal rulemaking process. We begin with the notice of proposed rulemaking, which in many ways is the foundational document in the informal rulemaking process. In particular, the materials focus on substantive notice, whether agencies have explained their contemplated actions in a way that gives the public a meaningful opportunity for participation in the rulemaking process. Next, the materials focus on the creation of the rulemaking record, without which judicial review would be difficult if not impossible. Of particular interest here is the issue of *ex parte* contacts. Can agencies have conversations with parties—companies, public interest groups, officials at other agencies, politicians—outside of and apart from the comment mechanism set by the agency? If so, when and under what form must those conversations be disclosed to the public? Finally, we discuss the final rule and, more specifically, the concise general statement of basis and purpose. How much must agencies explain the reasons supporting a final rule to avoid its invalidation by the courts?

1. The Notice of Proposed Rulemaking

The public's right to participate in informal rulemaking would be of little practical import were agencies permitted to issue notices after regulatory actions had already been taken, to publish notices in places difficult for the public to access, or to couch their notices in language that obscures or conceals their policymaking substance. It is for this reason that adequate notice is the foundation of responsive, informed, and fair policymaking. It empowers the regulated public to understand, participate in, and challenge the factual and analytical premises on which agencies base their policies. This, in turn, supports the fundamental legitimacy of administrative rulemaking by making the administrators directly (albeit not entirely) accountable to the people.

Accordingly, § 553 imposes a general requirement that NPRMs state the "time, place and nature" of their informal rulemaking proceedings. *See* 5 U.S.C. § 553(b)(1). NPRMs—under APA § 553(b) and the Federal Register Act, 44 U.S.C. § 1501-1511—must also be published in the Federal Register. Figure 5.3, the first page of the NPRM at issue in *Chocolate Manufacturers Association v. Block*, below, provides a standard NPRM example. The first column indicates the issuing agency, the proposed action (in this instance a "Proposed rule"), the date by which and where interested parties must send comments, and an agency contact person. In addition to these largely logistical details, NPRMs must provide the public with *substantive* notice. Notices must include enough specificity to identify the proposed rule's subject matter, the actions the agency plans to take regarding it, and the facts and analysis informing those actions. *See* § 553(b)(3). The underlying intention here is straightforward: an agency's failure to disclose pertinent information makes meaningful public engagement with policymaking impossible. As in the example in Figure 5.3, most NPRMs provide this information in the Supplementary Information section, which, depending on the complexity of the issues involved, can be brief or several pages long.

It is here we see one of the key practical differences between formal and informal rulemaking. Whereas the former allows for interactive questioning that may elicit information the agency may not have thought relevant or sufficiently important to self-disclose, the latter provides for no such iterative inquiries. Disclosure at the front end is all the public gets, unless the agency decides or is statutorily required to hold hearings or to reopen the comment period after receiving an initial round of public commentary. Accordingly, the stakes can be much higher for ensuring that NPRMs share information that is pertinent to the agency's policymaking plans.

This concern has come up repeatedly in the context of agencies' obligations to disclose technical data and scientific studies on which they base rulemaking action. Agencies on occasion have been accused of cherry-picking the studies or findings that best support their preferred policy outcomes, while failing to reveal other studies and findings that might undermine them. Courts in such circumstances have often found that agencies must err on the side of greater disclosure. As the D.C. Circuit said in its highly influential *Portland Cement Association v. Ruckelshaus* decision, "[i]t is not consonant with the purpose of a rule-making proceeding to promulgate rules on the basis of inadequate data, or on data that, [to a] critical degree, is known only to the agency." 486 F.2d 375, 393 (D.C. Cir. 1973); *see also Connecticut Light & Power Co. v. Nuclear Regulatory Commission*, 673 F.2d 525, 530-31 (D.C. Cir. 1982) ("To allow an agency to play hunt the peanut with

Figure 5.3

69254   Federal Register / Vol. 44, No. 232 / Friday, November 30, 1979 / Proposed Rules

DEPARTMENT OF AGRICULTURE

Food and Nutrition Service

7 CFR Part 246

Special Supplemental Food Program for Women, Infants and Children

AGENCY: Food and Nutrition Service, USDA.

ACTION: Proposed rule.

SUMMARY: This notice proposes various changes in requirements for the Special Supplemental Food Program for Women, Infants and Children (WIC Program), in order to comply with Section 3 of Pub. L. 95-627 which amends Section 17 of the Child Nutrition Act of 1966 and extends the authorization for the WIC Program through FY 1982. This proposal deals with the kinds and quantities of supplemental foods provided under the WIC Program.

DATES: To be assured of consideration comments must be received on or before January 28, 1980.

ADDRESS: Send comments to Supplemental Food Programs Division, Food and Nutrition Service, U.S. Department of Agriculture, Washington, D.C. 20250.

FOR FURTHER INFORMATION CONTACT: Jane McNeil, Acting Director, Supplemental Food Programs Division, Food and Nutrition Service, U.S. Department of Agriculture, Washington, D.C. 20250, (202) 447-8206.

SUPPLEMENTARY INFORMATION: Pub. L. 94-105 specified key nutrients which were to be provided by WIC Program supplemental foods. New WIC Program legislation enacted by Pub. L. 95-627 requires the Secretary to design food packages to contain nutrients which, based on the latest nutritional research, are shown to be lacking in the diets of the WIC Program target population. The Secretary is required to ensure to the degree possible that the fat, sugar and salt content of the prescribed foods is appropriate. State agencies may request substitutions in the WIC food packages to allow for different cultural eating patterns. The substitution must provide as nearly as possible the nutritional equivalent of the target nutrients offered through the supplemental food which is replaced, and the substitution must be approved by FNS. Pub. L. 95-627 allows the Secretary to donate commodities at a State agency's request for use in the Program.

These requirements are proposed to become effective 6 months after final publication to allow State agencies that period of time to phase these changes into their food delivery systems. These proposals will ensure that the food

packages are closely aligned to participants' needs for supplemental foods, will encourage breastfeeding and will result in improved services to WIC participants. As required by Executive Order 12004 and Department regulations, a draft Impact Analysis Statement concerning the major proposals is available from the address listed above.

The Department believes that public participation in policy development serves as a valuable information source for developing and assessing program alternatives. The Department further believes that any program which it administers should reflect the needs and viewpoints of the public served by the program. Because public participation serves as a means of improving the effectiveness of the Department programs, public input is particularly important prior to the development of regulations. Consequently, prior to issuing this proposal the Department actively sought the advice and assistance of knowledgeable individuals, groups and organizations which were willing to offer assistance and expertise in developing regulations that would most effectively satisfy the health and nutritional needs of the eligible population. The following steps were taken in the development of this proposal.

National Advisory Council on Maternal, Infant and Fetal Nutrition

Input on the WIC food packages has been periodically received from the Advisory Council established by Pub. L. 94-105. The members of the Council have widely diversified backgrounds. The membership includes State and local health officials and administrators of the WIC and Commodity Supplemental Food (CSF) Programs, representatives of the Department of Health, Education and Welfare, three parent participants in the programs, a pediatrician, an obstetrician, representatives from migrant farmworker and advocacy organizations, and a person involved in the retail sale of foods used in the Program. This council has the ability and expertise to consider all aspects of the food packages and is extremely helpful in providing insight into how the food packages are viewed by persons involved with the Program.

The council biennially submits a written report to the Congress and the President with recommendations for administrative and legislative changes. Advisory Council meetings were held in June 1977; February 1978; June 1978; February 1979; May 1979; and September 1979. Prior to each meeting a

notice was published in the **Federal Register** announcing the dates of each meeting and advising that the meetings were open to the public. At these meetings the nutritional needs of the target population and the specific WIC food packages were discussed.

Public Hearings. In June 1977 public hearings were held in seven cities to consider public comments regarding possible legislative and regulatory changes for the WIC Program. The hearings were held to solicit public testimony concerning the future structure and administration of the Program. The Washington Supplemental Food Programs Division, the Regional Administrators and their staffs, and the Information Division worked together to ensure that all interested parties were aware of the hearings and were encouraged to attend and testify. The Supplemental Food Programs Division published a notice in the **Federal Register** and worked with the Information Division to produce a public release, posters, and other forms of communication to bring media attention to the hearings. In addition, the supplemental Food Programs Division sent over 750 invitations to individuals as well as to every Governor, the House Education and Labor Committee, the Senate Select Committee on Nutrition, all members of the Advisory Council and Advisory Committee on Nutrition Evaluation, advocacy groups, grass roots organizations, industry representatives and professional groups. Regional Administrators wrote to all State Chief Health Officers and to all State WIC Coordinators. All individuals who desired to testify were allowed to do so. Time was allowed at the end of each speaker's testimony for questions from the floor. Public testimony on the food package covered the addition of new food items, the sugar levels of WIC cereal, the variety of cereals available, and the allowance of non-iron fortified infant formula.

Advisory Panel Meeting. The Department convened a Food Package Avisory Panel in October 1978 to review the current WIC Food packages and recommend changes. Members of the Advisory Panel included State health officials, representatives from the nutrition community and advocacy groups and a parent participant.

Public Comment. The preamble to the final WIC regulations published on August 26, 1977, included a discussion of the WIC authorized cereals. Specifically, the sugar and fortification levels of the cereals, the iron requirement for the cereals, and the issues of whole grains and artificial flavors and colors were

First Page of Food and Nutrition Service NPRM on Supplemental Foods, November 30, 1979.

technical information, hiding or disguising the information that it employs, is to condone a practice in which the agency treats what should be genuine interchange as mere bureaucratic sport.").

A related notice issue arises when interested members of the public claim that they could never have anticipated the content of the final rule based on what the agency said in its NPRM. The claim here is that the content of the final rule and the NPRM are so different that the NPRM failed to provide adequate notice of the agency's policymaking intentions. *See, e.g., CSX Transportation, Inc. v. Surface Transportation Board,* 584 F.3d 1076, 1079-80 (D.C. Cir. 2009) ("A final rule fails the logical outgrowth test and thus violates the APA's notice and comment requirement where interested parties would have to divine [the agency's] unspoken thoughts, because the final rule was surprisingly distant from the proposed rule.") (internal quotations and citations omitted). This is the concern addressed by the Fourth Circuit in the following case, *Chocolate Manufacturers Association v. Block.* To resolve it, the court applied the "logical outgrowth" test, which gauges whether and to what extent the contents of a final rule could have been anticipated from the notice that preceded it.

Chocolate Manufacturers Association v. Block
755 F.2d 1098 (4th Cir. 1985)

Before RUSSELL and SPROUSE, Circuit Judges, and HARGROVE, United States District Judge for the District of Maryland, sitting by designation.

SPROUSE, Circuit Judge:

Chocolate Manufacturers Association (CMA) appeals from the decision of the district court denying it relief from a rule promulgated by the Food and Nutrition Service (FNS) of the United States Department of Agriculture (USDA or Department). CMA protests that part of the rule that prohibits the use of chocolate flavored milk in the federally funded Special Supplemental Food Program for Women, Infants and Children (WIC Program). Holding that the Department's proposed rulemaking did not provide adequate notice that the elimination of flavored milk would be considered in the rulemaking procedure, we reverse.

I

Since 1946 USDA has administered a variety of child nutrition programs under the National School Lunch Act and the Child Nutrition Act of 1966. Besides the WIC Program, these programs are the National School Lunch Program, the Special Milk Program for Children, the School Breakfast Program, the Summer Food Service Program, and the Child Care Food Program.

The WIC Program was established by Congress in 1972 to assist pregnant, postpartum, and breastfeeding women, infants and young children from families with inadequate income whose physical and mental health is in danger because of inadequate nutrition or health care. Under the program, the Department designs food packages reflecting the different nutritional needs of women, infants, and children and provides cash grants to state or local agencies, which distribute cash or vouchers to qualifying individuals in accordance with Departmental regulations as to the type and quantity of food.

In 1975 Congress revised and extended the WIC Program through fiscal year 1978 and, for the first time, defined the "supplemental foods" which the program was established to provide. The term

> shall mean those foods containing nutrients known to be lacking in the diets of populations at nutritional risk and, in particular, those foods and food products containing high-quality protein, iron, calcium, vitamin A, and vitamin C. . . . The contents of the food package shall be made available in such a manner as to provide flexibility, taking into account medical and nutritional objectives and cultural eating patterns.

Pub. L. No. 94-105, § 17(g)(3), 89 Stat. 511, 520 (1975) (codified at 42 U.S.C. § 1786(g)(3) (1976)) (replaced by 42 U.S.C. § 1786(b)(14) (1982)).

Pursuant to this statutory definition, the Department promulgated new regulations specifying the contents of WIC Program food packages. These regulations specified that flavored milk was an acceptable substitute for fluid whole milk in the food packages for women and children, but not infants. This regulation formalized the Department's practice of permitting the substitution of flavored milk, a practice observed in the WIC Program since its inception in 1973 as well as in several of the other food programs administered by the Department.

In 1978 Congress, in extending the WIC Program through fiscal year 1982, redefined the term "supplemental foods" to mean:

> those foods containing nutrients determined by nutritional research to be lacking in the diets of pregnant, breastfeeding, and postpartum women, infants, and children, as prescribed by the Secretary. State agencies may, with the approval of the Secretary, substitute different foods providing the nutritional equivalent of foods prescribed by the Secretary, to allow for different cultural eating patterns.

PUB. L. No. 95-627, § 17(b)(14), 92 Stat. 3603, 3613 (1978) (codified at 42 U.S.C. § 1786(b)(14) (1982)). Congress stated further:

> The Secretary shall prescribe by regulation supplemental foods to be made available in the program under this section. To the degree possible, the Secretary shall assure that the fat, sugar, and salt content of the prescribed foods is appropriate.

Id. at § 17(f)(12), 92 Stat. at 3616 (codified at 42 U.S.C. § 1786(f)(12) (1982)). To comply with this statutory redefinition, the Department moved to redraft its regulations specifying the WIC Program food packages. In doing so it relied upon information collected during an extensive investigative effort which had begun in 1977. In June 1977 the Department held public hearings in seven cities and elicited testimony on the structure and administration of the WIC Program. The Department invited many interested and informed parties to attend these hearings — the governor and chief health officer of every state, the House Education and Labor Committee, the Senate Select Committee on Nutrition Evaluation, state WIC coordinators, industry representatives, and professional and advocacy groups. In addition to information gathered at the public hearings, the Department received periodic reports from the National Advisory Council on Maternal, Infant, and Fetal Nutrition, as well as recommendations from a Food Package Advisory Panel convened in October 1978.

Using this information as well as its own research as a basis, the Department in November 1979 published for comment the proposed rule at issue in this case. 44 Fed. Reg. 69254 (1979). Along with the proposed rule, the Department published a preamble discussing the general purpose of the rule and acknowledging the congressional directive that the Department design food packages containing the requisite nutritional value and appropriate levels of fat, sugar, and salt. *Id.* at 69254. Discussing the issue of sugar at length, it noted, for example, that continued inclusion of high sugar cereals may be "contrary to nutrition education principles and may lead to unsound eating practices." *Id.* at 69263. It also noted that high sugar foods are more expensive than foods with lower sugar content, and that allowing them would be "inconsistent with the goal of teaching participants economical food buying patterns." *Id.*

The rule proposed a maximum sugar content specifically for authorized cereals. The preamble also contained a discussion of the sugar content in juice, but the Department did not propose to reduce the allowable amount of sugar in juice because of technical problems involved in any reduction. Neither the rule nor the preamble discussed sugar in relation to flavoring in milk. Under the proposed rule, the food packages for women and children without special dietary needs included milk that could be "flavored or unflavored." *Id.*

The notice allowed sixty days for comment and specifically invited comment on the entire scope of the proposed rules: "The public is invited to submit written comments in favor of or in objection to the proposed regulations or to make recommendations for alternatives not considered in the proposed regulations." *Id.* at 69255. Over 1,000 comments were received from state and local agencies, congressional offices, interest groups, and WIC Program participants and others. Seventy-eight commenters, mostly local WIC administrators, recommended that the agency delete flavored milk from the list of approved supplemental foods.

In promulgating the final rule, the Department, responding to these public comments, deleted flavored milk from the list, explaining:

> In the previous regulations, women and children were allowed to receive flavored or unflavored milk. No change in this provision was proposed by the Department. However, 78 commenters requested the deletion of flavored milk from the food packages since flavored milk has a higher sugar

content than unflavored milk. They indicated that providing flavored milk contradicts nutrition education and the Department's proposal to limit sugar in the food packages. Furthermore, flavored milk is more expensive than unflavored milk. The Department agrees with these concerns. There are significant differences in the sugar content of fluid whole milk and low fat chocolate milk. Fluid whole milk supplies 12.0 grams of carbohydrate per cup compared to 27.3 grams of carbohydrate per cup provided by low fat chocolate milk. If we assume that the major portion of carbohydrate in milk is in the form of simple sugar, fluid whole milk contains 4.9% sugar contrasted with 10.9% sugar in low fat chocolate milk. Therefore, to reinforce nutrition education, for consistency with the Department's philosophy about sugar in the food packages, and to maintain food package costs at economic levels, the Department is deleting flavored milk from the food packages for women and children. Although the deletion of flavored milk was not proposed, the comments and the Department's policy on sugar validate this change.

45 Fed. Reg. 74854, 74865-66 (1980).

After the final rule was issued, CMA petitioned the Department to reopen the rulemaking to allow it to comment, maintaining that it had been misled into believing that the deletion of flavored milk would not be considered. In a letter to CMA dated November 18, 1981, the Department indicated that it would reopen the issue of flavored milk for "further public comments" and would request "rationale both supporting and opposing the disallowance of flavored milk in the WIC Program." It subsequently reversed this position, however, and declined to reopen the rulemaking procedure.

On this appeal, CMA contends first that the Department did not provide notice that the disallowance of flavored milk would be considered, and second that the Department gave no reasoned justification for changing its position about the nutritional value of chocolate in the food distributed under its authority. The Department responds to the first contention by arguing that its notice advised the public of its general concern about high sugar content in the proposed food packages and that this should have alerted potentially interested commenters that it would consider eliminating any food with high sugar content. It also argues in effect that the inclusion of flavored milk in the proposed rule carried with it the implication that both inclusion and exclusion would be considered in the rulemaking process. Because we agree with CMA that the Department provided inadequate notice and, therefore, that it must reopen the comment period on the rule, we do not reach the issue of the reasonable justification for its change of position.

II

The requirement of notice and a fair opportunity to be heard is basic to administrative law. *See* 1 Kenneth Culp Davis, Administrative Law Treatise § 6.1 at 450 (2d ed. 1978). Our single chore is to determine if the Department's notice provided interested persons, including CMA, with that opportunity. We must decide whether inclusion of flavored milk in the allowable food packages under the proposed rule should have alerted interested persons that the Department might reverse its position and exclude flavored milk if adverse comments recommended its deletion from the program.

Section 4 of the Administrative Procedure Act (APA) requires that the notice in the Federal Register of a proposed rulemaking contain "either the terms or substance of the proposed rule or a description of the subjects and issues involved." 5 U.S.C. § 553(b)(3) (1982). The purpose of the notice-and-comment procedure is both "to allow the agency to benefit from the experience and input of the parties who file comments . . . and to see to it that the agency maintains a flexible and open-minded attitude towards its own rules." *National Tour Brokers Ass'n v. United States*, 591 F.2d 896, 902 (D.C. Cir. 1978). The notice-and-comment procedure encourages public participation in the administrative process and educates the agency, thereby helping to ensure informed agency decisionmaking.

The Department's published notice here consisted of the proposed rule and a preamble discussing the negative effect of high sugar content in general and specifically in relation to some foods such as cereals and juices, but it did not mention high sugar content in flavored milk. The proposed rule eliminated certain foods with high sugar content but specifically authorized flavored milk as part of the permissible diet. In a discussion characterized by pointed identification of foods with high sugar content, flavored milk was [conspicuous] by its exclusion. If after comments the agency had adopted without change the proposed rule as its final rule, there could have been no possible objection to the adequacy of notice. The public was fully notified as to what the Department considered to be a healthy and adequate diet for its target group. The final rule, however, dramatically altered the proposed rule, changing for the first time the milk content of the diet by deleting flavored milk. The agency concedes that the elimination of flavored milk by the final rule is a complete reversal from its treatment in the proposed rule, but it explains that the reversal was caused by the comments received from 78 interested parties — primarily professional administrators of the WIC Program.

This presents then not the simple question of whether the notice of a proposed rule adequately informs the public of its intent, but rather the question of how to judge the adequacy of the notice when the proposal it describes is replaced by a final rule which reaches a conclusion exactly opposite to that proposed, on the basis of comments received from parties representing only a single view of a controversy. In reviewing the propriety of such agency action, we are not constrained by the same degree of deference we afford most agency determinations. "Though our review of an agency's final decision is relatively narrow, we must be strict in reviewing an agency's compliance with procedural rules." *BASF Wyandotte Corp. v. Costle*, 598 F.2d at

641; *see also Weyerhauser Co. v. Costle*, 590 F.2d 1011, 1025-28 (D.C. Cir. 1978) (whereas a court defers to an agency's technical judgments, it is less hesitant to reject the agency's interpretation of statutes, and in reviewing an agency's procedural integrity, the court relies on its own independent judgment). "The question of adequacy of notice where a proposed rule is changed after comment . . . requires careful consideration on a case-by-case basis." *BASF*, 598 F.2d at 642.

There is no question that an agency may promulgate a final rule that differs in some particulars from its proposal. Otherwise the agency "can learn from the comments on its proposals only at the peril of starting a new procedural round of commentary." *International Harvester Co. v. Ruckelshaus*, 478 F.2d 615, 632 note 51 (D.C. Cir. 1973). An agency, however, does not have carte blanche to establish a rule contrary to its original proposal simply because it receives suggestions to alter it during the comment period. An interested party must have been alerted by the notice to the possibility of the changes eventually adopted from the comments. Although an agency, in its notice of proposed rulemaking, need not identify precisely every potential regulatory change, the notice must be sufficiently descriptive to provide interested parties with a fair opportunity to comment and to participate in the rulemaking.

There can be no doubt that the final rule in the instant case was the "outgrowth" of the original rule proposed by the agency, but the question of whether the change in it was in character with the original scheme and whether it was a "logical outgrowth" is not easy to answer. In resolving this difficult issue, we recognize that, although helpful, verbal formulations are not omnipotent talismans, and we agree that in the final analysis each case "must turn on how well the notice that the agency gave serves the policies underlying the notice requirement." *Small Refiner Lead Phase-Down Task Force v. EPA*, 705 F.2d 506, 547 (D.C. Cir. 1983). Under either view, we do not feel that CMA was fairly treated or that the administrative rulemaking process was well served by the drastic alteration of the rule without an opportunity for CMA to be heard.

It is apparent that for many years the Department of Agriculture has permitted the use of chocolate in some form in the food distribution programs that it administers. The only time the Department has proposed to remove chocolate in any form from its programs was in April 1978 when it sought to characterize chocolate as a candy and remove it from the School Lunch Program. That proposal was withdrawn after CMA commented, supporting chocolate as a part of the diet. Chocolate flavored milk has been a permissible part of the WIC Program diet since its inception and there have been no proposals for its removal until the present controversy.

The Department sponsored commendable information-gathering proceedings prior to publishing its proposed rule. Together with its own research, the information gathered in the pre-publication information solicitations formed the basis for the proposed rule. Most of the same information was presented to Congress prior to enactment of the 1978 statute that pre-cipitated the 1979 rulemaking here in controversy. The National Advisory Council on Maternal, Infant, and Fetal Nutrition provided information and advice. Regional council meetings were open to the public and held in diverse areas of the country. Department of Agriculture personnel attended a number of regional, state, and local meetings and gathered opinions con-cerning possible changes in the food packages. The agency also gathered a food package advisory panel of experts seeking their recommendations. Food packages were designed based on the information and advice gleaned from these sources. In all of these activities setting out and discussing food pack-ages, including the proposed rule and its preamble, the Department never suggested that flavored milk be removed from the WIC Program.

The published preamble to the proposed rule consisted of twelve pages in the Federal Register discussing in detail factors that would be considered in making the final rule. Two pages were devoted to a general discussion of nutrients, including protein, iron, calcium, vitamin A, vitamin C, folic acid, zinc, and fiber, and the dangers of overconsumption of sugar, fat, and salt. The preamble discussed some foods containing these ingredients and foods posing specific problems. It did not discuss flavored milk.

In the next eight pages of the preamble, the nutrition content of food packages was discussed — under the general headings of "cereal" and "juice" for infants; and "eggs," "milk," "cheese," "peanut butter and mature dried beans and peas," "juice," "additional foods," "cereals," "iron," "sugar," "whole grain cereals," "highly fortified cereals," and "artificial flavors and colors" for women and children. The only reference to milk concerned the correct quan-tity to be provided to children, *i.e.*, 24 quarts per month instead of 28 quarts. Although there was considerable discussion of the sugar content of juice and cereal, there was none concerning flavored milk. Likewise, there was consid-erable discussion of artificial flavor and color in cereal but none concerning flavored milk. The only reference to flavored milk was in the two-page dis-cussion of the individual food packages, which noted that the proposed rule would permit the milk to be flavored or unflavored. The proposed rule which followed the preamble expressly noted that flavored or unflavored milk was permitted in the individual food packages for women and children without special dietary needs.

At the time the proposed rulemaking was published, neither CMA nor the public in general could have had any indication from the history of either the WIC Program or any other food distribution programs that flavored milk was not part of the acceptable diet for women and children without special dietary needs. The discussion in the preamble to the proposed rule was very detailed and identified specific foods which the agency was examining for excess sugar. This specificity, together with total silence concerning any sug-gestion of eliminating flavored milk, strongly indicated that flavored milk was not at issue. The proposed rule positively and unqualifiedly approved the continued use of flavored milk. Under the specific circumstances of this case, it cannot be said that the ultimate changes in the proposed rule were in character with the original scheme or a logical outgrowth of the notice. We can well accept that, in general, an approval of a practice in a proposed rule may properly alert interested parties that the practice may be disapproved in the final rule in the event of adverse comments. The total effect of the history of the use of flavored milk, the preamble discussion, and the proposed rule, however, could have led interested persons only to conclude that a change in flavored milk would not be considered. Although ultimately their comments may well have been futile, CMA and other interested persons at least should have had the opportunity to make them. We believe that there was insufficient notice that the deletion of flavored milk from the WIC Program would be considered if adverse comments were received, and, therefore, that affected parties did not receive a fair opportunity to contribute to the administrative rulemaking process. That process was ill-served by the misleading or inadequate notice concerning the permissibility of chocolate flavored milk in the WIC Program and "does not serve the policy underlying the notice requirement."

The judgment of the district court is therefore reversed, and the case is remanded to the administrative agency with instructions to reopen the comment period and thereby afford interested parties a fair opportunity to comment on the proposed changes in the rule.

Reversed and Remanded with Instructions.

QUESTION SET 5.6

Review & Synthesis

1. The USDA clearly indicated that it was considering elimination of foods high in salt, fat, and sugar from the WIC program. It provided examples of such foods, including cereals and juices. The notice mentioned that flavored milk was an accepted food in packages for WIC recipients. Additionally, 78 commentators recognized that flavored milk fit the general profile of foods targeted for greater scrutiny during the rulemaking. Given all of this why, precisely, does the USDA's supplemental foods rule fail to satisfy the notification standard established by APA § 553(b)(3)? Stated differently, precisely what information was CMA entitled to receive that the supplemental foods NPRM failed to provide? Is the problem here less failure to notify and more detrimental reliance?

2. APA § 553(b)(3) provides that "notice shall include . . . either the terms or substance of the proposed rule or a description of the subjects and issues involved." Does the logical outgrowth test grow logically from this language? In the landmark case of *Vermont Yankee Nuclear Power Corp.*

v. National Resource Defense Council (discussed below at page 331), the Supreme Court held that agencies need only follow those procedures imposed on them by the Constitution, by statute, or by their own regulations. Federal courts have no authority to fashion new procedures for agencies to follow. At what point does the "interpretation" of a statutorily required procedure transform into an impermissible judicially imposed requirement? Consider the following argument made by Judge (now Justice) Brett Kavanaugh regarding the D.C. Circuit's *Portland Cement* doctrine, described in the introduction to this subsection:

> . . . *Portland Cement* stands on a shaky legal foundation (even though it may make sense as a policy matter in some cases). Put bluntly, the *Portland Cement* doctrine cannot be squared with the text of § 553 of the APA. And *Portland Cement*'s lack of roots in the statutory text creates a serious jurisprudential problem because the Supreme Court later rejected this kind of free-form interpretation of the APA. In its landmark *Vermont Yankee* decision, which came a few years after *Portland Cement*, the Supreme Court forcefully stated that the text of the APA binds courts: Section 553 of the APA established the maximum procedural requirements which Congress was willing to have the courts impose upon agencies in conducting rulemaking procedures. . . . Because there is nothing in the bare text of § 553 that could remotely give rise to the *Portland Cement* requirement, some commentators argue that *Portland Cement* is "a violation of the basic principle of *Vermont Yankee* that Congress and the agencies, but not the courts, have the power to decide on proper agency procedures. At the very least, others say, the Supreme Court's decision in *Vermont Yankee* raises a question concerning the continuing vitality of the Portland Cement requirement that an agency provide public notice of the data on which it proposes to rely in a rulemaking."

American Radio Relay League, Inc. v. FCC, 524 F.3d 227, 246 (D.C. Cir. 2008) (Kavanaugh, J., concurring in part, dissenting in part, concurring in judgment). Can the same criticism be lobbed at the Fourth Circuit's use of the logical outgrowth test in *Chocolate Manufacturers Association*?

3. Does *Chocolate Manufacturers Association* say that agencies can *never* deviate from the policy proposals in their NPRM when promulgating final rules? Apart from the seemingly easy cases at the two ends of the analytical spectrum — those in which the agency adopts a final rule identical to the one it proposed, and those in which the agency adopts a final rule that repudiates the one it proposed — how helpful is the logical outgrowth test in separating adequate notices from inadequate ones?

4. What overall effect would you expect the logical outgrowth test to have on agencies' willingness to pursue informal rulemaking? Would it lead them

to seek other, less visible ways of adopting regulatory policies? Would it shift agencies' information-gathering efforts to the pre-notice phase, inducing them to have more interaction with interested parties before publishing NPRMs? Would it lead to multiple reopenings of public comment periods, increasing both the costs and delays of rulemakings?

5. Short of reopening the notice-and-comment period to full public participation on the flavored milk question (which it declined to do), is there anything the USDA could have done to avoid the notice challenge in this case?

---

2. The Rulemaking Record: *Ex Parte* Contacts

Factual record-development is an integral aspect of the judicial decision-making process. Opposing parties gather evidence, judges assess its admissibility, and fact-finders judge its credibility and establish facts based on it. Courts then reach legal conclusions based on those facts. Thus the record-building requirement in judicial proceedings, among other things, keeps decision-makers grounded in the particulars of the disputes before them, limits the scope of their decision-making authority to the considerations deemed pertinent by law, and facilitates effective formal review of their decisions by appellate bodies. Contrast this with the absence of record development requirements in the legislative context. Congress may draw information from almost any source, need not resort to the Federal Rules of Evidence (or any other code for that matter) to determine its admissibility, has broad discretion to deem it probative, and is under no legal obligation to maintain records supporting its factual determinations.

We now turn to the question of which of these two models of record development—the judicial model or the legislative model—best describes agency rulemaking under the APA. The answer, to some extent, is "both." Formal rulemaking under APA §§ 556 and 557 adopts several of the judicial process' record-development requirements. Rules promulgated pursuant to it must be supported by "reliable, probative, and substantial evidence." 5 U.S.C. § 556(d). The "transcript of testimony and exhibits, together with all papers and requests filed in the proceeding, constitutes the exclusive record for decision." § 556(e). Critically, *ex parte* contacts—conversations or other exchanges of information with agency decision-makers outside of official proceedings—are flatly prohibited. § 557(d).

Informal rulemaking, at least according to the text of the APA, features no such restrictions. As originally conceived, agencies engaged in APA notice-and-comment rulemaking "were generally free, in the absence of special statute, to develop factual materials or not to develop them, as they saw fit, unless a party subject to a rule attempted to rebut the presumption [that the rule had a sound factual basis] on judicial review." *See* LUBBERS, A GUIDE TO FEDERAL AGENCY RULEMAKING 287 (citing 2 KENNETH CULP DAVIS, ADMINISTRATIVE LAW TREATISE § 6:1 (1978)). In other words, agencies operating under § 553 enjoyed a presumption that facts supported the rules they promulgated, and the burden was on the rule's challenger to rebut that presumption. It was thus left largely to agencies' discretion whether to develop formal factual records as the rulemaking proceeded. Only after their rules were challenged in court would they have to assemble for judicial inspection whatever materials and information informed their final rules. *See* William F. Pedersen, Jr., *Formal Records and Informal Rulemaking*, 85 YALE L.J. 38 (1975). This is not the case for formal rulemaking; there, agencies have the burden of proving that their rules are supported by substantial evidence. Also, and in contrast to formal rulemaking, the APA imposes no explicit *ex parte* contact restrictions on agencies engaged in informal rulemaking.

Nevertheless, the story of informal rulemaking record development does not end with a reading of the APA's history or its text. Pursuant to the Supreme Court's seminal decision in *Citizens to Preserve Overton Park, Inc. v. Volpe, see infra* page 395, courts began conducting more searching reviews of agency informal adjudications. Like informal rulemakings, the APA does not require agencies to compile formal factual records when engaged in informal adjudication. Rather than simply presuming the rationality of decisions reached through informal adjudication, however, courts insisted on testing them for administrative arbitrariness or capriciousness. To conduct this review, courts needed access to whatever information or materials were before the agency at the time it made its decision. Only then could they search for possible errors. Agencies, in turn, came to recognize their obligation to produce factual records, regardless of what the APA might otherwise require.

Lower courts translated *Overton Park* for use in the informal rulemaking context. *See* Pedersen, *supra*, at 48. They reasoned that public participation in the process could be meaningful only if the public had access to the "whole record" on which the agency planned to base its policymaking. Unfortunately, courts could not agree on what the "whole record" of informal rulemaking was. Some concluded that it consisted of "comments received, hearings held, if any, and the basis and purpose statement." *Rodway v. United States Dep't of Agriculture*, 514 F.2d 809, 817 (D.C. Cir. 1975). Others included additional information, such as responses to comments and agency data and research. *See, e.g., Portland Cement Association v. Ruckelshaus*, 486 F.2d 375 (D.C. Cir. 1973) (technical and scientific data part of the public rulemaking record).

It thus remained an open question heading into the early 1980s whether the public record had to include all of the conversations between an agency and interested parties, including those conducted outside of the formal comment process (i.e., *ex parte* contacts). Posed interrogatively, could agencies engaged in informal rulemaking have side conversations with interested parties before issuing final rules and not tell the public or courts about them?

Again, the text of APA § 553 provided no direct answer. It does not prohibit *ex parte* contacts and makes no mention of an informal rulemaking record. Today, many agencies have adopted their own guidelines on *ex parte* contacts in the hopes of avoiding actual or apparent impropriety. *See, e.g., Ex parte Communications in Informal Rulemaking Proceedings*, Fed. Reg. 9,222-01 (Mar. 5, 2018). At the time, however, courts intent on facilitating meaningful public participation and judicial review felt obliged to develop their own standards.

The D.C. Circuit cases that follow explore different aspects of the quandary. It addressed the question as it relates to private parties in *Home Box Office, Inc. (HBO) v. FCC*. In *Sierra Club v. Costle*, it dealt with governmental *ex parte* contacts, asking what obligations (if any) do agencies have to disclose their conversations with federal officials and politicians.

Home Box Office, Inc. v. Federal Communications Commission
567 F.2d 9 (D.C. Cir. 1977)

Before WRIGHT and MACKINNON, Circuit Judges, and WEIGEL,* District judge.

PER CURIAM:
In these 15 cases, consolidated for purposes of argument and decision, petitioners challenge various facets of four orders of the Federal Communications Commission which, taken together, regulate and limit the program fare "cablecasters" and "subscription broadcast television stations" may offer to the public for a fee set on a per-program or per-channel basis. . . . We . . . uphold the orders challenged here insofar as they relate to subscription broadcast television and vacate the orders as arbitrary, capricious, and unauthorized by law in all other respects.

I. THE FACTUAL BACKGROUND

At the heart of these cases are the Commission's "pay cable" rules. . . . The effect of these rules is to restrict sharply the ability of cablecasters to present feature film and sports programs if a separate program or channel charge is made for this material. In addition, the rules prohibit cablecasters from devoting more than 90 percent of their cablecast hours to movie and sports programs and further bar cablecasters from showing commercial advertising

---

* Of the United States District Court for the Northern District of California, sitting by designation pursuant to 28 U.S.C. § 292(d) (1970).

on cable channels on which programs are presented for a direct charge to the viewer. Virtually identical restrictions apply to subscription broadcast television. . . .

[The first subscription broadcast television licenses issued by the FCC in 1959 included a number of operating limitations, including] restrictions on feature films, sports events, and series programs that could be shown for a fee, and prohibited commercial advertising during subscription operations. The purpose of these limitations was twofold. First, the Commission had agonized over both its authority to dedicate one or more channels from the electronic spectrum to subscription operations and the desirability of doing so. Such channels are scarce, and opponents of subscription television had argued that they should be used for conventional programming which would, of course, be free to all viewers. The Commission ultimately concluded that it had the required authority, a position sustained by this Court . . ., but that subscription service would not be desirable unless the programming presented was distinct from that on conventional advertiser-supported television. As a result, the Commission placed restrictions on the number of hours of feature films and sports programs, both [of which were] readily available on conventional television, that could be shown and prohibited commercial advertising in an effort to remove any economic pressure to appeal to a mass audience, a pressure to which the Commission attributed the sameness of conventional television fare. A second reason for restricting the feature films, sports events, and series programs that could be shown on subscription television was the Commission's fear that the revenue derived from subscription operations would be sufficient to allow subscription operators to bid away the best programs in these categories, thus reducing the quality of conventional television. By limiting the subscription operator to material that would not otherwise be shown on [broadcast] television, the Commission hoped both to prevent such "siphoning" and to enhance the diversity of program offerings on broadcast television as a whole. . . .

The Commission's regulation of cable television [("CATV")] reflects its technological development. At first the Commission eschewed regulation altogether. However, as CATV systems with multiple channels developed, the Commission asserted jurisdiction over cable operations to prevent fragmentation of audiences and revenues between local broadcasters and competing cable systems which were bringing distant broadcast signals into local markets. In 1968 the Commission launched a further, broad-ranging inquiry into the uses to which cable television might be put in the national communications network. The outcome of these proceedings was a series of regulations which, among other things, required cable systems in major markets to provide cablecasting services, to set aside "access channels" on which members of the public could rent time to produce and transmit their own shows, and to furnish channels for government and educational use. The Commission specifically declined, however, to promulgate rules for cable television similar to those adopted for subscription broadcast television. The reasons given were that the Commission had no information which would indicate that pay cable television could penetrate any television market to the extent needed to "siphon" programming, and that the Commission would in any event be able to act in time to correct any adverse effects on conventional broadcasting.

> ### In Context
>
> Although the opinion refers to the FCC's "orders," these are not the orders agencies issue pursuant to formal adjudications (or any other adjudications). Rather, the FCC issues a "Report and Order" ("R&O") after considering public input received during the informal rulemaking comment period. These R&Os may develop new rules, amend existing rules, or announce the FCC's decision not to move forward with the rulemaking at all. R&Os are published in the Federal Register.

Nine months later the Commission reversed its course and applied the rules developed in the subscription broadcast field to cable television. The reasons for such a quick reversal are not clear in the Order and a number of the petitioners here filed petitions to reconsider imposition of the subscription broadcast rules on the ground that the Commission's abrupt change of course was arbitrary and not adequately explained. These petitions for reconsideration were denied. In this same order Docket 19554, which spawned the orders reviewed here, was established. In its *First Report and Order* in this docket, the Commission re-adopted, with minor modifications, the pay cable rules originally announced. Petitions for reconsideration of this *Report and Order* were denied, except to the extent that some petitioners sought to establish reporting requirements designed to enhance enforcement of the rules. Contemporaneously the Commission issued a *Second Further Notice of Proposed Rule Making* eliciting additional information on the rules relating to series programming. On the basis of that information the Commission deleted any restriction on subscription use of series programs. . . .

. . . Siphoning is said to occur when an event or program currently shown on conventional free television is purchased by a cable operator for showing on a subscription cable channel. If such a transfer occurs, the Commission believes, the program or event will become unavailable for showing on the free television system or its showing on free television will be delayed (since the commercial appeal of the cable showing is the assurance of earlier access to program material, an assurance that might itself be brought about by agreement between the seller of the program or event and the subscription cablecaster). In either case a segment of the American people those in areas not served by cable or those too poor to afford subscription cable service could receive delayed access to the program or could be denied access altogether. The ability of the half-million cable subscribers thus to preempt the other 70 million television homes is said to arise from the fact that subscribers are willing to pay more to see certain types of features than are advertisers to spread their messages by attaching them to those same features. . . .

Whether such a siphoning scenario is in fact likely to occur and, if so, whether the result of siphoning would be to lower the quality of free television programming available to certain areas of the country or to certain economic strata of the population are matters of great dispute among the Commission and the various petitioners and intervenors seeking review of the Commission's regulations in this case. Other petitioners both here and before the Commission argue that the rules which ostensibly place cable in a subordinate role in order to increase program diversity[—]a goal which has been basic to a number of Commission regulations[—]in fact diminish diversity by prohibiting subscription cable operators from showing the programs that are most likely to be the financial backbone of a successful cable operation. As a result, it is claimed, cultural and minority programming that could otherwise "piggyback" on a cable system supported by more broadly popular fare is precluded. . . .

IV. *EX PARTE* CONTACTS

During the pendency of this proceeding Mr. Henry Geller, a participant before the Commission and an amicus here, filed with the Commission a "Petition for Revision of Procedures or for Issuance of Notice of Inquiry or Proposed Rule Making." In this petition amicus Geller sought to call the Commission's attention to what were alleged to be violations in these proceedings of the *ex parte* communications doctrine set out by this court in *Sangamon Valley Television Corp. v. United States*, 269 F.2d 221 (D.C. Cir. 1959). The Commission took no action in response to the petition, and amicus now presses us to set aside the orders under review here because of procedural infirmity in their promulgation.

It is apparently uncontested that a number of participants before the Commission sought out individual commissioners or Commission employees for the purpose of discussing *ex parte* and in confidence the merits of the rules under review here. In fact, the Commission itself solicited such communications in its notices of proposed rulemaking and, without discussing the nature, substance, or importance of what was said, argues before us that we should simply ignore these communications because amicus' petition was untimely, because amicus is estopped from complaining about a course of conduct in which he also participated, or, alternatively, because *Sangamon* does not apply. In an attempt to clarify the facts this court *sua sponte* ordered the Commission to provide "a list of all of the *ex parte* presentations, together with the details of each, made to it, or to any of its members or representatives, during the rulemaking proceedings." In response to this order the Commission filed a document over 60 pages long which revealed, albeit imprecisely, widespread *ex parte*

> ### In Context
> *Sangamon Valley Television Corp. v. United States*, 269 F.2d 221 (D.C. Cir. 1959), involved an FCC rule reallocating a VHF television channel from Springfield, Illinois, to St. Louis, Missouri, and two UHF channels from St. Louis to Springfield. The St. Louis licensee benefited, as the VHF was an upgrade in signal strength from UHF. Although the FCC settled on the transfer through a rulemaking procedure, the court said it was actually resolving "conflicting private claims to a valuable privilege." *Id.* at 224. In other words, the court viewed the decision as quasi-adjudicative.

communications involving virtually every party before this court, including amicus Geller.

Unfortunately, the document filed with this court does not allow an assessment of what was said to the Commission by the various persons who engaged in *ex parte* contacts. . . . [Nevertheless, it] is important to note that many contacts occurred in the crucial period between the close of oral argument on October 25, 1974 and the adoption of the *First Report and Order* on March 20, 1975, when the rulemaking record should have been closed while the Commission was deciding what rules to promulgate. The information submitted to this court by the Commission indicates that during this period broadcast interests met some 18 times with Commission personnel, cable interests some nine times, motion picture and sports interests five times each, and "public interest" intervenors not at all.

Although it is impossible to draw any firm conclusions about the effect of *ex parte* presentations upon the ultimate shape of the pay cable rules, the evidence is certainly consistent with often-voiced claims of undue industry influence over Commission proceedings, and we are particularly concerned that the final shaping of the rules we are reviewing here may have been by compromise among the contending industry forces, rather than by exercise of the independent discretion in the public interest the Communications Act vests in individual commissioners. Our concern is heightened by the submission of the Commission's Broadcast Bureau to this court which states that in December 1974 broadcast representatives "described the kind of pay cable regulation that, in their view, broadcasters 'could live with.'" If actual positions were not revealed in public comments, as this statement would suggest, and, further, if the Commission relied on these apparently more candid private discussions in framing the final pay cable rules, then the elaborate public discussion in these dockets has been reduced to a sham.

Even the possibility that there is here one administrative record for the public and this court and another for the Commission and those "in the know" is intolerable. Whatever the law may have been in the past, there can now be no doubt that implicit in the decision to treat the promulgation of rules as a "final" event in an ongoing process of administration is an assumption that an act of reasoned judgment has occurred, an assumption which further contemplates the existence of a body of material documents, comments, transcripts, and statements in various forms declaring agency expertise or policy with reference to which such judgment was exercised. Against this material, "the full administrative record that was before (an agency official) at the time he made his decision," *Citizens to Preserve Overton Park, Inc. v. Volpe*, 401 U.S. at 420, it is the obligation of this court to test the actions of the Commission for arbitrariness or inconsistency with delegated authority. Yet here agency secrecy stands between us and fulfillment of our obligation. As a practical matter, *Overton Park's* mandate means that the public record must reflect what representations were made to an agency so that relevant information supporting or refuting those representations may be brought to the attention of the reviewing courts by persons participating in agency proceedings. This course is obviously foreclosed if communications are made to the agency in secret and the agency itself does not disclose the information presented. Moreover, where, as here, an agency justifies its actions by reference only to information in the public file while failing to disclose the substance of other relevant information that has been presented to it, a reviewing court cannot presume that the agency has acted properly, [*Citizens to Preserve Overton Park, Inc.*, at 415] but must treat the agency's justifications as a fictional account of the actual decisionmaking process and must perforce find its actions arbitrary.

The failure of the public record in this proceeding to disclose all the information made available to the Commission is not the only inadequacy we find here. Even if the Commission had disclosed to this court the substance of what was said to it *ex parte*, it would still be difficult to judge the truth of what the Commission asserted it knew about the television industry because we would not have the benefit of an adversarial discussion among the parties. The importance of such discussion to the proper functioning of the agency decisionmaking and judicial review processes is evident in our cases. . . . This requirement not only allows adversarial critique of the agency but is perhaps one of the few ways that the public may be apprised of what the agency thinks it knows in its capacity as a repository of expert opinion. From a functional standpoint, we see no difference between assertions of fact and expert opinion tendered by the public, as here, and that generated internally in an agency: each may be biased, inaccurate, or incomplete failings which adversary comment may illuminate. Indeed, the potential for bias in private presentations in rulemakings which resolve "conflicting private claims to a valuable privilege," [*Sangamon Valley*,] 269 F.2d at 224, seems to us greater than in cases where we have reversed agencies for failure to disclose internal studies. We do not understand the rulemaking procedures adopted by the Commission to be inconsistent with these views since those procedures provide for a dialogue among interested parties through provisions for comment, reply-comment, and subsequent oral argument. What we do find baffling is why the Commission, which apparently recognizes that ready availability of private contacts saps the efficacy of the public proceedings, nonetheless continues the practice of allowing public and private comments to exist side by side.

Equally important is the inconsistency of secrecy with fundamental notions of fairness implicit in due process and with the ideal of reasoned decisionmaking on the merits which undergirds all of our administrative law. This inconsistency was recognized in *Sangamon*, and we would have thought that the principles announced there so clearly governed the instant proceeding that there could be no question of the impropriety of *ex parte* contacts here. . . .

From what has been said above, it should be clear that information gathered *ex parte* from the public which becomes relevant to a rulemaking will have to be disclosed at some time. On the other hand, we recognize that informal contacts between agencies and the public are the "bread and butter" of the process of administration and are completely appropriate so long as they do not frustrate judicial review or raise serious questions of fairness. Reconciliation of these considerations in a manner which will reduce procedural uncertainty leads us to conclude that communications which are received prior to issuance of a formal notice of rulemaking do not, in general, have to be put in a public file. Of course, if the information contained in such a communication forms the basis for agency action, then, under well established principles, that information must be disclosed to the public in some form. Once a notice of proposed rulemaking has been issued, however, any agency official or employee who is or may reasonably be expected to be involved in the decisional process of the rulemaking proceeding, should refuse to discuss matters relating to the disposition of a rulemaking proceeding with any interested private party, or an attorney or agent for any such party, prior to the agency's decision. If *ex parte* contacts nonetheless occur, we think that any written document or a summary of any oral communication must be placed in the public file established for each rulemaking docket immediately after the communication is received so that interested parties may comment thereon.

For the foregoing reasons, we must consider what steps should be taken to cure the procedural defect introduced by *ex parte* contacts. One option would be simply to vacate all of the rules under review and remand them to the Commission for consideration *de novo*. This approach has two defects, however. First, it is not possible for us to expunge from the Commission's collective memory what was said to it *ex parte*. Consequently, information untested by public scrutiny could influence the outcome of future proceedings if steps are not now taken to put this information on the public record. Second . . . we find it possible to uphold the Commission's rules relating to subscription broadcast television on the basis of the public record as it now stands. We further find no indication in the material already submitted to this court that the subscription broadcast rule amendments benefit persons who participated in *ex parte* contacts. We think the subscription broadcast rules ought, therefore, to remain in effect pending clarification of what was said to the Commission *ex parte*. Such clarification would, of course, require further proceedings to be held to determine what was said to the Commission. . . . Therefore, we today remand the record to the Commission for supplementation with instructions to hold, with the aid of a specially appointed hearing examiner, an evidential hearing to determine the nature and source of all *ex parte* pleas and other approaches that were made to the Commission or its employees after the issuance of the first notice of proposed rulemaking in these dockets. All parties to the former proceeding and to the present review may on request participate fully in the evidential hearing, and may further participate in any proceedings before the Commission which it may hold for the purpose of evaluating the report of the hearing examiner. The

Commission is further instructed to file the supplemented record with this court within 120 days of the date of this opinion, together with its recommendations concerning our disposition of the subscription broadcast television segment of this review. . . . *So ordered.*

[The concurring opinions of Judges MacKinnon and Weigel are omitted].

Sierra Club v. Costle
657 F.2d 298 (D.C. Cir. 1981)

Before ROBB, WALD and GINSBURG, Circuit Judges.

WALD, Circuit Judge:

This case concerns the extent to which new coal-fired steam generators that produce electricity must control their emissions of sulfur dioxide and particulate matter into the air. In June of 1979 EPA revised the regulations called "new source performance standards" ("NSPS" or "standards") governing emission control by coal burning power plants. On this appeal we consider challenges to the revised NSPS brought by environmental groups which contend that the standards are too lax and by electric utilities which contend that the standards are too rigorous. . . . For the reasons stated below, we hold that EPA did not exceed its statutory authority under the Clean Air Act in promulgating the NSPS, and we decline to set aside the standards.

I. INTRODUCTION
A. *The Challenged Standards*

The Clean Air Act provides for direct federal regulation of emissions from new stationary sources of air pollution by authorizing EPA to set performance standards for significant sources of air pollution which may be reasonably anticipated to endanger public health or welfare. In June 1979 EPA promulgated the NSPS involved in this case. The new standards increase pollution controls for new coal-fired electric power plants by tightening restrictions on emissions of sulfur dioxide and particulate matter. Sulfur dioxide emissions are limited to a maximum of 1.2 lbs./MBtu (or 520 ng/j) and a 90 percent reduction of potential uncontrolled sulfur dioxide emissions is required except when emissions to the atmosphere are less than 0.60 lbs./MBtu (or 260 ng/j). When sulfur dioxide emissions are less than 0.60 lbs./MBtu potential emissions must be reduced by no less than 70 percent. In addition, emissions of particulate matter are limited to 0.03 lbs./MBtu (or 13 ng/j). . . .

C. Background

The importance of the challenged standards arises not only from the magnitude of the environmental and health interests involved, but also from the critical implications the new pollution controls have for the economy at the local and national levels. Further heightening the significance of this controversy is the crucial role coal burning power plants are expected to play in our nation's effort to cope with the problems associated with energy scarcity.

Coal is the dominant fuel used for generating electricity in the United States. When coal is burned, it releases sulfur dioxide and particulate matter into the atmosphere. At the very least these pollutants are known to cause or contribute to respiratory illnesses. In 1975 alone electric power plants emitted 18.6 million tons of sulfur dioxide. If the former NSPS had not been changed the total annual national sulfur dioxide emissions could have exceeded 23 million tons by 1995: a 27 percent increase. . . . In 1976 power plant emissions accounted for 64 percent of the total estimated sulfur dioxide emissions and 24 percent of the total estimated particulate matter emissions in the entire country.

EPA's revised NSPS are designed to curtail these emissions. EPA predicts that the new standards would reduce national sulfur dioxide emissions from new plants by 50 percent and national particulate matter emissions by 70 percent by 1995. The cost of the new controls, however, is substantial. EPA estimates that utilities will have to spend tens of billions of dollars by 1995 on pollution control under the new NSPS. Consumers will ultimately bear these costs, both directly in the form of residential utility bills, and indirectly in the form of higher consumer prices due to increased energy costs. Coinciding with these trends the utility industry is expected to have continued and significant growth. Under the new NSPS EPA projects that overall utility capacity should increase by about 50 percent with approximately 300 new fossil-fuel fired power plants to begin operation within the next ten years. And approximately 350 new plants (capable of generating 250 Gigawatts ("GW")) are expected to be constructed by 1995. Present levels of national coal production and consumption will triple by 1995. With oil scarce, the future of nuclear and solar energy uncertain, and hydro limited, "the nation's rich and cheap coal reserves call for exploitation." Not surprisingly, coal burning power plants' already preeminent share of electric power produced in the United States will grow over the remainder of this century. . . .

D. Procedural History

In 1970 Congress for the first time authorized the federal government to set performance standards limiting emissions from newly built or modified sources of air pollution. These sources to be controlled were those that EPA determined emitted pollution contributing substantially to the endangerment of the public health or welfare. EPA decided that large coal-fired generators fell within that category. In December 1971 EPA issued a NSPS for these sources. That first NSPS applied to units capable of firing more than 250 MBtu per hour, and limited sulfur dioxide emissions to 1.2 lbs./MBtu and particulate matter emissions to 0.10 lbs./MBtu. Under this standard it was possible to satisfy the emission limitations simply by burning coal with a low sulfur content.

In 1976 the Sierra Club and the Oljato and Red Mesa Chapters of the Navajo Tribe petitioned EPA to revise the NSPS so as to require a 90 percent reduction in sulfur dioxide emissions. The petition claimed that advances in technology since 1971 justified a revision of the standard. In response to the petition EPA began an investigation of whether the standard should be changed.

While EPA's decision was pending the Clean Air Act Amendments of 1977 were signed into law. Section 111 of the amendments . . . required EPA to revise the standards of performance for electric power plants within one year after the August 1977 enactment date. When it appeared that EPA would not meet this deadline, the Sierra Club filed a complaint in the District Court for the District of Columbia. The court approved a stipulation requiring the proposed regulations to issue in September 1978, and promulgation of final regulations within six months after the proposal. Eventually, after further delay, the final NSPS were promulgated in June 1979.

Several parties petitioned EPA for reconsideration of the revised NSPS. In February of 1980 EPA denied all the petitions for reconsideration.

The present appeal followed. . . .

V. THE 1.2 LBS./MBTU EMISSION CEILING

EPA proposed and ultimately adopted a 1.2 lbs./MBtu ceiling for total sulfur dioxide emissions which is applicable regardless of the percentage of sulfur dioxide reduction attained. The 1.2 lbs./MBtu standard is identical to the emission ceiling required by the former standard. The achievability of the standard is undisputed.

[The Environmental Defense Fund ("EDF")] challenges this part of the final NSPS on procedural grounds, contending that although there may be evidence supporting the 1.2 lbs./MBtu standard, EPA should have and would have adopted a stricter standard if it had not engaged in post-comment period irregularities and succumbed to political pressures. EDF raises its procedural objections in the context of its view that a more stringent emission ceiling would have been better than the 1.2 lbs./MBtu limit because it would decrease total emissions significantly without impeding the production or use of coal. . . .

> **In Context**
>
> As discussed below, the EPA adopts new source performance standards through "statutory hybrid" rulemaking. For the most part, the EPA does not follow the informal rulemaking procedures set out in APA § 553 when promulgating NSPSs. It is instead required to follow the specific informal rulemaking provisions set out in the Clean Air Act § 307(d) (42 U.S.C. § 7607), unless specifically instructed to follow § 553. One such instruction directs that the EPA publish NPRMs falling under § 307(d) in the Federal Register, as required by § 553(b).

B. EDF's Procedural Attack

EDF alleges that as a result of an *"ex parte* blitz" by coal industry advocates conducted after the close of the comment period, EPA backed away from adopting the .55 lbs./MBtu limit, and instead adopted the higher 1.2 lbs./MBtu restriction. EDF asserts that even before the comment period had ended EPA had already narrowed its focus to include only options which provided for the .55 lbs./MBtu ceiling. EDF also claims that as of March 9, 1979, the three proposals which EPA had under active consideration all included the more stringent .55 lbs./MBtu ceiling, and the earlier 1.2 lbs./ MBtu ceiling had been discarded. Whether or not EDF's scenario is credible, it is true that EPA did circulate a draft NSPS with an emissions ceiling below the 1.2 lbs./MBtu level for interagency comment during February, 1978. Following a "leak" of this proposal, EDF says, the so-called *"ex parte* blitz" began. "Scores" of pro-industry *"ex parte"* comments were received by EPA in the post-comment period, states EDF, and various meetings with coal industry advocates including Senator Robert Byrd of West Virginia took place during that period. These communications, EDF asserts, were unlawful and prejudicial to its position. . . .

1. Late Comments

The comment period for the NSPS began on September 19, 1978, and closed on January 15, 1979. After January 15, EPA received almost 300 written submissions on the proposed rule from a broad range of interests. EPA accepted these comments and entered them all on its administrative docket. EPA did not, however, officially reopen the comment period, nor did it notify the public through the Federal Register or by other means that it had received and was entering the "late" comments. According to EDF, most of the approximately 300 late comments were received after the "leak" of the new .55 lbs./MBtu proposal. EDF claims that of the 138 late comments from non-government sources, at least 30 were from "representatives of the coal or utility industries," and of the 53 comments from members of Congress, 22 were either forwarded by the Congressmen from industry interests, or else were prepared and submitted by Congressmen as advocates of those interests.

2. Meetings

EDF objects to nine different meetings. A chronological list and synopsis of the challenged meetings follows:

March 14, 1979—This was a one and a half hour briefing at the White House for high-level officials from the Department of Energy (DOE), the Council of Economic Advisers (CEA), the White House staff, the Department of Interior, the Council on Environmental Quality (CEQ), the Office of Management and Budget (OMB), and the National Park Service. . . . A summary of the meeting and the materials distributed were docketed on May 30, 1979. EDF also obtained, after promulgation of the final rule, a copy of the memorandum to Senator Muskie in response to its Freedom of Information Act ("FOIA") request.

April 5, 1979—. . . The meeting was attended by representatives of EPA, DOE, NCA, EDF, Congressman Paul Simon's office, ICF, Inc. . . . , and Hunton & Williams (who represented the Electric Utilities). The participants were notified in advance of the agenda for the meeting. Materials relating to EPA's and NCA's presentations during the meeting were distributed and copies were later put into the docket along with detailed minutes of the meeting. Followup calls and letters between NCA and EPA came on April 20, 23, and 29, commenting or elaborating upon the April 5 data. All of these followup contacts were recorded in the docket.

April 23, 1979—This was a 30-45 minute meeting held at then Senate Majority Leader Robert Byrd's request, in his office, attended by EPA Administrator Douglas Costle, Chief Presidential Assistant Stuart Eizenstat, and NCA officials. A summary of this meeting was put in the docket on May 1, 1979, and copies of the summary were sent to EDF and to other parties. In its denial of the petition for reconsideration, EPA was adamant that no new information was transmitted to EPA at this meeting.

April 27, 1979—This was a briefing on dry scrubbing technology conducted by EPA for representatives of the Office of Science and Technology Policy, the Council on Wage and Price Stability, DOE, the President's domestic policy staff, OMB, and various offices within EPA. A description of this briefing and copies of the material distributed were docketed on May 1, 1979.

April 30, 1979—At 10:00 a.m., a one hour White House briefing was held for the President, the White House staff, and high ranking members of the Executive Branch "concerning the issues and options presented by the rulemaking." This meeting was noted on an EPA official's personal calendar which EDF obtained after promulgation in response to its FOIA request, but was never noted in the rulemaking docket.

April 30, 1979—At 2:30 p.m., a technical briefing on dry scrubbing technology at the White House was conducted by EPA for the White House staff. A short memorandum describing this briefing was docketed on May 30, 1979.

May 1, 1979—Another White House briefing was held on the subject of FGD technology. A description of the meeting and materials distributed were docketed on May 30, 1979.

May 1, 1979—EPA conducted a one hour briefing of staff members of the Senate Committee on Environmental and Public Works concerning EPA's analysis of the effect of alternative emission ceilings on coal reserves. The briefing was "substantially the same as the briefing given to Senator Byrd on May 2, 1980." No persons other than Committee staff members and EPA officials attended the briefing. This meeting, like the one at 10:00 a.m. on April 30, was never entered on the rulemaking docket but was listed on an EPA official's calendar obtained by EDF in response to its FOIA request. This EPA official has since stated that it was an oversight not to have a memorandum of this briefing prepared for the docket.

May 2, 1979—This was a brief meeting between Senator Byrd, EPA, DOE and NCA officials held ostensibly for Senator Byrd to hear EPA's comments on the NCA data. A 49 word, not very informative, memorandum describing the meeting was entered on the docket on June 1, 1979.

On June 16, 1980, responding to motions filed by EDF, this court ordered EPA to file affidavits providing additional information regarding five of these nine meetings (March 14, April 23, April 27, April 30, and May 2, 1979). After EPA complied with the order, EDF argued that the other meetings held on April 30 and May 1 were still undocumented, whereupon EPA voluntarily filed an affidavit describing them.

EDF believes that the communications just outlined, when taken as a whole, were so extensive and had such a serious impact on the NSPS rulemaking, that they violated EDF's rights to due process in the proceeding, and that these "*ex parte*" contacts were procedural errors of such magnitude that this court must reverse. EDF does not specify which particular features in each of the above-enumerated communications violated due process or constituted errors under the statute; indeed, EDF nowhere lists the communications in a form designed to clarify why any particular communication was unlawful. Instead, EDF labels all post-comment communications with EPA from whatever source and in whatever form as "*ex parte*," and claims that "this court has repeatedly stated that *ex parte* contacts of substance violate due process."

At the outset, we decline to begin our task of reviewing EPA's procedures by labeling all post-comment communications with the agency as "*ex parte*." Such an approach essentially begs the question whether these particular communications in an informal rulemaking proceeding were unlawful. Instead of beginning with a conclusion that these communications were "*ex parte*," we must evaluate the various communications in terms of their timing, source, mode, content, and the extent of their disclosure on the docket, in order to discover whether any of them violated the procedural requirements of the Clean Air Act, or of due process.

C. Standard for Judicial Review of EPA Procedures

This court's scope of review is delimited by the special procedural provisions of the Clean Air Act, which declare that we may reverse the Administrator's decision for procedural error only if (i) his failure to observe procedural requirements was arbitrary and capricious, (ii) an objection was raised during the comment period, or the grounds for such objection arose only after the comment period and the objection is "of central relevance to the outcome of the rule," and (iii) "the errors were so serious and related to matters of such central relevance to the rule that there is a substantial likelihood that the rule would have been significantly changed if such errors had not been made." The essential message of so rigorous a standard is that Congress was concerned that EPA's rulemaking not be casually overturned for procedural reasons, and we of course must respect that judgment.

Our authority to reverse informal administrative rulemaking for procedural reasons is also informed by *Vermont Yankee Nuclear Power Corp. v. Natural Resources Defense Council, Inc.* In its unanimous opinion, the Supreme Court unambiguously cautioned this court against imposing its own notions of proper procedures upon an administrative agency entrusted with substantive functions by Congress. The Court declared that so long as an agency abided by the minimum procedural requirements laid down by statute, this court was not free to impose additional procedural rights if the agency did not choose to grant them. Except in "extremely rare" circumstances, the Court stated, there is no justification for a reviewing court to overturn agency action because of the failure to employ procedures beyond those required by Congress. . . .

D. Statutory Provisions Concerning Procedure

The procedural provisions of the Clean Air Act specifying the creation and content of the administrative rulemaking record are contained in section 307. Responding in part to criticism that there was no formalized record which courts could rely upon when reviewing EPA rules, Congress enacted new procedures which represented "(b)y and large . . . a legislative adoption of the suggestions for a rulemaking record set forth in a law review article dealing with EPA. [William F. Pedersen], *Formal Records and Informal Rulemaking*, 85 YALE L.J. 38 (1975). . . .

Following Pedersen's recommendations, the 1977 Amendments required the agency to establish a "rulemaking docket" for each proposed rule which would form the basis of the record for judicial review. The docket must contain, *inter alia*, (1) "notice of the proposed rulemaking . . . accompanied by a statement of its basis and purpose," and a specification of the public comment period; (2) "all written comments and documentary information on the proposed rule received from any person . . . during the comment period(;) (t)he transcript of public hearings, if any(;) and (a)ll documents . . . which become available after the proposed rule has been published and which the Administrator determines are of central relevance to the rulemaking. . . ."; (3) drafts of proposed rules submitted for interagency review, and all documents accompanying them and responding to them; and (4) the promulgated rule and the various accompanying agency documents which explain and justify it.

In contrast to other recent statutes, there is no mention of any restrictions upon "*ex parte*" contacts. However, the statute apparently did envision that participants would normally submit comments, documentary material, and oral presentations during a prescribed comment period. . . .

. . . [T]his court can reverse an agency on procedural grounds only if it finds a failure to observe procedures "required by law," [so] we must first decide whether the procedures followed by EPA between January 15 and June 1, 1979 were unlawful. Only if we so find would we then face the second issue whether the unlawful errors were "of such central relevance to the rule that there is a substantial likelihood that the rule would have been significantly changed if such errors had not been made." 42 U.S.C. § 7607(d)(8). We now hold that EPA's procedures during the post-comment period were lawful, and therefore do not face the issue whether any alleged errors were of "central relevance" to the outcome.

E. Validity of EPA's Procedures During the Post-Comment Period

The post-comment period communications about which EDF complains vary widely in their content and mode; some are written documents or letters, others are oral conversations and briefings, while still others are meetings where alleged political arm-twisting took place. For analytical purposes we have grouped the communications into categories and shall discuss each of them separately. As a general matter, however, we note at the outset that nothing in the statute prohibits EPA from admitting all post-comment communications into the record; nothing expressly requires it, either. Most likely the drafters envisioned promulgation of a rule soon after the close of the public comment period, and did not envision a months-long hiatus where continued outside communications with the agency would continue unabated. We must therefore attempt to glean the law for this case by inference from the procedural framework provided in the statute.

1. Written Comments Submitted During Post-Comment Period

Although no express authority to admit post-comment documents exists, the statute does provide that:

> All documents which become available after the proposed rule has been published and which the Administrator determines are of central relevance to the rulemaking shall be placed in the docket as soon as possible after their availability.

This provision, in contrast to others in the same subparagraph, is not limited to the comment period. Apparently it allows EPA not only to put documents into the record after the comment period is over, but also to define which documents are "of central relevance" so as to require that they be placed in the docket. The principal purpose of the drafters was to define in advance, for the benefit of reviewing courts, the record upon which EPA would rely in defending the rule it finally adopted; it was not their purpose to guarantee that every piece of paper or phone call related to the rule which was received by EPA during the post-comment period be included in the docket. EPA thus has authority to place post-comment documents into the docket, but it need not do so in all instances. . . .

If . . . documents of central importance upon which EPA intended to rely had been entered on the docket too late for any meaningful public comment prior to promulgation, then both the structure and spirit of section 307 would have been violated. The Congressional drafters, after all, intended to provide "thorough and careful procedural safeguards . . . (to) insure an effective opportunity for public participation in the rulemaking process." H. Rep. No. 95-294. Indeed the Administrator is obligated by the statute to convene a proceeding to reconsider the rule where an objection of central importance to it is proffered, and the basis of the objection arose after the comment period had closed. Thus we do not hold that there are no circumstances in which reopening the comment period would ever be required.

The case before us, however, does not present an instance where documents vital to EPA's support for its rule were submitted so late as to preclude any effective public comment. The vast majority of the written comments referred to earlier . . . were submitted in ample time to afford an opportunity for response. Regarding those documents submitted closer to the promulgation date, our review does not reveal that they played any significant role in the agency's support for the rule. The decisive point, however, is that EDF itself has failed to show us any particular document or documents to which it lacked an opportunity to respond, and which also were vital to EPA's support for the rule. . . .

We therefore conclude that it was not improper in this case for EPA to docket and consider the post-comment documents submitted to it. Nor was it improper for EPA to decline to reopen the formal comment period and delay promulgation, since there was no proof that evidence crucial to the rule's validity was entered too late for any effective public comment.

2. Meetings Held With Individuals Outside EPA

The statute does not explicitly treat the issue of post-comment period meetings with individuals outside EPA. Oral face-to-face discussions are not prohibited anywhere, anytime, in the Act. The absence of such prohibition may have arisen from the nature of the informal rulemaking procedures Congress had in mind. Where agency action resembles judicial action, where it involves formal rulemaking, adjudication, or quasi-adjudication among "conflicting private claims to a valuable privilege,"[499] the insulation of the decisionmaker from *ex parte* contacts is justified by basic notions of due process to the parties involved. But where agency action involves informal rulemaking of a policymaking sort, the concept of *ex parte* contacts is of more questionable utility.

Under our system of government, the very legitimacy of general policymaking performed by unelected administrators depends in no small part upon the openness, accessibility, and amenability of these officials to the needs and ideas of the public from whom their ultimate authority derives, and upon whom their commands must fall. As judges we are insulated from these pressures because of the nature of the judicial process in which we participate; but we must refrain from the easy temptation to look askance at all face-to-face lobbying efforts, regardless of the forum in which they occur, merely because we see them as inappropriate in the judicial context. Furthermore, the importance to effective regulation of continuing contact with a regulated industry, other affected groups, and the public cannot be underestimated. Informal contacts may enable the agency to win needed support for its program, reduce future enforcement requirements by helping those regulated to anticipate and shape their plans for the future, and spur the provision of information which the agency needs. The possibility of course exists that in permitting *ex parte* communications with rulemakers we create the danger of "one administrative record for the public and this court and another for the Commission."[505] Under the Clean Air Act procedures, however, "(t)he promulgated rule may not be based (in part or whole) on any information or data which has not been placed in the docket. . . ." Thus EPA must justify its rulemaking solely on the basis of the record it compiles and makes public.

Regardless of this court's views on the need to restrict all post-comment contacts in the informal rulemaking context, however, it is clear to us that Congress has decided not to do so in the statute which controls this case. . . .

Lacking a statutory basis for its position, EDF would have us extend our decision in *Home Box Office, Inc. v. FCC* to cover all meetings with individuals outside EPA during the post-comment period. Later decisions of this court, however, have declined to apply *Home Box Office* to informal rulemaking of the general policymaking sort involved here, and there is no precedent for applying it to the procedures found in the Clean Air Act Amendments of 1977.

It still can be argued, however, that if oral communications are to be freely permitted after the close of the comment period, then at least some

---

[499] *Sangamon Valley Television Corp. v. United States,* 269 F.2d 221, 224 (D.C. Cir. 1959) (FCC channel assignment proceeding involved claims of this sort, and "basic fairness requires such proceeding to be carried on in the open").

[505] *Home Box Office, Inc. v. FCC,* 567 F.2d 9, 54 (D.C. Cir.), *cert. denied,* 434 U.S. 829 (1977).

adequate summary of them must be made in order to preserve the integrity of the rulemaking docket, which under the statute must be the sole repository of material upon which EPA intends to rely. The statute does not require the docketing of all post-comment period conversations and meetings, but we believe that a fair inference can be drawn that in some instances such docketing may be needed in order to give practical effect to section 307(d)(4)(B)(i), which provides that all documents "of central relevance to the rulemaking" shall be placed in the docket as soon as possible after their availability. This is so because unless oral communications of central relevance to the rulemaking are also docketed in some fashion or other, information central to the justification of the rule could be obtained without ever appearing on the docket, simply by communicating it by voice rather than by pen, thereby frustrating the command of section 307 that the final rule not be "based (in part or whole) on any information or data which has not been placed in the docket. . . ."

EDF is understandably wary of a rule which permits the agency to decide for itself when oral communications are of such central relevance that a docket entry for them is required. Yet the statute itself vests EPA with discretion to decide whether "documents" are of central relevance and therefore must be placed in the docket; surely EPA can be given no less discretion in docketing oral communications, concerning which the statute has no explicit requirements whatsoever. Furthermore, this court has already recognized that the relative significance of various communications to the outcome of the rule is a factor in determining whether their disclosure is required. A judicially imposed blanket requirement that all post-comment period oral communications be docketed would, on the other hand, contravene our limited powers of review, would stifle desirable experimentation in the area by Congress and the agencies, and is unnecessary for achieving the goal of an established, procedure-defined docket, *viz.*, to enable reviewing courts to fully evaluate the stated justification given by the agency for its final rule.

Turning to the particular oral communications in this case, we find that only two of the nine contested meetings were undocketed by EPA. The agency has maintained that, as to the May 1 meeting where Senate staff people were briefed on EPA's analysis concerning the impact of alternative emissions ceilings upon coal reserves, its failure to place a summary of the briefing in the docket was an oversight. We find no evidence that this oversight was anything but an honest inadvertence; furthermore, a briefing of this sort by EPA which simply provides background information about an upcoming rule is not the type of oral communication which would require a docket entry under the statute.

The other undocketed meeting occurred at the White House and involved the President and his White House staff. Because this meeting involves considerations unique to intra-executive meetings, it is discussed in the section immediately *infra*.

(a) Intra-executive branch meetings

We have already held that a blanket prohibition against meetings during the post-comment period with individuals outside EPA is unwarranted, and this perforce applies to meetings with White House officials. We have not yet addressed, however, the issue whether such oral communications with White House staff, or the President himself, must be docketed on the rulemaking record, and we now turn to that issue. The facts, as noted earlier, present us with a single undocketed meeting held on April 30, 1979, at 10:00 a.m., attended by the President, White House staff, other high ranking members of the Executive Branch, as well as EPA officials, and which concerned the issues and options presented by the rulemaking.

We note initially that section 307 makes specific provision for including in the rulemaking docket the "written comments" of other executive agencies along with accompanying documents on any proposed draft rules circulated in advance of the rulemaking proceeding. Drafts of the final rule submitted to an executive review process prior to promulgation, as well as all "written comments," "documents," and "written responses" resulting from such inter-agency review process, are also to be put in the docket prior to promulgation. This specific requirement does not mention informal meetings or conversations concerning the rule which are not part of the initial or final review processes, nor does it refer to oral comments of any sort. Yet it is hard to believe Congress was unaware that intra-executive meetings and oral comments would occur throughout the rulemaking process. We assume, therefore, that unless expressly forbidden by Congress, such intra-executive contacts may take place, both during and after the public comment period; the only real issue is whether they must be noted and summarized in the docket.

The court recognizes the basic need of the President and his White House staff to monitor the consistency of executive agency regulations with Administration policy. He and his White House advisers surely must be briefed fully and frequently about rules in the making, and their contributions to policymaking considered. . . .

The authority of the President to control and supervise executive policymaking is derived from the Constitution; the desirability of such control is demonstrable from the practical realities of administrative rulemaking. Regulations such as those involved here demand a careful weighing of cost, environmental, and energy considerations. They also have broad implications for national economic policy. Our form of government simply could not function effectively or rationally if key executive policymakers were isolated from each other and from the Chief Executive. Single mission agencies do not always have the answers to complex regulatory problems. An overworked administrator exposed on a 24-hour basis to a dedicated but zealous staff needs to know the arguments and ideas of policymakers in other agencies as well as in the White House.

We recognize, however, that there may be instances where the docketing of conversations between the President or his staff and other Executive Branch officers or rulemakers may be necessary to ensure due process. This may be true, for example, where such conversations directly concern the outcome of adjudications or quasi-adjudicatory proceedings; there is no inherent executive power to control the rights of individuals in such settings. Docketing may also be necessary in some circumstances where a statute like this one specifically requires that essential "information or data" upon which a rule is based be docketed. But in the absence of any further Congressional requirements, we hold that it was not unlawful in this case for EPA not to docket a face-to-face policy session involving the President and EPA officials during the post-comment period, since EPA makes no effort to base the rule on any "information or data" arising from that meeting. Where the President himself is directly involved in oral communications with Executive Branch officials, Article II considerations combined with the strictures of *Vermont Yankee* require that courts tread with extraordinary caution in mandating disclosure beyond that already required by statute.

The purposes of full-record review which underlie the need for disclosing *ex parte* conversations in some settings do not require that courts know the details of every White House contact, including a Presidential one, in this informal rulemaking setting. After all, any rule issued here with or without White House assistance must have the requisite factual support in the rulemaking record, and under this particular statute the Administrator may not base the rule in whole or in part on any "information or data" which is not in the record, no matter what the source. The courts will monitor all this, but they need not be omniscient to perform their role effectively. Of course, it is always possible that undisclosed Presidential prodding may direct an outcome that is factually based on the record, but different from the outcome that would have obtained in the absence of Presidential involvement. In such a case, it would be true that the political process did affect the outcome in a way the courts could not police. But we do not believe that Congress intended that the courts convert informal rulemaking into a rarified technocratic process, unaffected by political considerations or the presence of Presidential power. In sum, we find that the existence of intra-Executive Branch meetings during the post-comment period, and the failure to docket one such meeting involving the President, violated neither the procedures mandated by the Clean Air Act nor due process.

(b) Meetings involving alleged congressional pressure

Finally, EDF challenges the rulemaking on the basis of alleged Congressional pressure, citing principally two meetings with Senator Byrd. . . .

Senator Byrd requested a meeting in order to express "strongly" his already well-known views that the SO2 standards' impact on coal reserves was a matter of concern to him. EPA initiated a second responsive meeting to report its reaction to the reserve data submitted by the NCA. In neither meeting is there any allegation that EPA made any commitments to Senator Byrd. The meetings did underscore Senator Byrd's deep concerns for EPA, but there is no evidence he attempted actively to use "extraneous" pressures to further his position. Americans rightly expect their elected representatives to voice their grievances and preferences concerning the administration of our laws. We believe it entirely proper for Congressional representatives vigorously to represent the interests of their constituents before administrative agencies engaged in informal, general policy rulemaking, so long as individual Congressmen do not frustrate the intent of Congress as a whole as expressed in statute, nor undermine applicable rules of procedure. Where Congressmen keep their comments focused on the substance of the proposed rule and we have no substantial evidence to cause us to believe Senator Byrd did not do so here administrative agencies are expected to balance Congressional pressure with the pressures emanating from all other sources. To hold otherwise would deprive the agencies of legitimate sources of information and call into question the validity of nearly every controversial rulemaking.

* * *

In sum, we conclude that EPA's adoption of the 1.2 lbs./MBtu emissions ceiling was free from procedural error. . . .

Affirmed.

QUESTION SET 5.7

Review & Synthesis

1. Which APA provisions govern the creation and disclosure of factual records in formal and informal rulemaking? Which provisions govern the inclusion or exclusion of *ex parte* contacts specifically?

2. Did the D.C. Circuit in *Sierra Club* apply its precedent in *HBO v. FCC* when determining whether the Environmental Defense Fund was entitled to more procedural rights than provided by the EPA? Why or why not?

3. With regard to *HBO v. FCC*:
   a. The court heavily relied on two cases in reaching its decision. First, it invoked its *Sangamon Valley* precedent. *Sangamon Valley* involved the FCC's decision to reallocate VHF and UHF television channels. A D.C. Circuit panel viewed the decision as adjudicative even

though the FCC issued it through rulemaking. Second, the court frequently referred to the Supreme Court's decision in *Citizens to Preserve Overton Park, Inc. v. Volpe*, which involved an informal adjudication. This implies that the court viewed the FCC's pay TV proceedings as more adjudicative than legislative. Applying the Court's *Bi-Metallic Investment Co. v. State Board of Equalization* analysis, how would you characterize the FCC's proceedings here?

b. How far do you think the D.C. Circuit intended *HBO* to reach? Did the court intend to severely restrict *ex parte* contacts in *all* informal rulemakings, or just those involving "conflicting private claims to a valuable privilege" as in *Sangamon Valley*? A different panel of the D.C. Circuit seemed to think the former, and repudiated the implication. *See Action for Children's Television v. FCC*, 564 F.2d 458, 477 (D.C. Cir. 1977).

c. What was the source of the court's legal authority to order supplementation of the rulemaking record or the "evidential hearing" with a hearing examiner to determine the nature and sources of the proceedings' *ex parte* contacts? Was it a statute? The Due Process Clause? Something else?

d. What, precisely, was the *factual* harm suffered by the "public interest" intervenors here? In light of that factual harm, do you think the court's remedy—remand of the record to the FCC for supplementation, identification of all *ex parte* communications, additional opportunities for interested party commentary, etc.—was appropriate? Did it take appropriate account of the free-flowing exchange of information that the APA's drafters expected would characterize informal rulemakings? Was it more likely to hinder the flow of information to the FCC?

4. With regard to *Sierra Club*:
   a. Answer the following questions raised by the *ex parte* contacts at issue in the case:
      1. Does Clean Air Act § 307 permit the EPA to engage in *ex parte* contacts at all? If so, must those contacts be made part of the informal rulemaking record?
      2. What restrictions does § 307 place on *ex parte* contacts between the EPA and other government officials? Does the treatment of intra-governmental *ex parte* contacts depend on whether the official is in Congress or in the Executive Branch? On whether the official is a bureaucrat or a politician?
   b. The court observed that *ex parte* conversations between the EPA and Executive Branch officials regarding the NSPS are allowed "unless expressly forbidden by Congress." Does that include the President? The Article II Opinion Clause provides that the President "may require the Opinion, in writing, of the principal Officer in each of

the executive Departments, upon any Subject relating to the duties of their respective offices." U.S. Const. Art. II, § 2, cl. 1. The EPA is an executive independent agency whose Administrator answers directly to the President. Does the Opinions Clause divest Congress of the power to forbid off-the-record conversations between the President and the EPA Administrator? Assuming that Congress cannot prevent such dialogue, can Congress nevertheless force the EPA to disclose the content of such conversations in the public record? Could the President assert executive privilege to prevent that? *See* Peter L. Strauss, *The Place of Agencies in Government: Separation of Powers and the Fourth Branch*, 84 COLUM. L. REV. 573, 657-58 (1984).

Application & Analysis

1. You are an attorney for an executive independent agency that is preparing to issue a final rule, developed through APA § 553 notice-and-comment rulemaking, which will be published in the Federal Register. The official managing the rulemaking informs you that she and members of her team have received information, held meetings, and had informal conversations with members of industry, staff members from the agency's Senate oversight committee, and the news media since the comments period closed. She would like your advice on how to handle these communications, and you are scheduled to meet in her office next week. Think about how you would prepare for that meeting. What additional questions will be pertinent to providing solid guidance? What statutory, court decisions, or other materials might be relevant? What advice do you feel comfortable giving now, based on the little she has told you?

3. The Final Rule: Concise General Statements

APA § 553(c) provides that "after consideration of all relevant matter presented, the agency shall incorporate in the rules adopted a concise general statement of their basis and purpose." The APA's drafters understood that this statement, often referred to as the "preamble" to the final rule, would be critical for communicating a rule's content, coverage, and purpose to the public. It also appears that Congress did not intend for its formulation to be a particularly burdensome undertaking. Per the ATTORNEY GENERAL'S MANUAL, its drafters did not require "an elaborate analysis of the rules or of the considerations upon which the rules were issued. Rather, the statement [was] intended to advise the public of the general basis of the rules." ATTORNEY GENERAL'S MANUAL at 32.

As with other APA provisions, § 553 tells agencies what they must do but provides no further guidance on how they may do it. It does not reveal what subjects the preamble should cover, nor does it indicate the specificity with which it should cover them. Agencies have thus adopted two approaches to drafting them. The first focuses on the public. Officials use the preamble to "advise interested persons on how the rule will be applied, to respond to questions raised by comments received during the rulemaking, and as a 'legislative history' that can be referred to in future application of the rule." LUBBERS, A GUIDE TO FEDERAL AGENCY RULEMAKING at 337. The second focuses on the courts. Agencies are acutely aware that federal litigation often awaits the final rules they promulgate; they must prepare for the parties who will come forward to challenge them. Accordingly, they draft preambles to anticipate a host of substantive and procedural objections. They may include explanations for changes from the NPRM, considered but rejected alternative regulatory approaches, responses to significant criticisms received during the comments period, and additional information demonstrating analytical soundness (e.g., scientific, legal, and economic impact analyses).

For courts, the preamble often provides a focal point for legal analysis. As we saw in *Chocolate Manufacturers Association v. Block* (page 275), the preamble was critical to the Fourth Circuit's application of the "logical outgrowth" test. It contained the USDA's explanation for eliminating flavored milk from the WIC program. As we will see in *Reytblatt v. U.S. Nuclear Regulatory Commission* below, and in Part IV of this casebook, courts often focus on the preamble when testing an agency's final rule for reasonableness under the "arbitrary and capricious" standard of review (5 U.S.C. § 706(2)(A), discussed in Chapter 9). It should therefore come as little surprise that the preamble's importance has grown as the Judiciary's scrutiny of agency rulemaking has expanded. The preamble now has significance the APA's drafters likely did not anticipate, and agencies looking to protect their final rules from judicial invalidation must ensure that their preambles are adequately reasoned and documented. The expectations were clearly expressed in an oft-cited passage from the D.C. Circuit's decision in *Automotive Parts & Accessories Association v. Boyd*:

> [I]t is appropriate for us to remind the [Federal Highway] Administrator of the ever present possibility of judicial review, and to caution against an overly literal reading of the statutory terms "concise" and "general." These adjectives must be accommodated to the realities of judicial scrutiny, which do not contemplate that the court itself will, by a laborious examination of the record, formulate in the first instance the significant issues faced by the agency and articulate the rationale of their resolution. We do not expect the agency to discuss every item of fact or opinion included in the submissions made to it in informal rule making. We do expect that, if the judicial review which Congress has thought it important to provide is to be meaningful, the "concise general statement of . . . basis and purpose"

> mandated by Section 4 will enable us to see what major issues of policy
> were ventilated by the informal proceedings and why the agency reacted to
> them as it did.

407 F.2d 330, 338 (D.C. Cir. 1968).

As part of ensuring that "major issues of policy [are] ventilated" by agencies during the informal rulemaking process, courts look at their responses to comments submitted by the public. A recurring issue is the issuing agency's obligation to respond to such comments. Time was that agencies could do so with acknowledgments of receipt and cursory dismissals. Not so today. "The basis and purpose statement is not intended to be an abstract explanation addressed to imaginary complaints. Rather, its purpose is, at least in part, to respond in a reasoned manner to the comments received, to explain how the agency resolved any significant problems raised by the comments, and to show how that resolution led the agency to the ultimate rule." *Rodway v. Department of Agriculture*, 514 F.2d 809, 817 (D.C. Cir. 1975). Of course, courts interpreting § 553(c) have not insisted that agencies respond to every comment they receive; only "significant" ones warrant dedicated attention. *See City of Portland, Oregon v. EPA*, 507 F.3d 706, 715 (D.C. Cir. 2007) ("Significant comments are those 'which, if true, raise points relevant to the agency's decision and *which, if adopted, would require a change in an agency's proposed rule.*'") *citing HBO v. FCC*, 567 F.2d 9, 35 n.58 (D.C. Cir. 1977) (emphasis added by court). Nor must agencies respond individually to each comment raising significant issues. Courts have routinely held that addressing the issues themselves satisfies § 553(c).

The case that follows provides a standard example of how courts analyze claims of inadequate response to public comments under § 553(c).

Reytblatt v. U.S. Nuclear Regulatory Commission
105 F.3d 715 (D.C. Cir. 1997)

Before EDWARDS, Chief Judge, WALD, Circuit Judge, and BUCKLEY, Senior Circuit Judge.

BUCKLEY, Senior Judge:

Petitioners Dr. Zinovy Reytblatt and Ohio Citizens for Responsible Energy challenge the Nuclear Regulatory Commission's final rule amending the reporting requirements for performance-based containment leakage rate testing by nuclear power plants. Their primary contention is that the Commission acted arbitrarily and capriciously in failing to respond adequately to Dr. Reytblatt's comments. Because we find the Commission's response to be adequate, we deny the petition for review.

I. BACKGROUND

All nuclear power plants licensed in the United States must have a protective shielding structure, commonly called the "containment," which houses the nuclear reactor and its associated parts. If an accident damages the reactor, the containment is intended to confine the gaseous radioactive material that would otherwise be released into the environment. The Nuclear Regulatory Commission ("NRC" or "Commission") has issued rules governing the permissible rate of leakage from these containment systems and requiring periodic leakage rate tests. These are contained in Appendix J to the Commission's regulations. *See generally* 10 C.F.R. pt. 50 App. J (1996).

A. Appendix J's Testing Requirements

Prior to September 1995, Appendix J incorporated a "prescriptive approach" to the testing of containment leakage rates. Regulations implementing this approach specified the types of tests that were acceptable, the manner in which they were to be conducted, their frequency, and how they were to be reported. *See* 10 C.F.R. at 757-61.

The amendments to Appendix J adopted in September 1995 ("September Rule") gave licensees the option of adopting a "performance-based" approach to containment leakage rate testing as an alternative to compliance with the prescriptive requirements. *See id.* at 756, 761-63; *Primary Reactor Containment Leakage Testing for Water-Cooled Power Reactors*, 60 Fed. Reg. 49,495, 49,495 (1995). Under this approach, the frequency of leakage rate testing is not specified but is determined by the results of prior tests. 10 C.F.R. at 762.

B. Appendix J's Reporting Requirements

1. Reporting Requirements Under the Prescriptive Approach

Under the original prescriptive program, licensees were required to file a summary report of the results of all leakage rate tests, regardless of whether the licensee believed that the plant had failed or passed the test. 10 C.F.R. at 764 (1995). These reports were kept in the NRC's Public Document Room . . . and made available to the public pursuant to the Freedom of Information Act ("FOIA").

In March 1995, the NRC issued a final rule ("March Rule") that reduced the reporting requirements under the prescriptive program. *Reduction of Reporting Requirements Imposed on NRC Licensees*, 60 Fed. Reg. 13,615, 13,615 (1995) (codified at 10 C.F.R. pt. 50 App. J). Although, under the new rule, licensees were still obliged to prepare summary reports for all leakage rate test results and to make them available for the NRC's review and inspection at the respective plant sites, they were only required to file the reports of failed tests to the NRC. *Id.* at 13,615, 13,617. Therefore, only reports for failed tests were available for public inspection.

In the preamble to the March Rule, the NRC explained that, in determining whether to eliminate a reporting requirement, it

> first consider[ed] the public health and safety impact of the proposed elimination [and if] there [was] no direct impact on public health and safety, [it] also consider[ed] the reduced administrative burden on the licensee and the extent to which the proposed elimination [would] deprive the public of important health and safety information.

Id. at 13,615. The Commission concluded that limiting the filing requirements to reports of failed leakage rate tests would reduce the regulatory burden on licensees without adversely affecting the public health and safety. *Id.* All seven parties commenting on the proposed rule agreed with this conclusion. *Id.*

Dr. Reytblatt did not comment on the March Rule. Ohio Citizens for Responsible Energy ("OCRE"), however, filed a timely objection to the proposed modification of reporting requirements on the ground that it would diminish the public's access to information necessary for public participation in the regulatory process. *Id.* The NRC responded by referring to a previous OCRE petition that sought to establish a public right-to-know provision that would ensure public access to information held by licensees. That petition addressed the cumulative effect of various rulemakings that deprived the public of access to information previously available through the NRC. The Commission concluded that OCRE's comments on the March Rule raised a "generic issue [that was] better addressed in the context of [the earlier] petition." *Id.* at 13,616. It also found that "the loss of information in this particular case [would] not adversely affect the public interest in access to information regarding adequate protection of the public health and safety." *Id.*

2. Reporting Requirements Under the Performance-Based Approach

The September Rule provided licensees with a performance-based option whose reporting requirements were essentially identical to those previously adopted under the March Rule for the prescriptive approach. Thus, under the September Rule, licensees must make successful performance-based test results available to the NRC for inspection at plant sites. 60 Fed. Reg. at 49,505. If a containment system fails to meet its performance criteria, however, a report of the test results must be filed with the Commission pursuant to the "Emergency Notification System" provisions of 10 C.F.R. §§ 50.72(b)(1)(ii), 50.72(b)(2)(i), and 50.73(a)(2)(ii). *Id.*

The performance-based rule was proposed in a February 1995 notice in the Federal Register that established a 75-day comment period. *Primary*

Reactor Containment Leakage Testing for Water-Cooled Power Reactors, 60 Fed. Reg. 9634, 9634 (proposed Feb. 21, 1995). The NRC "assure[d] consideration only for comments received on or before [the May 8, 1995 deadline]," and indicated that those received after the deadline would be considered to the extent "practical." *Id.* Although the NRC received numerous comments on the technical aspects of the proposed rule, the only timely comment that mentioned the reporting requirements was contained in a letter dated May 4, 1995, from Dr. Reytblatt, an expert in nuclear reactor containment leakage rate testing who frequently commented on NRC proposals involving that subject. *See* 60 Fed. Reg. at 49,503.

In his seventeen-page submission regarding the September Rule, Dr. Reytblatt focused primarily on methodologies for conducting and analyzing leakage rate test results. Nevertheless, at five places he expressed a general concern regarding the reporting requirements under the performance-based option. The following excerpts from Addendum 1 to his comments describe both the nature of his concern and specific proposals for making test information available to the public:

> What the Standard [a reference to a guideline proposed by an industry group, American National Standards Institute ("ANSI"), that the Commission had not adopted] proposes to submit to NRC is just a cover letter.

> Section 5.11 is written with the clear intent to conceal from the public all essential information about a test.

> Section 5.11.2 is vague and unclear and contains no defined requirements. The idea of fair analysis without any public access is preposterous.

> The adequate requirement would be to hold a short, announced well ahead of time, seminar similar to a public hearing where utility analysts and consultants would have an opportunity to expose the test to their colleagues and to the public.

> Section 5.12.2 does not require retaining of computer programs controlling the test. It is written with a malicious intent to preclude [the] public from accessing the test data and processing thereof by filing FOIA requests to NRC. There is no essential propriet[a]ry information involved with this matter contrary to the industry position, and if there is, then specific petitions may be filed for exemptions.

> I propose that all Sections of the Standard concerned with reporting be replaced with one short requirement that all computer files pertaining to testing be submitted in a real-time mode to the NRC for permanent storage to prevent their alteration or destruction. This is the cheapest and technologically perfect way of reporting. It also puts an end to all attempts to deprive [the] public from information vital to [its] safety. This proposal is so important that it merits presentation for consideration to the United States Government.

Addendum 1 to comments on App. J. to 10 C.F.R. Part 50, NUREG–1493 & ANSI/ANS 56.8-94, by Dr. Zinovy Reytblatt, dated May 4, 1995, *reprinted in* Joint Appendix ("JA") at 398–99.

> The test reporting is reduced to a cover letter to prevent the American people from obtaining [] complete test data through FOIA. All test computer programs, calculations and files must be copied in real-time mode and deposited with the NRC. This is the most inexpensive and technically perfect way to secure an instant access to the test data.

Id. at 401 ¶ 7.

On July 7, 1995, the NRC sent Dr. Reytblatt a copy of its Public Comment Resolution, reprinted in JA at 410-43. In this document, the Commission responded to 26 letters addressing the proposed rule, including Dr. Reytblatt's May 4 submission. In a section entitled "Reporting Requirements," the Commission stated:

> 97. Only one comment was received on this issue. Dr. Z. Reytblatt noted that the proposed rule's reporting requirements consist only of a cover letter to the NRC, and suggested this is intended to conceal information from the public. It was suggested that a public hearing, in which utility analysts present the results of their tests to the general public, would constitute an adequate reporting requirement. Moreover, Dr. Reytblatt suggests that utilities should be required to submit all computer files related to testing to the NRC immediately after the tests have been completed to prevent their alteration or destruction. Dr. Reytblatt believes such brief reporting would not seem to be burdensome, does not add any additional costs, and will be extremely useful for any public member who is doing independent research in the field of leak rate testing to the public benefit.

> *NRC Response:*

> 98. It is not the intent of the NRC's reporting requirements to conceal information from the public; if tests fail, the information is required to be reported to the NRC, and the NRC will make such data available to the public. The NRC believes that its on-site inspections of Appendix J tests and the requirements to make such data accessible to the NRC provides adequate assurance of the integrity of the test data.

> *NRC Disposition[:]*

> 99. The NRC has decided, based on consideration of this public comment, to retain its reporting requirements as stated in the proposed rule.

Id. at 438-39. The NRC summarized paragraphs 98 and 99 of the Public Comment Resolution in the preamble to the September Rule. 60 Fed. Reg. at 49,503.

On July 28, 1995, two months after the deadline for comments had passed, Dr. Reytblatt wrote a second letter to the NRC addressing the Public

Comment Resolution, to which the NRC did not respond. OCRE, on the other hand, filed timely comments to the September Rule; but these did not deal with the reporting requirements for performance-based testing.

In this proceeding, petitioners do not challenge either the testing requirements of the performance-based option or the testing or reporting requirements under the prescriptive approach. They only question the reporting requirements under the performance-based option.

II. DISCUSSION

[In Section II.A. of its opinion, the court found that Dr. Reytblatt and OCRE met the constitutional, statutory, and prudential requirements for standing to sue the NRC.]

B. The Merits

Under the Administrative Procedure Act ("APA"), the September Rule must be set aside if it is "arbitrary, capricious, an abuse of discretion, or otherwise not in accordance with law." 5 U.S.C. § 706(2)(A) (1994). "When an agency rule is challenged as arbitrary and capricious, the scope of judicial review is narrow. Courts may not substitute their judgment for that of the agency." *Western Coal Traffic League v. United States*, 677 F.2d 915, 927 (D.C. Cir. 1982) (citations omitted). "But . . . courts must assure that the agency has provided a reasoned explanation for its rule." *Id.*

Section 553 of the APA requires an agency, after notice and comment on a proposed rule, to "incorporate in the rules adopted a concise general statement of their basis and purpose." 5 U.S.C. § 553(c) (1994). Thus, "[t]he basis and purpose statement is inextricably intertwined with the receipt of comments." *Action on Smoking & Health v. CAB*, 699 F.2d 1209, 1216 (D.C. Cir. 1983) (internal quotation marks and footnote omitted). An agency need not address every comment, but it must respond in a reasoned manner to those that raise significant problems. *See id.* Nevertheless, "[t]he detail required in a statement of basis and purpose depends on the subject of the regulation and the nature of the comments received." *Id.*

Petitioners' primary contention is that the NRC failed to respond adequately to Dr. Reytblatt's concerns about the reporting requirements under the performance-based approach. These concerns, however, were mentioned in the May 4, 1995, letter only in general (and highly abusive) terms. The letter did not explain why the public needed the information or how the reporting requirements would hinder Dr. Reytblatt's ability to file section 2.206 petitions alerting the NRC to possible violations. Indeed, the letter did not even mention that section. Rather, it referred to an irrelevant "Standard" that the NRC had not adopted and did not rely upon in establishing the reporting requirements for the performance-based option. Moreover, the letter failed to mention the reporting requirements under the March Rule and did not explain why the requirements under the performance-based option should differ from those already in effect for the prescriptive option.

Under the circumstances, we find the NRC's response to Dr. Reytblatt's concerns over the reporting rules and his accusation that the NRC had maliciously intended to preclude the public from obtaining access to test data to be entirely adequate. Given his substitution of invective for a reasoned explanation of why he opposed the proposed rule, it was appropriate for the NRC to simply affirm that its intent was not to conceal information from the public, that information concerning failed leakage rate tests would still be made available to the public, and that the combination of on-site inspections and the dissemination of data from failed tests would ensure the integrity of the test data.

Although the NRC did not directly respond to Dr. Reytblatt's suggested alternatives to the reporting requirements, which included holding seminars discussing test data and requiring licensees to submit a computer disk containing test data to the NRC, its explanation was adequate in light of the general nature of Dr. Reytblatt's comments and the fact that the primary focus of the September Rule was the establishment of a new performance-based approach rather than modification of existing reporting requirements. *See Thompson v. Clark*, 741 F.2d 401, 408 (D.C. Cir. 1984) (citation omitted) (Section 553(c) of the APA "has never been interpreted to require the agency to respond to every comment, or to analy[z]e every issue or alternative raised by the comments, no matter how insubstantial.").

Petitioners also contend that the NRC erred in failing to address Dr. Reytblatt's July 28, 1995, letter, which he wrote in response to the Public Comment Resolution. This second letter specifically raised Dr. Reytblatt's concern that decreasing the amount of testing data available to the public would hinder his ability to review nuclear power plants' compliance with NRC regulations. Although petitioners concede that the letter arrived more than two months after the close of the comment period, they assert that because the Commission represented that it had considered all comments, including those received after the deadline, 60 Fed. Reg. at 49,499, it was somehow obligated to respond to the untimely ones. We have previously determined that "[a]gencies are free to ignore . . . late filings." *Personal Watercraft Indus. Ass'n v. Department of Commerce*, 48 F.3d 540, 543 (D.C. Cir. 1995). We see no basis for obliging an agency to specifically address untimely comments merely because it has indicated that it would take them into consideration.

We note that Dr. Reytblatt and OCRE are free to petition the NRC, pursuant to 10 C.F.R. § 2.802, to conduct a new rulemaking that would increase the reporting requirements under both the prescriptive and the performance-based options. OCRE has already filed a separate petition urging the adoption of public right-to-know provisions that would give the public access to documents relevant to NRC-licensed or NRC-regulated activities that are in the possession of licensees and license applicants. *Ohio Citizens for Responsible Energy, Inc.; Receipt of Petition for Rulemaking,* 59 Fed. Reg. 30,308, 30,309 (1994). The NRC's counsel indicated at oral argument that a draft response is circulating within the agency and is expected to be released shortly. If the NRC grants OCRE's petition, both petitioners will be free to comment on any rule proposed as a consequence.

III. CONCLUSION

Because we find that the NRC did not act arbitrarily or capriciously when it amended Appendix J, the petition for review is
Denied.

QUESTION SET 5.8

Review & Synthesis

1. Did the D.C. Circuit adopt a clear test for distinguishing significant comments that warrant an agency's response from insignificant comments that do not? If not, how would you fashion such a test from the facts on which the court relied in rejecting Dr. Reytblatt's assertions?

2. Explain why, as the court says, "the basis and purpose statement is inextricably intertwined with the receipt of comments." How are the two connected?

3. Is it clear from the court's analysis from whose perspective relevance or irrelevance must be determined? This question raises the problems of "over-inclusivity" and "under-inclusivity." An over-inclusive rule would force agency responses to too many irrelevant comments, whereas an under-inclusive rule would force agency responses to too few. Presumably members of the public always think their comments are important enough to warrant dedicated responses. A rule that gives definitive weight to their views on relevance will almost certainly be over-inclusive. Should the agency's views be paramount then? It is true that agencies have the substantive expertise to identify significant problems raised by the comments they receive. But such a rule would likely be under-inclusive, since agencies have an incentive to protect their resources and policy preferences from external objections. Such a rule may also fail to facilitate an adequate degree of public accountability, one of the core purposes underlying § 553's comment requirement. Should the courts then rely on their own assessments of relevance? Do you think courts would be over-inclusive or

under-inclusive in determining comment significance? Could they better balance the competing considerations of public accountability and decision-making flexibility at the core of informal rulemaking?

4. What remedy do you think is appropriate for violations of the "concise general statement" requirement? Do you think that final rules should be invalidated for failing to comply with it? This would force agencies to go through the rulemaking process all over again. Should such rules be remanded to agencies with an instruction to better explain their views on the significant comments not properly addressed in the rule's preamble? In thinking about the appropriate remedy, consider the effect it would have on agency willingness to engage in rulemaking. If the consequences of eventual judicial invalidation are too high, agencies may forego the process altogether in favor of others that provide far fewer opportunities for public participation (e.g., case-by-case adjudication or policy statement issuance).

D. THE PRESIDENT'S ROLE IN RULEMAKING

Congress, the public, and the courts are not the only players in the administrative rulemaking game. The President, too, plays a critical role. As Figure 5.1 on page 270 shows, the Executive Office of the President — in the form of the Office of Management and Budget ("OMB") and the Office of Information and Regulatory Affairs ("OIRA") — scrutinize certain agency rules both at the beginning of the adoption process and again toward its end. Indeed, Executive regulatory oversight has steadily and dramatically increased since the early 1970s, as successive Presidents have exerted more control over agency policymaking and increased the analytical rigor and political palatability of social and economic regulation.

Modern Presidential oversight of rulemaking began with President Richard M. Nixon. In 1971, the Nixon Administration introduced the "Quality of Life" review process for agency actions, which largely dealt with EPA regulations. As described by an inter-agency memorandum issued by Nixon's OMB Director George P. Shultz, Quality of Life review instructed agencies to take consumer protection, environmental interests, industry requirements, and concerns of public health and safety into account when adopting regulatory policies. The stated purpose of this review was to ensure that "agencies make suitable analyses of benefits and costs [and] that outside viewpoints are taken into account in the decision process." Jim Tozzi, *OIRA's Formative Years: The Historical Record of Centralized Regulatory Review Preceding OIRA's Founding*, 63 ADMIN. L. REV. 37, 44 (2011) (internal citations omitted). Substantively, this initiative was the starting point for the Executive's insistence on cost-benefit analysis in rulemaking. It called for "a comparison of the expected benefits or accomplishments and the costs (Federal and non-Federal) associated with the alternatives considered." Memorandum from George P. Shultz, Dir., OMB, to the Heads of Departments and Agencies, Agency Regulations, Standards, and Guidelines Pertaining to Environmental Quality, Consumer Protection, and Occupational and Public Health and Safety (Oct. 5, 1971). Procedurally, the Shultz Memorandum portended future efforts to centralize administrative policymaking in the White House by granting OMB both oversight and auditing authority. With regard to oversight, it required agencies to submit to OMB "a schedule . . . covering the ensuring year showing estimated dates of future announcements of all proposed and final regulations, standards, guidelines, or similar matters in the subject areas shown above." *Id.* With respect to auditing, it gave OMB the authority to review individual regulations.

President Ford built on this move toward CBA and centralized regulatory management. Executive Order 11,821, issued by Ford, required "all major legislative proposals, regulations, and rules emanating from the executive branch of the Government include a statement certifying the inflationary impact of such actions on the Nation." It further instructed the OMB Director to "develop criteria for the identification" of such actions, "and to prescribe procedures for their evaluation." Ford later extended this directive to the end of 1977, and changed the name of the reports it required to "Economic Impact Statements." Exec. Order 11,949, 42 Fed. Reg. 1017 (Dec. 31, 1976).

Whatever his other policy differences with Ford, President Carter expressed similar concerns about the economic impact of federal regulations:

> Regulation has a large and increasing impact on the economy. Uncertainty about upcoming rules can reduce investment and productivity. Compliance with regulations absorbs large amounts of the capital investments of some industries, further restricting productivity. Inflexible rules and massive paperwork generate extra costs that are especially burdensome for small businesses, state and local governments, and non-profit groups. Regulations that impose needless costs add to inflation.
>
> If we are to continue our progress, we must ensure that regulation gives Americans their money's worth.

In Context

"Cost-benefit analysis" ("CBA") is often referenced in discussions about the analytical rigor of agency policymaking. It can have different meanings depending on the context. For present purposes, we can adopt the following functional CBA definition:

> Although members of the CBA family come in many shapes and sizes, they usually feature identification, quantification, monetization, aggregation, and comparison. Ideally, the conscientious analyst performing CBA identifies the available alternatives, quantifies the consequences that each alternative could be expected to have, monetizes the quantified expressions of these consequences, and then aggregates these monetized valuations according to some formula to assign a number to each alternative. These numbers may be compared to each other or they may be compared to some pre-defined baseline.

Benjamin Minhao Chen, *What's in a Number: Arguing About Cost-Benefit Analysis in Administrative Law*, 22 Lewis & Clark L. Rev. 923, 933 (2018).

President Carter's Regulatory Reform Message to the Congress, 1 PUB. PAPERS 492 (Mar. 26, 1979). His approach to addressing these concerns differed from Nixon's and Ford's, however, placing the onus of reviewing regulations on individual agencies rather than OMB. He issued Executive Order 12,044, which mandated regulatory analysis on "significant" regulations that resulted in "an annual effect on the economy of $100 million or more" or "a major increase in costs or prices for individual industries, levels of government or geographic regions." Exec. Order No. 12,044, 3 C.F.R. 152 (1978). The order also called for agencies to periodically review their existing regulations to ensure they were accomplishing their policy goals. OMB's role in this review process was limited; it was tasked with ensuring that the agencies followed the order, but it did not conduct any auditing of individual regulations itself. Carter created other centralized oversight mechanisms in addition to this. The Regulatory Analysis Review Group ("RARG"), convened in 1978, was staffed by representatives from OMB and other executive departments. Each year, RARG selected a small number of high-economic-impact regulations for additional scrutiny. Carter also established the Regulatory Council, which, among other things, published semiannual synopses of major regulations that were likely to have a substantial economic or public impact. *See generally* Harold H. Bruff, *Presidential Management of Agency Rulemaking*, 57 GEO. WASH. L. REV. 533, 548-49 (1989).

Although the President's involvement in the rulemaking process increased steadily throughout the 1970s, the American Bar Association in 1979 called for even more Presidential management of the federal regulatory regime. Finding that Congress could not manage agency rulemaking alone, it suggested that "[t]he President is the elected official most capable of making the needed balancing decisions as critical issues arise, while the most appropriate and effective role for Congress is to review and, where necessary, to curb unwise Presidential intervention." COMMISSION ON LAW AND THE ECONOMY, ABA, FEDERAL REGULATION: ROADS TO FREEDOM 73 (1979). President Reagan could not have agreed more.

Executive Order 12,291 was "the centerpiece of the administration's regulatory reform effort." MARC A. EISNER, REGULATORY POLITICS IN TRANSITION 182 (2000). Establishing the current framework for the White House's involvement in notice-and-comment rulemaking, E.O. 12,291 was an ambitious effort to increase the analytical rigor, reduce the volume, and centralize control of federal regulatory policymaking. It required executive agencies to apply CBA principles when implementing regulations (to the extent permitted by law). It also obligated executive agencies to prepare Regulatory Impact Analyses ("RIAs") for all "major rules" (those rules that had a significant impact on the economy). These RIAs had to include descriptions of potential benefits, including nonmonetary benefits and who was to receive those benefits; descriptions of the costs, including nonmonetary costs, and who was to bear those costs; determinations of the net benefits of rules; and descriptions of alternative approaches that could achieve the same goal at lower costs. *See* Exec. Order No. 12,291, 46 Fed. Reg. 13,193 (Feb. 19, 1981). Critically, it set a clear threshold for justifying regulatory action: "Regulatory action shall not be undertaken unless the potential benefits to society for the regulation *outweigh* the potential costs to society." *Id.* § 2(b) (emphasis added). The E.O. did not, however, extend to independent agencies. The Administration had initially planned to include them, but ultimately refrained over legal concerns that it lacked the authority to do so and political concerns that Congress would view the move as an overreach by the Executive Branch. The Administration nevertheless asked the independent agencies to voluntarily comply, and all of them declined to do so. *See* Cass R. Sunstein, The Cost-Benefit State 10 (2002).

Procedurally, agencies were required to submit their major rules and RIAs to OMB for review; agencies could not publish notices of proposed rulemaking or final rules until they considered and responded to OMB's comments. *See id.* § 3(f)(1). The Paperwork Reduction Act of 1980 established OIRA within OMB, and it was given responsibility to implement Executive Order 12,291. It now serves as the central federal authority for reviewing regulations. Several years thereafter, President Reagan issued Executive Order 12,498 establishing a centralized regulatory planning process. It required agencies to submit statements to OMB detailing their regulatory policies, goals, and objectives for the coming year, which OMB would review for consistency with Administration policy preferences. Exec. Order No. 12,498, 3 C.F.R. 323 (1985).

President Reagan's regulatory oversight regime brought about a "sea change" in the role of the President in the rulemaking process. Elena Kagan, *Presidential Administration*, 114 Harv. L. Rev. 2245, 2277 (2001). While the percentage of rules OMB returned to the agencies for reconsideration was not high, they tended toward greater regulatory significance. OMB's control over NPRM issuance solidified; agencies did not frequently proceed over its objections. OMB would block rules that were inconsistent with the Administration's priorities, until agencies changed them. While some welcomed this effort to better scrutinize, coordinate, and prioritize policies, others viewed this increased Presidential oversight (particularly its emphasis on cost-benefit analysis) as reflective of "anti-regulatory bias." *See id.* at 2278-81.

President Bill Clinton "came to view administration as perhaps the single most critical . . . vehicle to achieve his domestic policy goals. He accordingly developed a set of practices that enhanced his ability to influence or even dictate the content of administrative initiatives." *Id.* at 2282. Clinton repealed Executive Orders 12,291 and 12,498 and issued his own Executive Order 12,866. Executive Order 12,866 retained the centrality of CBA and OIRA in executive regulatory review. While doing so, it also sought to address several concerns about the process Executive Order 12,291 established. These include the use of OIRA review to stymie promulgation of rules rather than to simply review them, the potential influence of interest groups in the OIRA review process, the public's ability to understand the considerations informing OIRA review, and the CBA threshold for justifying regulation.

Executive Order 12,866
58 Fed. Reg. 51,735 (Sept. 30, 1993)

[B]y the authority vested in me as President by the Constitution and the laws of the United States of America, it is hereby ordered as follows:

Section 1. *Statement of Regulatory Philosophy and Principles.*
(a) *The Regulatory Philosophy.* Federal agencies should promulgate only such regulations as are required by law, are necessary to interpret the law, or are made necessary by compelling public need, such as material failures of private markets to protect or improve the health and safety of the public, the environment, or the well-being of the American people. In deciding whether and how to regulate, agencies should assess all costs and benefits of available regulatory alternatives, including the alternative of not regulating. Costs and benefits shall be understood to include both quantifiable measures (to the fullest extent that these can be usefully estimated) and qualitative measures of costs and benefits that are difficult to quantify, but nevertheless essential to consider. Further, in choosing among alternative regulatory approaches, agencies should select those approaches that maximize net benefits (including potential economic, environmental, public health and safety, and other advantages; distributive impacts; and equity), unless a statute requires another regulatory approach. . . .

Sec. 2. *Organization.* An efficient regulatory planning and review process is vital to ensure that the Federal Government's regulatory system best serves the American people. . . .
(b) *The Office of Management and Budget.* Coordinated review of agency rulemaking is necessary to ensure that regulations are consistent with applicable law, the President's priorities, and the principles set forth in this Executive order, and that decisions made by one agency do not conflict with the policies or actions taken or planned by another agency. The Office of Management and Budget (OMB) shall carry out that review function. Within OMB, the Office of Information and Regulatory Affairs (OIRA) is the repository of expertise concerning regulatory issues, including methodologies and procedures that affect more than one agency, this Executive order, and the President's regulatory policies. To the extent permitted by law, OMB shall provide guidance to agencies and assist the President, the Vice President, and other regulatory policy advisors to the President in regulatory

planning and shall be the entity that reviews individual regulations, as provided by this Executive order. . . .

Sec. 3. *Definitions.* For purposes of this Executive order. . . .

(d) "Regulation" or "rule" means an agency statement of general applicability and future effect, which the agency intends to have the force and effect of law, that is designed to implement, interpret, or prescribe law or policy or to describe the procedure or practice requirements of an agency. It does not, however, include:

(1) Regulations or rules issued in accordance with the formal rulemaking provisions of 5 U.S.C. 556, 557;

(2) Regulations or rules that pertain to a military or foreign affairs function of the United States, other than procurement regulations and regulations involving the import or export of non-defense articles and services;

(3) Regulations or rules that are limited to agency organization, management, or personnel matters; or

(4) Any other category of regulations exempted by the Administrator of OIRA.

(e) "Regulatory action" means any substantive action by an agency (normally published in the Federal Register) that promulgates or is expected to lead to the promulgation of a final rule or regulation, including notices of inquiry, advance notices of proposed rulemaking, and notices of proposed rulemaking.

(f) "Significant regulatory action" means any regulatory action that is likely to result in a rule that may:

(1) Have an annual effect on the economy of $100 million or more or adversely affect in a material way the economy, a sector of the economy, productivity, competition, jobs, the environment, public health or safety, or State, local, or tribal governments or communities;

(2) Create a serious inconsistency or otherwise interfere with an action taken or planned by another agency;

(3) Materially alter the budgetary impact of entitlements, grants, user fees, or loan programs or the rights and obligations of recipients thereof; or

(4) Raise novel legal or policy issues arising out of legal mandates, the President's priorities, or the principles set forth in this Executive order.

Sec. 4. *Planning Mechanism.* In order to have an effective regulatory program, to provide for coordination of regulations, to maximize consultation and the resolution of potential conflicts at an early stage, to involve the public and its State, local, and tribal officials in regulatory planning, and to ensure that new or revised regulations promote the President's priorities and the principles set forth in this Executive order, these procedures shall be followed, to the extent permitted by law:

(a) *Agencies' Policy Meeting.* Early in each year's planning cycle, the Vice President shall convene a meeting of the Advisors and the heads of agencies to seek a common understanding of priorities and to coordinate regulatory efforts to be accomplished in the upcoming year.

(b) *Unified Regulatory Agenda.* For purposes of this subsection, the term "agency" or "agencies" shall also include those considered to be independent regulatory agencies, as defined in 44 U.S.C. 3502(10). Each agency shall prepare an agenda of all regulations under development or review, at a time and in a manner specified by the Administrator of OIRA. . . .

(c) *The Regulatory Plan.* For purposes of this subsection, the term "agency" or "agencies" shall also include those considered to be independent regulatory agencies, as defined in 44 U.S.C. 3502(10).

> (1) As part of the Unified Regulatory Agenda, beginning in 1994, each agency shall prepare a Regulatory Plan (Plan) of the most important significant regulatory actions that the agency reasonably expects to issue in proposed or final form in that fiscal year or thereafter. The Plan shall be approved personally by the agency head and shall contain at a minimum:
>
>> (A) A statement of the agency's regulatory objectives and priorities and how they relate to the President's priorities;
>> (B) A summary of each planned significant regulatory action including, to the extent possible, alternatives to be considered and preliminary estimates of the anticipated costs and benefits;
>> (C) A summary of the legal basis for each such action, including whether any aspect of the action is required by statute or court order;
>> (D) A statement of the need for each such action and, if applicable, how the action will reduce risks to public health, safety, or the environment, as well as how the magnitude of the risk addressed by the action relates to other risks within the jurisdiction of the agency;
>> (E) The agency's schedule for action, including a statement of any applicable statutory or judicial deadlines. . . .

Sec. 5. *Existing Regulations.* . . .

(a) Within 90 days of the date of this Executive order, each agency shall submit to OIRA a program, consistent with its resources and regulatory priorities, under which the agency will periodically review its existing significant regulations to determine whether any such regulations should be modified or eliminated so as to make the agency's regulatory program more effective in achieving the regulatory objectives, less burdensome, or in greater alignment with the President's priorities and the principles set forth in this Executive order. Any significant regulations selected for review shall be included in the agency's annual Plan. The agency shall also identify any legislative mandates that require the agency to promulgate or continue to impose regulations that the agency believes are unnecessary or outdated by reason of changed circumstances. . . .

Sec. 6. *Centralized Review of Regulations.* The guidelines set forth below shall apply to all regulatory actions, for both new and existing regulations, by agencies other than those agencies specifically exempted by the Administrator of OIRA:

(a) *Agency Responsibilities.* . . .

(3) In addition to adhering to its own rules and procedures and to the requirements of the Administrative Procedure Act, the Regulatory Flexibility Act, the Paperwork Reduction Act, and other applicable law, each agency shall develop its regulatory actions in a timely fashion and adhere to the following procedures with respect to a regulatory action:

(A) Each agency shall provide OIRA, at such times and in the manner specified by the Administrator of OIRA, with a list of its planned regulatory actions, indicating those which the agency believes are significant regulatory actions within the meaning of this Executive order. Absent a material change in the development of the planned regulatory action, those not designated as significant will not be subject to review under this section unless, within 10 working days of receipt of the list, the Administrator of OIRA notifies the agency that OIRA has determined that a planned regulation is a significant regulatory action within the meaning of this Executive order. The Administrator of OIRA may waive review of any planned regulatory action designated by the agency as significant, in which case the agency need not further comply with subsection (a)(3)(B) or subsection (a)(3)(C) of this section.

(B) For each matter identified as, or determined by the Administrator of OIRA to be, a significant regulatory action, the issuing agency shall provide to OIRA:

(i) The text of the draft regulatory action, together with a reasonably detailed description of the need for the regulatory action and an explanation of how the regulatory action will meet that need; and

(ii) An assessment of the potential costs and benefits of the regulatory action, including an explanation of the manner in which the regulatory action is consistent with a statutory mandate and, to the extent permitted by law, promotes the President's priorities and avoids undue interference with State, local, and tribal governments in the exercise of their governmental functions.

(C) For those matters identified as, or determined by the Administrator of OIRA to be, a significant regulatory action within the scope of section 3(f)(1), the agency shall also provide to OIRA the following additional information developed as part of the agency's decision-making process (unless prohibited by law):

(i) An assessment, including the underlying analysis, of benefits anticipated from the regulatory action (such as, but not limited to, the promotion of the efficient functioning of the economy and private markets, the enhancement of health and safety, the protection of the natural environment, and the elimination or reduction of discrimination or bias) together with, to the extent feasible, a quantification of those benefits;

(ii) An assessment, including the underlying analysis, of costs anticipated from the regulatory action (such as, but not limited to, the direct cost both to the government in administering the regulation and to businesses and others in complying with the regulation, and any adverse effects on the efficient functioning of the economy, private markets (including productivity, employment, and competitiveness), health, safety, and the natural environment), together with, to the extent feasible, a quantification of those costs; and

(iii) An assessment, including the underlying analysis, of costs and benefits of potentially effective and reasonably feasible alternatives to the planned regulation, identified by the agencies or the public (including improving the current regulation and reasonably viable nonregulatory actions), and an explanation why the planned regulatory action is preferable to the identified potential alternatives. . . .

(b) *OIRA Responsibilities.* The Administrator of OIRA shall provide meaningful guidance and oversight so that each agency's regulatory actions are consistent with applicable law, the President's priorities, and the principles set forth in this Executive order and do not conflict with the policies or actions of another agency. OIRA shall, to the extent permitted by law, adhere to the following guidelines:

(1) OIRA may review only actions identified by the agency or by OIRA as significant regulatory actions under subsection (a)(3)(A) of this section.

(2) OIRA shall waive review or notify the agency in writing of the results of its review within the following time periods:

(A) For any notices of inquiry, advance notices of proposed rulemaking, or other preliminary regulatory actions prior to a Notice of Proposed Rulemaking, within 10 working days after the date of submission of the draft action to OIRA;

(B) For all other regulatory actions, within 90 calendar days after the date of submission of the information set forth in subsections (a)(3)(B) and (C) of this section, unless OIRA has previously reviewed this information and, since that review, there has been no material change in the facts and circumstances upon which the regulatory action is based, in which case, OIRA shall complete its review within 45 days; and

(C) The review process may be extended (1) once by no more than 30 calendar days upon the written approval of the Director and (2) at the request of the agency head.

(3) For each regulatory action that the Administrator of OIRA returns to an agency for further consideration of some or all of its provisions, the Administrator of OIRA shall provide the issuing agency a written explanation for such return, setting forth the pertinent provision of this Executive order on which OIRA is relying. If the agency head disagrees with some or all of the bases for the return, the agency head shall so inform the Administrator of OIRA in writing.

(4) Except as otherwise provided by law or required by a Court, in order to ensure greater openness, accessibility, and accountability in the regulatory review process, OIRA shall be governed by the following disclosure requirements:

(A) Only the Administrator of OIRA (or a particular designee) shall receive oral communications initiated by persons not employed by the executive branch of the Federal Government regarding the substance of a regulatory action under OIRA review;

(B) All substantive communications between OIRA personnel and persons not employed by the executive branch of the Federal Government regarding a regulatory action under review shall be governed by the following guidelines:

(i) A representative from the issuing agency shall be invited to any meeting between OIRA personnel and such person(s);

(ii) OIRA shall forward to the issuing agency, within 10 working days of receipt of the communication(s), all written communications, regardless of format, between OIRA personnel and any person who is not employed by the executive branch of the Federal Government, and the dates and names of individuals involved in all substantive oral communications (including meetings to which an agency representative was invited, but did not attend, and telephone conversations between OIRA personnel and any such persons); and

(iii) OIRA shall publicly disclose relevant information about such communication(s), as set forth below in subsection (b)(4)(C) of this section.

(C) OIRA shall maintain a publicly available log that shall contain, at a minimum, the following information pertinent to regulatory actions under review. . . .

(D) After the regulatory action has been published in the Federal Register or otherwise issued to the public, or after the agency has announced its decision not to publish or issue the regulatory action, OIRA shall make available to the public all documents exchanged between OIRA and the agency during the review by OIRA under this section. . . .

Sec. 10. *Judicial Review*. Nothing in this Executive order shall affect any otherwise available judicial review of agency action. This Executive order is intended only to improve the internal management of the Federal Government and does not create any right or benefit, substantive or procedural, enforceable at law or equity by a party against the United States, its agencies or instrumentalities, its officers or employees, or any other person.

Sec. 11. *Revocations*. Executive Orders Nos. 12291 and 12498; all amendments to those Executive orders; all guidelines issued under those orders; and any exemptions from those orders heretofore granted for any category of rule are revoked.

WILLIAM CLINTON
THE WHITE HOUSE, September 30, 1993.

* * *

For the most part, President Clinton's successors have retained the centralized oversight and review structure established by Executive Order 12,866 while tweaking operational details or points of analytical emphasis. President George W. Bush stressed clear identification of market failures in justifying new regulations, required aggregate CBA analysis for all regulations adopted by individual agencies each calendar year, and expanded OIRA review to include significant agency guidance documents. Executive Order 13,422. Exec. Order No. 13,422, 72 Fed. Reg. 2763 (Jan. 23, 2007). President Obama likewise reaffirmed the basic principles, structures, and definitions governing regulatory review established by Executive Order 12,866. Like his predecessors, he emphasized the importance of cost-benefit analysis, adding that the factors of "human dignity" and "fairness" were to be included in the calculus even though those values admittedly may be "difficult or impossible to quantify." Exec. Order No. 13,563 § 1(c) 76 Fed. Reg. 3821 (Jan. 21, 2011). Notably, President Obama also attempted to influence independent agencies more than did his predecessors. Other than requiring them to submit Unified Regulatory Agendas and Regulatory Plans, President Clinton exempted independent agencies from the CBA and review directives in Executive Order 12,866. By contrast, Executive Order 13,579, titled *Regulation and Independent Regulatory Agencies*, exhorted independent agencies to comply (albeit voluntarily) with the directives issued in Executive Order 13,563. Exec. Order 13,579, 76 Fed. Reg. 41,587 (July 11, 2011).

More recently, two Executive Orders issued by President Trump have taken a more overtly deregulatory bent than those issued by his predecessors, while retaining core commitments to CBA and centralized regulation management. In Executive Order 13,771, he deemed it "essential to manage costs" associated with regulation, and to that end he set the goal that "for every one new regulation issued, at least two prior regulations be identified for elimination." Exec. Order No. 13,771 § 1, 82 FR 9339 (Feb. 3, 2017). Executive Order 13,777 created mechanisms to accomplish this aggressive rule-reduction mandate. It instructed each agency to appoint Regulatory Reform Officers to "oversee the implementation of regulatory reform initiatives and policies to ensure that agencies effectively carry out regulatory reforms, consistent with applicable law." Exec. Order No. 13,777 § 2(a), 82 FR 12285 (Feb. 24, 2017).

QUESTION SET 5.9

Review & Synthesis

1. Review the basic substantive and procedural features of Executive Order 12,866. What requirements does it impose on agencies, and what tasks does it assign OIRA in the rulemaking review process?

2. Section 553 of the Administrative Procedure Act provides the default notice-and-comment rulemaking procedures that federal agencies must follow. Judicial review ensures that agencies follow those procedures and reviews the policies produced by them for basic rationality. What, then, does Executive Order 12,866 § 6 contribute to the informal rulemaking process? Is it merely a mechanism for Presidents to exercise political control over administrative policymaking, or does it enhance other values that inform § 553 (public participation, agency transparency, and accountability, etc.)?

3. Compare the regulatory justification thresholds adopted by President Reagan in Executive Order 12,291 with those adopted by President Clinton in 12,866. Which of the two imposes the more stringent standard? What relative practical effects on the rate of rule promulgation would you expect them to have?

4. What do you make of Executive Order 12,866 § 10? If, as it states, it creates no legally enforceable rights or obligations, why should the agencies

at whom it is directed feel obliged to follow it? Also consider that it, and the other executive orders discussed above, do not apply to independent agencies. Why do you think that is? What does it say about the President's power to enforce compliance with these executive orders?

5. As indicated above, Executive Order 12,866 § 6(b)(4) attempted to increase public transparency of OIRA review while shielding the process from undue influence by interest groups. What procedures does it adopt for achieving these goals? Would you expect them to be effective?

E. "JUDICIAL HYBRID" RULEMAKING

As noted earlier, Congress sometimes adds to the procedural mechanism otherwise required by 5 U.S.C. § 553. For example, § 655(b)(3) of the Occupational Safety and Health Act requires OSHA to hold public hearings at the request of an interested person objecting to a proposed rule, an obligation absent from § 553. As we saw in *Sierra Club v. Costle* (page 293), § 7607(d) of the Clean Air Act replaces many of the APA's default rulemaking procedures. While interpretive issues may arise with respect to these and similar provisions, no one questions Congress' authority to adopt them. The same is true of procedures voluntarily adopted by agencies themselves. The APA's rulemaking provisions are floors not ceilings; they set the minimum procedural protections afforded to interested members of the public, leaving agencies to adopt more if they wish. Several have done so.

The question whether *courts* may impose procedures on agencies not otherwise mandated by positive law—the Constitution, statutes, or their own regulations—has been much more controversial. Beginning in the late 1960s, the Supreme Court responded to the growing role of administrative policymaking by expanding opportunities for judicial review. It committed more fully to pre-enforcement review of rules in the seminal decision of *Abbott Laboratories v. Gardner* 387 U.S. 136 (1967). This exposed agency policymaking to judicial scrutiny before situation-specific fact development could occur. The Court also committed to scrutinizing informal agency decision-making much more closely in *Citizens to Preserve Overton Park, Inc. v. Volpe*, 401 U.S. 402, 420 (1971). The statutes governing such informal decision-making did not require agencies to develop formal administrative records. Nevertheless, the lower federal courts read these precedents as requiring them to engage in more frequent and more searching review of the evidence on which agencies based their decisions. This posed a basic logistical problem: how could courts review such evidence when agencies did not have the opportunity to, or were not required to, compile administrative records?

Courts solved this problem by identifying additional procedures for agencies to follow, most of which mimicked the information-gathering tools familiar to adjudication: presiding officers, oral hearings, cross-examination of witnesses, etc. They also began to police the types of information agencies were required to include in these administrative records. Due in part to the volume of administrative review it conducts, many of the leading precedents from this era were issued by the D.C. Circuit. *See, e.g., Rodway v. United States Dep't of Agriculture,* 514 F.2d 809, 817 (D.C. Cir. 1975); *Portland Cement Association v. Ruckelshaus,* 486 F.2d 375 (D.C. Cir. 1973); *International Harvestor Co. v. Ruckelshaus,* 478 F.2d 615 (D.C. Cir. 1973); *Automotive Parts & Accessories Association v. Boyd,* 407 F.2d 330 (D.C. Cir. 1968).

As too often seems to be the case, every solution has its attendant problems. These "judicial hybrid" rules of agency procedure certainly helped courts perform their review responsibilities by forcing agencies to produce the "whole record" on which they relied when making their decisions. The courts' imposition of these additional procedures also raised serious questions about their legal legitimacy. How could the courts require compilations of administrative records or other procedures absent constitutional, statutory, or regulatory directives? Despite such questions, the courts continued to fashion judicial hybrid rulemaking procedures throughout the 1970s. The Court's decision in *HBO v. FCC,* excerpted above, is but one well-known example. It wasn't until the end of the decade that the Supreme Court weighed in. And it did so with a seminal administrative law decision.

Vermont Yankee Nuclear Power Corp. v. Natural Resources Defense Council, Inc.

435 U.S. 519 (1978)

Mr. Justice REHNQUIST delivered the opinion of the Court.

. . . Interpreting [the rulemaking provisions of 5 U.S.C. § 553] in *United States v. Allegheny-Ludlum Steel Corp.,* 406 U.S. 742 (1972), and *United States v. Florida East Coast R. Co.,* 410 U.S. 224 (1973), we held that generally speaking this section of the Act established the maximum procedural requirements which Congress was willing to have the courts impose upon agencies in conducting rulemaking procedures. Agencies are free to grant additional procedural rights in the exercise of their discretion, but reviewing courts are generally not free to impose them if the agencies have not chosen to grant them. This is not to say necessarily that there are no circumstances which would ever justify a court in overturning agency action because of a failure to employ procedures beyond those required by the statute. But such circumstances, if they exist, are extremely rare.

Even apart from the Administrative Procedure Act this Court has for more than four decades emphasized that the formulation of procedures was basically to be left within the discretion of the agencies to which Congress had confided the responsibility for substantive judgments. . . .

It is in the light of this background of statutory and decisional law that we granted *certiorari* to review two judgments of the Court of Appeals for the District of Columbia Circuit because of our concern that they had seriously misread or misapplied this statutory and decisional law cautioning reviewing courts against engrafting their own notions of proper procedures upon agencies entrusted with substantive functions by Congress. We conclude that the Court of Appeals has done just that. . . .

[The Court consolidated two cases raising similar issues for consideration. The excerpt below contains only the portion of the Court's opinion relating to Vermont Yankee.]

I

A

Under the Atomic Energy Act of 1954, 68 Stat. 919, as amended, 42 U.S.C. § 2011 *et seq.*, the Atomic Energy Commission was given broad regulatory authority over the development of nuclear energy. Under the terms of the Act, a utility seeking to construct and operate a nuclear power plant must obtain a separate permit or license at both the construction and the operation stage of the project. *See* 42 U.S.C. §§ 2133, 2232, 2235, 2239. In order to obtain the construction permit, the utility must file a preliminary safety analysis report, an environmental report, and certain information regarding the antitrust implications of the proposed project. *See* 10 CFR §§ 2.101, 50.30(f), 50.33a, 50.34(a) (1977). This application then undergoes exhaustive review by the Commission's staff and by the Advisory Committee on Reactor Safeguards (ACRS), a group of distinguished experts in the field of atomic energy. Both groups submit to the Commission their own evaluations, which then become part of the record of the utility's application. *See* 42 U.S.C. §§ 2039, 2232(b). The Commission staff also undertakes the review required by the National Environmental Policy Act of 1969 (NEPA), 83 Stat. 852, 42 U.S.C. § 4321 *et seq.*, and prepares a draft environmental impact statement, which, after being circulated for comment, 10 CFR §§ 51.22–51.25 (1977), is revised and becomes a final environmental impact statement. § 51.26. Thereupon a three-member Atomic Safety and Licensing

Board conducts a public adjudicatory hearing, 42 U.S.C. § 2241, and reaches a decision which can be appealed to the Atomic Safety and Licensing Appeal Board, and currently, in the Commission's discretion, to the Commission itself. 10 CFR §§ 2.714, 2.721, 2.786, 2.787 (1977). The final agency decision may be appealed to the courts of appeals. 42 U.S.C. § 2239; 28 U.S.C. § 2342. The same sort of process occurs when the utility applies for a license to operate the plant, 10 CFR § 50.34(b) (1977), except that a hearing need only be held in contested cases and may be limited to the matters in controversy. *See* 42 U.S.C. § 2239(a); 10 CFR § 2.105 (1977); 10 CFR pt. 2, App. A, V(f) (1977). . . .

B

In December 1967, after the mandatory adjudicatory hearing and necessary review, the Commission granted petitioner Vermont Yankee a permit to build a nuclear power plant in Vernon, Vt. *See* 4 A.E.C. 36 (1967). Thereafter, Vermont Yankee applied for an operating license. Respondent Natural Resources Defense Council (NRDC) objected to the granting of a license, however, and therefore a hearing on the application commenced on August 10, 1971. Excluded from consideration at the hearings, over NRDC's objection, was the issue of the environmental effects of operations to reprocess fuel or dispose of wastes resulting from the reprocessing operations. This ruling was affirmed by the Appeal Board in June 1972.

In November 1972, however, the Commission, making specific reference to the Appeal Board's decision with respect to the Vermont Yankee license, instituted rulemaking proceedings that would specifically deal with the question of consideration of environmental effects associated with the uranium fuel cycle in the individual cost-benefit analyses for light water cooled nuclear power reactors. The notice of proposed rulemaking offered two alternatives, both predicated on a report prepared by the Commission's staff entitled Environmental Survey of the Nuclear Fuel Cycle. The first would have required no quantitative evaluation of the environmental hazards of fuel reprocessing or disposal because the Environmental Survey had found them to be slight. The second would have specified numerical values for the environmental impact of this part of the fuel cycle, which values would then be incorporated into a table, along with the other relevant factors, to determine the overall cost-benefit balance for each operating license.

Much of the controversy in this case revolves around the procedures used in the rulemaking hearing which commenced in February 1973. In a supplemental notice of hearing the Commission indicated that while discovery or cross-examination would not be utilized, the Environmental Survey would be available to the public before the hearing along with the extensive background documents cited therein. All participants would be given a reasonable opportunity to present their position and could be represented by counsel if they so desired. Written and, time permitting, oral statements would be received and incorporated into the record. All persons giving oral statements would be subject to questioning by the Commission. At the conclusion of the hearing, a transcript would be made available to the public and the record would remain open for 30 days to allow the filing of supplemental written statements. More than 40 individuals and organizations representing a wide variety of interests submitted written comments. On January 17, 1973, the Licensing Board held a planning session to schedule the appearance of witnesses and to discuss methods for compiling a record. The hearing was held on February 1 and 2, with participation by a number of groups, including the Commission's staff, the United States Environmental Protection Agency, a manufacturer of reactor equipment, a trade association from the nuclear industry, a group of electric utility companies, and a group called Consolidated National Intervenors which represented 79 groups and individuals including respondent NRDC.

After the hearing, the Commission's staff filed a supplemental document for the purpose of clarifying and revising the Environmental Survey. Then the Licensing Board forwarded its report to the Commission without rendering any decision. The Licensing Board identified as the principal procedural question the propriety of declining to use full formal adjudicatory procedures. The major substantive issue was the technical adequacy of the Environmental Survey.

In April 1974, the Commission issued a rule which adopted the second of the two proposed alternatives described above. The Commission also approved the procedures used at the hearing, and indicated that the record, including the Environmental Survey, provided an adequate data base for the regulation adopted. Finally, the Commission ruled that to the extent the rule differed from the Appeal Board decisions in Vermont Yankee those decisions have no further precedential significance, but that since the environmental effects of the uranium fuel cycle have been shown to be relatively insignificant it is unnecessary to apply the amendment to applicant's environmental reports submitted prior to its effective date or to Final Environmental Statements for which Draft Environmental Statements have been circulated for comment prior to the effective date.

Respondents appealed from both the Commission's adoption of the rule and its decision to grant Vermont Yankee's license to the Court of Appeals for the District of Columbia Circuit. . . .

D

... [T]he court ... ruled that in the absence of effective rulemaking proceedings, the Commission must deal with the environmental impact of fuel reprocessing and disposal in individual licensing proceedings. The court then examined the rulemaking proceedings and, despite the fact that it appeared that the agency employed all the procedures required by 5 U.S.C. § 553 (1976 ed.) and more, the court determined the proceedings to be inadequate and overturned the rule. Accordingly, the Commission's determination with respect to Vermont Yankee's license was also remanded for further proceedings. ...

II ....

B

... [B]efore determining whether the Court of Appeals reached a permissible result, we must determine exactly what result it did reach, and in this case that is no mean feat. Vermont Yankee argues that the court invalidated the rule because of the inadequacy of the procedures employed in the proceedings. Respondents, on the other hand, labeling petitioner's view of the decision a "straw man," argue to this Court that the court merely held that the record was inadequate to enable the reviewing court to determine whether the agency had fulfilled its statutory obligation. But we unfortunately have not found the parties' characterization of the opinion to be entirely reliable. ...

After a thorough examination of the opinion itself, we conclude that while the matter is not entirely free from doubt, the majority of the Court of Appeals struck down the rule because of the perceived inadequacies of the procedures employed in the rulemaking proceedings. The court first determined the intervenors' primary argument to be "that the decision to preclude 'discovery or cross-examination' denied them a meaningful opportunity to participate in the proceedings as guaranteed by due process." 547 F.2d at 643. The court then went on to frame the issue for decision thus:

> Thus, we are called upon to decide whether the procedures provided by the agency were sufficient to ventilate the issues. *Ibid.*

The court conceded that absent extraordinary circumstances it is improper for a reviewing court to prescribe the procedural format an agency must follow, but it likewise clearly thought it entirely appropriate

> **In Context**
>
> After finding the evidence in the record insufficient to support the NRC's rule, the D.C. Circuit suggested (but did not require) several means by which the NRC could create "a genuine dialogue" on environmental impact. These included "informal conferences between intervenors and staff, document discovery, interrogatories, technical advisory committees comprised of outside experts ..., limited cross-examination, funding independent research by intervenors, detailed annotation of technical reports, surveys of existing literature, [and] memoranda explaining methodology." NRDC v. NRC, 547 F.2d 633, 653 (D.C. Cir. 1976).

to "scrutinize the record as a whole to insure that genuine opportunities to participate in a meaningful way were provided. . . ." *Id.* at 644. The court also refrained from actually ordering the agency to follow any specific procedures, *id.* at 653-654, but there is little doubt in our minds that the ineluctable mandate of the court's decision is that the procedures afforded during the hearings were inadequate. This conclusion is particularly buttressed by the fact that after the court examined the record, particularly the testimony of Dr. Pittman, and declared it insufficient, the court proceeded to discuss at some length the necessity for further procedural devices or a more "sensitive" application of those devices employed during the proceedings. *Ibid.* The exploration of the record and the statement regarding its insufficiency might initially lead one to conclude that the court was only examining the sufficiency of the evidence, but the remaining portions of the opinion dispel any doubt that this was certainly not the sole or even the principal basis of the decision. Accordingly, we feel compelled to address the opinion on its own terms, and we conclude that it was wrong.

In prior opinions we have intimated that even in a rulemaking proceeding when an agency is making a " 'quasi-judicial' " determination by which a very small number of persons are " 'exceptionally affected, in each case upon individual grounds,' " in some circumstances additional procedures may be required in order to afford the aggrieved individuals due process.[16] . . . It might also be true, although we do not think the issue is presented in this case and accordingly do not decide it, that a totally unjustified departure from well-settled agency procedures of long standing might require judicial correction.

But this much is absolutely clear. Absent constitutional constraints or extremely compelling circumstances the "administrative agencies 'should be free to fashion their own rules of procedure and to pursue methods of inquiry capable of permitting them to discharge their multitudinous duties.' " *FCC v. Schreiber*, 381 U.S., at 290, quoting from *FCC v. Pottsville Broadcasting Co.*, 309 U.S. at 143. Indeed, our cases could hardly be more explicit in this regard. . . .

Respondent NRDC argues that § 4 of the Administrative Procedure Act, 5 U.S.C. § 553 (1976 ed.), merely establishes lower procedural bounds and that a court may routinely require more than the minimum when an agency's proposed rule addresses complex or technical factual issues or "Issues of Great Public Import." Brief for Respondents in No. 76-419, p. 49. We have, however, previously shown that our decisions reject this view. We also think the legislative history, even the part which it cites, does

---

[16] Respondent NRDC does not now argue that additional procedural devices were required under the Constitution. Since this was clearly a rulemaking proceeding in its purest form, we see nothing to support such a view. *See . . . Bi-Metallic Investment Co. v. State Board of Equalization*, 239 U.S. 441 (1915).

not bear out its contention. The Senate Report explains what eventually became § 4 thus:

> This subsection states . . . the minimum requirements of public rule making procedure short of statutory hearing. Under it agencies might in addition confer with industry advisory committees, consult organizations, hold informal "hearings," and the like. Considerations of practicality, necessity, and public interest . . . will naturally govern the agency's determination of the extent to which public proceedings should go. Matters of great import, or those where the public submission of facts will be either useful to the agency or a protection to the public, should naturally be accorded more elaborate public procedures. S. Rep. No. 79-752, at 4-15 (1945).

The House Report is in complete accord. . . .

And the Attorney General's Manual on the Administrative Procedure Act 31, 35 (1947), a contemporaneous interpretation previously given some deference by this Court because of the role played by the Department of Justice in drafting the legislation, further confirms that view. In short, all of this leaves little doubt that Congress intended that the discretion of the agencies and not that of the courts be exercised in determining when extra procedural devices should be employed.

There are compelling reasons for construing § 4 in this manner. In the first place, if courts continually review agency proceedings to determine whether the agency employed procedures which were, in the court's opinion, perfectly tailored to reach what the court perceives to be the "best" or "correct" result, judicial review would be totally unpredictable. And the agencies, operating under this vague injunction to employ the "best" procedures and facing the threat of reversal if they did not, would undoubtedly adopt full adjudicatory procedures in every instance. Not only would this totally disrupt the statutory scheme . . . but all the inherent advantages of informal rulemaking would be totally lost.

Secondly, it is obvious that the court in these cases reviewed the agency's choice of procedures on the basis of the record actually produced at the hearing, 547 F.2d, at 644, and not on the basis of the information available to the agency when it made the decision to structure the proceedings in a certain way. This sort of Monday morning quarterbacking not only encourages but almost compels the agency to conduct all rulemaking proceedings with the full panoply of procedural devices normally associated only with adjudicatory hearings.

Finally, and perhaps most importantly, this sort of review fundamentally misconceives the nature of the standard for judicial review of an agency rule. The court below uncritically assumed that additional procedures will automatically result in a more adequate record because it will give interested parties more of an opportunity to participate in and contribute to the proceedings. But informal rulemaking need not be based solely on the transcript of a hearing held before an agency. Indeed, the agency need not even hold a formal hearing. *See* 5 U.S.C. § 553(c) (1976 ed.). Thus, the adequacy of the "record" in this type of proceeding is not correlated directly to the type of procedural devices employed, but rather turns on whether the agency has followed the statutory mandate of the Administrative Procedure Act or other relevant statutes. If the agency is compelled to support the rule which it ultimately adopts with the type of record produced only after a full adjudicatory hearing, it simply will have no choice but to conduct a full adjudicatory hearing prior to promulgating every rule. In sum, this sort of unwarranted judicial examination of perceived procedural shortcomings of a rulemaking proceeding can do nothing but seriously interfere with that process prescribed by Congress.

Respondent NRDC also argues that the fact that the Commission's inquiry was undertaken in the context of NEPA somehow permits a court to require procedures beyond those specified in § 4 of the APA when investigating factual issues through rulemaking. The Court of Appeals was apparently also of this view, indicating that agencies may be required to "develop new procedures to accomplish the innovative task of implementing NEPA through rulemaking." 547 F.2d, at 653. But we search in vain for something in NEPA which would mandate such a result. . . . In fact, just two Terms ago, we emphasized that the only procedural requirements imposed by NEPA are those stated in the plain language of the Act. *Kleppe v. Sierra Club*, 427 U.S. 390, 405-406 (1976). Thus, it is clear NEPA cannot serve as the basis for a substantial revision of the carefully constructed procedural specifications of the APA.

In short, nothing in the APA, NEPA, the circumstances of this case, the nature of the issues being considered, past agency practice, or the statutory mandate under which the Commission operates permitted the court to review and overturn the rulemaking proceeding on the basis of the procedural devices employed (or not employed) by the Commission so long as the Commission employed at least the statutory minima, a matter about which there is no doubt in this case. . . .

Reversed and remanded.

Mr. Justice BLACKMUN and Mr. Justice POWELL took no part in the consideration or decision of these cases.

QUESTION SET 5.10

Review & Synthesis

1. Vermont Yankee and the Natural Resources Defense Council ("NRDC") disagreed vehemently on what the D.C. Circuit actually decided in the case below. Vermont Yankee argued that the court invalidated the Nuclear

Regulatory Commission's ("NRC") nuclear waste environmental impact rule because the agency's procedures were inadequate. The NRDC characterized the decision as rejecting the inadequacy of the record on which the NRC based its rule. Why did this disagreement matter, and how did the Court resolve it?

2. Why did the NRDC argue that using a table rather than case-by-case determinations to judge the environmental impact of nuclear waste disposal violated the National Environmental Protection Act? What statute-relevant information would be elicited from adjudication that would be lost by employing rulemaking? With respect to Dr. Pittman's testimony specifically, what relevant information could the NRDC have gotten from him in direct questioning that was not already contained in his testimony?

3. Think for a moment about the NRDC's advocacy strategy in challenging Vermont Yankee's nuclear plant operating license. Why would it be advantageous to the organization for the NRC to determine environmental impact on a license-by-license basis?

4. Several of the cases discussed or alluded to in the previous subsection on *ex parte* contacts in informal rulemaking—*Automotive Parts & Accessories Association, Portland Cement, Chocolate Manufacturers, HBO, Sierra Club*—involved judicial orders to change or supplement the procedures agencies used to promulgate regulations. What aspects of their holdings, if any, are still good law after *Vermont Yankee*? *Sierra Club* presents a special case; it was decided three years *after Vermont Yankee*. The D.C. Circuit did not vacate the EPA's sulfur dioxide NSPS in that case. However, it seemed to assume that it *could* do so if the EPA had mishandled the *ex parte* contacts at issue. Did *Sierra Club* misapply or simply ignore *Vermont Yankee*?

5. Do you agree with the Court's assessment that "judicial review would be totally unpredictable" if "courts continually review[ed] agency proceedings to determine whether the agency employed procedures which were, in the court's opinion, perfectly tailored to reach what the court perceives to be the 'best' or 'correct' result?" Based on the judicial hybrid procedures developed by the D.C. Circuit, does it appear to you that its precedents produced total unpredictability for agencies? Even if that were the case, is there no middle ground between unfettered judicial discretion to create new procedures and no judicial role in procedure creation whatsoever? Couldn't the Court have set some parameters for fashioning procedural remedies? Based on the reasoning in the case, why might the Court have eschewed that option?

F. NEGOTIATED RULEMAKING

The notice-and-comment rulemaking process was designed to be a flexible, substantive, fair, and efficient way for agencies to develop and adopt regulatory policy. Many believe that, by and large, it has achieved those goals. The process is not, however, without its (quite vocal) critics. For decades, scholars and commentators have pointed to proliferating executive, statutory, and judicial requirements that have pushed the process toward sclerosis. The President has added analytical checkpoints—like cost-benefit and federalism analyses—to the rulemaking process and has empowered OMB and OIRA to patrol them. Congress has layered expensive and time-consuming procedural requirements—like witness cross-examination rights—on top of the basic notice-and-comment framework. The courts have interpreted § 553 and the judicial review standards of § 706 (discussed in Chapter 9) in ways that dramatically decrease the likelihood that even the most diligently crafted rules will withstand scrutiny. *See, e.g.*, Richard J. Pierce, *Seven Ways to Deossify Agency Rulemaking*, 47 ADMIN. L. REV. 59, 62-66 (1995) (describing sources of rulemaking ossification); Jerry L. Mashaw & David Harfst, *Inside the NHTSA: Legal Determinants of Bureaucratic Organization and Performance*, 57 U. CHI. L. REV. 443 (1990) (arguing that the Supreme Court's application of "hard look review" to NHTSA's rescission of a seatbelt rule "burdened, dislocated, and ultimately paralyzed" the agency's rulemaking efforts). Critics have further insisted that the courts' apparent willingness to vacate and remand agency rules has increased incentives to challenge them. Critics assert that, as a result, rulemaking is little more than an occasion for litigants to preserve claims predestined for a federal complaint.

To address the "malaise" seizing administrative policymaking, Professor Philip Harter proposed an innovative alternative to the status quo: "regulatory negotiation." Rather than devising new legal commitments largely in isolation and then attempting to impose them on regulated parties, he suggested that representatives from industry and agency begin the policymaking process working side-by-side. In a negotiation stewarded by an impartial mediator, the camps could build policy together and then present it to the agency for publication as a notice of proposed rulemaking. *See* Philip J. Harter, *Negotiating Regulations: A Cure for the Malaise*, 71 GEO. L.J. 1 (1981). Among its benefits, Harter argued that affected parties would be less likely to mount judicial challenges against regulations they had a meaningful role in drafting. More substantively, he believed that the negotiated rulemaking process could allow more opportunities than notice-and-comment rulemaking for agency officials to learn about the potential impacts of their proposed regulations. His proposal was later adopted by the Administrative Conference of the United States, which issued a formal recommendation urging agencies to experiment with the procedure and for Congress to codify it. *See Recommendation 82-4: Procedures for Negotiating Proposed Regulations*, 47 Fed. Reg. 10,708 (July 15, 1982).

After gaining traction in scholarly and regulatory circles, Congress did adopt the idea in the Negotiated Rulemaking Act of 1990 ("NRA"), 5 U.S.C. §§ 561-570 (2018). The NRA establishes a negotiated rulemaking framework that supplements rather than replaces the APA's rulemaking provisions, and its provisions are advisory rather than mandatory. It sets guidelines for assessing the need for negotiated rulemaking (§ 563), for convening a negotiated rulemaking committee (§§ 564 and 565), and for conducting the committee's deliberations (§ 566). It also bars judicial review of how agencies establish, assist, or terminate the committees they convene, and makes clear that any rule that comes out of the process receives no particularized judicial deference (§ 570).

Even before its passage of the NRA, Congress included versions of negotiated rulemaking procedures in some statutory schemes. One of them, considered in the Seventh Circuit case below, required the Secretary of Education to work with the federal student loan servicing industry. The central question of the case was whether Department of Education was required to promulgate the rules upon which the working group agreed. Put another way, do agencies have a duty to negotiate "in good faith," and, if so, what does that duty oblige agencies to do with what they've negotiated?

USA Loan Group Services, Inc. v. Riley
82 F.3d 708 (7th Cir. 1996)

Before POSNER, Chief Judge, and DIANE P. WOOD and EVANS, Circuit Judges.

POSNER, Chief Judge.

The federal government has an enormous program, administered by the Department of Education, of subsidizing student loans. The loans are made by banks but are guaranteed by state and private agencies that have reinsurance contracts with the Department, making it the indirect guarantor of the loans and thus inducing banks to make what would otherwise be risky loans. The proceeds of the loans are used to pay tuition and other expenses; so the colleges and other schools whose students are receiving these loans are also involved in the federal program. Like so many government programs, the student loan program places heavy administrative burdens on the entities involved in it—the lenders, the guarantors, and the institutions. A whole industry of "servicers" has arisen to relieve these entities of some of the administrative burdens. As agents of the educational institutions, the servicers maintain records of the institution's student loans. As agents of the banks, they collect the loans from the students as the loans come due and dun the students when they are slow in paying. As agents of the guarantors, the servicers keep track of defaults and make sure that the banks comply with the various conditions for triggering the guarantees. In any of these roles a servicer who makes a mistake can end up costing the federal government money. If the servicer remits loan moneys to a school for the tuition of a student not eligible for a loan, or fails to pursue a defaulting student, or honors an invalid claim by a bank for reimbursement from a guarantor, federal money is disbursed in violation of the regulations governing the student loan program.

Mistakes and outright fraud by servicers, some resulting in large losses of federal money, led Congress in 1992 to amend Title IV of the Higher Education Act to authorize the Secretary of Education to "prescribe . . . regulations applicable to third party servicers (including regulations concerning financial responsibility standards for, and the assessment of liabilities for program violations against, such servicers) to establish minimum standards with respect to sound management and accountability." 20 U.S.C. § 1082(a)(1). . . . The Secretary has done this . . . and the servicers have brought this suit to invalidate portions of the regulations on substantive and procedural grounds. The district court rejected the challenge, and the servicers appeal.

[The court next considered and rejected several arguments raised by the loan services, which related among other things to the reasonableness, evidentiary support for, and possibly undesirable effects of the Department of Education's regulation.]

The remaining arguments are procedural and the main one is that the Secretary adopted the challenged regulation in violation of the conditions of "negotiated rulemaking," a novelty in the administrative process. The 1992 amendment to the Higher Education Act, under which the regulation was promulgated, required that the Secretary submit any draft regulation to a process of negotiated rulemaking, to be conducted in accordance with recommendations made by the Administrative Conference of the United States and codified in 1 C.F.R. §§ 305.82-4 and 305.85-5 and with "any successor recommendation, regulation, or law." 20 U.S.C. § 1098a(b). A "successor law" to the Administrative Conference's recommendations had in fact been enacted in 1990. It is the Negotiated Rulemaking Act, 5 U.S.C. §§ 561 *et seq.* . . . The Act and the Administrative Conference's recommendations authorize the agency, in advance of the notice and comment rulemaking proceeding, to submit draft regulations to the industry or other groups that are likely to be significantly affected by the regulations and to negotiate with them over the form and substance of the regulations. The hope is that these negotiations will produce a better draft as the basis for the notice and comment proceeding. The 1992 amendment to the Higher Education Act made negotiated rulemaking mandatory in proceedings implementing the amendment, as we have seen.

The servicers argue that the Department negotiated in bad faith with them. Neither the 1992 amendment nor the Negotiated Rulemaking Act specifies a remedy for such a case, and the latter act strongly implies there is none. 5 U.S.C. § 570. But even if a regulation could be invalidated because the agency had failed to negotiate in good faith, this would not carry the day for the servicers.

During the negotiations, an official of the Department of Education promised the servicers that the Department would abide by any consensus reached by them unless there were compelling reasons to depart. The propriety of such a promise may be questioned. It sounds like an abdication of regulatory authority to the regulated, the full burgeoning of the interest-group state, and the final confirmation of the "capture" theory of administrative regulation. At all events, although the servicers reached a firm consensus that they should not be liable for their mistakes the Department refused to abide by its official's promise. What is more, the draft regulations that the Department submitted to the negotiating process capped the servicers' liability at the amount of the fees they received from their customers, yet when it came time to propose a regulation as the basis for the notice and comment rulemaking the Department abandoned the cap. The breach of the promise to abide by consensus in the absence of compelling reasons not here suggested, and the unexplained withdrawal of the Department's proposal to cap the servicers' liability, form the basis for the claim that the Department negotiated in bad faith.

We have doubts about the propriety of the official's promise to abide by a consensus of the regulated industry, but we have no doubt that the Negotiated Rulemaking Act did not make the promise enforceable. The practical effect of enforcing it would be to make the Act extinguish notice and comment rulemaking in all cases in which it was preceded by negotiated rulemaking; the comments would be irrelevant if the agency were already bound by promises that it had made to the industry. There is no textual or other clue that the Act meant to do this. Unlike collective bargaining negotiations, to which the servicers compare negotiated rulemaking, the Act does not envisage that the negotiations will end in a binding contract. The Act simply creates a consultative process in advance of the more formal arms' length procedure of notice and comment rulemaking. *See* 5 U.S.C. § 566(f).

The complaint about the Secretary's refusal to adhere to the proposal to cap the servicers' liability misconceives the nature of negotiation. The Secretary proposed the cap in an effort to be accommodating and deflect the industry's wrath. The industry, in retrospect improvidently, rejected the proposal, holding out for no liability. So, naturally, the Secretary withdrew the proposal. A rule that a rejected offer places a ceiling on the offeror's demands would destroy negotiation. Neither party would dare make an offer, as the other party would be certain to reject it in order to limit the future demands that his opponent could make. This concern lies behind the principle that settlement offers are not admissible in litigation if the settlement effort breaks down. Fed. R. Evid. 408. By the same token, the negotiating position of the parties in negotiated rulemaking ought not be admissible in a challenge to the rule eventually promulgated when the negotiation failed.

The servicers argue that they should be allowed to conduct discovery to uncover the full perfidy of the Department's conduct in the negotiations. Discovery is rarely proper in the judicial review of administrative action. The court is supposed to make its decision on the basis of the administrative record, not create its own record. There are exceptions . . . and the main one has some potential applicability here: discovery is proper when it is necessary to create a record without which the challenge to the agency's action cannot be evaluated. E.g., *Citizens to Preserve Overton Park, Inc. v. Volpe*, 401 U.S. 402, 420 (1971). . . . Negotiated rulemaking does not usually produce a comprehensive administrative record, such as notice and comment rulemaking, or a cease and desist order proceeding, or a licensing proceeding would do, any more than a settlement conference will usually produce a full record. Some discovery was conducted in the district court in order to present a picture of what went on at the negotiations between the servicers and the Department. The servicers argue that if only they could get access to the notes of certain participants in the negotiating sessions they could demonstrate additional instances of bad faith on the part of the Department.

Their conception of "bad faith" reflects, as we have noted, a misconception of the negotiation process. It is not bad faith to withdraw an offer after the other side has rejected it. If as we doubt the Negotiated Rulemaking Act creates a remedy as well as a right, we suppose that a refusal to negotiate that really was in bad faith, because the agency was determined to stonewall, might invalidate the rule eventually adopted by the agency. But we do not think that the Act was intended to open the door wide to discovery in judicial proceedings challenging regulations issued after the notice and comment proceeding that followed the negotiations. If as in this case the public record discloses no evidence of bad faith on the part of the agency, that should be the end of the inquiry. A contrary conclusion would stretch out such judicial proceedings unconscionably. The Act's purpose—to reduce judicial challenges to regulations by encouraging the parties to narrow their differences in advance of the formal rulemaking proceeding—would be poorly served if the negotiations became a source and focus of litigation.

Affirmed.

QUESTION SET 5.11

Review & Synthesis

1. The court rightly pointed out that the Negotiated Rulemaking Act does not expressly adopt a duty of "good faith" negotiation. Nevertheless, Judge Posner said that courts may be led to invalidate rules promulgated after rejection of a negotiated proposal where "a refusal to negotiate that really was in bad faith, because the agency was determined to stonewall." On what legal basis could a court base such a ruling, if the NRA itself does

not provide for it? Why shouldn't private litigants be permitted discovery on whether an agency engaged in bad faith negotiations? *See Citizens to Preserve Overton Park, Inc. v. Volpe,* page 395.

2. Judge Posner responded with skepticism (and thinly veiled derision) to the assertion that the Department of Education should be required to adopt the rule proposed to it by the negotiating committee. Such an obligation sounded to the court "like an abdication of regulatory authority to the regulated, the full burgeoning of the interest-group state, and the final confirmation of the 'capture' theory of administrative regulation." This problem was avoided because the DOE could reject the proposal in its discretion. As the facts of the case also show, however, industries that engage in negotiated rulemaking expect to benefit from their labors—and may sue when they do not.

   a. One way to address this concern is for agencies to precommit to using the recommendations reached by negotiating committees. As the court made clear, however, such precommitment may raise the specter of agency capture that allows industry to write its own regulations at public expense. The legality of such an arrangement would also be an open question. How should policymakers, whether in Congress or in agencies, balance these concerns?

   b. Why isn't negotiated rulemaking a violation of the nondelegation doctrine? As discussed in Chapter 2, the Supreme Court in *A.L.A. Schechter* indicated its discomfort with allowing trade groups to fashion rules that could potentially be enforced against their competitors. It more explicitly rejected the idea of delegating legislative authority to private parties in *Carter v. Carter Coal,* describing it as delegation "in its most obnoxious form." Does the NRA overcome this concern? If so, how does it do so?

3. One (admittedly rough) measure of how successful negotiated rulemaking has been in addressing the "ossification" process is the number of times agencies have used it. Search for the term "negotiated rulemaking" over the past ten years in the online Federal Register database of your choice (e.g., www.federalregister.gov). How many results does that search return? Which agencies have made repeated use of the procedure during this time period? How many of these agencies are *required* to use the procedure, and how many may use it in their discretion?

CHAPTER 6

Adjudication

At this point in your legal studies, you are well acquainted with the judicial model of governmental decision-making. Almost all of your courses thus far—particularly Civil Procedure—orient strongly toward examining the process and policy implications of how judges decide cases. In particular, the federal civil litigation model—the form of judicial decision-making most studied in law schools—has several core features that readily identify it: opposing parties who vigorously advocate for different conceptions of the facts giving rise to their disputes and of the laws that apply to those facts; inclusive joinder rules that permit multiple claims from multiple parties to be litigated at the same time in a single court; generous discovery rules that allow wide-ranging pursuit of facts to support the parties' legal claims; restrictive evidence rules that protect fact-finders (whether they be judges or jurors) from being misled by irrelevant or confusing information; impartial, generalist judges who are insulated from political influence; and a multilayer appeals process that reduces the likelihood of decisional error. This system, overseen by federal judges and featuring numerous solemnities and protections, can be quite effective in producing fairness to parties and eliciting trust from the public. It can also be quite costly in terms of time to dispute resolution, consumption of governmental resources, and financial costs to the parties and to the taxpayers who fund the Judicial Branch. Nevertheless, it is considered the high-water mark for fair and thorough decision-making in the federal government.

Adjudication in the administrative state is so richly varied in formalities, contexts, and purposes that it cannot be reduced to a single model of any descriptive value. Sometimes it so closely resembles the civil litigation model that differences between the two are practically trivial. Sometimes it bears no resemblance to the civil litigation model at all. Much of this variety stems from how the Administrative Procedure Act

("APA") defines "adjudication": the "agency process for the formulation of an order." 5 U.S.C. § 551(7). It defines "order," in turn, as "the whole or a part of a final disposition, whether affirmative, negative, injunctive, or declaratory in form, of an agency in a matter other than rule making but including licensing." 5 U.S.C. § 551(6). These are broad definitions that encompass a vast array of decisions. Consider the following three examples:

- **Example 1:** A federal statute empowers the Secretary of Transportation to finance highway construction through public parks if she determines that there is no "feasible and prudent" alternative route, and if she also determines that the project takes all possible steps to minimize harm to the park through which the highway will be built. Where the Secretary finds that there is a feasible and prudent alternative route, or that the proposal being considered does not take all possible steps to the minimize harm, the statute prohibits granting construction funds. The Secretary is presented with a proposal to build an interstate highway through a large public park in a densely populated metropolitan area. In addition to the information included with the proposal, the Secretary studies information provided by agency staff members: maps, aerial photographs of the park and its surrounding area, analyses of the expected effects on traffic congestion and safety, project cost projections, and comments (both oral and written) from the city council and concerned citizens groups. The Secretary also discusses three alternative routes with agency personnel and the city council. Based on this information, the Secretary concludes that there is no feasible and prudent alternative to the route that runs through the park, and that the proposal meets the statutory standard for minimizing harm. She decides that the Department of Transportation will fund the project.
- **Example 2:** Smith suffers from chronic migraine headaches. She files an application for Social Security Disability Insurance ("DI") with the Social Security Administration ("SSA"). To qualify for the monthly Social Security DI benefit, Smith must prove that she worked for a specified time in a job covered by Social Security and that now, due to her disability, she cannot perform the work of her most recent job or any similar work. To support her application, Smith files evidence of her disability (its duration and severity), her work history, and her earnings history with a disability determination service ("DDS"), which is a state agency that provides initial DI benefits eligibility determinations for the SSA. In addition to the information Smith submits, the DDS gathers relevant information from Smith's past co-workers and medical providers. Upon concluding its investigation, the DDS determines that Smith is ineligible for DI benefits and sends her a letter denying the application. Smith disagrees with the DDS' initial decision

and exercises her right to a *de novo* review by an administrative law judge ("ALJ"). The ALJ holds an informal non-adversarial hearing, which Smith attends with a relative. The ALJ receives documentary evidence, hears sworn witness testimony, and questions Smith about the claimed impairment. Like the DDS, the ALJ concludes that Smith is ineligible for DI benefits and sends her a letter with a copy of the decision attached. Smith then seeks to appeal the ALJ's decision to the SSA's Appeals Council. However, review by the Appeals Council is discretionary; unlike her appeal to the ALJ, Smith has no right to have her case heard by the Council. Exercising its discretion, the Appeals Council declines to review the ALJ's decision.

- **Example 3:** ABC Loan Corp. ("ABC") is a "payday lender" that issues short-term, small-dollar loans. The annual percentage rate ABC charges can go as high as 800 percent. The Consumer Financial Protection Bureau ("CFPB") is an independent federal agency that, among other things, enforces the Truth in Lending Act ("TILA"). TILA requires lenders like ABC to clearly disclose the terms and total cost of the loans they issue. Believing that ABC has consistently failed to do this, the CFPB issued a Notice of Charges against the company alleging various TILA violations. The case was assigned to a CFPB administrative law judge ("ALJ") and placed on the agency's adjudicative docket. ABC moved to dismiss the Notice under CFPB Rule of Practice for Adjudication Procedure 212(c) (which is similar to Federal Rule of Civil Procedure 12(b)(6)). The ALJ denied the motion after oral arguments from the parties. The ALJ then held a hearing after limited discovery. At that hearing, the parties entered documents into evidence, objected to entry of certain documents by the opposition, and called and cross-examined expert and lay witnesses. Based on a review of the whole record, and by a preponderance of the evidence, the ALJ issued a detailed recommended decision finding that ABC violated TILA. ABC appealed the decision to the CFPB Director, who is empowered to review *de novo* all factual and legal issues raised in the appeal. After briefing from the parties and hearing oral arguments, the Director adopted the ALJ's recommendations in their entirety.

All three examples share important characteristics that led to their being grouped under the APA's "adjudication" umbrella. They all involve an agency's "final disposition" of discrete issues pertaining to clearly identified people or groups, although those issues vary considerably in subject matter and scope of effect. Relatedly, none of them can reasonably be described as "rulemaking," as none produce agency statements of general applicability and future effect. *See* 5 U.S.C. § 551(4). Instead, the decision-makers in each example applied preexisting government policies to the actions of particular persons or situations. Moreover, each example involves agency officials gathering evidence. Whether the officials received that evidence or heard those arguments orally or in writing does not matter; the APA's definitions of "adjudication" and "order" make room for both types of collection. Finally, the decisions reached in each example are, well, final. Each resolves its respective issue until it is overturned by a higher ranking agency official or by a federal court through judicial review.

Despite these and other similarities, these examples also exhibit features that distinguish them from civil litigation and from each other. The Secretary of Transportation's decision-making process in Example 1 looks almost nothing like federal civil litigation. Generally speaking, the Secretary's process was much more open and unstructured than the one employed by federal judges. For example, it did not feature adversarial parties who gathered probative evidence to inform the ultimate decision, who assisted the Secretary in framing the important issues in the case, or who could present the Secretary with competing arguments as to how those issues are best resolved. The Secretary bore sole responsibility for gathering, weighing, and applying the law to the evidence (likely with the assistance of agency staff).

Moreover, the statute providing for federal highway funding placed no limits on the sources of evidence the Secretary could use. She was free to consult with experts inside or outside of the agency, with laypersons, and with political and business leaders. Judges are much more limited in whom they may consult when deciding a case. Discussing material issues with persons other than the parties or without their knowledge is particularly problematic in the civil litigation context. The Secretary, in her discretion, could also receive information either orally or in person. By contrast, the Federal Rules of Evidence carefully curate the types and sources of information that fact-finders (whether they be judges or layperson jurors) are permitted to consider. The Secretary may (hopefully) be a subject matter expert with respect to transportation. If so, she walks into the situation with a significant amount of experience and insight (or, at a minimum, the staff that assists her does). Federal judges, by contrast, are not typically specialists in the subject matter of the cases they hear. Whereas federal judges are Article III appointees with life tenure, the Secretary is a member of the President's cabinet and serves only at the President's pleasure. The Secretary is therefore far less insulated from political and interest group pressure than is a federal judge. Moreover, the Secretary held no hearings during which interested parties could present evidence or cross-examine witnesses. Although trials are exceedingly rare in federal civil litigation these days, they will be held where there remain disputed issues of material fact after summary judgment and the parties fail to settle their differences. No such hearing requirement was imposed on the Secretary's decision to fund the highway construction proposed in Example 1. Finally, there is no intra-agency appeal from the Secretary's decision. While it could presumably be reviewed by a federal court to ensure conformance with federal law, no one within the agency has the authority to overrule her. Yet, despite all of these significant differences, the Secretary's decision to fund the proposed construction project would still (and quite clearly) be denominated "adjudication" by APA § 551(7).

Example 2 initially presents like Example 1. The disability determination service's ("DDS'") evaluation of Smith's DI application looks in many ways like the Secretary of Transportation's evaluation of the highway construction proposal. The DDS receives Smith's application with the required disclosures, conducts some additional fact-finding, and comes to an initial determination by applying the relevant legal rules (here, the disability insurance program's eligibility requirements) to those facts. It does not hear arguments from an opposing party; it does not hold an in-person hearing that allows for oral presentation of evidence or cross-examination of witnesses; the Federal Rules of Evidence do not restrict the sources or types of information on which it can rely; and the DDS staff member making the initial determination is not (presumably) insulated from political or other pressures by security of position.

However, Example 2 more closely resembles the formalized procedures of the civil litigation model as it moves past the DDS' initial determination of ineligibility. Most prominently, Smith has the right to an in-person hearing before an ALJ who reviews her application *de novo*. As discussed in the materials that follow, ALJs have substantially greater security of position than other agency staff members (or state-based agency contractors like DDS staffers), although they have fewer protections than federal judges. These protections insulate ALJs from the pressures—within and outside of their agencies—that could undermine (or be perceived as undermining) their impartiality and independence. Further, the ALJ in Example 2 presided over a live hearing that gave Smith the chance to orally challenge the DDS' initial decision. Such a hearing played no part in Example 1 or in the DDS initial decision process. Permitting oral presentation of evidence gives parties much more procedural protection than limiting arguments to written submissions, even if the presentation comes after benefits are denied, and even if the proceedings are informal and nonadversarial. Finally, Smith was permitted to bring someone along—in this case a relative—to assist at the hearing, mimicking the attorney representation that commonly accompanies civil litigation. These procedural features—an assisted in-person hearing before an ALJ with limited security of position—mirror civil litigation's procedural features without adopting all of its restrictions, protections, or formalities.

Clearly, Example 3 most closely resembles civil litigation. Indeed, the two seem almost identical. The proceedings begin with a Notice of Charges issued by the CFPB, which operates in much the same way as a complaint filed in federal court. The parties filed dispositive motions, the first by ABC to dismiss the suit and the others for summary disposition after the conclusion of discovery. A "trial"—or a hearing, in administrative parlance—was held, during which the parties entered documents and witness testimony into the record. The CFPB presumably had to prove its case by a preponderance of the evidence, the burden of persuasion often used in civil suits. The ALJ presiding over the hearing, as discussed above, enjoys security of position. As would a federal judge in a bench trial, a written decision detailed the ALJ's factual and legal conclusions and resolved the dispute by issuing an order. ABC was permitted an appeal to a reviewing authority—in this instance the CFPB Director—who upheld the ALJ's decision after receiving briefs and hearing oral arguments from the parties.

Despite these substantial similarities between Example 3's formal agency adjudication and the civil litigation we find in federal courts, the student of Administrative Law must recognize some significant differences. The procedural rules employed in Example 3 were those adopted by the CFPB itself; the Federal Rules of Civil Procedure do not, by their own force, apply to federal agency adjudications. The same is true for the Federal Rules of Evidence; comparatively speaking, the default rules for admission of evidence in administrative adjudications are much more relaxed. The discovery permitted in CFPB adjudications is more limited than it is in federal civil litigation and is not mandated by any federal statute. During the hearing, the ALJ actively questioned the parties and their witnesses, taking a more proactive role in framing and exploring the issues than would a federal judge, even in a bench trial. Moreover, the ALJ is a CFPB employee. Unlike federal judges whose appointments in the Judicial Branch separate them from any parties who might appear before them, the ALJ actually works for the agency that investigated and sought to enforce the TILA violations ABC allegedly committed. While the CFPB's adjudicative procedures provide for appeals, there are important differences there, too. The Director who heard ABC's appeal is not a judge, but the leader of the agency. As such, the Director is ultimately responsible for the CFPB fulfilling its statutory mandate, which includes investigative, enforcement, and adjudicative functions. The Director is also a political appointee with a five-year term in office. Unlike federal judges who can be removed only through the Constitution's impeachment process, the President can fire the Director at will. *See Seila Law LLC v. CFPB*, 140 S. Ct. 2183 (2020). The CFPB Director is susceptible to external political pressures, though succumbing to them would likely violate ABC's due process rights. Nevertheless, the Director is the final adjudicator within the agency.

The above examples and accompanying analyses highlight several issues addressed in greater depth in the materials that follow. The discussion is divided into two broad categories: formal adjudication and informal adjudication.

A. FORMAL ADJUDICATION

Governed by §§ 554, 556, and 557 of the Administrative Procedure Act ("APA"), formal adjudication is the most elaborate adjudicative process employed by federal administrative agencies. It incorporates many of the procedural features ordinarily found in federal and state judicial proceedings: hearings over which neutral decision-makers with some security of position typically preside, representation by counsel at the option of the parties, pre-hearing conferences, discovery-like exchanges of information, in-person presentations of evidence, cross-examination of adverse witnesses, formal written explanations of orders, etc. Taken together, formal adjudications under the APA provides more expansive procedural protection than those required by the Constitution's due process clauses, a topic explored more fully in the following chapter.

While it does protect parties from potentially erroneous or prejudicial decision-making, formal adjudication is also expensive and time-consuming. In recognition of this, Congress rarely requires its use. Even when it does, APA § 554(c) requires that agencies give parties the chance to informally resolve their disputes when practicable. At the time of the APA's passage, Members of Congress were well aware that the opportunity for settlement by consent order or decree was critical to effective administration of the laws, and so they wanted to make sure that agencies were given latitude to pursue such informal (less costly and time-consuming) resolutions when appropriate. *See* Attorney General's Manual at 49.

Settlement, of course, is not always possible. Accordingly, the following materials focus on several core aspects of formal adjudication under the Administrative Procedure Act. These include the statutory language requiring its use, the notice to which its parties are entitled, the protections given to its presiding officers (administrative law judges), and the sufficiency and admissibility of the evidence submitted during it.

Note the similarities to and differences between federal (particularly civil) court proceedings and the agency adjudications described below. Such a comparison leads to several system design questions. Do agencies and courts have similar or different missions in the adjudicative context? Based on your answer, do you think agencies should behave more like courts, such that agencies should be required to use formal adjudication more often? If you think that formal adjudication provides poor value for money, which specific procedural protections could agencies jettison without unduly endangering the fairness or accuracy of their adjudicative proceedings? Should Congress ideally require that agencies provide even more protections than formal adjudication affords? If so, should Congress provide these additional protections irrespective of cost because fundamental fairness demands it?

1. Required Use of Formal Adjudication

APA § 554(a) sets out when agencies must proceed by formal adjudication, and thus when they are precluded from utilizing informal adjudication or rulemaking (whether formal or informal). Unless one of the six exceptions listed in § 554(a)(1)-(6) applies,[1] Congress requires formal agency adjudication "in every case of adjudication required by statute to be determined on the record after opportunity for an agency hearing." 5 U.S.C. § 554(a). In other words, the APA's formal adjudication requirements are triggered only when a separate statute specifically requires it. Courts sometimes have little trouble finding that the requirement applies, either because a statute uses the familiar term of art "on the record" or because it otherwise clearly demonstrates an agency's obligation to provide a formal hearing. *See, e.g., National Labor Relations Board v. Curtin Matheson Scientific, Inc.,* 494 U.S. 775 (1990) (Scalia, J., dissenting) (noting that "[a]n NLRB unfair-labor-practice action is the form of administrative proceeding known as formal adjudication, governed by the Administrative Procedure Act (APA), 5 U.S.C. §§ 556, 557"); *Lane v. U.S. Department of Agriculture,* 120 F.3d 106, 108-109 (8th Cir. 1997) (finding that USDA's National Appeals Division proceedings were governed by § 557); Tariff Act of 1930, 19 U.S.C. § 1337 (requiring certain determinations be "made on the record after notice and opportunity for a hearing in conformity with the provisions of subchapter II of chapter 5 of title 5").

Most of the time, however, Congress provides courts with far less guidance. As with rulemaking, the question is whether courts will readily or reluctantly infer formal procedural requirements from ambiguous statutory text. Recall that in *United States v. Florida East Coast Railway Company,* 410 U.S. 224 (1973), the Court did not think use of the term "after hearing" in the Interstate Commerce Act was enough to force the Interstate Commerce Commission into formal rulemaking under APA §§ 556 and 557. *See* page 259. The Court has never explicitly extended *Florida East Coast*'s holding to administrative adjudications. The lower courts have done so nevertheless, adopting at least three differing approaches for applying it. Under one approach, courts do not require that federal statutes use the precise language "on the record" to trigger the formal adjudication requirement. *See, e.g., Seacoast Anti-Pollution League v. Costle,* 572 F.2d 872 (1st Cir. 1978) (stating formal adjudication requirement is triggered by the substantive nature of the hearing Congress requires, not by the term "on the record"), *overruled by Dominion Energy Brayton Point, LLC v. Johnson,* 443 F.3d 12 (1st Cir. 2006). Under a more restrictive approach, courts read statutes as triggering § 554(a) only if their text clearly requires that result, though even then the statute need not use the exact phrase "on the record." *See, e.g., City of West Chicago v. Nuclear Regulatory Commission,* 701 F.2d 632 (7th Cir. 1983). The third and prevailing approach, adopted by the First Circuit

---

[1] Section 554(a) exempts agencies from engaging in formal (i.e., "on the record") hearings if the underlying matter before the agency (1) is subject to a subsequent *de novo* trial in court; (2) involves the selection or tenure of an employee other than an administrative law judge appointed under 5 U.S.C. § 3105; (3) involves proceedings in which decisions rest solely on inspections, tests, or elections; (4) involves the conduct of military or foreign affairs functions; (5) is a case in which the agency is acting as an agency for a court; or (6) involves the certification of worker representatives.

in *Dominion Energy* (excerpted below), gives *Chevron* deference to agencies' reasonable interpretations of their organic statutes if there is a question whether those statutes trigger § 554(a). In other words, whether Congress requires formal adjudication is primarily determined not by the courts, but by the agencies when Congress has tasked them with resolving ambiguities in the statutes they administer.

Dominion Energy Brayton Point, LLC v. Johnson
443 F.3d 12 (1st Cir. 2006)

Before SELYA, LIPEZ and HOWARD, Circuit Judges.

SELYA, Circuit Judge.

USGen New England, Inc., now Dominion Energy Brayton Point, LLC (Dominion), filed suit against the U.S. Environmental Protection Agency, its administrator, and its regional office (collectively, the EPA), alleging that the EPA failed to perform a non-discretionary duty when it refused to grant Dominion's request for a formal evidentiary hearing after issuing a proposed final National Pollution Discharge Elimination System (NPDES) permit. The district court dismissed the case for want of subject matter jurisdiction. On appeal, the central question presented concerns the effect of this court's decision in *Seacoast Anti-Pollution League v. Costle*, 572 F.2d 872 (1st Cir. 1978), in light of the Supreme Court's subsequent decision in *Chevron U.S.A. Inc. v. Natural Resources Defense Council, Inc.* Concluding, as we do, that *Seacoast* does not control, we affirm the judgment below.

I. BACKGROUND

Dominion owns an electrical generating facility in Somerset, Massachusetts (the station). The station opened in the 1960s and, like most power plants of its era, utilizes an "open-cycle" cooling system. Specifically, the station withdraws water from the Lees and Taunton Rivers, circulates that water through the plant's generating equipment as a coolant, and then discharges the water (which, by then, has attained an elevated temperature) into Mount Hope Bay.

The withdrawals and discharges of water are regulated by the Clean Water Act (CWA), 33 U.S.C. §§ 1251-1387. For the last three decades, these actions have been authorized by a series of NPDES permits issued by the EPA pursuant to section 402(a) of the CWA. *See id.* § 1342(a). The standards incorporated into those permits are determined under the thermal variance procedures laid out in section 316(a). *See id.* § 1326(a).

In 1998, the station applied for renewal of its NPDES permit and thermal variance authorization. The EPA issued a proposed final permit on

October 6, 2003, in which it rejected the requested thermal variance. On November 4, Dominion sought review before the Environmental Appeals Board (the Board), *see* 40 C.F.R. § 124.19(a) (authorizing Board review), and asked for an evidentiary hearing. The Board accepted the petition for review but declined to convene an evidentiary hearing.

On August 11, 2004, Dominion notified the EPA of its intent to file a citizen's suit under section 505(a)(2) of the CWA, 33 U.S.C. § 1365(a)(2), to compel the Board to hold an evidentiary hearing. Receiving no reply, Dominion proceeded to file its complaint in the United States District Court for the District of Massachusetts. The EPA moved to dismiss.

The district court granted the motion on jurisdictional grounds [, concluding] that it was without subject matter jurisdiction because the suit, though billed as a citizen's suit, constituted a direct challenge to the EPA's hearing rule and, thus, came within the exclusive jurisdiction of the circuit court under 33 U.S.C. § 1369(b)(1)(E). This timely appeal followed.

II. THE LEGAL LANDSCAPE

We set the stage for our substantive discussion by undertaking a brief review of the legal rules that frame the controversy at hand.

Before the EPA either issues an NPDES permit or authorizes a thermal variance, it must offer an "opportunity for public hearing." 33 U.S.C. §§ 1326(a), 1342(a). No definition of "public hearing" is contained within the four corners of the CWA.

The Administrative Procedure Act (APA), 5 U.S.C. § 551 *et seq.*, is also part of the relevant legal landscape. Most pertinent here are those sections that combine to describe the procedures for formal administrative adjudications. *See id.* §§ 554, 556, 557. These procedures apply "in every case of adjudication required by statute to be determined on the record after opportunity for an agency hearing." *Id.* § 554(a). The APA does not directly address whether these procedures apply when a statute simply calls for an "opportunity for public hearing" without any specific indication that the hearing should be "on the record."

In *Seacoast*, this court interpreted "public hearing" (as used in sections 402(a) and 316(a) of the CWA) to mean "evidentiary hearing"—in other words, a hearing that comports with the APA's requirements for a formal adjudication. Examining the legislative history of the APA, we adopted a presumption that "unless a statute otherwise specifies, an adjudicatory hearing subject to judicial review must be [an evidentiary hearing] on the record." Applying that presumption to the CWA, we concluded that "the statute certainly does not indicate that the determination need *not* be on the record." [(Emphasis in original.)]

So viewed, *Seacoast* established a rebuttable presumption that, in the context of an adjudication, an organic statute that calls for a "public hearing" should be read to require an evidentiary hearing in compliance with the formal adjudication provisions of the APA.... Acquiescing in this construction, the EPA promulgated regulations that memorialized the use of formal evidentiary hearings in the NPDES permit process. *See* NPDES; Revision of Regulations, 44 Fed. Reg. 32,854, 32,938 (June 7, 1979).

In 1984, a sea change occurred in administrative law and, specifically, in the interpretation of organic statutes such as the CWA. The Supreme Court held that "[w]hen a court reviews an agency's construction of the statute which it administers," the reviewing court first must ask "whether Congress has directly spoken to the precise question at issue." *Chevron*, 467 U.S. at 842. If Congress's intent is clear, that intent governs—both the court and the agency must give it full effect. If, however, Congress has not directly addressed the question and the agency has stepped into the vacuum by promulgating an interpretive regulation, a reviewing court may "not simply impose its own construction on the statute," but, rather, ought to ask "whether the agency's answer is based on a permissible construction of the statute." *Id.* at 843.

> **Cross-Reference**
>
> *Chevron* and the long line of cases that it has spawned—including the Court's decision in *Brand X*, referenced below—are considered in Chapter 9.

This paradigm, sometimes called the *Chevron* two-step, increases the sphere of influence of agency action. If congressional intent is unclear and an agency's interpretation of a statute that it administers is reasonable, an inquiring court must defer to that interpretation. That is so even if the agency's interpretation is not the one that the court considers to be the best available interpretation.

Armed with the *Chevron* decision and a presidential directive to streamline regulatory programs ... the EPA advanced a proposal to eliminate formal evidentiary hearings from the NPDES permitting process. *See* Amendments to Streamline the NPDES Program Regulations: Round Two, 61 Fed. Reg. 65,268, 65,276 (Dec. 11, 1996). In due course, the EPA adopted that proposal as a final rule. *See* Amendments to Streamline the NPDES Program Regulations: Round Two, 65 Fed. Reg. 30,886, 30,900 (May 15, 2000).

This revision depended heavily on a *Chevron* analysis. The agency began by "finding no evidence that Congress intended to require formal evidentiary hearings or that the text [of section 402(a)] precludes informal adjudication of permit review petitions." *Id.* at 30,896. Then, it weighed the risks and benefits of employing informal hearing procedures for NPDES permit review, "determining that these procedures would not violate the Due Process Clause." *Id.* Finally, it "concluded that informal hearing procedures satisfy the hearing requirement of section 402(a)." *Id.*

It was under this new regulatory scheme that the EPA considered Dominion's request to renew its NPDES permit and to authorize a thermal variance. Thus, it was under this scheme that the EPA denied Dominion's request for an evidentiary hearing.

III. ANALYSIS....

. . . Dominion's claim on appeal rests on the premise that it has satisfied the jurisdictional requirements for a citizen's suit under section 505(a)(2) of the CWA. Subject to a notice requirement—suit may not be commenced "prior to sixty days after the plaintiff has given notice of such [proposed] action," 33 U.S.C. § 1365(b)(2)—the statute invoked by Dominion grants federal district courts jurisdiction over any citizen's suit brought "against the Administrator [of the EPA] where there is alleged a failure of the Administrator to perform any act or duty under [the CWA] which is not discretionary," *id.* § 1365(a)(2). There is no question but that Dominion satisfied the applicable notice requirement. The crux of the case, therefore, is whether Dominion has pleaded the flouting of a non-discretionary duty.

One thing is crystal clear: on their face, the current EPA regulations do not establish a non-discretionary duty to provide the evidentiary hearing that Dominion seeks. Prior to the date of Dominion's request, the EPA vitiated the preexisting rule introducing evidentiary hearings into the NPDES permitting process. *See* 40 C.F.R. § 124.21(b) (explaining that the "EPA eliminated the previous requirement for NPDES permits to undergo an evidentiary hearing after permit issuance . . . on June 14, 2000"). Dominion concedes this fact, but nonetheless relies on *Seacoast* as the source of a non-discretionary duty to convene an evidentiary hearing.

This reliance is misplaced. Even if *Seacoast* established a non-discretionary duty for section 505(a)(2) purposes when it was decided—a matter upon which we need not opine—Dominion's position ignores two important post-*Seacoast* changes in the legal landscape: the Supreme Court's decision in *Chevron* and the agency's subsequent promulgation of the current "no evidentiary hearing" rule....

For present purposes, the critical precedent is *National Cable & Telecommunications Ass'n v. Brand X Internet Services*, 545 U.S. 967 (2005). There, the Court examined the relationship between the *stare decisis* effect of an appellate court's statutory interpretation and the *Chevron* deference due to an administrative agency's subsequent, but contrary, interpretation. Echoing *Chevron*, the Court reiterated that "[f]illing [statutory] gaps . . . involves difficult policy choices that agencies are better equipped to make than courts." *Id.* at 2699. Then, concluding that *Chevron*'s application should not turn on the order in which judicial and agency interpretations issue, the Justices held squarely that "[a] court's prior judicial construction of a statute trumps an agency construction otherwise entitled to *Chevron* deference only if the prior court decision holds that its construction follows from the unambiguous terms of the statute and thus leaves no room for agency discretion." *Id.* at 2700. This approach "hold[s] judicial interpretations contained in precedents to the same demanding *Chevron* . . . standard that applies if the court is reviewing the agency's construction on a blank slate." *Id.*

Brand X demands that we reexamine pre-*Chevron* precedents through a *Chevron* lens. The *Chevron* two-step applies. At the first step, a court "must look primarily to the plain meaning of the statute, drawing its essence from the particular statutory language at issue, as well as the language and design of the statute as a whole." [Citation omitted.] At this step, the court may "examine the legislative history, albeit skeptically, in search of an unmistakable expression of congressional intent." [Citation omitted.] If the precedent at issue finds clarity at step one — that is, if the holding of the case rests on a perception of clear and unambiguous congressional intent — that precedent will govern. If, however, the precedent operates at *Chevron* step two — that is, if the case holds, in effect, that congressional intent is less than pellucid and proceeds to choose a "*best* reading" rather than "the *only permissible reading*," *Brand X* at 2701 (emphasis in original) — its *stare decisis* effect will, through *Chevron* deference, yield to a contrary but plausible agency interpretation.

Once this mode of analysis is understood and applied, Dominion's argument collapses. *Seacoast* simply does not hold that Congress clearly intended the term "public hearing" in sections 402(a) and 316(a) of the CWA to mean "evidentiary hearing." To the contrary, the *Seacoast* court based its interpretation of the CWA on a presumption derived from the legislative history of the APA — a presumption that would hold sway only in the absence of a showing of a contrary congressional intent. In other words, the court resorted to the presumption only because it could find no sign of a plainly discernible congressional intent. A statutory interpretation constructed on such a negative finding is antithetic to a conclusion that Congress's intent was clear and unambiguous.

The short of it is that the *Seacoast* court, faced with an opaque statute, settled upon what it sensibly thought was the best construction of the CWA's "public hearing" language. Such a holding is appropriate at step two of the *Chevron* pavane, not at step one. Consequently, under *Brand X*, *Seacoast* must yield to a reasonable agency interpretation of the CWA's "public hearing" requirement.

The only piece left to this puzzle is to confirm that the EPA's new regulations are, in fact, entitled to *Chevron* deference. This inquiry is a straightforward one. As our earlier discussion suggests (and as the *Seacoast* court correctly deduced), Congress has not spoken directly to the precise question at issue here. *See, e.g., United States v. Fla. E. Coast Ry. Co.,* 410 U.S. 224, 239 (1973) ("The term 'hearing' in its legal context undoubtedly has a host of meanings."). Accordingly, we must [give *Chevron* deference] to the EPA's interpretation of the CWA as long as that interpretation is reasonable.

In this instance, the administrative interpretation took into account the relevant universe of factors. *See* 65 Fed. Reg. at 30,898–30,900 (considering "(1) [t]he private interests at stake, (2) the risk of erroneous decision-making, and (3) the nature of the government interest," and concluding that its new regulation was a reasonable interpretation of the CWA). The agency's conclusion that evidentiary hearings are unnecessary and that Congress, in using the phrase "opportunity for public hearing," did not mean to mandate evidentiary hearings seems reasonable—and Dominion, to its credit, has conceded the point. . . .

IV. CONCLUSION

We summarize succinctly. Although we in no way disparage the soundness of *Seacoast's* reasoning, the *Chevron* and *Brand X* opinions and the interposition of a new and reasonable agency interpretation of the disputed statutory language have changed the picture. Because we, like the *Seacoast* court, cannot discern a clear and unambiguous congressional intent behind the words "public hearing" in the CWA and because the EPA's interpretation of that term constitutes a reasonable construction of the statute, deference is due. It follows inexorably that no non-discretionary duty to grant Dominion an evidentiary hearing on its permit application exists. Consequently, the jurisdictional requirements of section 505(a)(2) have not been satisfied.

We need go no further. For the reasons elucidated above, we conclude that the district court did not err in dismissing Dominion's action.

Affirmed.

QUESTION SET 6.1

Review & Synthesis

1. Describe the procedures the EPA afforded Dominion and identify the reasons Dominion may have been motivated to challenge those procedures as inadequate.

2. Explain why the court accepted the EPA's interpretation of the term "public hearing" as used in Clean Water Act §§ 1326(a) and 1342(a). Was it not the case that a prior First Circuit decision, *Seacoast Anti-Pollution League v. Costle*, had already determined that the EPA had a duty to convene an evidentiary hearing? What authority does an agency have to overrule a federal court's prior interpretation of a federal statute?

3. Should courts defer under the *Chevron* doctrine to agencies' interpretations of procedural statutes like §§ 1326(a) and 1342(a)? Such provisions limit agencies' substantive regulatory authority by setting the terms

on which they must exercise it. Relatedly, procedural provisions like §§ 1326(a) and 1342(a) establish the protections agencies must provide the individuals and entities they regulate. Should agencies be given discretion to choose which limits and protections they will acknowledge, and which they will ignore? Even if you believe that Congress has the authority to delegate such choices to agencies, in the absence of clear evidence should courts assume that it did?

Application & Analysis

1. An organic statute enacted last year states that Agency can assess civil penalties against trucking companies that fail to maintain their delivery trucks in accordance with Agency's regulations. The statute further states that Agency must conduct an "evidentiary hearing" before it can assess those civil penalties. Agency has commenced a civil penalty proceeding against ABC Trucking for failing to properly maintain its fleet of delivery trucks. For each of the following scenarios, identify the part of APA § 554 that applies, whether a formal adjudication is required, and why.

   a. Agency has promulgated regulations providing for the written submission of evidence and rebuttal to evidence submitted by Agency's investigators in its civil penalty proceedings. The regulations do not provide for in-person evidentiary hearings. ABC Trucking challenges the validity of the regulations.

   b. Agency has promulgated regulations providing for oral evidentiary hearings. However, Agency argues that these regulations and the procedural protections they afford do not apply to ABC Trucking because the company is a military contractor serving domestic bases for the United States Marine Corp. ABC Trucking disputes Agency's conclusion.

   c. Agency has promulgated regulations that allow its attorneys to take evidence, preside over, and issue initial decisions in its civil penalty hearings. ABC Trucking believes that the APA mandates that an administrative law judge ("ALJ") preside over the adjudication.

   d. Agency gives its ALJs the discretion to hold settlement conferences for the settlement of civil penalty proceedings. Shortly after receiving notice from Agency of its intent to pursue civil penalties against

> ### In Context
>
> APA § 556 states, in relevant part:
>
>   (b) There shall preside at the taking of evidence—
>   (1) the agency;
>   (2) one or more members of the body which comprises the agency; or
>   (3) one or more administrative law judges appointed under section 3105 of this title.
>
> 5 U.S.C. § 556. Although agency heads can preside over formal adjudications, they rarely do so. *See* Michael Asimow, *The Spreading Umbrella: Extending the APA's Adjudication Provisions to All Evidentiary Hearings Required by Statute*, 56 ADMIN. L. REV. 1003, 1005 n. 11 (2004).

it, ABC Trucking requests a conference to propose settlement terms. The presiding ALJ rejects ABC Trucking's conference request.

e. ABC Trucking argues that it is entitled to an in-person evidentiary hearing to determine whether an expert relied upon by Agency is biased. The company believes that limiting its questioning of the expert to written interrogatories is insufficient; it can only assess the expert's "motive, intent, and credibility" if it is allowed to orally cross-examine her. Agency argues, in response, that ABC Trucking has offered no evidence to support its claim of bias against the expert. The presiding ALJ denies ABC Trucking's request.

f. In an affidavit submitted as part of the civil penalties adjudication against ABC Trucking, its CEO admitted to omitting material information from forms submitted on the company's behalf pursuant to Agency's delivery truck maintenance regulations. If included, the omitted information would show that ABC Trucking failed to comply with the regulations. ABC Trucking is requesting an oral evidentiary hearing on whether it has violated Agency's regulations.

---

2. The Hearing Officers: Administrative Law Judges

According to the U.S. Office of Personnel Management ("OPM"), the federal government employed 1,931 administrative law judges ("ALJs") across 28 agencies as of March 2017. *See* U.S. Office of Personnel Management, Federal Administrative Law Judges by Agency and Level (EHRI-SDM March 2017), https://www.opm.gov/services-for-agencies/administrative -law-judges/#url=ALJs-by-Agency (last visited Sept. 15, 2019). The overwhelming majority were employed by the Social Security Administration (1,655 or 86 percent), where they hear appeals from across the country on retirement, survivors, disability insurance, and supplemental security income benefits determinations. The Postal Service employed the fewest (only 1). To put the size of the ALJ pool into some perspective, there were 860 authorized Article III judgeships as of 2017, roughly half the number employed by the Social Security Administration alone. *See* United States Courts, Authorized Judgeships—From 1789 to Present, http://www.uscourts.gov/judges-judgeships/authorized-judgeships (last visited Sept. 15, 2019). Aside from ALJs, federal agencies employ many thousands of administrative officials with varying titles who perform adjudicative functions: administrative judges, hearing officers, hearing examiners, trial examiners, immigration judges (naturally in the immigration context), etc. The precise number of these adjudicators remains an open question. However, the U.S. Patent and Trademark Officer reported that it employed 8,351 patent examiners (a type of administrative judge) at the end of Fiscal Year 2017. *See generally* Kent Barnett & Russell Wheeler, *Non-ALJ Adjudicators in Federal Agencies: Status, Selection, Oversight, and Removal*, 53 GA. L. REV. 1 (2018).

Pursuant to APA § 556, however, only ALJs may preside over formal adjudications. The reason for this seems straightforward when one understands that formal adjudications have a particular need for adjudicators who are shielded from undue influences. As the Supreme Court observed in *Butz v. Economou*, "the securing of fair and competent hearing personnel was viewed as the heart of formal administrative adjudication" prior to the APA, and so "the process of agency adjudication is currently structured [under the APA] so as to assure that the hearing examiner [now, the ALJ] exercises his independent judgment on the evidence before him, free from pressures by the parties or other officials within the agency." 438 U.S. 478, 513 (1978).

Congress accordingly granted ALJs substantial job protections to facilitate their impartiality and independence. While these protections are not as robust as those enjoyed by Article III judges, they are certainly more substantial than the ones held by other agency adjudicators. ALJs can only be removed for cause or under staffing reductions based on seniority and, before being removed for cause, they are entitled to an on-the-record hearing before the Merit Systems Protection Board. 5 U.S.C. § 3105, 7521. Their pay is set by statute, 5 U.S.C. § 5372, although it, along with their seniority, can be reduced through disciplinary action, 5 U.S.C. § 7521. Section 554(d)(2) forbids presiding ALJs from being supervised or directed by agency employees with investigative or prosecutorial responsibilities. By separating ALJs from other agency officials in this way, § 554(d)(2) tries to avoid the apparent conflicts of commitment that tend to taint decision-makers' perceived neutrality. It almost goes without saying that the losing party in a formal adjudication would question the proceeding's fairness if the presiding ALJ reported to the agency's chief of enforcement.

Section 554(d)(2) thus works in tandem with 5 U.S.C. § 3105, which forbids agencies from assigning ALJs "duties inconsistent with their duties and responsibilities as administrative law judges." 5 U.S.C. § 3105. The practical upshot of this, with a few exceptions, is the organizational separation of ALJs from the rest of their agencies' operations. For similar reasons, ALJs' units can be headed only by agency leadership or by officials with no investigative or prosecutorial responsibilities. *See* ATTORNEY GENERAL'S MANUAL at 55-56. Section 554(d)(2) likewise forbids (with a few exceptions) agency investigators and prosecutors in the case over which the ALJ presides, or in factually similar ones, from participating in that case's resolution unless they do so as witnesses or counsel in public hearings.

Other APA provisions with a slightly different focus also work in tandem with ALJs' statutory protections to ensure decisional integrity. Rather than protecting ALJs from undue external influences, they protect the process from errors the ALJs themselves might make. In particular, these provisions direct ALJs to personally familiarize themselves with the facts of the disputes over which they preside and to focus only on those facts and the relevant law when resolving them. These obligations were firmly established as maxims of administrative adjudication even before passage of the APA; as the Supreme Court stated in *Morgan v. United States*, 298 U.S. 468 (1936), the adjudicator's duty of reaching evidence-driven conclusions "cannot be performed by one who has not considered evidence or argument. It is not an impersonal obligation. It is a duty akin to that of a judge. *The one who decides must hear.*" *Id.* at 481 (emphasis added). APA Section 554(d) accordingly requires the ALJ who "presides at the reception of evidence" to "make the recommended decision or initial decision." Only in unusual circumstances, such as illness or departure from the agency, should someone other than the ALJ who managed development of the factual record issue the initial order or recommendation for resolving a dispute. Even when that situation does arise, the agency adjudicators—whether in an original or an appellate posture—still have a personal obligation to familiarize themselves with the case's legal and factual issues.

ALJs must not only focus on the evidence and the law when deciding cases, they must demonstrate that they have done so. APA § 557(c)(3)(A) requires that agency decisions in formal adjudications be accompanied by findings, conclusions, and explanations for all material issues of fact, law, and discretion. Requiring agencies to "show their work" leads them to think carefully through each step of the analytical process before reaching their decisions, lest they open themselves up to criticism (and possible reversal) by scrutinizing external observers (reviewing courts, the public, Members of Congress, etc.). The statement setting out the ALJ's analysis need not be lengthy and detailed to satisfy § 557(c)(3)(A), but it must be robust enough for a reviewing court to be confident that the ALJ took a "hard look" at the relevant issues in the case. Moreover, requiring that agencies explain themselves helps to bring closure to contested issues and informs third parties of how the agency will likely resolve similar disputes in future cases. *See* A GUIDE TO FEDERAL AGENCY ADJUDICATION 107 (Jeffrey Litwak, ed., 2d ed. 2012) (hereinafter FEDERAL AGENCY ADJUDICATION). Moreover, and before a decision or recommendation can be issued in an APA § 556 formal adjudication, § 557(c)(1)-(3) guarantees the parties an opportunity to propose findings and conclusions or to take exception to an agency's findings or conclusions.

The APA's preoccupation with ALJ independence and impartiality was also clearly reflected in the process for hiring them. In place for more than 70 years, this process was consciously apolitical and merit-driven. While ALJs were eventually hired by individual agencies, those agencies could only do so after thorough vetting by the U.S. Office of Personnel Management ("OPM"). ALJ candidates had to be licensed attorneys with at least seven-years' experience (though not necessarily in the area of law on which the hiring agency focused) and take an examination administered by OPM. OPM would then provide the hiring agency with a list of the top three candidates, whose rankings were based on their examination scores, experience, and veteran status. Accordingly, the process tried to eliminate neutrality-compromising factors—political bias, ideological leanings, nepotism, etc.—from ALJ appointments.

However effective a process such as this might be in identifying highly qualified and neutral adjudicators, it did raise a rather important question: is it constitutional? ALJs wield powers that closely resemble those of Article III judges. They rule on preliminary motions, conduct pre-hearing conferences, issue subpoenas, manage on-the-record hearings including through the imposition of sanctions, make evidentiary rulings (though these are not necessarily governed by the Federal Rules of Evidence), and issue initial or recommended decisions that can result in final agency orders. Given this range of judge-like powers, should their appointment be governed by the Article III Appointments Clause? As discussed in Part IV, so-called "principal" federal officers wield the federal government's "significant authority" (i.e., legislative, executive, or judicial) and must be nominated by the President with the advice and consent of the Senate. So-called "inferior officers" can be appointed by the President, the federal courts (though not limited to Article III courts), or agency heads. The OPM hiring model adopted neither of these selection methods. It instead treated ALJs as civil "competitive service" employees whose hiring the Appointments Clause did not govern. Of course, handing ALJ hiring over to the President or his political appointees could upend the merit-driven system so carefully constructed by Congress.

The Supreme Court had previously addressed a variant of this issue in *Freytag v. Commissioner of Internal Revenue*, 501 U.S. 868 (1991). By statute, the chief judge of the United States Tax Court was permitted to appoint "special trial judges" ("STJs") to preside over certain hearings and to submit proposed findings and opinions to Tax Court judges. The Tax Court judges (Article I administrative law judges) were then responsible for rendering decisions. Taxpayers challenged a determination of deficiencies recommended by an STJ and adopted by the chief judge as the opinion of the court. The Supreme Court, *sua sponte*, raised the issue whether STJs were constitutionally appointed. In answering in the affirmative, the Court concluded that STJs are "inferior officers" of the United States, rather than employees, whose appointment could be vested in the chief judge.

The Supreme Court returned to this issue in *Lucia v. SEC*, a case with potentially far-reaching implications that closely scrutinized the adjudicative powers wielded by ALJs.

Lucia v. Securities Exchange Commission
138 S. Ct. 2044 (2018)

Justice KAGAN delivered the opinion of the Court.

The Appointments Clause of the Constitution lays out the permissible methods of appointing "Officers of the United States," a class of government officials distinct from mere employees. Art. II, § 2, cl. 2. This case requires us to decide whether administrative law judges (ALJs) of the Securities and Exchange Commission (SEC or Commission) qualify as such "Officers." In keeping with *Freytag v. Commissioner*, 501 U.S. 868 (1991), we hold that they do.

I

The SEC has statutory authority to enforce the nation's securities laws. One way it can do so is by instituting an administrative proceeding against an alleged wrongdoer. By law, the Commission may itself preside over such a proceeding. *See* 17 C.F.R. § 201.110 (2017). But the Commission also may, and typically does, delegate that task to an ALJ. *See ibid.*; 15 U.S.C. § 78d-1(a). The SEC currently has five ALJs. Other staff members, rather than the Commission proper, selected them all.

An ALJ assigned to hear an SEC enforcement action has extensive powers—the "authority to do all things necessary and appropriate to discharge his or her duties" and ensure a "fair and orderly" adversarial proceeding. §§ 201.111, 200.14(a). Those powers "include, but are not limited to," supervising discovery; issuing, revoking, or modifying subpoenas; deciding motions; ruling on the admissibility of evidence; administering oaths; hearing and examining witnesses; generally "[r]egulating the course of" the proceeding and the "conduct of the parties and their counsel"; and imposing sanctions for "[c]ontemptuous conduct" or violations of procedural requirements. §§ 201.111, 201.180; *see* §§ 200.14(a), 201.230. As that list suggests, an SEC ALJ exercises authority "comparable to" that of a federal district judge conducting a bench trial. *Butz v. Economou*, 438 U.S. 478, 513 (1978).

After a hearing ends, the ALJ issues an "initial decision." § 201.360(a)(1). That decision must set out "findings and conclusions" about all "material issues of fact [and] law"; it also must include the "appropriate order, sanction, relief, or denial thereof." § 201.360(b). The Commission can then review the ALJ's decision, either upon request or *sua sponte*. *See* § 201.360(d)(1). But if it opts against review, the Commission "issue[s] an order that the [ALJ's] decision has become final." § 201.360(d)(2). At that point, the initial decision is "deemed the action of the Commission." § 78d-1(c).

This case began when the SEC instituted an administrative proceeding against petitioner Raymond Lucia and his investment company. Lucia marketed a retirement savings strategy called "Buckets of Money." In the SEC's view, Lucia used misleading slideshow presentations to deceive prospective clients. The SEC charged Lucia under the Investment Advisers Act, § 80b-1 *et seq.*, and assigned ALJ Cameron Elliot to adjudicate the case. After nine days of testimony and argument, Judge Elliot issued an initial decision concluding that Lucia had violated the Act and imposing sanctions, including civil penalties of $300,000 and a lifetime bar from the investment industry. In his decision, Judge Elliot made factual findings about only one of the four ways the SEC thought Lucia's slideshow misled investors. The Commission thus remanded for factfinding on the other three claims, explaining that an ALJ's "personal experience with the witnesses" places him "in the best position to make findings of fact" and "resolve any conflicts in the evidence." Judge Elliot then made additional findings of deception and issued a revised initial decision, with the same sanctions.

On appeal to the SEC, Lucia argued that the administrative proceeding was invalid because Judge Elliot had not been constitutionally appointed. According to Lucia, the Commission's ALJs are "Officers of the United States" and thus subject to the Appointments Clause. Under that Clause, Lucia noted, only the President, "Courts of Law," or "Heads of Departments" can appoint "Officers." *See* Art. II, § 2, cl. 2. And none of those actors had made Judge Elliot an ALJ. To be sure, the Commission itself counts as a "Head[ ] of Department[ ]." *See Free Enterprise Fund v. Public Company Accounting Oversight Bd.,* 561 U.S. 477, 511-513 (2010). But the Commission had left the task of appointing ALJs, including Judge Elliot, to SEC staff members. As a result, Lucia contended, Judge Elliot lacked constitutional authority to do his job.

The Commission rejected Lucia's argument. It held that the SEC's ALJs are not "Officers of the United States." Instead, they are "mere employees"— officials with lesser responsibilities who fall outside the Appointments Clause's ambit. The Commission reasoned that its ALJs do not "exercise significant authority independent of [its own] supervision." Because that is so (said the SEC), they need no special, high-level appointment.

Lucia's claim fared no better in the Court of Appeals for the D.C. Circuit. A panel of that court seconded the Commission's view that SEC ALJs are employees rather than officers, and so are not subject to the Appointments Clause. Lucia then petitioned for rehearing en banc.... [T]he ten members of the en banc court divided evenly, resulting in a *per curiam* order denying Lucia's claim. That decision conflicted with one from the Court of Appeals for the Tenth Circuit. *See Bandimere v. SEC,* 844 F.3d 1168, 1179 (2016).

[We granted certiorari and] now reverse.

II

The sole question here is whether the Commission's ALJs are "Officers of the United States" or simply employees of the Federal Government. The Appointments Clause prescribes the exclusive means of appointing

"Officers." Only the President, a court of law, or a head of department can do so. *See* Art. II, § 2, cl. 2. And as all parties agree, none of those actors appointed Judge Elliot before he heard Lucia's case; instead, SEC staff members gave him an ALJ slot. So if the Commission's ALJs are constitutional officers, Lucia raises a valid Appointments Clause claim. The only way to defeat his position is to show that those ALJs are not officers at all, but instead non-officer employees — part of the broad swath of "lesser functionaries" in the Government's workforce. *Buckley v. Valeo*, 424 U.S. 1, 126, note 162 (1976) (*per curiam*). For if that is true, the Appointments Clause cares not a whit about who named them. *See United States v. Germaine*, 99 U.S. 508, 510 (1879).

Two decisions set out this Court's basic framework for distinguishing between officers and employees. *Germaine* held that "civil surgeons" (doctors hired to perform various physical exams) were mere employees because their duties were "occasional or temporary" rather than "continuing and permanent." *Id.* at 511-512. Stressing "ideas of tenure [and] duration," the Court there made clear that an individual must occupy a "continuing" position established by law to qualify as an officer. *Id.* at 511. *Buckley* then set out another requirement, central to this case. It determined that members of a federal commission were officers only after finding that they "exercis[ed] significant authority pursuant to the laws of the United States." 424 U.S., at 126. The inquiry thus focused on the extent of power an individual wields in carrying out his assigned functions.

Both the amicus and the Government urge us to elaborate on *Buckley*'s "significant authority" test, but another of our precedents makes that project unnecessary.... [M]aybe one day we will see a need to refine or enhance the test *Buckley* set out so concisely. But that day is not this one, because in *Freytag v. Commissioner*, 501 U.S. 868 (1991), we applied the unadorned "significant authority" test to adjudicative officials who are near-carbon copies of the Commission's ALJs. As we now explain, our analysis there (sans any more detailed legal criteria) necessarily decides this case.

The officials at issue in *Freytag* were the "special trial judges" (STJs) of the United States Tax Court. The authority of those judges depended on the significance of the tax dispute before them. In "comparatively narrow and minor matters," they could both hear and definitively resolve a case for the Tax Court. In more major matters, they could preside over the hearing, but could not issue the final decision; instead, they were to "prepare proposed findings and an opinion" for a regular Tax Court judge to consider. [*Id.* at 873.] The proceeding challenged in *Freytag* was a major one, involving $1.5 billion in alleged tax deficiencies. After conducting a 14-week trial, the STJ drafted a proposed decision in favor of the Government. A regular judge then adopted the STJ's work as the opinion of the Tax Court. The losing parties argued on appeal that the STJ was not constitutionally appointed.

This Court held that the Tax Court's STJs are officers, not mere employees. Citing *Germaine*, the Court first found that STJs hold a continuing office established by law. *See* 501 U.S., at 881. They serve on an ongoing, rather than a "temporary [or] episodic [,] basis"; and their "duties, salary, and means of appointment" are all specified in the Tax Code. *Ibid.* The Court then considered, as *Buckley* demands, the "significance" of the "authority" STJs wield. 501 U.S., at 881. In addressing that issue, the Government had argued that STJs are employees, rather than officers, in all cases (like the one at issue) in which they could not "enter a final decision." *Ibid.* But the Court thought the Government's focus on finality "ignore[d] the significance of the duties and discretion that [STJs] possess." *Ibid.* Describing the responsibilities involved in presiding over adversarial hearings, the Court said: STJs "take testimony, conduct trials, rule on the admissibility of evidence, and have the power to enforce compliance with discovery orders." *Id. at* 881-882. And the Court observed that "[i]n the course of carrying out these important functions, the [STJs] exercise significant discretion." *Id.* at 882. That fact meant they were officers, even when their decisions were not final.

Freytag says everything necessary to decide this case. To begin, the Commission's ALJs, like the Tax Court's STJs, hold a continuing office established by law. *See id.* at 881. Indeed, everyone here—Lucia, the Government, and the amicus—agrees on that point. Far from serving temporarily or episodically, SEC ALJs "receive[ ] a career appointment." 5 C.F.R. § 930.204(a) (2018). And that appointment is to a position created by statute, down to its "duties, salary, and means of appointment." *Freytag*, 501 U.S., at 878; *see* 5 U.S.C. §§ 556-557, 5372, 3105.

Still more, the Commission's ALJs exercise the same "significant discretion" when carrying out the same "important functions" as STJs do. *Freytag*, 501 U.S., at 878. Both sets of officials have all the authority needed to ensure fair and orderly adversarial hearings—indeed, nearly all the tools of federal trial judges. *See Butz*, 438 U.S., at 513. Consider in order the four specific (if overlapping) powers *Freytag* mentioned. First, the Commission's ALJs (like the Tax Court's STJs) "take testimony." 501 U.S., at 881. More precisely, they "[r]eceiv[e] evidence" and "[e]xamine witnesses" at hearings, and may also take pre-hearing depositions. 17 C.F.R. §§ 201.111(c), 200.14(a)(4); *see* 5 U.S.C. § 556(c)(4). Second, the ALJs (like STJs) "conduct trials." 501 U.S., at 882. As detailed earlier, they administer oaths, rule on motions, and generally "regulat[e] the course of" a hearing, as well as the conduct of parties and counsel. § 201.111; *see* §§ 200.14(a)(1), (a)(7). Third, the ALJs (like STJs) "rule on the admissibility of evidence." 501 U.S., at 882; *see* § 201.111(c). They thus critically shape the administrative record (as they also do when issuing document subpoenas). *See* § 201.111(b). And fourth, the ALJs (like STJs) "have the power to enforce compliance with discovery orders." 501 U.S., at 882. In particular, they may punish all "[c]ontemptuous conduct," including violations of those orders, by means as severe as excluding the offender from the hearing. *See* § 201.180(a)(1). So point for point—straight from *Freytag*'s list—the Commission's ALJs have equivalent duties and powers as STJs in conducting adversarial inquiries.

And at the close of those proceedings, ALJs issue decisions much like that in *Freytag*—except with potentially more independent effect. As the *Freytag* Court recounted, STJs "prepare proposed findings and an opinion" adjudicating charges and assessing tax liabilities. 501 U.S., at 873. Similarly, the Commission's ALJs issue decisions containing factual findings, legal conclusions, and appropriate remedies. *See* § 201.360(b). And what happens next reveals that the ALJ can play the more autonomous role. In a major case like *Freytag*, a regular Tax Court judge must always review an STJ's opinion. And that opinion counts for nothing unless the regular judge adopts it as his own. *See* 501 U.S., at 873. By contrast, the SEC can decide against reviewing an ALJ decision at all. And when the SEC declines review (and issues an order saying so), the ALJ's decision itself "becomes final" and is "deemed the action of the Commission." § 201.360(d)(2); 15 U.S.C. § 78d–1(c). That last-word capacity makes this an *a fortiori* case: If the Tax Court's STJs are officers, as *Freytag* held, then the Commission's ALJs must be too....

The only issue left is remedial.... [Lucia] contested the validity of Judge Elliot's appointment before the Commission, and continued pressing that claim in the Court of Appeals and this Court. So what relief follows? This Court has also held that the "appropriate" remedy for an adjudication tainted with an appointments violation is a new "hearing before a properly appointed" official. [*Ryder v. United States*, 515 U.S. 177, 183, 188 (1995).] And we add today one thing more. That official cannot be Judge Elliot, even if he has by now received (or receives sometime in the future) a constitutional appointment. Judge Elliot has already both heard Lucia's case and issued an initial decision on the merits. He cannot be expected to consider the matter as though he had not adjudicated it before. To cure the constitutional error, another ALJ (or the Commission itself) must hold the new hearing to which Lucia is entitled.[6]

We accordingly reverse the judgment of the Court of Appeals and remand the case for further proceedings consistent with this opinion.

It is so ordered.

[The separate opinions by Justices BREYER and SOTOMAYOR are omitted.]

* * *

---

[6] While this case was on judicial review, the SEC issued an order "ratif[ying]" the prior appointments of its ALJs. Order (Nov. 30, 2017), online at https://www.sec.gov/litigation/opinions/2017/33-10440.pdf (as last visited June 18, 2018). Lucia argues that the order is invalid. *See* Brief for Petitioners 50-56. We see no reason to address that issue. The Commission has not suggested that it intends to assign Lucia's case on remand to an ALJ whose claim to authority rests on the ratification order. The SEC may decide to conduct Lucia's rehearing itself. Or it may assign the hearing to an ALJ who has received a constitutional appointment independent of the ratification.

The Court's ruling in *Lucia* may endanger the OPM-managed ALJ hiring system, as well as the ALJ independence it is believed to protect. This possibility was certainly not lost on the Justices. During oral argument, Justice Kagan (a former Administrative Law professor) readily accepted the centrality of ALJ independence in the APA's formal adjudication scheme and the OPM hiring system's role in facilitating it. She accordingly expressed particular concern about ALJs being political appointees rather than civil servants. Rejecting the position taken by the Obama Administration, the Trump Administration agreed with Lucia that the ALJ hearing his case was unconstitutionally appointed. Going further, the Solicitor General argued that the "for cause" removal protections granted to ALJs were also unconstitutional. Justice Kagan asked him whether the Administration's position would "interfere[e] with [ALJs'] decisional independence." The Solicitor General essentially responded that the Framers had already chosen the balance between independence and accountability when it comes to officers of the United States. The Appointment Clause requires that there be a clear line of accountability between the People's elected leaders and the government officials who wield significant federal authority (including judicial authority). Without that line, the solicitor general asserted, politicians would take no responsibility for those officials' actions. While it is unclear whether she found this argument persuasive, Justice Kagan clearly felt that the Appointments Clause compelled the result reached in the case.

Mere weeks after the Supreme Court announced its decision, President Donald J. Trump issued Executive Order 13,843. Citing *Lucia*, it significantly altered not just the process for appointing ALJs, but also the minimum qualifications for holding those positions.

Executive Order 13,843: Excepting Administrative Law Judges from the Competitive Service

July 10, 2018

By the authority vested in me as President by the Constitution and the laws of the United States of America, including sections 3301 and 3302 of title 5, United States Code, it is hereby ordered as follows:

Section 1. *Policy.* The Federal Government benefits from a professional cadre of administrative law judges (ALJs) appointed under section 3105 of title 5, United States Code, who are impartial and committed to the rule of law. As illustrated by the Supreme Court's recent decision in *Lucia v. Securities and Exchange Commission*, No. 17-130 (June 21, 2018), ALJs are often called upon to discharge significant duties and exercise significant discretion in conducting proceedings under the laws of the United States. As part of their adjudications, ALJs interact with the public on issues of significance. Especially given the importance of the functions they discharge — which may range from taking testimony and conducting trials to ruling on the admissibility of evidence and enforcing compliance with their orders — ALJs must display appropriate temperament, legal acumen, impartiality, and sound judgment. They must also clearly communicate their decisions to the parties who appear before them, the agencies that oversee them, and the public that entrusts them with authority.

Previously, appointments to the position of ALJ have been made through competitive examination and competitive service selection procedures. The role of ALJs, however, has increased over time and ALJ decisions have, with increasing frequency, become the final word of the agencies they serve. Given this expanding responsibility for important agency adjudications, and as recognized by the Supreme Court in *Lucia*, at least some — and perhaps all — ALJs are "Officers of the United States" and thus subject to the Constitution's Appointments Clause, which governs who may appoint such officials.

As evident from recent litigation, *Lucia* may also raise questions about the method of appointing ALJs, including whether competitive examination and competitive service selection procedures are compatible with the discretion an agency head must possess under the Appointments Clause in selecting ALJs. Regardless of whether those procedures would violate the Appointments Clause as applied to certain ALJs, there are sound policy reasons to take steps to eliminate doubt regarding the constitutionality of the method of appointing officials who discharge such significant duties and exercise such significant discretion.

Pursuant to my authority under section 3302(1) of title 5, United States Code, I find that conditions of good administration make necessary an exception to the competitive hiring rules and examinations for the position of ALJ. These conditions include the need to provide agency heads with additional flexibility to assess prospective appointees without the limitations imposed by competitive examination and competitive service selection procedures. Placing the position of ALJ in the excepted service will mitigate concerns about undue limitations on the selection of ALJs, reduce the likelihood of successful Appointments Clause challenges, and forestall litigation in which such concerns have been or might be raised. This action will also give agencies greater ability and discretion to assess critical qualities in ALJ candidates, such as work ethic, judgment, and ability to meet the particular needs of the agency. These are all qualities individuals should have before wielding the significant authority conferred on ALJs, and each agency should be able to assess them without proceeding through complicated and elaborate examination processes or rating procedures that do not necessarily reflect the agency's particular needs. This change will also promote confidence in, and the durability of, agency adjudications.

Sec. 2. *Excepted Service.* Appointments of ALJs shall be made under Schedule E of the excepted service, as established by section 3 of this order.

Sec. 3. *Implementation.* (a) Civil Service Rule VI is amended as follows: . . . (b) To the extent permitted by law and the provisions of this part, and subject to the suitability and fitness requirements of the applicable Civil Service Rules and Regulations, appointments and position changes in the excepted service shall be made in accordance with such regulations and practices as the head of the agency concerned finds necessary. These shall include, for the position of administrative law judge appointed under 5 U.S.C. [§] 3105, the requirement that, at the time of application and any new appointment, the individual, other than an incumbent administrative law judge, must possess a professional license to practice law and be authorized to practice law under the laws of a State, the District of Columbia, the Commonwealth of Puerto Rico, or any territorial court established under the United States Constitution. For purposes of this requirement, judicial status is acceptable in lieu of "active" status in States that prohibit sitting judges from maintaining "active" status to practice law, and being in "good standing" is also acceptable in lieu of "active" status in States where the licensing authority considers "good standing" as having a current license to practice law. This requirement shall constitute a minimum standard for appointment to the position of administrative law judge, and such appointments may be subject to additional agency requirements where appropriate. . . .

DONALD J. TRUMP
THE WHITE HOUSE

July 10, 2018

QUESTION SET 6.2

Review & Synthesis

1. What, precisely, was the constitutional problem with the merit-based ALJ hiring system? Was it that the OPM vetting system unlawfully cabined the SEC's discretion in choosing candidates? That the Commissioners delegated ALJ hiring decisions to staff members? That OPM hiring infringed on ALJs' decisional independence? Something else?

2. Agencies have responded to the Appointments Clause issue addressed in *Lucia* by attempting, as did the SEC (see footnote 6 in the opinion), to "ratify" prior ALJ appointments. *See, e.g.*, International Trade Commission, *The Appointment of the Commission's Administrative Law Judges for Section 337 Investigations*, 83 Fed. Reg. 45,678 (Sept. 10, 2018); Federal Deposit Insurance Corp., *Resolution of Board of Directors* (July 19, 2018). Even agencies that doubted their administrative judges were covered by *Lucia* have pursued ratification out of an abundance

of caution. *See, e.g.,* Commodity Futures Trading Commission, *In re: Pending Administrative Proceedings,* 2018 WL 1966116 (Apr. 9, 2018) (ratifying appointment of "Judgment Officer" even though "[t]he Commission employs no administrative law judges"). Assuming that the judges employed by these agencies are covered by *Lucia,* is such post-appointment confirmation of their employment sufficient to address the Appointment Clause problems addressed in the case? What do you make of the Court's observation in footnote 6 that, on remand, the SEC should decide the case itself or assign it to an ALJ whose appointment does not depend on the ratification order? Does this imply that the power to appoint Officers of the United States must be personally exercised because it is nondelegable?

3. Executive Order 13,843 excepted ALJs from the merit-based OPM hiring and vetting system. Was doing so necessary to comply with *Lucia?* In other words, do the changes effected by the Executive Order respond solely to the constitutional problems identified by *Lucia?*

4. The President of the Association of Administrative Law Judges published an op-ed in response to Executive Order 13,843, making the following assertion: "Now, as a result of the president's executive order, an agency that wants to employ an ALJ can recruit any attorney regardless of skill or experience. Competence and impartiality apparently are no longer essential; cronyism and political interference will no longer be taboo." Marilyn Zahm, *Do you have a Social Security card? Then take this executive order personally,* Wash. Post (July 18, 2018). Do you agree or disagree? At least one agency has adopted ALJ eligibility criteria similar to those adopted by the OPM system. *See* Department of Labor, *Procedures for Appointment of Administrative Law Judges for the Department of Labor,* 83 Fed. Reg. 44,307 (Aug. 30, 2018) (requiring, among other things, at least ten years of bar membership in "good standing" and seven years of relevant litigation or administrative law experience).

Application & Analysis

1. The Social Security Administration ("SSA") houses one of the largest administrative judicial systems in the world, comprising over 1,600 administrative law judges, 168 hearing offices, five national hearing centers, and two national case centers. The SSA issues over 700,000 decisions to disability claimants each year. It is supervised by a chief administrative law judge ("CALJ") who develops, disseminates, and coordinates compliance with the Administration's claims adjudication procedures and policies.

Concerned about mounting case backlogs, the CALJ issued a directive setting ALJ case clearance "goals." It states that ALJs should "manage their docket in such a way that they will be able to issue 500-700 legally sufficient decisions each year." When the directive was issued, 56 percent of the administrative law judges were deciding fewer than 500 cases a year. The CALJ has taken formal and informal disciplinary measures to enforce the directive.

The Association of Administrative Law Judges is a union representing the SSA's ALJs in collective bargaining negotiations with the Administration. It has filed suit in the U.S. District Court for the Northern District of Illinois, asserting that the directive is a veiled attempt to increase benefits awards to claimants. It claims that ALJs can more easily award benefits than deny them, because awards are not judicially appealable. Denials, by contrast, take much more time to process. By placing pressure on ALJs to clear more cases, the union believes that the directive forces its members to award more benefits than they otherwise would. Such pressure unlawfully infringes on ALJs' decisional independence in violation of the Administrative Procedure Act, which provides that when conducting hearings ALJs are not subject to the direction or supervision of other employees in their agencies and that they cannot be employed by and may not be assigned duties inconsistent with their duties and responsibilities as ALJs. 5 U.S.C. §§ 554(d)(2), 3105.

You are clerking for the federal district judge hearing this case. Research the case law relating to interference with ALJ independence and write a brief memorandum analyzing the union's claim.

3. *Ex Parte* Contacts

As in civil litigation in federal and state courts, *ex parte* communications are forbidden in federal formal adjudications. APA § 551(14) defines an *ex parte* communication as "an oral or written communication not on the public record with respect to which reasonable prior notice to all parties is not given, but it shall not include requests for status reports on any matter or proceeding covered by this subchapter." APA § 557(d)(1) applies this definition directly to formal adjudications. It prohibits off-the-record communications relevant to the merits between "any interested person outside the agency" and any agency employee (agency heads, ALJs, etc.) reasonably expected to be involved in the proceedings (except to the extent authorized by law). Importantly, the prohibition does not prevent interested outside parties from discussing procedural issues with agency adjudicators, as such inquiries do not go to the substance of their decisions. *See, e.g., Louisiana Ass'n of Independent Producers and Royalty Owners v. FERC*, 958 F.2d 1101, 1111 (D.C. Cir. 1992). Still, the D.C. Circuit has also warned that "even a procedural inquiry may be a subtle effort to influence an agency decision." *Professional Air Traffic*

Controllers Organization (PATCO) v. Federal Labor Relations Authority, 685 F.2d 547, 568 (D.C. Cir. 1982).

The reasons for the off-the-record communications ban are clear. Parties in formal adjudications are entitled to hear, interrogate, and rebut the evidence presented against them. Moreover, ALJs (or agency heads when they preside) must decide formal adjudications solely on the evidence included in the official record. These protections would ring hollow if the adjudicator could receive and rely on information adverse to a party's interests without providing a meaningful opportunity to rebut it. Permitting *ex parte* contacts could also undermine effective judicial review. A court can hardly be expected competently to test the legality of an agency's order if the agency hides its factual foundation from view. The same is true if the agency publicly discloses that foundation for the first time on appeal, as it could not have benefited from adversarial development.

Where prohibited off-the-record communications nevertheless occur, APA § 557(d)(1)(C) requires that they be disclosed on the official record of the proceeding. Additionally, a party who has or causes prohibited communication might have its claims dismissed or may have an adverse judgment entered against it. *See, e.g., Press Broadcasting Co., Inc. v. FCC*, 59 F.3d 1365, 1370-71 (D.C. Cir. 1995). In its influential *PATCO* decision, the D.C. Circuit crafted the following test for whether these sanctions should be levied against an offending party:

> [A] court must consider whether, as a result of improper *ex parte* communications, the agency's decisionmaking process was irrevocably tainted so as to make the ultimate judgment of the agency unfair, either to an innocent party or to the public interest that the agency was obliged to protect. In making this determination, a number of considerations may be relevant: the gravity of the *ex parte* communications; whether the contacts may have influenced the agency's ultimate decision; whether the party making the improper contacts benefited from the agency's ultimate decision; whether the contents of the communications were unknown to opposing parties, who therefore had no opportunity to respond; and whether vacation of the agency's decision and remand for new proceedings would serve a useful purpose.

PATCO, 685 F.2d at 564-65 (internal citations omitted). In that case, the court found prohibited *ex parte* communications between interested parties and the Federal Labor Relations Authority but, applying the test above, concluded that those communications did not irrevocably taint the Authority's decision-making. *See id.* at 566.

While the *ex parte* communications provisions in APA § 557(d)(1) are quite detailed, they do not answer all questions that might arise from their application. Importantly, the provision warns against off-the-record contacts with any "interested person outside the agency," but does not tell us how to identify an "interested party," nor how we should determine whether such a party is "outside of the agency." There are some clear cases, of course; private parties appearing in an adjudication have legal interests in the dispute, and they obviously come from outside of the agency. On the flip side, many agency staffers who support the ALJ presiding over the dispute are certainly not outsiders nor are they (unless we are looking at highly unusual circumstances) personally interested in its outcome. A potential exception here would be agency employees with investigative or prosecutorial functions, who would be "outsiders" based on the APA's separation-of-function provisions. *See* APA § 554(d).

But what about the President and his or her staff? After all, administrative agencies organizationally fall within the Executive Branch, which the President oversees. Even assuming that White House personnel are not agency insiders, are they nevertheless "interested persons" such that they must be barred from having off-the-record communications with adjudicators? Whatever types of interests trigger § 557(d)(1), they must apparently amount to more than the general public's as a whole. On the one hand, the White House is indirectly accountable to the People for the decisions made within the Executive Branch. That accountability should, presumably, make the President and White House staffers *very* interested in how cases are decided. On the other hand, the same can be said of *all* administrative adjudications. One could surmise that the White House's interest would vary little from case to case, such that no particular case should prove more important than any other. The following case, decided by the Ninth Circuit, addressed these issues.

Portland Audubon Society v. Endangered Species Committee
984 F.2d 1534 (9th Cir. 1993)

Before: GOODWIN, D.W. NELSON, and REINHARDT, Circuit Judges.

REINHARDT, Circuit Judge:

We consider here a motion filed in a most important and controversial case. The motion itself raises a significant issue of first impression. In the underlying proceeding, petitioners Portland Audubon Society *et al.* (collectively "the environmental groups") challenge the decision of the statutorily-created Endangered Species Committee ("the Committee"), known popularly as "The God Squad," to grant an exemption from the requirements of the Endangered Species Act to the Bureau of Land Management for thirteen timber sales in western Oregon. The environmental groups complain of numerous procedural and substantive flaws in the Committee's decision.

In the motion before us the environmental groups seek . . . leave to conduct discovery into allegedly improper *ex parte* communications between the White House and individual Committee members.... The Committee opposes the motion on the ground that our review must be limited to the record before the agency and that supplementation of that record on appeal would be inappropriate. The Committee argues further that *ex parte* communications between the White House and its members are permissible under applicable law, and therefore, there is no legal justification for any inquiry into whether the alleged communications occurred.

We agree with the environmental groups that *ex parte* communications between the White House and the God Squad are contrary to law. We further hold that a record that does not include all matters on which the Committee relied does not constitute the "whole record" required for judicial review and that the failure to include all materials in the record violates the Administrative Procedure Act ("APA").... [W]e remand the matter to the Committee for an evidentiary hearing before an administrative law judge ("ALJ") (and for such other procedures as the ALJ may find necessary) on the questions whether any improper communications with the White House occurred during the Committee's decision-making process, and, if so, what remedy is required....

I. BACKGROUND

The Endangered Species Act requires that "[e]ach Federal agency shall . . . insure that any action authorized, funded or carried out by such agency . . . is not likely to jeopardize the continued existence of any endangered species . . . or result in the destruction or adverse modification of [critical] habitat of such species." 16 U.S.C. § 1536(a)(2) (1988). However, if the Secretary of the Interior ("Secretary") finds that a proposed agency action would violate § 1536(a)(2), an agency may apply to the Committee for an exemption from the Endangered Species Act. §§ 1536(a)(2), (g)(1)-(2). The Committee was created by the Endangered Species Act for the sole purpose of making final decisions on applications for exemptions from the Act, § 1536(e), and it is composed of high level officials.[1] Because it is the ultimate arbiter of the fate of an endangered species, the Committee is known as "The God Squad."

The Secretary must initially consider any exemption application, publish a notice and summary of the application in the Federal Register, and

---

[1] The seven-member Committee is composed of: the Secretary of Agriculture, the Secretary of the Army, the Chairman of the Council of Economic Advisors, the Administrator of the Environmental Protection Agency, the Secretary of the Interior, the Administrator of the National Oceanic and Atmospheric Administration, and "one individual from each affected State" appointed by the President. 16 U.S.C. § 1536(e)(3). The Committee members from the affected states have one collective vote. 50 C.F.R. § 453.05(d) (Oct. 1, 1991).

determine whether certain threshold requirements have been met. 16 U.S.C. §§ 1536(g)(1)-(3). If so, the Secretary shall, in consultation with the other members of the Committee, hold a hearing on the application (which is conducted by an ALJ), and prepare a written report to the Committee. § 1536(g)(4); 50 C.F.R. § 452.05(a)(2) (Oct. 1, 1991). Within thirty days of receiving the Secretary's report, the Committee shall make a final determination whether or not to grant the exemption from the Endangered Species Act based on the report, the record of the Secretary's hearing, and any additional hearings or written submissions for which the Committee itself may call. § 1536(h)(1)(A); 50 C.F.R. § 453.04. An exemption requires the approval of five of the seven members of the Committee. § 1536(h)(1).

On May 15, 1992, the Committee approved an exemption for the Bureau of Land Management for thirteen of forty-four timber sales. It was only the second exemption ever granted by the Committee. The environmental groups filed a timely petition for review in this court on June 10, 1992. The environmental groups have Article III standing if for no other reason than that they allege procedural violations in an agency process in which they participated. *Cf. Lujan v. Defenders of Wildlife*, 504 U.S. 555 (1992) (Article III requires that plaintiff filing suit under the Endangered Species Act possess more than a "generally available grievance about government" in order to have standing).

Both in their petition and in this motion the environmental groups contend that improper *ex parte* contacts between the White House and members of the Committee tainted the decision-making process. They base their charges on two press reports, one by Associated Press ("AP") and one by Reuters, and on the facts stated in the declaration of Victor Sher, lead counsel for the environmental groups. Published on May 6, 1992, the AP and Reuters accounts reported that, according to two anonymous administration sources, at least three Committee members had been "summoned" to the White House and pressured to vote for the exemption. In his declaration filed August 25, 1992, Sher stated that his conversations with "several sources within the Administration," who asked for anonymity, revealed that the media reports were accurate, and further that the pressure exerted by the White House may have changed the vote of at least one Committee member. Sher declared that his sources indicated that, in addition to in-person meetings, at least one Committee member had "substantial on-going contacts with White House staff concerning the substance of his decision on the application for exemption by telephone and facsimile, as well as through staff intermediaries." He also declared that he had learned from his sources that White House staff members had made substantial comments and recommendations on draft versions of the "Endangered Species Committee Amendment," a part of the Committee's final decision. For the purposes of the present motion, the Committee neither admits nor denies that these communications occurred....

II. *EX PARTE* COMMUNICATIONS BETWEEN THE COMMITTEE AND THE PRESIDENT AND MEMBERS OF HIS STAFF ARE PROHIBITED BY LAW

This case raises two important and closely related questions of statutory construction: 1) Are Committee proceedings subject to the *ex parte* communications ban of 5 U.S.C. § 557(d)(1)? and, 2) are communications from the President and his staff covered by that provision? For the reasons that follow, we answer both questions in the affirmative.

A. *The Committee's Proceedings are Subject to the APA's Prohibition on* Ex parte *Communications*

The environmental groups contend that the Endangered Species Act incorporates by reference the *ex parte* communications ban of the APA and forbids *ex parte* contacts with members of the Committee regarding an exemption application. The *ex parte* prohibition is set forth at 5 U.S.C. § 557(d)(1). Section 557(d)(1) is a broad provision that prohibits any *ex parte* communications relevant to the merits of an agency proceeding between "any member of the body comprising the agency" or any agency employee who "is or may reasonably be expected to be involved in the decisional process" and any "interested person outside the agency." 5 U.S.C. §§ 557(d)(1)(A)-(B). The purpose of the *ex parte* communications prohibition is to ensure that "'agency decisions required to be made on a public record are not influenced by private, off-the-record communications from those personally interested in the outcome.'" *Raz Inland Navigation Co. v. Interstate Commerce Comm'n,* 625 F.2d 258, 260 (9th Cir. 1980) (quoting legislative history).

It is of no consequence that the sections of the Endangered Species Act governing the operations of the Committee fail to mention the APA. The APA itself mandates that its provisions govern certain administrative proceedings. By its terms, section 554 of the APA, which pertains to formal adjudications, applies to "every case of adjudication required by statute to be determined on the record after [the] opportunity for an agency hearing." 5 U.S.C. § 554(a). That section also provides that any hearing conducted and any decision made in connection with such an adjudication shall be "in accordance with sections 556 and 557 of this title." 5 U.S.C. § 554(c)(2).

In other words, by virtue of the terms of APA § 554, sections 556 and 557 are applicable whenever that section applies. Accordingly, the *ex parte* communications prohibition applies whenever the three requirements set forth in APA § 554(a) are satisfied: The administrative proceeding must be 1) an adjudication; 2) determined on the record; and 3) after the opportunity for an agency hearing. The question is, therefore, are those three conditions met here? We find our answer primarily in the language of section 1536(h)(1)(A) of the Endangered Species Act.

We conclude that the first requirement of APA § 554(a) is satisfied. Certain administrative decisions closely resemble judicial determinations and, in the interests of fairness, require similar procedural protections. Where an agency's task is "to adjudicate disputed facts in particular cases," an administrative determination is quasi-judicial. By contrast, rulemaking concerns policy judgments to be applied generally in cases that may arise in the future; it is sometimes guided by more informal procedures. Under the Endangered Species Act the Committee decides whether to grant or deny specific requests for exemptions based upon specific factual showings. Thus, the Committee's determinations are quasi-judicial. Accordingly, they constitute "adjudications" within the meaning of § 554(a).

The legislative history of the Endangered Species Act confirms our conclusion in this respect. The Senate committee report accompanying the 1982 amendments to the Endangered Species Act stated that "the Endangered Species Committee is designed to function as an *administrative court of last resort.*" S. Rep. No. 418, 97th Congress, 2d Sess. 17 (1982) (emphasis added). The Report states that the Committee's decision will be based, in part, upon a "formal adjudicatory hearing." *Id.* at 18. The Report also makes clear that the Committee's duty is to be the ultimate arbiter of conflicts that the parties involved have been unable to resolve. *Id.* at 16-17.

The language of the Endangered Species Act explicitly meets the second requirement of section 554(a). Section 1536(h)(1)(A) of the Act mandates that the Committee make its final determination of an exemption application "on the record." No further discussion is required on this point.

It is equally clear that the third requirement of APA § 554(a) is satisfied here. Section 1536(h)(1)(A) of the Endangered Species Act also requires that the Committee's final decision be "*based on* the report of the Secretary, *the hearing* held under (g)(4) of this section [(the Secretary's hearing)] and on such other testimony or evidence as it may receive." 16 U.S.C. § 1536(h)(1)(A) (emphasis added). Wherever the outer bounds of the "after opportunity for an agency hearing" requirement may lie, we hold that where, as here, a statute provides that an adjudication be determined at least in part based on an agency hearing, that requirement is fulfilled.

Because Committee decisions are adjudicatory in nature, are required to be on the record, and are made after an opportunity for an agency hearing, we conclude that the APA's *ex parte* communication prohibition is applicable....

B. *The President and the White House Staff are Subject to the APA's Prohibition on* Ex parte *Communications*

The APA prohibits an "interested person outside the agency" from making, or knowingly causing to be made, an *ex parte* communication relevant to the merits of the proceeding with a member of the body comprising the agency. 5 U.S.C. § 557(d)(1)(A). Likewise, agency members are prohibited from engaging in such *ex parte* communication. § 557(d)(1)(B). Although the APA's ban on *ex parte* communications is absolute and includes no special exemption for White House officials, the government advances three arguments in support of its position that section 557(d)(1) does not apply to the President and his staff.

First, the government argues that because the President is the center of the Executive Branch and does not represent or act on behalf of a particular agency, he does not have an interest in Committee proceedings greater than the interest of the public as a whole. Therefore, the government contends, neither the President nor his staff is an "interested person." Next, the government maintains that the President and his staff do not fall within the terms of section 557(d)(1) because the President's interest as the Chief of the Executive Branch is no different from that of his subordinates on the Committee. Specifically, the government claims that by placing the Chairman of the President's Council of Economic Advisors on the Committee, Congress directly and expressly involved the Executive Office of the President in the decision-making process. In other words, it is the government's position that because the Committee members are Executive Branch officials, communications between them and the White House staff cannot be considered to come from "outside the agency." Finally, the government argues that if the APA's *ex parte* communications ban encompasses the President and his aides, the provision violates the doctrine of separation of powers. We find all three of the government's arguments to be without merit.

There is little decisional law on the meaning of the term "interested person." Nor is the meaning of the term clear on the face of the statute. A person can be "interested" in at least three different senses. First, an interested person can be someone who has a curiosity or a concern about a matter, although he may be neutral with respect to the outcome. Second, an interested person can have a preference or a bias regarding a matter's outcome but no direct stake in the proceedings. Finally, a person can be "interested" in a matter in the sense of having a legal interest that will be determined or affected by the decision.

Ultimately, the *ex parte* communication provision must be interpreted in a commonsense fashion. Its purposes are to insure open decision-making and the appearance thereof, to preserve the opportunity for effective response, and to prevent improper influences upon agency decision-makers. To achieve these ends we must give the provision a broad scope rather than a constricted interpretation. The essential purposes of the APA require that all communications that might improperly influence an agency be encompassed within the *ex parte* contacts prohibition or else the public and the parties will be denied indirectly their guaranteed right to meaningful participation in agency decisional processes.

The legislative history of the *ex parte* communication provision confirms the breadth of the ban:

> The term "interested person" is intended to be a wide, inclusive term covering any individual or other person with an interest in the agency proceeding that is greater than the general interest the public as a whole may have. The interest need not be monetary, nor need a person to [sic] be a party to, or intervenor in, the agency proceeding to come under this section. The term includes, but is not limited to, parties, competitors, *public officials*, and nonprofit or public interest organizations and associations with a special interest in the matter regulated. The term does not include a member of the public at large who makes a casual or general expression of opinion about a pending proceeding.

H.R. Rep. No. 880, Pt. I, 94th Cong., 2d Sess. 19-20 (1976), reprinted in 1976 U.S.C.C.A.N. 2183, 2201 (emphasis added). The legislative history of APA § 557(d) makes clear that the term "interested person" was intended to have a broad scope. In particular, the provision's history makes it clear that the *ex parte* communication prohibition was meant to include public officials. . . .

[The government] . . . argues that the President's broader policy role places him beyond the reach of the "interested person" language. We strongly disagree. In fact, we believe the proper argument is quite the opposite from the one the government advances. We believe the President's position at the center of the Executive Branch renders him, *ex officio*, an "interested person" for the purposes of APA § 557(d)(1). As the head of government and chief executive officer, the President necessarily has an interest in every agency proceeding. No *ex parte* communication is more likely to influence an agency than one from the President or a member of his staff. No communication from any other person is more likely to deprive the parties and the public of their right to effective participation in a key governmental decision at a most crucial time. The essential purposes of the statutory provision compel the conclusion that the President and his staff are "interested persons" within the meaning of 5 U.S.C. § 557(d)(1).

The government's next argument — that because the President and the members of the Committee are all members of the executive branch the President is, for all intents and purposes, a "member" of the Committee and may attempt to influence its decisions — amounts to a contention that the President is not "outside the agency" for the purposes of APA § 557(d)(1). The Supreme Court soundly rejected the basic logic of this argument in *United States ex rel. Accardi v. Shaughnessy*, 347 U.S. 260 (1954). The Court held that where legally binding regulations delegated a particular discretionary decision to the Board of Immigration Appeals, the Attorney General could not dictate a decision of the Board, even though the Board was appointed by the Attorney General, its members served at his pleasure, and its decision was subject to his ultimate review. Here, the Endangered Species Act explicitly vests discretion to make exemption decisions in the Committee and does not contemplate that the President or the White House will become involved in Committee deliberations. The President and his aides are not a part of the Committee decision-making process. They are "outside the agency" for the purposes of the *ex parte* communications ban.

The government then argues that *Sierra Club v. Costle* determined that contacts with the White House do not constitute *ex parte* communications that would contaminate the Committee's decision-making process, and that we should follow that precedent. 657 F.2d 298, 400-10 (D.C. Cir. 1981). We disagree. *Costle* is inapplicable because that case did not consider and, indeed, could not have considered, whether the APA's definition of *ex parte* communications includes White House contacts. The decision in *Costle* that the contacts were not impermissible was based explicitly on the fact that the proceeding involved was informal rulemaking to which the APA restrictions on *ex parte* communications are not applicable. *Id.* at 400-02, 402 note 507. In fact, while the *Costle* court recognized that political pressure from the President may not be inappropriate in informal rulemaking proceedings, it acknowledged that the contrary is true in formal adjudications. *See id.* at 406-07. Because Congress has decided that Committee determinations are formal adjudications, *Costle* supports, rather than contradicts, the conclusion that the President and his staff are subject to the APA's *ex parte* communication ban.

Accordingly, the President and his staff are covered by section 557's prohibition and are not free to attempt to influence the decision-making processes of the Committee through *ex parte* communications. The APA's ban on such communications is fully applicable to the President and his White House aides, and *ex parte* contacts by them relevant to the merits of an agency proceeding would be in violation of that Act.

The government next contends that any construction of APA § 557(d)(1) that includes presidential communications within the ban on *ex parte* contacts would constitute a violation of the separation of powers doctrine. It relies on language in *Myers v. United States* that states that the President has the constitutional authority to "supervise and guide" Executive Branch officials in "their construction of the statutes under which they act." 272 U.S. 52, 135 (1926). The government argues that including the President and his staff within the APA's *ex parte* communication ban would represent Congressional interference with the President's constitutional duty to provide such supervision and guidance to inferior officials. We reject this argument out of hand....

We conclude that Congress in no way invaded any legitimate constitutional power of the President in providing that he may not attempt to influence the outcome of administrative adjudications through *ex parte* communications and that Congress' important objectives reflected in the enactment of the APA would, in any event, outweigh any *de minimis* impact on presidential power.

While the government's argument to the contrary arises in the context of Committee decisions regarding Endangered Species Act exemption applications, carried to its logical conclusion the government's position would effectively destroy the integrity of all federal agency adjudications. It is a fundamental precept of administrative law that . . . when an agency performs a quasi-judicial (or a quasi-legislative) function its independence must be protected. There is no presidential prerogative to influence quasi-judicial administrative agency proceedings through behind-the-scenes lobbying. *Myers* itself clearly recognizes that "there may be duties of a quasi-judicial character imposed on executive officers and members of executive tribunals whose decisions after hearing affect interests of individuals, the discharge of which the President can not in a particular case properly influence or control." 272 U.S. at 135. And in *Humphrey's Executor v. United States* the Court observed that "[t]he authority of Congress, in creating quasi-legislative or quasi-judicial agencies, to require them to act in discharge of their duties independently of executive control cannot well be doubted." 295 U.S. 602, 629 (1935). The government's position in this case is antithetical to and destructive of these elementary legal precepts, and we unequivocally reject it. . . .

[In the remainder of its opinion, the Ninth Circuit remanded the case to the Committee to hold additional evidentiary hearings, with the assistance of an administrative law judge, to determine the nature, content, extent, sources, and effects of any *ex parte* contacts between the Committee's members or its staff and the White House and its staff.]

QUESTION SET 6.3

Review & Synthesis

1. Consider the procedures followed by the "God Squad" to consider Endangered Species Act exemptions, including the means by which it was permitted to gather evidence to inform its decisions. Is it clear to you that the God Squad's deliberations constituted "adjudications" as that term is defined by 5 U.S.C. § 551(7)? Apart from the APA definition, did the Committee rely on "legislative" facts, or on "adjudicative" facts? Additionally, administrative law judges (and to a lesser extent administrative judges) have a measure of job security that protects their independence. That independence is a fundamental feature of the administrative hearings over which they preside. Can the same be said for the members of the God Squad?

2. Assume that the Endangered Species Act § 1536(h)(1)(A) did not include the term "on the record," but was otherwise identical to the provision interpreted and applied by the Ninth Circuit. Do you think the court would have inferred that Congress intended to require formal proceedings in light of the other procedural features of the statute?

3. Judge Reinhardt rejected the idea that the President has any right to "listen in" or to otherwise be involved in the Committee's deliberations because the President is necessarily, by virtue of holding the office, an "interested person" in every adjudication. How much of this bar turns on mere formalities? Could the President (or, more likely, someone on the President's staff), ask for leave to submit on-the-record comments disclosing the Administration's views on particular exemptions (like the routine practice of submitting amicus briefs)? If so, couldn't such a submission be as coercive as an Oval Office conversation sharing the same concerns? Is the salient difference simply that one communication would be "out in the open" and other would not be? Is the intuition that political coercion is more likely to be expressed in private than in public?

Application & Analysis

1. Hospitality LLC owns and operates several restaurants and hotels in Omaha, Nebraska. Early last year, a union began an effort to organize the company's employees. When the company fired several workers involved in that effort, the fired employees filed charges with the National Labor Relations Board ("NLRB") Regional Director, alleging that the company had engaged in unfair labor practices in violation of the National Labor Relations Act ("NLRA"). Determining that formal action should be taken, the regional director issued a complaint and notice of hearing. On the second day of the ensuing hearing, the ALJ advised the parties that she had consulted "with a colleague" as to the best procedure to follow in ruling on one of Hospitality LLC's motions. Although the ALJ did not name the colleague with whom she had consulted, the context of her statements strongly suggested she was referring to a fellow judge. Hospitality LLC responded that the consultation constituted grounds for the ALJ to disqualify herself. The ALJ declined and, the following day, found that the company had violated the NLRA. The company appealed to the Board, which agreed with the ALJ. It ordered Hospitality LLC to cease and desist its unfair practices and to offer full reinstatement to its fired former employees.

   Hospitality LLC has petitioned for review of the NLRB's order in the D.C. Circuit. It claims that the ALJ's consultation with a colleague was an *ex parte* contact prohibited by 5 U.S.C. § 557. You are a clerk for one of the judges hearing the case. Write a brief memorandum assessing Hospitality LLC's claim.

4. Admissibility and Sufficiency of Evidence

APA Section 556 addresses several evidentiary concerns that arise in formal agency adjudication. Subsection (e) recognizes that ALJs can take "official" or "administrative" notice of particular facts. If the agency's decision relies on those facts, and they do not otherwise appear in the record, the agency must give the parties an opportunity to rebut them. Pursuant to § 556(d), parties are entitled to present their cases or defenses by oral or documentary evidence. Despite this specific reference to oral (i.e., "live") presentations of evidence, § 556(d) allows agencies to limit parties to documentary evidence in some circumstances, provided that doing so does not prejudice them. "The instances in which the agency can dispense with oral proceedings are formal rulemaking, determinations relating to claims for money or benefits, and applications for initial licenses." FEDERAL AGENCY ADJUDICATION at 100 (citing *Seacoast Anti-Pollution League v. Costle*, 572 F.2d 872, 879 (1st Cir. 1978)). While a party may still request the opportunity to present oral evidence in such cases, they may be required to show why being limited to documentary evidence would prejudice their case. *Id.*

Section 556(d) also addresses cross-examination, entitling a party "to conduct such cross-examination as may be required for a full and true disclosure of the facts." This is not an unqualified entitlement, however. A party seeking to cross-examine witnesses may have to show that doing so is necessary to properly present her case, and agencies still have discretion to limit its availability.

Among the more complicated (and hence interesting) issues addressed by § 556 is the admissibility and sufficiency of evidence in on-the-record proceedings. With respect to admissibility, the Federal Rules of Evidence do not apply to administrative hearings unless specifically required by statute or agency rules. Courts and commentators have long reasoned that the Federal Rules of Evidence were intended to protect inexperienced factfinders, such as layperson jurors, from being confused or misled by prejudicial, unreliable, or irrelevant information. Agency adjudicators are, by contrast, assumed to be experts in their respective fields. As such, they can capably identify probative information even if it is well hidden, and presumably do not require the level of protection afforded laypersons by the Federal Rules of Evidence. Moreover, and as pointed out by the Seventh Circuit, evidence the Federal Rules would otherwise exclude may be "essential to the exercise of expert judgment by a specialized professional adjudicator." *Peabody Coal Co. v. Director, Office of Workers' Compensation Programs*, 165 F.3d 1126, 1129 (7th Cir. 1999). Accordingly, § 556(d) allows agencies to consider a wider variety of evidence than can federal district courts, so long as that evidence is probative, reliable, and its admission comports with due process. Further, the judicial review standard applied to agencies' decisions to admit evidence supports the latitude they enjoy in considering information that would be excluded in a federal district court. When challenged in federal court, an agency adjudicator's decision to admit evidence is reviewed for abuse of discretion, a permissive standard that will uphold adjudicators' decisions in most cases. *See* FEDERAL AGENCY ADJUDICATION at 91.

With respect to the burden of proof, § 556(d) assigns it to the proponent of an order by default. For example, an agency will bear the burden of proof in enforcement actions brought against private parties to impose civil penalties, and the applicant will bear the burden of proof in a dispute over his or her entitlement to a government benefit or license. Provided they are granted the authority to do so by statute, § 556(d) also permits agencies to reallocate burdens of proofs. Relatedly, nothing in § 556(d) prevents agencies from setting rebuttable presumptions that a private party seeking an order must overcome.

The standard of proof—as distinct from the burden of proof—is addressed in § 556(d) by the following language: "A sanction may not be imposed or rule or order issued except on consideration of the whole record or those parts thereof cited by a party and supported by and in accordance with the reliable, probative, and substantial evidence." The following case carefully details the Supreme Court's understanding of this provision. It also explicates the conceptually tricky distinction between the standard of *proof* (covered in § 556) and the standard of *review* (codified in § 706(2)(E)). As you will see, both provisions use the term "substantial evidence," but they do so in very different ways. Additionally, the case deals with a critical question about the standard of proof: should it correlate with the severity of the sanction faced by the regulated party?

Steadman v. Securities and Exchange Commission
450 U.S. 91 (1981)

Justice BRENNAN delivered the opinion of the Court.

In administrative proceedings, the Securities and Exchange Commission applies a preponderance-of-the-evidence standard of proof in determining whether the antifraud provisions of the federal securities laws have been violated. The question presented is whether such violations must be proved by clear and convincing evidence rather than by a preponderance of the evidence.

I

In June 1971, the Commission initiated a disciplinary proceeding against petitioner and certain of his wholly owned companies. The proceeding against petitioner was brought pursuant to § 9(b) of the Investment Company Act of 1940 and § 203(f) of the Investment Advisers Act of 1940. The Commission alleged that petitioner had violated numerous provisions of the federal securities laws in his management of several mutual funds registered under the Investment Company Act.

After a lengthy evidentiary hearing before an Administrative Law Judge and review by the Commission in which the preponderance-of-the-evidence standard was employed,[3] the Commission held that between December 1965 and June 1972, petitioner had violated antifraud, reporting, conflict of interest, and proxy provisions of the federal securities laws. Accordingly, it entered an order permanently barring petitioner from associating with any investment adviser or affiliating with any registered investment company, and suspending him for one year from associating with any broker or dealer in securities.

Petitioner sought review of the Commission's order in the United States Court of Appeals for the Fifth Circuit on a number of grounds, only one of which is relevant for our purposes. Petitioner challenged the Commission's use of the preponderance-of-the-evidence standard of proof in determining whether he had violated antifraud provisions of the securities laws. He contended that, because of the potentially severe sanctions that the Commission was empowered to impose and because of the circumstantial and inferential nature of the evidence that might be used to prove intent to defraud, the Commission was required to weigh the evidence against a clear-and-convincing standard of proof. The Court of Appeals rejected petitioner's argument, holding that in a disciplinary proceeding before the Commission violations of the antifraud provisions of the securities laws may be established by a preponderance of the evidence. 603 F.2d 1126, 1143 (1979).... We affirm.

II

Where Congress has not prescribed the degree of proof which must be adduced by the proponent of a rule or order to carry its burden of persuasion in an administrative proceeding, this Court has felt at liberty to prescribe the standard, for "[i]t is the kind of question which has traditionally been left to the judiciary to resolve." *Woodby v. INS*, 385 U.S. 276, 284 (1966). However, where Congress has spoken, we have deferred to "the traditional powers of Congress to prescribe rules of evidence and standards of proof in the federal courts" absent countervailing constitutional constraints. *Vance v. Terrazas*, 444 U.S. 252, 265 (1980). For Commission disciplinary proceedings initiated pursuant to 15 U.S.C. § 80a-9(b) and § 80b-3(f), we

---

[3] Disciplinary proceedings before the Securities and Exchange Commission are governed by the Commission's Rules of Practice, 17 CFR § 201.1 *et seq.* (1980), which enlarge, in certain respects, protections afforded by the Administrative Procedure Act (APA), 5 U.S.C. § 551 *et seq.*

Cross-Reference

Section 10(e) (5 U.S.C. § 706(2)(E)) provides the standard by which federal courts review agency factual findings and policy judgments in formal agency adjudications. For a fuller discussion of § 706(2)(E) and the substantial evidence test, see Chapter 9, page 955.

conclude that Congress has spoken, and has said that the preponderance-of-the-evidence standard should be applied.

The securities laws provide for judicial review of Commission disciplinary proceedings in the federal courts of appeals and specify the scope of such review. Because they do not indicate which standard of proof governs Commission adjudications, however, we turn to § 5 of the Administrative Procedure Act (APA), 5 U.S.C. § 554, which "applies . . . in every case of adjudication required by statute to be determined on the record after opportunity for an agency hearing," except in instances not relevant here. Section 5(b), 5 U.S.C. § 554(c)(2), makes the provisions of § 7, 5 U.S.C. § 556, applicable to adjudicatory proceedings. The answer to the question presented in this case turns therefore on the proper construction of § 7.

The search for congressional intent begins with the language of the statute. Section 7(c), 5 U.S.C. § 556(d), states in pertinent part:

> Except as otherwise provided by statute, the proponent of a rule or order has the burden of proof. Any oral or documentary evidence may be received, but the agency as a matter of policy shall provide for the exclusion of irrelevant, immaterial, or unduly repetitious evidence. A sanction may not be imposed or rule or order issued except on consideration of the whole record or those parts thereof cited by a party and supported by and *in accordance with* the reliable, probative, and *substantial evidence*. (Emphasis added.)

The language of the statute itself implies the enactment of a standard of proof. By allowing sanctions to be imposed only when they are "in accordance with . . . substantial evidence," Congress implied that a sanction must rest on a minimum quantity of evidence. The word "substantial" denotes quantity. The phrase "in accordance with . . . substantial evidence" thus requires that a decision be based on a certain quantity of evidence. Petitioner's contention that the phrase "reliable, probative, and substantial evidence" sets merely a standard of quality of evidence is, therefore, unpersuasive.

The phrase "in accordance with" lends further support to a construction of § 7(c) as establishing a standard of proof. Unlike § 10(e), the APA's explicit "Scope of review" provision that declares that agency action shall be held unlawful if "unsupported by substantial evidence," § 7(c), provides that an agency may issue an order only if that order is "supported by and *in accordance with* . . . substantial evidence" (emphasis added). The additional words

---

Cf. Vermont Yankee Nuclear Power Corp. v. Natural Resources Defense Council, Inc., 435 U.S. 519, 524 (1978) (as to 5 U.S.C. § 553, "[a]gencies are free to grant additional procedural rights in the exercise of their discretion, but reviewing courts are generally not free to impose them if the agencies have not chosen to grant them")....

"in accordance with"[19] suggest that the adjudicating agency must weigh the evidence and decide, based on the weight of the evidence, whether a disciplinary order should be issued. The language of § 7(c), therefore, requires that the agency decision must be "in accordance with" the weight of the evidence, not simply supported by enough evidence "'to justify, if the trial were to a jury, a refusal to direct a verdict when the conclusion sought to be drawn from it is one of fact for the jury.'" *Consolo v. FMC*, 383 U.S. 607, 620 (1966), quoting *NLRB v. Columbian Enameling & Stamping Co.*, 306 U.S. 292, 300 (1939). Obviously, weighing evidence has relevance only if the evidence on each side is to be measured against a standard of proof which allocates the risk of error. Section 10(e), by contrast, does not permit the reviewing court to weigh the evidence, but only to determine that there is in the record "'such relevant evidence as a reasonable mind might accept as adequate to support a conclusion,'" *Consolo v. FMC, supra*, at 620, quoting *Consolidated Edison Co. v. NLRB*, 305 U.S. 197, 229 (1938). It is not surprising, therefore, in view of the entirely different purposes of § 7(c) and § 10(e), that Congress intended the words "substantial evidence" to have different meanings in context. Thus, petitioner's argument that § 7(c) merely establishes the scope of judicial review of agency orders is unavailing.[20]

While the language of § 7(c) suggests, therefore, that Congress intended the statute to establish a standard of proof, the language of the statute is somewhat opaque concerning the precise standard of proof to be used. The legislative history, however, clearly reveals the Congress' intent. The original Senate version of § 7(c) provided that "no sanction shall be imposed . . . except as supported by relevant, reliable, and probative evidence." S. 7, 79th Cong., 1st Sess. (1945). After the Senate passed this version, the House passed the language of the statute as it reads today, and the Senate accepted the amendment. Any doubt as to the intent of Congress is removed by the House Report, which expressly adopted a preponderance-of-the-evidence standard:

> [W]here a party having the burden of proceeding has come forward with a *prima facie* and substantial case, he will prevail unless his evidence is discredited or rebutted. In any case the agency must decide "in accordance with the evidence." Where there is evidence pro and con, the agency must

---

[19] Section 10(e) expressly refers to § 7. Addition of the words "in accordance with" could not have been inadvertent. This is especially true in light of the House Report's discussion of the relationship between § 7(c) and § 10(e): "'Substantial evidence' [in § 10(e)] means evidence which on the whole record is clearly substantial, plainly sufficient to support a finding or conclusion under the requirements of section 7(c), and material to the issues." H.R. Rep. No. 1980, 79th Cong., 2d Sess., 45 (1946).

[20] It is true that the phrase "substantial evidence" is often used to denote the scope of judicial review. But to conclude that the phrase "substantial evidence" in § 7(c) defines the scope of judicial review would make the "substantial evidence" language of § 10(e) redundant. Moreover, it is implausible to think that the drafters of the APA would place a scope-of-review standard in the middle of a statutory provision designed to govern evidentiary issues in adjudicatory proceedings. . . .

weigh it and decide in *accordance with the preponderance*. In short, these provisions require a conscientious and rational judgment on the whole record in accordance with the proofs adduced. H.R. Rep. No. 1980, 79th Cong., 2d Sess., 37 (1946) (emphasis added).

Nor is there any suggestion in the legislative history that a standard of proof higher than a preponderance of the evidence was ever contemplated, much less intended. Congress was primarily concerned with the elimination of agency decisionmaking premised on evidence which was of poor quality— irrelevant, immaterial, unreliable, and nonprobative—and of insufficient quantity—less than a preponderance. *See id.*, at 36-37 and 45; S. Doc. No. 248, 79th Cong., 2d Sess., 320-322 and 376-378 (1946); n. 21, *supra*.

The language and legislative history of § 7(c) lead us to conclude, therefore, that § 7(c) was intended to establish a standard of proof and that the standard adopted is the traditional preponderance-of-the-evidence standard.

III

Our view of congressional intent is buttressed by the Commission's long-standing practice of imposing sanctions according to the preponderance of the evidence. As early as 1938, the Commission rejected the argument that in a proceeding to determine whether to suspend, expel, or otherwise sanction a brokerage firm and its principals for, *inter alia*, manipulation of security prices in violation of § 9 of the Securities Exchange Act of 1934, 15 U.S.C. § 78i, a standard of proof greater than the preponderance-of-the-evidence standard was required. Use of the preponderance standard continued after passage of the APA, and persists today. The Commission's consistent practice, which is in harmony with § 7(c) and its legislative history, is persuasive authority that Congress intended that Commission disciplinary proceedings, subject to § 7 of the APA, be governed by a preponderance-of-the-evidence standard.

In *Vermont Yankee Nuclear Power Corp. v. Natural Resources Defense Council, Inc.*, 435 U.S. 519, 524 (1978) we stated that § 4 of the APA, 5 U.S.C. § 553, established the "maximum procedural requirements which Congress was willing to have the courts impose upon agencies in conducting rulemaking procedures." In § 7(c), Congress has similarly expressed its intent that adjudicatory proceedings subject to the APA satisfy the statute where determinations are made according to the preponderance of the evidence. Congress was free to make that choice, *Vance v. Terrazas*, 444 U.S., at 265-266, and, in the absence of countervailing constitutional considerations, the courts are not free to disturb it.

Affirmed.

[The dissenting opinion of Justice POWELL, joined by Justice STEWART, is omitted.]

QUESTION SET 6.4

Review & Synthesis

1. Based on Justice Brennan's analysis, how is the term "substantial evidence" used differently in 5 U.S.C. § 556(d) than in § 706(2)(E)?

2. Through a close reading of the APA's legislative history, the Court concluded that Congress intended the standard of proof under § 556(d) to be a preponderance of the evidence, and not the more onerous "clear and convincing" standard. From a policy (rather than a statutory) perspective, do you agree with Steadman that agencies should have to carry a heavier burden when seeking to impose severe sanctions on regulated parties? Should the standard of judicial review (as distinguished from the standard of proof) be taken into account, such that the courts have more leeway to reject agency sanctions the more severe they are?

B. INFORMAL ADJUDICATION

"Informal adjudication" is the process by which administrative agencies issue orders (5 U.S.C. § 551(6)) when formal adjudication is not required. Admittedly this definition is not all that helpful, since it defines informal adjudication by what it is *not* rather than by what it is. It is nevertheless accurate, since it captures all of the adjudications conducted by agencies that do not employ the trial-like procedures governed by 5 U.S.C. §§ 554, 556, and 557. To put things in some perspective, the overwhelming majority of federal agency adjudications fall into the informal category; one study estimated the proportion to be as high as 90 percent. *See* Paul R. Verkuil, *A Study of Informal Adjudication Procedures*, 43 U. Chi. L. Rev. 739, 741 (1976). Moreover, agencies take a staggering variety of actions through informal adjudication. These include:

- Eligibility determinations for grants, benefits, loans, and subsidies (e.g., Example 2 on page 348);
- Licensing and accrediting;
- Inspections, grading, and auditing;
- Planning and policymaking for economic development and public works (e.g., Example 1 on page 348);
- Orders imposing penalties and fines, or requiring a regulated party to remedy a statutory or rule violation; and
- Internal agency interpretations of statutory or regulatory provisions.

See FEDERAL AGENCY ADJUDICATION at 176-77; *see also* Verkuil, *supra,* at 757-59.

Given the number of adjudications that fall into the "informal" category, and given the variety of agency actions taken through informal adjudication, you might be surprised to learn that the APA adopts few requirements for how to conduct them. Section 555 (which applies to all agency decision-making procedures) gives parties several rights, including the right to be represented by counsel, to have an agency render its decision in a reasonable time period, and to have the agency provide a statement of reasons for its decisions. Section 558 provides procedural protections for those engaged in the licensing process, which the APA considers a form of adjudication.

Apart from these few requirements or those that may be contained in organic or other statutes, agencies are largely left to adopt (or not to adopt) the informal adjudication procedures they deem best. They may accordingly adopt decision-making processes that would be verboten in more regimented adjudicative contexts, like permitting *ex parte* contacts (a la Example 1 on page 348), accepting only written submissions of evidence, deciding cases through conferences or other informal meetings, and allowing the adjudicator to perform both investigative and adjudicative functions.

Another important difference between formal and informal adjudications relates to the agency officials who are permitted to preside over them. As already discussed, APA § 556(b) requires that ALJs preside over all formal adjudications covered by APA § 554 (unless the matter is before the head(s) of the agency). ALJs enjoy numerous statutory protections that facilitate their independence from investigators, prosecutors, and other policymakers within their agencies. Additionally, ALJs must be functionally segregated within their agencies; they cannot participate in any non-adjudicative duties. By contrast, ALJs do not preside over informal adjudications. Those are instead conducted by other officials, including so-called "administrative judges" ("AJs"). In sum, there are generally few statutory checks on how agencies conduct informal adjudications.

Given that Congress has declined to exercise tight control over informal agency adjudications, the minimal procedural protections they afford mostly come from two other sources: the regulations the agencies themselves adopt and the Fifth Amendment Due Process Clause. With respect to regulations, courts will enforce agencies' own informal procedures against them, even if the adoption of those procedures was entirely discretionary. *See generally* Rodney A. Smolla, *The Erosion of the Principle that the Government Must Follow Self-Imposed Rules,* 52 FORDHAM L. REV. 472 (1984).

With respect to the Constitution, agencies must always conform their adjudicative procedures to the requirements of due process where protected interests or entitlements are at issue. Whereas the granular provisions of APA §§ 554, 556, and 557 do much of this work in formal adjudications, the APA mostly leaves federal agencies engaged in informal adjudication to fend for the themselves. While agencies can always take the safe route by simply adopting formal procedures for their informal adjudications, they very rarely do so. They instead prefer to take advantage of the potential efficiencies and cost savings that can come from procedural simplicity (and fewer protections for the regulated). Agencies must then think carefully about the informal procedures they choose, as the Supreme Court has developed elaborate methods for testing the constitutionality of those choices. The same can be said of state agencies engaged in informal adjudications which, of course, are not governed by the APA. The constitutionality of federal (and state) informal adjudicative procedures is exhaustively considered in Chapter 7, below.

The following cases focus on two practical but important issues that arise when courts are asked to review agency decisions reached through informal adjudication. The first—addressed in *Citizens to Preserve Overton Park, Inc. v. Volpe*—is whether they must create formal records of the findings that support their orders and, if they do, where that obligation comes from. If an agency engaged in informal adjudication has no statutory obligation to create a formal fact-finding record —as was true in *Overton Park*—how can courts conduct a meaningful review of its decisions? How can affected members of the public be sure that the decision is sound?

The second, closely related issue—addressed in *Pension Benefit Guaranty Corp. v. LTV*—is whether courts have independent authority to impose new or different procedures on federal agencies engaged in informal adjudication. Congress can clearly do so, as can the agencies themselves when permitted by statute. *Vermont Yankee Nuclear Power Corp. v. Natural Resources Defense Council,* 435 U.S. 519 (1978)—a seminal administrative law decision considered in Chapter 5—ruled that the courts have no procedure-imposing authority in the informal *rulemaking* context. "In short, . . . Congress intended that the discretion of the agencies and not that of the courts be exercised in determining when extra procedural devices should be employed." *Id.* at 546. The issue in *PBGC* was whether *Vermont Yankee* also applies to informal adjudications.

When reading the cases, pay attention to the justifications the Court provided for ordering agencies to reconsider how they performed their work. Can you tie the Court's decisions back to specific sources of law? To the Constitution? To the APA? To the Court's inherent authority? To something else? Also, what do the Court's decisions say about the respective decision-making responsibilities of the Judiciary and the administrative state, and about their relationship to one another?

Citizens to Preserve Overton Park, Inc. v. Volpe
401 U.S. 402 (1971)

Opinion of the Court by Mr. Justice MARSHALL, announced by MR. JUSTICE STEWART.

The growing public concern about the quality of our natural environment has prompted Congress in recent years to enact legislation designed to curb the accelerating destruction of our country's natural beauty. We are concerned in this case with § 4(f) of the Department of Transportation Act of 1966, as amended,[2] and § 18(a) of the Federal-Aid Highway Act of 1968, 82 Stat. 823, 23 U.S.C. § 138 (1964 ed., Supp. V) (hereafter § 138).[3] These statutes prohibit the Secretary of Transportation from authorizing the use of federal funds to finance the construction of highways through public parks if a "feasible and prudent" alternative route exists. If no such route is available, the statutes allow him to approve construction through parks only if there has been "all possible planning to minimize harm" to the park.

Petitioners, private citizens as well as local and national conservation organizations, contend that the Secretary has violated these statutes by authorizing the expenditure of federal funds for the construction of a six-lane interstate highway through a public park in Memphis, Tennessee. Their claim was rejected by the District Court, which granted the Secretary's motion for summary judgment, and the Court of Appeals for the Sixth Circuit affirmed. After oral argument, this Court granted a stay that halted construction and, treating the application for the stay as a petition for certiorari, granted review. We now reverse the judgment below and remand for further proceedings in the District Court.

Overton Park is 342-acre city park located near the center of Memphis. The park contains a zoo, a nine-hole municipal golf course, an outdoor theater, nature trails, a bridle path, an art academy, picnic areas, and 170 acres of forest. The proposed highway, which is to be a six-lane, high-speed, expressway, will sever the zoo from the rest of the park. Although the road-way will be depressed below ground level except where it crosses a small creek, 26 acres of the park will be destroyed. The highway is to be a segment of Interstate Highway I-40, part of the National System of Interstate and Defense Highways. I-40 will provide Memphis with a major east-west expressway which will allow easier access to downtown Memphis from the residential areas on the eastern edge of the city.

Although the route through the park was approved by the Bureau of Public Roads in 1956 and by the Federal Highway Administrator in 1966,

---

[2] "It is hereby declared to be the national policy that special effort should be made to preserve the natural beauty of the countryside and public park and recreation lands, wildlife and waterfowl refuges, and historic sites. The Secretary of Transportation shall cooperate and consult with the Secretaries of the Interior, Housing and Urban Development, and Agriculture, and with the States in developing transportation plans and programs that include measures to maintain or enhance the natural beauty of the lands traversed. After August 23, 1968, the Secretary shall not approve any program or project which requires the use of any publicly owned land from a public park, recreation area, or wildlife and waterfowl refuge of national, State, or local significance as determined by the Federal, State, or local officials having jurisdiction thereof, or any land from an historic site of national, State, or local significance as so determined by such officials unless (1) there is no feasible and prudent alternative to the use of such land, and (2) such program includes all possible planning to minimize harm to such park, recreational area, wildlife and waterfowl refuge, or historic site resulting from such use." 82 Stat. 824, 49 U.S.C. § 1653(f) (1964 ed., Supp. V).

[3] [This statute is almost identical to § 4(f) of the Department of Transportation Act of 1966.]

the enactment of § 4(f) of the Department of Transportation Act prevented distribution of federal funds for the section of the highway designated to go through Overton Park until the Secretary of Transportation determined whether the requirements of § 4(f) had been met. Federal funding for the rest of the project was, however, available; and the state acquired a right-of-way on both sides of the park. In April 1968, the Secretary announced that he concurred in the judgment of local officials that I-40 should be built through the park. And in September 1969 the State acquired the right-of-way inside Overton Park from the city.[15] Final approval for the project—the route as well as the design—was not announced until November 1969, after Congress had reiterated in § 138 of the Federal-Aid Highway Act that highway construction through public parks was to be restricted. Neither announcement approving the route and design of I-40 was accompanied by a statement of the Secretary's factual findings. He did not indicate why he believed there were no feasible and prudent alternative routes or why design changes could not be made to reduce the harm to the park.

Petitioners contend that the Secretary's action is invalid without such formal findings and that the Secretary did not make an independent determination but merely relied on the judgment of the Memphis City Council.[17] They also contend that it would be "feasible and prudent" to route I-40 around Overton Park either to the north or to the south. And they argue that if these alternative routes are not "feasible and prudent," the present plan does not include "all possible" methods for reducing harm to the park. Petitioners claim that I-40 could be built under the park by using either of two possible tunneling methods, and they claim that, at a minimum, by using advanced drainage techniques the expressway could be depressed below ground level along the entire route through the park including the section that crosses the small creek.

Respondents argue that it was unnecessary for the Secretary to make formal findings, and that he did, in fact, exercise his own independent judgment which was supported by the facts. In the District Court, respondents introduced affidavits, prepared specifically for this litigation, which indicated that the Secretary had made the decision and that the decision was supportable. These affidavits were contradicted by affidavits introduced by petitioners, who also sought to take the deposition of a former Federal Highway Administrator who had participated in the decision to route I-40 through Overton Park.

---

[15] The regulation was promulgated pursuant to Executive Order 11514, dated March 5, 1970, 35 Fed. Reg. 4247, which instructed all federal agencies to initiate procedures needed to direct their policies and programs toward meeting national environmental goals.

[17] Petitioners contend that former Federal Highway Administrator Bridwell's account of an April 3, 1968, meeting with the Memphis City Council given to the Senate Subcommittee on Roads of the Senate Committee on Public Works supports this charge. *See* Hearings on Urban Highway Planning, Location, and Design before the Subcommittee on Roads of the Senate Committee on Public Works, 90th Cong., 1st and 2d Sess., pt. 2, pp. 478-480 (1968).

The District Court and the Court of Appeals found that formal findings by the Secretary were not necessary and refused to order the deposition of the former Federal Highway Administrator because those courts believed that probing of the mental processes of an administrative decisionmaker was prohibited. And, believing that the Secretary's authority was wide and reviewing courts' authority narrow in the approval of highway routes, the lower courts held that the affidavits contained no basis for a determination that the Secretary had exceeded his authority.

We agree that formal findings were not required. But we do not believe that in this case judicial review based solely on litigation affidavits was adequate.

[The Court provided a detailed — and seminal — discussion of the various judicial review standards enumerated in 5 U.S.C § 706 and how they apply to the Secretary's informal adjudication at issue in this case. It concluded that it must determine whether the Secretary acted within the scope of his statutory authority, and whether the choice he made within the scope of that authority was "arbitrary and capricious." This part of the Court's opinion is excerpted in Chapter 9 at page 395, which analyzes in detail the judicial review standards applicable to various types of administrative decision-making.]

The final inquiry is whether the Secretary's action followed the necessary procedural requirements. Here the only procedural error alleged is the failure of the Secretary to make formal findings and state his reason for allowing the highway to be built through the park.

Undoubtedly, review of the Secretary's action is hampered by his failure to make such findings, but the absence of formal findings does not necessarily require that the case be remanded to the Secretary. Neither the Department of Transportation Act nor the Federal-Aid Highway Act requires such formal findings. Moreover, the Administrative Procedure Act requirements that there be formal findings in certain rulemaking and adjudicatory proceedings do not apply to the Secretary's action here. *See* 5 U.S.C. §§ 553(a)(2), 554(a) (1964 ed., Supp. V). And, although formal findings may be required in some cases in the absence of statutory directives when the nature of the agency action is ambiguous, those situations are rare. *See City of Yonkers v. United States,* 320 U.S. 685 (1944); *American Trucking Assn's v. United States,* 344 U.S. 298, 320 (1953). Plainly, there is no ambiguity here; the Secretary has approved the construction of I-40 through Overton Park and has approved a specific design for the project.

Petitioners contend that although there may not be a statutory requirement that the Secretary make formal findings and even though this may not be a case for the reviewing court to impose a requirement that findings be made, Department of Transportation regulations require them. This argument is based on DOT Order 5610.1,[31] which requires the Secretary

---

[31] The regulation was promulgated pursuant to Executive Order 11514, dated March 5, 1970, 35 Fed. Reg. 4247, which instructed all federal agencies to initiate procedures needed to direct their policies and programs toward meeting national environmental goals.

to make formal findings when he approves the use of parkland for highway construction but which was issued after the route for I-40 was approved.[32] Petitioners argue that even though the order was not in effect at the time approval was given to the Overton Park project and even though the order was not intended to have retrospective effect the order represents the law at the time of this Court's decision and under *Thorpe v. Housing Authority*, 393 U.S. 268, 281-282 (1969), should be applied to this case.

The *Thorpe* litigation resulted from an attempt to evict a tenant from a federally funded housing project under circumstances that suggested that the eviction was prompted by the tenant's objections to the management of the project. Despite repeated requests, the Housing Authority would not give an explanation for its action. The tenant claimed that the eviction interfered with her exercise of First Amendment rights and that the failure to state the reasons for the eviction and to afford her a hearing denied her due process. After denial of relief in the state courts, this Court granted certiorari "to consider whether (the tenant) was denied due process by the Housing Authority's refusal to state the reasons for her eviction and to afford her a hearing at which she could contest the sufficiency of those reasons." 393 U.S., at 272.

While the case was pending in this Court, the Department of Housing and Urban Development issued regulations requiring Housing Authority officials to inform tenants of the reasons for an eviction and to give a tenant the opportunity to reply. The case was then remanded to the state courts to determine if the HUD regulations were applicable to that case. The state court held them not to be applicable and this Court reversed on the ground that the general rule is "that an appellate court must apply the law in effect at the time it renders its decision." 393 U.S., at 281.

While we do not question that DOT Order 5610.1 constitutes the law in effect at the time of our decision, we do not believe that *Thorpe* compels us to remand for the Secretary to make formal findings.[33] Here, unlike the situation in *Thorpe*, there has been a change in circumstances—additional right-of-way has been cleared and the 26-acre right-of-way inside Overton Park has been purchased by the State. Moreover, there is an administrative record that allows the full, prompt review of the Secretary's action that is sought without additional delay which would result from having a remand to the Secretary.

That administrative record is not, however, before us. The lower courts based their review on the litigation affidavits that were presented. These affidavits were merely "*post hoc*" rationalizations, *Burlington Truck Lines v. United States*, 371 U.S. 156, 168-69 (1962), which have traditionally been found

[32] DOT Order 5610.1 was issued on October 7, 1970.
[33] Even if formal findings by the Secretary were mandatory, the proper course would be to remand the case to the District Court directing that court to order the Secretary to make formal findings. Of course, the District Court is not prohibited from remanding the case to the Secretary.

to be an inadequate basis for review. *Burlington Truck Lines v. United States, supra*; *SEC v. Chenery Corp.*, 318 U.S. 80, 87 (1943) [*Chenery I*]. And they clearly do not constitute the "whole record" compiled by the agency: the basis for review required by § 706 of the Administrative Procedure Act.

Thus it is necessary to remand this case to the District Court for plenary review of the Secretary's decision. That review is to be based on the full administrative record that was before the Secretary at the time he made his decision. But since the bare record may not disclose the factors that were considered or the Secretary's construction of the evidence it may be necessary for the District Court to require some explanation in order to determine if the Secretary acted within the scope of his authority and if the Secretary's action was justifiable under the applicable standard.

The court may require the administrative officials who participated in the decision to give testimony explaining their action. Of course, such inquiry into the mental processes of administrative decisionmakers is usually to be avoided. *United States v. Morgan*, 313 U.S. 409, 422 (1941). And where there are administrative findings that were made at the same time as the decision, as was the case in *Morgan*, there must be a strong showing of bad faith or improper behavior before such inquiry may be made. But here there are no such formal findings and it may be that the only way there can be effective judicial review is by examining the decisionmakers themselves.

The District Court is not, however, required to make such an inquiry. It may be that the Secretary can prepare formal findings including the information required by DOT Order 5610.1 that will provide an adequate explanation for his action. Such an explanation will, to some extent, be a "*post hoc* rationalization" and thus must be viewed critically. If the District Court decides that additional explanation is necessary, that court should consider which method will prove the most expeditious so that full review may be had as soon as possible.

Reversed and remanded.

Mr. Justice DOUGLAS took no part in the consideration or decision of this case.

Separate opinion of Mr. Justice BLACK, with whom Mr. Justice BRENNAN joins.

I agree with the Court that the judgment of the Court of Appeals is wrong and that its action should be reversed. I do not agree that the whole matter should be remanded to the District Court. I think the case should be sent back to the Secretary of Transportation. It is apparent from the Court's opinion today that the Secretary of Transportation completely failed to comply with the duty imposed upon him by Congress not to permit a federally financed public highway to run through a public park "unless (1) there is no feasible and prudent alternative to the use of such land, and (2) such program includes all possible planning to minimize harm to such park...." 23 U.S.C. § 138 (1964 ed., Supp. V); 49 U.S.C. § 1653(f) (1964 ed., Supp. V). That congressional command should not be taken lightly by the Secretary or by this Court. It represents a solemn determination of the highest law-making body of this Nation that the beauty and health-giving facilities of our parks are not to be taken away for public roads without hearings, factfindings, and policy determinations under the supervision of a Cabinet officer—the Secretary of Transportation. The Act of Congress in connection with other federal highway aid legislation, it seems to me, calls for hearings—hearings that a court can review, hearings that demonstrate more than mere arbitrary defiance by the Secretary. Whether the findings growing out of such hearings are labeled "formal" or "informal" appears to me to be no more than an exercise in semantics. Whatever the hearing requirements might be, the Department of Transportation failed to meet them in this case. I regret that I am compelled to conclude for myself that, except for some too-late formulations, apparently coming from the Solicitor General's office, this record contains not one word to indicate that the Secretary raised even a finger to comply with the command of Congress. It is our duty, I believe, to remand this whole matter back to the Secretary of Transportation for him to give this matter the hearing it deserves in full good-faith obedience to the Act of Congress. That Act was obviously passed to protect our public parks from forays by road builders except in the most extraordinary and imperative circumstances. This record does not demonstrate the existence of such circumstances. I dissent from the Court's failure to send the case back to the Secretary, whose duty has not yet been performed.

Mr. Justice BLACKMUN.

I fully join the Court in its opinion and in its judgment. I merely wish to state the obvious: (1) The case comes to this Court as the end product of more than a decade of endeavor to solve the interstate highway problem at Memphis. (2) The administrative decisions under attack here are not those of a single Secretary; some were made by the present Secretary's predecessor and, before him, by the Department of Commerce's Bureau of Public Roads. (3) The 1966 Act and the 1968 Act have cut across former methods and here have imposed new standards and conditions upon a situation that already was largely developed.

This undoubtedly is why the record is sketchy and less than one would expect if the project were one which had been instituted after the passage of the 1966 Act.

Pension Benefit Guaranty Corp. v. LTV Corp.
496 U.S. 633 (1990)

Justice BLACKMUN delivered the opinion of the Court.

I

Petitioner PBGC is a wholly owned United States Government corporation, *see* 29 U.S.C. § 1302, modeled after the Federal Deposit Insurance Corporation. *See* 120 Cong. Rec. 29950 (1974) (statement of Sen. Bentsen). The Board of Directors of the PBGC consists of the Secretaries of the Treasury, Labor, and Commerce. 29 U.S.C. § 1302(d). The PBGC administers and enforces Title IV of ERISA. Title IV includes a mandatory Government insurance program that protects the pension benefits of over 30 million private-sector American workers who participate in plans covered by the Title. In enacting Title IV, Congress sought to ensure that employees and their beneficiaries would not be completely "deprived of anticipated retirement benefits by the termination of pension plans before sufficient funds have been accumulated in the plans." *Pension Benefit Guaranty Corporation v. R.A. Gray & Co.,* 467 U.S. 717, 720 (1984).

When a plan covered under Title IV terminates with insufficient assets to satisfy its pension obligations to the employees, the PBGC becomes trustee of the plan, taking over the plan's assets and liabilities. The PBGC then uses the plan's assets to cover what it can of the benefit obligations. *See* 29 U.S.C. § 1344 (1982 ed. and Supp. IV). The PBGC then must add its own funds to ensure payment of most of the remaining "nonforfeitable" benefits, *i.e.,* those benefits to which participants have earned entitlement under the plan terms as of the date of termination. §§ 1301(a)(8), 1322(a) and (b). ERISA does place limits on the benefits PBGC may guarantee upon plan termination, however, even if an employee is entitled to greater benefits under the terms of the plan. *See* 29 CFR § 2621.3(a)(2) and App. A (1989); 29 U.S.C. § 1322(b)(3)(B). In addition, benefit increases resulting from plan amendments adopted within five years of the termination are not paid in full. Finally, active plan participants (current employees) cease to earn additional benefits under the plan upon its termination and lose entitlement to most benefits not yet fully earned as of the date of plan termination. 29 U.S.C. §§ 1322(a) and (b), 1301(a)(8); 29 CFR § 2613.6 (1989)....

. . . [P]lan termination is the insurable event under Title IV. Plans may be terminated "voluntarily" by an employer or "involuntarily" by the PBGC. An employer may terminate a plan voluntarily in one of two ways. It may proceed with a "standard termination" only if it has sufficient assets to pay all benefit commitments. A standard termination thus does not implicate PBGC insurance responsibilities. If an employer wishes to terminate a plan whose assets are insufficient to pay all benefits, the employer must demonstrate that it is in financial "distress" as defined in 29 U.S.C. § 1341(c) (1982 ed., Supp. IV). Neither a standard nor a distress termination by the employer, however, is permitted if termination would violate the terms of an existing collective-bargaining agreement. 29 U.S.C. § 1341(a)(3).

The PBGC, though, may terminate a plan "involuntarily," notwithstanding the existence of a collective-bargaining agreement.... Termination can be undone by PBGC.... When a plan is restored, full benefits are reinstated, and the employer, rather than the PBGC, again is responsible for the plan's unfunded liabilities.

II

This case arose after respondent The LTV Corporation (LTV Corp.) and many of its subsidiaries, including LTV Steel Company Inc. (LTV Steel), (collectively LTV), in July 1986 filed petitions for reorganization under Chapter 11 of the Bankruptcy Code. At that time, LTV Steel was the sponsor of three defined benefit pension plans (Plans) covered by Title IV of ERISA. Two of the Plans were the products of collective-bargaining negotiations with the United Steelworkers of America (Steelworkers). The third was for nonunion salaried employees. Chronically underfunded, the Plans, by late 1986, had unfunded liabilities for promised benefits of almost $2.3 billion. Approximately $2.1 billion of this amount was covered by PBGC insurance.

It is undisputed that one of LTV Corp.'s principal goals in filing the Chapter 11 petitions was the restructuring of LTV Steel's pension obligations, a goal which could be accomplished if the Plans were terminated and responsibility for the unfunded liabilities was placed on the PBGC. LTV Steel then could negotiate with its employees for new pension arrangements. LTV, however, could not voluntarily terminate the Plans because two of them had been negotiated in collective bargaining. LTV therefore sought to have the PBGC terminate the Plans.

To that end, LTV advised the PBGC in 1986 that it could not continue to provide complete funding for the Plans.... Confronted with this information, the PBGC, invoking § 4042(a)(4) of ERISA, 29 U.S.C. § 1342(a)(4), determined that the Plans should be terminated in order to protect the insurance program from the unreasonable risk of large losses, and commenced termination proceedings in the District Court. With LTV's consent, the Plans were terminated effective January 13, 1987....

In early August 1987, the PBGC determined that the financial factors on which it had relied in terminating the Plans had changed significantly. Of particular significance to the PBGC was its belief that the steel industry, including LTV Steel, was experiencing a dramatic turnaround. As a result, the PBGC concluded it no longer faced the imminent risk, central to its original termination decision, of large unfunded liabilities stemming from plant shutdowns. Later that month, the PBGC's internal working group made a recommendation, based upon LTV's improved financial circumstances and its follow-on plans, to the PBGC's Executive Director to restore the Plans under the PBGC's § 4047 powers. After consulting the PBGC's Board of Directors, which agreed with the working group that restoration was appropriate, the Executive Director decided to restore the Plans.

The Director issued a notice of restoration on September 22, 1987, indicating the PBGC's intent to restore the terminated Plans. The PBGC notice explained that the restoration decision was based on (1) LTV's establishment of "a retirement program that results in an abuse of the pension plan termination insurance system established by Title IV of ERISA," and (2) LTV's "improved financial circumstances." *See* App. to Pet. for Cert. 182a. Restoration meant that the Plans were ongoing, and that LTV again would be responsible for administering and funding them.

LTV refused to comply with the restoration decision. This prompted the PBGC to initiate an enforcement action in the District Court. The court vacated the PBGC's restoration decision, finding, among other things, that the PBGC had exceeded its authority under § 4047.

The Court of Appeals for the Second Circuit affirmed, holding that the PBGC's restoration decision was "arbitrary and capricious" or contrary to law under the APA, 5 U.S.C. § 706(2)(A), in various ways.... [T]he court concluded that the agency's restoration decision was arbitrary and capricious because the PBGC's decisionmaking process of informal adjudication lacked adequate procedural safeguards. *Id. at* 1021.

Because of the significant administrative law questions raised by this case, and the importance of the PBGC's insurance program, we granted certiorari.

III

[In Section III.A. and B. of its opinion, the Court rejected the Second Circuit's conclusion that the substantive foundations of PBGC's restoration decision were arbitrary and capricious.]

C.

Finally, we consider the Court of Appeals' ruling that the agency procedures were inadequate in this particular case. Relying upon a passage in *Bowman Transportation, Inc. v. Arkansas-Best Freight System, Inc.*, 419 U.S. 281, 288, note 4 (1974), the court held that the PBGC's decision was arbitrary and capricious because the "PBGC neither apprised LTV of the material on which it was to base its decision, gave LTV an adequate opportunity to offer contrary evidence, proceeded in accordance with ascertainable standards . . ., nor provided [LTV] a statement showing its reasoning in applying those standards." 875 F.2d, at 1021. The court suggested that on remand the agency was required to do each of these things.

The PBGC argues that this holding conflicts with *Vermont Yankee Nuclear Power Corp. v. Natural Resources Defense Council, Inc.*, 435 U.S. 519 (1978), where, the PBGC contends, this Court made clear that when the Due Process Clause is not implicated and an agency's governing statute contains no specific procedural mandates, the APA establishes the maximum procedural requirements a reviewing court may impose on agencies. Although *Vermont Yankee* concerned additional procedures imposed by the Court of Appeals for the District of Columbia Circuit on the Atomic Energy Commission when the agency was engaging in informal rulemaking, the PBGC argues that the informal adjudication process by which the restoration decision was made should be governed by the same principles.

Respondents counter by arguing that courts, under some circumstances, do require agencies to undertake additional procedures. As support for this proposition, they rely on *Citizens to Preserve Overton Park, Inc. v. Volpe*, 401 U.S. 402 (1971). In *Overton Park*, the Court concluded that the Secretary of Transportation's "*post hoc* rationalizations" regarding a decision to authorize the construction of a highway did not provide "an [a]dequate basis for [judicial] review" for purposes of the APA, 5 U.S.C. § 706. *Id.* at 419. Accordingly, the Court directed the District Court on remand to consider evidence that shed light on the Secretary's reasoning at the time he made the decision. Of particular relevance for present purposes, the Court in *Overton Park* intimated that one recourse for the District Court might be a remand to the agency for a fuller explanation of the agency's reasoning at the time of the agency action. *See id.* at 420-421. Subsequent cases have made clear that remanding to the agency in fact is the preferred course. *See Florida Power & Light Co. v. Lorion*, 470 U.S. 729, 744 (1985) ("[I]f the reviewing court simply cannot evaluate the challenged agency action on the basis of the record before it, the proper course, except in rare circumstances, is to remand to the agency for additional investigation or explanation"). Respondents contend that the instant case is controlled by *Overton Park* rather than *Vermont Yankee*, and that the Court of Appeals' ruling was thus correct.

We believe that respondents' argument is wide of the mark. We begin by noting that although one initially might feel that there is some tension between *Vermont Yankee* and *Overton Park*, the two cases are not necessarily inconsistent. *Vermont Yankee* stands for the general proposition that courts are not free to impose upon agencies specific procedural requirements that have no basis in the APA. *See* 435 U.S., at 524. At most, *Overton Park* suggests that § 706(2)(A), which directs a court to ensure that an agency action is not arbitrary and capricious or otherwise contrary to law, imposes a general "procedural" requirement of sorts by mandating that an agency take whatever steps it needs to provide an explanation that will enable the court to evaluate the agency's rationale at the time of decision.

Here, unlike in *Overton Park*, the Court of Appeals did not suggest that the administrative record was inadequate to enable the court to fulfill its duties under § 706. Rather, to support its ruling, the court focused on "fundamental fairness" to LTV. 875 F.2d, at 1020-1021. With the possible exception of the absence of "ascertainable standards" — by which we are not exactly sure what the Court of Appeals meant — the procedural inadequacies cited by the court all relate to LTV's role in the PBGC's decisionmaking process. But the court did not point to any provision in ERISA or the APA which gives LTV the procedural rights the court identified. Thus, the court's holding runs afoul of *Vermont Yankee* and finds no support in *Overton Park*.

Nor is *Arkansas-Best*, the case on which the Court of Appeals relied, to the contrary. The statement relied upon (which was dictum) said: "A party is entitled, of course, to know the issues on which decision will turn and to be apprised of the factual material on which the agency relies for decision so that he may rebut it." 419 U.S., at 288, note 4. That statement was entirely correct in the context of *Arkansas-Best*, which involved a formal adjudication by the Interstate Commerce Commission pursuant to the trial-type procedures set forth in §§ 5, 7 and 8 of the APA, 5 U.S.C. §§ 554, 556-557, which include requirements that parties be given notice of "the matters of fact and law asserted," § 554(b)(3), an opportunity for "the submission and consideration of facts [and] arguments," § 554(c)(1), and an opportunity to submit "proposed findings and conclusions" or "exceptions," § 557(c)(1), (2). The determination in this case, however, was lawfully made by informal adjudication, the minimal requirements for which are set forth in the APA, 5 U.S.C. § 555, and do not include such elements. A failure to provide them where the Due Process Clause itself does not require them (which has not been asserted here) is therefore not unlawful.

IV

. . . [W]e find the procedures employed by the PBGC to be consistent with the APA. Accordingly, the judgment of the Court of Appeals is reversed, and the case is remanded for further proceedings consistent with this opinion.

It is so ordered.

[The opinion of Justice White concurring in part and dissenting in part, is omitted, as is the dissenting opinion of Justice Stevens.]

QUESTION SET 6.5

Review & Synthesis

1. Putting *Overton Park*, *Vermont Yankee*, and *LTV Corp.* together, what is the rule regarding an agency's obligation to compile a decision-making record when engaged in informal adjudication?

2. What is the apparent "tension" between *Overton Park* and *Vermont Yankee* the Court identified in *LTV Corp.*, and how did the Court resolve it?

3. With respect to *Overton Park:*

   a. During your weekly study group, your classmate Karim makes the following observation: "I don't see why what happened in *Overton Park* is an adjudication. It doesn't look anything like any kind of adjudication we've ever studied. It didn't even have plaintiffs or defendants, just the Transportation Secretary. What am I missing?" How would you respond to Karim?

   b. What was the legal basis on which the Court issued its order requiring that the Secretary of Transportation compile an "administrative record" for the courts to review? Was there a statute that required it? A Department of Transportation regulation? Is this an example of a "judicial hybrid" procedure, whereby the Court, under its own authority, simply imposed a new procedural requirement (compilation and production of a factual record) on the agency? If this is the description that best fits the Court's decision, do you think it is still permissible after the Court's decision in *Vermont Yankee*, decided approximately seven years later?

   c. Identify the statutory basis for Justice Black's assertion that the Secretary of Transportation was required to hold hearings to determine whether the I-40 highway should have been built through Overton Park. On reversing the Secretary's decision, did Justice Black agree with the majority that the Secretary simply needed to gather the information on which he relied so the district court could review it, or was he arguing that the Secretary could not have gathered the information needed to make a reasonable decision because he failed to hold hearings? Could there have been another reason Justice Black believed a hearing was necessary, having nothing to do with statutory or fact-gathering requirements?

   d. Justice Blackmun pointed to a hard reality of complicated administrative decision-making; it may take many years, multiple administrations, and successive decision-makers to complete implementation of some regulatory policies. In light of that reality, was it fair to ask the Secretary to compile the "administrative record" that informed the Overton Park highway funding decision? Should the Secretary (or his legal staff) have anticipated that his decision would be challenged in court? Before you answer, consider *Automotive Parts & Accessories Association v. Boyd*, 407 F.2d 330, 338 (D.C. Cir. 1968) (warning Secretary Volpe's *immediate predecessor* of the "ever present possibility of judicial review" in the informal rulemaking context). Is it obvious that the holding in *Automotive Parts* should apply to informal adjudication? Could you make an argument that courts should have more license to impose additional procedural constraints on agency adjudications than on agency rulemakings?

4. With respect to *LTV Corp.*, your classmate Jasmine offers the following summary of the case during your Administrative Law study group session: "The Court concluded that the procedures used by the PBGC in making its restoration decision were wholly adequate, both under the APA and under the Due Process Clause. It also concluded that, under *Overton Park*, agencies engaged in informal adjudication have an automatic obligation to create a formal record that lets courts review their decisions later." Do you accept Jasmine's summary? If not, how would you change it?

Application & Analysis

1. Pursuant to the Indian Gaming Regulatory Act, a Native American tribe applied to the Interior Department's National Indian Gaming Commission for approval to conduct gaming operations on its lands. Under the Act, the Commission may not approve such an application if the anticipated gaming will be conducted on "newly acquired" land, i.e., land that the Interior Department took into trust for a tribe's benefit after October 17, 1988. While the tribe's application was pending, the county in which the tribe's lands are located challenged it by arguing that the tribe had no historical connection to the land on which it planned to locate its casino. The county also alleged that the land had been acquired after the cutoff date set by the Act. It submitted a lengthy memorandum in support of its challenge, supported by extensive documentary evidence and affidavits. After a yearslong delay, the Commission sent the county a letter rejecting its challenge. The entirety of its explanation consisted of a single sentence: "The Commission is not inclined to sustain your challenge." The county believes that the Commission's response was procedurally inadequate under the Administrative Procedure Act. Is that right?

2. Assume the same facts as presented in Question 1. The county now would like to challenge the Commission's determination in federal court on the theory that it is arbitrary and capricious under APA § 706(2)(A). How does the focus of this argument differ from the argument raised in Question 1, which claimed that the Commission's response was procedurally inadequate?

CHAPTER 7

Due Process and Administrative Adjudication

In the previous chapter, we focused on the procedural requirements Congress imposes on federal administrative adjudication through the Administrative Procedure Act. Given that most of these protections apply solely to formal adjudications, we have had comparatively little occasion to consider the minimal required procedures for informal adjudications. We have likewise had little chance to consider the protections agency adjudicators at the state level must afford affected parties, as the APA does not apply to them. We now turn to the Constitution's Due Process Clauses, which apply to all administrative adjudications, whether formal or informal, whether state or federal. Because formal adjudications typically clear the due process hurdle by adopting a full complement of procedural protections, the issues addressed below arise primarily in the context of informal federal and state adjudications.

The Fifth Amendment Due Process Clause, which applies to federal adjudications, states that "No person shall . . . be deprived of life, liberty, or property, without due process of law." The Fourteenth Amendment Due Process Clause applies to the states, using similar language. The Constitution does not define the term "due process," but at its most basic level it refers to the essential fairness of the government's adjudicative procedures. Prior to the 1960s, the Court did little to systematize its approach to due process questions, insisting that the flexibility of the concept made such efforts futile. It instead opted for a context-driven "fairness under the circumstances" approach. This changed dramatically with the Court's decision in *Goldberg v. Kelly*, which found that beneficiaries of government welfare programs have a property interest in their support payments that is protected by due process. 397 U.S. 254 (1970). Expanding the concept of "property" to include a host of government-supplied benefits (welfare payments, public sector employment, public education) led the Court to seriously reconsider how much process the government must follow before depriving a person of it. *Id.* at 262. Concurrently, the Court began to reassess how it approached government deprivations of "liberty," a second interest protected by the Due Process Clauses. In doing so, it developed the modern approach to "procedural due process": the government must provide notice, a meaningful opportunity to be heard, and a decision made by a neutral decision-maker when depriving someone of their life, liberty, or property.

The following materials focus on four recurring issues courts face when applying the Due Process Clauses to agency adjudications: (1) what constitutes adequate notice; (2) what are the interests protected by due process; (3) to which procedural protections is the holder of a protected interest entitled; and (4) whether the decision-maker presiding over an agency adjudication is impartial (i.e., whether she was a neutral decision-maker). While difficult questions can certainly arise regarding fair notice and neutral decision-making, the courts' approach to them has been fairly consistent. The same cannot be said for how the Supreme Court has identified the interests due process protects, or for how it has identified the procedural protections owed to a due process rights holder. Accordingly, most of the materials that follow focus on these issues.

A. NOTICE

As the Supreme Court made clear in *Mullane v. Central Hanover Bank & Trust Co.* almost 70 years ago, "[a]n elementary and fundamental requirement of due process in any proceeding which is to be accorded finality is notice reasonably calculated, under all the circumstances, to apprise interested parties of the pendency of the action and afford them an opportunity to present their objections." 339 U.S. 306, 314 (1950) (internal citations omitted). There are temporal and substantive aspects to the notice required by due process. Temporally speaking, the defendant in federal or state court must be given sufficiently advanced warning of the allegations against it if it is to have any hope of mounting an adequate defense. Notice of a lawsuit does little good if received only minutes before being expected to present a responsive answer. Substantively speaking, notice to the defendant must be informative as well as timely. Simply telling the defendant that it is the target of some unspecified legal claim does nothing to help it understand the allegations to which it must formally object. In sum, "[t]he notice [given] must be of such nature as reasonably to convey the required information, and it must afford a reasonable time for those interested to make their appearance." *Id.* (internal citations omitted).

This idea—that a party subject to the government's adjudicative power is entitled to sufficiently timely and informative notice—has been incorporated into the administrative context through a combination of statutes and judicial decisions applying the Fifth and Fourteenth

Amendment Due Process Clauses. APA § 554(b), which applies to formal adjudications conducted by federal agencies, adopts the same protections deemed elemental by the *Mullane* Court. It directs agencies to inform "[p]ersons entitled to notice of an agency's hearing" of "the time, place, and nature of [that] hearing," the legal authority under which the hearing will be conducted, and "the matters of fact and law" that it will address. It also instructs agencies to pay "due regard" to the parties' convenience when setting hearing times and places. The provision is silent on some notice questions, such as who is entitled to notice and the precise amount of advanced warning sufficient to constitute "timely" notice. Congress left these context-driven problems for the agencies, who it believed could better resolve them on a case-by-case basis. *See* ATTORNEY GENERAL'S MANUAL at 46.

> **In Context**
>
> Congress does on occasion use organic statutes to mandate the timing of notices in administrative adjudications. For example, the Federal Trade Commission Act requires the Federal Trade Commission to provide at least 30 days' notice after serving a complaint in a cease and desist hearings. *See* 15 U.S.C. § 45(b).

With respect to the sufficiency of a notice's content, the courts have construed § 554(b) as adopting the requirements of the Due Process Clause and of the notice pleading standard applied in federal civil litigation. In other words, the notice must contain enough information to give its subject fair warning of both the conduct under adjudicative review and the law governing that conduct. *See, e.g., Wallaesa v. Federal Aviation Administration*, 824 F.3d 1071, 1083-84 (D.C. Cir. 2016), *citing Public Service Commission of Kentucky v. Federal Energy Regulatory Commission*, 397 F.3d 1004, 1012 (D.C. Cir. 2005) ("The Due Process Clause and the APA require that an agency setting a matter for hearing provide parties with adequate notice of the issues that would be considered, and ultimately resolved, at that hearing.") (internal quotation omitted). As one might expect, a finding of inadequate notice can lead a reviewing court to overturn the results of an administrative adjudication.

In contrast to the attention it pays to notice in formal adjudications, the APA is silent on the notice required in informal adjudications. This is not so surprising, since the APA says little about informal adjudication as a general matter. For the most part, Congress has left development of informal procedures to individual agencies. It is also the case that much of the business federal agencies conduct through informal adjudication is not adversarial in the traditional sense, as it involves neither in-person hearings nor opposing parties. It would therefore fit uncomfortably within the prior-warning model adopted by *Mullane* and § 554(b). As Example 1 on page 348 illustrates, an informal adjudication under the APA may involve government decision-making in the context of a particular government program or, as Example 2 illustrates, determination of an applicant's eligibility for government benefits in non-adversarial proceeding. While these proceedings may adversely affect interests held by members of the public, their purpose is not to determine the legal liability of private persons or entities. Accordingly, the need for proper notice to defendants that is so central to the traditional litigation model may not apply with the same force.

The more apt and closely related procedural protection in this context is that of "prompt notice" provided by APA § 555(e), which requires an agency to inform "interested person[s]" when it denies their "written application[s], petition[s], or other request[s]." While federal agencies cannot always provide prior notice of the actions they may take, they can certainly provide explanations for the actions they have taken or declined to take. The Supreme Court has made clear that such adjudicative reason-giving falls within the procedural protections guaranteed by the Fifth and Fourteenth Amendment Due Process Clauses, separate and apart from what the APA may require. *Cf. Goldberg v. Kelly*, 397 U.S. 254, 271 (1970) (noting that "the decisionmaker's conclusion as to a recipient's eligibility must rest solely on the legal rules and evidence adduced at the hearing," and "[t]o demonstrate compliance with this elementary requirement, the decision maker should state the reasons for his determination and indicate the evidence he relied on").

In any event, a critical due process protection that applies to all adjudications—formal and informal, state and federal, adversarial and non-adversarial—is so-called "fair notice." The case that follows—*General Electric Co. v. U.S. Environmental Protection Agency*—presents a typical fact pattern. Administrative agencies sometimes police conduct not clearly covered by the language of their regulations. This raises the "fair notice" issue: whether a regulated party could reasonably have known that an agency's regulations proscribed its actions. Stated interrogatively, when are agency rules so unclear that they fail adequately to warn a regulated party that its activities might be illegal? The fair notice doctrine finds its origins in criminal law. It was subsequently expanded to the civil context where a party would be subject to quasi-criminal penalties like heavy fines or other severe sanctions. The lower federal courts have since required fair notice in administrative adjudication as well, particularly where an agency imposes penalties so severe as to cause a possible property deprivation. The animating fairness concern here is that the agency may have used vague regulations to surreptitiously expand its enforcement powers. In other words, promulgating a vague regulation gives the agency the chance to "clarify" it during a future adjudication—to the surprise and detriment of regulated parties.

The Supreme Court has not weighed in on administrative fair notice, and the circuit courts have adopted varying approaches for addressing it. *See generally* Albert C. Lin, *Refining Fair Notice Doctrine: What Notice Is Required of Civil Regulations?*, 55 BAYLOR L. REV. 991 (2003). The case below presents the leading approach, developed by the D.C. Circuit. In studying the D.C. Circuit's reasoning, note the difference between two legal issues: whether the EPA properly interpreted its own regulations, and whether the EPA's regulations clearly indicated what they required of General Electric before it incurred a fine. Only the latter issue relates to fair notice; the former relates to the deference reviewing courts must give when agencies resolve ambiguities in the statutes they administer, a topic given detailed consideration in Chapter 9. After reading the case, can you succinctly explain the difference between these issues? Relatedly, why did the D.C. Circuit regard fair notice as a "due process" issue?

General Electric Co. v. U.S. Environmental Protection Agency
53 F.3d 1324 (D.C. Cir. 1995)

Before: WALD, SILBERMAN, and TATEL, Circuit Judges.

TATEL, Circuit Judge:

The Environmental Protection Agency fined the General Electric Company $25,000 after concluding that it had processed polychlorinated biphenyls in a manner not authorized under EPA's interpretation of its regulations. We conclude that EPA's interpretation of those regulations is permissible, but because the regulations did not provide GE with fair warning of the agency's interpretation, we vacate the finding of liability and set aside the fine.

I.

GE's Apparatus Service Shop in Chamblee, Georgia decommissioned large electric transformers. Inside these transformers was a "dielectric fluid" that contained high concentrations of polychlorinated biphenyls ("PCBs"), which are good conductors of electricity. PCBs are also dangerous pollutants. "[A]mong the most stable chemicals known," they are extremely persistent in the environment and have both acute and chronic effects on human health. Recognizing the dangers of PCBs, Congress has required their regulation under the Toxic Substances Control Act. 15 U.S.C. §§ 2601-29 (1988 & Supp. V 1993) ("TSCA"); *id.* at § 2605(e). Pursuant to TSCA, the EPA promulgated detailed regulations governing the manufacture, use, and disposal of PCBs. *See* 40 C.F.R. pt. 761 (1994).

Because GE's transformers were contaminated with PCBs, the company had to comply with the disposal requirements of 40 C.F.R. § 761.60. Section 761.60(b)(1) requires the disposal of transformers by either incinerating the transformer, 40 C.F.R. § 761.60(b)(1)(i)(A), or by placing it into a chemical waste landfill after the PCB-laced dielectric fluid has been drained and the transformer rinsed with a PCB solvent, *id.* at (B). GE chose the "drain-and-landfill" option of section 761.60(b)(1)(i)(B).

The drain-and-landfill alternative required GE to dispose of the liquid drained from the transformer "in accordance with" the terms of section 761.60(a). Since the dielectric fluid contained extremely high concentrations of PCBs, the relevant provision of section 761.60(a) was section (1), a catch-all section applicable to liquids contaminated with more than 500 parts per million ("ppm") of PCBs. This section required those disposing of these particularly dangerous materials to do so solely by incineration in an approved facility. 40 C.F.R. § 761.60(a). In accord with that requirement, GE incinerated the dielectric fluid after draining it from the transformers. It then soaked the transformers in a PCB solvent — in this case, freon — for 18 hours, drained the contaminated solvent, and immediately incinerated it as well.

In March, 1987, GE changed these procedures, beginning a process that ultimately led to the EPA complaint in this case. While GE continued to incinerate the dielectric fluid, it began a recycling process that recovered a portion of the dirty solvent through distillation. After soaking the transformer, GE poured the dirty solvent into a still that heated the freon, boiling off about 90% of it. The 10% of the liquid that was left, which was highly contaminated with presumably all the PCBs that had been rinsed from the transformer, was immediately incinerated. Meanwhile, the vapor from the still was cooled, recondensing into nearly pure liquid freon that contained less than the regulatory threshold of 50 ppm PCBs and, as an administrative law judge later found, probably less than the detectable level of 2 ppm. See General Electric Co., EPA Docket No. TSCA–IV–89–0016, 1992 TSCA LEXIS 2, at *69 (Feb. 7, 1992) [hereinafter ALJ Decision]. GE then used this recycled solvent to rinse other transformers.

GE and EPA agree that the regulations require the incineration of the solvent. They disagree about whether the intervening distillation and recycling process violated the regulations. EPA argues that section 761.60(b)(1)(i)(B) required GE to dispose of all the dirty solvent "in accordance with the requirements of [section 761.60(a)(1)]" — i.e., by immediate incineration. § 761.60(b)(1)(i)(B). GE did not think that section prohibited it from taking intermediate steps like distillation prior to incinerating the PCBs. To GE, distillation was permitted by section 761.20(c)(2), which allows the processing and distribution of PCBs "for purposes of disposal in accordance with the requirements of § 761.60." 40 C.F.R. § 761.20(c)(2). GE believed that this section authorized intermediate processing "for purposes of disposal" — processing such as distillation — as long as it complied with the other requirements of the PCB regulations like those relating to the management of spills, storage, and labelling of PCB materials. EPA has not alleged that GE's distillation process failed to comply with those requirements. In fact, as the ALJ later concluded, distillation reduced the amount of contaminated materials, thus producing environmental benefits. See ALJ Decision, 1992 TSCA LEXIS 2, at *73.

Despite those benefits, EPA charged the company with violating the PCB disposal regulations. After a hearing, an ALJ agreed and assessed a $25,000 fine. On appeal, the Environmental Appeals Board modified the ALJ's reasoning, but agreed with the disposition of the complaint and upheld the $25,000 penalty. *See* General Electric Co., TSCA Appeal No. 92-2a, 1993 TSCA LEXIS 265 (Envtl. App. Bd., Nov. 1, 1993). In other proceedings, the agency found the company liable for distillation it performed in six other locations, but suspended the fines for those violations pending the outcome of this appeal.

II.

[In this part of the court's opinion, it upheld the EPA's interpretation of its regulations. The court said it would find the EPA's interpretation permissible unless it is plainly wrong, even if that interpretation "diverge[d] significantly from what a first-time reader of the regulations might conclude was the 'best' interpretation of their language." Indeed, the court said it would defer to the agency even where "the agency's reading of the statute would not be obvious to the most astute reader." The court went on to clarify that "this case would be over" if the EPA only required GE to *comply* with its interpretation. However, EPA's decision to *fine* GE raised due process concerns that required separate consideration.]

III.

Due process requires that parties receive fair notice before being deprived of property. *See Mullane v. Central Hanover Bank & Trust Co.*, 339 U.S. 306, 314 (1950). The due process clause thus "prevents . . . deference from validating the application of a regulation that fails to give fair warning of the conduct it prohibits or requires." *Gates & Fox Co. v. OSHRC*, 790 F.2d 154, 156 (D.C. Cir. 1986). In the absence of notice—for example, where the regulation is not sufficiently clear to warn a party about what is expected of it—an agency may not deprive a party of property by imposing civil or criminal liability. Of course, it is in the context of criminal liability that this "no punishment without notice" rule is most commonly applied. *See, e.g., United States v. National Dairy Corp.*, 372 U.S. 29, 32-33 (1963) ("[C]riminal responsibility should not attach where one could not reasonably understand that his contemplated conduct is proscribed."). But as long ago as 1968, we recognized this "fair notice" requirement in the civil administrative context. In *Radio Athens, Inc. v. FCC*, we held that when sanctions are drastic—in that case, the FCC dismissed the petitioner's application for a radio station license—"elementary fairness compels clarity" in the statements and regulations setting forth the actions with which the agency expects the public to comply. 401 F.2d 398, 404 (D.C. Cir. 1968). This requirement has now been thoroughly "incorporated into administrative law." *Satellite Broadcasting Co. v. FCC,* 824 F.2d 1, 3 (D.C. Cir. 1987).

Although the agency must always provide "fair notice" of its regulatory interpretations to the regulated public, in many cases the agency's pre-enforcement efforts to bring about compliance will provide adequate notice. If, for example, an agency informs a regulated party that it must seek a permit for a particular process, but the party begins processing without seeking a permit, the agency's pre-violation contact with the regulated party has provided notice, and we will enforce a finding of liability as long as the agency's interpretation was permissible. In some cases, however, the agency will provide no pre-enforcement warning, effectively deciding "to use a citation [or other punishment] as the initial means for announcing a particular interpretation"—or for making its interpretation clear. *E.g. Martin v. OSHRC,* 499 U.S. 144, 158 (1991) (noting that such a decision may raise a question about "the adequacy of notice to regulated parties"). This, GE claims, is what happened here. In such cases, we must ask whether the regulated party received, or should have received, notice of the agency's interpretation in the most obvious way of all: by reading the regulations. If, by reviewing the regulations and other public statements issued by the agency, a regulated party acting in good faith would be able to identify, with "ascertainable certainty," the standards with which the agency expects parties to conform, then the agency has fairly notified a petitioner of the agency's interpretation. . . .

. . . GE has clearly raised the due process "notice" issue in this case. Although we defer to EPA's interpretation regarding distillation because it is "logically consistent with the language of the regulation[s]," [*Rollins Environmental Services, Inc. v. EPA,* 937 F.2d 649, 652 (D.C. Cir. 1991)], we must, because the agency imposed a fine, nonetheless determine whether that interpretation is "ascertainably certain" from the regulations. As in *Gates & Fox* and *Satellite Broadcasting,* we conclude that the interpretation is so far from a reasonable person's understanding of the regulations that they could not have fairly informed GE of the agency's perspective. We therefore reverse the agency's finding of liability and the related fine.

On their face, the regulations reveal no rule or combination of rules providing fair notice that they prohibit pre-disposal processes such as distillation. To begin with, such notice would be provided only if it was "reasonably comprehensible to people of good faith" that distillation is indeed a means of "disposal." *McElroy Electronics Corp. v. FCC,* 990 F.2d 1351, 1358 (D.C. Cir. 1993) (internal punctuation, citations, and emphasis omitted). While EPA can permissibly conclude, given the sweeping regulatory definition of "disposal," that distillation is a means of disposal, such a characterization nonetheless strays far from the common understanding of the word's meaning. *Cf. American Mining Congress v. EPA,* 824 F.2d 1177, 1184 (D.C. Cir. 1987) (noting that the plain meaning of the term "discarded" was "disposed of," "thrown away," or "abandoned"). A person "of good faith," *McElroy,*

990 F.2d at 1358, would not reasonably expect distillation—a process which did not and was not intended to prevent the ultimate destruction of PCBs—to be barred as an unapproved means of "disposal."

Not only do the regulations fail clearly to bar distillation, they apparently permit it. Section 761.20(c)(2) permits processing and distribution of PCBs "for purposes of disposal." This language would seem to allow parties to conduct certain pre-disposal processes without authorization as long as they facilitate the ultimate disposal of PCBs and are done "in compliance with the requirements of this Part"—i.e., in accordance with other relevant regulations governing the handling, labelling, and transportation of PCBs. § 761.20(c)(2). EPA argues—permissibly, as we concluded above—that the section allows parties to "use" PCBs in the described manner, but that those uses must still comply with the disposal requirements of section 761.60, including the requirement that unauthorized methods of disposal receive a disposal permit from the agency. This permissible interpretation, however, is by no means the most obvious interpretation of the regulation, particularly since, under EPA's view, section 761.20(c)(2) would not need to exist at all. If every process "for purposes of disposal" also requires a disposal permit, section 761.20(c)(2) does nothing but lull regulated parties into a false sense of security by hinting that their processing "for purposes of disposal" is authorized. While the mere presence of such a regulatory trap does not reflect an irrational agency interpretation, it obscures the agency's interpretation of the regulations sufficiently to convince us that GE did not have fair notice that distillation was prohibited.

GE points out that if section 761.20(c)(2) is applied as EPA interprets it, the regulations apparently would not authorize, on their face, any steps between the draining of the fluid and its incineration even though such steps are clearly necessary. Drained fluids, for example, must be stored and transported to the incinerator. According to GE, section 761.20(c)(2) provides explicit permission for these pre-disposal processes, while under EPA's view, such incidental processes would require permits. But the agency has never imposed such a broad permit requirement on this type of intermediate PCB "processing." To avoid this inconsistency, the agency argues that while storage, transportation, and other "processing steps that are truly incidental and necessary to the disposal methods prescribed by the regulations" do require authorization other than that in section 761.20(c)(2), authorization for such steps is nonetheless "implicit" in section 761.60's disposal regulations. Government Brief at 27. Although this reading is certainly permissible, the agency presents it for the first time in this appeal, and it represents a further stretching of the regulations, reinforcing our conclusion that GE did not have fair notice of the agency's interpretation. Indeed, the agency itself has recognized that its interpretation of section 761.20(c)(2) is not apparent. It has recently proposed new regulations that would make this implicit waiver for incidental pre-disposal processing explicit by "clarifying" section 761.20(c)(2).

The location in which EPA has proposed to codify these new regulations adds to our concern about the clarity of the present ones. The new regulations apply to section 761.20(c)(2), and are intended, according to the agency, to "clarify[] how [§ 761.20(c)(2)] applies to the disposal of all PCBs." 59 Fed. Reg. at 62802 (emphasis added). To us, this seems to contradict EPA's assertion here that section 761.20(c)(2) does not apply to disposal of PCBs, but only to their use. If, as the agency asserts, section 761.20(c)(2) merely authorizes the "use" of pre-disposal activities, and that it is section 761.60 which "implicitly" permits incidental processing, then the agency should have added the recent language making that permission explicit to section 761.60, not to section 761.20(c)(2). By "clarifying" that section 761.20(c)(2) fully authorizes incidental pre-disposal activities, EPA lends support to GE's argument that, prior to the amendments, section 761.20(c)(2) fully authorized all pre-disposal processing "for purposes of disposal," and that the company could not therefore have been on notice of the agency's contrary interpretation. . . .

We thus conclude that EPA did not provide GE with fair warning of its interpretation of the regulations. Where, as here, the regulations and other policy statements are unclear, where the petitioner's interpretation is reasonable, and where the agency itself struggles to provide a definitive reading of the regulatory requirements, a regulated party is not "on notice" of the agency's ultimate interpretation of the regulations, and may not be punished. EPA thus may not hold GE responsible in any way — either financially or in future enforcement proceedings — for the actions charged in this case. Although we conclude that EPA's interpretation of the regulations is permissible, we grant the petition for review, vacate the agency's finding of liability, and remand for further proceedings consistent with this opinion.

So ordered.

QUESTION SET 7.1

Review & Synthesis

1. State the test the D.C. Circuit adopted for determining whether an agency regulation fails to provide the "fair notice" required by due process. Did the EPA's regulations pass or fail that test?

2. Is it not the case that *every* ambiguous statute or regulation poses a notice problem of the kind addressed in *General Electric*? By definition, an ambiguous rule is susceptible to more than a single reasonable interpretation.

A. Notice   **419**

Accordingly, regulated entities seeking to comply with it may not know what the rule requires of them prior to clarification by the agency. Do you understand the D.C. Circuit as adopting a bright-line rule that all ambiguous statutes fail to provide the "fair notice" due process requires? Also, isn't the fair notice issue here replicated any time a common law court applies a rule in the case that creates it? Why is that not a due process violation?

Application & Analysis

1. The Federal Communications Commission ("FCC") is empowered to consider and grant applications from radio stations to use certain frequencies. As part of that power, the FCC was charged with allocating certain "fixed microwave service channels" ("FMSCs") in the Chicago and Sacramento areas. The FCC solicited applications from interested companies and received numerous applications, including an application that the Satellite Broadcasting Company ("SBC") sent to the FCC's Washington, D.C. office. The FCC held two lotteries to rank the order of the competing applicants and SBC won both lotteries.

   The FCC promulgated rules about how applicants were supposed to submit applications for radio channels, but it never clearly indicated where to send applications for FMSCs. This left applicants to determine which of two FCC rules controlled. Section 1.912 of the FCC rules directed that all applications, with only several exceptions that did not include FMSCs, be filed with the FCC's Gettysburg office. Section 1.972 of the FCC's rules, which specifically covered applications for FMSCs, said that applications should be filed according to the rules and policies established in Section 94.25 for FMSCs. Section 94.25 explained that all correspondence related to FMSCs should be submitted to the FCC's Washington office. Faced with this conflict between Section 1.912 and Section 94.25, SBC's counsel determined that its applications had to be sent to the Washington office in accordance with 94.25. The company submitted a complete application before the submission deadline.

   After SBC won the lotteries, FCC staff attorneys reviewed the application process and interpreted the agency's rules as requiring that FMSC applications be sent to the Gettysburg office. The FCC thus dismissed SBC's applications as untimely filed because they were first sent to Washington before being forwarded to Gettysburg. SBC now challenges the agency's decision, arguing it denied the company due process because the FCC failed to give fair notice of the FCC filing requirements. Analyze the merits of SBC's claim.

B. THE INTERESTS PROTECTED BY DUE PROCESS

Beginning in the 1960s, and as discussed in the historical overview provided in Chapter 1, the Supreme Court extended judicial protections to the government-provided entitlements Professor Charles A. Reich famously dubbed "the new property." "For a large number of people, government is a direct source of income although they hold no public job. Their eligibility arises from legal status. Examples are Social Security benefits, unemployment compensation, aid to dependent children, veterans benefits, and the whole scheme of state and local welfare." *See* Charles A. Reich, *The New Property*, 73 YALE L.J. 733, 734 (1964). This reflected a considerable shift in the federal government's relationship with the People, which had largely been limited to regulation of private conduct: investigations, enforcement actions, sanctions, and similar administrative activities. The emergence of the new property also triggered the emergence of the Supreme Court's "procedural due process" jurisprudence. Whereas government entitlements had previously been treated as mere privileges the government could rescind in its discretion, the Supreme Court came to view them as legislatively conferred property interests protected by the Fifth and Fourteenth Amendments. Before the government could take them away—before the government could "deprive" the recipient of them—it had to provide minimal procedural protections established by the Constitution.

During the same period, the Court also explored the contours of the "liberty" interests protected by the Fifth and Fourteenth Amendment Due Process Clauses. Like the property interest, the government's conduct could infringe on one's liberty and thus rights holders were owed certain procedural protections. The jurisprudential challenge was defining the scope and source of the interests liberty embodies. How do they differ from property interests? Is "liberty," like welfare payments or a job as a police officer, something that exists only if the government first provides it? Is it instead "pre-governmental" in the sense that it does not depend on legislative action for its existence? How many such liberty interests are there? How direct an effect must the government's conduct on them be before constitutional protections are triggered?

The materials that follow address how courts identify the presence or absence of property and liberty interests. As you read through the cases, pay particular attention to the sources of the rights claimed. Do they come from the Constitution? From federal or state statutes? From federal or state common law? In determining whether the claimants have a procedural due process right, does it matter where the underlying property or liberty interest comes from? Also pay attention to how property and liberty interests are described by the courts. Are they interests that must (or even can) be created by the government, or are they brought into being by some other means? Can someone have a property or liberty interest in *someone else's* status or circumstances? Must the decision to provide procedures to protect these interests—whatever their number and sources—be balanced against other considerations?

Goldberg v. Kelly
397 U.S. 254 (1970).

Mr. Justice BRENNAN delivered the opinion of the Court.

The question for decision is whether a State that terminates public assistance payments to a particular recipient without affording him the opportunity for an evidentiary hearing prior to termination denies the recipient procedural due process in violation of the Due Process Clause of the Fourteenth Amendment.

This action was brought in the District Court for the Southern District of New York by residents of New York City receiving financial aid under the federally assisted program of Aid to Families with Dependent Children (AFDC) or under New York State's general Home Relief program.[1] Their complaint alleged that the New York State and New York City officials administering these programs terminated, or were about to terminate, such aid without prior notice and hearing, thereby denying them due process of law.[2] At the time the suits were filed there was no requirement of prior notice or hearing of any kind before termination of financial aid. However, the State and city adopted procedures for notice and hearing after the suits were brought, and

> **In Context**
>
> Pursuant to the Personal Responsibility and Work Opportunity Reconciliation Act of 1996, Congress replaced AFDC with the Temporary Assistance for Needy Families ("TANF") program. States have been primarily responsible for implementing both AFDC and TANF. Unlike AFDC, however, TANF imposes lifetime limits on recipient benefits and requires that recipients engage in work activities as a condition of receiving benefits. Additionally, TANF is partially funded through fixed federal block grants to states, whereas the federal government paid a percentage of states' AFDC costs. TANF is currently administered by the Office of Family Assistance of the Administration for Children and Families within the Department of Health and Human Services.

---

[1] AFDC was established by the Social Security Act of 1935, 49 Stat. 627, as amended, 42 U.S.C. §§ 601-610 (1964 ed. and Supp. IV). It is a categorical assistance program supported by federal grants-in-aid but administered by the States according to regulations of the Secretary of Health, Education, and Welfare. *See* N.Y. Social Welfare Law §§ 343-362 (1966). . . . Home Relief is a general assistance program financed and administered solely by New York state and local governments. N.Y. Social Welfare Law §§ 157-165 (1966), since July 1, 1967, Social Services Law §§ 157-166. It assists any person unable to support himself or to secure support from other sources. *Id.* § 158.

[2] Two suits were brought and consolidated in the District Court. The named plaintiffs were 20 in number, including intervenors. Fourteen had been or were about to be cut off from AFDC, and six from Home Relief. During the course of this litigation most, though not all, of the plaintiffs either received a "fair hearing" or were restored to the rolls without a hearing. However, even in many of the cases where payments have been resumed, the underlying questions of eligibility that resulted in the bringing of this suit have not been resolved. . . .

the plaintiffs, appellees here, then challenged the constitutional adequacy of those procedures.

The State Commissioner of Social Services amended the State Department of Social Services' Official Regulations to require that local social services officials proposing to discontinue or suspend a recipient's financial aid do so according to a procedure that conforms to either subdivision (a) or subdivision (b) of § 351.26 of the regulations as amended. The City of New York elected to promulgate a local procedure according to subdivision (b). That subdivision, so far as here pertinent, provides that the local procedure must include the giving of notice to the recipient of the reasons for a proposed discontinuance or suspension at least seven days prior to its effective date, with notice also that upon request the recipient may have the proposal reviewed by a local welfare official holding a position superior to that of the supervisor who approved the proposed discontinuance or suspension, and, further, that the recipient may submit, for purposes of the review, a written statement to demonstrate why his grant should not be discontinued or suspended. The decision by the reviewing official whether to discontinue or suspend aid must be made expeditiously, with written notice of the decision to the recipient. The section further expressly provides that "(a)ssistance shall not be discontinued or suspended prior to the date such notice of decision is sent to the recipient and his representative, if any, or prior to the proposed effective date of discontinuance or suspension, whichever occurs later."

Pursuant to subdivision (b), the New York City Department of Social Services promulgated Procedure No. 68-18. A caseworker who has doubts about the recipient's continued eligibility must first discuss them with the recipient. If the caseworker concludes that the recipient is no longer eligible, he recommends termination of aid to a unit supervisor. If the latter concurs, he sends the recipient a letter stating the reasons for proposing to terminate aid and notifying him that within seven days he may request that a higher official review the record, and may support the request with a written statement prepared personally or with the aid of an attorney or other person. If the reviewing official affirms the determination of ineligibility, aid is stopped immediately and the recipient is informed by letter of the reasons for the action. Appellees' challenge to this procedure emphasizes the absence of any provisions for the personal appearance of the recipient before the reviewing official, for oral presentation of evidence, and for confrontation and cross-examination of adverse witnesses. However, the letter does inform the recipient that he may request a post-termination "fair hearing." This is a proceeding before an independent state hearing officer at which the recipient may appear personally, offer oral evidence, confront and cross-examine the witnesses against him, and have a record made of the hearing. If the recipient prevails at the "fair hearing" he is paid all funds erroneously withheld. A recipient whose aid is not restored by a "fair hearing" decision may have judicial review. The recipient is so notified.

I. . . .

Appellant does not contend that procedural due process is not applicable to the termination of welfare benefits. Such benefits are a matter of statutory entitlement for persons qualified to receive them.[8] Their termination involves state action that adjudicates important rights. The constitutional challenge cannot be answered by an argument that public assistance benefits are "a 'privilege' and not a 'right.'" *Shapiro v. Thompson*, 394 U.S. 618, 627 note 6 (1969). Relevant constitutional restraints apply as much to the withdrawal of public assistance benefits as to disqualification for unemployment compensation, *Sherbert v. Verner*, 374 U.S. 398 (1963); or to denial of a tax exemption, *Speiser v. Randall*, 357 U.S. 513 (1958); or to discharge from public employment, *Slochower v. Board of Higher Education*, 350 U.S. 551 (1956). The extent to which procedural due process must be afforded the recipient is influenced by the extent to which he may be "condemned to suffer grievous loss," *Joint Anti-Fascist Refugee Committee v. McGrath*, 341 U.S. 123, 168 (1951) (Frankfurter, J., concurring), and depends upon whether the recipient's interest in avoiding that loss outweighs the governmental interest in summary adjudication. Accordingly, as we said in *Cafeteria & Restaurant Workers Union, etc. v. McElroy*, 367 U.S. 886, 895 (1961), "consideration of what procedures due process may require under any given set of circumstances must begin with a determination of the precise nature of the government function involved as well as of the private interest that has been affected by governmental action."

It is true, of course, that some governmental benefits may be administratively terminated without affording the recipient a pre-termination evidentiary hearing. But we agree with the District Court that when welfare is discontinued, only a pre-termination evidentiary hearing provides the recipient with procedural due process. For qualified recipients, welfare provides the means to obtain essential food, clothing, housing, and medical care. Thus the crucial factor in this context—a factor not present in the case of the blacklisted government contractor, the discharged government employee,

---

[8] It may be realistic today to regard welfare entitlements as more like "property" than a "gratuity." Much of the existing wealth in this country takes the form of rights that do not fall within traditional common-law concepts of property. It has been aptly noted that

> [S]ociety today is built around entitlement. The automobile dealer has his franchise, the doctor and lawyer their professional licenses, the worker his union membership, contract, and pension rights, the executive his contract and stock options; all are devices to aid security and independence. Many of the most important of these entitlements now flow from government: subsidies to farmers and businessmen, routes for airlines and channels for television stations; long term contracts for defense, space, and education; social security pensions for individuals. Such sources of security, whether private or public, are no longer regarded as luxuries or gratuities; to the recipients they are essentials, fully deserved, and in no sense a form of charity. It is only the poor whose entitlements, although recognized by public policy, have not been effectively enforced.

Charles A. Reich, *Individual Rights and Social Welfare: The Emerging Legal Issues*, 74 Yale L.J. 1245, 1255 (1965). *See also* Charles A. Reich, *The New Property*, 73 Yale L.J. 733 (1964).

the taxpayer denied a tax exemption, or virtually anyone else whose governmental entitlements are ended—is that termination of aid pending resolution of a controversy over eligibility may deprive an *eligible* recipient of the very means by which to live while he waits. Since he lacks independent resources, his situation becomes immediately desperate. His need to concentrate upon finding the means for daily subsistence, in turn, adversely affects his ability to seek redress from the welfare bureaucracy.

Moreover, important governmental interests are promoted by affording recipients a pre-termination evidentiary hearing. From its founding the Nation's basic commitment has been to foster the dignity and well-being of all persons within its borders. We have come to recognize that forces not within the control of the poor contribute to their poverty. This perception, against the background of our traditions, has significantly influenced the development of the contemporary public assistance system. Welfare, by meeting the basic demands of subsistence, can help bring within the reach of the poor the same opportunities that are available to others to participate meaningfully in the life of the community. At the same time, welfare guards against the societal malaise that may flow from a widespread sense of unjustified frustration and insecurity. Public assistance, then, is not mere charity, but a means to "promote the general Welfare, and secure the Blessings of Liberty to ourselves and our Posterity." The same governmental interests that counsel the provision of welfare, counsel as well its uninterrupted provision to those eligible to receive it; pre-termination evidentiary hearings are indispensable to that end.

Appellant does not challenge the force of these considerations but argues that they are outweighed by countervailing governmental interests in conserving fiscal and administrative resources. These interests, the argument goes, justify the delay of any evidentiary hearing until after discontinuance of the grants. Summary adjudication protects the public fisc by stopping payments promptly upon discovery of reason to believe that a recipient is no longer eligible. Since most terminations are accepted without challenge, summary adjudication also conserves both the fisc and administrative time and energy by reducing the number of evidentiary hearings actually held.

We agree with the District Court, however, that these governmental interests are not overriding in the welfare context. The requirement of a prior hearing doubtless involves some greater expense, and the benefits paid to ineligible recipients pending decision at the hearing probably cannot be recouped, since these recipients are likely to be judgment-proof. But the State is not without weapons to minimize these increased costs. Much of the drain on fiscal and administrative resources can be reduced by developing procedures for prompt pre-termination hearings and by skillful use of personnel and facilities. Indeed, the very provision for a post-termination evidentiary hearing in New York's Home Relief program is itself cogent evidence that the State recognizes the primacy of the public interest in correct eligibility determinations and therefore in the provision of procedural safeguards.

Thus, the interest of the eligible recipient in uninterrupted receipt of public assistance, coupled with the State's interest that his payments not be erroneously terminated, clearly outweighs the State's competing concern to prevent any increase in its fiscal and administrative burdens. As the District Court correctly concluded, "(t)he stakes are simply too high for the welfare recipient, and the possibility for honest error or irritable misjudgment too great, to allow termination of aid without giving the recipient a chance, if he so desires, to be fully informed of the case against him so that he may contest its basis and produce evidence in rebuttal." 294 F. Supp., at 904-905.

II

We also agree with the District Court, however, that the pre-termination hearing need not take the form of a judicial or quasi-judicial trial. We bear in mind that the statutory "fair hearing" will provide the recipient with a full administrative review.[14] Accordingly, the pre-termination hearing has one function only: to produce an initial determination of the validity of the welfare department's grounds for discontinuance of payments in order to protect a recipient against an erroneous termination of his benefits. Thus, a complete record and a comprehensive opinion, which would serve primarily to facilitate judicial review and to guide future decisions, need not be provided at the pre-termination stage. We recognize, too, that both welfare authorities and recipients have an interest in relatively speedy resolution of questions of eligibility, that they are used to dealing with one another informally, and that some welfare departments have very burdensome caseloads. These considerations justify the limitation of the pre-termination hearing to minimum procedural safeguards, adapted to the particular characteristics of welfare recipients, and to the limited nature of the controversies to be resolved. We wish to add that we, no less than the dissenters, recognize the importance of not imposing upon the States or the Federal Government in this developing field of law any procedural requirements beyond those demanded by rudimentary due process.

"The fundamental requisite of due process of law is the opportunity to be heard." *Grannis v. Ordean*, 234 U.S. 385, 394 (1914). The hearing must be "at a meaningful time and in a meaningful manner." *Armstrong v. Manzo*, 380 U.S. 545, 552 (1965). In the present context these principles require that a recipient have timely and adequate notice detailing the reasons for a proposed termination, and an effective opportunity to defend by confronting any adverse witnesses and by presenting his own arguments and evidence orally. These rights are important in cases such as those before us, where recipients have challenged proposed terminations as resting on incorrect or

---

[14] Due process does not, of course, require two hearings. If, for example, a State simply wishes to continue benefits until after a "fair" hearing there will be no need for a preliminary hearing.

misleading factual premises or on misapplication of rules or policies to the facts of particular cases.

We are not prepared to say that the seven-day notice currently provided by New York City is constitutionally insufficient *per se*, although there may be cases where fairness would require that a longer time be given. Nor do we see any constitutional deficiency in the content or form of the notice. New York employs both a letter and a personal conference with a caseworker to inform a recipient of the precise questions raised about his continued eligibility. Evidently the recipient is told the legal and factual bases for the Department's doubts. This combination is probably the most effective method of communicating with recipients.

The city's procedures presently do not permit recipients to appear personally with or without counsel before the official who finally determines continued eligibility. Thus a recipient is not permitted to present evidence to that official orally, or to confront or cross-examine adverse witnesses. These omissions are fatal to the constitutional adequacy of the procedures.

The opportunity to be heard must be tailored to the capacities and circumstances of those who are to be heard. It is not enough that a welfare recipient may present his position to the decision maker in writing or second-hand through his caseworker. Written submissions are an unrealistic option for most recipients, who lack the educational attainment necessary to write effectively and who cannot obtain professional assistance. Moreover, written submissions do not afford the flexibility of oral presentations; they do not permit the recipient to mold his argument to the issues the decision maker appears to regard as important. Particularly where credibility and veracity are at issue, as they must be in many termination proceedings, written submissions are a wholly unsatisfactory basis for decision. The second-hand presentation to the decisionmaker by the caseworker has its own deficiencies; since the caseworker usually gathers the facts upon which the charge of ineligibility rests, the presentation of the recipient's side of the controversy cannot safely be left to him. Therefore a recipient must be allowed to state his position orally. Informal procedures will suffice; in this context due process does not require a particular order of proof or mode of offering evidence.

In almost every setting where important decisions turn on questions of fact, due process requires an opportunity to confront and cross-examine adverse witnesses. . . .

Welfare recipients must therefore be given an opportunity to confront and cross-examine the witnesses relied on by the department.

"The right to be heard would be, in many cases, of little avail if it did not comprehend the right to be heard by counsel." *Powell v. Alabama*, 287 U.S. 45, 68-69 (1932). We do not say that counsel must be provided at the pretermination hearing, but only that the recipient must be allowed to retain an attorney if he so desires. Counsel can help delineate the issues, present the factual contentions in an orderly manner, conduct cross-examination, and generally safeguard the interests of the recipient. We do not anticipate that this assistance will unduly prolong or otherwise encumber the hearing. Evidently [the Department of Health, Education, and Welfare] has reached the same conclusion. *See* 45 CFR § 205.10, 34 Fed. Reg. 1144 (1969); 45 CFR § 220.25, 34 Fed. Reg. 13595 (1969).

Finally, the decisionmaker's conclusion as to a recipient's eligibility must rest solely on the legal rules and evidence adduced at the hearing. *Ohio Bell Tel. Co. v. PUC*, 301 U.S. 292 (1937); *United States v. Abilene & S.R. Co.*, 265 U.S. 274, 288-289 (1924). To demonstrate compliance with this elementary requirement, the decision maker should state the reasons for his determination and indicate the evidence he relied on, though his statement need not amount to a full opinion or even formal findings of fact and conclusions of law. And, of course, an impartial decision maker is essential. *Cf. In re Murchison*, 349 U.S. 133 (1955); *Wong Yang Sung v. McGrath*, 339 U.S. 33, 45-46 (1950). We agree with the District Court that prior involvement in some aspects of a case will not necessarily bar a welfare official from acting as a decision maker. He should not, however, have participated in making the determination under review.

Affirmed.

Mr. Justice BLACK, dissenting. . . .

Representatives of the people of the Thirteen Original Colonies spent long, hot months in the summer of 1787 in Philadelphia, Pennsylvania, creating a government of limited powers. They divided it into three departments—Legislative, Judicial, and Executive. The Judicial Department was to have no part whatever in making any laws. In fact proposals looking to vesting some power in the Judiciary to take part in the legislative process and veto laws were offered, considered, and rejected by the Constitutional Convention. In my judgment there is not one word, phrase, or sentence from the beginning to the end of the Constitution from which it can be inferred that judges were granted any such legislative power. True, *Marbury v. Madison*, [5 U.S. (1 Cranch) 137 (1803)], held, and properly, I think, that courts must be the final interpreters of the Constitution, and I recognize that the holding can provide an opportunity to slide imperceptibly into constitutional amendment and law making. But when federal judges use this judicial power for legislative purposes, I think they wander out of their field of vested powers and transgress into the area constitutionally assigned to the

> **In Context**
> The Department of Health, Education, and Welfare ("HEW"), created by a 1953 reorganization plan adopted by President Dwight D. Eisenhower, was the first new cabinet-level department since the Department of Labor's creation in 1913. HEW's subdivisions included the Public Health Service, the Office of Education, the Food and Drug Administration, and the Social Security Administration. In 1979, HEW was divided into two cabinet-level departments, the Department of Health and Human Services ("HHS") and the Department of Education. HHS retained control over the Social Security Administration until Congress established it as an executive independent agency in 1995.

Congress and the people. That is precisely what I believe the Court is doing in this case. . . .

The more than a million names on the relief rolls in New York, and the more than nine million names on the rolls of all the 50 States were not put there at random. The names are there because state welfare officials believed that those people were eligible for assistance. Probably in the officials' haste to make out the lists many names were put there erroneously in order to alleviate immediate suffering, and undoubtedly some people are drawing relief who are not entitled under the law to do so. Doubtless some draw relief checks from time to time who know they are not eligible, either because they are not actually in need or for some other reason. Many of those who thus draw undeserved gratuities are without sufficient property to enable the government to collect back from them any money they wrongfully receive. But the Court today holds that it would violate the Due Process Clause of the Fourteenth Amendment to stop paying those people weekly or monthly allowances unless the government first affords them a full "evidentiary hearing" even though welfare officials are persuaded that the recipients are not rightfully entitled to receive a penny under the law. In other words, although some recipients might be on the lists for payment wholly because of deliberate fraud on their part, the Court holds that the government is helpless and must continue, until after an evidentiary hearing, to pay money that it does not owe, never has owed, and never could owe. I do not believe there is any provision in our Constitution that should thus paralyze the government's efforts to protect itself against making payments to people who are not entitled to them. . . .

I would have little, if any, objection to the majority's decision in this case if it were written as the report of the House Committee on Education and Labor, but as an opinion ostensibly resting on the language of the Constitution I find it woefully deficient. Once the verbiage is pared away it is obvious that this Court today adopts the views of the District Court "that to cut off a welfare recipient in the face of . . . brutal need' without a prior hearing of some sort is unconscionable," and therefore, says the Court, unconstitutional. The majority reaches this result by a process of weighing "the recipient's interest in avoiding" the termination of welfare benefits against "the governmental interest in summary adjudication." Today's balancing act requires a "pre-termination evidentiary hearing," yet there is nothing that indicates what tomorrow's balance will be. Although the majority attempts to bolster its decision with limited quotations from prior cases, it is obvious that today's result doesn't depend on the language of the Constitution itself or the principles of other decisions, but solely on the collective judgment of the majority as to what would be a fair and humane procedure in this case. . . .

The Court apparently feels that this decision will benefit the poor and needy. In my judgment the eventual result will be just the opposite. While today's decision requires only an administrative, evidentiary hearing, the inevitable logic of the approach taken will lead to constitutionally imposed, time-consuming delays of a full adversary process of administrative and judicial review. In the next case the welfare recipients are bound to argue that cutting off benefits before judicial review of the agency's decision is also a denial of due process. Since, by hypothesis, termination of aid at that point may still "deprive an eligible recipient of the very means by which to live while he waits," I would be surprised if the weighing process did not compel the conclusion that termination without full judicial review would be unconscionable. After all, at each step, as the majority seems to feel, the issue is only one of weighing the government's pocketbook against the actual survival of the recipient, and surely that balance must always tip in favor of the individual. Similarly today's decision requires only the opportunity to have the benefit of counsel at the administrative hearing, but it is difficult to believe that the same reasoning process would not require the appointment of counsel, for otherwise the right to counsel is a meaningless one since these people are too poor to hire their own advocates. *Cf. Gideon v. Wainwright,* 372 U.S. 335, 344 (1963). Thus the end result of today's decision may well be that the government, once it decides to give welfare benefits, cannot reverse that decision until the recipient has had the benefits of full administrative and judicial review, including, of course, the opportunity to present his case to this Court. Since this process will usually entail a delay of several years, the inevitable result of such a constitutionally imposed burden will be that the government will not put a claimant on the rolls initially until it has made an exhaustive investigation to determine his eligibility. While this Court will perhaps have insured that no needy person will be taken off the rolls without a full "due process" proceeding, it will also have insured that many will never get on the rolls, or at least that they will remain destitute during the lengthy proceedings followed to determine initial eligibility.

For the foregoing reasons I dissent from the Court's holding. . . .

QUESTION SET 7.2

Review & Synthesis

1. Define the concept of "procedural due process" and explain why it is applicable to the claims raised in this case.

2. Retrace the procedural steps the New York City Department of Social Services took before terminating a recipient's benefits under the Aid to Families with Dependent Children and Home Relief programs. What, precisely, did the Court find constitutionally deficient about this process?

3. Justice Brennan developed a balancing test for determining whether a benefits recipient is entitled to an in-person hearing before the government can terminate her benefits. Balancing tests generally require (1) identification of relevant facts or considerations, (2) a way of measuring them, and (3) a method by which to consistently compare those measurements. What did Justice Brennan say about each of these three test elements? What was Justice Black's concern with respect to the third element?

4. Did Justice Brennan seem concerned about the decisional error rate in New York City's welfare termination decisions? In other words, did he point to any evidence that its caseworkers were generating an unacceptably high number of "false negatives," people who were eligible but had their benefits stripped anyway? Assume a study reported that New York City's procedures (pre-*Goldberg*) resulted in few eligible recipients being denied benefits. Why or why shouldn't such a finding factor into whether New York City was ordered to provide an in-person pre-deprivation hearing?

5. What legal point was Justice Black making when he remarked that the majority opinion read like it "were written as the report of the House Committee on Education and Labor"? How did this connect to his description of the Constitutional Convention?

6. How far do you think the Court's decision in *Goldberg* reaches? For example, do you think it would entitle a benefits *applicant* to a pre-*rejection* hearing? Why or why not?

7. As indicated in the In Context box on page 421, Congress replaced the AFDC program in 1996 with the Temporary Assistance for Needy Families ("TANF") program. It effected this change in the Personal Responsibility and Work Opportunity Reconciliation Act of 1996, which also included the following provision: "NO INDIVIDUAL ENTITLEMENT — This part shall not be interpreted to entitle any individual . . . to assistance under any state program funded under this part." What legal effect would you expect this provision to have on program recipients' procedural due process rights?

Application & Analysis

1. Despite his best efforts to find consistent work, Ronald has been unemployed for most of the last two years. As a result, he finds himself in dire financial straits. After applying for and being deemed eligible to participate in his state's public assistance program, Ronald begins to receive monthly support payments. It is clear that Ronald, a single father, would not be able to adequately care for his two children without these support

payments. However, the governor of Ronald's state recently signed a law that completely eliminates the public assistance program in which Ronald participates. According to the governor, the state can no longer afford the program and, in any case, public assistance robs recipients of the personal dignity that comes from earning a paycheck. Based on *Goldberg v. Kelly*, could Ronald successfully claim that the governor's veto deprived him of property without due process of law?

2. Assume the same facts as Question 1, except that the governor signs an amendment to the program giving its officials the discretion to increase or decrease the amount eligible beneficiaries receive based on changes in recipients' personal circumstances. Pursuant to this new authority, a program official decides to reduce Ronald's monthly benefit by 20 percent because his oldest child turned 18 the previous month. Under the terms of the program, children who have reached the age of majority are excluded from the recipient's benefits calculation. Is Ronald entitled to a pre-deprivation hearing under *Goldberg* to challenge the amount of this reduction?

3. Assume that Doreen, Ronald's neighbor, applies for and is denied benefits under their state's public assistance program. She then successfully proves her right to due process protection in federal district court. She asks the court to order the state to admit her to the public assistance program and to pay her the full amount of benefits retroactive to the time she says her application should have been approved. Should the court give her the remedy she has requested?

4. During your weekly Administrative Law study session, the members of your group wonder about the general effects that *Goldberg* would have had on benefits programs. Jasmine speculates that requiring pre-deprivation hearings probably got very expensive for the states administering public assistance programs. "Those hearings aren't cheap," she soberly informs the group. Karim has a different perspective, arguing that *Goldberg* would have made the distribution of benefits much fairer, which would ultimately benefit eligible recipients and the communities in which they live. "If more people can buy what they need, if their kids don't have to worry about where they're going to live or how they're going to get food to eat, that improves their lives and the local economy." Jasmine retorts that the default of a pre-deprivation hearing before benefits can be taken away means that even ineligible recipients will continue to be paid for a long time. "That takes money away from the people who actually need it and rewards fraudsters. Where's the fairness in that?" They turn to you to break their stalemate. Whose side do you take? Is there a third position that you would adopt instead?

C. THE INTERESTS PROTECTED: PROPERTY INTERESTS

Early in the nation's history, courts defined the property interests protected by due process fairly narrowly; they were the property interests traditionally recognized by the common law. Accordingly, the government would have to afford "due process of law" before taking a person's home, money, or other worldly possessions. By contrast, the government did *not* owe a person due process if it merely deprived them of a so-called "privilege," a government-created benefit one enjoyed but was not owed under the common law. Thus, a government employee could be fired without notice, a hearing, or any other due process protection; the courts recognized no right to work for the government.

As you have already seen from *Goldberg v. Kelly*, the Court seemingly abandoned this traditional approach to defining property during the latter half of the twentieth century. Under the traditional approach, courts would have viewed public assistance payments as a privilege rather than property, and thus their deprivation would not have implicated due process. In *Goldberg*, New York City's Commissioner of Social Services *conceded* that cutting off public assistance triggers Fourteenth Amendment procedural due process rights. The Court accepted this concession, relying on Professor Charles Reich's argument that public assistance should be considered less like a gratuity and more like property.

Thus, in one sense, *Goldberg* was a very easy case; all parties agreed that the claimants had a constitutionally protected property interest in their government benefits. But how should courts identify the presence or absence of such interests when the point is contested by the government? The Supreme Court wrestled with that question in the two cases that follow.

Board of Regents of State Colleges v. Roth
408 U.S. 564 (1972)

Mr. Justice STEWART delivered the opinion of the Court.

In 1968 the respondent, David Roth, was hired for his first teaching job as assistant professor of political science at Wisconsin State University-Oshkosh. He was hired for a fixed term of one academic year. The notice of his faculty appointment specified that his employment would begin on September 1, 1968, and would end on June 30, 1969.[1] The respondent

---

[1] The respondent had no contract of employment. Rather, his formal notice of appointment was the equivalent of an employment contract.

completed that term. But he was informed that he would not be rehired for the next academic year.

The respondent had no tenure rights to continued employment. Under Wisconsin statutory law a state university teacher can acquire tenure as a "permanent" employee only after four years of year-to-year employment. Having acquired tenure, a teacher is entitled to continued employment "during efficiency and good behavior." A relatively new teacher without tenure, however, is under Wisconsin law entitled to nothing beyond his one-year appointment.[2] There are no statutory or administrative standards defining eligibility for re-employment. State law thus clearly leaves the decision whether to rehire a nontenured teacher for another year to the unfettered discretion of university officials.

The procedural protection afforded a Wisconsin State University teacher before he is separated from the University corresponds to his job security. As a matter of statutory law, a tenured teacher cannot be "discharged except for cause upon written charges" and pursuant to certain procedures. A nontenured teacher, similarly, is protected to some extent during his one-year term. Rules promulgated by the Board of Regents provide that a nontenured teacher "dismissed" before the end of the year may have some opportunity for review of the "dismissal." But the Rules provide no real protection for a nontenured teacher who simply is not re-employed for the next year. He must be informed by February 1 "concerning retention or non-retention for the ensuing year." But "no reason for non-retention need be given. No review or appeal is provided in such case."

In conformance with these Rules, the President of Wisconsin State University-Oshkosh informed the respondent before February 1, 1969, that he would not be rehired for the 1969-1970 academic year. He gave the respondent no reason for the decision and no opportunity to challenge it at any sort of hearing.

The respondent then brought this action in Federal District Court alleging that the decision not to rehire him for the next year infringed his Fourteenth Amendment rights. He attacked the decision both in substance and procedure. First, he alleged that the true reason for the decision was to

---

The notice of his appointment provided that: "*David F. Roth* is hereby appointed to the faculty of the Wisconsin State University Position number 0262. (Location:) *Oshkosh* as (Rank:) *Assistant Professor* of (Department:) *Political Science* this (Date:) *first day* of (Month:) *September* (Year:) *1968*." The notice went on to specify that the respondent's "appointment basis" was for the "academic year." And it provided that "(r)egulations governing tenure are in accord with Chapter 37.31, Wisconsin Statutes. The employment of any staff member for an academic year shall not be for a term beyond June 30th of the fiscal year in which the appointment is made." *See* note 2 *infra*.

[2] Wis. Stat. § 37.31(1) (1967), in force at the time, provided in pertinent part that: "All teachers in any state university shall initially be employed on probation. The employment shall be permanent, during efficiency and good behavior after 4 years of continuous service in the state university system as a teacher."

punish him for certain statements critical of the University administration, and that it therefore violated his right to freedom of speech. Second, he alleged that the failure of University officials to give him notice of any reason for nonretention and an opportunity for a hearing violated his right to procedural due process of law.

The District Court granted summary judgment for the respondent on the procedural issue, ordering the University officials to provide him with reasons and a hearing. The Court of Appeals, with one judge dissenting, affirmed this partial summary judgment. We granted certiorari. The only question presented to us at this stage in the case is whether the respondent had a constitutional right to a statement of reasons and a hearing on the University's decision not to rehire him for another year. We hold that he did not.

I

The requirements of procedural due process apply only to the deprivation of interests encompassed by the Fourteenth Amendment's protection of liberty and property. When protected interests are implicated, the right to some kind of prior hearing is paramount. But the range of interests protected by procedural due process is not infinite.

The District Court decided that procedural due process guarantees apply in this case by assessing and balancing the weights of the particular interests involved. It concluded that the respondent's interest in re-employment at Wisconsin State University-Oshkosh outweighed the University's interest in denying him re-employment summarily. Undeniably, the respondent's re-employment prospects were of major concern to him—concern that we surely cannot say was insignificant. And a weighing process has long been a part of any determination of the form of hearing required in particular situations by procedural due process. But, to determine whether due process requirements apply in the first place, we must look not to the "weight" but to the nature of the interest at stake. We must look to see if the interest is within the Fourteenth Amendment's protection of liberty and property.

"Liberty" and "property" are broad and majestic terms. They are among the "(g)reat (constitutional) concepts . . . purposely left to gather meaning from experience. . . . (T)hey relate to the whole domain of social and economic fact, and the statesmen who founded this Nation knew too well that only a stagnant society remains unchanged." *National Mutual Ins. Co. v. Tidewater Transfer Co.*, 337 U.S. 582, 646 (1949) (Frankfurter, J., dissenting). For that reason, the Court has fully and finally rejected the wooden distinction between "rights" and "privileges" that once seemed to govern the applicability of procedural due process rights. The Court has also made clear that the property interests protected by procedural due process extend well beyond actual ownership of real estate, chattels, or money. By the same token, the Court has required due process protection for deprivations of liberty beyond the sort of formal constraints imposed by the criminal process.

Yet, while the Court has eschewed rigid or formalistic limitations on the protection of procedural due process, it has at the same time observed certain boundaries. For the words "liberty" and "property" in the Due Process Clause of the Fourteenth Amendment must be given some meaning.

II

[The Court in this section rejected Roth's claim that his nonretention damaged his liberty interest in his "good name, reputation, honor, or integrity," finding "there [was] no suggestion whatever" that they were endangered by the University's decision. It also rejected the notion that Roth's nonretention could somehow damage a liberty interest in finding future work as a professor. The record contained no evidence that his nonretention so substantially impacted his employment prospects that it constituted a deprivation of his liberty. The issue of liberty interests protected by the Due Process Clause is explored more fully later in this chapter. Additionally, the Court refused to consider Roth's claim that the University infringed on his First Amendment right to freedom of speech, as the issue had not been argued before the district court.]

III

The Fourteenth Amendment's procedural protection of property is a safeguard of the security of interests that a person has already acquired in specific benefits. These interests — property interests — may take many forms.

Thus, the Court has held that a person receiving welfare benefits under statutory and administrative standards defining eligibility for them has an interest in continued receipt of those benefits that is safeguarded by procedural due process. *Goldberg v. Kelly*, 397 U.S. 254 (1970). Similarly, in the area of public employment, the Court has held that a public college professor dismissed from an office held under tenure provisions, *Slochower v. Board of Education*, 350 U.S. 551 (1956), and college professors and staff members dismissed during the terms of their contracts, *Wieman v. Updegraff*, 344 U.S. 183 (1952), have interests in continued employment that are safeguarded by due process. Only last year, the Court held that this principle "proscribing summary dismissal from public employment without hearing or inquiry required by due process" also applied to a teacher recently hired without tenure or a formal contract, but nonetheless with a clearly implied promise of continued employment. *Connell v. Higginbotham*, 403 U.S. 207, 208 (1971).

Certain attributes of "property" interests protected by procedural due process emerge from these decisions. To have a property interest in a benefit, a person clearly must have more than an abstract need or desire for it. He must have more than a unilateral expectation of it. He must, instead, have a legitimate claim of entitlement to it. It is a purpose of the ancient institution of property to protect those claims upon which people rely in their daily lives, reliance that must not be arbitrarily undermined. It is a purpose of the constitutional right to a hearing to provide an opportunity for a person to vindicate those claims.

Property interests, of course, are not created by the Constitution. Rather they are created and their dimensions are defined by existing rules or understandings that stem from an independent source such as state law—rules or understandings that secure certain benefits and that support claims of entitlement to those benefits. Thus, the welfare recipients in *Goldberg v. Kelly*, *supra*, had a claim of entitlement to welfare payments that was grounded in the statute defining eligibility for them. The recipients had not yet shown that they were, in fact, within the statutory terms of eligibility. But we held that they had a right to a hearing at which they might attempt to do so.

Just as the welfare recipients' "property" interest in welfare payments was created and defined by statutory terms, so the respondent's "property" interest in employment at Wisconsin State University-Oshkosh was created and defined by the terms of his appointment. Those terms secured his interest in employment up to June 30, 1969. But the important fact in this case is that they specifically provided that the respondent's employment was to terminate on June 30. They did not provide for contract renewal absent "sufficient cause." Indeed, they made no provision for renewal whatsoever.

Thus, the terms of the respondent's appointment secured absolutely no interest in re-employment for the next year. They supported absolutely no possible claim of entitlement to re-employment. Nor, significantly, was there any state statute or University rule or policy that secured his interest in re-employment or that created any legitimate claim to it. In these circumstances, the respondent surely had an abstract concern in being rehired, but he did not have a property interest sufficient to require the University authorities to give him a hearing when they declined to renew his contract of employment.

IV

Our analysis of the respondent's constitutional rights in this case in no way indicates a view that an opportunity for a hearing or a statement of reasons for nonretention would, or would not, be appropriate or wise in public colleges and universities. For it is a written Constitution that we apply. Our role is confined to interpretation of that Constitution.

We must conclude that the summary judgment for the respondent should not have been granted, since the respondent has not shown that he was deprived of liberty or property protected by the Fourteenth Amendment. The judgment of the Court of Appeals, accordingly, is reversed and the case is remanded for further proceedings consistent with this opinion. It is so ordered. Reversed and remanded.

Mr. Justice POWELL took no part in the decision of this case.

[The dissenting opinion of Justice Douglas is omitted.]

Mr. Justice MARSHALL, dissenting. . . .

The prior decisions of this Court, discussed at length in the opinion of the Court, establish a principle that is as obvious as it is compelling—i.e., federal and state governments and governmental agencies are restrained by the Constitution from acting arbitrarily with respect to employment opportunities that they either offer or control. Hence, it is now firmly established that whether or not a private employer is free to act capriciously or unreasonably with respect to employment practices, at least absent statutory or contractual controls, a government employer is different. The government may only act fairly and reasonably.

This Court has long maintained that "the right to work for a living in the common occupations of the community is of the very essence of the personal freedom and opportunity that it was the purpose of the (Fourteenth) Amendment to secure." *Truax v. Raich,* 239 U.S. 33, 41 (1915) (Hughes, J.). *See also Meyer v. Nebraska,* 262 U.S. 390, 399 (1923). It has also established that the fact that an employee has no contract guaranteeing work for a specific future period does not mean that as the result of action by the government he may be "discharged at any time, for any reason or for no reason." *Truax v. Raich, supra,* 239 U.S., at 38.

In my view, every citizen who applies for a government job is entitled to it unless the government can establish some reason for denying the employment. This is the "property" right that I believe is protected by the Fourteenth Amendment and that cannot be denied "without due process of law." And it is also liberty—liberty to work—which is the "very essence of the personal freedom and opportunity" secured by the Fourteenth Amendment.

This Court has often had occasion to note that the denial of public employment is a serious blow to any citizen. Thus, when an application for public employment is denied or the contract of a government employee is not renewed, the government must say why, for it is only when the reasons underlying government action are known that citizens feel secure and protected against arbitrary government action.

Employment is one of the greatest, if not the greatest, benefits that governments offer in modern-day life. When something as valuable as the opportunity to work is at stake, the government may not reward some citizens and not others without demonstrating that its actions are fair and equitable. And it is procedural due process that is our fundamental guarantee of fairness, our protection against arbitrary, capricious, and unreasonable government action. . . .

Where there are numerous applicants for jobs, it is likely that few will choose to demand reasons for not being hired. But, if the demand for reasons is exceptionally great, summary procedures can be devised that would provide fair and adequate information to all persons. As long as the government has a good reason for its actions it need not fear disclosure. It is only where the government acts improperly that procedural due process is truly burdensome. And that is precisely when it is most necessary. . . .

Accordingly, I dissent.

Perry v. Sindermann
408 U.S. 593 (1972)

Mr. Justice STEWART delivered the opinion of the Court.

From 1959 to 1969 the respondent, Robert Sindermann, was a teacher in the state college system of the State of Texas. After teaching for two years at the University of Texas and for four years at San Antonio Junior College, he became a professor of Government and Social Science at Odessa Junior College in 1965. He was employed at the college for four successive years, under a series of one-year contracts. He was successful enough to be appointed, for a time, the cochairman of his department.

During the 1968-1969 academic year, however, controversy arose between the respondent and the college administration. The respondent was elected president of the Texas Junior College Teachers Association. In this capacity, he left his teaching duties on several occasions to testify before committees of the Texas Legislature, and he became involved in public disagreements with the policies of the college's Board of Regents. In particular, he aligned himself with a group advocating the elevation of the college to four-year status—a change opposed by the Regents. And, on one occasion, a newspaper advertisement appeared over his name that was highly critical of the Regents.

Finally, in May 1969, the respondent's one-year employment contract terminated and the Board of Regents voted not to offer him a new contract for the next academic year. The Regents issued a press release setting forth allegations of the respondent's insubordination.[1] But they provided him no official statement of the reasons for the nonrenewal of his contract. And they allowed him no opportunity for a hearing to challenge the basis of the nonrenewal. . . .

---

[1] The press release stated, for example, that the respondent had defied his superiors by attending legislative committee meetings when college officials had specifically refused to permit him to leave his classes for that purpose.

I

[In this section of its opinion, the Court concluded that the Board of Regents would have violated Sindermann's First Amendment rights if it had terminated his contract because of his public criticism of its policies. "[T]his Court has made clear that even though a person has no 'right' to a valuable governmental benefit and even though the government may deny him the benefit for any number of reasons, . . . [i]t may not deny a benefit to a person on a basis that infringes his constitutionally protected interests—especially, his interest in freedom of speech." Because the district court decided that Sindermann had no property interest in his job, it granted the Regents summary judgment before he could fully explore the merits of his First Amendment claim. Agreeing with the Court of Appeals, the Court found the district court's decision improper.]

II

The respondent's lack of formal contractual or tenure security in continued employment at Odessa Junior College, though irrelevant to his free speech claim, is highly relevant to his procedural due process claim. But it may not be entirely dispositive.

We have held today in *Board of Regents v. Roth*, 408 U.S. 564 (1972), that the Constitution does not require opportunity for a hearing before the nonrenewal of a nontenured teacher's contract, unless he can show that the decision not to rehire him somehow deprived him of an interest in "liberty" or that he had a "property" interest in continued employment, despite the lack of tenure or a formal contract. In *Roth* the teacher had not made a showing on either point to justify summary judgment in his favor.

Similarly, the respondent here has yet to show that he has been deprived of an interest that could invoke procedural due process protection. As in *Roth*, the mere showing that he was not rehired in one particular job, without more, did not amount to a showing of a loss of liberty. Nor did it amount to a showing of a loss of property.

But the respondent's allegations—which we must construe most favorably to the respondent at this stage of the litigation—do raise a genuine issue as to his interest in continued employment at Odessa Junior College. He alleged that this interest, though not secured by a formal contractual tenure provision, was secured by a no less binding understanding fostered by the college administration. In particular, the respondent alleged that the college had a *de facto* tenure program, and that he had tenure under that program. He claimed that he and others legitimately relied upon an unusual provision that had been in the college's official Faculty Guide for many years:

"Teacher Tenure: Odessa College has no tenure system. The Administration of the College wishes the faculty member to feel that he has permanent tenure as long as his teaching services are satisfactory and as long as he displays a cooperative attitude toward his co-workers and his superiors, and as long as he is happy in his work."

Moreover, the respondent claimed legitimate reliance upon guidelines promulgated by the Coordinating Board of the Texas College and University System that provided that a person, like himself, who had been employed as a teacher in the state college and university system for seven years or more has some form of job tenure. Thus, the respondent offered to prove that a teacher with his long period of service at this particular State College had no less a "property" interest in continued employment than a formally tenured teacher at other colleges, and had no less a procedural due process right to a statement of reasons and a hearing before college officials upon their decision not to retain him.

We have made clear in *Roth* . . . that "property" interests subject to procedural due process protection are not limited by a few rigid, technical forms. Rather, "property" denotes a broad range of interests that are secured by "existing rules or understandings." *Id. at* 577. A person's interest in a benefit is a "property" interest for due process purposes if there are such rules or mutually explicit understandings that support his claim of entitlement to the benefit and that he may invoke at a hearing. *Ibid.*

A written contract with an explicit tenure provision clearly is evidence of a formal understanding that supports a teacher's claim of entitlement to continued employment unless sufficient "cause" is shown. Yet absence of such an explicit contractual provision may not always foreclose the possibility that a teacher has a "property" interest in reemployment. For example, the law of contracts in most, if not all, jurisdictions long has employed a process by which agreements, though not formalized in writing, may be "implied." 3 Corbin on Contracts §§ 561-572A (1960). Explicit contractual provisions may be supplemented by other agreements implied from "the promisor's words and conduct in the light of the surrounding circumstances." *Id. at* § 562. And, "(t)he meaning of (the promisor's) words and acts is found by relating them to the usage of the past." *Ibid.*

A teacher, like the respondent, who has held his position for a number of years, might be able to show from the circumstances of this service — and from other relevant facts — that he has a legitimate claim of entitlement to job tenure. . . . [T]here may be an unwritten "common law" in a particular university that certain employees shall have the equivalent of tenure. This is particularly likely in a college or university, like Odessa Junior College, that has no explicit tenure system even for senior members of its faculty, but that nonetheless may have created such a system in practice.

In this case, the respondent has alleged the existence of rules and understandings, promulgated and fostered by state officials, that may justify his legitimate claim of entitlement to continued employment absent "sufficient cause." We disagree with the Court of Appeals insofar as it held that a mere subjective "expectancy" is protected by procedural due process, but we agree that the respondent must be given an opportunity to prove the legitimacy of his claim of such entitlement in light of "the policies and practices of the institution." 430 F.2d, at 943. Proof of such a property interest would not, of course, entitle him to reinstatement. But such proof would obligate college officials to grant a hearing at his request, where he could be informed of the grounds for his nonretention and challenge their sufficiency. . . .

Affirmed.

Mr. Justice POWELL took no part in the decision of this case.

[The dissenting opinion of Justice MARSHALL is omitted.]

QUESTION SET 7.3

Review & Synthesis

1. Putting *Roth* and *Sindermann* together, what test did the Supreme Court develop for determining whether a claimant has a property interest protected by the Due Process Clause? What is a "legitimate claim of entitlement"?

2. How did the Court distinguish the test it applied in *Goldberg v. Kelly* from the one it applied in *Roth*? How do the facts informing the two inquiries differ?

3. *Roth* and *Sindermann* have very similar facts, but very different results. What are the salient factual differences between the two cases that explain their opposing outcomes?

Application & Analysis

1. A state statute authorizes the provision of state-funded medical services to physically disabled children. Program eligibility and benefit amounts, which are determined by the State Health Commission, are based on family income as well as other criteria. The statute states: "The Commission shall on its own initiative provide, within the limits of the appropriations made therefor, such medical service for children with physical disabilities as in the judgment of the Commission is needed." Claire, a disabled child seeking medical services, applies for and is denied assistance under the program. The statutory scheme affords her neither a pre-determination

hearing before the Commission nor a means to appeal the Commission's decision. Her parents file suit on her behalf in federal district court, arguing that the lack of a hearing and Claire's inability to appeal the Commission's decision violate her procedural due process rights under the Fourteenth Amendment. The Commission responds that the program does not create any property rights, and therefore Claire has no procedural due process rights to assert. You are a clerk for the judge before whom this case is pending. She has asked for your input on the merits of the parties' arguments. How would you respond?

2. State Legislature enacts a statute providing up to 50 percent of community college tuition for state residents pursuing Associate's degrees in fields for which the state has a shortage of skilled labor. Eligibility for this tuition support ends with the earlier of the recipient's graduation from her supported degree program (provided she graduates no more than 48 months after the start of the first semester for which support is provided) or her securing at least 15 hours of "employment" per week in a field related to her or his degree program. The statute itself does not define the term "employment." The statute's conference committee report states that one of its primary purposes is to support small business growth within the state. Additionally, a prior draft of the statute placed the word "gainful" immediately before "employment," but the word was removed from the final version. Felicia, a program recipient, is pursuing a two-year Associate's degree in automotive collision repair at her local community college. Before the end of her first year, she starts a 15-hour/week unpaid internship at a small automotive dealership in her town, with the expectation that she would continue until she graduates. She properly disclosed this fact in the forms she is required to submit to the state agency administering the tuition support program. After reviewing her forms, the agency informs her by letter that she is no longer eligible for tuition support because she has secured "employment." Although the statute gives her the right to file a post-deprivation appeal, Felicia wants a hearing before the agency. She also wants to continue receiving tuition support until the agency renders a decision based on that hearing. She has asked for your advice on whether she should challenge the agency's decision. Does she have a protected interest?

3. The Surface Transportation Assistance Act ("STAA") authorizes the Department of Labor ("DOL") to order a trucking company to reinstate a previously fired employee if the agency determines that the company fired that employee for reporting a safety violation to the Department of Transportation ("DOT"). Domenic is a truck driver for Truck Co. The terms of his employment are governed by a collective bargaining agreement between Truck Co. and his labor union, which entitles the company to discharge drivers for cause. Earlier this year, Domenic reported to

the DOT several ongoing safety problems at Truck Co. Truck Co. fired him shortly thereafter, citing Domenic's frequent absences from work. Domenic immediately filed a complaint with DOL, alleging that Truck Co. fired him for STAA-protected whistleblowing. After conducting an investigation, and despite Truck Co.'s assertions to the contrary, DOL found reason to believe that the company had retaliated against Domenic in violation of the STAA. It then ordered Domenic's immediate reinstatement with backpay. Truck Co. could have requested an evidentiary hearing before the Secretary of Labor but doing so would not have stayed DOL's preliminary order of reinstatement. Truck Co. instead filed suit in federal district court, arguing that its rights under the collective bargaining agreement created a Fifth Amendment procedural due process entitlement to a pre-reinstatement evidentiary hearing. Domenic responded that any rights Truck Co. has under the agreement would be governed by state contract law, not the Fifth Amendment. You are a clerk for the judge presiding over this case. He has asked you whether procedural due process rights attach in a contractual dispute between private parties. How do you respond?

Roth and *Sindermann* involved governmental actions that directly impacted the property interests asserted in those cases. For both plaintiffs, their schools purposely ended their employment. Do procedural due process protections attach when the government's actions *indirectly*, though nevertheless severely, impact a person's interest in a government-conferred entitlement? What about when government conduct lessens or removes an indirect *benefit* being received by a government beneficiary? The next case addresses these questions.

O'Bannon v. Town Court Nursing Center
447 U.S. 773 (1980)

Mr. Justice STEVENS delivered the opinion of the Court.

The question presented is whether approximately 180 elderly residents of a nursing home operated by Town Court Nursing Center, Inc., have a constitutional right to a hearing before a state or federal agency may revoke the home's authority to provide them with nursing care at government expense. Although we recognize that such a revocation may be harmful to some patients, we hold that they have no constitutional right to participate in the revocation proceedings.

Town Court Nursing Center, Inc. (Town Court), operates a 198-bed nursing home in Philadelphia, Pa. In April 1976 it was certified by the Department of Health, Education, and Welfare (HEW) as a "skilled nursing facility," thereby becoming eligible to receive payments from HEW and from the Pennsylvania Department of Public Welfare (DPW), for providing nursing care services to aged, disabled, and poor persons in need of medical care. After receiving its certification, Town Court entered into formal "provider agreements" with both HEW and DPW. In those agreements HEW and DPW agreed to reimburse Town Court for a period of one year for care provided to persons eligible for Medicare or Medicaid benefits under the Social Security Act, on the condition that Town Court continue to qualify as a skilled nursing facility.

On May 17, 1977, HEW notified Town Court that it no longer met the statutory and regulatory standards for skilled nursing facilities and that, consequently, its Medicare provider agreement would not be renewed. The HEW notice stated that no payments would be made for services rendered after July 17, 1977, explained how Town Court might request reconsideration of the decertification decision, and directed it to notify Medicare beneficiaries that payments were being discontinued. Three days later DPW notified Town Court that its Medicaid provider agreement would also not be renewed.

Town Court requested HEW to reconsider its termination decision. While the request was pending, Town Court and six of its Medicaid patients filed a complaint in the United States District Court for the Eastern District of Pennsylvania alleging that both the nursing home and the patients were entitled to an evidentiary hearing on the merits of the decertification decision before the Medicaid payments were discontinued. The complaint alleged that termination of the payments would require Town Court to close and would cause the individual plaintiffs to suffer both a loss of benefits and "immediate and irreparable psychological and physical harm.

The District Court granted a preliminary injunction against DPW and HEW, requiring payments to be continued for new patients as well as for patients already in the home and prohibiting any patient transfers until HEW acted on Town Court's petition for reconsideration. After HEW denied that petition, the District Court dissolved the injunction and denied the plaintiffs any further relief, except that it required HEW and DPW to pay for services actually provided to patients.

Town Court and the six patients filed separate appeals from the denial of the preliminary injunction, as well as a motion, which was subsequently granted, for reinstatement of the injunction pending appeal. The Secretary of HEW cross-appealed from the portion of the District Court's order requiring payment for services rendered after the effective date of the termination. The Secretary of DPW took no appeal and, though named as an appellee, took no position on the merits.

The United States Court of Appeals for the Third Circuit, sitting *en banc*, unanimously held that there was no constitutional defect in the HEW procedures that denied Town Court an evidentiary hearing until after the termination had become effective and the agency had ceased paying benefits.[6] The Court of Appeals came to a different conclusion, however, with respect to the patients' claim to a constitutional right to a pretermination hearing. . . .

. . . [S]ix judges held that the patients were entitled to a pretermination hearing on the issue of whether Town Court's Medicare and Medicaid provider agreements should be renewed. The court thus reinstated that portion of the preliminary injunction that prohibited patient transfers until after the patients had been granted a hearing and affirmed that portion that required HEW and DPW to continue paying benefits on behalf of Town Court residents. It then remanded, leaving the nature of the hearing to be accorded the patients to be determined, in the first instance, by the District Court. Three judges dissented, concluding that neither the statutes nor the regulations granted the patients any substantive interest in decertification proceedings and that they had no constitutionally protected property right in uninterrupted occupancy.

. . . We now reverse. . . .

At the outset, it is important to remember that this case does not involve the question whether HEW or DPW should, as a matter of administrative efficiency, consult the residents of a nursing home before making a final decision to decertify it. Rather, the question is whether the patients have an interest in receiving benefits for care in a particular facility that entitles them, as a matter of constitutional law, to a hearing before the Government can decertify that facility. The patients have identified two possible sources of such a right. First, they contend that the Medicaid provisions relied upon by the Court of Appeals give them a property right to remain in the home of their choice absent good cause for transfer and therefore entitle them to a hearing on whether such cause exists. Second, they argue that a transfer may have such severe physical or emotional side effects that it is tantamount to a deprivation of life or liberty, which must be preceded by a due process hearing.[16] We find both argument[s] unpersuasive.[17]

---

[6] Relying on this Court's decision in *Mathews v. Eldridge*, 424 U.S. 319 (1976), the Court of Appeals held that Town Court's property interests were sufficiently protected by informal pretermination procedures and by the opportunity for an administrative hearing and federal-court review after benefits had been terminated. . . .

[16] The patients cite a number of studies indicating that removal to another home may cause "transfer trauma," increasing the possibility of death or serious illness for elderly, infirm patients. They also argue that associational interests, such as friendship among patients and staff and family ties, may be disrupted if the patients are scattered to other nursing homes, perhaps in other areas of the country. In denying the motion for a preliminary injunction, the District Court did not take evidence or make any findings on the harm that might result from a transfer. Nevertheless, we assume for purposes of this decision that there is a risk that some residents may encounter severe emotional and physical hardship as a result of a transfer.

[17] The patients also argue that they are third-party beneficiaries of the provider agreement between DPW and Town Court and that this status somehow entitles them to more than Town Court itself is entitled to-namely, a pretermination hearing. They also argue that a legitimate entitlement to continued care in the home of their choice arises out of Pennsylvania's long history of providing

Whether viewed singly or in combination, the Medicaid provisions relied upon by the Court of Appeals do not confer a right to continued residence in the home of one's choice. Title 42 U.S.C. § 1396a(a)(23) (1976 ed., Supp. II) gives recipients the right to choose among a range of qualified providers, without government interference. By implication, it also confers an absolute right to be free from government interference with the choice to remain in a home that continues to be qualified. But it clearly does not confer a right on a recipient to enter an unqualified home and demand a hearing to certify it, nor does it confer a right on a recipient to continue to receive benefits for care in a home that has been decertified. Second, although the regulations do protect patients by limiting the circumstances under which a home may transfer or discharge a Medicaid recipient, they do not purport to limit the Government's right to make a transfer necessary by decertifying a facility. Finally, since decertification does not reduce or terminate a patient's financial assistance, but merely requires him to use it for care at a different facility, regulations granting recipients the right to a hearing prior to a reduction in financial benefits are irrelevant. . . .

In the Medicare and the Medicaid Programs the Government has provided needy patients with both direct benefits and indirect benefits. The direct benefits are essentially financial in character; the Government pays for certain medical services and provides procedures to determine whether and how much money should be paid for patient care. The net effect of these direct benefits is to give the patients an opportunity to obtain medical services from providers of their choice that is comparable, if not exactly equal, to the opportunity available to persons who are financially independent. The Government cannot withdraw these direct benefits without giving the patients notice and an opportunity for a hearing on the issue of their eligibility for benefits.

This case does not involve the withdrawal of direct benefits. Rather, it involves the Government's attempt to confer an indirect benefit on Medicaid patients by imposing and enforcing minimum standards of care on facilities like Town Court. When enforcement of those standards requires decertification of a facility, there may be an immediate, adverse impact on some residents. But surely that impact, which is an indirect and incidental result of the Government's enforcement action, does not amount to a deprivation of any interest in life, liberty, or property.

Medicaid patients who are forced to move because their nursing home has been decertified are in no different position for purposes of due process analysis than financially independent residents of a nursing home who are forced to move because the home's state license has been revoked. Both groups of patients are indirect beneficiaries of government programs

---

free medical care for those who are indigent. Nothing in the cited Pennsylvania statutes or court decisions, however, purports to create the kind of broad entitlement that the patients claim. In any event, neither of these state-law arguments was advanced in the courts below and therefore neither may provide the basis for an affirmance in this Court.

designed to guarantee a minimum standard of care for patients as a class. Both may be injured by the closing of a home due to revocation of its state license or its decertification as a Medicaid provider. Thus, whether they are private patients or Medicaid patients, some may have difficulty locating other homes they consider suitable or may suffer both emotional and physical harm as a result of the disruption associated with their move. Yet none of these patients would lose the ability to finance his or her continued care in a properly licensed or certified institution. And, while they might have a claim against the nursing home for damages, none would have any claim against the responsible governmental authorities for the deprivation of an interest in life, liberty, or property. Their position under these circumstances would be comparable to that of members of a family who have been dependent on an errant father; they may suffer serious trauma if he is deprived of his liberty or property as a consequence of criminal proceedings, but surely they have no constitutional right to participate in his trial or sentencing procedures. . . .

Whatever legal rights these patients may have against Town Court for failing to maintain its status as a qualified skilled nursing home — and we express no opinion on that subject — we hold that the enforcement by HEW and DPW of their valid regulations did not directly affect the patients' legal rights or deprive them of any constitutionally protected interest in life, liberty, or property.

The judgment of the Court of Appeals is reversed, and the case is remanded for further proceedings consistent with this opinion.

It is so ordered.

Mr. Justice MARSHALL took no part in the consideration or decision of this case.

Mr. Justice BLACKMUN, concurring in the judgment.

Although the Court reaches the result I reach, I find its analysis simplistic and unsatisfactory. I write separately to explain why and to set forth the approach I feel should be followed.

The patients rest their due process claim on two distinct foundations. First, they assert a property interest in continued residence at their home. Second, they claim life and liberty interests tied to their physical and psychological well-being. According to the patients, because each of these interests is threatened directly by decertification, they are constitutionally entitled to a hearing on the propriety of that action. Unlike the Court, I find it necessary to treat these distinct arguments separately.

I

In my view, the Court deals far too casually with § 1902(a)(23) of the Social Security Act, 42 U.S.C. § 1396(a)(23) (1976 ed., Supp. II), in rejecting the patients' "property" claim. That provision guarantees that a patient may receive nursing home care "from any institution . . . qualified to perform the . . . services . . . who undertakes to provide him such services." The statute thus vests each patient with a broad right to resist governmental removal, which can be disrupted only when the Government establishes the home's noncompliance with program participation requirements. Given this fact and our precedents, one can easily understand why seven judges of the Court of Appeals adopted the patients' argument. . . .

I have no quarrel with the Court's observation that the Due Process Clause generally is unconcerned with "indirect" losses. I fear, however, that such platitudes often submerge analytical complexities in particular cases. I also question whether that generalization has relevance here. Even assuming it does, the Court's treatment of it leaves me unimpressed. To say that the decertification decision directly affects the home is not to say that it "indirectly" affects the patients. Transfer is not only the "inevitabl[e]," clearly foreseeable consequence of decertification; a basic purpose of decertification is to force patients to relocate. Thus, not surprisingly, § 1396(a)(23) specifically ties the patients' right to continued residence in a home to qualification of the facility. Under these circumstances, I have great difficulty concluding that the patients' loss of their home should be characterized as "indirect and incidental," . . . But so are a wide range of other governmental acts that invoke due process protections for the intended beneficiary. Indeed a basic purpose of affording a hearing in such cases is to test the Government's judgment that its action will in fact prove to be beneficial.

In my view, there exists a more principled and sensible analysis of the patients' "property" claim. Given § 1396(a)(23), I am forced to concede that the patients have some form of property interest in continued residence at Town Court. And past decisions compel me to observe that where, as here, a substantial restriction inhibits governmental removal of a presently enjoyed benefit, a property interest normally will be recognized. To state a general rule, however, is not to decide a specific case. The Court never has held that any substantive restriction upon removal of any governmental benefit gives rise to a generalized property interest in its continued enjoyment. Indeed, a majority of the Justices of this Court are already on record as concluding that the term "property" sometimes incorporates limiting characterizations of statutorily bestowed interests. Common sense and sound policy support this recognition of some measure of flexibility in defining "new property" expectancies. Public benefits are not held in fee simple. And even if we analogize the patients' claim to "continued residence" to holdings more familiar to the law of private property — even to interests in homes, such as life tenancies — we would find that those interests are regularly subject to easements, conditions subsequent, possibilities of reverter, and other similar limitations. In short, it does not suffice to say that a litigant holds property. The inquiry also must focus on the dimensions of that interest. *See Board of Regents v. Roth*, 408 U.S. 564, 577 (1972).

The determinative question is whether the litigant holds such a legitimate "claim of entitlement" that the Constitution, rather than the political branches, must define the procedures attending its removal. *Id.* at 578. Claims of entitlement spring from expectations that are "justifiable," "protectible," "sufficient," or "proper" [citations omitted]. In contrast, the Constitution does not recognize expectancies that are "unilateral," or "too ephemeral and insubstantial."

. . . [F]our distinct considerations convince me that—even though the statutes place a significant substantive restriction on transferring patients—their expectancy in remaining in their home is conditioned upon its status as a qualified provider.

(1) The lengthy process of deciding the disqualification question has intimately involved Town Court. The home has been afforded substantial procedural protections, and, throughout the process, has shared with the patients who wish to stay there an intense interest in keeping the facility certified. . . . In this case, since the home had the opportunity and incentive to make the very arguments the patients might make, their due process interest in accurate and informed decisionmaking already, in large measure was satisfied. . . .

(2) Town Court is more than a *de facto* representative of the patients' interests; it is the underlying source of the benefit they seek to retain. Again, this fact is important, for the property of a recipient of public benefits must be limited, as a general rule, by the governmental power to remove, through prescribed procedures, the underlying source of those benefits. The Constitution would not have entitled John Kelly to a fair hearing if New York had chosen to disband its public assistance programs rather than to cut off his particular award. *See Goldberg v. Kelly*, 397 U.S. 254 (1970). Nor would Texas have had to afford process to Professor Sindermann had it decided for budgetary reasons to close Odessa Junior College. *See Perry v. Sindermann*, 408 U.S. 593 (1972). . . .

(3) That the asserted deprivation of property extends in a nondiscriminatory fashion to some 180 patients also figures in my calculus. "Where a rule of conduct applies to more than a few people, it is impracticable that every one should have a direct voice in its adoption. The Constitution does not require all public acts to be done in town meeting or an assembly of the whole." *Bi-Metallic Investment Co. v. State Board*, 239 U.S. 441, 445 (1915). When governmental action affects more than a few individuals, concerns beyond economy, efficiency and expedition tip the balance against finding that due process attaches. . . "[T]the case for due protection grows stronger as the identity of the persons affected by a government choice becomes clearer; and the case becomes stronger still as the precise nature of the effect on each individual comes more determinately within the decisionmaker's purview. For when government acts in a way that singles out identifiable individuals—in a way that is likely to be premised on suppositions about specific persons—it activates the special concern about being personally

talked to about the decision rather than simply being *dealt with.*" Laurence Tribe, American Constitutional Law § 10-7, pp. 503-504 (1978) (emphasis in original). I agree with this general statement and find its "flipside" informative here.

(4) Finally I find it important that the patients' interest has been jeopardized not at all because of alleged shortcomings on their part. Frequently, significant interests are subjected to adverse action upon a contested finding of fault, impropriety or incompetence. In these contexts the Court has seldom hesitated to require that a hearing be afforded the "accused." It may be that patients' participation in the decertification decision would vaguely heighten their and others' sense of the decision's legitimacy, even though the decision follows extensive government inspections undertaken with the very object of protecting the patients' interest. Even so, that interest is far less discernible in this context than when a stigmatizing determination of wrongdoing or fault supplements removal of a presently enjoyed benefit.

For these reasons, I am willing to recognize in this case that "the very legislation which 'defines' the 'dimension' of the [patient's] entitlement, while providing a right to [remain in a home] generally, does not establish this right free of [disqualification of the home] in accord with [federal statutory] law." *Goss v. Lopez*, 419 U.S. 565, 586-587 (1975) (Powell, J., dissenting).

QUESTION SET 7.4

Review & Synthesis

1. Why did the Court conclude that the nursing home residents lacked a protectable property interest in their continued residence at Town Court? What entitlements comprised their property interests, and how did the Court identify them?

2. Based on the Court's analysis, can indirect harms (including removal of indirect benefits) caused by government conduct ever trigger procedural due process protections? What if the harm was explicitly anticipated by Congress, as shown by the legislative history of the statute creating the entitlement? What if the harm was not explicitly anticipated, but was instead reasonably foreseeable?

Application & Analysis

1. Under a state statute that has been in effect for decades, public school principals are granted tenure after three years of continuous service in their positions. Carlos has been the principal of City High School, located

in the state capital, for the past eight years. Last week, the state significantly cut its education budget. Citing a sizable budgetary shortfall, the school board closed Carlos' high school (its students will now attend a neighboring school) and terminated Carlos. He believes that he was terminated because of his opposition to several curricular innovations recently adopted by the board, and not because of the school district's budget situation. His high school was the only one the board closed, and most of the teachers and staff he once supervised have been moved to similar positions elsewhere in the school district. Does he have any interests protected by due process?

As the cases we have considered up to this point show, courts must look to the government's words and actions when identifying the property interests that trigger procedural due process protections. In *Goldberg*, federal and state statutes created and set the terms of the welfare programs at issue in that case. In *Roth* and *Sindermann*, the sources of the putative job entitlements weren't statutes, but documents generated by state "agencies" (i.e., a state university in *Roth* and a state college in *Sindermann*). In *O'Bannon*, again, the nursing home residents' procedural due process claims were anchored in federal statutes. The Court carefully construed the legal sources relevant to each case to understand the substantive benefits they conferred. Each of those cases also implied that creation of "new property" is a volitional act; the government *may* create it, but is under no obligation to do so. Accordingly, the substantive benefits the government grants are the sum total of what eligible beneficiaries receive; they have no legal basis to demand more than what the government has, in its discretion, agreed to provide.

The question we turn to now is just how far the government's discretion extends. Clearly, it has broad control over the *substance* of the property interests it creates. Can the same be said of the *procedures* it adopts to vindicate those interests? Consider the following argument made by then-Professor Frank Easterbrook:

> Substance and process are intimately related. The procedures one uses determine how much substance is achieved, and by whom. Procedural rules are just a measure of how much the substantive entitlements are worth, of what we are willing to sacrifice to see a given goal attained. The body that creates a substantive rule is the logical judge of how much should be spent to avoid errors in the process of disposing of claims to that right. The substantive rule itself is best seen as a promised benefit coupled with a promised rate of mistake: the legislature sets up an X% probability that a person will receive a certain boon. The Court cannot logically be reticent about revising the substantive rules but unabashed about rewriting the procedures to be followed in administering those rules.

Frank Easterbrook, *Substance and Due Process*, 1982 Sup. Ct. Rev. 85, 112-13 (1982). The implications of this argument for the new property are far-reaching. If the substantive value of an entitlement—as measured by the amount the government is willing to expend to provide it—is inextricably intertwined with the procedures used to facilitate its distribution, then governments must be free to fashion those procedures. Where the government deems a particular entitlement to be highly valuable, it will expend the resources necessary to ensure a low decisional error rate in providing it. Stated differently, the government will provide considerable procedural protections—pre-deprivation in-person hearings, discovery, cross-examination of witnesses, representation by counsel, etc.—to make sure those who are eligible for the entitlement receive it. For those entitlements the government values less, the procedures for its provision need not be elaborate or expensive; a high error rate in its provision (or its denial) is acceptable. In either case, the upshot of Easterbrook's argument is this: the process due to someone holding a property interest should be determined by the governmental body that created it, and not by judicial interpretations of what the Due Process Clauses require.

In a series of cases decided from the mid-1970s through the mid-1980s, the Justices on the Supreme Court wrestled with this notion that governmental will, rather than constitutional decree, determines the minimal amount of procedural protection property rights holders receive. In *Arnett v. Kennedy*, 416 U.S. 134 (1974), the Court considered the claim of a "nonprobationary" civil service employee in the federal Office of Economic Opportunity who asserted that he was fired for making defamatory remarks about his supervisor. He argued that he was entitled to a pre-termination hearing, whereas the civil service statutes (derived from the Lloyd-LaFollete Act of 1912) and regulations in place at that time provided only for a post-termination hearing. The Court, in plurality, disagreed. Justice Rehnquist, writing for himself and two others, argued that Kennedy had received all the process he was owed.

> Here appellee did have a statutory expectancy that he not be removed other than for "such cause as will promote the efficiency of (the) service." But the very section of the statute which granted him that right, a right which had previously existed only by virtue of administrative regulation, expressly provided also for the procedure by which "cause" was to be determined, and expressly omitted the procedural guarantees which appellee insists are mandated by the Constitution. Only by bifurcating the very sentence of the Act of Congress which conferred upon appellee the right not to be removed save for cause could it be said that he had an expectancy of that substantive right without the procedural limitations which Congress attached to it. In the area of federal regulation of government employees, where in the absence of statutory limitation the governmental employer has had virtually uncontrolled latitude in decisions as to hiring and firing . . . we do not believe that a statutory enactment such as the Lloyd-La Follette Act

may be parsed as discretely as appellee urges. Congress was obviously intent on according a measure of statutory job security to governmental employees which they had not previously enjoyed, but was likewise intent on excluding more elaborate procedural exquirements which it felt would make the operation of the new scheme unnecessarily burdensome in practice. Where the focus of legislation was thus strongly on the procedural mechanism for enforcing the substantive right which was simultaneously conferred, we decline to conclude that the substantive right may be viewed wholly apart from the procedure provided for its enforcement. The employee's statutorily defined right is not a guarantee against removal without cause in the abstract, but such a guarantee as enforced by the procedures which Congress has designated for the determination of cause.

"It is an elementary rule of constitutional law that one may not 'retain the benefits of an Act while attacking the constitutionality of one of its important conditions.'["] *United States v. San Francisco*, 310 U.S. 16, 29 [(1940)]. . . .

This doctrine has unquestionably been applied unevenly in the past, and observed as often as not in the breach. We believe that at the very least it gives added weight to our conclusion that where the grant of a substantive right is inextricably intertwined with the limitations on the procedures which are to be employed in determining that right, a litigant in the position of appellee must take the bitter with the sweet.

416 U.S. at 151-54. Again, this reasoning commanded only three votes. Justice Powell, joined by Justice Blackmun, rejected it while agreeing in the result.

The plurality would . . . conclude that the statute governing federal employment determines not only the nature of appellee's property interest, but also the extent of the procedural protections to which he may lay claim. It seems to me that this approach is incompatible with the principles laid down in *Roth* and *Sindermann*. Indeed, it would lead directly to the conclusion that whatever the nature of an individual's statutorily created property interest, deprivation of that interest could be accomplished without notice or a hearing at any time. This view misconceives the origin of the right to procedural due process. That right is conferred, not by legislative grace, but by constitutional guarantee. While the legislature may elect not to confer a property interest in federal employment, it may not constitutionally authorize the deprivation of such an interest, once conferred, without appropriate procedural safeguards. As our cases have consistently recognized, the adequacy of statutory procedures for deprivation of a statutorily created property interest must be analyzed in constitutional terms.

416 U.S. at 166-67 (Powell, J., concurring in part and concurring in the result).

The Court returned to this topic two years later, in *Bishop v. Wood*, 426 U.S. 341 (1976). There a police officer asserted his right to a pre-termination hearing. Rejecting his claim, the five-member majority observed the following:

> A property interest in employment can, of course, be created by ordinance, or by an implied contract. In either case, however, the sufficiency of the claim of entitlement must be decided by reference to state law. The North Carolina Supreme Court has held that an enforceable expectation of continued public employment in that State can exist only if the employer, by statute or contract, has actually granted some form of guarantee. *Still v. Lance*, 279 N.C. 254, 182 S.E.2d 403 (1971). Whether such a guarantee has been given can be determined only by an examination of the particular statute or ordinance in question.
>
> On its face the ordinance on which petitioner relies may fairly be read as conferring such a guarantee. However, such a reading is not the only possible interpretation; the ordinance may also be construed as granting no right to continued employment but merely conditioning an employee's removal on compliance with certain specified procedures. We do not have any authoritative interpretation of this ordinance by a North Carolina state court. We do, however, have the opinion of the United States District Judge who, of course, sits in North Carolina and practiced law there for many years. Based on his understanding of state law, he concluded that petitioner "held his position at the will and pleasure of the city." This construction of North Carolina law was upheld by the Court of Appeals for the Fourth Circuit, albeit by an equally divided court. In comparable circumstances, this Court has accepted the interpretation of state law in which the District Court and the Court of Appeals have concurred even if an examination of the state-law issue without such guidance might have justified a different conclusion.
>
> In this case, as the District Court construed the ordinance, the City Manager's determination of the adequacy of the grounds for discharge is not subject to judicial review; the employee is merely given certain procedural rights which the District Court found not to have been violated in this case. The District Court's reading of the ordinance is tenable; it derives some support from a decision of the North Carolina Supreme Court, *Still v. Lance, supra*; and it was accepted by the Court of Appeals for the Fourth Circuit. These reasons are sufficient to foreclose our independent examination of the state-law issue.
>
> Under that view of the law, petitioner's discharge did not deprive him of a property interest protected by the Fourteenth Amendment.

426 U.S. at 344-47. Writing in dissent, Justice White viewed the majority's decision as validation of the "bitter with the sweet" view of procedural due process.

> I dissent because the decision of the majority rests upon a proposition which was squarely addressed and in my view correctly rejected by six Members of this Court in *Arnett v. Kennedy*, 416 U.S. 134 (1974).

The second sentence of this ordinance plainly conditions petitioner's dismissal on cause—i.e., failure to perform up to standard, negligence, inefficiency, or unfitness to perform the job. The District Court below did not otherwise construe this portion of the ordinance. . . .

The majority . . . implicitly concedes that the ordinance supplies the "grounds" for discharge and that the City Manager must determine them to be "adequate" before he may fire an employee. The majority's holding that petitioner had no property interest in his job in spite of the unequivocal language in the city ordinance that he may be dismissed only for certain kinds of cause rests, then, on the fact that state law provides no *procedures* for assuring that the City Manager dismiss him only for cause. The right to his job apparently given by the first two sentences of the ordinance is thus redefined, according to the majority, by the procedures provided for in the third sentence and as redefined is infringed only if the procedures are not followed.

This is precisely the reasoning which was embraced by only three and expressly rejected by six Members of this Court in *Arnett v. Kennedy*. . . .

Id. at 355-57 (White, J., dissenting). Neary a decade later, Justice White was able to write a majority opinion more to his liking.

Cleveland Board of Education v. Loudermill
470 U.S. 532 (1985)

Justice WHITE delivered the opinion of the Court.

In these cases we consider what pretermination process must be accorded a public employee who can be discharged only for cause.

I

In 1979 the Cleveland Board of Education, petitioner in No. 83-1362, hired respondent James Loudermill as a security guard. On his job application, Loudermill stated that he had never been convicted of a felony. Eleven months later, as part of a routine examination of his employment records, the Board discovered that in fact Loudermill had been convicted of grand larceny in 1968. By letter dated November 3, 1980, the Board's Business Manager informed Loudermill that he had been dismissed because of his dishonesty in filling out the employment application. Loudermill was not afforded an opportunity to respond to the charge of dishonesty or to challenge his dismissal. On November 13, the Board adopted a resolution officially approving the discharge.

Under Ohio law, Loudermill was a "classified civil servant." Ohio Rev. Code Ann. § 124.11 (1984). Such employees can be terminated only for cause, and may obtain administrative review if discharged. § 124.34. Pursuant to this provision, Loudermill filed an appeal with the Cleveland Civil Service Commission on November 12. The Commission appointed a referee, who held a hearing on January 29, 1981. Loudermill argued that he had thought that his 1968 larceny conviction was for a misdemeanor rather than a felony. The referee recommended reinstatement. On July 20, 1981, the full Commission heard argument and orally announced that it would uphold the dismissal. Proposed findings of fact and conclusions of law followed on August 10, and Loudermill's attorneys were advised of the result by mail on August 21.

Although the Commission's decision was subject to judicial review in the state courts, Loudermill instead brought the present suit in the Federal District Court for the Northern District of Ohio. The complaint alleged that § 124.34 was unconstitutional on its face because it did not provide the employee an opportunity to respond to the charges against him prior to removal. As a result, discharged employees were deprived of liberty and property without due process. The complaint also alleged that the provision was unconstitutional as applied because discharged employees were not given sufficiently prompt postremoval hearings.

Before a responsive pleading was filed, the District Court dismissed for failure to state a claim on which relief could be granted. *See* Fed. Rule Civ. Proc. 12(b)(6). It held that because the very statute that created the property right in continued employment also specified the procedures for discharge, and because those procedures were followed, Loudermill was, by definition, afforded all the process due. The post-termination hearing also adequately protected Loudermill's liberty interests. Finally, the District Court concluded that, in light of the Commission's crowded docket, the delay in processing Loudermill's administrative appeal was constitutionally acceptable.

The other case before us arises on similar facts and followed a similar course. Respondent Richard Donnelly was a bus mechanic for the Parma Board of Education. In August 1977, Donnelly was fired because he had failed an eye examination. He was offered a chance to retake the examination but did not do so. Like Loudermill, Donnelly appealed to the Civil Service Commission. After a year of wrangling about the timeliness of his appeal, the Commission heard the case. It ordered Donnelly reinstated, though without backpay. In a complaint essentially identical to Loudermill's, Donnelly challenged the constitutionality of the dismissal procedures. The District Court dismissed for failure to state a claim, relying on its opinion in *Loudermill*.

. . . [The Sixth Circuit] Court of Appeals found that both respondents had been deprived of due process. [I]t concluded that the compelling private interest in retaining employment, combined with the value of presenting evidence prior to dismissal, outweighed the added administrative burden of a pretermination hearing. *Id. at* 561-562. . . .

Both employers petitioned for certiorari. In a cross-petition, Loudermill sought review of the rulings adverse to him. We granted all three petitions, and now affirm in all respects.

II

Respondents' federal constitutional claim depends on their having had a property right in continued employment. *Board of Regents v. Roth*, 408 U.S. 564, 576-578 (1972). If they did, the State could not deprive them of this property without due process. *See Goss v. Lopez*, 419 U.S. 565, 573-574 (1975).

Property interests are not created by the Constitution, "they are created and their dimensions are defined by existing rules or understandings that stem from an independent source such as state law. . . ." *Board of Regents v. Roth, supra*, 408 U.S., at 577. *See also Paul v. Davis*, 424 U.S. 693, 709 (1976). The Ohio statute plainly creates such an interest. Respondents were "classified civil service employees," Ohio Rev. Code Ann. § 124.11 (1984), entitled to retain their positions "during good behavior and efficient service," who could not be dismissed "except . . . for . . . misfeasance, malfeasance, or nonfeasance in office," § 124.34.4 The statute plainly supports the conclusion, reached by both lower courts, that respondents possessed property rights in continued employment. Indeed, this question does not seem to have been disputed below.

The Parma Board argues, however, that the property right is defined by, and conditioned on, the legislature's choice of procedures for its deprivation. The Board stresses that in addition to specifying the grounds for termination, the statute sets out procedures by which termination may take place. The procedures were adhered to in these cases. According to petitioner, "[t]o require additional procedures would in effect expand the scope of the property interest itself."

This argument, which was accepted by the District Court, has its genesis in the plurality opinion in *Arnett v. Kennedy*, 416 U.S. 134 (1974). *Arnett* involved a challenge by a former federal employee to the procedures by which he was dismissed. The plurality reasoned that where the legislation conferring the substantive right also sets out the procedural mechanism for enforcing that right, the two cannot be separated. . . .

This view garnered three votes in *Arnett*, but was specifically rejected by the other six Justices. *See id.* at 166-167 (Powell, J., joined by Blackmun, J.,); *id.* at 177-178, 185 (White, J.,); *id.* at 211 (Marshall, J., joined by Douglas and Brennan, JJ.). Since then, this theory has at times seemed to gather some additional support. *See Bishop v. Wood*, 426 U.S. 341, 355-361 (1976) (White, J., dissenting); *Goss v. Lopez*, 419 U.S., at 586-587 (Powell, J., joined by Burger, C.J., and Blackmun and Rehnquist, JJ., dissenting). More recently, however, the Court has clearly rejected it. In *Vitek v. Jones*,

445 U.S. 480, 491 (1980), we pointed out that "minimum [procedural] requirements [are] a matter of federal law, they are not diminished by the fact that the State may have specified its own procedures that it may deem adequate for determining the preconditions to adverse official action." This conclusion was reiterated in *Logan v. Zimmerman Brush Co.*, 455 U.S. 422, 432 (1982), where we reversed the lower court's holding that because the entitlement arose from a state statute, the legislature had the prerogative to define the procedures to be followed to protect that entitlement.

In light of these holdings, it is settled that the "bitter with the sweet" approach misconceives the constitutional guarantee. If a clearer holding is needed, we provide it today. The point is straightforward: the Due Process Clause provides that certain substantive rights—life, liberty, and property— cannot be deprived except pursuant to constitutionally adequate procedures. The categories of substance and procedure are distinct. Were the rule otherwise, the Clause would be reduced to a mere tautology. "Property" cannot be defined by the procedures provided for its deprivation any more than can life or liberty. The right to due process "is conferred, not by legislative grace, but by constitutional guarantee. While the legislature may elect not to confer a property interest in [public] employment, it may not constitutionally authorize the deprivation of such an interest, once conferred, without appropriate procedural safeguards." *Arnett v. Kennedy, supra*, 416 U.S., at 167 (Powell, J., concurring in part and concurring in result in part); *see id. at* 185 (White, J., concurring in part and dissenting in part).

In short, once it is determined that the Due Process Clause applies, "the question remains what process is due." *Morrissey v. Brewer*, 408 U.S. 471, 481 (1972). The answer to that question is not to be found in the Ohio statute.

[In Sections III and IV of its opinion, the Court applied the test it developed in *Mathews v. Eldridge*, 424 U.S. 319 (1976), to identify the procedural protections to which Loudermill was entitled. This issue is addressed beginning on p. 502].

[The concurring opinions of Justices BRENNAN and MARSHALL are omitted.]

Justice REHNQUIST, dissenting.

In *Arnett v. Kennedy*, 416 U.S. 134 (1974), six Members of this Court agreed that a public employee could be dismissed for misconduct without a full hearing prior to termination. A plurality of Justices agreed that the employee was entitled to exactly what Congress gave him, and no more. . . .

[Here,] in one legislative breath Ohio has conferred upon civil service employees such as respondents in these cases a limited form of tenure during good behavior, and prescribed the procedures by which that tenure may be terminated. Here, as in *Arnett*, "[t]he employee's statutorily defined right is not a guarantee against removal without cause in the abstract, but such a guarantee as enforced by the procedures which [the Ohio Legislature] has designated for the determination of cause." 416 U.S., at 152 (opinion of Rehnquist, J.)....

We ought to recognize the totality of the State's definition of the property right in question, and not merely seize upon one of several paragraphs in a unitary statute to proclaim that in that paragraph the State has inexorably conferred upon a civil service employee something which it is powerless under the United States Constitution to qualify in the next paragraph of the statute. This practice ignores our duty under *Roth* to rely on state law as the source of property interests for purposes of applying the Due Process Clause of the Fourteenth Amendment. While it does not impose a federal definition of property, the Court departs from the full breadth of the holding in *Roth* by its selective choice from among the sentences the Ohio Legislature chooses to use in establishing and qualifying a right....

Because I believe that the Fourteenth Amendment of the United States Constitution does not support the conclusion that Ohio's effort to confer a limited form of tenure upon respondents resulted in the creation of a "property right" in their employment, I dissent.

QUESTION SET 7.5

Review & Synthesis

1. Summarize the "bitter with the sweet" interpretation of procedural due process as described by Justice Rehnquist's plurality opinion in *Arnett v. Kennedy*. Under this interpretation, do policymakers (legislators or administrators) or courts determine how much procedural protection is provided to government benefits recipients?

2. Do you agree with Justice White's observation in *Loudermill* that substantive property interests cannot be defined by the procedures afforded for their protection any more than life or liberty can be? Is it not the case that life and liberty can only be *recognized* by the government, whereas property can be *created* by it? Should this distinction matter when addressing procedural due process claims?

3. Under the "bitter with the sweet" view of procedural due process, procedures matter only to the extent that they affect the value of an underlying substantive entitlement. Procedures, in other words, have no independent value of their own. Some scholars have rejected this view, arguing instead that procedures have *intrinsic* value. Not only are they a means by which governments reach decisions, they show the governments' respect for its people and reaffirm human worth and dignity. It is for this reason, they argue, that procedural due process should be set by the Constitution

and the courts, rather than by policymakers in statutes or regulations. *See generally*, Lawrence B. Solum, *Procedural Justice*, 78 S. CAL. L. REV. 181 (2004); JERRY L. MASHAW, DUE PROCESS IN THE ADMINISTRATIVE STATE (1985). With which of these positions do you most agree?

Application & Analysis

1. Fearing for her and her minor son's safety, Melinda sought and received a restraining order against Fred, her ex-boyfriend. The TRO instructed Fred to remain at least 500 feet from Melinda's home at all times and ordered him not to "interfere with or disturb the peace of [Melinda] or of [her son], directly or indirectly, for any purpose." The back of the TRO included the following preprinted language:

> **Warning: A Knowing Violation of a Restraining Order is a Crime.** A violation will also constitute contempt of court. You may be arrested without notice if a law enforcement officer has probable cause to believe that you have knowingly violated this order. . . .

> **Notice to Law Enforcement Officials:** You shall use every reasonable means to enforce this restraining order. You shall arrest, or, if arrest would be impractical under the circumstances, seek a warrant for the arrest of the restrained person when you have information amounting to probable cause that the restrained person has violated or attempted to violate any provision of this order and the restrained person has been properly served with a copy of this order or has received actual notice of the existence of this order.

After arriving home from work early one afternoon, Melinda did not see her son as she had expected. She immediately went to her son's school, thinking he might have remained there for activities or to play with friends. Failing to find him there and becoming increasingly alarmed, Melinda immediately drove home and called the Police Department. When an officer arrived shortly thereafter, Melinda showed her the TRO and demanded that it be enforced by finding Fred and immediately returning her son. The officer responded that there was nothing she could do at that point and suggested that Melinda call the Police Department again in a few hours if her son did not come back home. Melinda called again well after sunset when her son had not returned home and asked that the police search for him and Fred. The officer to whom she spoke refused to do so, and again suggested that she wait several more hours. Just after midnight, Melinda drove to the Police Department and filed a report, on which the Department's officers did not immediately act. Shortly before dawn, Fred entered the Police Department with Melinda's son. Fred immediately admitted that he had kidnapped the boy and had physically injured him in the course of doing so.

Melinda has filed a 42 U.S.C. § 1983 lawsuit against the Police Department, alleging that it has an official policy or custom of refusing properly to enforce TROs. She argues that this alleged policy or custom resulted in the violation of her procedural due process rights because the TRO gave her and her son a legitimate claim of entitlement to its enforcement against Fred, and the Department failed to hear or to seriously consider her repeated requests for that enforcement. The Police Department has responded that, contrary to Melinda's interpretation of the language printed on the back of the TRO, its enforcement is discretionary rather than mandatory.

You are a clerk for the judge before whom Melinda's lawsuit is pending. She has asked you to assess the legal merits of Melinda's argument.

D. THE INTERESTS PROTECTED: LIBERTY INTERESTS

As illustrated by the cases excerpted above, the Supreme Court has adopted a positive-law approach to defining property interests. It has told us that the government must affirmatively, and in its discretion, create the property interests to which procedural due process protections attach. We accordingly look to statutes, regulations, policies, and practices to figure out whether federal, state, or local governments have created legitimate claims of entitlement to government benefits. By contrast, the Court's liberty interest jurisprudence is defined by its erraticism. It is riddled with inconsistencies, contradictions, and retreats from seemingly settled law. As one commentator laments, "[t]he result has been an inconsistent pattern of decisions that cannot be explained by reference to any coherent principles." 2 RICHARD J. PIERCE, JR., ADMINISTRATIVE LAW TREATISE § 9.4 (2010).

Nevertheless, one can roughly outline two approaches for identifying constitutionally cognizable liberty interests. The first is a concept-based approach, in which the Court asks whether an asserted interest falls within the concept of "liberty" as used in the Fifth and Fourteenth Amendment Due Process Clauses. To answer this question, the Court has referred to natural rights, its own common sense (i.e., *ipsa dixitism*), and evidence of what the Founders would have understood the concept to include. Much of the Court's development of the concept-based approach has come in the context of alleged reputational harms caused by government decision-making. Plaintiffs in these cases claim that they have a liberty interest in their "good names" and that government officials deprived them of that interest by spreading negative information about them. In addition to modeling the Court's concept-based approach, the reputational harm cases introduce the "stigma-plus" test which the Court currently applies to liberty interest claims based on reputational harm.

Our consideration of the concept-based approach ends with the recent decision of *Kerry v. Din*, 135 S. Ct. 2128 (2015), among the last in which Justice Scalia delivered the opinion of the Court. It arises not in the context of reputational harm, but in the interesting intersection of immigration and marriage. The dueling opinions of the Court's former Administrative Law professors—Justice Scalia for the plurality and Justice Breyer for the dissent—provide excellent illustrations of the concept-based approach and the evidentiary disagreements it can generate. It also points to how the Court may understand and apply the approach going forward.

The second approach—which we shall call the positive law approach—is very similar to the Court's property interest analysis. Here, the Court recognizes only those liberty interests already recognized by federal or state law. We can trace the development of this approach through the Court's correctional facilities jurisprudence, which explores prisoners' liberty interest in being free from unnecessary physical restraint.

As you consider the materials that follow, try to identify the types of evidence on which the Justices rely when determining whether a protected liberty interest is implicated. Do they look for evidence that such interests were recognized and accepted in some other historical period? If so, to whose history does the Court most frequently refer: American, English, someone else's? Also, to what time period should such an inquiry be limited? Should the question even be empirically based? In other words, should the Justices recognize an alleged liberty interest based on whether it fits within abstract principles, and not on whether jurists or politicians in some earlier period demonstrably recognized it? Is the evidence the Court considered persuasive to be found in contemporaneous rather than in historical sources? With respect to the positive law approach in particular, do you think whether a person has a liberty interest under the *federal* Constitution should turn on a *state*'s decision to recognize it? Would you be more comfortable if the authority to recognize liberty interests rested with Congress, rather than with the states? If neither of these options appeal to you, are you comfortable with federal judges deciding the existence or nonexistence of these interests? If so, what principles would you adopt to limit their discretion?

1. The Concept-Based Approach

A seminal example of the concept-based approach comes in *Meyer v. Nebraska*, 262 U.S. 390 (1923). There, the Court said the following about the scope of liberty interests protected by procedural due process:

> While this court has not attempted to define with exactness the liberty thus guaranteed, the term has received much consideration and some of the included things have been definitely stated. Without doubt, it denotes not merely freedom from bodily restraint but also the right of

the individual to contract, to engage in any of the common occupations of life, to acquire useful knowledge, to marry, establish a home and bring up children, to worship God according to the dictates of his own conscience, and generally to enjoy those privileges long recognized at common law as essential to the orderly pursuit of happiness by free men.

Id. at 399 (citations omitted). As you can see, the Court disavowed any attempt to populate an exhaustive list of liberties the Constitution may protect, opting instead for a brief survey of liberties it has recognized in its prior decisions. The Court provided no concrete explanation for why these liberties triggered due process protections, offering only that they did so "without doubt" (i.e., "please don't ask us how we know this"), and that they had been "long recognized at common law" (i.e., "look back to English and early American experience").

Despite the innumerable liberties that could be identified by this approach, the Court has explored the contours of two more frequently than it has others: one's liberty interest in her reputation, and one's liberty interest in being free from physical restraint. With respect to the first of these, the Court has often queried what procedural due process protections the government owes if it stigmatizes someone.

In *Wisconsin v. Constantineau*, 400 U.S. 433 (1971), the respondent challenged a state statute that allowed her town's police chief, without notice or hearing, to post her name in retail liquor stores as an alcoholic to whom they should not give or sell inebriating beverages. The Court found that the "'[p]osting' under the Wisconsin Act may to some be . . . a stigma, an official branding of a person" that is "degrading." *Id.* at 437. In such instances, "[w]here a person's good name, reputation, honor, or integrity is at stake because of what the government is doing to him, notice and an opportunity to be heard are essential." *Id.* The Court pointed to no sources of evidence, other than its own perception of the obvious, to support its conclusion that reputation falls within the ambit of constitutionally protected liberty interests.

The Court reached a similar conclusion in *Goss v. Lopez*, 419 U.S. 565 (1975). There, public school officials suspended the respondent students for alleged misconduct without affording them pre-suspension hearings. Citing both *Constantineau* and *Board of Regents v. Roth*, the Court deemed the students' suspensions stigmatizing and hence a violation of their liberty interests in their reputations. The charges of wrongdoing on which the school based the suspensions "could seriously damage the students' standing with their fellow pupils and their teachers as well as interfere with later opportunities for higher education and employment." *Id.* at 575. Importantly, the Court distinguished the students' liberty interests in their reputations from their property interests in receiving the free education to which they were entitled under state law; either would have been independently sufficient to trigger the Fourteenth Amendment Due Process Clause. *Id.*

That a person has a liberty interest in her reputation seemed a settled issue until the Court's about face a little more than a year later. The petitioners in *Paul v. Davis*, 424 U.S. 693 (1976), police officials in Louisville, Kentucky, distributed fliers to local retail businesses warning them to look out for "active shoplifters." *Id.* at 695. The fliers included Davis' name and photo (among those of others), after he had been arrested for (though not convicted of) shoplifting, and even though he was never given the chance to challenge his inclusion.

The *Davis* Court reframed its prior holdings in both *Constantineau* and in *Roth*. Though *Constantineau*'s language seemed to say otherwise, the Court concluded that it did "not think that . . . defamation, standing alone, deprived Constantineau of any 'liberty' protected by the procedural guarantees of the Fourteenth Amendment." *Id.* at 709. Rather, it was her stigmatization *plus* a resulting infringement of her legal rights (the right to purchase alcohol) that triggered the procedural due process concerns in that case. The Court likewise reinterpreted *Roth*; the Due Process Clause could only protect Roth against stigma that *also* denied him other employment opportunities. *Id.* at 709-10. Now, the Court will find a procedural due process violation based on reputational harm only if that harm is accompanied by curtailed enjoyment of some *other* interest.

Accordingly, lower courts have interpreted *Paul* as establishing the so-called "stigma-plus" test; an asserted liberty interest is sufficient to trigger procedural due process protections if the government stigmatizes the claimant in connection with the denial of some state or federally recognized right or status. *See, e.g., Dennis v. S & S Consolidated Rural High School District*, 577 F.2d 338, 341 (5th Cir. 1978). In other words, courts after *Paul* now ask (1) whether the claimant has been stigmatized; (2) whether she has been or will be deprived of some "interest" recognized by state or federal law; and (3) whether there is a causal connection between her stigmatization and her deprivation. The reporters are filled with cases litigating the meaning of each prong of this test, with many being brought as civil rights cases against state and local governments under 42 U.S.C. § 1983. In particular, courts have grappled with the type of "interest" that, when coupled with stigmatization, is sufficient to implicate procedural due process rights. Must the claimant have a *property* interest? Is some lesser interest, plus stigmatization, enough?

The Third Circuit's influential decision in *Hill v. Borough of Kutztown*, 455 F.3d 225 (3d Cir. 2006), excerpted below, serves as an instructive example of how courts have applied the "stigma-plus" test. It also provides a helpful review of basic property interest analysis which, it turns out, figures heavily in the court's resolution of the liberty interest issue.

Hill v. Borough of Kutztown
455 F.3d 225 (3d Cir. 2006)

Before McKee and Garth, Circuit Judges, and Lifland, District Judge.*

Garth, Circuit Judge.

On this appeal we review whether the District Court erred when it dismissed Keith A. Hill's complaint charging Gennaro Marino (the former Mayor of the Borough of Kutztown[, Pennsylvania]), and the Borough itself, with violating his rights under the United States Constitution, federal and state statutes, and the common law of Pennsylvania. The District Court dismissed Hill's 6-count complaint in its entirety. We will affirm in part, and reverse in part.

I.

Appellant Hill, a licensed professional engineer, was appointed Borough Manager of Kutztown in early 1991. In this capacity, he reported to the Borough Council (which consisted of six elected members) and, "in respect to some subjects," to Gennaro Marino, the elected Mayor of the Borough. As Borough Manager, Hill was responsible for the administration of all departments within the Borough.

In short, Hill's complaint alleges that Mayor Marino harassed him and other Borough employees. When he reported the Mayor's harassment to the Borough Council, the Mayor intensified his attacks on Hill as retaliation for this reporting (and for positions Hill took that were contrary to the Mayor's positions). As a result of the Mayor's conduct, Hill's workplace became so intolerable that he had no choice but to resign.[2]

More specifically, the complaint alleges as follows: Shortly after he took office in 2002, Mayor Marino "began orally to spread the word that he intended to get rid of" Hill and "other high-priced senior staff employees." The Borough Council became aware of, and disapproved of, the things Marino was saying. . . .

Marino's conduct and behavior nevertheless continued. He told the Chief of Police that he "would make life difficult for him as a means to get him to resign as chief." Further, he behaved in a hostile and intimidating

---

* The Honorable John C. Lifland, Senior District Judge for the District of New Jersey, sitting by designation.

[2] Hill's employment was the responsibility of the Borough Council. He could only be appointed and fired by the Borough Council. 53 Pa. Cons. Stat. § 46141.

manner toward several other Borough employees, each of whom approached Hill and told him about this treatment at the hands of the Mayor.

In addition to his threats to "get rid of"—and his hostile treatment of—Borough employees, Mayor Marino also made several false accusations against Hill. At a meeting of the Borough Council on April 23, 2002, Mayor Marino demanded Hill's resignation, purportedly because of his involvement in certain appointments by the Council which the Mayor described as a "'plot' that was corrupt and criminal." Mayor Marino also told Borough employee Frank Caruso that Hill was "illegally moving funds to confuse everyone."

As part of his duties as Manager, Hill reported Mayor Marino's conduct towards him and towards the other Borough employees to the Borough Council.

Apparently at the same time that all of the above was occurring, Mayor Marino began to attack the Borough's telecommunications project, with which Hill was identified, and which had traditionally enjoyed the support of the Borough Council. The Mayor made clear his utter distaste for the project. In response, Hill advocated for the project's continuation.

As retaliation (1) for Hill's reporting the Mayor's conduct to the Borough Council, (2) for Hill's advocacy in support of the telecommunications project, and (3) for Hill's support of other unspecified positions that were associated with the previous mayor, Mayor Marino continued his persecution of Hill. Specifically, the Mayor engaged in a series of harassing, intimidating and oppressive confrontations with Hill at his workplace and at Council meetings, and defamed Hill to Borough employees, and to consultants present at Hill's workplace, and to the public.

Hill sent a number of letters to the Borough Solicitor and had multiple conversations with the Personnel Committee of the Borough Council, asking each to remedy the course of conduct by [Mayor] Marino. In July 2002, Hill made oral complaints to the Pennsylvania Human Relations Commission ("PHRC") and the Equal Employment Opportunity Commission ("EEOC"). He subsequently filed a written complaint with the PHRC.

The Mayor's conduct nevertheless persisted. On August 22, 2002, Mayor Marino published a "newspaper commentary" in which he accused Hill of "irregular or illegal" allocations of funds, and of "recklessly handling our money." This accusation was false. The Borough of Kutztown actually possessed a AAA credit rating. Moreover, a bond attorney, a bond underwriter and Borough auditors had verified the Borough's solid financial condition and its efficient management.

Prior to Mayor Marino's public attacks on him, Hill had enjoyed a reputation for honesty, integrity and professionalism. After Marino's attacks, Hill was subjected to scorn and ridicule, including one incident where Hill's son's employer confronted Hill and Hill's wife and told them that he, the employer, had heard the Mayor "was pursuing [Hill] concerning corruption."

The Mayor's conduct, and the Borough Council's failure to stop it, made life so intolerable for Hill that he eventually had no choice but to resign. Hill submitted a letter of resignation on August 29, 2002, which stated that he would cease work on October 12, 2002.

The Borough Council continued to be upset about Mayor Marino's conduct, and the effect it was having. It asked Hill to reconsider and stay on as Borough Manager. Hill refused, but did agree to postpone his departure until October 27, 2002.

Hill then accepted a position with the engineering consulting firm that had for years served in the role of Borough engineer. The Borough Council (by unanimous vote) initiated and worked out a part-time emergency "consulting" arrangement with that firm so that Hill could be made available to assist with certain urgent Borough tasks, such as budget preparation, in the period of transition to the new Manager. Hill worked in this capacity, without receiving any additional salary for it, until January 2003, when the Borough hired a replacement. The replacement was twenty-seven years old, some fifteen or sixteen years younger than Hill, who was over 40 years of age when he left the Borough's employ.

Hill brought this lawsuit against Mayor Marino (in his individual and official capacities) and the Borough of Kutztown. The complaint alleged that the Mayor's campaign of harassment, defamation and retaliation deprived Hill of his job (through constructive discharge[7]), and did damage to his reputation and his ability to earn a living as a licensed professional engineer and a public servant. He further alleged that the Borough Council "did not halt, reverse or lessen or otherwise materially affect the alleged offending conduct of the Mayor."

Hill's complaint asserted § 1983 claims against both the Mayor and the Borough for violation of his (1) procedural due process rights, (2) substantive due process rights, (3) equal protection rights, and (4) First Amendment rights under the U.S. Constitution. The complaint also asserted against the Borough (5) a claim under the Age Discrimination in Employment Act ("ADEA"), 29 U.S.C. § 621,

> **In Context**
>
> Provided in 42 U.S.C. § 1983 is a federal private right of action against any person acting "under color of" state or local law when those actions violate the plaintiff's federal rights.

et seq., and state law claims for (6) violation of the Pennsylvania Human Relations Act ("PHRA"), 43 PA. CONS. STAT. § 951, *et seq.* and (7) indemnification and restitution. Finally, the complaint asserted against the Mayor a (8) state law malicious prosecution claim.

---

[7] "Under the constructive discharge doctrine, an employee's reasonable decision to resign because of unendurable working conditions is assimilated to a formal discharge for remedial purposes." *Pennsylvania State Police v. Suders*, 542 U.S. 129, 141 (2004) (discussing constructive discharge in the context of a Title VII sexual harassment suit). "The inquiry is objective: Did working conditions become so intolerable that a reasonable person in the employee's position would have felt compelled to resign?" *Id.*

Pursuant to Rule 12(b)(6), the District Court dismissed all of the federal claims against both the Mayor and the Borough, and the PHRA claim against the Borough. It then declined to exercise jurisdiction over the remaining pendent state common law claims.

[In Section II of the court's opinion, it established its appellate jurisdiction over the district court's dismissal of Hill's complaint and described the applicable standard of review.]

III.

A.

We first address Hill's § 1983 claims against Mayor Marino. . . .

1. Procedural Due Process Claims[10]

To state a claim under § 1983 for deprivation of procedural due process rights, a plaintiff must allege that (1) he was deprived of an individual interest that is encompassed within the Fourteenth Amendment's protection of "life, liberty, or property," and (2) the procedures available to him did not provide "due process of law." *Alvin v. Suzuki*, 227 F.3d 107, 116 (3d Cir. 2000).

Hill advances two procedural due process claims. He first raises a classic property-based procedural due process claim, arguing that when Mayor Marino constructively discharged him, he was deprived of his right to continued employment without due process. He then raises a so-called "stigma-plus" claim, arguing that when Marino defamed him in the course of discharging him, he was deprived of his liberty interest in his reputation "without opportunity for any meaningful procedure."

a. Property Interest

The District Court properly concluded that Hill failed to state a claim for deprivation of his right to retain his job without due process because Hill's interest in retaining his job was not "encompassed within the Fourteenth Amendment's protection of property." "To have a property interest in a job . . . a person must have more than a unilateral expectation of continued

---

[10] We have held that a resignation will be deemed involuntary (i.e., deemed a constructive discharge) and will thus trigger the protections of the due process clause, and form the basis of a § 1983 due process claim, under only two circumstances: (1) when the employer forces the employee's resignation or retirement by coercion or duress, or (2) when the employer obtains the resignation or retirement by deceiving or misrepresenting a material fact to the employee. *Leheny v. City of Pittsburgh*, 183 F.3d 220, 228 (3d Cir. 1999).

employment; rather, she must have a legitimate entitlement to such continued employment." *Elmore v. Cleary*, 399 F.3d 279, 282 (3d Cir. 2005) (citing *Bd. of Regents v. Roth*, 408 U.S. 564, 577 (1972)). Whether a person has a legitimate entitlement to — and hence a property interest in — his government job is a question answered by state law. *Id.*

Pursuant to Pennsylvania law, Hill was an at-will employee. "The decisional law is clear that an at-will employee does not have a legitimate entitlement to continued employment because [he] serves solely at the pleasure of [his] employer." *Elmore*, 399 F.3d at 282. Hill thus lacked a property interest in retaining his position as Borough Manager that was "sufficient to trigger due process concerns." *Id.* We therefore need not consider whether the procedures available to him provided due process in order to conclude that the District Court should be affirmed on Hill's claim that he was deprived of employment without due process.

b. Liberty Interest

In his second procedural due process claim, Hill alleges that he suffered harm to his reputation and ability to earn a living in his chosen profession as a result of the defamatory statements Marino made about him in the process of constructively discharging him; he claims Marino's scurrilous and false charges deprived him of a liberty interest protected by the due process clause. The District Court dismissed this claim for this same reason it denied Hill's other procedural due process claim: because Hill lacked a property interest in retaining his job.

[T]he District Court held that defamation such as that with which Hill charges Marino, does not implicate a liberty interest protected by the due process clause unless it "occurs in the course of or is accompanied by . . . extinguishment of a right or status guaranteed by law or the Constitution." Because Hill lacked a property interest in retaining his job under state law, the District Court held, Hill was not deprived of such a right or status when he was constructively discharged. Accordingly, Hill's due process claim failed.

This court has yet to decide the question of whether a public employee who is defamed in the course of being discharged, fails to state a claim for deprivation of a liberty interest merely because he lacked a property interest in continued employment that is independently protected by the due process clause. Hill's appeal now presents that issue squarely.

The Supreme Court held in *Wisconsin v. Constantineau*, 400 U.S. 433 (1971) that an individual has a protectable interest in reputation. "Where a person's good name, reputation, honor, or integrity is at stake because of what the government is doing to him, notice and an opportunity to be heard are essential." *Id.* at 437.

Courts have subsequently clarified, however, that "reputation *alone* is not an interest protected by the Due Process Clause." *Versarge v. Township of Clinton, New Jersey*, 984 F.2d 1359, 1371 (3d Cir. 1993) (citing *Paul v. Davis*, 424 U.S. 693, 701-712 (1976)) (emphasis added). Rather, to make out a due process claim for deprivation of a liberty interest in reputation, a plaintiff must show a stigma to his reputation *plus* deprivation of some additional right or interest. *Paul v. Davis*, 424 U.S. 693, 701 (1976). *Accord, e.g., Siegert v. Gilley*, 500 U.S. 226, 233-234 (1991). We have referred to this as the "stigma-plus" test.

In the public employment context, the "stigma-plus" test has been applied to mean that when an employer "creates and disseminates a false and defamatory impression about the employee in connection with his termination," it deprives the employee of a protected liberty interest. *Codd v. Velger*, 429 U.S. 624, 628 (1977). The creation and dissemination of a false and defamatory impression is the "stigma," and the termination is the "plus." When such a deprivation occurs, the employee is entitled to a name-clearing hearing.

To satisfy the "stigma" prong of the test, it must be alleged that the purportedly stigmatizing statement(s) (1) were made publicly, *Bishop v. Wood*, 426 U.S. 341, 348 (1976), and (2) were false. *Codd*, 429 U.S. at 627–629.

Hill has clearly alleged that Marino defamed him by accusing him of wrongdoing. He alleges that the accusations were made publicly—before his colleagues and before the general public (at Borough Council meetings and in newspaper articles). He alleges that the accusations were false, and that they tarnished his reputation and "subjected [him] to scorn and ridicule."[16] His complaint thus adequately alleges the "stigma" prong of the "stigma-plus" test.

What is required to satisfy the "plus" prong of the test in the public employment context is more equivocal. The Supreme Court precedent is not crystal clear on whether termination from government employment constitutes a sufficient "plus" when, as a matter of state law, the plaintiff lacked a property interest in retaining his job.

In *Paul v. Davis*, the Court stated, somewhat enigmatically, that the "plus" had to be an alteration or extinguishment of "a right or status previously recognized by state law." 424 U.S. at 711. That Court's treatment of *Board of Regents v. Roth*, 408 U.S. 564, 573 (1972) suggests that, under this standard, a person's loss of employment to which he did not hold a state law-created property interest is a sufficient "plus."

---

[16] The Mayor suggests that his statements about which Hill complains could not be sufficiently stigmatizing because they addressed "matters of public concern" (a phrase of art relevant in the First Amendment context), or because they were one public servant's statements about another public servant's performance of his public job. The statements about which Hill complains are not statements of opinion about the issues of the day, however, or standard comments made among politicians in the rough-and-tumble that is local politics. He complains about factual allegations of illegal conduct, that allegedly were false, and that the Mayor allegedly knew were false. They are not protected as a matter of law by any exception for "matters of public concern" or "public servant" exception.

In *Roth*, a non-tenured professor who had not been reappointed after his initial one-year term ended claimed he had been deprived of a right to continued employment without due process. The Court denied his claim, finding that the professor, because he was not tenured, did not have a property right to continued employment. It noted, however, that had the University defamed the professor in the course of declining to rehire him, it would have deprived the professor of a liberty interest. *Id.* at 573. It came to this conclusion despite the fact that the professor lacked a property interest in his job. The Court in *Paul v. Davis*—and then in later opinions—impliedly endorsed this conclusion. 424 U.S. at 709-710. *See also Siegert*, 500 U.S. at 233; *Owen v. City of Independence*, 445 U.S. 622, 633 note 13 (1980).

Though it has never again taken this issue on directly, the Court in subsequent opinions has reiterated that the "plus" in "stigma-plus" claims arising out of public employment decisions, may be loss of a job in which the plaintiff held no property interest under state law. In *Owen*, the Eighth Circuit had held that the police chief petitioner "possessed no property interest in continued employment," but that allegedly false accusations the city made incident to his discharge "had blackened petitioner's name and reputation, thus depriving him of liberty without due process of law." 445 U.S. at 631. Citing *Roth* and *Paul v. Davis*, the Supreme Court held that it had "no doubt that the Court of Appeals" was correct in this conclusion. *Id.* at 633 note 13. Similarly, in *Codd v. Velger*, the Court stated that "where a non-tenured employee has been stigmatized in the course of a decision to terminate his employment," he is entitled to a name-clearing hearing. 429 U.S. at 627.[18]

We, too, have never clearly answered the question whether termination from a government job constitutes a sufficient "plus" under the "stigma-plus" test when, as a matter of state law, the plaintiff lacked a property interest in retaining the job. . . .

We have in several cases used language that could be read broadly to require that the "plus" be loss of a job in which the plaintiff had a protectible property interest. These cases, however, are all factually distinguishable. In each of them, we held that the deprivation the plaintiff suffered along with stigma to his reputation was not sufficiently weighty to satisfy the "plus" requirement. We so held because the plaintiff did not lose his job, and instead complained about some adverse employment action less drastic than discharge. Here, however, Hill did lose his job. The "plus," consisting of Hill's constructive discharge was substantial—so substantial, in fact, that we can comfortably hold that Hill has met all requirements of "stigma-plus."

We therefore conclude today that a public employee who is defamed in the course of being terminated or constructively discharged satisfies the

---

[18] In *Codd v. Velger*, the Court denied the claim of the petitioner—a probationary employee who lacked a property interest in his job—not because he was probationary, but because he failed to allege that the information that had been disclosed was false. 429 U.S. at 627–628.

"stigma-plus" test even if, as a matter of state law, he lacks a property interest in the job he lost.

We note that other courts have come to this conclusion, mostly based on Supreme Court language in *Paul v. Davis. See, e.g., Doe v. U.S. Dept. of Justice,* 753 F.2d 1092, 1104-1112 (D.C. Cir. 1985); *Dennis v. S & S Consol. Rural High Sch. Dist.,* 577 F.2d 338, 342-343 (5th Cir. 1978); *Colaizzi v. Walker,* 542 F.2d 969, 973 (7th Cir.1976).

We believe that this conclusion makes good sense, and is logical. To hold otherwise—that a government employee must be deprived of a state law-created property interest in continued employment in order to satisfy the "plus" in a "stigma-plus" claim—would

> equate the interests protected by the property clause of the [fourteenth] amendment with those protected by the liberty clause . . . [T]he liberty clause would be stripped of any independent meaning in the context of government defamation. Government employees who enjoy an independent property interest in continued employment, of course, must be afforded due process upon termination regardless of whether they are discharged in connection with stigmatizing allegations. That process will ordinarily afford those employees an opportunity to refute stigmatizing allegations. The liberty clause, by contrast, protects reputation, not job tenure, in the government employment context. Although *Paul* requires the alteration of some governmentally recognized status in addition to defamation, the *Paul* court plainly declined to equate that additional component with an independent, constitutionally protected property interest.

Doe, 753 F.2d at 1108 n. 15.

Hill has alleged that Marino's defamation occurred in connection with his discharge. Under our holding today, this is sufficient to satisfy the "plus" prong of the "stigma-plus" test, despite the fact that Hill was an at-will employee and did not have a property interest in continued employment under state law.

Hill has thus alleged deprivation of a liberty interest protectible under the due process clause. Hill was not given the process he was due—a name-clearing hearing. He has consequently stated a claim for deprivation of his liberty interest in his reputation without the process the U.S. constitution [sic] requires.

[In the remainder of its opinion, the court affirmed the district court's dismissal of most of Hill's other claims.]

. . . We will remand for further proceedings consistent with this opinion. On remand, the District Court will have to address the state claims over which it declined to exercise jurisdiction.

* * *

Since the late nineteenth century, the Supreme Court has made clear that Congress and the President have broad discretion under the

Constitution to set the nation's immigration policies. This is particularly true when dealing with the admission or exclusion of noncitizens. *See, e.g., Chae Chan Ping v. United States,* 130 U.S. 581 (1889), including those seeking entry to the United States for the first time. Moreover, the political Branches' near total immigration authority extends to questions of both substance and procedure. In terms that foreshadowed the "bitter with the sweet" procedural due process debates of the 1970s and 1980s (*see Cleveland Board of Education v. Loudermill, supra*), the Court has stated flatly that "the decisions of executive or administrative officers, acting within powers expressly conferred by Congress, *are* due process of law." *Nishimura Ekiu v. United States,* 142 U.S. 651, 660 (1892) (emphasis added). The Court has accordingly turned away noncitizens seeking entry to the United States who claim that either the substance or the enforcement of federal immigration policy violated their right to procedural due process. It has framed these disputes as political rather than judicial and thus as constitutionally committed to Congress and the President instead of the courts. *See, e.g., Fong Yue Ting v. United States,* 149 U.S. 698, 713-14 (1893) (quoting *Murray's Lessee v. Hoboken Land & Improvement Co.,* 59 U.S. (18 How.) 272, 284 (1856)).

It was not until 1903 that the Court recognized that the political Branches' plenary immigration power could be tempered by procedural due process and that pronouncement arose in the case of a noncitizen who was already in the country. *See Yamataya v. Fischer,* 189 U.S. 86, 101 (1903) ("[I]t is not competent for . . . any executive officer . . . arbitrarily to cause an alien, who has entered the country, and has become subject in all respects to its jurisdiction, and a part of its population, although alleged to be illegally here, to be taken into custody and deported without giving him all opportunity to be heard upon the question involving his right to be and remain in the United States."). It is true that the Court has been more open in recent years to procedural due process claims raised by noncitizens in some immigration contexts, such as when they begin to develop ties to the country through their presence in it. *See, e.g., Landon v. Plascencia,* 459 U.S. 21, 32-33 (1982) (recognizing procedural due process right of lawful permanent resident denied re-admission to the United States). *Cf. Shaughnessy v. United States ex rel. Mezei,* 345 U.S. 206, 212 (1953) (holding that noncitizens "who have once passed through our gates, even illegally," must be afforded procedural due process protections, and "may be expelled only after proceedings conforming to traditional standards of fairness"). Nevertheless, it retains a stingy procedural due process view when it comes to noncitizens seeking first-time entry into the country, deeming such entry a mere privilege to which the noncitizen can claim no right. *See, e.g., id.* at 32 ("This Court has long held that an alien seeking initial admission to the United States requests a privilege and has no constitutional rights regarding his application, for the power to admit or exclude aliens is a sovereign prerogative.") (citing *Fiallo v. Bell,* 430 U.S. 787, 792 (1977); *Kleindienst v. Mandel,* 408 U.S. 753 (1972)).

It is against this legal and historical backdrop that the Court decided *Kerry v. Din* in 2015. There a State Department consular officer denied an American citizen's husband's visa application. The husband was afforded no pre-denial process (other than consideration of his written application by the consular officer) and was provided little in the way of an explanation for the denial. Understanding that Supreme Court case law gave the husband practically no hope of successfully pressing his own procedural due process claim, his citizen wife asserted that the State Department's decision infringed *her* liberty interest in living with him in the United States. In effect, she argued that the government's treatment of her husband harmed her so grievously that it deprived her of liberty in violation of the Fifth Amendment Due Process Clause.

In addition to describing the (almost nonexistent) procedural due process rights afforded to noncitizens seeking first-time entry into the United States, *Din* provides an excellent and fairly recent working example of how the Court wrestles with the concept-based approach to liberty interests. Take note of how Justices Scalia and Breyer identify the contours of the respondent's liberty interest in her marriage. What types of evidence do they think are relevant to the inquiry? Who has the more persuasive argument?

Kerry v. Din
135 S. Ct. 2128 (2015)

Justice Scalia announced the judgment of the Court and delivered an opinion, in which The Chief Justice and Justice Thomas join.

Fauzia Din is a citizen and resident of the United States. Her husband, Kanishka Berashk, is an Afghan citizen and former civil servant in the Taliban regime who resides in that country. When the Government declined to issue an immigrant visa to Berashk, Din sued.

The state action of which Din complains is the denial of Berashk's visa application. Naturally, one would expect him—not Din—to bring this suit. But because Berashk is an unadmitted and nonresident alien, he has no right of entry into the United States, and no cause of action to press in furtherance of his claim for admission. *See Kleindienst v. Mandel*, 408 U.S. 753, 762 (1972). So, Din attempts to bring suit on his behalf, alleging that the Government's denial of her husband's visa application violated *her* constitutional rights [emphasis added]. In particular, she claims that the Government denied her due process of law when, without adequate explanation of the reason for the visa denial, it deprived her of her constitutional right to live in the United States with her spouse. There is no such constitutional right. What Justice Breyer's dissent strangely describes as a "deprivation of her freedom to live together with her spouse in America" is, in any world other than the artificial world of ever-expanding constitutional rights, nothing more than a deprivation of her spouse's freedom to immigrate into America.

For the reasons given in this opinion and in the opinion concurring in the judgment, we vacate and remand.

I

A

Under the Immigration and Nationality Act (INA), 66 Stat. 163, as amended, 8 U.S.C. § 1101 *et seq.*, an alien may not enter and permanently reside in the United States without a visa. § 1181(a). The INA creates a special visa-application process for aliens sponsored by "immediate relatives" in the United States. §§ 1151(b), 1153(a). Under this process, the citizen-relative first files a petition on behalf of the alien living abroad, asking to have the alien classified as an immediate relative. See §§ 1153(f), 1154(a)(1). If and when a petition is approved, the alien may apply for a visa by submitting the required documents and appearing at a United States Embassy or consulate for an interview with a consular officer. *See* §§ 1201(a)(1), 1202. Before issuing a visa, the consular officer must ensure the alien is not inadmissible under any provision of the INA. § 1361.

One ground for inadmissibility, § 1182(a)(3)(B), covers "[t]errorist activities." In addition to the violent and destructive acts the term immediately brings to mind, the INA defines "terrorist activity" to include providing material support to a terrorist organization and serving as a terrorist organization's representative. § 1182(a)(3)(B)(i), (iii)-(vi).

B

Fauzia Din came to the United States as a refugee in 2000, and became a naturalized citizen in 2007. She filed a petition to have Kanishka Berashk, whom she married in 2006, classified as her immediate relative. The petition was granted, and Berashk filed a visa application. The U.S. Embassy in Islamabad, Pakistan, interviewed Berashk and denied his application. A consular officer informed Berashk that he was inadmissible under § 1182(a)(3)(B) but provided no further explanation.

Din then brought suit in Federal District Court seeking a writ of mandamus directing the United States to properly adjudicate Berashk's visa application. . . . The District Court granted the Government's motion to dismiss, but the Ninth Circuit reversed. The Ninth Circuit concluded that Din "has a protected liberty interest in marriage that entitled [her] to review of the denial of [her] spouse's visa," 718 F.3d 856, 860 (2013), and that the Government's citation of § 1182(a)(3)(B) did not provide Din with the "limited judicial review" to which she was entitled under the Due Process Clause, *Id. at* 868. This Court granted certiorari.

II

The Fifth Amendment provides that "[n]o person shall be . . . deprived of life, liberty, or property, without due process of law." Although the amount and quality of process that our precedents have recognized as "due" under the Clause has changed considerably since the founding, it remains the case that no process is due if one is not deprived of "life, liberty, or property." The first question that we must ask, then, is whether the denial of Berashk's visa application deprived Din of any of these interests. Only if we answer in the affirmative must we proceed to consider whether the Government's explanation afforded sufficient process.

A

The Due Process Clause has its origin in Magna Carta. As originally drafted, the Great Charter provided that "[n]o freeman shall be taken, or imprisoned, or be disseised of his freehold, or liberties, or free customs, or be outlawed, or exiled, or any otherwise destroyed; nor will we not pass upon him, nor condemn him, but by lawful judgment of his peers, or *by the law of the land.*" Magna Carta, ch. 29, in 1 E. Coke, The Second Part of the Institutes of the Laws of England 45 (1797) (emphasis added). The Court has recognized that at the time of the Fifth Amendment's ratification, the words "due process of law" were understood "to convey the same meaning as the words 'by the law of the land'" in Magna Carta. *Murray's Lessee v. Hoboken Land & Improvement Co.,* 18 How. 272, 276 (1856). Although the terminology associated with the guarantee of due process changed dramatically between 1215 and 1791, the general scope of the underlying rights protected stayed roughly constant.

Edward Coke, whose Institutes "were read in the American Colonies by virtually every student of law," *Klopfer v. North Carolina,* 386 U.S. 213, 225 (1967), thoroughly described the scope of the interests that could be deprived only pursuant to "the law of the land." Magna Carta, he wrote, ensured that, without due process, "no man [may] be taken or imprisoned"; "disseised of his lands, or tenements, or dispossessed of his goods, or chattels"; "put from his livelihood without answer"; "barred to have the benefit of the law"; denied "the franchises, and priviledges, which the subjects have of the gift of the king"; "exiled"; or "forejudged of life, or limbe, disherited, or put to torture, or death." 1 Coke, *supra,* at 46-48. Blackstone's description of the rights protected by Magna Carta is similar, although he discusses them in terms much closer to the "life, liberty, or property" terminology used in the Fifth Amendment. He described first an interest in "personal security," "consist[ing] in a person's legal and uninterrupted enjoyment of his life, his limbs, his body, his health, and his reputation." 1 William Blackstone, Commentaries on the Laws of England 125 (1769). Second, the "personal liberty of individuals" "consist[ed] in the power of locomotion, of changing situation, or removing one's person to whatsoever place one's own inclination may direct; without imprisonment or restraint." *Id. at* 130. And finally, a person's right to property included "the free use, enjoyment, and disposal of all his acquisitions." *Id. at* 134.

Din, of course, could not conceivably claim that the denial of Berashk's visa application deprived her — or for that matter even Berashk — of life or property; and under the above described historical understanding, a claim that it deprived her of liberty is equally absurd. The Government has not "taken or imprisoned" Din, nor has it "confine[d]" her, either by "keeping [her] against h[er] will in a private house, putting h[er] in the stocks, arresting or forcibly detaining h[er] in the street." *Id.* at 132. Indeed, not even Berashk has suffered a deprivation of liberty so understood.

B

Despite this historical evidence, this Court has seen fit on several occasions to expand the meaning of "liberty" under the Due Process Clause to include certain implied "fundamental rights." (The reasoning presumably goes like this: If you have a right to do something, you are free to do it, and deprivation of freedom is a deprivation of "liberty" — never mind the original meaning of that word in the Due Process Clause.) These implied rights have been given more protection than "life, liberty, or property" properly understood. While one may be dispossessed of property, thrown in jail, or even executed so long as proper procedures are followed, the enjoyment of implied constitutional rights cannot be limited at all, except by provisions that are "narrowly tailored to serve a compelling state interest." *Reno v. Flores,* 507 U.S. 292, 301-302 (1993). Din does not explicitly argue that the Government has violated this absolute prohibition of the substantive component of the Due Process Clause, likely because it is obvious that a law barring aliens engaged in terrorist activities from entering this country is narrowly tailored to serve a compelling state interest. She nevertheless insists that, because enforcement of the law affects her enjoyment of an implied fundamental liberty, the Government must first provide her a full battery of procedural-due-process protections.

I think it worth explaining why, even if one accepts the textually unsupportable doctrine of implied fundamental rights, Din's arguments would fail. Because "extending constitutional protection to an asserted right or liberty interest . . . place[s] the matter outside the arena of public debate and legislative action," *Washington v. Glucksberg,* 521 U.S. 702, 720 (1997), and because the "guideposts for responsible decisionmaking in this unchartered area are scarce and open-ended," *Collins v. Harker Heights,* 503 U.S. 115,

125 (1992), "[t]he doctrine of judicial self-restraint requires us to exercise the utmost care whenever we are asked to break new ground in this field," *ibid.* Accordingly, before conferring constitutional status upon a previously unrecognized "liberty," we have required "a careful description of the asserted fundamental liberty interest," as well as a demonstration that the interest is "objectively, deeply rooted in this Nation's history and tradition, and implicit in the concept of ordered liberty, such that neither liberty nor justice would exist if [it was] sacrificed." *Glucksberg, supra,* at 720-721 (citations and internal quotation marks omitted).

Din describes the denial of Berashk's visa application as implicating, alternately, a "liberty interest in her marriage," a "right of association with one's spouse," "a liberty interest in being reunited with certain blood relatives," and "the liberty interest of a U.S. citizen under the Due Process Clause to be free from arbitrary restrictions on his right to live with his spouse." To be sure, this Court has at times indulged a propensity for grandiloquence when reviewing the sweep of implied rights, describing them so broadly that they would include not only the interests Din asserts but many others as well. For example: "Without doubt, [the liberty guaranteed by the Due Process Clause] denotes not merely freedom from bodily restraint but also the right of the individual to contract, to engage in any of the common occupations of life, to acquire useful knowledge, to marry, establish a home and bring up children, [and] to worship God according to the dictates of his own conscience." *Meyer v. Nebraska,* 262 U.S. 390, 399 (1923). But this Court is not bound by dicta, especially dicta that have been repudiated by the holdings of our subsequent cases. And the actual holdings of the cases Din relies upon hardly establish the capacious right she now asserts.

Unlike the States in *Loving v. Virginia,* 388 U.S. 1 (1967), *Zablocki v. Redhail,* 434 U.S. 374 (1978), and *Turner v. Safley,* 482 U.S. 78 (1987), the Federal Government here has not attempted to forbid a marriage. Although Din and the dissent borrow language from those cases invoking a fundamental right to marriage, they both implicitly concede that no such right has been infringed in this case. Din relies on the "associational interests in marriage that necessarily are protected by the right to marry," and that are "presuppose[d]" by later cases establishing a right to marital privacy. The dissent supplements the fundamental right to marriage with a fundamental right to live in the United States in order to find an affected liberty interest. . . .

Nothing in the cases Din cites establishes a free-floating and categorical liberty interest in marriage (or any other formulation Din offers) sufficient to trigger constitutional protection whenever a regulation in any way touches upon an aspect of the marital relationship. . . .

Here, a long practice of regulating spousal immigration precludes Din's claim that the denial of Berashk's visa application has deprived her of a fundamental liberty interest. Although immigration was effectively unregulated prior to 1875, as soon as Congress began legislating in this area it enacted a complicated web of regulations that erected serious impediments to a person's ability to bring a spouse into the United States. . . .

To be sure, these early regulations were premised on the derivative citizenship of women, a legacy of the law of coverture that was already in decline at the time. Modern equal-protection doctrine casts substantial doubt on the permissibility of such asymmetric treatment of women citizens in the immigration context, and modern moral judgment rejects the premises of such a legal order. Nevertheless, this all-too-recent practice repudiates any contention that Din's asserted liberty interest is "deeply rooted in this Nation's history and tradition, and implicit in the concept of ordered liberty." *Glucksberg*, *supra*, at 720 (citations and internal quotations marks omitted).

Indeed, the law showed little more solicitude for the marital relationship when it was a male resident or citizen seeking admission for his fiancée or wife. . . . [A] citizen could move his spouse forward in the line, but once all the quota spots were filled for the year, the spouse was barred without exception. . . .

. . . Even where Congress has provided special privileges to promote family immigration, it has also written in careful checks and qualifications. This Court has consistently recognized that these various distinctions are "policy questions entrusted exclusively to the political branches of our Government, and we have no judicial authority to substitute our political judgment for that of the Congress." *Fiallo v. Bell*, 430 U.S. 787, 798. Only by diluting the meaning of a fundamental liberty interest and jettisoning our established jurisprudence could we conclude that the denial of Berashk's visa application implicates any of Din's fundamental liberty interests.

C

Justice BREYER suggests that procedural due process rights attach to liberty interests that either are (1) created by nonconstitutional law, such as a statute, or (2) "sufficiently important" so as to "flow 'implicit[ly]' from the design, object, and nature of the Due Process Clause."

The first point is unobjectionable, at least given this Court's case law. *See, e.g., Goldberg v. Kelly*, 397 U.S. 254, 262, and note 8 (1970). But it is unhelpful to Din, who does not argue that a statute confers on her a liberty interest protected by the Due Process Clause. Justice Breyer attempts to make this argument for Din, latching onto language in *Wilkinson v. Austin*, 545 U.S. 209, 221 (2005), saying that a liberty interest "may arise from an expectation or interest created by state laws or policies." Such an "expectation" has been created here, he asserts, because "the law . . . surrounds marriage with a host of legal protections to the point that it creates a strong expectation that government will not deprive married individuals of their freedom to live together without strong reasons and (in individual cases) without fair procedure." But what *Wilkinson* meant by an "expectation or interest" was not that sort of judicially unenforceable substantial hope, but a present and legally recognized substantive entitlement. . . . The legal benefits afforded to marriages and the preferential treatment accorded to visa applicants with citizen relatives are insufficient to confer on Din a right that can be deprived only pursuant to procedural due process.

Justice Breyer's second point—that procedural due process rights attach even to some nonfundamental liberty interests that have not been created by statute—is much more troubling. He relies on the implied-fundamental-rights cases discussed above to divine a "right of spouses to live together and to raise a family," along with "a citizen's right to live within this country." But perhaps recognizing that our established methodology for identifying fundamental rights cuts against his conclusion, he argues that the term "liberty" in the Due Process Clause includes implied rights that, although not so fundamental as to deserve substantive-due-process protection, are important enough to deserve procedural-due-process protection. In other words, there are two categories of implied rights protected by the Due Process Clause: really fundamental rights, which cannot be taken away at all absent a compelling state interest; and not-so-fundamental rights, which can be taken away so long as procedural due process is observed.

The dissent fails to cite a single case supporting its novel theory of implied nonfundamental rights. . . .

[Moreover, holding that there are implied nonfundamental rights protected by procedural due process would create] a dangerous doctrine. It [would vastly expand] the scope of our implied-rights jurisprudence by setting it free from the requirement that the liberty interest be "objectively, deeply rooted in this Nation's history and tradition, and implicit in the concept of ordered liberty," *Glucksberg*, 521 U.S., at 720-721 (internal quotation marks omitted). Even shallow-rooted liberties would, thanks to this new procedural-rights-only notion of quasi-fundamental rights, qualify for judicially imposed procedural requirements. Moreover, Justice Breyer gives no basis for distinguishing the fundamental rights recognized in the cases he depends on from the nonfundamental right he believes they give rise to in the present case.

Neither Din's right to live with her spouse nor her right to live within this country is implicated here. There is a "simple distinction between government action that directly affects a citizen's legal rights, or imposes a direct restraint on his liberty, and action that is directed against a third party and affects the citizen only indirectly or incidentally." *O'Bannon v. Town Court Nursing Center*, 447 U.S. 773, 788 (1980). The Government has not refused to recognize Din's marriage to Berashk, and Din remains free to live with her husband anywhere in the world that both individuals are permitted to reside. And the Government has not expelled Din from the country. It has simply determined that Kanishka Berashk engaged in terrorist activities within the meaning of the Immigration and Nationality Act, and has therefore denied him admission into the country. This might, indeed, deprive Din of something "important," but if that is the criterion for Justice Breyer's new pairing of substantive and procedural due process, we are in for quite a ride.

* * *

Because Fauzia Din was not deprived of "life, liberty, or property" when the Government denied Kanishka Berashk admission to the United States, there is no process due to her under the Constitution. To the extent that she received any explanation for the Government's decision, this was more than the Due Process Clause required. The judgment of the Ninth Circuit is vacated, and the case is remanded for further proceedings.

It is so ordered.

Justice KENNEDY, with whom Justice ALITO joins, concurring in the judgment.

[Justices Kennedy and Alito agreed with the plurality's conclusion that Din lacked a procedural due process claim. Thus, five Justices were able to cobble together enough votes to vacate the Ninth Circuit's prior judgment. Kennedy and Alito did not believe, however, that the Court needed to decide whether Din had a protected liberty interest in her husband's visa denial or immigration status. Even assuming she did, they felt that the process already afforded to her by the State Department's consular officers satisfied the requirements of procedural due process. The issue of the process due to a holder of procedural due process rights — the one on which Justices Kennedy and Alito would have decided this case — is addressed below, beginning with the Court's decision in *Mathews v. Eldridge*.]

Justice BREYER, with whom Justice GINSBURG, Justice SOTOMAYOR, and Justice KAGAN join, dissenting.

I

The plurality opinion (which is not controlling) concludes that Ms. Din lacks the kind of liberty interest to which the Due Process Clause provides procedural protections. . . . I believe that Ms. Din possesses that kind of constitutional interest.

The liberty interest that Ms. Din seeks to protect consists of her freedom to live together with her husband in the United States. She seeks procedural, not substantive, protection for this freedom.

Our cases make clear that the Due Process Clause entitles her to such procedural rights as long as (1) she seeks protection for a liberty interest sufficiently important for procedural protection to flow "implicit[ly]" from the design, object, and nature of the Due Process Clause, or (2) nonconstitutional law (a statute, for example) creates "an expectation" that a person will not be deprived of that kind of liberty without fair procedures. *Wilkinson, supra,* at 221.

The liberty for which Ms. Din seeks protection easily satisfies both standards. As this Court has long recognized, the institution of marriage, which encompasses the right of spouses to live together and to raise a family, is central to human life, requires and enjoys community support, and plays a central role in most individuals' "orderly pursuit of happiness," *Meyer v. Nebraska*, 262 U.S. 390, 399 (1923). Similarly, the Court has long recognized that a citizen's right to live within this country, being fundamental, enjoys basic procedural due process protection.

At the same time, the law, including visa law, surrounds marriage with a host of legal protections to the point that it creates a strong expectation that government will not deprive married individuals of their freedom to live together without strong reasons and (in individual cases) without fair procedure. Justice Scalia's response—that nonconstitutional law creates an "expectation" that merits procedural protection under the Due Process Clause only if there is an unequivocal statutory right—is sorely mistaken. His argument rests on the rights/privilege distinction that this Court rejected almost five decades ago, in the seminal case of *Goldberg v. Kelly*, 397 U.S. 254, 262 (1970). *See generally Board of Regents of State Colleges v. Roth*, 408 U.S. 564, 571 (1972) ("[T]he Court has fully and finally rejected the wooden distinction between 'rights' and 'privileges' that once seemed to govern the applicability of procedural due process rights"); *id. at* 572 ("In a Constitution for a free people, there can be no doubt that the meaning of 'liberty' must be broad indeed").

Justice Scalia's more general response—claiming that I have created a new category of constitutional rights—misses the mark. I break no new ground here. Rather, this Court has already recognized that the Due Process Clause guarantees that the government will not, without fair procedure, deprive individuals of a host of rights, freedoms, and liberties that are no more important, and for which the state has created no greater expectation of continued benefit, than the liberty interest at issue here. [Here Justice Breyer cited a host of liberty interests the Court has previously recognized as warranting procedural due process protection the significance of which, in his view, the plurality questionably minimized.] How could a Constitution that protects individuals against the arbitrary deprivation of so diverse a set of interests not also offer some form of procedural protection to a citizen threatened with governmental deprivation of her freedom to live together with her spouse in America? As compared to reputational harm [recognized in *Roth Constantineau*, and *Goss*], for example, how is Ms. Din's liberty interest any less worthy of due process protections?

[In Section II of his dissent, Justice Breyer concluded that procedural due process entitled Din to a statement of the State Department's reasons for denying her husband a visa.]

* * *

For these reasons, with respect, I dissent.

QUESTION SET 7.6

Review & Synthesis

1. With regard to *Hill. v. Borough of Kutztown*:
   a. Describe the "stigma-plus" test. Does it require a claimant to assert that her stigmatization resulted in injury to a property interest before she can claim procedural due process protections?
   b. If a claimant's property interest has been harmed by government conduct, why bother pleading harm to a liberty interest at all? Why not base the claim directly on the harm to the property interest itself? Consider that the Supreme Court has consistently held that procedural due process protections are not triggered by indirect harms to property interests.

2. With regard to *Kerry v. Din*:
   a. How did Din describe the liberty interest she claimed was protected by procedural due process? In what respects was it similar to the property interests asserted by the nursing home residents in *O'Bannon v. Town Court Nursing Center*?
   b. What test did Justice Scalia apply in rejecting Din's procedural due process claim? What evidence did he consider? In applying that test and considering that evidence, did he conclude that Din's claimed liberty interest does not exist, or did he find that it exists but that it failed to encompass all of the rights she asserted?
   c. Concern over judicial overreach clearly animated Justice Scalia's plurality opinion. He insisted that matters of public concern will be placed beyond the reach of policymakers (politicians and administrators) if courts were permitted to expand fundamental liberties beyond the bounds clearly set by historical or textual constraints. Consider the substance of Justice Breyer's dissent. Does his analysis illustrate judicial overreach, as Justice Scalia argued it did?
   d. As explained in the introduction to *Din* and in *Din* itself, the Supreme Court has been especially deferential to policy decisions rendered in the immigration context. This deference reaches its apex when the government deals with noncitizens seeking first-time entry to the United States. Should *whether* someone possesses a procedural due process right depend on the legal context in which that right is claimed? In other words, should courts be less willing to find that a claimant's interests trigger due process protections if, say, she claims them in an immigration case? Instead, do you think that the legal context should impact the *amount* of process the government is required to provide a claimant? For instance, should raising a procedural due process claim in an immigration case impact whether a person has a protectable interest, or should it only impact whether the court affords the claimant an in-person hearing or a chance to cross-examine witnesses?

Application & Analysis

1. Brooks, a City Manager, initiated an investigation into his city's police department due to his concern that Tang, the police chief, had been mismanaging it. The investigation uncovered several issues, but it produced no evidence of criminal wrongdoing. During a City Council meeting one of its members, citing the report, issued a public statement accusing Tang of various acts of malfeasance, including illegally misappropriating police property for his personal use. The Council then approved the member's motion to release the report to the news media, to refer the matter to local prosecutors, and to ask Brooks to take all necessary actions against anyone responsible for the problems detailed in the report. Brooks fired Tang the next day. He provided no reason for his decision other than pointing to the City's charter, which gives him sole authority to "appoint, and when deemed necessary for the good of the service, lay off, suspend, demote, or remove all directors, or heads, of administrative departments and all other administrative officers and employees of the city," including the chief of police. Nor did Brooks speak with Tang about his job performance before firing him. The local press prominently covered Tang's firing, linking it to the findings in the report. Tang believes that he should have at least been given a name-clearing hearing to challenge those findings before Brooks fired him. He has asked you, a local attorney, whether he has a viable claim. What do you think?

2. Boggs was a good cop. He was respected by his peers, made more arrests than any other officer on the force over the last several years, and responded well when his superiors suggested ways for him to improve his job performance. Nevertheless, the new Chief of Police recommended to the City Manager that Boggs be fired, and the City Manager promptly accepted and acted upon that recommendation. Shocked, Boggs asked for an explanation. In a private meeting, the Chief of Police told Boggs that he was insubordinate, routinely failed to attend mandatory training sessions, and was a drag on the morale of the department. You are a local attorney whom Boggs has approached about filing a lawsuit. He believes that the Chief of Police is either mistaken or is lying and that he should have been given a pre-termination hearing to counter the falsehoods that resulted in his dismissal. Among other things, Boggs believes that his firing has destroyed his good name and reputation in the community. Do you think he has a viable procedural due process claim?

3. Dr. Cyrus Cole was a clinical psychologist for Regents Hospital, a federally operated mental health-care facility near Washington, D.C. After more than ten years of employment, Regents informed Cole of its intention to fire him for his inability reliably to report for work and for his repeated failures to follow his supervisor's instructions. Cole and the hospital

agreed that he would resign rather than be fired, in an effort to prevent damage to his professional reputation. Several weeks later, Cole began work as a clinical psychologist at Naval Hospital Jacksonville ("NHJ") in Florida. Although Cole has already begun work on a probationary basis, NHJ required information on his past job performance before it could finalize his appointment and give him full hospital privileges. Cole provided contact information for Dr. Evelyn Craine, his direct supervisor at Regents. Craine responded to NHJ's request for information by letter, informing it that Cole was "inept, unethical, and perhaps the least trustworthy individual I have supervised in my 20 years at Regents." NHJ fired Cole after receiving Craine's letter, explaining that the reports about him were "unfavorable." After learning about the letter, Cole filed a damages action against Craine in federal district court alleging that she had caused an infringement of his "liberty interests" in violation of the Fifth Amendment Due Process Clause. Specifically, Cole alleged that Craine "maliciously and in bad faith published defamatory statements [about him] which she knew at the time to be false." Craine responded that Cole's complaint should be dismissed because it failed to allege any liberty interests that could be protected by the Fifth Amendment. You are a clerk for the judge before whom this lawsuit is pending. She has asked for your opinion of Cole's legal argument. How do you respond?

4. Marta Lopez is a 20-year-old Salvadoran citizen who recently fled her home country, seeking asylum at the U.S. port of entry in Hidalgo, Texas. She claims that she had been threatened by gangsters who said they would kill her if she did not pay them $2,000. According to Marta, one of her younger cousins had been killed by the same gangsters only a few days before they started to threaten her. She further alleges that she repeatedly contacted her local police department, but its officers did nothing to help. Pursuant to her asylum application, an Immigration Judge ("IJ") conducted an asylum hearing late last year, during which Marta presented several documents, including signed statements from family members and neighbors attesting to the threats against her and the gang's recent extortion attempts directed at young people in Marta's area. Following 8 C.F.R. § 208.11, the IJ allowed the government to request a State Department investigation of Marta's claims. The investigation was conducted by the U.S. embassy in Antiguo Cuscatlán and summarized in a letter signed by Mark Mattson, Director of the Department of State's Office of Country Reports and Asylum Affairs. The Mattson Letter pointed to several factual discrepancies between Marta's claims and the information gathered by the Embassy. While it did confirm her home address, the Embassy could not locate the family members or neighbors whose statements Marta provided and could not confirm that one of her cousins had been murdered prior to her departure. Additionally, the local police flatly denied that Marta had ever

contacted them about her safety concerns. Marta's attorney provided rebuttal evidence. He also argued that the Letter was hearsay, and its admission would violate Marta's procedural due process rights absent the chance to cross-examine the Embassy's investigator. The government asked for an interview with the investigator but the State Department refused, citing its policy against providing more specific information about its overseas investigations. Based on the Mattson Letter, the IJ made an adverse credibility determination against Marta and denied her asylum application. The Board of Immigration Appeals ("BIA") sustained this judgment, also finding (based on the Mattson Letter) that the documents Marta submitted were fraudulent. Marta has filed an appeal from the BIA's decision with the U.S. Court of Appeals for the Fifth Circuit, arguing that the BIA's reliance on the Mattson Letter denied her procedural due process in violation of the Fifth Amendment. You are a clerk for one of the Fifth Circuit judges before whom this appeal is pending. She has asked you to write a brief memo assessing the merits of Marta's claim. What do you think?

2. The Positive Law Approach

As explained above, one approach to identifying liberty interests protected by procedural due process analysis is determining whether a claimed right originates in the Due Process Clauses themselves. Courts ascertain this by identifying inherent aspects of the concept of liberty or by studying historical understandings of what liberty entails. This is not, however, the only method. State statutes and regulations can also create liberty interests not already evident in the Fifth and Fourteenth Amendment Due Process Clauses themselves or in their histories. We will refer to this second identification method as the "positive law" approach.

One of the contexts in which the Court has worked hardest to develop its positive law approach is incarceration of prisoners. As a general matter, the right to be free from governmentally imposed physical restraint is inherent to the liberty protected by the Fifth and Fourteenth Amendment Due Process Clauses. It accordingly fits comfortably within the concept-based approach to identifying liberty interests discussed in the prior subsection. Prisoners find themselves in far different circumstances than the population as a whole. "Lawful incarceration brings about the necessary withdrawal or limitation of many privileges and rights, a retraction justified by the considerations underlying our penal system." *Price v. Johnston*, 334 U.S. 266, 285 (1948).

Having lost the general freedom from restraint that inheres in the Due Process Clauses, do prisoners have any liberty interests left relating to the conditions of their confinement? For example, are there procedural due process limits on the punishments prison officials can impose on the inmates under their control? Can they, without notice or prior hearing, restrict outside visitor or library privileges, impose solitary confinement, or revoke early release credits? If so, from what legal source do these protections originate? The Court has consistently held that due process by itself does not protect inmates from such impositions on their liberty. What's more, the Court has often acknowledged that the difficulties involved in running correctional facilities require that prison officials have broad administrative and discretionary power over the lives of the inmates they guard. It has therefore said that any procedural due process rights relating to the circumstances of inmates' imprisonment must come, if at all, from state statutes or regulations.

The question then becomes how one knows when a statute or regulation creates a liberty interest that triggers procedural due process protections. The Court's earlier correctional facilities jurisprudence coalesced around the idea that liberty interests could be created in a fashion similar to property interests. Just as the government can create a property interest by establishing legal criteria for receiving an entitlement (*see, e.g., Goldberg v. Kelly,* 397 U.S. 254 (1970)), it can also create a liberty interest by placing limits on prison officials' discretion to further reduce the freedoms inmates had already lost by virtue of their incarceration. Thus, in *Wolff v. McDonnell,* 418 U.S. 539 (1974), the Court considered whether a Nebraska prisoner could be stripped, without a hearing, of earned "good-time" credits entitling him to early release. The Court conceded that "the Constitution itself does not guarantee good-time credit for satisfactory behavior while in prison." *Id.* at 557. However, Nebraska of its own volition created the good-time credit system and mandated that those credits be revoked only upon proof of an inmate's "major misconduct." *Id.* Put another way, state officials did not have unfettered discretion to revoke inmates' credits; such revocation had to be based on the evidence required by Nebraska law. Accordingly, Nebraska created for the respondent prisoner a Fourteenth Amendment liberty interest of "real substance" that it could not "arbitrarily abrogate[]." *Id.*

The Court applied similar reasoning in *Meachum v. Fano,* 427 U.S. 215 (1976), although doing so produced a far different result. The Massachusetts inmates in that case challenged their transfers, without prior hearings, to maximum security prisons with less favorable conditions. Through Justice White, the Court again held that the Due Process Clause itself afforded the inmates no protection from the harm they complained of. "[W]e cannot agree that *any* change in the conditions of confinement having a substantial adverse impact on the prisoner involved is sufficient to invoke the protections of the Due Process Clause." *Id.* at 224. Nor had the Court found that Massachusetts created such a liberty interest through its statutes or regulations.

> . . . Massachusetts law conferred no right on the prisoner to remain in the prison to which he was initially assigned, defeasible only upon proof of specific acts of misconduct. Insofar as we are advised, transfers between

Massachusetts prisons are not conditioned upon the occurrence of specified events. On the contrary, transfer in a wide variety of circumstances is vested in prison officials. The predicate for invoking the protection of the Fourteenth Amendment as construed and applied in *Wolff v. McDonnell* is totally nonexistent in this case.

Id. at 226-27. In subsequent cases, courts looked to the extent of prison officials' administrative discretion to determine whether inmates had any liberty interests in avoiding further diminishment of their already limited freedoms. Where prison regulations imposed few or no restrictions on officials' discretion, courts found no state-created liberty interests and refused to order additional procedural protections. By contrast, courts found such liberty interests where prison regulations imposed substantive conditions on officials' use of their discretion.

For example, in *Hewitt v. Helms*, 459 U.S. 460 (1983), the Court held for the first time that regulations governing day-to-day prison operations could (and did) give an allegedly dangerous inmate a liberty interest in avoiding administrative segregation from the general prison population. Pennsylvania created this liberty interest by adopting "unmistakably mandatory" language requiring prison officials to use particular procedures, and by requiring that prison officials establish "specified substantive predicates-*viz.*, 'the need for control,' or 'the threat of a serious disturbance,'" before imposing administrative segregation. *Id.* at 471-72. Importantly, the Court made clear that it would not have found a liberty interest had Pennsylvania simply adopted procedural guidelines for imposing administrative segregation that lacked these discretion-cabining features. Later cases affirmed *Hewitt*'s approach. *See Kentucky Department of Corrections. v. Thompson*, 490 U.S. 454, 461 (1989) (explaining that the Court's "method of inquiry in these [prisoner liberty interest] cases always has been to examine closely the language of the relevant statutes and regulations.").

Relying on *Hewitt*, inmates routinely claimed the right to be spared even small negative changes to the conditions of their confinement. This in turn led courts to scour prison regulations in search of mandatory limitations on official discretion which, according to the complaining inmates, impliedly entitled them to be free from punishment unless prison officials could first prove misconduct in an evidentiary hearing. The result was far greater judicial involvement in mundane prison administration than the *Hewitt* Court likely foresaw or intended. It is against this backdrop that the Court decided *Sandin v. Conner*, 515 U.S. 472 (1995), and dramatically changed its approach to finding liberty interests in the correctional facilities context.

As you read the case, be sure to note how the Court has reoriented its analysis. Has it completely abandoned or simply refined the positive law approach applied in its prior cases? Can you identify the types of facts or policy considerations it now says are relevant to the liberty interest inquiry? Are those facts and policy considerations inclusive or exclusive of the mandatory/

discretionary distinction deemed so important in cases like *Hewitt*? Lastly, do you think the *Sandin* approach protects inmates' procedural due process rights more or less appropriately than does the *Hewitt* approach?

Sandin v. Conner
515 U.S. 472 (1995)

Chief Justice REHNQUIST delivered the opinion of the Court.

I

DeMont Conner was convicted of numerous state crimes, including murder, kidnaping, robbery, and burglary, for which he is currently serving an indeterminate sentence of 30 years to life in a Hawaii prison. He was confined in the Halawa Correctional Facility, a maximum security prison in central Oahu. In August 1987, a prison officer escorted him from his cell to the module program area. The officer subjected Conner to a strip search, complete with an inspection of the rectal area. Conner retorted with angry and foul language directed at the officer. Eleven days later he received notice that he had been charged with disciplinary infractions. The notice charged Conner with "high misconduct" for using physical interference to impair a correctional function, and "low moderate misconduct" for using abusive or obscene language and for harassing employees.[1]

Conner appeared before an adjustment committee on August 28, 1987. The committee refused Conner's request to present witnesses at the hearing, stating that "[w]itnesses were unavailable due to move [sic] to the medium facility and being short staffed on the modules." At the conclusion of proceedings, the committee determined that Conner was guilty of the alleged misconduct. It sentenced him to 30 days' disciplinary segregation

---

[1] Hawaii's prison regulations establish a hierarchy of misconduct ranging from "greatest misconduct," Haw. Admin. Rule § 17-201-6(a) (1983), to "minor misconduct," § 17-201-10. Section 17-201-7 enumerates offenses punishable as "high misconduct" and sets available punishment for such offenses at disciplinary segregation up to 30 days or any sanction other than disciplinary segregation. Section 17-01-9 lists offenses punishable as "low moderate misconduct" and sets punishment at disciplinary segregation up to four hours in cell, monetary restitution, or any sanction other than disciplinary segregation. In addition to the levels of misconduct which classify various misdeeds, the regulations also define "serious misconduct" as "that which poses a serious threat to the safety, security, or welfare of the staff, other inmates or wards, or the institution and subjects the individual to the imposition of serious penalties such as segregation for longer than four hours." § 17-201-12. Such misconduct is punished through adjustment committee procedures. *Ibid.* The parties apparently concede that the physical obstruction allegation constituted serious misconduct, but that the low moderate misconduct charges did not.

in the Special Holding Unit for the physical obstruction charge, and four hours segregation for each of the other two charges to be served concurrent with the 30 days. Conner's segregation began August 31, 1987, and ended September 29, 1987.

Conner sought administrative review within 14 days of receiving the committee's decision. Haw. Admin. Rule § 17-201-20(a) (1983). Nine months later, the deputy administrator found the high misconduct charge unsupported and expunged Conner's disciplinary record with respect to that charge. But before the deputy administrator decided the appeal, Conner had brought this suit against the adjustment committee chair and other prison officials in the United States District Court for the District of Hawaii based on Rev. Stat. § 1979, 42 U.S.C. § 1983. His amended complaint prayed for injunctive relief, declaratory relief, and damages for, among other things, a deprivation of procedural due process in connection with the disciplinary hearing. The District Court granted summary judgment in favor of the prison officials.

The Court of Appeals for the Ninth Circuit reversed the judgment. It concluded that Conner had a liberty interest in remaining free from disciplinary segregation and that there was a disputed question of fact with respect to whether Conner received all of the process due under this Court's pronouncement in *Wolff v. McDonnell*, 418 U.S. 539 (1974). . . . We granted the State's petition for certiorari, and now reverse.

II

[The Court began its analysis with a lengthy discussion of its prison procedural due process jurisprudence since *Wolff v. McDonnell*. Toward the end of this recapitulation, it emphasized that "since *Hewitt*, [it] has wrestled with the language of intricate, often rather routine prison guidelines to determine whether mandatory language and substantive predicates created an enforceable expectation that the State would produce a particular outcome with respect to the prisoner's conditions of confinement."]

By shifting the focus of the liberty interest inquiry to one based on the language of a particular regulation, and not the nature of the deprivation, the Court encouraged prisoners to comb regulations in search of mandatory language on which to base entitlements to various state-conferred privileges. Courts have, in response, and not altogether illogically, drawn negative inferences from mandatory language in the text of prison regulations. The Court of Appeals' approach in this case is typical: It inferred from the mandatory directive that a finding of guilt "shall" be imposed under certain conditions the conclusion that the absence of such conditions prevents a finding of guilt.

Such a conclusion may be entirely sensible in the ordinary task of construing a statute defining rights and remedies available to the general public. It is a good deal less sensible in the case of a prison regulation primarily designed to guide correctional officials in the administration of a prison. Not only are such regulations not designed to confer rights on inmates, but the result of the negative implication jurisprudence is not to require the prison officials to follow the negative implication drawn from the regulation, but is instead to attach procedural protections that may be of quite a different nature. Here, for example, the Court of Appeals did not hold that a finding of guilt could not be made in the absence of substantial evidence. Instead, it held that the "liberty interest" created by the regulation entitled the inmate to the procedural protections set forth in *Wolff.*

Hewitt has produced at least two undesirable effects. First, it creates disincentives for States to codify prison management procedures in the interest of uniform treatment. Prison administrators need be concerned with the safety of the staff and inmate population. Ensuring that welfare often leads prison administrators to curb the discretion of staff on the front line who daily encounter prisoners hostile to the authoritarian structure of the prison environment. Such guidelines are not set forth solely to benefit the prisoner. They also aspire to instruct subordinate employees how to exercise discretion vested by the State in the warden, and to confine the authority of prison personnel in order to avoid widely different treatment of similar incidents. The approach embraced by *Hewitt* discourages this desirable development: States may avoid creation of "liberty" interests by having scarcely any regulations, or by conferring standardless discretion on correctional personnel.

Second, the *Hewitt* approach has led to the involvement of federal courts in the day-to-day management of prisons, often squandering judicial resources with little offsetting benefit to anyone. In so doing, it has run counter to the view expressed in several of our cases that federal courts ought to afford appropriate deference and flexibility to state officials trying to manage a volatile environment. *Wolff,* 418 U.S., at 561-563; *Hewitt,* 459 U.S., at 470-471. Such flexibility is especially warranted in the fine-tuning of the ordinary incidents of prison life, a common subject of prisoner claims since *Hewitt.*

In light of the above discussion, we believe that the search for a negative implication from mandatory language in prisoner regulations has strayed from the real concerns undergirding the liberty protected by the Due Process Clause. The time has come to return to the due process principles we believe were correctly established and applied in *Wolff* and *Meachum.* Following *Wolff,* we recognize that States may under certain circumstances create liberty interests which are protected by the Due Process Clause. But these interests will be generally limited to freedom from restraint which, while not exceeding the sentence in such an unexpected manner as to give rise to protection by the Due Process Clause of its own force, nonetheless imposes atypical and significant hardship on the inmate in relation to the ordinary incidents of prison life. . . .

This case, though concededly punitive, does not present a dramatic departure from the basic conditions of Conner's indeterminate sentence. Although Conner points to dicta in cases implying that solitary confinement automatically triggers due process protection, *Wolff, supra*, at 571, n. 19, this Court has not had the opportunity to address in an argued case the question whether disciplinary confinement of inmates itself implicates constitutional liberty interests. We hold that Conner's discipline in segregated confinement did not present the type of atypical, significant deprivation in which a State might conceivably create a liberty interest. The record shows that, at the time of Conner's punishment, disciplinary segregation, with insignificant exceptions, mirrored those conditions imposed upon inmates in administrative segregation and protective custody. We note also that the State expunged Conner's disciplinary record with respect to the "high misconduct" charge nine months after Conner served time in segregation. Thus, Conner's confinement did not exceed similar, but totally discretionary, confinement in either duration or degree of restriction. Indeed, the conditions at Halawa involve significant amounts of "lockdown time" even for inmates in the general population. Based on a comparison between inmates inside and outside disciplinary segregation, the State's actions in placing him there for 30 days did not work a major disruption in his environment.

Nor does Conner's situation present a case where the State's action will inevitably affect the duration of his sentence. Nothing in Hawaii's code requires the parole board to deny parole in the face of a misconduct record or to grant parole in its absence, Haw. Rev. Stat. §§ 353-68, 353-69 (1985), even though misconduct is by regulation a relevant consideration, Haw. Admin. Rule § 23-700-33(b) (effective Aug. 1992). The decision to release a prisoner rests on a myriad of considerations. And, the prisoner is afforded procedural protection at his parole hearing in order to explain the circumstances behind his misconduct record. Haw. Admin. Rule §§ 23-700–31(a), 23-700-35(c), 23-700-36 (1983). The chance that a finding of misconduct will alter the balance is simply too attenuated to invoke the procedural guarantees of the Due Process Clause. The Court rejected a similar claim in *Meachum*, 427 U.S., at 229, n. 8 (declining to afford relief on the basis that petitioner's transfer record might affect his future confinement and possibility of parole).

We hold, therefore, that neither the Hawaii prison regulation in question, nor the Due Process Clause itself, afforded Conner a protected liberty interest that would entitle him to the procedural protections set forth in *Wolff*. The regime to which he was subjected as a result of the misconduct hearing was within the range of confinement to be normally expected for one serving an indeterminate term of 30 years to life.

The judgment of the Court of Appeals is accordingly
Reversed.

[The dissenting opinions of Justices Ginsburg and Breyer are omitted.]

* * *

Sandin made clear that, moving forward, a change to an inmate's conditions of confinement will implicate the Due Process Clause only if it "imposes atypical and significant hardship on the inmate in relation to the ordinary incidents of prison life." This new standard immediately raised two questions that the Court did not definitively answer. First, what constitutes the baseline "ordinary incidents of prison life" against which courts must compare the conditions of a complaining inmate? Is ordinariness determined by what other inmates in the same facility experience, by some common experience of all similarly situated inmates regardless of facility, or by something else? Second, what degree of deviance from the "ordinary" suffices to constitute hardship that is both atypical and significant?

The case that follows, *Wilkinson v. Austin*, 545 U.S. 209 (2005), is the Court's lengthiest discussion and application of *Sandin* to date. How many of its unanswered questions does Justice Kennedy's opinion resolve, if any?

Wilkinson v. Austin
545 U.S. 209 (2005)

Justice KENNEDY delivered the opinion of the Court.

I

The use of Supermax prisons has increased over the last 20 years, in part as a response to the rise in prison gangs and prison violence. About 30 States now operate Supermax prisons, in addition to the two somewhat comparable facilities operated by the Federal Government. In 1998, Ohio opened its only Supermax facility, the Ohio State Penitentiary (OSP), after a riot in one of its maximum-security prisons. OSP has the capacity to house up to 504 inmates in single-inmate cells and is designed to "'separate the most predatory and dangerous prisoners from the rest of the . . . general [prison] population.'" *See* 189 F. Supp.2d 719, 723 (N.D. Ohio 2002) (*Austin I*).

Conditions at OSP are more restrictive than any other form of incarceration in Ohio, including conditions on its death row or in its administrative control units. The latter are themselves a highly restrictive form of solitary confinement. In OSP almost every aspect of an inmate's life is controlled and monitored. Inmates must remain in their cells, which measure 7 by 14 feet, for 23 hours per day. A light remains on in the cell at all times, though it is sometimes dimmed, and an inmate who attempts to shield the light to sleep is subject to further discipline. During the one hour per day that an inmate may leave his cell, access is limited to one of two indoor recreation cells.

Incarceration at OSP is synonymous with extreme isolation. In contrast to any other Ohio prison, including any segregation unit, OSP cells have solid metal doors with metal strips along their sides and bottoms which prevent conversation or communication with other inmates. All meals are taken alone in the inmate's cell instead of in a common eating area. Opportunities for visitation are rare and in all events are conducted through glass walls. It is fair to say OSP inmates are deprived of almost any environmental or sensory stimuli and of almost all human contact.

Aside from the severity of the conditions, placement at OSP is for an indefinite period of time, limited only by an inmate's sentence. For an inmate serving a life sentence, there is no indication how long he may be incarcerated at OSP once assigned there. Inmates otherwise eligible for parole lose their eligibility while incarcerated at OSP.

Placement at OSP is determined in the following manner: Upon entering the prison system, all Ohio inmates are assigned a numerical security classification from level 1 through level 5, with 1 the lowest security risk and 5 the highest. The initial security classification is based on numerous factors (e.g., the nature of the underlying offense, criminal history, or gang affiliation) but is subject to modification at any time during the inmate's prison term if, for instance, he engages in misconduct or is deemed a security risk. Level 5 inmates are placed in OSP, and levels 1 through 4 inmates are placed at lower security facilities throughout the State.

Ohio concedes that when OSP first became operational, the procedures used to assign inmates to the facility were inconsistent and undefined. For a time, no official policy governing placement was in effect. Haphazard placements were not uncommon, and some individuals who did not pose high-security risks were designated, nonetheless, for OSP. In an effort to establish guidelines for the selection and classification of inmates suitable for OSP, Ohio issued Department of Rehabilitation and Correction Policy 111-07 (Aug. 31, 1998). This policy has been revised at various points but relevant here are two versions: the "Old Policy" and the "New Policy." The Old Policy took effect on January 28, 1999, but problems with assignment appear to have persisted even under this written set of standards. After forming a committee to study the matter and retaining a national expert in prison security, Ohio promulgated the New Policy in early 2002. The New Policy provided more guidance regarding the factors to be considered in placement decisions and afforded inmates more procedural protection against erroneous placement at OSP.

Although the record is not altogether clear regarding the precise manner in which the New Policy operates, we construe it based on the policy's text, the accompanying forms, and the parties' representations at oral argument and in their briefs. The New Policy appears to operate as follows: A classification review for OSP placement can occur either (1) upon entry into the prison system if the inmate was convicted of certain offenses, e.g., organized crime, or (2) during the term of incarceration if an inmate engages in specified conduct, e.g., leads a prison gang. The review process begins when a prison official prepares a "Security Designation Long Form" (Long Form). This three-page form details matters such as the inmate's recent violence, escape attempts, gang affiliation, underlying offense, and other pertinent details.

A three-member Classification Committee (Committee) convenes to review the proposed classification and to hold a hearing. At least 48 hours before the hearing, the inmate is provided with written notice summarizing the conduct or offense triggering the review. At the time of notice, the inmate also has access to the Long Form, which details why the review was initiated. The inmate may attend the hearing, may "offer any pertinent information, explanation and/or objections to [OSP] placement," and may submit a written statement. He may not call witnesses.

If the Committee does not recommend OSP placement, the process terminates. If the Committee does recommend OSP placement, it documents the decision on a "Classification Committee Report" (CCR), setting forth the nature of the threat the inmate presents and the committee's reasons for the recommendation, as well as a summary of any information presented at the hearing. The Committee sends the completed CCR to the warden of the prison where the inmate is housed or, in the case of an inmate just entering the prison system, to another designated official.

If, after reviewing the CCR, the warden (or the designated official) disagrees and concludes that OSP is inappropriate, the process terminates and the inmate is not placed in OSP. If the warden agrees, he indicates his approval on the CCR, provides his reasons, and forwards the annotated CCR to the Bureau of Classification (Bureau) for a final decision. (The Bureau is a body of Ohio prison officials vested with final decisionmaking authority over all Ohio inmate assignments.) The annotated CCR is served upon the inmate, notifying him of the Committee's and warden's recommendations and reasons. *Id.* at 65. The inmate has 15 days to file any objections with the Bureau.

After the 15-day period, the Bureau reviews the CCR and makes a final determination. If it concludes OSP placement is inappropriate, the process terminates. If the Bureau approves the warden's recommendation, the inmate is transferred to OSP. The Bureau's chief notes the reasons for the decision on the CCR, and the CCR is again provided to the inmate.

Inmates assigned to OSP receive another review within 30 days of their arrival. That review is conducted by a designated OSP staff member, who examines the inmate's file. If the OSP staff member deems the inmate inappropriately placed, he prepares a written recommendation to the OSP warden that the inmate be transferred to a lower security institution. If the OSP warden concurs, he forwards that transfer recommendation to the Bureau for appropriate action. If the inmate is deemed properly placed, he remains in OSP and his placement is reviewed on at least an annual basis according to the initial three-tier classification review process outlined above.

[In Section II of its opinion, the Court recounts the procedural history of the case. The inmates challenged the Old Policy, seeking declaratory and injunctive relief. While the case was pending, Ohio promulgated the New Policy, and it's the one on which the district court, court of appeals, and the Supreme Court focused. The district court found that the inmates had a liberty interest to avoid assignment to OSP under *Sandin v. Connor*, and the Sixth Circuit affirmed.]

III

Withdrawing from the position taken in the Court of Appeals, Ohio in its briefs to this Court conceded that the inmates have a liberty interest in avoiding assignment at OSP. The United States, supporting Ohio as *amicus curiae*, disagrees with Ohio's concession and argues that the inmates have no liberty interest in avoiding assignment to a prison facility with more restrictive conditions of confinement. At oral argument Ohio initially adhered to its earlier concession, but when pressed, the State backtracked. We need reach the question of what process is due only if the inmates establish a constitutionally protected liberty interest, so it is appropriate to address this threshold question at the outset.

The Fourteenth Amendment's Due Process Clause protects persons against deprivations of life, liberty, or property; and those who seek to invoke its procedural protection must establish that one of these interests is at stake. A liberty interest may arise from the Constitution itself, by reason of guarantees implicit in the word "liberty," *see, e.g., Vitek v. Jones*, 445 U.S. 480, 493-494 (1980) (liberty interest in avoiding involuntary psychiatric treatment and transfer to mental institution), or it may arise from an expectation or interest created by state laws or policies, *see, e.g., Wolff v. McDonnell*, 418 U.S. 539, 556-558 (1974) (liberty interest in avoiding withdrawal of state-created system of good-time credits).

We have held that the Constitution itself does not give rise to a liberty interest in avoiding transfer to more adverse conditions of confinement. *Meachum v. Fano*, 427 U.S. 215, 225 (1976) (no liberty interest arising from Due Process Clause itself in transfer from low-to maximum-security prison because "[c]onfinement in any of the State's institutions is within the normal limits or range of custody which the conviction has authorized the State to impose"). We have also held, however, that a liberty interest in avoiding particular conditions of confinement may arise from state policies or regulations, subject to the important limitations set forth in *Sandin v. Conner*, 515 U.S. 472 (1995).

Sandin involved prisoners' claims to procedural due process protection before placement in segregated confinement for 30 days, imposed as discipline for disruptive behavior. *Sandin* observed that some of our earlier cases, *Hewitt v. Helms*, 459 U.S. 460 (1983), in particular, had employed a methodology for identifying state-created liberty interests that emphasized "the language of a particular [prison] regulation" instead of "the nature of the deprivation." *Sandin*, 515 U.S., at 481. In *Sandin*, we criticized this methodology as creating a disincentive for States to promulgate procedures for prison management, and as involving the federal courts in the day-to-day management of prisons. *Id. at* 482-483. . . .

After *Sandin*, it is clear that the touchstone of the inquiry into the existence of a protected, state-created liberty interest in avoiding restrictive conditions of confinement is not the language of regulations regarding those conditions but the nature of those conditions themselves "in relation to the ordinary incidents of prison life." *Id. at* 484.

Applying this refined inquiry, *Sandin* found no liberty interest protecting against a 30-day assignment to segregated confinement because it did not "present a dramatic departure from the basic conditions of [the inmate's] sentence." *Id. at* 485. We noted, for example, that inmates in the general population experienced "significant amounts of 'lockdown time'" and that the degree of confinement in disciplinary segregation was not excessive. *Id. at* 486. We did not find, moreover, the short duration of segregation to work a major disruption in the inmate's environment. *Ibid.*

The *Sandin* standard requires us to determine if assignment to OSP "imposes atypical and significant hardship on the inmate in relation to the ordinary incidents of prison life." *Id. at* 484. In *Sandin*'s wake the Courts of Appeals have not reached consistent conclusions for identifying the baseline from which to measure what is atypical and significant in any particular prison system. This divergence indicates the difficulty of locating the appropriate baseline, an issue that was not explored at length in the briefs. We need not resolve the issue here, however, for we are satisfied that assignment to OSP imposes an atypical and significant hardship under any plausible baseline.

For an inmate placed in OSP, almost all human contact is prohibited, even to the point that conversation is not permitted from cell to cell; the light, though it may be dimmed, is on for 24 hours; exercise is for 1 hour per day, but only in a small indoor room. Save perhaps for the especially severe limitations on all human contact, these conditions likely would apply to most solitary confinement facilities, but here there are two added components. First is the duration. Unlike the 30-day placement in *Sandin*, placement at OSP is indefinite and, after an initial 30-day review, is reviewed just annually. Second is that placement disqualifies an otherwise eligible inmate for parole consideration. While any of these conditions standing alone might not be sufficient to create a liberty interest, taken together they impose an atypical and significant hardship within the correctional context. It follows that respondents have a liberty interest in avoiding assignment to OSP. *Sandin, supra,* at 483.

OSP's harsh conditions may well be necessary and appropriate in light of the danger that high-risk inmates pose both to prison officials and to other prisoners. That necessity, however, does not diminish our conclusion that the conditions give rise to a liberty interest in their avoidance.

[In Section IV of its opinion, the Court agreed with the Sixth Circuit that the procedures Ohio adopted in the New Policy satisfied due process, but disagreed that it should have sustained the procedural modifications ordered by the district court.]

* * *

. . . The judgment of the Court of Appeals is affirmed in part and reversed in part, and the case is remanded for further proceedings consistent with this opinion.

It is so ordered.

QUESTION SET 7.7

Review & Synthesis

1. What is the test for determining whether an inmate has a liberty interest in avoiding more restrictive confinement after *Sandin*? How does this test differ from the one that preceded it, as emblematized by *Hewitt*, and why did the Court decide to change it?

2. What, precisely, was the legal basis for the Court's abandonment of the *Hewitt* test in favor of the *Sandin* test? What rules, doctrines, or legal principles informed the change?

3. The Court acknowledged that its decision in *Sandin* left lower courts struggling to identify the appropriate baseline for whether a change in confinement "imposes atypical and significant hardship on the inmate in relation to the ordinary incidents of prison life." The result, also acknowledged by the Court, was inconsistent decisions. How did the Court resolve this issue in *Wilkinson*? What facts did it emphasize in holding that Austin's (the inmate plaintiff) liberty interests were infringed?

Application & Analysis

1. State's administrative code provides for so-called "TLU" (temporary lock-up) of inmates held in its prisons. Pursuant to the code, TLU is a "nonpunitive segregated status that segregates an inmate from the general population pending further administrative action." The code further explains that TLU's main purpose is to detain an inmate temporarily "until it is possible to complete an investigation, cool down a volatile situation or hold a disciplinary hearing." Accordingly, prison officials have the discretion to place an inmate in TLU if they suspect that the inmate "may impede a pending investigation." No hearing is held prior to an inmate's relocation to TLU and, in keeping with its "temporary" aspect, inmates may initially be segregated for no more than 21 days with a possible extension to a maximum of 63 days. Several guards at one of State's prisons were severely injured in a riot instigated by one of the

prison's gangs. Prison officials placed 150 inmates in TLU as part of their subsequent search for those responsible. Gary, one of those inmates, was released back into the general population after 61 days without any further disciplinary action and with no impact on the length of his sentence. During his segregation, Gary was forced to share a small cell designed to accommodate only one inmate at a time and had to sleep on a thin mattress on the cell's concrete floor. The mattress quickly became wet, moldy, and foul-smelling because the cell's shower drained in the middle of the floor. Gary has exhausted his administrative remedies and would now like to file a federal civil rights action against the prison. He would like to allege that the prison officials' decision to place him in TLU infringed his liberty interests in violation of the Fourteenth Amendment Due Process Clause. You are a summer clerk for a prisoners' rights organization. The attorney with whom you are working would like to know whether Gary has a viable claim under *Sandin v. Conner* and *Wilkinson v. Austin*.

2. State's law requires that criminal defendants judged mentally unfit to stand trial be placed in the custody of State's Office of Mental Health ("OMH") for care and treatment. To be involuntarily retained in a State mental health facility for more than 90 days, OMH must find that the defendant is mentally ill and in need of involuntary care treatment. The defendant is entitled to challenge OMH's determinations in a judicial proceeding. However, OMH has sole discretion to choose the facility that will retain the defendant if retention is deemed warranted (or if the defendant chooses not to challenge OMH's mental illness determination). State's law further provides that OMH's facility choice is subject to very limited judicial review. While there are certain procedures it must follow and factors it must consider, a court can overturn OMH's facility choice only if it is arbitrary and capricious, an abuse of discretion, or based on an error of law. Reed, prosecuted for several minor nonviolent felonies, was judged mentally unfit to stand trial and accordingly placed in OMH custody. After unsuccessfully challenging OMH's determination that he requires involuntary care treatment, OMH committed Reed to the Morgan Psychiatric Hospital, a high-security facility that is far more restrictive than any of the others controlled by State. You are a summer clerk at the law firm Reed has approached to represent him in a possible lawsuit against OMH. The partner with whom you are working thinks Reed may have a procedural due process claim. Given the amount of discretion over facility choices State's law gives OMH, however, she is concerned that Reed's claim may be precluded by the Supreme Court's correctional facilities jurisprudence. She has asked you to look into it and give her your thoughts over lunch tomorrow. What do you think?

E. THE PROCESS DUE

In *Goldberg v. Kelly*, the Court listed several hearing elements that protect a defendant's due process rights: (1) "timely and adequate notice detailing the reasons for a proposed termination"; (2) "an effective opportunity (for the recipient) to defend by confronting any adverse witnesses and by presenting his own arguments and evidence orally"; (3) retained counsel, if desired; (4) an "impartial" decision-maker; (5) a decision resting "solely on the legal rules and evidence adduced at the hearing"; and (6) a statement of reasons for the decision and identification of the evidence on which it relies. *Goldberg*, 397 U.S. at 267-71. Judicial trials (particularly in the criminal context) feature all of these hearing elements, and accordingly provide the most formal type of adjudicative decision-making offered by federal or state governments. *Goldberg* also emphasized, however, that the government need not provide all of these protections to comply with the requirements of Due Process. Depending on the situation, the government need only provide "rudimentary due process" protections. *Goldberg* did not, however, indicate how the government was to identify this procedural minimum.

The idea that administrative adjudication did not need to adopt all the formalities of trial-type proceedings was not new when the Court decided *Goldberg*. Nor was the Court's reticence in identifying a procedural due process floor, apart from indicating that doing so is a case-by-case endeavor. Take, for example, a case we considered in the previous chapter: *Londoner v. Denver*, 210 U.S. 373 (1908). *Londoner*, decided in the early twentieth century and thus decades before *Goldberg*, concluded that the demands of due process in a state administrative context could be satisfied by procedures less exhaustive than those typically employed at trial:

> But where the legislature of a state, instead of fixing the tax itself, commits to some subordinate body the duty of determining whether, in what amount, and upon whom it shall be levied, and of making its assessment and apportionment, due process of law requires that, at some stage of the proceedings, before the tax becomes irrevocably fixed, the taxpayer shall have an opportunity to be heard, of which he must have notice, either personal, by publication, or by a law fixing the time and place of the hearing. . . . If it is enough that, under such circumstances, an opportunity is given to submit in writing all objections to and complaints of the tax to the board, then there was a hearing afforded in the case at bar. But we think that something more than that, even in proceedings for taxation, is required by due process of law. Many requirements essential in strictly judicial proceedings may be dispensed with in proceedings of this nature. But even here a hearing, in its very essence, demands that he who is entitled to it shall have the right to support his allegations by argument, however brief: and, if need be, by proof, however informal.

Id. at 385-86 (citations omitted).

The Court did little to elaborate on the conception of "hearing" it adopted in *Londoner* in the decades that followed. *See, e.g., Greene v. McElroy*, 360 U.S. 474, 496-97 (1959) (observing that a "relatively immutable" aspect of the Court's due process jurisprudence is its insistence that individuals injured by government action be shown and afforded a chance to rebut the facts supporting the government's conduct, including through cross-examination of witnesses). According to one learned commentator, the Court did not require the full measure of procedural due process afforded in judicial proceedings for the vast majority of government decisions, reserving it for the relatively few instances involving the endangerment of individual rights. *See* RICHARD J. PIERCE, JR., ADMINISTRATIVE TREATISE § 9.5 (2010).

After *Goldberg*, however, government-conferred entitlements the Court previously regarded as mere "privileges" (e.g., public assistance benefits) instead became due process-triggering property interests. *Id.* This shift led the Court more seriously to consider the practicality of imposing court-like "hearings" on agency decision-makers. Due process claimants would frequently demand two costly procedural protections typically featured at trial: oral presentations of evidence and opportunities for cross-examination of witnesses. However effective they might be at facilitating full presentation of issues or engendering in parties a sense of decisional fairness and legitimacy, oral hearings and cross-examination could be manipulated to obscure important issues, substantially increase monetary costs, and cause substantial delays in decision-making.

The *Goldberg* Court insisted that oral presentation and cross-examination were not constitutionally required for all administrative adjudications. Nevertheless, it required them for the entitlement eligibility decisions at issue in that case. "The only procedural safeguards urged in *Goldberg* and rejected by the Court were the right to counsel provided at government expense and the right to formal findings of fact." *Id.* The implications of such procedural generosity were not lost on Justice Black who, as we will recall, warned of the costs that would result if agencies were prevented from quickly removing ineligible assistance recipients from the rolls. *See* pages 427-28. Critics sounded similar notes of concern in *Goldberg*'s wake, *see, e.g.,* Jerry L. Mashaw, *The Management Side of Due Process: Some Theoretical and Litigation Notes on the Assurance of Accuracy, Fairness, and Timeliness in the Adjudication of Social Welfare Claims*, 59 CORNELL L. REV. 772 (1974), and state and federal agencies struggled to calibrate their procedures to conform with the decision. It was against this backdrop that the Court decided the seminal case of *Mathews v. Eldridge*, which established the modern test for determining the hearing elements due process requires.

As you read the case, critically assess the constitutive elements of the test the Court establishes. What types of information does it require? Are they the types of information appropriately gathered by administrative agencies? What does the Court suggest agencies do with that information once it is gathered? Is that suggestion reasonable given agencies' budgetary and structural limitations? What values—efficiency or accuracy of decision-making, protection or promotion of human dignity—appear imbedded in the *Eldridge* test?

Mathews v. Eldridge
424 U.S. 319 (1976)

Mr. Justice POWELL delivered the opinion of the Court.

The issue in this case is whether the Due Process Clause of the Fifth Amendment requires that prior to the termination of Social Security disability benefit payments the recipient be afforded an opportunity for an evidentiary hearing.

I

Cash benefits are provided to workers during periods in which they are completely disabled under the disability insurance benefits program created by the 1956 amendments to Title II of the Social Security Act. 70 Stat. 815, 42 U.S.C. § 423. Respondent Eldridge was first awarded benefits in June 1968. In March 1972, he received a questionnaire from the state agency charged with monitoring his medical condition. Eldridge completed the questionnaire, indicating that his condition had not improved and identifying the medical sources, including physicians, from whom he had received treatment recently. The state agency then obtained reports from his physician and a psychiatric consultant. After considering these reports and other information in his file the agency informed Eldridge by letter that it had made a tentative determination that his disability had ceased in May 1972. The letter included a statement of reasons for the proposed termination of benefits, and advised Eldridge that he might request reasonable time in which to obtain and submit additional information pertaining to his condition.

In his written response, Eldridge disputed one characterization of his medical condition and indicated that the agency already had enough evidence to establish his disability.[2] The state agency then made its final determination that he had ceased to be disabled in May 1972. This determination

------

[2] Eldridge originally was disabled due to chronic anxiety and back strain. He subsequently was found to have diabetes. The tentative determination letter indicated that aid would be terminated because available medical evidence indicated that his diabetes was under control, that there existed no limitations on his back movements which would impose severe functional restrictions, and that he no longer suffered emotional problems that would preclude him from all work for which he was qualified. In his reply letter he claimed to have arthritis of the spine rather than a strained back.

was accepted by the Social Security Administration (SSA), which notified Eldridge in July that his benefits would terminate after that month. The notification also advised him of his right to seek reconsideration by the state agency of this initial determination within six months.

Instead of requesting reconsideration Eldridge commenced this action challenging the constitutional validity of the administrative procedures established by the Secretary of Health, Education, and Welfare for assessing whether there exists a continuing disability. He sought an immediate rein-statement of benefits pending a hearing on the issue of his disability. The Secretary moved to dismiss on the grounds that Eldridge's benefits had been terminated in accordance with valid administrative regulations and proce-dures and that he had failed to exhaust available remedies. In support of his contention that due process requires a pretermination hearing, Eldridge relied exclusively upon this Court's decision in *Goldberg v. Kelly*, 397 U.S. 254 (1970), which established a right to an "evidentiary hearing" prior to termination of welfare benefits. The Secretary contended that *Goldberg* was not controlling since eligibility for disability benefits, unlike eligibility for welfare benefits, is not based on financial need and since issues of credibility and veracity do not play a significant role in the disability entitlement deci-sion, which turns primarily on medical evidence.

The District Court concluded that the administrative procedures pursu-ant to which the Secretary had terminated Eldridge's benefits abridged his right to procedural due process. The court viewed the interest of the disabil-ity recipient in uninterrupted benefits as indistinguishable from that of the welfare recipient in *Goldberg*. It further noted that decisions subsequent to *Goldberg* demonstrated that the due process requirement of pretermination hearings is not limited to situations involving the deprivation of vital neces-sities. *See Fuentes v. Shevin*, 407 U.S. 67, 88-89 (1972); *Bell v. Burson*, 402 U.S. 535, 539 (1971). Reasoning that disability determinations may involve subjective judgments based on conflicting medical and nonmedical evi-dence, the District Court held that prior to termination of benefits Eldridge had to be afforded an evidentiary hearing of the type required for welfare beneficiaries under Title IV of the Social Security Act. Relying entirely upon the District Court's opinion, the Court of Appeals for the Fourth Circuit affirmed the injunction barring termination of Eldridge's benefits prior to an evidentiary hearing. We reverse.

[In Section II of the Court's opinion, it rejectd the government's claim that the district court below lacked jurisdiction to hear Eldridge's case.]

III

A

Procedural due process imposes constraints on governmental decisions which deprive individuals of "liberty" or "property" interests within the meaning of the Due Process Clause of the Fifth or Fourteenth Amendment. The Secretary does not contend that procedural due process is inapplicable to terminations of Social Security disability benefits. He recognizes . . . that the interest of an individual in continued receipt of these benefits is a statutorily created "property" interest protected by the Fifth Amendment. *Cf. Arnett v. Kennedy*, 416 U.S. 134, 166 (Powell, J., concurring in part) (1974); *Board of Regents v. Roth*, 408 U.S. 564, 576-578 (1972); *Bell v. Burson*, 402 U.S., at 539; *Goldberg v. Kelly*, 397 U.S., at 261-262. Rather, the Secretary contends that the existing administrative procedures, detailed below, provide all the process that is constitutionally due before a recipient can be deprived of that interest.

This Court consistently has held that some form of hearing is required before an individual is finally deprived of a property interest. *Wolff v. McDonnell*, 418 U.S. 539, 557-558 (1974). The "right to be heard before being condemned to suffer grievous loss of any kind, even though it may not involve the stigma and hardships of a criminal conviction, is a principle basic to our society." *Joint Anti-Fascist Comm. v. McGrath*, 341 U.S. 123, 168 (1951) (Frankfurter, J., concurring). The fundamental requirement of due process is the opportunity to be heard "at a meaningful time and in a meaningful manner." *Armstrong v. Manzo*, 380 U.S. 545, 552 (1965). Eldridge agrees that the review procedures available to a claimant before the initial determination of ineligibility becomes final would be adequate if disability benefits were not terminated until after the evidentiary hearing stage of the administrative process. The dispute centers upon what process is due prior to the initial termination of benefits, pending review.

In recent years this Court increasingly has had occasion to consider the extent to which due process requires an evidentiary hearing prior to the deprivation of some type of property interest even if such a hearing is provided thereafter. In only one case, *Goldberg v. Kelly*, 397 U.S., at 266-271, has the Court held that a hearing closely approximating a judicial trial is necessary. In other cases requiring some type of pretermination hearing as a matter of constitutional right the Court has spoken sparingly about the requisite procedures. . . . *Bell v. Burson, supra*, at 540, held, in the context of the revocation of a state-granted driver's license, that due process required only that the prerevocation hearing involve a probable-cause determination as to the fault of the licensee, noting that the hearing "need not take the form of a full adjudication of the question of liability." More recently, in *Arnett v. Kennedy, supra*, we sustained the validity of procedures by which a federal employee could be dismissed for cause. They included notice of the action sought, a copy of the charge, reasonable time for filing a written response, and an opportunity for an oral appearance. Following dismissal, an evidentiary hearing was provided. 416 U.S., at 142-146.

These decisions underscore the truism that "'(d)ue process,' unlike some legal rules, is not a technical conception with a fixed content unrelated to time, place and circumstances." *Cafeteria Workers v. McElroy*, 367

U.S. 886, 895 (1961). "(D)ue process is flexible and calls for such procedural protections as the particular situation demands." *Morrissey v. Brewer*, 408 U.S. 471, 481 (1972). Accordingly, resolution of the issue whether the administrative procedures provided here are constitutionally sufficient requires analysis of the governmental and private interests that are affected. More precisely, our prior decisions indicate that identification of the specific dictates of due process generally requires consideration of three distinct factors: First, the private interest that will be affected by the official action; second, the risk of an erroneous deprivation of such interest through the procedures used, and the probable value, if any, of additional or substitute procedural safeguards; and finally, the Government's interest, including the function involved and the fiscal and administrative burdens that the additional or substitute procedural requirement would entail. *See, e. g., Goldberg v. Kelly, supra*, 397 U.S., at 263-271.

We turn first to a description of the procedures for the termination of Social Security disability benefits and thereafter consider the factors bearing upon the constitutional adequacy of these procedures.

B

The disability insurance program is administered jointly by state and federal agencies. State agencies make the initial determination whether a disability exists, when it began, and when it ceased. 42 U.S.C. § 421(a).[13] The standards applied and the procedures followed are prescribed by the Secretary, *see* § 421(b), who has delegated his responsibilities and powers under the Act to the SSA. *See* 40 Fed. Reg. 4473 (1975).

In order to establish initial and continued entitlement to disability benefits a worker must demonstrate that he is unable

> to engage in any substantial gainful activity by reason of any medically determinable physical or mental impairment which can be expected to result in death or which has lasted or can be expected to last for a continuous period of not less than 12 months . . . . 42 U.S.C. § 423(d)(1)(A).

To satisfy this test the worker bears a continuing burden of showing, by means of "medically acceptable clinical and laboratory diagnostic

---

[13] In all but six States the state vocational rehabilitation agency charged with administering the state plan under the Vocational Rehabilitation Act of 1920, 41 Stat. 735, as amended, 29 U.S.C. § 701 *et seq.* (1970 ed., Supp. III), acts as the "state agency" for purposes of the disability insurance program. Staff of the House Comm. on Ways and Means, Report on the Disability Insurance Program, 93d Cong., 2d Sess., 148 (1974). This assignment of responsibility was intended to encourage rehabilitation contacts for disabled workers and to utilize the well-established relationships of the local rehabilitation agencies with the medical profession. H.R. Rep. No.1698, 83d Cong., 2d Sess., 23-24 (1954).

techniques," § 423(d)(3), that he has a physical or mental impairment of such severity that

> he is not only unable to do his previous work but cannot, considering his age, education, and work experience, engage in any other kind of substantial gainful work which exists in the national economy, regardless of whether such work exists in the immediate area in which he lives, or whether a specific job vacancy exists for him, or whether he would be hired if he applied for work. § 423(d)(2)(A).[14]

The principal reasons for benefits terminations are that the worker is no longer disabled or has returned to work. As Eldridge's benefits were terminated because he was determined to be no longer disabled, we consider only the sufficiency of the procedures involved in such cases.

The continuing-eligibility investigation is made by a state agency acting through a "team" consisting of a physician and a nonmedical person trained in disability evaluation. The agency periodically communicates with the disabled worker, usually by mail in which case he is sent a detailed questionnaire or by telephone, and requests information concerning his present condition, including current medical restrictions and sources of treatment, and any additional information that he considers relevant to his continued entitlement to benefits.[16]

Information regarding the recipient's current condition is also obtained from his sources of medical treatment. If there is a conflict between the information provided by the beneficiary and that obtained from medical sources such as his physician, or between two sources of treatment, the agency may arrange for an examination by an independent consulting physician.[17] Whenever the agency's tentative assessment of the beneficiary's condition differs from his own assessment, the beneficiary is informed that benefits may be terminated, provided a summary of the evidence upon which the proposed determination to terminate is based, and afforded an opportunity to review the medical reports and other evidence in his case file.[18] He also may respond in writing and submit additional evidence.

---

[14] Work which "exists in the national economy" is in turn defined as "work which exists in significant numbers either in the region where such individual lives or in several regions of the country." § 423(d)(2)(A).

[16] Information is also requested concerning the recipient's belief as to whether he can return to work, the nature and extent of his employment during the past year, and any vocational services he is receiving.

[17] All medical-source evidence used to establish the absence of continuing disability must be in writing, with the source properly identified.

[18] The disability recipient is not permitted personally to examine the medical reports contained in his file. This restriction is not significant since he is entitled to have any representative of his choice, including a lay friend or family member, examine all medical evidence. The Secretary informs us that this curious limitation is currently under review.

The state agency then makes its final determination, which is reviewed by an examiner in the SSA Bureau of Disability Insurance. 42 U.S.C. § 421(c); CM §§ 6701(b), (c).[19] If, as is usually the case, the SSA accepts the agency determination it notifies the recipient in writing, informing him of the reasons for the decision, and of his right to seek *de novo* reconsideration by the state agency. 20 CFR §§ 404.907, 404.909 (1975). Upon acceptance by the SSA, benefits are terminated effective two months after the month in which medical recovery is found to have occurred. 42 U.S.C. (Supp. III) § 423(a) (1970 ed., Supp. III).

If the recipient seeks reconsideration by the state agency and the determination is adverse, the SSA reviews the reconsideration determination and notifies the recipient of the decision. He then has a right to an evidentiary hearing before an SSA administrative law judge. The hearing is nonadversary, and the SSA is not represented by counsel. As at all prior and subsequent stages of the administrative process, however, the claimant may be represented by counsel or other spokesmen. If this hearing results in an adverse decision, the claimant is entitled to request discretionary review by the SSA Appeals Council, and finally may obtain judicial review.[21]

Should it be determined at any point after termination of benefits, that the claimant's disability extended beyond the date of cessation initially established, the worker is entitled to retroactive payments. If, on the other hand, a beneficiary receives any payments to which he is later determined not to be entitled, the statute authorizes the Secretary to attempt to recoup these funds in specified circumstances.

C

Despite the elaborate character of the administrative procedures provided by the Secretary, the courts below held them to be constitutionally inadequate, concluding that due process requires an evidentiary hearing prior to termination. In light of the private and governmental interests at stake here and the nature of the existing procedures, we think this was error.

Since a recipient whose benefits are terminated is awarded full retroactive relief if he ultimately prevails, his sole interest is in the uninterrupted receipt of this source of income pending final administrative decision on his claim. His potential injury is thus similar in nature to that of the welfare recipient in *Goldberg*. . . .

---

[19] The SSA may not itself revise the state agency's determination in a manner more favorable to the beneficiary. If, however, it believes that the worker is still disabled, or that the disability lasted longer than determined by the state agency, it may return the file to the agency for further consideration in light of the SSA's views. The agency is free to reaffirm its original assessment.

[21] Unlike all prior levels of review, which are de novo, the district court is required to treat findings of fact as conclusive if supported by substantial evidence.

Only in *Goldberg* has the Court held that due process requires an evidentiary hearing prior to a temporary deprivation. It was emphasized there that welfare assistance is given to persons on the very margin of subsistence:

> The crucial factor in this context a factor not present in the case of . . . virtually anyone else whose governmental entitlements are ended is that termination of aid pending resolution of a controversy over eligibility may deprive an *eligible* recipient of the very means by which to live while he waits. 397 U.S., at 264 (emphasis in original).

Eligibility for disability benefits, in contrast, is not based upon financial need.[24] Indeed, it is wholly unrelated to the worker's income or support from many other sources, such as earnings of other family members, workmen's compensation awards, tort claims awards, savings, private insurance, public or private pensions, veterans' benefits, food stamps, public assistance, or the "many other important programs, both public and private, which contain provisions for disability payments affecting a substantial portion of the work force. . . ." *Richardson v. Belcher*, 404 U.S., at 85-87 (1971) (Douglas, J., dissenting).

As *Goldberg* illustrates, the degree of potential deprivation that may be created by a particular decision is a factor to be considered in assessing the validity of any administrative decisionmaking process. The potential deprivation here is generally likely to be less than in *Goldberg*, although the degree of difference can be overstated. As the District Court emphasized, to remain eligible for benefits a recipient must be "unable to engage in substantial gainful activity." 42 U.S.C. § 423. Thus, in contrast to the discharged federal employee in *Arnett*, there is little possibility that the terminated recipient will be able to find even temporary employment to ameliorate the interim loss.

As we recognized last Term in *Fusari v. Steinberg*, 419 U.S. 379, 389 (1975), "the possible length of wrongful deprivation of . . . benefits (also) is an important factor in assessing the impact of official action on the private interests." The Secretary concedes that the delay between a request for a hearing before an administrative law judge and a decision on the claim is currently between 10 and 11 months. Since a terminated recipient must first obtain a reconsideration decision as a prerequisite to invoking his right to an evidentiary hearing, the delay between the actual cutoff of benefits and final decision after a hearing exceeds one year.

In view of the torpidity of this administrative review process, and the typically modest resources of the family unit of the physically disabled worker, the hardship imposed upon the erroneously terminated disability recipient may be significant. Still, the disabled worker's need is likely to be less than that of a welfare recipient. In addition to the possibility of access to private

---

[24] The level of benefits is determined by the worker's average monthly earnings during the period prior to disability, his age, and other factors not directly related to financial need . . . .

resources, other forms of government assistance will become available where the termination of disability benefits places a worker or his family below the subsistence level. In view of these potential sources of temporary income, there is less reason here than in *Goldberg* to depart from the ordinary principle, established by our decisions, that something less than an evidentiary hearing is sufficient prior to adverse administrative action.

D

An additional factor to be considered here is the fairness and reliability of the existing pretermination procedures, and the probable value, if any, of additional procedural safeguards. Central to the evaluation of any administrative process is the nature of the relevant inquiry. *See* Friendly, *Some Kind of Hearing*, 123 U. PA. L. REV. 1267, 1281 (1975). In order to remain eligible for benefits the disabled worker must demonstrate by means of "medically acceptable clinical and laboratory diagnostic techniques," 42 U.S.C. § 423(d)(3), that he is unable "to engage in any substantial gainful activity by reason of any *medically determinable* physical or mental impairment. . . ." § 423(d)(1)(A) (emphasis supplied). In short, a medical assessment of the worker's physical or mental condition is required. This is a more sharply focused and easily documented decision than the typical determination of welfare entitlement. In the latter case, a wide variety of information may be deemed relevant, and issues of witness credibility and veracity often are critical to the decisionmaking process. *Goldberg* noted that in such circumstances "written submissions are a wholly unsatisfactory basis for decision." 397 U.S., at 269.

By contrast, the decision whether to discontinue disability benefits will turn, in most cases, upon "routine, standard, and unbiased medical reports by physician specialists," *Richardson v. Perales*, 402 U.S. 389, 404 (1971), concerning a subject whom they have personally examined.[28] In *Richardson* the Court recognized the "reliability and probative worth of written medical reports," emphasizing that while there may be "professional disagreement with the medical conclusions" the "specter of questionable credibility and

---

[28] The decision is not purely a question of the accuracy of a medical diagnosis since the ultimate issue which the state agency must resolve is whether in light of the particular worker's "age, education, and work experience" he cannot "engage in any . . . substantial gainful work which exists in the national economy . . . ." 42 U.S.C. § 423(d)(2)(A). Yet information concerning each of these worker characteristics is amenable to effective written presentation. The value of an evidentiary hearing, or even a limited oral presentation, to an accurate presentation of those factors to the decisionmaker does not appear substantial. Similarly, resolution of the inquiry as to the types of employment opportunities that exist in the national economy for a physically impaired worker with a particular set of skills would not necessarily be advanced by an evidentiary hearing. The statistical information relevant to this judgment is more amenable to written than to oral presentation.

veracity is not present." *Id. at* 405, 407. To be sure, credibility and veracity may be a factor in the ultimate disability assessment in some cases. But procedural due process rules are shaped by the risk of error inherent in the truthfinding process as applied to the generality of cases, not the rare exceptions. The potential value of an evidentiary hearing, or even oral presentation to the decisionmaker, is substantially less in this context than in *Goldberg*.

The decision in *Goldberg* also was based on the Court's conclusion that written submissions were an inadequate substitute for oral presentation because they did not provide an effective means for the recipient to communicate his case to the decisionmaker. Written submissions were viewed as an unrealistic option, for most recipients lacked the "educational attainment necessary to write effectively" and could not afford professional assistance. In addition, such submissions would not provide the "flexibility of oral presentations" or "permit the recipient to mold his argument to the issues the decision maker appears to regard as important." 397 U.S., at 269. In the context of the disability-benefits-entitlement assessment the administrative procedures under review here fully answer these objections.

The detailed questionnaire which the state agency periodically sends the recipient identifies with particularity the information relevant to the entitlement decision, and the recipient is invited to obtain assistance from the local SSA office in completing the questionnaire. More important, the information critical to the entitlement decision usually is derived from medical sources, such as the treating physician. Such sources are likely to be able to communicate more effectively through written documents than are welfare recipients or the lay witnesses supporting their cause. The conclusions of physicians often are supported by X-rays and the results of clinical or laboratory tests, information typically more amenable to written than to oral presentation.

A further safeguard against mistake is the policy of allowing the disability recipient's representative full access to all information relied upon by the state agency. In addition, prior to the cutoff of benefits the agency informs the recipient of its tentative assessment, the reasons therefor, and provides a summary of the evidence that it considers most relevant. Opportunity is then afforded the recipient to submit additional evidence or arguments, enabling him to challenge directly the accuracy of information in his file as well as the correctness of the agency's tentative conclusions. These procedures, again as contrasted with those before the Court in *Goldberg*, enable the recipient to "mold" his argument to respond to the precise issues which the decisionmaker regards as crucial.

Despite these carefully structured procedures, amici point to the significant reversal rate for appealed cases as clear evidence that the current process is inadequate. Depending upon the base selected and the line of analysis followed, the relevant reversal rates urged by the contending parties vary from a high of 58.6% for appealed reconsideration decisions to an overall reversal rate of only 3.3%. Bare statistics rarely provide a satisfactory measure of the fairness of a decisionmaking process. Their adequacy is especially suspect here since the administrative review system is operated on an open-file basis. A recipient may always submit new evidence, and such submissions may result in additional medical examinations. Such fresh examinations were held in approximately 30% to 40% of the appealed cases, in fiscal 1973, either at the reconsideration or evidentiary hearing stage of the administrative process. In this context, the value of reversal rate statistics as one means of evaluating the adequacy of the pretermination process is diminished. Thus, although we view such information as relevant, it is certainly not controlling in this case.

E

In striking the appropriate due process balance the final factor to be assessed is the public interest. This includes the administrative burden and other societal costs that would be associated with requiring, as a matter of constitutional right, an evidentiary hearing upon demand in all cases prior to the termination of disability benefits. The most visible burden would be the incremental cost resulting from the increased number of hearings and the expense of providing benefits to ineligible recipients pending decision. No one can predict the extent of the increase, but the fact that full benefits would continue until after such hearings would assure the exhaustion in most cases of this attractive option. Nor would the theoretical right of the Secretary to recover undeserved benefits result, as a practical matter, in any substantial offset to the added outlay of public funds. The parties submit widely varying estimates of the probable additional financial cost. We only need say that experience with the constitutionalizing of government procedures suggests that the ultimate additional cost in terms of money and administrative burden would not be insubstantial.

Financial cost alone is not a controlling weight in determining whether due process requires a particular procedural safeguard prior to some administrative decision. But the Government's interest, and hence that of the public, in conserving scarce fiscal and administrative resources is a factor that must be weighed. At some point the benefit of an additional safeguard to the individual affected by the administrative action and to society in terms of increased assurance that the action is just, may be outweighed by the cost. Significantly, the cost of protecting those whom the preliminary administrative process has identified as likely to be found undeserving may in the end come out of the pockets of the deserving since resources available for any particular program of social welfare are not unlimited. *See* Friendly, *supra*, 123 U. PA. L. REV., at 1276, 1303.

But more is implicated in cases of this type than ad hoc weighing of fiscal and administrative burdens against the interests of a particular category of claimants. The ultimate balance involves a determination as to when, under our constitutional system, judicial-type procedures must be imposed upon administrative action to assure fairness. . . . The judicial model of an evidentiary hearing is neither a required, nor even the most effective, method of decisionmaking in all circumstances. The essence of due process is the requirement that "a person in jeopardy of serious loss (be given) notice of the case against him and opportunity to meet it." *Joint Anti-Fascist Comm. v. McGrath*, 341 U.S., at 171-172 (Frankfurter, J., concurring). All that is necessary is that the procedures be tailored, in light of the decision to be made, to "the capacities and circumstances of those who are to be heard," *Goldberg v. Kelly*, 397 U.S., at 268-269 (footnote omitted), to insure that they are given a meaningful opportunity to present their case. In assessing what process is due in this case, substantial weight must be given to the good-faith judgments of the individuals charged by Congress with the administration of social welfare programs that the procedures they have provided assure fair consideration of the entitlement claims of individuals. This is especially so where, as here, the prescribed procedures not only provide the claimant with an effective process for asserting his claim prior to any administrative action, but also assure a right to an evidentiary hearing, as well as to subsequent judicial review, before the denial of his claim becomes final.

We conclude that an evidentiary hearing is not required prior to the termination of disability benefits and that the present administrative procedures fully comport with due process.

The judgment of the Court of Appeals is
Reversed.

Mr. Justice STEVENS took no part in the consideration or decision of this case.

Mr. Justice BRENNAN, with whom Mr. Justice MARSHALL concurs, dissenting.

. . . I agree with the District Court and the Court of Appeals that, prior to termination of benefits, Eldridge must be afforded an evidentiary hearing of the type required for welfare beneficiaries under Title IV of the Social Security Act, 42 U.S.C. § 601 *et seq. See Goldberg v. Kelly*, 397 U.S. 254 (1970). I would add that the Court's consideration that a discontinuance of disability benefits may cause the recipient to suffer only a limited deprivation is no argument. It is speculative. Moreover, the very legislative determination to provide disability benefits, without any prerequisite determination of need in fact, presumes a need by the recipient which is not this Court's function to denigrate. Indeed, in the present case, it is indicated that because disability benefits were terminated there was a foreclosure upon the Eldridge home and the family's furniture was repossessed, forcing Eldridge, his wife, and their children to sleep in one bed. Finally, it is also no argument that a worker, who has been placed in the untenable position of having been denied disability benefits, may still seek other forms of public assistance.

* * *

In developing its three-factor balancing test, *Mathews* tried to synthesize and lend consistency to how courts approach the procedural adequacy question. It isolated the basic factual inputs for any such due process inquiry (the individual's interest affected by the government's decision, the government's interests in keeping the procedures it has chosen, and the risk of decisional error posed by those procedures as compared to more robust ones) and explained what to do with those inputs (weigh each one and balance them). However, neither the test itself nor the Court's description of it provide definitive guidance on how to establish any of these facts. What unit of measurement, for instance, should courts use when assigning weight to an individual's private interests? By what *common* unit of measurement can courts credibly weigh that interest against the government's? How are they to calculate a procedural scheme's probability of decisional error?

It seems safe to say that the *Mathews* Court did not (and could not) have intended the degree of analytical precision implied by these questions. The *Mathews* test instead insists on a seemingly intuitive, commonsensical balancing of particular facts when judging the adequacy of adjudicative procedures. The legal conclusions drawn from that balancing will, inevitably, differ from case to case. Put another way, the *Mathews* test calls for consistency in inputs and analytical approach, but not necessarily consistency in results. Accordingly, the outcomes it produces will differ depending on (sometimes subtle) situational distinctions.

The next case—*Ingraham v. Wright*—addressed such a distinction, and in doing so addressed an issue left unanswered by *Mathews*. To what extent should courts applying the balancing test account for extra-administrative processes—e.g., the availability of a civil damages action in state court—when determining whether to order the extra procedural protections sought by plaintiffs? Does the claimant's ability to seek redress in an alternate forum impact the need for new or additional procedures?

Ingraham v. Wright
430 U.S. 651 (1977)

Mr. Justice POWELL delivered the opinion of the Court.

[In Section I of its opinion, the Court recounted the basic facts and procedural history of the case. Petitioners James Ingraham and Roosevelt Andrews, Florida junior high school students, filed a civil rights action against various school officials. They alleged that they were subjected to physical punishment (paddling) before being afforded pre-punishment hearings in violation of their Fourteenth Amendment procedural due process rights. They also argued that their paddlings violated their Eighth Amendment rights to be protected from cruel and unusual punishment. Corporal punishment was permitted under Florida law at the time, as long as it was not "degrading or unduly severe" and inflicted with prior consultation with the principal or teacher in charge of the school. Fla. Stat. Ann. § 232.27 (1961). Imposition of this punishment was further regulated by Dade County School Board Policy 5144, which permitted paddling on the buttocks with a flat wooden paddle measuring less than two feet long, three to four inches wide, and about one-half inch thick. The normal punishment was limited to one to five "licks" or blows with the paddle and resulted in no apparent physical injury to the student. Contrary to the procedural requirements of the statute and regulation, teachers often paddled students on their own authority without first consulting the principal. Ingraham was subjected to more than 20 licks with a paddle while being held over a table in the principal's office. His paddling was so severe that he suffered a hematoma requiring medical attention and keeping him out of school for several days. Andrews was paddled several times for minor infractions. On two occasions he was struck on his arms, once depriving him of the full use of his arm for a week.

The district court dismissed their claims. The Fifth Circuit reversed, finding the punishment to be so severe and oppressive that it violated the Eighth Amendment. It also found that the procedures outlined in Policy 5144 failed to satisfy the requirements of due process. The Fifth Circuit, sitting *en banc,* rejected these conclusions and affirmed the judgment of the district court.

In Sections II and III of the Court's opinion, it reviewed the history of corporal discipline in American public schools and of the Eighth Amendment's protection against cruel and unusual punishment. It concluded that the Eighth Amendment does not apply to corporal punishment administered in schools.

In Section IV.A, the Court concluded that the plaintiffs had liberty interests in being free from bodily restraint and punishment that were protected by procedural due process.]

IV. . . .

B

"(T)he question remains what process is due." *Morrissey v. Brewer, supra,* at 481. Were it not for the common-law privilege permitting teachers, to inflict reasonable corporal punishment on children in their care, and the availability of the traditional remedies for abuse, the case for requiring advance procedural safeguards would be strong indeed. But here we deal with a punishment — paddling — within that tradition, and the question is whether the common-law remedies are adequate to afford due process.

> "(D)ue process," unlike some legal rules, is not a technical conception with a fixed content unrelated to time, place and circumstances. . . . Representing a profound attitude of fairness . . . "due process" is compounded of history, reason, the past course of decisions, and stout confidence in the strength of the democratic faith which we profess. . . . *Anti-Fascist Comm. v. McGrath*, 341 U.S. 123, 162-163 (1951) (Frankfurter, J., concurring).

Whether in this case the common-law remedies for excessive corporal punishment constitute due process of law must turn on an analysis of the competing interests at stake, viewed against the background of "history, reason, (and) the past course of decisions." The analysis requires consideration of three distinct factors: "First, the private interest that will be affected . . .; second, the risk of an erroneous deprivation of such interest . . . and the probable value, if any, of additional or substitute procedural safeguards; and, finally, the (state) interest, including the function involved and the fiscal and administrative burdens that the additional or substitute procedural requirement would entail." *Mathews v. Eldridge*, 424 U.S. 319, 335 (1976).

1

Because it is rooted in history, the child's liberty interest in avoiding corporal punishment while in the care of public school authorities is subject to historical limitations. Under the common law, an invasion of personal security gave rise to a right to recover damages in a subsequent judicial proceeding. 3 William Blackstone, Commentaries *120-121. But the right of recovery was qualified by the concept of justification. Thus, there could be no recovery against a teacher who gave only "moderate correction" to a child. *Id. at* *120. To the extent that the force used was reasonable in light of its purpose, it was not wrongful, but rather "justifiable or lawful." *Ibid.*

The concept that reasonable corporal punishment in school is justifiable continues to be recognized in the laws of most States. It represents the balance struck by this country, between the child's interest in personal security and the traditional view that some limited corporal punishment may be necessary in the course of a child's education. Under that longstanding accommodation of interests, there can be no deprivation of substantive rights as long as disciplinary corporal punishment is within the limits of the common-law privilege.

This is not to say that the child's interest in procedural safeguards is insubstantial. The school disciplinary process is not "a totally accurate, unerring process, never mistaken and never unfair. . . ." *Goss v. Lopez*, 419 U.S. 565, 579-580 (1975). In any deliberate infliction of corporal punishment on a child who is restrained for that purpose, there is some risk that the intrusion on the child's liberty will be unjustified and therefore unlawful. In these circumstances the child has a strong interest in procedural safeguards that minimize the risk of wrongful punishment and provide for the resolution of disputed questions of justification. . . .

2

Florida has continued to recognize, and indeed has strengthened by statute, the common-law right of a child not to be subjected to excessive corporal punishment in school. Under Florida law the teacher and principal of the school decide in the first instance whether corporal punishment is reasonably necessary under the circumstances in order to discipline a child who has misbehaved. But they must exercise prudence and restraint. For Florida has preserved the traditional judicial proceedings for determining whether the punishment was justified. If the punishment inflicted is later found to have been excessive not reasonably believed at the time to be necessary for the child's discipline or training the school authorities inflicting it may be held liable in damages to the child and, if malice is shown, they may be subject to criminal penalties.

Although students have testified in this case to specific instances of abuse, there is every reason to believe that such mistreatment is an aberration. The uncontradicted evidence suggests that corporal punishment in the Dade County schools was, "(w)ith the exception of a few cases, . . . unremarkable in physical severity." Moreover, because paddlings are usually inflicted in response to conduct directly observed by teachers in their presence, the risk that a child will be paddled without cause is typically insignificant. In the ordinary case, a disciplinary paddling neither threatens seriously to violate any substantive rights nor condemns the child "to suffer grievous loss of any kind." *Anti-Fascist Comm. v. McGrath*, 341 U.S., at 168 (Frankfurter, J., concurring).

In those cases where severe punishment is contemplated, the available civil and criminal sanctions for abuse considered in light of the openness of the school environment afford significant protection against unjustified corporal punishment. Teachers and school authorities are unlikely to inflict corporal punishment unnecessarily or excessively when a possible consequence of doing so is the institution of civil or criminal proceedings against them.

It still may be argued, of course, that the child's liberty interest would be better protected if the common-law remedies were supplemented by the administrative safeguards of prior notice and a hearing. We have found frequently that some kind of prior hearing is necessary to guard against arbitrary impositions on interests protected by the Fourteenth Amendment. *See, e. g., Board of Regents v. Roth*, 408 U.S., at 569-570; *Wolff v. McDonnell*, 418 U.S. 539, 557-558. But where the State has preserved what "has always been the law of the land," the case for administrative safeguards is significantly less compelling. . . .

3

But even if the need for advance procedural safeguards were clear, the question would remain whether the incremental benefit could justify the cost. Acceptance of petitioners' claims would work a transformation in the law governing corporal punishment in Florida and most other States. Given the impracticability of formulating a rule of procedural due process that varies with the severity of the particular imposition, the prior hearing petitioners seek would have to precede any paddling, however moderate or trivial.

Such a universal constitutional requirement would significantly burden the use of corporal punishment as a disciplinary measure. Hearings—even informal hearings—require time, personnel, and a diversion of attention from normal school pursuits. School authorities may well choose to abandon corporal punishment rather than incur the burdens of complying with the procedural requirements. Teachers, properly concerned with maintaining authority in the classroom, may well prefer to rely on other disciplinary measures which they may view as less effective rather than confront the possible disruption that prior notice and a hearing may entail. Paradoxically, such an alteration of disciplinary policy is most likely to occur in the ordinary case where the contemplated punishment is well within the common-law privilege.

Elimination or curtailment of corporal punishment would be welcomed by many as a societal advance. But when such a policy choice may result from this Court's determination of an asserted right to due process, rather than from the normal processes of community debate and legislative action, the societal costs cannot be dismissed as insubstantial. We are reviewing here a legislative judgment, rooted in history and reaffirmed in the laws of many States, that corporal punishment serves important educational interests. This judgment must be viewed in light of the disciplinary problems commonplace in the schools. As noted in *Goss v. Lopez*, 419 U.S., at 580: "Events calling for discipline are frequent occurrences and sometimes require immediate, effective action." Assessment of the need for, and the appropriate means of maintaining, school discipline is committed generally to the discretion of school authorities subject to state law. The Court has repeatedly emphasized the need for affirming the comprehensive authority of the States and of school officials, consistent with fundamental constitutional safeguards, to prescribe and control conduct in the schools.

"At some point the benefit of an additional safeguard to the individual affected . . . and to society in terms of increased assurance that the action is just, may be outweighed by the cost." *Mathews v. Eldridge*, 424 U.S., at 348. We think that point has been reached in this case. In view of the low incidence of abuse, the openness of our schools, and the common-law safe-guards that already exist, the risk of error that may result in violation of a schoolchild's substantive rights can only be regarded as minimal. Imposing additional administrative safeguards as a constitutional requirement might reduce that risk marginally, but would also entail a significant intrusion into an area of primary educational responsibility. We conclude that the Due Process Clause does not require notice and a hearing prior to the imposition of corporal punishment in the public schools, as that practice is authorized and limited by the common law. . . .

Affirmed.

Mr. Justice WHITE, with whom Mr. Justice BRENNAN, Mr. Justice MARSHALL, and Mr. Justice STEVENS join, dissenting. . . .

The Court now holds that . . . "rudimentary precautions against unfair or mistaken findings of misconduct," are not required if the student is pun-ished with "appreciable physical pain" rather than with a suspension, even though both punishments deprive the student of a constitutionally protected interest. Although the respondent school authorities provide absolutely no process to the student before the punishment is finally inflicted, the majority concludes that the student is nonetheless given due process because he can later sue the teacher and recover damages if the punishment was "excessive."

This tort action is utterly inadequate to protect against erroneous inflic-tion of punishment for two reasons. First, under Florida law, a student pun-ished for an act he did not commit cannot recover damages from a teacher proceeding in utmost good faith on the reports and advice of others; the stu-dent has no remedy at all for punishment imposed on the basis of mistaken facts, at least as long as the punishment was reasonable from the point of view of the disciplinarian, uninformed by any prior hearing. The "traditional common-law remedies" on which the majority relies thus do nothing to pro-tect the student from the danger that concerned the Court in *Goss*, the risk of reasonable, good-faith mistake in the school disciplinary process.

Second, and more important, even if the student could sue for good-faith error in the infliction of punishment, the lawsuit occurs after the pun-ishment has been finally imposed. The infliction of physical pain is final and irreparable; it cannot be undone in a subsequent proceeding. There is every reason to require, as the Court did in *Goss*, a few minutes of "informal give-and-take between student and disciplinarian" as a "meaningful hedge" against the erroneous infliction of irreparable injury. 419 U.S., at 583-584.

The majority's conclusion that a damages remedy for excessive corporal punishment affords adequate process rests on the novel theory that the State may punish an individual without giving him any opportunity to present his side of the story, as long as he can later recover damages from a state official if he is innocent. The logic of this theory would permit a State that punished speeding with a one-day jail sentence to make a driver serve his sentence first without a trial and then sue to recover damages for wrongful imprisonment. Similarly, the State could finally take away a prisoner's good-time credits for alleged disciplinary infractions and require him to bring a damages suit after he was eventually released. There is no authority for this theory, nor does the majority purport to find any, in the procedural due process decisions of this Court. Those cases have "consistently held that *some kind of hearing is required at some time before a person is finally deprived* of his property interests . . . (and that) a person's liberty is equally protected. . . ." *Wolff v. McDonnell*, 418 U.S. 539, 557-558 (1974). (Emphasis added.). . .

There is . . . no basis in logic or authority for the majority's suggestion that an action to recover damages for excessive corporal punishment "afford(s) substantially greater protection to the child than the informal conference mandated by *Goss*." The majority purports to follow the settled principle that what process is due depends on "'the risk of an erroneous deprivation of (the protected) interest . . . and the probable value, if any, of additional or substitute procedural safeguards'"; it recognizes, as did *Goss*, the risk of error in the school disciplinary process and concedes that "the child has a strong interest in procedural safeguards that minimize the risk of wrongful punishment . . . ," but it somehow concludes that this risk is adequately reduced by a damages remedy that never has been recognized by a Florida court, that leaves unprotected the innocent student punished by mistake, and that allows the State to punish first and hear the student's version of events later. I cannot agree.

The majority emphasizes, as did the dissenters in *Goss*, that even the "rudimentary precautions" required by that decision would impose some burden on the school disciplinary process. But those costs are no greater if the student is paddled rather than suspended; the risk of error in the punishment is no smaller; and the fear of "a significant intrusion" into the disciplinary process is just as exaggerated. The disciplinarian need only take a few minutes to give the student "notice of the charges against him and, if he denies them, an explanation of the evidence the authorities have and an opportunity to present his side of the story." *Goss*, 419 U.S., at 581. In this context the Constitution requires, "if anything, less than a fair-minded school principal would impose upon himself" in order to avoid injustice. *Id. at* 583.

I would reverse the judgment below.

[The dissenting opinion of Justice STEVENS is omitted.]

QUESTION SET 7.8

Review & Synthesis

1. With regard to *Mathews v. Eldridge*:
    a. Review the Social Security Administration process for determining eligibility for disability insurance payments. In your estimation, did

this process provide for careful consideration of disability insurance eligibility? Was Eldridge's challenge to this process based on its failure to provide him with a pre-deprivation hearing?

b. What is the three-part balancing test established by *Mathews v. Eldridge*, and what question is it designed to answer?

c. In applying the first part of the balancing test, the Court concluded Social Security disability insurance benefits are not "need-based," and thus eligibility for them signals a lesser degree of financial desperation than does eligibility for welfare payments. What aspects of the disability insurance program's eligibility requirements led the Court to this conclusion? Is it not the case that a person who is eligible for disability insurance is unable to work and is accordingly dependent on those insurance benefits to sustain themselves?

d. The Court points to two basic questions the SSA must answer to determine Eldridge's eligibility for disability insurance. First, is he medically unable to engage in substantial gainful activity? Second, is there any work in the national economy he is able to perform given his disabilities, age, education, and work experience? In applying the second part of the due process balancing test, the Court focused on whether the additional procedural protection Eldridge requested—an in-person pre-deprivation hearing—would produce evidence that reduced the risk of erroneous answers to these questions. What information relevant to these questions could be produced by an in-person hearing that would not be uncovered by relying solely on documents and questionnaires?

e. To what extent should exigent circumstances impact the *Mathews* calculus? Should the government be excused from conducting pre-deprivation hearings when, for example, it confiscates or destroys property to avoid an immediate threat to public health and safety?

2. With regard to *Ingraham v. Wright*:

a. The plaintiffs argued that the Fourteenth Amendment entitled them to a pre-punishment hearing. How, precisely, does a *post-punishment* tort action provide an adequate substitute? Is the Court saying, in effect, that schoolchildren who may be subject to physical punishment by their teachers are never entitled to advanced procedural safeguards? Consider what the Court observed in *Goss v. Lopez*, another school discipline case decided before *Mathews*, about the adequacy of post-punishment administrative review:

> . . . Appellants do not cite any case in which this general administrative review statute has been used to appeal from a disciplinary decision by a school official. If it be assumed that it could be so used, it is for two reasons insufficient to save inadequate procedures at the school level. First, although new proof may be offered in [the

administrative review] proceeding, . . . the proceeding is not *de
novo.* . . . Thus the decision by the school—even if made upon inadequate procedures—is entitled to weight in the court proceeding.
Second, without a demonstration to the contrary, we must assume
that delay will attend any proceeding, that the suspension will not be
stayed pending hearing, and that the student meanwhile will irreparably lose his educational benefit.

419 U.S. 565, 581 n.10 (1975). The Court emphasized that the Due
Process "[C]lause requires at least . . . rudimentary precautions against
unfair or mistaken findings of misconduct and arbitrary exclusion from
school." *Id.* at 581. How does this square with the holding in *Ingraham*?

b. When considering whether alternative review procedures can substitute for those requested by a claimant in a procedural due process case,
should those alternatives be available as a conceptual or as a practical
matter? What if, for example, the statute of limitations has run on the
alternative state tort action? What if the government officials would
have the benefit of state-based immunities that would likely result in
dismissal of the lawsuit before the state court could reach the merits?
What if, as pointed out in *Goss*, the state court would treat factual
findings made by the government officials deferentially? What if the
standard of proof in the state court was higher than the one that would
otherwise apply in a pre-deprivation administrative hearing?

Application & Analysis

1. Bob is an inmate at the state penitentiary. His mother ordered him a
painting kit and arranged for it to be delivered to him by mail. When the
kit did not arrive, Bob asked one of the prison guards to look for it. The
guard later informed Bob that the kit had indeed arrived at the prison.
Unfortunately, one of the mailroom workers accidently discarded it when
he failed to follow the prison's established procedures for receiving and
distributing packages. Pursuant to prison regulations, Bob lodged a written complaint with the warden, who rejected it. Having exhausted his
administrative remedies, Bob has filed a 42 U.S.C. § 1983 lawsuit arguing
that prison officials deprived him of his property without due process of
law. You are a law clerk for the judge before whom the suit is pending.
She has asked you to assess the strength of Bob's claim. How do you
respond?

2. Imogen is an undergraduate student at State University ("SU"). Wayne,
one of her classmates, tells the Dean of Students that Imogen tried to steal
his laptop while he left it unattended at a campus library. Based solely
on Wayne's accusation, and without speaking with Imogen, the Dean
of Students suspended her for the remainder of the semester, with fewer

than three weeks before her first final exam. SU's student code provides that the Dean of Students may suspended students based on theft allegations, but is silent on the procedures that should attend such a decision. Imogen has asked you, a law school friend, whether the Dean of Students should have gotten her side of the story before suspending her. What do you think?

3. Assume the same facts as Question 2, except that Imogen confesses to the attempted laptop theft. She nevertheless demands a pre-suspension hearing with the Dean of Students to explain that Wayne's laptop contains proof of his collaboration with several students who plan to cheat on their final exams. Once she "acquired" the laptop, she intended to turn it over to the Dean for inspection. Do you think the Fourteenth Amendment Due Process Clause entitles her to a pre-suspension hearing?

4. Assume the same facts as Question 2, except that Wayne presses charges against Imogen with the State University Police Department ("SUPD") before going to the Dean of Students. The SUPD finds that there is a reasonable basis for believing that Imogen attempted to steal the laptop and arrests her on attempted petty theft (a misdemeanor punishable by a $1,000 fine and no more than two months' jail time). Learning of Imogen's arrest, the Dean of Students immediately suspends her. Imogen believes that she is entitled to an informal hearing before her suspension can take effect. She asks for your opinion.

5. Assume the same facts as Question 2, except that the Dean of Students concludes that Imogen is entitled to a pre-suspension hearing. She tells Imogen that she may submit whatever evidence she deems relevant, such as a written statement detailing her understanding of the facts. The Dean makes clear that she will not grant Imogen any kind of in-person, oral hearing. Imogen would strongly prefer to have her say in person. Does the Due Process Clause entitle her to that?

F. THE RIGHT TO A NEUTRAL DECISION-MAKER

As is clear from the *Mathews v. Eldridge* line of cases, the procedures that secure parties the meaningful opportunity to be heard required by the Fifth and Fourteenth Amendments depend on several factors and therefore vary from one case to another. Indeed, the government may even deny an affected party of pre-deprivation notice and an opportunity to be heard if it has a sufficiently weighty reason for doing so. *See Gilbert v. Homar*, 520 U.S. 924, 930 (1997) ("This Court has recognized, on many occasions, that where a State must act quickly, or where it would be impractical to provide pre-deprivation process, postdeprivation process satisfies the requirements of the Due Process Clause."). Despite this, certain procedural due process protections are not subject to *Mathews* balancing and must therefore be provided regardless of the weight of the affected party's interests, the weight of the government's interests, or the protections' effectiveness in reducing the risk of erroneous decision-making. One such protection is the right to a neutral decision-maker, which the *Goldberg* Court described as an essential element of procedural due process. Parties' disputes must be resolved through a fair-minded application of relevant legal rules to reliable evidence, and not by resort to adjudicators' preconceptions or personal biases.

The neutral decision-maker requirement applies with equal force to judicial and administrative adjudication, though the latter raises conceptual and practical challenges atypical of the former. To ward off even the potential appearance of bias, state and federal governments conspicuously insulate their judges from other officials. Their judges are not employed by, do not answer to, and have tightly regulated interactions with those performing investigative, prosecutorial, or legislative functions. Contrast that with the organizational relationship between adjudicators and other personnel within an administrative agency. It is not uncommon for adjudicators, investigators, prosecutors, and rulemakers to be employees of a single agency that is headed by political appointees. The institutional loyalties that could develop from this commonality of employer, and the political pressure agency leaders are positioned to exert, might create an appearance of partiality if not carefully monitored and managed. Moreover, agency leaders may serve an adjudicative role despite the fact that they are political appointees removable by the President, and even though they may also perform investigative tasks.

As already detailed earlier in this chapter, Congress has paid close attention to this issue in the context of formal adjudications. The APA contains numerous provisions insulating administrative law judges ("ALJs") from their agencies' nonadjudicative functions and personnel. To review, ALJs preside over all formal adjudications not conducted by agency leadership (5 U.S.C. § 556), enjoy security of position approaching what is granted to federal judges (5 U.S.C. §§ 3105, 5372, 7521), cannot be supervised by agency employees (apart from agency heads) with investigative or prosecutorial responsibilities (5 U.S.C. § 554(d)(2)), and cannot be assigned duties that are inconsistent with their adjudicative function (5 U.S.C. § 3105). When faithfully followed, these provisions resolve the neutral decision-maker problem in the situations to which they apply. Of course, the APA's formal adjudication rules do not apply to informal adjudications conducted by federal agencies, or to any adjudications conducted by states. Accordingly, courts must often resort directly to constitutional due process principles to assure neutral decision-making.

The cases that follow coalesce around two recurring neutrality problems. The first involves pre-judgment, wherein the administrative adjudicator is alleged to have decided the merits of a legal claim either before hearing the relevant evidence or in disregard of that evidence after hearing it. The second involves self-dealing, wherein the adjudicator appears to have a personal interest in the disposition of a legal question. That impermissible interest can take a variety of forms, including pecuniary, professional, or familial. Both problems threaten one of due process' most basic guarantees: a judgment based on nothing other than the relevant facts and the applicable law.

1. The Problem of Pre-Judgment

Withrow v. Larkin
421 U.S. 35 (1975)

Mr. Justice WHITE delivered the opinion for a unanimous Court.

I

Appellee, a resident of Michigan and licensed to practice medicine there, obtained a Wisconsin license in August 1971 under a reciprocity agreement between Michigan and Wisconsin governing medical licensing. His practice in Wisconsin consisted of performing abortions at an office in Milwaukee. On June 20, 1973, the [Wisconsin Medical Examining] Board sent to appellee a notice that it would hold an investigative hearing on July 12, 1973, under Wis. Stat. Ann. § 448.17, to determine whether he had engaged in certain proscribed acts. The hearing would be closed to the public, although appellee and his attorney could attend. They would not, however, be permitted to cross-examine witnesses. Based upon the evidence presented at the hearing, the Board would decide whether to warn or reprimand if it finds such practice and whether to institute criminal action or action to revoke license if probable cause therefor exists under criminal or revocation statutes.

On July 6, 1973, appellee filed his complaint in this action under 42 U.S.C. § 1983 seeking preliminary and permanent injunctive relief and a temporary restraining order preventing the Board from investigating him and from conducting the investigative hearing. The District Court denied the motion for a temporary restraining order. . . .

The Board proceeded with its investigative hearing on July 12 and 13, 1973; numerous witnesses testified and appellee's counsel was present throughout the proceedings. Appellee's counsel was subsequently informed that appellee could if he wished, appear before the Board to explain any of the evidence which had been presented.

On September 18, 1973, the Board sent to appellee a notice that a "contested hearing" would be held on October 4, 1973, to determine whether appellee had engaged in certain prohibited acts and that based upon the evidence adduced at the hearing the Board would determine whether his license would be suspended temporarily under Wis. Stat. § 448.18(7). Appellee moved for a restraining order against the contested hearing. The District Court granted the motion on October 1, 1973. Because the Board had moved from purely investigative proceedings to a hearing aimed at deciding whether suspension of appellee's license was appropriate, the District Court concluded that a substantial federal question had arisen, namely, whether the authority given to appellants both "to investigate physicians and present charges (and) to rule on those charges and impose punishment, at least to the extent of reprimanding or temporarily suspending" violated appellee's due process rights. . . .

The Board complied and did not go forward with the contested hearing. Instead, it noticed and held a final investigative session on October 4, 1973, at which appellee's attorney, but not appellee, appeared. The Board thereupon issued "Findings of Fact," "Conclusions of Law," and a "Decision" in which the Board found that appellee had engaged in specified conduct proscribed by the statute. [The Decision found probable cause to believe that Dr. Larkin had engaged in unprofessional conduct violating the criminal provisions of sec. 448 and ordered the filing of a complaint with the Milwaukee district attorney to revoke his medical license and to initiate criminal proceedings against him. The district court initially found sec. 448.18(7) unconstitutional. It subsequently modified its order to enjoin the section's enforcement against Larkin only, finding that he was likely to succeed on the merits of his constitutional claim and that he would suffer irreparable injury if not granted injunctive relief.]

III

The District Court framed the constitutional issue, which it addressed as being whether "for the board temporarily to suspend Dr. Larkin's license at its own contested hearing on charges evolving from its own investigation would constitute a denial to him of his rights to procedural due process." 368 F. Supp., at 797. The question was initially answered affirmatively, and in its amended judgment the court asserted that there was a high probability that appellee would prevail on the question. Its opinion stated that the "state medical examining board (did) not qualify as (an independent) decisionmaker (and could not) properly rule with regard to the merits of the same charges it investigated and, as in this case, presented to the district attorney." *Id.* at 798. We disagree. On the present record, it is quite unlikely that appellee would ultimately prevail on the merits of the due process issue presented to the District Court, and it was an abuse of discretion to issue the preliminary injunction.

Concededly, a "fair trial in a fair tribunal is a basic requirement of due process." *In re Murchison,* 349 U.S. 133, 136 (1955). This applies to administrative agencies which adjudicate as well as to courts. *Gibson v. Berryhill*, 411 U.S. 564, 579 (1973). Not only is a biased decisionmaker constitutionally unacceptable but "our system of law has always endeavored to prevent even the probability of unfairness." *In re Murchison, supra,* 349 U.S., at 136; *cf. Tumey v. Ohio,* 273 U.S. 510, 532 (1927). In pursuit of this end, various situations have been identified in which experience teaches that the probability of actual bias on the part of the judge or decisionmaker is too high to be constitutionally tolerable. Among these cases are those in which the adjudicator has a pecuniary interest in the outcome and in which he has been the target of personal abuse or criticism from the party before him.

The contention that the combination of investigative and adjudicative functions necessarily creates an unconstitutional risk of bias in administrative adjudication has a much more difficult burden of persuasion to carry. It must overcome a presumption of honesty and integrity in those serving as adjudicators; and it must convince that, under a realistic appraisal of psychological tendencies and human weakness, conferring investigative and adjudicative powers on the same individuals poses such a risk of actual bias or prejudgment that the practice must be forbidden if the guarantee of due process is to be adequately implemented. . . .

That is not to say that there is nothing to the argument that those who have investigated should not then adjudicate. The issue is substantial, it is not new, and legislators and others concerned with the operations of administrative agencies have given much attention to whether and to what extent distinctive administrative functions should be performed by the same persons. No single answer has been reached. Indeed, the growth, variety, and complexity of the administrative processes have made any one solution highly unlikely. Within the Federal Government itself, Congress has addressed the issue in several different ways, providing for varying degrees of separation from complete separation of functions to virtually none at all. For the generality of agencies, Congress has been content with § 5 of the Administrative Procedure Act, 5 U.S.C. § 554(d), which provides that no employee engaged in investigating or prosecuting may also participate or advise in the adjudicating function, but which also expressly exempts from this prohibition "the agency or a member or members of the body comprising the agency."

It is not surprising, therefore, to find that "(t)he case law, both federal and state, generally rejects the idea that the combination (of) judging (and) investigating functions is a denial of due process. . . ." 2 Kenneth Culp Davis, Administrative Law Treatise § 13.02, p. 175 (1958). Similarly, our cases, although they reflect the substance of the problem, offer no support for the bald proposition applied in this case by the District Court that agency members who participate in an investigation are disqualified from adjudicating. The incredible variety of administrative mechanisms in this country will not yield to any single organizing principle. . . .

When the Board instituted its investigative procedures, it stated only that it would investigate whether proscribed conduct had occurred. Later in noticing the adversary hearing, it asserted only that it would determine if violations had been committed which would warrant suspension of appellee's license. Without doubt, the Board then anticipated that the proceeding would eventuate in an adjudication of the issue; but there was no more evidence of bias or the risk of bias or prejudgment than inhered in the very fact that the Board had investigated and would now adjudicate. Of course, we should be alert to the possibilities of bias that may lurk in the way particular procedures actually work in practice. The processes utilized by the Board, however, do not in themselves contain an unacceptable risk of bias. The investigative proceeding had been closed to the public, but appellee and his counsel were permitted to be present throughout; counsel actually attended the hearings and knew the facts presented to the Board. No specific foundation has been presented for suspecting that the Board had been prejudiced by its investigation or would be disabled from hearing and deciding on the basis of the evidence to be presented at the contested hearing. The mere exposure to evidence presented in nonadversary investigative procedures is insufficient in itself to impugn the fairness of the board members at a later adversary hearing. Without a showing to the contrary, state administrators "are assumed to be men of conscience and intellectual discipline, capable of judging a particular controversy fairly on the basis of its own circumstances." *United States v. Morgan*, 313 U.S. 409, 421 (1941).

We are of the view, therefore, that the District Court was in error when it entered the restraining order against the Board's contested hearing and when it granted the preliminary injunction based on the untenable view that it would be unconstitutional for the Board to suspend appellee's license "at its own contested hearing on charges evolving from its own investigation. . . ." The contested hearing should have been permitted to proceed.

IV

Nor do we think the situation substantially different because the Board, when it was prevented from going forward with the contested hearing, proceeded to make and issue formal findings of fact and conclusions of law asserting that there was probable cause to believe that appellee had engaged in various acts prohibited by the Wisconsin statutes. These findings and conclusions were verified and filed with the district attorney for the purpose of initiating revocation and criminal proceedings. Although the District Court did not emphasize this aspect of the case before it, appellee stresses it in attempting to show prejudice and prejudgment. We are not persuaded.

Judges repeatedly issue arrest warrants on the basis that there is probable cause to believe that a crime has been committed and that the person named in the warrant has committed it. Judges also preside at preliminary hearings where they must decide whether the evidence is sufficient to hold a defendant for trial. Neither of these pretrial involvements has been thought to raise any constitutional barrier against the judge's presiding over the criminal trial and, if the trial is without a jury, against making the necessary determination of guilt or innocence. Nor has it been thought that a judge is disqualified from presiding over injunction proceedings because he has initially assessed the facts in issuing or denying a temporary restraining order or a preliminary injunction. It is also very typical for the members of administrative agencies to receive the results of investigations, to approve the filing of charges or formal complaints instituting enforcement proceedings, and then to participate in the ensuing hearings. This mode of procedure does not violate the Administrative Procedure Act, and it does not violate due process of law. We should also remember that it is not contrary to due process to allow judges and administrators who have had their initial decisions reversed on appeal to confront and decide the same questions a second time around.

Here, the Board stayed within the accepted bounds of due process. Having investigated, it issued findings and conclusions asserting the commission of certain acts and ultimately concluding that there was probable cause to believe that appellee had violated the statutes.

The risk of bias or prejudgment in this sequence of functions has not been considered to be intolerably high or to raise a sufficiently great possibility that the adjudicators would be so psychologically wedded to their complaints that they would consciously or unconsciously avoid the appearance of having erred or changed position. Indeed, just as there is no logical inconsistency between a finding of probable cause and an acquittal in a criminal proceeding, there is no incompatibility between the agency filing a complaint based on probable cause and a subsequent decision, when all the evidence is in, that there has been no violation of the statute. Here, if the Board now proceeded after an adversary hearing to determine that appellee's license to practice should not be temporarily suspended, it would not implicitly be admitting error in its prior finding of probable cause. Its position most probably would merely reflect the benefit of a more complete view of the evidence afforded by an adversary hearing.

The initial charge or determination of probable cause and the ultimate adjudication have different bases and purposes. The fact that the same agency makes them in tandem and that they relate to the same issues does not result in a procedural due process violation. Clearly, if the initial view of the facts based on the evidence derived from nonadversarial processes as a practical or legal matter foreclosed fair and effective consideration at a subsequent adversary hearing leading to ultimate decision, a substantial due process question would be raised. But in our view, that is not this case. . . .

The judgment of the District Court is reversed and the case is remanded to that court for further proceedings consistent with this opinion.

So ordered.

Cinderella Career and Finishing Schools, Inc. v. Federal Trade Commission
425 F.2d 583 (D.C. Cir. 1970)

Before: TAMM, MacKINNON and ROBB, Circuit Judges.

TAMM, Circuit Judge:

This is a petition to review orders of the Federal Trade Commission which required petitioners Cinderella Career College and Finishing Schools, Inc. (hereinafter Cinderella), Stephen Corporation (the corporate entity which operates Cinderella), and Vincent Melzac (the sole owner of the stock of Cinderella and Stephen Corporation), to cease and desist from engaging in certain practices which were allegedly unfair and deceptive.[1]

After the Commission filed its complaint under section 5 of the Federal Trade Commission Act, 15 U.S.C. § 45 (1964), which charged Cinderella with making representations and advertising in a manner which was false,

---

[1] The Commission's complaint alleged that advertising used by petitioners contained the following false representations: 1. Petitioners make educational loans to students who register for courses at the Cinderella Career and Finishing School. 2. School Services, Inc. is a government or public nonprofit organization that has officially approved the Cinderella School or its courses. 3. Dianna Batts, "Miss U.S.A. 1965," and Carol Ness, "Miss Cinderella 1965," were graduates of the Cinderella School and owe their success to the courses they took there. 4. and 5. Petitioners offer courses of instruction which qualify students to become airline stewardesses and buyers for retail stores. 6. Petitioners find jobs for their students in almost all cases through their job placement service. 7. Graduates of petitioners' courses are qualified to assume executive positions. 8. Cinderella Career and Finishing School is the official Washington, D.C., headquarters for the Miss Universe Beauty Pageant. 9. Cinderella Career College and Finishing School is a college.

The complaint also alleged that the following practices were deceptive: 10. Prospective students who visit petitioners' school are frequently led to believe that they will be qualified to compete in certain beauty contests if they sign up for courses. 11. Petitioners frequently add that completion of their courses will enable applicants in most cases to obtain better jobs. 12. Prospective students are subjected to constant pressure to persuade them to enroll in petitioners' courses. 13. Petitioners fail to disclose the nature of the commitments the students are expected to assume or to provide them with sufficient time or opportunity to read and consider them.

misleading and deceptive, a hearing examiner held a lengthy series of hearings which consumed a total of sixteen days; these proceedings are reported in 1,810 pages of transcript. After the Commission had called twenty-nine witnesses and the petitioners twenty-three, and after the FTC had introduced 157 exhibits and petitioners 90, the hearing examiner ruled in a ninety-three page initial decision that the charges in the complaint should be dismissed.

Complaint counsel appealed the hearing examiner's initial decision to the full Commission; oral argument was heard on the appeal on May 28, 1968, and the Commission's final order was issued on October 10, 1968. The full Commission reversed the hearing examiner as to six of the original thirteen charges and entered a cease and desist order against the petitioners, who then brought this appeal. For the reasons which follow we remand to the Commission for further proceedings. . . .

[In Section I of its opinion, the court concluded that, under the FTC's regulations, the Commissioners could not ignore the hearing examiner's factual findings and substitute their own. While they could disagree with the hearing examiner's factual conclusions, they could not completely disregard them.]

II. DISQUALIFICATION OF CHAIRMAN DIXON

An additional ground which requires remand of these proceedings — and which would have required reversal even in the absence of the above-described procedural irregularities — is participation in the proceedings by the then Chairman of the Federal Trade Commission, Paul Rand Dixon.

Notice that the hearing examiner's dismissal of all charges would be appealed was filed by the Commission staff on February 1, 1968. On March 12, 1968, this court's decision was handed down in a prior appeal arising from this same complaint, in which we upheld the Commission's issuance of press releases which called attention to the pending proceedings. Then, on March 15, 1968, while the appeal from the examiner's decision was pending before him, Chairman Dixon made a speech before the Government Relations Workshop of the National Newspaper Association in which he stated:

> What kind of vigor can a reputable newspaper exhibit? The quick answer, of course, pertains to its editorial policy, its willingness to present the news without bias. However, that is only half the coin. How about ethics on the business side of running a paper? What standards are maintained on advertising acceptance? What would be the attitude toward accepting good money for advertising by a merchant who conducts a "going out of business" sale every five months? What about carrying ads that offer

college educations in five weeks, fortunes by raising mushrooms in the basement, getting rid of pimples with a magic lotion, or becoming an airline's hostess by attending a charm school? Or, to raise the target a bit, how many newspapers would hesitate to accept an ad promising an unqualified guarantee for a product when the guarantee is subject to many limitations? Without belaboring the point, I'm sure you're aware that advertising acceptance standards could stand more tightening by many newspapers. Granted that newspapers are not in the advertising policing business, their advertising managers are savvy enough to smell deception when the odor is strong enough. And it is in the public interest, as well as their own, that their sensory organs become more discriminating. The Federal Trade Commission, even where it has jurisdiction, could not protect the public as quickly.

It requires no superior olfactory powers to recognize that the danger of unfairness through prejudgment is not diminished by a cloak of self-righteousness. We have no concern for or interest in the public statements of government officers, but we are charged with the responsibility of making certain that the image of the administrative process is not transformed from a Rubens to a Modigliani.

We indicated in our earlier opinion in this case that "there is in fact and law authority in the Commission, acting in the public interest, to alert the public to suspected violations of the law by factual press releases whenever the Commission shall have reason to believe that a respondent is engaged in activities made unlawful by the Act. . . ." *FTC v. Cinderella Career & Finishing Schools, Inc.,* 404 F.2d 1308, 1314 (D.C. Cir. 1968). This does not give individual Commissioners license to prejudge cases or to make speeches which give the appearance that the case has been prejudged. Conduct such as this may have the effect of entrenching a Commissioner in a position which he has publicly stated, making it difficult, if not impossible, for him to reach a different conclusion in the event he deems it necessary to do so after consideration of the record. There is a marked difference between the issuance of a press release which states that the Commission has filed a complaint because it has "reason to believe" that there have been violations, and statements by a Commissioner after an appeal has been filed which give the appearance that he has already prejudged the case and that the ultimate determination of the merits will move in predestined grooves. While these two situations—Commission press releases and a Commissioner's pre-decision public statements—are similar in appearance, they are obviously of a different order of merit.

As we noted in our earlier opinion, Congress has specifically vested the administrative agencies both with the "power to act in an accusatory capacity" and with the "responsibility of ultimately determining the merits of the charges so presented." 404 F.2d at 315.

Chairman Dixon, sensitive to theory but insensitive to reality, made the following statement in declining to recuse himself from this case after petitioners requested that he withdraw:

> ["]As . . . I have stated . . . this principle "is not a rigid command of the law, compelling disqualification for trifling causes, but a consideration addressed to the discretion and sound judgment of the administrator himself in determining whether, irrespective of the law's requirements, he should disqualify himself."

(App. 143.) To this tenet of self-appraisal we apply Lord Macaulay's evaluation more than 100 years ago of our American government: "It has one drawback — it is all sail and no anchor." We find it hard to believe that former Chairman Dixon is so indifferent to the dictates of the Courts of Appeals that he has chosen once again to put his personal determination of what the law requires ahead of what the courts have time and again told him the law requires. If this is a question of "discretion and judgment," Commissioner Dixon has exercised questionable discretion and very poor judgment indeed, in directing his shafts and squibs at a case awaiting his official action. We can use his own words in telling Commissioner Dixon that he has acted "irrespective of the law's requirements"; we will spell out for him once again, avoiding tired cliché and weary generalization, in no uncertain terms, exactly what those requirements are, in the fervent hope that this will be the last time we have to travel this wearisome road.

The test for disqualification has been succinctly stated as being whether "a disinterested observer may conclude that (the agency) has in some measure adjudged the facts as well as the law of a particular case in advance of hearing it." *Gilligan, Will & Co. v. SEC,* 267 F.2d 461, 469 (2d Cir.), *cert. denied,* 361 U.S. 896 (1959). . . .

We further stated that such an administrative hearing "must be attended, not only with every element of fairness but with the very appearance of complete fairness," citing *Amos Treat & Co. v. SEC,* 306 F.2d 260, 267 (D.C. Cir. 1962). We therefore concluded that Chairman Dixon's participation in the Texaco case amounted to a denial of due process.

After our decision in Texaco the United States Court of Appeals for the Sixth Circuit was required to reverse a decision of the FTC because Chairman Dixon refused to recuse himself from the case even though he had served as Chief Counsel and Staff Director to the Senate Subcommittee which made the initial investigation into the production and sale of the "wonder drug" tetracycline. *American Cyanamid Co. v. FTC,* 363 F.2d 757 (6th Cir. 1966). Incredible though it may seem, the court was compelled to note in that case that:

> The Commission is a fact-finding body. As Chairman, Mr. Dixon sat with the other members as triers of the facts and joined in making the factual determination upon which the order of the Commission is based. As

counsel for the Senate Subcommittee, he had investigated and developed many of these same facts.

363 F.2d at 767. It is appalling to witness such insensitivity to the requirements of due process; it is even more remarkable to find ourselves once again confronted with a situation in which Mr. Dixon, pounding on the most convenient victim, has determined either to distort the holdings in the cited cases beyond all reasonable interpretation or to ignore them altogether. We are constrained to this harshness of language because of Mr. Dixon's flagrant disregard of prior decisions.

The rationale for remanding the case despite the fact that former Chairman Dixon's vote was not necessary for a majority is well established:

> Litigants are entitled to an impartial tribunal whether it consists of one man or twenty and there is no way which we know of whereby the influence of one upon the others can be quantitatively measured.

Berkshire Employees Ass'n of Berkshire Knitting Mills v. NLRB, 121 F.2d 235, 239 (3d Cir. 1941). This rationale was cited with approval in the *American Cyanamid* opinion; we adopt the position of our sister circuits on this point.

III. CONCLUSION

For the reasons set forth above we vacate the order of the Commission and remand with instructions that the Commissioners consider the record and evidence in reviewing the initial decision, without the participation of Commissioner Dixon.

Vacated and remanded.

QUESTION SET 7.9

Review & Synthesis

1. In *Withrow*, what test did the Court adopt for identifying prejudgment that violates of the Due Process Clauses? What test did the D.C. Circuit adopt in *Cinderella*? How do they compare?

2. Explain why prejudgment of a dispute by a government adjudicator constitutes a violation of the constitutional right to procedural due process.

3. The Court in *Withrow* analogized the Wisconsin Medical Examining Board's investigation and subsequent judgment of Larkin's conduct to a judge hearing a preliminary injunction and then presiding over the

534

534 Chapter 7: Due Process and Administrative Adjudication

subsequent case. Although the adjudicator in both situations makes initial factual and legal determinations, doing so precludes neither adjudicator from rendering judgment on ultimate legal culpability. Think about the organizational differences between courts and agencies. Do these differences strengthen or undermine the argumentative power of the Court's analogy? Now revisit the organizational arrangements relating to administrative law judges that are required by 5 U.S.C. § 554(d) (*see* Chapter 6, page 363). How do they reduce the problem of prejudgment?

Application & Analysis

1. Wisconsin state law grants state school boards the power to employ and dismiss teachers, a power that includes negotiating and agreeing to collective bargaining agreements with teachers' unions. Near the end of a recent school year, the Outagamie School Board realized that its collective bargaining agreement with the local teachers' union was going to expire. The School Board and teachers' union commenced negotiations on a new agreement over the summer. The negotiations stretched into the start of the next school year with the teachers agreeing to work while the negotiations continued.

    One month into the new school year, the negotiations broke down and the teachers went on strike in violation of Wisconsin law. The district superintendent invited the 86 striking teachers to return to their jobs, but very few did. The ongoing strike led the School Board to begin scheduling individual disciplinary hearings for the striking teachers. The Board sent notices to the teachers and, several days later, most of the teachers appeared before the Board with counsel. They requested the Board treat them as a group for disciplinary purposes and raised several procedural objections. Their main objection, however, was that the Board was not a neutral decision-maker under the Fourteenth Amendment Due Process Clause. The teachers argued that the Board was biased because it was intimately involved with—indeed, it took an oppositional stance regarding—the negotiations for a new collective bargaining agreement before the strike.

    The Board's members had no official or financial stake in the outcome of the disciplinary actions and were empowered by state law to conduct the disciplinary hearings. The Board allowed the teachers to submit proof in support of their allegations that the strike had been provoked by the Board's failure to meet teacher demands, that the Board's contract offers were unsatisfactory, and that the Board used coercive and illegal bargaining tactics. The Board weighed the evidence and ultimately voted to terminate the striking teachers.

    Analyze the merits of the teachers' claim that they were deprived of an unbiased decision-maker.

2. The Tahoe Regional Planning Association ("TRPA") is a ten-member agency established through an interstate compact between California

and Nevada. The agency is made up of an equal number of individuals from each state and is designed to oversee proposed new developments in the Lake Tahoe area. Any planned development in the area needs TRPA approval before it can move forward.

Last year, TRPA reviewed a proposal from Sahara Corp. to build a six-story parking garage next to an existing casino in the Lake Tahoe area. The state of California and the California Regional Planning Agency ("CRPA") both opposed construction of the parking garage. The TRPA members debated the Sahara Corp. proposal and, with a majority of members supporting the proposal, allowed it to be "deemed approved." A proposal before TRPA is "deemed approved" if the agency has not acted on it for 60 days. California and the CRPA then challenged the TRPA decision, arguing the agency was not an unbiased, independent decision-maker as due process requires.

The challenge was based on alleged gifts that three members of TRPA received from Sahara. The first TRPA member, Mr. Henry, won a Cadillac in a golfing contest Sahara and one other company sponsored a year before the parking structure proposal came before TRPA. Mr. Henry paid his own entry fee for the golf contest and won the car by coming closest to getting a hole-in-one out of the 354 people who entered. There was no evidence that the contest was organized to give Mr. Henry an unfair advantage. Mr. Henry originally voted against authorizing the Sahara project but changed his vote when he realized there were not enough votes to defeat the proposal.

The two other TRPA members identified by the plaintiffs, Mr. Stewart and Ms. Stoess, previously received campaign contributions from Sahara while they were running for local office. Ms. Stoess and Mr. Stewart received contributions of $300 and $450, respectively, three years before the proposal in question. The plaintiffs could not furnish any evidence that the contributions biased either member's decision-making.

Analyze the plaintiffs' claim that the TRPA decision did not conform to due process requirements.

---

2. The Problem of Self-Interest

Gibson v. Berryhill
411 U.S. 564 (1973)

Mr. Justice WHITE delivered the opinion of the Court.

Prior to 1965, the laws of Alabama relating to the practice of optometry permitted any person, including a business firm or corporation, to maintain a department in which "eyes are examined or glasses fitted," provided that such department was in the charge of a duly licensed optometrist. The permission was expressly conferred by § 210 of Title 46 of the Alabama Code of 940, and also inferentially by § 211 of the Code which regulates the advertising practices of optometrists, and which, until 1965, appeared to contemplate the existence of commercial stores with optical departments. In 1965, § 210 was repealed in its entirety by the Alabama Legislature, and § 211 was amended so as to eliminate any direct reference to optical departments maintained by corporations or other business establishments under the direction of employee optometrists.

Soon after these statutory changes, the Alabama Optometric Association, a professional organization whose membership is limited to independent practitioners of optometry not employed by others, filed charges against various named optometrists, all of whom were duly licensed under Alabama law but were the salaried employees of Lee Optical Co. The charges were filed with the Alabama Board of Optometry, the statutory body with authority to issue, suspend, and revoke licenses for the practice of optometry. The gravamen of these charges was that the named optometrists, by accepting employment from Lee Optical, a corporation, had engaged in "unprofessional conduct" within the meaning of § 206 of the Alabama optometry statute and hence were practicing their profession unlawfully. More particularly, the Association charged the named individuals with, among other things, aiding and abetting a corporation in the illegal practice of optometry; practicing optometry under a false name, that is, Lee Optical Co.; unlawfully soliciting the sale of glasses; lending their licenses to Lee Optical Co.; and splitting or dividing fees with Lee Optical. It was apparently the Association's position that, following the repeal of § 210 and the amendment of § 211, the practice of optometry by individuals as employees of business corporations was no longer permissible in Alabama, and that, by accepting such employment the named optometrists had violated the ethics of their profession. It was prayed that the Board revoke the licenses of the individuals charged following due notice and a proper hearing.

Two days after these charges were filed by the Association in October 1965, the Board filed a suit of its own in state court against Lee Optical, seeking to enjoin the company from engaging in the "unlawful practice of optometry." The Board's complaint also named 13 optometrists employed by Lee Optical as parties defendant, charging them with aiding and abetting the company in its illegal activities, as well as with other improper conduct very similar to that charged by the Association in its complaint to the Board.

Proceedings on the Association's charges were held in abeyance by the Board while its own state court suit progressed. The individual defendants in that suit were dismissed on grounds that do not adequately appear in the record before us; and, eventually, on March 17, 1971, the state trial court rendered judgment for the Board, and enjoined Lee Optical both from practicing optometry without a license and from employing licensed optometrists. The company appealed this judgment.

Meanwhile, following its victory in the trial court, the Board reactivated the proceedings pending before it since 1965 against the individual optometrists employed by Lee, noticing them for hearings to be held on May 26 and 27, 1971. Those individuals countered on May 14, 1971, by filing a complaint in the United States District Court naming as defendants the Board of Optometry and its individual members, as well as the Alabama Optometric Association and other individuals. The suit, brought under the Civil Rights Act of 1871, 42 U.S.C. § 1983, sought an injunction against the scheduled hearings on the grounds that the statutory scheme regulating the practice of optometry in Alabama was unconstitutional insofar as it permitted the Board to hear the pending charges against the individual plaintiffs in the federal suit. The thrust of the complaint was that the Board was biased and could not provide the plaintiffs with a fair and impartial hearing in conformity with due process of law.

A three-judge court was convened in August 1971, and shortly thereafter entered judgment for plaintiffs, enjoining members of the State Board and their successors 'from conducting a hearing on the charges heretofore preferred against the Plaintiffs' and from revoking their licenses to practice optometry in the State of Alabama. . . .

[In Sections I and II of its opinion, the Court affirmed the district court's conclusion that it was not precluded from enjoining the state proceedings under the Anti-Injunction Act (28 U.S.C. § 2283), by principles of equity or federalism established by the Supreme Court's decision in *Younger v. Harris*, 401 U.S. 37 (1971), or by a failure to exhaust administrative remedies.]

III

It is appropriate, therefore, that we consider the District Court's conclusions that the State Board of Optometry was so biased by prejudgment and pecuniary interest that it could not constitutionally conduct hearings looking toward the revocation of appellees' licenses to practice optometry. . . .

The District Court thought the Board to be impermissibly biased for two reasons. First, the Board had filed a complaint in state court alleging that appellees had aided and abetted Lee Optical Co. in the unlawful practice of optometry and also that they had engaged in other forms of "unprofessional conduct" which, if proved, would justify revocation of their licenses. These charges were substantially similar to those pending against appellees before the Board and concerning which the Board had noticed hearings following its successful prosecution of Lee Optical in the state trial court.

Secondly, the District Court determined that the aim of the Board was to revoke the licenses of all optometrists in the State who were employed by business corporations such as Lee Optical, and that these optometrists accounted for nearly half of all the optometrists practicing in Alabama. Because the Board of Optometry was composed solely of optometrists in private practice for their own account, the District Court concluded that success in the Board's efforts would possibly redound to the personal benefit of members of the Board, sufficiently so that in the opinion of the District Court the Board was constitutionally disqualified from hearing the charges filed against the appellees.

The District Court apparently considered either source of possible bias—prejudgment of the facts or personal interest—sufficient to disqualify the members of the Board. Arguably, the District Court was right on both scores, but we need reach, and we affirm, only the latter ground of possible personal interest.

It is sufficiently clear from our cases that those with substantial pecuniary interest in legal proceedings should not adjudicate these disputes. *Tumey v. Ohio*, 273 U.S. 510 (1927). And *Ward v. Village of Monroeville*, 409 U.S. 57 (1972), indicates that the financial stake need not be as direct or positive as it appeared to be in *Tumey*. It has also come to be the prevailing view that "(m)ost of the law concerning disqualification because of interest applies with equal force to . . . administrative adjudicators." Kenneth Culp Davis, Administrative Law Text § 12.04, p. 250 (1972), and cases cited. The District Court proceeded on this basis and, applying the standards taken from our cases, concluded that the pecuniary interest of the members of the Board of Optometry had sufficient substance to disqualify them, given the context in which this case arose. As remote as we are from the local realities underlying this case and it being very likely that the District Court has a firmer grasp of the facts and of their significance to the issues presented, we have no good reason on this record to overturn its conclusion and we affirm it.

[In Section IV of its opinion, the Court rejected the argument that the district court abused its discretion by not staying its proceedings under until unsettled state law questions could be presented to the state courts, pursuant to *Railroad Comm'n v. Pullman Co.*, 312 U.S. 496 (1941) and related precedents.]

[The concurring opinions of Chief Justice Burger and Justice Marshall are omitted.]

QUESTION SET 7.10

Review & Synthesis

1. Is it not the case that the rules against corporate optometry adopted in Alabama applied equally to all optometrists in the state? If that is the case, how could the Court conclude that enforcement of those rules evidenced bias on the part of the State Board of Optometry?

2. Assume that the Board's proceedings had no precedential value. In other words, it would have to enforce the state proscription against corporate optometry on a case-by-case basis, and the result in one case would have no bearing on the results in others. Do you think this should have any impact on a judicial determination of whether the Board's members were biased?

3. Are concerns over biased decision-makers strengthened, weakened, or unaffected by the availability of an appeals process? In other words, could one persuasively argue that bias at the initial stages of an adjudicative process does not trigger due process concerns as long as the *system* of adjudication ultimately provides unbiased decision-making?

4. Do you get the sense that the Supreme Court is skeptical about the legality of commercial self-regulation? In addition to *Gibson* (a case of occupational self-regulation), we have seen two other cases (*Schechter Poultry* and *Carter Coal*) where the Court had harsh words for federal statutes empowering industrial self-regulation. In your opinion, is there an inherent problem with giving industry groups the authority to create industry-wide rules that govern the conduct of their competitors? Even if such rules point toward a conflict of interest, would their *implementation* (in enforcement actions or adjudications) necessarily result in bias that violates procedural due process?

Application & Analysis

1. State recently passed legislation containing aggressive measures against public drunkenness within its borders. As part of this legislation, judges would be compensated with additional money beyond their normal pay whenever they convicted and fined someone for violating it. Specifically, judges would receive an additional $150 for every successful conviction that resulted in a fine. Is this compensation scheme constitutionally permissible under the Fourteenth Amendment Due Process Clause?

2. A state statute authorizes mayors to sit as judges in cases of ordinance violations and certain traffic offenses. Any fines or penalties assessed in such proceedings are deposited in the town's accounts. In one town, fees generated by its "mayor's court" total over $50,000 each year and account for almost half of the town's annual revenue. A driver who was caught speeding while passing through the town was convicted in mayor's court and fined $500. She would like to appeal the decision in state court. She has contacted a local law firm at which you are clerking

during the academic year. The attorney considering the case has asked you to assess whether the driver's procedural due process rights under the Fourteenth Amendment have been violated. Write a brief memo analyzing this potential claim.

3. The Natural Gas Act requires companies to obtain a "certificate of public convenience and necessity" before constructing facilities to transport natural gas in interstate commerce. 15 U.S.C. § 717f(c)(1)(A). The Federal Energy Regulatory Commission ("FERC") issues certificates to qualified applicants if the projects they propose are "required by the present or future public convenience and necessity," subject to any reasonable terms and conditions imposed by the Commission. § 717f(e). Although FERC receives annual appropriations fixed by Congress, the Omnibus Budget Reconciliation Act of 1986 requires FERC to assess and collect fees and annual charges from the various industries that it regulates, including the natural-gas industry. § 7178(a)(1). The amounts FERC collects are credited to the general fund of the Treasury. § 7178(f).

A party aggrieved by an order issued by the Commission in a proceeding under the Natural Gas Act may seek rehearing. Unless the Commission acts upon the application for rehearing within 30 days after it is filed, that application is deemed denied. The aggrieved party then may seek review in the court of appeals within 60 days.

Last year, Natural Gas Distributors, LLC ("NGD") applied for a certificate to build a 100-mile natural-gas pipeline through Pennsylvania and West Virginia. Protectors of Water and Wildlife ("POWW"), a Pennsylvania-based environmental group, intervened to oppose the project. Recently, while FERC was still reviewing NGD's proposal, POWW filed a complaint in federal district court seeking declaratory relief against the Commission and its members. The complaint alleges that FERC's funding structure creates structural bias, in violation of the Due Process Clause of the Fifth Amendment, by incentivizing the Commission to approve new pipelines in order to secure additional sources for its future funding.

Write up a brief analysis of POWW's due process claim.

PART IV

Control of Administrative Decision-Making

As we have seen, agencies are endowed with massive amounts of policymaking and adjudicative power over a seemingly unlimited variety of economic and social activities. Part III studied the work of administrative bodies and, most particularly, the procedures administrative officials must follow when performing that work. Even when agencies follow these procedures perfectly, however, they still have broad discretion in how they perform their policymaking and adjudicative functions. Who ensures that agencies operate within their prescribed jurisdictions, follow mandated procedures, undertake their functions with the requisite level of analytical rigor, and ensure that they responsibly exercise their discretion? What laws empower these supervisors to do so? In short, how is administrative decision-making to be controlled? These are the questions to which Part IV turns. To answer them, the materials that follow are organized around four sources of bureaucratic control.

The first is political, as exercised by Congress and the President. As discussed in Part II, Congress and the President exercise some political control when they create agencies and assign them governmental powers. An agency's ability to regulate private conduct, whether social or economic, is necessarily cabined by the organizational structure, jurisdiction, and substantive authority set out in its enabling act and other statutes (the FTC Act, the Administrative Procedure Act, etc.). Other forms of political control—those studied in this part—are exercised *after* the point of creation. They operate more on agency decision-making and decision-makers than they do on agency design. The various forms of political control studied here—the legislative veto, the line-item veto, appointment and removal of officials—ask a common question: how does the Constitution distribute control over the administrative state between Congress and the President? Separation-of-powers concepts figure heavily in how the Supreme Court answers this question. It may therefore be beneficial to review the separation-of-powers materials provided in Part I.

Judicial review is the second source of control discussed in this part, and the one to which most of the pages that follow are dedicated. To some extent, we have been studying this issue throughout the casebook; each case we have read involves judicial review in some form or fashion. In the materials presented below, we focus specifically on its availability and the standards governing how it is conducted.

Next, this part turns to how the public holds bureaucratic decision-makers accountable. Understanding that legislative, executive, and judicial oversight would be insufficient to control or to facilitate trust in bureaucratic decision-making, Congress has provided numerous ways for interested members of the public to participate in and gather information about those decisions. One such mechanism discussed in Part III is the notice-and-comment process set out in 5 U.S.C. § 553. Here, we will focus on two other public accountability tools: the Freedom of Information Act (5 U.S.C. § 552) and the Government in the Sunshine Act (5 U.S.C. § 552b).

Finally, this part touches on intra-bureaucracy controls, those managerial measures imposed not from external sources but from within the administrative state itself. The focal point here is the operation of the civil service system, which provides certain employment-related protections for federal employees.

CHAPTER 8

The President and Congress

"[T]he Constitution provides few details about the departments and agencies of government." . . . JENNIFER L. SELIN & DAVID E. LEWIS, ADMINISTRATIVE CONFERENCE OF THE UNITED STATES, SOURCEBOOK OF UNITED STATES EXECUTIVE AGENCIES 87 (2d ed. 2018). Among the questions it does not explicitly address is who within the federal government is responsible for its oversight. Certainly, one can reasonably infer from the basic structure of the Executive Branch set out in Article II that the President plays the central managerial role. The President is vested with the federal government's executive power (Art. II, § 1), and charged with ensuring faithful execution of federal laws (Art. II, § 3). In addition to being commander in chief of the armed forces, the President may demand information from "the principal Officer in each of the executive Departments, upon any Subject relating to the Duties of their respective Offices" (Art. II, § 2, cl. 1). Moreover, he or she has the authority to nominate principal "Officers of the United States" and, at Congress' behest, the power to appoint "inferior Officers" as well (Art. II, § 2, cl. 2). Taken together, these provisions imply that the federal government is structured hierarchically; the President sits at the top of the Executive Branch, there are departments located within it, and the leaders of those departments are hired by and must provide reports on their activities to the President. Beyond this, the Constitution is largely silent on a number of definitional, organizational, and managerial issues. For instance, it does not define the term "department," does not require that Executive Branch subunits be limited to that organizational form (however defined), places no express limits on the number or powers of such subunits, and does not expressly insist that they adopt a particular leadership structure or follow particular decision-making procedures. Additionally, and while the Article II provisions enumerated above clearly secure a central role in Executive Branch management for the President, none of them explicitly *excludes* Congress from retaining some supervisory authority for itself.

In light of these and other ambiguities, Congress has sometimes treated the hierarchy apparent in Article II as a default rather than as a requirement. While strict adherence to the "President-oversees-department" model would certainly satisfy the Constitution, Congress occasionally has experimented with other models that it believed the Constitution would countenance. This structural adventurism has also brought Congress and the President into conflict, as they have tussled over control of the federal bureaucracy.

The cases in this chapter address three distinct ways that Congress has tried to involve itself in the management of administrative officials or decision-making. The first set of cases relates to the procedures it must follow when invalidating agency actions. It asks whether Congress may deviate, or empower the President to deviate, from constitutionally specified procedures when doing so facilitates more effective supervision of administrative action. The key constitutional provisions here are the Bicameralism and Presentment Clauses (Art. I, § 7, cls. 2 and 3). The second set of cases explores Congress' and the President's respective constitutional roles in appointing agency leadership. These cases apply the Appointments Clause. The third set of cases focuses on Congress' authority to participate in or to limit the President's decisions to *remove* Executive Branch officials. No constitutional provision establishes the parameters for removal, but the Supreme Court has derived standards from the Appointments Clause.

The chapter ends with consideration of whether generalized separation-of-powers principles—those derived from but not explicitly stated in the Constitution—limit Congress' involvement in administrative management or law implementation.

A. THE LEGISLATIVE VETO

As discussed in Chapter 2, delegation of policymaking authority to federal agencies provides a measure of regulatory flexibility and nimbleness that Congress, as an institution, cannot match. In recognition of this reality, Congress has steadily increased both the number and the breadth of such delegations over the past several decades. Whatever the benefits of this gradual shift of federal policymaking discretion from Congress to agencies, many have expressed deep-seated concerns about its effects on democratic self-governance. Agency officials almost certainly pursue their duties with good-faith and public spiritedness. Unlike Members of Congress, however, they do not stand for election and thus are not directly accountable to the people whom they serve. Focused as they are on the individual missions of their respective agencies, they may also have fewer personal or institutional incentives to consider policy priorities that compete with those of their agencies. The balancing of such priorities is a hallmark of the political decision-making, but not always a feature of its administrative counterpart.

As discussed in Part III, Congress and the President have built into the administrative policymaking process a number of steps to mitigate these problems of public accountability and prioritization. When these measures prove insufficient to halt the administrative decisions of which it disapproves, Congress always retains the authority to override agencies by passing new legislation. The irony, of course, is that the ponderousness and high failure rate of the normal legislative process is what led Congress to delegate so much policymaking power to agencies in the first place. It is thus easy to understand why the normal legislative process often proves to be a suboptimal check on bureaucratic power.

These and other considerations led Congress to develop a more effective device for constraining agency conduct: the legislative veto. The details of its operation varied some from statute to statute. Some veto provisions provided that both chambers of Congress had to pass concurrent resolutions approving an agency action before it could take effect. The concurrent resolution process could be completed more quickly than the normal legislative process; it did not require the President's approval, and thus avoided the risk of the President's veto. Another device, the unicameral (or "one-house") veto, allowed either the House or the Senate, acting entirely on its own, to block disfavored administrative measures. It, too, bypassed involvement by the President. Congress adopted the veto beginning in the 1930s, often in connection with Presidential reorganization plans and tariff provisions.

One might wonder why Presidents would not veto legislation granting Congress this kind of power. After all, these devices were specifically calculated to cabin Executive Branch power and to limit the President's involvement in agency policymaking. The answer, it appears, was straightforward: Congress was willing to delegate expanded powers to agencies as long as the President accepted Congress' expanded control over the use of those delegations. Although frequently expressing skepticism about the device's constitutionality, and occasionally vetoing the legislation containing it, Presidents by and large accepted the bargain. *See* RICHARD J. ELLIS, JUDGING EXECUTIVE POWER: SIXTEEN SUPREME COURT CASES THAT HAVE SHAPED THE AMERICAN PRESIDENCY 59-60 (2009); Louis Fisher, *The Legislative Veto: Invalidated, It Survives*, 56 L. & CONTEMP. PROBS. 273 (1993).

One area in which Congress insisted on legislative veto power was administration of the nation's immigration laws. As early as 1940, Congress gave the Attorney General discretionary authority to suspend deportation orders against deportable noncitizens. *See* Alien Registration Act of June 28, 1940, 54 Stat. 672 (1940). Prior to that time, Congress provided such relief itself through the cumbersome, inconsistent, and ultimately ineffective private bills process. Congress would pass legislation for individual noncitizens allowing them to remain in the country and then present that legislation to the President for signature or veto. It was hoped that transferring this responsibility to the Attorney General would make relief from the country's draconian immigration laws both more humane and more consistent. However, Congress attached a unicameral veto provision to this grant of discretion to facilitate oversight of its use. Subsequent immigration statutes, including the Immigration and Nationality Act of 1952 and its amendments, retained these relief and veto provisions.

The constitutionality of the legislative veto was tested in the seminal case below, *INS v. Chadha*. In essence, the claim in the case was that the unicameral veto violated the Constitution's Bicameralism and Presentment Clauses, which establish the procedures by which Congress can pass legislation. *Chadha* is a complex decision, with many moving parts and competing opinions. As you read it, be sure to track how the Justices answer the following question: Is suspension of a deportation order a "legislative" act? The answer largely determines the outcome of the case.

Immigration and Naturalization Service v. Chadha
462 U.S. 919 (1983)

Chief Justice BURGER delivered the opinion of the Court. . . .

Chadha is an East Indian who was born in Kenya and holds a British passport. He was lawfully admitted to the United States in 1966 on a nonimmigrant student visa. His visa expired on June 30, 1972. On October 11, 1973, the District Director of the Immigration and Naturalization Service ordered Chadha to show cause why he should not be deported for having "remained in the United States for a longer time than permitted." App. 6. Pursuant to § 242(b) of the Immigration and Nationality Act (Act), 8 U.S.C. § 1252(b), a deportation hearing was held before an immigration judge on January 11, 1974. Chadha conceded that he was deportable for overstaying his visa and the hearing was adjourned to enable him to file an application for suspension of deportation under § 244(a)(1) of the Act, 8 U.S.C. § 1254(a)(1). Section 244(a)(1) provides:

> (a) As hereinafter prescribed in this section, the Attorney General may, in his discretion, suspend deportation and adjust the status to that of an alien lawfully admitted for permanent residence, in the case of an alien who applies to the Attorney General for suspension of deportation and—
>
> (1) is deportable under any law of the United States except the provisions specified in paragraph (2) of this subsection; has been physically present in the United States for a continuous period of not less than seven years immediately preceding the date of such application, and proves that during

all of such period he was and is a person of good moral character; and is a person whose deportation would, in the opinion of the Attorney General, result in extreme hardship to the alien or to his spouse, parent, or child, who is a citizen of the United States or an alien lawfully admitted for permanent residence.[1]

After Chadha submitted his application for suspension of deportation, the deportation hearing was resumed on February 7, 1974. On the basis of evidence adduced at the hearing, affidavits submitted with the application, and the results of a character investigation conducted by the INS, the immigration judge, on June 25, 1974, ordered that Chadha's deportation be suspended. The immigration judge found that Chadha met the requirements of § 244(a)(1): he had resided continuously in the United States for over seven years, was of good moral character, and would suffer "extreme hardship" if deported.

Pursuant to § 244(c)(1) of the Act, 8 U.S.C. § 1254(c)(1), the immigration judge suspended Chadha's deportation and a report of the suspension was transmitted to Congress. Section 244(c)(1) provides:

> Upon application by any alien who is found by the Attorney General to meet the requirements of subsection (a) of this section the Attorney General may in his discretion suspend deportation of such alien. If the deportation of any alien is suspended under the provisions of this subsection, a complete and detailed statement of the facts and pertinent provisions of law in the case shall be reported to the Congress with the reasons for such suspension. Such reports shall be submitted on the first day of each calendar month in which Congress is in session.

Once the Attorney General's recommendation for suspension of Chadha's deportation was conveyed to Congress, Congress had the power under § 244(c)(2) of the Act, 8 U.S.C. § 1254(c)(2), to veto the Attorney General's determination that Chadha should not be deported. Section 244(c)(2) provides:

> (2) In the case of an alien specified in paragraph (1) of subsection (a) of this subsection—
>
> if during the session of the Congress at which a case is reported, or prior to the close of the session of the Congress next following the session at which a case is reported, either the Senate or the House of Representatives passes a resolution stating in substance that it does not favor the suspension of such deportation, the Attorney General shall thereupon deport such

---

[1] Congress delegated the major responsibilities for enforcement of the Immigration and Nationality Act to the Attorney General. 8 U.S.C. § 1103(a). The Attorney General discharges his responsibilities through the Immigration and Naturalization Service, a division of the Department of Justice. *Ibid.* [These responsibilities are now undertaken by the Department of Homeland Security.]

alien or authorize the alien's voluntary departure at his own expense under the order of deportation in the manner provided by law. If, within the time above specified, neither the Senate nor the House of Representatives shall pass such a resolution, the Attorney General shall cancel deportation proceedings.

The June 25, 1974 order of the immigration judge suspending Chadha's deportation remained outstanding as a valid order for a year and a half. For reasons not disclosed by the record, Congress did not exercise the veto authority reserved to it under § 244(c)(2) until the first session of the 94th Congress. This was the final session in which Congress, pursuant to § 244(c)(2), could act to veto the Attorney General's determination that Chadha should not be deported. The session ended on December 19, 1975. 121 Cong. Rec. 42014, 42277 (1975). Absent Congressional action, Chadha's deportation proceedings would have been cancelled after this date and his status adjusted to that of a permanent resident alien. *See* 8 U.S.C. § 1254(d).

On December 12, 1975, Representative Eilberg, Chairman of the Judiciary Subcommittee on Immigration, Citizenship, and International Law, introduced a resolution opposing "the granting of permanent residence in the United States to [six] aliens", including Chadha. H.R. Res. 926, 94th Cong., 1st Sess.; 121 Cong. Rec. 40247 (1975). The resolution was referred to the House Committee on the Judiciary. On December 16, 1975, the resolution was discharged from further consideration by the House Committee on the Judiciary and submitted to the House of Representatives for a vote. 121 Cong. Rec. 40800. The resolution had not been printed and was not made available to other Members of the House prior to or at the time it was voted on. *Ibid.* So far as the record before us shows, the House consideration of the resolution was based on Representative Eilberg's statement from the floor that

> [i]t was the feeling of the committee, after reviewing 340 cases, that the aliens contained in the resolution [Chadha and five others] did not meet these statutory requirements, particularly as it relates to hardship; and it is the opinion of the committee that their deportation should not be suspended. *Ibid.*

The resolution was passed without debate or recorded vote.[3] Since the House action was pursuant to § 244(c)(2), the resolution was not treated as

[3] It is not at all clear whether the House generally, or Subcommittee Chairman Eilberg in particular, correctly understood the relationship between H.R. Res. 926 and the Attorney General's decision to suspend Chadha's deportation. Exactly one year previous to the House veto of the Attorney General's decision in this case, Representative Eilberg introduced a similar resolution disapproving the Attorney General's suspension of deportation in the case of six other aliens. H.R. Res. 1518, 93d Cong., 2d Sess. The following colloquy occurred on the floor of the House:

> "Mr. WYLIE. Mr. Speaker, further reserving the right to object, is this procedure to expedite the ongoing operations of the Department of Justice, as far as these people are

an Article I legislative act; it was not submitted to the Senate or presented to the President for his action.

After the House veto of the Attorney General's decision to allow Chadha to remain in the United States, the immigration judge reopened the deportation proceedings to implement the House order deporting Chadha. Chadha moved to terminate the proceedings on the ground that § 244(c)(2) is unconstitutional. The immigration judge held that he had no authority to rule on the constitutional validity of § 244(c)(2). On November 8, 1976, Chadha was ordered deported pursuant to the House action.

Chadha appealed the deportation order to the Board of Immigration Appeals again contending that § 244(c)(2) is unconstitutional. The Board held that it had "no power to declare unconstitutional an act of Congress" and Chadha's appeal was dismissed. App. 55-56.

Pursuant to § 106(a) of the Act, 8 U.S.C. § 1105a(a), Chadha filed a petition for review of the deportation order in the United States Court of Appeals for the Ninth Circuit. The Immigration and Naturalization Service agreed with Chadha's position before the Court of Appeals and joined him in arguing that § 244(c)(2) is unconstitutional. In light of the importance of the question, the Court of Appeals invited both the Senate and the House of Representatives to file briefs *amici curiae*.

After full briefing and oral argument, the Court of Appeals held that the House was without constitutional authority to order Chadha's deportation; accordingly it directed the Attorney General "to cease and desist from

---

concerned. Is it in any way contrary to whatever action the Attorney General has taken on the question of deportation; does the gentleman know?

"Mr. EILBERG. Mr. Speaker, the answer is no to the gentleman's final question. These aliens have been found to be deportable and the Special Inquiry Officer's decision denying suspension of deportation has been reversed by the Board of Immigration Appeals. We are complying with the law since all of these decisions have been referred to us for approval or disapproval, and there are hundreds of cases in this category. In these six cases however, we believe it would be grossly improper to allow these people to acquire the status of permanent resident aliens.

"Mr. WYLIE. In other words, the gentleman has been working with the Attorney General's office?

"Mr. EILBERG. Yes.

"Mr. WYLIE. This bill then is in fact a confirmation of what the Attorney General intends to do?

"Mr. EILBERG. The gentleman is correct insofar as it relates to the determination of deportability which has been made by the Department of Justice in these cases.

"Mr. WYLIE. Mr. Speaker, I withdraw my reservation of objection." 120 Cong. Rec. 41412 (1974).

Clearly, this was an obfuscation of the effect of a veto under § 244(c)(2). Such a veto in no way constitutes "a confirmation of what the Attorney General intends to do." To the contrary, such a resolution was meant to overrule and set aside, or "veto," the Attorney General's determination that, in a particular case, cancellation of deportation would be appropriate under the standards set forth in § 244(a)(1).

taking any steps to deport this alien based upon the resolution enacted by the House of Representatives." *Chadha v. INS,* 634 F.2d 408, 436 (9th Cir. 1980). The essence of its holding was that § 244(c)(2) violates the constitutional doctrine of separation of powers.

We granted certiorari . . . and we now affirm.

[In Section II of its opinion, the Court rejected various challenges to its jurisdiction and the justiciability of Chadha's claims.]

III

A

We turn now to the question whether action of one House of Congress under § 244(c)(2) violates strictures of the Constitution. We begin, of course, with the presumption that the challenged statute is valid. Its wisdom is not the concern of the courts; if a challenged action does not violate the Constitution, it must be sustained. . . .

By the same token, the fact that a given law or procedure is efficient, convenient, and useful in facilitating functions of government, standing alone, will not save it if it is contrary to the Constitution. Convenience and efficiency are not the primary objectives — or the hallmarks — of democratic government and our inquiry is sharpened rather than blunted by the fact that Congressional veto provisions are appearing with increasing frequency in statutes which delegate authority to executive and independent agencies. . . .

Justice White undertakes to make a case for the proposition that the one-House veto is a useful "political invention," and we need not challenge that assertion. We can even concede this utilitarian argument although the long range political wisdom of this "invention" is arguable. . . . But policy arguments supporting even useful "political inventions" are subject to the demands of the Constitution which defines powers and, with respect to this subject, sets out just how those powers are to be exercised.

Explicit and unambiguous provisions of the Constitution prescribe and define the respective functions of the Congress and of the Executive in the legislative process. Since the precise terms of those familiar provisions are critical to the resolution of this case, we set them out verbatim. Art. I provides:

> All legislative Powers herein granted shall be vested in a Congress of the United States, which shall consist of a Senate *and* a House of Representatives. Art. I, § 1. (Emphasis added).

> Every Bill which shall have passed the House of Representatives *and* the Senate, *shall,* before it becomes a Law, be presented to the President of the United States; . . . Art. I, § 7, cl. 2. (Emphasis added).

> *Every* Order, Resolution, or Vote to which the Concurrence of the Senate and House of Representatives may be necessary (except on a question of

Adjournment) *shall be* presented to the President of the United States; and before the Same shall take Effect, *shall be* approved by him, or being disapproved by him, *shall be* repassed by two thirds of the Senate and House of Representatives, according to the Rules and Limitations prescribed in the Case of a Bill. Art. I, § 7, cl. 3. (Emphasis added).

These provisions of Art. I are integral parts of the constitutional design for the separation of powers. We have recently noted that "[t]he principle of separation of powers was not simply an abstract generalization in the minds of the Framers: it was woven into the documents that they drafted in Philadelphia in the summer of 1787." *Buckley v. Valeo*, 424 U.S., at 124. Just as we relied on the textual provision of Art. II, § 2, cl. 2, to vindicate the principle of separation of powers in *Buckley*, we find that the purposes underlying the Presentment Clauses, Art. I, § 7, cls. 2, 3, and the bicameral requirement of Art. I, § 1 and § 7, cl. 2, guide our resolution of the important question presented in this case. The very structure of the articles delegating and separating powers under Arts. I, II, and III exemplify the concept of separation of powers and we now turn to Art. I.

B

The Presentment Clauses

The records of the Constitutional Convention reveal that the requirement that all legislation be presented to the President before becoming law was uniformly accepted by the Framers.[14] Presentment to the President and the Presidential veto were considered so imperative that the draftsmen took special pains to assure that these requirements could not be circumvented. During the final debate on Art. I, § 7, cl. 2, James Madison expressed concern that it might easily be evaded by the simple expedient of calling a proposed law a "resolution" or "vote" rather than a "bill." 2 M. Farrand, The Records of the Federal Convention of 1787 301-302. As a consequence, Art. I, § 7, cl. 3 . . . was added. *Id.* at 304-305.

The decision to provide the President with a limited and qualified power to nullify proposed legislation by veto was based on the profound conviction of the Framers that the powers conferred on Congress were the powers to

---

[14] The widespread approval of the delegates was commented on by Joseph Story:

> In the convention there does not seem to have been much diversity of opinion on the subject of the propriety of giving to the president a negative on the laws. The principal points of discussion seem to have been, whether the negative should be absolute, or qualified; and if the latter, by what number of each house the bill should subsequently be passed, in order to become a law; and whether the negative should in either case be exclusively vested in the president alone, or in him jointly with some other department of government. 1 Joseph Story, Commentaries on the Constitution of the United States 611 (1858). *See* 1 Max Farrand, The Records of the Federal Convention of 1787 21, 97-104, 138-140; *id.*, at 73-80, 181, 298, 301-305.

be most carefully circumscribed. It is beyond doubt that lawmaking was a power to be shared by both Houses and the President. . . .

The President's role in the lawmaking process also reflects the Framers' careful efforts to check whatever propensity a particular Congress might have to enact oppressive, improvident, or ill-considered measures. The President's veto role in the legislative process was described later during public debate on ratification:

> It establishes a salutary check upon the legislative body, calculated to guard the community against the effects of faction, precipitancy, or of any impulse unfriendly to the public good which may happen to influence a majority of that body. . . . The primary inducement to conferring the power in question upon the Executive is to enable him to defend himself; the secondary one is to increase the chances in favor of the community against the passing of bad laws through haste, inadvertence, or design. The Federalist No. 73, *supra*, at 458 (A. Hamilton).

See also The Pocket Veto Case, 279 U.S. 655 (1929); *Myers v. United States*, 272 U.S. 52, 123 (1926). The Court also has observed that the Presentment Clauses serve the important purpose of assuring that a "national" perspective is grafted on the legislative process:

> The President is a representative of the people just as the members of the Senate and of the House are, and it may be, at some times, on some subjects, that the President elected by all the people is rather more representative of them all than are the members of either body of the Legislature whose constituencies are local and not countrywide. . . .

Myers, 272 U.S., at 123.

C

Bicameralism

The bicameral requirement of Art. I, §§ 1, 7 was of scarcely less concern to the Framers than was the Presidential veto and indeed the two concepts are interdependent. By providing that no law could take effect without the concurrence of the prescribed majority of the Members of both Houses, the Framers reemphasized their belief, already remarked upon in connection with the Presentment Clauses, that legislation should not be enacted unless it has been carefully and fully considered by the Nation's elected officials. In the Constitutional Convention debates on the need for a bicameral legislature, James Wilson, later to become a Justice of this Court, commented:

> Despotism comes on mankind in different shapes. Sometimes in an Executive, sometimes in a military, one. Is there danger of a Legislative despotism? Theory & practice both proclaim it. If the Legislative authority

be not restrained, there can be neither liberty nor stability; and it can only be restrained by dividing it within itself, into distinct and independent branches. In a single house there is no check, but the inadequate one, of the virtue & good sense of those who compose it.

1 Farrand at 254.

[This observation is] consistent with what many of the Framers expressed, none more cogently than Madison in pointing up the need to divide and disperse power in order to protect liberty:

> In republican government, the legislative authority necessarily predominates. The remedy for this inconveniency is to divide the legislature into different branches; and to render them, by different modes of election and different principles of action, as little connected with each other as the nature of their common functions and their common dependence on the society will admit.

The Federalist No. 51, at 324. *See also* The Federalist No. 62.

However familiar, it is useful to recall that apart from their fear that special interests could be favored at the expense of public needs, the Framers were also concerned, although not of one mind, over the apprehensions of the smaller states. Those states feared a commonality of interest among the larger states would work to their disadvantage; representatives of the larger states, on the other hand, were skeptical of a legislature that could pass laws favoring a minority of the people. See 1 Farrand, *supra,* 176-177, 484-491. It need hardly be repeated here that the Great Compromise, under which one House was viewed as representing the people and the other the states, allayed the fears of both the large and small states.

We see therefore that the Framers were acutely conscious that the bicameral requirement and the Presentment Clauses would serve essential constitutional functions. The President's participation in the legislative process was to protect the Executive Branch from Congress and to protect the whole people from improvident laws. The division of the Congress into two distinctive bodies assures that the legislative power would be exercised only after opportunity for full study and debate in separate settings. The President's unilateral veto power, in turn, was limited by the power of two thirds of both Houses of Congress to overrule a veto thereby precluding final arbitrary action of one person. It emerges clearly that the prescription for legislative action in Art. I, §§ 1, 7 represents the Framers' decision that the legislative power of the Federal government be exercised in accord with a single, finely wrought and exhaustively considered, procedure.

IV

The Constitution sought to divide the delegated powers of the new federal government into three defined categories, legislative, executive and judicial, to assure, as nearly as possible, that each Branch of government would confine itself to its assigned responsibility. The hydraulic pressure inherent within each of the separate Branches to exceed the outer limits of its power, even to accomplish desirable objectives, must be resisted.

Although not "hermetically" sealed from one another, *Buckley v. Valeo*, 424 U.S. at 121, the powers delegated to the three Branches are functionally identifiable. When any Branch acts, it is presumptively exercising the power the Constitution has delegated to it. *See Hampton & Co. v. United States*, 276 U.S. 394, 406 (1928). When the Executive acts, it presumptively acts in an executive or administrative capacity as defined in Art. II. And when, as here, one House of Congress purports to act, it is presumptively acting within its assigned sphere.

Beginning with this presumption, we must nevertheless establish that the challenged action under § 244(c)(2) is of the kind to which the procedural requirements of Art. I, § 7 apply. Not every action taken by either House is subject to the bicameralism and presentment requirements of Art. I. Whether actions taken by either House are, in law and fact, an exercise of legislative power depends not on their form but upon "whether they contain matter which is properly to be regarded as legislative in its character and effect." S. Rep. No. 1335, 54th Cong., 2d Sess., 8 (1897).

Examination of the action taken here by one House pursuant to § 244(c)(2) reveals that it was essentially legislative in purpose and effect. In purporting to exercise power defined in Art. I, § 8, cl. 4 to "establish an uniform Rule of Naturalization," the House took action that had the purpose and effect of altering the legal rights, duties and relations of persons, including the Attorney General, Executive Branch officials and Chadha, all outside the legislative branch. Section 244(c)(2) purports to authorize one House of Congress to require the Attorney General to deport an individual alien whose deportation otherwise would be cancelled under § 244. The one-House veto operated in this case to overrule the Attorney General and mandate Chadha's deportation; absent the House action, Chadha would remain in the United States. Congress has acted and its action has altered Chadha's status.

The legislative character of the one-House veto in this case is confirmed by the character of the Congressional action it supplants. Neither the House of Representatives nor the Senate contends that, absent the veto provision in § 244(c)(2), either of them, or both of them acting together, could effectively require the Attorney General to deport an alien once the Attorney General, in the exercise of legislatively delegated authority,[16] had determined the alien

---

[16] Congress protests that affirming the Court of Appeals in this case will sanction "lawmaking by the Attorney General. . . . Why is the Attorney General exempt from submitting his proposed changes in the law to the full bicameral process?" Brief of the United States House of Representatives 40. To be sure, some administrative agency action — rule making, for example — may resemble "lawmaking. . . ." This Court has referred to agency activity as being "quasi-legislative" in character. *Humphrey's Executor v. United States*, 295 U.S. 602 (1935). Clearly, however, "[i]n the framework

should remain in the United States. Without the challenged provision in § 244(c)(2), this could have been achieved, if at all, only by legislation requiring deportation. Similarly, a veto by one House of Congress under § 244(c)(2) cannot be justified as an attempt at amending the standards set out in § 244(a)(1), or as a repeal of § 244 as applied to Chadha. Amendment and repeal of statutes, no less than enactment, must conform with Art. I.

The nature of the decision implemented by the one-House veto in this case further manifests its legislative character. After long experience with the clumsy, time consuming private bill procedure, Congress made a deliberate choice to delegate to the Executive Branch, and specifically to the Attorney General, the authority to allow deportable aliens to remain in this country in certain specified circumstances. It is not disputed that this choice to delegate authority is precisely the kind of decision that can be implemented only in accordance with the procedures set out in Art. I. Disagreement with the Attorney General's decision on Chadha's deportation—that is, Congress' decision to deport Chadha—no less than Congress' original choice to delegate to the Attorney General the authority to make that decision, involves determinations of policy that Congress can implement in only one way; bicameral passage followed by presentment to the President. Congress must abide by its delegation of authority until that delegation is legislatively altered or revoked.[19]

---

of our Constitution, the President's power to see that the laws are faithfully executed refutes the idea that he is to be a lawmaker." *Youngstown Sheet & Tube Co. v. Sawyer* (The Steel Seizure Case), 343 U.S. 579, 587 (1952). *See Buckley v. Valeo*, 424 U.S. 1, 123 (1976). When the Attorney General performs his duties pursuant to § 244, he does not exercise "legislative" power. The bicameral process is not necessary as a check on the Executive's administration of the laws because his administrative activity cannot reach beyond the limits of the statute that created it—a statute duly enacted pursuant to Art. I, §§ 1, 7. The constitutionality of the Attorney General's execution of the authority delegated to him by § 244 involves only a question of delegation doctrine. The courts, when a case or controversy arises, can always "ascertain whether the will of Congress has been obeyed," *Yakus v. United States*, 321 U.S. 414, 425 (1944), and can enforce adherence to statutory standards. It is clear, therefore, that the Attorney General acts in his presumptively Art. II capacity when he administers the Immigration and Nationality Act. Executive action under legislatively delegated authority that might resemble "legislative" action in some respects is not subject to the approval of both Houses of Congress and the President for the reason that the Constitution does not so require. That kind of Executive action is always subject to check by the terms of the legislation that authorized it; and if that authority is exceeded it is open to judicial review as well as the power of Congress to modify or revoke the authority entirely. A one-House veto is clearly legislative in both character and effect and is not so checked; the need for the check provided by Art. I, §§ 1, 7 is therefore clear. Congress' authority to delegate portions of its power to administrative agencies provides no support for the argument that Congress can constitutionally control administration of the laws by way of a Congressional veto.

[19] This does not mean that Congress is required to capitulate to "the accretion of policy control by forces outside its chambers." Jacob Javits and Gary J. Klein, *Congressional Oversight and the Legislative Veto: A Constitutional Analysis*, 52 N.Y.U. L. REV. 455, 462 (1977). The Constitution provides Congress with abundant means to oversee and control its administrative creatures. Beyond the obvious fact that Congress ultimately controls administrative agencies in the legislation that creates them, other means of control, such as durational limits on authorizations and

Finally, we see that when the Framers intended to authorize either House of Congress to act alone and outside of its prescribed bicameral legislative role, they narrowly and precisely defined the procedure for such action. There are but four provisions in the Constitution, explicit and unambiguous, by which one House may act alone with the unreviewable force of law, not subject to the President's veto:

> The House of Representatives alone was given the power to initiate impeachments. Art. I, § 2, cl. 6;

> The Senate alone was given the power to conduct trials following impeachment on charges initiated by the House and to convict following trial. Art. I, § 3, cl. 5;

> The Senate alone was given final unreviewable power to approve or to disapprove presidential appointments. Art. II, § 2, cl. 2;

> The Senate alone was given unreviewable power to ratify treaties negotiated by the President. Art. II, § 2, cl. 2.

Clearly, when the Draftsmen sought to confer special powers on one House, independent of the other House, or of the President, they did so in explicit, unambiguous terms. These carefully defined exceptions from presentment and bicameralism underscore the difference between the legislative functions of Congress and other unilateral but important and binding one-House acts provided for in the Constitution. These exceptions are narrow, explicit, and separately justified; none of them authorize the action challenged here. On the contrary, they provide further support for the conclusion that Congressional authority is not to be implied and for the conclusion that the veto provided for in § 244(c)(2) is not authorized by the constitutional design of the powers of the Legislative Branch.

Since it is clear that the action by the House under § 244(c)(2) was not within any of the express constitutional exceptions authorizing one House to act alone, and equally clear that it was an exercise of legislative power, that action was subject to the standards prescribed in Article I.[22] The

---

formal reporting requirements, lie well within Congress' constitutional power. *See id.,* at 460-461; Frederick M. Kaiser, *Congressional Action to Overturn Agency Rules: Alternatives to the "Legislative Veto",* 32 ADMIN. L. REV. 667 (1980).

[22] Justice Powell's position is that the one-House veto in this case is a judicial act and therefore unconstitutional as beyond the authority vested in Congress by the Constitution. We agree that there is a sense in which one-House action pursuant to § 244(c)(2) has a judicial cast, since it purports to "review" Executive action. In this case, for example, the sponsor of the resolution vetoing the suspension of Chadha's deportation argued that Chadha "did not meet [the] statutory requirements" for suspension of deportation. To be sure, it is normally up to the courts to decide whether an agency has complied with its statutory mandate. But the attempted analogy between judicial action and the one-House veto is less than perfect. Federal courts do not enjoy a roving mandate to correct alleged excesses of administrative agencies; we are limited by Art. III to hearing cases and

bicameral requirement, the Presentment Clauses, the President's veto, and Congress' power to override a veto were intended to erect enduring checks on each Branch and to protect the people from the improvident exercise of power by mandating certain prescribed steps. To preserve those checks, and maintain the separation of powers, the carefully defined limits on the power of each Branch must not be eroded. To accomplish what has been attempted by one House of Congress in this case requires action in conformity with the express procedures of the Constitution's prescription for legislative action: passage by a majority of both Houses and presentment to the President.

The veto authorized by § 244(c)(2) doubtless has been in many respects a convenient shortcut; the "sharing" with the Executive by Congress of its authority over aliens in this manner is, on its face, an appealing compromise. In purely practical terms, it is obviously easier for action to be taken by one House without submission to the President; but it is crystal clear from the records of the Convention, contemporaneous writings and debates, that the Framers ranked other values higher than efficiency. The records of the Convention and debates in the States preceding ratification underscore the common desire to define and limit the exercise of the newly created federal powers affecting the states and the people. There is unmistakable expression of a determination that legislation by the national Congress be a step-by-step, deliberate and deliberative process.

The choices we discern as having been made in the Constitutional Convention impose burdens on governmental processes that often seem clumsy, inefficient, even unworkable, but those hard choices were consciously made by men who had lived under a form of government that permitted arbitrary governmental acts to go unchecked. There is no support in the Constitution or decisions of this Court for the proposition that the cumbersomeness and delays often encountered in complying with explicit Constitutional standards may be avoided, either by the Congress or by the President. With all the obvious flaws of delay, untidiness, and potential for abuse, we have not yet found a better way to preserve freedom than by making the exercise of power subject to the carefully crafted restraints spelled out in the Constitution.

---

controversies and no justiciable case or controversy was presented by the Attorney General's decision to allow Chadha to remain in this country. We are aware of no decision, and Justice Powell has cited none, where a federal court has reviewed a decision of the Attorney General suspending deportation of an alien pursuant to the standards set out in § 244(a)(1). This is not surprising, given that no party to such action has either the motivation or the right to appeal from it. As Justice White correctly notes, "the courts have not been given the authority to review whether an alien should be given permanent status; review is limited to whether the Attorney General has properly applied the statutory standards for" denying a request for suspension of deportation. . . . We are satisfied that the one-House veto is legislative in purpose and effect and subject to the procedures set out in Art. I.

V

We hold that the Congressional veto provision in § 244(c)(2) is severable from the Act and that it is unconstitutional. Accordingly, the judgment of the Court of Appeals is
Affirmed.

Justice POWELL, concurring in the judgment.

The Court's decision, based on the Presentment Clauses, Art. I, § 7, cls. 2 and 3, apparently will invalidate every use of the legislative veto. The breadth of this holding gives one pause. Congress has included the veto in literally hundreds of statutes, dating back to the 1930s. Congress clearly views this procedure as essential to controlling the delegation of power to administrative agencies. One reasonably may disagree with Congress' assessment of the veto's utility, but the respect due its judgment as a coordinate branch of Government cautions that our holding should be no more extensive than necessary to decide this case. In my view, the case may be decided on a narrower ground. . . .

On its face, the House's action appears clearly adjudicatory.[7] The House did not enact a general rule; rather it made its own determination that six specific persons did not comply with certain statutory criteria. It thus undertook the type of decision that traditionally has been left to other branches. Even if the House did not make a *de novo* determination, but simply reviewed the Immigration and Naturalization Service's findings, it still assumed a function ordinarily entrusted to the federal courts.[8] *See* 5 U.S.C. § 704 (providing

---

[7] The Court concludes that Congress' action was legislative in character because each branch "presumptively act[s] within its assigned sphere." The Court's presumption provides a useful starting point, but does not conclude the inquiry. Nor does the fact that the House's action alters an individual's legal status indicate, as the Court reasons, that the action is legislative rather than adjudicative in nature. In determining whether one branch unconstitutionally has assumed a power central to another branch, the traditional characterization of the assumed power as legislative, executive, or judicial may provide some guidance. But reasonable minds may disagree over the character of an act and the more helpful inquiry, in my view, is whether the act in question raises the dangers the Framers sought to avoid.

[8] The Court reasons in response to this argument that the one-house veto exercised in this case was not judicial in nature because the decision of the Immigration and Naturalization Service did not present a justiciable issue that could have been reviewed by a court on appeal. The Court notes that since the administrative agency decided the case in favor of Chadha, there was no aggrieved party who could appeal. Reliance by the Court on this fact misses the point. Even if review of the particular decision to suspend deportation is not committed to the courts, the House of Representatives assumed a function that generally is entrusted to an impartial tribunal. In my view, the legislative branch in effect acted as an appellate court by overruling the Service's application of established law to Chadha. And unlike a court or an administrative agency, it did not provide Chadha with the right to counsel or a hearing before acting. Although the parallel is not entirely complete, the effect on Chadha's personal rights would not have been different in principle had he been acquitted of a federal crime and thereafter found by one House of Congress to have been guilty.

generally for judicial review of final agency action); *cf. Foti v. INS*, 375 U.S. 217 (1963) (holding that courts of appeals have jurisdiction to review INS decisions denying suspension of deportation). Where, as here, Congress has exercised a power "that cannot possibly be regarded as merely in aid of the legislative function of Congress," *Buckley v. Valeo*, 424 U.S. at 138, the decisions of this Court have held that Congress impermissibly assumed a function that the Constitution entrusted to another branch, *see id.* at 138-141.

The impropriety of the House's assumption of this function is confirmed by the fact that its action raises the very danger the Framers sought to avoid—the exercise of unchecked power. In deciding whether Chadha deserves to be deported, Congress is not subject to any internal constraints that prevent it from arbitrarily depriving him of the right to remain in this country. Unlike the judiciary or an administrative agency, Congress is not bound by established substantive rules. Nor is it subject to the procedural safeguards, such as the right to counsel and a hearing before an impartial tribunal, that are present when a court or an agency adjudicates individual rights. The only effective constraint on Congress' power is political, but Congress is most accountable politically when it prescribes rules of general applicability. When it decides rights of specific persons, those rights are subject to "the tyranny of a shifting majority."

Chief Justice Marshall observed: "It is the peculiar province of the legislature to prescribe general rules for the government of society; the application of those rules would seem to be the duty of other departments." *Fletcher v. Peck*, 6 Cranch 87, 136 (1810). In my view, when Congress undertook to apply its rules to Chadha, it exceeded the scope of its constitutionally prescribed authority. I would not reach the broader question whether legislative vetoes are invalid under the Presentment Clauses.

Justice WHITE, dissenting.

Today the Court not only invalidates § 244(c)(2) of the Immigration and Nationality Act, but also sounds the death knell for nearly 200 other statutory provisions in which Congress has reserved a "legislative veto." For this reason, the Court's decision is of surpassing importance. And it is for this reason that the Court would have been well-advised to decide the case, if possible, on the narrower grounds of separation of powers, leaving for full consideration the constitutionality of other congressional review statutes operating on such varied matters as war powers and agency rulemaking, some of which concern the independent regulatory agencies.

The prominence of the legislative veto mechanism in our contemporary political system and its importance to Congress can hardly be overstated. It has become a central means by which Congress secures the accountability of executive and independent agencies. Without the legislative veto, Congress is faced with a Hobson's choice: either to refrain from delegating the necessary authority, leaving itself with a hopeless task of writing laws with the requisite specificity to cover endless special circumstances across the entire policy landscape, or in the alternative, to abdicate its law-making function to the executive branch and independent agencies. To choose the former leaves major national problems unresolved; to opt for the latter risks unaccountable policymaking by those not elected to fill that role. Accordingly, over the past five decades, the legislative veto has been placed in nearly 200 statutes. The device is known in every field of governmental concern: reorganization, budgets, foreign affairs, war powers, and regulation of trade, safety, energy, the environment and the economy.

I

[Justice WHITE summarized the history of the legislative veto, from its earliest uses in the Hoover and Roosevelt Administrations through the 1970s.]

Even this brief review suffices to demonstrate that the legislative veto is more than "efficient, convenient, and useful." It is an important if not indispensable political invention that allows the President and Congress to resolve major constitutional and policy differences, assures the accountability of independent regulatory agencies, and preserves Congress' control over lawmaking. Perhaps there are other means of accommodation and accountability, but the increasing reliance of Congress upon the legislative veto suggests that the alternatives to which Congress must now turn are not entirely satisfactory.[10]

The history of the legislative veto also makes clear that it has not been a sword with which Congress has struck out to aggrandize itself at the expense of the other branches—the concerns of Madison and Hamilton. Rather, the veto has been a means of defense, a reservation of ultimate authority necessary if Congress is to fulfill its designated role under Article I as the nation's lawmaker. While the President has often objected to particular legislative vetoes, generally those left in the hands of congressional committees, the

---

[10] While Congress could write certain statutes with greater specificity, it is unlikely that this is a realistic or even desirable substitute for the legislative veto. "Political volatility and the controversy of many issues would prevent Congress from reaching agreement on many major problems if specificity were required in their enactments." Ralph F. Fuchs, *Administrative Agencies and the Energy Problem*, 47 IND. L.J. 606, 608 (1972); Richard B. Stewart, *Reformation of American Administrative Law*, 88 HARV. L. REV. 1667, 1695-1696 (1975). For example, in the deportation context, the solution is not for Congress to create more refined categorizations of the deportable aliens whose status should be subject to change. In 1979, the Immigration and Naturalization Service proposed regulations setting forth factors to be considered in the exercise of discretion under numerous provisions of the Act, but not including § 244, to ensure "fair and uniform" adjudication "under appropriate discretionary criteria." 44 Fed. Reg. 36187 (1979). The proposed rule was canceled in 1981, because "[t]here is an inherent failure in any attempt to list those factors which should be considered in the exercise of discretion. It is impossible to list or foresee all of the adverse or favorable factors which may be present in a given set of circumstances." 46 Fed. Reg. 9119 (1981).

Executive has more often agreed to legislative review as the price for a broad delegation of authority. To be sure, the President may have preferred unrestricted power, but that could be precisely why Congress thought it essential to retain a check on the exercise of delegated authority.

II

. . . [T]he apparent sweep of the Court's decision today is regretable [*sic*]. The Court's Article I analysis appears to invalidate all legislative vetoes irrespective of form or subject. . . . If the legislative veto were as plainly unconstitutional as the Court strives to suggest, its broad ruling today would be more comprehensible. But, the constitutionality of the legislative veto is anything but clearcut. The issue divides scholars, courts, attorneys general, and the two other branches of the National Government. If the veto devices so flagrantly disregarded the requirements of Article I as the Court today suggests, I find it incomprehensible that Congress, whose members are bound by oath to uphold the Constitution, would have placed these mechanisms in nearly 200 separate laws over a period of 50 years.

The reality of the situation is that the constitutional question posed today is one of immense difficulty over which the executive and legislative branches—as well as scholars and judges—have understandably disagreed. That disagreement stems from the silence of the Constitution on the precise question: The Constitution does not directly authorize or prohibit the legislative veto. Thus, our task should be to determine whether the legislative veto is consistent with the purposes of Art. I and the principles of Separation of Powers which are reflected in that Article and throughout the Constitution. We should not find the lack of a specific constitutional authorization for the legislative veto surprising, and I would not infer disapproval of the mechanism from its absence. . . .

. . . In my view, neither Article I of the Constitution nor the doctrine of separation of powers is violated by this mechanism by which our elected representatives preserve their voice in the governance of the nation. . . .

III. . . .

B

. . . The Court's holding today that all legislative-type action must be enacted through the lawmaking process ignores that legislative authority is routinely delegated to the Executive branch, to the independent regulatory agencies, and to private individuals and groups. . . . This Court's decisions sanctioning such delegations make clear that Article I does not require all action with the effect of legislation to be passed as a law. . . .

If Congress may delegate lawmaking power to independent and executive agencies, it is most difficult to understand Article I as forbidding Congress from also reserving a check on legislative power for itself. Absent the veto, the agencies receiving delegations of legislative or quasi-legislative power may issue regulations having the force of law without bicameral approval and without the President's signature. It is thus not apparent why the reservation of a veto over the exercise of that legislative power must be subject to a more exacting test. In both cases, it is enough that the initial statutory authorizations comply with the Article I requirements. . . .

The Court's opinion in the present case comes closest to facing the reality of administrative lawmaking in considering the contention that the Attorney General's action in suspending deportation under § 244 is itself a legislative act. The Court posits that the Attorney General is acting in an Article II enforcement capacity under § 244. This characterization is at odds with *Mahler v. Eby*, 264 U.S. 32 (1924), where the power conferred on the Executive to deport aliens was considered a delegation of legislative power. The Court suggests, however, that the Attorney General acts in an Article II capacity because the courts when a case or controversy arises, can always "ascertain whether the will of Congress has been obeyed, and can enforce adherence to statutory standards." [*See* note 16 of the Majority Opinion.] This assumption is simply wrong [because no party would have the motivation or the right to appeal from an Attorney General's decision to suspend a deportation order under § 244]. It is perhaps on the erroneous premise that judicial review may check abuses of the § 244 power that the Court also submits that "The bicameral process is not necessary as a check on the Executive's administration of the laws because his administrative activity cannot reach beyond the limits of the statute that created it — a statute duly enacted pursuant to Art. I, §§ 1, 7." [*See* note 16 of the Majority Opinion.] On the other hand, the Court's reasoning does persuasively explain why a resolution of disapproval under § 244(c)(2) need not again be subject to the bicameral process. Because it serves only to check the Attorney General's exercise of the suspension authority granted by § 244, the disapproval resolution — unlike the Attorney General's action — "cannot reach beyond the limits of the statute that created it — a statute duly enacted pursuant to Article I."

More fundamentally, even if the Court correctly characterizes the Attorney General's authority under § 244 as an Article II Executive power, the Court concedes that certain administrative agency action, such as rulemaking, "may resemble lawmaking" and recognizes that "[t]his Court has referred to agency activity as being 'quasi-legislative' in character. *Humphrey's Executor v. United States*, 295 U.S. 602, 628 (1935)." Such rules and adjudications by the agencies meet the Court's own definition of legislative action for they "alter [] the legal rights, duties, and relations of persons . . . outside the legislative branch," and involve "determinations of policy." Under the Court's analysis, the Executive Branch and the independent agencies may make rules with the effect of law while Congress, in whom the Framers confided the legislative power, Art. I, § 1, may not exercise a veto which precludes such rules from having operative force. If the effective functioning of a complex modern government requires the delegation of vast authority which, by virtue of its breadth, is legislative or "quasi-legislative" in character, I cannot accept that Article I—which is, after all, the source of the non-delegation doctrine—should forbid Congress from qualifying that grant with a legislative veto.[21]

C

The Court also takes no account of perhaps the most relevant consideration: However resolutions of disapproval under § 244(c)(2) are formally characterized, in reality, a departure from the status quo occurs only upon the concurrence of opinion among the House, Senate, and President. Reservations of legislative authority to be exercised by Congress should be upheld if the exercise of such reserved authority is consistent with the distribution of and limits upon legislative power that Article I provides.

1

[After summarizing numerous, decades-long attempts by Congress and the Executive Branch to find a mutually agreeable approach to making deportation decisions, Justice White concludes that the] history of the Immigration Act makes clear that § 244(c)(2) did not alter the division of actual authority between Congress and the Executive. At all times, whether

---

[21] The Court's other reasons for holding the legislative veto subject to the presentment and bicameral passage requirements require but brief discussion. First, the Court posits that the resolution of disapproval should be considered equivalent to new legislation because absent the veto authority of § 244(c)(2) neither House could, short of legislation, effectively require the Attorney General to deport an alien once the Attorney General has determined that the alien should remain in the United States. The statement is neither accurate nor meaningful. The Attorney General's power under the Act is only to "suspend" the order of deportation; the "suspension" does not cancel the deportation or adjust the alien's status to that of a permanent resident alien. Cancellation of deportation and adjustment of status must await favorable action by Congress. More important, the question is whether § 244(c)(2) as written is constitutional and no law is amended or repealed by the resolution of disapproval which is, of course, expressly authorized by that section.

The Court also argues that "the legislative character of the challenged action of one House is confirmed by the fact that when the Framers intended to authorize either House of Congress to act alone and outside of its prescribed bicameral legislative role, they narrowly and precisely defined the procedure for such action." Leaving aside again the above-refuted premise that all action with a legislative character requires passage in a law, the short answer is that all of these carefully defined exceptions to the presentment and bicameralism strictures do not involve action of the Congress pursuant to a duly-enacted statute. Indeed, for the most part these powers—those of impeachment, review of appointments, and treaty ratification—are not legislative powers at all. The fact that it was essential for the Constitution to stipulate that Congress has the power to impeach and try the President hardly demonstrates a limit upon Congress' authority to reserve itself a legislative veto, through statutes, over subjects within its lawmaking authority.

through private bills, or through affirmative concurrent resolutions, or through the present one-House veto, a permanent change in a deportable alien's status could be accomplished only with the agreement of the Attorney General, the House, and the Senate.

2

The central concern of the presentation and bicameralism requirements of Article I is that when a departure from the legal status quo is undertaken, it is done with the approval of the President and both Houses of Congress — or, in the event of a presidential veto, a two-thirds majority in both Houses. This interest is fully satisfied by the operation of § 244(c)(2). The President's approval is found in the Attorney General's action in recommending to Congress that the deportation order for a given alien be suspended. The House and the Senate indicate their approval of the Executive's action by not passing a resolution of disapproval within the statutory period. Thus, a change in the legal status quo — the deportability of the alien — is consummated only with the approval of each of the three relevant actors. The disagreement of any one of the three maintains the alien's pre-existing status: the Executive may choose not to recommend suspension; the House and Senate may each veto the recommendation. The effect on the rights and obligations of the affected individuals and upon the legislative system is precisely the same as if a private bill were introduced but failed to receive the necessary approval. "The President and the two Houses enjoy exactly the same say in what the law is to be as would have been true for each without the presence of the one-House veto, and nothing in the law is changed absent the concurrence of the President and a majority in each House." *Atkins v. United States*, 556 F.2d 1028, 1064 (Ct. Claims, 1977), *cert. denied*, 434 U.S. 1009 (1978).

. . . [I]t may be asserted that Chadha's status before legislative disapproval is one of nondeportation and that the exercise of the veto, unlike the failure of a private bill, works a change in the status quo. This position plainly ignores the statutory language. At no place in § 244 has Congress delegated to the Attorney General any final power to determine which aliens shall be allowed to remain in the United States. Congress has retained the ultimate power to pass on such changes in deportable status. By its own terms, § 244(a) states that whatever power the Attorney General has been delegated to suspend deportation and adjust status is to be exercisable only "as hereinafter prescribed in this section." Subsection (c) is part of that section. A grant of "suspension" does not cancel the alien's deportation or adjust the alien's status to that of a permanent resident alien. A suspension order is merely a "deferment of deportation," *McGrath v. Kristensen*, 340 U.S. 162, 168 (1950), which can mature into a cancellation of deportation and adjustment of status only upon the approval of Congress — by way of silence — under

§ 244(c)(2). Only then does the statute authorize the Attorney General to "cancel deportation proceedings" § 244(c)(2), and "record the alien's lawful admission for permanent residence . . ." § 244(d). . . . Until [such] ratification occurs, the executive's action is simply a recommendation that Congress finalize the suspension — in itself, it works no legal change. . . .

. . . [I]t may [also] be objected that Congress cannot indicate its approval of legislative change by inaction. In the Court of Appeals' view, inaction by Congress "could equally imply endorsement, acquiescence, passivity, indecision or indifference." 634 F.2d, at 435, and the Court appears to echo this concern. This objection appears more properly directed at the wisdom of the legislative veto than its constitutionality. The Constitution does not and cannot guarantee that legislators will carefully scrutinize legislation and deliberate before acting. In a democracy it is the electorate that holds the legislators accountable for the wisdom of their choices. It is hard to maintain that a private bill receives any greater individualized scrutiny than a resolution of disapproval under § 244(c)(2). Certainly the legislative veto is no more susceptible to this attack than the Court's increasingly common practice of according weight to the failure of Congress to disturb an Executive or independent agency's action. . . .

IV

The Court of Appeals struck § 244(c)(2) as violative of the constitutional principle of separation of powers. It is true that the purpose of separating the authority of government is to prevent unnecessary and dangerous concentration of power in one branch. For that reason, the Framers saw fit to divide and balance the powers of government so that each branch would be checked by the others. Virtually every part of our constitutional system bears the mark of this judgment.

But the history of the separation of powers doctrine is also a history of accommodation and practicality. Apprehensions of an overly powerful branch have not led to undue prophylactic measures that handicap the effective working of the national government as a whole. The Constitution does not contemplate total separation of the three branches of Government. . . .

Only where the potential for disruption is present must we then determine whether that impact is justified by an overriding need to promote objectives within the constitutional authority of Congress." [*United States v. Nixon*, 433 U.S. 418, 443 (1974).]

Section 244(c)(2) survives this test. The legislative veto provision does not "prevent the Executive Branch from accomplishing its constitutionally assigned functions." First, it is clear that the Executive Branch has no "constitutionally assigned" function of suspending the deportation of aliens. "'Over no conceivable subject is the legislative power of Congress more complete than it is over' the admission of aliens." *Kleindienst v. Mandel*, 408

U.S. 753, 766 (1972), quoting *Oceanic Steam Navigation Co. v. Stranahan*, 214 U.S. 320, 339 (1909). Nor can it be said that the inherent function of the Executive Branch in executing the law is involved. *The Steel Seizure Case* resolved that the Article II mandate for the President to execute the law is a directive to enforce the law which Congress has written. *Youngstown Sheet & Tube Co. v. Sawyer*, 343 U.S. 579 (1952). "The duty of the President to see that the laws be executed is a duty that does not go beyond the laws or require him to achieve more than Congress sees fit to leave within his power." *Myers v. United States*, 272 U.S., at 177 (Holmes, J., dissenting); 272 U.S., at 247 (Brandeis, J., dissenting). Here, § 244 grants the executive only a qualified suspension authority and it is only that authority which the President is constitutionally authorized to execute.

Moreover, the Court believes that the legislative veto we consider today is best characterized as an exercise of legislative or quasi-legislative authority. Under this characterization, the practice does not, even on the surface, constitute an infringement of executive or judicial prerogative. The Attorney General's suspension of deportation is equivalent to a proposal for legislation. The nature of the Attorney General's role as recommendatory is not altered because § 244 provides for congressional action through disapproval rather than by ratification. In comparison to private bills, which must be initiated in the Congress and which allow a Presidential veto to be overridden by a two-thirds majority in both Houses of Congress, § 244 augments rather than reduces the executive branch's authority. So understood, congressional review does not undermine, as the Court of Appeals thought, the "weight and dignity" that attends the decisions of the Executive Branch.

Nor does § 244 infringe on the judicial power, as Justice Powell would hold. Section 244 makes clear that Congress has reserved its own judgment as part of the statutory process. Congressional action does not substitute for judicial review of the Attorney General's decisions. The Act provides for judicial review of the refusal of the Attorney General to suspend a deportation and to transmit a recommendation to Congress. *INS v. Wang*, 450 U.S. 139 (1981) (per curiam). But the courts have not been given the authority to review whether an alien should be given permanent status; review is limited to whether the Attorney General has properly applied the statutory standards for essentially denying the alien a recommendation that his deportable status be changed by the Congress. . . .

I do not suggest that all legislative vetoes are necessarily consistent with separation of powers principles. A legislative check on an inherently executive function, for example that of initiating prosecutions, poses an entirely different question. But the legislative veto device here — and in many other settings — is far from an instance of legislative tyranny over the Executive. It is a necessary check on the unavoidably expanding power of the agencies, both executive and independent, as they engage in exercising authority delegated by Congress.

Justice REHNQUIST, with whom Justice WHITE joins, dissenting.

A severability clause creates a presumption that Congress intended the valid portion of the statute to remain in force when one part is found to be invalid. *Carter v. Carter Coal Co.*, 298 U.S. 238, 312 (1936). . . .

The Court finds that the legislative history of § 244 shows that Congress intended § 244(c)(2) to be severable because Congress wanted to relieve itself of the burden of private bills. But the history elucidated by the Court shows that Congress was unwilling to give the Executive Branch permission to suspend deportation on its own. Over the years, Congress consistently rejected requests from the Executive for complete discretion in this area. Congress always insisted on retaining ultimate control, whether by concurrent resolution, as in the 1948 Act, or by one-House veto, as in the present Act. Congress has never indicated that it would be willing to permit suspensions of deportation unless it could retain some sort of veto.

It is doubtless true that Congress has the power to provide for suspensions of deportation without a one-House veto. But the Court has failed to identify any evidence that Congress intended to exercise that power. On the contrary, Congress' continued insistence on retaining control of the suspension process indicates that it has never been disposed to give the Executive Branch a free hand. . . .

Because I do not believe that § 244(c)(2) is severable, I would reverse the judgment of the Court of Appeals.

* * *

After *Chadha*. It took Congress over a decade to adopt a replacement for the legislative veto. The Congressional Review Act of 1996, 5 U.S.C. §§ 801-808 (included in the Appendix), established an expedited procedure for Congress to disapprove certain rules promulgated by federal agencies. As illustrated by Figure 5.1 on page 270, before certain rules can take effect their promulgating agencies must submit them to Congress for review. The Act provides that all "major rules" (those having a significant economic impact as determined by the Office of Information Regulatory Affairs) submitted for review do not become effective for 60 days. This waiting period allows Congress time to review the rule and, if it chooses, pass a joint resolution disapproving it. To ensure it can act within the 60-day window, Congress conducts its review through "fast track" parliamentary procedures that facilitate faster action than is possible with normal legislation. If Congress passes the joint resolution the rule is then sent to the President for signature or veto, just like other legislation. It is this procedural feature—approval in both chambers of Congress and presentment to the President—that brings Congress' review of agency rules in line with the Supreme Court's holding in *Chadha*. If the resolution becomes law, the rule it disapproves cannot take effect or continue in effect. Additionally, the agency is barred from reissuing the same rule or one that is substantially similar to it, unless Congress subsequently enacts a statute that would permit the agency to do so.

The first successful use of the CRA was to disapprove of a rule submitted by the Department of Labor during the final months of the Clinton Administration. The rule would have required employers to take certain measures to combat musculoskeletal disorders caused by repeated motions, lifting heavy objects, and other work-related physical activities. The Occupational Safety and Health Administration ("OSHA") estimated that it would save billions in lost productivity. Nevertheless, the rule was opposed by industry, Congress disapproved it, and President George W. Bush signed the resolution into law in March 2001. It was not until 16 years later that Congress again used the CRA to disapprove an agency rule, but it certainly made up for lost time. Congress overturned 14 regulations promulgated toward the end of the Obama Administration in 2017 alone. As of this writing, Congress and the Trump Administration have used the CRA to repeal a total of 16 regulations promulgated by a variety of agencies, including the Departments of Labor, Agriculture, Education, Interior, Health and Human Services, OSHA, the Securities and Exchange Commission, and the Consumer Financial Protection Bureau.

QUESTION SET 8.1

Review & Synthesis

1. Describe how the legislative veto improved Congress' ability to supervise administrative conduct.

2. The legislative veto provision was part of the Immigration and Nationality Act of 1952, as amended ("INA"). The INA, in turn, was enacted pursuant to the requirements of bicameralism and presentment. Why, then, was the legislative veto unconstitutional? Did the Court imply that the Attorney General's deportation suspension power constituted an unconstitutional delegation of legislative authority, in violation of the nondelegation doctrine (*see* Chapter 2)? Why or why not?

3. How did Chief Justice Burger, writing for the majority, define what it means to take "legislative" action, and what legislative actions did he conclude were taken in this case?

4. Compare Chief Justice Burger's reasoning with Justice White's. Which actions did Justice White conclude were "legislative," and why did he disagree with Chief Justice Burger's conclusions in that respect?

5. Justice Powell characterized the House's actions in this case as "judicial." On what facts did he base this characterization? Why did Chief Justice Burger disagree with him? How do you characterize what the House did in this case?

6. Do you agree with Justice Rehnquist that Congress would not have wanted the Attorney General's deportation suspension power to remain in the INA absent the check provided by the unicameral veto? How did Chief Justice Burger justify preserving that power in light of its connection to the unicameral veto?

7. In his dissent, Justice White forcefully argued that the Framers designed the federal government around the notion that no Branch should be permitted to expand its own powers at the expense of the others. In his view, INA § 244 respected this organizing principle by requiring that all three federal political actors—the President, the House, and the Senate—agreed on whether an immigrant in Chadha's position should be deported. Based on your review of the separation-of-powers materials provided in Chapter 1, do you agree with Justice White's understanding of the Framer's intentions? Is Chief Justice Burger's majority opinion *inconsistent* with this understanding of the Framers' intent? If so, in what way? If not, what is the crux of his and Justice White's disagreement?

Application & Analysis

1. Federal law allows private entities to purchase mining rights on public lands owned and controlled by the federal government. Pursuant to the Federal Land Policy Management Act ("FLPMA"), the Interior Secretary may temporarily "withdraw" tracts of land, making them unavailable for private mining activities. Goals and objectives contained in the FLPMA guide the Secretary's discretion in exercising this withdrawal authority, and the Act requires the Secretary to send a detailed report to Congress about planned withdrawals. The Act also gives Congress the authority to veto any large-tract withdrawal of which it disapproves. 43 U.S.C. § 1714(c)(1). Vetoes are effected through concurrent resolutions passed by both the House of Representatives and the Senate and are not presented to the President for signature or veto. Congress has never used this veto power. The FLPMA's severability clause provides that the remainder of the Act is not affected if any of its provisions are held to be invalid. 43 U.S.C. § 1701.

    The Secretary recently withdrew a 25,000-acre tract near Grand Canyon National Park in northern Arizona from new uranium mining claims. Mining companies and local governments concerned about the withdrawal's economic impact filed suit in federal court to challenge the

Secretary's decision. Among other claims, the plaintiffs assert that 43 U.S.C. § 1714(c)(1) contains an unconstitutional legislative veto provision that is not severable from the remainder of the subsection. They accordingly ask that the FLPMA be struck down in its entirety. Assess the legal merits of the plaintiffs' claim.

2. The U.S. Senate Committee on Health, Education, Labor, and Pensions is considering a bill that would significantly expand protections against respiratory diseases caused by poor ventilation in indoor workspaces. The responsibility for providing these additional protections would fall on employers. As currently written, the bill would direct the Occupational Safety and Health Administration ("OSHA") to promulgate rules to enforce its provisions. A Senator on the subcommittee agrees with the measure and expects that it will produce significant long-term savings in the form of reduced worker sick days and healthcare expenditures. However, she is skeptical that OSHA will promulgate implementing rules that minimize compliance costs for employers, which have the potential of being quite high. She has asked that the draft bill be amended to include a "report and wait" provision. This provision would require OSHA to report any rules promulgated under the bill to the Committee. OSHA would then have to wait for up to two years before putting the rule into effect, during which time Congress would consider whether to disapprove it. The disapproval process would be identical to the one established by the Congressional Review Act.

   You are legal counsel for the Committee, and the bill's sponsor has asked whether this "report and wait" provision would be constitutional. In light of *INS v. Chadha*, how do you respond?

B. THE LINE-ITEM VETO

The legislative veto and the expedited disapproval procedures established by the Congressional Review Act are far from the only mechanisms by which Congress has attempted to control bureaucratic decision-making. The most long-standing, and perhaps the most effective, is the appropriations process. Article I, section 9, clause 7 of the Constitution provides that "[n]o money shall be drawn from the Treasury, but in Consequence of Appropriations made by Law." Pursuant to this power, the government is not permitted to spend any funds—regardless of their source—without Congress' authorization. *See* Kate Stith, *Congress' Power of the Purse*, 97 YALE L.J. 1343, 1345 (1988). By reducing or completely cutting funding, Congress can eliminate disfavored programs and even abolish entire agencies. Conversely, Congress can increase appropriations to agencies when it approves of their performance or regulatory agendas. In either instance, the spending power gives Congress enormous leverage to influence how agencies pursue their regulatory mandates. The Framers were well aware of the practical authority they were handing Congress. *See* THE FEDERALIST NO. 58 (James Madison) ("This power over the purse may, in fact, be regarded as the most complete and effectual weapon with which any constitution can arm the immediate representatives of the people, for obtaining a redress of every grievance, and for carrying into effect every just and salutary measure.").

As with other forms of legislation, appropriations bills are subject to veto by the President. The Framers thought this power to negate legislation was critical to protecting the "weaker" Executive Branch from being controlled by the Legislative Branch, which, as we will remember James Madison also observing in *The Federalist No.* 51, "necessarily predominates" in any republican government. Despite clearly recognizing the need to grant veto power to the President, the records of the Constitutional Convention give no indication that the delegates considered conferring the lesser power of vetoing specific provisions within legislative acts. Presidents have nevertheless pursued that power, whether through executive fiat or statutory enactment.

An oft-cited early example of the former is a statement President Andrew Jackson attached to a bill involving road construction from Detroit to Chicago. Even though he signed the bill into law, Jackson flatly refused to extend the road beyond the Michigan border. The House of Representatives condemned the move, describing it as an impermissible item veto. *See* LOUIS FISHER, CONSTITUTIONAL CONFLICTS BETWEEN CONGRESS AND THE PRESIDENT 139 (6th ed. 2014). Since the early nineteenth century, Presidents have used such "signing statements" to advance their interpretations of statutory language, to assert constitutional objections to provisions within statutes, and to signal that they would enforce those statutes only in accordance with their understandings of what the Constitution permits. Presidents in the modern era have used the device more frequently than their predecessors. According to one study, Ronald Reagan issued 86 signing statements objecting to particular statutory provisions, President George H. W. Bush issued 107 (in four years), Bill Clinton issued 70, George W. Bush issued 127, and Barack Obama issued 10 (in his first four years). *See* TODD GARVEY, CONG. RSCH. SERV., RL33667, PRESIDENTIAL SIGNING STATEMENTS: CONSTITUTIONAL AND INSTITUTIONAL IMPLICATIONS (2012).

Alternatively, and since at least the mid-nineteenth century, Presidents have sought *statutory* authority to veto discrete legislative items. According to one source, "[t]he practice of attaching nongermane riders to bills became so commonplace that, in 1873, President Ulysses Grant recommended, in a message to Congress, an amendment to the Constitution 'to authorize the Executive to approve of so much of any measure passing the two Houses of Congress as his judgment may dictate, without approving the whole, the disapproved portions or portion to be subject to the same rules as now.'" STAFF OF HOUSE COMM. ON THE BUDGET, 98TH CONG. 1ST SESS. THE LINE-ITEM

Veto: An Appraisal 11 (Comm. Print 1984). Although that request was revived by several of Grant's successors, Congress never adopted it. President Franklin D. Roosevelt offered an alternative to a constitutional amendment several decades later. He suggested appropriations bills include provisions allowing him to reduce specific spending provisions by executive order, while also allowing Congress to legislatively veto those reductions within a specified time period. This proposal, too, failed to gain traction.

In the 1970s, President Nixon adopted the practice of "impounding"—or refusing to release—Congressionally appropriated funds when he disagreed with the programs they supported. He asserted that the Constitution implicitly granted this discretion to the President; although Congress possessed the power to make appropriations, the Constitution left their actual expenditure to the Executive Branch. While this fact gave the President some undiminishable discretion in using the monies appropriated by Congress, Nixon took matters one step further by explicitly refusing to spend line-items: monies designated by Congress to support particular programs. To curtail these impoundments, Congress passed the Congressional Budget and Impoundment Control Act of 1974. The Act allowed the President to impound funds upon transmitting a "special message" to Congress. The amounts proposed for rescission (i.e., for permanent cancellation) could be impounded for up to 45 legislative session days. The default position was expenditure rather than impoundment; the funds would be released if no statute was enacted approving the impoundment within the allotted time.

The Impoundment Act and other budget control measures (e.g., the Gramm-Rudman-Hollings Act of 1985) proved insufficient to curtail "earmarks" or "pork barrel" spending, appropriations for local projects that sent money to individual legislators' states or districts. The size and complexity of appropriations bills (they run into the thousands of pages and are separated into multiple acts) made it easy for individual legislators to bury funding for pet projects. The incentives for engaging in such stealth funding was strong, as it conspicuously demonstrated what a legislator was "accomplishing" for his or her constituents or for influential special interests. The opportunities to discover and perhaps eliminate such spending were few; Congress typically operates under tremendous time pressure when compiling budget bills and, given their length, there is almost no opportunity to comb through their provisions for unpalatable expenditures. What's more, the President's ability to control profligate spending of this type was practically nil. He or she would have to veto an entire appropriations bill just to eliminate a handful of earmarks that, no matter how objectionable, ultimately amounted to a miniscule percentage of the total federal budget.

It was not until 1994 that a fiscally conservative Congress agreed to give line-item veto power to President Clinton. The Line Item Veto Act gave the President authority to "cancel" certain spending measures and tax benefits within five days of signing an appropriations bill into law. Congress retained the authority to override the cancellation by passing a "disapproval" bill enacted through expedited legislative processes. Clinton used the line-item veto to cancel 82 expenditures and tax benefits. The following case tested the constitutionality of two of them.

Clinton v. City of New York
524 U.S. 417 (1998)

Justice STEVENS delivered the opinion of the Court.

[President Clinton used his line-item veto authority to cancel a provision in the Balanced Budget Act of 1997 that terminated a Medicaid repayment claim by the Department of Health and Human Services against New York State. The practical effect of the cancellation was to reinstate the State's responsibility for paying the claim, which totaled as much as $2.6 billion. President Clinton also cancelled a provision in the Taxpayer Relief Act of 1997, which granted a "limited tax benefit" to farmers' cooperatives, refiners, and food processors. The thwarted beneficiaries challenged the cancellations in federal district court, which found them unconstitutional. The Administration sought expedited review in the Supreme Court via a provision in the Line Item Veto Act allowing it to bypass the courts of appeals.]

IV

The Line Item Veto Act gives the President the power to "cancel in whole" three types of provisions that have been signed into law: "(1) any dollar amount of discretionary budget authority; (2) any item of new direct spending; or (3) any limited tax benefit." 2 U.S.C. § 691(a) (1994 ed., Supp. II). It is undisputed that the [provisions cancelled by the President that are at issue in this case involve an "item of new direct spending" and a "limited tax benefit"] as those terms are defined in the Act. It is also undisputed that each of those provisions had been signed into law pursuant to Article I, § 7, of the Constitution before it was canceled.

The Act requires the President to adhere to precise procedures whenever he exercises his cancellation authority. In identifying items for cancellation he must consider the legislative history, the purposes, and other relevant information about the items. *See* 2 U.S.C. § 691(b) (1994 ed., Supp. II). He must determine, with respect to each cancellation, that it will "(i) reduce the Federal budget deficit; (ii) not impair any essential Government functions; and (iii) not harm the national interest." § 691(a)(3)(A). Moreover, he must transmit a special message to Congress notifying it of each cancellation within five calendar days (excluding Sundays) after the enactment of the canceled provision. *See* § 691(a)(3)(B). It is undisputed that the President meticulously followed these procedures in these cases.

A cancellation takes effect upon receipt by Congress of the special message from the President. *See* § 691b(a). If, however, a "disapproval bill" pertaining to a special message is enacted into law, the cancellations set forth in that message become "null and void." *Ibid.* The Act sets forth a detailed expedited procedure for the consideration of a "disapproval bill," *see* § 691d, but no such bill was passed for either of the cancellations involved in these cases. A majority vote of both Houses is sufficient to enact a disapproval bill. The Act does not grant the President the authority to cancel a disapproval bill, *see* § 691(c), but he does, of course, retain his constitutional authority to veto such a bill.

The effect of a cancellation is plainly stated in § 691e, which defines the principal terms used in the Act. With respect to both an item of new direct spending and a limited tax benefit, the cancellation prevents the item "from having legal force or effect." §§ 691e(4)(B)-(C). Thus, under the plain text of the statute, the two actions of the President that are challenged in these cases prevented one section of the Balanced Budget Act of 1997 and one section of the Taxpayer Relief Act of 1997 "from having legal force or effect." The remaining provisions of those statutes, with the exception of the second canceled item in the latter, continue to have the same force and effect as they had when signed into law.

In both legal and practical effect, the President has amended two Acts of Congress by repealing a portion of each. "[R]epeal of statutes, no less than enactment, must conform with Art. I." *INS v. Chadha*, 462 U.S. 919, 954 (1983). There is no provision in the Constitution that authorizes the President to enact, to amend, or to repeal statutes. Both Article I and Article II assign responsibilities to the President that directly relate to the lawmaking process, but neither addresses the issue presented by these cases. The President "shall from time to time give to the Congress Information on the State of the Union, and recommend to their Consideration such Measures as he shall judge necessary and expedient. . . ." Art. II, § 3. Thus, he may initiate and influence legislative proposals. Moreover, after a bill has passed both Houses of Congress, but "before it become[s] a Law," it must be presented to the President. If he approves it, "he shall sign it, but if not he shall return it, with his Objections to that House in which it shall have originated, who shall enter the Objections at large on their Journal, and proceed to reconsider it." Art. I, § 7, cl. 2. His "return" of a bill, which is usually described as a "veto," is subject to being overridden by a two-thirds vote in each House.

There are important differences between the President's "return" of a bill pursuant to Article I, § 7, and the exercise of the President's cancellation authority pursuant to the Line Item Veto Act. The constitutional return takes place before the bill becomes law; the statutory cancellation occurs after the bill becomes law. The constitutional return is of the entire bill; the statutory cancellation is of only a part. Although the Constitution expressly authorizes the President to play a role in the process of enacting statutes, it is silent on the subject of unilateral Presidential action that either repeals or amends parts of duly enacted statutes.

There are powerful reasons for construing constitutional silence on this profoundly important issue as equivalent to an express prohibition. The procedures governing the enactment of statutes set forth in the text of Article I were the product of the great debates and compromises that produced the Constitution itself. Familiar historical materials provide abundant support for the conclusion that the power to enact statutes may only "be exercised in accord with a single, finely wrought and exhaustively considered, procedure." *Chadha*, 462 U.S. 951. Our first President understood the text of the Presentment Clause as requiring that he either "approve all the parts of a Bill, or reject it in toto." What has emerged in these cases from the President's exercise of his statutory cancellation powers, however, are truncated versions of two bills that passed both Houses of Congress. They are not the product of the "finely wrought" procedure that the Framers designed. . . .

V

The Government advances two related arguments to support its position that despite the unambiguous provisions of the Act, cancellations do not amend or repeal properly enacted statutes in violation of the Presentment Clause. First, relying primarily on *Field v. Clark*, 143 U.S. 649 (1892), the Government contends that the cancellations were merely exercises of discretionary authority granted to the President by the Balanced Budget Act and the Taxpayer Relief Act read in light of the previously enacted Line Item Veto Act. Second, the Government submits that the substance of the authority to cancel tax and spending items "is, in practical effect, no more and no less than the power to 'decline to spend' specified sums of money, or to 'decline to implement' specified tax measures." Neither argument is persuasive.

> **Cross-Reference**
>
> *Field v. Clark*, along with the Supreme Court's other seminal nondelegation decisions, is considered in Chapter 2.

In *Field v. Clark*, the Court upheld the constitutionality of the Tariff Act of 1890. Act of Oct. 1, 1890, 26 Stat. 567. That statute contained a "free list" of almost 300 specific articles that were exempted from import duties "unless otherwise specially provided for in this act." *Id.* at 602. Section 3 was a special provision that directed the President to suspend that exemption for sugar, molasses, coffee, tea, and hides "whenever, and so often" as he should be satisfied that any country producing and exporting those products imposed duties on the agricultural products of the United States that he deemed to be "reciprocally unequal and unreasonable . . ." *Id.* at 612. The section then specified the duties to be imposed on those products during any such suspension.

[The *Field* Court identified] three critical differences between the power to suspend the exemption from import duties and the power to cancel portions of a duly enacted statute. First, the exercise of the suspension power was contingent upon a condition that did not exist when the Tariff Act was passed: the imposition of "reciprocally unequal and unreasonable" import duties by other countries. In contrast, the exercise of the cancellation power within five days after the enactment of the Balanced Budget and Tax Reform Acts necessarily was based on the same conditions that Congress evaluated when it passed those statutes. Second, under the Tariff Act, when the President determined that the contingency had arisen, he had a duty to suspend; in contrast, while it is true that the President was required by the Act to make three determinations before he canceled a provision, *see* 2 U.S.C. § 691(a)(A) (1994 ed., Supp. II), those determinations did not qualify his discretion to cancel or not to cancel. Finally, whenever the President suspended an exemption under the Tariff Act, he was executing the policy that Congress had embodied in the statute. In contrast, whenever the President cancels an item of new direct spending or a limited tax benefit he is rejecting the policy judgment made by Congress and relying on his own policy judgment. Thus, the conclusion in *Field v. Clark* that the suspensions mandated by the Tariff Act were not exercises of legislative power does not undermine our opinion that cancellations pursuant to the Line Item Veto Act are the functional equivalent of partial repeals of Acts of Congress that fail to satisfy Article I, § 7. . . .

. . . More important, when enacting the statutes discussed in *Field*, Congress itself made the decision to suspend or repeal the particular provisions at issue upon the occurrence of particular events subsequent to enactment, and it left only the determination of whether such events occurred up to the President. The Line Item Veto Act authorizes the President himself to effect the repeal of laws, for his own policy reasons, without observing the procedures set out in Article I, § 7. The fact that Congress intended such a result is of no moment. Although Congress presumably anticipated that the President might cancel some of the items in the Balanced Budget Act and in the Taxpayer Relief Act, Congress cannot alter the procedures set out in Article I, § 7, without amending the Constitution.

Neither are we persuaded by the Government's contention that the President's authority to cancel new direct spending and tax benefit items is no greater than his traditional authority to decline to spend appropriated funds. The Government has reviewed in some detail the series of statutes in which Congress has given the Executive broad discretion over the expenditure of appropriated funds. For example, the First Congress appropriated "sum[s] not exceeding" specified amounts to be spent on various Government operations. *See, e.g.,* Act of Sept. 29, 1789, ch. 23, § 1, 1 Stat. 95; Act of Mar. 26, 1790, ch. 4, 1 Stat. 104; Act of Feb. 11, 1791, ch. 6, 1 Stat. 190. In those statutes, as in later years, the President was given wide discretion with respect to both the amounts to be spent and how the money would be allocated among different functions. It is argued that the Line Item Veto Act merely confers comparable discretionary authority over the expenditure of appropriated funds. The critical difference between this statute and all of its predecessors, however, is that unlike any of them, this Act gives the President the unilateral power to change the text of duly enacted statutes. None of the Act's predecessors could even arguably have been construed to authorize such a change. . . .

The judgment of the District Court is affirmed.
It is so ordered.

[The concurring opinion of Justice KENNEDY is omitted.]

Justice SCALIA, with whom Justice O'CONNOR joins, and with whom Justice BREYER joins as to Part III, concurring in part and dissenting in part. . . .

III

. . . Unlike the Court . . . I do not believe that Executive cancellation of . . . direct spending violates the Presentment Clause.

The Presentment Clause requires, in relevant part, that "[e]very Bill which shall have passed the House of Representatives and the Senate, shall, before it become a Law, be presented to the President of the United States; If he approve he shall sign it, but if not he shall return it." U.S. CONST., Art. I, § 7, cl. 2. There is no question that enactment of the Balanced Budget Act complied with these requirements: the House and Senate passed the bill, and the President signed it into law. It was only after the requirements of the Presentment Clause had been satisfied that the President exercised his authority under the Line Item Veto Act to cancel the spending item. Thus, the Court's problem with the Act is not that it authorizes the President to veto parts of a bill and sign others into law, but rather that it authorizes him to "cancel" — prevent from "having legal force or effect" — certain parts of duly enacted statutes.

Article I, § 7, of the Constitution obviously prevents the President from canceling a law that Congress has not authorized him to cancel. Such action cannot possibly be considered part of his execution of the law, and if it is legislative action, as the Court observes, "'repeal of statutes, no less than enactment, must conform with Art. I[,]'" quoting from *INS v. Chadha*, 462 U.S. 919, 954 (1983). But that is not this case. It was certainly arguable, as an original matter, that Art. I, § 7, also prevents the President from canceling a law which itself authorizes the President to cancel it. But as the Court acknowledges, that argument has long since been made and rejected. In 1809, Congress passed a law authorizing the President to cancel trade restrictions against Great Britain and France if either revoked edicts directed at the United States. Act of Mar. 1, 1809, § 11, 2 Stat. 528. Joseph Story regarded the conferral of that authority as entirely unremarkable in *The Orono*, 18 F. Cas. 830, No. 10,585 (C.C.D. Mass. 1812). The Tariff Act of 1890 authorized the President to "suspend, by proclamation to that effect" certain of its provisions if he determined that other countries were imposing "reciprocally unequal and unreasonable" duties. Act of Oct. 1, 1890, § 3, 26 Stat. 612. This Court upheld the constitutionality of that Act in *Field v. Clark*, 143 U.S. 649 (1892). . . .

As much as the Court goes on about Art. I, § 7, therefore, that provision does not demand the result the Court reaches. It no more categorically prohibits the Executive reduction of congressional dispositions in the course of implementing statutes that authorize such reduction, than it categorically prohibits the Executive augmentation of congressional dispositions in the course of implementing statutes that authorize such augmentation—generally known as substantive rulemaking. There are, to be sure, limits upon the former just as there are limits upon the latter—and I am prepared to acknowledge that the limits upon the former may be much more severe. Those limits are established, however, not by some categorical prohibition of Art. I, § 7, which our cases conclusively disprove, but by what has come to be known as the doctrine of unconstitutional delegation of legislative authority: When authorized Executive reduction or augmentation is allowed to go too far, it usurps the nondelegable function of Congress and violates the separation of powers.

It is this doctrine, and not the Presentment Clause, that was discussed in the *Field* opinion, and it is this doctrine, and not the Presentment Clause, that is the issue presented by the statute before us here. That is why the Court is correct to distinguish prior authorizations of Executive cancellation, such as the one involved in *Field*, on the ground that they were contingent upon an Executive finding of fact, and on the ground that they related to the field of foreign affairs, an area where the President has a special " 'degree of discretion and freedom. . . .' " These distinctions have nothing to do with whether the details of Art. I, § 7, have been complied with, but everything to do with whether the authorizations went too far by transferring to the Executive a degree of political, lawmaking power that our traditions demand be retained by the Legislative Branch.

I turn, then, to the crux of the matter: whether Congress's authorizing the President to cancel an item of spending gives him a power that our history and traditions show must reside exclusively in the Legislative Branch. I may note, to begin with, that the Line Item Veto Act is not the first statute to authorize the President to "cancel" spending items. In *Bowsher v. Synar*, 478 U.S. 714, (1986), we addressed the constitutionality of the Balanced Budget and Emergency Deficit Control Act of 1985, 2 U.S.C. § 901 et seq. (1982 ed., Supp. III), which required the President, if the federal budget deficit exceeded a certain amount, to issue a "sequestration" order mandating spending reductions specified by the Comptroller General, § 902. The effect of sequestration was that "amounts sequestered . . . shall be *permanently cancelled.*" § 902(a)(4) (emphasis added). We held that the Act was unconstitutional, not because it impermissibly gave the Executive legislative power, but because it gave the Comptroller General, an officer of the Legislative Branch over whom Congress retained removal power, "the ultimate authority to determine the budget cuts to be made," 478 U.S., at 733, "functions . . . *plainly entailing execution of the law in constitutional terms,*" *id.* at 732–733 (emphasis added). The President's discretion under the Line Item Veto Act is certainly broader than the Comptroller General's discretion was under the 1985 Act, but it is no broader than the discretion traditionally granted the President in his execution of spending laws.

Insofar as the degree of political, "lawmaking" power conferred upon the Executive is concerned, there is not a dime's worth of difference between Congress's authorizing the President to cancel a spending item, and Congress's authorizing money to be spent on a particular item at the President's discretion. And the latter has been done since the founding of the Nation. . . . Examples of appropriations committed to the discretion of the President abound in our history. . . . The constitutionality of such appropriations has never seriously been questioned. . . .

Certain Presidents have claimed Executive authority to withhold appropriated funds even absent an express conferral of discretion to do so. . . .

The short of the matter is this: Had the Line Item Veto Act authorized the President to "decline to spend" any item spending contained in the Balanced Budget Act of 1997, there is not the slightest doubt that authorization would have been constitutional. What the Line Item Veto Act does instead— authorizing the President to "cancel" an item of spending—is technically different. But the technical difference does not relate to the technicalities of the Presentment Clause, which have been fully complied with; and the doctrine of unconstitutional delegation, which is at issue here, is preeminently not a doctrine of technicalities. The title of the Line Item Veto Act, which was perhaps designed to simplify for public comprehension, or perhaps merely to comply with the terms of a campaign pledge, has succeeded in faking out the Supreme Court. The President's action it authorizes in fact is not a line-item veto and thus does not offend Art. I, § 7; and insofar as the substance of that action is concerned, it is no different from what Congress has permitted the President to do since the formation of the Union. . . .

For the foregoing reasons, I respectfully dissent.

Justice BREYER, with whom Justice O'CONNOR and Justice SCALIA join as to Part III, dissenting.

. . . In my view the Line Item Veto Act (Act) does not violate any specific textual constitutional command, nor does it violate any implicit separation-of-powers principle. Consequently, I believe that the Act is constitutional. . . .

IV

. . . There are three relevant separation-of-powers questions here: (1) Has Congress given the President the wrong kind of power, i.e., "non-Executive" power? (2) Has Congress given the President the power to "encroach" upon Congress' own constitutionally reserved territory? (3) Has Congress given the President too much power, violating the doctrine of "nondelegation"? [W]ith respect to this Act, the answer to all these questions is "no."

A

Viewed conceptually, the power the Act conveys is the right kind of power. It is "executive." . . . [A]n exercise of that power "executes" the Act. Conceptually speaking, it closely resembles the kind of delegated authority—to spend or not to spend appropriations, to change or not to change tariff rates—that Congress has frequently granted the President, any differences being differences in degree, not kind.

The fact that one could also characterize this kind of power as "legislative," say, if Congress itself (by amending the appropriations bill) prevented a provision from taking effect, is beside the point. This Court has frequently found that the exercise of a particular power, such as the power to make rules of broad applicability, or to adjudicate claims, can fall within the constitutional purview of more than one branch of Government. The Court does not "carry out the distinction between legislative and executive action with mathematical precision" or "divide the branches into watertight compartments," *Springer v. Philippine Islands*, 277 U.S. 189, 211 (1928) (Holmes, J., dissenting), for, as others have said, the Constitution "blend[s]" as well as "separat[es]" powers in order to create a workable government. 1 K. Davis, Administrative Law § 1.09, p. 68 (1958). . . .

If there is a separation-of-powers violation, then, it must rest, not upon purely conceptual grounds, but upon some important conflict between the Act and a significant separation-of-powers objective.

B

The Act does not undermine what this Court has often described as the principal function of the separation-of-powers, which is to maintain the tripartite structure of the Federal Government—and thereby protect individual liberty—by providing a "safeguard against the encroachment or aggrandizement of one branch at the expense of the other." *Buckley v. Valeo*, 424 U.S. 1, 122 (1976) (per curiam). *See* The Federalist No. 51, p. 349

(J. Cooke ed. 1961) (J. Madison) (separation of powers confers on each branch the means "to resist encroachments of the others").

In contrast to [*Buckley* and similar cases], one cannot say that the Act "encroaches" upon Congress' power, when Congress retained the power to insert, by simple majority, into any future appropriations bill, into any section of any such bill, or into any phrase of any section, a provision that says the Act will not apply. *See* 2 U.S.C. § 691f(c)(1) (1994 ed., Supp. II). Congress also retained the power to "disapprov[e]," and thereby reinstate, any of the President's cancellations. *See* 2 U.S.C. § 691b(a). And it is Congress that drafts and enacts the appropriations statutes that are subject to the Act in the first place—and thereby defines the outer limits of the President's cancellation authority. . . . Indeed, the President acts only in response to, and on the terms set by, the Congress.

Nor can one say that the Act's basic substantive objective is constitutionally improper, for the earliest Congresses could, and often did, confer on the President this sort of discretionary authority over spending. . . . And, if an individual Member of Congress, who, say, favors aid to Country A but not to Country B, objects to the Act on the ground that the President may "rewrite" an appropriations law to do the opposite, one can respond: "But a majority of Congress voted that he have that power; you may vote to exempt the relevant appropriations provision from the Act; and if you command a majority, your appropriation is safe." Where the burden of overcoming legislative inertia lies is within the power of Congress to determine by rule. Where is the encroachment?

Nor can one say the Act's grant of power "aggrandizes" the Presidential office. The grant is limited to the context of the budget. It is limited to the power to spend, or not to spend, particular appropriated items, and the power to permit, or not to permit, specific limited exemptions from generally applicable tax law from taking effect. These powers . . . resemble those the President has exercised in the past on other occasions. The delegation of those powers to the President may strengthen the Presidency, but any such change in Executive Branch authority seems minute when compared with the changes worked by delegations of other kinds of authority that the Court in the past has upheld.

C

The "nondelegation" doctrine represents an added constitutional check upon Congress' authority to delegate power to the Executive Branch. And it raises a more serious constitutional obstacle here. The Constitution permits Congress to "see[k] assistance from another branch" of Government, the "extent and character" of that assistance to be fixed "according to common sense and the inherent necessities of the governmental co-ordination."

J.W. Hampton, 276 U.S., at 406. But there are limits on the way in which Congress can obtain such assistance. . . . [I]n Chief Justice Taft's more familiar words, the Constitution permits only those delegations where Congress "shall lay down by legislative act an *intelligible principle* to which the person or body authorized to [act] is directed to conform." *J.W. Hampton*, 276 U.S., at 409 (emphasis added). . . .

. . . [The (a)] broadly phrased limitations in the Act, together with (b) its evident deficit reduction purpose, and (c) a procedure that guarantees Presidential awareness of the reasons for including a particular provision in a budget bill, taken together, guide the President's exercise of his discretionary powers.

1. . . .

. . . The President, unlike most agency decisionmakers, is an elected official. He is responsible to the voters, who, in principle, will judge the manner in which he exercises his delegated authority. Whether the President's expenditure decisions, for example, are arbitrary is a matter that in the past has been left primarily to those voters to consider. And this Court has made clear that judicial review is less appropriate when the President's own discretion, rather than that of an agency, is at stake. . . . [This reflects] in part the Constitution's own delegation of "executive Power" to "a President," Art. II, § 1, and we must take this into account when applying the Constitution's nondelegation doctrine to questions of Presidential authority.

Consequently I believe that the power the Act grants the President to prevent spending items from taking effect does not violate the "nondelegation" doctrine. . . .

V

In sum, I recognize that the Act before us is novel. In a sense, it skirts a constitutional edge. But that edge has to do with means, not ends. The means chosen do not amount literally to the enactment, repeal, or amendment of a law. Nor, for that matter, do they amount literally to the "line item veto" that the Act's title announces. Those means do not violate any basic separation-of-powers principle. They do not improperly shift the constitutionally foreseen balance of power from Congress to the President. Nor, since they comply with separation-of-powers principles, do they threaten the liberties of individual citizens. They represent an experiment that may, or may not, help representative government work better. The Constitution, in my view, authorizes Congress and the President to try novel methods in this way. Consequently, with respect, I dissent.

QUESTION SET 8.2

Review & Synthesis

1. Restate the test the majority applied in judging the constitutionality of the Line Item Veto Act, and identify the specific actions permitted by the Act that failed that test.

2. Was the majority's holding in *Clinton* overly formalistic? If the President already had authority to veto entire bills, and already had discretion not to spend monies appropriated for the Executive Branch, was the Court's objection simply that the Constitution did not *explicitly* permit the President to excise statutory provisions after they have been passed into law?

3. Was Justice Scalia right that *Clinton* was better understood as a nondelegation case, rather than as a Bicameralism and Presentment case? The Court specifically compared the Line Item Veto Act to the Tariff Act considered in *Field v. Clark*. Didn't this comparison reveal the real issues with the Line Item Veto Act: it permitted Presidential policymaking separate and apart from Congress' intent, whereas the Tariff Act permitted Presidential policymaking only when consistent with Congress' intent?

4. Should separation-of-powers questions, such as those at issue in *INS v. Chadha* and *Clinton v. New York*, be answered formalistically or functionally? In other words, should courts judge the constitutionality of Congress' actions exclusively by whether they adhered to the specific procedures set out in the Constitution, or should courts instead judge its actions by the underlying principles that are reflected in those specific procedures? In thinking through your answer, consider the practical effects each position might generally produce. Would it allow Congress to usurp the President's constitutional authority to implement federal law? Would it hamper Congress' ability to check Presidential efforts to usurp Congress' lawmaking authority? Do you find Justice Breyer's arguments in this regard persuasive or unpersuasive?

5. In his majority opinion, Justice Stevens observed that "whenever the President cancels an item of new direct spending or a limited tax benefit he is rejecting the policy judgment made by Congress and relying on his own policy judgment." Was that necessarily true and, even if it was, should it have mattered? Is it not possible that President Clinton exercised the line-item veto when his policy preferences *aligned* with those of Congress? In other words, was it not the case that Clinton could only

use the veto when Congress' budget-reduction priorities were followed, whatever his other internal motivations may have been?

6. From a political rather than a legal perspective, why would President Clinton have wanted the line-item veto power? Didn't it give Members of Congress license to be irresponsible in their earmarking, leaving President Clinton to take the blame if he failed to reign them in? Wouldn't the power also have led President Clinton to eliminate earmarks inserted by members of his own political party, possibly reducing their chances at reelection?

Application & Analysis

1. Under specified conditions, § 802 of the Foreign Intelligence Surveillance Act Amendments of 2008 ("FISA") immunizes telecommunications companies from all civil liability arising from the assistance they lend the government's intelligence gathering activities. The section dovetails with other statutory provisions that grant the Executive Branch authority to enlist those companies for intelligence gathering, to protect them from suit, and to keep their efforts secret. This immunization is provided on a case-by-case basis. The Attorney General is empowered to certify that a defendant company has provided surveillance assistance covered by FISA. Upon receiving the Attorney General's certification, courts are required to dismiss any claims arising from that assistance.

   After learning from national news reports that their local telephone company cooperated with the National Security Agency's warrantless eavesdropping program, a group of the company's customers sued it in federal district court. When the Attorney General filed a § 802 immunity certification on the company's behalf, the plaintiffs challenged the provision's constitutionality. They argued that it operated similarly to the Line Item Veto Act because it permitted the Attorney General to partially repeal or preempt federal and state laws against electronic surveillance.

   You are a clerk for the judge presiding over the lawsuit. Write a brief memorandum assessing the plaintiffs' argument.

C. APPOINTMENTS

As discussed in Chapter 2, Congress has primary responsibility for drafting regulatory blueprints—for making regulatory policy choices and creating federal agencies to implement them. Of course, this is but an early step toward eventual policy implementation, as even the most carefully drafted regulatory plan cannot execute itself. Actual administration requires the establishment of administrative positions and the appointment of officials to fill them. Here, the Constitution divides responsibility between Congress and the President.

Congress has the initial responsibility for creating Executive Branch offices and for setting the statutory qualifications to hold them. The Constitution vests it with the legislative power (Art. I, § 1), and the Necessary and Proper Clause (Art. I, § 8, cl. 18) vests it with general authority to structure the federal government. *See, e.g.,* John F. Manning, *Foreword: The Means of Constitutional Power,* 128 HARV. L. REV. 1, 81 (2014) ("When it comes to composing the government . . . the Constitution is not neutral between Congress and the coordinate branches. Rather, the Necessary and Proper Clause . . . gives Congress power to implement not only its own powers, but also 'all other Powers vested . . . *in any* Department or Officer' of the federal government.").

Once Congress has created an Executive Branch office, the Appointments Clause (Art. II, § 2, cl. 2) gives it a critical but limited role in selecting the person appointed to it. The Clause outlines the basic procedures for appointing two categories of senior decision-makers. The first category is comprised of so-called "Officers of the United States." The Clause makes no attempt to define who these officers are, but it does establish a clear procedure by which they are to be hired: They must be nominated by the President and confirmed by the Senate. Notably, the Constitution leaves no task here for the House of Representatives to perform. The second category is comprised of "inferior Officers." Again, the Clause does not define who these folks are. Moreover, the Clause sets out a process for their selection that is different in two respects from the one it establishes for "principal" officers. First, it does not assign nomination of inferior officers to President. It instead gives Congress discretion to delegate that responsibility to "the President alone, [to] the Courts of Law, or [to] the Heads of Departments." Second, it requires no Congressional approval of that delegate's choice; the appointment presumably becomes effective upon the appointee's acceptance of it.

The materials that follow address two issues that have arisen from the procedures set out in the Appointments Clause. The first, addressed by the Supreme Court in *Buckley v. Valeo,* is whether Congress can have any role in appointing Officers of the United States apart from the one specifically reserved for it by the Appointments Clause. Stated differently, does the Appointments Clause set the sum total of Congress' involvement in hiring officials who execute federal law? Why Congress might want a greater role is clear, as its ability to control administrators' decisions is limited to *ex ante* office creation, qualification setting, and budgetary measures. Apart from this, Congress has few opportunities for direct *ex post* control over individual appointees once they take office. To be sure, appointment is an imperfect method of bureaucratic control; appointees do not always adopt the policy preferences of those who appoint them. Nevertheless, the likelihood that an appointee will undertake his or her responsibilities in a way that Congress prefers is greater if Congress does the hiring itself. This serious separation-of-powers concern—that Congress aggrandizes its own power when it tries to appoint officials who execute the laws—is the one the Court tackles in *Buckley*. As you read it, pay close attention to how the Court defined the Appointment Clause's operative terms: "Officers of the United States," "Heads of Departments," and "Courts of Law." Also be sure to note how the Court defined another critical term that is not used in the Appointments Clause: "significant authority."

The second issue, addressed by the Court's decision in *NLRB v. Noel Canning*, involves a very different aspect of Congress' involvement in the appointments process. The Appointments Clause establishes the "normal" process for filling Executive Branch vacancies. Sometimes, however, use of this process is impracticable because vacancies need to be filled quickly. This is especially true when the President needs to appoint a principal officer and the Senate is not in session to provide its advice and consent. The Recess Appointments Clause (Art. II, § 2, cl. 3) addresses this concern by permitting the President to "to fill up all Vacancies that may happen during the Recess of the Senate, by granting Commissions which shall expire at the End of their next Session." The question in *Noel Canning* was whether the Senate can avoid going into recess—and thus prevent the President from making recess appointments—simply by holding *pro forma* sessions during which it conducts no business.

Buckley v. Valeo
424 U.S. 1 (1975)

PER CURIAM.

[In 1974, Congress significantly amended the Federal Election Campaign Act of 1971 (the "FECA" or the "Act"), creating what the D.C. Circuit called "by far the most comprehensive [] reform legislation passed by Congress concerning the election of the President, Vice-President, and members of Congress." *Buckley v. Valeo*, 519 F.2d 821, 831 (D.C. Cir. 1975). The amended Act provided for the public financing of Presidential elections, capped contributions to candidates for federal elected office, and required the disclosure of federal campaign contributions. Additionally, and most importantly for present purposes, the FECA created the Federal Election Commission (the "FEC" or the "Commission"), an independent agency invested with broad-ranging powers to enforce the Act's provisions. In the Supreme Court, candidates for national political office, their campaigns, and numerous political and legal advocacy groups argued, among other things, that the FECA's method for appointing the agency's Commissioners violated the Appointments Clause.]

IV. THE FEDERAL ELECTION COMMISSION

The 1974 amendments to the Act create an eight-member Federal Election Commission (Commission), and vest in it primary and substantial responsibility for administering and enforcing the Act. The question that we address in this portion of the opinion is whether, in view of the manner in which a majority of its members are appointed, the Commission may under the Constitution exercise the powers conferred upon it. . . .

Chapter 14 of Title 2148 makes the Commission the principal repository of the numerous reports and statements which are required by that chapter to be filed by those engaging in the regulated political activities. Its duties under § 438(a) with respect to these reports and statements include filing and indexing, making them available for public inspection, preservation, and auditing and field investigations. It is directed to "serve as a national clearinghouse for information in respect to the administration of elections." § 438(b).

Beyond these recordkeeping, disclosure, and investigative functions, however, the Commission is given extensive rulemaking and adjudicative powers. Its duty under § 438(a)(10) is "to prescribe suitable rules and regulations to carry out the provisions of . . . chapter (14)." Under § 437d(a)(8) the Commission is empowered to make such rules "as are necessary to carry out the provisions of this Act." Section 437d(a)(9) authorizes it to "formulate general policy with respect to the administration of this Act" and enumerated sections of Title 18's Criminal Code, as to all of which provisions the Commission "has primary jurisdiction with respect to (their) civil enforcement." § 437c(b). The Commission is authorized under § 437f(a) to render advisory opinions with respect to activities possibly violating the Act, the Title 18 sections, or the campaign funding provisions of Title 26, the effect of which is that "(n)otwithstanding any other provision of law, any person with respect to whom an advisory opinion is rendered . . . who acts in good faith in accordance with the provisions and findings (thereof) shall be presumed to be in compliance with the (statutory provision) with respect to which such advisory opinion is rendered." § 437f(b). In the course of administering the provisions for Presidential campaign financing, the Commission may authorize convention expenditures which exceed the statutory limits. 26 U.S.C. § 9008(d)(3) (1970 ed., Supp. IV).

The Commission's enforcement power is both direct and wide ranging. It may institute a civil action for (i) injunctive or other relief against "any acts or practices which constitute or will constitute a violation of this Act," § 437g(a)(5); (ii) declaratory or injunctive relief "as may be appropriate to implement or con(s)true any provisions" of Chapter 95 of Title 26, governing administration of funds for Presidential election campaigns and national party conventions, 26 U.S.C. § 9011(b)(1) (1970 ed., Supp. IV); and (iii) "such injunctive relief as is appropriate to implement any provision" of Chapter 96 of Title 26, governing the payment of matching funds for Presidential primary campaigns, 26 U.S.C. § 9040(c) (1970 ed., Supp. IV). If after the Commission's post-disbursement audit of candidates receiving payments under Chapter 95 or 96 it finds an overpayment, it is empowered to seek repayment of all funds due the Secretary of the Treasury. 26 U.S.C. §§ 9010(b), 9040(b) (1970 ed., Supp. IV). In no respect do the foregoing civil actions require the concurrence of or participation by the Attorney General; conversely, the decision not to seek judicial relief in the above respects would appear to rest solely with the Commission. With respect to the referenced Title 18 sections, § 437g(a)(7) provides that if, after notice and opportunity for a hearing before it, the Commission finds an actual or threatened criminal violation, the Attorney General "upon request by the Commission . . . shall institute a civil action for relief." Finally, as "(a)dditional enforcement authority," § 456(a) authorizes the Commission, after notice and opportunity for hearing, to make "a finding that a person . . . while a candidate for Federal office, failed to file" a required report of contributions or expenditures. If that finding is made within the applicable limitations period for prosecutions, the candidate is thereby "disqualified from becoming a candidate in any future election for Federal office for a period of time beginning on the date of such finding and ending one year after the expiration of the term of the Federal office for which such person was a candidate."

The body in which this authority is reposed consists of eight members. The Secretary of the Senate and the Clerk of the House of Representatives are *ex officio* members of the Commission without the right to vote. Two members are appointed by the President *pro tempore* of the Senate "upon the recommendations of the majority leader of the Senate and the minority leader of the Senate." Two more are to be appointed by the Speaker of the House of Representatives, likewise upon the recommendations of its respective majority and minority leaders. The remaining two members are appointed by the President. Each of the six voting members of the Commission must be confirmed by the majority of both Houses of Congress, and each of the three appointing authorities is forbidden to choose both of their appointees from the same political party. . . .

B. The Merits

Appellants urge that since Congress has given the Commission wide-ranging rulemaking and enforcement powers with respect to the substantive provisions of the Act, Congress is precluded under the principle of separation of powers from vesting in itself the authority to appoint those who will exercise such authority. Their argument is based on the language of Art. II, § 2, cl. 2, of the Constitution, which provides in pertinent part as follows:

(The President) shall nominate, and by and with the Advice and Consent of the Senate, shall appoint . . . all other Officers of the United States, whose

Appointments are not herein otherwise provided for, and which shall be established by Law: but the Congress may by Law vest the Appointment of such inferior Officers, as they think proper, in the President alone, in the Courts of Law, or in the Heads of Departments.

Appellants' argument is that this provision is the exclusive method by which those charged with executing the laws of the United States may be chosen. Congress, they assert, cannot have it both ways. If the Legislature wishes the Commission to exercise all of the conferred powers, then its members are in fact "Officers of the United States" and must be appointed under the Appointments Clause. But if Congress insists upon retaining the power to appoint, then the members of the Commission may not discharge those many functions of the Commission which can be performed only by "Officers of the United States," as that term must be construed within the doctrine of separation of powers.

Appellee Commission and *amici* in support of the Commission urge that the Framers of the Constitution, while mindful of the need for checks and balances among the three branches of the National Government, had no intention of denying to the Legislative Branch authority to appoint its own officers. Congress, either under the Appointments Clause or under its grants of substantive legislative authority and the Necessary and Proper Clause in Art. I, is in their view empowered to provide for the appointment to the Commission in the manner which it did because the Commission is performing "appropriate legislative functions." . . .

2. *The Appointments Clause*

The principle of separation of powers was not simply an abstract generalization in the minds of the Framers: it was woven into the document that they drafted in Philadelphia in the summer of 1787. Article I, § 1, declares: "All legislative Powers herein granted shall be vested in a Congress of the United States." Article II, § 1, vests the executive power "in a President of the United States of America," and Art. III, § 1, declares that "The judicial Power of the United States, shall be vested in one supreme Court, and in such inferior Courts as the Congress may from time to time ordain and establish." The further concern of the Framers of the Constitution with maintenance of the separation of powers is found in the so-called "Ineligibility" and "Incompatibility" Clauses contained in Art. I, § 6:

No Senator or Representative shall, during the Time for which he was elected, be appointed to any civil Office under the Authority of the United States, which shall have been created, or the Emoluments whereof shall have been increased during such time; and no Person holding any Office under the United States, shall be a Member of either House during his Continuance in Office.

It is in the context of these cognate provisions of the document that we must examine the language of Art. II, § 2, cl. 2, which appellants contend provides the only authorization for appointment of those to whom substantial executive or administrative authority is given by statute. . . .

The Appointments Clause could, of course, be read as merely dealing with etiquette or protocol in describing "Officers of the United States," but the drafters had a less frivolous purpose in mind. . . .

We think that the term "Officers of the United States" as used in Art. II . . . is a term intended to have substantive meaning. We think its fair import is that any appointee exercising significant authority pursuant to the laws of the United States is an "Officer of the United States," and must, therefore, be appointed in the manner prescribed by § 2, cl. 2, of that Article.

If "all persons who can be said to hold an office under the government about to be established under the Constitution were intended to be included within one or the other of these modes of appointment," *United States v. Germaine*[, 99 U.S. 508, 510 (1878),] it is difficult to see how the members of the Commission may escape inclusion. If a postmaster first class, *Myers v. United States*, 272 U.S. 52 (1926), and the clerk of a district court, *Ex parte Hennen*, 38 U.S. 225, 13 Pet. 230 (1839), are inferior officers of the United States within the meaning of the Appointments Clause, as they are, surely the Commissioners before us are at the very least such "inferior Officers" within the meaning of that Clause.

Although two members of the Commission are initially selected by the President, his nominations are subject to confirmation not merely by the Senate, but by the House of Representatives as well. The remaining four voting members of the Commission are appointed by the President *pro tempore* of the Senate and by the Speaker of the House. While the second part of the Clause authorizes Congress to vest the appointment of the officers described in that part in "the Courts of Law, or in the Heads of Departments," neither the Speaker of the House nor the President *pro tempore* of the Senate comes within this language.

The phrase "Heads of Departments," used as it is in conjunction with the phrase "Courts of Law," suggests that the Departments referred to are themselves in the Executive Branch or at least have some connection with that branch. While the Clause expressly authorizes Congress to vest the appointment of certain officers in the "Courts of Law," the absence of similar language to include Congress must mean that neither Congress nor its officers were included within the language "Heads of Departments" in this part of cl. 2.

Thus with respect to four of the six voting members of the Commission, neither the President, the head of any department, nor the Judiciary has any voice in their selection.

The Appointments Clause specifies the method of appointment only for "Officers of the United States" whose appointment is not "otherwise provided for" in the Constitution. But there is no provision of the Constitution remotely providing any alternative means for the selection of the members of the Commission or for anybody like them. . . .

3. The Commission's Powers

. . . [O]n the assumption that all of the powers granted in the statute may be exercised by an agency whose members have been appointed in accordance with the Appointments Clause, the ultimate question is which, if any, of those powers may be exercised by the present voting Commissioners, none of whom was appointed as provided by that Clause. Our previous description of the statutory provisions disclosed that the Commission's powers fall generally into three categories: functions relating to the flow of necessary information receipt, dissemination, and investigation; functions with respect to the Commission's task of fleshing out the statute rulemaking and advisory opinions; and functions necessary to ensure compliance with the statute and rules informal procedures, administrative determinations and hearings, and civil suits.

Insofar as the powers confided in the Commission are essentially of an investigative and informative nature, falling in the same general category as those powers which Congress might delegate to one of its own committees, there can be no question that the Commission as presently constituted may exercise them. . . . As this Court stated in *McGrain, supra*, 273 U.S., at 175:

> A legislative body cannot legislate wisely or effectively in the absence of information respecting the conditions which the legislation is intended to affect or change; and where the legislative body does not itself possess the requisite information which not infrequently is true recourse must be had to others who do possess it. Experience has taught that mere requests for such information often are unavailing, and also that information which is volunteered is not always accurate or complete; so some means of compulsion are essential to obtain what is needed. All this was true before and when the Constitution was framed and adopted. In that period the power of inquiry, with enforcing process, was regarded and employed as a necessary and appropriate attribute of the power to legislate, indeed, was treated as inhering in it.

But when we go beyond this type of authority to the more substantial powers exercised by the Commission, we reach a different result. The Commission's enforcement power, exemplified by its discretionary power to seek judicial relief, is authority that cannot possibly be regarded as merely in aid of the legislative function of Congress. A lawsuit is the ultimate remedy for a breach of the law, and it is to the President, and not to the Congress, that the Constitution entrusts the responsibility to "take Care that the Laws be faithfully executed." Art. II, § 3.

Congress may undoubtedly under the Necessary and Proper Clause create "offices" in the generic sense and provide such method of appointment to those "offices" as it chooses. But Congress' power under that Clause is inevitably bounded by the express language of Art. II, § 2, cl. 2, and unless the method it provides comports with the latter, the holders of those offices will not be "Officers of the United States." They may, therefore, properly perform duties only in aid of those functions that Congress may carry out by itself, or in an area sufficiently removed from the administration and enforcement of the public law as to permit their being performed by persons not "Officers of the United States." . . .

We hold that these provisions of the Act, vesting in the Commission primary responsibility for conducting civil litigation in the courts of the United States for vindicating public rights, violate Art. II, § 2, cl. 2, of the Constitution. Such functions may be discharged only by persons who are "Officers of the United States" within the language of that section.

All aspects of the Act are brought within the Commission's broad administrative powers: rulemaking, advisory opinions, and determinations of eligibility for [campaign] funds and even for federal elective office itself. These functions, exercised free from day-to-day supervision of either Congress or the Executive Branch, are more legislative and judicial in nature than are the Commission's enforcement powers, and are of kinds usually performed by independent regulatory agencies or by some department in the Executive Branch under the direction of an Act of Congress. Congress viewed these broad powers as essential to effective and impartial administration of the entire substantive framework of the Act. Yet each of these functions also represents the performance of a significant governmental duty exercised pursuant to a public law. While the President may not insist that such functions be delegated to an appointee of his removable at will, *Humphrey's Executor v. United States*, 295 U.S. 602 (1935), none of them operates merely in aid of congressional authority to legislate or is sufficiently removed from the administration and enforcement of public law to allow it to be performed by the present Commission. These administrative functions may therefore be exercised only by persons who are "Officers of the United States . . . ."

CONCLUSION

. . . [W]e hold that most of the powers conferred by the Act upon the Federal Election Commission can be exercised only by "Officers of the United States," appointed in conformity with Art. II, § 2, cl. 2, of the Constitution, and therefore cannot be exercised by the Commission as presently constituted. . . .

So ordered.

Mr. Justice STEVENS took no part in the consideration or decision of these cases.

QUESTION SET 8.3

Review & Synthesis

1. Why did the appointments of the FEC Commissioners violate the Appointments Clause? In other words, how did the Supreme Court connect the manner of their appointments to the "significant authority" vested in them by the Federal Election Campaign Act?

2. Consider the FEC's appointment structure. Each of the federal government's political "departments"—the House, the Senate, and the White House—picked two Commissioners. Both chambers of Congress had to approve each of these appointments by majority vote. No "department" could select both of its nominees from the same political party. Taken together, do you think the FEC was more susceptible to or insulated from Congress' political influence?

3. Would you characterize the Court's reasoning here as functionalistic (applying the underlying principles evident in the Constitution's text) or as formalistic (adhering strictly to the precise procedures laid out in the Constitution's text)? Would the constitutional defect found by the Court have been eliminated had the Federal Election Campaign Act strictly limited the post-appointment contact members of Congress could have with the Commissioners?

4. Two FEC Commissioners—the Secretary of the Senate and the Clerk of the House of Representatives—were appointed *ex officio* and did not vote. Accordingly, it appeared that they did not share the "significant authority" wielded by the rest of the Commission. Assuming that the other six Commissioners were reappointed in accordance with the Appointments Clause, could they remain on the Commission as nonvoting members?

5. One could imagine Congress placing qualifications on an Executive Branch position that are so stringent that almost no one is eligible for appointment to it. Such a maneuver would effectively negate the President's appointment power for that position. Did *Buckley* place any limits on Congress' ability to do this? Do generalized separation-of-powers principles?

Application & Analysis

1. The Securities and Exchange Commission has statutory authority to enforce the nation's securities laws. It often does so through adversarial administrative proceedings against alleged scofflaws. One of the

Commission's five administrative law judges ("ALJs") usually presides over these proceedings. All of these ALJs were hired by SEC staff members rather than by the Commissioners themselves, and all of them hold career appointments. They have the "authority to do all things necessary and appropriate" to ensure a fair and orderly adversarial proceeding. 17 C.F.R. §§ 201.111, 200.14(a). This includes the power to take testimony, conduct trials, rule on the admissibility of evidence, and enforce compliance with discovery and other orders. At the conclusion of these proceedings, the ALJs issue initial decisions that the Commission can review on administrative appeal or adopt as final decisions without prior review.

The SEC charged Ron Loria with violating various securities laws and assigned an ALJ to adjudicate his case. After a hearing, the ALJ issued an initial decision concluding that Loria had violated the law and suggesting that sanctions be imposed on him. On appeal, the Commissioners rejected Loria's argument that the initial decision was void because the ALJ was an "Officer of the United States" who had not been constitutionally appointed.

Loria now appeals the SEC's decision to the D.C. Circuit, making the same argument. You are a clerk for one of the judges assigned to the appeal. Write a brief memorandum addressing its merits.

2. Created by executive order, the President's Commission on Organized Crime conducts national analyses of organized crime, including its nature, its sources and amounts of income, information on participants, and evaluation of pertinent federal laws. The President appointed 19 individuals to the Commission, including an active United States Court of Appeals judge to serve as chairperson. All of the appointees are volunteers; none of them are paid for their service. To support the Commission in its work, Congress enacted a statute that grants it the authority to hold hearings and issue subpoenas. The statute designates the Commission a "law enforcement agency" and deems its members investigative or law enforcement officers for purposes of access to wiretap information. These designations give the Commission access to documents and other evidence not available to the Judiciary or the general public. Further, the statute authorizes the Commission to issue subpoenas that may be enforced by the federal district courts, and authorizes it to request immunity for its witnesses from the Attorney General. The statute also instructs the Attorney General to provide the Commission with administrative services, funds, facilities, staff, and other supports.

The Commission issued a subpoena to Jay Jones, ordering him to appear at a hearing in Chicago, Illinois, at the end of next month. Rather than responding, Jones filed a motion in the U.S. District Court for the Northern District of Illinois to quash the subpoena. He argues that the

Commission lacks the authority to issue it because its members were unconstitutionally appointed under the separation-of-powers principles discussed in *Buckley v. Valeo*.

You clerk for the district judge who must rule on Jones' motion. Write a brief memorandum analyzing his argument.

In *The Federalist No. 76*, Alexander Hamilton explained that the Appointment Clause's Senate confirmation requirement worked to prevent Presidential appointments based on bias or favoritism. In *The Federalist No. 67*, he explained that the purpose of the Recess Appointments Clause was somewhat different. It served as a supplement to the Appointments Clause and ensured the President's ability to quickly fill government positions when the Senate was not in session.

Of course, this authority could be abused by either the President or the Senate. A broad interpretation of what it means for the Senate to be "in recess" would expand opportunities for the President to bypass the advice-and-consent procedure and the check it places on his or her hiring discretion along with it. A narrow interpretation of "in recess," by contrast, could cripple the President's ability to fill vacancies when circumstances warrant expediency. Congress schedules its time in two-year increments, which coincides with the election of all House Representatives and one-third of Senators. Congress refers to each two-year increment by number (i.e., the "116th Congress"). Within each two-year period, Congress generally schedules two regular "sessions" to satisfy the constitutional requirement that the body meet every year. The breaks between those regular sessions are called "inter-session" breaks, and they have generally been accepted as recesses for purposes of the Recess Appointments Clause. Over time, Congress began to take breaks of differing lengths *within* its regular yearly sessions. Less clear was whether these breaks, called "intra-session" breaks, also constituted recesses for Recess Appointments Clause purposes.

Another interpretive problem appears with respect to the timing of vacancies. Is the President's recess appointment power triggered whenever a vacancy arises? If so, he or she could simply wait until the Senate was in recess—whether intra-session or inter-session—then appoint someone to fill a vacancy, and have that person serve until the end of the following session. If the President's recess appointment power is triggered only when a vacancy happens to first arise during a recess, then his or her opportunities to utilize it are much more limited.

President Obama and the Republican-led Senate disagreed on these points. Obama had tried in vain to get Senate confirmation for three nominees to the National Labor Relations Board. The Board is a five-member body so, without these appointments, it lacked the quorum needed to officially conduct business. Using his power under the Recess Appointments Clause, the President appointed the stalled nominees during a three-day break between two "*pro forma*" Senate sessions. The following case resulted.

National Labor Relations Board v. Noel Canning
573 U.S. 513 (2014)

Justice BREYER delivered the opinion of the Court.

Ordinarily the President must obtain "the Advice and Consent of the Senate" before appointing an "Office[r] of the United States." U.S. Const., Art. II, § 2, cl. 2. But the Recess Appointments Clause creates an exception. It gives the President alone the power "to fill up all Vacancies that may happen during the Recess of the Senate, by granting Commissions which shall expire at the End of their next Session." Art. II, § 2, cl. 3. We here consider three questions about the application of this Clause.

The first concerns the scope of the words "recess of the Senate." Does that phrase refer only to an inter-session recess (i.e., a break between formal sessions of Congress), or does it also include an intra-session recess, such as a summer recess in the midst of a session? We conclude that the Clause applies to both kinds of recess.

The second question concerns the scope of the words "vacancies that may happen." Does that phrase refer only to vacancies that first come into existence during a recess, or does it also include vacancies that arise prior to a recess but continue to exist during the recess? We conclude that the Clause applies to both kinds of vacancy.

The third question concerns calculation of the length of a "recess." The President made the appointments here at issue on January 4, 2012. At that time the Senate was in recess pursuant to a December 17, 2011, resolution providing for a series of brief recesses punctuated by "*pro forma* session[s]," with "no business . . . transacted," every Tuesday and Friday through January 20, 2012. S.J., 112th Cong., 1st Sess., 923 (2011) (hereinafter 2011 S.J.). In calculating the length of a recess are we to ignore the *pro forma* sessions, thereby treating the series of brief recesses as a single, month-long recess? We conclude that we cannot ignore these *pro forma* sessions.

Our answer to the third question means that, when the appointments before us took place, the Senate was in the midst of a 3-day recess. Three days is too short a time to bring a recess within the scope of the Clause. Thus we conclude that the President lacked the power to make the recess appointments here at issue.

I

The case before us arises out of a labor dispute. The National Labor Relations Board (NLRB) found that a Pepsi-Cola distributor, Noel Canning, had unlawfully refused to reduce to writing and execute a collective-bargaining agreement with a labor union. The Board ordered the distributor to execute the agreement and to make employees whole for any losses.

The Pepsi-Cola distributor subsequently asked the Court of Appeals for the District of Columbia Circuit to set the Board's order aside. It claimed that three of the five Board members had been invalidly appointed, leaving the Board without the three lawfully appointed members necessary for it to act.

The three members in question were Sharon Block, Richard Griffin, and Terence Flynn. In 2011 the President had nominated each of them to the Board. As of January 2012, Flynn's nomination had been pending in the Senate awaiting confirmation for approximately a year. The nominations of each of the other two had been pending for a few weeks. On January 4, 2012, the President, invoking the Recess Appointments Clause, appointed all three to the Board.

The distributor argued that the Recess Appointments Clause did not authorize those appointments. It pointed out that on December 17, 2011, the Senate, by unanimous consent, had adopted a resolution providing that it would take a series of brief recesses beginning the following day. Pursuant to that resolution, the Senate held *pro forma* sessions every Tuesday and Friday until it returned for ordinary business on January 23, 2012. The President's January 4 appointments were made between the January 3 and January 6 *pro forma* sessions. In the distributor's view, each *pro forma* session terminated the immediately preceding recess. Accordingly, the appointments were made during a 3-day adjournment, which is not long enough to trigger the Recess Appointments Clause. . . .

III

. . . In our view, the phrase "the recess" includes an intra-session recess of substantial length. Its words taken literally can refer to both types of recess. Founding-era dictionaries define the word "recess," much as we do today, simply as "a period of cessation from usual work." 13 The Oxford English Dictionary 322-323 (2d ed. 1989) (hereinafter OED) (citing 18th- and 19th-century sources for that definition of "recess"). The Founders themselves used the word to refer to intra-session, as well as to inter-session, breaks. *See, e.g.*, 3 Records of the Federal Convention of 1787, p. 76 (M. Farrand rev. 1966) (hereinafter Farrand) (letter from George Washington to John Jay using "the recess" to refer to an intra-session break of the Constitutional Convention); id., at 191 (speech of Luther Martin with a similar usage).

We recognize that the word "the" in "the recess" might suggest that the phrase refers to the single break separating formal sessions of Congress. That is because the word "the" frequently (but not always) indicates "a particular thing." 2 Johnson 2003. But the word can also refer "to a term used generically or universally." 17 OED 879. . . .

The constitutional text is . . . ambiguous. And we believe the Clause's purpose demands the broader interpretation. The Clause gives the President authority to make appointments during "the recess of the Senate" so that the President can ensure the continued functioning of the Federal Government when the Senate is away. The Senate is equally away during both an inter-session and an intra-session recess, and its capacity to participate in the appointments process has nothing to do with the words it uses to signal its departure. . . .

The greater interpretive problem is determining how long a recess must be in order to fall within the Clause. Is a break of a week, or a day, or an hour too short to count as a "recess"? The Clause itself does not say. And Justice Scalia claims that this silence itself shows that the Framers intended the Clause to apply only to an inter-session recess.

We disagree. For one thing, the most likely reason the Framers did not place a textual floor underneath the word "recess" is that they did not foresee the need for one. They might have expected that the Senate would meet for a single session lasting at most half a year. The Federalist No. 84, at 596 (A. Hamilton). And they might not have anticipated that intra-session recesses would become lengthier and more significant than inter-session ones. The Framers' lack of clairvoyance on that point is not dispositive. Unlike Justice Scalia, we think it most consistent with our constitutional structure to presume that the Framers would have allowed intra-session recess appointments where there was a long history of such practice.

Moreover, the lack of a textual floor raises a problem that plagues both interpretations — Justice Scalia's and ours. Today a brief inter-session recess is just as possible as a brief intra-session recess. And though Justice Scalia says that the "notion that the Constitution empowers the President to make unilateral appointments every time the Senate takes a half-hour lunch break is so absurd as to be self-refuting," he must immediately concede (in a footnote) that the President "can make recess appointments during any break between sessions, *no matter how short.*"

Even the Solicitor General, arguing for a broader interpretation, acknowledges that there is a lower limit applicable to both kinds of recess. He argues that the lower limit should be three days by analogy to the Adjournments Clause of the Constitution. That Clause says: "Neither House, during the Session of Congress, shall, without the Consent of the other, adjourn for more than three days." Art. I, § 5, cl. 4.

We agree with the Solicitor General that a 3-day recess would be too short. The Adjournments Clause reflects the fact that a 3-day break is not a significant interruption of legislative business. As the Solicitor General says, it is constitutionally *de minimis*. A Senate recess that is so short that it does not require the consent of the House is not long enough to trigger the President's recess-appointment power.

That is not to say that the President may make recess appointments during any recess that is "more than three days." Art. I, § 5, cl. 4. The Recess Appointments Clause seeks to permit the Executive Branch to function smoothly when Congress is unavailable. And though Congress has taken short breaks for almost 200 years, and there have been many thousands of recess appointments in that time, we have not found a single example of a recess appointment made during an intra-session recess that was shorter than 10 days. Nor has the Solicitor General. Indeed, the Office of Legal Counsel once informally advised against making a recess appointment during a 6-day intra-session recess. The lack of examples suggests that the recess-appointment power is not needed in that context.

. . . We therefore conclude, in light of historical practice, that a recess of more than 3 days but less than 10 days is presumptively too short to fall within the Clause. We add the word "presumptively" to leave open the possibility that some very unusual circumstance—a national catastrophe, for instance, that renders the Senate unavailable but calls for an urgent response—could demand the exercise of the recess-appointment power during a shorter break. . . .

IV

The second question concerns the scope of the phrase "vacancies *that may happen* during the recess of the Senate." Art. II, § 2, cl. 3 (emphasis added). All agree that the phrase applies to vacancies that initially occur during a recess. But does it also apply to vacancies that initially occur before a recess and continue to exist during the recess? In our view the phrase applies to both kinds of vacancy.

We believe that the Clause's language, read literally, permits, though it does not naturally favor, our broader interpretation. We concede that the most natural meaning of "happens" as applied to a "vacancy" (at least to a modern ear) is that the vacancy "happens" when it initially occurs. *See* 1 Johnson 913 (defining "happen" in relevant part as meaning "[t]o fall out; to chance; to come to pass"). But that is not the only possible way to use the word. . . .

The Clause's purpose strongly supports the broader interpretation. That purpose is to permit the President to obtain the assistance of subordinate officers when the Senate, due to its recess, cannot confirm them. . . .

Examples are not difficult to imagine: An ambassadorial post falls vacant too soon before the recess begins for the President to appoint a replacement; the Senate rejects a President's nominee just before a recess, too late to select another. [Attorney General William] Wirt explained that the "substantial purpose of the constitution was to keep these offices filled," and "if the President shall not have the power to fill a vacancy thus circumstanced, . . . the substance of the constitution will be sacrificed to a dubious construction of its letter." [1 Op. Atty. Gen. 631, 632 (1832).] Thus the broader construction, encompassing vacancies that initially occur before the beginning of a recess, is the "only construction of the constitution which is compatible with its spirit, reason, and purposes; while, at the same time, it offers no violence to its language." *Id.*, at 633. . . .

Historical practice over the past 200 years strongly favors the broader interpretation. The tradition of applying the Clause to pre-recess vacancies dates at least to President James Madison. There is no undisputed record of Presidents George Washington, John Adams, or Thomas Jefferson making such an appointment. . . .

The upshot is that the President has consistently and frequently interpreted the Recess Appointments Clause to apply to vacancies that initially occur before, but continue to exist during, a recess of the Senate. The Senate as a body has not countered this practice for nearly three-quarters of a century, perhaps longer. The tradition is long enough to entitle the practice "to great regard in determining the true construction" of the constitutional provision. *The Pocket Veto Case*, 279 U.S. 655, 690 (1929). And we are reluctant to upset this traditional practice where doing so would seriously shrink the authority that Presidents have believed existed and have exercised for so long.

In light of some linguistic ambiguity, the basic purpose of the Clause, and the historical practice we have described, we conclude that the phrase "all vacancies" includes vacancies that come into existence while the Senate is in session.

V

The third question concerns the calculation of the length of the Senate's "recess." On December 17, 2011, the Senate by unanimous consent adopted a resolution to convene "*pro forma* session[s]" only, with "no business . . . transacted," on every Tuesday and Friday from December 20, 2011, through January 20, 2012. 2011 S.J. 923. At the end of each *pro forma* session, the Senate would "adjourn until" the following *pro forma* session. *Ibid.* During that period, the Senate convened and adjourned as agreed. It held *pro forma* sessions on December 20, 23, 27, and 30, and on January 3, 6, 10, 13, 17, and 20; and at the end of each *pro forma* session, it adjourned until the time and date of the next. *Id.*, at 923-924.

The President made the recess appointments before us on January 4, 2012, in between the January 3 and the January 6 *pro forma* sessions. We must determine the significance of these sessions—that is, whether, for purposes of the Clause, we should treat them as periods when the Senate was in session or as periods when it was in recess. . . .

In our view . . . the *pro forma* sessions count as sessions, not as periods of recess. We hold that, for purposes of the Recess Appointments Clause, the Senate is in session when it says it is, provided that, under its own rules, it retains the capacity to transact Senate business. The Senate met that standard here.

The standard we apply is consistent with the Constitution's broad delegation of authority to the Senate to determine how and when to conduct its business. The Constitution explicitly empowers the Senate to "determine the Rules of its Proceedings." Art. I, § 5, cl. 2. And we have held that "all matters of method are open to the determination" of the Senate, as long as there is "a reasonable relation between the mode or method of proceeding established by the rule and the result which is sought to be attained" and the rule does not "ignore constitutional restraints or violate fundamental rights." *United States v. Ballin*, 144 U.S. 1, 5 (1892).

In addition, the Constitution provides the Senate with extensive control over its schedule. . . . The Constitution thus gives the Senate wide latitude to determine whether and when to have a session, as well as how to conduct the session. This suggests that the Senate's determination about what constitutes a session should merit great respect.

Furthermore, this Court's precedents reflect the breadth of the power constitutionally delegated to the Senate. We generally take at face value the Senate's own report of its actions. When, for example, "the presiding officers" of the House and Senate sign an enrolled bill (and the President "approve[s]" it), "its authentication as a bill that has passed Congress should be deemed complete and unimpeachable." *Marshall Field & Co. v. Clark*, 143 U.S. 649, 672 (1892). By the same principle, when the Journal of the Senate indicates that a quorum was present, under a valid Senate rule, at the time the Senate passed a bill, we will not consider an argument that a quorum was not, in fact, present. *Ballin, supra*, at 9. The Constitution requires the Senate to keep its Journal, and "if reference may be had to" it, "it must be assumed to speak the truth," *Ballin, supra*, at 4.

For these reasons, we conclude that we must give great weight to the Senate's own determination of when it is and when it is not in session. But our deference to the Senate cannot be absolute. When the Senate is without the capacity to act, under its own rules, it is not in session even if it so declares. In that circumstance, the Senate is not simply unlikely or unwilling to act upon nominations of the President. It is unable to do so. The purpose of the Clause is to ensure the continued functioning of the Federal Government while the Senate is unavailable. This purpose would count for little were we to treat the Senate as though it were in session even when it lacks the ability to provide its "advice and consent." Art. II, § 2, cl. 2. Accordingly, we conclude that when the Senate declares that it is in session and possesses the capacity, under its own rules, to conduct business, it is in session for purposes of the Clause.

Applying this standard, we find that the *pro forma* sessions were sessions for purposes of the Clause. First, the Senate said it was in session. . . .

Second, the Senate's rules make clear that during its *pro forma* sessions, despite its resolution that it would conduct no business, the Senate retained the power to conduct business. During any *pro forma* session, the Senate could have conducted business simply by passing a unanimous consent agreement. Senate rules presume that a quorum is present unless a present Senator questions it. And when the Senate has a quorum, an agreement is unanimously passed if, upon its proposal, no present Senator objects. It is consequently unsurprising that the Senate has enacted legislation during *pro forma* sessions even when it has said that no business will be transacted. . . .

By way of contrast, we do not see how the Senate could conduct business during a recess. It could terminate the recess and then, when in session, pass a bill. But in that case, of course, the Senate would no longer be in recess. It would be in session. And that is the crucial point. Senate rules make clear that, once in session, the Senate can act even if it has earlier said that it would not.

. . . [T]he Solicitor General warns that our holding may "'disrup[t] the proper balance between the coordinate branches by preventing the Executive Branch from accomplishing its constitutionally assigned functions.'" Brief for Petitioner 64 (quoting *Morrison v. Olson*, 487 U.S. 654, 695 (1988); alteration in original). We do not see, however, how our holding could significantly alter the constitutional balance. Most appointments are not controversial and do not produce friction between the branches. Where political controversy is serious, the Senate unquestionably has other methods of preventing recess appointments. As the Solicitor General concedes, the Senate could preclude the President from making recess appointments by holding a series of twice-a-week ordinary (not *pro forma*) sessions. . . .

Regardless, the Recess Appointments Clause is not designed to overcome serious institutional friction. It simply provides a subsidiary method for appointing officials when the Senate is away during a recess. Here, as in other contexts, friction between the branches is an inevitable consequence of our constitutional structure. . . .

VI

. . . Given our answer to the last question before us, we conclude that the Recess Appointments Clause does not give the President the constitutional authority to make the appointments here at issue. Because the Court of Appeals reached the same ultimate conclusion (though for reasons we reject), its judgment is affirmed.

It is so ordered.

Justice SCALIA, with whom THE CHIEF JUSTICE, Justice THOMAS, and Justice ALITO join, concurring in the judgment. . . .

I. OUR RESPONSIBILITY

Today's majority disregards two overarching principles that ought to guide our consideration of the questions presented here.

First, the Constitution's core, government-structuring provisions are no less critical to preserving liberty than are the later adopted provisions of the Bill of Rights. . . . Those structural provisions reflect the founding generation's deep conviction that "checks and balances were the foundation of a structure of government that would protect liberty." *Bowsher v. Synar*, 478 U.S. 714, 722 (1986). . . .

Second and relatedly, when questions involving the Constitution's government-structuring provisions are presented in a justiciable case, it is the solemn responsibility of the Judicial Branch " 'to say what the law is.' " *Zivotofsky v. Clinton*, 566 U.S. 189, 196 (2012) (quoting *Marbury v. Madison*, 1 Cranch 137, 177 (1803)). This Court does not defer to the other branches' resolution of such controversies. . . .

Of course, where a governmental practice has been open, widespread, and unchallenged since the early days of the Republic, the practice should guide our interpretation of an ambiguous constitutional provision. That is a necessary corollary of the principle that the political branches cannot by agreement alter the constitutional structure. Plainly, then, a self-aggrandizing practice adopted by one branch well after the founding, often challenged, and never before blessed by this Court—in other words, the sort of practice on which the majority relies in this case—does not relieve us of our duty to interpret the Constitution in light of its text, structure, and original understanding. . . .

II. INTRA–SESSION BREAKS

A sensible interpretation of the Recess Appointments Clause should start by recognizing that the Clause uses the term "Recess" in contradistinction to the term "Session." As Alexander Hamilton wrote: "The time within which the power is to operate 'during the recess of the Senate' and the duration of the appointments 'to the end of the next session' of that body, conspire to elucidate the sense of the provision." The Federalist No. 67, p. 455 (J. Cooke ed. 1961).

In the founding era, the terms "recess" and "session" had well-understood meanings in the marking-out of legislative time. The life of each elected Congress typically consisted (as it still does) of two or more formal sessions separated by adjournments "*sine die,*" that is, without a specified return date. The period between two sessions was known as "the recess." By contrast, other provisions of the Constitution use the verb "adjourn" rather than "recess" to refer to the commencement of breaks during a formal legislative session.

The dictionary definitions of "recess" on which the majority relies provide no such principle. On the contrary, they make clear that in colloquial usage, a recess could include any suspension of legislative business, no matter how short. . . . The notion that the Constitution empowers the President to make unilateral appointments every time the Senate takes a half-hour lunch break is so absurd as to be self-refuting. But that, in the majority's view, is what the text authorizes. . . .

To avoid the absurd results that follow from its colloquial reading of "the Recess," the majority is forced to declare that some intra-session breaks—though undisputedly within the phrase's colloquial meaning—are simply "too short to trigger the Recess Appointments Clause." But it identifies no textual basis whatsoever for limiting the length of "the Recess," nor does it point to any clear standard for determining how short is too short. It is inconceivable that the Framers would have left the circumstances in which the President could exercise such a significant and potentially dangerous power so utterly indeterminate. . . . [O]n the majority's view, when the first Senate considered taking a 1-month break, a 3-day weekend, or a half-hour siesta, it had no way of knowing whether the President would be constitutionally authorized to appoint officers in its absence. . . .

An interpretation that calls for this kind of judicial adventurism cannot be correct. Indeed, if the Clause really did use "Recess" in its colloquial sense, then there would be no "judicially discoverable and manageable standard for resolving" whether a particular break was long enough to trigger the recess-appointment power, making that a nonjusticiable political question.

III. PRE-RECESS VACANCIES

. . . [N]o reasonable reader would have understood the Recess Appointments Clause to use the word "happen" in the majority's "happen to be" sense, and thus to empower the President to fill all vacancies that might exist during a recess, regardless of when they arose. For one thing, the Clause's language would have been a surpassingly odd way of giving the President that power. The Clause easily could have been written to convey that meaning clearly: It could have referred to "all Vacancies that may exist during the Recess," or it could have omitted the qualifying phrase entirely and simply authorized the President to "fill up all Vacancies during the Recess." Given those readily available alternative phrasings, the reasonable reader might have wondered, why would any intelligent drafter intending the majority's reading have inserted the words "that may happen"—words that, as the majority admits, make the majority's desired reading awkward and unnatural, and that must be effectively read out of the Clause to achieve that reading?

For another thing, the majority's reading not only strains the Clause's language but distorts its constitutional role, which was meant to be subordinate. As Hamilton explained, appointment with the advice and consent of the Senate was to be "the general mode of appointing officers of the United States." The Federalist No. 67, at 455. The Senate's check on the President's appointment power was seen as vital because "'manipulation of official appointments' had long been one of the American revolutionary generation's greatest grievances against executive power." *Freytag*, 501 U.S., at 883. The unilateral power conferred on the President by the Recess Appointments Clause was therefore understood to be "nothing more than a supplement" to the "general method" of advice and consent. The Federalist No. 67, at 455 . . . .

IV. CONCLUSION

The real tragedy of today's decision is not simply the abolition of the Constitution's limits on the recess-appointment power and the substitution of a novel framework invented by this Court. It is the damage done to our separation-of-powers jurisprudence more generally. It is not every day that we encounter a proper case or controversy requiring interpretation of the Constitution's structural provisions. Most of the time, the interpretation of those provisions is left to the political branches—which, in deciding how much respect to afford the constitutional text, often take their cues from this Court. We should therefore take every opportunity to affirm the primacy of the Constitution's enduring principles over the politics of the moment. Our failure to do so today will resonate well beyond the particular dispute at hand. Sad, but true: The Court's embrace of the adverse-possession theory of executive power (a characterization the majority resists but does not refute) will be cited in diverse contexts, including those presently unimagined, and will have the effect of aggrandizing the Presidency beyond its constitutional bounds and undermining respect for the separation of powers.

I concur only in the judgment.

QUESTION SET 8.4

Review & Synthesis

1. Justice Breyer, writing for the majority, and Justice Scalia, writing for the concurrence, disagreed on how the term "recess" should be interpreted for purposes of the Recess Appointments Clause. Justice Breyer concluded that a "recess" can occur both during and in between annual sessions of Congress. Justice Scalia rejected this view, arguing instead that "recess" refers only to breaks between official sessions of Congress whereas

"adjournments" refer to the breaks taken during them. Which interpretation do you find more persuasive?

    a. Consider the possible effect of each interpretation on the President's ability to fill Executive Branch vacancies. Which interpretation runs the greater risk of allowing the President to bypass the normal appointments process, and the Senate's check on Presidential discretion that comes with it? Alternatively, is the more pressing concern that the Senate could thwart the President's execution of the laws by remaining in session and refusing to confirm his or her nominees?

    b. Would you characterize Justice Breyer's analysis as functionalistic or formalistic? Justice Scalia's? How does the reasoning in *Noel Canning* compare with the Court's reasoning in *INS v. Chadha* and *Clinton v. New York*?

2. Consider the Court's conclusion that a vacancy can "happen" either before or during a Senate recess. Does this interpretation of the Recess Appointments Clause have the potential to make its use the rule, rather than the exception it was intended to be? What would stop a president—regardless of when a vacancy opens up—from simply waiting until the Senate goes into recess to make his or her appointments? Relatedly, the Court adopted this interpretation while conceding that the most natural interpretation of the term "happens" would restrict the Clause's application to when a vacancy *initially* opens up. What reasons does the Court give for not adopting this interpretation? Are you persuaded by them?

D. REMOVAL

It is understandable that Congress would want to secure for itself a significant role in appointing Officers of the United States. With such authority firmly in hand, Congress would have a powerful additional tool by which to influence federal administrative policy formation and implementation. Even if the Constitution permitted Congress to wield such appointments power, however, that power would be an incomplete method of control at best. After all, its chosen administrator could act quite differently than expected once firmly ensconced in the agency. In such a circumstance, the power of appointment taken alone may not provide Congress (or the President for that matter) with a sufficient means of disciplining the wayward administrator's conduct. An arguably more potent—and hence more desirable—control mechanism is the authority to remove Executive Branch officials.

As we have seen, Article II expressly addresses the appointments power. It vests the President with the authority to appoint "principal" or "superior" officers subject to the advice and consent of the Senate. It then gives Congress discretion as to whether "inferior officers" are appointed by the President, the "Heads of Departments," or the "Courts of Law." Contrast this with how little the document says about the power to remove these officers. Apart from the Impeachment and Removal Clauses (Art. I, § 3, cls. 6, 7), the Constitution does not indicate how or by whom these officials may be stripped of their positions. Curiously, records indicate that the subject was not discussed by the delegates to the Constitutional Convention of 1787. Rather, debate on it was not held until the First Congress, in what is now referred to as the Decision of 1789.

Early in Congress' first session, a plan was introduced in the House of Representatives to create the first executive departments of the new federal government. James Madison moved for the creation of three—Treasury, War, and Foreign Affairs (i.e., the State Department)—each led by secretaries appointable by the President (with the Senate's advice and consent), but removable by the President alone. The motion sparked several days of debate over how the Constitution distributed the removal power between Congress and the President. In essence, the Members tried to draw definitive meaning from the document's ambiguities and silences. Some argued that the Impeachment and Removal Clauses were the exclusive means by which such officers could be relieved of their duties. Others judged that the Constitution's silence on the issue indicated that its resolution was left to Congress' discretion. Still others believed that removal should track appointments, and so the Senate should have to give its advice and consent before a removal could be effected by the President. Finally, several Representatives (including Madison) argued that the President alone must have the power to remove Executive Branch officers. Per Madison: "If the president should possess alone the power of removal from office, those who are employed in the execution of the law will be in their proper situation, and the chain of dependence be preserved; the lowest officers, the middle grade, and the highest, will depend, as they ought, on the president, and the president on the community. The chain of dependence therefore terminates in the supreme body, namely, in the people." CHARLES C. THACH, JR., THE CREATION OF THE PRESIDENCY, 1775-1789: A STUDY IN CONSTITUTIONAL HISTORY 147 (1922) (citing 1 ANNALS OF CONGRESS 518 (1789)). *See generally* Saikrishna Prakash, *New Light on the Decision of 1789,* 91 CORNELL L. REV. 1021 (2006). Madison later added: "I conceive that if any power whatsoever is in its nature executive it is the power of appointing, overseeing, and controlling those who execute the laws." THACH, *supra,* at 152 (citing 1 ANNALS OF CONG. 481-82 (June 16, 1789)).

Ultimately, the Decision of 1789's "decision" was to leave resolution of the constitutional issue for another day. Congress allowed the President to hold exclusive removal power over the Secretaries of Treasury, War, and Foreign Affairs. Doing so accommodated those who thought the Constitution vested that discretion in the President anyway. It also accommodated those who thought the Constitution's silence on the matter was an implicit delegation of authority to Congress; granting the President at-will removal did not foreclose the possibility that Congress could strip or encumber that authority later on.

During the following century, the Supreme Court opined on the President's general authority to direct the actions of Executive Branch officials. One if its most notable cases in this regard was *Kendall v. United States*, 37 U.S. (12 Pet.) 524 (1838). There, Postmaster General Amos Kendall refused to pay monies owed to a Mr. Stokes, who had performed delivery services for the Post Office Department. Stokes sought a writ of mandamus in federal court ordering Kendall to make payment. Kendall countered that he was acting under President Martin Van Buren's orders. The Court rejected this argument. It concluded that the President has inherent authority to direct the "political" action of Executive Branch subordinates. However, it observed, "it would be an alarming doctrine, that Congress cannot impose upon any executive officer any duty they may think proper, which is not repugnant to any rights secured and protected by the constitution." *Id.* at 610. When Congress imposes such nondiscretionary, "ministerial" duties, they "grow out of and are subject to the control of the law, and not the direction of the President." *Id.* Thus, the President does not have unfettered discretion to control the actions of his or her subordinates while they hold office.

By contrast, the nineteenth-century Court said comparatively little about the President's power to *remove* those officials from office. In *Marbury v. Madison*, Chief Justice John Marshall indirectly signaled that Congress could limit the authority to fire government officials. 5 U.S. (1 Cranch) 137, 162 (1803). In discussing the legal effects of the President signing and sealing a commission for federal office, he observed that "[w]here an officer is removable at the will of the executive, the circumstance which completes his appointment is of no concern; because the act is at any time revocable; and the commission may be arrested, if still in the office. *But when the officer is not removable at the will of the executive,* the appointment is not revocable, and cannot be annulled. It has conferred legal rights which cannot be resumed." *Id.* (emphasis added). The implications of this statement were unclear. Marshall recognized that the President did not have unfettered discretion to remove all government officials, but he did so when discussing a position (justice of the peace) that was essentially judicial in character. *See* Act of Feb. 27, 1801, 2 Stat. 103. Did the limitation to which he alluded extend to those holding office in the Executive Branch? Did it mean that Congress could participate in the President's removal decisions by, say, requiring the President to seek its prior approval?

After the Civil War, Congress sought to resolve the issue the Decision of 1789 left open. But it did so in the political arena rather than in the courts. Over President Andrew Johnson's veto, Congress passed the Tenure of Office Act in 1867. It barred the President from removing any executive officer who had been appointed with the Senate's advice and consent—including members of the Cabinet—unless the Senate first approved. In violation of the Act, Johnson attempted to remove Secretary of War Edwin M. Stanton without Senate approval. This led to Johnson's impeachment in 1868 (the first of a President in the country's history); he survived removal by a single Senate vote. Congress repealed the Act in 1887, though others like it remained in the United States Code.

The cases that follow addressed questions left unanswered by the Decision of 1789. Although they are presented in chronological order, note that they ask two distinct question related to the President's removal power. The first question—addressed in *Myers v. United States* and *Bowsher v. Synar*—is whether the Constitution permits Congress to give itself a role in the decision to remove Executive Branch officials. The second question—addressed in *Humphrey's Executor v. United States* and *Morrison v. Olson*—is whether and to what extent Congress can limit the President's discretion to remove Executive Branch officials.

As you read the cases, be sure to note the Court's method for determining Congress' authority to participate in or limit the President's exercise of the removal power. Does the resolution of the issue turn on the nature of the powers being exercised by the officer? Does it turn on the degree to which Congress encumbers the President's ability to take care that the laws are faithfully executed? Does it turn on something else?

Myers v. United States, **272 U.S. 52 (1926).** An 1876 statute provided that "Postmasters of the first, second, and third classes shall be appointed and may be removed by the President by and with the advice and consent of the Senate, and shall hold their offices for four years unless sooner removed or suspended according to law." July 12, 1876, 19 Stat. 80, 81, c. 179. Frank S. Myers was appointed to a four-year term as postmaster first class for Portland, Oregon. Acting on President Woodrow Wilson's instructions, Postmaster General Albert S. Burleson ordered Myers be removed from his post in 1920. Myers then sued unsuccessfully in the Court of Claims for pay he would have received had he been permitted to stay in office. He argued that his removal was effected without the Senate's consent in violation of the 1876 statute. He died in 1924, but his estate pursued his claim all the way to the Supreme Court.

In finding the statute unconstitutional, Chief Justice Taft recounted, and largely endorsed, the Madisonian view of presidential removal power advanced in the Decision of 1789. As importantly for present purposes, Taft connected that view with an expansive understanding of the President's constitutional authority to supervise Executive Branch officials. As the Court did in *Kendall v. United States,* Taft

In Context

William Howard Taft is the only person to hold both the Presidency and a spot on the Supreme Court. Interestingly, Taft disliked the Presidency. He often stated, in public and private, that he loved the Court and is believed to have admitted that "[t]here is nothing I would have loved more than being Chief Justice of the United States." Taft eventually got his wish. Nine years after winning less than 25 percent of the popular vote and losing his reelection bid to Woodrow Wilson, President Warren G. Harding nominated Taft, age 63, to the Court.

distinguished between two categories of executive actions: those to which the Constitution delegates broad discretion, and those in which Congress has provided clear statutory instructions for the President's subordinates to follow. He recognized that the extent of Presidential supervision and control may vary depending on the category. With respect to the first category, Taft explained:

> Made responsible under the Constitution for the effective enforcement of the law, the President needs as an indispensable aid to meet it the disciplinary influence upon those who act under him of a reserve power of removal. But it is contended that executive officers appointed by the President with the consent of the Senate are bound by the statutory law, and are not his servants to do his will, and that his obligation to care for the faithful execution of the laws does not authorize him to treat them as such. The degree of guidance in the discharge of their duties that the President may exercise over executive officers varies with the character of their service as prescribed in the law under which they act. The highest and most important duties which his subordinates perform are those in which they act for him. In such cases they are exercising not their own but his discretion. This field is a very large one. It is sometimes described as political. *Kendall v. United States*, 37 U.S. (12 Pet.) 524, 610 (1838). Each head of a department is and must be the President's alter ego in the matters of that department where the President is required by law to exercise authority. [Here, Taft cited relations with foreign governments, protection of the mails and of the public domain, and governance of territories absent guidance from Congress as examples of the President's "political" executive responsibilities.]
>
> In all such cases, the discretion to be exercised is that of the President in determining the national public interest and in directing the action to be taken by his executive subordinates to protect it. In this field his cabinet officers must do his will. He must place in each member of his official family, and his chief executive subordinates, implicit faith. The moment that he loses confidence in the intelligence, ability, judgment, or loyalty of any one of them, he must have the power to remove him without delay. To require him to file charges and submit them to the consideration of the Senate might make impossible that unity and co-ordination in executive administration essential to effective action.
>
> The duties of the heads of departments and bureaus in which the discretion of the President is exercised and which we have described are the most important in the whole field of executive action of the government. There is nothing in the Constitution which permits a distinction between the removal of the head of a department or a bureau, when he discharges a political duty of the President or exercises his discretion, and the removal of executive officers engaged in the discharge of their other normal duties. The imperative reasons requiring an unrestricted power to remove the most important of his subordinates in their most important duties must therefore control the interpretation of the Constitution as to all appointed by him.

Myers, 272 U.S. at 134-35. With regard to the second category, Taft likewise found that the President must be able to remove Executive Branch officials without Congress' interference. However, he acknowledged an important caveat:

> . . . [T]his is not to say that there are not strong reasons why the President should have a like power to remove his appointees charged with other duties than those above described. The ordinary duties of officers prescribed by statute come under the general administrative control of the President by virtue of the general grant to him of the executive power, and he may properly supervise and guide their construction of the statutes under which they act in order to secure that unitary and uniform execution of the laws which article 2 of the Constitution evidently contemplated in vesting general executive power in the President alone. Laws are often passed with specific provision for adoption of regulations by a department or bureau head to make the law workable and effective. The ability and judgment manifested by the official thus empowered, as well as his energy and stimulation of his subordinates, are subjects which the President must consider and supervise in his administrative control. Finding such officers to be negligent and inefficient, the President should have the power to remove them. *Of course there may be duties so peculiarly and specifically committed to the discretion of a particular officer as to raise a question whether the President may overrule or revise the officer's interpretation of his statutory duty in a particular instance.* Then there may be duties of a quasi-judicial character imposed on executive officers and members of executive tribunals whose decisions after hearing affect interests of individuals, the discharge of which the President cannot in a particular case properly influence or control. But even in such a case he may consider the decision after its rendition as a reason for removing the officer, on the ground that the discretion regularly entrusted to that officer by statute has not been on the whole intelligently or wisely exercised. Otherwise he does not discharge his own constitutional duty of seeing that the laws be faithfully executed.

Id. at 135 (emphasis added). Finally, Taft addressed whether Congress has any more right to participate in the removal of "inferior officers" appointed by "heads of departments" than it does in the removal of superior ones. He answered that question in the negative.

> The power to remove inferior executive officers, like that to remove superior executive officers, is an incident of the power to appoint them, and is in its nature an executive power. The authority of Congress given by the excepting clause to vest the appointment of such inferior officers in the heads of departments carries with it authority incidentally to invest the heads of departments with power to remove. It has been the practice of Congress to do so and this court has recognized that power. The court also has recognized . . . that Congress, in committing the appointment of such inferior officers to the heads of departments, may prescribe incidental regulations controlling and restricting the latter in the exercise of the

power of removal. But the court never has held, nor reasonably could hold, although it is argued to the contrary on behalf of the appellant, that the excepting clause enables Congress to draw to itself, or to either branch of it, the power to remove or the right to participate in the exercise of that power. To do this would be to go beyond the words and implications of that clause, and to infringe the constitutional principle of the separation of governmental powers.

Id. at 161.

Humphrey's Executor v. United States, 295 U.S. 602 (1935). Less than a decade after *Myers*, the Court tested the removal implications of Chief Justice Taft's observation that "there may be duties so peculiarly and specifically committed to the discretion of a particular officer as to raise a question whether the President may overrule or revise the officer's interpretation of his statutory duty in a particular instance." Early in his first term, President Franklin D. Roosevelt asked for the resignation of Federal Trade Commission Commissioner William Humphrey. Humphrey had been appointed to the FTC by President Calvin Coolidge in 1925 and was reappointed by President Herbert Hoover in 1931. Although the FTC was an independent agency, Roosevelt felt that its law-enforcement powers necessarily placed it under his constitutional supervision. Humphrey refused to leave office, whereupon Roosevelt again insisted that he do so. "I do not feel that your mind and my mind go along together on either policies or the administering of the Federal Trade Commission, and frankly, I think it best for the people of this country that I should have full confidence." *Id.* at 619. In October 1933, and after Humphrey continued to refuse to step down, Roosevelt finally fired him. Humphrey then sued for lost salary. He argued that the Federal Trade Commission Act permitted commissioners to be dismissed for "inefficiency, neglect of duty, or malfeasance in office," but not because the President would simply feel more comfortable with a different appointee. The government responded by arguing that the President had inherent authority, granted by Article II, to remove FTC commissioners. After Humphrey died in 1934, his executor assumed control of the lawsuit.

In ruling for Humphrey's executor, the Court found a situation to which Chief Justice Taft's dicta in *Myers* applied. Note a subtle but important difference between the two cases. *Myers* involved an attempt by Congress to participate in the removal decision—like the Tenure of Office Act, the Act of 1876 required that the President get Senate approval before removing a postmaster. Here, Congress was not trying to insinuate itself into the removal process. Rather, it placed an *ex ante* restriction on the President's discretion to remove FTC commissioners. The question, then, was whether the FTC's responsibilities were—like those of a postmaster general—so "executive" in nature that the Constitution granted the President unfettered removal authority over its commissioners.

To support its contention that the removal provision of [FTC Act § 1] . . . is an unconstitutional interference with the executive power of the President, the government's chief reliance is *Myers v. United States*, 272 U.S. 52 [(1926)]. . . . [T]he narrow point actually decided [in that case] was only that the President had power to remove a postmaster of the first class, without the advice and consent of the Senate as required by act of Congress. In the course of the opinion of the court, expressions occur which tend to sustain the government's contention, but these are beyond the point involved and, therefore, do not come within the rule of *stare decisis*. In so far as they are out of harmony with the views here set forth, these expressions are disapproved. . . .

The office of a postmaster is so essentially unlike the office now involved that the decision in the *Myers* Case cannot be accepted as controlling our decision here. A postmaster is an executive officer restricted to the performance of executive functions. He is charged with no duty at all related to either the legislative or judicial power. The actual decision in the *Myers* Case finds support in the theory that such an officer is merely one of the units in the executive department and, hence, inherently subject to the exclusive and illimitable power of removal by the Chief Executive, whose subordinate and aid he is. Putting aside dicta, which may be followed if sufficiently persuasive but which are not controlling, the necessary reach of the decision goes far enough to include all purely executive officers. It goes no farther; much less does it include an officer who occupies no place in the executive department and who exercises no part of the executive power vested by the Constitution in the President.

The Federal Trade Commission is an administrative body created by Congress to carry into effect legislative policies embodied in the statute in accordance with the legislative standard therein prescribed, and to perform other specified duties as a legislative or as a judicial aid. Such a body cannot in any proper sense be characterized as an arm or an eye of the executive. Its duties are performed without executive leave and, in the contemplation of the statute, must be free from executive control. In administering the provisions of the statute in respect of "unfair methods of competition," that is to say, in filling in and administering the details embodied by that general standard, the commission acts in part quasi-legislatively and in part quasi-judicially. In making investigations and reports thereon for the information of Congress under section 6, in aid of the legislative power, it acts as a legislative agency. Under section 7, which authorizes the commission to act as a master in chancery under rules prescribed by the court, it acts as an agency of the judiciary. To the extent that it exercises any executive function, as distinguished from executive power in the constitutional sense, it does so in the discharge and effectuation of its quasi-legislative or quasi-judicial powers, or as an agency of the legislative or judicial departments of the government. . . .

The fundamental necessity of maintaining each of the three general departments of government entirely free from the control or coercive influence, direct or indirect, of either of the others, has often been stressed and is hardly open to serious question. So much is implied in the very fact of the separation of the powers of these departments by the Constitution; and in the rule which recognizes their essential coequality. . . .

The power of removal here claimed for the President falls within this principle, since its coercive influence threatens the independence of a commission, which is not only wholly disconnected from the executive department, but which, as already fully appears, was created by Congress as a means of carrying into operation legislative and judicial powers, and as an agency of the legislative and judicial departments. . . .

The result of what we now have said is this: Whether the power of the President to remove an officer shall prevail over the authority of Congress to condition the power by fixing a definite term and precluding a removal except for cause will depend upon the character of the office; the *Myers* decision, affirming the power of the President alone to make the removal, is confined to purely executive officers; and as to officers of the kind here under consideration, we hold that no removal can be made during the prescribed term for which the officer is appointed, except for one or more of the causes named in the applicable statute. . . .

Id. at 626-32.

Bowsher v. Synar, 478 U.S. 714 (1986). About a decade before Congress passed the Line Item Veto Act (considered above in *Clinton v. New York*), it passed the Balanced Budget and Emergency Deficit Control Act of 1985 (99 Stat. 103). The Gramm-Rudman-Hollings Act, as it was more colloquially known, set a series of deficit targets to balance the federal budget by 1991. If these targets were not met in any given year, the Act required across-the-board spending cuts ("sequestration") until the targets were met. The Act tasked the Comptroller General—head of the General Accounting Office within the Legislative Branch—with implementing its provisions. The OMB Director and the Congressional Budget Office were required to submit deficit estimates and program-by-program budget reduction calculations to the Comptroller General who, after reviewing this information, reported reduction measures to the President. The President was then obligated to issue a sequestration order mandating the spending reductions specified by the Comptroller General. The sequestration order became effective unless, within a specified time, Congress legislated the necessary reductions itself.

Congressman Michael Synar (D-OK), along with several other Members of Congress, challenged Gramm-Rudman-Hollings in federal court. They argued that the Act's deficit reduction measures could not be implemented by the Comptroller General, a legislative official answerable to Congress. The Court agreed. It stressed an axiomatic constitutional principle gleaned from its prior decisions: Congress may never implement the laws.

The Constitution does not contemplate an active role for Congress in the supervision of officers charged with the execution of the laws it enacts. The President appoints "Officers of the United States" with the "Advice and Consent of the Senate. . . ." Art. II, § 2. Once the appointment has been made and confirmed, however, the Constitution explicitly provides for removal of Officers of the United States by Congress only upon impeachment by the House of Representatives and conviction by the Senate. An impeachment by the House and trial by the Senate can rest only on "Treason, Bribery or other high Crimes and Misdemeanors." Article II, § 4. A direct congressional role in the removal of officers charged with the execution of the laws beyond this limited one is inconsistent with separation of powers.

This was made clear in debate in the First Congress in 1789. When Congress considered an amendment to a bill establishing the Department of Foreign Affairs, the debate centered around whether the Congress "should recognize and declare the power of the President under the Constitution to remove the Secretary of Foreign Affairs without the advice and consent of the Senate." *Myers*, 272 U.S., at 114. James Madison urged rejection of a congressional role in the removal of Executive Branch officers, other than by impeachment. . . .

. . . Chief Justice Taft, writing for the Court [in *Myers*], declared the [Act of July 12, 1876] unconstitutional on the ground that for Congress to "draw to itself, or to either branch of it, the power to remove or the right to participate in the exercise of that power . . . would be . . . to infringe the constitutional principle of the separation of governmental powers." *Id.*, at 161.

. . . *Humphrey's Executor* involved an issue not presented either in the *Myers* case or in this case—i.e., the power of Congress to limit the President's powers of removal of a Federal Trade Commissioner. . . . The Court distinguished *Myers*, reaffirming its holding that congressional participation in the removal of executive officers is unconstitutional. . . .

In light of these precedents, we conclude that Congress cannot reserve for itself the power of removal of an officer charged with the execution of the laws except by impeachment. To permit the execution of the laws to be vested in an officer answerable only to Congress would, in practical terms, reserve in Congress control over the execution of the laws. . . . The structure of the Constitution does not permit Congress to execute the laws; it follows that Congress cannot grant to an officer under its control what it does not possess. . . .

478 U.S. at 722-26. The Court then turned to the Comptroller General, specifically:

Although the Comptroller General is nominated by the President from a list of three individuals recommended by the Speaker of the House of Representatives and the President *pro tempore* of the Senate, and confirmed by the Senate, he is removable only at the initiative of Congress. He may be removed not only by impeachment but also by joint resolution of Congress "at any time" resting on any one of the following bases: (i) permanent disability; (ii) inefficiency; (iii) neglect of duty; (iv) malfeasance; or (v) a felony or conduct involving moral turpitude." 31 U.S.C. § 703(e)(1)B. This provision was included . . . because Congress "felt that [the Comptroller General] should be brought under the sole control of Congress, so that Congress at any moment when it found he was inefficient and was not carrying on the duties of his office as he should and as the Congress expected, could remove him without the long, tedious process of a trial by impeachment." 61 Cong. Rec. 1081 (1921).

. . . These terms ["inefficiency," "neglect of duty," and "malfeasance"] are very broad and, as interpreted by Congress, could sustain removal of a Comptroller General for any number of actual or perceived transgressions of the legislative will. The Constitutional Convention chose to permit impeachment of executive officers only for "Treason, Bribery, or other high Crimes and Misdemeanors." It rejected language that would have permitted impeachment for "maladministration," with Madison arguing that "[s]o vague a term will be equivalent to a tenure during pleasure of the Senate." 2 M. Farrand, Records of the Federal Convention of 1787, p. 550 (1911). . . .

We conclude that . . . the powers vested in the Comptroller General . . . violate the command of the Constitution that the Congress play no direct role in the execution of the laws. . . .

Id. at 727-36. Justice White, writing in dissent, took a very different position on Congress' control over the Comptroller General.

. . . That the agent enforcing the standard is Congress may be of some significance to the Comptroller, but Congress' substantively limited removal power will undoubtedly be less of a spur to subservience than Congress' unquestionable and unqualified power to enact legislation reducing the Comptroller's salary, cutting the funds available to his department, reducing his personnel, limiting or expanding his duties, or even abolishing his position altogether.

More importantly, the substantial role played by the President in the process of removal through joint resolution reduces to utter insignificance the possibility that the threat of removal will induce subservience to the Congress. . . . [A] joint resolution must be presented to the President and is ineffective if it is vetoed by him, unless the veto is overridden by the constitutionally prescribed two-thirds majority of both Houses of Congress. The requirement of Presidential approval obviates the possibility that the Comptroller will perceive himself as so completely at the mercy of Congress that he will function as its tool. . . .

The practical result of the removal provision is not to render the Comptroller unduly dependent upon or subservient to Congress, but to render him one of the most independent officers in the entire federal establishment. . . .

Id. at 771-73 (White, J., dissenting).

Before moving on to *Morrison v. Olson*, it would be beneficial to take stock of the removal jurisprudence covered up to this point.

QUESTION SET 8.5

Review & Synthesis

1. Compare the Supreme Court's decisions in *Myers, Humphrey's Executor,* and *Bowsher.*

   a. According to *Myers,* what is the constitutional rationale for granting the President expansive removal powers over Executive Branch officials? Is that rationale consistent with *Humphrey's Executor* and *Bowsher*?

   b. What role does the Constitution leave for Congress in removing Executive Branch officials?

   c. What test does the Court apply for determining whether Congress has exceeded its constitutional bounds relating to the removal of Executive Branch officials? Does that test focus on the nature of the administrative power exercised by the official? Does it focus on the effect that Congress' involvement in the removal decision will have on the President's capacity to supervise the Executive Branch? Both? Something else?

   d. Were the postmaster first class in *Myers,* the FTC Commissioner in *Humphrey's Executor,* and the Comptroller General in *Bowsher* Officers of the United States who wielded significant authority?

2. In *Humphrey's Executor,* the Court drew a distinction between "executive function" and "executive power." Does this distinction make sense? More specifically, the FTC had authority to enforce the FTC Act against regulated entities at the time of the Court's decision. Is it plausible to say that the agency did not have executive power?

3. Based on *Myers, Humphrey's Executor,* and *Bowsher,* could Congress adopt "for cause" removal protections—for inefficiency, neglect of duty, or malfeasance—for a Cabinet Secretary, like the Secretary of Labor? Note that Congress vests heads of executive departments with quasi-legislative and quasi-judicial authority, and so they do not wield exclusively executive power. Does that mean that Congress can shield them from the President's removal discretion, just as it shields heads of independent agencies like the FTC?

On June 17, 1972, several burglars were arrested after breaking into the Democratic National Committee's offices at the Watergate Hotel in Washington, D.C. It was soon discovered that the wrongdoers were associated with Richard M. Nixon's presidential reelection campaign. During his attorney general confirmation hearing in the Senate, Elliot Richardson promised that his first official act would be to hire a special prosecutor—law professor Archibald Cox—to investigate the break-in. In addition, he promised that he would only remove Cox for "extraordinary improprieties." True to his word, Richardson appointed Cox to a position in the Justice Department, answerable directly to him. After it was revealed that President Nixon had recorded Oval Office conversations of potential relevance to his investigation, Cox sought and received a subpoena to secure the tapes. Nixon challenged the subpoena on grounds of executive privilege, but the D.C. Circuit ultimately ordered him to produce them. Nixon's subsequent attempts to avoid production of the tapes failed. On October 20, 1973, in what is now known as the Saturday Night Massacre, Nixon ordered Richardson and Deputy Attorney General William Ruckelshaus to fire Cox. Both refused and resigned. Nixon then turned to Solicitor General Robert Bork, third in the Justice Department chain of command and by default the Acting Attorney General. Bork followed Nixon's order and fired Cox. Public pressure forced Nixon to allow Bork to appoint a new special counsel, Leon Jaworski. The rest, as they say, is history. Jaworski's investigation contributed to Nixon's resignation in 1974.

This debacle spurred Congress to pass several statutory reforms to make governmental decision-makers more accountable. One such piece of legislation was the Ethics in Government Act of 1978, 28 U.S.C. § 591, *et seq.*, which was designed to address the classic "who guards the guardians" problem. If the President or his close advisors are suspected of illegal conduct can the Attorney General, who answers to the President, be trusted to credibly investigate them? Elliot Richardson had made principled decisions during his brief tenure as Attorney General, but Congress apparently felt that firmer assurances of propriety were needed moving forward.

The Act created the position of "independent counsel" ("IC") to investigate and prosecute allegations of wrongdoing by federal officials. An IC investigation began with the Attorney General receiving an allegation of wrongdoing, a complaint, or a request for the appointment of an IC from a Member of Congress. The Act then required the Attorney General to conduct a preliminary investigation upon concluding that the allegations were "sufficient to constitute grounds to investigate." If the preliminary investigation revealed "reasonable grounds to believe that further investigation or prosecution [was] warranted," the Act required the Attorney General to apply to a special court called the "Special Division" for the appointment of an IC. The Special Division was staffed by three D.C. Circuit judges or Supreme Court Justices appointed by the Chief Justice of the United States.

The Special Division would then appoint an IC and define the scope of his or her jurisdiction. Once appointed, the IC had all the investigative and prosecutorial functions and powers of the Department of Justice, the Attorney General, and any other officer or employee of the Department of Justice. The Attorney General could refer additional matters to the IC relevant to his or her charge, and the IC could seek permission from the Special Division to expand his or her jurisdiction. With regard to removal, the IC could be relieved of his or her duties in either of two ways. First, the Special Division could terminate the position when the IC's work was completed. Second, the Attorney General could fire the IC "for good cause, physical or mental disability . . . or any other condition that substantially impairs the performance of such independent counsel's duties." 28 U.S.C. § 596 (a)(1).

The following case—*Morrison v. Olson*—tested the constitutionality of the IC appointment and removal provisions. It originated in a document disclosure dispute between the House of Representatives and the Environmental Protection Agency ("EPA"). The House had requested that the EPA turn over documents relating to its administration of the "Superfund" law. Pursuant to advice given by the Department of Justice, the President instructed the EPA to invoke executive privilege and withhold the documents demanded by the House. The House held the EPA Administrator in contempt, but eventually the dispute was resolved when the Administration gave the House limited access to the documents it sought. The House Judiciary Committee held hearings on the Justice Department's role in the dispute the following year, during which it received testimony from Assistant Attorney General for the Office of Legal Counsel Theodore Olson. The Committee issued a report criticizing DOJ's role in the executive privilege dispute and accusing Olsen of giving false testimony during its investigation. It requested an IC be appointed to investigate Olson, and the Attorney General complied. The Special Division appointed Alexia Morrison, giving her jurisdiction to investigate "whether the testimony of . . . Olson and his revision of such testimony on March 10, 1983, violated either 18 U.S.C. § 1505 or § 1001, or any other provision of federal law." Order, Div. No. 86-1 (CADC Special Division, April 23, 1986). When Morrison caused a grand jury to subpoena documents and testimony from Olson, he moved to quash them on the ground that the IC provisions were unconstitutional, and she therefore had no authority to investigate him.

Morrison v. Olson was a watershed decision in which the Court substantially changed its approach to removal questions. As you read it, be sure to note how the Court's analysis both tracks and departs from the cases we have considered thus far.

> ### In Context
>
> The "Superfund Law" is the Comprehensive Environmental Response, Compensation, and Liability Act, also referred to at CERCLA. It imposes a tax on the chemical and petroleum industries, assigns responsibility to the federal government for responding to environmental and public health dangers caused by the release of hazardous substances, establishes a trust fund for hazardous substance clean up, and makes liable those responsible for releasing hazardous waste into the environment.

Morrison v. Olson
487 U.S. 654 (1988)

Chief Justice REHNQUIST delivered the opinion of the Court.

This case presents us with a challenge to the independent counsel provisions of the Ethics in Government Act of 1978, 28 U.S.C. §§ 49, 591 *et seq.* (1982 ed., Supp. V). We hold today that these provisions of the Act do not violate the Appointments Clause of the Constitution, Art. II, § 2, cl. 2, or the limitations of Article III, nor do they impermissibly interfere with the President's authority under Article II in violation of the constitutional principle of separation of powers. . . .

III. . . .

. . . The parties do not dispute that "[t]he Constitution for purposes of appointment . . . divides all its officers into two classes." *United States v. Germaine*, 99 U.S. (9 Otto) 508 (1879). As we stated in *Buckley v. Valeo*, 424 U.S. 1, 132 (1976): "[P]rincipal officers are selected by the President with the advice and consent of the Senate. Inferior officers Congress may allow to be appointed by the President alone, by the heads of departments, or by the Judiciary." The initial question is, accordingly, whether appellant is an "inferior" or a "principal" officer. If she is the latter, then the Act is in violation of the Appointments Clause.

The line between "inferior" and "principal" officers is one that is far from clear, and the Framers provided little guidance into where it should be drawn. . . . We need not attempt here to decide exactly where the line falls between the two types of officers, because in our view appellant clearly falls on the "inferior officer" side of that line. Several factors lead to this conclusion.

First, appellant is subject to removal by a higher Executive Branch official. Although appellant may not be "subordinate" to the Attorney General (and the President) insofar as she possesses a degree of independent discretion to exercise the powers delegated to her under the Act, the fact that she can be removed by the Attorney General indicates that she is to some degree "inferior" in rank and authority. Second, appellant is empowered by the Act to perform only certain, limited duties. An independent counsel's role is restricted primarily to investigation and, if appropriate, prosecution for certain federal crimes. Admittedly, the Act delegates to appellant "full power and independent authority to exercise all investigative and prosecutorial functions and powers of the Department of Justice," § 594(a), but this grant of authority does not include any authority to formulate policy for the Government or the Executive Branch, nor does it give appellant any administrative duties outside of those necessary to operate her office. The Act specifically provides that in policy matters appellant is to comply to the extent possible with the policies of the Department. § 594(f).

Third, appellant's office is limited in jurisdiction. Not only is the Act itself restricted in applicability to certain federal officials suspected of certain serious federal crimes, but an independent counsel can only act within the scope of the jurisdiction that has been granted by the Special Division pursuant to a request by the Attorney General. Finally, appellant's office is limited in tenure. There is concededly no time limit on the appointment of a particular counsel. Nonetheless, the office of independent counsel is "temporary" in the sense that an independent counsel is appointed essentially to accomplish a single task, and when that task is over the office is terminated, either by the counsel herself or by action of the Special Division. Unlike other prosecutors, appellant has no ongoing responsibilities that extend beyond the accomplishment of the mission that she was appointed for and authorized by the Special Division to undertake. In our view, these factors relating to the "ideas of tenure, duration . . . and duties" of the independent counsel, [*Germaine*, 99 U.S. at 511], are sufficient to establish that appellant is an "inferior" officer in the constitutional sense. . . .

This does not, however, end our inquiry under the Appointments Clause. Appellees argue that even if appellant is an "inferior" officer, the Clause does not empower Congress to place the power to appoint such an officer outside the Executive Branch. They contend that the Clause does not contemplate congressional authorization of "interbranch appointments," in which an officer of one branch is appointed by officers of another branch. The relevant language of the Appointments Clause is worth repeating. It reads: ". . . but the Congress may by Law vest the Appointment of such inferior Officers, as they think proper, in the President alone, in the courts of Law, or in the Heads of Departments." On its face, the language of this "excepting clause" admits of no limitation on interbranch appointments. Indeed, the inclusion of "as they think proper" seems clearly to give Congress significant discretion to determine whether it is "proper" to vest the appointment of, for example, executive officials in the "courts of Law." . . .

We do not mean to say that Congress' power to provide for interbranch appointments of "inferior officers" is unlimited. In addition to separation-of-powers concerns, which would arise if such provisions for appointment had the potential to impair the constitutional functions assigned to one of the branches, [we have previously suggested that] Congress' decision to vest the appointment power in the courts would be improper if there was some "incongruity" between the functions normally performed by the courts and the performance of their duty to appoint. In this case, however, we do not think it impermissible for Congress to vest the power to appoint independent counsel in a specially created federal court. We thus disagree with the [D.C. Circuit's] conclusion that there is an inherent incongruity about a court having the power to appoint prosecutorial officers.[13] We have recognized that courts may appoint private attorneys to act as prosecutor for judicial contempt judgments . . . [W]e approved court appointment of United States commissioners, who exercised certain limited prosecutorial powers . . . [We have] indicated that judicial appointment of federal marshals, who are [executive officers] would not be inappropriate. Lower courts have also upheld interim judicial appointments of United States Attorneys, and Congress itself has vested the power to make these interim appointments in the district courts. Congress, of course, was concerned when it created the office of independent counsel with the conflicts of interest that could arise in situations when the Executive Branch is called upon to investigate its own high-ranking officers. If it were to remove the appointing authority from the Executive Branch, the most logical place to put it was in the Judicial Branch. In the light of the Act's provision making the judges of the Special Division ineligible to participate in any matters relating to an independent counsel they have appointed, we do not think that appointment of the independent counsel by the court runs afoul of the constitutional limitation on "incongruous" interbranch appointments.

IV

[In this Section, the Court rejected appellees' contention that allowing the Special Division to appoint the independent counsel constituted a violation of Article III.]

V

We now turn to consider whether the Act is invalid under the constitutional principle of separation of powers. Two related issues must be addressed: The first is whether the provision of the Act restricting the Attorney General's power to remove the independent counsel to only those instances in which he can show "good cause," taken by itself, impermissibly interferes with the President's exercise of his constitutionally appointed functions. The second is whether, taken as a whole, the Act violates the separation of powers by reducing the President's ability to control the prosecutorial powers wielded by the independent counsel.

---

[13] Indeed, in light of judicial experience with prosecutors in criminal cases, it could be said that courts are especially well qualified to appoint prosecutors. This is not a case in which judges are given power to appoint an officer in an area in which they have no special knowledge or expertise, as in, for example, a statute authorizing the courts to appoint officials in the Department of Agriculture or the Federal Energy Regulatory Commission.

A

Two Terms ago we had occasion to consider whether it was consistent with the separation of powers for Congress to pass a statute that authorized a Government official who is removable only by Congress to participate in what we found to be "executive powers." *Bowsher v. Synar*, 478 U.S. 714, 730 (1986). We held in *Bowsher* that "Congress cannot reserve for itself the power of removal of an officer charged with the execution of the laws except by impeachment." *Bowsher*, 478 U.S. at 726. A primary antecedent for this ruling was our 1926 decision in *Myers v. United States*, 272 U.S. 52 (1926). *Myers* had considered the propriety of a federal statute by which certain post-masters of the United States could be removed by the President only "by and with the advice and consent of the Senate." There too, Congress' attempt to involve itself in the removal of an executive official was found to be sufficient grounds to render the statute invalid. As we observed in *Bowsher*, the essence of the decision in *Myers* was the judgment that the Constitution prevents Congress from "draw[ing] to itself . . . the power to remove or the right to participate in the exercise of that power. To do this would be to go beyond the words and implications of the [Appointments Clause] and to infringe the constitutional principle of the separation of governmental powers." 272 U.S. at 161.

Unlike both *Bowsher* and *Myers*, this case does not involve an attempt by Congress itself to gain a role in the removal of executive officials other than its established powers of impeachment and conviction. The Act instead puts the removal power squarely in the hands of the Executive Branch; an independent counsel may be removed from office, "only by the personal action of the Attorney General, and only for good cause." § 596(a)(1).[23] There is no requirement of congressional approval of the Attorney General's removal decision, though the decision is subject to judicial review. § 596(a)(3). In our view, the removal provisions of the Act make this case more analogous to *Humphrey's Executor v. United States*, 295 U.S. 602 (1935), and *Wiener v. United States*, 357 U.S. 349 (1958), than to *Myers* or *Bowsher*.

In *Humphrey's Executor*, the issue was whether a statute restricting the President's power to remove the Commissioners of the Federal Trade Commission (FTC) only for "inefficiency, neglect of duty, or malfeasance in office" was consistent with the Constitution. 295 U.S. at 619. We stated that whether Congress can "condition the [President's power of removal] by fixing a definite term and precluding a removal except for cause, will depend upon the character of the office." *Id.* at 631. Contrary to the implication of

---

[23] As noted, an independent counsel may also be removed through impeachment and conviction. In addition, the Attorney General may remove a counsel for "physical disability, mental incapacity, or any other condition that substantially impairs the performance" of his or her duties. § 596(a)(1).

some dicta in *Myers*,[24] the President's power to remove Government officials simply was not "all-inclusive in respect of civil officers with the exception of the judiciary provided for by the Constitution." *Id.* at 629. At least in regard to "quasi-legislative" and "quasi-judicial" agencies such as the FTC, "[t]he authority of Congress, in creating [such] agencies, to require them to act in discharge of their duties independently of executive control . . . includes, as an appropriate incident, power to fix the period during which they shall continue in office, and to forbid their removal except for cause in the meantime." *Id.* In *Humphrey's Executor*, we found it "plain" that the Constitution did not give the President "illimitable power of removal" over the officers of independent agencies. Were the President to have the power to remove FTC Commissioners at will, the "coercive influence" of the removal power would "threate[n] the independence of [the] commission." *Id.* at 630.

Similarly, in *Wiener* we considered whether the President had unfettered discretion to remove a member of the War Claims Commission, which had been established by Congress in the War Claims Act of 1948, 62 Stat. 1240. The Commission's function was to receive and adjudicate certain claims for compensation from those who had suffered personal injury or property damage at the hands of the enemy during World War II. Commissioners were appointed by the President, with the advice and consent of the Senate, but the statute made no provision for the removal of officers, perhaps because the Commission itself was to have a limited existence. As in *Humphrey's Executor*, however, the Commissioners were entrusted by Congress with adjudicatory powers that were to be exercised free from executive control. In this context, "Congress did not wish to have hang over the Commission the Damocles' sword of removal by the President for no reason other than that he preferred to have on that Commission men of his own choosing." 357 U.S. at 356. Accordingly, we rejected the President's attempt to remove a Commissioner "merely because he wanted his own appointees on [the] Commission," stating that "no such power is given to the President directly by the Constitution, and none is impliedly conferred upon him by statute." *Id.*

Appellees contend that *Humphrey's Executor* and *Wiener* are distinguishable from this case because they did not involve officials who performed a "core executive function." They argue that our decision in *Humphrey's Executor* rests on a distinction between "purely executive" officials and officials who exercise "quasi-legislative" and "quasi-judicial" powers. In their view, when a "purely executive" official is involved, the governing precedent is *Myers*, not *Humphrey's Executor*. And, under *Myers*, the President must have absolute discretion to discharge "purely" executive officials at will.

---

[24] The Court expressly disapproved of any statements in *Myers* that "are out of harmony" with the views expressed in *Humphrey's Executor*. 295 U.S., at 626. We recognized that the only issue actually decided in *Myers* was that "the President had power to remove a postmaster of the first class, without the advice and consent of the Senate as required by act of Congress." 295 U.S., at 626.

We undoubtedly did rely on the terms "quasi-legislative" and "quasi-judicial" to distinguish the officials involved in *Humphrey's Executor* and *Wiener* from those in *Myers*, but our present considered view is that the determination of whether the Constitution allows Congress to impose a "good cause"–type restriction on the President's power to remove an official cannot be made to turn on whether or not that official is classified as "purely executive." The analysis contained in our removal cases is designed not to define rigid categories of those officials who may or may not be removed at will by the President,[28] but to ensure that Congress does not interfere with the President's exercise of the "executive power" and his constitutionally appointed duty to "take care that the laws be faithfully executed" under Article II. *Myers* was undoubtedly correct in its holding, and in its broader suggestion that there are some "purely executive" officials who must be removable by the President at will if he is to be able to accomplish his constitutional role. But as the Court noted in *Wiener*: "The assumption was short-lived that the *Myers* case recognized the President's inherent constitutional power to remove officials no matter what the relation of the executive to the discharge of their duties and no matter what restrictions Congress may have imposed regarding the nature of their tenure." 357 U.S. at 352.

At the other end of the spectrum from *Myers*, the characterization of the agencies in *Humphrey's Executor* and *Wiener* as "quasi-legislative" or "quasi-judicial" in large part reflected our judgment that it was not essential to the President's proper execution of his Article II powers that these agencies be headed up by individuals who were removable at will. We do not mean to suggest that an analysis of the functions served by the officials at issue is irrelevant. But the real question is whether the removal restrictions are of such a nature that they impede the President's ability to perform his constitutional duty, and the functions of the officials in question must be analyzed in that light.

---

[28] The difficulty of defining such categories of "executive" or "quasi-legislative" officials is illustrated by a comparison of our decisions in cases such as *Humphrey's Executor*, *Buckley v. Valeo*, 424 U.S. 1 (1976), and *Bowsher*. In *Buckley*, we indicated that the functions of the Federal Election Commission are "administrative," and "more legislative and judicial in nature," and are "of kinds usually performed by independent regulatory agencies or by some department in the Executive Branch under the direction of an Act of Congress." 42 U.S., at 140-141. In *Bowsher*, we found that the functions of the Comptroller General were "executive" in nature, in that he was required to "exercise judgment concerning facts that affect the application of the Act," and he must "interpret the provisions of the Act to determine precisely what budgetary calculations are required." 478 U.S., at 733. Compare this with the description of the FTC's powers in *Humphrey's Executor*, which we stated "occupie[d] no place in the executive department": "The [FTC] is an administrative body created by Congress to carry into effect legislative policies embodied in the statute in accordance with the legislative standard therein prescribed, and to perform other specified duties as a legislative or as a judicial aid." 295 U.S., at 628. As Justice White noted in his dissent in *Bowsher*, it is hard to dispute that the powers of the FTC at the time of *Humphrey's Executor* would at the present time be considered "executive," at least to some degree. *See* 478 U.S., at 761 n. 3.

Considering for the moment the "good cause" removal provision in isolation from the other parts of the Act at issue in this case, we cannot say
that the imposition of a "good cause" standard for removal by itself unduly
trammels on executive authority. There is no real dispute that the functions
performed by the independent counsel are "executive" in the sense that they
are law enforcement functions that typically have been undertaken by officials within the Executive Branch. . . . [H]owever, the independent counsel is
an inferior officer under the Appointments Clause, with limited jurisdiction
and tenure and lacking policymaking or significant administrative authority.
Although the counsel exercises no small amount of discretion and judgment
in deciding how to carry out his or her duties under the Act, we simply do
not see how the President's need to control the exercise of that discretion is
so central to the functioning of the Executive Branch as to require as a matter
of constitutional law that the counsel be terminable at will by the President.

Nor do we think that the "good cause" removal provision at issue here
impermissibly burdens the President's power to control or supervise the
independent counsel, as an executive official, in the execution of his or her
duties under the Act. This is not a case in which the power to remove an
executive official has been completely stripped from the President, thus providing no means for the President to ensure the "faithful execution" of the
laws. Rather, because the independent counsel may be terminated for "good
cause," the Executive, through the Attorney General, retains ample authority to assure that the counsel is competently performing his or her statutory
responsibilities in a manner that comports with the provisions of the Act.
Although we need not decide in this case exactly what is encompassed within
the term "good cause" under the Act, the legislative history of the removal
provision also makes clear that the Attorney General may remove an independent counsel for "misconduct." *See* H.R. Conf. Rep. No. 100-452, p. 37
(1987). Here, as with the provision of the Act conferring the appointment
authority of the independent counsel on the special court, the congressional
determination to limit the removal power of the Attorney General was essential, in the view of Congress, to establish the necessary independence of the
office. We do not think that this limitation as it presently stands sufficiently
deprives the President of control over the independent counsel to interfere
impermissibly with his constitutional obligation to ensure the faithful execution of the laws.

B

The final question to be addressed is whether the Act, taken as a whole,
violates the principle of separation of powers by unduly interfering with the
role of the Executive Branch. Time and again we have reaffirmed the importance in our constitutional scheme of the separation of governmental powers
into the three coordinate branches. As we stated in *Buckley v. Valeo*, 424 U.S.

1 (1976), the system of separated powers and checks and balances established in the Constitution was regarded by the Framers as "a self-executing safeguard against the encroachment or aggrandizement of one branch at the expense of the other." . . . We have not hesitated to invalidate provisions of law which violate this principle. *Id.*, at 122. On the other hand, we have never held that the Constitution requires that the three branches of Government "operate with absolute independence." *United States v. Nixon*, 418 U.S. 683, 707 (1974). . . .

We observe first that this case does not involve an attempt by Congress to increase its own powers at the expense of the Executive Branch. *Cf. Commodity Futures Trading Commission v. Schor*, 478 U.S. 833, 856 (1986). Unlike some of our previous cases, most recently *Bowsher v. Synar*, this case simply does not pose a "dange[r] of congressional usurpation of Executive Branch functions." 478 U.S. at 727; *see also INS v. Chadha*. Indeed, with the exception of the power of impeachment—which applies to all officers of the United States—Congress retained for itself no powers of control or supervision over an independent counsel. . . . Congress' role under the Act is [almost entirely] limited to receiving reports or other information and oversight of the independent counsel's activities, functions that we have recognized generally as being incidental to the legislative function of Congress.

Similarly, we do not think that the Act works any judicial usurpation of properly executive functions. As should be apparent from our discussion of the Appointments Clause above, the power to appoint inferior officers such as independent counsel is not in itself an "executive" function in the constitutional sense, at least when Congress has exercised its power to vest the appointment of an inferior office in the "courts of Law." We note nonetheless that under the Act the Special Division has no power to appoint an independent counsel *sua sponte*; it may only do so upon the specific request of the Attorney General, and the courts are specifically prevented from reviewing the Attorney General's decision not to seek appointment. In addition, once the court has appointed a counsel and defined his or her jurisdiction, it has no power to supervise or control the activities of the counsel. As we pointed out in our discussion of the Special Division in relation to Article III, the various powers delegated by the statute to the Division are not supervisory or administrative, nor are they functions that the Constitution requires be performed by officials within the Executive Branch. The Act does give a federal court the power to review the Attorney General's decision to remove an independent counsel, but in our view this is a function that is well within the traditional power of the Judiciary.

Finally, we do not think that the Act impermissibly undermines the powers of the Executive Branch, or disrupts the proper balance between the coordinate branches by preventing the Executive Branch from accomplishing its constitutionally assigned functions. It is undeniable that the Act reduces the amount of control or supervision that the Attorney General and, through him, the President exercises over the investigation and prosecution of a certain class of alleged criminal activity. The Attorney General is not allowed to appoint the individual of his choice; he does not determine the counsel's jurisdiction; and his power to remove a counsel is limited. Nonetheless, the Act does give the Attorney General several means of supervising or controlling the prosecutorial powers that may be wielded by an independent counsel. Most importantly, the Attorney General retains the power to remove the counsel for "good cause," a power that we have already concluded provides the Executive with substantial ability to ensure that the laws are "faithfully executed" by an independent counsel. No independent counsel may be appointed without a specific request by the Attorney General, and the Attorney General's decision not to request appointment if he finds "no reasonable grounds to believe that further investigation is warranted" is committed to his unreviewable discretion. The Act thus gives the Executive a degree of control over the power to initiate an investigation by the independent counsel. In addition, the jurisdiction of the independent counsel is defined with reference to the facts submitted by the Attorney General, and once a counsel is appointed, the Act requires that the counsel abide by Justice Department policy unless it is not "possible" to do so. Notwithstanding the fact that the counsel is to some degree "independent" and free from executive supervision to a greater extent than other federal prosecutors, in our view these features of the Act give the Executive Branch sufficient control over the independent counsel to ensure that the President is able to perform his constitutionally assigned duties.

VI

In sum, we conclude today that it does not violate the Appointments Clause for Congress to vest the appointment of independent counsel in the Special Division; that the powers exercised by the Special Division under the Act do not violate Article III; and that the Act does not violate the separation-of-powers principle by impermissibly interfering with the functions of the Executive Branch. The decision of the Court of Appeals is therefore

Reversed.

Justice KENNEDY took no part in the consideration or decision of this case.

Justice SCALIA, dissenting. . . .

The Framers of the Federal Constitution . . . viewed the principle of separation of powers as the absolutely central guarantee of a just Government. In No. 47 of The Federalist, Madison wrote that "[n]o political truth is certainly of greater intrinsic value, or is stamped with the authority of more enlightened patrons of liberty." The Federalist No. 47, p. 301 (C. Rossiter ed. 1961) (hereinafter Federalist). Without a secure structure of separated powers, our Bill of Rights would be worthless, as are the bills of rights of many nations of the world that have adopted, or even improved upon, the mere words of ours. . . .

But just as the mere words of a Bill of Rights are not self-effectuating, the Framers recognized "[t]he insufficiency of a mere parchment delineation of the boundaries" to achieve the separation of powers. Federalist No. 73, p. 442 (A. Hamilton). "[T]he great security," wrote Madison, "against a gradual concentration of the several powers in the same department consists in giving to those who administer each department the necessary constitutional means and personal motives to resist encroachments of the others. The provision for defense must in this, as in all other cases, be made commensurate to the danger of attack." Federalist No. 51, pp. 321-322. Madison continued:

> But it is not possible to give to each department an equal power of self-defense. In republican government, the legislative authority necessarily predominates. The remedy for this inconveniency is to divide the legislature into different branches; and to render them, by different modes of election and different principles of action, as little connected with each other as the nature of their common functions and their common dependence on the society will admit. . . . As the weight of the legislative authority requires that it should be thus divided, the weakness of the executive may require, on the other hand, that it should be fortified. *Id.* at 322-323.

The major "fortification" provided, of course, was the veto power. But in addition to providing fortification, the Founders conspicuously and very consciously declined to sap the Executive's strength in the same way they had weakened the Legislature: by dividing the executive power. Proposals to have multiple executives, or a council of advisers with separate authority were rejected. Thus, while "[a]ll legislative Powers herein granted shall be vested in a Congress of the United States, which shall consist of a Senate *and* House of Representatives," U.S. CONST., Art. I, § 1 (emphasis added), "[t]he executive Power shall be vested in a *President of the United States*," Art. II, § 1, cl. 1 (emphasis added).

That is what this suit is about. Power. The allocation of power among Congress, the President, and the courts in such fashion as to preserve the equilibrium the Constitution sought to establish — so that "a gradual concentration of the several powers in the same department," Federalist No. 51, (J. Madison), can effectively be resisted. Frequently an issue of this sort will come before the Court clad, so to speak, in sheep's clothing: the potential of the asserted principle to effect important change in the equilibrium of power is not immediately evident, and must be discerned by a careful and perceptive analysis. But this wolf comes as a wolf. . . .

II

If to describe this case is not to decide it, the concept of a government of separate and coordinate powers no longer has meaning. The Court devotes most of its attention to such relatively technical details as the Appointments Clause and the removal power, addressing briefly and only at the end of its opinion the separation of powers. As my prologue suggests, I think that has it backwards. Our opinions are full of the recognition that it is the principle of separation of powers, and the inseparable corollary that each department's "defense must . . . be made commensurate to the danger of attack," Federalist No. 51, p. 322 (J. Madison), which gives comprehensible content to the Appointments Clause, and determines the appropriate scope of the removal power. Thus, while I will subsequently discuss why our appointments and removal jurisprudence does not support today's holding, I begin with a consideration of the fountainhead of that jurisprudence, the separation and equilibration of powers. . . .

To repeat, Article II, § 1, cl. 1, of the Constitution provides:

"The executive Power shall be vested in a President of the United States."

As I described at the outset of this opinion, this does not mean *some of* the executive power, but *all of* the executive power. It seems to me, therefore, that the decision of the Court of Appeals invalidating the present statute must be upheld on fundamental separation-of-powers principles if the following two questions are answered affirmatively: (1) Is the conduct of a criminal prosecution (and of an investigation to decide whether to prosecute) the exercise of purely executive power? (2) Does the statute deprive the President of the United States of exclusive control over the exercise of that power? Surprising to say, the Court appears to concede an affirmative answer to both questions, but seeks to avoid the inevitable conclusion that since the statute vests some purely executive power in a person who is not the President of the United States it is void.

The Court concedes that "[t]here is no real dispute that the functions performed by the independent counsel are 'executive'," though it qualifies that concession by adding "in the sense that they are law enforcement functions that typically have been undertaken by officials within the Executive Branch." The qualifier adds nothing but atmosphere. In what other sense can one identify "the executive Power" that is supposed to be vested in the President (unless it includes everything the Executive Branch is given to do) except by reference to what has always and everywhere—if conducted by government at all—been conducted never by the legislature, never by the courts, and always by the executive. There is no possible doubt that the independent counsel's functions fit this description. She is vested with the "full power and independent authority to exercise all *investigative and prosecutorial* functions and powers of the Department of Justice [and] the Attorney General." 28 U.S.C. § 594(a) (1982 ed., Supp. V) (emphasis added). Governmental investigation and prosecution of crimes is a quintessentially executive function.

As for the second question, whether the statute before us deprives the President of exclusive control over that quintessentially executive activity: The Court does not, and could not possibly, assert that it does not. That is indeed the whole object of the statute. Instead, the Court points out that the President, through his Attorney General, has at least some control. That concession is alone enough to invalidate the statute, but I cannot refrain from pointing out that the Court greatly exaggerates the extent of that "some" Presidential control. "Most importan[t]" among these controls, the Court asserts, is the Attorney General's "power to remove the counsel for 'good cause.'" This is somewhat like referring to shackles as an effective means of locomotion. As we recognized in [*Humphrey's Executor*] — indeed, what *Humphrey's Executor* was all about — a limiting removal power to "good cause" is an impediment to, not an effective grant of, Presidential control. We said that limitation was necessary with respect to members of the Federal Trade Commission, which we found to be "an agency of the legislative and judicial departments," and "wholly disconnected from the executive department," 295 U.S., at 630, because "it is quite evident that one who holds his office only during the pleasure of another, cannot be depended upon to maintain an attitude of independence against the latter's will." *Id.* at 629. What we in *Humphrey's Executor* found to be a means of eliminating Presidential control, the Court today considers the "most importan[t]" means of assuring Presidential control. Congress, of course, operated under no such illusion when it enacted this statute, describing the "good cause" limitation as "protecting the independent counsel's ability to act independently of the President's direct control" since it permits removal only for "misconduct." H.R. Conf. Rep. 100-452, p. 37 (1987).

Moving on to the presumably "less important" controls that the President retains, the Court notes that no independent counsel may be appointed without a specific request from the Attorney General. As I have discussed above, the condition that renders such a request mandatory (inability to find "no reasonable grounds to believe" that further investigation is warranted) is so insubstantial that the Attorney General's discretion is severely confined. And once the referral is made, it is for the Special Division to determine the scope and duration of the investigation. And in any event, the limited power over referral is irrelevant to the question whether, once appointed, the independent counsel exercises executive power free from the President's control. Finally, the Court points out that the Act directs the independent counsel to abide by general Justice Department policy, except when not "possible." The exception alone shows this to be an empty promise. . . .

632 Chapter 8: The President and Congress

As I have said, however, it is ultimately irrelevant how much the statute reduces Presidential control. The case is over when the Court acknowledges, as it must, that "[i]t is undeniable that the Act reduces the amount of control or supervision that the Attorney General and, through him, the President exercises over the investigation and prosecution of a certain class of alleged criminal activity." It effects a revolution in our constitutional jurisprudence for the Court, once it has determined that (1) purely executive functions are at issue here, and (2) those functions have been given to a person whose actions are not fully within the supervision and control of the President, nonetheless to proceed further to sit in judgment of whether "the President's need to control the exercise of [the independent counsel's] discretion is so *central* to the functioning of the Executive Branch" as to require complete control, whether the conferral of his powers upon someone else "*sufficiently* deprives the President of control over the independent counsel to interfere impermissibly with [his] constitutional obligation to ensure the faithful execution of the laws," and whether "the Act give[s] the Executive Branch *sufficient* control over the independent counsel to ensure that the President is able to perform his constitutionally assigned duties[.]" It is not for us to determine, and we have never presumed to determine, how much of the purely executive powers of government must be within the full control of the President. The Constitution prescribes that they all are.

Is it unthinkable that the President should have such exclusive power, even when alleged crimes by him or his close associates are at issue? . . . While the separation of powers may prevent us from righting every wrong, it does so in order to ensure that we do not lose liberty. The checks against any branch's abuse of its exclusive powers are twofold: First, retaliation by one of the other branch's use of its exclusive powers: Congress, for example, can impeach the executive who willfully fails to enforce the laws; the executive can decline to prosecute under unconstitutional statutes; and the courts can dismiss malicious prosecutions. Second, and ultimately, there is the political check that the people will replace those in the political branches . . . who are guilty of abuse. . . .

The Court has, nonetheless, replaced the clear constitutional prescription that the executive power belongs to the President with a "balancing test." What are the standards to determine how the balance is to be struck, that is, how much removal of Presidential power is too much? . . . The most amazing feature of the Court's opinion is that it does not even purport to give an answer. It simply announces, with no analysis, that the ability to control the decision whether to investigate and prosecute the President's closest advisers, and indeed the President himself, is not "so central to the functioning of the Executive Branch" as to be constitutionally required to be within the President's control. Apparently that is so because we say it is so. . . .

In my view, moreover, even as an ad hoc, standardless judgment the Court's conclusion must be wrong. Before this statute was passed, the President, in taking action disagreeable to the Congress, or an executive officer giving advice to the President or testifying before Congress concerning one of those many matters on which the two branches are from time to time at odds, could be assured that his acts and motives would be adjudged — insofar as the decision whether to conduct a criminal investigation and to prosecute is concerned — in the Executive Branch, that is, in a forum attuned to the interests and the policies of the Presidency. That was one of the natural advantages the Constitution gave to the Presidency, just as it gave Members of Congress (and their staffs) the advantage of not being prosecutable for anything said or done in their legislative capacities. It is the very object of this legislation to eliminate that assurance of a sympathetic forum. . . . Perhaps the boldness of the President himself will not be affected — though I am not even sure of that. . . . But as for the President's high-level assistants, who typically have no political base of support, it is as utterly unrealistic to think that they will not be intimidated by this prospect, and that their advice to him and their advocacy of his interests before a hostile Congress will not be affected, as it would be to think that the Members of Congress and their staffs would be unaffected by replacing the Speech or Debate Clause with a similar provision. It deeply wounds the President, by substantially reducing the President's ability to protect himself and his staff. . . .

III. . . .

. . . Because appellant . . . was not appointed by the President with the advice and consent of the Senate, but rather by the Special Division of the United States Court of Appeals, her appointment is constitutional only if (1) she is an "inferior" officer within the meaning of the above Clause, and (2) Congress may vest her appointment in a court of law.

As to the first of these inquiries, the Court does not attempt to "decide exactly" what establishes the line between principal and "inferior" officers, but is confident that, whatever the line may be, appellant "clearly falls on the 'inferior officer' side" of it. The Court gives three reasons: *First*, she "is subject to removal by a higher Executive Branch official," namely, the Attorney General. *Second*, she is "empowered by the Act to perform only certain, limited duties." *Third*, her office is "limited in jurisdiction" and "limited in tenure."

. . . [I]t is not clear from the Court's opinion why the factors it discusses . . . are determinative of the question of inferior officer status. . . . I think it preferable to look to the text of the Constitution and the division of power that it establishes. These demonstrate, I think, that the independent counsel is not an inferior officer because she is not subordinate to any officer in the Executive Branch (indeed, not even to the President). . . .

That "inferior" means "subordinate" is also consistent with what little we know about the evolution of the Appointments Clause. As originally reported to the Committee on Style, the Appointments Clause provided no "exception" from the standard manner of appointment (President with the advice and consent of the Senate) for inferior officers. 2 M. Farrand, Records of the Federal Convention of 1787, pp. 498-499, 599 (rev. ed. 1966). Gouverneur Morris [subsequently] moved to add the exceptions clause. No great debate ensued; the only disagreement was over whether it was necessary at all. It is perfectly obvious, therefore, both from the relative brevity of the discussion this addition received, and from the content of that discussion, that it was intended merely to make clear (what Madison thought already was clear) that those officers appointed by the President with Senate approval could on their own appoint their subordinates, who would, of course, by chain of command still be under the direct control of the President. . . .

To be sure, it is not a *sufficient* condition for "inferior" officer status that one be subordinate to a principal officer. . . . But it is surely a *necessary* condition for inferior officer status that the officer be subordinate to another officer.

The independent counsel is not even subordinate to the President. The Court essentially admits as much, noting that "appellant may not be 'subordinate' to the Attorney General (and the President) insofar as she possesses a degree of independent discretion to exercise the powers delegated to her under the Act." As noted earlier, the Act specifically grants her the "full power and independent authority to exercise all investigative and prosecutorial functions of the Department of Justice," and makes her removable only for "good cause," a limitation specifically intended to ensure that she be independent of, not subordinate to, the President and the Attorney General.

Because appellant is not subordinate to another officer, she is not an "inferior" officer and her appointment other than by the President with the advice and consent of the Senate is unconstitutional.

IV

. . . There is . . . no provision in the Constitution stating who may remove executive officers, except the provisions for removal by impeachment. Before the present decision it was established, however, (1) that the President's power to remove principal officers who exercise purely executive powers could not be restricted, see *Myers*, 272 U.S., at 127, and (2) that his power to remove inferior officers who exercise purely executive powers, and whose appointment Congress had removed from the usual procedure of Presidential appointment with Senate consent, could be restricted, at least where the appointment had been made by an officer of the Executive Branch, *id.*

The Court could have resolved the removal power issue in this case by simply relying upon its erroneous conclusion that the independent counsel was an inferior officer, and then extending our holding that the removal of inferior officers appointed by the Executive can be restricted, to a new holding that even the removal of inferior officers appointed by the courts can be restricted. That would in my view be a considerable and unjustified extension, giving the Executive full discretion in neither the selection nor the removal of a purely executive officer. The course the Court has chosen, however, is even worse.

Since our 1935 decision in [*Humphrey's Executor*] — which was considered by many at the time the product of an activist, anti-New Deal Court bent on reducing the power of President Franklin Roosevelt — it has been established that the line of permissible restriction upon removal of principal officers lies at the point at which the powers exercised by those officers are no longer purely executive. . . . It has often been observed, correctly in my view, that the line between "purely executive" functions and "quasi-legislative" or "quasi-judicial" functions is not a clear one or even a rational one. But at least it permitted the identification of certain officers, and certain agencies, whose functions were entirely within the control of the President. Congress had to be aware of that restriction in its legislation. Today, however, *Humphrey's Executor* is swept into the dustbin of repudiated constitutional principles. . . . What *Humphrey's Executor* (and presumably *Myers*) really means, we are now told [by the majority], is not that there are any "rigid categories of those officials who may or may not be removed at will by the President," but simply that Congress cannot "[interfere] with the President's exercise of the 'executive power' and his constitutionally appointed duty to 'take care that the laws be faithfully executed.' "

One can hardly grieve for the shoddy treatment given today to *Humphrey's Executor*, which, after all, accorded the same indignity (with much less justification) to Chief Justice Taft's opinion 10 years earlier in [*Myers*] — gutting, in six quick pages devoid of textual or historical precedent for the novel principle it set forth, a carefully researched and reasoned 70-page opinion. It is in fact comforting to witness the reality that he who lives by the *ipse dixit* dies by the *ipse dixit*. But one must grieve for the Constitution. *Humphrey's Executor* at least had the decency formally to observe the constitutional principle that the President had to be the repository of *all* executive power, which, as *Myers* carefully explained, necessarily means that he must be able to discharge those who do not perform executive functions according to his liking. . . . By contrast, "our present considered view" is simply that any executive officer's removal can be restricted, so long as the President remains "able to accomplish his constitutional role." There are now no lines. . . .

V

The purpose of the separation and equilibration of powers in general, and of the unitary Executive in particular, was not merely to assure effective government but to preserve individual freedom. Those who hold or have held offices covered by the Ethics in Government Act are entitled to that

In Context

In essence, the "unitary executive theory" posits that the President has direct control over all federal officers wielding executive power. As Professors Lawrence Lessig and Cass Sunstein have pointed out, there are strong and weak forms of the theory. In its strong form, the President has unlimited power to control the decisions of all officers in the Executive Branch. The President also has largely unrestricted discretion to fire administrative officials. In its weak form, the President has plenary power over certain administrative functions, but Congress retains significant latitude in structuring the workings of the administrative agencies it creates. For further reading, *see* Lessig & Sunstein, *The President and the Administration,* 94 Colum. L. Rev. 1 (1994); Calabresi & Prakash, *The President's Power to Execute the Laws,* 104 Yale L.J. 541, 549-50 (1994).

protection as much as the rest of us, and I conclude my discussion by considering the effect of the Act upon the fairness of the process they receive.

. . . Under our system of government, the primary check against prosecutorial abuse is a political one. The prosecutors who exercise this awesome discretion are selected and can be removed by a President, whom the people have trusted enough to elect. Moreover, when crimes are not investigated and prosecuted fairly, nonselectively, with a reasonable sense of proportion, the President pays the cost in political damage to his administration. . . .

. . . It is, in other words, an [advantage] of the unitary Executive that it can achieve a more uniform application of the law. Perhaps that is not always achieved, but the mechanism to achieve it is there. The mini-Executive that is the independent counsel, however, operating in an area where so little is law and so much is discretion, is intentionally cut off from the unifying influence of the Justice Department, and from the perspective that multiple responsibilities provide. What would normally be regarded as a technical violation (there are no rules defining such things), may in his or her small world assume the proportions of an indictable offense. What would normally be regarded as an investigation that has reached the level of pursuing such picayune matters that it should be concluded, may to him or her be an investigation that ought to go on for another year. How frightening it must be to have your own independent counsel and staff appointed, with nothing else to do but to investigate you until investigation is no longer worthwhile—with whether it is worthwhile not depending upon what such judgments usually hinge on, competing responsibilities. And to have that counsel and staff decide, with no basis for comparison, whether what you have done is bad enough, willful enough, and provable enough, to warrant an indictment. How admirable the constitutional system that provides the means to avoid such a distortion. And how unfortunate the judicial decision that has permitted it. . . .

The ad hoc approach to constitutional adjudication has real attraction, even apart from its work-saving potential. It is guaranteed to produce a result, in every case, that will make a majority of the Court happy with the law. The law is, by definition, precisely what the majority thinks, taking all things into account, it *ought* to be. I prefer to rely upon the judgment of the wise men who constructed our system, and of the people who approved it, and of two centuries of history that have shown it to be sound. Like it or not, that judgment says, quite plainly, that "[t]he executive Power shall be vested in a President of the United States."

* * *

Requiem for the Independent Counsel. The independent counsel provisions of the Ethics in Government Act stayed on the books for a little over 20 years and produced some notable investigations (including Kenneth Starr's investigation of President Clinton, which eventuated in the latter's impeachment). It was slated for reauthorization by Congress in 1999, pursuant to its sunset provision. Congress declined to extend it. The Department of Justice under Attorney General Janet Reno later promulgated rules that established a similar position: the "special counsel." 28 C.F.R. § 600.1. Unlike the independent counsel provisions, these regulations gave the Attorney General power to define the special counsel's jurisdiction. They also allowed the Attorney General to remove the special counsel for good cause. These are the provisions (in addition to 28 U.S.C. § 515) under which Deputy Attorney General Rod Rosenstein appointed former FBI Director Robert Mueller as special counsel to investigate possible interference by Russia in the 2016 Presidential election. *See* Office of the Deputy Attorney General, Appointment of Special Counsel to Investigate Russian Interference with the 2016 Presidential Election and Related Matters, Order No. 3915-2017 (2017).

QUESTION SET 8.6

Review & Synthesis

1. How did the Court determine that the independent counsel was an "inferior" officer rather than a "principal" one? What indicia of "inferiority" did it emphasize? Do you agree or disagree with Justice Scalia that the independent counsel was not subordinate to the Attorney General or the President because the Ethics in Government Act granted her a measure of investigative and prosecutorial discretion?

2. What test did the *Morrison* Court adopt for identifying unconstitutional encumbrances on the President's removal power? How is this test fundamentally different than the ones applied in *Myers v. United States* and *Humphrey's Executor*?

3. How do you think *Morrison* affects the balance of power between Congress and the President when it comes to supervising and controlling the administrative state? Is it more or less favorable to the President than the tests adopted in *Myers* and *Humphrey's Executor*?

4. Why did the Court conclude that the most logical place to situate appointment of the independent counsel, outside of the Executive Branch, was in the Judicial Branch? Was it because there is some natural affinity between the executive and judicial functions? Was it because courts had appointed officials with prosecutorial and investigative responsibilities in

the past? Was it because, given the independent counsel's responsibilities, appointment by the President or a member of his or her Cabinet would be self-defeating?

5. Justice Scalia argued that the Constitution vests *all* of the federal government's executive power in the President and therefore the President has unfettered discretion to remove Executive Branch officials. Does his argument also imply that the President can lawfully order a subordinate not to carry out a nondiscretionary duty required by statute? How would such a position square with the distinction between "political" decision-making and ministerial decision-making advanced in both *Kendall v. United States* and *Myers v. United States*?

Application & Analysis

1. In the wake of the 2008 financial crisis, Congress established the Consumer Financial Protection Bureau ("CFPB"), an independent regulatory agency tasked with ensuring that consumer debt products are safe and transparent. *See* Dodd-Frank Wall Street Reform and Consumer Protection Act, Pub. L. No. 111-203, 124 Stat. 1376 (2010). The CFPB administers 18 existing federal statutes, including the Fair Credit Reporting Act and the Truth in Lending Act. It also has rulemaking, enforcement, and adjudicatory powers, including the authority to conduct investigations, issue subpoenas, initiate administrative adjudications, prosecute civil actions in federal court, and issue binding decisions in administrative proceedings. The agency is led by a single Director, who is appointed to a five-year term by the President, with the advice and consent of the Senate. The President may remove the Director only for "inefficiency, neglect of duty, or malfeasance in office." 12 U.S.C. §§ 5491(c)(3). The CFPB is not funded through the normal appropriations process. It instead receives funding from the Federal Reserve, which is itself funded outside the appropriations process through assessments paid by banks.

   In 2017, the CFPB issued a subpoena to Seila Law LLC, a California-based law firm that provides debt-related legal services to clients. The subpoena sought information and documents related to the firm's business practices. Seila Law asked the CFPB to drop the subpoena on the ground that the agency's leadership by a single Director removable only for cause violated the separation of powers. The CFPB refused and Seila Law declined to comply with the subpoena.

   The CFPB has filed a petition to enforce the subpoena in federal district court. Seila Law has again asserted that the agency's structure violates the separation of powers. You are a clerk for the judge assigned to the case. Write a brief memorandum analyzing Seila Law's claim.

2. The Public Company Accounting Oversight Board was established as part of several accounting reforms in the Sarbanes-Oxley Act of 2002. The Board is composed of five members, all of whom are appointed by the SEC. Every accounting firm that audits public companies under federal securities laws must register with the Board, pay it an annual fee, and comply with its rules and oversight. The Board may inspect registered firms, initiate formal investigations, and issue severe sanctions in its disciplinary proceedings. While the SEC oversees the Board's activities, it cannot remove Board members at will. Rather, the SEC may only remove Board members "for good cause shown," "in accordance with" specified procedures. 15 U.S.C. §§ 7211(e)(6), 7217(d)(3). The SEC's Commissioners, in turn, cannot themselves be removed by the President except for inefficiency, neglect of duty, or malfeasance in office.

The Board inspected Johnson LLC, a registered accounting firm, several months ago. After the inspection it released a public report criticizing the firm's auditing procedures and then launched a formal investigation into its practices. The firm responded by suing the Board in federal district court. It seeks a declaratory judgment that the Board's structure is unconstitutional and an injunction preventing the Board from exercising its powers. Specifically, Johnson LLC makes two arguments. First, it claims that the Board cannot wield the executive power granted it by Sarbanes-Oxley because it is unconstitutionally insulated from the President's removal power. Second, it claims that the Board's members are principal Officers of the United States and thus could not have been lawfully appointed by the SEC.

You clerk for the judge hearing the case. Write a brief memorandum analyzing Johnson LLC's claims.

E. GENERALIZED SEPARATION OF POWERS PRINCIPLES

Thus far, we have discussed textually driven challenges to Congress' efforts to oversee and control administrative agencies. To be sure, the Court has demonstrated its comfort with relying on those provisions to invalidate federal statutes. As numerous commentators have observed, however, the separation of powers is an idea that permeates the original Constitution. It is reflected not just in the document's explicit provisions, but also in the underlying relational structure of the Legislative, Executive, and Judicial Branches. Since separation of powers is uniformly accepted as a foundational constitutional principle, does the Court need to rely on specific constitutional text to invoke it? In other words, can the Court strike down federal legislation on separation of powers grounds, even if it can point to no text in the Constitution that the challenged legislation has violated? Even if it can, should it do so?

The case that follows — *Metropolitan Washington Airports Authority v. Citizens for Abatement of Aircraft Noise, Inc.* — addresses these questions. As in other cases we have considered, the plaintiffs disagreed with decisions being made by an administrative body (here, the Metropolitan Washington Airports Authority ("MWAA")), and so they sought to nullify those decisions by attacking the constitutionality of the legislation — the Transfer Act — that created it. The specific issue before the Court was whether Congress violated the separation of powers by creating a Board of Review staffed exclusively by sitting members of Congress to oversee the MWAA's operations. Rather than pointing to explicit constitutional provisions that might forbid sitting Members of Congress from staffing an administrative oversight body, Justice Stevens (writing for the majority) inferred general separation of powers principles from the Constitution's text and several of the cases we have previously considered — *Bowsher v. Synar* and *INS v. Chadha* figure prominently in his analysis.

Writing in dissent, Justice White rejected the Court's conclusion on the Transfer Act's constitutionality and took particular issue with the Court's reliance on inferred separation of powers principles. To the extent the Transfer Act might be thought to violate the Constitution — a conclusion that he, Justice Marshall, and Chief Justice Burger rejected — White did not think it ran afoul of the generalized separation of powers principles the Court identified. He felt that the only possible separation of powers limitation implicated by the Transfer Act was the Ineligibility Clause (Art. I, § 6, cl. 2). Even that provision, to Justice White's mind, was inapplicable to the administrative scheme established by the Act.

Note three features as you read the case. First, the Court acknowledged that it typically characterizes administrative actions as "legislative" or "executive." Once it has done so, it identifies and applies the relevant constitutional limitations. Here, however, the Court observed that labeling the Board of Review's actions as "legislative" or "executive" did nothing to answer the constitutional question presented to it. Second, the duties undertaken by the MWAA Review Board were performed not by Congress' designees or agents under its control, but by Members of Congress themselves (purportedly in their individual rather than elected capacities). Third, the Board of Review was not created by Congress. Rather, it was created by the Commonwealth of Virginia and the District of Columbia. It was superficially a state agency, and so one of the questions in the case was whether it was *substantively* a federal entity to which the federal Constitution's separation-of-powers principles applied.

Metropolitan Washington Airports Authority v. Citizens for the Abatement of Aircraft Noise, Inc.
501 U.S. 252 (1991)

Justice STEVENS delivered the opinion of the Court.

An Act of Congress authorizing the transfer of operating control of two major airports from the Federal Government to the Metropolitan Washington Airports Authority (MWAA) conditioned the transfer on the creation by MWAA of a unique "Board of Review" composed of nine Members of Congress and vested with veto power over decisions made by MWAA's Board of Directors. The principal question presented is whether this unusual statutory condition violates the constitutional principle of separation of powers, as interpreted in *INS v. Chadha*, 462 U.S. 919 (1983), *Bowsher v. Synar*, 478 U.S. 714 (1986), and *Springer v. Philippine Islands*, 277 U.S. 189 (1928). We conclude, as did the Court of Appeals for the District of Columbia Circuit, that the condition is unconstitutional.

I....

. . . National and Dulles are the only two major commercial airports owned by the Federal Government. A third airport, Baltimore Washington International (BWI), which is owned by the State of Maryland, also serves the Washington metropolitan area. Like Dulles, it is larger than National and located in a rural area many miles from the Capitol. Because of its location, National is by far the busiest and most profitable of the three. Although proposals for the joint operating control of all three airports have been considered, the plan that gave rise to this litigation involves only National and Dulles, both of which are located in Virginia. Maryland's interest in the overall problem explains its representation on the Board of Directors of MWAA.

Throughout its history, National has been the subject of controversy. Its location at the center of the metropolitan area is a great convenience for air travelers, but flight paths over densely populated areas have generated concern among local residents about safety, noise, and pollution. Those living closest to the airport have provided the strongest support for proposals to close National or to transfer some of its operations to Dulles.

Despite the FAA's history of profitable operation of National and excellent management of both airports, the Secretary of Transportation concluded that necessary capital improvements could not be financed for either National or Dulles unless control of the airports was transferred to a regional authority with power to raise money by selling tax-exempt bonds. In 1984, she therefore appointed an advisory commission to develop a plan for the creation of such a regional authority. . . .

In 1985, Virginia and the District both passed legislation authorizing the establishment of the recommended regional authority. [Bills were also drafted in the House and Senate to surrender control of the airports to the MWAA. The bills also provided] for the establishment of a review board with veto power over major actions of MWAA's Board of Directors. Under two of the proposals, the board of review would clearly have acted as an agent of the Congress. After Congress received an opinion from the Department of Justice that a veto of MWAA action by such a board of review "would plainly be legislative action that must conform to the requirements of Article 1, section 7 of the Constitution," the Senate adopted a version of the review board that required Members of Congress to serve in their individual capacities as representatives of users of the airports. The provision was further amended in the House, and the Senate concurred. Ultimately, § 2456(f) of the Transfer Act, as enacted, defined the composition and powers of the Board of Review in much greater detail than the Board of Directors.

Subparagraph (1) of § 2456(f) specifies that the Board of Review "shall consist" of nine Members of the Congress, eight of whom serve on committees with jurisdiction over transportation issues and none of whom may be a Member from Maryland, Virginia, or the District of Columbia. Subparagraph (4)(B) details the actions that must be submitted to the Board of Review for approval, which include adoption of a budget, authorization of bonds, promulgation of regulations, endorsement of a master plan, and appointment of the chief executive officer of the Authority. Subparagraph (4)(D) explains that disapproval by the Board will prevent submitted actions from taking effect. Other significant provisions of the Act include subparagraph (5), which authorizes the Board of Review to require Authority directors to consider any action relating to the airports; subsection (g), which requires that any action changing the hours of operation at either National or Dulles be taken by regulation and therefore be subject to veto by the Board of Review; and subsection (h), which contains a provision disabling MWAA's Board of Directors from performing any action subject to the veto power if a court should hold that the Board of Review provisions of the Act are invalid.

. . . MWAA's Board of Directors adopted bylaws providing for the Board of Review, and Virginia and the District of Columbia amended their legislation to give MWAA power to establish the Board of Review. On September 2, 1987, the directors appointed the nine members of the Board of Review from lists that had been submitted by the Speaker of the House of Representatives and the President pro tempore of the Senate.

On March 16, 1988, MWAA's Board of Directors adopted a master plan providing for the construction of a new terminal at National with gates capable of handling larger aircraft, an additional taxiway turnoff to reduce aircraft time on the runway and thereby improve airport capacity, a new dual-level roadway system, and new parking facilities. On April 13, the Board of Review met and voted not to disapprove the master plan.

II

In November 1988, Citizens for the Abatement of Aircraft Noise, Inc., and two individuals who reside under flight paths of aircraft departing from, and arriving at, National (collectively CAAN) brought this action. CAAN sought a declaration that the Board of Review's power to veto actions of MWAA's Board of Directors is unconstitutional and an injunction against any action by the Board of Review as well as any action by the Board of Directors that is subject to Board of Review approval. The complaint alleged that most of the members of CAAN live under flight paths to and from National and that CAAN's primary purpose is to develop and implement a transportation policy for the Washington area that would include balanced service among its three major airports, thus reducing the operations at National and alleviating noise, safety, and air pollution problems associated with such operations. The complaint named MWAA and its Board of Review as defendants. [The District Court for the District of Columbia granted summary judgment for the defendants. A divided D.C. Circuit panel reversed on appeal, concluding that the MWAA was an agent of Congress because of its power to disapprove key MWAA operational decisions.]

[In Section III of its opinion, the Court considered and rejected the defendants' argument that the plaintiffs' complaint failed to allege facts demonstrating their constitutional standing to sue.]

IV

Petitioners argue that this case does not raise any separation-of-powers issue because the Board of Review neither exercises federal power nor acts as an agent of Congress. Examining the origin and structure of the Board, we conclude that petitioners are incorrect.

Petitioners lay great stress on the fact that the Board of Review was established by the bylaws of MWAA, which was created by legislation enacted by the Commonwealth of Virginia and the District of Columbia. Putting aside the unsettled question whether the District of Columbia acts as a State or as an agent of the Federal Government for separation-of-powers purposes, we believe the fact that the Board of Review was created by state enactments is not enough to immunize it from separation-of-powers review. Several factors combine to mandate this result.

Control over National and Dulles was originally in federal hands, and was transferred to MWAA only subject to the condition that the States create the Board of Review. Congress placed such significance on the Board that it required that the Board's invalidation prevent MWAA from taking any action that would have been subject to Board oversight. Moreover, the Federal Government has a strong and continuing interest in the efficient operation of the airports, which are vital to the smooth conduct of Government business, especially to the work of Congress, whose Members must maintain offices in both Washington and the districts that they represent and must shuttle back and forth according to the dictates of busy and often unpredictable schedules. This federal interest was identified in the preamble to the Transfer Act, justified a Presidential appointee on the Board of Directors, and motivated the creation of the Board of Review, the structure and the powers of which Congress mandated in detail. Most significant, membership on the Board of Review is limited to federal officials, specifically members of congressional committees charged with authority over air transportation.

That the Members of Congress who serve on the Board nominally serve "in their individual capacities, as representatives of users" of the airports does not prevent this group of officials from qualifying as a congressional agent exercising federal authority for separation-of-powers purposes. As we recently held, "separation-of-powers analysis does not turn on the labeling of an activity," *Mistretta v. United States*, 488 U.S. 361, 393 (1989). The Transfer Act imposes no requirement that the Members of Congress who are appointed to the Board actually be users of the airports. Rather, the Act imposes the requirement that the Board members have congressional responsibilities related to the federal regulation of air transportation. These facts belie the *ipse dixit* that the Board members will act "in their individual capacities." . . .

Congress as a body also exercises substantial power over the appointment and removal of the particular Members of Congress who serve on the Board. The Transfer Act provides that the Board "shall consist" of "two members of the Public Works and Transportation Committee and two members of the Appropriations Committee of the House of Representatives from a list provided by the Speaker of the House," "two members of the Commerce, Science, and Transportation Committee and two members of the Appropriations Committee of the Senate from a list provided by the President pro tempore of the Senate," and "one member chosen alternately . . . from a list provided by the Speaker of the House or the President pro tempore of the Senate, respectively." 49 U.S.C. App. § 2456(f)(1). Significantly, appointments must be made from the lists, and there is no requirement that the lists contain more recommendations than the number of Board openings. . . . The list system, combined with congressional authority over committee assignments, guarantees Congress effective control over appointments. Control over committee assignments also gives Congress effective removal power over Board members because depriving a Board member of membership in the relevant committees deprives the member of authority to sit on the Board.

We thus confront an entity created at the initiative of Congress, the powers of which Congress has delineated, the purpose of which is to protect an acknowledged federal interest, and membership in which is restricted to congressional officials. Such an entity necessarily exercises sufficient federal power as an agent of Congress to mandate separation-of-powers scrutiny. Any other conclusion would permit Congress to evade the "carefully crafted" constraints of the Constitution, *INS v. Chadha*, 462 U.S. 919, 959 (1983), simply by delegating primary responsibility for execution of national policy to the States, subject to the veto power of Members of Congress acting "in their individual capacities."

V

Because National and Dulles are the property of the Federal Government and their operations directly affect interstate commerce, there is no doubt concerning the ultimate power of Congress to enact legislation defining the policies that govern those operations. Congress itself can formulate the details, or it can enact general standards and assign to the Executive Branch the responsibility for making necessary managerial decisions in conformance with those standards. The question presented is only whether the Legislature has followed a constitutionally acceptable procedure in delegating decision-making authority to the Board of Review.

The structure of our Government as conceived by the Framers of our Constitution disperses the federal power among the three branches—the Legislative, the Executive, and the Judicial—placing both substantive and procedural limitations on each. The ultimate purpose of this separation of powers is to protect the liberty and security of the governed. . . .

Violations of the separation-of-powers principle have been uncommon because each branch has traditionally respected the prerogatives of the other two. Nevertheless, the Court has been sensitive to its responsibility to enforce the principle when necessary.

> Time and again we have reaffirmed the importance in our constitutional scheme of the separation of governmental powers into the three coordinate branches. *See, e.g., Bowsher v. Synar*, 478 U.S., at 725 (citing *Humphrey's Executor*, 295 U.S. [602], 629-630). As we stated in *Buckley v. Valeo*, 424 U.S. 1 (1976), the system of separated powers and checks and balances established in the Constitution was regarded by the Framers as "a self-executing safeguard against the encroachment or aggrandizement of one branch at the expense of the other." *Id.* at 122. We have not hesitated to invalidate provisions of law which violate this principle. *See id.* at 123. *Morrison v. Olson*, 487 U.S. 654, 693 (1988). . . .

To forestall the danger of encroachment "beyond the legislative sphere," the Constitution imposes two basic and related constraints on the Congress. It may not "invest itself or its Members with either executive power or judicial power." *J.W. Hampton, Jr., & Co. v. United States*, 276 U.S. 394, 406 (1928). And, when it exercises its legislative power, it must follow the "single, finely wrought and exhaustively considered, procedures" specified in Article I. *INS v. Chadha*, 462 U.S., at 951.

The first constraint is illustrated by the Court's holdings in *Springer v. Philippine Islands*, 277 U.S. 189 (1928), and *Bowsher v. Synar*, 478 U.S. 714 (1986). *Springer* involved the validity of Acts of the Philippine Legislature that authorized a committee of three—two legislators and one executive—to vote corporate stock owned by the Philippine Government. Because the Organic Act of the Philippine Islands incorporated the separation-of-powers principle, and because the challenged statute authorized two legislators to perform the executive function of controlling the management of the government-owned corporations, the Court held the statutes invalid. Our more recent decision in *Bowsher* involved a delegation of authority to the Comptroller General to revise the federal budget. After concluding that the Comptroller General was in effect an agent of Congress, the Court held that he could not exercise executive powers. . . . The second constraint is illustrated by our decision in *Chadha*. That case involved the validity of a statute that authorized either House of Congress by resolution to invalidate a decision by the Attorney General to allow a deportable alien to remain in the United States. Congress had the power to achieve that result through legislation, but the statute was nevertheless invalid because Congress cannot exercise its legislative power to enact laws without following the bicameral and presentment procedures specified in Article I. For the same reason, an attempt to characterize the budgetary action of the Comptroller General in *Bowsher* as legislative action would not have saved its constitutionality because Congress may not delegate the power to legislate to its own agents or to its own Members.

Respondents rely on both of these constraints in their challenge to the Board of Review. The Court of Appeals found it unnecessary to discuss the second constraint because the court was satisfied that the power exercised by the Board of Review over "key operational decisions is quintessentially executive." We need not agree or disagree with this characterization by the Court of Appeals to conclude that the Board of Review's power is constitutionally impermissible. If the power is executive, the Constitution does not permit an agent of Congress to exercise it. If the power is legislative, Congress must exercise it in conformity with the bicameralism and presentment requirements of Art. I, § 7. In short, when Congress "[takes] action that ha[s] the purpose and effect of altering the legal rights, duties, and relations of persons . . . outside the Legislative Branch," it must take that action by the procedures authorized in the Constitution. *See Chadha*, 462 U.S., at 952-955.[21]

. . . As James Madison presciently observed, the legislature "can with greater facility, mask under complicated and indirect measures, the encroachments which it makes on the co-ordinate departments." The

[21] The Constitution does permit Congress or a part of Congress to take some actions with effects outside the Legislative Branch by means other than the provisions of Art. I, § 7. These include at least the power of the House alone to initiate impeachments, Art. I, § 2, cl. 5; the power of the Senate alone to try impeachments, Art. I, § 3, cl. 6; the power of the Senate alone to approve or disapprove Presidential appointments, Art. II, § 2, cl. 2; and the power of the Senate alone to ratify treaties, Art. II, § 2, cl. 2. *See also* Art. II, § 1, and Amdt. 12 (congressional role in Presidential election process); Art. V (congressional role in amendment process). Moreover, Congress can, of course, manage its own affairs without complying with the constraints of Art. I, § 7. *See Chadha*, 462 U.S., at 954, n. 16; *Bowsher*, 478 U.S., at 753-756 (Stevens, J., concurring in judgment).

Federalist No. 48. Heeding his warning that legislative "power is of an encroaching nature," we conclude that the Board of Review is an impermissible encroachment.[23]

The judgment of the Court of Appeals is affirmed.

It is so ordered.

Justice WHITE, with whom THE CHIEF JUSTICE and Justice MARSHALL join, dissenting.

Today the Court strikes down yet another innovative and otherwise lawful governmental experiment in the name of separation of powers. To reach this result, the majority must strain to bring state enactments within the ambit of a doctrine hitherto applicable only to the Federal Government and strain again to extend the doctrine even though both Congress and the Executive argue for the constitutionality of the arrangement which the Court invalidates. These efforts are untenable because they violate the "'cardinal principle that this Court will first ascertain whether a construction of [a] statute is fairly possible by which the [constitutional] question may be avoided.'" *Ashwander v. TVA*, 297 U.S. 288, 348 (1936) (Brandeis, J., concurring), (quoting *Crowell v. Benson*, 285 U.S. 22, 62 (1932)). They are also untenable because the Court's separation-of-powers cases in no way compel the decision the majority reaches.

I

[In addition to arguing that the Transfer Act could have been read to avoid any separation-of-powers problems, and that Congress was permitted to transfer control of Dulles and National Airports to Virginia and the District of Columbia under the Property Clause (Art. IV, § 3, cl. 2.), Justice White insisted that the Board of Review was created (and thus controlled by) state rather than federal law. He then observed:]

Considered as a creature of state law, the Board offends no constitutional provision or doctrine. The Court does not assert that congressional membership on a state-created entity, without more, violates the Incompatibility or Ineligibility Clauses. U.S. Const., Art. I, § 6, cl. 2. By their express terms, these provisions prohibit Members of Congress from serving in another federal office. They say nothing to bar congressional service in state or state-created offices. To the contrary, the Framers considered and rejected such a bar. 1 Max Farrand,

---

[23] Because we invalidate the Board of Review under basic separation-of-powers principles, we need not address respondents' claim that Members of Congress serve on the Board in violation of the Incompatibility and Ineligibility Clauses. *See* U.S. Const., Art. I, § 6. We also express no opinion on whether the appointment process of the Board of Review contravenes the Appointments Clause, U.S. Const., Art. II, § 2, cl. 2.

Records of the Federal Convention of 1787, pp. 20-21, 217, 386, 389, 428-429 (1966 ed.). As Roger Sherman observed, maintaining a state-ineligibility requirement would amount to "erecting a Kingdom at war with itself." The historical practice of the First Congress confirms the Conventions [*sic*] sentiments, insofar as several Members simultaneously sat as state legislators and judges. As the Court has held, actions by Members of the First Congress provide weighty evidence on the Constitution's meaning. *Bowsher v. Synar*, 478 U.S. 714, 723-724 (1986). Constitutional text and history leave no question but that Virginia and the District of Columbia could constitutionally agree to pass reciprocal legislation creating a body to which nonfederal officers would appoint Members of Congress functioning in their individual capacities. No one in this case contends otherwise. . . .

II

Even assuming that separation-of-powers principles apply, the Court can hold the Board to be unconstitutional only by extending those principles in an unwarranted fashion. The majority contends otherwise, reasoning that the Constitution requires today's result whether the Board exercises executive or legislative power. Yet never before has the Court struck down a body on separation-of-powers grounds that neither Congress nor the Executive oppose. It is absurd to suggest that the Board's power represents the type of "legislative usurpatio[n] . . . which, by assembling all power in the same hands . . . must lead to the same tyranny," that concerned the Framers. The Federalist No. 48 (J. Madison). More to the point, it is clear that the Board does not offend separation-of-powers principles either under our cases dealing with executive power or our decisions concerning legislative authority.[3]

---

[3] For these reasons, the Court's historical exposition is not entirely relevant. The majority attempts to clear the path for its decision by stressing the Framers' fear of overweening legislative authority. It cannot be seriously maintained, however, that the basis for fearing legislative encroachment has increased or even persisted rather than substantially diminished. At one point Congress may have reigned as the pre-eminent branch, much as the Framers predicted. *See* W. Wilson, Congressional Government 40-57 (1885). It does so no longer. This century has witnessed a vast increase in the power that Congress has transferred to the Executive. *See INS v. Chadha*, 462 U.S. 919, 968-974 (1983) (White, J., dissenting). Given this shift in the constitutional balance, the Framers' fears of legislative tyranny ring hollow when invoked to portray a body like the Board as a serious encroachment on the powers of the Executive.

A

Based on its faulty premise that the Board is exercising federal power, the Court first reasons that "[i]f the [Board's] power is executive, the Constitution does not permit an agent of Congress to exercise it." The majority does not, however, rely on the constitutional provisions most directly on point. Under the Incompatibility and Ineligibility Clauses, Members of Congress may not serve in another office that is under the authority of the United States. U.S. Const., Art. I, § 6, cl. 2. If the Board did exercise executive authority that is federal in nature, the Court would have no need to say anything other than that congressional membership on the Board violated these express constitutional limitations. The majority's failure is either unaccountable or suggests that it harbors a certain discomfort with its own position that the Board in fact exercises significant federal power. Whichever is the case, the Court instead relies on expanding nontextual principles as articulated in *Bowsher v. Synar*, 478 U.S. 714 (1986). *Bowsher*, echoing *Springer v. Philippine Islands*, 277 U.S. 189 (1928), held that the Constitution prevented legislative agents from exercising executive authority. *Bowsher*, 478 U.S., at 726. The Court asserts that the Board, again in effect, is controlled by Congress. The analysis the Court has hitherto employed to recognize congressional control, however, show this not to be the case. . . .

. . . Accordingly, I dissent.

QUESTION SET 8.7

Review & Synthesis

1. Before the Court could test the Board of Review's constitutionality, it first had to establish that the Board exercised federal power (whether executive or legislative). The Board was created by state actions: bylaws adopted by the MWAA and legislation passed by Virginia and the District of Columbia. Why, then, did the Court conclude that it wielded federal power? Didn't the legal force behind the Board's actions derive from state rather than from federal authority? Was it enough that the Board was composed of Members of Congress? Put another way, is wielding the Board's authority to *serve* Congress' interests the same as *deriving* that authority from Congress?

2. Assuming that the Board wielded federal authority subject to constitutional limitations, would characterizing it as an independent agency to which Congress had delegated quasi-legislative authority have saved it? Why or why not?

3. Rather than invalidating the Board based on a specific constitutional doctrine or provision, the Court pointed to "two basic and related constraints on the Congress" that prevent it from usurping the authority of the Executive and Judicial Branches. What are those specific constraints? How do they address the concerns expressed by James Madison in *The Federalist No.* 48? *See* Chapter 1.

4. Do you agree with Justice White's view, expressed in footnote 3 of his dissent, that the Framers' fear of an "overweening legislative authority" is no longer relevant? If so, do you think the legislative power is less insidious than *The Federalist No.* 48 described it to be? Are the other Branches inherently stronger than Madison thought they were? Or did he simply underestimate how much Congress would be willing to cede its power to the other Branches? Which of the other Branches is currently, in your view, more of a danger to "liberty"?

5. Justice White did not believe that the Board exercised any federal powers. Accordingly, he argued that the Incompatibility Clause presented the only possible problem for the Board's structure under the federal Constitution. Why, in his view, did the Board not violate this provision, either?

F. THE PRESIDENT WITHOUT CONGRESS: INHERENT EXECUTIVE SUPERVISORY AUTHORITY

As we have discussed, the Constitution grants Congress substantial discretion to shape the federal bureaucracy. Through legislation it creates Executive Branch agencies, assigns them regulatory powers, establishes the offices to which their administrators are appointed, sets qualifications and terms of employment for those administrators, and provides appropriations to fund their activities. The President has constitutional authority to supervise the administrative state, but the scope of that authority is heavily dependent on the type of administrative state Congress chooses to create.

The question to which we now turn is whether the President has any *independent* authority to direct the actions of administrative officials. Put another way, to what extent may the President direct the actions of Executive Branch officers in the absence of, or even contrary to, clear instructions from Congress? As we saw in the removal materials, the Supreme Court has narrowly construed the President's authority to direct nondiscretionary, ministerial duties imposed on his or her subordinates by statute. *See, e.g., Kendall v. United States*, 37 U.S. (12 Pet.) 524 (1838), discussed on page 608. Somewhat more successfully, Presidents have acted unilaterally to exercise greater control over informal rulemaking under 5 U.S.C. § 553. *See* Chapter 5. In a series of memoranda and executive orders, Presidents since Richard M. Nixon have inserted White House review into the agency policymaking process for a host of reasons: to increase its analytical rigor, to slow its rate of promulgation, to ensure its fidelity with their policy priorities. These exercises of supervisory authority, though important, are focused on management of the government's *internal* operations; they do not create or eliminate any legal rights or obligations, and they only indirectly affect the life, liberty, or property interests of private parties. The question then remains whether the President has any inherent authority to affect individual rights without Congress' authorization or against its manifest wishes.

The Supreme Court addressed this question in *The Steel Seizure Case, Youngstown Sheet & Tube Co. v. Sawyer*, 343 U.S. 579 (1952). Concerned that steel workers would cripple the country's ability to fight the Korean War by going on strike, President Harry S. Truman ordered Secretary of Commerce Charles Sawyer to commandeer most of the nation's steel mills. Presidents had seized private production facilities before, but they had always done so pursuant some federal statute. Unlike his predecessors, President Truman rested his order solely on his independent authority as President, separate and apart from any statute. The Court tested the constitutionality of Truman's gambit. In a famous and highly influential concurrence, excerpted below, Justice Robert H. Jackson described the constitutional framework for understanding the President's inherent authority.

Youngstown Sheet & Tube Co. v. Sawyer
(The Steel Seizure Case)
343 U.S. 579 (1952)

Mr. Justice BLACK delivered the opinion of the Court. . . .

In the latter part of 1951, a dispute arose between the steel companies and their employees over terms and conditions that should be included in new collective bargaining agreements. Long-continued conferences failed to resolve the dispute. On December 18, 1951, the employees' representative, United Steelworkers of America, C.I.O., gave notice of an intention to strike when the existing bargaining agreements expired on December 31. The Federal Mediation and Conciliation Service then intervened in an effort to get labor and management to agree. This failing, the President on December 22, 1951, referred the dispute to the Federal Wage Stabilization Board to investigate and make recommendations for fair and equitable terms of settlement. This Board's report resulted in no settlement. On April 4, 1952, the Union gave notice of a nation-wide strike called to begin at 12:01 a.m. April 9. The indispensability of steel as a component of substantially all weapons and other war materials led the President to believe that the proposed work stoppage would immediately jeopardize our national defense and that governmental seizure of the steel mills was necessary in order to assure the continued availability of steel. Reciting these considerations for his action, the President, a few hours before the strike was to begin, issued Executive Order 10340. . . . The order directed the Secretary of Commerce to take possession of most of the steel mills and keep them running. The Secretary immediately issued his own possessory orders, calling upon the presidents of the various seized companies to serve as operation managers for the United States. They were directed to carry on their activities in accordance with regulations and directions of the Secretary. The next morning the President sent a message to Congress reporting his action. Twelve days later he sent a second message. Congress has taken no action.

Obeying the Secretary's orders under protest, the companies brought proceedings against him in the District Court. Their complaints charged that the seizure was not authorized by an act of Congress or by any constitutional provisions. . . .

[In Section I of its opinion, the Court found ripe for determination whether the President had the constitutional authority to seize the plaintiffs' steel mills.]

II.

The President's power, if any, to issue the order must stem either from an act of Congress or from the Constitution itself. There is no statute that expressly authorizes the President to take possession of property as he did here. Nor is there any act of Congress to which our attention has been directed from which such a power can fairly be implied. Indeed, we do not understand the Government to rely on statutory authorization for this seizure. There are two statutes which do authorize the President to take both personal and real property under certain conditions.[2] However, the Government admits that these conditions were not met and that the President's order was not rooted in either of the statutes. The Government refers to the seizure provisions of one of these statutes (§ 201(b) of the Defense Production Act) as "much too cumbersome, involved, and time-consuming for the crisis which was at hand."

Moreover, the use of the seizure technique to solve labor disputes in order to prevent work stoppages was not only unauthorized by any congressional

---

[2] The Selective Service Act of 1948, 62 Stat. 604, 625-627, 50 U.S.C. App. (Supp. IV) § 468; the Defense Production Act of 1950, Tit. II, 64 Stat. 798, as amended, 65 Stat. 132, 50 U.S.C.A. Appendix, § 2081.

enactment; prior to this controversy, Congress had refused to adopt that method of settling labor disputes. When the Taft-Hartley Act was under consideration in 1947, Congress rejected an amendment which would have authorized such governmental seizures in cases of emergency. . . .

It is clear that if the President had authority to issue the order he did, it must be found in some provisions of the Constitution. And it is not claimed that express constitutional language grants this power to the President. The contention is that presidential power should be implied from the aggregate of his powers under the Constitution. Particular reliance is placed on provisions in Article II which say that "the executive Power shall be vested in a President . . ."; that "he shall take Care that the Laws be faithfully executed"; and that he "shall be Commander in Chief of the Army and Navy of the United States."

The order cannot properly be sustained as an exercise of the President's military power as Commander in Chief of the Armed Forces. The Government attempts to do so by citing a number of cases upholding broad powers in military commanders engaged in day-to-day fighting in a theater of war. Such cases need not concern us here. Even though "theater of war" be an expanding concept, we cannot with faithfulness to our constitutional system hold that the Commander in Chief of the Armed Forces has the ultimate power as such to take possession of private property in order to keep labor disputes from stopping production. This is a job for the Nation's lawmakers, not for its military authorities.

Nor can the seizure order be sustained because of the several constitutional provisions that grant executive power to the President. In the framework of our Constitution, the President's power to see that the laws are faithfully executed refutes the idea that he is to be a lawmaker. The Constitution limits his functions in the lawmaking process to the recommending of laws he thinks wise and the vetoing of laws he thinks bad. And the Constitution is neither silent nor equivocal about who shall make laws which the President is to execute. The first section of the first article says that "All legislative Powers herein granted shall be vested in a Congress of the United States. . . ." After granting many powers to the Congress, Article I goes on to provide that Congress may "make all Laws which shall be necessary and proper for carrying into Execution the foregoing Powers and all other Powers vested by this Constitution in the Government of the United States, or in any Department or Officer thereof."

The President's order does not direct that a congressional policy be executed in a manner prescribed by Congress—it directs that a presidential policy be executed in a manner prescribed by the President. The preamble of the order itself, like that of many statutes, sets out reasons why the President believes certain policies should be adopted, proclaims these policies as rules of conduct to be followed, and again, like a statute, authorizes a government official to promulgate additional rules and regulations consistent with the policy proclaimed and needed to carry that policy into execution. The power of Congress to adopt such public policies as those proclaimed by the order is beyond question. It can authorize the taking of private property for public use. It can make laws regulating the relationships between employers and employees, prescribing rules designed to settle labor disputes, and fixing wages and working conditions in certain fields of our economy. The Constitution did not subject this law-making power of Congress to presidential or military supervision or control.

It is said that other Presidents without congressional authority have taken possession of private business enterprises in order to settle labor disputes. But even if this be true, Congress has not thereby lost its exclusive constitutional authority to make laws necessary and proper to carry out the powers vested by the Constitution "in the Government of the United States, or in any Department or Officer thereof."

The Founders of this Nation entrusted the law making power to the Congress alone in both good and bad times. It would do no good to recall the historical events, the fears of power and the hopes for freedom that lay behind their choice. Such a review would but confirm our holding that this seizure order cannot stand.

The judgment of the District Court is affirmed.

Mr. Justice JACKSON, concurring in the judgment and opinion of the Court.

. . . The actual art of governing under our Constitution does not and cannot conform to judicial definitions of the power of any of its branches based on isolated clauses or even single Articles torn from context. While the Constitution diffuses power the better to secure liberty, it also contemplates that practice will integrate the dispersed powers into a workable government. It enjoins upon its branches separateness but interdependence, autonomy but reciprocity. Presidential powers are not fixed but fluctuate, depending upon their disjunction or conjunction with those of Congress. We may well begin by a somewhat over-simplified grouping of practical situations in which a President may doubt, or others may challenge, his powers, and by distinguishing roughly the legal consequences of this factor of relativity.

1. When the President acts pursuant to an express or implied authorization of Congress, his authority is at its maximum, for it includes all that he possesses in his own right plus all that Congress can delegate. In these circumstances, and in these only, may he be said (for what it may be worth), to personify the federal sovereignty. If his act is held unconstitutional under these circumstances, it usually means that the Federal Government as an undivided whole lacks power. A seizure executed by the President pursuant to an Act of Congress would be supported by the strongest of presumptions and the widest latitude of judicial interpretation, and the burden of persuasion would rest heavily upon any who might attack it.

2. When the President acts in absence of either a congressional grant or denial of authority, he can only rely upon his own independent powers, but

there is a zone of twilight in which he and Congress may have concurrent authority, or in which its distribution is uncertain. Therefore, congressional inertia, indifference or quiescence may sometimes, at least as a practical matter, enable, if not invite, measures on independent presidential responsibility. In this area, any actual test of power is likely to depend on the imperatives of events and contemporary imponderables rather than on abstract theories of law.

3. When the President takes measures incompatible with the expressed or implied will of Congress, his power is at its lowest ebb, for then he can rely only upon his own constitutional powers minus any constitutional powers of Congress over the matter. Courts can sustain exclusive Presidential control in such a case only by disabling the Congress from acting upon the subject. Presidential claim to a power at once so conclusive and preclusive must be scrutinized with caution, for what is at stake is the equilibrium established by our constitutional system.

Into which of these classifications does this executive seizure of the steel industry fit? It is eliminated from the first by admission, for it is conceded that no congressional authorization exists for this seizure. That takes away also the support of the many precedents and declarations which were made in relation, and must be confined, to this category.

Can it then be defended under flexible tests available to the second category? It seems clearly eliminated from that class because Congress has not left seizure of private property an open field but has covered it by three statutory policies inconsistent with this seizure. In cases where the purpose is to supply needs of the Government itself, two courses are provided: one, seizure of a plant which fails to comply with obligatory orders placed by the Government, another, condemnation of facilities, including temporary use under the power of eminent domain. The third is applicable where it is the general economy of the country that is to be protected rather than exclusive governmental interests. None of these were invoked. In choosing a different and inconsistent way of his own, the President cannot claim that it is necessitated or invited by failure of Congress to legislate upon the occasions, grounds and methods for seizure of industrial properties.

This leaves the current seizure to be justified only by the severe tests under the third grouping, where it can be supported only by any remainder of executive power after subtraction of such powers as Congress may have over the subject. In short, we can sustain the President only by holding that seizure of such strike-bound industries is within his domain and beyond control by Congress. Thus, this Court's first review of such seizures occurs under circumstances which leave Presidential power most vulnerable to attack and in the least favorable of possible constitutional postures. . . .

[The separate opinions of Justices Douglas, Frankfurter, Burton, and Clark are omitted.]

QUESTION SET 8.8

Review & Synthesis

1. In light of Justice Black's opinion on the Court's behalf, what power, if any, does the President have to affect private property interests without Congress' authorization? Does the framing of the issue matter? Although he mentioned (and quickly dismissed) the President's powers as commander in chief, Justice Black primarily framed President Truman's actions as settling a domestic labor dispute. Would Truman's actions have been constitutionally permissible had the Court instead framed the labor dispute as incidental to addressing a national security matter?

2. How certain could the Court have been that Congress did not approve of Truman's actions? As the recitation of the facts made clear, Truman sent notice to Congress both before and after ordering Commerce Secretary Sawyer to seize the steel mills. Is the problem that Congress' acquiescence was constitutionally insufficient to authorize them?

3. Consider the second category of Presidential action identified by Justice Jackson, the famed "zone of twilight." Do you agree with his conclusion that it did not apply to President Truman's actions because Congress had already passed legislation in the field of domestic labor relations? Should the constitutional test as to whether the President "and Congress may have concurrent authority, or in which its distribution is uncertain" turn simply on whether Congress moved first?

CHAPTER 9

The Judiciary

As the historical overview presented in Part I illustrates, the tension between law and discretion has been central to the development both of administrative law and the administrative state. It was evident in the conflict between King's Bench and Chancery in seventeenth- and eighteenth-century England, in judicial refusals to directly review most administrative conduct throughout the nineteenth century, in resistance to the New Deal in the early twentieth century, and in the assertion of more searching judicial review by the Supreme Court and the D.C. Circuit in the early 1970s and retrenchment of the same by the end of the decade. Accordingly, politicians, judges, administrators, scholars, and students have posed varying forms of the following question for the past several centuries: to what extent should regulatory policy be determined by the discretion of bureaucrats, by the laws passed by politicians, or by the decisions rendered by judges?

The answer has direct institutional consequences. The more administrative policies and practices are governed by law—substantive or procedural—the more likely it will be that courts are empowered to exercise control over administrative policymaking. This makes sense; where the Constitution or Congress gives administrators clear instructions, the courts should ensure that those administrators follow them. By contrast, the more the bureaucracy is free to act by discretion, the more limited a supervisory role courts are likely to play. Here, considerations of institutional competence come forward. Congress sometimes asks agencies to resolve issues requiring their peculiar analytical expertise and/or practical experience, neither of which generalist judges possess. Courts in such situations are understandably leery of substituting their own judgments for those of expert agencies, and so may interpret their supervisory responsibilities more narrowly. Understanding the critical role the Judicial Branch plays in supervising the administrative state requires study of the constitutional provisions, statutes, and doctrines that calibrate judicial review of agency action. It is to that subject we now turn.

It is no exaggeration that one could spend an entire career studying the seemingly innumerable nuances of how courts supervise administrative decision-making. Thankfully, our immediate goal is the much more modest (though still challenging) one of surveying the topic's core conceptual and doctrinal features. Specifically, the materials that follow focus on two aspects of judicial review. The first relates to its availability. When are courts empowered to review the decisions made by administrative officials? The second relates to scope. When courts are tasked with reviewing administrative conduct, how searching must (or should) that review be?

A. AVAILABILITY OF JUDICIAL REVIEW

As the Supreme Court made clear in *Citizens to Preserve Overton Park, Inc. v. Volpe*, a "threshold question" federal courts must answer when considering a plaintiff's lawsuit against an administrative agency is whether that plaintiff is "entitled to any judicial review." 401 U.S. 402, 410 (1971). You might assume that the answer to this question is obvious. If an administrative agency injures you by, say, taking possession of your property and refusing to return it, the courts will surely be available to provide you a remedy. If the courts would hear your suit against a private person, they would naturally have the power to hold agencies equally accountable. Right?

Until the late nineteenth century, and with respect to direct review by a federal court, the answer was almost always "no." Congress had given the federal courts no general statutory power to review Executive Branch decision-making. Nor did the federal courts seem eager to assume such authority themselves. Although plaintiffs could seek review of administrative orders or rules by petitioning for a writ of mandamus (a judicial order commanding a government official to perform official duties), courts narrowly construed the writ as applying only to "ministerial" (i.e., nondiscretionary) acts. *See Kendall v. United States*, 37 U.S. (12 Pet.) 524 (1838). Decisions for which administrative officials enjoyed even a modicum of discretion—i.e., the lion's share of agency actions—were thus placed outside the scope of the writ. Courts similarly circumscribed on technical grounds the availability of other writs that could have been useful to litigants, such as certiorari and injunction. Hence, much administrative decision-making was judicially unreviewable during this period. *See* Frederic P. Lee, *The Origins of Judicial Control of Federal Executive Action*, 36 Geo. L.J. 287, 295-96 (1948). In any case, courts seemed to regard such requests for review with some hostility. This sentiment was summed up by the Supreme Court in *Decatur v. Paulding*, 39 U.S. (14 Pet.) 497, 515 (1840): "interference of the courts with performance of the ordinary duties of the executive departments of the government, would be productive of nothing but mischief."

That is not to say that litigants objecting to administrative actions were wholly bereft of legal recourse. Courts had long entertained collateral review of agency conduct through state common lawsuits brought against agency officials in their personal capacities. *See, e.g., Little v. Barreme*, 6 U.S. (2 Cranch) 170 (1804) (holding naval officer personally liable in trespass for seizing Dutch vessel pursuant to statutorily invalid orders issued by the Secretary of the Navy); Ann Woolhandler, *Judicial Deference to Administrative Action—A Revisionist History*, 43 ADMIN. L. REV. 197 (1991) (describing nineteenth-century suits for damages and suits in assumpsit, replevin, and trespass brought by private parties against government officials). These suits were generally initiated in state courts and subsequently removed to federal court. While state laws often granted officials some immunity from suit, those protections were not as robust as the ones available today. Accordingly, federal officials typically had to defend themselves by framing their actions as within the scope of their statutory duties (in other words, by arguing that federal law gave them the right to do what they did).

With the emergence of the modern administrative state—customarily pegged to the creation of the Interstate Commerce Commission in 1887—and its accompanying rapid expansion of economic and social regulation, the Supreme Court revisited the hands-off approach to agency decision-making that characterized its nineteenth-century reviewability jurisprudence. In doing so, it exhibited greater openness to directly reviewing and redressing agency conduct.

A watershed case in this regard was *American School of Magnetic Healing v. McAnnulty*, 187 U.S. 94 (1902). There the Court considered a challenge to the Postmaster General's refusal to honor any postal money orders payable to the petitioners, or to deliver any mail sent to them, based on his determination that they were engaged in fraudulent business practices. Breaking with its prior approach to such cases, the Court concluded that the statutes under which the Postmaster General acted did not give him the authority to denominate the petitioners' business a fraud. Although conceding that Congress had given the Postmaster General conclusive authority to decide all factual matters relating to the statutes he was appointed to administer, the Court concluded that it had the power to grant the petitioners relief where the Postmaster General had "assumed and exercised jurisdiction in a case not covered by the statutes." *Id.* at 107-08. In other words, the Court concluded that it had the power to review and to remedy the Postmaster General's erroneous decision based solely on its own authority, not derived from any statute. Although the Court did not explicitly reject its long-standing presumption against reviewability of administrative decision-making, it did make clear that where a government official like the Postmaster General makes "a clear mistake of law," federal courts "must have power in a proper proceeding to grant relief." *Id.* at 110. If courts have no such authority, the Court emphasized, "the individual is left to the absolutely uncontrolled and arbitrary action of a public and administrative officer, whose action is unauthorized by any law, and is in violation of the rights of the individual." *Id.* Decisions citing *American School* indicated that judicial review would be available where "a Federal officer [is found to have acted] in excess of his authority or under an authority not validly conferred." *Philadelphia v. Stimson*, 223 U.S. 605, 620 (1912); *see also Public Clearing House v. Coyne*, 194 U.S. 497, 509 (1904) (stating that courts will grant relief where a government official "has exceeded his authority, or his action is palpably wrong"). In the years following *American School*, the Court exhibited greater willingness to review administrative actions and to grant relief when it found that those actions fell outside federal officials' statutorily granted authority. *See, e.g., Dismuke v. United States*, 297 U.S. 167, 171-73 (1936); *Stark v. Wickard*, 321 U.S. 288, 309-10 (1944).

By the middle of the twentieth century, both Congress and the Supreme Court had largely abandoned the nineteenth-century presumption against judicial review of administrative decision-making. Section 10 of the Administrative Procedure Act of 1946 (5 U.S.C. §§ 701-706), constituted a "general restatement of the principles of judicial review embodied in many statutes and judicial decisions." ATTORNEY GENERAL'S MANUAL at 93. As the Supreme Court made clear in *Abbott Laboratories v. Gardner*, 387 U.S. 136, 140 (1967), the APA "embodies the basic presumption of judicial review to one 'suffering legal wrong because of agency action, or adversely affected or aggrieved by agency action within the meaning of a relevant statute . . . so long as no statute precludes such relief or the action is not one committed by law to agency discretion.'" *Id.* at 140 (quoting 5 U.S.C. §§ 701(a) and 702). *See also Citizens to Preserve Overton Park, Inc. v. Volpe*, 401 U.S. 402 (1971). "Indeed, judicial review of . . . administrative action is the rule, and nonreviewability an exception which must be demonstrated." *Barlow v. Collins*, 397 U.S. 159, 166 (1970).

Four sections in APA Chapter 7—§§ 701-704—address core reviewability questions: which agency decisions Congress permits federal courts to review, who may properly request that review, where that review may be had, and when courts may undertake review. Each section contains operative terms—"affected or aggrieved" persons, "agency action," etc.—that courts must construe and apply before deciding whether to review an agency's conduct.

It would be the quintessence of understatement to say that reviewability of agency decision-making is a complicated and sometimes confusing area of administrative law. The questions that one could ask, and the puzzles one could attempt to solve, are legion. Accordingly, the materials that follow focus on only a handful of critical topics: (1) how APA Chapter 7 defines the critical term "agency action;" (2) when courts are expressly or impliedly precluded from reviewing agency conduct; (3) which potential plaintiffs have the "standing" to challenge an agency's actions (almost a whole course by itself); (4) when a plaintiff's grievances against an agency are sufficiently developed for judicial resolution ("finality" and "ripeness"); and (5) whether courts or agencies have initial authority to decide a matter when their jurisdictions overlap ("primary jurisdiction").

1. Defining "Agency Action"

Plaintiffs mounting a judicial challenge to an agency's decision must, as a threshold matter, make sure the action they are targeting is covered by APA Chapter 7's review provisions. APA § 704 (titled "Actions Reviewable") specifies that Chapter 7 applies only to "agency action." This may seem obvious given the context, but the term has a specific meaning and a plaintiff may fail to satisfy it in at least two ways.

> **In Context**
>
> APA § 551(13) defines "agency action" as "the whole or a part of an agency rule, order, license, sanction, relief, or the equivalent or denial thereof, or failure to act." 5 U.S.C. § 551(13).

First, the plaintiff may name a defendant that is not an "agency" for purposes of Chapter 7. Section 701(b)(1) defines "agency" as "each authority of the Government of the United States, whether or not it is within or subject to review by another agency." Given the breadth of this definition, Congress saw fit to exempt several federal entities that might otherwise fall within it. These include Congress, the federal courts, governments of U.S. territories and possessions (e.g., Puerto Rico and American Samoa) and the District of Columbia, military courts and commissions, and agencies in which party or organization representatives form a dispute resolution body (e.g., the National Railroad Adjustment Board, which arbitrates minor railroad industry labor disputes pursuant to the Railway Labor Act). The Supreme Court has also added to this list; the President is not an "agency." *See Dalton v. Specter*, 511 U.S. 462, 470 (1994); *Franklin v. Massachusetts*, 505 U.S. 788, 801 (1992). Thus, despite § 704's silence on the matter, Chapter 7 does not empower the federal courts to review the President's decisions when acting pursuant to congressionally delegated authority. Nor does it allow courts to review the actions of White House staff who advise and assist the President if they do not have substantial independent authority when performing specific functions. *See Soucie v. David*, 448 F.2d 1067, 1073 (D.C. Cir. 1971); *cf. Armstrong v. Executive Office of the President*, 90 F.3d 553, 558 (D.C. Cir. 1996) (stating in the context of FOIA that "[t]he closer an entity is to the President, the more it is like the White House staff, which solely advises and assists the President, and the less it is like an agency to which substantial independent authority has been delegated").

Second, plaintiffs may mistakenly challenge conduct that does not in fact constitute an "agency action" for Chapter 7 purposes. Section 704's use of the term "agency action" in this regard is intertwined with both § 551(13) and § 706. Section 551(13) defines "agency action," and "includes the whole or a part of an agency rule, order, license, sanction, relief or the equivalent or denial thereof, or failure to act." Section 706 sets out the

> **Cross-Reference**
>
> APA § 706 and the topic of standards of judicial review of agency actions will be discussed at length beginning on page 896.

standards of review courts must apply when scrutinizing those actions, and commands that they be set aside when failing to pass muster.

The question as to whether an agency has actually taken a reviewable action sometimes arises in the context of its decision not to take any action at all. Put another way, can *inaction* count as *action*, thereby falling within courts' review power? The Supreme Court tangled with this interesting conceptual issue in *Norton v. Southern Utah Wilderness Alliance*, 542 U.S. 55 (2004), the seminal case on this topic. Its resolution turned largely on whether the agency (here the Bureau of Land Management) unlawfully withheld action required of it by law. As you read *SUWA*, note the interpretive approach taken by Justice Antonin Scalia, who wrote the opinion for a unanimous Court, to fit §§ 551(13), 704, and 706(1) together. Do you agree with his use of the interpretive canon *ejusdem generis*? Do you think that he interpreted §§ 551(13), 704, and 706(1) in a way that gives plausible meaning to the term "agency action"? Finally, pay attention to whether the APA provisions analyzed in the case permit review of discretionary and ministerial actions. Does this distinction sound familiar? Is it still applicable?

Norton v. Southern Utah Wilderness Alliance
542 U.S. 55 (2004)

Justice SCALIA delivered the opinion of the Court.

In this case, we must decide whether the authority of a federal court under the Administrative Procedure Act (APA) to "compel agency action unlawfully withheld or unreasonably delayed," 5 U.S.C. § 706(1), extends to the review of the United States Bureau of Land Management's stewardship of public lands under certain statutory provisions and its own planning documents.

I

Almost half the State of Utah, about 23 million acres, is federal land administered by the Bureau of Land Management (BLM), an agency within the Department of Interior. For nearly 30 years, BLM's management of public lands has been governed by the Federal Land Policy and Management Act of 1976 (FLPMA), 90 Stat. 2744, 43 U.S.C. § 1701 *et seq.*, which "established a policy in favor of retaining public lands for multiple use management." *Lujan v. National Wildlife Federation*, 497 U.S. 871, 877 (1990). "Multiple use management" is a deceptively simple term that describes the enormously complicated task of striking a balance among the many competing uses to which land can be put, "including, but not limited to, recreation, range, timber, minerals, watershed, wildlife and fish, and [uses serving] natural scenic, scientific and historical values." 43 U.S.C. § 1702(c). A second management goal, "sustained yield," requires BLM to control depleting uses over time, so as to ensure a high level of valuable uses in the future.

§ 1702(h). To these ends, FLPMA establishes a dual regime of inventory and planning. Sections 1711 and 1712, respectively, provide for a comprehensive, ongoing inventory of federal lands, and for a land use planning process that "project[s]" "present and future use," § 1701(a)(2), given the lands' inventoried characteristics.

Of course not all uses are compatible. Congress made the judgment that some lands should be set aside as wilderness at the expense of commercial and recreational uses. A pre-FLPMA enactment, the Wilderness Act of 1964, 78 Stat. 890, provides that designated wilderness areas, subject to certain exceptions, "shall [have] no commercial enterprise and no permanent road," no motorized vehicles, and no manmade structures. 16 U.S.C. § 1133(c). The designation of a wilderness area can be made only by Act of Congress, *see* 43 U.S.C. § 1782(b).

Pursuant to § 1782, the Secretary of the Interior (Secretary) has identified so-called "wilderness study areas" (WSAs), roadless lands of 5,000 acres or more that possess "wilderness characteristics," as determined in the Secretary's land inventory. § 1782(a); *see* 16 U.S.C. § 1131(c). As the name suggests, WSAs (as well as certain wild lands identified prior to the passage of FLPMA) have been subjected to further examination and public comment in order to evaluate their suitability for designation as wilderness. In 1991, out of 3.3 million acres in Utah that had been identified for study, 2 million were recommended as suitable for wilderness designation. 1 U.S. Dept. of Interior, BLM, Utah Statewide Wilderness Study Report 3 (Oct. 1991). This recommendation was forwarded to Congress, which has not yet acted upon it. Until Congress acts one way or the other, FLPMA provides that "the Secretary shall continue to manage such lands . . . in a manner so as not to impair the suitability of such areas for preservation as wilderness." 43 U.S.C. § 1782(c). This nonimpairment mandate applies to all WSAs identified under § 1782, including lands considered unsuitable by the Secretary. *See* §§ 1782(a), (b).

Aside from identification of WSAs, the main tool that BLM employs to balance wilderness protection against other uses is a land use plan—what BLM regulations call a "resource management plan." 43 CFR § 1601.0-5(k) (2003). Land use plans, adopted after notice and comment, are "designed to guide and control future management actions," § 1601.0-2. *See* 43 U.S.C. § 1712; 43 CFR § 1610.2 (2003). Generally, a land use plan describes, for a particular area, allowable uses, goals for future condition of the land, and specific next steps. § 1601.0-5(k). Under FLPMA, "[t]he Secretary shall manage the public lands under principles of multiple use and sustained yield, in accordance with the land use plans . . . when they are available." 43 U.S.C. § 1732(a).

Protection of wilderness has come into increasing conflict with another element of multiple use, recreational use of so-called off-road vehicles (ORVs), which include vehicles primarily designed for off-road use, such as lightweight, four-wheel "all-terrain vehicles," and vehicles capable of such use, such as sport utility vehicles. *See* 43 CFR § 8340.0-5(a) (2003). According to the United States Forest Service's most recent estimates, some 42 million Americans participate in off-road travel each year, more than double the number two decades ago. H. KEN CORDELL, OUTDOOR RECREATION FOR 21ST CENTURY AMERICA 40 (2004). United States sales of all-terrain vehicles alone have roughly doubled in the past five years, reaching almost 900,000 in 2003. The use of ORVs on federal land has negative environmental consequences, including soil disruption and compaction, harassment of animals, and annoyance of wilderness lovers. Thus, BLM faces a classic land use dilemma of sharply inconsistent uses, in a context of scarce resources and congressional silence with respect to wilderness designation.

In 1999, respondents Southern Utah Wilderness Alliance and other organizations (collectively SUWA) filed this action in the United States District Court for Utah against petitioners BLM, its Director, and the Secretary. In its second amended complaint, SUWA sought declaratory and injunctive relief for BLM's failure to act to protect public lands in Utah from damage caused by ORV use. SUWA made three claims that are relevant here: (1) that BLM had violated its nonimpairment obligation under § 1782(c) by allowing degradation in certain WSAs; (2) that BLM had failed to implement provisions in its land use plans relating to ORV use; and (3) that BLM had failed to take a "hard look" at whether, pursuant to the National Environmental Policy Act of 1969 (NEPA), 83 Stat. 852, 42 U.S.C. § 4321 *et seq.*, it should undertake supplemental environmental analyses for areas in which ORV use had increased. SUWA contended that it could sue to remedy these three failures to act pursuant to the APA's provision of a cause of action to "compel agency action unlawfully withheld or unreasonably delayed." 5 U.S.C. § 706(1). . . .

II

All three claims at issue here involve assertions that BLM failed to take action with respect to ORV use that it was required to take. Failures to act are sometimes remediable under the APA, but not always. We begin by considering what limits the APA places upon judicial review of agency inaction.

The APA authorizes suit by "[a] person suffering legal wrong because of agency action, or adversely affected or aggrieved by agency action within the meaning of a relevant statute." 5 U.S.C. § 702. Where no other statute provides a private right of action, the "agency action" complained of must be "*final* agency action." § 704 (emphasis added). "[A]gency action" is defined in § 551(13) to include "the whole or a part of an agency rule, order, license, sanction, relief, or the equivalent or denial thereof, or *failure to act*." (Emphasis added.) The APA provides relief for a failure to act in

§ 706(1): "The reviewing court shall . . . compel agency action unlawfully withheld or unreasonably delayed."

Sections 702, 704, and 706(1) all insist upon an "agency action," either as the action complained of (in §§ 702 and 704) or as the action to be compelled (in § 706(1)). The definition of that term begins with a list of five categories of decisions made or outcomes implemented by an agency— "agency rule, order, license, sanction [or] relief." § 551(13). All of those categories involve circumscribed, discrete agency actions, as their definitions make clear: "an agency statement of . . . future effect designed to implement, interpret, or prescribe law or policy" (rule); "a final disposition . . . in a matter other than rule making" (order); a "permit . . . or other form of permission" (license); a "prohibition . . . or . . . taking [of] other compulsory or restrictive action" (sanction); or a "grant of money, assistance, license, authority," etc., or "recognition of a claim, right, immunity," etc., or "taking of other action on the application or petition of, and beneficial to, a person" (relief). §§ 551(4), (6), (8), (10), (11).

The terms following those five categories of agency action are not defined in the APA: "or the equivalent or denial thereof, or failure to act." § 551(13). But an "equivalent . . . thereof" must also be discrete (or it would not be equivalent), and a "denial thereof" must be the denial of a discrete listed action (and perhaps denial of a discrete equivalent).

The final term in the definition, "failure to act," is in our view properly understood as a failure to take an agency action—that is, a failure to take one of the agency actions (including their equivalents) earlier defined in § 551(13). Moreover, even without this equation of "act" with "agency action" the interpretive canon of *ejusdem generis* would attribute to the last item ("failure to act") the same characteristic of discreteness shared by all the preceding items. *See, e.g., Washington State Dept. of Social and Health Servs. v. Guardianship Estate of Keffeler*, 537 U.S. 371, 384-385 (2003). A "failure to act" is not the same thing as a "denial." The latter is the agency's act of saying no to a request; the former is simply the omission of an action without formally rejecting a request—for example, the failure to promulgate a rule or take some decision by a statutory deadline. The important point is that a "failure to act" is properly understood to be limited, as are the other items in § 551(13), to a discrete action.

A second point central to the analysis of the present case is that the only agency action that can be compelled under the APA is action legally *required*. This limitation appears in § 706(1)'s authorization

> **In Context**
>
> BLACK'S LAW DICTIONARY defines *ejusdem generis* as follows:
>
> A canon of construction holding that when a general word or phrase follows a list of specifics, the general word or phrase will be interpreted to include only items of the same class as those listed. For example, in the phrase horses, cattle, sheep, pigs, goats, or any other farm animals, the general language or any other farm animals—despite its seeming breadth—would probably be held to include only four-legged, hoofed mammals typically found on farms, and thus would exclude chickens.
>
> BLACK'S LAW DICTIONARY (10th ed. 2014).

for courts to "compel agency action *unlawfully* withheld."[1] (Emphasis added.) In this regard the APA carried forward the traditional practice prior to its passage, when judicial review was achieved through use of the so-called prerogative writs—principally writs of mandamus under the All Writs Act, now codified at 28 U.S.C. § 1651(a). The mandamus remedy was normally limited to enforcement of "a specific, unequivocal command," *ICC v. New York, N.H. & H.R. Co.*, 287 U.S. 178, 204 (1932), the ordering of a "'precise, definite act . . . about which [an official] had no discretion whatever,'" *United States ex rel. Dunlap v. Black*, 128 U.S. 40, 46 (1888) (quoting *Kendall v. United States ex rel. Stokes*, 12 Pet. 524, 613 (1838)). As described in the Attorney General's Manual on the APA, a document whose reasoning we have often found persuasive, § 706(1) empowers a court only to compel an agency "to perform a ministerial or non-discretionary act," or "to take action upon a matter, without directing *how* it shall act." Attorney General's Manual on the Administrative Procedure Act 108 (1947) (emphasis added).

Thus, a claim under § 706(1) can proceed only where a plaintiff asserts that an agency failed to take a *discrete* agency action that it is *required to take*. . . .

The limitation to required agency action rules out judicial direction of even discrete agency action that is not demanded by law (which includes, of course, agency regulations that have the force of law). Thus, when an agency is compelled by law to act within a certain time period, but the manner of its action is left to the agency's discretion, a court can compel the agency to act, but has no power to specify what the action must be. For example, 47 U.S.C. § 251(d)(1), which required the Federal Communications Commission "to establish regulations to implement" interconnection requirements "[w]ithin 6 months" of the date of enactment of the Telecommunications Act of 1996, would have supported a judicial decree under the APA requiring the prompt issuance of regulations, but not a judicial decree setting forth the content of those regulations.

III

A

With these principles in mind, we turn to SUWA's first claim, that by permitting ORV use in certain WSAs, BLM violated its mandate to "continue to manage [WSAs] . . . in a manner so as not to impair the suitability of such areas for preservation as wilderness," 43 U.S.C. § 1782(c). SUWA relies not only upon § 1782(c) but also upon a provision of BLM's Interim Management Policy for Lands Under Wilderness Review, which interprets

---

[1] Of course § 706(1) also authorizes courts to "compel agency action . . . unreasonably delayed"—but a delay cannot be unreasonable with respect to action that is not required.

the nonimpairment mandate to require BLM to manage WSAs so as to prevent them from being "degraded so far, compared with the area's values for other purposes, as to significantly constrain the Congress's prerogative to either designate [it] as wilderness or release it for other uses." App. 65.

Section 1782(c) is mandatory as to the object to be achieved, but it leaves BLM a great deal of discretion in deciding how to achieve it. It assuredly does not mandate, with the clarity necessary to support judicial action under § 706(1), the total exclusion of ORV use.

SUWA argues that § 1782 does contain a categorical imperative, namely, the command to comply with the nonimpairment mandate. It contends that a federal court could simply enter a general order compelling compliance with that mandate, without suggesting any particular manner of compliance. It relies upon the language from the Attorney General's Manual quoted earlier, that a court can "take action upon a matter, without directing how [the agency] shall act," and upon language in a case cited by the Manual noting that "mandamus will lie . . . even though the act required involves the exercise of judgment and discretion," *Safeway Stores, Inc. v. Brown*, 138 F.2d 278, 280 (Emerg. Ct. App. 1943). The action referred to in these excerpts, however, is discrete agency action, as we have discussed above. General deficiencies in compliance, unlike the failure to issue a ruling that was discussed in *Safeway Stores*, lack the specificity requisite for agency action.

The principal purpose of the APA limitations we have discussed — and of the traditional limitations upon mandamus from which they were derived — is to protect agencies from undue judicial interference with their lawful discretion, and to avoid judicial entanglement in abstract policy disagreements which courts lack both expertise and information to resolve. If courts were empowered to enter general orders compelling compliance with broad statutory mandates, they would necessarily be empowered, as well, to determine whether compliance was achieved — which would mean that it would ultimately become the task of the supervising court, rather than the agency, to work out compliance with the broad statutory mandate, injecting the judge into day-to-day agency management. To take just a few examples from federal resources management, a plaintiff might allege that the Secretary had failed to "manage wild free-roaming horses and burros in a manner that is designed to achieve and maintain a thriving natural ecological balance," or to "manage the [New Orleans Jazz National] [H]istorical [P]ark in such a manner as will preserve and perpetuate knowledge and understanding of the history of jazz," or to "manage the [Steens Mountain] Cooperative Management and Protection Area for the benefit of present and future generations." 16 U.S.C. §§ 1333(a), 410bbb-2(a)(1), 460nnn-12(b). The prospect of pervasive oversight by federal courts over the manner and pace of agency compliance with such congressional directives is not contemplated by the APA.

[In the remainder of its opinion, the Court rejected SUWA's claims that the BLM failed to comply with its land use plans in violation of

43 U.S.C. § 1732(a), and that the agency failed to comply with certain National Environmental Protection Act requirements.]

The judgment of the Court of Appeals is reversed, and the case is remanded for further proceedings consistent with this opinion.

It is so ordered.

QUESTION SET 9.1

Review & Synthesis

1. During your weekly study group:
   a. Jasmine raises the following questions about the Court's decision in *SUWA*:

   > I don't understand how Justice Scalia could say that only "discrete" actions fall in APA § 551(13)'s definition of "agency action." That term doesn't appear anywhere in the text of the statute, and he doesn't mention any legislative history that includes it. Where did it come from? In any case, SUWA *did* want BLM to do something discrete. It wanted BLM to protect public lands from ORVs, right?

   What is your response?
   b. Karim also had a question about the majority's reasoning:

   > It seems like Congress already made the failure to issue a rule, order, license, sanction or relief reviewable when it included the term "denial thereof" in § 551(13). If an agency denies a request to do one of these things, then it's failed to act. Are there failures to act that are not also denials of one of the actions listed in § 551(13)?

   What do you think?

Application & Analysis

1. The La Sal Mountain Range, located in southeastern Utah on the Colorado Plateau, encompasses the vast acreage of the Manti-La Sal National Forest. A few years ago, the United States Forest Service ("FS") designated a 2,380-acre portion of the Manti-La Sal National Forest's highest elevations, namely the summits and ridges of Mt. Peale, as the Mt. Peale Research Natural Area ("RNA"). According to an FS regulation, an RNA should "illustrate adequately or typify for research or educational purposes, the important forest and range types in each forest region, as well as other plant communities that have special or unique characteristics of scientific interest and importance." 36 C.F.R. § 251.23. The regulation further states that an RNA "will be retained in a virgin or

unmodified condition except where measures are required to maintain a plant community which the area is intended to represent."

Last year, the State of Utah's Division of Wildlife Resources ("UDWR") initiated the Utah Mountain Goat Statewide Management Plan. Pursuant to this plan, the UDWR anticipated release of 200 mountain goats on state-controlled land adjacent to the Mt. Peale RNA. Concerned that these goats would migrate into the RNA and damage it, FS asked the UDWR to delay action until its potential ramifications for the RNA could be studied. The UDWR refused, and it released the goats shortly thereafter. Within a few weeks, the goats were wandering around and foraging in the RNA, consuming much of its flora.

Noting ongoing harm to the RNA, and citing 36 C.F.R. § 251.23, the Grand Canyon Trust ("GCT") sent a letter to FS demanding that it remove or destroy all of the goats currently squatting there. FS denied the request, at least temporarily. In a letter to GCT, FS explained that it had decided to monitor the goat situation before deciding what action to take, if any. GCT then sued FS in federal district court, seeking relief under APA § 706(1). It alleged that FS failed to act when it refused to comply with § 251.23's mandate that RNAs "be retained in a virgin or unmodified condition."

You are a clerk for the district court judge hearing GCT's case. Write a brief memorandum analyzing whether FS' inaction is reviewable.

---

2. Express Preclusion of Judicial Review

As discussed above, both Congress and the Supreme Court have embraced a presumption in favor of making administrative decision-making reviewable by federal courts. Nevertheless, there are instances in which Congress, either expressly or by implication, has decided to shield agency actions from judicial scrutiny. In fact, Congress clearly signaled the possibility of such statutory preclusion in APA § 701(a)(1), which makes Chapter 7 judicial review unavailable if some other federal statute precludes it. Before proceeding with its case, therefore, an aspiring plaintiff must be sure that its suit isn't barred by some preclusion provision located outside of the APA.

This task seems straightforward where Congress has adopted clearly preclusive language. After all, if Congress has unequivocally stated that a subset of administrative decisions will not be subject to judicial second-guessing, any reasonable person would consider that the end of the matter. Of course, as law students, you are now well acquainted with the siren's song of easy interpretation. Even when Congress settles on clearly preclusive statutory language, questions may linger about the preclusive *scope* of that language.

This leaves administrators, litigants, and courts to divine whether or not Congress has in fact provided for review of an agency's actions.

One finds a notable example of Congress explicitly shielding agency decision-making from judicial review in benefit determinations by the Department of Veterans Affairs (commonly referred to as the "VA"). *See* Attorney General's Manual at 94. Originally called the Veterans' Administration, the VA was redesignated a cabinet-level Executive department in the Department of Veterans Affairs Act of 1988. The VA was the largest federal cabinet-level agency by number of employees as of Fiscal Year 2017. *See* United States Office of Personnel, *Sizing Up the Executive Branch: Fiscal Year 2017* 6 (Feb. 2018) (reporting 342,111 employees). It is responsible for administering a wide array of benefits for and services to the nation's eligible military veterans, their families, and their survivors. To facilitate compassionate treatment, to reduce costs, and to avoid undesirable decisional delays, Congress has sought to make the VA benefits process as nonadversarial as possible. Until 1988, for instance, attorneys representing veterans in VA proceedings were prohibited from receiving more than a $10 fee per claim. That restriction has since been slackened, but even now attorneys are limited to receiving no more than 20 percent of the total amount of past-due benefits recovered in a successful claim. *See* 38 U.S.C. § 5904(d). Another such statutory feature, one of direct relevance here, is Congress' long-standing protection of VA benefits determinations from judicial review.

In a continuous chain of statutes dating back to the VA's creation, Congress has explicitly precluded federal judicial review of its veteran benefits determinations. After all, what could more clearly signal the intended nonadversarial character of such determinations than forbidding them from ever being scrutinized in court? Perhaps unsurprisingly, courts and commentators found significant fault with the breadth of this exemption. What if, for instance, an unsuccessful benefits applicant claimed that the agency violated her constitutional rights? Would the VA still get the last word, even on constitutional questions? The Supreme Court initially appeared to answer this question with a shrug, addressing the issue in dictum as follows: "Pensions, compensation allowances and privileges are gratuities. They involve no agreement of the parties; and the grant of them creates no vested right. The benefits conferred by gratuities may be redistributed or withdrawn at any time in the discretion of Congress." *Lynch v. United States*, 292 U.S. 571, 576-77 (1934).

Nevertheless, the D.C. Circuit in a string of opinions from the late 1950s through the 1960s construed the VA preclusion provision as barring judicial review only of the agency's initial claim determinations, while permitting review for subsequent benefit reduction determinations. *See Tracy v. Gleason*, 379 F.2d 469 (D.C. Cir. 1967); *Thompson v. Gleason*, 317 F.2d 901 (D.C. Cir. 1962); *Wellman v. Whittier*, 259 F.2d 163 (D.C. Cir. 1958). *See generally* Stephen Van Dolsen, *Judicial Review of Allegedly* Ultra Vires *Actions of the Veterans' Administration: Does 38 U.S.C. § 211(a) Preclude Review*, 55 FORDHAM L. REV. 579 (1987). Congress overruled these decisions by statute in 1970. In a harshly worded rebuke, the House Veterans' Affairs Committee observed that Congress "did not intend the fairly tortured construction adopted by the court of appeals in the *Wellman, Thompson*, and *Tracy* holdings." H.R. REP. NO. 91-1166, at 3731 (1970). The revised preclusion provision accordingly read as follows:

> [T]he decisions of the [Veterans'] Administrator on any question of law or fact under any law administered by the Veterans' Administration providing benefits for veterans and their dependents or survivors shall be final and conclusive and no other official or any court of the United States shall have power or jurisdiction to review any such decision by an action in the nature of mandamus or otherwise.

38 U.S.C. § 211(a) (1970).

This did not settle matters, however. In *Johnson v. Robison*, the leading case on the subject, the Supreme Court directly addressed whether Congress could insulate the VA's pension benefits determinations from constitutional review by the courts.

Johnson v. Robison
415 U.S. 361 (1974)

Mr. Justice BRENNAN delivered the opinion of the Court.

A draftee accorded Class I-O conscientious objector status and completing performance of required alternative civilian service does not qualify under 38 U.S.C. § 1652(a)(1) as a "veteran who . . . served on active duty" (defined in 38 U.S.C. § 101(21) as "full-time duty in the Armed Forces"), and is therefore not an "eligible veteran" entitled under 38 U.S.C. § 1661(a) to veterans' educational benefits provided by the Veterans' Readjustment Benefits Act of 1966. Appellants, the Veterans' Administration and the Administrator of Veterans' Affairs, for that reason, denied the application for educational assistance of appellee Robison, a conscientious objector who filed his application after he satisfactorily completed two years of alternative civilian service at the Peter Bent Brigham Hospital, Boston. Robison thereafter commenced this class action in the United States District Court for the District of Massachusetts, seeking a declaratory judgment that 38 U.S.C. §§ 101(21), 1652(a)(1), and 1661(a), read together, violated the First Amendment's guarantee of religious freedom and the Fifth Amendment's guarantee of equal protection of the laws. Appellants moved to dismiss the action on the ground, among others, that the District Court lacked jurisdiction because of 38 U.S.C. § 211(a) which prohibits judicial review of decisions of the Administrator. The District Court denied the motion, and, on the merits, rejected appellee's First Amendment claim, but sustained the equal protection claim. . . . We hold, in agreement with the District Court, that § 211(a) is inapplicable to this action and therefore that appellants' motion to dismiss for lack of jurisdiction of the subject matter was properly denied. . . .

I

We consider first appellants' contention that § 211(a) bars federal courts from deciding the constitutionality of veterans' benefits legislation. Such a construction would, of course, raise serious questions concerning the constitutionality of § 211(a), and in such case "it is a cardinal principle that this Court will first ascertain whether a construction of the statute is fairly possible by which the [constitutional] question[s] may be avoided." *United States v. Thirty-seven Photographs*, 402 U.S. 363, 369 (1971).

Plainly, no explicit provision of § 211(a) bars judicial consideration of appellee's constitutional claims. That section provides that "the *decisions* of the Administrator on any question of law or fact *under* any law administered by the Veterans' Administration providing benefits for veterans . . . shall be final and conclusive and no . . . court of the United States shall have power or jurisdiction to review any such decision. . . ." (Emphasis added.) The prohibitions would appear to be aimed at review only of those decisions of law or fact that arise in the *administration* by the Veterans' Administration of a *statute* providing benefits for veterans. A decision of law or fact "under" a statute is made by the Administrator in the interpretation or application of a particular provision of the statute to a particular set of facts[.] Appellee's constitutional challenge is not to any such decision of the *Administrator*, but rather to a decision *of Congress* to create a statutory class entitled to benefits that does not include I-O conscientious objectors who performed alternative civilian service. Thus, as the District Court stated: "The questions of law presented in these proceedings arise under the Constitution, not under the statute whose validity is challenged." 352 F. Supp., at 853.

This construction is also supported by the administrative practice of the Veterans' Administration. "When faced with a problem of statutory construction, this Court shows great deference to the interpretation given the statute by the officers or agency charged with its administration." *Udall v. Tallman*, 380 U.S. 1, 16 (1965). The Board of Veterans' Appeals expressly disclaimed authority to decide constitutional questions in *Appeal of Sly*, C-27 593 725 (May 10, 1972). There the Board, denying a claim for educational assistance by a I-O conscientious objector, held that "[t]his decision does not reach the issue of the constitutionality of the pertinent laws as this matter is not within the jurisdiction of this Board." *Sly* thus accepts and follows the principle that "(a)djudication of the constitutionality of congressional enactments has generally been thought beyond the jurisdiction of administrative agencies." *See Public Utilities Comm'n v. United States*, 355 U.S. 534, 539 (1958); Louis L. Jaffe, *Judicial Review: Question of Law*, 69 HARV. L. REV. 239, 271-275 (1955).

Nor does the legislative history accompanying the 1970 amendment of § 211(a) demonstrate a congressional intention to bar judicial review even of constitutional questions. No-review clauses similar to § 211(a) have been a part of veterans' benefits legislation since 1933. While the legislative history accompanying these precursor no-review clauses is almost nonexistent, the Administrator, in a letter written in 1952 in connection with a revision of the clause under consideration by the Subcommittee of the House Committee on Veterans' Affairs, comprehensively explained the policies necessitating the no-review clause and identified two primary purposes: (1) to insure that veterans' benefits claims will not burden the courts and the Veterans' Administration with expensive and time-consuming litigation, and (2) to insure that the technical and complex determinations and applications of Veterans' Administration policy connected with veterans' benefits decisions will be adequately and uniformly made.

The legislative history of the 1970 amendment indicates nothing more than a congressional intent to preserve these two primary purposes. Before amendment, the no-review clause made final "the decisions of the Administrator on any question of law or fact *concerning a claim for benefits or payments* under [certain] law[s] administered by the Veterans' Administration" (emphasis added), 38 U.S.C. § 211(a) (1964 ed.). In a series of decisions, e.g., *Wellman v. Whittier*, 259 F.2d 163 (D.C. Cir. 1958); *Thompson v. Gleason*, 317 F.2d 901 (D.C. Cir. 1962); and *Tracy v. Gleason*, 379 F.2d 469 (D.C. Cir. 1967), the Court of Appeals for the District of Columbia Circuit interpreted the term "claim" as a limitation upon the reach of § 211(a), and as a consequence held that judicial review of actions by the Administrator *subsequent* to an original grant of benefits was not barred.

Congress perceived this judicial interpretation as a threat to the dual purposes of the no-review clause. First, the interpretation would lead to an inevitable increase in litigation with consequent burdens upon the courts and the Veterans' Administration. In its House Report, the Committee on Veterans' Affairs stated that "[s]ince the decision in the *Tracy* case—and as the result of that decision and the *Wellman* and *Thompson* decisions—suits in constantly increasing numbers have been filed in the U.S. District Court for the District of Columbia by plaintiffs seeking a resumption of terminated benefits." H.R. Rep. No. 91-1166, p. 10 (1970). . . .

Second, Congress was concerned that the judicial interpretation of § 211(a) would involve the courts in day-to-day determination and interpretation of Veterans' Administration policy. The House Report states that the cases already filed in the courts in response to *Wellman*, *Thompson*, and *Tracy*

[I]nvolve a large variety of matters—a 1930's termination of a widow's pension payments under a statute then extant, because of her open and

notorious adulterous cohabitation; invalid marriage to a veteran; severance
of a veteran's service connection for disability compensation; reduction of
such compensation because of lessened disability . . . [and] suits . . . brought
by [Filipino] widows of World War II servicemen seeking restoration of
death compensation or pension benefits terminated after the Administrator
raised a presumption of their remarriage on the basis of evidence gathered
through field examination. Notwithstanding the 1962 endorsement by the
Congress of the Veterans' Administration's [sic] administrative presumption of remarriage rule, most of [the suits brought by Filipino widows]
have resulted in judgments adverse to the Government. *Id.* at 10.

The Administrator voiced similar concerns, stating that "it seems obvious
that suits similar to the several hundred already filed can — and undoubtedly
will — subject nearly every aspect of our benefit determinations to judicial
review, including rating decisions, related Veterans' Administration regulations, Administrator's decisions, and various adjudication procedures."
Letter to the Committee on Veterans' Affairs 23-24, U.S. Code Cong. &
Admin. News 1970, p. 3742.

Thus, the 1970 amendment was enacted to overrule the interpretation of
the Court of Appeals for the District of Columbia Circuit, and thereby restore
vitality to the two primary purposes to be served by the no-review clause.
Nothing whatever in the legislative history of the 1970 amendment, or predecessor no-review clauses, suggests any congressional intent to preclude judicial
cognizance of constitutional challenges to veterans' benefits legislation. Such
challenges obviously do not contravene the purposes of the no-review clause,
for they cannot be expected to burden the courts by their volume, nor do
they involve technical considerations of Veterans' Administration policy. We
therefore conclude, in agreement with the District Court, that a construction
of § 211(a) that does not extend the prohibitions of that section to actions
challenging the constitutionality of laws providing benefits for veterans is
not only "fairly possible" but is the most reasonable construction, for neither
the text nor the scant legislative history of § 211(a) provides the "clear and
convincing" evidence of congressional intent required by this Court before
a statute will be construed to restrict access to judicial review. *See Abbott
Laboratories v. Gardner*, 387 U.S. 136, 141 (1967).

[In Section II of its opinion, the Court found that Robison's First and
Fifth Amendment claims were without merit, reversing the decision of the
district court.]

Reversed.

[The dissenting opinion of Justice DOUGLAS is omitted.]

After *Robison.* In response to the Court's decision, a number of lower
courts concluded that § 211(a) applied only to VA adjudications, reasoning that the Court had intended to limit the provision to "interpretation or
application of a particular provision of the statute to a particular set of facts."

VA *regulations*, by contrast, were fair game for judicial review. The Supreme Court confirmed this view, holding in *Traynor v. Turnage*, 485 U.S. 535 (1988), that § 211(a) did *not* preclude judicial review of whether regulations promulgated by the VA violated the Rehabilitation Act of 1973. The Court noted that the Rehabilitation Act was a statute "applicable to all federal agencies" and enacted after § 211(a), and that the VA had no "special expertise in assessing the validity of its regulations construing veterans' benefits statutes under a later passed statute of general application." *Id.* at 544.

Congress amended the veterans' benefits statutes yet again in the Veterans' Judicial Review Act of 1988, P.L. 100-687, 102 Stat. 4105 (1988) (codified at 38 U.S.C. § 7253(c) *et seq.*). Acknowledging the need for some kind of judicial review of individual benefits determinations but largely resisting the federal judiciary's gravitational pull, the Act created a new Article I appellate body called the United States Court of Appeals for Veterans Claims (the "CAVC"). The CAVC has exclusive jurisdiction over appeals from the Board of Veterans Appeals, an administrative appellate body housed within the VA. The CAVC's decisions are, in turn, subject to limited review in the United States Court of Appeals for the Federal Circuit. *See* 38 U.S.C. § 7292; *Fugere v. Derwinski*, 972 F.2d 331 (Fed. Cir. 1992). With regard to regulations, the Act requires the VA to use the notice and comment rulemaking procedures laid out in APA § 553 when promulgating rules relating to "rules, grants, or benefits." *See* 38 U.S.C. § 501(d). It also subjects those regulations to exclusive judicial review in the Federal Circuit. *See* 38 U.S.C. § 502. Given Congress' historical interest in making the veterans' benefits process nonadversarial and economical, why do you think it adopted these judicial review procedures? What would an Article I Court—the CAVC—be able to do that an Article III court like the Federal Circuit can't? And why create a special appeals body for the VA's adjudications but not for its regulations?

QUESTION SET 9.2

Review & Synthesis

1. What type of agency action—rulemaking or adjudication, formal or informal—gave rise to Robison's legal claim against the VA? Was that action the actual target of Robison's lawsuit?

2. What test did the Court adopt for determining whether Congress has expressly precluded judicial review of agency actions that raise constitutional questions? Does it appear from the Court's opinion that Congress has the power to preclude *all* judicial review of administrative decision-making, effectively leaving Executive Branch officials with the final word on whether their actions comply with the Constitution?

3. To what extent should the reasoning in *Robison* apply to nonconstitutional claims? For example, do you read § 211(a) as precluding judicial review when the VA interprets and applies provisions of the Administrative Procedure Act? The VA must adhere to certain APA procedures when making certain decisions, but is the APA a "a law administered by" the VA? In formulating your answer, think through some of the downstream consequences. Would construing § 211(a) narrowly lead courts to be more or less involved in VA benefits adjudications? Would that result be consistent or inconsistent with what appeared to be Congress' intent in revising § 211(a)'s language? Would construing it broadly to include the APA really interfere with the VA's ability to inexpensively and consistently decide benefits claims? Would doing so interfere with the uniformity in administrative procedure the APA was enacted to foster?

Application & Analysis

1. The Federal Employees' Compensation Act, 5 U.S.C. §§ 8101 *et seq.* ("FECA"), provides workers' compensation coverage to federal and postal workers around the world for employment-related injuries and occupational diseases. It provides that "[a]n employee shall submit to examination by a medical officer of the United States, or by a physician designated or approved by the Secretary of Labor, after the injury and as frequently and at the times and places as may be reasonably required." 5 U.S.C. § 8123(a). Employees who refuse to submit to or obstruct an examination may have their benefits stopped. § 8123(d). Additionally, "[t]he action of the Secretary or [his or her] designee in allowing or denying a payment under this subchapter is—(1) final and conclusive for all purposes and with respect to all questions of law and fact; and (2) not subject to review by another official of the United States or by a court by mandamus or otherwise." 5 U.S.C. § 8128(b).

   Anibal Gonzalez was a federal corrections officer in Beckley, West Virginia. He suffered a lower back injury in January 2018 when a prisoner struck him with a wooden industrial floor broom. Gonzalez filed for disability benefits with the Department of Labor's Office of Workers' Compensation Programs ("OWCP"), which awarded him FECA wage loss benefits. He received regular payments from February 2018 through June 2019. In a letter dated July 1, 2019, and addressed to "Anibal Gonzalez," OWCP stated that Gonzalez had to see a physician on July 31 to "clarify the cause and extent of [his] injury-related impairment." The letter warned that failure to do so "may result in the suspension of your right to compensation under Title 5 U.S.C. § 8123(d)." Gonzalez did not attend the medical appointment. In a follow-up letter addressed to "Aniball Gonsales," OWCP asked Gonzalez to explain why he did not attend the medical appointment and reiterated that "any action on [his] part short of full cooperation could result in suspension of benefits." OWCP never received a response. Finally, in a letter addressed to "Anibal Gonsales," dated September 18, 2019, OWCP informed Gonzalez that his benefits were suspended because of his failure to attend or explain his nonattendance at the scheduled medical examination. OWCP sent each of these letters to the same address it used for all correspondence relating to Gonzalez's disability benefits. When he did not receive his regular payment, Gonzalez requested that OWCP reconsider its decision. He also asked that it send future correspondence by certified mail to a new address. The agency refused both requests.

Gonzalez appealed to the Employee's Compensation Appeals Board, arguing that he had not been notified of the required medical appointment and that he was willing submit to one. In rejecting his appeal, the Board relied on the federal "mailbox rule." Notice is presumed to be received by an individual when it is properly addressed and duly mailed in the ordinary course of business.

Gonzalez now seeks review of the Board's decision in federal district court. He argues that its application of the mailbox rule denied him procedural due process in violation of the Fifth Amendment Due Process Clause. The Board counters that the court lacks jurisdiction to hear the challenge under 5 U.S.C. § 8128(b). You are a clerk for the judge before whom the matter is pending. Write a brief memorandum analyzing the parties' claims.

---

3. Implied Preclusion of Judicial Review

As suggested above, the Supreme Court only begrudgingly reads statutes as precluding judicial review of agency decision-making. It has accordingly sought to narrow the scope of even categorically preclusive language. The lower courts have followed suit. *See, e.g., Alvarez v. U.S. Immigration and Customs Enforcement*, 818 F.3d 1194, 1200-05 (11th Cir. 2016) (claims of unconstitutional detention brought by lawful permanent resident subject to removal held reviewable despite provision stating "no court shall have jurisdiction to hear any cause or claim by or on behalf of any alien arising from the decision or action by the Attorney General to commence proceedings, adjudicate cases, or execute removal orders against any alien"). Part of the reason is what the *Robison* Court described as the "serious questions" that comprehensively preclusive statutes would raise about Congress' power to bar judicial review of all administrative decision-making. Absent "clear and convincing" evidence to the contrary, it is better to read preclusion statutes narrowly than to mediate a constitutional showdown. It thus seems that nothing short of statutory language expressly forbidding judicial review of allegedly unconstitutional agency conduct would force the courts into a confrontation with Congress.

You might be surprised to learn, then, that the Court has entertained the possibility that Congress has precluded judicial review of agency decision-making through *implication*, rather than through express statutory language. The two cases that follow — *Block v. Community Nutrition Institute* and *Bowen v. Michigan Academy of Family Physicians* — address this implied preclusion issue. As you read them, think about the relationship between a dedicated administrative scheme for reviewing agency decisions and judicial review. Does Congress' provision of the former necessarily mean that it intended to foreclose the latter? Could Congress' provision of the former simply affect the *timing* of review or *development of issues* for the latter?

Block v. Community Nutrition Institute
467 U.S. 340 (1984)

Justice O'CONNOR delivered the opinion of the Court.

This case presents the question whether ultimate consumers of dairy products may obtain judicial review of milk market orders issued by the Secretary of Agriculture (Secretary) under the authority of the Agricultural Marketing Agreement Act of 1937 (Act), ch. 296, 50 Stat. 246, as amended, 7 U.S.C. § 601 *et seq*. We conclude that consumers may not obtain judicial review of such orders.

I

A

In the early 1900's, dairy farmers engaged in intense competition in the production of fluid milk products. To bring this destabilizing competition under control, the 1937 Act authorizes the Secretary to issue milk market orders setting the minimum prices that handlers (those who process dairy products) must pay to producers (dairy farmers) for their milk products. 7 U.S.C. § 608c. The "essential purpose [of this milk market order scheme is] to raise producer prices," S. Rep. No. 1011, 74th Cong., 1st Sess., 3 (1935), and thereby to ensure that the benefits and burdens of the milk market are fairly and proportionately shared by all dairy farmers.

Under the scheme established by Congress, the Secretary must conduct an appropriate rulemaking proceeding before issuing a milk market order. The public must be notified of these proceedings and provided an opportunity for public hearing and comment. *See* 7 U.S.C. § 608c(3). An order may be issued only if the evidence adduced at the hearing shows "that [it] will tend to effectuate the declared policy of this chapter with respect to such commodity." 7 U.S.C. § 608c(4). Moreover, before any market order may become effective, it must be approved by the handlers of at least 50% of the volume of milk covered by the proposed order and at least two-thirds of the affected dairy producers in the region. 7 U.S.C. §§ 608c(8), 608c(5)(B)(i). If the handlers withhold their consent, the Secretary may nevertheless impose the order. But the Secretary's power to do so is conditioned upon at least two-thirds of the producers consenting to its promulgation and upon his making an administrative determination that the order is "the only practical means of advancing the interests of the producers." 7 U.S.C. § 608c(9)(B).

The Secretary currently has some 45 milk market orders in effect. *See* 7 CFR pts. 1001-1139 (1984). Each order covers a different region of the country, and collectively they cover most, though not all, of the United States. The orders divide dairy products into separately priced classes based on the uses to which raw milk is put. *See* 44 Fed. Reg. 65990 (1979). Raw milk that is processed and bottled for fluid consumption is termed "Class I" milk. Raw milk that is used to produce milk products such as butter, cheese, or dry milk powder is termed "Class II" milk.

For a variety of economic reasons, fluid milk products would command a higher price than surplus milk products in a perfectly functioning market. Accordingly, the Secretary's milk market orders require handlers to pay a higher order price for Class I products than for Class II products. To discourage destabilizing competition among producers for the more desirable fluid milk sales, the orders also require handlers to submit their payments for either class of milk to a regional pool. Administrators of these regional pools are then charged with distributing to dairy farmers a weighted average price for each milk product they have produced, irrespective of its use. *See* 7 U.S.C. § 608c(5)(B)(ii).

In particular, the Secretary has regulated the price of "reconstituted milk" — that is, milk manufactured by mixing milk powder with water — since 1964. *See* 29 Fed. Reg. 9002, 9010 (1964); *see also* 34 Fed. Reg. 16548, 16551 (1969). The Secretary's orders assume that handlers will use reconstituted milk to manufacture surplus milk products. Handlers are therefore required to pay only the lower Class II minimum price. *See* 44 Fed. Reg. 65989, 65990 (1979). However, handlers are required to make a "compensatory payment" on any portion of the reconstituted milk that their records show has not been used to manufacture surplus milk products. 7 CFR §§ 1012.44(a)(5)(i), 1012.60(e) (1984). The compensatory payment is equal to the difference between the Class I and Class II milk product prices. Handlers make these payments to the regional pool, from which moneys are then distributed to producers of fresh fluid milk in the region where the reconstituted milk was manufactured and sold. § 1012.71(a)(1).

B

In December 1980, respondents brought suit in District Court, contending that the compensatory payment requirement makes reconstituted milk uneconomical for handlers to process. Respondents, as plaintiffs in the District Court, included three individual consumers of fluid dairy products, a handler regulated by the market orders, and a nonprofit organization. The District Court concluded that the consumers and the nonprofit organization did not have standing to challenge the market orders. In addition, it found that Congress had intended by the Act to preclude such persons from obtaining judicial review. The District Court dismissed the milk handler's complaint because he had failed to exhaust his administrative remedies.

The Court of Appeals affirmed in part and reversed in part, and remanded the case for a decision on the merits. The Court of Appeals agreed that the milk handler and the nonprofit organization had been properly dismissed by the District Court. But the court concluded that the individual consumers had standing: they had suffered an injury-in-fact, their injuries were redressable, and they were within the zone of interests arguably protected by the Act. The Court also concluded that the statutory structure and purposes of the Act did not reveal "the type of clear and convincing evidence of congressional intent needed to overcome the presumption in favor of judicial review." . . .

. . . We now reverse the judgment of the Court of Appeals in this case.

II

Respondents filed this suit under the Administrative Procedure Act (APA), 5 U.S.C. § 701 *et seq.* The APA confers a general cause of action upon persons "adversely affected or aggrieved by agency action within the meaning of a relevant statute," 5 U.S.C. § 702, but withdraws that cause of action to the extent the relevant statute "preclude[s] judicial review," 5 U.S.C. § 701(a)(1). Whether and to what extent a particular statute precludes judicial review is determined not only from its express language, but also from the structure of the statutory scheme, its objectives, its legislative history, and the nature of the administrative action involved. Therefore, we must examine this statutory scheme "to determine whether Congress precluded all judicial review, and, if not, whether Congress nevertheless foreclosed review to the class to which the [respondents] belon[g]." *Barlow v. Collins*, 397 U.S. 159, 173 (1970).

It is clear that Congress did not intend to strip the judiciary of all authority to review the Secretary's milk market orders. The Act's predecessor, the Agricultural Adjustment Act of 1933, 48 Stat. 31, contained no provision relating to administrative or judicial review. In 1935, however, Congress added a mechanism by which dairy handlers could obtain review of the Secretary's market orders. 49 Stat. 760. That mechanism was retained in the

1937 legislation and remains in the Act as § 608c(15) today. Section 608c(15) requires handlers first to exhaust the administrative remedies made available by the Secretary. 7 U.S.C. § 608c(15)(A); *see* 7 CFR §§ 900.50900.71 (1984). After these formal administrative remedies have been exhausted, handlers may obtain judicial review of the Secretary's ruling in the federal district court in any district "in which [they are] inhabitant[s], or ha[ve their] principal place[s] of business." 7 U.S.C. § 608c(15)(B). These provisions for handler-initiated review make evident Congress' desire that some persons be able to obtain judicial review of the Secretary's market orders.

The remainder of the statutory scheme, however, makes equally clear Congress' intention to limit the classes entitled to participate in the development of market orders. The Act contemplates a cooperative venture among the Secretary, handlers, and producers the principal purposes of which are to raise the price of agricultural products and to establish an orderly system for marketing them. Handlers and producers—but not consumers—are entitled to participate in the adoption and retention of market orders. 7 U.S.C. §§ 608c(8), (9), (16)(B). The Act provides for agreements among the Secretary, producers, and handlers, 7 U.S.C. § 608(2), for hearings among them, §§ 608(5), 608c(3), and for votes by producers and handlers, §§ 608c(8)(A), (9)(B), (12), 608c(19). Nowhere in the Act, however, is there an express provision for participation by consumers in any proceeding. In a complex scheme of this type, the omission of such a provision is sufficient reason to believe that Congress intended to foreclose consumer participation in the regulatory process. *See Switchmen v. National Mediation Board*, 320 U.S. 297, 305-306 (1943).

To be sure, the general purpose sections of the Act allude to general consumer interests. *See* 7 U.S.C. §§ 602(2), (4). But the preclusion issue does not only turn on whether the interests of a particular class like consumers are implicated. Rather, the preclusion issue turns ultimately on whether Congress intended for that class to be relied upon to challenge agency disregard of the law. *See Barlow v. Collins, supra*, at 167. The structure of this Act indicates that Congress intended only producers and handlers, and not consumers, to ensure that the statutory objectives would be realized.

Respondents would have us believe that, while Congress unequivocally directed handlers first to complain to the Secretary that the prices set by milk market orders are too high, it was nevertheless the legislative judgment that the same challenge, if advanced by consumers, does not require initial administrative scrutiny. There is no basis for attributing to Congress the intent to draw such a distinction. The regulation of agricultural products is a complex, technical undertaking. Congress channeled disputes concerning marketing orders to the Secretary in the first instance because it believed that only he has the expertise necessary to illuminate and resolve questions about them. Had Congress intended to allow consumers to attack provisions of marketing orders, it surely would have required them to pursue the administrative remedies provided in § 608c(15)(A) as well. The restriction of the administrative remedy to handlers strongly suggests that Congress intended a similar restriction of judicial review of market orders.

Allowing consumers to sue the Secretary would severely disrupt this complex and delicate administrative scheme. It would provide handlers with a convenient device for evading the statutory requirement that they first exhaust their administrative remedies. A handler may also be a consumer and, as such, could sue in that capacity. Alternatively, a handler would need only to find a consumer who is willing to join in or initiate an action in the district court. The consumer or consumer-handler could then raise precisely the same exceptions that the handler must raise administratively. Consumers or consumer-handlers could seek injunctions against the operation of market orders that "impede, hinder, or delay" enforcement actions, even though such injunctions are expressly prohibited in proceedings properly instituted under 7 U.S.C. § 608c(15). Suits of this type would effectively nullify Congress' intent to establish an "equitable and expeditious procedure for testing the validity of orders, without hampering the Government's power to enforce compliance with their terms." S. REP. No. 1011, 74th Cong., 1st Sess., 14 (1935). For these reasons, we think it clear that Congress intended that judicial review of market orders issued under the Act ordinarily be confined to suits brought by handlers in accordance with 7 U.S.C. § 608c(15).

III

The Court of Appeals viewed the preclusion issue from a somewhat different perspective. First, it recited the presumption in favor of judicial review of administrative action that this Court usually employs. It then noted that the Act has been interpreted to authorize producer challenges to the administration of market order settlement funds, and that no legislative history or statutory language directly and specifically supported the preclusion of consumer suits. In these circumstances, the Court of Appeals reasoned that the Act could not fairly be interpreted to overcome the presumption favoring judicial review and to leave consumers without a judicial remedy. We disagree with the Court of Appeals' analysis.

The presumption favoring judicial review of administrative action is just that—a presumption. This presumption, like all presumptions used in interpreting statutes, may be overcome by specific language or specific legislative history that is a reliable indicator of congressional intent. The congressional intent necessary to overcome the presumption may also be inferred from contemporaneous judicial construction barring review and the congressional acquiescence in it, or from the collective import of legislative and judicial history behind a particular statute. More important for purposes of this case, the presumption favoring judicial review of administrative action may be overcome by inferences of intent drawn from the statutory scheme as a whole. See *Switchmen v. National Mediation Board*, 320 U.S. 297 (1943). In particular, at least when a statute provides a detailed mechanism for judicial consideration of particular issues at the behest of particular persons, judicial review of those issues at the behest of other persons may be found to be impliedly precluded. *See Barlow v. Collins*, 397 U.S., at 168, and note 2, 175, and note 9 (opinion of Brennan, J.); *Switchmen v. National Mediation Board, supra*, at 300-01. . . .

In this case, the Court of Appeals did not take [a] balanced approach to statutory construction. . . . Rather, it recited this Court's oft-quoted statement that "only upon a showing of 'clear and convincing evidence' of a contrary legislative intent should the courts restrict access to judicial review." *Abbott Laboratories v. Gardner*, 387 U.S. 136, 141. According to the Court of Appeals, the "clear and convincing evidence" standard required it to find unambiguous proof, in the traditional evidentiary sense, of a congressional intent to preclude judicial review at the consumers' behest. Since direct statutory language or legislative history on this issue could not be found, the Court of Appeals found the presumption favoring judicial review to be controlling.

This Court has, however, never applied the "clear and convincing evidence" standard in the strict evidentiary sense the Court of Appeals thought necessary in this case. Rather, the Court has found the standard met, and the presumption favoring judicial review overcome, whenever the congressional intent to preclude judicial review is "fairly discernible in the statutory scheme." *Data Processing Service v. Camp*, 397 U.S. 150, 157 (1970). In the context of preclusion analysis, the "clear and convincing evidence" standard is not a rigid evidentiary test but a useful reminder to courts that, where substantial doubt about the congressional intent exists, the general presumption favoring judicial review of administrative action is controlling. That presumption does not control in cases such as this one, however, since the congressional intent to preclude judicial review is "fairly discernible" in the detail of the legislative scheme. Congress simply did not intend for consumers to be relied upon to challenge agency disregard of the law. . . .

. . . [P]reclusion of consumer suits will not threaten realization of the fundamental objectives of the statute. Handlers have interests similar to those of consumers. Handlers, like consumers, are interested in obtaining reliable supplies of milk at the cheapest possible prices. Handlers can therefore be expected to challenge unlawful agency action and to ensure that the statute's objectives will not be frustrated. Indeed, as noted above, consumer suits might themselves frustrate achievement of the statutory purposes. The Act contemplates a cooperative venture among the Secretary, producers, and handlers; consumer participation is not provided for or desired under the complex scheme enacted by Congress. Consumer suits would undermine the congressional preference for administrative remedies and provide a mechanism for disrupting administration of the congressional scheme. . . .

IV

The structure of this Act implies that Congress intended to preclude consumer challenges to the Secretary's market orders. Preclusion of such suits does not pose any threat to realization of the statutory objectives; it means only that those objectives must be realized through the specific remedies provided by Congress and at the behest of the parties directly affected by the statutory scheme. Accordingly, the judgment of the Court of Appeals is reversed.

It is so ordered.

Justice STEVENS took no part in the decision of this case.

Bowen v. Michigan Academy of Family Physicians
476 U.S. 667 (1986)

Justice STEVENS delivered the opinion of the Court.

The question presented in this case is whether Congress, in either § 1395ff or § 1395ii of Title 42 of the United States Code, barred judicial review of regulations promulgated under Part B of the Medicare program.

Respondents, who include an association of family physicians and several individual doctors, filed suit to challenge the validity of 42 C.F.R. § 405.504(b) (1985), which authorizes the payment of benefits in different amounts for similar physicians' services. The District Court held that the regulation contravened several provisions of the statute governing the Medicare program:

> There is no basis to justify the segregation of allopathic family physicians from all other types of physicians. Such segregation is not rationally related to any legitimate purpose of the Medicare statute. To lump MDs who are family physicians, but who have chosen not to become board certified family physicians for whatever motive, with chiropractors, dentists, and podiatrists for the purpose of determining Medicare reimbursement defies all reason.

Michigan Academy of Family Physicians v. Blue Cross and Blue Shield of Michigan, 502 F. Supp. 751, 755 (E.D. Mich. 1980).

Because it ruled in favor of respondents on statutory grounds, the District Court did not reach their constitutional claims. The Court of Appeals agreed with the District Court that the Secretary's regulation was "obvious[ly] inconsisten[t] with the plain language of the Medicare statute" and held that "this regulation is irrational and is invalid." *Michigan Academy of Family*

Physicians v. Blue Cross and Blue Shield of Michigan, 728 F.2d 326, 332 (6th Cir. 1984). Like the District Court, it too declined to reach respondents' constitutional claims.

The Secretary of Health and Human Services has not sought review of the decision on the merits invalidating the regulation. Instead, he renews the contention, rejected by both the District Court and the Court of Appeals, that Congress has forbidden judicial review of all questions affecting the amount of benefits payable under Part B of the Medicare program. Because the question is important and has divided the Courts of Appeals, we granted the petition for a writ of certiorari. We now affirm.

I

We begin with the strong presumption that Congress intends judicial review of administrative action. From the beginning "our cases [have established] that judicial review of a final agency action by an aggrieved person will not be cut off unless there is persuasive reason to believe that such was the purpose of Congress." *Abbott Laboratories v. Gardner,* 387 U.S. 136, 140 (1967) (citing cases). *See generally* Louis L. Jaffe, Judicial Control of Administrative Action 339-353 (1965). . . .

Committees of both Houses of Congress have endorsed this view. In undertaking the comprehensive rethinking of the place of administrative agencies in a regime of separate and divided powers that culminated in the passage of the Administrative Procedure Act (APA), 5 U.S.C. §§ 551-559, 701-706, the Senate Committee on the Judiciary remarked:

> Very rarely do statutes withhold judicial review. It has never been the policy of Congress to prevent the administration of its own statutes from being judicially confined to the scope of authority granted or to the objectives specified. Its policy could not be otherwise, for in such a case statutes would in effect be blank checks drawn to the credit of some administrative officer or board." S. Rep. No. 752, 79th Cong., 1st Sess., 26 (1945).

Accord, H.R. Rep. No. 1980, 79th Cong., 2d Sess., 41 (1946). The Committee on the Judiciary of the House of Representatives agreed that Congress ordinarily intends that there be judicial review, and emphasized the clarity with which a contrary intent must be expressed:

> The statutes of Congress are not merely advisory when they relate to administrative agencies, any more than in other cases. To preclude judicial review under this bill a statute, if not specific in withholding such review, must upon its face give clear and convincing evidence of an intent to withhold it. The mere failure to provide specially by statute for judicial review is certainly no evidence of intent to withhold review. *Ibid.* . . .

Subject to constitutional constraints, Congress can, of course, make exceptions to the historic practice whereby courts review agency action. The presumption of judicial review is, after all, a presumption, and "like all presumptions used in interpreting statutes, may be overcome by," *inter alia*, "specific language or specific legislative history that is a reliable indicator of congressional intent," or a specific congressional intent to preclude judicial review that is "'fairly discernible' in the detail of the legislative scheme." *Block v. Community Nutrition Institute*, 467 U.S. 340, 349, 351 (1984).

In this case, the Government asserts that two statutory provisions remove the Secretary's regulation from review under the grant of general federal-question jurisdiction found in 28 U.S.C. § 1331. First, the Government contends that 42 U.S.C. § 1395ff(b) (1982 ed., Supp. II), which authorizes "Appeal by individuals," impliedly forecloses administrative or judicial review of any action taken under Part B of the Medicare program by failing to authorize such review while simultaneously authorizing administrative and judicial review of "any determination . . . as to . . . the amount of benefits under part A," § 1395ff(b)(1)(C). Second, the Government asserts that 42 U.S.C. § 1395ii (1982 ed., Supp. II), which makes applicable 42 U.S.C. § 405(h) (1982 ed., Supp. II), of the Social Security Act to the Medicare program, expressly precludes all administrative or judicial review not otherwise provided in that statute. We find neither argument persuasive.

II

Section 1395ff on its face is an explicit authorization of judicial review, not a bar.[5] As a general matter, "'[t]he mere fact that some acts are made reviewable should not suffice to support an implication of exclusion as to others. The right to review is too important to be excluded on such slender and indeterminate evidence of legislative intent.'" *Abbott Laboratories v.*

---

[5] The pertinent text of § 1395ff reads as follows:

   (a) Entitlement to and amount of benefits

   "The determination of whether an individual is entitled to benefits under part A or part B, and the determination of the amount of benefits under part A, shall be made by the Secretary in accordance with regulations prescribed by him.

   (b) Appeal by individuals

   (1) Any individual dissatisfied with any determination under subsection (a) of this section as to-

      (A) whether he meets the conditions of section 426 or section 426a of this title [which set forth eligibility requirements to be satisfied before an individual is permitted to participate in Part A of the Medicare program], or

      (B) whether he is eligible to enroll and has enrolled pursuant to the provisions of part B of [the Medicare program] . . . , or

      (C) the amount of the benefits under part A (including a determination where such amount is determined to be zero)
        shall be entitled to a hearing thereon by the Secretary to the same extent as is provided in section 405(b) of this title and to judicial review of the Secretary's final decision after such hearing as is provided in section 405(g) of this title.

Gardner, 387 U.S., at 141 (quoting Louis L. Jaffe, Judicial Control of Administrative Action 357 (1965)). *See Barlow v. Collins*, 397 U.S. 159, 166.

In the Medicare program, however, the situation is somewhat more complex. Under Part B of that program, which is at issue here, the Secretary contracts with private health insurance carriers to provide benefits for which individuals voluntarily remit premiums. This optional coverage, which is federally subsidized, supplements the mandatory institutional health benefits (such as coverage for hospital expenses) provided by Part A. Subject to an amount-in-controversy requirement, individuals aggrieved by delayed or insufficient payment with respect to benefits payable under Part B are afforded an "opportunity for a fair hearing by the *carrier*," 42 U.S.C. § 1395u(b)(3)(C) (emphasis added); in comparison, and subject to a like amount-in-controversy requirement, a similarly aggrieved individual under Part A is entitled "to a hearing thereon by the *Secretary* . . . and to judicial review," 42 U.S.C. §§ 1395ff(b)(1)(C), (b)(2) (1982 ed. and Supp. II). "In the context of the statute's precisely drawn provisions," we held in *United States v. Erika, Inc.*, 456 U.S. 201, 208 (1982), that the failure "to authorize further review for determinations of the amount of Part B awards . . . provides persuasive evidence that Congress deliberately intended to foreclose further review of such claims." Not limiting our consideration to the statutory text, we investigated the legislative history which "confirm[ed] this view," *ibid.*, and disclosed a purpose to " 'avoid overloading the courts' " with " 'trivial matters,' " a consequence which would " 'unduly ta[x]' " the federal court system with " 'little real value' " to be derived by participants in the program, *id.* at 210, note 13.

Respondents' federal-court challenge to the validity of the Secretary's regulation is not foreclosed by § 1395ff as we construed that provision in *Erika*. The reticulated statutory scheme, which carefully details the forum and limits of review of "any determination . . . of . . . the amount of benefits under part A," 42 U.S.C. § 1395ff(b)(1)(C) (1982 ed., Supp. II), and of the "amount of . . . payment" of benefits under Part B, 42 U.S.C. § 1395u(b)(3)(C), simply does not speak to challenges mounted against the method by which such amounts are to be determined rather than the determinations themselves. As the Secretary has made clear, "the legality, constitutional or otherwise, of any provision of the Act or regulations relevant to the Medicare Program" is not considered in a "fair hearing" held by a carrier to resolve a grievance related to a determination of the amount of a Part B award. As a result, an attack on the validity of a regulation is not the kind of administrative action that we described in *Erika* as an "amount determination" which decides "the amount of the Medicare payment to be made on a particular claim" and with respect to which the Act impliedly denies judicial review. 456 U.S., at 208. . . .

Careful analysis of the governing statutory provisions and their legislative history thus reveals that Congress intended to bar judicial review only of determinations of the amount of benefits to be awarded under Part B.

Congress delegated this task to carriers who would finally determine such matters in conformity with the regulations and instructions of the Secretary. We conclude, therefore, that those matters which Congress did not leave to be determined in a "fair hearing" conducted by the carrier — including challenges to the validity of the Secretary's instructions and regulations — are not impliedly insulated from judicial review by 42 U.S.C. § 1395ff (1982 ed. and Supp. II).

III

In light of Congress' express provision for carrier review of millions of what it characterized as "trivial" claims, it is implausible to think it intended that there be no forum to adjudicate statutory and constitutional challenges to regulations promulgated by the Secretary. The Government nevertheless maintains that this is precisely what Congress intended to accomplish in 42 U.S.C. § 1395ii (1982 ed., Supp. II). That section states that 42 U.S.C. § 405(h) (1982 ed., Supp. II), along with a string citation of 10 other provisions of Title II of the Social Security Act, "shall also apply with respect to this subchapter to the same extent as they are applicable with respect to subchapter II of this chapter." Section 405(h), in turn, reads in full as follows:

> (h) Finality of Secretary's decision
>   The findings and decision of the Secretary after a hearing shall be binding upon all individuals who were parties to such hearing. No findings of fact or decision of the Secretary shall be reviewed by any person, tribunal, or governmental agency except as herein provided. No action against the United States, the Secretary, or any officer or employee thereof shall be brought under section 1331 or 1346 of title 28 to recover on any claim arising under this subchapter.

The Government contends that the third sentence of § 405(h) by its terms prevents any resort to the grant of general federal-question jurisdiction contained in 28 U.S.C. § 1331. . . . Respondents counter that . . . Congress' purpose was to make clear that whatever specific procedures it provided for judicial review of final action by the Secretary were exclusive, and could not be circumvented by resort to the general jurisdiction of the federal courts.

. . . [W]e need not pass on the meaning of § 405(h) in the abstract to resolve this case. Section 405(h) does not apply on its own terms to Part B of the Medicare program, but is instead incorporated *mutatis mutandis* by § 1395ii. The legislative history of both the statute establishing the Medicare program and the 1972 amendments thereto provides specific evidence of Congress' intent to foreclose review only of "amount determinations" — i.e., those "quite minor matters," 118 Cong. Rec. 33992 (1972) (remarks of Sen. Bennett), remitted finally and exclusively to adjudication by private insurance carriers in a "fair hearing." By the same token, matters which Congress did not delegate to private carriers, such as challenges to the validity of the Secretary's instructions and regulations, are cognizable in courts of law. In the face of this persuasive evidence of legislative intent, we will not indulge the Government's assumption that Congress contemplated review by carriers of "trivial" monetary claims, *ibid.*, but intended no review at all of substantial statutory and constitutional challenges to the Secretary's administration of Part B of the Medicare program. This is an extreme position, and one we would be most reluctant to adopt without "a showing of 'clear and convincing evidence,'" *Abbott Laboratories v. Gardner*, 387 U.S., at 141, to overcome the "strong presumption that Congress did not mean to prohibit all judicial review" of executive action, *Dunlop v. Bachowski*, 421 U.S., at 567. We ordinarily presume that Congress intends the executive to obey its statutory commands and, accordingly, that it expects the courts to grant relief when an executive agency violates such a command. That presumption has not been surmounted here.[12]

The judgment of the Court of Appeals is
Affirmed.

Justice REHNQUIST took no part in the consideration or decision of this case.

QUESTION SET 9.3

Review & Synthesis

1. In contrast to *Robison*, the lawsuits in *Block* and *Bowen* were targeted at agency rather than congressional actions. How did this difference impact the Court's analyses in the cases? Do you think that preclusion of review by implication is even possible given *Robison*'s reasoning? Why or why not?

2. The government in both *Block* and in *Bowen* argued that Congress intended to preclude judicial review of the regulatory decisions at issue. Additionally, in neither case did the applicable statutes expressly preclude the plaintiffs from seeking judicial review. In light of the presumption in favor of reviewability, why were the plaintiffs barred from suing the Agriculture Secretary in *Block* but allowed to sue the HHS Secretary in *Bowen*?

---

[12] Our disposition avoids the "serious constitutional question" that would arise if we construed § 1395ii to deny a judicial forum for constitutional claims arising under Part B of the Medicare program. . . .

3. What standard of proof did *Block* and *Bowen* adopt for overcoming the presumption in favor of reviewability? Was it the "clear and convincing" evidence standard or the "fairly discernable" standard? Are they the same?

4. Whatever the standard of proof applied to questions of implied preclusion, what evidence did the Court deem probative of the issue in each case? Do you think the weight of that evidence was greater in *Block* than it was in *Bowen*?

5. Do you think the standard of proof to overcome the presumption of reviewability should be set at clear and convincing evidence or at something like a preponderance of the evidence? In making up your mind, consider whether each standard would generally increase or decrease the involvement of courts in bureaucratic decision-making. Also think about the types of decisions at issue in *Block* and *Bowen*. Do you think that managing milk prices or setting physician payments are suitable subjects for judicial review, or are they better left to the discretion of agency officials? Are there other factors that you would weigh in formulating an answer?

Application & Analysis

1. The Randolph-Sheppard Act of 1936 ("RSA"), 20 U.S.C. §§ 107-107f, was designed to provide blind persons with remunerative employment, enlarge their economic opportunities, and enable them to become self-supporting. To effectuate these aims, the RSA provides a "priority . . . to blind persons licensed by a State agency" in "the operation of vending facilities on Federal property." § 107(b). The Education Secretary is responsible for implementing RSA's preference for blind vendors and promulgating regulations in accordance with the statute. §§ 107(b), § 107a(a). Specifically, the RSA directs the Secretary to designate a licensing agency in each state. §§ 107a(a)(5), 107b. These state licensing agencies seek vending contracts from federal agencies, and then award them to blind vendors. § 107a(a)(5), (b). Congress included an arbitration provision in the RSA to resolve conflicts between state licensing agencies and the federal agencies from which they seek contracts. State licensing agencies may compel the Secretary to convene an arbitration panel when they conclude that a federal agency is violating the RSA or its regulations. § 107d-1(b). Arbitration decisions constitute final agency action for purposes of the Administrative Procedure Act's judicial review provisions. The RSA also authorizes blind vendors to initiate arbitration proceedings to resolve disputes with state licensing agencies. §§ 107d-1(a), 107d-2(b)(1).

   Pursuant to the RSA, the Kansas Department for Children and Families ("KDCF") secured a vending contract from the Department of the Army to provide cleaning services for the dining facilities on one of its bases. KDCF then awarded that contract to a local vendor. When the contract came up for renewal, the Army concluded that it would not be subject to the RSA's preference for blind vendors. Accordingly, the Army instead procured a contract from a different local vendor not covered by the RSA. Believing that the new contract was subject to the RSA, KDCF filed a request with the Secretary for arbitration with the Army. As required by the RSA, the Secretary convened a three-member panel to arbitrate the dispute. The panel then ruled against KDCF.

KDCF now seeks review of the panel's decision in the United States District Court for the District of Kansas, arguing that the panel misinterpreted and misapplied the RSA's requirements. The Army argues that the panel's decision is not judicially reviewable because the RSA provides exclusively for arbitration. You are a clerk for the district court judge hearing the case. Write a brief memorandum analyzing the parties' claims.

4. Decisions Committed to Agency Discretion by Law

Section 701(a)(2) precludes judicial review if an "agency action is committed to agency discretion by law." But what does this verbal formulation really mean? Unfortunately, the APA itself does not tell us. Perhaps the best place to start looking for answers is a case we have already encountered several times: *Citizens to Preserve Overton Park, Inc. v. Volpe*. As you will remember, the Court in that case was asked to review the Secretary of Transportation's decision to fund the purchase of public parkland for a highway construction project. A statute permitted the Secretary to release these funds only if "(1) there is no feasible and prudent alternative to the use of such land, and (2) such program includes all possible planning to minimize harm to the park. . . ." 401 U.S. 402, 411 (1971). The Court rejected the Secretary's contention that APA § 701(a)(2) precluded its review of his decision. In doing so the Court, through Justice Thurgood Marshall, observed that the "committed to agency discretion" provision is "a very narrow exception," limited to "'statutes [that] are drawn in such broad terms that in a given case there is no law to apply.'" 401 U.S. 402, 410-11 (1971) (quoting S. Rep. No. 752, 79th Cong., 1st Sess., 26 (1945)). Applying this "no law to apply" gloss, the Court held that "[p]lainly, there is 'law to apply' and thus the exemption for action 'committed to agency discretion' [was] inapplicable" to the Secretary's decision.

Justice Marshall's attempts to clarify the § 701(a)(2) exemption may have simply substituted one puzzle for another. Whereas the uncertainty before *Overton Park* had centered on what it means for a decision to be committed to agency discretion by law, afterwards it shifted to what it means for "no law to apply" to an agency's decision-making. As it seems that courts can always find *some* statutory restraints on agency decision-making, is it likely that Congress adopted *no* law that could be applied to a given agency's actions? Did *Overton Park*'s gloss mean that the APA contemplated two categories of agency discretion, one subject to "abuse of discretion" judicial review under § 706(2)(A) and another that is exempt from judicial review altogether? How do we square § 701(a)(2) with the strong presumption in favor of reviewability of agency actions (*see Abbott Laboratories v. Gardner*, 387 U.S. 136, 141 (1967))?

Each of the three cases that follow apply § 701(a)(2) to different types of agency discretion and attempt to address these questions. As you read them, try to identify the evidence on which the Court relied when determining whether the decisions under review were committed to agency discretion. How would you categorize that evidence? Is it historical? Assumptive? Legislative? Something else?

a. Enforcement Discretion

Discretion is an integral part of law enforcement. Indeed, critical steps in the criminal justice process are rooted in governmental discretion. Police exercise it when deciding whether to conduct an arrest. Prosecutors exercise it when deciding whether to investigate possible criminal conduct and whether to charge those who may have engaged in it. Because these actions are often left to the judgments of law enforcement officials, there is normally no cause of action by which a private party can ask a court to require them. Nor do private parties have civil recourse against government officials guilty of prosecutorial abuses. When performing prosecutorial functions, government officials are absolutely immune from personal damages judgments. *See, e.g., Imbler v. Pachtman*, 424 U.S. 409, 427 (1976) (acknowledging that the immunity "leave[s] the genuinely wronged defendant without civil redress against a prosecutor whose malicious or dishonest action deprives him of liberty").

> **Cross-Reference**
>
> Agencies also have substantial discretion whether to engage in notice-and-comment rulemaking. However, the APA provisions governing that decision do not apply to initiation of enforcement proceedings. Accordingly, judicial review of rulemaking initiation is considered separately. *See infra* page 945.

Several justifications have been offered for shielding prosecutorial decisions from judicial scrutiny. Government officials have finite resources, and so they must be given wide latitude in deciding where and when to deploy those resources. Vigorous and fearless performance of prosecutorial functions may be chilled if prosecutions are subject to judicial micro-management. Law enforcement officials are best positioned to gauge the sufficiency of the evidence they have gathered, and judging that sufficiency is central to deciding when and if to initiate enforcement proceedings against private parties. Discretion serves as a bulwark against undisciplined and overreaching lawmakers whose statutes, if fully enforced, would result in abuses of the public.

Like prosecutors in the criminal context, administrative agencies with enforcement mandates must choose when to initiate enforcement actions against regulated parties. Also like criminal prosecutors, these officials operate under budgetary, evidentiary, civic, and moral constraints.

The question addressed by *Heckler v. Chaney* is the extent to which agency enforcement decisions benefit from the deference typically afforded other law enforcement officials. As you read it, think about whether there are meaningful differences between agency officials and other law enforcement agents—like prosecutors—that would warrant giving the former more or less freedom from judicial review.

<hr>

Heckler v. Chaney
470 U.S. 821 (1985)

Justice REHNQUIST delivered the opinion of the Court.

This case presents the question of the extent to which a decision of an administrative agency to exercise its "discretion" not to undertake certain enforcement actions is subject to judicial review under the Administrative Procedure Act, 5 U.S.C. § 501 *et seq.* (APA). Respondents are several prison inmates convicted of capital offenses and sentenced to death by lethal injection of drugs. They petitioned the Food and Drug Administration (FDA), alleging that under the circumstances the use of these drugs for capital punishment violated the Federal Food, Drug, and Cosmetic Act, 52 Stat. 1040, as amended, 21 U.S.C. § 301 *et seq.* (FDCA), and requesting that the FDA take various enforcement actions to prevent these violations. The FDA refused their request. We review here a decision of the Court of Appeals for the District of Columbia Circuit, which held the FDA's refusal to take enforcement actions both reviewable and an abuse of discretion, and remanded the case with directions that the agency be required "to fulfill its statutory function." 718 F.2d 1174, 1191 (D.C. Cir. 1983).

I

Respondents have been sentenced to death by lethal injection of drugs under the laws of the States of Oklahoma and Texas. Those States, and several others, have recently adopted this method for carrying out the capital sentence. Respondents first petitioned the FDA, claiming that the drugs used by the States for this purpose, although approved by the FDA for the medical purposes stated on their labels, were not approved for use in human executions. They alleged that the drugs had not been tested for the purpose for which they were to be used, and that, given that the drugs would likely be administered by untrained personnel, it was also likely that the drugs would not induce the quick and painless death intended. They urged that use of these drugs for human execution was the "unapproved use of an approved drug" and constituted a violation of the Act's prohibitions against "misbranding." They also suggested that the FDCA's requirements for approval of "new drugs" applied, since these drugs were now being used for a new purpose. Accordingly, respondents claimed that the FDA was required to approve the drugs as "safe and effective" for human execution before they could be distributed in interstate commerce. *See* 21 U.S.C. § 355. They therefore requested the FDA to take various investigatory and enforcement actions to prevent these perceived violations; they requested the FDA to affix warnings to the labels of all the drugs stating that they were unapproved and unsafe for human execution, to send statements to the drug manufacturers and prison administrators stating that the drugs should not be so used, and to adopt procedures for seizing the drugs from state prisons and to recommend the prosecution of all those in the chain of distribution who knowingly distribute or purchase the drugs with intent to use them for human execution.

The FDA Commissioner responded, refusing to take the requested actions. The Commissioner first detailed his disagreement with respondents' understanding of the scope of FDA jurisdiction over the unapproved use of approved drugs for human execution, concluding that FDA jurisdiction in the area was generally unclear but in any event should not be exercised to interfere with this particular aspect of state criminal justice systems. He went on to state:

> Were FDA clearly to have jurisdiction in the area, moreover, we believe we would be authorized to decline to exercise it under our inherent discretion to decline to pursue certain enforcement matters. The unapproved use of approved drugs is an area in which the case law is far from uniform. Generally, enforcement proceedings in this area are initiated only when there is a serious danger to the public health or a blatant scheme to defraud. We cannot conclude that those dangers are present under State lethal injection laws, which are duly authorized statutory enactments in furtherance of proper State functions. . . .

Respondents then filed the instant suit in the United States District Court for the District of Columbia, claiming the same violations of the FDCA and asking that the FDA be required to take the same enforcement actions requested in the prior petition.[2] Jurisdiction was grounded in the general federal-question jurisdiction statute, 28 U.S.C. § 1331, and review of the agency action was sought under the judicial review provisions of the APA,

---

[2] Although respondents also requested an evidentiary hearing, the District Court regarded this hearing as having "no purpose apart from serving as a prelude to the pursuit of the very enforcement steps that plaintiffs demanded in their administrative petition." *Chaney v. Schweiker*, Civ. No. 81–2265 (DC, Aug. 30, 1982). Respondents have not challenged the statement that all they sought were certain enforcement actions, and this case therefore does not involve the question of agency discretion not to invoke rulemaking proceedings.

5 U.S.C. §§ 701-706. . . . [The district court granted summary judgment for the petition and the D.C. Circuit reversed.]

II

. . . [T]his case turns on the important question of the extent to which determinations by the FDA not to exercise its enforcement authority over the use of drugs in interstate commerce may be judicially reviewed. That decision in turn involves the construction of two separate but necessarily interrelated statutes, the APA and the FDCA.

The APA's comprehensive provisions for judicial review of "agency actions," are contained in 5 U.S.C. §§ 701-706. Any person "adversely affected or aggrieved" by agency action; *see* § 702, including a "failure to act," is entitled to "judicial review thereof," as long as the action is a "final agency action for which there is no other adequate remedy in a court," *see* § 704. The standards to be applied on review are governed by the provisions of § 706. But before any review at all may be had, a party must first clear the hurdle of § 701(a). That section provides that the chapter on judicial review "applies, according to the provisions thereof, except to the extent that— (1) statutes preclude judicial review; or (2) agency action is committed to agency discretion by law." Petitioner urges that the decision of the FDA to refuse enforcement is an action "committed to agency discretion by law" under § 701(a)(2).

This Court has not had occasion to interpret this second exception in § 701(a) in any great detail. On its face, the section does not obviously lend itself to any particular construction; indeed, one might wonder what difference exists between § (a)(1) and § (a)(2). The former section seems easy in application; it requires construction of the substantive statute involved to determine whether Congress intended to preclude judicial review of certain decisions. . . . But one could read the language "committed to agency discretion by law" in § (a)(2) to require a similar inquiry. In addition, commentators have pointed out that construction of § (a)(2) is further complicated by the tension between a literal reading of § (a)(2), which exempts from judicial review those decisions committed to agency "discretion," and the primary scope of review prescribed by § 706(2)(A) — whether the agency's action was "arbitrary, capricious, or an abuse of discretion." How is it, they ask, that an action committed to agency discretion can be unreviewable and yet courts still can review agency actions for abuse of that discretion? *See* 5 KENNETH CULP DAVIS, ADMINISTRATIVE LAW § 28:6 (1984) (hereafter DAVIS); Raoul Berger, *Administrative Arbitrariness and Judicial Review*, 65 COLUM. L. REV. 55, 58 (1965). The APA's legislative history provides little help on this score. Mindful, however, of the common-sense principle of statutory construction that sections of a statute generally should be read "to give effect, if possible, to every clause . . . ," *see United States v. Menasche*, 348 U.S. 528, 538-539

(1955), we think there is a proper construction of § (a)(2) which satisfies each of these concerns.

This Court first discussed § (a)(2) in *Citizens to Preserve Overton Park v. Volpe*, 401 U.S. 402 (1971). That case dealt with the Secretary of Transportation's approval of the building of an interstate highway through a park in Memphis, Tennessee. The relevant federal statute provided that the Secretary "shall not approve" any program or project using public parkland unless the Secretary first determined that no feasible alternatives were available. *Id.* at 411. Interested citizens challenged the Secretary's approval under the APA, arguing that he had not satisfied the substantive statute's requirements. This Court first addressed the "threshold question" of whether the agency's action was at all reviewable. . . .

[The *Overton Park* Court's analysis] answers several of the questions raised by the language of § 701(a), although it raises others. First, it clearly separates the exception provided by § (a)(1) from the § (a)(2) exception. The former applies when Congress has expressed an intent to preclude judicial review. The latter applies in different circumstances; even where Congress has not affirmatively precluded review, review is not to be had if the statute is drawn so that a court would have no meaningful standard against which to judge the agency's exercise of discretion. In such a case, the statute ("law") can be taken to have "committed" the decisionmaking to the agency's judgment absolutely. This construction avoids conflict with the "abuse of discretion" standard of review in § 706—if no judicially manageable standards are available for judging how and when an agency should exercise its discretion, then it is impossible to evaluate agency action for "abuse of discretion." In addition, this construction satisfies the principle of statutory construction mentioned earlier, by identifying a separate class of cases to which § 701(a)(2) applies.

To this point our analysis does not differ significantly from that of the Court of Appeals. That court purported to apply the "no law to apply" standard of *Overton Park*. We disagree, however, with that court's insistence that the "narrow construction" of § (a)(2) required application of a presumption of reviewability even to an agency's decision not to undertake certain enforcement actions. Here we think the Court of Appeals broke with tradition, case law, and sound reasoning.

Overton Park did not involve an agency's refusal to take requested enforcement action. It involved an affirmative act of approval under a statute that set clear guidelines for determining when such approval should be given. Refusals to take enforcement steps generally involve precisely the opposite situation, and in that situation we think the presumption is that judicial review is not available. This Court has recognized on several occasions over many years that an agency's decision not to prosecute or enforce, whether through civil or criminal process, is a decision generally committed to an agency's absolute discretion. This recognition of the existence of discretion is attributable in no small part to the general unsuitability for judicial review of agency decisions to refuse enforcement.

The reasons for this general unsuitability are many. First, an agency decision not to enforce often involves a complicated balancing of a number of factors which are peculiarly within its expertise. Thus, the agency must not only assess whether a violation has occurred, but whether agency resources are best spent on this violation or another, whether the agency is likely to succeed if it acts, whether the particular enforcement action requested best fits the agency's overall policies, and, indeed, whether the agency has enough resources to undertake the action at all. An agency generally cannot act against each technical violation of the statute it is charged with enforcing. The agency is far better equipped than the courts to deal with the many variables involved in the proper ordering of its priorities. Similar concerns animate the principles of administrative law that courts generally will defer to an agency's construction of the statute it is charged with implementing, and to the procedures it adopts for implementing that statute. *See Vermont Yankee Nuclear Power Corp. v. Natural Resources Defense Council, Inc.,* 435 U.S. 519, 543 (1978).

In addition to these administrative concerns, we note that when an agency refuses to act it generally does not exercise its coercive power over an individual's liberty or property rights, and thus does not infringe upon areas that courts often are called upon to protect. Similarly, when an agency does act to enforce, that action itself provides a focus for judicial review, inasmuch as the agency must have exercised its power in some manner. The action at least can be reviewed to determine whether the agency exceeded its statutory powers. Finally, we recognize that an agency's refusal to institute proceedings shares to some extent the characteristics of the decision of a prosecutor in the Executive Branch not to indict — a decision which has long been regarded as the special province of the Executive Branch, inasmuch as it is the Executive who is charged by the Constitution to "take Care that the Laws be faithfully executed." U.S. Const., Art. II, § 3.

We of course only list the above concerns to facilitate understanding of our conclusion that an agency's decision not to take enforcement action should be presumed immune from judicial review under § 701(a)(2). For good reasons, such a decision has traditionally been "committed to agency discretion," and we believe that the Congress enacting the APA did not intend to alter that tradition. *Cf.* 5 DAVIS § 28:5 (APA did not significantly alter the "common law" of judicial review of agency action). In so stating, we emphasize that the decision is only presumptively unreviewable; the presumption may be rebutted where the substantive statute has provided guidelines for the agency to follow in exercising its enforcement powers. Thus, in establishing this presumption in the APA, Congress did not set agencies free to disregard legislative direction in the statutory scheme that the agency administers. Congress may limit an agency's exercise of enforcement power if it wishes, either by setting substantive priorities, or by otherwise circumscribing an agency's power to discriminate among issues or cases it will pursue. How to determine when Congress has done so is the question left open by *Overton Park.*

Dunlop v. Bachowski, 421 U.S. 560 (1975) . . . presents an example of statutory language which supplied sufficient standards to rebut the presumption of unreviewability. *Dunlop* involved a suit by a union employee, under the Labor-Management Reporting and Disclosure Act, 29 U.S.C. § 481 *et seq.* (LMRDA), asking the Secretary of Labor to investigate and file suit to set aside a union election. Section 482 provided that, upon filing of a complaint by a union member, "[t]he Secretary shall investigate such complaint and, if he finds probable cause to believe that a violation . . . has occurred . . . he shall . . . bring a civil action. . . ." After investigating the plaintiff's claims the Secretary of Labor declined to file suit, and the plaintiff sought judicial review under the APA. This Court held that review was available. It rejected the Secretary's argument that the statute precluded judicial review, and in a footnote it stated its agreement with the conclusion of the Court of Appeals that the decision was not an unreviewable exercise of prosecutorial discretion. Our textual references to the "strong presumption" of reviewability in *Dunlop* were addressed only to the § (a)(1) exception; we were content to rely on the Court of Appeals' opinion to hold that the § (a)(2) exception did not apply. The Court of Appeals, in turn, had found the "principle of absolute prosecutorial discretion" inapplicable, because the language of the LMRDA indicated that the Secretary was required to file suit if certain "clearly defined" factors were present. The decision therefore was not beyond the judicial capacity to supervise.

Dunlop is thus consistent with a general presumption of unreviewability of decisions not to enforce. The statute being administered quite clearly withdrew discretion from the agency and provided guidelines for exercise of its enforcement power. Our decision that review was available was not based on "pragmatic considerations," such as those cited by the Court of Appeals, that amount to an assessment of whether the interests at stake are important enough to justify intervention in the agencies' decisionmaking. The danger that agencies may not carry out their delegated powers with sufficient vigor does not necessarily lead to the conclusion that courts are the most appropriate body to police this aspect of their performance. That decision is in the first instance for Congress, and we therefore turn to the FDCA to determine whether in this case Congress has provided us with "law to apply." If it has indicated an intent to circumscribe agency enforcement discretion, and has provided meaningful standards for defining the limits of that discretion, there is "law to apply" under § 701(a)(2), and courts may require that the agency follow that law; if it has not, then an agency refusal to institute proceedings is a decision "committed to agency discretion by law" within the meaning of that section.

III

To enforce the various substantive prohibitions contained in the FDCA, the Act provides for injunctions, 21 U.S.C. § 332, criminal sanctions,

§§ 333 and 335, and seizure of any offending food, drug, or cosmetic article, § 334. The Act's general provision for enforcement, § 372, provides only that "[t]he Secretary is *authorized* to conduct examinations and investigations . . ." (emphasis added). Unlike the statute at issue in *Dunlop*, § 332 gives no indication of when an injunction should be sought, and § 334, providing for seizures, is framed in the permissive—the offending food, drug, or cosmetic "shall be liable to be proceeded against." The section on criminal sanctions states baldly that any person who violates the Act's substantive prohibitions "shall be imprisoned . . . or fined." Respondents argue that this statement mandates criminal prosecution of every violator of the Act but they adduce no indication in case law or legislative history that such was Congress' intention in using this language, which is commonly found in the criminal provisions of Title 18 of the United States Code. We are unwilling to attribute such a sweeping meaning to this language, particularly since the Act charges the Secretary only with recommending prosecution; any criminal prosecutions must be instituted by the Attorney General. The Act's enforcement provisions thus commit complete discretion to the Secretary to decide how and when they should be exercised.

Respondents nevertheless present three separate authorities that they claim provide the courts with sufficient indicia of an intent to circumscribe enforcement discretion. Two of these may be dealt with summarily. First, we reject respondents' argument that the Act's substantive prohibitions of "misbranding" and the introduction of "new drugs" absent agency approval, *see* 21 U.S.C. §§ 352(f)(1), 355, supply us with "law to apply." These provisions are simply irrelevant to the agency's discretion to refuse to initiate proceedings.

We also find singularly unhelpful the agency "policy statement" on which the Court of Appeals placed great reliance. We would have difficulty with this statement's vague language even if it were a properly adopted agency rule. Although the statement indicates that the agency considered itself "obligated" to take certain investigative actions, that language did not arise in the course of discussing the agency's discretion to exercise its enforcement power, but rather in the context of describing agency policy with respect to unapproved uses of approved drugs by physicians. In addition, if read to circumscribe agency enforcement discretion, the statement conflicts with the agency rule on judicial review, 21 CFR § 10.45(d)(2) (1984), which states that "[t]he Commissioner shall object to judicial review . . . if (i) [t]he matter is committed by law to the discretion of the Commissioner, e.g., a decision to recommend or not to recommend civil or criminal enforcement action. . . ." But in any event the policy statement was attached to a rule that was never adopted. Whatever force such a statement might have, and leaving to one side the problem of whether an agency's rules might under certain circumstances provide courts with adequate guidelines for informed judicial review of decisions not to enforce, we do not think the language of the agency's "policy statement" can plausibly be read to override the agency's express assertion of unreviewable discretion contained in the above rule.

Respondents' third argument, based upon § 306 of the FDCA, merits only slightly more consideration. That section provides:

> Nothing in this chapter shall be construed as requiring the Secretary to report for prosecution, or for the institution of libel or injunction proceedings, minor violations of this chapter whenever he believes that the public interest will be adequately served by a suitable written notice or ruling. 21 U.S.C. § 336.

Respondents seek to draw from this section the negative implication that the Secretary is required to report for prosecution all "major" violations of the Act, however those might be defined, and that it therefore supplies the needed indication of an intent to limit agency enforcement discretion. We think that this section simply does not give rise to the negative implication which respondents seek to draw from it. The section is not addressed to agency proceedings designed to discover the existence of violations, but applies only to a situation where a violation has already been established to the satisfaction of the agency. We do not believe the section speaks to the criteria which shall be used by the agency for investigating possible violations of the Act.

IV

We therefore conclude that the presumption that agency decisions not to institute proceedings are unreviewable under 5 U.S.C. § 701(a)(2) is not overcome by the enforcement provisions of the FDCA. The FDA's decision not to take the enforcement actions requested by respondents is therefore not subject to judicial review under the APA. The general exception to reviewability provided by § 701(a)(2) for action "committed to agency discretion" remains a narrow one, *see Citizens to Preserve Overton Park v. Volpe*, 401 U.S. 402 (1971), but within that exception are included agency refusals to institute investigative or enforcement proceedings, unless Congress has indicated otherwise. In so holding, we essentially leave to Congress, and not to the courts, the decision as to whether an agency's refusal to institute proceedings should be judicially reviewable. No colorable claim is made in this case that the agency's refusal to institute proceedings violated any constitutional rights of respondents, and we do not address the issue that would be raised in such a case. *Cf. Johnson v. Robison*, 415 U.S. 361, 366 (1974). The fact that the drugs involved in this case are ultimately to be used in imposing the death penalty must not lead this Court or other courts to import profound differences of opinion over the meaning of the Eighth Amendment to the United States Constitution into the domain of administrative law.

The judgment of the Court of Appeals is
Reversed.

Justice MARSHALL, concurring in the judgment.

Easy cases at times produce bad law, for in the rush to reach a clearly ordained result, courts may offer up principles, doctrines, and statements that calmer reflection, and a fuller understanding of their implications in concrete settings, would eschew. In my view, the "presumption of unreviewability" announced today is a product of that lack of discipline that easy cases make all too easy. The majority, eager to reverse what it goes out of its way to label as an "implausible result," not only does reverse, as I agree it should, but along the way creates out of whole cloth the notion that agency decisions not to take "enforcement action" are unreviewable unless Congress has rather specifically indicated otherwise. Because this "presumption of unreviewability" is fundamentally at odds with rule-of-law principles firmly embedded in our jurisprudence, because it seeks to truncate an emerging line of judicial authority subjecting enforcement discretion to rational and principled constraint, and because, in the end, the presumption may well be indecipherable, one can only hope that it will come to be understood as a relic of a particular factual setting in which the full implications of such a presumption were neither confronted nor understood.

I write separately to argue for a different basis of decision: that refusals to enforce, like other agency actions, are reviewable in the absence of a "clear and convincing" congressional intent to the contrary, but that such refusals warrant deference when, as in this case, there is nothing to suggest that an agency with enforcement discretion has abused that discretion.

I

In response to respondents' petition, the FDA Commissioner stated that the FDA would not pursue the complaint. . . . The FDA may well have been legally required to provide this statement of basis and purpose for its decision not to take the action requested. Under the Administrative Procedure Act, such a statement is required when an agency denies a "written application, petition, or other request of an interested person made in connection with any agency proceedings." 5 U.S.C. § 555(e). Whether this written explanation was legally required or not, however, it does provide a sufficient basis for holding, on the merits, that the FDA's refusal to grant the relief requested was within its discretion. . . .

. . . As long as the agency is choosing how to allocate finite enforcement resources, the agency's choice will be entitled to substantial deference, for the choice among valid alternative enforcement policies is precisely the sort of choice over which agencies generally have been left substantial discretion by their enabling statutes. On the merits, then, a decision not to enforce that is based on valid resource-allocation decisions will generally not be "arbitrary, capricious, an abuse of discretion, or otherwise not in accordance with law," 5 U.S.C. § 706(2)(A). The decision in this case is no exception to this principle.

The Court, however, is not content to rest on this ground. Instead, the Court transforms the arguments for deferential review on the merits into the wholly different notion that "enforcement" decisions are presumptively unreviewable altogether—unreviewable whether the resource-allocation rationale is a sham, unreviewable whether enforcement is declined out of vindictive or personal motives, and unreviewable whether the agency has simply ignored the request for enforcement. *But cf. Logan v. Zimmerman Brush Co.,* 455 U.S. 422 (1982) (due process and equal protection may prevent agency from ignoring complaint). But surely it is a far cry from asserting that agencies must be given substantial leeway in allocating enforcement resources among valid alternatives to suggesting that agency enforcement decisions are presumptively unreviewable no matter what factor caused the agency to stay its hand.

This "presumption of unreviewability" is also a far cry from prior understandings of the Administrative Procedure Act. As the Court acknowledges, the APA presumptively entitles any person "adversely affected or aggrieved by agency action," 5 U.S.C. § 702—which is defined to include the "failure to act," 5 U.S.C. § 551(13)—to judicial review of that action. That presumption can be defeated if the substantive statute precludes review, § 701(a)(1), or if the action is committed to agency discretion by law, § 701(a)(2), but as Justice Harlan's opinion in *Abbott Laboratories v. Gardner,* 387 U.S. 136 (1967), made clear in interpreting the APA's judicial review provisions[, that access to judicial review should be restricted only with clear and convincing evidence of Congress' intent].

. . . Rather than confront *Abbott Laboratories,* perhaps the seminal case on judicial review under the APA, the Court chooses simply to ignore it. Instead, to support its newfound "presumption of unreviewability," the Court resorts to completely undefined and unsubstantiated references to "tradition," and to citation of four cases. . . .

. . . [F]or at least two reasons it is inappropriate to rely on notions of prosecutorial discretion to hold agency inaction unreviewable. First, since the dictum in [*United States v. Nixon,* 418 U.S. 683 (1974)], the Court has made clear that prosecutorial discretion is not as unfettered or unreviewable as . . . *Nixon* suggests. . . . In *Blackledge v. Perry,* 417 U.S. 21, 28 (1974), instead of invoking notions of "absolute" prosecutorial discretion, we held that certain potentially vindictive exercises of prosecutorial discretion were both reviewable and impermissible. The "retaliatory use" of prosecutorial power is no longer tolerated. *Thigpen v. Roberts,* 468 U.S. 27, 30 (1984). Nor do prosecutors have the discretion to induce guilty pleas through promises that are not kept. *Blackledge v. Allison,* 431 U.S. 63 (1977); *Santobello v. New York,* 404 U.S. 257, 262 (1971). And in rejecting on the merits a claim of improper prosecutorial conduct in *Bordenkircher v. Hayes,* 434 U.S. 357 (1978), we clearly laid to rest any notion that prosecutorial discretion is unreviewable no matter what the basis is upon which it is exercised . . .

Second, arguments about prosecutorial discretion do not necessarily translate into the context of agency refusals to act. . . . Criminal prosecutorial decisions vindicate only intangible interests, common to society as a whole, in the enforcement of the criminal law. The conduct at issue has already occurred; all that remains is society's general interest in assuring that the guilty are punished. In contrast, requests for administrative enforcement typically seek to prevent concrete and future injuries that Congress has made cognizable—injuries that result, for example, from misbranded drugs, such as alleged in this case, or unsafe nuclear power plants—or to obtain palpable benefits that Congress has intended to bestow—such as labor union elections free of corruption, *see Dunlop v. Bachowski*, 421 U.S. 560 (1975). Entitlements to receive these benefits or to be free of these injuries often run to specific classes of individuals whom Congress has singled out as statutory beneficiaries. The interests at stake in review of administrative enforcement decisions are thus more focused and in many circumstances more pressing than those at stake in criminal prosecutorial decisions. . . .

Perhaps most important, the *sine qua non* of the APA was to alter inherited judicial reluctance to constrain the exercise of discretionary administrative power—to rationalize and make fairer the exercise of such discretion. Since passage of the APA, the sustained effort of administrative law has been to "continuously narro[w] the category of actions considered to be so discretionary as to be exempted from review." Shapiro, *Administrative Discretion: The Next Stage*, 92 YALE L.J. 1487, 1489, note 11 (1983). Discretion may well be necessary to carry out a variety of important administrative functions, but discretion can be a veil for laziness, corruption, incompetency, lack of will, or other motives, and for that reason "the presence of discretion should not bar a court from considering a claim of illegal or arbitrary use of discretion." Louis L. Jaffe, Judicial Control of Administrative Action 375 (1965). . . .

QUESTION SET 9.4

Review & Synthesis

1. Like APA § 701(a)(2), § 706(2)(A) is directed at discretionary agency decisions. Specifically, it provides that courts must "hold unlawful and set aside agency action, findings, and conclusions found to be . . . an abuse of discretion. . . ." If discretionary decisions are unreviewable under § 701(a)(2), under what circumstances would courts find them unlawful and set them aside under § 706(2)(A)?

2. The Court acknowledged that it had little occasion to interpret APA § 701(a)(2) prior to its decision in *Heckler*, and that the APA's legislative

history said little about the provision's scope. How, then, did the Court arrive at the conclusion that § 701(a)(2) applies to agency enforcement decisions (prosecutorial discretion)?

3. Why does the *Heckler* Court adopt a *presumption* against reviewing decisions to initiate enforcement actions? What type of evidence did the Court say is required to overcome the presumption?

4. What practical effect does the presumption have on seeking review of these decisions? Wouldn't the Court's test allow most abusive exercises of agency enforcement discretion to go unredressed by courts? Wouldn't it similarly allow agencies to refuse to enforce statutes or regulations for illegitimate or corrupt reasons? Would the presumption against reviewability be overcome if a plaintiff were able to make a *prima facie* case that an agency's nonenforcement decision raised such concerns?

5. Contrast the Court's approach to § 701(a)(2) with the one advanced by Justice Marshall, concurring in the judgment (and the author of the *Overton Park* decision). He would have adopted a "clear and convincing" standard of proof for all unreviewability claims without a presumption against review of enforcement decisions specifically. Wouldn't Justice Marshall's test invite the kind of substantive review § 701(a)(2) appears to preclude?

---

b. Statutory vs. Constitutional Challenges to Discretionary Agency Decisions

The Court in *Heckler* concluded that administrative decisions not to institute enforcement proceedings are presumptively unreviewable under § 701(a)(2). The next case dealt with some issues *Heckler* left unresolved. The first relates to the relationship between § 701(a)(1) and § 701(a)(2). Under a natural reading of the provisions, the "statutes" referenced in the former seem to be a subset of the "law" referenced in the latter. The Court tried to explain their relationship. The second, more important issue relates to the legal source of challenges to discretionary agency decisions. Can a statute that clearly leaves certain decisions to the discretion of an administrative official—as does § 102(c) of the National Security Act—shield decisions made pursuant to it from *constitutional* challenges? If so, how does Congress signal that it intended that result? Finally, and as addressed by the dissent filed by Justice Scalia, are there regulatory areas like national security in which unreviewability is particularly appropriate?

Webster v. Doe

486 U.S. 592 (1988)

Chief Justice REHNQUIST delivered the opinion of the Court.

Section 102(c) of the National Security Act of 1947, 61 Stat. 498, as amended, provides that:

> [T]he Director of Central Intelligence may, in his discretion, terminate the employment of any officer or employee of the Agency whenever he shall deem such termination necessary or advisable in the interests of the United States. . . . 50 U.S.C. § 403(c).

In this case we decide whether, and to what extent, the termination decisions of the Director under § 102(c) are judicially reviewable.

I

Respondent John Doe was first employed by the Central Intelligence Agency (CIA or Agency) in 1973 as a clerk-typist. He received periodic fitness reports that consistently rated him as an excellent or outstanding employee. By 1977, respondent had been promoted to a position as a covert electronics technician.

In January 1982, respondent voluntarily informed a CIA security officer that he was a homosexual. Almost immediately, the Agency placed respondent on paid administrative leave pending an investigation of his sexual orientation and conduct. On February 12 and again on February 17, respondent was extensively questioned by a polygraph officer concerning his homosexuality and possible security violations. Respondent denied having sexual relations with any foreign nationals and maintained that he had not disclosed classified information to any of his sexual partners. After these interviews, the officer told respondent that the polygraph tests indicated that he had truthfully answered all questions. The polygraph officer then prepared a five-page summary of his interviews with respondent, to which respondent was allowed to attach a two-page addendum.

On April 14, 1982, a CIA security agent informed respondent that the Agency's Office of Security had determined that respondent's homosexuality posed a threat to security, but declined to explain the nature of the danger. Respondent was then asked to resign. When he refused to do so, the Office of Security recommended to the CIA Director (petitioner's predecessor) that respondent be dismissed. After reviewing respondent's records and the evaluations of his subordinates, the Director "deemed it necessary and advisable in the interests of the United States to terminate [respondent's] employment with this Agency pursuant to section 102(c) of the National

Security Act. . . ." Respondent was also advised that, while the CIA would give him a positive recommendation in any future job search, if he applied for a job requiring a security clearance the Agency would inform the prospective employer that it had concluded that respondent's homosexuality presented a security threat.

Respondent then filed an action against petitioner in the United States District Court for the District of Columbia. Respondent's amended complaint asserted a variety of statutory and constitutional claims against the Director. Respondent alleged that the Director's decision to terminate his employment violated the Administrative Procedure Act (APA), 5 U.S.C. § 706, because it was arbitrary and capricious, represented an abuse of discretion, and was reached without observing the procedures required by law and CIA regulations. He also complained that the Director's termination of his employment deprived him of constitutionally protected rights to property, liberty, and privacy in violation of the First, Fourth, Fifth, and Ninth Amendments. Finally, he asserted that his dismissal transgressed the procedural due process and equal protection of the laws guaranteed by the Fifth Amendment. Respondent requested a declaratory judgment that the Director had violated the APA and the Constitution, and asked the District Court for an injunction ordering petitioner to reinstate him to the position he held with the CIA prior to his dismissal. As an alternative remedy, he suggested that he be returned to paid administrative leave and that petitioner be ordered to reevaluate respondent's employment termination and provide a statement of the reasons for any adverse final determination. Respondent sought no monetary damages in his amended complaint.

Petitioner moved to dismiss respondent's amended complaint on the ground that § 102(c) of the National Security Act (NSA) precludes judicial review of the Director's termination decisions under the provisions of the APA set forth in 5 U.S.C. §§ 701, 702, and 706 (1982 ed., Supp. IV). Section 702 provides judicial review to any "person suffering legal wrong because of agency action, or adversely affected or aggrieved by agency action within the meaning of a relevant statute." The section further instructs that "[a]n action in a court of the United States seeking relief other than money damages and stating a claim that an agency or an officer or employee thereof acted or failed to act in an official capacity or under color of legal authority shall not be dismissed nor relief therein be denied on the ground that it is against the United States or that the United States is an indispensable party." The scope of judicial review under § 702, however, is circumscribed by § 706, and its availability at all is predicated on satisfying the requirements of § 701, which provides:

> (a) This chapter applies, according to the provisions thereof, except to the extent that—
>
> (1) statutes preclude judicial review; or
> (2) agency action is committed to agency discretion by law.

. . . The Court of Appeals first decided that judicial review under the APA of the Agency's decision to terminate respondent was not precluded by §§ 701(a)(1) or (a)(2). Turning to the merits, the Court of Appeals found that, while an agency must normally follow its own regulations, the CIA regulations cited by respondent do not limit the Director's discretion in making termination decisions. Moreover, the regulations themselves state that, with respect to terminations pursuant to § 102(c), the Director need not follow standard discharge procedures, but may direct that an employee "be separated immediately and without regard to any suggested procedural steps." The majority thus concluded that the CIA regulations provide no independent source of procedural or substantive protection.

The Court of Appeals went on to hold that respondent must demonstrate that the Director's action was an arbitrary and capricious exercise of his power to discharge employees under § 102(c). Because the record below was unclear on certain points critical to respondent's claim for relief, the Court of Appeals remanded the case to District Court for a determination of the reason for the Director's termination of respondent. We granted certiorari to decide the question whether the Director's decision to discharge a CIA employee under § 102(c) of the NSA is judicially reviewable under the APA.

II

The APA's comprehensive provisions, set forth in 5 U.S.C. §§ 701-706 (1982 ed. and Supp. IV), allow any person "adversely affected or aggrieved" by agency action to obtain judicial review thereof, so long as the decision challenged represents a "final agency action for which there is no other adequate remedy in a court." Typically, a litigant will contest an action (or failure to act) by an agency on the ground that the agency has neglected to follow the statutory directives of Congress. Section 701(a), however, limits application of the entire APA to situations in which judicial review is not precluded by statute, *see* § 701(a)(1), and the agency action is not committed to agency discretion by law, *see* § 701(a)(2).

In *Citizens to Preserve Overton Park, Inc. v. Volpe*, 401 U.S. 402 (1971), this Court explained the distinction between §§ 701(a)(1) and (a)(2). Subsection (a)(1) is concerned with whether Congress expressed an intent to prohibit judicial review; subsection (a)(2) applies "in those rare instances where 'statutes are drawn in such broad terms that in a given case there is no law to apply.'" 401 U.S., at 410 (citing S. REP. No. 752, 79th Cong., 1st Sess., 26 (1945)).

We further explained what it means for an action to be "committed to agency discretion by law" in *Heckler v. Chaney*, 470 U.S. 821 (1985). *Heckler* required the Court to determine whether the Food and Drug Administration's decision not to undertake an enforcement proceeding against the use of certain drugs in administering the death penalty was subject to judicial review.

We noted that, under § 701(a)(2), even when Congress has not affirmatively precluded judicial oversight, "review is not to be had if the statute is drawn so that a court would have no meaningful standard against which to judge the agency's exercise of discretion." 470 U.S., at 830. Since the statute conferring power on the Food and Drug Administration to prohibit the unlawful misbranding or misuse of drugs provided no substantive standards on which a court could base its review, we found that enforcement actions were committed to the complete discretion of the FDA to decide when and how they should be pursued.

Both *Overton Park* and *Heckler* emphasized that § 701(a)(2) requires careful examination of the statute on which the claim of agency illegality is based (the Federal-Aid Highway Act of 1968 in *Overton Park* and the Federal Food, Drug, and Cosmetic Act in *Heckler*). In the present case, respondent's claims against the CIA arise from the Director's asserted violation of § 102(c) of the NSA. As an initial matter, it should be noted that § 102(c) allows termination of an Agency employee whenever the Director "shall *deem* such termination necessary or advisable in the interests of the United States" (emphasis added), not simply when the dismissal is necessary or advisable to those interests. This standard fairly exudes deference to the Director, and appears to us to foreclose the application of any meaningful judicial standard of review. Short of permitting cross-examination of the Director concerning his views of the Nation's security and whether the discharged employee was inimical to those interests, we see no basis on which a reviewing court could properly assess an Agency termination decision. The language of § 102(c) thus strongly suggests that its implementation was "committed to agency discretion by law."

So too does the overall structure of the NSA. Passed shortly after the close of the Second World War, the NSA created the CIA and gave its Director the responsibility "for protecting intelligence sources and methods from unauthorized disclosure." *See* 50 U.S.C. § 403(d)(3). Section 102(c) is an integral part of that statute, because the Agency's efficacy, and the Nation's security, depend in large measure on the reliability and trustworthiness of the Agency's employees. . . . [E]mployment with the CIA entails a high degree of trust that is perhaps unmatched in Government service.

. . . Section 102(c), that portion of the NSA under consideration in the present case, is part and parcel of the entire Act, and likewise exhibits the Act's extraordinary deference to the Director in his decision to terminate individual employees.

We thus find that the language and structure of § 102(c) indicate that Congress meant to commit individual employee discharges to the Director's discretion, and that § 701(a)(2) accordingly precludes judicial review of these decisions under the APA. We reverse the Court of Appeals to the extent that it found such terminations reviewable by the courts.

III

In addition to his claim that the Director failed to abide by the statutory dictates of § 102(c), respondent also alleged a number of constitutional violations in his amended complaint. Respondent charged that petitioner's termination of his employment deprived him of property and liberty interests under the Due Process Clause of the Fifth Amendment, denied him equal protection of the laws, and unjustifiably burdened his right to privacy. Respondent asserts that he is entitled, under the APA, to judicial consideration of these claimed violations.

We share the confusion of the Court of Appeals as to the precise nature of respondent's constitutional claims. It is difficult, if not impossible, to ascertain from the amended complaint whether respondent contends that his termination, based on his homosexuality, is constitutionally impermissible, or whether he asserts that a more pervasive discrimination policy exists in the CIA's employment practices regarding all homosexuals. This ambiguity in the amended complaint is no doubt attributable in part to the inconsistent explanations respondent received from the Agency itself regarding his termination. Prior to his discharge, respondent had been told by two CIA security officers that his homosexual activities themselves violated CIA regulations. In contrast, the Deputy General Counsel of the CIA later informed respondent that homosexuality was merely a security concern that did not inevitably result in termination, but instead was evaluated on a case-by-case basis.

Petitioner maintains that, no matter what the nature of respondent's constitutional claims, judicial review is precluded by the language and intent of § 102(c). In petitioner's view, all Agency employment termination decisions, even those based on policies normally repugnant to the Constitution, are given over to the absolute discretion of the Director, and are hence unreviewable under the APA. We do not think § 102(c) may be read to exclude review of constitutional claims. We emphasized in *Johnson v. Robison*, 415 U.S. 361 (1974), that where Congress intends to preclude judicial review of constitutional claims its intent to do so must be clear. . . . We require this heightened showing in part to avoid the "serious constitutional question" that would arise if a federal statute were construed to deny any judicial forum for a colorable constitutional claim. *See Bowen v. Michigan Academy of Family Physicians*, 476 U.S. 667, 681, note 12 (1986).

Our review of § 102(c) convinces us that it cannot bear the preclusive weight petitioner would have it support. As detailed above, the section does commit employment termination decisions to the Director's discretion, and precludes challenges to these decisions based upon the statutory language of § 102(c). A discharged employee thus cannot complain that his termination was not "necessary or advisable in the interests of the United States," since that assessment is the Director's alone. Subsections (a)(1) and (a)(2) of § 701, however, remove from judicial review only those determinations specifically identified by Congress or "committed to agency discretion by law." Nothing in § 102(c) persuades us that Congress meant to preclude consideration of colorable constitutional claims arising out of the actions of the Director pursuant to that section; we believe that a constitutional claim based on an individual discharge may be reviewed by the District Court. We agree with the Court of Appeals that there must be further proceedings in the District Court on this issue.

. . . On remand, the District Court should thus address respondent's constitutional claims and the propriety of the equitable remedies sought.

The judgment of the Court of Appeals is affirmed in part, reversed in part, and the case is remanded for further proceedings consistent with this opinion.

It is so ordered.

Justice KENNEDY took no part in the consideration or decision of this case.

Justice SCALIA, dissenting.

I agree with the Court's apparent holding in Part II of its opinion, that the Director's decision to terminate a CIA employee is "committed to agency discretion by law" within the meaning of 5 U.S.C. § 701(a)(2). But because I do not see how a decision can, either practically or legally, be both unreviewable and yet reviewable for constitutional defect, I regard Part III of the opinion as essentially undoing Part II. I therefore respectfully dissent from the judgment of the Court.

I

Before proceeding to address Part III of the Court's opinion, which I think to be in error, I must discuss one significant element of the analysis in Part II. Though I subscribe to most of that analysis, I disagree with the Court's description of what is required to come within subsection (a)(2) of § 701, which provides that judicial review is unavailable "to the extent that . . . agency action is committed to agency discretion by law."* The Court's discussion suggests that the Court of Appeals below was correct in

---

* Technically, this provision merely precludes judicial review under the judicial review provisions of the Administrative Procedure Act (APA), that is, under Chapter 7 of Title 5 of the United States Code. However, at least with respect to all entities that come within the Chapter's definition of "agency," *see* 5 U.S.C. § 701(b), if review is not available under the APA it is not available at all. Chapter 7 (originally enacted as § 10 of the APA) is an umbrella statute governing judicial review of all federal agency action. While a right to judicial review of agency action may be created by a separate statutory or constitutional provision, once created it becomes subject to the judicial review provisions of the APA unless specifically excluded, *see* 5 U.S.C. § 559. To my knowledge, no specific exclusion exists.

holding that this provision is triggered only when there is "no law to apply." Our precedents amply show that "commit[ment] to agency discretion by law" includes, but is not limited to, situations in which there is "no law to apply."

The Court relies for its "no law to apply" formulation upon our discussion in *Heckler v. Chaney*, 470 U.S. 821 (1985)—which, however, did not apply that as the sole criterion of § 701(a)(2)'s applicability, but to the contrary discussed the subject action's "general unsuitability" for review, and adverted to "tradition, case law, and sound reasoning." 470 U.S., at 831. Moreover, the only supporting authority for the "no law to apply" test cited in *Chaney* was our observation in *Citizens to Preserve Overton Park, Inc. v. Volpe*, 401 U.S. 402 (1971), that "[t]he legislative history of the Administrative Procedure Act indicates that [§ 701(a)(2)] is applicable in those rare instances where 'statutes are drawn in such broad terms that in a given case there is no law to apply.' S. Rep. No. 752, 79th Cong., 1st Sess., 26 (1945)," *id.* at 410. Perhaps *Overton Park* discussed only the "no law to apply" factor because that was the only basis for nonreviewability that was even arguably applicable. It surely could not have believed that factor to be exclusive, for that would contradict the very legislative history, both cited and quoted in the opinion, from which it had been derived, which read in full: "The basic exception of matters committed to agency discretion would apply even if not stated at the outset [of the judicial review Chapter]. If, *for example*, statutes are drawn in such broad terms that in a given case there is no law to apply, courts of course have no statutory question to review." S. Rep. No. 752, 79th Cong., 1st Sess., 26 (1945) (emphasis added).

The "no law to apply" test can account for the nonreviewability of certain issues, but falls far short of explaining the full scope of the areas from which the courts are excluded. For the fact is that there is no governmental decision that is not subject to a fair number of legal constraints precise enough to be susceptible of judicial application—beginning with the fundamental constraint that the decision must be taken in order to further a public purpose rather than a purely private interest; yet there are many governmental decisions that are not at all subject to judicial review. A United States Attorney's decision to prosecute, for example, will not be reviewed on the claim that it was prompted by personal animosity. Thus, "no law to apply" provides much less than the full answer to whether § 701(a)(2) applies.

The key to understanding the "committed to agency discretion by law" provision of § 701(a)(2) lies in contrasting it with the "statutes preclude judicial review" provision of § 701(a)(1). Why "statutes" for preclusion, but the much more general term "law" for commission to agency discretion? The answer is, as we implied in *Chaney*, that the latter was intended to refer to "the 'common law' of judicial review of agency action," 470 U.S., at 832—a body of jurisprudence that had marked out, with more or less precision, certain issues and certain areas that were beyond the range of judicial review. That jurisprudence included principles ranging from the "political question" doctrine, to sovereign immunity (including doctrines determining when a suit against an officer would be deemed to be a suit against the sovereign), to official immunity, to prudential limitations upon the courts' equitable powers, to what can be described no more precisely than a traditional respect for the functions of the other branches reflected in the statement in *Marbury v. Madison*, 5 U.S. (1 Cranch) 137, 170-171 (1803), that "[w]here the head of a department acts in a case, in which executive discretion is to be exercised; in which he is the mere organ of executive will; it is again repeated, that any application to a court to control, in any respect, his conduct, would be rejected without hesitation." Only if all that "common law" were embraced within § 701(a)(2) could it have been true that, as was generally understood, "[t]he intended result of [§ 701(a)] is to restate the existing law as to the area of reviewable agency action." Attorney General's Manual on the Administrative Procedure Act 94 (1947). Because that is the meaning of the provision, we have continued to take into account for purposes of determining reviewability, post-APA as before, not only the text and structure of the statute under which the agency acts, but such factors as whether the decision involves "a sensitive and inherently discretionary judgment call," *Department of Navy v. Egan*, 484 U.S. 518, 527 (1988), whether it is the sort of decision that has traditionally been nonreviewable, *ICC v. Locomotive Engineers*, 482 U.S. 270, 282 (1987); *Chaney, supra*, 470 U.S., at 832, and whether review would have "disruptive practical consequences," *see Southern R. Co. v. Seaboard Allied Milling Corp.*, 442 U.S. 444, 457 (1979). This explains the seeming contradiction between § 701(a)(2)'s disallowance of review to the extent that action is "committed to agency discretion," and § 706's injunction that a court shall set aside agency action that constitutes "an abuse of discretion." Since, in the former provision, "committed to agency discretion by law" means "of the sort that is traditionally unreviewable," it operates to keep certain categories of agency action out of the courts; but when agency action is appropriately in the courts, abuse of discretion is of course grounds for reversal.

All this law, shaped over the course of centuries and still developing in its application to new contexts, cannot possibly be contained within the phrase "no law to apply." It is not surprising, then, that although the Court recites the test it does not really apply it. Like other opinions relying upon it, this one essentially announces the test, declares victory and moves on. It is not really true "'that a court would have no meaningful standard against which to judge the agency's exercise of discretion,'" quoting *Chaney*, 470 U.S., at 830. The standard set forth in § 102(c) of the National Security Act of 1947, 50 U.S.C. § 403(c), "necessary or advisable in the interests of the United States," at least excludes dismissal out of personal vindictiveness, or because the Director wants to give the job to his cousin. Why, on the Court's theory, is respondent not entitled to assert the presence of such excesses, under the "abuse of discretion" standard of § 706? . . .

III

I turn, then, to whether that executive action is, within the meaning of § 701(a)(2), "committed to agency discretion by law." . . .

It is baffling to observe that the Court seems to agree . . . that "the language and structure of § 102(c) indicate that Congress meant to commit individual employee discharges to the Director's discretion." Nevertheless, without explanation the Court reaches the conclusion that "a constitutional claim based on an individual discharge may be reviewed by the District Court." It seems to me the Court is attempting the impossible feat of having its cake and eating it too. The opinion states that "[a] discharged employee . . . cannot complain that his termination was not 'necessary or advisable in the interests of the United States,' *since that assessment is the Director's alone*" (emphasis added). But two sentences later it says that "[n]othing in § 102(c) persuades us that Congress meant to preclude consideration of colorable constitutional claims arising out of the actions of the Director pursuant to that section." Which are we to believe? If the former, the case should be at an end. If the § 102(c) assessment is really "the Director's alone," the only conceivable basis for review of respondent's dismissal (which is what this case is about) would be that the dismissal was not *really* the result of a § 102(c) assessment by the Director. But respondent has never contended that, nor could he. . . . Even if the basis for the Director's assessment was the respondent's homosexuality, and even if the connection between that and the interests of the United States is an irrational and hence an unconstitutional one, if that assessment is really "the Director's alone" there is nothing more to litigate about. I cannot imagine what the Court expects the "further proceedings in the District Court" which it commands, to consist of, unless perhaps an academic seminar on the relationship of homosexuality to security risk. For even were the District Court persuaded that no such relationship exists, "that assessment is the Director's alone."

Since the Court's disposition contradicts its fair assurances, I must assume that the § 102(c) judgment is no longer "the Director's alone," but rather only "the Director's alone except to the extent it is colorably claimed that his judgment is unconstitutional." I turn, then, to the question of where this exception comes from. As discussed at length earlier, the Constitution assuredly does not require it. Nor does the text of the statute. True, it only gives the Director absolute discretion to dismiss "[n]otwithstanding . . . the provisions of any other *law*" (emphasis added). But one would hardly have expected it to say "[n]otwithstanding the provisions of any other law or of the Constitution." What the provision directly addresses is the authority to dismiss, not the authority of the courts to review the dismissal. And the Director does not have the authority to dismiss in violation of the Constitution, nor could Congress give it to him. The implication of nonreviewability in this text, its manifestation that the action is meant to be "committed to agency discretion," is no weaker with regard to constitutional claims than nonconstitutional claims, unless one accepts the unacceptable proposition that the only basis for such committal is "no law to apply."

Perhaps, then, a constitutional right is by its nature so much more important to the claimant than a statutory right that a statute which plainly excludes the latter should not be read to exclude the former unless it says so. That principle has never been announced—and with good reason, because its premise is not true. . . . A citizen would much rather have his statutory entitlement correctly acknowledged after a constitutionally inadequate hearing, than have it incorrectly denied after a proceeding that fulfills all the requirements of the Due Process Clause. The only respect in which a constitutional claim is necessarily more significant than any other kind of claim is that, regardless of how trivial its real-life importance may be in the case at hand, it can be asserted against the action of the legislature itself, whereas a nonconstitutional claim (no matter how significant) cannot. That is an important distinction, and one relevant to the constitutional analysis that I conducted above. But it has no relevance to the question whether, as between executive violations of statute and executive violations of the Constitution—both of which are equally unlawful, and neither of which can be said, a priori, to be more harmful or more unfair to the plaintiff—one or the other category should be favored by a presumption against exclusion of judicial review.

Even if we were to assume, however, contrary to all reason, that every constitutional claim is *ipso facto* more worthy, and every statutory claim less worthy, of judicial review, there would be no basis for writing that preference into a statute that makes no distinction between the two. We have rejected such judicial rewriting of legislation even in the more appealing situation where particular applications of a statute are not merely less desirable but in fact raise "grave constitutional doubts." That, we have said, only permits us to adopt one rather than another permissible reading of the statute, but not, by altering its terms, "to ignore the legislative will in order to avoid constitutional adjudication." *Commodity Futures Trading Comm'n v. Schor*, 478 U.S. 833, 841 (1986). . . .

The harm done by today's decision is that, contrary to what Congress knows is preferable, it brings a significant decision-making process of our intelligence services into a forum where it does not belong. Neither the Constitution, nor our laws, nor common sense gives an individual a right to come into court to litigate the reasons for his dismissal as an intelligence agent. It is of course not just valid constitutional claims that today's decision makes the basis for judicial review of the Director's action, but all colorable constitutional claims, whether meritorious or not. And in determining whether what is colorable is in fact meritorious, a court will necessarily have to review the entire decision. If the Director denies, for example, respondent's contention in the present case that he was dismissed because he was a homosexual, how can a court possibly resolve the dispute without knowing what other good, intelligence-related reasons there might have been? I do not see how any "latitude to control any discovery process" could justify the refusal to permit such an inquiry, at least *in camera*. Presumably the court would be expected to evaluate whether the agent really did fail in this or that secret mission. The documents needed will make interesting reading for district judges (and perhaps others) throughout the country. Of course the Agency can seek to protect itself, ultimately, by an authorized assertion of executive privilege, but that is a power to be invoked only *in extremis*, and any scheme of judicial review of which it is a central feature is extreme. I would, in any event, not like to be the agent who has to explain to the intelligence services of other nations, with which we sometimes cooperate, that they need have no worry that the secret information they give us will be subjected to the notoriously broad discovery powers of our courts, because, although we have to litigate the dismissal of our spies, we have available a protection of somewhat uncertain scope known as executive privilege, which the President can invoke if he is willing to take the political damage that it often entails.

Today's result, however, will have ramifications far beyond creation of the world's only secret intelligence agency that must litigate the dismissal of its agents. If constitutional claims can be raised in this highly sensitive context, it is hard to imagine where they cannot. The assumption that there are any executive decisions that cannot be hauled into the courts may no longer be valid. Also obsolete may be the assumption that we are capable of preserving a sensible common law of judicial review.

I respectfully dissent.

QUESTION SET 9.5

Review & Synthesis

1. What distinction did the Court draw between statutory unreviewability under § 701(a)(1) and decisions "committed to agency discretion by law" under § 701(a)(2)? Put another way, what is the difference between implied preclusion cases (*Block v. Community Nutrition Institute* and *Bowen v. Michigan Academy of Family Physicians*) and § 701(a)(2) cases (*Webster v. Doe*) in which "there is no law to apply"?

2. In his dissent, Justice Scalia argued that the "law" to which § 701(a)(2) adverts is the " 'common law' of judicial review of agency action" as it existed at the time of the APA's passage in 1946. By his account, this body of common law was distinguishable from "statutes" referenced in § 701(a)(1), which were subsequently passed by Congress and could likewise preclude judicial review of discretionary agency action. Even assuming that Justice Scalia was correct, how are we to know what the content of that common

law is? Relatedly, do you think the APA codified dynamic or static common law? In other words, did Congress memorialize the common law of unreviewability as it stood at that time, or did it delegate to courts the task of incrementally adjusting the unreviewability rules?

3. Is it in fact the case that § 102(c) contained "no law to apply"? The provision stated that the CIA Director could terminate a CIA employee if he or she deemed "termination necessary or advisable in the interests of the United States." At a minimum, the Court could have inquired into whether the Director had actually formulated such a rationale prior to firing Doe. Why did it not do so? Relatedly, why wouldn't a statutory provision containing no law for courts to apply also lack intelligible principles, and thus be an unconstitutional delegation of legislative authority in violation of the Article I Vesting Clause?

4. If § 102(c) "exhibits the Act's extraordinary deference to the Director in his decision to terminate individual employees," and thereby makes that decision unreviewable, why was Doe permitted to move forward with his constitutional claim? Was it because Congress is without power to vest bureaucrats with the discretion to violate the Constitution, or because Congress has that authority but did not clearly use it in § 102(c)? Within a part of his dissent not excerpted above, Justice Scalia argued that Congress has the authority to make even constitutional injuries unreviewable by any federal court. Do you agree? Even if Congress could eliminate lower court jurisdiction to review the Director's personnel decisions, could it prevent appellate review in the Supreme Court?

5. Should the availability of constitutional review under § 701(a)(2) depend on the nature of the power being exercised by the Executive Branch? In other words, should there be a stronger presumption against reviewability when an Executive Branch official exercises discretion in areas adjacent to foreign or military affairs (e.g., immigration or national security) than in areas of domestic regulation (e.g., workplace safety or the environment)? What rationales might support such a difference?

c. Discretionary Use of Appropriations

As touched on in the line-item veto materials above (Chapter 8, page 570), no money can be drawn out of the federal treasury without an appropriation from Congress. *See United States v. MacCollom*, 426 U.S. 317, 321 (1976) ("The established rule is that the expenditure of public funds is proper only when authorized by Congress, not that public funds may be expended unless prohibited by Congress."). Sometimes those appropriations are targeted at particular programs or activities. When that is the case, agencies must use the allocated funds for the purposes specified by Congress, either in the appropriation or in an authorizing statute. In contrast to such line-item appropriations, Congress often funds federal administrative agencies through so-called "lump-sum" appropriations. A lump-sum appropriation is a general fund allocation intended to cover multiple agency expenditures, including those for programs, projects, salaries, and basic operations. Agencies generally have broad discretion in using these funds, though they may develop informal understandings with oversight committees in Congress about how they do so. The following case asked whether the discretionary decisions of an agency—the Indian Health Service—to spend a lump-sum appropriation were unreviewable within the meaning of § 701(a)(2).

Lincoln v. Vigil
508 U.S. 182 (1993)

JUSTICE SOUTER delivered the opinion of the Court.

For several years in the late 1970's and early 1980's, the Indian Health Service provided diagnostic and treatment services, referred to collectively as the Indian Children's Program (Program), to handicapped Indian children in the Southwest. In 1985, the Service decided to reallocate the Program's resources to a nationwide effort to assist such children. We hold that the Service's decision to discontinue the Program was "committed to agency discretion by law" and therefore not subject to judicial review under the Administrative Procedure Act, 5 U.S.C. § 701(a)(2), and that the Service's exercise of that discretion was not subject to the notice-and-comment rulemaking requirements imposed by § 553.

I

The Indian Health Service, an agency within the Public Health Service of the Department of Health and Human Services, provides health care for some 1.5 million American Indian and Alaska Native people. The Service receives yearly lump-sum appropriations from Congress and expends the funds under authority of the Snyder Act, 42 Stat. 208, as amended, 25 U.S.C. § 13, and the Indian Health Care Improvement Act, 90 Stat. 1400, as amended, 25 U.S.C. § 1601 *et seq.* So far as it concerns us here, the Snyder Act authorizes the Service to "expend such moneys as Congress may from time to time appropriate, for the benefit, care, and assistance of the Indians," for the "relief of distress and conservation of health." 25 U.S.C. § 13. The Improvement Act authorizes expenditures for, *inter alia,* Indian mental-health care, and specifically for "therapeutic and residential treatment centers." § 1621(a)(4)(D).

The Service employs roughly 12,000 people and operates more than 500 health-care facilities in the continental United States and Alaska. This case concerns a collection of related services, commonly known as the Indian Children's Program, that the Service provided from 1978 to 1985. In the words of the Court of Appeals, a "clou[d] [of] bureaucratic haze" obscures the history of the Program, *Vigil v. Rhoades,* 953 F.2d 1225, 1226 (10th Cir. 1992), which seems to have grown out of a plan "to establish therapeutic and residential treatment centers for disturbed Indian children." H.R. Rep. No. 94–1026, pt. 1, p. 80 (1976) (prepared in conjunction with enactment of the Improvement Act). These centers were to be established under a "major cooperative care agreement" between the Service and the Bureau of Indian Affairs, and would have provided such children "with intensive care in a residential setting." *Id.* at 80.

Congress never expressly appropriated funds for these centers. In 1978, however, the Service allocated approximately $292,000 from its fiscal year 1978 appropriation to its office in Albuquerque, New Mexico, for the planning and development of a pilot project for handicapped Indian children, which became known as the Indian Children's Program. The pilot project apparently convinced the Service that a building was needed, and, in 1979, the Service requested $3.5 million from Congress to construct a diagnostic and treatment center for handicapped Indian children. *See* Hearings on Department of the Interior and Related Agencies Appropriations for 1980 before a Subcommittee of the House Committee on Appropriations, 96th Cong., 1st Sess., pt. 8, p. 250 (1979) (hereinafter House Hearings (Fiscal Year 1980)). The appropriation for fiscal year 1980 did not expressly provide the requested funds, however, and legislative reports indicated only that Congress had increased the Service's funding by $300,000 for nationwide expansion and development of the Program in coordination with the Bureau.

Plans for a national program to be managed jointly by the Service and the Bureau were never fulfilled, however, and the Program continued simply as an offering of the Service's Albuquerque office, from which the Program's staff of 11 to 16 employees would make monthly visits to Indian communities in New Mexico and southern Colorado and on the Navajo and Hopi Reservations. The Program's staff provided "diagnostic, evaluation, treatment planning and followup services" for Indian children with emotional, educational, physical, or mental handicaps. "For parents, community groups, school personnel and health care personnel," the staff provided "training in child development, prevention of handicapping conditions, and care of the handicapped child." Hearings on Department of the Interior and Related Agencies Appropriations for 1984 before a Subcommittee of the House Committee on Appropriations, 98th Cong., 1st Sess., pt. 3, p. 374 (1983) (Service submission) (hereinafter House Hearings (Fiscal Year 1984)). Congress never authorized or appropriated moneys expressly for the Program, and the Service continued to pay for its regional activities out of annual lump-sum appropriations from 1980 to 1985, during which period the Service repeatedly apprised Congress of the Program's continuing operation.

Nevertheless, the Service had not abandoned the proposal for a nation-wide treatment program, and in June 1985 it notified those who referred patients to the Program that it was re-evaluating the Program's purpose as a national mental health program for Indian children and adolescents. In August 1985, the Service determined that Program staff hitherto assigned to provide direct clinical services should be reassigned as consultants to other nationwide Service programs, and discontinued the direct clinical services to Indian children in the Southwest. The Service announced its decision in a memorandum, dated August 21, 1985, addressed to Service offices and Program referral sources. . . .

Respondents, handicapped Indian children eligible to receive services through the Program, subsequently brought this action for declaratory and injunctive relief against petitioners, the Director of the Service and others (collectively, the Service), in the United States District Court for the District of New Mexico. Respondents alleged, *inter alia*, that the Service's decision to discontinue direct clinical services violated the federal trust responsibility to Indians, the Snyder Act, the Improvement Act, the Administrative Procedure Act, various agency regulations, and the Fifth Amendment's Due Process Clause.

The District Court granted summary judgment for respondents. . . .

The Court of Appeals affirmed. Like the District Court, it rejected the Service's argument that the decision to discontinue the Program was com-mitted to agency discretion under the APA. Although the court conced-edly could identify no statute or regulation even mentioning the Program, it believed that the repeated references to it in the legislative history of the annual appropriations Acts, "in combination with the special relationship between the Indian people and the federal government," 953 F.2d, at 1230, provided a basis for judicial review. . . . We granted certiorari to address the narrow questions presented by the Court of Appeals's decision.

II

First is the question whether it was error for the Court of Appeals to hold the substance of the Service's decision to terminate the Program reviewable under the APA. The APA provides that "[a] person suffering legal wrong because of agency action, or adversely affected or aggrieved by agency action within the meaning of a relevant statute, is entitled to judicial review thereof," 5 U.S.C. § 702, and we have read the APA as embodying a "basic presumption of judicial review," *Abbott Laboratories v. Gardner*, 387 U.S. 136, 140 (1967). This is "just" a presumption, however, *Block v.*

Community Nutrition Institute, 467 U.S. 340, 349 (1984), and under § 701(a)(2) agency action is not subject to judicial review "to the extent that" such action "is committed to agency discretion by law."[3] As we explained in *Heckler v. Chaney*, 470 U.S. 821, 830 (1985), § 701(a)(2) makes it clear that "review is not to be had" in those rare circumstances where the relevant statute "is drawn so that a court would have no meaningful standard against which to judge the agency's exercise of discretion." *See also Webster v. Doe*, 486 U.S. 592, 599-600 (1988); *Citizens to Preserve Overton Park, Inc. v. Volpe*, 401 U.S. 402, 410 (1971). "In such a case, the statute ('law') can be taken to have 'committed' the decisionmaking to the agency's judgment absolutely." *Heckler, supra*, at 830.

Over the years, we have read § 701(a)(2) to preclude judicial review of certain categories of administrative decisions that courts traditionally have regarded as "committed to agency discretion." *See Webster, supra*, at 609 (Scalia, J., dissenting). In *Heckler* itself, we held an agency's decision not to institute enforcement proceedings to be presumptively unreviewable under § 701(a)(2). 470 U.S., at 831. An agency's "decision not to enforce often involves a complicated balancing of a number of factors which are peculiarly within its expertise," *ibid.*, and for this and other good reasons, we concluded, "such a decision has traditionally been 'committed to agency discretion,'" *id.* at 832. . . . [I]n *Webster, supra*, at 599-601, we held that § 701(a)(2) precludes judicial review of a decision by the Director of Central Intelligence to terminate an employee in the interests of national security, an area of executive action "in which courts have long been hesitant to intrude."

The allocation of funds from a lump-sum appropriation is another administrative decision traditionally regarded as committed to agency discretion. After all, the very point of a lump-sum appropriation is to give an agency the capacity to adapt to changing circumstances and meet its statutory responsibilities in what it sees as the most effective or desirable way. For this reason, a fundamental principle of appropriations law is that where "Congress merely appropriates lump-sum amounts without statutorily restricting what can be done with those funds, a clear inference arises that it does not intend to impose legally binding restrictions, and indicia in committee reports and other legislative history as to how the funds should or are expected to be spent do not establish any legal requirements on" the agency. *LTV Aerospace Corp.*, 55 Comp. Gen. 307, 319 (1975); *cf. American Hospital Assn. v. NLRB*, 499 U.S. 606, 616 (1991) (statements in committee reports do not have the force of law). Put another way, a lump-sum appropriation reflects a congressional recognition that an agency must be allowed "flexibility to shift . . . funds within a particular . . . appropriation account so that"

---

[3] In full, § 701(a) provides: "This chapter [relating to judicial review] applies, according to the provisions thereof, except to the extent that — (1) statutes preclude judicial review; or (2) agency action is committed to agency discretion by law." The parties have not addressed, and we have no occasion to consider, the application of § 701(a)(1) in this case.

the agency "can make necessary adjustments for 'unforeseen developments' " and " 'changing requirements.' " *LTV Aerospace Corp., supra*, at 318 (citation omitted).

Like the decision against instituting enforcement proceedings, then, an agency's allocation of funds from a lump-sum appropriation requires "a complicated balancing of a number of factors which are peculiarly within its expertise": whether its "resources are best spent" on one program or another; whether it "is likely to succeed" in fulfilling its statutory mandate; whether a particular program "best fits the agency's overall policies"; and, "indeed, whether the agency has enough resources" to fund a program "at all." *Heckler*, 470 U.S., at 831. As in *Heckler*, so here, the "agency is far better equipped than the courts to deal with the many variables involved in the proper ordering of its priorities." *Id.* at 831-832. Of course, an agency is not free simply to disregard statutory responsibilities: Congress may always circumscribe agency discretion to allocate resources by putting restrictions in the operative statutes (though not, as we have seen, just in the legislative history). And, of course, we hardly need to note that an agency's decision to ignore congressional expectations may expose it to grave political consequences. But as long as the agency allocates funds from a lump-sum appropriation to meet permissible statutory objectives, § 701(a)(2) gives the courts no leave to intrude. "[T]o [that] extent," the decision to allocate funds "is committed to agency discretion by law." § 701(a)(2).

The Service's decision to discontinue the Program is accordingly unreviewable under § 701(a)(2). As the Court of Appeals recognized, the appropriations Acts for the relevant period do not so much as mention the Program, and both the Snyder Act and the Improvement Act likewise speak about Indian health only in general terms. It is true that the Service repeatedly apprised Congress of the Program's continued operation, but, as we have explained, these representations do not translate through the medium of legislative history into legally binding obligations. The reallocation of agency resources to assist handicapped Indian children nationwide clearly falls within the Service's statutory mandate to provide health care to Indian people, and respondents, indeed, do not seriously contend otherwise. The decision to terminate the Program was committed to the Service's discretion.

The Court of Appeals saw a separate limitation on the Service's discretion in the special trust relationship existing between Indian people and the Federal Government. We have often spoken of this relationship, and the law is "well established that the Government in its dealings with Indian tribal property acts in a fiduciary capacity," *United States v. Cherokee Nation of Okla.*, 480 U.S. 700, 707 (1987). Whatever the contours of that relationship, though, it could not limit the Service's discretion to reorder its priorities from serving a subgroup of beneficiaries to serving the broader class of all Indians nationwide.

One final note: although respondents claimed in the District Court that the Service's termination of the Program violated their rights under the Fifth Amendment's Due Process Clause, that court expressly declined to address respondents' constitutional arguments, as did the Court of Appeals. Thus, while the APA contemplates, in the absence of a clear expression of contrary congressional intent, that judicial review will be available for colorable constitutional claims, *see Webster*, 486 U.S., at 603-604, the record at this stage does not allow mature consideration of constitutional issues, which we leave for the Court of Appeals on remand.

[In Section III of its opinion, the Court concluded that the Indian Health Service was not required to follow the notice-and-comment procedures of § 553 before terminating the Indian Children's Program.]

IV

The judgment of the Court of Appeals is reversed, and the case is remanded for further proceedings consistent with this opinion.

It is so ordered.

QUESTION SET 9.6

Review & Synthesis

1. A unanimous Court in *Vigil* concluded that Congress left the discontinuation of the Indian Children's Program to the Indian Health Service's discretion. On what facts did it rely in reaching this conclusion? Was its application of § 701(a)(2) consistent with *Webster v. Doe*?

2. Assume that the legislative history in the Snyder Act and the Indian Health Care Improvement Act made clear that Congress expected that the Indian Health Service would provide the Indian Children's Program. Would that fact alone have been sufficient to establish that its creation was not committed to the Indian Health Service's discretion under § 701(a)(2)?

3. It is not necessarily the case that unreviewable agency decisions under § 701(a)(1) or (a)(2) escape external supervision. Oversight committees in both the House of Representatives and in the Senate will retain jurisdiction over those decisions not susceptible to judicial review. Some might argue that Congress' oversight committees can provide a more appropriate and effective check on discretionary agency decisions because they require policymakers to balance policy and resource priorities. Consider, however, the following: A court concludes that an agency's decision to fund a particular program is committed to agency discretion by law, and is thus unreviewable under § 701(a)(2). The House and Senate committee reports for the authorizing legislation under which the agency established

the program expressly disapproved of the program, and those committees reiterate that disapproval in oversight hearings in which the agency's leaders are called to testify. What recourse is there to prevent the expenditure, and how effective do you anticipate it would be?

4. Even if neither the Snyder Act nor the Indian Healthcare Improvement Act provided substantive rules applicable to the Indian Health Service's lump-sum appropriation, does it necessarily follow that the agency's decision to discontinue the Indian Children's Program is immune from *procedural* attack under the APA? The respondents argued that IHS' decision constituted a "rule" under APA § 551(4), and therefore had to be promulgated through § 553 notice-and-comment rulemaking. The Court rejected this challenge, concluding that the decision was either a rule of agency organization or a general policy statement, and thus exempt from the APA's rulemaking requirements. *Lincoln*, 508 U.S. at 197.

Application & Analysis

1. The Army Board for Correction of Military Records (the "Board") is composed of civilians who evaluate former servicemembers' allegations of errors or injustices in their military records. The Board derives its authority from 10 U.S.C. § 1552(a)(1), which provides that "[t]he Secretary of [of the Army] may correct any military record of the Secretary's department when the Secretary considers it necessary to correct an error or remove an injustice. . . . [S]uch corrections shall be made by the Secretary acting through boards of civilians of the executive part of that military department." Servicemembers seeking record corrections must file for them within three years after discovery of the error or injustice, although the Board "may excuse a failure to file within three years after discovery if it finds it to be in the interest of justice." 10 U.S.C. § 1552(b).

Bucky Batson voluntarily enlisted in the Army in 1995, and after approximately nine months of service was granted a two-week leave. He was court-martialed and convicted when he returned from leave one week late. He was absent without leave two more times in the 18 months immediately following his release from the stockade. In 1997, he was discharged for inability to adapt to military life under "other than honorable conditions."

Batson recently applied to the Board for an upgrade of his discharge classification. He claimed that his discharge had been unjust because he was not counseled before signing his discharge papers. The Board denied his application. It concluded that Batson could have, "with reasonable diligence," discovered the issue on the date of his discharge. Accordingly, it ruled: "The subject application was not submitted within the time required. The applicant has not submitted, nor do the records contain, sufficient justification to establish that it would be in the interest of justice to excuse the failure to file within the time prescribed by law."

Batson now petitions for review of the Board's decision, asserting that it was arbitrary and capricious. Among other things, the government argues that waiver determinations are not reviewable because they involve matters committed to agency discretion under APA § 701(a)(2). It maintains that 10 U.S.C. § 1552(b) contains no judicially manageable standards against which a court may analyze the Board's exercise of discretion, and thus does not permit review. You clerk for the judge before whom the petition is pending. Write a brief memorandum on whether the Board's decision is reviewable.

2. The Civil Service Reform Act of 1978 ("CSRA"), 5 U.S.C. § 1101 *et seq.*, established a comprehensive system for reviewing personnel actions taken against federal employees, including dismissals. A qualifying employee has the right to a hearing before the Merit Systems Protection Board ("MSPB"), which is authorized to order reinstatement, back pay, and attorney's fees. An employee who is dissatisfied with the MSPB's decision is entitled to judicial review in the United States Court of Appeals for the Federal Circuit, which has exclusive jurisdiction over such appeals. The Federal Circuit must vacate any MSPB decisions it finds arbitrary and capricious, an abuse of discretion, or otherwise not in accordance with law. § 7703(a)(1), (c).

Christopher Chen, a former federal competitive service employee at the Treasury Department, failed to comply with the Military Selective Service Act, 50 U.S.C. App. § 453. The Act requires male citizens and lawful permanent residents between the ages of 18 and 26 to register for the Selective Service. Federal law bars anyone who has knowingly and willfully failed to register from employment by an Executive Branch agency. 5 U.S.C. § 3328. The Treasury Department discharged Chen when it discovered that he had failed to register.

Chen appealed his dismissal to the MSPB. He asserted that Section 3328 is an unconstitutional bill of attainder and unconstitutionally discriminates on the basis of sex when combined with the registration requirement of the Military Selective Service Act. The MSPB referred the case to an ALJ. The ALJ dismissed it for lack of jurisdiction, finding that Chen's dismissal was unreviewable because it was based on an absolute statutory bar to employment. Additionally, the ALJ held that the MSPB could not hear Chen's constitutional claims because it lacks authority to determine the constitutionality of statutes.

Rather than appealing to the Federal Circuit, Chen has filed a new lawsuit in federal district court, raising the same constitutional claims. The government argues that the adjudicative procedure set by the CSRA is exclusive, and therefore Chen's dismissal is not reviewable in federal district court. Chen counters that, under *Webster v. Doe*, a "heightened showing" is required before any federal court can be denied jurisdiction over a colorable constitutional claim. The CSRA, Chen asserts, does not meet *Doe's* "heightened showing" standard.

You are a clerk for the district court judge assigned to Chen's suit. Analyze the merits of the parties' claims.

---

5. Standing to Challenge Agency Decision-Making

A party must do more than establish that an agency's decisions are judicially reviewable. It must also show that it has "standing" to file its federal lawsuit against an agency. The standing doctrine's general purpose is easy enough to state: it prevents federal litigants from challenging conduct in federal court to which they have little or no connection. Put another way, standing doctrine ensures that federal plaintiffs actually have some stake or interest in the disputes they ask courts to resolve. Federal plaintiffs who do not have "a dog in the fight" will get their claims dismissed.

However simply we can state standing's general purpose, federal courts have struggled mightily to apply it consistently (or sometimes even coherently). Indeed, the Supreme Court's standing jurisprudence is a multileveled labyrinth of early Anglo-American judicial history, constitutional language and theory, statutory interpretation, and common law reasoning. The doctrine's maze-like contours led Justice William O. Douglas to remark (with some resignation) that "[g]eneralizations about standing to sue are largely worthless as such." *Association of Data Processing Service Organizations, Inc. v. Camp*, 397 U.S. 150, 151 (1970).

Nevertheless, the Supreme Court has made standing an absolute requirement for invoking federal judicial power. Unfortunately, the Justices have held diverse and sometimes irreconcilable views on what the test for standing should be. As a result, they have also held diverse and sometimes irreconcilable views on what standing doctrine requires plaintiffs to show. As you will see, these doctrinal disagreements often reflect much deeper philosophical disputes about the proper roles of Congress, the President, the courts, and private parties in ensuring that government actors follow the law.

In the specific context of federal lawsuits against agencies, standing disputes often begin with how one answers the following question: Can a federal plaintiff sue an agency when it has no *personal legal right* to be protected from that agency's actions? Say, for example, the plaintiff is a business and an agency grants an operating license to a new competitor. This new competitor increases competition which, in turn, causes the plaintiff harm by decreasing its profitability. The business's managers do not believe the new competitor meets the legal requirements for receiving an operating license and would like a federal court to review the agency's decision granting it. However, there is no law—constitutional, statutory, or common—giving the business an exclusive right to operate in its chosen market. Can the business sue when no law grants it a personal legal right to be protected from increased competition? Does the fact that it has directly suffered factual harm—in the form of reduced profits—create enough of an interest in the agency's decision for it to mount a federal court challenge?

In one form or another, the cases below reflect how the Supreme Court has tried to answer these questions. By way of brief preview, the Court has separated its modern standing doctrine into constitutional and prudential requirements. It traces the constitutional requirements to Article III, which establishes the jurisdiction of the federal court system. According to the Court, the Constitution requires federal plaintiffs to show that they have personally suffered an *injury-in-fact*, that the defendant's conduct *caused* that injury, and that a ruling in the plaintiff's favor will *redress* (make the plaintiff whole for) that injury. By contrast, the Court has identified no textual basis for its prudential standing requirements. Rather, these requirements seem to come from the Judiciary's inherent (though limited) authority to choose the cases it hears. Congress can play an important role here; the Supreme Court has acknowledged that legislation can override the prudential standing requirements and mandate that courts hear cases they would otherwise refuse. To further complicate matters, the Court has at times blurred the line between what it considers a "constitutional" requirement and what it deems a "prudential" one. In any event, it remains clear that plaintiffs must satisfy both the constitutional and the prudential standing requirements to maintain a suit in federal court.

This section begins with a brief history of standing. Familiarity with this history is invaluable for understanding why the Justices continue fiercely to debate what standing should require of federal plaintiffs. The section ends with a study of the modern doctrine, including cases that exhibit those disagreements.

a. Standing from Early America to the Early Twentieth Century

(Possible) Origins. Scholars looking to understand the origins of modern standing doctrine often begin their search with the practice of the English courts and colonial period American courts. Which plaintiffs did these courts allow to file lawsuits? Prior to the Constitution's ratification, these courts routinely assumed that plaintiffs who possessed substantive personal legal rights under the common law necessarily held the related procedural right to file suits to protect them. In other words, these courts seldom distinguished between the substantive rights on which plaintiffs based their claims and their right to sue. The plaintiff's procedural right to file a lawsuit implicitly traveled with its possession of a substantive legal right. The reasoning here is fairly straightforward: the right would be a dead letter if its possessor did not also have the means to enforce it against violators. Hence the maxim *ubi jus ibi remedium* ("for every wrong, the law provides a remedy") frequently invoked by English courts. Hence the confidence with which Chief Justice John Marshall acknowledged a similar and by then well-established precept in American law. Pointing to those instances when "mere operation of law" gives litigants the right to file suit, he observed that "it is a general and indisputable rule, that where there is a legal right, there is also a legal remedy by suit or action at law, whenever that right is invaded." *Marbury v. Madison*, 5 U.S. (1 Cranch) 137, 163 (1803) (internal quotations omitted).

The question then arises whether plaintiffs with legally protected personal interests were the *only* ones who could come to a pre-constitutional English or American court. Would these courts accept suits from plaintiffs who did *not* claim injuries to their personal interests? The history indicates that the answer is "yes." Scholars point to petitions for prerogative writs—e.g., prohibition and *quo warranto*—filed in eighteenth-century English and colonial courts to challenge allegedly illegal government conduct as examples. These petitions did not always protect the personal interests of their petitioners, nor did they always seek to redress any personal injuries they may have suffered. These writs could be used instead to check governmental encroachments and thus to vindicate ostensibly communal interests. *Qui tam* and informers' actions similarly allowed those without concrete personal interests to file suit in federal courts. *See* Cass R. Sunstein, *What's Standing after* Lujan? *Of Citizen Suits, "Injuries," and Article III*, 91 MICH. L. REV. 163, 174-75 (1992). In other words, and unlike those suits brought under the common law, petitioners were not asked to show any personally suffered harms or point to invasions of personal rights to obtain judicial relief. *See* Louis Jaffe, *Standing to Secure Judicial Review: Public Actions*, 74 HARV. L. REV. 1265, 1308 (1961); Raoul Berger, *Standing to Sue in Public Actions: Is It a Constitutional Requirement?*, 78 YALE L.J. 816, 840 (1969). This writ practice points to a much broader conception of standing—of who may properly invoke judicial power—than one that embraces only those plaintiffs who can claim injuries to personal interests secured by the common law.

Scholars disagree as to whether such suits were generally reflective of how English and pre-constitutional American courts viewed plaintiffs' right to sue, or whether they were simply in a class by themselves. Some have argued that such "stranger" suits—suits in which plaintiffs asserted no personal injuries or legal rights—were far from typical. Much to the contrary, these scholars argue that they were actively limited by English and early American courts even before the formal development of standing doctrine. Accordingly, they warn against thinking that standing was readily recognized in plaintiffs with no personal interests at stake. *See, e.g.,* Ann Woolhandler & Caleb Nelson, *Does History Defeat Standing Doctrine?*, 102 MICH. L. REV. 689 (2004); Bradley S. Clanton, *Standing and the English Prerogative Writs: The Original Understanding*, 63 BROOK. L. REV. 1001 (1997).

Note that there was no discussion of standing as such by the Framers, nor was the topic addressed in the state ratification debates. Article III extends the federal judicial power to "cases" or "controversies," but does not say anything about standing. Indeed, the term "standing" appears nowhere in the text of the Constitution. As discussed in greater detail below, standing as a constitutional requirement is a relatively recent invention by the Supreme Court.

The Early Twentieth Century: The Primacy of Personal Interests. While reasonable people can disagree about what the historical record shows, it is certainly true that the Supreme Court began to focus more intently on the concept of standing during the early twentieth century. Whereas the Court paid almost no attention to the issue before that time, it paid far more attention to it thereafter. It is also true that the Court of this period began to solidify one of the core elements of its standing jurisprudence: plaintiffs must show harm to some personally held interest to invoke federal judicial jurisdiction. *See, e.g., McCabe v. Atchison*, 235 U.S. 151, 162 (1914) ("It is the fact, clearly established, of injury to the complainant—not to others—which justifies judicial intervention."); *Braxton County Court v. West Virginia*, 208 U.S. 192, 197 (1908) (holding that standing requires plaintiffs to "be interested in and affected adversely by the decision . . . and [their] interest must . . . be of a personal, and not of an official, nature"); *Clark v. City of Kansas City*, 176 U.S. 114, 118 (1900) ("'A court will not listen to an objection made to the constitutionality of an act by a party whose rights it does not affect and who has therefore no interest in defeating it.'" (quoting THOMAS M. COOLEY, TREATISE ON CONSTITUTIONAL LIMITATIONS 196 (1871)). Although the Court would eventually dilute the personal interest requirement (see below), at the time it operated to significantly narrow the types of cases plaintiffs could bring. Suits filed ostensibly on behalf of the public—like the writ petitions discussed above—would find a cold reception in the federal judicial system. Similarly, third-party claims—those filed to vindicate the rights of parities who were not themselves litigants in the case—were explicitly rejected by the Court.

In addition to establishing the personal interest requirement, the Court during this period began exploring the amount of personal injury that was needed to sustain a federal standing claim. It found that an alleged harm could be too small, too speculative, and/or too widely shared among the general public for a federal plaintiff to base a lawsuit on it. The Court's decision in *Frothingham v. Mellon*, 262 U.S. 447 (1923) is instructive here. The plaintiff in that case challenged the constitutionality of the federal Maternity Act of 1921, which provided grants to states that established welfare programs to help infants and mothers. Among other things, she argued that the Act personally injured her by increasing her tax burden; she would have to pay higher taxes in the future if Congress were permitted to unconstitutionally fund the Maternity

Act's grants. The Court declined to test the merits of her claim, holding instead that a federal taxpayer's "interest in the moneys of the treasury . . . is shared with millions of others; is comparatively minute and indeterminable; and the effect upon future taxation, of a payment out of the funds, so remote, fluctuating and uncertain, that no basis is afforded for an appeal to the preventive powers of a court of equity." *Id.* at 487. *See also id.* at 488 (observing that a federal plaintiff "must be able to show . . . that he has sustained or is immediately in danger of sustaining some direct injury as the result of its enforcement, and not merely that he suffers in some indefinite way in common with people generally"). Further, the Court stated that injuries shared by vast swaths of the public—such as those suffered by all federal taxpayers—are essentially public disputes that should be resolved by political rather than by judicial processes. *Id.* at 487-88.

The New Deal Era: From the Rights-Based Model to the Harm-Based Model. So the Court determined that a plaintiff must demonstrate injury to some personally held interest to sue in federal court. Moreover, it indicated that some injuries could be too minute, too speculative, or too widely shared to sustain a federal claim. What remained unclear was whether a plaintiff had to show that its *legal rights* were violated by the government's conduct in order to establish standing to sue. In other words, did the Court's emerging standing doctrine require a federal plaintiff to show that the law protected it from the harm it suffered, or could it answer the standing inquiry simply by showing that it suffered the harm? These questions indicated a growing tension between the Court's views on standing and changes to how the federal government did business. Congress delegated more and more governing authority to newly formed administrative agencies, dramatically increasing the scope of federal regulation. Citizens at large would invoke the Constitution when attempting to invalidate these statutes, but they held no common law rights and Congress passed few statutes providing a right to bring suit. As a result, the private law standing approach—where plaintiffs brought claims under the common law for concrete and personally

In Context

The Court had previously come to a different conclusion regarding the ability of taxpayers to challenge appropriations of municipal funds. In *Crampton v. Zabriskie*, 101 U.S. 601 (1879), it stated that "the right of resident taxpayers to invoke the interposition of a court of equity to prevent an illegal disposition of the moneys of the county or the illegal creation of a debt which they in common with other propertyholders of the county may otherwise be compelled to pay, there is at this day no serious question." *Id.* at 609. *See also Roberts v. Bradfield*, 12 App. D.C. 453, 459-60 (1898) (citing *Crampton*). As *Frothingham* made clear, this decision is limited to the municipal context, and thus does not indicate what suits Article III might permit. *Frothingham*, 262 U.S. at 486-87.

Cross-Reference

Recall the Supreme Court's decisions in *Bi-Metallic Investment Co. v. State Board of Equalization*, 239 U.S. 441 (1915), which involved taxpayer challenges to municipal tax policy. *See* Chapter 4. The Court decided *Bi-Metallic* during the same period in which it developed its standing jurisprudence. Like the standing cases discussed here, the *Bi-Metallic* Court indicated that government decisions affecting broad swaths of the public are not suitable for judicial resolution. *Londoner*, however, made no mention of the personal interest requirement. Is *Londoner* really a standing case in disguise?

suffered injuries—began to strain with the emergence of the administrative state. *See generally* Cass R. Sunstein, *Standing and the Privatization of Public Law*, 88 COLUM. L. REV. 1432 (1988).

The Court initially responded to this tension by adopting a "rights-based" standing model. A plaintiff challenging agency conduct had to show a factual injury—loss of money, damage to or loss of personal property, etc.—and that it held a legal right to be protected from whatever injury the agency had allegedly caused. That legal right could come from the common law, statute, or from some interest Congress intended an administrative agency to consider and protect when making decisions. Assume, for example, that a government official seizes a business' property to satisfy an unpaid tax liability. If that seizure could have constituted a common law tort (conversion, for example) had the official been acting as a private person, then the property owner would have standing to sue under the rights-based model. The official would likely defend against the suit by arguing that she had the legal authority to act as she did. Contrast this with the government official who, acting pursuant to her statutorily granted authority, declines to award a government contract to a vendor in a competitive bidding process. Though the vendor would assuredly suffer significant personal harm from being denied the contract, neither the applicable statute nor the common law gives her any legally enforceable rights to it. She would accordingly lack standing to challenge the official's decision under the rights-based model.

Justices Louis Brandeis and Felix Frankfurter are often credited with guiding the Court's adoption of the rights-based model. *See, e.g., Joint Anti-Fascist Refugee Committee v. McGrath*, 341 U.S. 123 (1951) (Frankfurter, J., concurring); *Alexander Sprunt & Son, Inc. v. United States*, 281 U.S. 249 (1930); *The Chicago Junction Case*, 264 U.S. 258 (1924). Both appeared to favor President Franklin D. Roosevelt's energetic expansion of social and economic regulation in response to the Great Depression and wanted to protect it through more restrictive standing rules. "The Court was well aware that the politically accountable Branches of government were experimenting with a wide array of interventionalist strategies in their desperate attempt to extricate the nation from the Great Depression. The Court was also aware that many conservative judges were hostile to these radical experiments. It is fair to infer that the Court adopted the [rights-based model] in part to minimize the potential for constant conflicts between federal judges and the Legislative and Executive Branches." 3 RICHARD J. PIERCE, JR., ADMINISTRATIVE LAW TREATISE § 16.2 (2010). By requiring that plaintiffs hold personal legal rights to be protected from their alleged injuries, the rights-based model reduced the number of plaintiffs who could challenge administrative decision-making. This, in turn, facilitated growth of economic regulation without judicial interference during the 1930s.

We find a well-known application of the rights-based model in *Alabama Power Co. v. Ickes*, 302 U.S. 464 (1938). Pursuant to the Emergency Relief Appropriation Act of 1935 ("ERAA"), the Federal Emergency Administrator of Public Works (Harold Ickes) approved loans to two Alabama towns to establish public power plants. A private power plant serving the area, Alabama Power, sued to enjoin issuance of the loans by arguing that the ERAA violated the Commerce Clause. The Court, speaking through Justice George Sutherland, rejected the company's claim of standing. The Court conceded that Alabama Power had an interest in preventing issuance of the loans; the funds they made available would facilitate increased competition where the company operated, thereby decreasing its expected profits. This "competitive" economic injury, though almost certain, was nevertheless insufficient to support Alabama Power's standing. The reason was straightforward under the rights-based model; Alabama Power held no legal right (under the common law or from any other source) to be free from increased competition. "[W]here, although there is damage, there is no violation of a right no action can be maintained." *Id.* at 479. *See also Tennessee Electric Power Co. v. TVA*, 306 U.S. 118, 139 (1939); *Alexander Sprunt & Son, Inc. v. United States*, 281 U.S. 249, 254-55 (1930).

Note the basic fact pattern here. Alabama Power sued a federal official (the Public Works Administrator) rather than the towns seeking funds under the federal program the administrator administered. Accordingly, the parties directly causing Alabama Power's alleged economic injuries were not litigants in the case. Why? Because the towns did nothing illegal; they simply followed the law by seeking assistance from a government program. Alabama Power could only indirectly eliminate its potential competitors by attacking the Public Works Administrator's legal authority to issue loans. Many administrative standing cases similarly involve a separation between personal legal rights and alleged factual injuries. The plaintiff cannot sue the party most directly responsible for its alleged harms—such as the loan-receiving towns in *Alabama Power*—because that party is simply following the law. The lawsuit instead attacks the agency's regulatory authority. By essentially requiring the impossible—a showing of a personal legal right to be protected from entirely lawful conduct—the rights-based model thwarted standing in these suits.

Compare the Court's application of the rights-based model with its analysis in *FCC v. Sanders Bros. Radio Station*, 309 U.S. 470 (1940), below. Does the Court retain the rights-based model, or does it change its standing approach? What does Congress provide in the Communications Act (analyzed in *Sanders Brothers.*) that it did not provide in the ERAA (analyzed in *Alabama Power*)?

Federal Communications Commission v. Sanders Brothers Radio Station
309 U.S. 470 (1940)

Mr. Justice [Owen] ROBERTS delivered the opinion of the Court.

We took this case to resolve important issues of substance and procedure arising under the Communications Act of 1934. . . .

January 20, 1936, the Telegraph Herald, a newspaper published in Dubuque, Iowa, filed with the petitioner an application for a construction permit to erect a broadcasting station in that city. May 14, 1936, the respondent, who had for some years held a broadcasting license for, and had operated, Station WKBB at East Dubuque, Illinois, directly across the Mississippi River from Dubuque, Iowa, applied for a permit to move its transmitter and studios to the last named city and to install its station there. August 18, 1936, respondent asked leave to intervene in the Telegraph Herald proceeding, alleging in its petition, *inter alia*, that there was an insufficiency of advertising revenue to support an additional station in Dubuque and insufficient talent to furnish programs for an additional station; that adequate service was being rendered to the community by Station WKBB and there was no need for any additional radio outlet in Dubuque and that the granting of the Telegraph Herald application would not serve the public interest, convenience, and necessity. Intervention was permitted and both applications were set for consolidated hearing.

The respondent and the Telegraph Herald offered evidence in support of their respective applications. The respondent's proof showed that its station had operated at a loss; that the area proposed to be served by the Telegraph Herald was substantially the same as that served by the respondent and that, of the advertisers relied on to support the Telegraph Herald station, more than half had used the respondent's station for advertising.

An examiner reported that the application of the Telegraph Herald should be denied and that of the respondent granted. On exceptions of the Telegraph Herald, and after oral argument, the broadcasting division of petitioner made an order granting both applications, reciting that 'public interest, convenience, and necessity would be served' by such action. The division promulgated a statement of the facts and of the grounds of decision, reciting that both applicants were legally, technically, and financially qualified to undertake the proposed construction and operation; that there was need in Dubuque and the surrounding territory for the services of both stations, and that no question of electrical interference between the two stations was involved. A rehearing was denied and respondent appealed to the Court of Appeals for the District of Columbia. That court entertained the appeal and held that one of the issues which the Commission should have tried was that of alleged economic injury to the respondent's station by the establishment of an additional station and that the Commission had erred in failing to make findings on that issue. It decided that, in the absence of such findings, the Commission's action in granting the Telegraph Herald permit must be set aside as arbitrary and capricious.

The petitioner's contentions are that under the Communications Act economic injury to a competitor is not a ground for refusing a broadcasting license and that, since this is so, the respondent was not a person aggrieved or whose interests were adversely affected, by the Commission's action, within the meaning of Section 402(b) of the Act, 47 U.S.C.A. § 402(b), which authorizes appeals from the Commission's orders.

The respondent asserts that the petitioner in argument below contended itself with the contention that the respondent had failed to produce evidence requiring a finding of probable economic injury to it. It is consequently insisted that the petitioner is not in a position here to defend its failure to make such findings on the ground that it is not required by the Act to consider any such issue. By its petition for rehearing in the court below, the Commission made clear its position as now advanced. The decision of the court below, and the challenge made in petition for rehearing and here by the Commission, raise a fundamental question as to the function and powers of the Commission and we think that, on the record, it is open here.

First. We hold that resulting economic injury to a rival station is not in and of itself, and apart from considerations of public convenience, interest, or necessity, an element the petitioner must weigh and as to which it must make findings in passing on an application for a broadcasting license.

Section 307(a) of the Communications Act, 47 U.S.C.A. § 307(a), directs that "the Commission, if public convenience, interest, or necessity will be served thereby, subject to the limitations of this Act (chapter), shall grant to any applicant therefor a station license provided for by this Act (chapter)." This mandate is given meaning and contour by the other provisions of the statute and the subject matter with which it deals. The Act contains no express command that in passing upon an application the Commission must consider the effect of competition with an existing station. Whether the Commission should consider the subject must depend upon the purpose of the Act and the specific provisions intended to effectuate that purpose.

. . . [T]he Act recognizes that the field of broadcasting is one of free competition. The sections dealing with broadcasting demonstrate that Congress has not, in its regulatory scheme, abandoned the principle of free competition, as it has done in the case of railroads, in respect of which regulation involves the suppression of wasteful practices due to competition, the regulation of rates and charges, and other measures which are unnecessary if free competition is to be permitted.

An important element of public interest and convenience affecting the issue of a license is the ability of the licensee to render the best practicable service to the community reached by his broadcasts. That such ability may be assured the Act contemplates inquiry by the Commission, *inter alia*, into an applicant's financial qualifications to operate the proposed station.

But the Act does not essay to regulate the business of the licensee. The Commission is given no supervisory control of the programs, of business management or of policy. In short, the broadcasting field is open to anyone, provided there be an available frequency over which he can broadcast without interference to others, if he shows his competency, the adequacy of his equipment, and financial ability to make good use of the assigned channel.

The policy of the Act is clear that no person is to have anything in the nature of a property right as a result of the granting of a license. Licenses are limited to a maximum of three years' duration, may be revoked, and need not be renewed. Thus the channels presently occupied remain free for a new assignment to another licensee in the interest of the listening public.

Plainly it is not the purpose of the Act to protect a licensee against competition but to protect the public. Congress intended to leave competition in the business of broadcasting where it found it, to permit a licensee who was not interfering electrically with other broadcasters to survive or succumb according to his ability to make his programs attractive to the public. . . .

We conclude that economic injury to an existing station is not a separate and independent element to be taken into consideration by the Commission in determining whether it shall grant or withhold a license.

Second. It does not follow that, because the licensee of a station cannot resist the grant of a license to another, on the ground that the resulting competition may work economic injury to him, he has no standing to appeal from an order of the Commission granting the application.

Section 402(b) of the Act, 47 U.S.C.A. § 402(b), provides for an appeal to the Court of Appeals of the District of Columbia (1) by an applicant for a license or permit, or (2) "by any other person aggrieved or whose interests are adversely affected by any decision of the Commission granting or refusing any such application."

The petitioner insists that as economic injury to the respondent was not a proper issue before the Commission it is impossible that § 402(b) was intended to give the respondent standing to appeal, since absence of right implies absence of remedy. This view would deprive subsection (2) of any substantial effect.

Congress had some purpose in enacting section 402(b)(2). It may have been of opinion that one likely to be financially injured by the issue of a license would be the only person having a sufficient interest to bring to the attention of the appellate court errors of law in the action of the Commission in granting the license. It is within the power of Congress to confer such standing to prosecute an appeal.

We hold, therefore, that the respondent had the requisite standing to appeal and to raise, in the court below, any relevant question of law in respect of the order of the Commission. . . .

The judgment of the Court of Appeals is reversed.

Mr. Justice McREYNOLDS took no part in the decision of this case.

QUESTION SET 9.7

Review & Synthesis

1. What are the basic elements of the rights-based model of Article III standing?

2. What is the fundamental difference between the rights-based model applied in *Alabama Power* and the Court's holding in *Sanders Brothers*? Of the two, which is more likely to generate judicial challenges to agency decision-making?

3. Based on the discussion above, do you think Article III allows federal lawsuits brought by plaintiffs who do not have personal legal rights to be protected from the factual harms they suffer? Isn't the absence of a personal legal right a strong indication that the harm allegedly suffered by the plaintiff is not particular to her, but shared by members of the public more generally? Why not leave such injured parties to seek recourse in the political process, either through private bills passed by Congress addressed to their individual circumstances or by lobbying for rescission of the agency actions that led to their injuries?

4. The Communications Act § 402(b) stated that a federal lawsuit could be maintained by "any . . . person aggrieved or whose interests are adversely affected by any decision of the Commission granting or refusing any such application." What kind of interests do you think could be contemplated by such a provision? Would the interests affected be limited to economic injuries? Could someone have sued the FCC if its licensing decisions resulted in their favorite radio programs being canceled? If it resulted in the building of a transmitter that ruined the aesthetic quality of a park they frequented?

---

b. Standing: From the New Deal to the Early 1970s

The complaint in *Sanders Brothers* sounded very much like the one filed in *Alabama Power*. Agency action in both cases would allegedly have caused economic injury to the complaining parties by increasing competition in their respective markets. Moreover, neither of the complaining parties in these cases held any substantive legal right—under the common law or otherwise—to be free from the economic consequences of increased competition. The Court's analysis and conclusion, however, ended up in two different places. Writing for the Court in *Sanders Brothers*, Justice Owen Roberts made the following observation, which, in light of the recently decided *Alabama Power*, was a fairly stunning about face: "It does not follow that, because the license of a station cannot resist the grant of a license of another, on the ground that the resulting competition may work economic injury to him, he has no standing to appeal from an order of the Commission granting the application." Rather, the Court said, "[i]t is within the power of Congress to confer such standing to prosecute an appeal." Curiously, Justice Roberts's opinion does not even mention *Alabama Power*.

Note five features of the *Sanders Brothers* holding that foreshadow the standing debates that would follow it. First, the Court established the core premise of the harm-based model: federal plaintiffs who are injured by agency decisions can have standing *despite* their lack of personal legal rights protecting them from those injuries. In effect, the Court rejected the notion that the lack of personal legal rights necessarily forecloses the plaintiffs' ability to seek federal judicial remedies. This also implies that nothing in Article III of the Constitution requires plaintiffs to have personal legal rights to maintain lawsuits in federal courts. Sanders Brothers clearly would have been unable to meet such a requirement, and the Court certainly would have dismissed its case had there been one.

Second, the Court made no attempt to explain precisely why standing—under any model—requires federal plaintiffs to show that they have been harmed. Congress required that plaintiffs be "aggrieved" or "adversely affected" by the FCC's orders to invoke Communications Act § 402(b). But did Congress include this requirement because, as the *Sanders Brothers* Court suggested, it believed injured parties would be better positioned to litigate against the FCC than uninjured parties? This would imply that Congress could have chosen to leave the requirement out while still granting plaintiffs the ability to file suit against the FCC. Or did § 402(b) instead reflect Congress' understanding that it was *obligated*—by the Constitution or something else—to limit standing to factually (though not legally) aggrieved or adversely affected parties? The *Sanders Brothers* Court did not say.

In Context

APA § 702 provides in part that "[a] person suffering legal wrong because of agency action, or adversely affected or aggrieved by agency action within the meaning of a relevant statute, is entitled to judicial review thereof." 5 U.S.C. § 702. It is the general federal citizen suit provision. It applies where Congress has not passed a more specific judicial review provision (such as in an organic statute).

Third, the *Sanders Brothers* Court implied that a personally suffered factual harm, though necessary to establish a plaintiff's standing, was nonetheless insufficient to do so. The plaintiff also had to have a *procedural* right to file a lawsuit, which simply suffering an injury did not automatically confer. Typically, and based on Anglo-American judicial history and the case law up to that point, the procedural right traveled with a personal legal right under the common law or some other source (e.g., the Constitution or a statute). *Sanders Brothers* established that there was a second way: Congress could also confer procedural rights through so-called "citizen suit provisions" that allowed federal plaintiffs with factual injuries but no personal legal rights access to federal district courts. The provision at issue in *Sanders Brothers*, Communications Act § 402(b), is one example. Congress has also provided a general citizen suit provision in Section 702 of the Administrative Procedure Act, with some caveats discussed below. Without either a personal legal right or a citizen suit provision, plaintiffs filing in federal district court would get their claims dismissed for lack of standing.

Fourth, the Court's adoption of the harm-based standing model acknowledged Congress' power to create causes of action to facilitate judicial review of agency action. Through citizen suit provisions like Communications Act § 402(b) and APA § 702, Congress can empower "private attorneys general" who will alert the judiciary to administrative wrongdoing. While these private attorneys general must be personally affected by an agency's actions to have standing, their suits vindicate the *public's* interest in ensuring lawful administration of the laws (or, at least, that's the theory). Put another way, Congress can choose to police the administrative state by deputizing injured (and hence interested) private parties. Accordingly, the harm-based model opens opportunities for checking administrative decision-making that the rights-based model foreclosed.

Fifth, *Sanders Brothers* left unspecified the *extent* of Congress' power to create standing. It decided that Congress clearly has the authority to let plaintiffs file suit who have relevant factual injuries but lack personal legal rights to be protected from them. On the flip side, it seems highly unlikely that the Court believed Congress could grant standing to parties who had suffered no harms whatsoever. But can Congress both create a substantive right and establish, as a matter of statutory law, that violation of that right *by itself* permits standing? In other words, can Congress create factual injuries where none would have otherwise existed? Yet again, the *Sanders Brothers* Court left resolution of this puzzle for another day.

The APA and *Data Processing*. The APA's general citizen suit provision, currently codified at 5 U.S.C. § 702, grants standing to three types of federal plaintiffs. First are those suffering a "legal wrong" as a result of agency action. "The phrase 'legal wrong' . . . means that something more than mere adverse personal effect must be shown in order to prevail — that is, that the adverse effect must be an *illegal* effect." SENATE COMM. ON THE JUDICIARY, ADMINISTRATIVE PROCEDURE ACT: LEGISLATIVE HISTORY, S. DOC. No. 248, 79th Cong., 2d Sess. 276 (1946) (emphasis added).

There were two senses in which a plaintiff could claim to have suffered a "legal wrong" under the provision. First, she could assert that the agency's actions had violated some personally held legal right traditionally protected under the common law. Second, she could show that some statutory interest she held was negatively impacted by an agency's actions. Such an interest was distinguishable from a personal legal right; it was recognized by a statute but created no substantive entitlements. Say, for instance, a statute requires its implementing agency to consider prevailing levels of competition before granting operating licenses to new market entrants. If the agency issued a new license but failed to factor competition levels into its decision, a current market participant could invoke § 702 to challenge the agency's licensing decision in court. It is enough that the market participant had an interest in the competition level, and that the statute explicitly recognized that interest by requiring the agency to factor it into its decision-making. Section 702 did not require a further showing that the statute gave the market participant a legally enforceable entitlement to a particular competition level.

The third category of plaintiffs was covered by § 702's second clause, under which any person "adversely affected or aggrieved by agency action within the meaning of a relevant statute" could file suit. These plaintiffs did not have to demonstrate that they had suffered a legal wrong of any kind. Rather, this clause adopted the harm-based standing model reflected in Communications Act § 402(b) and recognized by the Supreme Court in *Sanders Brothers*. Whereas the "legal wrong" test asked whether the agency's actions *illegally* impacted the plaintiff, here the inquiry was whether the agency's decisions had *factually* impacted the plaintiff. Thus § 702 also allowed a plaintiff to challenge an agency's decisions when she held no personal legal right to different treatment and when the agency was under no statutory obligation to consider her interests. In essence, she could operate as a private attorney general who, despite having no personal legal interest in the dispute, sues to vindicate the public's interest in lawful administrative decision-making.

In the years after the APA's passage, there was some disagreement as to what "within the meaning of a relevant statute" meant. The prevailing view in the circuit courts was that Congress did not want § 702 to be a general grant of standing to everyone adversely affected by agency action. Instead, the "relevant statutes" to which the clause referred were organic statutes apart from the APA that contained their own citizen-suit provisions. *See, e.g., South Suburban Safeway Lines, Inc. v. City of Chicago*, 416 F.2d 535, 537 & n.8 (7th Cir. 1969) (citing cases). This interpretation echoed the Department of Justice's view that § 702 made no fundamental changes to the law of standing that existed prior to the APA's passage. According to DOJ, the parties who counted as "adversely affected or aggrieved" were to be "marked out largely by the gradual judicial process of inclusion and exclusion, aided at times by the courts' judgment as to the probable legislative intent derived from the spirit of the statutory scheme." *See* ATTORNEY GENERAL'S MANUAL at 96. As far as DOJ and the circuit courts were concerned, Congress did not mean for the APA to create a blanket right to standing. Congress instead intended to pass individual citizen-suit provisions (like Communications Act § 402(b)) whenever it wanted to empower private plaintiffs to sue agencies for the benefit of society generally. Absent a separate "relevant statute" identifying a "party in interest" who was empowered to seek judicial review, anyone wanting to challenge agency actions would need to have suffered a legal wrong. By contrast, at least one prominent commentator felt that the "relevant statute" language placed no such "legal wrong" limitation on administrative standing. Instead, he argued that courts should read § 702 generously to provide standing to *any* private party negatively affected by an agency's decision-making, not just members of groups specifically identified in citizen-suit provisions outside of the APA. *See, e.g.*, Kenneth Culp Davis, *Standing: Taxpayers and Others*, 35 U. CHI. L. REV. 601, 618-20 (1968).

So things stood until 1970, when the Court created a new standing test in the surprisingly short opinion that follows, authored by Justice William O. Douglas.

Association of Data Processing Service
Organizations, Inc. v. Camp
397 U.S. 150 (1970)

Mr. Justice Douglas delivered the opinion of the Court.

Petitioners sell data processing services to businesses generally. In this suit they seek to challenge a ruling by respondent Comptroller of the Currency that, as an incident to their banking services, national banks, including respondent American National Bank & Trust Company, may make data processing services available to other banks and to bank customers. The District Court dismissed the complaint for lack of standing of petitioners to bring the suit. The Court of Appeals affirmed. The case is here on a petition for writ of certiorari which we granted.

Generalizations about standing to sue are largely worthless as such. One generalization is, however, necessary and that is that the question of standing in the federal courts is to be considered in the framework of Article III which restricts judicial power to "cases" and "controversies." As we recently stated in *Flast v. Cohen*, 392 U.S. 83, 101 (1968) "[I]n terms of Article III limitations on federal court jurisdiction, the question of standing is related only to whether the dispute sought to be adjudicated will be presented in an adversary context and in a form historically viewed as capable of judicial resolution." *Flast* was a taxpayer's suit. The present is a competitor's suit. And while the two have the same Article III starting point, they do not necessarily track one another.

The first question is whether the plaintiff alleges that the challenged action has caused him injury in fact, economic or otherwise. There can be no doubt but that petitioners have satisfied this test. The petitioners not only allege that competition by national banks in the business of providing data processing services might entail some future loss of profits for the petitioners, they also allege that respondent American National Bank & Trust Company was performing or preparing to perform such services for two customers for whom petitioner Data Systems, Inc., had previously agreed or negotiated to perform such services. The petitioners' suit was brought not only against the American National Bank & Trust Company, but also against the Comptroller of the Currency. The Comptroller was alleged to have caused petitioners injury in fact by his 1966 ruling which stated:

> Incidental to its banking services, a national bank may make available its data processing equipment or perform data processing services on such equipment for other banks and bank customers. COMPTROLLER'S MANUAL FOR NATIONAL BANKS 3500 (October 15, 1966).

The Court of Appeals viewed the matter differently, stating:

> [A] plaintiff may challenge alleged illegal competition when as complainant
> it pursues (1) a legal interest by reason of public charter or contract, . . .
> (2) a legal interest by reason of statutory protection, . . . or (3) a "public
> interest" in which Congress has recognized the need for review of admin-
> istrative action and plaintiff is significantly involved to have standing to
> represent the public. . . . 406 F.2d, at 842-843.[1]

Those tests were based on prior decisions of this Court. . . .

The "legal interest" test goes to the merits. The question of standing is
different. It concerns, apart from the "case" or "controversy" test, the question whether the interest sought to be protected by the complainant is arguably within the zone of interests to be protected or regulated by the statute or
constitutional guarantee in question. Thus the Administrative Procedure Act
grants standing to a person "aggrieved by agency action within the meaning
of a relevant statute." 5 U.S.C. § 702 (1964 ed., Supp. IV). That interest, at
times, may reflect "aesthetic, conservational, and recreational" as well as economic values. *Scenic Hudson Preservation Conference v. FPC*, 354 F.2d 608,
616 (2d Cir. 1965); *Office of Communication of United Church of Christ v.
FCC*, 359 F.2d 994, 1000-1006 (D.C. Cir. 1966). A person or a family may
have a spiritual stake in First Amendment values sufficient to give standing
to raise issues concerning the Establishment Clause and the Free Exercise
Clause. *Abington School District v. Schempp*, 374 U.S. 203 (1963). We mention these noneconomic values to emphasize that standing may stem from
them as well as from the economic injury in which petitioners rely here.
Certainly he who is "likely to be financially" injured, *FCC v. Sanders Bros.
Radio Station*, 309 U.S. 470, at 477 (1940), may be a reliable private attorney general to litigate the issues of the public interest in the present case.

Apart from Article III jurisdictional questions, problems of standing, as
resolved by this Court for its own governance, have involved a "rule of self-
restraint." *Barrows v. Jackson*, 346 U.S. 249, 255 (1953). Congress can, of
course, resolve the question one way or another, save as the requirements of
Article III dictate otherwise.

Where statutes are concerned, the trend is toward enlargement of the
class of people who may protest administrative action. The whole drive for
enlarging the category of aggrieved "persons" is symptomatic of that trend.
In a closely analogous case we held that an existing entrepreneur had standing to challenge the legality of the entrance of a newcomer into the business, because the established business was allegedly protected by a valid city

[1] The first two tests applied by the Court of Appeals required a showing of a "legal interest." But
the existence or non-existence of a "legal interest" is a matter quite distinct from the problem of
standing. The third test mentioned by the Court of Appeals, which rests on an explicit provision
in a regulatory statute conferring standing and is commonly referred to in terms of allowing suits
by "private attorneys general," is inapplicable to the present case. *See FCC v. Sanders Bros. Radio
Station*, 309 U.S. 470 (1940).

ordinance that protected it from unlawful competition. *Chicago v. Atchison, T. & S.F.R. Co.*, 357 U.S. 77, 83-84 (1958). In that tradition was *Hardin v. Kentucky Utilities Co.*, 390 U.S. 1 (1968), which involved a section of the TVA Act designed primarily to protect, through area limitations, private utilities against TVA competition. We held that no explicit statutory provision was necessary to confer standing, since the private utility bringing suit was within the class of persons that the statutory provision was designed to protect. . . .

It is argued that the *Chicago* case and the *Hardin* case are relevant here because of § 4 of the Bank Service Corporation Act of 1962, 76 Stat. 1132, 12 U.S.C. § 1864, which provides:

> No bank service corporation may engage in any activity other than the performance of bank services for banks.

The Court of Appeals for the First Circuit held in *Arnold Tours, Inc. v. Camp*, 408 F.2d 1147, 1153 (1st Cir. 1969), that by reason of § 4 a data processing company has standing to contest the legality of a national bank performing data processing services for other banks and bank customers:

> Section 4 had a broader purpose than regulating only the service corporations. It was also a response to the fears expressed by a few senators, that without such a prohibition, the bill would have enabled "banks to engage in a nonbanking activity," S. Rep. No. 2105, (87th Cong., 2d Sess., 7-12) (Supplemental views of Senators Proxmire, Douglas, and Neuberger), and thus constitute "a serious exception to the accepted public policy which strictly limits banks to banking." (Supplemental views of Senators Muskie and Clark). We think Congress has provided the sufficient statutory aid to standing even though the competition may not be the precise kind Congress legislated against.

We do not put the issue in those words, for they implicate the merits. We do think, however, that § 4 arguably brings a competitor within the zone of interests protected by it. . . .

We hold that petitioners have standing to sue and that the case should be remanded for a hearing on the merits.

Reversed and remanded.

QUESTION SET 9.8

Review & Synthesize

1. Explain the distinction Justice Douglas drew between standing and "the merits." Why did the Court say that the "legal interest" test spoke to the latter and not to the former? Also, is it possible to answer the standing

question without analyzing the claim being brought by the plaintiff? If not, how distinct is standing from a merits inquiry?

2. What is the "zone of interests" test, and how does it relate to citizen suit provisions in non-APA statutes? Does a plaintiff have to show that it is in the zone of interests protected by a non-APA citizen suit provision or a substantive provision in a non-APA statute? Is the zone of interests test a substitute for explicit citizen suit provisions in non-APA statutes, such that courts will infer from statutory language, purpose, and structure the right to sue without a personal legal interest? Is it something else?

3. What function does the zone of interests test perform? Why is it important for the Court to understand whether the interest held by the plaintiff is arguably within the zone of those Congress intended to protect or regulate in an enabling act or other legislation?

4. How limiting is the zone of interests test? Would someone whose interests are hostile to those regulated or protected by a regulatory statute be within the zone? Is it simply enough for the plaintiff's interests to be affected by those addressed in legislation, regardless of whether that affect is positive or negative? Based on *Data Processing*, does it appear that the relevant interests for the zone test have to be based on particular provisions within a statutory scheme, or can they be based on protected or regulated interests evident in the statutory scheme as a whole?

---

c. Standing in the Modern Era: The Constitution, Prudence, and Congress

Data Processing established the modern two-part standing analysis that determines which private parties can challenge agency actions in a federal court. The first part—constitutional standing—identifies the plaintiffs who have an Article III case or controversy fit for adjudication in federal court. Broadly introduced in *Data Processing*, the Supreme Court has tried to refine its constitutional standing analysis in dozens of cases since. As it stands today, the Court requires that federal plaintiffs make three showings, which are presented as allegations at the complaint stage, require factual support at the summary judgment stage, and require persuasive evidence at the trial stage: (1) she has personally suffered an injury-in-fact; (2) the defendant's conduct caused her injury; and (3) a ruling in her favor will redress that injury. As the Court traces these requirements to Article III, Congress can neither alter them nor grant standing to a plaintiff who fails to satisfy them.

The second part—prudential standing—consists of judge-made limitations on the plaintiffs who can file suit in federal court. In effect, prudential standing shrinks the universe of federal cases to something smaller than what Article III would otherwise allow. These limitations are "prudential" in the sense that they are interpretive norms informed by the Judiciary's collective wisdom and experience. They are also voluntary; no statutory or constitutional provision required the Judiciary to adopt them. Although *Data Processing* did not refer to it as such, it established the first prudential standing doctrine: the "zone of interests" test. It asks whether a plaintiff's asserted interests fall within the zone of those protected or regulated by a relevant organic statute. The Court has since added others, including prohibitions on so-called "generalized grievances" (harms shared by broad swaths of the public) and third-party suits (lawsuits attempting to vindicate the interests of nonparties). Unlike constitutional standing requirements, these prudential standing limitations can be altered or abrogated by Congress. Put another way, Congress can choose to expand federal standing beyond prudential standing limits as long as it stays within the boundaries set by Article III.

> **In Context**
>
> There is some dispute as to whether the zone of interests test is properly called "prudential" rather than simply a method of statutory interpretation. Put another way, the Court has not always been clear on whether the test is federal common law or a principle of statutory interpretation. The Court first explicitly referred to the zone of interests test as "prudential" in *Valley Forge Christian College v. Americans United for Separation of Church and State*, 454 U.S. 464 (1982). A few years later, however, it framed the test as an interpretive gloss on APA § 702. *See Clarke v. Securities Industry Association*, 479 U.S. 388 (1987). It again seemed to change its mind in *Bennett v. Spear*, 520 U.S. 154 (1997), excerpted below. The Court now seems to consider the test a rule of statutory interpretation. *Lexmark Int'l, Inc. v. Static Control, Inc.*, 572 U.S. 118 (2014). Regardless, the test's operation appears unaffected by the label assigned to it.

Some of administrative law's core concerns are clearly evident in how broadly or narrowly the Supreme Court construes its constitutional and prudential standing tests. What role should courts play in reviewing the decisions of agency officials? Is private party litigation an effective method of ensuring lawful and reasoned administrative decision-making? If so, what is the optimal level of such private litigation? If not, are the available alternatives—administrative review processes, political processes, public disclosure requirements, etc. — any better? Does empowering or disempowering judicial review of agency conduct shift the balance of power among the Branches in a way that is normatively desirable?

Take federal citizen-suit provisions as an example. If citizen-suit provisions like APA § 702 are generously worded by Congress and/or expansively interpreted by the courts, they can vest enormous prosecutorial discretion in members of the public who want to police administrative conduct. The "private attorneys general" to whom these provisions grant standing choose the agency actions the Judiciary will scrutinize based largely on interests that may or may not reflect those of the public at large. A private litigation-focused oversight regime of this type might also send a strong signal about competing forms of oversight. Control by political appointees in the Executive Branch and congressional committees, or required disclosures to the public, might be deemed comparatively ineffective at properly policing the administrative state. Conversely, drawing or construing citizen-suit provisions narrowly may inadequately redress harms caused by unlawful and injurious agency conduct. It also signals that Congress and the Court believe in the oversight effectiveness of nonjudicial processes or, at a minimum, that they believe checking agency conduct is better left to someone other than judges. One would encounter similar push-pull trade-offs depending on how rigorously or laxly courts enforce the constitutional standing requirements.

The materials that follow begin with one of the most important standing cases decided after *Data Processing*—*Lujan v. Defenders of Wildlife*. As with many post–*Data Processing* standing cases, *Lujan* arose in the environmental context (the Endangered Species Act of 1973). It provides an excellent over-view of the Supreme Court's constitutional and prudential standing require-ments and thus serves as a sound introduction to the materials that follow it. *Lujan* also illustrates many of the conceptual flashpoints discussed above, which have driven the Court's standing jurisprudence for several decades.

The materials then explore each of the constitutional standing doctrines, with particular emphasis on injury-in-fact. Finally, they consider the "zone of interests" test and a second prudential standing limitation—the prohibition against "generalized grievances"—which is very closely related to the consti-tutional injury-in-fact requirement and is therefore considered along with it.

* * *

It should come as little surprise that some are less comfortable with the pri-vate litigation oversight model than others. Among the most vocal modern skeptics was Justice Antonin Scalia, who warned against it first as a law pro-fessor and then as a jurist. He framed the empowerment of private attorneys general as a separation of powers problem, arguing that it drains power away from the President who Article II, Section 3 makes solely responsible for "tak[ing] Care that the Laws be faithfully executed." Relatedly, he was leery of asking courts to scrutinize political branch decisions (including adminis-trative ones) because doing so took them too far away from their traditional role of protecting individual rights. He accordingly resisted standing asser-tions that expanded private challenges to agency conduct, particularly when plaintiffs alleged undifferentiated harms suffered by broad cross-sections of the public. Consider, for example, the following excerpt from a speech he delivered prior to his appointment to the Supreme Court:

> Is standing functionally related to the distinctive role that we expect the courts to perform? The question is not of purely academic interest, because if there is a functional relationship it may have some bearing upon how issues of standing are decided in particular cases. There is, I think, a func-tional relationship, which can best be described by saying that the law of standing roughly restricts courts to their traditional undemocratic role of protecting individuals and minorities against impositions of the majority, and excludes them from the even more undemocratic role of prescribing how the other two branches should function in order to serve the interest *of the majority itself.* . . .

[W]hen an individual who is the very *object* of a law's requirement or prohibition seeks to challenge it, he always has standing. . . . Contrast that classic form of court challenge with the increasingly frequent administrative law cases in which the plaintiff is complaining of an agency's unlawful *failure* to impose a requirement or prohibition upon *someone else.* Such a failure harms the plaintiff, by depriving him, as a citizen, of governmental acts which the Constitution and laws require. But that harm alone is, so to speak, a *majoritarian* one. The plaintiff may *care* more about it; he may be a more ardent proponent of constitutional regularity or of the necessity of the governmental act that has been wrongfully omitted. But that does not establish that he has been harmed distinctively—only that he assesses the harm as more grave, which is a fair subject for democratic debate in which he may persuade the rest of us. Since our readiness to be persuaded is no less than his own (we are harmed just as much) there is no reason to remove the matter from the political process and place it in the courts. Unless the plaintiff can show some respect in which he is harmed *more* than the rest of us . . . he has not established any basis for concern that the majority is suppressing or ignoring the rights of a minority that wants protection, and thus has not established the prerequisites for judicial intervention.

That explains, I think, why "concrete injury"—an injury apart from the mere breach of the social contract, so to speak, effected by the very fact of unlawful government action—is the indispensable prerequisite of standing. Only that can separate the plaintiff from all the rest of us who also claim benefit of the social contract, and can thus entitle him to some special protection from the democratic manner in which we ordinarily run our social-contractual affairs. . . .

Antonin Scalia, *The Doctrine of Standing as an Essential Element of the Separation of Powers*, 17 SUFFOLK L. REV. 881, 894-95 (1983).

Justice Scalia pushed the Court hard to adopt these views on standing and the separation of powers. Perhaps his most notable effort in this regard was his majority opinion in a seminal standing case, *Lujan v. Defenders of Wildlife*, 504 U.S. 555 (1992).

Lujan v. Defenders of Wildlife
504 U.S. 555 (1992)

Justice SCALIA delivered the opinion of the Court with respect to Parts I, II, III–A, and IV. . . .

This case involves a challenge to a rule promulgated by the Secretary of the Interior interpreting § 7 of the Endangered Species Act of 1973 (ESA), 87 Stat. 884, 892, as amended, 16 U.S.C. § 1536, in such fashion as to render it applicable only to actions within the United States or on the high seas.

The preliminary issue, and the only one we reach, is whether respondents here, plaintiffs below, have standing to seek judicial review of the rule.

I

The ESA, 87 Stat. 884, as amended, 16 U.S.C. § 1531 *et seq.*, seeks to protect species of animals against threats to their continuing existence caused by man. *See generally TVA v. Hill*, 437 U.S. 153 (1978). The ESA instructs the Secretary of the Interior to promulgate by regulation a list of those species which are either endangered or threatened under enumerated criteria, and to define the critical habitat of these species. 16 U.S.C. §§ 1533, 1536. Section 7(a)(2) of the Act then provides, in pertinent part:

> Each Federal agency shall, in consultation with and with the assistance of the Secretary [of the Interior], insure that any action authorized, funded, or carried out by such agency . . . is not likely to jeopardize the continued existence of any endangered species or threatened species or result in the destruction or adverse modification of habitat of such species which is determined by the Secretary, after consultation as appropriate with affected States, to be critical. 16 U.S.C. § 1536(a)(2).

In 1978, the Fish and Wildlife Service (FWS) and the National Marine Fisheries Service (NMFS), on behalf of the Secretary of the Interior and the Secretary of Commerce respectively, promulgated a joint regulation stating that the obligations imposed by § 7(a)(2) extend to actions taken in foreign nations. 43 Fed. Reg. 874 (1978). The next year, however, the Interior Department began to reexamine its position. A revised joint regulation, reinterpreting § 7(a)(2) to require consultation only for actions taken in the United States or on the high seas, was proposed in 1983, 48 Fed. Reg. 29990, and promulgated in 1986, 51 Fed. Reg. 19926; 50 CFR 402.01 (1991).

Shortly thereafter, respondents, organizations dedicated to wildlife conservation and other environmental causes, filed this action against the Secretary of the Interior, seeking a declaratory judgment that the new regulation is in error as to the geographic scope of § 7(a)(2) and an injunction requiring the Secretary to promulgate a new regulation restoring the initial interpretation. The District Court granted the Secretary's motion to dismiss for lack of standing. The Court of Appeals for the Eighth Circuit reversed by a divided vote. On remand, the Secretary moved for summary judgment on the standing issue, and respondents moved for summary judgment on the merits. The District Court denied the Secretary's motion, on the ground that the Eighth Circuit had already determined the standing question in this case; it granted respondents' merits motion, and ordered the Secretary to publish a revised regulation. The Eighth Circuit affirmed. We granted certiorari.

II

While the Constitution of the United States divides all power conferred upon the Federal Government into "legislative Powers," Art. I, § 1, "[t]he executive Power," Art. II, § 1, and "[t]he judicial Power," Art. III, § 1, it does not attempt to define those terms. To be sure, it limits the jurisdiction of federal courts to "Cases" and "Controversies," but an executive inquiry can bear the name "case" (the *Hoffa* case) and a legislative dispute can bear the name "controversy" (the *Smoot-Hawley* controversy). Obviously, then, the Constitution's central mechanism of separation of powers depends largely upon common understanding of what activities are appropriate to legislatures, to executives, and to courts.

In The Federalist No. 48, Madison expressed the view that "[i]t is not infrequently a question of real nicety in legislative bodies whether the operation of a particular measure will, or will not, extend beyond the legislative sphere," whereas "the executive power [is] restrained within a narrower compass and . . . more simple in its nature," and "the judiciary [is] described by landmarks still less uncertain." The Federalist No. 48, p. 256 (Carey and McClellan eds. 1990). One of those landmarks, setting apart the "Cases" and "Controversies" that are of the justiciable sort referred to in Article III — "serv[ing] to identify those disputes which are appropriately resolved through the judicial process," *Whitmore v. Arkansas*, 495 U.S. 149, 155 (1990) — is the doctrine of standing. Though some of its elements express merely prudential considerations that are part of judicial self-government, the core component of standing is an essential and unchanging part of the case-or-controversy requirement of Article III.

Over the years, our cases have established that the irreducible constitutional minimum of standing contains three elements. First, the plaintiff must have suffered an "injury in fact" — an invasion of a legally protected interest which is (a) concrete and particularized, and (b) "actual or imminent, not 'conjectural' or 'hypothetical,'" *Whitmore, supra*, 495 U.S., at 155 (quoting *Los Angeles v. Lyons*, 461 U.S. 95, 102 (1983)). Second, there must be a causal connection between the injury and the conduct complained of — the injury has to be "fairly . . . trace[able] to the challenged action of the defendant, and not . . . th[e] result [of] the independent action of some third party not before the court." *Simon v. Eastern Ky. Welfare Rights Organization*, 426 U.S. 26, 41-42 (1976). Third, it must be "likely," as opposed to merely "speculative," that the injury will be "redressed by a favorable decision." *Id.* at 38, 43.

The party invoking federal jurisdiction bears the burden of establishing these elements. Since they are not mere pleading requirements but rather an indispensable part of the plaintiff's case, each element must be supported in the same way as any other matter on which the plaintiff bears the burden of proof, i.e., with the manner and degree of evidence required at the successive stages of the litigation. At the pleading stage, general factual allegations of injury resulting from the defendant's conduct may suffice, for on a motion to dismiss we "presum[e] that general allegations embrace those specific facts that are necessary to support the claim." *Lujan v. National Wildlife Federation*, 497 U.S. 871, 889 (1990). In response to a summary judgment motion, however, the plaintiff can no longer rest on such "mere allegations," but must "set forth" by affidavit or other evidence "specific facts," Fed. Rule Civ. Proc. 56(e), which for purposes of the summary judgment motion will be taken to be true. And at the final stage, those facts (if controverted) must be "supported adequately by the evidence adduced at trial." *Gladstone, Realtors v. Village of Bellwood*, 441 U.S. 91 115, note 31 (1979).

When the suit is one challenging the legality of government action or inaction, the nature and extent of facts that must be averred (at the summary judgment stage) or proved (at the trial stage) in order to establish standing depends considerably upon whether the plaintiff is himself an object of the action (or forgone action) at issue. If he is, there is ordinarily little question that the action or inaction has caused him injury, and that a judgment preventing or requiring the action will redress it. When, however, as in this case, a plaintiff's asserted injury arises from the government's allegedly unlawful regulation (or lack of regulation) of *someone else*, much more is needed. In that circumstance, causation and redressability ordinarily hinge on the response of the regulated (or regulable) third party to the government action or inaction — and perhaps on the response of others as well. The existence of one or more of the essential elements of standing "depends on the unfettered choices made by independent actors not before the courts and whose exercise of broad and legitimate discretion the courts cannot presume either to control or to predict," *ASARCO Inc. v. Kadish*, 490 U.S. 605, 615 (1989) (opinion of Kennedy, J.); and it becomes the burden of the plaintiff to adduce facts showing that those choices have been or will be made in such manner as to produce causation and permit redressability of injury. Thus, when the plaintiff is not himself the object of the government action or inaction he challenges, standing is not precluded, but it is ordinarily "substantially more difficult" to establish. *Allen v. Wright*, 468 U.S. 737, 758 (1984); *Simon, supra*, 426 U.S., at 44-45.

III

We think the Court of Appeals failed to apply the foregoing principles in denying the Secretary's motion for summary judgment. Respondents had not made the requisite demonstration of . . . injury. . . .

A

Respondents' claim to injury is that the lack of consultation with respect to certain funded activities abroad "increas[es] the rate of extinction of endangered and threatened species." Of course, the desire to use or observe an animal species, even for purely esthetic purposes, is undeniably a cognizable interest for purpose of standing. *See,* e.g., *Sierra Club v. Morton,* 405 U.S. 727, 734 (1972). "But the 'injury in fact' test requires more than an injury to a cognizable interest. It requires that the party seeking review be himself among the injured." *Id.* at 734-735. To survive the Secretary's summary judgment motion, respondents had to submit affidavits or other evidence showing, through specific facts, not only that listed species were in fact being threatened by funded activities abroad, but also that one or more of respondents' members would thereby be "directly" affected apart from their " 'special interest' in th[e] subject." *Id.* at 735, 739.

With respect to this aspect of the case, the Court of Appeals focused on the affidavits of two Defenders' members — Joyce Kelly and Amy Skilbred. Ms. Kelly stated that she traveled to Egypt in 1986 and "observed the traditional habitat of the endangered Nile crocodile there and intend[s] to do so again, and hope[s] to observe the crocodile directly," and that she "will suffer harm in fact as the result of [the] American . . . role . . . in overseeing the rehabilitation of the Aswan High Dam on the Nile . . . and [in] develop[ing] . . . Egypt's . . . Master Water Plan." Ms. Skilbred averred that she traveled to Sri Lanka in 1981 and "observed th[e] habitat" of "endangered species such as the Asian elephant and the leopard" at what is now the site of the Mahaweli project funded by the Agency for International Development (AID), although she "was unable to see any of the endangered species"; "this development project," she continued, "will seriously reduce endangered, threatened, and endemic species habitat including areas that I visited . . . [, which] may severely shorten the future of these species"; that threat, she concluded, harmed her because she "intend[s] to return to Sri Lanka in the future and hope[s] to be more fortunate in spotting at least the endangered elephant and leopard." When Ms. Skilbred was asked at a subsequent deposition if and when she had any plans to return to Sri Lanka, she reiterated that "I intend to go back to Sri Lanka," but confessed that she had no current plans: "I don't know [when]. There is a civil war going on right now. I don't know. Not next year, I will say. In the future."

We shall assume for the sake of argument that these affidavits contain facts showing that certain agency-funded projects threaten listed species — though that is questionable. They plainly contain no facts, however, showing how damage to the species will produce "imminent" injury to Mses. Kelly and Skilbred. That the women "had visited" the areas of the projects before the projects commenced proves nothing. As we have said in a related context, " 'Past exposure to illegal conduct does not in itself show a present case or controversy regarding injunctive relief . . . if unaccompanied by any continuing, present adverse effects.' " *Lyons,* 461 U.S., at 102 (quoting *O'Shea v. Littleton,* 414 U.S. 488, 495-496 (1974)). And the affiants' profession of an "inten[t]" to return to the places they had visited before — where they will presumably, this time, be deprived of the opportunity to observe animals of the endangered species — is simply not enough. Such "some day" intentions — without any description of concrete plans, or indeed even any specification of when the some day will be—do not support a finding of the "actual or imminent" injury that our cases require.

Besides relying upon the Kelly and Skilbred affidavits, respondents propose a series of novel standing theories. The first, inelegantly styled "ecosystem nexus," proposes that any person who uses any part of a "contiguous ecosystem" adversely affected by a funded activity has standing even if the activity is located a great distance away. This approach . . . is inconsistent with our opinion in *National Wildlife Federation*, which held that a plaintiff claiming injury from environmental damage must use the area affected by the challenged activity and not an area roughly "in the vicinity" of it. 497 U.S., at 887-889; *see also Sierra Club*, 405 U.S., at 735. It makes no difference that the general-purpose section of the ESA states that the Act was intended in part "to provide a means whereby the ecosystems upon which endangered species and threatened species depend may be conserved," 16 U.S.C. § 1531(b). To say that the Act protects ecosystems is not to say that the Act creates (if it were possible) rights of action in persons who have not been injured in fact, that is, persons who use portions of an ecosystem not perceptibly affected by the unlawful action in question.

Respondents' other theories are called, alas, the "animal nexus" approach, whereby anyone who has an interest in studying or seeing the endangered animals anywhere on the globe has standing; and the "vocational nexus" approach, under which anyone with a professional interest in such animals can sue. Under these theories, anyone who goes to see Asian elephants in the Bronx Zoo, and anyone who is a keeper of Asian elephants in the Bronx Zoo, has standing to sue because the Director of the Agency for International Development (AID) did not consult with the Secretary regarding the AID-funded project in Sri Lanka. This is beyond all reason. Standing is not "an ingenious academic exercise in the conceivable," *United States v. Students Challenging Regulatory Agency Procedures (SCRAP)*, 412 U.S. 669, 688 (1973), but as we have said requires, at the summary judgment stage, a factual showing of perceptible harm. It is clear that the person who observes or works with a particular animal threatened by a federal decision is facing perceptible harm, since the very subject of his interest will no longer exist. It is even plausible—though it goes to the outermost limit of plausibility—to think that a person who observes or works with animals of a particular species in the very area of the world where that species is threatened by a federal decision is facing such harm, since some animals that might have been the subject of his interest will no longer exist. It goes beyond the limit, however, and into pure speculation and fantasy, to say that anyone who observes or works with an endangered species, anywhere in the world, is appreciably harmed by a single project affecting some portion of that species with which he has no more specific connection. . . .

IV

The Court of Appeals found that respondents had standing for an additional reason: because they had suffered a "procedural injury." The so-called "citizen-suit" provision of the ESA provides, in pertinent part, that "any person may commence a civil suit on his own behalf (A) to enjoin any person, including the United States and any other governmental instrumentality or agency . . . who is alleged to be in violation of any provision of this chapter." 16 U.S.C. § 1540(g). The court held that, because § 7(a)(2) requires interagency consultation, the citizen-suit provision creates a "procedural righ[t]" to consultation in all "persons"—so that anyone can file suit in federal court to challenge the Secretary's (or presumably any other official's) failure to follow the assertedly correct consultative procedure, notwithstanding his or her inability to allege any discrete injury flowing from that failure. 911 F.2d, at 121-122. To understand the remarkable nature of this holding one must be clear about what it does not rest upon: This is not a case where plaintiffs are seeking to enforce a procedural requirement the disregard of which could impair a separate concrete interest of theirs (e.g., the procedural requirement for a hearing prior to denial of their license application, or the procedural requirement for an environmental impact statement before a federal facility is constructed next door to them). Nor is it simply a case where concrete injury has been suffered by many persons, as in mass fraud or mass tort situations. Nor, finally, is it the unusual case in which Congress has created a concrete private interest in the outcome of a suit against a private party for the government's benefit, by providing a cash bounty for the victorious plaintiff. Rather, the court held that the injury-in-fact requirement had been satisfied by congressional conferral upon all persons of an abstract, self-contained, noninstrumental "right" to have the Executive observe the procedures required by law. We reject this view.

We have consistently held that a plaintiff raising only a generally available grievance about government—claiming only harm to his and every citizen's interest in proper application of the Constitution and laws, and seeking relief that no more directly and tangibly benefits him than it does the public at large—does not state an Article III case or controversy. . . .

To be sure, our generalized-grievance cases have typically involved Government violation of procedures assertedly ordained by the Constitution rather than the Congress. But there is absolutely no basis for making the Article III inquiry turn on the source of the asserted right. Whether the courts were to act on their own, or at the invitation of Congress, in ignoring the concrete injury requirement described in our cases, they would be discarding a principle fundamental to the separate and distinct constitutional role of the Third Branch—one of the essential elements that identifies those "Cases" and "Controversies" that are the business of the courts rather than of the political branches. . . . If the concrete injury requirement has the separation-of-powers significance we have always said, the answer must be obvious: To permit Congress to convert the undifferentiated public interest in executive officers' compliance with the law into an "individual right" vindicable in the courts is to permit Congress to transfer from the President to the courts the Chief Executive's most important constitutional duty, to "take Care that the Laws be faithfully executed," Art. II, § 3. It would enable the courts, with the permission of Congress, "to assume a position of authority over the governmental acts of another and co-equal department," *Massachusetts [Frothingham] v. Mellon*, 262 U.S., at 489, and to become " 'virtually continuing monitors of the wisdom and soundness of Executive action.' " *Allen, supra,* 468 U.S., at 760 (quoting *Laird v. Tatum,* 408 U.S. 1, 15 (1972)). We have always rejected that vision of our role. . . .

* * *

We hold that respondents lack standing to bring this action and that the Court of Appeals erred in denying the summary judgment motion filed by the United States. The opinion of the Court of Appeals is hereby reversed, and the cause is remanded for proceedings consistent with this opinion.

It is so ordered.

Justice KENNEDY, with whom Justice SOUTER joins, concurring in part and concurring in the judgment.

Although I agree with the essential parts of the Court's analysis, I write separately to make several observations.

I agree with the Court's conclusion in Part III–A that, on the record before us, respondents have failed to demonstrate that they themselves are "among the injured." *Sierra Club v. Morton,* 405 U.S. 727, 735 (1972). . . .

While it may seem trivial to require that Mses. Kelly and Skilbred acquire airline tickets to the project sites or announce a date certain upon which they will return, this is not a case where it is reasonable to assume that the affiants will be using the sites on a regular basis, *see Sierra Club v. Morton, supra,* 405 U.S., at 735, note 8, nor do the affiants claim to have visited the sites since the projects commenced. . . .

I also join Part IV of the Court's opinion with the following observations. As Government programs and policies become more complex and far-reaching, we must be sensitive to the articulation of new rights of action that do not have clear analogs in our common-law tradition. Modern litigation has progressed far from the paradigm of Marbury suing Madison to get his commission . . . In my view, Congress has the power to define injuries and articulate chains of causation that will give rise to a case or controversy where none existed before, and I do not read the Court's opinion to suggest a contrary view. In exercising this power, however, Congress must at the very least identify the injury it seeks to vindicate and relate the injury to the class of persons entitled to bring suit. The citizen-suit provision of the Endangered

Species Act does not meet these minimal requirements, because while the statute purports to confer a right on "any person . . . to enjoin . . . the United States and any other governmental instrumentality or agency . . . who is alleged to be in violation of any provision of this chapter," it does not of its own force establish that there is an injury in "any person" by virtue of any "violation." 16 U.S.C. § 1540(g)(1)(A).

The Court's holding that there is an outer limit to the power of Congress to confer rights of action is a direct and necessary consequence of the case and controversy limitations found in Article III. I agree that it would exceed those limitations if, at the behest of Congress and in the absence of any showing of concrete injury, we were to entertain citizen suits to vindicate the public's nonconcrete interest in the proper administration of the laws. While it does not matter how many persons have been injured by the challenged action, the party bringing suit must show that the action injures him in a concrete and personal way. This requirement is not just an empty formality. It preserves the vitality of the adversarial process by assuring both that the parties before the court have an actual, as opposed to professed, stake in the outcome, . . . In addition, the requirement of concrete injury confines the Judicial Branch to its proper, limited role in the constitutional framework of Government. . . .

With these observations, I concur in Parts I, II, III-A, and IV of the Court's opinion and in the judgment of the Court.

Justice STEVENS, concurring in the judgment. . . .

In my opinion a person who has visited the critical habitat of an endangered species has a professional interest in preserving the species and its habitat, and intends to revisit them in the future has standing to challenge agency action that threatens their destruction. Congress has found that a wide variety of endangered species of fish, wildlife, and plants are of "aesthetic, ecological, educational, historical, recreational, and scientific value to the Nation and its people." 16 U.S.C. § 1531(a)(3). Given that finding, we have no license to demean the importance of the interest that particular individuals may have in observing any species or its habitat, whether those individuals are motivated by esthetic enjoyment, an interest in professional research, or an economic interest in preservation of the species. Indeed, this Court has often held that injuries to such interests are sufficient to confer standing, and the Court reiterates that holding today.

The Court nevertheless concludes that respondents have not suffered "injury in fact" because they have not shown that the harm to the endangered species will produce "imminent" injury to them. I disagree. An injury to an individual's interest in studying or enjoying a species and its natural habitat occurs when someone (whether it be the Government or a private party) takes action that harms that species and habitat. In my judgment, therefore, the "imminence" of such an injury should be measured by the timing and likelihood of the threatened environmental harm, rather than — as the Court seems to suggest — by the time that might elapse between the present and the time when the individuals would visit the area if no such injury should occur.

. . . Concerned about "the proper — and properly limited — role of the courts in a democratic society," we have long held that "Art. III judicial power exists only to redress or otherwise to protect against injury to the complaining party." *Warth v. Seldin*, 422 U.S. 490, 498-499 (1975). . . . For that reason, "[a]bstract injury is not enough. It must be alleged that the plaintiff 'has sustained or is immediately in danger of sustaining some direct injury' as the result of the challenged statute or official conduct. . . . The injury or threat of injury must be both 'real and immediate,' not 'conjectural,' or 'hypothetical.'" *O'Shea v. Littleton*, 414 U.S. 488, 494 (1974) (quoting *Golden v. Zwickler*, 394 U.S. 103, 109-110 (1969)).

Consequently, we have denied standing to plaintiffs whose likelihood of suffering any concrete adverse effect from the challenged action was speculative. In this case, however, the likelihood that respondents will be injured by the destruction of the endangered species is not speculative. If respondents are genuinely interested in the preservation of the endangered species and intend to study or observe these animals in the future, their injury will occur as soon as the animals are destroyed. Thus the only potential source of "speculation" in this case is whether respondents' intent to study or observe the animals is genuine. In my view, Joyce Kelly and Amy Skilbred have introduced sufficient evidence to negate petitioner's contention that their claims of injury are "speculative" or "conjectural." . . .

Justice BLACKMUN, with whom Justice O'CONNOR joins, dissenting. . . .

I think a reasonable finder of fact could conclude from the information in the affidavits and deposition testimony that either Kelly or Skilbred will soon return to the project sites, thereby satisfying the "actual or imminent" injury standard. The Court dismisses Kelly's and Skilbred's general statements that they intended to revisit the project sites as "simply not enough." But those statements did not stand alone. A reasonable finder of fact could conclude, based not only upon their statements of intent to return, but upon their past visits to the project sites, as well as their professional backgrounds, that it was likely that Kelly and Skilbred would make a return trip to the project areas. Contrary to the Court's contention that Kelly's and Skilbred's past visits "prov[e] nothing," the fact of their past visits could demonstrate to a reasonable factfinder that Kelly and Skilbred have the requisite resources and personal interest in the preservation of the species endangered by the Aswan and Mahaweli projects to make good on their intention to return again. Similarly, Kelly's and Skilbred's professional backgrounds in wildlife preservation also make it likely — at least far more likely than for the average citizen—that they would choose to visit these areas of the world where species are vanishing.

By requiring a "description of concrete plans" or "specification of when the some day [for a return visit] will be," the Court, in my view, demands what is likely an empty formality. No substantial barriers prevent Kelly or Skilbred from simply purchasing plane tickets to return to the Aswan and Mahaweli projects. This case differs from other cases in which the imminence of harm turned largely on the affirmative actions of third parties beyond a plaintiff's control. To be sure, a plaintiff's unilateral control over his or her exposure to harm does not necessarily render the harm nonspeculative. Nevertheless, it suggests that a finder of fact would be far more likely to conclude the harm is actual or imminent, especially if given an opportunity to hear testimony and determine credibility.

I fear the Court's demand for detailed descriptions of future conduct will do little to weed out those who are genuinely harmed from those who are not. More likely, it will resurrect a code-pleading formalism in federal court summary judgment practice, as federal courts, newly doubting their jurisdiction, will demand more and more particularized showings of future harm. . . .

II. . . .

The Court expresses concern that allowing judicial enforcement of "agencies' observance of a particular, statutorily prescribed procedure" would "transfer from the President to the courts the Chief Executive's most important constitutional duty, to 'take Care that the Laws be faithfully executed,' Art. II, § 3." In fact, the principal effect of foreclosing judicial enforcement of such procedures is to transfer power into the hands of the Executive at the expense—not of the courts—but of Congress, from which that power originates and emanates.

Under the Court's anachronistically formal view of the separation of powers, Congress legislates pure, substantive mandates and has no business structuring the procedural manner in which the Executive implements these mandates. To be sure, in the ordinary course, Congress does legislate in black-and-white terms of affirmative commands or negative prohibitions on the conduct of officers of the Executive Branch. In complex regulatory areas, however, Congress often legislates, as it were, in procedural shades of gray. That is, it sets forth substantive policy goals and provides for their attainment by requiring Executive Branch officials to follow certain procedures, for example, in the form of reporting, consultation, and certification requirements. . . .

Congress legislates in procedural shades of gray not to aggrandize its own power but to allow maximum Executive discretion in the attainment of Congress' legislative goals. . . . [It] sets forth substantive guidelines and allows the Executive, within certain procedural constraints, to decide how best to effectuate the ultimate goal. The Court never has questioned Congress' authority to impose such procedural constraints on Executive power. Just as Congress does not violate separation of powers by structuring the procedural manner in which the Executive shall carry out the laws, surely the federal courts do not violate separation of powers when, at the very instruction and command of Congress, they enforce these procedures.

To prevent Congress from conferring standing for "procedural injuries" is another way of saying that Congress may not delegate to the courts authority deemed "executive" in nature. Here Congress seeks not to delegate "executive" power but only to strengthen the procedures it has legislatively mandated. "We have long recognized that the nondelegation doctrine does not prevent Congress from seeking assistance, within proper limits, from its coordinate Branches." *Touby v. United States*, 500 U.S. 160, 165 (1991). "Congress does not violate the Constitution merely because it legislates in broad terms, leaving a certain degree of discretion to executive *or judicial actors*." *Ibid.* (emphasis added). . . .

QUESTION SET 9.9

Review & Synthesis

1. According to Justice Scalia's majority opinion in *Lujan*, how do the constitutional standing requirements advance the separation-of-powers principles described by James Madison in *The Federalist No.* 48? Stated differently, how does the requirement prevent the Judiciary from encroaching on the legislative and executive powers vested by the Constitution in Congress and the President, respectively? What was Justice Blackmun's perspective on how the Court's standing ruling would affect the balance of power among the three Branches?

2. How does the plaintiff's burden of establishing the core elements of constitutional standing—injury-in-fact, causation, and redressability—differ at the pleading, summary judgment, and trial phases of federal litigation?

3. In a lawsuit brought under citizen-suit provisions—like APA § 702 or § 7(a)(2) of the Endangered Species Act—the plaintiff does not file suit against the person or entity directly causing that plaintiff's alleged factual injuries. Rather, the plaintiff files suit against the federal agency that regulates the person or entity allegedly causing the plaintiff's harm. This was the situation in *Lujan*: rather than suing the persons or entities directly involved in the foreign development projects they opposed, the plaintiffs

sued the Interior Department for failing to consult with the agencies responsible for authorizing those projects.

a. Why didn't the plaintiffs simply sue those directly responsible for the habitat destruction they alleged (e.g., the contractors working on the rehabilitation of the Aswan High Dam)?

b. The Court observed that when "a plaintiff's asserted injury arises from the government's allegedly unlawful regulation (or lack of regulation) of *someone else*, much more is needed." What more is needed, and why?

4. What is a "generalized grievance," and how is it distinguishable from the type of lawsuits normally heard in federal district courts? How is it distinguishable from a mass tort class action lawsuit, which may have thousands of plaintiffs? How did *Lujan* describe the separation-of-powers problem raised by generalized grievances?

5. The Court concluded that the plaintiffs' injuries were not "imminent," and thus they had not demonstrated the injury-in-fact required for constitutional standing.

a. How much was that conclusion informed by the nature of the harm alleged? Are intangible harms—like infringements on opportunities for aesthetic enjoyment—inherently more difficult to demonstrate than tangible harms—like physical damage to property? Is that difficulty compounded when the plaintiff alleges that the intangible harm has not yet occurred, but will occur at some future time if a court does not intercede?

b. What do you make of Justice Kennedy's suggestion that the plaintiffs buy "plane tickets" to support their standing claims? Should federal plaintiffs have to monetize their claims of intangible harms to get them heard? Do you agree with Justice Blackmun that requiring the plaintiffs show concrete plans to visit the potentially endangered habitats would amount to little more than an empty formality?

c. Justices Stevens disagreed with the Court's conclusion that the plaintiffs had failed to show "imminent" harm from the Interior Department's narrowed interpretation of the ESA's consultation requirement. He asserted instead that imminence "should be measured by the timing and likelihood of the threatened environmental harm" and not "by the time that might elapse between the present and the time when the individuals would visit the area if no such injury should occur." Do you agree? Why not point to the plaintiffs' lack of concrete plans to visit the habitats allegedly endangered by the government's actions as evidence that they were unlikely to suffer any harm? Under Justice Stevens' approach, would courts simply have to accept a plaintiff's uncorroborated assertion that she will be affected by future governmental conduct?

6. Justice Kennedy observed that "Congress has the power to define injuries and articulate chains of causation that will give rise to a case or controversy where none existed before." Did he mean that Congress has the authority to attach litigation rights to factual injuries, or did he mean that Congress could create factual injuries *and* attach litigation rights to them? In other words, did he assert that injury to an abstract legislative right, without any real-world impact on the plaintiff, could satisfy the Article III injury-in-fact requirement?

---

6. Constitutional Standing Requirements

a. Injuries-in-Fact

We turn now to the first constitutional standing requirement which requires federal plaintiffs to allege and eventually prove that they have or soon will suffer a factual injury. The Court in *Data Processing* did not state the matter as plainly as it could have, but it clearly tied the injury-in-fact requirement to the Case or Controversy Clause of Article III. It was much more explicit in *Barlow v. Collins*, 397 U.S. 159 (1970), a standing decision issued the same day as *Data Processing*. In an opinion also written by Justice Douglas, the Court stated that complainants must "have the personal stake and interest that impart the concrete adverseness required by Article III." *Id.* at 164. In other words, plaintiffs must have some "skin in the game," actual or threatened loss of something personally valuable, to litigate in an Article III court. Though prior decisions hinted that standing and Article III were linked, *Barlow* was the Court's first clear acknowledgment of that connection. As several scholars have argued, however, the historical record does not clearly establish that the Framers thought of injury to personal interests as a constitutional requirement for invoking federal judicial power. The Court nevertheless concluded that it is, and with surprisingly little elaboration. As *Lujan v. Defenders of Wildlife* showed, the Court now has an unwavering commitment to standing's constitutionalization, the injury-in-fact requirement included.

Apart from identifying the source of the injury-in-fact requirement, courts have also had to identify the types of harms it includes. The *Data Processing* Court spent little time assessing whether the plaintiffs satisfied this prong of the standing test it established. As it did in *Sanders Brothers* decades earlier (*see supra*, page 731), the Court readily recognized economic harms caused by increased competition. Nevertheless, Justice Douglas made clear that economic injuries are not the only ones on which federal plaintiffs can rest their standing claims. Intangible injuries (e.g., to aesthetic, conservational, recreational, or spiritual interests) are just as valid a basis for standing as tangible ones (economic, physical, etc.), even though they are more difficult to observe and to measure. *Lujan* reaffirmed Article III's recognition of noneconomic harms, including intangible ones.

The materials that follow focus on two recurring injury-in-fact issues. The first asks whether a "generalized grievance" can ever be a harm recognized by Article III. Again, a generalized grievance is a harm that is widely shared by broad swaths of the public. Recall that Justice Scalia made the following observation in *Lujan*:

> We have consistently held that a plaintiff raising only a generally available grievance about government—claiming only harm to his and every citizen's interest in proper application of the Constitution and laws, and seeking relief that no more directly and tangibly benefits him than it does the public at large—does not state an Article III case or controversy. . . .

See supra, page 751. To the *Lujan* majority, "generalized grievances" were not merely ill-suited for judicial resolution for prudential reasons. They were *constitutionally* inadequate under Article III. *Federal Election Commission v. Akins*, decided several years after *Lujan* and excerpted below, revisited this issue. In an opinion by Justice Breyer, the Court explored not only the legal source of the prohibition against hearing generalized grievances, it asked whether *all* generalized grievances should be prohibited.

After considering *Akins*, we turn to a more practical injury-in-fact problem: how does a plaintiff convince a court that she has suffered one? As noted above, the Court in *Lujan* accepted the constitutional cognizability of the plaintiffs' intangible injuries. Aesthetic harms count as much as economic harms as far as Article III is concerned. The plaintiffs' attempts to establish standing faltered for a different reason; they failed to *demonstrate* that they were going to suffer those intangible harms. Because their standing was assessed at summary judgment, they had to do more than simply allege harm; they had to offer corroborating evidence of it. It was their inability to do so that resulted in the dismissal of their case. Compare this with the harm alleged in *Data Processing*. The plaintiffs there had it much easier. Their injury claim was challenged in a motion to dismiss, which, as you learned in Civil Procedure, looks only to the allegations in the complaint that courts assume to be true. Additionally, they alleged potential economic harms, which are more tangible and thus easier to corroborate. This challenge of corroborating intangible harms is addressed in *Spokeo, Inc. v. Robins*.

i. Conceptual Puzzle: Injuries-in-Fact and Generalized Grievances

Can an injury be both particular to a person and undifferentiated among the people? Can it affect large parts of the public in the same way and still be considered personal? This is a conceptual puzzle noted by the *Lujan* majority. Article III injuries-in-fact must be "particular," that is, a federal plaintiff must have personally suffered the injury allegedly caused by the defendant's conduct. Particularity is rarely a problem in run-of-the-mill lawsuits. For instance, a plaintiff who disputes the IRS's calculation of her federal income tax liability is essentially arguing that the agency has applied the Internal Revenue Code differently to her than to everyone else who is similarly situated. Her harm is particularized because the IRS's alleged error differentiates her from the rest of the taxpaying public.

By contrast, widely shared, undifferentiated harms — the factual basis for generalized grievances — raise particularity concerns. What if, for example, Congress appropriated funds to support religious organizations in alleged violation of the Establishment Clause? This would be a classic generalized grievance directed at broadly applicable government policy. Congress does not force a single taxpayer to support these organizations through her tax payments, it forces *all* taxpayers to do so. In such a scenario, the violation of one taxpayer's Establishment Clause right is no different than the violation of everyone else's. *See Flast v. Cohen*, 392 U.S. 83, 117-18 (1968) (Harlan, J., dissenting). Nevertheless, all taxpayers are, in fact, *affected*; each is personally touched by Congress' allegedly illegal appropriation, even if it might be hard to measure the degree to which they are.

Two pertinent questions arise from this. The first is whether an injury-in-fact can be both particularized *and* undifferentiated. Stated differently, is the fact that each individual taxpayer suffers an Establishment Clause violation rendered irrelevant by the fact that the violation affects all taxpayers in common? The Justices have disagreed on the answer. The second question is whether this insistence on particularized harms comes from Article III, or whether it is part of the Court's prudential concerns. If the former, particularity sets the outer bounds of federal judicial power that Congress has no authority to expand. If the latter, Congress can override the particularity requirement by statute. Again, the Justices have disagreed on the answer.

In a string of cases going back to the late 1960s, the Court considered whether plaintiffs' status as injured taxpayers, citizens, or voters could grant them standing to challenge the constitutionality of government conduct. As in the previous hypothetical, the injuries plaintiffs claimed in these cases were shared by everyone of the same status. Further, these plaintiffs did not have citizen-suit statutes they could rely on; Congress had provided them with no statutory means to challenge the government's conduct. Accordingly, the Court determined their standing based on whether there was a "logical nexus" between (1) their claimed status — e.g., as a taxpayer — and the type of governmental action they were challenging, and (2) their claimed status and the precise nature of the constitutional infringement they alleged. *See Flast*, 392 U.S. at 102-03. In *Flast*, the Court acknowledged the taxpayer plaintiffs' standing after finding that they satisfied the logical nexus test.

Unfortunately for plaintiffs looking to challenge the constitutionality of government decision-making, *Flast* has turned out to be something of a unicorn. Contrary to the trend of statutorily empowering private attorneys general to challenge administrative actions, the Supreme Court now consistently denies standing to "status" plaintiffs whose claims deviate even trivially from those asserted in *Flast*. *See, e.g., Schlesinger v. Reservists*, 418 U.S. 208 (1974) (citizens and taxpayers claiming service by Members of Congress in the armed forces reserves violates the Incompatibility Clause); *Valley Forge Christian College v. Americans United*, 454 U.S. 464 (1982) (taxpayers claiming conveyance of federal property to religiously affiliated college violates the Establishment Clause); *Hein v. Freedom from Religion Foundation*, 551 U.S. 587 (2007) (taxpayers claiming creation of White House Office of Faith-Based Initiatives violated the Establishment Clause); *Arizona Christian School Tuition Organization v. Winn*, 563 U.S. 125 (2011) (taxpayers claiming that Arizona tuition tax credit violated the Establishment Clause).

United States v. Richardson, 418 U.S. 166 (1974) is among the most notable examples. The complainant there was a taxpayer who filed a mandamus action demanding that the Treasury Secretary publish details of the Central Intelligence Agency ("CIA") budget. He argued that the Central Intelligence Agency Act, which essentially shielded the CIA's expenditures from public view, violated the public funds reporting requirement of the Accounts Clause (Art. I, § 9, cl. 7). The Court rejected Richardson's standing claim, concluding that he failed to satisfy the requirements of *Flast's* logical nexus test. *Id.* at 174-76. In doing so, it stated the following:

> The respondent's claim is that without detailed information on CIA expenditures—and hence its activities—he cannot intelligently follow the actions of Congress or the Executive, nor can he properly fulfill his obligations as a member of the electorate in voting for candidates seeking national office.
> This is surely the kind of a generalized grievance described in both *Frothingham* and *Flast* since the impact on him is plainly undifferentiated and common to all members of the public. [internal quotations omitted] While we can hardly dispute that this respondent has a genuine interest in the use of funds and that his interest may be prompted by his status as a taxpayer, he has not alleged that, as a taxpayer, he is in danger of suffering any particular concrete injury as a result of the operation of this statute.

Id. at 176-77. While *Richardson* and the other post-*Flast* generalized grievances shared the same dismal fate, the Court's reasoning was opaque on whether an undifferentiated injury is constitutionally insufficient to support standing. *Richardson* cited *Flast* as involving a generalized grievance, but the cases reached opposite conclusions on the standing question. Did *Richardson* simply overrule *Flast* on this point? The Court has never indicated that it did and still insists that the logical nexus test is good law. Do the different results in *Flast* and *Richardson* mean that undifferentiated harms *can* satisfy the Constitution but will be rejected on prudential grounds absent satisfaction of the logical nexus test or a statutory override like a citizen-suit provision?

The following standing case—*Federal Election Commission v. Akins*—dealt directly with these questions. It arose under a citizen-suit provision rather than the Constitution and was therefore analyzed under the "zone of interests" analysis rather than the logical nexus test. Nevertheless, *Richardson* figured heavily in both the majority's and dissent's analyses. The case also features dueling opinions by former administrative law professors Stephen Breyer and Antonin Scalia.

As you read, note how the Court situates particularity within its injury-in-fact analysis, and whether the Court viewed it as a constitutional or prudential requirement. More broadly, think about whether the Court's decision on balance increased or decreased judicial oversight of administrative conduct. Finally, what view on the relationship between standing and separation of powers did Justice Breyer adopt in his majority opinion, and how did that view differ from Justice Scalia's?

Federal Election Commission v. Akins
524 U.S. 11 (1998)

Justice BREYER delivered the opinion of the Court.

The Federal Election Commission (FEC) has determined that the American Israel Public Affairs Committee (AIPAC) is not a "political committee" as defined by the Federal Election Campaign Act of 1971 (FECA or Act), and, for that reason, the FEC has refused to require AIPAC to make disclosures regarding its membership, contributions, and expenditures that FECA would otherwise require. We hold that respondents, a group of voters, have standing to challenge the Commission's determination in court, and we remand this case for further proceedings.

I. . . .

This case arises out of an effort by respondents, a group of voters with views often opposed to those of AIPAC, to persuade the FEC to treat AIPAC as a "political committee." Respondents filed a complaint with the FEC, stating that AIPAC had made more than $1,000 in qualifying "expenditures" per year, and thereby became a "political committee." They added that AIPAC had violated the FEC provisions requiring "political committee[s]" to register and to make public the information about members, contributions, and expenditures to which we have just referred. Respondents also claimed that AIPAC had violated [the FECA by making] corporate campaign "contribution[s]" and "expenditure[s]." They asked the FEC to find that AIPAC had violated the Act, and, among other things, to order AIPAC to make public the information that FECA demands of a "political committee." . . .

The FEC . . . held that AIPAC was not subject to the disclosure requirements. . . . In the FEC's view, the Act's definition of "political committee" includes only those organizations that have as a "major purpose" the nomination or election of candidates. AIPAC, it added, was fundamentally an issue-oriented lobbying organization, not a campaign-related organization, and hence AIPAC fell outside the definition of a "political committee". . . . The FEC consequently dismissed respondents' complaint.

Respondents filed a petition in Federal District Court seeking review of the FEC's determination dismissing their complaint. The District Court granted summary judgment for the FEC, and a divided panel of the Court of Appeals affirmed. The *en banc* Court of Appeals reversed, however, on the ground that the FEC's "major purpose" test improperly interpreted the Act's definition of a "political committee." We granted the FEC's petition for certiorari. . . .

II

The Solicitor General argues that respondents lack standing to challenge the FEC's decision not to proceed against AIPAC. He claims that they have failed to satisfy the "prudential" standing requirements upon which this Court has insisted. *See, e.g., National Credit Union Admin. v. First Nat. Bank & Trust Co.*, 522 U.S. 479, 488 (1998) (*NCUA*); *Association of Data Processing Service Organizations, Inc. v. Camp*, 397 U.S. 150, 153 (1970). He adds that respondents have not shown that they "suffe[r] injury in fact," that their injury is "fairly traceable" to the FEC's decision, or that a judicial decision in their favor would "redres[s]" the injury. *E.g., Bennett v. Spear*, 520 U.S. 154, 162, (1997) (internal quotation marks omitted); *Lujan v. Defenders of Wildlife*, 504 U.S. 555, 560–61 (1992). In his view, respondents' District Court petition consequently failed to meet Article III's demand for a "case" or "controversy."

We do not agree with the FEC's "prudential standing" claim. Congress has specifically provided in FECA that "[a]ny person who believes a violation of this Act . . . has occurred, may file a complaint with the Commission." § 437g(a)(1). It has added that "[a]ny party aggrieved by an order of the Commission dismissing a complaint filed by such party . . . may file a petition" in district court seeking review of that dismissal. § 437g(a)(8)(A). History associates the word "aggrieved" with a congressional intent to cast the standing net broadly—beyond the common-law interests and substantive statutory rights upon which "prudential" standing traditionally rested. *FCC v. Sanders Brothers Radio Station*, 309 U.S. 470 (1940). *Cf.* Administrative Procedure Act, 5 U.S.C. § 702 (stating that those "suffering legal wrong" or "adversely affected or aggrieved . . . within the meaning of a relevant statute" may seek judicial review of agency action).

Moreover, prudential standing is satisfied when the injury asserted by a plaintiff " 'arguably [falls] within the zone of interests to be protected or regulated by the statute . . . in question.'" *NCUA*, 522 U.S. at 488 (quoting *Data Processing*, 397 U.S. at 153). The injury of which respondents complain — their failure to obtain relevant information — is injury of a kind that FECA seeks to address. We have found nothing in the Act that suggests Congress intended to exclude voters from the benefits of these provisions, or otherwise to restrict standing, say, to political parties, candidates, or their committees.

Given the language of the statute and the nature of the injury, we conclude that Congress, intending to protect voters such as respondents from suffering the kind of injury here at issue, intended to authorize this kind of suit. Consequently, respondents satisfy "prudential" standing requirements.

Nor do we agree with the FEC or the dissent that Congress lacks the constitutional power to authorize federal courts to adjudicate this lawsuit. Article III, of course, limits Congress' grant of judicial power to "cases" or "controversies." That limitation means that respondents must show, among other things, an "injury in fact" — a requirement that helps assure that courts will not "pass upon . . . abstract, intellectual problems," but adjudicate "concrete, living contest[s] between adversaries." *Coleman v. Miller*, 307 U.S. 433, 460 (1939) (Frankfurter, J., dissenting); *see also Bennett, supra*, at 167; *Lujan, supra*, at 560-561. In our view, respondents here have suffered a genuine "injury in fact."

The "injury in fact" that respondents have suffered consists of their inability to obtain information — lists of AIPAC donors (who are, according to AIPAC, its members), and campaign-related contributions and expenditures — that, on respondents' view of the law, the statute requires that AIPAC make public. There is no reason to doubt their claim that the information would help them (and others to whom they would communicate it) to evaluate candidates for public office, especially candidates who received assistance from AIPAC, and to evaluate the role that AIPAC's financial assistance might play in a specific election. Respondents' injury consequently seems concrete and particular. Indeed, this Court has previously held that a plaintiff suffers an "injury in fact" when the plaintiff fails to obtain information which must be publicly disclosed pursuant to a statute.

The dissent refers to *United States v. Richardson*, 418 U.S. 166 (1974), a case in which a plaintiff sought information (details of Central Intelligence Agency (CIA) expenditures) to which, he said, the Constitution's Accounts Clause, Art. I, § 9, cl. 7, entitled him. The Court held that the plaintiff there lacked Article III standing. The dissent says that *Richardson* and this case are "indistinguishable." But as the parties' briefs suggest — for they do not mention *Richardson* — that case does not control the outcome here.

Richardson's plaintiff claimed that a statute permitting the CIA to keep its expenditures nonpublic violated the Accounts Clause, which requires that "a regular Statement and Account of the Receipts and Expenditures of all public Money shall be published from time to time." 418 U.S., at 167-169. The Court held that the plaintiff lacked standing because there was "no 'logical nexus' between the [plaintiff's] asserted status of taxpayer and the claimed failure of the Congress to require the Executive to supply a more detailed report of the [CIA's] expenditures." *Id.* at 175.

In this case, however, the "logical nexus" inquiry is not relevant. Here, there is no constitutional provision requiring the demonstration of the "nexus" the Court believed must be shown in *Richardson* and *Flast.* Rather, there is a statute which, as we previously pointed out, does seek to protect individuals such as respondents from the kind of harm they say they have suffered, i.e., failing to receive particular information about campaign-related activities.

The fact that the Court in *Richardson* focused upon taxpayer standing, not voter standing, places that case at still a greater distance from the case before us. We are not suggesting, as the dissent implies, that *Richardson* would have come out differently if only the plaintiff had asserted his standing to sue as a voter, rather than as a taxpayer. Faced with such an assertion, the *Richardson* Court would simply have had to consider whether "the Framers . . . ever imagined that *general directives* [of the Constitution] . . . would be subject to enforcement by an individual citizen." 418 U.S., at 178, note 11 (emphasis added). But since that answer (like the answer to whether there was taxpayer standing in *Richardson*) would have rested in significant part upon the Court's view of the Accounts Clause, it still would not control our answer in this case. All this is to say that the legal logic which critically determined *Richardson*'s outcome is beside the point here.

The FEC's strongest argument is its contention that this lawsuit involves only a "generalized grievance." (Indeed, if *Richardson* is relevant at all, it is because of its broad discussion of this matter, not its basic rationale.) The FEC points out that respondents' asserted harm (their failure to obtain information) is one which is " 'shared in substantially equal measure by all or a large class of citizens.' " This Court, the FEC adds, has often said that "generalized grievance[s]" are not the kinds of harms that confer standing. *See, e.g., Lujan,* 504 U.S., at 573-574; *Valley Forge Christian College v. Americans United for Separation of Church and State, Inc.,* 454 U.S. 464, 475-479 (1982); *Richardson, supra,* at 176-178; *Frothingham v. Mellon,* decided with *Massachusetts v. Mellon,* 262 U.S. 447, 487 (1923). Whether styled as a constitutional or prudential limit on standing, the Court has sometimes determined that where large numbers of Americans suffer alike, the political process, rather than the judicial process, may provide the more appropriate remedy for a widely shared grievance. *Schlesinger v. Reservists Comm. to Stop the War,* 418 U.S. 208, 222 (1974); *Richardson,* 418 U.S., at 179 (Powell, J., concurring); *see also Flast, supra,* at 131 (Harlan, J., dissenting).

The kind of judicial language to which the FEC points, however, invariably appears in cases where the harm at issue is not only widely shared, but is also of an abstract and indefinite nature—for example, harm to the "common concern for obedience to law." The abstract nature of the harm—for example, injury to the interest in seeing that the law is obeyed—deprives the case of the concrete specificity that characterized those controversies which were "the traditional concern of the courts at Westminster," *Coleman*, 307 U.S., at 460 (Frankfurter, J., dissenting); and which today prevents a plaintiff from obtaining what would, in effect, amount to an advisory opinion.

Often the fact that an interest is abstract and the fact that it is widely shared go hand in hand. But their association is not invariable, and where a harm is concrete, though widely shared, the Court has found "injury in fact." Thus the fact that a political forum may be more readily available where an injury is widely shared (while counseling against, say, interpreting a statute as conferring standing) does not, by itself, automatically disqualify an interest for Article III purposes. Such an interest, where sufficiently concrete, may count as an "injury in fact. This conclusion seems particularly obvious where (to use a hypothetical example) large numbers of individuals suffer the same common-law injury (say, a widespread mass tort), or where large numbers of voters suffer interference with voting rights conferred by law. We conclude that, similarly, the informational injury at issue here, directly related to voting, the most basic of political rights, is sufficiently concrete and specific such that the fact that it is widely shared does not deprive Congress of constitutional power to authorize its vindication in the federal courts. . . .

[In the remainder of his opinion, Justice Breyer concluded that the plaintiffs had satisfied the other constitutional standing requirements, that the FECA explicitly made reviewable the FEC's decision not to enforce the Act against AIPAC, and that the FEC should have the first opportunity to decide whether AIPAC fell outside FECA's regulatory scope.]

It is so ordered.

Justice SCALIA, with whom Justice O'CONNOR and Justice THOMAS join, dissenting.

The provision of law at issue in this case is an extraordinary one, conferring upon a private person the ability to bring an Executive agency into court to compel its enforcement of the law against a third party. Despite its liberality, the Administrative Procedure Act does not allow such suits, since enforcement action is traditionally deemed "committed to agency discretion by law." 5 U.S.C. § 701(a)(2); *Heckler v. Chaney*, 470 U.S. 821, 827-835 (1985). If provisions such as the present one were commonplace, the role of the Executive Branch in our system of separated and equilibrated powers would be greatly reduced, and that of the Judiciary greatly expanded.

Because this provision is so extraordinary, we should be particularly careful not to expand it beyond its fair meaning. In my view the Court's opinion does that. Indeed, it expands the meaning beyond what the Constitution permits.

I

It is clear that the Federal Election Campaign Act of 1971 (FECA or Act) does not intend that all persons filing complaints with the Federal Election Commission have the right to seek judicial review of the rejection of their complaints. This is evident from the fact that the Act permits a complaint to be filed by "[a]ny *person* who believes a violation of this Act . . . has occurred," 2 U.S.C. § 437g(a)(1) (emphasis added), but accords a right to judicial relief only to "[a]ny *party aggrieved* by an order of the Commission dismissing a complaint filed by such party," § 437g(a)(8)(A) (emphasis added). The interpretation that the Court gives the latter provision deprives it of almost all its limiting force. Any voter can sue to compel the agency to require registration of an entity as a political committee, even though the "aggrievement" consists of nothing more than the deprivation of access to information whose public availability would have been one of the consequences of registration.

This seems to me too much of a stretch. It should be borne in mind that the agency action complained of here is not the refusal to make available information in its possession that the Act requires to be disclosed. A person demanding provision of information that the law requires the agency to furnish—one demanding compliance with the Freedom of Information Act or the Federal Advisory Committee Act, for example—can reasonably be described as being "aggrieved" by the agency's refusal to provide it. What the respondents complain of in this suit, however, is not the refusal to provide information, but the refusal (for an allegedly improper reason) to commence an agency enforcement action against a third person. That refusal itself plainly does not render respondents "aggrieved" within the meaning of the Act, for in that case there would have been no reason for the Act to differentiate between "person" in subsection (a)(1) and "party aggrieved" in subsection (a)(8). Respondents claim that each of them is elevated to the special status of a "party aggrieved" by the fact that the requested enforcement action (if it was successful) would have had the effect, among others, of placing certain information in the agency's possession, where respondents, along with everyone else in the world, would have had access to it. It seems to me most unlikely that the failure to produce that effect—both a secondary consequence of what respondents immediately seek, and a consequence that affects respondents no more and with no greater particularity than it affects virtually the entire population—would have been meant to set apart each respondent as a "party aggrieved" (as opposed to just a rejected complainant) within the meaning of the statute.

This conclusion is strengthened by the fact that this citizen-suit provision was enacted two years after this Court's decision in *United States v. Richardson*, 418 U.S. 166 (1974), which, as I shall discuss at greater length below, gave Congress every reason to believe that a voter's interest in information helpful to his exercise of the franchise was constitutionally inadequate to confer standing. *Richardson* had said that a plaintiff's complaint that the Government was unlawfully depriving him of information he needed to "properly fulfill his obligations as a member of the electorate in voting" was "surely the kind of a generalized grievance" that does not state an Article III case or controversy. *Id.* at 176.

And finally, a narrower reading of "party aggrieved" is supported by the doctrine of constitutional doubt, which counsels us to interpret statutes, if possible, in such fashion as to avoid grave constitutional questions. As I proceed to discuss, it is my view that the Court's entertainment of the present suit violates Article III. Even if one disagrees with that judgment, however, it is clear from *Richardson* that the question is a close one, so that the statute ought not be interpreted to present it.

II

In *Richardson*, we dismissed for lack of standing a suit whose "aggrievement" was precisely the "aggrievement" respondents assert here: the Government's unlawful refusal to place information within the public domain. The only difference, in fact, is that the aggrievement there was more direct, since the Government already had the information within its possession, whereas here respondents seek enforcement action that will bring information within the Government's possession and then require the information to be made public. The plaintiff in *Richardson* challenged the Government's failure to disclose the expenditures of the Central Intelligence Agency (CIA), in alleged violation of the constitutional requirement, Art. I, § 9, cl. 7, that "a regular Statement and Account of the Receipts and Expenditures of all public Money shall be published from time to time." We held that such a claim was a nonjusticiable "generalized grievance" because "the impact on [plaintiff] is plainly undifferentiated and common to all members of the public." 418 U.S., at 176-177 (internal quotation marks and citations omitted).

It was alleged in *Richardson* that the Government had denied a right conferred by the Constitution, whereas respondents here assert a right conferred by statute — but of course "there is absolutely no basis for making the Article III inquiry turn on the source of the asserted right." *Lujan v. Defenders of Wildlife*, 504 U.S. 555, 576 (1992). The Court today distinguishes *Richardson* on a different basis — a basis that reduces it from a landmark constitutional holding to a curio. According to the Court, "*Richardson* focused upon taxpayer standing, . . . not voter standing." In addition to being a silly distinction, given the weighty governmental purpose underlying the "generalized grievance" prohibition . . . this is also a distinction that the Court in *Richardson* went out of its way explicitly to eliminate. It is true enough that the narrow question presented in *Richardson* was "'[w]hether a federal taxpayer has standing,'" *Id.* at 167, note 1. But the *Richardson* Court did not hold only, as the Court today suggests, that the plaintiff failed to qualify for the exception to the rule of no taxpayer standing established by the "logical nexus" test of *Flast v. Cohen*, 392 U.S. 83 (1968). The plaintiff's complaint in *Richardson* had also alleged that he was "'a member of the electorate,'" 418 U.S., at 167, note 1, and he asserted injury in that capacity as well. The *Richardson* opinion treated that as fairly included within the taxpayer-standing question, or at least as plainly indistinguishable from it. . . .

The Court's opinion asserts that our language disapproving generalized grievances "invariably appears in cases where the harm at issue is not only widely shared, but is also of an abstract and indefinite nature." "Often," the Court says, "the fact that an interest is abstract and the fact that it is widely shared go hand in hand. But their association is not invariable, and where a harm is concrete, though widely shared, the Court has found 'injury in fact.'" If that is so—if concrete generalized grievances (like concrete particularized grievances) are OK, and abstract generalized grievances (like abstract particularized grievances) are bad—one must wonder why we ever developed the superfluous distinction between generalized and particularized grievances at all. But of course the Court is wrong to think that generalized grievances have only concerned us when they are abstract. One need go no further than Richardson to prove that—unless the Court believes that deprivation of information is an abstract injury, in which event this case could be disposed of on that much broader ground.

What is noticeably lacking in the Court's discussion of our generalized-grievance jurisprudence is all reference to two words that have figured in it prominently: "particularized" and "undifferentiated." *See Richardson, supra,* at 177; *Lujan,* 504 U.S., at 560, and note 1. "Particularized" means that "the injury must affect the plaintiff in a personal and individual way." *Id.* at 560, note 1. If the effect is "undifferentiated and common to all members of the public," *Richardson, supra,* at 177, the plaintiff has a "generalized grievance" that must be pursued by political, rather than judicial, means. These terms explain why it is a gross oversimplification to reduce the concept of a generalized grievance to nothing more than "the fact that [the grievance] is widely shared," thereby enabling the concept to be dismissed as a standing principle by such examples as "large numbers of individuals suffer[ing] the same common-law injury (say, a widespread mass tort), or . . . large numbers of voters suffer[ing] interference with voting rights conferred by law." The exemplified injuries are widely shared, to be sure, but each individual suffers a particularized and differentiated harm. One tort victim suffers a burnt leg, another a burnt arm—or even if both suffer burnt arms they are different arms. One voter suffers the deprivation of his franchise, another the deprivation of hers. With the generalized grievance, on the other hand, the injury or deprivation is not only widely shared but it is undifferentiated. The harm caused to Mr. Richardson by the alleged disregard of the Statement-of-Accounts Clause was precisely the same as the harm caused to everyone else: unavailability of a description of CIA expenditures. Just as the (more indirect) harm caused to Mr. Akins by the allegedly unlawful failure to enforce FECA is precisely the same as the harm caused to everyone else: unavailability of a description of AIPAC's activities.

The Constitution's line of demarcation between the Executive power and the judicial power presupposes a common understanding of the type of interest needed to sustain a "case or controversy" against the Executive in the courts. A system in which the citizenry at large could sue to compel Executive compliance with the law would be a system in which the courts, rather than the President, are given the primary responsibility to "take Care that the Laws be faithfully executed," Art. II, § 3. We do not have such a system because the common understanding of the interest necessary to sustain suit has included the requirement, affirmed in *Richardson*, that the complained-of injury be particularized and differentiated, rather than common to all the electorate. When the Executive can be directed by the courts, at the instance of any voter, to remedy a deprivation that affects the entire electorate in precisely the same way — and particularly when that deprivation (here, the unavailability of information) is one inseverable part of a larger enforcement scheme — there has occurred a shift of political responsibility to a branch designed not to protect the public at large but to protect individual rights. "To permit Congress to convert the undifferentiated public interest in executive officers' compliance with the law into an 'individual right' vindicable in the courts is to permit Congress to transfer from the President to the courts the Chief Executive's most important constitutional duty. . . ." *Lujan, supra*, at 577. If today's decision is correct, it is within the power of Congress to authorize any interested person to manage (through the courts) the Executive's enforcement of any law that includes a requirement for the filing and public availability of a piece of paper. This is not the system we have had, and is not the system we should desire. . . .

QUESTION SET 9.10

Review & Synthesis

1. According to the *Akins* majority:
   a. What status did the plaintiffs claim and what injury did they allegedly suffer?
   b. Is the Supreme Court's prohibition against "generalized grievances" constitutional or prudential in origin?
   c. Can an injury-in-fact be both particular to an individual plaintiff and widely shared by the public?
   d. What are the descriptive and doctrinal differences between concrete and abstract injuries-in-fact?
   e. Is a widely shared injury-in-fact necessarily abstract?

2. Does the Court's decision positively or negatively affect the power of the President to oversee agency conduct? In what ways?

3. Why did the *Akins* Court reach a different standing conclusion than the *Lujan* Court?

4. Was the respondents' asserted right to receive information regarding AIPAC's activities from the FEC procedural or substantive in nature? In other words, did they claim a statutory entitlement to that information (as the majority concluded), or did they assert a right to have the FEC follow certain enforcement procedures that would have enabled them to ask the FEC for that information (as Justice Scalia argued)? Is the latter any less a factual injury than the former?

5. According to Justice Scalia's dissent:
   a. Did *United States v. Richardson* hold that the prohibition against hearing generalized grievances is constitutional or prudential in origin?
   b. What was the injury-in-fact allegedly suffered by the plaintiffs?
   c. Why was this alleged injury insufficient to satisfy Article III?

Application & Analysis

1. "[I]n order to protect the privacy of individuals identified in information systems maintained by Federal agencies," the Privacy Act of 1974 provides that "it is necessary . . . to regulate the collection, maintenance, use, and dissemination of information by such agencies." § 2(a)(5). The Act gives agencies detailed instructions for managing their records. It also allows individuals who suffer "adverse effect[s]" from an agency's failure to follow those instructions to sue that agency for damages. § 2(g)(1)(D). If a court determines that the agency's failure was willful or intentional, the Act sets the minimum recovery at $1,000 plus costs and reasonable attorneys' fees.

   Casey Cornish filed for benefits under the Black Lung Benefits Act, Pub. L. No. 91-173, 83 Stat. 792 (1969), with the Office of Workers' Compensation Programs ("OWCP") in the Department of Labor. The application form called for a Social Security number ("SSN"), which OWCP used to identify the applicant's claim. OWCP printed applicants' SSNs on documents like "multi-captioned" hearing notices, which it sent to groups of claimants, their employers, and lawyers involved in their cases. As a result of this practice, Cornish's SSN was disclosed beyond the limits set by the Privacy Act.

   Invoking § 2(g)(1)(D) of the Act, Cornish filed a civil suit against the OWCP in federal district court. OWCP concedes that it violated the Privacy Act when it disclosed Cornish's SSN, but argues that her complaint must be dismissed because she suffered no factual injuries as a result. In her complaint, Cornish alleges that she was "torn all to pieces" and "greatly concerned and worried" about OWCP's unlawful disclosure of her SSN, and that these allegations alone satisfy the Article III injury-in-fact requirement.

You clerk for the judge hearing the case. Write a brief memorandum on whether Cornish has standing to sue OWCP.

2. The United States Forest Service ("FS"), is entrusted with maintaining and administering the country's system of national parks. This includes evaluating bids for limited private development of and construction in those parks. Last year, a private developer proposed the construction and operation of a massive resort complex—complete with restaurants, swimming pools, parking lots, and utilities stations—in North Cascades National Park in Washington State. FS accepted the proposal and granted the developer a three-year permit to conduct surveys and explorations in the park in connection with its preparation of a complete master plan for the resort. When completed, the complex will accommodate 14,000 daily visitors, which is significantly higher than the number the park currently accommodates. To ensure easy access to the complex, the plan calls for construction of a 30-mile four-lane highway.

Save the Parks ("STP") is an environmental group opposed to the development plan. After unsuccessful attempts to have FS solicit public feedback on the proposal through public hearings, it petitioned for a preliminary injunction against the agency in the United States District Court for the Western District of Washington. The group alleges that FS's approval of the proposal violates numerous provisions in Title 16 of the United States Code governing commercial use of federal lands. It bases its right to sue on APA § 702 and alleges that the developer's plan, if completed, "would destroy or otherwise adversely affect the scenery, natural and historic objects and wildlife of the park and would impair recreational and aesthetic enjoyment of the park for future generations." Rather than identifying individual members who would be affected by completion of the development plan, STP filed its complaint on behalf of its entire membership. FS moves to dismiss the complaint, arguing that STP lacks standing. Analyze the merits of FS's motion.

3. IRS policies deny tax-exempt status—and hence eligibility to receive charitable contributions deductible from income taxes—to racially discriminatory private schools. Its policies require that schools applying for tax-exempt status show that they "admit the students of any race to all the rights, privileges, programs, and activities generally accorded or made available to students at that school" and that they do not "discriminate on the basis of race in administration of its educational policies [or] admissions policies." Rev. Rul. 71-447 (1971). The IRS has adopted procedures to determine whether a school is racially nondiscriminatory, and failure

to comply with those procedures "will ordinarily result in the proposed revocation" of tax-exempt status. Rev. Proc. 75-50 (1975). Among other things, the Revenue Procedure 75-50 requires schools to show that they have adopted racially nondiscriminatory student admissions policies, that they have in fact complied with those policies since adoption, and that they have stated their policies in all of their admissions materials. The guidelines further provide that, once given an exemption, a school must keep specified records to demonstrate its continued compliance. Finally, the procedures expressly request that anyone with information concerning discrimination at a tax-exempt school to share it with the IRS.

African American parents have filed a class action lawsuit against the IRS Commissioner to challenge the IRS's implementation of Revenue Procedure 75-50. The class is comprised of the plaintiffs themselves and all other African American parents whose children currently attend racially segregated public schools in the United States. They allege that the IRS continues, unlawfully, to grant tax-exempt status to private schools with racially discriminatory admissions practices. Although the class representatives' children have not applied for, and hence have not been rejected by, any allegedly discriminatory private schools, they claim that the IRS's unlawful conduct harms them in three ways. First, they claim to be harmed by the fact that the IRS has failed to enforce its own procedures. Second, they claim that they are denigrated based on race when the federal government enables discrimination by tax-exempt private schools. These private schools would have to close without the charitable contributions generated by their tax-exempt status, so the IRS's failure to strip the schools of that status facilitates their discriminatory behavior. Third, they argue that the IRS's failures diminish their children's ability to be educated in racially integrated public schools. The Commissioner has moved to dismiss the complaint, countering that the plaintiffs lack standing because they have failed to allege injuries recognized by Article III of the Constitution. Assess the merits of the Commissioner's motion.

---

ii. A Practical Puzzle: Stage of Litigation and Intangible Harms

Now a practical puzzle. As made clear by *Lujan, Akins,* and the other standing cases referenced above, a federal plaintiff must demonstrate that her injury is "concrete." That is, her injury must be "real," rather than abstract, hypothetical, or speculative. How she shows this depends in part on the litigation stage at which the court tests her standing. At the motion to dismiss stage, the plaintiff need only allege in her complaint enough facts which, if true, would satisfy all the elements of the standing tests. No corroborating evidence is needed. At the summary judgment stage, she must offer more than mere allegations. She must instead produce some factual support of her injuries or, alternatively, demonstrate that there is a genuine issue of material fact regarding those injuries sufficient to avoid dismissal of her suit. At the trial stage, she must produce evidence of her injuries that convinces the fact-finder of their actuality.

The difficulty of these undertakings depends to a large extent on the type of injuries the plaintiff claims. There are two types for present purposes: tangible harms and intangible harms. Comparatively speaking, tangible harms are easier to demonstrate. They can be directly observed from evidence; the evidence itself indicates loss or damage. For example, a plaintiff who claims property damage can present that property as direct evidence of loss. The same is generally true of economic injuries which easily can be demonstrated through financial statements. Few would argue that these harms fail to satisfy Article III, however small in magnitude they are alleged to be (e.g., a bruise on the arm, a penny's worth of financial loss).

By contrast, intangible harms can be difficult to show because they cannot be directly observed or measured. It is for this reason Justice Scalia derided them as "psychic" harms existing solely in the complainant's mind. *See, e.g., Hein v Freedom from Religion Foundation*, 551 U.S. 587, 619-20 (2007) (Scalia, J., concurring). Examples include emotional harms, damage to personal or professional reputation, or lost opportunities for educational enrichment or aesthetic enjoyment. None of these interests manifest physically and thus are not susceptible to direct observation or measurement. Corroborating their diminishment therefore involves an inferential step away from whatever evidence the plaintiff offers. The best the plaintiff can do is identify evidentiary proxies that indirectly indicate loss or damage. This task becomes even more difficult where the plaintiff asserts an *imminent* intangible harm, a harm with no independent physical presence that hasn't happened yet.

Recall that the Court in *Lujan* reviewed the plaintiffs' standing at the summary judgment stage of the litigation. It concluded that they had failed to provide enough evidence to corroborate their imminent intangible harm — future inability to observe threatened animals protected by the Endangered Species Act. Had they produced some tangible markers of their intangible loss — such as plane tickets to visit the animals' habitat or concrete travel plans on specific dates — the Court might have viewed their claims more sympathetically. Of course, reasonable minds can (and did) disagree on the sufficiency of the plaintiffs' evidence. Justices Blackmun and O'Connor found the plaintiffs' affidavits (a form of testimonial evidence) sufficient to demonstrate their standing claim.

Note the broader implications of permissive or demanding evidentiary expectations for showing intangible harms. A permissive expectation gives private parties more opportunities to challenge administrative decision-making in court, whereas a more demanding expectation funnels complainants to political or other processes. One can read *Lujan* as showing how a judge's assumptions about the proper role of the courts—and on separation of powers more generally—can affect how much evidence a plaintiff will be expected to produce in support of her intangible injury claims. Also keep in mind that a harm's tangibility or intangibility does not implicate its Article III status. Recall that *Data Processing*, *Lujan*, and *Akins* all made clear that either type of harm can support a successful standing claim.

Among the Court's more recent pronouncements on the relationship between intangible harms and standing—*Spokeo, Inc. v. Robins*—arises outside of the administrative standing context. Nevertheless, many of the precedents on which it relies come out of challenges to agency action. It is therefore instructive in what plaintiffs challenging agency conduct must show to keep their lawsuits in federal court.

Spokeo, Inc. v. Robins
578 U.S. ___, 136 S. Ct. 1540 (2016)

Justice ALITO delivered the opinion of the Court.

This case presents the question whether respondent Robins has standing to maintain an action in federal court against petitioner Spokeo under the Fair Credit Reporting Act of 1970 (FCRA or Act), 84 Stat. 1127, as amended, 15 U.S.C. § 1681 *et seq.* . . .

I

The FCRA seeks to ensure "fair and accurate credit reporting." § 1681(a)(1). . . .

[It] imposes a host of requirements concerning the creation and use of consumer reports. As relevant here, the Act requires consumer reporting agencies to "follow reasonable procedures to assure maximum possible accuracy of" consumer reports, § 1681e(b); to notify providers and users of consumer information of their responsibilities under the Act, § 1681e(d); to limit the circumstances in which such agencies provide consumer reports "for employment purposes," § 1681b(b)(1); and to post toll-free numbers for consumers to request reports, § 1681j(a).

The Act also provides that "[a]ny person who willfully fails to comply with any requirement [of the Act] with respect to any [individual] is liable to that [individual]" for, among other things, either "actual damages" or statutory damages of $100 to $1,000 per violation, costs of the action and attorney's fees, and possibly punitive damages. § 1681n(a).

Spokeo is alleged to qualify as a "consumer reporting agency" under the FCRA. It operates a Web site that allows users to search for information about other individuals by name, e-mail address, or phone number. . . . According to Robins, Spokeo markets its services to a variety of users, including not only "employers who want to evaluate prospective employees," but also "those who want to investigate prospective romantic partners or seek other personal information." Persons wishing to perform a Spokeo search need not disclose their identities, and much information is available for free.

At some point in time, someone (Robins' complaint does not specify who) made a Spokeo search request for information about Robins, and Spokeo trawled its sources and generated a profile. By some means not detailed in Robins' complaint, he became aware of the contents of that profile and discovered that it contained inaccurate information. . . .

Robins filed a class-action complaint in the United States District Court for the Central District of California, claiming, among other things, that Spokeo willfully failed to comply with the FCRA requirements enumerated above.

The District Court . . . dismissed the complaint with prejudice. The court found that Robins had not "properly pled" an injury in fact, as required by Article III.

The Court of Appeals for the Ninth Circuit reversed . . . The court recognized that "the Constitution limits the power of Congress to confer standing." But the court held that those limits were honored in this case because Robins alleged that "Spokeo violated *his* statutory rights, not just the statutory rights of other people," and because his "personal interests in the handling of his credit information are individualized rather than collective" (emphasis in original). The court thus concluded that Robins' "alleged violations of [his] statutory rights [were] sufficient to satisfy the injury-in-fact requirement of Article III."

We granted certiorari.

II

A

The Constitution confers limited authority on each branch of the Federal Government. It vests Congress with enumerated "legislative Powers," Art. I, § 1; it confers upon the President "[t]he executive Power," Art. II, § 1, cl. 1; and it endows the federal courts with "[t]he judicial Power of the United States," Art. III, § 1. In order to remain faithful to this tripartite structure, the power of the Federal Judiciary may not be permitted to intrude upon the powers given to the other branches. *See Lujan v. Defenders of Wildlife*, 504 U.S. 555, 559-560 (1992).

Although the Constitution does not fully explain what is meant by "[t]he judicial Power of the United States," Art. III, § 1, it does specify that this power extends only to "Cases" and "Controversies," Art. III, § 2. And

" '[n]o principle is more fundamental to the judiciary's proper role in our system of government than the constitutional limitation of federal-court jurisdiction to actual cases or controversies.' " *Raines v. Byrd*, 521 U.S. 811, 818 (1997).

Standing to sue is a doctrine rooted in the traditional understanding of a case or controversy. The doctrine developed in our case law to ensure that federal courts do not exceed their authority as it has been traditionally understood. The doctrine limits the category of litigants empowered to maintain a lawsuit in federal court to seek redress for a legal wrong. In this way, "[t]he law of Article III standing . . . serves to prevent the judicial process from being used to usurp the powers of the political branches," *Clapper v. Amnesty Int'l USA*, 568 U.S. [398, 408] (2013); *Lujan, supra,* at 576-577 and confines the federal courts to a properly judicial role.

Our cases have established that the "irreducible constitutional minimum" of standing consists of three elements. *Lujan*, 504 U.S., at 560. The plaintiff must have (1) suffered an injury in fact, (2) that is fairly traceable to the challenged conduct of the defendant, and (3) that is likely to be redressed by a favorable judicial decision. *Id.* at 560-561; *Friends of the Earth, Inc. v. Laidlaw Environmental Services (TOC)*, 528 U.S. 167, 180-181 (2000). The plaintiff, as the party invoking federal jurisdiction, bears the burden of establishing these elements. Where, as here, a case is at the pleading stage, the plaintiff must "clearly . . . allege facts demonstrating" each element. [*Warth v. Seldin*, 422 U.S. 490, 518 (1975).]

B

This case primarily concerns injury in fact, the "[f]irst and foremost" of standing's three elements. *Steel Co. v. Citizens for Better Environment*, 523 U.S. 83, 103 (1998). Injury in fact is a constitutional requirement, and "[i]t is settled that Congress cannot erase Article III's standing requirements by statutorily granting the right to sue to a plaintiff who would not otherwise have standing." *Raines, supra,* at 820, note 3.

To establish injury in fact, a plaintiff must show that he or she suffered "an invasion of a legally protected interest" that is "concrete and particularized" and "actual or imminent, not conjectural or hypothetical." *Lujan*, 504 U.S., at 560 (internal quotation marks omitted). We discuss the particularization and concreteness requirements below.

1

For an injury to be "particularized," it "must affect the plaintiff in a personal and individual way." *Lujan*, note 1; *see also, e.g., Valley Forge, supra,* at 472 (standing requires that the plaintiff " 'personally has suffered some actual or threatened injury'"); *United States v. Richardson*, 418 U.S. 166, 177 (1974) (not "undifferentiated").[7]

Particularization is necessary to establish injury in fact, but it is not sufficient. An injury in fact must also be "concrete." Under the Ninth Circuit's analysis, however, that independent requirement was elided. As previously noted, the Ninth Circuit concluded that Robins' complaint alleges "concrete, *de facto*" injuries for essentially two reasons. First, the court noted that Robins "alleges that Spokeo violated *his* statutory rights, not just the statutory rights of other people." Second, the court wrote that "Robins's personal interests in the handling of his credit information are *individualized rather than collective*" (emphasis added). Both of these observations concern particularization, not concreteness. We have made it clear time and time again that an injury in fact must be both concrete and particularized.

A "concrete" injury must be "*de facto*"; that is, it must actually exist. When we have used the adjective "concrete," we have meant to convey the usual meaning of the term — "real," and not "abstract." Webster's Third New International Dictionary 472 (1971); Random House Dictionary of the English Language 305 (1967). Concreteness, therefore, is quite different from particularization.

2

"Concrete" is not, however, necessarily synonymous with "tangible." Although tangible injuries are perhaps easier to recognize, we have confirmed in many of our previous cases that intangible injuries can nevertheless be concrete.

In determining whether an intangible harm constitutes injury in fact, both history and the judgment of Congress play important roles. Because the doctrine of standing derives from the case-or-controversy requirement, and because that requirement in turn is grounded in historical practice, it is instructive to consider whether an alleged intangible harm has a close relationship to a harm that has traditionally been regarded as providing a basis for a lawsuit in English or American courts. In addition, because Congress is well positioned to identify intangible harms that meet minimum Article III requirements, its judgment is also instructive and important. Thus, we said in *Lujan* that Congress may "elevat[e] to the status of legally cognizable injuries concrete, *de facto* injuries that were previously inadequate in law." 504 U.S., at 578. Similarly, Justice Kennedy's concurrence in that case explained that "Congress has the power to define injuries and articulate chains of causation

---

[7] The fact that an injury may be suffered by a large number of people does not of itself make that injury a nonjusticiable generalized grievance. The victims' injuries from a mass tort, for example, are widely shared, to be sure, but each individual suffers a particularized harm.

that will give rise to a case or controversy where none existed before." *Id.* at 580 (opinion concurring in part and concurring in judgment).

Congress' role in identifying and elevating intangible harms does not mean that a plaintiff automatically satisfies the injury-in-fact requirement whenever a statute grants a person a statutory right and purports to authorize that person to sue to vindicate that right. Article III standing requires a concrete injury even in the context of a statutory violation. For that reason, Robins could not, for example, allege a bare procedural violation, divorced from any concrete harm, and satisfy the injury-in-fact requirement of Article III.

This does not mean, however, that the risk of real harm cannot satisfy the requirement of concreteness. For example, the law has long permitted recovery by certain tort victims even if their harms may be difficult to prove or measure. Just as the common law permitted suit in such instances, the violation of a procedural right granted by statute can be sufficient in some circumstances to constitute injury in fact. In other words, a plaintiff in such a case need not allege any additional harm beyond the one Congress has identified. *See Federal Election Comm'n v. Akins*, 524 U.S. 11, 20-25 (1998) (confirming that a group of voters' "inability to obtain information" that Congress had decided to make public is a sufficient injury in fact to satisfy Article III).

In the context of this particular case, these general principles tell us two things: On the one hand, Congress plainly sought to curb the dissemination of false information by adopting procedures designed to decrease that risk. On the other hand, Robins cannot satisfy the demands of Article III by alleging a bare procedural violation. A violation of one of the FCRA's procedural requirements may result in no harm. For example, even if a consumer reporting agency fails to provide the required notice to a user of the agency's consumer information, that information regardless may be entirely accurate. In addition, not all inaccuracies cause harm or present any material risk of harm. An example that comes readily to mind is an incorrect zip code. It is difficult to imagine how the dissemination of an incorrect zip code, without more, could work any concrete harm.

Because the Ninth Circuit failed to fully appreciate the distinction between concreteness and particularization, its standing analysis was incomplete. It did not address the question framed by our discussion, namely, whether the particular procedural violations alleged in this case entail a degree of risk sufficient to meet the concreteness requirement. We take no position as to whether the Ninth Circuit's ultimate conclusion — that Robins adequately alleged an injury in fact — was correct.

* * *

The judgment of the Court of Appeals is vacated, and the case is remanded for proceedings consistent with this opinion.

It is so ordered.

Justice GINSBURG, with whom Justice SOTOMAYOR joins, dissenting. . . .

I agree with much of the Court's opinion. Robins, the Court holds, meets the particularity requirement for standing under Article III. The Court acknowledges that Congress has the authority to confer rights and delineate claims for relief where none existed before. *See Federal Election Comm'n v. Akins*, 524 U.S. 11, 19-20 (1998) (holding that inability to procure information to which Congress has created a right in the Federal Election Campaign Act of 1971 qualifies as concrete injury satisfying Article III's standing requirement). Congress' connection of procedural requirements to the prevention of a substantive harm, the Court appears to agree, is "instructive and important." *See Lujan v. Defenders of Wildlife*, 504 U.S. 555, 580 (1992) (Kennedy, J., concurring in part and concurring in judgment) ("As Government programs and policies become more complex and far reaching, we must be sensitive to the articulation of new rights of action. . . .").

I part ways with the Court, however, on the necessity of a remand to determine whether Robins' particularized injury was "concrete." Judged by what we have said about "concreteness," Robins' allegations carry him across the threshold. The Court's opinion observes that time and again, our decisions have coupled the words "concrete and particularized." True, but true too, [many of the Court's] opinions do not discuss the separate offices of the terms "concrete" and "particularized."

Inspection of the Court's decisions suggests that the particularity requirement bars complaints raising generalized grievances, seeking relief that no more benefits the plaintiff than it does the public at large. *See,* e.g., *Lujan*, 504 U.S., at 573-574 (a plaintiff "seeking relief that no more directly and tangibly benefits him than it does the public at large does not state an Article III case or controversy" (punctuation omitted)). Robins' claim does not present a question of that character. He seeks redress, not for harm to the citizenry, but for Spokeo's spread of misinformation specifically about him.

Concreteness as a discrete requirement for standing, the Court's decisions indicate, refers to the reality of an injury, harm that is real, not abstract, but not necessarily tangible. Illustrative opinions include *Akins*, 524 U.S., at 20 ("[C]ourts will not pass upon abstract, intellectual problems, but adjudicate concrete, living contests between adversaries." (internal quotation marks and alterations omitted)); *Simon v. Eastern Ky. Welfare Rights Organization*, 426 U.S. 26, 40 (1976) ("organization's abstract concern . . . does not substitute for the concrete injury required by Art. III"); *Coleman v. Miller*, 307 U.S. 433, 460 (1939) (opinion of Frankfurter, J.) ("[I]t [is] not for courts to pass upon . . . abstract, intellectual problems but only . . . concrete, living contest[s] between adversaries call[ing] for the arbitrament of law.").

Robins would not qualify, the Court observes, if he alleged a "bare" procedural violation, one that results in no harm, for example, "an incorrect zip code." Far from an incorrect zip code, Robins complains of misinformation about his education, family situation, and economic status, inaccurate representations that could affect his fortune in the job market. The FCRA's procedural requirements aimed to prevent such harm. I therefore see no utility in returning this case to the Ninth Circuit to underscore what Robins' complaint already conveys concretely: Spokeo's misinformation "cause[s] actual harm to [his] employment prospects."

* * *

For the reasons stated, I would affirm the Ninth Circuit's judgment.

QUESTION SET 9.11

Review & Synthesis

1. Justice Alito (writing for the majority) and Justice Ginsburg (writing in dissent) disagreed on whether Robins' injury was sufficiently "concrete" to be recognized by Article III. Is this because they had different views on whether failure to follow the procedures established by the FCRA constituted a factual injury for constitutional purposes? Did Justice Alito seem to believe that such failures did not automatically cause diminishment, whereas Justice Ginsburg did? In this respect, how does Justice Alito's reasoning compare with the majority opinion in *FEC v. Akins*?

2. Do you think that separating the "concreteness" inquiry from the "particularity" inquiry for injury-in-fact analysis serves the separation-of-powers goal of preventing the Judiciary from encroaching on the prerogatives of the other federal Branches? Note that this is a different question than whether separating the two requirements serves to reduce the cases heard by the Judiciary; increasing the rigor of any jurisdictional test would have that effect. Rather, does insisting on a distinct concreteness inquiry stop the courts from exercising executive or legislative power, or from diminishing the powers of the other Branches?

Application & Analysis

1. For each of the following scenarios, indicate whether the plaintiff's alleged harm is: (1) actual or imminent; (2) tangible or intangible; (3) particular and/or undifferentiated; and (4) abstract or concrete.
   a. Physical harm to property caused by defendant driving into plaintiff's car with his truck.
   b. Economic harm caused by expected agency refusal to pay statutorily created subsidy. Plaintiff qualifies for subsidy but has not submitted the required application for it.

c. Expected increase in competition caused by agency's decision to license competitor in plaintiff's geographic market. Plaintiff was sole market participant before agency's decision and believes that the licensee does not meet the statutory requirements for receiving the license.

d. Aesthetic harm caused by agency's decision to permit private drilling in a national park. Plaintiff has traveled to that national park in the past, would like to do so again, and has purchased plane tickets to the airport nearest the park. Drilling has not yet commenced.

e. Procedural harm caused by agency's failure to notify plaintiff of the date of an upcoming evidentiary hearing before an administrative law judge in the form required by statute. Plaintiff learned of the hearing date through unrelated correspondence with agency attorneys.

---

b. Causation

Whereas the injury-in-fact requirement deals with the particularity, actuality, and imminence of the harm alleged by a federal plaintiff, causation addresses the connection between that alleged harm and an agency's actions (or failures to act). Whatever the type of injury claimed by the plaintiff—actual tangible, actual intangible, imminent tangible, imminent intangible—she must show a causal connection between it and the agency's alleged conduct. That connection is established where the defendant's conduct substantially increases the risk of injury to the plaintiff. Courts have adopted no definitive set of factors for establishing it, nor have they adopted a consistent method for weighing the factors they consider from case to case. Courts approach causation intuitively and probabilistically. Scientific certainty is never required. Instead, the ageny's actions must *seem*, based on experience and common sense, to have resulted in the plaintiff's claimed injury. Courts are accordingly much more likely to find causation where "the causal chain is relatively direct, and the sequence of events between the act and the injury is based on logically plausible relationships." 3 Richard Pierce, Jr., Administrative Law Treatise § 16.5 (2010). By contrast, courts are more likely to reject causation claims where the connection between the defendant's alleged conduct and the claimed harm is "insubstantial, remote, tenuous, or speculative." *Id.*

Courts require relatively little proof of causation in run-of-the-mill disputes. To return to a previous example, suppose a plaintiff contests the IRS's calculation of her federal income tax liability. Her alleged factual harm (a reduction in her financial resources) flows directly from the IRS's alleged actions (its miscalculation of her income taxes). It seems clear that the IRS's miscalculation is itself the reason for her increased tax bill, so courts will not ask for additional evidence to support the causal chain.

Now suppose the plaintiff sues not to challenge her personal tax liability, but to challenge how the IRS has decided to tax some third party. Say she believes that the IRS has improperly granted tax-exempt status to a private organization. She argues that the IRS's mistake led the organization to act in some way that has damaged her interests. In other words, the organization would not have caused her harm had the IRS denied it tax-exempt status. This is the type of indirect causal chain routinely seen in citizen suits against agencies, which looks quite different than those we see in run-of-the-mill cases. The plaintiff can't sue the organization directly because the organization has broken no law; it has simply followed the rules as interpreted by the IRS. She is therefore left to proffer a more attenuated causal chain: the IRS's conduct affected the organization, which responded in a way that negatively affected her. Arguments like this — which would be brought under APA § 702 or some other citizen-suit provision — involve choices by some party (here, the organization) who is not itself before the court. How does the court know that the organization's injurious actions resulted from the IRS's conduct? Could the organization's actions have been influenced by factors completely unrelated to its tax-exempt status? Is it possible that the organization would have acted exactly the same way had the IRS refused to grant it tax-exempt status in the first place? As such causal uncertainties pile up, the link between the agency's decision and the plaintiff's injury grows more speculative. The more speculative the claim of causation, the less likely its acceptance by the courts. At least, that's how a reasonable person might expect things to work.

In reality, the Court's approach to causation in citizen suits has fallen short of perfect consistency. It has clearly concluded that competitor claims of indirect harm do not necessarily pose fatal constitutional causation problems. *See, e.g., Sanders Brothers.* It has seemingly reached the same conclusion in suits brought by citizens, taxpayers, voters, and environmental organizations. *See, e.g., FEC v. Akins, Flast v. Cohen, Lujan v. National Wildlife Foundation.* Like the example in the preceding paragraph, the strength of the causal link in each of these cases depended on at least one discretionary choice by a party other than the plaintiff or the defendant. The Court nevertheless felt comfortable assuming that these third-party choices would be made in a way that supported, rather than undermined, the plaintiffs' respective standing claims.

The Court's approach to more attenuated causation claims is harder to characterize, as it has rejected some and accepted others. Two cases illustrate this point. The first is the case of *United States v. Students Challenging Regulatory Agency Procedures (SCRAP)*, 412 U.S. 669 (1973). The now-defunct Interstate Commerce Commission ("ICC") allowed railroads to levy a freight surcharge without first determining the environmental impact of doing so. Pursuant to APA § 702, SCRAP (a group of George Washington University Law School students) claimed the ICC's decision caused its members aesthetic, recreational, and economic injury. SCRAP's complaint employed the following causal syllogism to connect the agency's actions with these alleged harms: "a general rate increase would allegedly cause increased use of nonrecyclable commodities as compared to recyclable goods, thus resulting in the need to use more natural resources to produce such goods, some of which resources might be taken from the Washington area, and resulting in more refuse that might be discarded in national parks in the Washington area." *Id.* at 688.

In Context

As with injuries-in-fact, there's a practical component to asserting causation. It's easier to simply allege causation in a complaint than it is to prove causation at summary judgment or trial. Accordingly, the difficulty of showing a causal chain depends in some measure on the stage of the judicial proceedings.

At the outset, the Court emphasized that "pleadings must be something more than an ingenious academic exercise in the conceivable" and that SCRAP must do more than simply "imagine circumstances in which [its members] could be affected by the agency's action." Rather, "the allegations [in the complaint] must be true and capable of proof at trial." *Id.* at 688-89. It may have been that SCRAP's assertions were untrue or impossible to support with evidence, as the ICC argued. This would have mattered had the district court ruled for the ICC on summary judgment. Since the district court dismissed the case at the motion to dismiss phase, however, the Supreme Court only considered the adequacy of SCRAP's causal chain *allegations.* Those allegations, the Court said, were sufficient. The implication was that SCRAP's causal argument was plausible as a legal matter. The Court clearly believed that the causal chain here was attenuated, as it hinged on the likelihood of numerous third-party reactions and decisions about which the Court could have no certainty. It nevertheless concluded that each step in SCRAP's proffered causal chain could ultimately connect the ICC's decision to SCRAP's alleged harm in a way that satisfied Article III. Whatever the conceptual minimum for constitutionally plausible causation, SCRAP had cleared it.

Compare this with the Court's well-known decision in *Allen v. Wright*, 468 U.S. 737 (1984). Plaintiffs, African American parents with children attending segregated public schools, claimed that the IRS failed to deny tax-exempt status to racially discriminatory private schools as required by federal law. They argued that they and their children suffered from this failure in two distinct ways: (1) they experienced denigration because the government provided financial aid and other support to racially discriminatory schools; and (2) their children had fewer opportunities to attend racially desegregated schools as required by federal law. The Court dismissed the first harm as no harm at all. Writing for the majority, Justice O'Connor characterized it as an equal treatment injury, which federal courts entertain only if a plaintiff has individually suffered it. She found no indication that the plaintiffs had done so. *Id.* at 755. While the Court agreed that the second harm constituted an Article III injury-in-fact, it found insufficient indication that the IRS caused it. As with *SCRAP*, *Allen* was not a case about direct causal harm. The private schools simply enjoyed the tax-exempt status the IRS had not rescinded. What's more, the plaintiff-parents had never sought admission of their children to those allegedly discriminatory private schools. According to the complaint, the children's opportunity for desegregated education was instead caused by white school children leaving the public schools, which was enabled by the operation of the private schools, which was in turn enabled by the IRS's failure to enforce federal desegregation policy against the private schools. This causal chain seemed no more speculative (and perhaps even more plausible) than the one the Court accepted in *SCRAP*. Justice O'Connor nevertheless found numerous reasons to reject it: there was no allegation that enough private schools adopted racially discriminatory admissions policies to appreciably affect the level of white public school attendance in the plaintiffs' communities; it was speculative whether the withdrawal of the tax exemption from any particular school would lead it to change its admissions policies; it was unknown whether any parent would transfer his or her child to a public school if that child's private school lost its tax-exempt status; it was unclear whether enough parents and school officials would make decisions to significantly impact the demographics of the public schools if the private schools lost their exemptions. *Id.* at 758-59. In sum, the Court did not feel comfortable assuming that third parties—the parents of white school children and the officials running the private schools they attended—would make discretionary decisions that supported the plaintiffs' standing. Frustratingly, the Court made no attempt to explain why these uncertainties caused it such discomfort. It simply assumed that their legal insufficiency was self-evident.

Allen is also notable for its discussion of how separation of powers affects the law of standing. Like generous injury-in-fact approaches, expansive views of causation may lead federal courts into disputes they are ill-suited to resolve. Justice O'Connor observed that allowing standing in a case like this "would pave the way generally for suits challenging, not specifically identifiable Government violations of law, but the particular programs agencies establish to carry out their legal obligations. Such suits, even when premised on allegations of several instances of violations of law, are rarely if ever appropriate for federal-court adjudication." *Id.* at 759-60. She added that a broader pernicious effect would have been the erosion of Presidential power: "[S]eparation of powers [] counsels against recognizing standing in a case brought, not to enforce specific legal obligations whose violation works a direct harm, but to seek a restructuring of the apparatus established by the Executive Branch to fulfill its legal duties." *Id.* at 760. Of course, any limitation on standing would leave the President free to execute the laws as he or she sees fit. The question, it seems, is not *whether* there should be such limitations but *how extensive* those limitations should be.

Consider the following case, on which Justice O'Connor drew much of her reasoning in *Allen*. As you read it, try to identify the factors that inform the Court's causation judgment. How did the Court weigh the uncertainties that necessarily come with the plaintiff's claims of indirect injury? Can you infer a test or glean some guidance from its analysis, or do you think the Court's approach to the causation claims was more a matter of judgment that cannot be systematized? What role, if any, did separation-of-powers concerns play in the majority's conclusions?

Simon v. Eastern Kentucky Welfare Rights Organization ["EKWRO"]
426 U.S. 26 (1976)

Mr. Justice POWELL delivered the opinion of the Court.

Several indigents and organizations composed of indigents brought this suit against the Secretary of the Treasury and the Commissioner of Internal Revenue. They asserted that the Internal Revenue Service (IRS) violated the Internal Revenue Code of 1954 (Code) and the Administrative Procedure Act (APA) by issuing a Revenue Ruling allowing favorable tax treatment to a nonprofit hospital that offered only emergency-room services to indigents. We conclude that these plaintiffs lack standing to bring this suit.

I

The Code . . . accords advantageous treatment to several types of non-profit corporations, including exemption of their income from taxation and deductibility by benefactors of the amounts of their donations. Nonprofit hospitals have never received these benefits as a favored general category, but an individual nonprofit hospital has been able to claim them if it could qualify as a corporation "organized and operated exclusively for . . . charitable . . . purposes" within the meaning of § 501(c)(3) of the Code, 26 U.S.C. § 501(c)(3). As the Code does not define the term "Charitable," the status of each nonprofit hospital is determined on a case-by-case basis by the IRS.

In recognition of the need of nonprofit hospitals for some guidelines on qualification as "charitable" corporations, the IRS in 1956 issued Revenue Ruling 56-185. This Ruling [stated] "that the term 'charitable' in its legal sense and as it is used in § 501(c) (3) of the Code contemplates an implied public trust constituted for some public benefit. . . ." In addition, the Ruling set out [that a hospital would be considered "charitable" if, among other things, it was "operated to the extent of its financial ability for those not able to pay for the services rendered and not exclusively for those who are able and expected to pay."]

Revenue Ruling 56-185 remained the announced policy with respect to a nonprofit hospital's "charitable" status for 13 years, until the IRS issued Revenue Ruling 69-545 on November 3, 1969. This new Ruling described two unidentified hospitals, referred to simply as Hospital A and Hospital B, which differed significantly in both corporate structure and operating policies. The description of Hospital A included the following paragraph:

> The hospital operates a full time emergency room and no one requiring emergency care is denied treatment. The hospital otherwise ordinarily limits admissions to those who can pay the cost of their hospitalization, either themselves, or through private health insurance, or with the aid of public programs such as Medicare. Patients who cannot meet the financial requirements for admission are ordinarily referred to another hospital in the community that does serve indigent patients.

Despite Hospital A's apparent failure to operate "to the extent of its financial ability for those not able to pay for the services rendered," as required by Revenue Ruling 56-185, the IRS in this new Ruling held Hospital A exempt as a charitable corporation under s 501(c)(3). Noting that Revenue Ruling 56-185 had set out requirements for serving indigents "more restrictive" than those applied to Hospital A, the IRS stated that "Revenue Ruling 56-185 is hereby modified to remove therefrom the requirements relating to caring for patients without charge or at rates below cost."

II

Issuance of Revenue Ruling 69-545 led to the filing of this suit . . . in the United States District Court for the District of Columbia, by a group of organizations and individuals. The plaintiff organizations described themselves as an unincorporated association and several nonprofit corporations each of which included low-income persons among its members and represented the interests of all such persons in obtaining hospital care and services. The 12 individual plaintiffs described themselves as subsisting below the poverty income levels established by the Federal Government and suffering from medical conditions requiring hospital services. The organizations sued on behalf of their members, and each individual sued on his own behalf and as representative of all other persons similarly situated.

Each of the individuals described an occasion on which he or a member of his family had been disadvantaged in seeking needed hospital services because of indigency. Most involved the refusal of a hospital to admit the person because of his inability to pay a deposit or an advance fee, even though in some instances the person was enrolled in the Medicare program. At least one plaintiff was denied emergency-room treatment because of his inability to pay immediately. And another was treated in the emergency room but then billed and threatened with suit although his indigency had been known at the time of treatment.

According to the complaint, each of the hospitals involved in these incidents had been determined by the Secretary and the Commissioner to be a tax-exempt charitable corporation, and each received substantial private contributions. The Secretary and the Commissioner were the only defendants. The complaint alleged that by extending tax benefits to such hospitals despite their refusals fully to serve the indigent, the defendants were "encouraging" the hospitals to deny services to the individual plaintiffs and to the members and clients of the plaintiff organizations. Those persons were alleged to be suffering "injury in their opportunity and ability to receive hospital services in nonprofit hospitals which receive . . . benefits . . . as 'charitable' organizations" under the Code. They also were alleged to be among the intended beneficiaries of the Code sections that grant favorable tax treatment to "charitable" organizations.

Plaintiffs made two principal claims. The first was that in issuing Revenue Ruling 69-545 the defendants had violated the Code, and that in granting charitable-corporation treatment to nonprofit hospitals that refused fully to serve indigents the defendants continued the violation. . . . [The] second claim was that the issuance of Revenue Ruling 69-545 without a public hearing and an opportunity for submission of views had violated the rulemaking procedures of the APA, 5 U.S.C. § 553. The theory of this claim was that the Ruling should be considered a "substantive" rule as opposed to the "interpretative" type of rule that is exempted from the requirements of § 553. Plaintiffs sought various forms of declaratory and injunctive relief. . . .

IV

No principle is more fundamental to the judiciary's proper role in our system of government than the constitutional limitation of federal-court jurisdiction to actual cases or controversies. See *Flast v. Cohen*, 392 U.S. 83, 95 (1968). The concept of standing is part of this limitation. Unlike other associated doctrines, for example, that which restrains federal courts from deciding political questions, standing "focuses on the party seeking to get his complaint before a federal court and not on the issues he wishes to have adjudicated." *Id.* at 99. . . . [W]hen a plaintiff's standing is brought into issue the relevant inquiry is whether, assuming justiciability of the claim, the plaintiff has shown an injury to himself that is likely to be redressed by a favorable decision. Absent such a showing, exercise of its power by a federal court would be gratuitous and thus inconsistent with the Art. III limitation.

Respondents brought this action under § 10 of the APA, 5 U.S.C. § 702, which gives a right to judicial review to any person "adversely affected or aggrieved by agency action within the meaning of a relevant statute." In *Data Processing Service v. Camp*, 397 U.S. 150 (1969), this Court held the constitutional standing requirement under this section to be allegations which, if true, would establish that the plaintiff had been injured in fact by the action he sought to have reviewed. Reduction of the threshold requirement to actual injury redressable by the court represented a substantial broadening of access to the federal courts over that previously thought to be the constitutional minimum under this statute. But, as this Court emphasized in *Sierra Club v. Morton*, 405 U.S. 727, 738 (1972), "broadening the categories of injury that may be alleged in support of standing is a different matter from abandoning the requirement that the party seeking review must himself have suffered an injury." *See also United States v. Richardson*, 418 U.S. 166, 194 (1974) (Powell, J., concurring). The necessity that the plaintiff who seeks to invoke judicial power stand to profit in some personal interest remains an Art. III requirement. A federal court cannot ignore this requirement without overstepping its assigned role in our system of adjudicating only actual cases and controversies. It is according to this settled principle that the allegations of both the individual respondents and the respondent organizations must be tested for sufficiency. . . .

B

The obvious interest of all respondents, to which they claim actual injury, is that of access to hospital services. In one sense, of course, they have suffered injury to that interest. The complaint alleges specific occasions on which each of the individual respondents sought but was denied hospital services solely due to his indigency, and in at least some of the cases it is clear that the needed treatment was unavailable, as a practical matter, anywhere else. The complaint also alleges that members of the respondent organizations need hospital services but live in communities in which the private hospitals do not serve indigents. We thus assume, for purpose of analysis, that some members have been denied service. But injury at the hands of a hospital is insufficient by itself to establish a case or controversy in the context of this suit, for no hospital is a defendant. The only defendants are officials of the Department of the Treasury, and the only claims of illegal action respondents desire the courts to adjudicate are charged to those officials. . . . [T]he "case or controversy" limitation of Art. III still requires that a federal court act only to redress injury that fairly can be traced to the challenged action of the defendant, and not injury that results from the independent action of some third party not before the court.

The complaint here alleged only that petitioners, by the adoption of Revenue Ruling 69-545, had "encouraged" hospitals to deny services to indigents. The implicit corollary of this allegation is that a grant of respondents' requested relief, resulting in a requirement that all hospitals serve indigents as a condition to favorable tax treatment, would "discourage" hospitals from denying their services to respondents. But it does not follow from the allegation and its corollary that the denial of access to hospital services in fact results from petitioners' new Ruling, or that a court-ordered return by petitioners to their previous policy would result in these respondents' receiving the hospital services they desire. It is purely speculative whether the denials of service specified in the complaint fairly can be traced to petitioners' "encouragement" or instead result from decisions made by the hospitals without regard to the tax implications. . . .

. . . As stated in *Warth*, [the controlling] principle is that indirectness of injury, while not necessarily fatal to standing, "may make it substantially more difficult to meet the minimum requirement of Art. III: To establish that, in fact, the asserted injury was the consequence of the defendants' actions, or that prospective relief will remove the harm." 422 U.S., at 505. Respondents have failed to carry this burden. Speculative inferences are necessary to connect their injury to the challenged actions of petitioners.[25] . . . A federal court, properly cognizant the Art. III limitation upon its jurisdiction, must require more than respondents have shown before proceeding to the merits.

Accordingly, the judgment of the Court of Appeals is vacated, and the cause is remanded to the District Court with instructions to dismiss the complaint.

It is so ordered.

[Justice STEVENS did not participate in the Court's decision, and Justice STEWART's concurring opinion is omitted.]

Mr. Justice BRENNAN, with whom Mr. Justice MARSHALL joins, concurring in the judgment.

I agree that in this litigation as it is presently postured, respondents have not met their burden of establishing a concrete and reviewable controversy between themselves and the Government with respect to the disputed Revenue Ruling. That is, however, the full extent of my agreement with the

[25] The courts below erroneously believed that *United States v. SCRAP*, supported respondents' standing. In *SCRAP*, although the injury was indirect and "the Court was asked to follow (an) attenuated line of causation," 412 U.S., at 688, the complaint nevertheless "alleged a specific and perceptible harm" flowing from the agency action. *Id.* at 689. Such a complaint withstood a motion to dismiss, although it might not have survived challenge on a motion for summary judgment. *Id.*, and n. 15. But in this case the complaint is insufficient even to survive a motion to dismiss, for it fails to allege an injury that fairly can be traced to petitioners' challenged action.

Our decision is also consistent with *Data Processing Service v. Camp*, 397 U.S. 150 (1969). . . . The complaint in *Data Processing* alleged injury that was directly traceable to the action of the defendant federal official, for it complained of injurious competition that would have been illegal without that action. Similarly, the complaint in . . . *Barlow v. Collins*, 397 U.S. 159, was sufficient because it alleged extortionate demands by plaintiffs' landlord made possible only by the challenged action of the defendant federal official. In the instant case respondents' injuries might have occurred even in the absence of the IRS Ruling that they challenge; whether the injuries fairly can be traced to that Ruling depends upon unalleged and unknown facts about the relevant hospitals.

Court in this case. I must dissent from the Court's reasoning on the standing issue, reasoning that is unjustifiable under any proper theory of standing and clearly contrary to the relevant precedents. . . .

Our previous decisions concerning standing to sue under the Administrative Procedure Act conclusively show that the injury in fact demanded is the constitutional minimum . . . the allegation of such a "personal stake in the outcome of the controversy as to assure" concrete adverseness. *Sierra Club v. Morton, supra,* 405 U.S., at 732-733; *Data Processing Service v. Camp, supra,* 397 U.S., at 151-152. True, the Court has required that the person seeking review allege that he personally has suffered or will suffer the injury sought to be avoided. But there can be no doubt that respondents here, by demonstrating a connection between the disputed Ruling and the hospitals affecting them, could have adequately served the policy implicated by [this] pleading requirement of *Sierra Club* putting "the decision as to whether review will be sought in the hands of those who have a direct stake in the outcome." *Ibid.* In such a case respondents would not be attempting merely to "vindicate their own value preferences through the judicial process." *Ibid.* If such a showing were made, a real and recognizable harm to a tangible interest would have been alleged, indeed more so than we have required in other circumstances. *United States v. SCRAP, supra,* 412 U.S. 669; *Sierra Club v. Morton, supra,* 405 U.S. 727; *cf. Barlow v. Collins, supra,* 397 U.S., at 163. . . .

Furthermore, our decisions regarding standing to sue in actions brought under the Administrative Procedure Act make plain that standing is not to be denied merely because the ultimate harm alleged is a threatened future one rather than an accomplished fact. *United States v. SCRAP, supra; Sierra Club v. Morton, supra.* Nor has the fact that the administrative action ultimately affects the complaining party only through responses to incentives by third parties been fatal to the standing of those who would challenge that action. *United States v. SCRAP, supra; Barlow v. Collins, supra.* And the ultimate harm to respondents threatened here is obviously much more "direct and perceptible" and the "line of causation" less "attenuated" than that found sufficient for standing in *United States v. SCRAP,* 412 U.S., at 688.

Certainly the Court's attempted distinction of *SCRAP* will not "wash." The Court states that in *SCRAP,* "although the injury was indirect and 'the Court was asked to follow (an) attenuated line of causation,' . . . the complaint nevertheless 'alleged a specific and perceptible harm' flowing from the agency action." The instant case is different, the Court says, because the complaint "fails to allege an injury that fairly can be traced" to the allegedly wrongful action. I find it simply impossible fairly and meaningfully to differentiate between the allegations of the two sets of pleadings. The Court complains that "whether the injuries fairly can be traced to (the disputed) Ruling depends upon unalleged and unknown facts about the relevant hospitals." It is obvious that the complaint in *SCRAP* lacked precisely the same specific factual allegations; there, however, the Court's response was much more in keeping with modern notions of civil procedure. 412 U.S., at 689-690, and note 15. . . .

QUESTION SET 9.12

Review & Synthesis

1. Describe the injury-in-fact EKWRO alleged the IRS caused with its tax ruling. Why did EKWRO not file a lawsuit against the hospitals that denied care to the indigent patients it represented?

2. Did the indigent patients represented by EKWRO have personal legal rights to be protected from the harm caused by being denied medical care by the hospitals? If not, what was the source of EKWRO's procedural right to file suit?

3. List all of the links in the causal chain between EKWRO's alleged injury-in-fact and the IRS' conduct. Identify the discretionary third-party choices within this causal chain. Why did the Court conclude EKWRO's causation narrative was constitutionally insufficient? Do you agree with the majority that EKWRO's argument is distinguishable from the one the Court accepted in *SCRAP*?

Application & Analysis

1. Carmen Li is a restauranteur and hotelier. She owns numerous high-end hotels, restaurants, and event spaces in New York City, one of the most dynamic, competitive, and expensive hospitality markets in the world. Travel writers in numerous high-circulation publications have often acknowledged the desirability of Li's hotels, describing them as "downtown landmarks known for their stylish accommodations and nightlife," "essential New York" hotels, and "neighborhood gamechangers." Her restaurants have received similar praise, with one being described as one of New York City's best hotel restaurants with "essential fresco dining." Diners at Li's restaurants and guests at her hotels frequently include diplomats and other foreign officials traveling on official business. When they do so, they use their governments' funds to pay for their meals and accommodations.

    Li has filed a lawsuit in the United States District Court for the Southern District of New York against Treasury Secretary Gordon Ward. Her complaint first asserts that her New York properties and restaurants directly compete with those owned by the Secretary or those from which the Secretary currently derives personal financial benefit. An expert hired by Li to conduct a market analysis filed a sworn declaration that Li's hotels directly compete with the Secretary's because they attract customers from the same pool of foreign government officials. Second, the complaint alleges that Li's properties—while still profitable—are losing and will continue to lose business as a direct result of their competition with the Secretary's properties. Third, Li asserts that this lost business and resultant revenue decline is directly and primarily traceable to the Secretary's attainment of high federal office, rather than to other competitive dynamics in the New York City hospitality market. She claims that the Secretary has publicly encouraged government officials to patronize his properties rather than those owned by his competitors (though the complaint does not allege that he made any public references to Li's properties) and that the Secretary is inclined to favor those governments who respond positively to that encouragement. The complaint then cites purported admissions by foreign officials that they have been influenced by the Secretary's statements. It also alleges that foreign officials' patronage of Mr. Ward's establishments has increased since he was appointed Treasury Secretary.

Finally, the complaint asserts that the Secretary's receipt of these increased revenues violates the Foreign Influence Prevention Act of 1975 ("FIPA"). FIPA states, in relevant part, that "[N]o Person holding any office under the United States shall, without the explicit consent of Congress, accept any present, salary, fee, honorarium, profit, office, or title, of any kind whatever, from any foreign government, or any official, representative, or consul of any foreign government." The complaint asserts that the Secretary has never sought, let alone received, such congressional consent. The legislative history produced in connection with FIPA's passage repeatedly expressed concern over the custom in some countries of bestowing gifts and money on foreign officials. More specifically, the conference report reconciling the House and Senate versions of the bill stated that Congress was chiefly motivated to protect Executive Branch decision-making from actual or apparent foreign corruption or undue influence. Li asks the district court to "enjoin Defendant from violating the FIPA" and to "require Defendant to release any and all financial records sufficient to confirm that Defendant is not engaging in any further transactions that would violate the FIPA."

You are an associate at the law firm representing the Secretary in this matter, and your firm is preparing a motion to dismiss the complaint. The lead partner is confident that Li's claim is nonjusticiable, and so doubts it would survive a well-argued motion. She accordingly has asked you to scrutinize both the strengths and the weaknesses of Li's claim for whether it satisfies the requirements of constitutional standing. Write a memorandum to the partner detailing your analysis.

c. Redressability

Redressability—the last of the constitutional standing requirements—asks whether a judicial decision in the plaintiff's favor would prevent or compensate for the harm she claims. The Supreme Court originally framed it as simply an aspect of causation. If the defendant had caused the plaintiff's injury, it seemed safe to assume that ordering the defendant to compensate her or to behave a certain way toward her would necessarily remedy it. *See, e.g., Duke Power Co. v. Carolina Environmental Study Group, Inc.*, 438 U.S. 59, 74 (1978) (equating causation and redressability). One would find this direct link between the plaintiff's harm and a favorable court decision in almost all traditional lawsuits between private parties.

The Court eventually separated causation and redressability when it became clear that they address different concerns. The Court first distinguished the two in *Allen v. Wright*, explaining that "the former examines the causal connection between the assertedly unlawful conduct and the alleged injury, whereas the latter examines the causal connection between the alleged injury and the judicial relief requested." 468 U.S. 737, 753 n.19 (1984). This connection between injury and relief has two aspects. First, unsuccessful defendants must redress the harms they cause, not the harms they had no hand in causing. Second, the relief requested must be likely (though not necessarily certain) to prevent or ameliorate the plaintiff's stated injury. Article III won't be satisfied if the requested relief is unlikely to address the plaintiff's concerns.

A notable example of this second point is *Linda R.S. v. Richard D.*, 410 U.S. 614 (1973). A Texas district attorney allegedly had a policy of bringing nonsupport prosecutions exclusively against fathers of children born in wedlock. A mother of a child born out of wedlock sought a declaration that this alleged policy violated the Fourteenth Amendment's Equal Protection Clause and an injunction preventing the district attorney from refusing to prosecute fathers of children born out of wedlock. The Court rejected her standing claim. Writing for the majority, Justice Thurgood Marshall found a constitutionally insufficient nexus between what he believed was the plaintiff's real injury (nonpayment of child support) and her requested remedy (a declaration and an injunction against the district attorney). According to Justice Marshall, "the requested relief . . . would result only in the jailing of the child's father. The prospect that prosecution will, at least in the future, result in payment of support can, at best, be termed only speculative." *Id.* at 618. Put another way, the Court was unwilling to assume that the father would respond to his prosecution—or even its threat—by paying child support. As he was not a party to the case and thus not subject to the court's jurisdiction, whether he paid or not was a matter of his discretion. The Court apparently thought it was unlikely that a judgment for Linda R. S. would redress her injury.

Justice Marshall also pointed to another basis for his conclusion, noting that "a citizen lacks standing to contest the policies of the prosecuting authority when he himself is neither prosecuted nor threatened with prosecution." *Id.* at 619. Accordingly, "in American jurisprudence . . . a private citizen lacks a judicially cognizable interest in the prosecution or nonprosecution of another." *Id. Linda R.S.* involved a state (Texas) prosecution policy. Applied in the federal context, this principle could be an argument against judicial adoption of a generous redressability approach. Prosecutorial discretion is the quintessence of the federal executive power vested in the President by Article II. Aside from the fact that the APA does not generally allow judicial review of decisions committed to agency discretion by law—*see* APA § 701(a)(2), *Heckler v. Chaney*, and discussion starting on page 693— permitting private parties to challenge the exercise of this discretion could raise separation of powers concerns.

As in *Linda R.S.*, courts often question the link between alleged harms and requested remedies in citizen-suits against agencies. Recall how causal chains in citizen-suits work: the plaintiff alleges that an agency's decision permitted or incentivized some third party to cause her factual harm. Redressability chains in citizen-suits similarly run through third parties: if a court orders the agency to reverse its decision, the third party will respond by refraining from or ceasing its allegedly harmful conduct. Because redress of the plaintiff's injury depends on how the third party responds to the agency's course reversal, it is possible that a judgment for the plaintiff against the agency would prove unavailing. Since the effectiveness of the plaintiff's requested remedy would depend on the reactions of a third party who is outside of the court's direct control, a court might deem the requested remedy too speculative to satisfy Article III.

Lujan v. Defenders of Wildlife—one of the citizen-suits we considered in the injury-in-fact portion of this chapter—touched on how third parties might respond to judgments rendered against agencies. Recall the plaintiffs' claim that the Endangered Species Act ("ESA") required federal agencies to consult with the Interior Secretary before taking any domestic or foreign actions that might jeopardize protected animal species. The Secretary interpreted the ESA more narrowly and promulgated regulations limiting required consultation to domestic agency actions. The plaintiffs sued, arguing that the Secretary's erroneous interpretation would hasten the extinction of species living outside of the United States. This, in turn, would harm their interest in observing those species in the future. *Lujan v. Defenders of Wildlife*, 504 U.S. 555, 562 (1992). Part III-B of the Court's opinion—for which Justice Scalia could secure only three other votes—emphasized that "[t]he most obvious problem in the present case is redressability."

Cross-Reference

Justice Scalia's argument here—that non-parties are not legally bound to follow a court's rulings—sounds like the argument made by Justice Fortas in the *Wyman-Gordon* case. *See* Chapter 4. While this may be true as a technical matter, is it true as a practical matter?

Id. at 568. Rather than suing the agencies that partially funded or over-saw the allegedly damaging projects—e.g., the Agency for International Development ("AID") and the U.S. Bureau of Reclamation—the plaintiffs sued the Interior Secretary. Justice Scalia wasn't convinced that the agencies were required to follow the Secretary's regulation implementing the ESA consultation requirement. The statutory language did not provide a clear answer on the Secretary's power to bind other agencies, and both the Solicitor General and AID had argued that the regulation was not binding. If the Secretary lacked this legal authority, ordering him to include foreign agency actions in his regulation would not necessarily have resulted in the consultation sought by the plaintiffs. Justice Scalia then went further: even a determination that the agencies *were* statutorily obligated to follow the Secretary's regulation would not have availed the plaintiffs. "[The agencies] were not parties to the suit, and there is no reason they should be obliged to honor an incidental legal determination the suit produced." *Id.* at 569. In other words, the legal conclusions reached in this case would be binding on the Secretary but not on the non-party agencies more directly responsible for the foreign projects. Justice Scalia accordingly assumed that the agencies would ignore those conclusions. Finally, Justice Scalia pointed to the funding level (less than 10 percent) of one of AID's projects. Even if AID consulted with the Secretary as plaintiffs demanded, and even if that consultation resulted in AID rescinding its financial support, the amount was too small to assume that its removal would result in the project's suspension or elimination. Again, the project's continuation would be up to non-agency third parties not subject to the Court's jurisdiction. As with the Court's causation analysis, the *Lujan* plurality provided no benchmarks for gauging when requested remedies are too speculative to satisfy Article III.

Doubts about how third parties might respond to judicial orders against agencies is only one potential reason for questioning the constitutionality of attenuated redressability chains. Another arises when plaintiffs can benefit *only incidentally* from the remedies they seek. For example, there might be a constitutional standing problem if the plaintiff claims that she will benefit indirectly from the defendant being ordered to do something for a non-party. As you can probably see, this is not an issue in typical cases. In an action at law, a plaintiff is made whole when she receives payment from the defendant. In equity actions, the defendant is ordered to behave in a certain way toward the plaintiff. Redress seems fairly certain in both situations; the defendant's remedial conduct is directed at the plaintiff who, presumably, will be made better off by it. By contrast, it is far less clear whether and how a plaintiff's alleged injuries are cured when the defendant's court-ordered conduct is directed toward *someone else*.

The following case, one of the most important in the Court's redressability jurisprudence, addressed this issue. It asked whether a private party has standing to seek payment of a civil penalty to a third party—here the U.S.

Treasury—that indirectly redresses its injuries by deterring the defendant's future bad conduct. As you read the Court's analysis, identify how it gauged the likelihood that deterring the defendant's future bad conduct would benefit the plaintiff. Is gauging that likelihood even a judicial task, or is it something better suited for Congress' determination?

Friends of the Earth, Inc. v. Laidlaw Environmental Services (TOC), Inc.
528 U.S. 167 (2000)

Justice GINSBURG delivered the opinion of the Court.

This case presents an important question concerning the operation of the citizen-suit provisions of the Clean Water Act. Congress authorized the federal district courts to entertain Clean Water Act suits initiated by "a person or persons having an interest which is or may be adversely affected." 33 U.S.C. §§ 1365(a), (g). To impel future compliance with the Act, a district court may prescribe injunctive relief in such a suit; additionally or alternatively, the court may impose civil penalties payable to the United States Treasury. § 1365(a). In the Clean Water Act citizen suit now before us, the District Court determined that injunctive relief was inappropriate because the defendant, after the institution of the litigation, achieved substantial compliance with the terms of its discharge permit. The court did, however, assess a civil penalty of $405,800. The "total deterrent effect" of the penalty would be adequate to forestall future violations, the court reasoned, taking into account that the defendant "will be required to reimburse plaintiffs for a significant amount of legal fees and has, itself, incurred significant legal expenses."

The Court of Appeals vacated the District Court's order. The case became moot, the appellate court declared, once the defendant fully complied with the terms of its permit and the plaintiff failed to appeal the denial of equitable relief. "[C]ivil penalties payable to the government," the Court of Appeals stated, "would not redress any injury Plaintiffs have suffered." Nor were attorneys' fees in order, the Court of Appeals noted, because absent relief on the merits, plaintiffs could not qualify as prevailing parties.

We reverse the judgment of the Court of Appeals. The appellate court erred in concluding that a citizen suitor's claim for civil penalties must be dismissed as moot when the defendant, albeit after commencement of the litigation, has come into compliance. . . .The Court of Appeals . . . misperceived the remedial potential of civil penalties. Such penalties may serve, as an alternative to an injunction, to deter future violations and thereby redress the injuries that prompted a citizen suitor to commence litigation.

I

A

In 1972, Congress enacted the Clean Water Act (Act), also known as the Federal Water Pollution Control Act, 86 Stat. 816, as amended, 33 U.S.C. § 1251 *et seq.* Section 402 of the Act, 33 U.S.C. § 1342, provides for the issuance, by the Administrator of the Environmental Protection Agency (EPA) or by authorized States, of National Pollutant Discharge Elimination System (NPDES) permits. NPDES permits impose limitations on the discharge of pollutants, and establish related monitoring and reporting requirements, in order to improve the cleanliness and safety of the Nation's waters. Noncompliance with a permit constitutes a violation of the Act. § 1342(h).

Under § 505(a) of the Act, a suit to enforce any limitation in an NPDES permit may be brought by any "citizen," defined as "a person or persons having an interest which is or may be adversely affected." 33 U.S.C. §§ 1365(a), (g). Sixty days before initiating a citizen suit, however, the would-be plaintiff must give notice of the alleged violation to the EPA, the State in which the alleged violation occurred, and the alleged violator. § 1365(b)(1)(A). "[T]he purpose of notice to the alleged violator is to give it an opportunity to bring itself into complete compliance with the Act and thus . . . render unnecessary a citizen suit." *Gwaltney of Smithfield, Ltd. v. Chesapeake Bay Foundation, Inc.*, 484 U.S. 49, 60 (1987). Accordingly, we have held that citizens lack statutory standing under § 505(a) to sue for violations that have ceased by the time the complaint is filed. *Id.* at 56-63. The Act also bars a citizen from suing if the EPA or the State has already commenced, and is "diligently prosecuting," an enforcement action. 33 U.S.C. § 1365(b)(1)(B).

The Act authorizes district courts in citizen-suit proceedings to enter injunctions and to assess civil penalties, which are payable to the United States Treasury. § 1365(a). In determining the amount of any civil penalty, the district court must take into account "the seriousness of the violation or violations, the economic benefit (if any) resulting from the violation, any history of such violations, any good-faith efforts to comply with the applicable requirements, the economic impact of the penalty on the violator, and such other matters as justice may require." § 1319(d). . . .

B

In 1986, defendant-respondent Laidlaw Environmental Services (TOC), Inc., bought a hazardous waste incinerator facility in Roebuck, South Carolina, that included a wastewater treatment plant. . . . Shortly after Laidlaw acquired the facility, the South Carolina Department of Health and Environmental Control (DHEC), acting under 33 U.S.C. § 1342(a)(1), granted Laidlaw an NPDES permit authorizing the company to discharge treated water into the North Tyger River. The permit, which became effective on January 1, 1987, placed limits on Laidlaw's discharge of several pollutants into the river, including—of particular relevance to this case—mercury, an extremely toxic pollutant. The permit also regulated the flow, temperature, toxicity, and pH of the effluent from the facility, and imposed monitoring and reporting obligations.

Once it received its permit, Laidlaw began to discharge various pollutants into the waterway; repeatedly, Laidlaw's discharges exceeded the limits set by the permit. In particular, despite experimenting with several technological fixes, Laidlaw consistently failed to meet the permit's stringent 1.3 ppb (parts per billion) daily average limit on mercury discharges. The District Court later found that Laidlaw had violated the mercury limits on 489 occasions between 1987 and 1995.

On April 10, 1992, plaintiff-petitioners Friends of the Earth (FOE) and Citizens Local Environmental Action Network, Inc. (CLEAN) (referred to collectively in this opinion, together with later joined plaintiff-petitioner Sierra Club, as "FOE") took the preliminary step necessary to the institution of litigation. They sent a letter to Laidlaw notifying the company of their intention to file a citizen suit against it under § 505(a) of the Act after the expiration of the requisite 60-day notice period, i.e., on or after June 10, 1992. Laidlaw's lawyer then contacted DHEC to ask whether DHEC would consider filing a lawsuit against Laidlaw. The District Court later found that Laidlaw's reason for requesting that DHEC file a lawsuit against it was to bar FOE's proposed citizen suit through the operation of 33 U.S.C. § 1365(b)(1)(B). DHEC agreed to file a lawsuit against Laidlaw; the company's lawyer then drafted the complaint for DHEC and paid the filing fee. On June 9, 1992, the last day before FOE's 60-day notice period expired, DHEC and Laidlaw reached a settlement requiring Laidlaw to pay $100,000 in civil penalties and to make "'every effort'" to comply with its permit obligations.

On June 12, 1992, FOE filed this citizen suit against Laidlaw under § 505(a) of the Act, alleging noncompliance with the NPDES permit and seeking declaratory and injunctive relief and an award of civil penalties. Laidlaw moved for summary judgment on the ground that FOE had failed to present evidence demonstrating injury in fact, and therefore lacked Article III standing to bring the lawsuit. . . . After examining [the] evidence, the District Court denied Laidlaw's summary judgment motion, finding— albeit "by the very slimmest of margins"—that FOE had standing to bring the suit. . . .

On January 22, 1997, the District Court issued its judgment. It found that Laidlaw had gained a total economic benefit of $1,092,581 as a result of its extended period of noncompliance with the mercury discharge limit in its permit. The court concluded, however, that a civil penalty of $405,800 was adequate in light of the guiding factors listed in 33 U.S.C. § 1319(d). In particular, the District Court stated that the lesser penalty was appropriate taking into account the judgment's "total deterrent effect." In reaching this determination, the court "considered that Laidlaw will be required to reimburse plaintiffs for a significant amount of legal fees." The court declined to grant FOE's request for injunctive relief, stating that an injunction was inappropriate because "Laidlaw has been in substantial compliance with all parameters in its NPDES permit since at least August 1992."

FOE appealed the District Court's civil penalty judgment, arguing that the penalty was inadequate, but did not appeal the denial of declaratory or injunctive relief. Laidlaw cross-appealed, arguing, among other things, that FOE lacked standing to bring the suit. . . .

. . . [T]he Court of Appeals reasoned that the case had become moot because "the only remedy currently available to [FOE]—civil penalties payable to the government—would not redress any injury [FOE has] suffered." The court therefore vacated the District Court's order and remanded with instructions to dismiss the action. . . .

II

A

The Constitution's case-or-controversy limitation on federal judicial authority, Art. III, § 2, underpins both our standing and our mootness jurisprudence, but the two inquiries differ in respects critical to the proper resolution of this case, so we address them separately. Because the Court of Appeals was persuaded that the case had become moot and so held, it simply assumed without deciding that FOE had initial standing. But because we hold that the Court of Appeals erred in declaring the case moot, we have an obligation to assure ourselves that FOE had Article III standing at the outset of the litigation. . . .

In *Lujan v. Defenders of Wildlife*, 504 U.S. 555, 560-561 (1992), we held that, to satisfy Article III's standing requirements, a plaintiff must show (1) it has suffered an "injury in fact" that is (a) concrete and particularized and (b) actual or imminent, not conjectural or hypothetical; (2) the injury is fairly traceable to the challenged action of the defendant; and (3) it is likely, as opposed to merely speculative, that the injury will be redressed by a favorable decision. An association has standing to bring suit on behalf of its members when its members would otherwise have standing to sue in their own right, the interests at stake are germane to the organization's purpose, and neither the claim asserted nor the relief requested requires the participation of individual members in the lawsuit. *Hunt v. Washington State Apple Advertising Comm'n*, 432 U.S. 333, 343 (1977). . . .

Laidlaw argues . . . that even if FOE had standing to seek injunctive relief, it lacked standing to seek civil penalties. Here the asserted defect is not injury but redressability. Civil penalties offer no redress to private plaintiffs, Laidlaw argues, because they are paid to the Government, and therefore a citizen plaintiff can never have standing to seek them.

Laidlaw is right to insist that a plaintiff must demonstrate standing separately for each form of relief sought. *See,* e.g., *City of Los Angeles v. Lyons,* 461 U.S. 95, 109 (1983) (notwithstanding the fact that plaintiff had standing to pursue damages, he lacked standing to pursue injunctive relief). But it is wrong to maintain that citizen plaintiffs facing ongoing violations never have standing to seek civil penalties.

We have recognized on numerous occasions that "all civil penalties have some deterrent effect." *Hudson v. United States,* 522 U.S. 93, 102 (1997). More specifically, Congress has found that civil penalties in Clean Water Act cases do more than promote immediate compliance by limiting the defendant's economic incentive to delay its attainment of permit limits; they also deter future violations. This congressional determination warrants judicial attention and respect. "The legislative history of the Act reveals that Congress wanted the district court to consider the need for retribution and deterrence, in addition to restitution, when it imposed civil penalties. . . . [The district court may] seek to deter future violations by basing the penalty on its economic impact." *Tull v. United States,* 481 U.S. 412, 422-423 (1987).

It can scarcely be doubted that, for a plaintiff who is injured or faces the threat of future injury due to illegal conduct ongoing at the time of suit, a sanction that effectively abates that conduct and prevents its recurrence provides a form of redress. Civil penalties can fit that description. To the extent that they encourage defendants to discontinue current violations and deter them from committing future ones, they afford redress to citizen plaintiffs who are injured or threatened with injury as a consequence of ongoing unlawful conduct.

The dissent argues that it is the availability rather than the imposition of civil penalties that deters any particular polluter from continuing to pollute. This argument misses the mark in two ways. First, it overlooks the interdependence of the availability and the imposition; a threat has no deterrent value unless it is credible that it will be carried out. Second, it is reasonable for Congress to conclude that an actual award of civil penalties does in fact bring with it a significant quantum of deterrence over and above what is achieved by the mere prospect of such penalties. A would-be polluter may or may not be dissuaded by the existence of a remedy on the books, but a defendant once hit in its pocketbook will surely think twice before polluting again.

We recognize that there may be a point at which the deterrent effect of a claim for civil penalties becomes so insubstantial or so remote that it cannot support citizen standing. The fact that this vanishing point is not easy to ascertain does not detract from the deterrent power of such penalties in the ordinary case. . . . In this case we need not explore the outer limits of the principle that civil penalties provide sufficient deterrence to support redressability. Here, the civil penalties sought by FOE carried with them a deterrent effect that made it likely, as opposed to merely speculative, that the penalties would redress FOE's injuries by abating current violations and preventing future ones—as the District Court reasonably found when it assessed a penalty of $405,800. . . .

Laidlaw contends that the reasoning of our decision in *Steel Co.* [*v. Citizens for a Better Environment*, 523 U.S. 83 (1998)] directs the conclusion that citizen plaintiffs have no standing to seek civil penalties under the Act. We disagree. *Steel Co.* established that citizen suitors lack standing to seek civil penalties for violations that have abated by the time of suit. 523 U.S., at 106-107. We specifically noted in that case that there was no allegation in the complaint of any continuing or imminent violation, and that no basis for such an allegation appeared to exist. *Id.* at 108. In short, *Steel Co.* held that private plaintiffs, unlike the Federal Government, may not sue to assess penalties for wholly past violations, but our decision in that case did not reach the issue of standing to seek penalties for violations that are ongoing at the time of the complaint and that could continue into the future if undeterred.[4] . . .

[In the remainder of its opinion, the Court concluded that FOE's case was not moot, and that the district court should determine in the first instance whether FOE was entitled to reimbursement of its attorneys fees and other costs.]

* * *

For the reasons stated, the judgment of the United States Court of Appeals for the Fourth Circuit is reversed, and the case is remanded for further proceedings consistent with this opinion.

It is so ordered.

---

[4] In insisting that the redressability requirement is not met, the dissent relies heavily on *Linda R.S. v. Richard D.*, 410 U.S. 614 (1973). That reliance is sorely misplaced. In *Linda R. S.*, the mother of an out-of-wedlock child filed suit to force a district attorney to bring a criminal prosecution against the absentee father for failure to pay child support. In finding that the mother lacked standing to seek this extraordinary remedy, the Court drew attention to "the special status of criminal prosecutions in our system," and carefully limited its holding to the "unique context of a challenge to [the nonenforcement of] a criminal statute." Furthermore, as to redressability, the relief sought in *Linda R. S.*—a prosecution which, if successful, would automatically land the delinquent father in jail for a fixed term, with predictably negative effects on his earning power—would scarcely remedy the plaintiff's lack of child support payments. In this regard, the Court contrasted "the civil contempt model whereby the defendant 'keeps the keys to the jail in his own pocket' and may be released whenever he complies with his legal obligations." The dissent's contention that "precisely the same situation exists here" as in *Linda R. S.* is, to say the least, extravagant.

Putting aside its mistaken reliance on *Linda R. S.*, the dissent's broader charge that citizen suits for civil penalties under the Act carry "grave implications for democratic governance," seems to us overdrawn. Certainly the Federal Executive Branch does not share the dissent's view that such suits dissipate its authority to enforce the law. In fact, the Department of Justice has endorsed this citizen suit from the outset, submitting amicus briefs in support of FOE in the District Court, the Court of Appeals, and this Court. As we have already noted, the Federal Government retains the power to foreclose a citizen suit by undertaking its own action. And if the Executive Branch opposes a particular citizen suit, the statute allows the Administrator of the EPA to "intervene as a matter of right" and bring the Government's views to the attention of the court.

[The concurring opinions of Justice STEVENS and Justice KENNEDY are omitted.]

Justice SCALIA, with whom Justice THOMAS joins, dissenting. . . .

II

The Court's treatment of the redressability requirement—which would have been unnecessary if it resolved the injury-in-fact question correctly—is equally cavalier. [P]etitioners allege ongoing injury consisting of diminished enjoyment of the affected waterways and decreased property values. They allege that these injuries are caused by Laidlaw's continuing permit violations. But the remedy petitioners seek is neither recompense for their injuries nor an injunction against future violations. Instead, the remedy is a statutorily specified "penalty" for past violations, payable entirely to the United States Treasury. Only last Term, we held that such penalties do not redress any injury a citizen plaintiff has suffered from past violations. *Steel Co. v. Citizens for a Better Environment*, 523 U.S. 83, 106-107 (1998). The Court nonetheless finds the redressability requirement satisfied here, distinguishing *Steel Co.* on the ground that in this case petitioners allege ongoing violations; payment of the penalties, it says, will remedy petitioners' injury by deterring future violations by Laidlaw. It holds that a penalty payable to the public "remedies" a threatened private harm, and suffices to sustain a private suit.

That holding has no precedent in our jurisprudence, and takes this Court beyond the "cases and controversies" that Article III of the Constitution has entrusted to its resolution. Even if it were appropriate, moreover, to allow Article III's remediation requirement to be satisfied by the indirect private consequences of a public penalty, those consequences are entirely too speculative in the present case. The new standing law that the Court makes—like all expansions of standing beyond the traditional constitutional limits—has grave implications for democratic governance. . . .

A

In *Linda R.S. v. Richard D.*, 410 U.S. 614 (1973), the plaintiff, mother of an illegitimate child, sought, on behalf of herself, her child, and all others similarly situated, an injunction against discriminatory application of Art. 602 of the Texas Penal Code. Although that provision made it a misdemeanor for "any parent" to refuse to support his or her minor children under 18 years of age, it was enforced only against married parents. That refusal, the plaintiff contended, deprived her and her child of the equal protection of the law by denying them the deterrent effect of the statute upon the father's failure to fulfill his support obligation. The Court held that there was no

Article III standing. There was no "'direct' relationship," it said, "between the alleged injury and the claim sought to be adjudicated," since "[t]he prospect that prosecution will, at least in the future, result in payment of support can, at best, be termed only speculative." *Id.* at 618. "[Our cases] demonstrate that, in American jurisprudence at least, a private citizen lacks a judicially cognizable interest in the prosecution or nonprosecution of another." *Id.* at 619.

Although the Court in *Linda R.S.* recited the "logical nexus" analysis of *Flast v. Cohen*, 392 U.S. 83 (1968), which has since fallen into desuetude, "it is clear that standing was denied . . . because of the unlikelihood that the relief requested would redress appellant's claimed injury." *Duke Power Co. v. Carolina Environmental Study Group, Inc.*, 438 U.S. 59, 79, note 24 (1978). There was no "logical nexus" between nonenforcement of the statute and Linda R. S.'s failure to receive support payments because "[t]he prospect that prosecution will . . . result in payment of support" was "speculative," *Linda R.S., supra,* at 618—that is to say, it was uncertain whether the relief would prevent the injury.[1] Of course precisely the same situation exists here. The principle that "in American jurisprudence . . . a private citizen lacks a judicially cognizable interest in the prosecution or nonprosecution of another" applies no less to prosecution for civil penalties payable to the State than to prosecution for criminal penalties owing to the State.

The Court's opinion reads as though the only purpose and effect of the redressability requirement is to assure that the plaintiff receive some of the benefit of the relief that a court orders. That is not so. If it were, a federal tort plaintiff fearing repetition of the injury could ask for tort damages to be paid not only to himself but to other victims as well, on the theory that those damages would have at least some deterrent effect beneficial to him. Such a suit is preposterous because the "remediation" that is the traditional business of Anglo-American courts is relief specifically tailored to the plaintiff's injury, and not any sort of relief that has some incidental benefit to the plaintiff. Just as a "generalized grievance" that affects the entire citizenry cannot satisfy the injury-in-fact requirement even though it aggrieves the plaintiff along with everyone else, *see Lujan*, 504 U.S., at 573-574, so also a generalized remedy that deters all future unlawful activity against all persons cannot satisfy the remediation requirement, even though it deters (among other things) repetition of this particular unlawful activity against these particular plaintiffs.

---

[1] The decision in *Linda R.S.* did not turn, as today's opinion imaginatively suggests, on the father's short-term inability to pay support if imprisoned. The Court's only comment upon the imprisonment was that, unlike imprisonment for civil contempt, it would not condition the father's release upon payment. The Court then continued: "The prospect that prosecution will, at least in the future"—i.e., upon completion of the imprisonment—"result in payment of support can, at best, be termed only speculative." *Linda R. S.*, 410 U.S., at 618.

Thus, relief against prospective harm is traditionally afforded by way of an injunction, the scope of which is limited by the scope of the threatened injury. In seeking to overturn that tradition by giving an individual plaintiff the power to invoke a public remedy, Congress has done precisely what we have said it cannot do: convert an "undifferentiated public interest" into an "individual right" vindicable in the courts. *Lujan, supra,* at 577; *Steel Co.,* 523 U.S., at 106. . . .

B. . . .

The Court recognizes . . . that to satisfy Article III, it must be "likely," as opposed to "merely speculative," that a favorable decision will redress plaintiffs' injury. Further, the Court recognizes that not all deterrent effects of all civil penalties will meet this standard—though it declines to "explore the outer limits" of adequate deterrence. It concludes, however, that in the present case "the civil penalties sought by FOE carried with them a deterrent effect" that satisfied the "likely [rather than] speculative" standard. There is little in the Court's opinion to explain why it believes this is so.

The Court cites the District Court's conclusion that the penalties imposed, along with anticipated fee awards, provided "adequate deterrence." There is absolutely no reason to believe, however, that this meant "deterrence adequate to prevent an injury to these plaintiffs that would otherwise occur." The statute does not even mention deterrence in general (much less deterrence of future harm to the particular plaintiff) as one of the elements that the court should consider in fixing the amount of the penalty. . . . The statute does require the court to consider "the seriousness of the violation or violations, the economic benefit (if any) resulting from the violation, any history of such violations, any good-faith efforts to comply with the applicable requirements, [and] the economic impact of the penalty on the violator. . . ." [33 U.S.C. § 1319(d).] The District Court['s opinion makes no mention]—in this portion of the opinion or anywhere else—of the degree of deterrence necessary to prevent future harm to these particular plaintiffs. Indeed . . . the District Court's final opinion . . . displayed *[no] awareness* that deterrence of *future injury to the plaintiffs* was necessary to support standing. . . .

If the Court had undertaken the necessary inquiry into whether significant deterrence of the plaintiffs' feared injury was "likely," it would have had to reason something like this: Strictly speaking, no polluter is deterred by a penalty for past pollution; he is deterred by the fear of a penalty for future pollution. That fear will be virtually nonexistent if the prospective polluter knows that all emissions violators are given a free pass; it will be substantial under an emissions program such as the federal scheme here, which is regularly and notoriously enforced; it will be even higher when a prospective polluter subject to such a regularly enforced program has, as here, been the object of public charges of pollution and a suit for injunction; and it will surely be near the top of the graph when, as here, the prospective polluter has already been subjected to state penalties for the past pollution. The deterrence on which the plaintiffs must rely for standing in the present case is the marginal increase in Laidlaw's fear of future penalties that will be achieved by adding federal penalties for Laidlaw's past conduct.

I cannot say for certain that this marginal increase is zero; but I can say for certain that it is entirely speculative whether it will make the difference between these plaintiffs' suffering injury in the future and these plaintiffs' going unharmed. In fact, the assertion that it will "likely" do so is entirely farfetched. The speculativeness of that result is much greater than the speculativeness we found excessive in *Simon v. Eastern Ky. Welfare Rights Organization*, 426 U.S. 26, 43 (1976), where we held that denying § 501(c)(3) charitable-deduction tax status to hospitals that refused to treat indigents was not sufficiently likely to assure future treatment of the indigent plaintiffs to support standing. And it is much greater than the speculativeness we found excessive in *Linda R.S. v. Richard D.*, where we said that "[t]he prospect that prosecution [for nonsupport] will . . . result in payment of support can, at best, be termed only speculative," 410 U.S., at 618.

In sum, if this case is, as the Court suggests, within the central core of "deterrence" standing, it is impossible to imagine what the "outer limits" could possibly be. The Court's expressed reluctance to define those "outer limits" serves only to disguise the fact that it has promulgated a revolutionary new doctrine of standing that will permit the entire body of public civil penalties to be handed over to enforcement by private interests.

C

Article II of the Constitution commits it to the President to "take Care that the Laws be faithfully executed," Art. II, § 3, and provides specific methods by which all persons exercising significant executive power are to be appointed, Art. II, § 2. . . . [T]he question of the conformity of this legislation with Article II has not been argued—and I, like the Court, do not address it. But Article III, no less than Article II, has consequences for the structure of our government, and it is worth noting the changes in that structure which today's decision allows.

By permitting citizens to pursue civil penalties payable to the Federal Treasury, the Act does not provide a mechanism for individual relief in any traditional sense, but turns over to private citizens the function of enforcing the law. A Clean Water Act plaintiff pursuing civil penalties acts as a self-appointed mini-EPA. Where, as is often the case, the plaintiff is a national association, it has significant discretion in choosing enforcement targets. Once the association is aware of a reported violation, it need not look long for an injured member, at least under the theory of injury the Court applies today. And once the target is chosen, the suit goes forward without meaningful public control. The availability of civil penalties vastly disproportionate to the individual injury gives citizen plaintiffs massive bargaining power—which is often used to achieve settlements requiring the defendant to support environmental projects of the plaintiffs' choosing. Thus is a public fine diverted to a private interest. . . .

QUESTION SET 9.13

Review & Synthesis

1. How do the concepts of redressability and causation differ in their relationship to injuries-in-fact?

2. On what basis did the Court conclude that civil penalties made available by the Clean Water Act—paid to the federal treasury rather than to Friends of the Earth—would deter Laidlaw from polluting in the future? What test, if any, did it adopt for (1) gauging whether civil penalties were likely to alter Laidlaw's future conduct, and (2) the degree to which that altered conduct remedied the harms alleged by Friends of the Earth?

3. Just how different was the deterrence theory advanced by Friends of the Earth from the one raised by Linda R. S. in her suit against Richard D.? Justice Ginsburg rightly pointed out that sending Richard D. to prison would not have generated the child support payments Linda R. S. claimed he owed her. That assumed, of course, that the deterrence effect of judicial procedures comes primarily (perhaps even solely) from the actual imposition of punishment. Is that a sound assumption? If the threat of an enforcement action is capable of changing behavior, how is Linda R. S.'s position any different than Friends of the Earth's?

4. Do you agree with Justice Scalia that allowing standing for deterrence cases unduly infringes on the Executive Branch's constitutional authority to implement federal law? Part of the concern is that expanding opportunities for "private attorneys-general" to file federal lawsuits against agencies or the parties they regulate erodes the President's prosecutorial discretion, his or her ability to choose the timing and manner of federal law enforcement. Was Justice Ginsburg's response—that the Clean Water Act allows the federal government to take over privately initiated enforcement actions—persuasive?

5. Consider the prosecutorial discretion issue raised by Justice Scalia from a different perspective. Assume he was correct that empowering

private attorneys-general to enforce federal environmental laws shrinks the President's enforcement authority. Is it not possible that what the President loses in unfettered discretion the public gains in greater legal accountability? Doesn't allowing private parties to file civil enforcement actions against scofflaws provide a meaningful check on the Executive's failures or refusals to enforce laws duly enacted by Congress? Doesn't it, as evidenced by the facts in this case, provide a bulwark against agency capture?

Application & Analysis

1. The Solomon Amendment, 10 U.S.C. § 983, prohibits colleges and universities from receiving certain federal funds if they do not give military recruiters access to their campuses and students that at least equals the access afforded other employers. On several occasions during the last two academic years, students and faculty protesters at University prevented or disrupted military recruiting at on-campus job fairs. In two instances, disruptive protests caused military recruiters to leave campus. In another, protesters physically blocked students' access to military recruiters. Additionally, protests caused University to cancel one job fair and caused some military recruiters to withdraw from another.

   Students for a Strong Military ("SSM") is a nonprofit organization that supports military recruitment of college students. Several of its members attend University and were prevented from meeting with military recruiters due to the incidents described above. SSM sent a letter to the Defense Secretary describing the incidents and expressing its concerns about the military's inability to recruit at University. The Secretary took no action. SSM subsequently sued the Secretary in federal district court. Its complaint recounted the disruptions at University and sought a writ of mandamus and an injunction ordering the Secretary to determine that University's federal funds should be withheld because it is in violation of the Solomon Amendment.

   You are a clerk with the district court hearing SSM's suit. The judge has asked you to write a brief memorandum assessing whether SSM's complaint satisfies the redressability prong of the constitutional standing inquiry.

---

7. Prudential Standing Requirements: The Zone of Interests Test

***Data Processing* Revisited.** Prudential standing constitutes the second part of the modern standing test established by *Association of Data Processing Service Organizations, Inc. v. Camp*. It is comprised of several "rule[s] of self-restraint" the Court has adopted "for its own governance," 397 U.S. 150, 154 (1970), the first of which is commonly referred to as the "zone of interests" or simply the "zone" test. It asks "whether the interest sought to be protected by the complainant is arguably within the zone of interests to be protected or regulated by the statute or constitutional guarantee in question." *Id.* at 153. Recall that the *Data Processing* plaintiffs claimed they were harmed by the Comptroller of the Currency's decision allowing national banks to compete in the data processing services market. Although they satisfied the constitutional standing requirements, the plaintiffs had no personal legal right to be protected from the increased competition that would result from Comptroller's decision. What's more, the statutes the Comptroller allegedly violated—the Bank Service Corporation Act ("BSCA") and the National Bank Act ("NBA")—did not include citizen-suit provisions. The plaintiffs instead relied on the citizen-suit provision of APA § 702, which grants standing to "[a] person . . . adversely affected or aggrieved within the meaning of a relevant statute." The Court accordingly had to determine whether the plaintiffs could properly invoke this provision.

The Court could have interpreted § 702 in a few ways. It could have adopted the narrow interpretation preferred by the Justice Department and the circuit courts at that time, which would have made § 702 available only when agency actions affected plaintiffs' personal legal interests or when Congress passed a citizen-suit provision *specifically* identifying the group of plaintiffs who could sue in the absence of personal legal rights. This approach would have thwarted the *Data Processing* plaintiffs' standing claim; they had no personal legal interests to advance, and neither the BSCA nor the NBA specifically identified data processors as eligible to file suit against the Comptroller. Alternatively, the Court could have interpreted § 702 expansively. Recall Professor Kenneth Culp Davis' argument that § 702 extended standing to any private party *factually injured* by an agency's action. Under this reading, plaintiffs would have two separate paths to standing: they could claim to be "adversely affected" by an agency's conduct, or they could claim to be "aggrieved within the meaning of a relevant statute." Assuming that "adversely affected" is synonymous with "injury in fact," any plaintiff with an alleged factual injury would be able to successfully invoke § 702 without having to rely on an organic statute. *See* Kenneth Culp Davis, *Standing: Taxpayers and Others*, 35 U. Chi. L. Rev. 601, 618-20 (1968); *see also* 3 Richard J. Pierce, Jr., Administrative Law Treatise § 16.9 (2010) (arguing that § 702 should grant standing to any private party factually injured by agency conduct because, grammatically, "within the meaning of a relevant statute" modifies "aggrieved" but not "adversely affected"). The implication of this interpretation, of course, is that Congress has the authority to stretch standing to the outermost limits of Article III, and it did so in APA § 702. A narrower interpretation would leave many private parties harmed by agency action—and thus fully motivated to litigate their cases—with no judicial recourse.

The Court rejected these interpretations in favor of a middle-ground approach. It effectively concluded that plaintiffs must show that their interests fall "within the meaning of a relevant statute" regardless of whether they claim to be "adversely affected" or they claim to be "aggrieved." In other words, the *Data Processing* Court concluded that § 702 requires plaintiffs to show more than bare harm to their interests; they must also show that Congress has given them statutory permission to vindicate those interests in court. Moreover, Congress need not give that permission by specifically identifying a class of private parties who are permitted to bring suit. Instead, the plaintiffs' asserted interests must simply overlap with the general policy concerns evident in a regulatory statute. The Court then used the zone of interests test to determine whether the plaintiffs' interests overlapped those regulated or protected by the BSCA or the NBA:

> We find no evidence that Congress in either the Bank Service Corporation Act or the National Bank Act sought to preclude judicial review of administrative rulings by the Comptroller as to the legitimate scope of activities available to national banks under those statutes. Both Acts are clearly "relevant" statutes within the meaning of § 702. The Acts do not in terms protect a specified group. But their general policy is apparent; and those whose interests are directly affected by a broad or narrow interpretation of the Acts are easily identifiable. It is clear that petitioners, as competitors of national banks which are engaging in data processing services, are within that class of "aggrieved" persons who, under § 702, are entitled to judicial review of "agency action."

Data Processing, 397 U.S. at 155.

As one commentator noted around the time of the decision, the Court's approach "would seem to work primarily to reduce the clarity with which plaintiff must show a legislative purpose to protect those in his position: perhaps indications of mere congressional awareness of their interests might suffice." Kenneth E. Scott, *Standing in the Supreme Court—A Functional Analysis*, 86 HARV. L. REV. 645, 663 (1973). As a practical matter, *Data Processing* found that standing under APA § 702 was easier to show than the DOJ and the circuit courts had thought, but not as easy as simply requiring that plaintiffs allege an injury-in-fact.

After *Data Processing*. Why didn't the Court read § 702 to grant all of the jurisdiction otherwise permitted by Article III? A strong argument can be made that this is what Congress actually wanted. As discussed earlier in this chapter, Congress made agency actions presumptively reviewable, such that review is available absent some clear indication to the contrary. What's more, § 702 could have been read as requiring that plaintiffs only allege injuries-in-fact (i.e., matching the statutory standing limit to the constitutional standing limit). Again, Professor Davis suggested this approach prior to *Data Processing*. It was also suggested from within the Court itself. Justice

Brennan concurred in the results in *Data Processing* and *Barlow* but dissented "from the Court's treatment of the question of standing to challenge agency action." *Barlow*, 397 U.S. at 159, 167 (Brennan, J., concurring in part and dissenting in part). He would have limited the inquiry to whether the plaintiffs had alleged an injury-in-fact, jettisoning the additional requirement that they show that their interests arguably fell within the zone of those protected or regulated by the statute or constitutional guarantee in question. *Id.* at 168. Rather than following the statutory cues or Justice Brennan's advice, the *Data Processing* majority developed the zone of interests test to place an additional restriction on the Judiciary's power to review administrative conduct.

By requiring an overlap of plaintiffs' allegedly injured interests and those an organic statute protects or regulates, the zone test becomes one of degrees and of kinds. Just *how much* of an overlap must there be to support a standing claim, and *what kinds* of interests does it recognize? With respect to the requisite degree of overlap, the answer must reside somewhere between the opposite ends of a range. At its most restrictive end, the zone test could require substantial harmony between plaintiffs' asserted interests and those addressed in a relevant organic statute. At its most permissive end, the test could seek a passing similarity of interests that would make the requirement largely irrelevant. The *Data Processing* Court appeared to land closer to the latter than to the former. It selected a permissive adverb — "arguably" — to describe the level of congruity the zone test expects. It is satisfied as long as the plaintiffs' interests arguably (possibly, conceivably, feasibly, plausibly) accord with those in the organic statute at issue.

This leaves in question the kinds of interests the zone test will recognize. The Court engaged with this issue in a line of cases from the 1970s through the end of the 1990s. It focused on whether plaintiffs' asserted interests had to be ones Congress *specifically intended* to protect or regulate through legislation, or whether those interests merely had to be *evident* in the legislation regardless of whether Congress focused on them. An illustration may clarify the concern. Assume that Congress passes a law directing a federal agency to protect the habitat of an endangered animal species. That legislation also instructs the agency to take economic impact into consideration when doing so. The agency promulgates regulations that will severely impact the profitability of a timber company by causing it to cease operations near one of the protected habitats. The company sues, claiming standing under APA § 702. The company is unlikely to have standing if the zone test recognizes only those interests Congress specifically intended to protect or regulate. While the legislation arguably considers economic interests like the company's, it does so incidentally; its clear purpose is to protect an endangered animal species. By contrast, the company might have more luck if the zone test can be satisfied by incidentally considered interests. In sum, and somewhat intuitively, standing opportunities expand with the variety of interests the zone test accepts.

Consider the following closely divided and highly influential zone-of-interests decision. It addressed whether plaintiffs' interests must be those

Congress specifically intended to address or whether Congress' incidental consideration of those interests sufficed. How did the Court interpret *Data Processing* and the decisions interpreting it? Did it choose a more restrictive or a more permissive zone-of-interests approach? Do you think its conclusion allows too many private parties to invoke citizen-suit provisions, or too few?

National Credit Union Administration v. First National Bank & Trust Co.
522 U.S. 479 (1998)

Justice THOMAS delivered the opinion of the Court. . . .

I

A

In 1934, during the Great Depression, Congress enacted the [Federal Credit Union Act ("FCUA")], which authorizes the chartering of credit unions at the national level and provides that federal credit unions may, as a general matter, offer banking services only to their members. Section 109 of the FCUA, which has remained virtually unaltered since the FCUA's enactment, expressly restricts membership in federal credit unions. . . .

Until 1982, the [National Credit Union Administration ("NCUA")] and its predecessors consistently interpreted § 109 to require that the same common bond of occupation unite every member of an occupationally defined federal credit union. In 1982, however, the NCUA reversed its longstanding policy in order to permit credit unions to be composed of multiple unrelated employer groups. It thus interpreted § 109's common bond requirement to apply only to each employer group in a multiple-group credit union, rather than to every member of that credit union. Under the NCUA's new interpretation, all of the employer groups in a multiple-group credit union had to be located "within a well-defined area," but the NCUA later revised this requirement to provide that each employer group could be located within "an area surrounding the [credit union's] home or a branch office that can be reasonably served by the [credit union] as determined by NCUA." Since 1982, therefore, the NCUA has permitted federal credit unions to be composed of wholly unrelated employer groups, each having its own distinct common bond.

B

After the NCUA revised its interpretation of § 109, petitioner AT&T Family Federal Credit Union (ATTF) expanded its operations considerably by adding unrelated employer groups to its membership. As a result, ATTF now has approximately 110,000 members nationwide, only 35% of whom are employees of AT&T and its affiliates. The remaining members are employees of such diverse companies as the Lee Apparel Company, the Coca-Cola Bottling Company, the Ciba–Geigy Corporation, the Duke Power Company, and the American Tobacco Company.

In 1990, after the NCUA approved a series of amendments to ATTF's charter that added several such unrelated employer groups to ATTF's membership, respondents brought this action. Invoking the judicial review provisions of the Administrative Procedure Act (APA), 5 U.S.C. § 702, respondents claimed that the NCUA's approval of the charter amendments was contrary to law because the members of the new groups did not share a common bond of occupation with ATTF's existing members, as respondents alleged § 109 required. ATTF and petitioner Credit Union National Association were permitted to intervene in the action as defendants.

The District Court dismissed the complaint. It held that respondents lacked prudential standing to challenge the NCUA's chartering decision because their interests were not within the "zone of interests" to be protected by § 109, as required by this Court's cases interpreting the APA. The District Court rejected as irrelevant respondents' claims that the NCUA's interpretation had caused them competitive injury, stating that the legislative history of the FCUA demonstrated that it was passed "to establish a place for credit unions within the country's financial market, and specifically not to protect the competitive interest of banks." The District Court also determined that respondents were not "suitable challengers" to the NCUA's interpretation, as that term had been used in prior prudential standing cases from the Court of Appeals for the District of Columbia Circuit.

The Court of Appeals for the District of Columbia Circuit reversed. [It] agreed that "Congress did not, in 1934, intend to shield banks from competition from credit unions," and hence respondents could not be said to be "intended beneficiaries" of § 109. Relying on two of our prudential standing cases involving the financial services industry . . . the Court of Appeals nonetheless concluded that respondents' interests were sufficiently congruent with the interests of § 109's intended beneficiaries that respondents were "suitable challengers" to the NCUA's chartering decision; therefore, their suit could proceed. . . .

II

Respondents claim a right to judicial review of the NCUA's chartering decision under § 10(a) of the APA, which provides:

> A person suffering legal wrong because of agency action, or adversely affected or aggrieved by agency action within the meaning of a relevant statute, is entitled to judicial review thereof. 5 U.S.C. § 702.

We have interpreted § 10(a) of the APA to impose a prudential standing requirement in addition to the requirement, imposed by Article III of the Constitution, that a plaintiff have suffered a sufficient injury in fact. *See, e.g., Association of Data Processing Service Organizations, Inc. v. Camp*, 397 U.S. 150, 152 (1970) (*Data Processing*). For a plaintiff to have prudential standing under the APA, "the interest sought to be protected by the complainant [must be] arguably within the zone of interests to be protected or regulated by the statute . . . in question." *Id.* at 153.

Based on four of our prior cases finding that competitors of financial institutions have standing to challenge agency action relaxing statutory restrictions on the activities of those institutions, we hold that respondents' interest in limiting the markets that federal credit unions can serve is arguably within the zone of interests to be protected by § 109. Therefore, respondents have prudential standing under the APA to challenge the NCUA's interpretation.

A

Although our prior cases have not stated a clear rule for determining when a plaintiff's interest is "arguably within the zone of interests" to be protected by a statute, they nonetheless establish that we should not inquire whether there has been a congressional intent to benefit the would-be plaintiff. In *Data Processing, supra*, the Office of the Comptroller of the Currency (Comptroller) had interpreted the National Bank Act's incidental powers clause, Rev. Stat. § 5136, 12 U.S.C. § 24 Seventh, to permit national banks to perform data processing services for other banks and bank customers. *See Data Processing, supra*, at 151. The plaintiffs, a data processing corporation and its trade association, alleged that this interpretation was impermissible because providing data processing services was not, as was required by the statute, "[an] incidental powe[r] . . . necessary to carry on the business of banking." *See* 397 U.S., at 157, note 2.

In holding that the plaintiffs had standing, we stated that § 10(a) of the APA required only that "the interest sought to be protected by the complainant [be] arguably within the zone of interests to be protected or regulated by the statute . . . in question." *Id.* at 153. In determining that the plaintiffs' interest met this requirement, we noted that although the relevant federal statutes—the National Bank Act, 12 U.S.C. § 24 Seventh, and the Bank Service Corporation Act, 76 Stat. 1132, 12 U.S.C. § 1864—did not "in terms protect a specified group[,] . . . their general policy is apparent; and those whose interests are directly affected by a broad or narrow interpretation of the Acts are easily identifiable." *Data Processing*, 397 U.S., at 157. "[A]s competitors of national banks which are engaging in data processing services," the plaintiffs were within that class of "aggrieved persons" entitled to judicial review of the Comptroller's interpretation. *Ibid.*

Less than a year later, we applied the "zone of interests" test in *Arnold Tours, Inc. v. Camp*, 400 U.S. 45 (1970) (per curiam) (*Arnold Tours*). There, certain travel agencies challenged a ruling by the Comptroller, similar to the one contested in *Data Processing*, that permitted national banks to operate travel agencies. *See* 400 U.S., at 45. In holding that the plaintiffs had prudential standing under the APA, we noted that it was incorrect to view our decision in *Data Processing* as resting on the peculiar legislative history of § 4 of the Bank Service Corporation Act, which had been passed in part at the behest of the data processing industry. *See* 400 U.S., at 46. We stated explicitly that "we did not rely on any legislative history showing that Congress desired to protect data processors alone from competition." *Ibid.* We further explained:

> In *Data Processing* . . . [w]e held that § 4 arguably brings a competitor within the zone of interests protected by it. Nothing in the opinion limited § 4 to protecting only competitors in the data-processing field. When national banks begin to provide travel services for their customers, they compete with travel agents no less than they compete with data processors when they provide data-processing services to their customers. *Ibid.* (internal citations and quotation marks omitted).

A year later, we decided *Investment Company Institute v. Camp*, 401 U.S. 617 (1971) (*ICI*). In that case, an investment company trade association and several individual investment companies alleged that the Comptroller had violated, *inter alia*, § 21 of the Glass-Steagall Act, 1932, by permitting national banks to establish and operate what in essence were early versions of mutual funds. We held that the plaintiffs, who alleged that they would be injured by the competition resulting from the Comptroller's action, had standing under the APA and stated that the case was controlled by *Data Processing*. *See* 401 U.S., at 621. Significantly, we found unpersuasive Justice Harlan's argument in dissent that the suit should be dismissed because "neither the language of the pertinent provisions of the Glass-Steagall Act nor the legislative history evince[d] any congressional concern for the interests of petitioners and others like them in freedom from competition." *Id.* at 640.

Our fourth case in this vein was *Clarke v. Securities Industry Assn.*, 479 U.S. 388 (1987) (*Clarke*). There, a securities dealers trade association sued the Comptroller, this time for authorizing two national banks to offer discount brokerage services both at their branch offices and at other locations inside and outside their home States. *See id.* at 391. The plaintiff contended that the Comptroller's action violated the McFadden Act, which permits national banks to carry on the business of banking only at authorized branches, and to open new branches only in their home States and only to the extent that state-chartered banks in that State can do so under state law. *See id.* at 391-392.

We again held that the plaintiff had standing under the APA. Summarizing our prior holdings, we stated that although the "zone of interests" test "denies a right of review if the plaintiff's interests are . . . marginally related to or inconsistent with the purposes implicit in the statute," *Id.* at 399, "there need be no indication of congressional purpose to benefit the would-be plaintiff," *Id.* at 399-400 (citing *ICI*). We then determined that by limiting the ability of national banks to do business outside their home States, "Congress ha[d] shown a concern to keep national banks from gaining a monopoly control over credit and money." 479 U.S., at 403. The interest of the securities dealers in preventing national banks from expanding into the securities markets directly implicated this concern because offering discount brokerage services would allow national banks "access to more money, in the form of credit balances, and enhanced opportunities to lend money, viz., for margin purchases." *Ibid.* The case was thus analogous to *Data Processing* and *ICI*: "In those cases the question was what activities banks could engage in at all; here, the question is what activities banks can engage in without regard to the limitations imposed by state branching law." 479 U.S., at 403.

B

Our prior cases, therefore, have consistently held that for a plaintiff's interests to be arguably within the "zone of interests" to be protected by a statute, there does not have to be an "indication of congressional purpose to benefit the would-be plaintiff." *Id.* at 399-400 (citing *ICI*); *see also Arnold Tours*, 400 U.S., at 46 (citing *Data Processing*). The proper inquiry is simply "whether the interest sought to be protected by the complainant is *arguably* within the zone of interests to be protected . . . by the statute." *Data Processing*, 397 U.S., at 153 (emphasis added). Hence in applying the "zone of interests" test, we do not ask whether, in enacting the statutory provision at issue, Congress specifically intended to benefit the plaintiff. Instead, we first discern the interests "arguably . . . to be protected" by the statutory provision at issue; we then inquire whether the plaintiff's interests affected by the agency action in question are among them.

Section 109 provides that "[f]ederal credit union membership shall be limited to groups having a common bond of occupation or association, or to groups within a well-defined neighborhood, community, or rural district." 12 U.S.C. § 1759. By its express terms, § 109 limits membership in every federal credit union to members of definable "groups." Because federal credit unions may, as a general matter, offer banking services only to members, *see*, e.g., 12 U.S.C. §§ 1757(5)-(6), § 109 also restricts the markets that every federal credit union can serve. Although these markets need not be small, they unquestionably are limited. The link between § 109's regulation of federal credit union membership and its limitation on the markets that federal credit unions can serve is unmistakable. Thus, even if it cannot be said that Congress had the specific purpose of benefiting commercial banks, one of the interests "arguably . . . to be protected" by § 109 is an interest in limiting the markets that federal credit unions can serve. This interest is precisely the interest of respondents affected by the NCUA's interpretation of § 109. As competitors of federal credit unions, respondents certainly have an interest in limiting the markets that federal credit unions can serve, and the NCUA's interpretation has affected that interest by allowing federal credit unions to increase their customer base.[7] . . .

C

Petitioners attempt to distinguish this action principally on the ground that there is no evidence that Congress, when it enacted the FCUA, was at all concerned with the competitive interests of commercial banks, or indeed at all concerned with competition. Indeed, petitioners contend that the very reason Congress passed the FCUA was that banks were simply not in the picture as far as small borrowers were concerned, and thus Congress believed it necessary to create a new source of credit for people of modest means.

The difficulty with this argument is that similar arguments were made unsuccessfully in each of *Data Processing*, *Arnold Tours*, *ICI*, and *Clarke*. . . .

We therefore cannot accept petitioners' argument that respondents do not have standing because there is no evidence that the Congress that enacted § 109 was concerned with the competitive interests of commercial banks. To accept that argument, we would have to reformulate the "zone of interests" test to require that Congress have specifically intended to benefit a particular class of plaintiffs before a plaintiff from that class could have standing under the APA to sue. We have refused to do this in our prior cases, and we refuse to do so today. . . .

---

[7] Contrary to the dissent's contentions, our formulation does not "eviscerat[e]" or "abolis[h]" the zone of interests requirement. Nor can it be read to imply that, in order to have standing under the APA, a plaintiff must merely have an interest in enforcing the statute in question. The test we have articulated — discerning the interests "arguably . . . to be protected" by the statutory provision at issue and inquiring whether the plaintiff's interests affected by the agency action in question are among them — differs only as a matter of semantics from the formulation that the dissent has accused us of "eviscerating" or "abolishing," (stating that the plaintiff must establish that "the injury he complains of . . . falls within the zone of interests sought to be protected by the statutory provision whose violation forms the legal basis for his complaint" (internal quotation marks and citation omitted)).

Our only disagreement with the dissent lies in the application of the "zone of interests" test. Because of the unmistakable link between § 109's express restriction on credit union membership and the limitation on the markets that federal credit unions can serve, there is objectively "some indication in the statute," that respondents' interest is "arguably within the zone of interests to be protected" by § 109. Hence respondents are more than merely incidental beneficiaries of § 109's effects on competition.

Respondents' interest in limiting the markets that credit unions can serve is "arguably within the zone of interests to be protected" by § 109. Under our precedents, it is irrelevant that in enacting the FCUA, Congress did not specifically intend to protect commercial banks. Although it is clear that respondents' objectives in this action are not eleemosynary in nature, under our prior cases that, too, is beside the point.[9]

[In Section III of its opinion, the Court concludes that the NCUA's interpretation of § 109 is contrary to the unambiguously expressed intent of Congress and is thus impermissible under the first step of *Chevron U.S.A. Inc. v. Natural Resources Defense Council, Inc.*, 467 U.S. 837 (1984). The *Chevron* analysis is discussed later in this chapter.]

The judgment of the Court of Appeals is therefore affirmed.
It is so ordered.

Justice O'CONNOR, with whom Justice STEVENS, Justice SOUTER, and Justice BREYER join, dissenting.

In determining that respondents have standing under the zone-of-interests test to challenge the National Credit Union Administration's (NCUA's) interpretation of the "common bond" provision of the Federal Credit Union Act (FCUA), 12 U.S.C. § 1759, the Court applies the test in a manner that is contrary to our decisions and, more importantly, that all but eviscerates the zone-of-interests requirement. In my view, under a proper conception of the inquiry, "the interest sought to be protected by" respondents in this action is not "arguably within the zone of interests to be protected" by the common bond provision. *Association of Data Processing Service Organizations, Inc. v. Camp*, 397 U.S. 150, 153 (1970). Accordingly, I respectfully dissent.

I. . . .

. . . The "injury respondents complain of," as the Court explains, is that the NCUA's interpretation of the common bond provision "allows persons who might otherwise be their customers to be . . . customers" of petitioner AT&T Family Federal Credit Union. Put another way, the injury is a loss of respondents' customer base to a competing entity, or more generally, an injury to respondents' commercial interest as a competitor. The relevant question under the zone-of-interests test, then, is whether injury to respondents' commercial interest as a competitor "falls within the zone of interests sought to be

---

[9] Unlike some of our prudential standing cases, no suggestion is made in this action that Congress has sought to preclude judicial review of agency action. *See, e.g., Block v. Community Nutrition Institute*, 467 U.S. 340 (1984).

protected by the [common bond] provision." *E.g.*, [*Air Courier Conference of America v. American Postal Workers Union, AFL-CIO*, 498 U.S. 517, 523-24 (1991)]. For instance, in *Data Processing*, where the plaintiffs—like respondents here—alleged competitive injury to their commercial interest, we found that the plaintiffs had standing because "their commercial interest was sought to be protected by the . . . provision which they alleged had been violated." *Bennett v. Spear*, 520 U.S. 154, 176 (1997) (discussing *Data Processing*).

The Court adopts a quite different approach to the zone-of-interests test today, eschewing any assessment of whether the common bond provision was intended to protect respondents' commercial interest. The Court begins by observing that the terms of the common bond provision—"[f]ederal credit union membership shall be limited to groups having a common bond of occupation or association, or to groups within a well-defined neighborhood, community, or rural district," 12 U.S.C. § 1759—expressly limit membership in federal credit unions to persons belonging to certain "groups." Then, citing other statutory provisions that bar federal credit unions from serving nonmembers, *see* §§ 1757(5)-(6), the Court reasons that one interest sought to be protected by the common bond provision "is an interest in limiting the markets that federal credit unions can serve." The Court concludes its analysis by observing simply that respondents, "[a]s competitors of federal credit unions, . . . certainly have [that] interest . . . , and the NCUA's interpretation has affected that interest."

Under the Court's approach, every litigant who establishes injury in fact under Article III will automatically satisfy the zone-of-interests requirement, rendering the zone-of-interests test ineffectual. *See Air Courier, supra*, at 524 ("mistak[e]" to "conflat[e] the zone-of-interests test with injury in fact"). That result stems from the Court's articulation of the relevant "interest." In stating that the common bond provision protects an "interest in limiting the markets that federal credit unions can serve," the Court presumably uses the term "markets" in the sense of customer markets, as opposed to, for instance, product markets: The common bond requirement and the provisions prohibiting credit unions from serving nonmembers combine to limit the customers a credit union can serve, not the services a credit union can offer.

With that understanding, the Court's conclusion that respondents "have" an interest in "limiting the [customer] markets that federal credit unions can serve" means little more than that respondents "have" an interest in enforcing the statute. The common bond requirement limits a credit union's membership, and hence its customer base, to certain groups, 12 U.S.C. § 1759, and in the Court's view, it is enough to establish standing that respondents "have" an interest in limiting the customers a credit union can serve. The Court's additional observation that respondents' interest has been "affected" by the NCUA's interpretation adds little to the analysis; agency interpretation of a statutory restriction will of course affect a party who has an interest in the restriction. Indeed, a party presumably will bring suit to vindicate an interest only if the interest has been affected by the challenged action. The crux of the Court's zone-of-interests inquiry, then, is simply that the plaintiff must "have" an interest in enforcing the pertinent statute.

A party, however, will invariably have an interest in enforcing a statute when he can establish injury in fact caused by an alleged violation of that statute. An example we used in *National Wildlife Federation* illustrates the point. There, we hypothesized a situation involving "the failure of an agency to comply with a statutory provision requiring 'on the record' hearings." *Lujan v. National Wildlife Federation*, 497 U.S. 871, 883 (1990). That circumstance "would assuredly have an adverse effect upon the company that has the contract to record and transcribe the agency's proceedings," and so the company would establish injury in fact. *Ibid.* But the company would not satisfy the zone-of-interests test, because "the provision was obviously enacted to protect the interests of the parties to the proceedings and not those of the reporters." *Ibid.*; *see Air Courier*, 498 U.S., at 524. Under the Court's approach today, however, the reporting company would have standing under the zone-of-interests test: Because the company is injured by the failure to comply with the requirement of on-the-record hearings, the company would certainly "have" an interest in enforcing the statute. . . .

In short, requiring simply that a litigant "have" an interest in enforcing the relevant statute amounts to hardly any test at all. That is why our decisions have required instead that a party "establish that *the injury he complains of* . . . falls within the 'zone of interests' sought to be protected by the statutory provision" in question. *National Wildlife Federation, supra*, at 883 (emphasis added); *see Bennett*, 520 U.S., at 176. . . .

II. . . .

It is true, as the Court emphasizes repeatedly, that we did not require in [*Data Processing, Arnold Tours, ICI*, and *Clarke*], that the statute at issue was designed to benefit the particular party bringing suit. *See Clarke, supra*, at 399-400. In *Arnold Tours* and *Data Processing*, for instance, it was sufficient that Congress desired to protect the interests of competitors generally through § 4 of the Bank Service Corporation Act, even if Congress did not have in mind the particular interests of travel agents or data processors. *See Arnold Tours, supra*, at 46. In *Clarke*, likewise, the antibranching provisions of the McFadden Act may have been intended primarily to protect state banks, and not the securities industry, from competitive injury. Respondents thus need not establish that the common bond provision was enacted specifically to benefit commercial banks, any more than they must show that the provision was intended to benefit Lexington State Bank, Piedmont State Bank, or any of the particular banks that filed this suit.

In each of the competitor standing cases, though, we found that Congress had enacted an "anti-competition limitation," *see Bennett*, 520 U.S., at 176 (discussing *Data Processing*), or, alternatively, that Congress had "legislated against . . . competition," *see Clarke, supra*, at 403; *ICI, supra*, at 620-621, and accordingly, that the plaintiff-competitor's "commercial interest was sought to be protected by the anti-competition limitation" at issue, *Bennett, supra*, at 176. We determined, in other words, that "the injury [the plaintiff] complain[ed] of . . . [fell] within the zone of interests sought to be protected by the [relevant] statutory provision." *National Wildlife Federation*, 497 U.S., at 883. The Court fails to undertake that analysis here. . . .

QUESTION SET 9.14

Review & Synthesis

1. According to the Court, how did the "unmistakable link" between the FCUA's limits on credit union membership and its limits on the markets credit unions are permitted to serve demonstrate the interests Congress intended to protect in the common bond provision? How did that statutory interest compare with the interests asserted by the banks in the case?

2. Under the Court's formulation of the zone-of-interests test, must vindication of the banks' interests advance the regulatory goals of the common bond provision? Was it enough that the banks wanted the credit unions' membership limited, even if Congress adopted the common bond provision for reasons having nothing to do with competition between credit unions and banks? In effect, the dissenters read the Court's opinion as stripping a critical policy judgment out of the zone-of-interests analysis. By disregarding the reason Congress adopted the common bond provision, the Court in their view focused the inquiry solely on the factual effect the NCUA's reinterpretation of the provision had on the banks. Were they right and, if so, was that a deviation from the test as applied in *Data Processing*?

3. How broadly should the zone-of-interests test be interpreted? Should a plaintiff be permitted to sue for review of agency decision-making even when Congress did not intend it to benefit from the statutory provision it invokes? Should courts only permit suit when Congress intended a plaintiff to benefit from the statutory provision it invokes? Only when Congress has granted plaintiff a personal legal right to be protected from the harms caused by the defendant (i.e., eliminate the zone-of-interests test and citizen-suit provisions altogether)?

Application & Analysis

1. The Indian Reorganization Act ("IRA") authorizes the Interior Secretary to acquire property "for the purpose of providing land for Indians." 25 U.S.C. § 465. Section 465 is the capstone of the IRA's land provisions. According to Interior Department regulations, the provision plays a key role in the IRA's overall goal of facilitating tribal self-determination, economic development, and housing development. 25 CFR § 151.3(a)(3) (2012).

   A Native American tribe requested that the Interior Secretary take into trust on its behalf a tract of land known as the Radley Property, which the tribe intends to use "for gaming purposes." Specifically, the tribe's request stated that the casino it plans to build would produce "revenue necessary to promote tribal economic development, self-sufficiency and a strong tribal government capable of providing its members with sorely needed social and educational programs." Pursuant to § 465, the Secretary took title to the Radley Property.

   Gale Suarez, who lives near the Radley Property, filed suit in federal district court under APA § 702, asserting that § 465 did not authorize the Secretary to acquire the property because the tribe was not federally recognized under the IRA. She alleged a variety of economic, environmental, and aesthetic harms that would result from the tribe's proposed use of the property to operate a casino, and she requested injunctive and declaratory relief reversing the Secretary's decision to take title to the land. The Secretary argues that Suarez lacks standing because § 465 focuses on land acquisition, whereas Suarez's interests relate to the land's use. Assess the merits of the Secretary's argument.

---

a. Congressional Power and the Zone of Interests Test

What power does Congress have to override or alter the zone-of-interests requirements? Can Congress grant a class of plaintiffs the right to sue that is broader than the zone-of-interests test might otherwise allow? When a statutory provision is written so broadly as even to include interests that are *hostile* to the general policy evident in the legislative scheme, should courts nevertheless deny standing under the zone test? Even assuming that Congress has the power to override the Court's zone test, at what point does Congress so alter the terms on which plaintiffs gain standing that it endangers the constitutional limits imposed by Article III?

   In the following case, a unanimous Court addressed these questions in the context of the Endangered Species Act.

Bennett v. Spear
520 U.S. 154 (1997)

Justice SCALIA delivered the opinion of the Court. . . .

I

The [Endangered Species Act] requires the Secretary of the Interior to promulgate regulations listing those species of animals that are "threatened" or "endangered" under specified criteria, and to designate their "critical habitat." 16 U.S.C. § 1533. The ESA further requires each federal agency to "insure that any action authorized, funded, or carried out by such agency . . . is not likely to jeopardize the continued existence of any endangered species or threatened species or result in the destruction or adverse modification of habitat of such species which is determined by the Secretary . . . to be critical." § 1536(a)(2). If an agency determines that action it proposes to take may adversely affect a listed species, it must engage in formal consultation with the Fish and Wildlife Service, as delegate of the Secretary, *ibid.*; 50 CFR § 402.14 (1995), after which the Service must provide the agency with a written statement (the Biological Opinion) explaining how the proposed action will affect the species or its habitat, 16 U.S.C. § 1536(b)(3)(A). If the Service concludes that the proposed action will "jeopardize the continued existence of any [listed] species or threatened species or result in the destruction or adverse modification of [critical habitat]," § 1536(a)(2), the Biological Opinion must outline any "reasonable and prudent alternatives" that the Service believes will avoid that consequence, § 1536(b)(3)(A). Additionally, if the Biological Opinion concludes that the agency action will not result in jeopardy or adverse habitat modification, or if it offers reasonable and prudent alternatives to avoid that consequence, the Service must provide the agency with a written statement (known as the Incidental Take Statement) specifying the "impact of such incidental taking on the species," any "reasonable and prudent measures that the [Service] considers necessary or appropriate to minimize such impact," and setting forth "the terms and conditions . . . that must be complied with by the Federal agency . . . to implement [those measures]." § 1536(b)(4).

The Klamath Project, one of the oldest federal reclamation schemes, is a series of lakes, rivers, dams, and irrigation canals in northern California and southern Oregon. The project was undertaken by the Secretary of the Interior pursuant to the Reclamation Act of 1902, 32 Stat. 388, as amended, 43 U.S.C. § 371 *et seq.*, and the Act of Feb. 9, 1905, 33 Stat. 714, and is administered by the Bureau of Reclamation, which is under the Secretary's jurisdiction. In 1992, the Bureau notified the Service that operation of the project might affect the Lost River Sucker (Deltistes luxatus) and Shortnose Sucker (Chasmistes brevirostris), species of fish that were listed as endangered in 1988, *see* 53 Fed. Reg. 27130-27133 (1988). After formal consultation with the Bureau in accordance with 50 CFR § 402.14 (1995), the Service issued a Biological Opinion which concluded that the long-term operation of the Klamath Project was likely to jeopardize the continued existence of the Lost River and shortnose suckers. The Biological Opinion identified "reasonable and prudent alternatives" the Service believed would avoid jeopardy, which included the maintenance of minimum water levels on Clear Lake and Gerber reservoirs. The Bureau later notified the Service that it intended to operate the project in compliance with the Biological Opinion.

Petitioners, two Oregon irrigation districts that receive Klamath Project water and the operators of two ranches within those districts, filed the present action against the director and regional director of the Service and the Secretary of the Interior. Neither the Bureau [of Reclamation] nor any of its officials is named as defendant. The complaint asserts that the Bureau "has been following essentially the same procedures for storing and releasing water from Clear Lake and Gerber reservoirs throughout the twentieth century"; that "[t]here is no scientifically or commercially available evidence indicating that the populations of endangered suckers in Clear Lake and Gerber reservoirs have declined, are declining, or will decline as a result" of the Bureau's operation of the Klamath Project; that "[t]here is no commercially or scientifically available evidence indicating that the restrictions on lake levels imposed in the Biological Opinion will have any beneficial effect on the . . . populations of suckers in Clear Lake and Gerber reservoirs"; and that the Bureau nonetheless "will abide by the restrictions imposed by the Biological Opinion."

Petitioners' complaint included three claims for relief that are relevant here. The first and second claims allege that the Service's jeopardy determination with respect to Clear Lake and Gerber reservoirs, and the ensuing imposition of minimum water levels, violated § 7 of the ESA, 16 U.S.C. § 1536. The third claim is that the imposition of minimum water elevations constituted an implicit determination of critical habitat for the suckers, which violated § 4 of the ESA, 16 U.S.C. § 1533(b)(2), because it failed to take into consideration the designation's economic impact. . . .

The complaint asserts that petitioners' use of the reservoirs and related waterways for "recreational, aesthetic and commercial purposes, as well as for their primary sources of irrigation water," will be "irreparably damaged" by the actions complained of, and that the restrictions on water delivery "recommended" by the Biological Opinion "adversely affect plaintiffs by substantially reducing the quantity of available irrigation water." In essence, petitioners claim a competing interest in the water the Biological Opinion declares necessary for the preservation of the suckers.

The District Court . . . concluded that petitioners did not have standing because their "recreational, aesthetic, and commercial interests . . . do not fall within the zone of interests sought to be protected by ESA." The Court of Appeals for the Ninth Circuit affirmed. It held that the "zone of interests" test limits the class of persons who may obtain judicial review not only under the APA, but also under the citizen-suit provision of the ESA, 16 U.S.C. § 1540(g), and that "only plaintiffs who allege an interest in the *preservation* of endangered species fall within the zone of interests protected by the ESA." [*Bennett v. Plenert*, 63 F.3d 915, 919 (9th Cir. 1995) (emphasis in original).]

In this Court, petitioners raise two questions: first, whether the prudential standing rule known as the "zone of interests" test applies to claims brought under the citizen-suit provision of the ESA; and second, if so, whether petitioners have standing under that test notwithstanding that the interests they seek to vindicate are economic rather than environmental. . . .

II

We first turn to the question the Court of Appeals found dispositive: whether petitioners lack standing by virtue of the zone-of-interests test. Although petitioners contend that their claims lie both under the ESA and the APA, we look first at the ESA because it may permit petitioners to recover their litigation costs, *see* 16 U.S.C. § 1540(g)(4), and because the APA by its terms independently authorizes review only when "there is no other adequate remedy in a court," 5 U.S.C. § 704.

The question of standing "involves both constitutional limitations on federal-court jurisdiction and prudential limitations on its exercise." *Warth v. Seldin*, 422 U.S. 490, 498 (1975). To satisfy the "case" or "controversy" requirement of Article III, which is the "irreducible constitutional minimum" of standing, a plaintiff must, generally speaking, demonstrate that he has suffered "injury in fact," that the injury is "fairly traceable" to the actions of the defendant, and that the injury will likely be redressed by a favorable decision. *Lujan v. Defenders of Wildlife*, 504 U.S. 555, 560-561 (1992). In addition to the immutable requirements of Article III, "the federal judiciary has also adhered to a set of prudential principles that bear on the question of standing." *Id.* at 474-475. Like their constitutional counterparts, these "judicially self-imposed limits on the exercise of federal jurisdiction," *Allen v. Wright*, 468 U.S. 737, 751 (1984), are "founded in concern about the proper — and properly limited — role of the courts in a democratic society," *Warth, supra*, at 498; but unlike their constitutional counterparts, they can be modified or abrogated by Congress. Numbered among these prudential requirements is the doctrine of particular concern in this case: that a plaintiff's grievance must arguably fall within the zone of interests protected or regulated by the statutory provision or constitutional guarantee invoked in the suit.

. . . We have made clear . . . that the breadth of the zone of interests varies according to the provisions of law at issue, so that what comes within the zone of interests of a statute for purposes of obtaining judicial review of administrative action under the "'generous review provisions'" of the APA may not do so for other purposes.

Congress legislates against the background of our prudential standing doctrine, which applies unless it is expressly negated. The first question in the present case is whether the ESA's citizen-suit provision, set forth in pertinent part in the margin,[2] negates the zone-of-interests test (or, perhaps more accurately, expands the zone of interests). We think it does. The first operative portion of the provision says that "any person may commence a civil suit"—an authorization of remarkable breadth when compared with the language Congress ordinarily uses. Even in some other environmental statutes, Congress has used more restrictive formulations, such as "[any person] having an interest which is or may be adversely affected," 33 U.S.C. § 1365(g) (Clean Water Act); *see also* 30 U.S.C. § 1270(a) (Surface Mining Control and Reclamation Act) (same); "[a]ny person suffering legal wrong," 15 U.S.C. § 797(b)(5) (Energy Supply and Environmental Coordination Act); or "any person having a valid legal interest which is or may be adversely affected . . . whenever such action constitutes a case or controversy," 42 U.S.C. § 9124(a) (Ocean Thermal Energy Conversion Act). And in contexts other than the environment, Congress has often been even more restrictive. In statutes concerning unfair trade practices and other commercial matters, for example, it has authorized suit only by "[a]ny person injured in his business or property," 7 U.S.C. § 2305(c); *see also* 15 U.S.C. § 72 (same), or only by "competitors, customers, or subsequent purchasers," § 298(b).

Our readiness to take the term "any person" at face value is greatly augmented by two interrelated considerations: that the overall subject matter of this legislation is the environment (a matter in which it is common to think all persons have an interest) and that the obvious purpose of the particular provision in question is to encourage enforcement by so-called "private attorneys general"—evidenced by its elimination of the usual amount-in-controversy and diversity-of-citizenship requirements, its provision for recovery of the costs of litigation (including even expert witness fees), and its reservation to the Government of a right of first refusal to pursue the action initially and a right to intervene later. Given these factors, we think

---

[2] (1) Except as provided in paragraph (2) of this subsection any person may commence a civil suit on his own behalf—

> (A) to enjoin any person, including the United States and any other governmental instrumentality or agency (to the extent permitted by the eleventh amendment to the Constitution), who is alleged to be in violation of any provision of this chapter or regulation issued under the authority thereof; or . . . .

> (C) against the Secretary where there is alleged a failure of the Secretary to perform any act or duty under section 1533 of this title which is not discretionary with the Secretary.

The district courts shall have jurisdiction, without regard to the amount in controversy or the citizenship of the parties, to enforce any such provision or regulation, or to order the Secretary to perform such act or duty, as the case may be. . . .

the conclusion of expanded standing follows *a fortiori* from our decision in *Trafficante v. Metropolitan Life Ins. Co.*, 409 U.S. 205 (1972), which held that standing was expanded to the full extent permitted under Article III by § 810(a) of the Civil Rights Act of 1968, 82 Stat. 85, 42 U.S.C. § 3610(a) (1986 ed.), that authorized "[a]ny person who claims to have been injured by a discriminatory housing practice" to sue for violations of the Act. There also we relied on textual evidence of a statutory scheme to rely on private litigation to ensure compliance with the Act. The statutory language here is even clearer, and the subject of the legislation makes the intent to permit enforcement by everyman even more plausible.

It is true that the plaintiffs here are seeking to prevent application of environmental restrictions rather than to implement them. But the "any person" formulation applies to all the causes of action authorized by § 1540(g) — not only to actions against private violators of environmental restrictions, and not only to actions against the Secretary asserting underenforcement under § 1533, but also to actions against the Secretary asserting overenforcement under § 1533. As we shall discuss below, the citizen-suit provision does favor environmentalists in that it covers all private violations of the ESA but not all failures of the Secretary to meet his administrative responsibilities; but there is no textual basis for saying that its expansion of standing requirements applies to environmentalists alone. The Court of Appeals therefore erred in concluding that petitioners lacked standing under the zone-of-interests test to bring their claims under the ESA's citizen-suit provision.

[In Section III of its opinion, the Court reached three conclusions. First, the plaintiffs satisfied all Article III standing requirements. Second, their first and second claims under § 1536 were not reviewable under § 1540(g)(1)(A) or (C). Section 1540(g)(1)(A) applies to regulated entities (private parties and other agencies) but not to the Secretary's enforcement of the ESA, and § 1540(g)(1)(C), by its terms, applies only to the Secretary's failure to perform non-discretionary acts "under section 1533." Third, their claim under § 1533(b)(2) was reviewable under § 1540(g)(1)(C) because it alleged that the Secretary failed to perform a non-discretionary duty.]

IV

The foregoing analysis establishes that the principal statute invoked by petitioners, the ESA, does authorize review of their § 1533 claim, but does not support their claims based upon the Secretary's alleged failure to comply with § 1536. To complete our task, we must therefore inquire whether these § 1536 claims may nonetheless be brought under the Administrative Procedure Act, which authorizes a court to "set aside agency action, findings, and conclusions found to be . . . arbitrary, capricious, an abuse of discretion, or otherwise not in accordance with law," 5 U.S.C. § 706.

A

No one contends (and it would not be maintainable) that the causes of action against the Secretary set forth in the ESA's citizen-suit provision are exclusive, supplanting those provided by the APA. The APA, by its terms, provides a right to judicial review of all "final agency action for which there is no other adequate remedy in a court," § 704, and applies universally "except to the extent that — (1) statutes preclude judicial review; or (2) agency action is committed to agency discretion by law," § 701(a). Nothing in the ESA's citizen-suit provision expressly precludes review under the APA, nor do we detect anything in the statutory scheme suggesting a purpose to do so. And any contention that the relevant provision of 16 U.S.C. § 1536(a)(2) is discretionary would fly in the face of its text, which uses the imperative "shall."

In determining whether the petitioners have standing under the zone-of-interests test to bring their APA claims, we look not to the terms of the ESA's citizen-suit provision, but to the substantive provisions of the ESA, the alleged violations of which serve as the gravamen of the complaint. The classic formulation of the zone-of-interests test is set forth in *Data Processing*, 397 U.S., at 153: "whether the interest sought to be protected by the complainant is arguably within the zone of interests to be protected or regulated by the statute or constitutional guarantee in question." The Court of Appeals concluded that this test was not met here, since petitioners are neither directly regulated by the ESA nor seek to vindicate its overarching purpose of species preservation. That conclusion was error.

Whether a plaintiff's interest is "arguably . . . protected . . . by the statute" within the meaning of the zone-of-interests test is to be determined not by reference to the overall purpose of the Act in question (here, species preservation), but by reference to the particular provision of law upon which the plaintiff relies. It is difficult to understand how the Ninth Circuit could have failed to see this from our cases. In *Data Processing* itself, for example, we did not require that the plaintiffs' suit vindicate the overall purpose of the Bank Service Corporation Act of 1962, but found it sufficient that their commercial interest was sought to be protected by the anticompetition limitation contained in § 4 of the Act — the specific provision which they alleged had been violated. *See Data Processing, supra,* at 155-156. As we said with the utmost clarity in *National Wildlife Federation*, "the plaintiff must establish that the injury he complains of . . . falls within the 'zone of interests' sought to be protected *by the statutory provision whose violation forms the legal basis for his complaint*." 497 U.S., at 883 (emphasis added).

In the claims that we have found not to be covered by the ESA's citizen-suit provision, petitioners allege a violation of § 7 of the ESA, 16 U.S.C. § 1536, which requires, *inter alia,* that each agency "use the best scientific and commercial data available," § 1536(a)(2). Petitioners contend that the available scientific and commercial data show that the continued operation of the Klamath Project will not have a detrimental impact on the endangered suckers, that the imposition of minimum lake levels is not necessary to protect the fish, and that by issuing a Biological Opinion which makes unsubstantiated findings to the contrary the defendants have acted arbitrarily and in violation of § 1536(a)(2). The obvious purpose of the requirement that each agency "use the best scientific and commercial data available" is to ensure that the ESA not be implemented haphazardly, on the basis of speculation or surmise. While this no doubt serves to advance the ESA's overall goal of species preservation, we think it readily apparent that another objective (if not indeed the primary one) is to avoid needless economic dislocation produced by agency officials zealously but unintelligently pursuing their environmental objectives. That economic consequences are an explicit concern of the ESA is evidenced by § 1536(h), which provides exemption from § 1536(a)(2)'s no-jeopardy mandate where there are no reasonable and prudent alternatives to the agency action and the benefits of the agency action clearly outweigh the benefits of any alternatives. We believe the "best scientific and commercial data" provision is similarly intended, at least in part, to prevent uneconomic (because erroneous) jeopardy determinations. Petitioners' claim that they are victims of such a mistake is plainly within the zone of interests that the provision protects.

[In Section IV.B of the Court's opinion, it concluded that the Biological Opinion was a "final action" under 5 U.S.C. § 704.]

* * *

The Court of Appeals erred in affirming the District Court's dismissal of petitioners' claims for lack of jurisdiction. Petitioners' complaint alleges facts sufficient to meet the requirements of Article III standing, and none of their ESA claims is precluded by the zone-of-interests test. Petitioners' § 1533 claim is reviewable under the ESA's citizen-suit provision, and petitioners' remaining claims are reviewable under the APA.

The judgment of the Court of Appeals is reversed, and the case is remanded for further proceedings consistent with this opinion.

It is so ordered.

QUESTION SET 9.15

Review & Synthesis

1. The Court acknowledged that Congress has the authority to supersede the zone-of-interests test when it stated that the Endangered Species Act's citizen-suit provision (§ 1540(g)) "negates the zone-of-interests test (or, perhaps more accurately, expands the zone of interests)." In what way, precisely, did § 1540(g) do this? What was the baseline of interests

normally recognized by the test, and how did § 1540(g) extend standing beyond it?

2. ESA § 1540(g)(1)(A) ("subsection (A)") allows private parties to sue "any person" who is alleged to have violated the ESA's provisions. Why did the Court conclude that this language excludes the Interior Secretary? In other words, didn't the plain meaning of the term "any person" necessarily include the Secretary, thus allowing plaintiffs to sue him for alleged ESA violations?

3. If ESA § 1540(g)(1)(A) does not permit private parties to sue the Interior Secretary for making discretionary decisions that allegedly violate the Act, are they completely forbidden from judicially challenging those decisions?

4. What did Justice Scalia mean when he observed "that the breadth of the zone of interests varies according to the provisions of law at issue, so that what comes within the zone of interests of a statute for purposes of obtaining judicial review of administrative action under the 'generous review provisions' of the APA may not do so for other purposes"?

5. The Court concluded that the plaintiffs—ranchers and irrigation districts—had satisfied the zone-of-interests test even though their interest in maintaining reservoir water levels could have undermined the government's efforts to save certain endangered fish species. The Court justified its conclusion, in part, by observing that "there is no textual basis for saying that [the term 'any person' as used in § 1540(g)(1)(A)] applies to environmentalists alone." Did there need to be one? Even if one accepts that § 1540(g) is much broader than most other citizen-suit provisions Congress enacts, does it necessarily follow that it must be read to allow suit by plaintiffs who are *hostile* to the ESA's overall purpose?

Application & Analysis

1. The Clean Water Act is the principal law governing pollution control and water quality of the nation's waterways. The CWA's purpose is to restore and maintain the chemical, physical, and biological integrity of the Nation's waters. Its citizen-suit provision, 33 U.S.C. § 1365(a), currently provides that "any citizen may commence a civil action on his own behalf (1) against any person . . . who is alleged to be in violation of (A) an effluent standard or limitation under this chapter or (B) an order issued by the [EPA] Administrator or a State with respect to such a standard or limitation, or; (2) against the Administrator where there is alleged a failure of the Administrator to perform any act or duty under this chapter which is not discretionary with the Administrator." Section § 1365(g)

defines "citizen" as "a person or persons having an interest which is or may be adversely affected."

The House of Representatives is considering the following revisions to this provision. For each one, discuss (1) whether and how it would expand or contract the current availability of judicial review currently provided by § 1365(a); (2) whether it would allow plaintiffs to sue whose interests are different from the CWA's overall statutory purpose; and (3) whether Congress has the constitutional authority to enact it. The following alternatives have been offered:

a. § 1365(a) revised to state "any *person* may commence a civil suit on *his or her* own behalf. . . ." Section § 1365(g) is eliminated.

b. § 1365(g) revised to state "a person or persons *having suffered or may suffer a legal wrong as a result of any violation or failure described in subsection (a) of this section.*"

c. § 1365(a)(1)(A) revised to state that a civil action may be commenced against any person alleged to have violated "an effluent standard or limitation under this chapter, *where such violation has caused or is likely to cause cumulative economic damage in excess of $5 million.*"

d. § 1365(a)(2) revised to eliminate "which is not discretionary with the Administrator."

8. The Timing of Judicial Review

Thus far, we have studied *whether* Congress permits judicial review of agency actions (reviewability), and, if so, *who* may initiate that review in federal court (standing). Next we consider another piece of the judicial oversight puzzle. Even if the federal courts are permitted to review agency conduct, and even if the plaintiff who files suit has standing, she must still file that suit *at the right time.* The courts will dismiss her case if she is either too early (the most frequent concern in agency review cases), or if she is too late. As is often said, timing is everything.

The Supreme Court has identified three doctrines to address the timing question: (1) exhaustion, (2) finality, and (3) ripeness. "Exhaustion" generally refers to the idea that litigants must give an agency the opportunity to address their complaints before heading to court. "Finality" refers to the requirement that an agency has concluded its consideration of a matter before courts are permitted to review it. "Ripeness" is both constitutional and prudential in nature. It "prevent[s] the courts, through avoidance of premature adjudication, from entangling themselves in abstract disagreements over administrative policies, and also [protects] the agencies from judicial interference until an administrative decision has been formalized and its effects felt in a concrete way by the challenging parties." *Abbott Laboratories v. Gardner*, 387 U.S. 136, 148-49 (1967).

A word of warning before you consider the materials that follow: Courts routinely blur the lines between these doctrines, mix them up, or use them interchangeably. For instance, ripeness is sometimes described as simply an aspect of finality, and some commentators have argued that finality and exhaustion are practically identical. Nevertheless, each doctrine has a distinct conceptual core that distinguishes it, at least to some extent, from the others.

a. Ripeness

i. Pre-enforcement Review

Before 1967, federal courts infrequently entertained constitutional or statutory challenges to agency policies unless the agency had already attempted to enforce them. Rather, courts would hear challenges only when the party asserted them as *defenses* to agency enforcement actions. Such postponement gave courts more developed, concrete records with which to work (or so the argument went). *International Longshoremen's and Warehouseman's Union, Local 37 v. Boyd*, 347 U.S. 222 (1954), serves as an apt example. According to the then-District Director of Immigration and Nationality in Seattle, § 212(d)(7) of the Immigration and Nationality Act of 1952 required him to treat noncitizens who resided in the continental United Sates and returned there from work in Alaska as if they were attempting to enter the United States for the first time. (Alaska was a U.S. territory at the time and would not gain statehood until January 3, 1959.) As a practical matter, treating noncitizens in this manner would have significantly increased the likelihood that they would be denied reentry to the continental United States; as is the case today, noncitizen first-time entry was subject to many more restrictions than noncitizen resident reentry. A labor union whose members spent summers working in Alaska's salmon and herring canneries sought judicial review of the Director's interpretation, arguing that it could result in some of its noncitizen members being denied reentry to the continental United States. The Court concluded that the union's claim was not ripe for adjudication because the Director had taken no steps to deny reentry to any of its members. It was, in the Court's view, a "hypothetical" controversy. *Id.* at 224. In his dissent, Justice Black pointed out (to no avail) that the union's noncitizen members were planning to work in Alaska the following summer, and that the Director had already announced they would be subject to examination and exclusion under the statute when they tried to return. Thus, as *International Longshoremen's* showed, a restrictive approach to ripeness could allow seemingly concrete controversies involving administrative decision-making to escape pre-enforcement review. Aspiring plaintiffs would accordingly be left with a difficult choice: they could accept agency policies that possibly infringed their rights or they could violate those policies and expose themselves to potentially ruinous legal consequences. *See also United Public Works of America v. Mitchell*, 330 U.S. 75 (1947); *Columbia Broadcasting System v. United States*, 316 U.S. 407 (1942) (Frankfurter, J. dissenting).

While the Court generally withheld judicial review until after agencies initiated enforcement proceedings, it did not always do so. It on occasion showed its willingness to entertain pre-enforcement review of agency action as well. Two decisions—*CBS* and *United States v. Storer Broadcasting Co.*, 351 U.S. 192 (1956)—involved challenges to Federal Communications Commission policies that could have negatively affected broadcast licensees but that the agency had taken no steps to enforce. The Court allowed those challenges to move forward, observing that the regulations were "not any less reviewable because their promulgation did not operate of their own force to deny or cancel a license." *Storer*, 351 U.S. at 198-99 (quoting *Columbia Broadcasting*, 316 U.S. at 417). Rather, it was "enough that, by setting controlling standards for the Commission's action, the regulations purport[ed] to operate to alter and affect adversely appellant's contractual rights and business relations with station owners whose applications for licenses the regulations will cause to be rejected and whose licenses the regulations may cause to be revoked." *Id* at 199 (quoting *Columbia Broadcasting*, 316 U.S. at 422). The FCC had taken "final agency action" as defined by APA § 704, *Storer*, 351 U.S. at 198, and the effect of that action was clear even in the absence of their specific enforcement against the plaintiffs. *See also Frozen Food Express v. United States*, 351 U.S. 40 (1956).

The following trilogy of cases decided on the same day and by the same Justice (John Marshall Harlan II)—*Abbott Laboratories v. Gardner, Toilet Goods Association v. Gardner*, and *Gardner v. Toilet Goods Association*—marked a definitive turning point in the Supreme Court's ripeness jurisprudence. As mentioned earlier in this casebook, these decisions also marked a turning point in the Judiciary's involvement in overseeing administrative decision-making. *See Chapter* 1, pages 27-29. Did the Court continue to insist that enforcement was necessary for courts properly to review administrative conduct? Did it adopt a more generous approach to ripeness that would increase opportunities for pre-enforcement review?

Abbott Laboratories v. Gardner
387 U.S. 136 (1967)

Mr. Justice HARLAN delivered the opinion of the Court.

In 1962 Congress amended the Federal Food, Drug, and Cosmetic Act, (52 Stat. 1040, as amended by the Drug Amendments of 1962, 76 Stat. 780, 21 U.S.C. § 301 *et seq.*), to require manufacturers of prescription drugs to print the "established name" of the drug "prominently and in type at least half as large as that used thereon for any proprietary name or designation for such drug," on labels and other printed material, § 502(e)(1)(B), 21 U.S.C. § 352(e)(1)(B). The "established name" is one designated by the Secretary of Health, Education, and Welfare pursuant to § 502(e)(2) of the Act, 21 U.S.C. § 352(e)(2); the "proprietary name" is usually a trade name under which a particular drug is marketed. The underlying purpose of the 1962 amendment was to bring to the attention of doctors and patients the fact that many of the drugs sold under familiar trade names are actually identical to drugs sold under their "established" or less familiar trade names at significantly lower prices. The Commissioner of Food and Drugs, exercising authority delegated to him by the Secretary, 22 Fed. Reg. 1051, 25 Fed. Reg. 8625, published proposed regulations designed to implement the statute, 28 Fed. Reg. 1448. After inviting and considering comments submitted by interested parties the Commissioner promulgated the following regulation for the "efficient enforcement" of the Act, § 701(a), 21 U.S.C. § 371(a):

> If the label or labeling of a prescription drug bears a proprietary name or designation for the drug or any ingredient thereof, the established name, if such there be, corresponding to such proprietary name or designation, shall accompany each appearance of such proprietary name or designation. 21 CFR § 1.104(g)(1).

A similar rule was made applicable to advertisements for prescription drugs, 21 CFR § 1.105(b)(1).

The present action was brought by a group of 37 individual drug manufacturers and by the Pharmaceutical Manufacturers Association, of which all the petitioner companies are members, and which includes manufacturers of more than 90% of the Nation's supply of prescription drugs. They challenged the regulations on the ground that the Commissioner exceeded his authority under the statute by promulgating an order requiring labels, advertisements, and other printed matter relating to prescription drugs to designate the established name of the particular drug involved every time its trade name is used anywhere in such material.

The District Court, on cross motions for summary judgment, granted the declaratory and injunctive relief sought, finding that the statute did not sweep so broadly as to permit the Commissioner's "every time" interpretation. The Court of Appeals for the Third Circuit reversed without reaching the merits of the case. It held first that under the statutory scheme provided by the Federal Food, Drug, and Cosmetic Act pre-enforcement review of these regulations was unauthorized and therefore beyond the jurisdiction of the District Court. Second, the Court of Appeals held that no "actual case or controversy" existed and, for that reason, that no relief under the Administrative Procedure Act, 5 U.S.C. §§ 701-704 (1964 ed., Supp. II), or under the Declaratory Judgment Act, 28 U.S.C. § 2201, was in any event available. . . .

[In Section I of its opinion, the Court concluded that nothing in the Food, Drug, and Cosmetic Act indicated congressional intent to prohibit pre-enforcement review of the Commissioner's labeling regulations.]

II.

. . . The injunctive and declaratory judgment remedies are discretionary, and courts traditionally have been reluctant to apply them to administrative determinations unless these arise in the context of a controversy "ripe" for judicial resolution. Without undertaking to survey the intricacies of the ripeness doctrine it is fair to say that its basic rationale is to prevent the courts, through avoidance of premature adjudication, from entangling themselves in abstract disagreements over administrative policies, and also to protect the agencies from judicial interference until an administrative decision has been formalized and its effects felt in a concrete way by the challenging parties. The problem is best seen in a twofold aspect, requiring us to evaluate both the fitness of the issues for judicial decision and the hardship to the parties of withholding court consideration.

As to the former factor, we believe the issues presented are appropriate for judicial resolution at this time. First, all parties agree that the issue tendered is a purely legal one: whether the statute was properly construed by the Commissioner to require the established name of the drug to be used every time the proprietary name is employed. Both sides moved for summary judgment in the District Court, and no claim is made here that further administrative proceedings are contemplated. It is suggested that the justification for this rule might vary with different circumstances, and that the expertise of the Commissioner is relevant to passing upon the validity of the regulation. This of course is true, but the suggestion overlooks the fact that both sides have approached this case as one purely of congressional intent, and that the Government made no effort to justify the regulation in factual terms.

Second, the regulations in issue we find to be "final agency action" within the meaning of § 10 of the Administrative Procedure Act, 5 U.S.C. § 704, as construed in judicial decisions. An "agency action" includes any "rule," defined by the Act as "an agency statement of general or particular applicability and future effect designed to implement, interpret, or prescribe law or policy," §§ 2(c), 2(g), 5 U.S.C. §§ 551(4), 551(13). The cases dealing with judicial review of administrative actions have interpreted the "finality" element in a pragmatic way. Thus in *Columbia Broadcasting System v. United States*, 316 U.S. 407, a suit under the Urgent Deficiencies Act, 38 Stat. 219, this Court held reviewable a regulation of the Federal Communications Commission setting forth certain proscribed contractual arrangements between chain broadcasters and local stations. The FCC did not have direct authority to regulate these contracts, and its rule asserted only that it would not license stations which maintained such contracts with the networks. Although no license had in fact been denied or revoked, and the FCC regulation could properly be characterized as a statement only of its intentions, the Court held that "Such regulations have the force of law before their sanctions are invoked as well as after. When as here they are promulgated by order of the Commission and the expected conformity to them causes injury cognizable by a court of equity, they are appropriately the subject of attack. . . ." 316 U.S., at 418-419.

Two more recent cases have taken a similarly flexible view of finality. In *Frozen Food Express v. United States*, 351 U.S. 40, at issue was an Interstate Commerce Commission order specifying commodities that were deemed to fall within the statutory class of "agricultural commodities." Vehicles carrying such commodities were exempt from ICC supervision. An action was brought by a carrier that claimed to be transporting exempt commodities, but which the ICC order had not included in its terms. Although the dissenting opinion noted that this ICC order had no authority except to give notice of how the Commission interpreted the Act and would have effect only if and when a particular action was brought against a particular carrier, and argued that "judicial intervention (should) be withheld until administrative action has reached its complete development," 351 U.S., at 45, the Court held the order reviewable.

Again, in *United States v. Storer Broadcasting Co.*, 351 U.S. 192, the Court held to be a final agency action within the meaning of the Administrative Procedure Act an FCC regulation announcing a Commission policy that it would not issue a television license to an applicant already owning five such licenses, even though no specific application was before the Commission. The Court stated: "The process of rulemaking was complete. It was final agency action . . . by which Storer claimed to be "aggrieved." 351 U.S. at 198.

We find decision in the present case following *a fortiori* from these precedents. The regulation challenged here, promulgated in a formal manner after announcement in the Federal Register and consideration of comments by interested parties is quite clearly definitive. There is no hint that this regulation is informal, or only the ruling of a subordinate official, or tentative. It was made effective upon publication, and the Assistant General Counsel for Food and Drugs stated in the District Court that compliance was expected.

The Government argues, however, that the present case can be distinguished from cases like *Frozen Food Express* on the ground that in those instances the agency involved could implement its policy directly, while here the Attorney General must authorize criminal and seizure actions for violations of the statute. In the context of this case, we do not find this argument persuasive. These regulations are not meant to advise the Attorney General, but purport to be directly authorized by the statute. Thus, if within the Commissioner's authority, they have the status of law and violations of them carry heavy criminal and civil sanctions. Also, there is no representation that the Attorney General and the Commissioner disagree in this area; the Justice Department is defending this very suit. It would be adherence to a mere technicality to give any credence to this contention. Moreover, the agency does have direct authority to enforce this regulation in the context of passing upon applications for clearance of new drugs, § 505, 21 U.S.C. § 355, or certification of certain antibiotics, § 507, 21 U.S.C. § 357.

This is also a case in which the impact of the regulations upon the petitioners is sufficiently direct and immediate as to render the issue appropriate for judicial review at this stage. These regulations purport to give an authoritative interpretation of a statutory provision that has a direct effect on the day-to-day business of all prescription drug companies; its promulgation puts petitioners in a dilemma that it was the very purpose of the Declaratory Judgment Act to ameliorate. As the District Court found on the basis of uncontested allegations, "Either they must comply with the every time requirement and incur the costs of changing over their promotional material and labeling or they must follow their present course and risk prosecution." The regulations are clear-cut, and were made effective immediately upon publication; as noted earlier the agency's counsel represented to the District Court that immediate compliance with their terms was expected. If petitioners wish to comply they must change all their labels, advertisements, and promotional materials; they must destroy stocks of printed matter; and they must invest heavily in new printing type and new supplies. The alternative to compliance—continued use of material which they believe in good faith meets the statutory requirements, but which clearly does not meet the regulation of the Commissioner—may be even more costly. That course would risk serious criminal and civil penalties for the unlawful distribution of "misbranded" drugs.

It is relevant at this juncture to recognize that petitioners deal in a sensitive industry, in which public confidence in their drug products is especially important. To require them to challenge these regulations only as a defense to an action brought by the Government might harm them severely and unnecessarily. Where the legal issue presented is fit for judicial resolution, and where a regulation requires an immediate and significant change in the plaintiffs' conduct of their affairs with serious penalties attached to noncompliance, access to the courts under the Administrative Procedure Act and the Declaratory Judgment Act must be permitted, absent a statutory bar or some other unusual circumstance, neither of which appears here. . . .

. . . [T]he Government urges that to permit resort to the courts in this type of case may delay or impede effective enforcement of the Act. We fully recognize the important public interest served by assuring prompt and unimpeded administration of the Pure Food, Drug, and Cosmetic Act, but we do not find the Government's argument convincing. First, in this particular case, a pre-enforcement challenge by nearly all prescription drug manufacturers is calculated to speed enforcement. If the Government prevails, a large part of the industry is bound by the decree; if the Government loses, it can more quickly revise its regulation.

The Government contends, however, that if the Court allows this consolidated suit, then nothing will prevent a multiplicity of suits in various jurisdictions challenging other regulations. The short answer to this contention is that the courts are well equipped to deal with such eventualities. The venue transfer provision, 28 U.S.C. § 1404(a), may be invoked by the Government to consolidate separate actions. Or, actions in all but one jurisdiction might be stayed pending the conclusion of one proceeding. A court may even in its discretion dismiss a declaratory judgment or injunctive suit if the same issue is pending in litigation elsewhere. In at least one suit for a declaratory judgment, relief was denied with the suggestion that the plaintiff intervene in a pending action elsewhere.

Further, the declaratory judgment and injunctive remedies are equitable in nature, and other equitable defenses may be interposed. If a multiplicity of suits are undertaken in order to harass the Government or to delay enforcement, relief can be denied on this ground alone. The defense of laches could be asserted if the Government is prejudiced by a delay. And courts may even refuse declaratory relief for the nonjoinder of interested parties who are not, technically speaking, indispensable.

In addition to all these safeguards against what the Government fears, it is important to note that the institution of this type of action does not by itself stay the effectiveness of the challenged regulation. There is nothing in the record to indicate that petitioners have sought to stay enforcement of the "every time" regulation pending judicial review. See 5 U.S.C. § 705. If the agency believes that a suit of this type will significantly impede enforcement or will harm the public interest, it need not postpone enforcement of the regulation and may oppose any motion for a judicial stay on the part of those challenging the regulation. *Ibid.* It is scarcely to be doubted that a court would refuse to postpone the effective date of an agency action if the Government could show, as it made no effort to do here, that delay would be detrimental to the public health or safety. . . .

Reversed and remanded.

Mr. Justice BRENNAN took no part in the consideration or decision of this case.

Toilet Goods Association v. Gardner
387 U.S. 158 (1967)

Mr. Justice HARLAN delivered the opinion of the Court.

Petitioners in this case are the Toilet Goods Association, an organization of cosmetics manufacturers accounting for some 90% of annual American sales in this field, and 39 individual cosmetics manufacturers and distributors. They brought this action in the United States District Court for the Southern District of New York seeking declaratory and injunctive relief against the Secretary of Health, Education, and Welfare and the Commissioner of Food and Drugs, on the ground that certain regulations promulgated by the Commissioner exceeded his statutory authority under the Color Additive Amendments to the Federal Food, Drug and Cosmetic Act, 74 Stat. 397, 21 U.S.C. §§ 321-376. The District Court held that the Act did not prohibit this type of pre-enforcement suit, that a case and controversy existed, that the issues presented were justiciable, and that no reasons had been presented by the Government to warrant declining jurisdiction on discretionary grounds. Recognizing that the subsequent decision of the Court of Appeals for the Third Circuit in *Abbott Laboratories v. Celebrezze*, 352 F.2d 286, appeared to conflict with its holding, the District Court reaffirmed its earlier rulings but certified the question of jurisdiction to the Court of Appeals for the Second Circuit under 28 U.S.C. § 1292(b). The Court of Appeals affirmed the judgment of the District Court that jurisdiction to hear the suit existed as to three of the challenged regulations, but sustained the Government's contention that judicial review was improper as to a fourth.

. . . In our decisions reversing the judgment in *Abbott Laboratories*, 387 U.S. 136, and affirming the judgment in *Gardner v. Toilet Goods Assn.*, 387 U.S. 167, both decided today, we hold that nothing in the Food, Drug, and Cosmetic Act, 52 Stat. 1040, as amended, bars a pre-enforcement suit under the Administrative Procedure Act, 5 U.S.C. §§ 701-704 (1964 ed., Supp. II), and the Declaratory Judgment Act, 28 U.S.C. § 2201. We nevertheless agree with the Court of Appeals that judicial review of this particular regulation in this particular context is inappropriate at this stage because, applying the standards set forth in *Abbott Laboratories v. Gardner*, the controversy is not presently ripe for adjudication.

The regulation in issue here was promulgated under the Color Additive Amendments of 1960, 74 Stat. 397, 21 U.S.C. §§ 321-376, a statute that revised and somewhat broadened the authority of the Commissioner to control the ingredients added to foods, drugs, and cosmetics that impart color to them. The Commissioner of Food and Drugs, exercising power delegated by the Secretary, under statutory authority "to promulgate regulations for the efficient enforcement" of the Act, § 701(a), 21 U.S.C. § 371(a), issued the following regulation after due public notice, and consideration of comments submitted by interested parties:

> (a) When it appears to the Commissioner that a person has:
> (4) Refused to permit duly authorized employees of the Food and Drug Administration free access to all manufacturing facilities, processes, and formulae involved in the manufacture of color additives and intermediates from which such color additives are derived; 'he may immediately suspend certification service to such person and may continue such

suspension until adequate corrective action has been taken.' 28 Fed. Reg. 6445-6446; 21 CFR § 8.28.

The petitioners maintain that this regulation is an impermissible exercise of authority, that the FDA has long sought congressional authorization for free access to facilities, processes, and formulae, but that Congress has always denied the agency this power except for prescription drugs. Framed in this way, we agree with petitioners that a "legal" issue is raised, but nevertheless we are not persuaded that the present suit is properly maintainable.

In determining whether a challenge to an administrative regulation is ripe for review a twofold inquiry must be made: first to determine whether the issues tendered are appropriate for judicial resolution, and second to assess the hardship to the parties if judicial relief is denied at that stage.

As to the first of these factors, we agree with the Court of Appeals that the legal issue as presently framed is not appropriate for judicial resolution. This is not because the regulation is not the agency's considered and formalized determination, for we are in agreement with petitioners that under this Court's decisions in *Frozen Food Express v. United States*, 351 U.S. 40, and *United States v. Storer Broadcasting Co.*, 351 U.S. 192, there can be no question that this regulation — promulgated in a formal manner after notice and evaluation of submitted comments — is a "final agency action" under § 10 of the Administrative Procedure Act, 5 U.S.C. § 704. *See Abbott Laboratories v. Gardner*, 387 U.S. 136. Also, we recognize the force of petitioners' contention that the issue as they have framed it presents a purely legal question: whether the regulation is totally beyond the agency's power under the statute, the type of legal issue that courts have occasionally dealt with without requiring a specific attempt at enforcement, *Columbia Broadcasting System v. United States*, 316 U.S. 407[,] or exhaustion of administrative remedies.

These points which support the appropriateness of judicial resolution are, however, outweighed by other considerations. The regulation serves notice only that the Commissioner may under certain circumstances order inspection of certain facilities and data, and that further certification of additives may be refused to those who decline to permit a duly authorized inspection until they have complied in that regard. At this juncture we have no idea whether or when such an inspection will be ordered and what reasons the Commissioner will give to justify his order. The statutory authority asserted for the regulation is the power to promulgate regulations "for the efficient enforcement" of the Act, § 701(a). Whether the regulation is justified thus depends not only, as petitioners appear to suggest, on whether Congress refused to include a specific section of the Act authorizing such inspections, although this factor is to be sure a highly relevant one, but also on whether the statutory scheme as a whole justified promulgation of the regulation. This will depend not merely on an inquiry into statutory purpose, but concurrently on an understanding of what types of enforcement problems are encountered by the FDA, the need for various sorts of supervision in order to effectuate the goals of the Act, and the safeguards devised to protect legitimate trade secrets (*see* 21 CFR § 130.14(c)). We believe that judicial appraisal of these factors is likely to stand on a much surer footing in the context of a specific application of this regulation than could be the case in the framework of the generalized challenge made here.

We are also led to this result by considerations of the effect on the petitioners of the regulation, for the test of ripeness, as we have noted, depends not only on how adequately a court can deal with the legal issue presented, but also on the degree and nature of the regulation's present effect on those seeking relief. The regulation challenged here is not analogous to those that were involved in *Columbia Broadcasting System, supra*, and *Storer, supra*, and those other color additive regulations with which we deal in *Gardner v. Toilet Goods Assn.*, 387 U.S. 167, where the impact of the administrative action could be said to be felt immediately by those subject to it in conducting their day-to-day affairs.

This is not a situation in which primary conduct is affected — when contracts must be negotiated, ingredients tested or substituted, or special records compiled. This regulation merely states that the Commissioner may authorize inspectors to examine certain processes or formulae; no advance action is required of cosmetics manufacturers, who since the enactment of the 1938 Act have been under a statutory duty to permit reasonable inspection of a "factory, warehouse, establishment, or vehicle and all pertinent equipment, finished and unfinished materials; containers, and labeling therein." § 704(a). Moreover, no irremediable adverse consequences flow from requiring a later challenge to this regulation by a manufacturer who refuses to allow this type of inspection. Unlike the other regulations challenged in this action, in which seizure of goods, heavy fines, adverse publicity for distributing "adulterated" goods, and possible criminal liability might penalize failure to comply, *see Gardner v. Toilet Goods Assn.*, 387 U.S. 167, a refusal to admit an inspector here would at most lead only to a suspension of certification services to the particular party, a determination that can then be promptly challenged through an administrative procedure, which in turn is reviewable by a court. Such review will provide an adequate forum for testing the regulation in a concrete situation.

. . . . For these reasons the judgment of the Court of Appeals is affirmed. Affirmed.

[Justice DOUGLAS's dissent is omitted.]

Mr. Justice BRENNAN took no part in the consideration or decision of this case.

Gardner v. Toilet Goods Association
387 U.S. 167 (1967)

Mr. Justice HARLAN delivered the opinion of the Court.

In *Toilet Goods Ass'n. v. Gardner*, 387 U.S. 158, we affirmed a judgment of the Court of Appeals for the Second Circuit holding that judicial review of a regulation concerning inspection of cosmetics factories was improper in a pre-enforcement suit for injunctive and declaratory judgment relief. The present case is brought here by the Government seeking review of the Court of Appeals' further holding that review of three other regulations in this type of action was proper. We likewise affirm.

For reasons stated in our opinion in *Abbott Laboratories v. Gardner*, 387 U.S. 136, we find nothing in the Federal Food, Drug, and Cosmetic Act, (52 Stat. 1040, as amended), 21 U.S.C. § 301 *et seq.*, that precludes resort to the courts for pre-enforcement relief under the Administrative Procedure Act, 5 U.S.C. §§ 701-704 (1964 ed., Supp. II), and the Declaratory Judgment Act, 28 U.S.C. § 2201. And for reasons to follow, we believe the Court of Appeals was correct in holding that the District Court did not err when it refused to dismiss the complaint with respect to these regulations.

The regulations challenged here were promulgated under the Color Additive Amendments of 1960, 74 Stat. 397, 21 U.S.C. §§ 321-376. These statutory provisions, in brief, allow the Secretary of Health, Education, and Welfare and his delegate, the Commissioner of Food and Drugs, to prescribe conditions for the of color additives in foods, drugs, and cosmetics. The Act requires clearance of every color additive in the form of a regulation prescribing conditions for use of that particular additive, and also certification of each "batch" unless exempted by regulation. A color additive is defined as "a dye, pigment, or other substance . . . (which) when added or applied to a food, drug, or cosmetic, or to the human body or any part thereof, is capable (alone or through reaction with other substance) of imparting color thereto . . . ," 21 U.S.C. § 321(t)(1).

Under his general rule-making power, § 701(a), 21 U.S.C. § 371(a), the Commissioner amplified the statutory definition to include as color additives all diluents, that is, "any component of a color additive mixture that is not of itself a color additive and has been intentionally mixed therein to facilitate the use of the mixture in coloring foods, drugs or cosmetics or in coloring the human body." 21 CFR § 8.1(m). By including all diluents as color additives, the Commissioner in respondents' view unlawfully expanded the number of items that must comply with the premarketing clearance procedure.

The Commissioner also included as a color additive within the coverage of the statute any "substance that, when applied to the human body results in coloring . . . unless the function of coloring is purely incidental to its intended use, such as in the case of deodorants. Lipstick, rouge, eye makeup colors, and related cosmetics intended for coloring the human body are 'color additives.'" 21 CFR § 8.1(f). Respondents alleged that in promulgating this regulation the Commissioner again impermissibly expanded the reach of the statute beyond the clear intention of Congress.

A third regulation challenged by these respondents concerns the statutory exemption for hair dyes that conform to a statutory requirement set out in § 601(e), 21 U.S.C. § 361(e). That requirement provides that hair dyes are totally exempt from coverage of the statute if they display a certain cautionary notice on their labels prescribing a "patch test" to determine whether the dye will cause skin irritation on the particular user. The Commissioner's regulation recognizes that the exemption applies to the Color Additive Amendments, but goes on to declare: "If the poisonous or deleterious substance in the 'hair dye' is one to which the caution is inapplicable and for which patch-testing provides no safeguard, the exemption does not apply; nor does the exemption extend to the poisonous or deleterious diluents that may be introduced as wetting agents, hair conditioners, emulsifiers, or other components in a color shampoo, rinse, tint, or similar dual-purpose cosmetics that alter the color of the hair." 21 CFR § 8.1(u).

Respondents contend that this regulation too is irreconcilable with the statute: whereas the statute grants an across-the-board exemption to all hair dyes meeting the patch-test notice requirement, the regulation purports to limit that exemption to cover only those dyes as to which the test is "effective." Moreover, it is said, the regulation appears to limit the exemption only to the coloring ingredient of the dye, and to require clearance for all other components of a particular hair dye.

We agree with the Court of Appeals that respondents' challenge to these regulations is ripe for judicial review under the standards elaborated in *Abbott Laboratories v. Gardner, supra*, namely the appropriateness of the issues for judicial determination and the immediate severity of the regulations' impact upon the plaintiffs.

The issue as framed by the parties is a straightforward legal one: what general classifications of ingredients fall within the coverage of the Color Additive Amendments? Both the Government and the respondents agree that for any color additive, distribution is forbidden unless the additive is (1) listed in a Food and Drug Administration regulation as safe for use under prescribed conditions, and (2) comes from a "certified" batch, unless specifically exempted from the certification requirement. The only question raised is what sort of items are "color additives." The three regulations outlined above purport to elaborate the statutory definition; they include within the statutory term certain classes of items, e.g., diluents, finished cosmetics, and hair dyes, that respondents assert are not within the purview of the statute at all. We agree with the District Court and the Court of Appeals that this is not a situation in which consideration of the underlying legal issues would necessarily be facilitated if they were raised in the context of a specific attempt to enforce the regulations. Rather, to the extent that they purport to apply premarketing requirements to broad categories like finished products and non-coloring ingredients and define the hair-dye exemption, they appear, *prima facie*, to be susceptible of reasoned comparison with the statutory mandate without inquiry into factual issues that ought to be first ventilated before the agency.

For these reasons we find no bar to consideration by the courts of these issues in their present posture. *Abbott Laboratories v. Gardner, supra; United States v. Storer Broadcasting Co.*, 351 U.S. 192 (1956); *Frozen Food Express v. United States*, 351 U.S. 40 (1956).

This result is supported as well by the fact that these regulations are self-executing, and have an immediate and substantial impact upon the respondents. *See Abbott Laboratories v. Gardner*, 386 U.S. pp. 152-153. The Act, as noted earlier, prescribes penalties for the distribution of goods containing color additives unless they have been cleared both by listing in a regulation and by certification of the particular batch. Faced with these regulations the respondents are placed in a quandary. On the one hand they can, as the Government suggests, refuse to comply, continue to distribute products that they believe do not fall within the purview of the Act, and test the regulations by defending against government criminal, seizure, or injunctive suits against them. We agree with the respondents that this proposed avenue of review is beset with penalties and other impediments rendering it inadequate as a satisfactory alternative to the present declaratory judgment action.

The penalties to which cosmetics manufacturers might be subject are extensive. A color additive that does not meet the premarketing clearance procedure is declared to be "unsafe," § 706(a), 21 U.S.C. § 376(a), and hence "adulterated," § 601, 21 U.S.C. § 361(e). It is a "prohibited act" to introduce such material into commerce, § 301, 21 U.S.C. § 331, subject to injunction, § 302, 21 U.S.C. § 332, criminal penalties, § 303, 21 U.S.C. § 333, and seizure of the goods, § 304(a), 21 U.S.C. § 334(a). The price of noncompliance is not limited to these formal penalties. Respondents note the importance of public good will in their industry, and not without reason fear the disastrous impact of an announcement that their cosmetics have been seized as "adulterated."

The alternative to challenging the regulations through noncompliance is, of course, to submit to the regulations and present the various ingredients embraced in them for premarketing clearance. We cannot say on this record that the burden of such a course is other than substantial, accepting, as we must on a motion to dismiss on the pleadings, the allegations of the complaint and supporting affidavits as true. The regulations in this area require separate petitions for listing each color additive, 21 CFR §§ 8.1(f), 8.1(m), 8.4(c), at an initial fee, subject to refunds, of $2,600, a listing. 21 CFR § 8.50(c). One respondent Kolmar Laboratories, Inc., in affidavits submitted to the District Court, asserted that more than 2,700 different formulae would fall under the Commissioner's regulations and would cost some $7,000,000 in listing fees alone. According to the allegations the company also uses 264 diluents which under the challenged regulations must be included as color additives as well. Moreover, a listing is not obtained by mere application alone. Physical and chemical tests must be made and their results submitted with each petition, 21 CFR § 8.4(c), at a cost alleged by Kolmar of up to $42,000,000. Detailed records must be maintained for each listed ingredient, 21 CFR § 8.26, and batches of listed items must ultimately be certified, again at a substantial fee, 21 CFR § 8.51.

Whether or not these cost estimates are exaggerated it is quite clear that if respondents, failing judicial review at this stage, elect to comply with the regulations and await ultimate judicial determination of the validity of them in subsequent litigation, the amount of preliminary paper work, scientific testing, and recordkeeping will be substantial. . . .

. . . [W]e think that this record supports those findings and conclusions. And as in *Abbott Laboratories, supra*, we have been shown no substantial governmental interest that should lead us to reach a conclusion different from the one we have reached in that case. We hold that this action is maintainable.

Affirmed.

Mr. Justice BRENNAN took no part in the consideration or decision of this case.

Mr. Justice FORTAS, with whom THE CHIEF JUSTICE and Mr. Justice CLARK join, concurring in [*Toilet Goods Association v. Gardner*], and dissenting in [*Abbott Laboratories v. Gardner* and *Gardner v. Toilet Goods Association*].

I am in agreement with the Court in . . . *Toilet Goods Ass'n v. Gardner*, 387 U.S. 158. . . .

. . . I am, however, compelled to dissent from the decisions of the Court in . . . *Abbott Laboratories v. Gardner*, 387 U.S. 136, and . . . *Gardner v. Toilet Goods Ass'n*, 387 U.S. 167. . . .

With all respect, I submit that established principles of jurisprudence, solidly rooted in the constitutional structure of our Government, require that the courts should not intervene in the administrative process at this stage, under these facts and in this gross, shotgun fashion. With all respect, I submit that the governing principles of law do not permit a different result in these cases than in [*Toilet Goods Association v. Gardner*]. In none of these cases is judicial interference warranted at this stage, in this fashion, and to test — on a gross, free-wheeling basis — whether the content of these regulations is within the statutory intendment. The contrary is dictated by a proper regard for the purpose of the regulatory statute and the requirements of effective administration; and by regard for the salutary rule that courts should pass upon concrete, specific questions in a particularized setting rather than upon a general controversy divorced from particular facts.

The Court, by today's decisions . . . has opened Pandora's box. Federal injunctions will now threaten programs of vast importance to the public welfare. The Court's holding here strikes at programs for the public health. The dangerous precedent goes even further. It is cold comfort—it is little more than delusion—to read in the Court's opinion that "It is scarcely to be doubted that a court would refuse to postpone the effective date of an agency action if the Government could show . . . that delay would be detrimental to the public health or safety." Experience dictates, on the contrary, that it can hardly be hoped that some federal judge somewhere will not be moved as the Court is here, by the cries of anguish and distress of those regulated, to grant a disruptive injunction. . . .

I.

Since enactment of the Federal Food, Drug, and Cosmetic Act in 1938, the mechanism for judicial review of agency actions under its provisions has been well understood. Except for specific types of agency regulations and actions . . . , judicial review has been confined to enforcement actions instituted by the Attorney General on recommendation of the agency. . . .

The present regulations concededly would be reviewable in the course of any [corresponding enforcement proceedings]. . . .

In effect, the Court says that the Food, Drug, and Cosmetic Act has always authorized threshold injunctions or declaratory judgement relief: that this relief has been available since the enactment of the law in 1938, and that it would have been granted in appropriate cases which are "ripe" for review. I must with respect characterize this as a surprising revelation. Despite the highly controversial nature of many provisions of such regulations under the Act, this possibility has not been realized by ingenious and aggressive counsel for the drug and food and cosmetics industries until this time. . . . The fact of the matter is that, except for the instances enumerated in §§ 701(e) and (f), the avenue for attack upon the statute and regulations has been by defense to specific enforcement actions by the agency. Congress has been well aware of this for more than a generation that the statute has been in effect. . . .

The limited applicability of the Administrative Procedure Act in these cases is entirely clear. That Act requires that unless precluded by Congress final agency action of the sorts involved here must be reviewable at some stage, and it recognizes that such review must be "adequate." It merely presents the question in these cases. It does not supply an answer. Certainly, it would be revolutionary doctrine that the Administrative Procedure Act authorizes threshold suits for injunction even where another and adequate review provision is available. The Court refers to the Administrative Procedure Act as "seminal." It is, in a real sense; but its seed may not produce the lush, tropical jungle of the doctrine that the Court will permit agency action to be attacked *in limine* by suit for injunction or declaratory action unless Congress expressly prohibits review of regulatory action. . . .

II.

. . . [T]he dilemma [faced by the petitioners in *Abbott Laboratories*] is no more than citizens face in connection with countless statutes and with the rules of the SEC, FTC, FCC, ICC, and other regulatory agencies. This has not heretofore been regarded as a basis for injunctive relief unless Congress has so provided. The overriding fact here is—or should be—that the public interest in avoiding the delay in implementing Congress' program far outweighs the private interest; and that the private interest which has so impressed the Court is no more than that which exists in respect of most regulatory statutes or agency rules. Somehow, the Court has concluded that the damage to petitioners if they have to engage in the required redesign and reprint of their labels and printed materials without threshold review outweighs the damage to the public of deferring during the tedious months and years of litigation a cure for the possible danger and asserted deceit of peddling plain medicine under fancy trademarks and for fancy prices which, rightly or wrongly, impelled the Congress to enact this legislation. I submit that a much stronger showing is necessary than the expense and trouble of compliance and the risk of defiance. . . .

. . . Those challenging the regulations have a remedy and there are no special reasons to relieve them of the necessity of deferring their challenge to the regulations until enforcement is undertaken. In this way, and only in this way, will the administrative process have an opportunity to function—to iron out differences, to accommodate special problems, to grant exemptions, etc. The courts do not and should not pass on these complex problems in the abstract and the general—because these regulations peculiarly depend for their quality and substance upon the facts of particular situations. We should confine ourselves—as our jurisprudence dictates—to actual, specific, particularized cases and controversies, in substance as well as in technical analysis. And we should repel these attacks, for we have no warrant and no reason to place these programs, essential to the public interest, and many others which this Court's action today will affect, at the peril of disruption by injunctive orders which can be issued by a single district judge. . . .

QUESTION SET 9.16

Review & Synthesis

1. What is the test for ripeness established by the Court in the *Abbott Labs* trilogy? As compared to the traditional method for challenging agency actions, how did it expand opportunities for judicial supervision of agency decision-making?

2. Justice Harlan purported to apply the same ripeness test to all three cases in the *Abbott Labs* trilogy. Why, precisely, did the Court's decision in *Toilet Goods* (the second of the three cases) differ from its decisions in *Abbott Labs* and *Gardner*?

3. The Declaratory Judgment Act permits "any court of the United States," "[i]n a case of actual controversy within its jurisdiction," to "declare the rights and other legal relations of any interested party seeking such declaration." According to Justice Harlan, what is the relationship between the Declaratory Judgment Act and the question of justiciability (i.e., whether the federal courts have authority to hear and resolve disputes under Article III) presented in the cases?

4. Even though *Toilet Goods* had a different result than *Abbott Labs* and *Gardner*, the Court found that the FDA's regulations were "final" in all three cases. What factual elements contributed to the Court's finality conclusions in each case, and why was a finding of finality not sufficient to authorize pre-enforcement review in *Toilet Goods*?

5. Justice Fortas rejected the idea that the FDA's rules should be subject to pre-enforcement review. He rested this determination on several arguments. First, he asserted that the traditional method of reviewing FDA's policies—enforcement and then defense by the regulated party—had long been considered adequate to address any legal missteps by the agency. Second, he argued that APA § 704 does not grant federal courts permission to hear pre-enforcement petitions for injunctions. Rather, it merely requires that "adequate" judicial review be available at some point, without specifying when such review must take place. Finally, he argued that the position of the companies in the cases was no different than any other regulatory party that must anticipate eventual enforcement of agency policies adverse to their interests. This final dynamic is a necessary part of the government's service to the public. Are you persuaded by his reasoning? Even if you are persuaded, do you also accept his solution: substantial elimination of pre-enforcement review? Can you think of at least one way to narrow availability of such review instead?

---

ii. *Contraction of Pre-enforcement Review?*

The *Abbott Labs* trilogy seemed to significantly increase private party opportunities for pre-enforcement review of agency conduct. What are the limits of the Court's generosity? For example, must an agency's interpretation of a statute have the force of law (e.g., like a duly promulgated rule) to make a challenge against it ripe? What if an agency simply announces how it plans to interpret a statute when the statutory interpretation included in that announcement will not be legally binding on private parties? Does it matter if that announcement and its interpretation, despite being non-binding, may lead private parties to alter their behavior? Consider Justice Thomas' answers in the following case. Did he adequately clarify the ripeness doctrine established in *Abbott Labs*, or did he instead restrict pre-enforcement review in an unexpected way?

National Park Hospitality Association v. Department of Interior
538 U.S. 803 (2003)

Justice THOMAS delivered the opinion of the Court.

Petitioner, a nonprofit trade association that represents concessioners doing business in the national parks, challenges a National Park Service (NPS) regulation that purports to render the Contract Disputes Act of 1978 (CDA), 92 Stat. 2383, 41 U.S.C. § 601 *et seq.*, inapplicable to concession contracts. We conclude that the controversy is not yet ripe for judicial resolution.

I

The CDA establishes rules governing disputes arising out of certain Government contracts. The statute provides that these disputes first be submitted to an agency's contracting officer. § 605. A Government contractor dissatisfied with the contracting officer's decision may seek review either from the United States Court of Federal Claims or from an administrative board in the agency. *See* §§ 606, 607(d), 609(a). Either decision may then be appealed to the United States Court of Appeals for the Federal Circuit. *See* 28 U.S.C. § 1295; 41 U.S.C. § 607(g).

Since 1916 Congress has charged NPS to "promote and regulate the use of the Federal areas known as national parks," "conserve the scenery and the natural and historic objects and the wild life therein," and "provide for [their] enjoyment [in a way that] will leave them unimpaired for the enjoyment of future generations." An Act to establish a National Park Service, 39 Stat. 535, 16 U.S.C. § 1. To make visits to national parks more enjoyable for the public, Congress authorized NPS to "grant privileges, leases, and permits for the use of land for the accommodation of visitors." § 3, 39 Stat. 535. Such "privileges, leases, and permits" have become embodied in national parks concession contracts.

The specific rules governing national parks concession contracts have changed over time. In 1998, however, Congress enacted the National Parks Omnibus Management Act of 1998 (1998 Act or Act), Pub. L. 105-391, 112 Stat. 3497 (codified with certain exceptions in 16 U.S.C. §§ 5951-5966), establishing a new and comprehensive concession management program for national parks. The 1998 Act authorizes the Secretary of the Interior to enact regulations implementing the Act's provisions, § 5965.

NPS, to which the Secretary has delegated her authority under the 1998 Act, promptly began a rulemaking proceeding to implement the Act. After notice and comment, final regulations were issued in April 2000. 65 Fed. Reg. 20630 (2000) (codified in 36 CFR pt. 51). The regulations define the term "concession contract" as follows:

> A concession contract (or contract) means a binding written agreement between the Director and a concessioner. . . . Concession contracts are not contracts within the meaning of 41 U.S.C. 601 *et seq.* (the Contract Disputes Act) and are not service or procurement contracts within the meaning of statutes, regulations or policies that apply only to federal service contracts or other types of federal procurement actions." 36 CFR § 51.3 (2002).

Through this provision NPS took a position with respect to a longstanding controversy with the Department of Interior's Board of Contract Appeals (IBCA). Beginning in 1989, the IBCA ruled that NPS concession contracts were subject to the CDA, *see* R & R Enterprises, 89-2 B.C.A., ¶ 21708, pp. 109145–109147 (1989), and subsequent attempts by NPS to convince the IBCA otherwise proved unavailing, National Park Concessions, Inc., 94-3 B.C.A., ¶ 27104, pp. 135096–135098 (1994).

II

[In Section II of its opinion, the Court recounted the procedural history of the case. The district court found NPS's interpretation of the CDA reasonable under the *Chevron* doctrine (discussed later in this chapter). The D.C. Circuit affirmed on different grounds, finding that NPS' interpretation was not entitled to *Chevron* deference but accepting it nonetheless.]

III

Ripeness is a justiciability doctrine designed "to prevent the courts, through avoidance of premature adjudication, from entangling themselves in abstract disagreements over administrative policies, and also to protect the agencies from judicial interference until an administrative decision has been formalized and its effects felt in a concrete way by the challenging parties." *Abbott Laboratories v. Gardner*, 387 U.S. 136, 148-149 (1967). The ripeness doctrine is "drawn both from Article III limitations on judicial power and from prudential reasons for refusing to exercise jurisdiction," *Reno v. Catholic Social Services*, Inc., 509 U.S. 43, 57, n. 18 (1993) (citations omitted), but, even in a case raising only prudential concerns, the question of ripeness may be considered on a court's own motion. *Ibid.*

Determining whether administrative action is ripe for judicial review requires us to evaluate (1) the fitness of the issues for judicial decision and (2) the hardship to the parties of withholding court consideration. *Abbott Laboratories, supra*, at 149. "Absent [a statutory provision providing for immediate judicial review], a regulation is not ordinarily considered the type of agency action 'ripe' for judicial review under the [Administrative Procedure Act (APA)] until the scope of the controversy has been reduced to more manageable proportions, and its factual components fleshed out, by some concrete action applying the regulation to the claimant's situation in a fashion that harms or threatens to harm him. (The major exception, of course, is a substantive rule which as a practical matter requires the plaintiff to adjust his conduct immediately. . . .)" *Lujan v. National Wildlife Federation*, 497 U.S. 871, 891 (1990). Under the facts now before us, we conclude this case is not ripe.

We turn first to the hardship inquiry. The federal respondents concede that, because NPS has no delegated rulemaking authority under the CDA, the challenged portion of § 51.3 cannot be a legislative regulation with the force of law. They note, though, that "agencies may issue interpretive rules 'to advise the public of the agency's construction of the statutes and rules *which it administers*,'" (quoting *Shalala v. Guernsey Memorial Hospital*, 514 U.S. 87, 99 (1995) (emphasis added)), and seek to characterize § 51.3 as such an interpretive rule.

We disagree. Unlike in *Guernsey Memorial Hospital*, where the agency issuing the interpretative guideline was responsible for administering the relevant statutes and regulations, NPS is not empowered to administer the CDA. Rather, the task of applying the CDA rests with agency contracting officers and boards of contract appeals, as well as the Federal Court of Claims, the Court of Appeals for the Federal Circuit, and, ultimately, this Court. Moreover, under the CDA, any authority regarding the proper arrangement of agency boards belongs to the Administrator for Federal Procurement Policy. *See* 41 U.S.C. § 607(h) ("Pursuant to the authority conferred under the Office of Federal Procurement Policy Act [41 U.S.C. § 401 *et seq.*], the Administrator is authorized and directed, as may be necessary or desirable to carry out the provisions of this chapter, to issue guidelines with respect to criteria for the establishment, functions, and procedures of the agency boards . . ."). Consequently, we consider § 51.3 to be nothing more than a "general statemen[t] of policy" designed to inform the public of NPS' views on the proper application of the CDA. 5 U.S.C. § 553(b)(3)(A).

Viewed in this light, § 51.3 does not create "adverse effects of a strictly legal kind," which we have previously required for a showing of hardship. *Ohio Forestry Assn., Inc.*, 523 U.S., at 733. Just like the Forest Service plan at issue in *Ohio Forestry*, § 51.3 "do[es] not command anyone to do anything or to refrain from doing anything; [it] do[es] not grant, withhold, or modify any formal legal license, power, or authority; [it] do[es] not subject anyone to any civil or criminal liability; [and it] create[s] no legal rights or obligations." *Ibid.*

Moreover, § 51.3 does not affect a concessioner's primary conduct. *Toilet Goods Assn., Inc. v. Gardner*, 387 U.S. 158, 164 (1967); *Ohio Forestry Assn., supra*, at 733–734. Unlike the regulation at issue in *Abbott Laboratories*, which required drug manufacturers to change the labels, advertisements, and promotional materials they used in marketing prescription drugs on pain of criminal and civil penalties, *see* 387 U.S., at 152-153, the regulation here leaves a concessioner free to conduct its business as it sees fit. *See also Gardner v. Toilet Goods Assn., Inc.*, 387 U.S. 167, 171 (1967) (regulations governing conditions for use of color additives in foods, drugs, and cosmetics were "self-executing" and had "an immediate and substantial impact upon the respondents").

We have previously found that challenges to regulations similar to § 51.3 were not ripe for lack of a showing of hardship. In *Toilet Goods Ass'n.*, for example, the Food and Drug Administration (FDA) issued a regulation requiring producers of color additives to provide FDA employees with access to all manufacturing facilities, processes, and formulae. 387 U.S., at 161-162. We concluded the case was not ripe for judicial review because the impact of the regulation could not "be said to be felt immediately by those subject to it in conducting their day-to-day affairs" and "no irremediabl[y] adverse consequences flow[ed] from requiring a later challenge." *Id.* at 164. Indeed, the FDA regulation was more onerous than § 51.3 because failure to comply with it resulted in the suspension of the producer's certification and, consequently, could affect production. Here, by contrast, concessioners suffer no practical harm as a result of § 51.3. All the regulation does is announce the position NPS will take with respect to disputes arising out of concession contracts. While it informs the public of NPS' view that concessioners are not entitled to take advantage of the provisions of the CDA, nothing in the regulation prevents concessioners from following the procedures set forth in the CDA once a dispute over a concession contract actually arises. And it appears that, notwithstanding § 51.3, the IBCA has been quite willing to apply the CDA to certain concession contracts.

Petitioner contends that delaying judicial resolution of this issue will result in real harm because the applicability *vel non* of the CDA is one of the factors a concessioner takes into account when preparing its bid for NPS concession contracts. Petitioner's argument appears to be that mere uncertainty as to the validity of a legal rule constitutes a hardship for purposes of the ripeness analysis. We are not persuaded. If we were to follow petitioner's logic, courts would soon be overwhelmed with requests for what essentially would be advisory opinions because most business transactions could be priced more accurately if even a small portion of existing legal uncertainties were resolved. In short, petitioner has failed to demonstrate that deferring judicial review will result in real hardship.

We consider next whether the issue in this case is fit for review. Although the question presented here is "a purely legal one" and § 51.3 constitutes "final agency action" within the meaning of § 10 of the APA, 5 U.S.C. § 704, *Abbott Laboratories, supra*, at 149 we nevertheless believe that further factual development would "significantly advance our ability to deal with the legal issues presented," *Duke Power Co. v. Carolina Environmental Study Group, Inc.*, 438 U.S. 59, 82 (1978); *accord, Ohio Forestry Assn., Inc.*, 523 U.S., at 736-737; *Toilet Goods Assn., supra*, at 163. While the federal respondents generally argue that NPS was correct to conclude that the CDA does not cover concession contracts, they acknowledge that certain types of concession contracts might come under the broad language of the CDA. Similarly, while petitioner . . . present[s] a facial challenge to § 51.3, [it relies] on specific characteristics of certain types of concession contracts to support [its] positions. In light of the foregoing, we conclude that judicial resolution of the question presented here should await a concrete dispute about a particular concession contract. . . .

Justice BREYER, with whom Justice O'CONNOR joins, dissenting.

. . . If the CDA does not apply to concession contract disagreements, as the Park Service regulation declares, then some of petitioner's members must plan now for higher contract implementation costs. Given the agency's regulation, bidders will likely be forced to pay more to obtain, or to retain, a concession contract than they believe the contract is worth. That is what petitioner argues. Certain general allegations in the underlying complaints support this claim. And several uncontested circumstances indicate that such allegations are likely to prove true.

. . . Given this threat of immediate concrete harm (primarily in the form of increased bidding costs), this case is also ripe for judicial review. . . . [T]he case now presents a legal issue — the applicability of the CDA to concession contracts — that is fit for judicial determination. That issue is a purely legal one, demanding for its resolution only use of ordinary judicial interpretive techniques. The relevant administrative action, i.e., the agency's definition of "concession contract" under the National Parks Omnibus Management Act of 1998, 16 U.S.C. §§ 5951-5966, has been "formalized," *Abbott Laboratories v. Gardner*, 387 U.S. 136, 148. It is embodied in an interpretive regulation issued after notice and public comment and pursuant to the Department of the Interior's formal delegation to the National Park Service of its own statutorily granted rulemaking authority, § 5965. (Unlike the majority, I would apply to the regulation the legal label "interpretive rule," not "general statement of policy," (internal quotation marks and alteration omitted), though I agree with the majority that, because the Park Service does not administer the CDA, we owe its conclusion less deference.) The Park Service's interpretation is definite and conclusive, not tentative or likely to change; as the majority concedes, the Park Service's determination constitutes "final agency action" within the meaning of the Administrative Procedure Act.

The only open question concerns the nature of the harm that refusing judicial review at this time will cause petitioner's members. *See Abbott Laboratories, supra,* at 149. The fact that concessioners can raise the legal question at a later time, after a specific contractual dispute arises, militates against finding this case ripe. So too does a precedential concern: Will present review set a precedent that leads to premature challenges in other cases where agency interpretations may be less formal, less final, or less well suited to immediate judicial determination?

But the fact of immediate and particularized (and not totally reparable) injury during the bidding process offsets the first of these considerations. And the second is more than offset by a related congressional statute that specifies that prospective bidders for Government contracts can obtain immediate judicial relief from agency determinations that unlawfully threaten precisely this kind of harm. *See* 28 U.S.C. § 1491(b)(1) (allowing prospective bidder to object, for instance, to "solicitation by a Federal agency for bids . . . for a proposed contract" and permitting review of related allegation of "any . . . violation of statute or regulation in connection with a procurement or a proposed procurement"). This statute authorizes a potential bidder to complain of a proposed contractual term that, in the bidder's view, is unlawful, say, because it formally incorporates a regulation that embodies a specific, allegedly unlawful, remedial requirement. That being so, i.e., the present injury in such a case being identical to the present injury at issue here, I can find no convincing prudential reason to withhold Administrative Procedure Act review. . . .

QUESTION SET 9.17

Review & Synthesis

1. Justice Thomas observed that the ripeness test is in part prudential and in part constitutional. Which part is prudential: the "hardship" prong or the "fitness" prong? Stated another way, which part of the test would it make more sense for Congress to be able to supersede by legislation?

2. Justice Thomas concluded that NPS's interpretation of the Contract Dispute Act did not have the force of law, and therefore it did not create "adverse effects of a strictly legal kind" that satisfy the ripeness inquiry established in *Abbott Labs*. Does this analysis strike you as a bit formalistic? As we discussed in Chapter 4, agency statements of policies and anticipated practices can be taken as legally binding by the regulated public. Should an agency's action be deemed not ripe because it has no legal effect as a technical matter, even if it has a demonstrable impact on the behavior of regulated parties? Wouldn't any reasonable test of "hardship" gauge the actual or likely impact of an agency's announced actions?

3. In his dissent, Justice Breyer argued that whether NPS had properly interpreted the CDA was an entirely legal question that could be answered without reference to the facts of any particular case. Assuming that NPS made clear its commitment to its interpretation of the CDA, should the Court have allowed NPHA's case to move forward? Would this ripeness approach—accepting an agency's stated commitment to an enforcement posture not otherwise compelled by statute—have been more, less, or just as generous as the one applied by the Court in the *Abbott Labs* trilogy?

In Context

Again, the action for which a litigant seeks judicial review must be taken by an "agency" for § 704 even to apply. In *Franklin v. Massachusetts*, 505 U.S. 788 (1992), the Commonwealth and two voters sought review of how the Secretary of Commerce calculated decennial census data used to apportion seats in the House of Representatives. The Supreme Court first found that the secretary's tabulation of census data was not final agency action under the APA. It stated she merely reports the results to the President, who may instruct her to amend the census, is not obliged to use the data in reporting the number of persons in each state to Congress, and is not obliged to share the report's results with Congress. *Id.* at 797. Nor is the President's report to Congress on the number of persons in each state a final agency action. The APA's definition of agency in § 551 makes no mention of the President. The Court accordingly found that respect for separation of powers principles and the presidency's unique constitutional position warranted its exclusion from the APA's judicial review provisions. *Id.* at 800-01. *See* page 661.

b. Finality

Section 704 of the Administrative Procedure Act requires that an agency action—defined in APA § 551(13) as "the whole or a part of an agency rule, order, license, sanction, relief, or the equivalent or denial thereof, or failure to act"—be "final" before a court can review it. Specifically, it provides:

> Agency action made reviewable by statute and final agency action for which there is no other adequate remedy in a court are subject to judicial review. A preliminary, procedural, or intermediate agency action or ruling not directly reviewable is subject to review on the review of the final agency action. Except as otherwise expressly required by statute, agency action

> otherwise final is final for the purposes of this section whether or not there has been presented or determined an application for a declaratory order, for any form of reconsideration, or, unless the agency otherwise requires by rule and provides that the action meanwhile is inoperative, for an appeal to superior agency authority.

In keeping with the APA drafters' goal of "constitut[ing] a general restatement of the principles of judicial review embodied in many statutes and judicial decisions," ATTORNEY GENERAL'S MANUAL at 93. Section 704 reflects the federal judiciary's long-standing reluctance to scrutinize the interim steps taken in governmental decision-making processes. *See, e.g., Rochester Telephone Corp. v. United States*, 307 U.S. 125 (1939).

While § 704 makes clear that judicial review under the APA is limited to final agency action, it is silent on how finality of action must be determined. The Supreme Court has developed a two-part test for this purpose, which it summarized in *Bennett v. Spear*, 520 U.S. 154, 177-78 (1997), a case we considered in the zone-of-interests materials. *See supra*, page 823. First, "the action must mark the 'consummation' of the agency's decision-making process—it must not be merely tentative or interlocutory in nature." *Bennett*, 520 U.S. at 177-78 (quoting *Chicago & Southern Air Lines, Inc. v. Waterman S.S. Corp.*, 333 U.S. 103, 113 (1948)). Stated differently, courts must figure out whether the challenged action reflects the end of the agency's process or just an intermediate or informal step that leaves the agency free to change course later on. The factual hallmarks of "consummation" necessarily vary from case to case, but courts have previously pointed to a host of factors: how thoroughly the agency considered a matter before acting on it, the formality with which it acted, whether the official communicating the decision had the authority to resolve it on the agency's behalf, whether the agency described its action as tentative, whether the head of the agency approved the action, whether the agency indicated any intention to take or typically takes further action, and whether the action is formally subject to further review within the agency. *See, e.g., Sackett v. EPA*, 566 U.S. 120, 127 (2012); *Sw. Airlines Co. v. U.S. Dep't of Transp.*, 832 F.3d 270, 275 (D.C. Cir. 2016).

Courts have also considered whether a petitioner's request for reconsideration of an otherwise final action tolls (suspends, delays) its finality. For instance, the Court in *Interstate Commerce Commission v. Locomotive Engineers*, 482 U.S. 270 (1987) held that the periods for seeking judicial review of otherwise final actions set by APA § 704 and the Hobbs Act, 28 U.S.C. §§ 2341-2344, are tolled while the agency considers a party's timely filed motion for reconsideration. *Interstate Commerce Comm'n*, 482 U.S. at 284-85. However, the Court later made clear that the tolling rule it applied in *Locomotive Engineers* is merely a default; it can be overcome by an organic statute that indicates Congress' interest in expediting rather than delaying judicial review. *See, e.g., Stone v. Immigration and Naturalization Service*, 514 U.S. 386, 398-401 (1995).

The second part of the Court's finality test requires that an action be "one by which 'rights or obligations have been determined,' or from which 'legal consequences will flow.'" *Bennett*, 520 U.S. at 178 (quoting *Port of Boston Marine Terminal Association v. Rederiaktiebolaget Transatlantic*, 400 U.S. 62, 71 (1970)). In determining whether "legal consequences will flow" from an agency action, the Court has often focused on its direct practical effects as well on whether it alters legal obligations. Recall, for example, the labeling rule under review in *Abbott Laboratories v. Gardner*, 387 U.S. 136 (1967). Promulgation of the rule had immediate legal and practical effects; it imposed a new obligation on drug companies to change their product labels at significant expense, and noncompliance could have subjected drug companies to significant civil and criminal penalties. The Court accordingly concluded that the rule was final agency action appropriate for judicial review.

Bennett presented a slightly different "legal consequences" problem, but ultimately reached the same result as *Abbott Labs*. Recall in that case the biological opinion issued by the Fish & Wildlife Service under the Endangered Species Act that concluded a Bureau of Reclamation project would jeopardize endangered species. The government argued that the opinion was merely advisory because it did not dictate to the Bureau how or whether to move forward with the project. In other words, and unlike the rule at issue in *Abbott Labs*, the government asserted that the biological opinion did not directly impose any new or different legal obligations on anyone. While this argument was true as a technical legal matter, the Court found it unpersuasive. An Incidental Take Statement included with the biological opinion "alter[ed] the legal regime to which the agency action [was] subject." *Bennett*, 520 U.S. at 169. In effect, the Statement functioned as a permit authorizing the Bureau to "take" listed endangered species as long as it followed the Statement's terms and conditions. While the Bureau was not obliged to comply with the Statement, failing to do so would subject it and its employees to substantial civil and criminal penalties for knowingly "taking" any endangered species the Statement listed. *Id.* at 169-70. As the biological opinion and the Statement changed the legal consequences for engaging with listed endangered species, they had a sufficiently coercive effect on agency conduct to satisfy the second part of the finality test. In fact, and based on the government's own admission, the Court found that "action agencies very rarely choose to engage in conduct that the Service has concluded is likely to jeopardize the continued existence of a listed species." *Id.* at 169.

Compare *Abbott Labs* and *Bennett* with the following case, recently decided by the D.C. Circuit. Why did the court reach a different result? What facts did it deem dispositive in reaching its conclusion? Also, consider the disagreement between the majority and the dissent on whether finality should be determined from an agency's or from a regulated industry's point of view. Since part of the finality test turns on the consequences that will flow from an agency's actions, doesn't it necessarily require a reviewing court to consider how a regulated industry is likely to react to what that agency does? If so, shouldn't the court consider the industry's assertions about how it is likely to react? How much weight should the court assign those assertions, if it does consider them?

Soundboard Association v. Federal Trade Commission
888 F.3d 1261 (D.C. Cir. 2018)

Before: ROGERS, MILLETT AND WILKINS, Circuit Judges.

WILKINS, Circuit Judge:

This appeal arises from Appellant Soundboard Association's ("SBA's") challenge to a November 10, 2016 informal opinion letter (the "2016 Letter") issued by Federal Trade Commission ("FTC" or "Commission") staff. The 2016 Letter stated it was the FTC staff's opinion that telemarketing technology used by SBA's members is subject to the FTC's regulation of so-called "robocalls," and it announced the rescission of a 2009 FTC staff letter (the "2009 Letter") that had reached the opposite conclusion.

SBA filed suit seeking to enjoin rescission of the 2009 Letter. It argued the 2016 Letter violated the Administrative Procedure Act ("APA") because it was a legislative rule issued without notice and comment and because the FTC's robocall regulation unconstitutionally restricted speech on the basis of content. The FTC opposed both these arguments and also disputed that the 2016 Letter was reviewable final agency action. The District Court concluded the 2016 letter qualified as reviewable final agency action, but the court granted summary judgment for the FTC on the grounds that the 2016 Letter was an interpretive rule not subject to notice and comment and that the interpretation stated in the letter survived First Amendment scrutiny.

We conclude that because the 2016 staff opinion letter does not constitute the consummation of the Commission's decisionmaking process by its own terms and under the FTC's regulations, it is not final agency action. As SBA concedes, its speech claims are pleaded as APA claims under 5 U.S.C. § 706(2)(B) and cannot proceed without final agency action. We therefore vacate the decision below and dismiss the case for failure to state a cause of action under the APA.

I.

A.

SBA is a trade association for companies that manufacture or use "soundboard" telemarketing technology ("soundboard"). Soundboard enables telemarketing agents to communicate with customers over the phone by playing prerecorded audio clips instead of using the agent's live voice. The agent can choose a pre-recorded clip to ask questions of or respond to a customer, while retaining the ability to break into the call and speak to the customer directly. Soundboard also enables agents to make and participate in multiple calls simultaneously. According to SBA, soundboard provides many advantages to telemarketers, including ensuring accurate communication of information and disclaimers, improving call-center performance and cost-effectiveness, and employing individuals who would otherwise have difficulty being understood over the phone due to accent or disability.

The FTC regulates telemarketing pursuant to the Telemarketing and Consumer Fraud and Abuse Prevention Act of 1994, which directs the Commission to "prescribe rules prohibiting deceptive . . . and other abusive telemarketing acts or practices." 15 U.S.C. § 6102(a)(1). In 1995, the Commission promulgated the Telemarketing Sales Rule ("TSR"), which restricts telemarketing to certain times of day, creates the "do-not-call" list, and imposes other requirements to prevent fraud, abuse, and intrusions on customer privacy. 60 Fed. Reg. 43842 (Aug. 23, 1995); 16 C.F.R. § 310.4(b)(ii), (c). In 2003, the Commission amended the TSR to more closely regulate "predictive dialing," which places multiple simultaneous calls for a single call-center agent and, therefore, can result in "call abandonment"— i.e., abruptly hanging up—when too many customers answer the phone. The 2003 amendment prohibited telemarketers from failing to connect a customer to an agent within two seconds of the customer's completed greeting. 16 C.F.R. § 310.4(b)(1)(iv). The amendment thus effectively prohibited outbound telemarketing campaigns consisting "solely of prerecorded messages"—colloquially known as robocalls—because "consumers who receive a prerecorded message would never be connected to a sales representative." 73 Fed. Reg. 51,164, 51,165 (Aug. 29, 2008).

In 2008, the Commission amended the TSR to prohibit telemarketers from "initiating any outbound telephone call that delivers a prerecorded message" without "an express agreement, in writing" from the consumer with language demonstrating the individual customer's consent to receiving such calls from that telemarketer. *Id.* at 51,184; 16 C.F.R. § 310.4(b)(1)(v)(A). The express-written-consent requirement does not apply to calls made on behalf of charitable organizations intended to "induce a charitable contribution from a member of, or previous donor to," the organization, as long as the donor can opt out of such calls. 16 C.F.R. § 310.4(b)(1)(v)(B). The Commission justified this exception on the grounds that members and prior donors have consented to receiving future charitable solicitation calls and, as a result, have a reduced privacy interest vis-à-vis a charitable organization's speech interest. *See* 73 Fed. Reg. at 51,193-94.

In promulgating the 2008 amendments, the Commission explained that the comments it received from customers and industry showed "the reasonable consumer would consider interactive prerecorded telemarketing messages to be coercive or abusive of such consumer's right to privacy. The mere ringing of the telephone to initiate such a call may be disruptive; the intrusion of such a call on a consumer's right to privacy may be exacerbated immeasurably when there is no human being on the other end of the line." *Id.* at 51,180. The Commission also rejected the industry's argument that an interactive opt-out mechanism for robocalls would adequately protect consumer privacy, reasoning that the "volume of telemarketing calls from multiple sources is so great that consumers find even an initial call from a telemarketer or seller to be abusive and invasive of privacy." *Id.* (quotation marks omitted).

B.

Before the TSR went into effect in September 2009, a telemarketer and soundboard user, Call Assistant LLC ("Call Assistant"), submitted a "request for a FTC Staff Opinion Letter" regarding whether Call Assistant's use of soundboard was subject to the 2008 amendments. In its request, Call Assistant represented that "[a]t all times" during a soundboard call, "even during the playing of any recorded segment, the agent retains the power to interrupt any recorded message." It also represented that during soundboard calls, "live agents hear every word spoken by the call recipient, and determine what is said" in response.

On September 11, 2009, FTC staff responded with an "informal staff opinion" letter from Lois Greisman, the FTC's Associate Director of the Division of Marketing Practices (the "2009 Letter"). The 2009 Letter stated that "[b]ased on the description of the technology included in [Call Assistant's] letter," "the staff of the [FTC] has concluded that the 2008 TSR Amendments . . . do not prohibit telemarketing calls using" soundboard. . . .

The 2009 Letter expressly conditioned this conclusion on the factual representations in Call Assistant's request for a staff opinion, and Greisman advised Call Assistant that the letter did not represent the views of the Commission. . . .

After issuing the 2009 Letter, the Commission began to receive consumer complaints and to observe media reports about the use of soundboard that conflicted with factual representations made by Call Assistant. This included complaints that consumers "are not receiving appropriate recorded responses to their questions or comments," that "no live telemarketer intervenes to provide a human response when requested to do so," and that "the call is terminated in response to consumers['] questions." FTC staff also collected evidence from consumers and industry stakeholders that "some companies are routinely using soundboard technology" to "conduct separate conversations with multiple consumers at the same time," and observed that companies engaging in these practices were using the 2009 Letter as a defense against consumer lawsuits.

The FTC staff began to reconsider the 2009 Letter. In early 2016, FTC staff contacted telemarketing industry groups for input and held meetings at which industry representatives made presentations about soundboard. In a February 2016 meeting, "representatives of [a telemarketing trade group] acknowledged that soundboard technology is frequently utilized in a matter to allow one live agent to handle multiple calls simultaneously." . . . During this time SBA argued to FTC staff that the practices described in consumer complaints were contrary to the trade groups' code of conduct, and that bad actors should be punished instead of the entire soundboard industry.

On November 10, 2016, FTC staff issued a letter (the "2016 Letter") concluding that the TSR did apply to soundboard calls and rescinding the 2009 Letter effective May 12, 2017. The 2016 Letter was from Greisman, as well. It noted the 2009 Letter was premised on factual representations made by Call Assistant. But based on consumer complaints, media reports, meetings with industry representatives, and other data points, by 2016 the FTC staff believed the factual bases of the 2009 Letter were faulty. . . .

The 2016 Letter also stated that because soundboard users play prerecorded audio files to communicate with customers, soundboard calls fall within the plain language of the TSR's prohibition on "any outbound telephone call that delivers a prerecorded message." Accordingly, the letter reasoned,

> Given the actual language used in the TSR, the increasing volume of consumer complaints, and all the abuses we have seen since we issued the September 2009 letter, we have decided to revoke the September 2009 letter. It is now staff's opinion that outbound telemarketing calls that utilize soundboard technology are subject to the TSR's prerecorded call provisions because such calls do, in fact, "deliver a prerecorded message" as set forth in the plain language of the rule. Accordingly, outbound telemarketing calls made using soundboard technology are subject to the provisions of 16 C.F.R. § 310.4(b)(1)(v), and can only be made legally if they comply with the requirements [applicable to robocalls].

The 2016 Letter provided that "[i]n order to give industry sufficient time to make any necessary changes to bring themselves into compliance, the revocation of the September 2009 Letter will be effective six months from today, on May 12, 2017. As of that date, the September 11, 2009 letter will no longer represent the opinions of FTC staff." The 2016 Letter concluded by stating that "the views expressed in this letter are those of the FTC staff, subject to the limitations of 16 C.F.R. § 1.3. They have not been approved or adopted by the Commission, and they are not binding upon the Commission. However, they do reflect the views of staff members charged with enforcement of the TSR."

C.

SBA sought to enjoin the revocation of the 2009 Letter and what it characterized as a compliance deadline of May 12, 2017. It argued before the District Court that the 2016 Letter is a legislative rule requiring notice and comment under 5 U.S.C. § 553 because it expanded the scope of the TSR to reach soundboard. It also argued that to the extent the 2016 Letter amends the TSR to apply to soundboard, it is a content-based speech restriction that "treat[s] speech tailored for first-time donors differently than speech tailored for previous donors." The Commission moved for summary judgment. It argued the 2016 Letter was not a reviewable final agency action. . . .

. . . The [district] court concluded the 2016 Letter was a final agency action but held it was an interpretive rule not subject to notice and comment, and that the TSR's application to SBA survived the intermediate scrutiny applicable to regulations of commercial speech. SBA timely appealed.

II.

. . . The APA limits judicial review to "final agency action for which there is no other adequate remedy in a court." 5 U.S.C. § 704. While the requirement of finality is not jurisdictional, without final agency action, "there is no doubt that appellant would lack a cause of action under the APA." *Reliable Automatic Sprinkler Co. v. Consumer Prod. Safety Comm'n*, 324 F.3d 726, 731 (D.C. Cir. 2003). Agency actions are final if two independent conditions are met: (1) the action "mark[s] the consummation of the agency's decisionmaking process" and is not "of a merely tentative or interlocutory nature"; and (2) it is an action "by which rights or obligations have been determined, or from which legal consequences will flow." *Bennett v. Spear*, 520 U.S. 154, 177-78 (1997) (internal quotation marks omitted). "An order must satisfy both prongs of the *Bennett* test to be considered final." *Sw. Airlines Co. v. U.S. Dep't of Transp.*, 832 F.3d 270, 275 (D.C. Cir. 2016).

In evaluating the first *Bennett* prong, this Court considers whether the action is "informal, or only the ruling of a subordinate official, or tentative." *Abbott Labs. v. Gardner*, 387 U.S. 136, 151 (1967) (internal citations omitted). The decisionmaking processes set out in an agency's governing statutes and regulations are key to determining whether an action is properly attributable to the agency itself and represents the culmination of that agency's consideration of an issue.

Because each prong of *Bennett* must be satisfied independently for agency action to be final, deficiency in either is sufficient to deprive SBA of a cause of action under the APA. *Sw. Airlines*, 832 F.3d at 275.

III.

A.

SBA argues, and the District Court concluded below, that the extensive investigative efforts by FTC staff and some definitive language in the 2016 Letter render it the consummation of agency decisionmaking for "all intents and purposes." We disagree.

There is no dispute that the 2016 Letter was "informal" and "only the ruling of a subordinate official," and not that of any individual Commissioner or of the full Commission. *Abbott Labs.*, 387 U.S. at 151 (citations omitted). It is readily distinguishable from the final agency action in *Frozen Food Express v. United States*, relied upon by SBA and the decision below. That case involved a formal, published report and order of the Interstate Commerce Commission, not its staff, following an investigation and formal public hearing. 351 U.S. 40, 41 (1956). Similarly, unlike the jurisdictional determination in *U.S. Army Corps of Engineers v. Hawkes Co.*, which was issued by the agency and expressly deemed "final agency action" by regulation, was "valid for a period of five years," and was "bind[ing on] the Corps for five years," —— U.S. ——, 136 S. Ct. 1807, 1814 (2016), the 2016 Letter is issued by staff under a regulation that distinguishes between Commission and staff advice, is subject to rescission at any time without notice, and is not binding on the Commission. 16 C.F.R. § 1.3(c). . . .

The 2016 Letter does not represent otherwise. It explicitly and repeatedly states that it expresses the views of "staff," and it explains that such views do not bind the Commission. While the letter does present a conclusive view that "outbound telemarketing calls made using soundboard are subject to [the TSR] . . . and can only be made legally if they required with [the TSR]," it characterizes this as "staff's opinion" and nowhere presents this as the conclusive view of the Commission. To the contrary, the 2016 Letter is clear that agency staff is "merely expressing *its* view of the law," *AT&T v. EEOC*, 270 F.3d 973, 976 (D.C. Cir. 2001) (emphasis added). Indeed, nonbinding staff advice is precisely what Call Assistant sought in its specific "request for a FTC *Staff Opinion Letter*."

True, the fact that staff and not an agency head has taken a challenged action does not end the finality inquiry. But the 2016 Letter differs significantly from decisions by subordinate officials we have deemed final agency action. Unlike the guidance at issue in *Appalachian Power v. EPA*, the 2016 Letter is not binding on Commission staff "in the field" or on third parties such as state permitting authorities. *Cf.* 208 F.3d 1015, 1022, 1023 (D.C. Cir. 2000) ("The short of the matter is that the Guidance, insofar as relevant here, is final agency action, reflecting a settled agency position which has legal consequences both for State agencies administering their permit programs and for companies like those represented by petitioners who must obtain Title V permits in order to continue operating."). Nor is SBA trapped without recourse due to the indefinite postponement of agency action. SBA concedes it could, but did not, seek an opinion from the Commission itself—and SBA remains free to do so today. *Cf. Sackett*, 566 U.S. at 127 (holding an order issued by the agency itself to be final when "not subject to further agency review").

The dissent repeatedly cites *Sackett* [*v. EPA*, 566 U.S. 120, 127 (2012)] as authority for its conclusion that informal staff advice is final agency action. *Sackett* is a very different case. There, the EPA Administrator issued a compliance order against the Sacketts under the "Enforcement" section of the Clean Water Act, 33 U.S.C. § 1319. The Administrator's order made enforceable factual findings and legal conclusions that the Sacketts' property included "waters of the United States" subject to the Clean Water Act, and that the Sacketts therefore had committed violations of the Clean Water Act. 566 U.S. at 124-25. The order directed the Sacketts "immediately [to] undertake activities to restore" their property "in accordance with [an EPA-created] Restoration Work Plan" and to provide to EPA employees "access to the Site . . . [and] access to all records and documentation related to the conditions at the Site." *Id.* at 125 (alterations in original). The Sacketts sought a hearing on the order from the EPA, which EPA denied, prompting the Sacketts (having no other recourse) to bring suit in the district court.

The Supreme Court analyzed the Administrator's order separately under each prong of *Bennett*. Under the first prong, the Administrator's order was the consummation of the agency's decisionmaking process because the Sacketts sought a hearing, and when that request was denied, "the 'Findings and Conclusions' that the compliance order contained were not subject to further agency review.'" 566 U.S. at 127. This alone sufficiently distinguishes the informal staff opinion in this case from the Administrator's enforcement order in *Sackett*, as the informal staff opinion is "subject to further agency review" in at least two ways. First, SBA is and has always been able to request an opinion from the Commission itself; given that Call Assistant specifically emphasized that they sought a "*Staff Opinion Letter*," a request for Commission advice remains an available alternative of which the requestors of the 2009 Letter were well aware—and which they chose not to pursue. Second, if at some future date the FTC staff make the further decision to recommend a TSR enforcement action against a soundboard user, proceeding on that recommendation would require the Commission to decide—itself, for the first time—whether the 2016 Letter's interpretation of the TSR is correct, and to vote on whether to issue a complaint. 16 C.F.R. § 3.11. SBA seeks a shortcut around both these decision points, but unlike the Sacketts, SBA is neither out of regulatory review options nor subject to an order or enforcement action issued from the head of the agency itself.

Further, the FTC regulations expressly delineate between advice from the Commission and advice from its staff. The manner in which an agency's governing statutes and regulations structure its decisionmaking processes is a touchstone of the finality analysis. Under FTC rules, when the

Commission itself gives advice, it may only rescind or revoke that advice upon "notice . . . to the requesting party so that he may discontinue the course of action taken pursuant to the Commission's advice." 16 C.F.R. § 1.3(b). Advice from the Commission also constrains its future enforcement authority: It "will not proceed against the requesting party with respect to any action taken in good faith reliance upon the Commission's advice under this section, where all the relevant facts were fully, completely, and accurately presented to the Commission. . . ." *Id.*

A separate provision governs "[a]dvice rendered by the staff." 16 C.F.R. § 1.3(c). Staff advice is given "without prejudice to the right of the Commission to later rescind the advice and, where appropriate, to commence an enforcement proceeding," and § 1.3(c) has no notice requirement and provides no safe harbor for reasonable reliance on the advice. *Id.* Unlike Commission opinions, staff advice cannot constrain the Commission's future enforcement authority. Thus, contrary to SBA's assertions, the 2016 Letter's disclaimer is not fairly read as meaningless "boilerplate." Rather, the 2016 Letter reflects and cites specific FTC regulations that structure the agency's decisionmaking processes. While an opinion from the Commission itself might constitute the consummation of its decisionmaking process, the 2016 Letter from FTC staff does not. . . .

B.

The dissent criticizes the majority for "measur[ing] finality exclusively from the Commission's vantage point" because we conclude that failure to meet *Bennett*'s first prong is sufficient to dismiss for want of finality. But it is undisputed that both prongs of *Bennett v. Spear* must be satisfied independently. *Sw. Airlines*, 832 F.3d at 275. *Bennett* directs courts to look at finality from the agency's perspective (whether the action represents the culmination of the agency's decisionmaking) and from the regulated parties' perspective (whether rights or obligations have been determined, and legal consequences flow). Deficiency from either perspective is sufficient to dismiss a claim. Thus, there is no need to reach the second *Bennett* prong if the action does not mark the consummation of agency decisionmaking. We therefore need not do so here.

We respond to some of the dissent's concerns out of respect for our colleague and to clarify the appropriate finality analysis. The dissent is troubled that judicial review of informal agency advice would be unavailable here where, according to SBA's characterization, companies have relied on the 2009 Letter in conducting and growing their operations. Certainly, reasonable reliance interests of regulated parties should often be considered when an agency changes course. But the facts matter. SBA's members do not have any significant or reasonable reliance interests in the 2009 Letter, either by the letter's own terms or under FTC regulations. Call Assistant specifically requested an informal *"Staff Opinion Letter"* (emphasis Call Assistant's) on the applicability of the TSR to soundboard; in that request, Call Assistant made representations about how it used soundboard in order to provide the staff with a factual basis for such an opinion. In express reliance on these factual representations, the FTC staff stated its opinion that, if these particular facts were true, the TSR would not prohibit the use of soundboard, at least for the uses described by Call Assistant. The 2009 Letter emphasized that the staff opinion extended only to soundboard use as factually portrayed in Call Assistant's letter soliciting the opinion. Call Assistant did not state anywhere in its letter or supporting materials that call-center agents would use soundboard to field multiple simultaneous calls; instead, Call Assistant highlighted how the technology would allow an agent to better interact with a caller and accurately convey information to a caller. Thus, even if the 2009 Letter had been binding on the Commission, it did not bless the practice of using soundboard to field multiple calls simultaneously, and it therefore does not appear to be reasonable for a company to rely upon the 2009 Letter for such uses. SBA members also did not take any affirmative steps to apprise the FTC that soundboard is frequently not used in the manner represented by Call Assistant, even after the issuance of the 2009 Letter; instead, the FTC had to learn this from its own investigation after receiving numerous consumer complaints and reviewing news reports. If industry actors such as Call Assistant had corrected the factual misrepresentations (by omission) as proactively as they solicited the staff opinion, seven years might not have passed before FTC staff reconsidered and rescinded the 2009 Letter.

Whether a regulated entity is a small business or a large trade association, the bottom line is the same for the finality of an agency's action. Both prongs of *Bennett* must be met. The dissent argues that somehow the impact on industry should have been accounted for in the staff's decisionmaking, and the failure to account for practical impacts somehow makes informal staff advice more final. That approach bootstraps *Bennett*'s second prong into its first. The point where an agency's decisionmaking process is complete cannot be pulled to and fro by the gravity of any particular decision for an industry. Such an unmoored approach to evaluating the finality an agency's decision would create uncertainty for everyone—the agency, the industry, and the courts. . . .

In addition, we do not believe finality can be measured by what the industry claims it will do or stop doing. The test is what legal and practical consequences will flow from the agency's action. Here, it is unclear that much, if any, of the claimed consequences for industry could properly be attributed to the 2016 Letter at all. Even from this underdeveloped record it appears that the practices that prompted the 2016 Letter—such as soundboard agents handling multiple calls at a time—may not be permissible under the 2009 Letter's interpretation of the TSR. In addition, even if the staff's interpretation were adopted or enforced by the Commission, many permissible soundboard uses remain. More importantly, if the soundboard industry built its business on practices that do not conform to the facts as represented by Call Assistant, they have no cause to complain about the impact of rescinding the 2009 Letter on those practices. In any event, under FTC regulations, the 2009 Letter is not and could not be a basis for legally cognizable reliance interests because it was not issued by the Commission. 16 C.F.R. § 1.3(b).

Finally, the dissent relies heavily again on *Sackett* to argue that the 2009 and 2016 Letters constitute final agency action under *Bennett*'s second prong. While we need not and do not conduct a full analysis of this prong, we note significant differences between the EPA Administrator's order setting out express legal obligations in *Sackett* and the informal staff advice here. The *Sackett* Court concluded that "through the order, the EPA 'determined' 'rights or obligations'" because, "[b]y reason of the order, the Sacketts have the legal obligation to 'restore' their property . . . and must give the EPA access to their property and to 'records and documentation related to the conditions at the Site.'" *Sackett*, 566 U.S. at 126. In contrast, the informal staff advice in the 2016 Letter offers an interpretation of the TSR, but it fixes no specific, legally enforceable rights or legal obligations of the kind created by the Administrator's order in *Sackett*. As the FTC conceded, the 2016 Letter might be used to show an SBA member's knowledge regarding the meaning of the TSR and, therefore, could be evidence of willfulness should an SBA member violate the TSR. But, unlike a violation of the Administrator's order in *Sackett*, a so-called "violation" of the 2016 Letter does not independently trigger any penalties.

We respect our dissenting colleague's concern for consequences to the soundboard industry in this case, but we cannot agree that these consequences are sufficient to render informal FTC staff advice final agency action.

* * *

Pursuant to FTC regulations and by its own terms, the 2016 Letter does not constitute the consummation of the Commission's decisionmaking process regarding the applicability of the TSR to soundboard technology. Without final agency action, SBA lacks a cause of action under the APA. We therefore vacate the decision below and dismiss the complaint for failure to state a claim.

So ordered.

MILLETT, Circuit Judge, dissenting.

Why let reality get in the way of a good bureaucratic construct? In holding that the 2016 Letter from the Federal Trade Commission's Division of Marketing Practices is not a judicially reviewable "final agency action," the court's opinion focuses on the Commission's structuring of its own regulations to preserve its right to disagree (or not) with the Division at some "later" date. 16 C.F.R. § 1.3(c). In so doing, the court's opinion measures finality exclusively from the Commission's vantage point.

But there are two sides to this story. Finality is supposed to look at both whether "the agency's decisionmaking process" has "consummat[ed]," and the reality of whether "rights or obligations have been determined" by or "legal consequences will flow" from the challenged agency action. *Bennett v. Spear*, 520 U.S. 154, 178 (1997) (internal quotation marks and citations omitted). And in deciding whether the agency process has ended for purposes of *Bennett*'s first prong, courts must look beyond the agency's say-so to objective and practical indicia of finality. *See, e.g., Sackett v. EPA*, 566 U.S. 120, 127 (2012) (holding that compliance order that triggers potential penalties is final even though agency provided for ongoing "informal discussion" and consideration of the accuracy of its findings).

In this case, the agency's emphatic and directive language in the 2016 Division Letter, combined with the absence of any avenue for internal administrative review, unleashes immediate legal and practical consequences for the industry, forcing its members to choose between complying by shuttering their businesses or exposing themselves to potentially significant financial penalties. When agency action threatens such severe repercussions, the "mere possibility that an agency might reconsider" does not deprive the action of finality. *Sackett*, 566 U.S. at 127.

In my view, the Administrative Procedure Act should not countenance an agency telling an individual or industry that its business must end, while fending off court review on the ground that its own internal administrative processes have not ended. Because the structure of the Commission's regulations, the substantive content of the Division's Letter, the absence of an internal appeal mechanism, and the consequences that flow from it together render the Division's 2016 Letter the end of the agency's process, I respectfully dissent. . . .

QUESTION SET 9.18

Review & Synthesis

1. Restate the test for finality applied by the *Soundboard* majority. On what facts did the majority base its conclusion that the FTC's staff opinion letter was not the consummation of the agency decision-making process, and on what facts did it conclude that no legal consequences flowed from the letter? How did these facts differ in legal significance from those at issue in *Abbott Labs* and *Bennett*?

2. Does the majority, as Judge Millett in dissent argued, approach the finality question solely from the FTC's perspective? If so, why did Judge Millett find that objectionable? Did he have a legal disagreement (i.e., different

view on what the finality test requires), or was his objection more practical (e.g., the consequences of the majority's analysis would produce undesirable results)? Do you find his reasoning persuasive, or are you persuaded by the majority?

3. Consider how the finality doctrine described and applied in *Soundboard* relates to the ripeness doctrine. Both gauge whether a dispute is appropriate for judicial consideration at the time of its filing. If ripeness (in part a constitutional inquiry) already addresses this concern, why do you think Congress added finality to the APA in § 704? Does finality address aspects of timeliness that ripeness does not? If so, what are they? In formulating your answer, be sure to review the respective elements of the ripeness and finality tests. Do they ask for the same or different information?

Application & Analysis

1. In order to participate in the Medicaid program, drug manufacturers must commit to the Centers for Medicare and Medicaid Services ("CMS") that they will provide rebates to states that elect to pay for outpatient prescription drugs. The rebate calculation for each drug depends on the average market price ("AMP") the manufacturer charges for it. Manufacturers that knowingly provide false information related to the rebate calculation are subject to civil penalties of up to $100,000 for each item of false information. 42 U.S.C. § 1396r-8(b)(3)(B)-(C). Review of rebate calculations is available in the U.S. Court of Appeals, but only as part of the court's review of enforcement proceedings brought by CMS. 42 U.S.C. § 1320a-7a(e).

    Pharma Corp. introduced Drug A, an outpatient drug, to the market in 2008. It based Drug A's rebate calculation on the AMP at that time. In 2015, Pharma Corp. sought and obtained FDA approval for a new outpatient drug, Drug A-1. In a letter to CMS, Pharma Corp. stated its belief that Drug A-1 is entitled to an AMP separate from Drug A's, and reporting what it believed to be Drug A-1's AMP. CMS responded several months later by stating that Drug A-1 must use the same AMP as Drug A. Pharma Corp. sent a second letter reiterating its position and requesting a meeting. CMS's Director of the Division of Pharmacy responded by letter, repeating CMS's view that a new AMP for Drug A-1 was not warranted. She explained that the FDA approved Drug A-1 based on an application that supplemented the one Pharma Corp. had previously filed for Drug A. As a result, the Director concluded, Pharma Corp. had to use the 2008 AMP for both Drug A and Drug A-1. The Director's letter expressly stated that it was not "a final agency action or even an initial determination on a reimbursement claim."

Pharma Corp. responded by filing suit in U.S. District Court for the District of Columbia. It asserts that legal consequences flowed from the Director's letter because the letter increased the probability that, in the future, it could be found to have "knowingly" supplied CMS with false information. CMS moved to dismiss the complaint, arguing that it had taken no final agency action to trigger judicial review under the APA. In doing so, CMS pointed to the D.C. Circuit's decision in *Soundboard* which stated that staff letters, even if they "could be [used as] evidence of willfulness," do not on their own produce any legal consequences.

Assess the merits of the parties' arguments.

---

c. Exhaustion of Administrative Remedies

That a petitioner must exhaust all of the remedies made available by an administrative agency before seeking review in federal court is among the most well-established principles in administrative law. *See, e.g., Myers v. Bethlehem Shipbuilding Corp.*, 303 U.S. 41, 50-51 (1938) ("[A] long settled rule of judicial administration [is] that no one is entitled to judicial relief for a supposed or threatened injury until the prescribed administrative remedy has been exhausted."). The Supreme Court has explained that the purpose of the doctrine is largely functional, and accordingly supports the distinctive role Congress has assigned administrative agencies. "The administrative agency is created as a separate entity and invested with certain powers and duties. The courts ordinarily should not interfere with an agency until it has completed its action, or else has clearly exceeded its jurisdiction." *McKart v. United States*, 395 U.S. 185, 194 (1969). Further, the Court has made clear that preventing courts from prematurely interfering with administrative decision-making can produce numerous benefits for the implementation of federal policy:

> The agency, like a trial court, is created for the purpose of applying a statute in the first instance. Accordingly, it is normally desirable to let the agency develop the necessary factual background upon which decisions should be based. And since agency decisions are frequently of a discretionary nature or frequently require expertise, the agency should be given the first chance to exercise that discretion or to apply that expertise. And of course it is generally more efficient for the administrative process to go forward without interruption than it is to permit the parties to seek aid from the courts at various intermediate stages.

Id. 193-94.

As indicated above, the doctrines governing when federal courts may review administrative decision-making can overlap and are sometimes used interchangeably by the courts applying them. *See, e.g., Ticor Title Insurance Co. v. Federal Trade Commission,* 814 F.2d 731 (D.C. Cir. 1987) (unanimously holding that court was precluded from hearing challenge to FTC's authority to prosecute, with each member of a three-judge panel relying on a different timing doctrine than the other two). This is especially true of exhaustion and finality. The two are nevertheless distinguishable. Whereas "the finality requirement is concerned with whether the initial decision-maker has arrived at a definitive position on the issue that inflicts an actual, concrete injury[,] the exhaustion requirement generally refers to administrative and judicial procedures by which an injured party may seek review of an adverse decision and obtain a remedy if the decision is found to be unlawful or otherwise inappropriate." *Williamson County Regional Planning Commission v. Hamilton Bank of Johnson City,* 473 U.S. 172, 193 (1985); *overruled on other grounds, Knick v. Township of Scott, Pennsylvania,* 139 S. Ct. 2162 (2019). It is therefore possible for an agency action to be final although administrative remedies have not been exhausted. Assume, for example, that an ALJ issues an initial decision against Smith that is a final agency action. Smith need not avail herself of the agency's internal review procedures before seeking federal judicial review if there is no requirement that she do so. If such an administrative appeal is merely optional, she need not exhaust it as a condition of moving the dispute to federal court. The question, then, is whether pursuing the administrative appeal is within her discretion or whether it is a mandatory precondition of judicial review.

The Supreme Court has recognized both common law and statutory sources of the exhaustion requirement. Developed by judges over the course of decades, common law exhaustion is discretionary and pragmatic. Even before passage of the APA, and without any statutory directive to do so, courts on their own initiative could require parties to exhaust any available administrative remedies — internal agency reviews, reopenings, rehearings, appeals, etc. — before they could seek judicial review. As is often the case with common law creations, judges have also developed a robust set of exceptions to the doctrine, greatly adding to their flexibility. These are discussed in *McCarthy v. Madigan,* 503 U.S. 140 (1992), excerpted below.

Federal statutory exhaustion requirements come (unsurprisingly) from Congress and supersede the common law doctrine whenever they apply. Importantly, "where Congress has not clearly required exhaustion, sound judicial discretion governs." *McCarthy,* 503 U.S. at 144. A notable example is the Prison Litigation Reform Act of 1996 ("PLRA"), enacted in response to complaints (particularly by the Department of Justice and federal judges) over the perceived frivolousness of many prisoner-initiated federal lawsuits. The PLRA states that "[n]o action shall be brought with respect to prison conditions under [42 U.S.C. § 1983], or any other Federal law, by a prisoner confined in jail, prison, or other correctional facility until such administrative remedies as are available are exhausted." *See* 42 U.S.C. § 1997e(a). *See generally Jones v. Bock,* 549 U.S. 199 (2007); Kermit Roosevelt III, *Exhaustion*

Under the Prison Litigation Reform Act: The Consequence of Procedural Error, 52 U. Emory L.J. 1771 (2003). Unlike common law exhaustion, which is discretionary on the part of the court and subject to numerous exceptions, statutory exhaustion is mandatory.

Given the common law and statutory sources for the exhaustion requirement, the question naturally arises as to how the two interact. If an organic statute is silent on exhaustion, are courts free to apply judicially created exhaustion requirements? In other words, do courts have the power to impose exhaustion on parties when Congress has not done so through an organic statute and an agency has not done so pursuant to a statutory delegation from Congress? What, if anything, has Congress said about exhaustion for judicial challenges brought under the Administrative Procedure Act? Consider the third sentence of APA § 704. Again, it states in relevant part:

> . . . Except as otherwise expressly required by statute, agency action otherwise final is final for the purposes of this section whether or not there has been presented or determined an application for a declaratory order, for any form of reconsideration, or, unless the agency otherwise requires by rule and provides that the action meanwhile is inoperative, for an appeal to superior agency authority.

5 U.S.C. § 704. The language of this provision refers explicitly to final agency action and to the review procedures that might follow it (application for a declaratory order, reconsideration, appeal to superior agency authority). Unless another statute expressly requires a party to seek review of its otherwise final action, that action is final and hence judicially reviewable even if the party does not pursue reconsideration within the agency. In other words, § 704 appears to say that finality under the APA does not depend on exhaustion of remedies unless some other statute specifically requires it. By indicating that resort to these procedures is *not* a prerequisite for finality unless expressly required by statute or regulation, could this provision plausibly be read as an explicit exhaustion provision? If it could be so read, what effect would it have on the applicability of common law exhaustion to lawsuits brought under the APA's judicial review provisions? The Court directly addressed these questions in *Darby v. Cisneros*, 509 U.S. 137 (1993), excerpted below, which it decided a little over a year after *McCarthy* and 47 years after passage of the APA.

McCarthy v. Madigan
503 U.S. 140 (1992)

Justice Blackmun delivered the opinion of the Court.

The issue in this case is whether a federal prisoner must resort to the internal grievance procedure promulgated by the Federal Bureau of Prisons before he may initiate a suit, pursuant to the authority of *Bivens v. Six Unknown Fed. Narcotics Agents*, 403 U.S. 388 (1971), solely for money damages. The Court of Appeals for the Tenth Circuit ruled that exhaustion of the grievance procedure was required. We granted certiorari to resolve a conflict among the Courts of Appeals.

I

While he was a prisoner in the federal penitentiary at Leavenworth, petitioner John J. McCarthy filed a *pro se* complaint in the United States District Court for the District of Kansas against four prison employees: the hospital administrator, the chief psychologist, another psychologist, and a physician. McCarthy alleged that respondents had violated his constitutional rights under the Eighth Amendment by their deliberate indifference to his needs and medical condition resulting from a back operation and a history of psychiatric problems. On the first page of his complaint, he wrote: "This Complaint seeks Money Damages Only."

The District Court dismissed the complaint on the ground that petitioner had failed to exhaust prison administrative remedies. Under 28 CFR pt. 542 (1991), setting forth the general "Administrative Remedy Procedure for Inmates" at federal correctional institutions, a prisoner may "seek formal review of a complaint which relates to any aspect of his imprisonment." § 542.10. When an inmate files a complaint or appeal, the responsible officials are directed to acknowledge the filing with a "signed receipt" which is returned to the inmate, to "[c]onduct an investigation," and to "[r]espond to and sign all complaints or appeals." §§ 542.11(a)(2) to (4). The general grievance regulations do not provide for any kind of hearing or for the granting of any particular type of relief.

To promote efficient dispute resolution, the procedure includes rapid filing and response timetables. An inmate first seeks informal resolution of his claim by consulting prison personnel. § 542.13(a). If this informal effort fails, the prisoner "may file a formal written complaint on the appropriate form, within fifteen (15) calendar days of the date on which the basis of the complaint occurred." § 542.13(b). Should the warden fail to respond to the inmate's satisfaction within 15 days, the inmate has 20 days to appeal to the Bureau's Regional Director, who has 30 days to respond. If the inmate still remains unsatisfied, he has 30 days to make a final appeal to the Bureau's general counsel, who has another 30 days to respond. §§ 542.14 and 542.15. If the inmate can demonstrate a "valid reason for delay," he "shall be allowed" an extension of any of these time periods for filing. § 542.13(b).

In Context

In *Bivens v. Six Unknown Named Agents of Federal Bureau of Narcotics*, the Supreme Court created a common law cause of action allowing plaintiffs to recover money damages against federal officers who, acting under color of federal authority, violate their constitutional rights. The Court has recognized several exceptions to *Bivens*. For example, the President and federal officials engaged in adjudicatory functions on behalf of administrative agencies are absolutely immune from *Bivens* suits. *See Nixon v. Fitzgerald*, 457 U.S. 731 (1982); *Butz v. Economou*, 438 U.S. 478 (1978).

Petitioner McCarthy filed with the District Court a motion for reconsideration under Federal Rule of Civil Procedure 60(b), arguing that he was not required to exhaust his administrative remedies, because he sought only money damages which, he claimed, the Bureau could not provide. The court denied the motion.

The Court of Appeals, in affirming, observed that because *Bivens* actions are a creation of the judiciary, the courts may impose reasonable conditions upon their filing. The exhaustion rule, the court reasoned, "is not keyed to the type of relief sought, but to the need for preliminary fact-finding" to determine "whether there is a possible *Bivens* cause of action." Accordingly, "'[a]lthough the administrative apparatus could not award money damages . . . , administrative consideration of the possibility of corrective action and a record would have aided a court in measuring liability and determining the extent of the damages.'" Exhaustion of the general grievance procedure was required notwithstanding the fact that McCarthy's request was solely for money damages.

II

The doctrine of exhaustion of administrative remedies is one among related doctrines—including abstention, finality, and ripeness—that govern the timing of federal-court decisionmaking. Of "paramount importance" to any exhaustion inquiry is congressional intent. *Patsy v. Board of Regents of Florida*, 457 U.S. 496, 501 (1982). Where Congress specifically mandates, exhaustion is required. *Coit Independence Joint Venture v. FSLIC*, 489 U.S. 561, 579 (1989); *Patsy*, 457 U.S., at 502, n. 4. But where Congress has not clearly required exhaustion, sound judicial discretion governs. *McGee v. United States*, 402 U.S. 479, 483, n. 6. *See also Patsy*, 457 U.S., at 518 (WHITE, J., concurring in part) ("[E]xhaustion is 'a rule of judicial administration,' . . . and unless Congress directs otherwise, rightfully subject to crafting by judges"). Nevertheless, even in this field of judicial discretion, appropriate deference to Congress' power to prescribe the basic procedural scheme under which a claim may be heard in a federal court requires fashioning of exhaustion principles in a manner consistent with congressional intent and any applicable statutory scheme. *Id.* at 501-502, and note 4.

A

This Court long has acknowledged the general rule that parties exhaust prescribed administrative remedies before seeking relief from the federal courts. *See, e.g., Myers v. Bethlehem Shipbuilding Corp.*, 303 U.S. 41, 50-51, and note 9 (1938) (discussing cases as far back as 1898). Exhaustion is required because it serves the twin purposes of protecting administrative agency authority and promoting judicial efficiency.

As to the first of these purposes, the exhaustion doctrine recognizes the notion, grounded in deference to Congress' delegation of authority to coordinate branches of Government, that agencies, not the courts, ought to have primary responsibility for the programs that Congress has charged them to administer. Exhaustion concerns apply with particular force when the action under review involves exercise of the agency's discretionary power or when the agency proceedings in question allow the agency to apply its special expertise. *McKart v. United States*, 395 U.S. 185, 194 (1969). The exhaustion doctrine also acknowledges the commonsense notion of dispute resolution that an agency ought to have an opportunity to correct its own mistakes with respect to the programs it administers before it is haled into federal court. Correlatively, exhaustion principles apply with special force when "frequent and deliberate flouting of administrative processes" could weaken an agency's effectiveness by encouraging disregard of its procedures. *McKart v. United States*, 395 U.S., at 195.

As to the second of the purposes, exhaustion promotes judicial efficiency in at least two ways. When an agency has the opportunity to correct its own errors, a judicial controversy may well be mooted, or at least piecemeal appeals may be avoided. *See, e.g., McKart v. United States*, 395 U.S., at 195. And even where a controversy survives administrative review, exhaustion of the administrative procedure may produce a useful record for subsequent judicial consideration, especially in a complex or technical factual context. *See, e.g., Weinberger v. Salfi*, 422 U.S. 749, 765 (1975) (exhaustion may allow agency "to compile a record which is adequate for judicial review").

B

Notwithstanding these substantial institutional interests, federal courts are vested with a "virtually unflagging obligation" to exercise the jurisdiction given them. *Colorado River Water Conservation Dist. v. United States*, 424 U.S. 800, 817-818 (1976). . . . Accordingly, this Court has declined to require exhaustion in some circumstances even where administrative and judicial interests would counsel otherwise. In determining whether exhaustion is required, federal courts must balance the interest of the individual in retaining prompt access to a federal judicial forum against countervailing institutional interests favoring exhaustion. "[A]dministrative remedies need not be pursued if the litigant's interests in immediate judicial review outweigh the government's interests in the efficiency or administrative autonomy that the exhaustion doctrine is designed to further." *West v. Bergland*, 611 F.2d 710, 715 (8th Cir. 1979), *cert. denied*, 449 U.S. 821 (1980). Application of this balancing principle is "intensely practical," *Bowen v. City of New York*, 476 U.S., at 484, *citing Mathews v. Eldridge*, 424 U.S. 319, 331, note 11 (1976), because attention is directed to both the nature of the claim presented and the characteristics of the particular administrative procedure provided.

C

This Court's precedents have recognized at least three broad sets of circumstances in which the interests of the individual weigh heavily against requiring administrative exhaustion. First, requiring resort to the administrative remedy may occasion undue prejudice to subsequent assertion of a court action. Such prejudice may result, for example, from an unreasonable or indefinite timeframe for administrative action. *See Gibson v. Berryhill,* 411 U.S. 564, 575, n. 14 (1973) (administrative remedy deemed inadequate "[m]ost often . . . because of delay by the agency"). Even where the administrative decisionmaking schedule is otherwise reasonable and definite, a particular plaintiff may suffer irreparable harm if unable to secure immediate judicial consideration of his claim. By the same token, exhaustion principles apply with less force when an individual's failure to exhaust may preclude a defense to criminal liability.

Second, an administrative remedy may be inadequate "because of some doubt as to whether the agency was empowered to grant effective relief." *Gibson v. Berryhill,* 411 U.S., at 575, note 14. For example, an agency, as a preliminary matter, may be unable to consider whether to grant relief because it lacks institutional competence to resolve the particular type of issue presented, such as the constitutionality of a statute. In a similar vein, exhaustion has not been required where the challenge is to the adequacy of the agency procedure itself, such that "'the question of the adequacy of the administrative remedy . . . [is] for all practical purposes identical with the merits of [the plaintiff's] lawsuit.'" *Barry v. Barchi,* 443 U.S. 55, 63, note 10 (1979) (quoting *Gibson v. Berryhill,* 411 U.S., at 575). Alternatively, an agency may be competent to adjudicate the issue presented, but still lack authority to grant the type of relief requested.

Third, an administrative remedy may be inadequate where the administrative body is shown to be biased or has otherwise predetermined the issue before it. *Gibson v. Berryhill,* 411 U.S., at 575.

III

In light of these general principles, we conclude that petitioner McCarthy need not have exhausted his constitutional claim for money damages. As a preliminary matter, we find that Congress has not meaningfully addressed the appropriateness of requiring exhaustion in this context. Although respondents' interests are significant, we are left with a firm conviction that, given the type of claim McCarthy raises and the particular characteristics of the Bureau's general grievance procedure, McCarthy's individual interests outweigh countervailing institutional interests favoring exhaustion.

A

Turning first to congressional intent, we note that the general grievance procedure was neither enacted nor mandated by Congress. Respondents, however, urge that Congress, in effect, has acted to require exhaustion by delegating power to the Attorney General and the Bureau of Prisons to control and manage the federal prison system. *See* 18 U.S.C. §§ 4001(b) and 4042. We think respondents confuse what Congress could be claimed to allow by implication with what Congress affirmatively has requested or required. By delegating authority, in the most general of terms, to the Bureau to administer the federal prison system, Congress cannot be said to have spoken to the particular issue whether prisoners in the custody of the Bureau should have direct access to the federal courts.

Respondents next argue that Congress, by enactment of § 7 of the Civil Rights of Institutionalized Persons Act, 94 Stat. 352, 42 U.S.C. § 1997e, has articulated a policy favoring exhaustion of the prison grievance procedure prior to the filing of a constitutional claim against prison officials. Section 1997e imposes a limited exhaustion requirement for a claim brought by a state prisoner under Rev. Stat. § 1979, 42 U.S.C. § 1983, provided that the underlying state prison administrative remedy meets specified standards. Section 1997e has no direct application in this case, because at issue here is a *Bivens* claim by a federal prisoner against federal prison officials. We find it significant that Congress, in enacting § 1997e, stopped short of imposing a parallel requirement in the federal prison context.*

Section 1997e is not only inapplicable to *Bivens* claims, but—by its own terms—cuts against respondents' claim that the particular procedure now at issue need be exhausted. First, unlike the rule of exhaustion proposed here, § 1997e does not authorize dismissal of an action for failure to exhaust. Instead, it provides that the action is to be stayed for a maximum of 90 days. *See* § 1997e(a)(1). Second, § 1997e does not mechanically require exhaustion in every case where an acceptable state procedure is in place. Rather, it directs federal courts to abstain "if the court believes that such a [waiting] requirement would be appropriate and in the interests of justice." § 1997e(a)(1). In other words, if an inmate fails to meet filing deadlines under an administrative scheme, a court has ample discretion to determine that exhaustion nonetheless should be forgone. Third, in contrast to the absence of any provision for the award of money damages under the

---

* [Congress amended § 1997e with its passage of the Prison Litigation Reform Act of 1996 ("PLRA"). The PLRA broadened § 1997e to include all prisoners (state and federal) and any federal law that would support a lawsuit challenging a prisoner's conditions of confinement (including *Bivens* actions). Whereas requiring exhaustion as a prerequisite to filing a *Bivens* claim was a matter of judicial discretion when *McCarthy* was decided, it is now mandated by statute. *See Porter v. Nussle*, 534 U.S. 516, 524 (2002).]

Bureau's general grievance procedure, the statute conditions exhaustion on the existence of "effective administrative remedies." It is difficult to see why a stricter rule of exhaustion than Congress itself has required in the state prison context should apply in the federal prison context.

Respondents also argue that requiring exhaustion is appropriate because *Bivens* relief gives way when necessary to accommodate either the effective functioning of Government or an articulated congressional policy. We have recognized that a *Bivens* remedy does not lie in two situations: (1) where Congress has provided an equally effective alternative remedy and declared it to be a substitute for recovery under the Constitution, and (2) where, in the absence of affirmative action by Congress, special factors counsel hesitation. *Carlson v. Green*, 446 U.S. 14, 18-19 (1980). As to the first exception, Congress did not create the remedial scheme at issue here and that scheme, in any case, as noted above, cannot be considered to be equally effective with respect to a claim for money damages. As to the second exception, respondents appear to confuse the presence of special factors with any factors counseling hesitation. In *Carlson*, the Court held that "special factors" do not free prison officials from *Bivens* liability, because prison officials do not enjoy an independent status in our constitutional scheme, nor are they likely to be unduly inhibited in the performance of their duties by the assertion of a *Bivens* claim. *Carlson v. Green*, 446 U.S., at 19. . . .

B

Because Congress has not required exhaustion of a federal prisoner's *Bivens* claim, we turn to an evaluation of the individual and institutional interests at stake in this case. The general grievance procedure heavily burdens the individual interests of the petitioning inmate in two ways. First, the procedure imposes short, successive filing deadlines that create a high risk of forfeiture of a claim for failure to comply. Second, the administrative "remedy" does not authorize an award of monetary damages—the only relief requested by McCarthy in this action. The combination of these features means that the prisoner seeking only money damages has everything to lose and nothing to gain from being required to exhaust his claim under the internal grievance procedure.

The filing deadlines for the grievance procedure require an inmate, within 15 days of the precipitating incident, not only to attempt to resolve his grievance informally but also to file a formal written complaint with the prison warden. 28 CFR § 542.13 (1991). Then, he must successively hurdle 20-day and 30-day deadlines to advance to the end of the grievance process. § 542.15. Other than the Bureau's general and quite proper interest in having early notice of any claim, we have not been apprised of any urgency or exigency justifying this timetable. As a practical matter, the filing deadlines, of course, may pose little difficulty for the knowledgeable inmate accustomed to grievances and court actions. But they are a likely trap for the inexperienced and unwary inmate, ordinarily indigent and unrepresented by counsel, with a substantial claim.

Respondents argue that the deadlines are not jurisdictional and may be extended for any "valid" reason. *See* 28 CFR §§ 542.13(b) and 542.15 (1991). Yet the regulations do not elaborate upon what a "valid" reason is. Moreover, it appears that prison officials — perhaps the very officials subject to suit — are charged with determining what is a "valid" reason.

All in all, these deadlines require a good deal of an inmate at the peril of forfeiting his claim for money damages. . . .

As we have noted, the grievance procedure does not include any mention of the award of monetary relief. Respondents argue that this should not matter, because "in most cases there are other things that the inmate wants." This may be true in some instances. But we cannot presume, as a general matter, that when a litigant has deliberately forgone any claim for injunctive relief and has singled out discrete past wrongs, specifically requesting monetary compensation only, that he is likely interested in "other things." The Bureau, in any case, is always free to offer an inmate administrative relief in return for withdrawal of his lawsuit. We conclude that the absence of any monetary remedy in the grievance procedure also weighs heavily against imposing an exhaustion requirement. . . .

We do not find the interests of the Bureau of Prisons to weigh heavily in favor of exhaustion in view of the remedial scheme and particular claim presented here. To be sure, the Bureau has a substantial interest in encouraging internal resolution of grievances and in preventing the undermining of its authority by unnecessary resort by prisoners to the federal courts. But other institutional concerns relevant to exhaustion analysis appear to weigh in hardly at all. The Bureau's alleged failure to render medical care implicates only tangentially its authority to carry out the control and management of the federal prisons. Furthermore, the Bureau does not bring to bear any special expertise on the type of issue presented for resolution here.

The interests of judicial economy do not stand to be advanced substantially by the general grievance procedure. No formal factfindings are made. The paperwork generated by the grievance process might assist a court somewhat in ascertaining the facts underlying a prisoner's claim more quickly than if it has only a prisoner's complaint to review. But the grievance procedure does not create a formal factual record of the type that can be relied on conclusively by a court for disposition of a prisoner's claim on the pleadings or at summary judgment without the aid of affidavits.

C

In conclusion, we are struck by the absence of supporting material in the regulations, the record, or the briefs that the general grievance procedure here was crafted with any thought toward the principles of exhaustion of claims for money damages. The Attorney General's professed concern for internal dispute resolution has not translated itself into a more effective grievance procedure that might encourage the filing of an administrative complaint as opposed to a court action. Congress, of course, is free to design or require an appropriate administrative procedure for a prisoner to exhaust his claim for money damages. Even without further action by Congress, we do not foreclose the possibility that the Bureau itself may adopt an appropriate administrative procedure consistent with congressional intent.

The judgment of the Court of Appeals is reversed.
It is so ordered.

Chief Justice REHNQUIST, with whom Justice SCALIA and Justice THOMAS join, concurring in the judgment.

I agree with the Court's holding that a federal prisoner need not exhaust the procedures promulgated by the Federal Bureau of Prisons. My view, however, is based entirely on the fact that the grievance procedure at issue does not provide for any award of monetary damages. As a result, in cases such as this one where prisoners seek monetary relief, the Bureau's administrative remedy furnishes no effective remedy at all, and it is therefore improper to impose an exhaustion requirement.

Because I would base the decision on this ground, I do not join the Court's extensive discussion of the general principles of exhaustion, nor do I agree with the implication that those general principles apply without modification in the context of a *Bivens* claim. In particular, I disagree with the Court's reliance on the grievance procedure's filing deadlines as a basis for excusing exhaustion. As the majority observes, we have previously refused to require exhaustion of administrative remedies where the administrative process subjects plaintiffs to unreasonable delay or to an indefinite timeframe for decision. This principle rests on our belief that when a plaintiff might have to wait seemingly forever for an agency decision, agency procedures are "inadequate" and therefore need not be exhausted.

But the Court makes strange use of this principle in holding that filing deadlines imposed by agency procedures may provide a basis for finding that those procedures need not be exhausted. Whereas before we have held that procedures without "reasonable time limit[s]" may be inadequate because they make a plaintiff wait too long, today the majority concludes that strict filing deadlines might also contribute to a finding of inadequacy because they make a plaintiff move too quickly. But surely the second proposition does not follow from the first. In fact, short filing deadlines will almost always promote quick decisionmaking by an agency, the very result that we have advocated repeatedly in the cases cited above. So long as there is an escape clause, as there is here, and the time limit is within a zone of reasonableness, as I believe it is here, the length of the period should not be a factor in deciding the adequacy of the remedy.

Darby v. Cisneros
509 U.S. 137 (1993)

Justice BLACKMUN delivered the opinion of the Court.*

This case presents the question whether federal courts have the authority to require that a plaintiff exhaust available administrative remedies before seeking judicial review under the Administrative Procedure Act (APA), 5 U.S.C. § 701 *et seq.*, where neither the statute nor agency rules specifically mandate exhaustion as a prerequisite to judicial review. At issue is the relationship between the judicially created doctrine of exhaustion of administrative remedies and the statutory requirements of § 10(c) [5 U.S.C. § 704] of the APA.

I

Petitioner R. Gordon Darby is a self-employed South Carolina real estate developer who specializes in the development and management of multifamily rental projects. In the early 1980s, he began working with Lonnie Garvin, Jr., a mortgage banker, who had developed a plan to enable multifamily developers to obtain single-family mortgage insurance from respondent Department of Housing and Urban Development (HUD). Respondent Secretary of HUD (Secretary) is authorized to provide single-family mortgage insurance under § 203(b) of the National Housing Act, 48 Stat. 1249, as amended, 12 U.S.C. § 1709(b). Although HUD also provides mortgage insurance for multifamily projects under § 207 of the National Housing Act, 12 U.S.C. § 1713, the greater degree of oversight and control over such projects makes it less attractive for investors than the single-family mortgage insurance option.

The principal advantage of Garvin's plan was that it promised to avoid HUD's "Rule of Seven." This rule prevented rental properties from receiving single-family mortgage insurance if the mortgagor already had financial interests in seven or more similar rental properties in the same project or subdivision. *See* 24 CFR § 203.42(a) (1992). Under Garvin's plan, a person seeking financing would use straw purchasers as mortgage insurance applicants. Once the loans were closed, the straw purchasers would transfer title

---

* The CHIEF JUSTICE, Justice SCALIA, and Justice THOMAS join all but Part III of this opinion.

back to the development company. Because no single purchaser at the time of purchase would own more than seven rental properties within the same project, the Rule of Seven appeared not to be violated. HUD employees in South Carolina apparently assured Garvin that his plan was lawful and that he thereby would avoid the limitation of the Rule of Seven.

Darby obtained financing for three separate multiunit projects, and, through Garvin's plan, Darby obtained single-family mortgage insurance from HUD. Although Darby successfully rented the units, a combination of low rents, falling interest rates, and a generally depressed rental market forced him into default in 1988. HUD became responsible for the payment of over $6.6 million in insurance claims.

HUD had become suspicious of Garvin's financing plan as far back as 1983. In 1986, HUD initiated an audit but concluded that neither Darby nor Garvin had done anything wrong or misled HUD personnel. Nevertheless, in June 1989, HUD issued a limited denial of participation (LDP) that prohibited petitioners for one year from participating in any program in South Carolina administered by respondent Assistant Secretary of Housing. Two months later, the Assistant Secretary notified petitioners that HUD was also proposing to debar them from further participation in all HUD procurement contracts and in any nonprocurement transaction with any federal agency. *See* 24 CFR § 24.200 (1992).

Petitioners' appeals of the LDP and of the proposed debarment were consolidated, and an Administrative Law Judge (ALJ) conducted a hearing on the consolidated appeals in December 1989. The judge issued an "Initial Decision and Order" in April 1990, finding that the financing method used by petitioners was "a sham which improperly circumvented the Rule of Seven." The ALJ concluded, however, that most of the relevant facts had been disclosed to local HUD employees, that petitioners lacked criminal intent, and that Darby himself "genuinely cooperated with HUD to try [to] work out his financial dilemma and avoid foreclosure." In light of these mitigating factors, the ALJ concluded that an indefinite debarment would be punitive and that it would serve no legitimate purpose; good cause existed, however, to debar petitioners for a period of 18 months.

Under HUD regulations,

> The hearing officer's determination shall be final unless, pursuant to 24 CFR part 26, the Secretary or the Secretary's designee, within 30 days of receipt of a request decides as a matter of discretion to review the finding of the hearing officer. The 30-day period for deciding whether to review a determination may be extended upon written notice of such extension by the Secretary or his designee. Any party may request such a review in writing within 15 days of receipt of the hearing officer's determination. 24 CFR § 24.314(c) (1992).

Neither petitioners nor respondents sought further administrative review of the ALJ's "Initial Decision and Order."

On May 31, 1990, petitioners filed suit in the United States District Court for the District of South Carolina. They sought an injunction and a declaration that the administrative sanctions were imposed for purposes of punishment, in violation of HUD's own debarment regulations, and therefore were "not in accordance with law" within the meaning of § 10(e)(B)(1) of the APA, 5 U.S.C. § 706(2)(A).

Respondents moved to dismiss the complaint on the ground that petitioners, by forgoing the option to seek review by the Secretary, had failed to exhaust administrative remedies. The District Court denied respondents' motion to dismiss, reasoning that the administrative remedy was inadequate and that resort to that remedy would have been futile. In a subsequent opinion, the District Court granted petitioners' motion for summary judgment, concluding that the "imposition of debarment in this case encroached too heavily on the punitive side of the line, and for those reasons was an abuse of discretion and not in accordance with the law."

The Court of Appeals for the Fourth Circuit reversed. It recognized that neither the National Housing Act nor HUD regulations expressly mandate exhaustion of administrative remedies prior to filing suit. The court concluded, however, that the District Court had erred in denying respondents' motion to dismiss, because there was no evidence to suggest that further review would have been futile or that the Secretary would have abused his discretion by indefinitely extending the time limitations for review.

. . . In order to resolve the tension between this and the APA, as well as to settle a perceived conflict among the Courts of Appeals, we granted certiorari.

II

Section 10(c) of the APA bears the caption "Actions reviewable." It provides in its first two sentences that judicial review is available for "final agency action for which there is no other adequate remedy in a court," and that "preliminary, procedural, or intermediate agency action . . . is subject to review on the review of the final agency action." The last sentence of § 10(c) reads:

> Except as otherwise expressly required by statute, agency action otherwise final is final for the purposes of this section whether or not there has been presented or determined an application for a declaratory order, for any form of reconsideration, or, unless the agency otherwise requires by rule and provides that the action meanwhile is inoperative, for an appeal to superior agency authority. 80 Stat. 392-393, 5 U.S.C. § 704.

Petitioners argue that this provision means that a litigant seeking judicial review of a final agency action under the APA need not exhaust available administrative remedies unless such exhaustion is expressly required by statute or agency rule. According to petitioners, since § 10(c) contains an explicit exhaustion provision, federal courts are not free to require further exhaustion as a matter of judicial discretion.

Respondents contend that § 10(c) is concerned solely with timing, that is, when agency actions become "final," and that Congress had no intention to interfere with the courts' ability to impose conditions on the timing of their exercise of jurisdiction to review final agency actions. Respondents concede that petitioners' claim is "final" under § 10(c), for neither the National Housing Act nor applicable HUD regulations require that a litigant pursue further administrative appeals prior to seeking judicial review. However, even though nothing in § 10(c) precludes judicial review of petitioners' claim, respondents argue that federal courts remain free under the APA to impose appropriate exhaustion requirements.

We have recognized that the judicial doctrine of exhaustion of administrative remedies is conceptually distinct from the doctrine of finality:

> [T]he finality requirement is concerned with whether the initial decision-maker has arrived at a definitive position on the issue that inflicts an actual, concrete injury; the exhaustion requirement generally refers to administrative and judicial procedures by which an injured party may seek review of an adverse decision and obtain a remedy if the decision is found to be unlawful or otherwise inappropriate." *Williamson County Regional Planning Comm'n v. Hamilton Bank of Johnson City*, 473 U.S. 172, 193 (1985).

Whether courts are free to impose an exhaustion requirement as a matter of judicial discretion depends, at least in part, on whether Congress has provided otherwise, for "[o]f 'paramount importance' to any exhaustion inquiry is congressional intent," *McCarthy v. Madigan*, 503 U.S. 140, 144 (1992), *quoting Patsy v. Board of Regents of Florida*, 457 U.S. 496, 501 (1982). We therefore must consider whether § 10(c), by providing the conditions under which agency action becomes "final for the purposes of" judicial review, limits the authority of courts to impose additional exhaustion requirements as a prerequisite to judicial review.

It perhaps is surprising that it has taken over 45 years since the passage of the APA for this Court definitively to address this question. Professor Davis noted in 1958 that § 10(c) had been almost completely ignored in judicial opinions, *see* 3 K. DAVIS, ADMINISTRATIVE LAW TREATISE § 20.08, p. 101 (1958); he reiterated that observation 25 years later, noting that the "provision is relevant in hundreds of cases and is customarily overlooked." 4 K. DAVIS, ADMINISTRATIVE LAW TREATISE § 26.12, pp. 468-469 (2d ed. 1983). Only a handful of opinions in the Courts of Appeals have considered the effect of § 10(c) on the general exhaustion doctrine.

. . . While some dicta in [our prior] cases might be claimed to lend support to respondents' interpretation of § 10(c), the text of the APA leaves little doubt that petitioners are correct. Under § 10(a) of the APA, "[a] person suffering legal wrong because of agency action, or adversely affected or aggrieved by agency action within the meaning of a relevant statute, *is entitled to judicial review thereof.*" 5 U.S.C. § 702 (emphasis added). Although § 10(a) provides the general right to judicial review of agency actions under the APA, § 10(c) establishes when such review is available. When an aggrieved party has exhausted all administrative remedies expressly prescribed by statute or agency rule, the agency action is "final for the purposes of this section" and therefore "subject to judicial review" under the first sentence. While federal courts may be free to apply, where appropriate, other prudential doctrines of judicial administration to limit the scope and timing of judicial review, § 10(c), by its very terms, has limited the availability of the doctrine of exhaustion of administrative remedies to that which the statute or rule clearly mandates.

The last sentence of § 10(c) refers explicitly to "any form of reconsideration" and "an appeal to superior agency authority." Congress clearly was concerned with making the exhaustion requirement unambiguous so that aggrieved parties would know precisely what administrative steps were required before judicial review would be available. If courts were able to impose additional exhaustion requirements beyond those provided by Congress or the agency, the last sentence of § 10(c) would make no sense. To adopt respondents' reading would transform § 10(c) from a provision designed to " 'remove obstacles to judicial review of agency action,' " *Bowen v. Massachusetts*, 487 U.S., at 904, quoting *Shaughnessy v. Pedreiro*, 349 U.S. 48, 51 (1955), into a trap for unwary litigants. Section 10(c) explicitly requires exhaustion of all intra-agency appeals mandated either by statute or by agency rule; it would be inconsistent with the plain language of § 10(c) for courts to require litigants to exhaust optional appeals as well. . . .

III

[In Section III of its opinion, the Court recounted the legislative history of § 10(c), and concluded that it supported its reading set forth in Section II of its opinion.]

IV

We noted just last Term in a non-APA case that

appropriate deference to Congress' power to prescribe the basic procedural scheme under which a claim may be heard in a federal court requires fashioning of exhaustion principles in a manner consistent with congressional intent and any applicable statutory scheme. *McCarthy v. Madigan*, 503 U.S., at 144.

Appropriate deference in this case requires the recognition that, with respect to actions brought under the APA, Congress effectively codified the doctrine of exhaustion of administrative remedies in § 10(c). Of course, the exhaustion doctrine continues to apply as a matter of judicial discretion in cases not governed by the APA. But where the APA applies, an appeal to "superior agency authority" is a prerequisite to judicial review only when expressly required by statute or when an agency rule requires appeal before review and the administrative action is made inoperative pending that review. Courts are not free to impose an exhaustion requirement as a rule of judicial administration where the agency action has already become "final" under § 10(c).

The judgment of the Court of Appeals is reversed, and the case is remanded for further proceedings consistent with this opinion.

It is so ordered.

QUESTION SET 9.19

Review & Synthesis

1. With regard to *McCarthy v. Madigan*:
   a. What test did the court adopt to determine whether McCarthy was required to exhaust available administrative remedies before filing suit in federal district court?
   b. The Court did not apply APA § 704 when determining whether McCarthy was required to exhaust his administrative remedies before filing his federal lawsuit. Why not? Did the absence of explicit statutory language requiring that he exhaust his administrative remedies alone determine whether Congress intended him to first seek redress within the federal prison system?
   c. McCarthy filed suit in federal district court because the grievance resolution procedures at his prison could not have afforded him monetary damages for his alleged mistreatment by prison officials. Should his obligation to exhaust administrative procedures have depended on his characterization of the relief best suited to redress his alleged injuries? Should the Court have at least considered whether other remedies available under the prison's procedures — like modified treatment of his physical and mental impairments — would have sufficed?

2. With respect to *Darby v. Cisneros*:
   a. What did the Court identify as the key conceptual difference between exhaustion and finality? Is APA § 704 a finality provision or an exhaustion provision?
   b. Restate the parties' respective positions on whether APA § 704 permits or precludes courts from imposing common law exhaustion requirements in cases brought under the APA. Why did the Court accept the petitioners' interpretation of § 704 over the respondent's?

3. What is the source of the courts' power to impose exhaustion requirements where Congress or agencies have not done so through adoption of positive law? If, as the Court said, courts have a "virtually unflagging obligation" to exercise the jurisdiction given to them by Congress, by what right do they shun plaintiffs who have received final determinations from administrative decision-makers? Apart from the sources of legal authority by which they do so, what of the rationales? The Court in *Madigan* observed that one purpose for imposing common law exhaustion is to ensure courts pay due deference to Congress' delegation of decision-making authority to agencies. If Congress did not see fit to codify such a concern, do you think it is the Judiciary's job to identify and act on it?

Application & Analysis

1. The Postal Service is authorized, "upon evidence satisfactory to" it, to deny the use of the mails to those engaged in schemes to obtain money by means of false representations. 39 U.S.C. § 3005. Procedures for using this authority are set out in regulations: the General Counsel of the Postal Service files a complaint, and a hearing is held before an administrative law judge, who then issues a decision. The ALJ's decision "shall become the final Agency decision unless an appeal is taken in accordance with § 952.25." 39 C.F.R. § 952.24(a) (2019). An appeal may be taken to the Judicial Officer of the Postal Service, who is authorized to render the "final Agency decision." *Id.* §§ 952.25, 952.26. The Postal Service may then issue a cease and desist order and may also order that mail addressed to the respondents be returned to its senders. 39 U.S.C. § 3005(a).

   MailSafe, Inc. is a self-described direct-mail solicitation company. In 2017, the General Counsel of the Postal Service initiated an administrative complaint against the company, alleging that its mailings contained false representations in violation of 39 U.S.C. § 3005. The complaint was settled by a consent agreement, which provided for a cease and desist order that placed conditions on any future mailings by the company. In 2018, the General Counsel filed an administrative breach petition against MailSafe, alleging violations of the 2017 consent agreement and cease and desist order. The Postal Service's Judicial Officer ruled that most of the MailSafe mailings at issue violated the 2017 agreement and order. The following year, the General Counsel initiated another complaint against MailSafe, alleging that further mailings contained fraudulent misrepresentations in violation of 39 U.S.C. § 3005.

In response to this latest administrative complaint, MailSafe filed suit in federal district court seeking an injunction. The company alleges that the latest complaint is barred by *res judicata* and collateral estoppel because it charges violations that were already addressed by the 2017 consent agreement and cease and desist order. It brings the suit under APA § 706(2)(A), asserting that the General Counsel's enforcement action is "not in accordance with law" because it exceeds the Postal Service's authority under 39 U.S.C. § 3005. The Postal Service counters that the lawsuit should be dismissed for lack of finality or, alternatively, for failure to exhaust administrative remedies.

You are a clerk for the judge hearing the dispute. Write a brief memorandum analyzing the merits of the parties' claims.

---

9. Selecting a Remedial Forum: The Doctrine of Primary Jurisdiction

Our review of the ripeness, finality, and exhaustion requirements shows the considerable time and attention that Congress and the courts have paid to properly allocating decisional responsibilities between administrative agencies and the Judiciary. Together, these doctrines manage when courts conduct their oversight of the administrative decision-making process.

The judicially created doctrine of primary jurisdiction also manages the boundaries between administrative and judicial decision-making, although it does so in a slightly different context. Sometimes courts and agencies have overlapping and simultaneous jurisdiction over a dispute which, if left unmanaged, can lead to conflict and confusion. Primary jurisdiction determines whether courts or agencies have initial decision-making authority when such conflicts arise. It provides that courts should refrain from hearing a dispute in the first instance if it falls within the "primary jurisdiction" of an agency. Stated differently, the doctrine identifies those issues and disputes that Congress intended agencies initially to resolve. Courts may afterwards consider the whole case if the agency does not completely dispose of it. Note that since primary jurisdiction addresses which decision-making body gets the first opportunity to resolve a dispute, it is not a judicial review doctrine like ripeness, finality, or exhaustion.

To understand the doctrine, it is important understand the situations to which it applies. It *does not* apply where an agency has exclusive statutory jurisdiction over a dispute. Courts must dismiss those disputes because they must be resolved by an agency rather than by the courts. Additionally, determining an agency's exclusive jurisdiction is a question of statutory interpretation, the resolution of which necessarily varies from statute to statute. Primary jurisdiction applies instead when a court's jurisdiction over a dispute is concurrent with an agency's or issues arise in a case within a court's exclusive jurisdiction that an agency is particularly competent to resolve. Stated differently, an agency need not possess exclusive or definitive authority over an issue for it to fall within that agency's primary jurisdiction. Rather, it applies when an agency "is best suited to make the initial decision on the issues in dispute, even though the district court has subject matter jurisdiction." *American Association of Cruise Passengers v. Cunard Line, Ltd.*, 31 F.3d 1184, 1186 (D.C. Cir. 1994) (citing *Allnet Commc'n Serv., Inc. v. Nat'l Exchange Carrier Ass'n*, Inc., 965 F.2d 1118, 1120 (D.C. Cir. 1992)).

As the Supreme Court has long made clear, there is no set formula for identifying when a court should abstain pursuant to primary jurisdiction. *See, e.g., United States v. Western Pacific R.R. Co.*, 352 U.S. 59, 64 (1956). It is largely a pragmatic analysis of several factors, including "(1) whether the question at issue is within the conventional expertise of judges; (2) whether the question at issue lies particularly within the agency's discretion or requires the exercise of agency expertise; (3) whether there exists a substantial danger of inconsistent rulings; and (4) whether a prior application to the agency has been made." *Lipton v. MCI Worldcom, Inc.*, 135 F. Supp. 2d 182, 190 (D.D.C. 2001). As the District Court for the District of Columbia further explained:

> In every case the question is whether the reasons for the existence of the doctrine are present and whether the purposes it serves will be aided by its application in the particular litigation. These purposes include the desirable uniformity which would obtain if initially a specialized agency passed on certain types of administrative questions and the expert and specialized knowledge of the agencies involved. Critically, whether there should be judicial forbearance hinges on the authority Congress delegated to the agency in the legislative scheme.

United States v. Philip Morris USA, Inc., 787 F. Supp. 2d 68, 77 (D.D.C. 2011) (internal quotations and alterations omitted). *See also* 2 RICHARD J. PIERCE, JR., ADMINISTRATIVE LAW TREATISE § 14.1 (2010). Accordingly, "[c]ourts frequently hold that an agency has primary jurisdiction . . . where [a] determination depends in part upon exercise of the agency's discretion or expert evaluation of facts that are more accessible and understandable to the agency than to a court." *Id.* When this is the case, courts will postpone final decision and refer the relevant issues to the appropriate federal agency for initial resolution. *See, e.g., United States v. Philadelphia National Bank*, 374

U.S. 321, 353 (1963). For example, courts have abstained on primary jurisdiction grounds when asked whether a tariff imposed by local exchange carriers complied with FCC regulations, *Allnet*, 965 F.2d at 1120, and whether FDA regulations deemed a new drug "safe and effective for interstate sale," *Israel v. Baxter Labs, Inc.*, 466 F.2d 272, 280 (D.C. Cir. 1972).

Given the purposes supporting the primary jurisdiction doctrine — facilitation of national uniformity in regulation, deference to superior institutional competence, fidelity to congressional intent, judicial efficiency, etc. — should agencies be *required* to resolve the issues federal courts refer to them? Note that in a similar context, state courts are not required to answer state law questions certified to them by the federal courts unless their states tell them to do so. For example, the Illinois Supreme Court may, in its discretion, answer questions of Illinois law certified to it by the U.S. Supreme Court or by the Seventh Circuit (but not by federal district courts). *See* Ill. S. Ct. R. 20. There is, however, no means by which the Supreme Court or the Seventh Circuit can *force* the Illinois Supreme Court to do so. What are courts to do if an agency refuses initially to resolve a seemingly pressing issue? For example, what if an agency simply declines to decide an issue referred to it by a court, or ignores that request altogether? Relatedly, what if an agency tries to get a court to initially decide an issue by filing a federal lawsuit? Consider the Fifth Circuit's answer in the following case.

Wagner & Brown v. ANR Pipeline Co.
837 F.2d 199 (5th Cir. 1988)

Before CLARK, Chief Judge, JOLLY and JONES, Circuit Judges.

CLARK, Chief Judge:

Wagner & Brown appeals the district court's dismissal of its action for damages for breach of a take-or-pay clause in a natural gas purchase contract. The district court did not abuse its discretion by deferring to the primary jurisdiction of the Federal Energy Regulatory Commission (FERC) for a determination of whether such take-or-pay issues affected the maximum lawful price of natural gas. The judgment appealed from is affirmed. However, to avoid possible prejudice to Wagner & Brown's rights under the contract, we direct the district court to modify its order dismissing the cause to provide that the action be stayed for 180 days to permit FERC to exercise its jurisdiction.

I.

This dispute arises from a contract for the sale of natural gas entered into between Wagner & Brown and ANR pipeline in August 1981. Under the terms of the contract, ANR Pipeline Company, a shipper and seller of natural gas, agreed to purchase natural gas produced by Wagner & Brown. Article IV of the contract contains a minimum purchase obligation, commonly known as a "take-or-pay" provision, under which ANR is obligated to take 75% of the gas produced at Wagner & Brown's wells or to pay Wagner & Brown as if this amount of gas was taken.

Wagner & Brown alleges that from January 1984 through April 1986, ANR failed to take the minimum volumes of gas and did not meet the payment requirements under the contract. On July 31, 1986, Wagner & Brown filed suit against ANR in state court, seeking damages for breach of the contract. ANR removed to the Southern District of Texas. ANR then filed a complaint with the Federal Energy Regulatory Commission (FERC), asking FERC to issue an order that the take-or-pay prepayments would constitute unlawful payments in excess of the maximum natural gas prices established in the Natural Gas Policy Act of 1978, 15 U.S.C. §§ 3301–3432 (1982) (the NGPA). ANR's complaint is currently pending before FERC.

On the day that it filed its complaint with FERC, ANR filed a motion to dismiss Wagner & Brown's suit pending in the Southern District of Texas. ANR argued that dismissal was proper because FERC has exclusive or primary jurisdiction to consider whether take-or-pay prepayments violate NGPA price ceilings.

After a hearing on the motion, the district court dismissed Wagner & Brown's suit, finding that the controlling issues in the case were within FERC's primary jurisdiction. Wagner & Brown appeals.

II.

Primary jurisdiction is a judicially created doctrine whereby a court of competent jurisdiction may dismiss or stay an action pending a resolution of some portion of the action by an administrative agency. The doctrine is invoked:

> whenever enforcement of the claim requires the resolution of issues which, under a regulatory scheme, have been placed within the special competence of an administrative body; in such a case the judicial process is suspended pending referral of such issues to the administrative body for its views.

United States v. Western Pacific R.R. Co., 352 U.S. 59, 63-64 (1956). It is a flexible doctrine to be applied at the discretion of the district court. *El Paso Natural Gas Co. v. Sun Oil Co.*, 708 F.2d 1011, 1020 (5th Cir. 1983), *cert. denied*, 468 U.S. 1219 (1984). Application of the doctrine is especially appropriate where:

> uniformity of certain types of administrative decisions is desirable, or where there is a need for the "expert and specialized knowledge of the agencies.

Avoyelles Sportsmen's League, Inc. v. Marsh, 715 F.2d 897, 919 (5th Cir. 1983) (quoting, *Western Pacific, supra*, 77 S. Ct. at 165).

A court considering deferring to an agency's primary jurisdiction must weigh the benefits of obtaining the agency's aid against the need to resolve the litigation expeditiously and may defer only if the benefits of agency review exceed the costs imposed on the parties. *Gulf States Utilities Co. v. Alabama Power Co.*, 824 F.2d 1465, 1473 (5th Cir. 1987).

In this case, the considerations of expertise and uniformity tip the scales in favor of deferral to FERC. FERC has acquired expertise on the subject of gas pricing while performing its rulemaking and price enforcement functions. The NGPA vested FERC with the power "to perform any and all acts (including any appropriate enforcement activity), and to prescribe, issue, amend, and rescind such rules and orders as it may find necessary or appropriate to carry out its functions under [the NGPA]." 15 U.S.C. § 3411(a) (1982). These activities have given FERC insight into why specific grades of gas should bear certain ceiling prices and how these ceilings contribute to the overall policy of natural gas price regulation. FERC's insight gives it special competence to determine what components should be included in the first sale price for natural gas.[4]

In addition, a ruling by FERC would create uniformity in the construction of take-or-pay clauses. Numerous district courts have ruled that take-or-pay payments do not violate federal NGPA price ceilings. The District of Columbia Circuit has recently indicated that Congress probably did not intend that take-or-pay provisions in producer contracts would violate the NGPA. *Associated Gas Distributors v. FERC*, 824 F.2d 981, 1022 note 26 (D.C. Cir. 1987). However, several district courts have considered that take-or-pay payments might be a component of price and have referred individual cases to FERC for resolution. *See, e.g., Gulf Oil Corp. v. Tenneco, Inc.*, 608 F. Supp. 1493, 1503 (E.D. La. 1985). These disparate interpretations underscore the need for a definitive pronouncement from FERC.

If resolution of the issue is left to district courts, they may make different rulings regarding whether prepayments will be considered a component of price. A uniform rule is preferable because the interstate market for gas is a nationwide market regulated under a single act of Congress. Conflicting decisions among the districts, even when brought into closer conformity by appellate decisions, are at best a patchwork solution to a problem that requires uniform resolution. The district court acted within

---

[4] FERC itself has recognized its competence to determine the components of the price of natural gas. *See e.g., Wisconsin Gas Co. v. FERC*, 770 F.2d 1144, 1152 (D.C. Cir. 1985), *cert. denied*, 476 U.S. 1114 (1986) (discussing FERC Order 380, 49 Fed. Reg. 22,778-01 (1984), in which FERC chose not to prohibit variable-cost components in take-or-pay clauses). It has expressed a willingness to hear individual rate cases filed by pipelines seeking a determination of "the amount of take-or-pay costs to be included as prudent costs in its just and reasonable rates." Congressional Letter from FERC Chairman Anthony G. Sousa to Honorable Frank Horton (June 27, 1986).

its discretion to rely on FERC to issue such a uniform ruling in the first instance.

Although we agree that FERC has primary jurisdiction, we do not accept ANR's further argument that FERC has exclusive jurisdiction over construction of take-or-pay contracts. FERC itself has recognized federal court jurisdiction over suits involving the construction of contracts for the sale of natural gas. *See, e.g., Hall v. FERC,* 691 F.2d 1184, 1188 (5th Cir. 1982), *cert. denied,* 464 U.S. 822 (1983). *Arkansas Louisiana Gas Co. v. Hall,* 55 F.P.C. 1018, 1020 (1976).

III.

Wagner & Brown presents essentially five objections to the district court's finding of primary jurisdiction. We will consider them in turn.

A) FERC's Jurisdiction over ANR's Complaint

Wagner & Brown argues that FERC lacks jurisdiction over its dispute with ANR because the dispute is purely contractual. Wagner & Brown states that FERC's authority under the NGPA does not encompass the interpretation of producer-pipeline contracts but rather is limited to determining whether a gas producer is entitled to increase his price to the level mandated by Congress in the NGPA. *Columbia Gas Development Corp. v. FERC,* 651 F.2d 1146, 1159 note 15 (5th Cir. 1981). We disagree.

The NGPA provides that "[i]t shall be unlawful for any person (1) to sell natural gas at a first sale price in excess of any applicable maximum lawful price under this chapter . . . " 15 U.S.C. § 3414(a)(1) (1982). The Act and the regulations duly promulgated give FERC the power to seek injunctions against sales of gas above the price ceilings. Hence, as Wagner & Brown argues, FERC's primary duty under the NGPA is to determine what price ceiling applies to a particular shipment of natural gas. However, implicit in this duty is FERC's authority to determine which payments required under producer-pipeline contracts will be included in the "price" of natural gas. For FERC to effectively exercise its authority to bring suit to enjoin violations of NGPA price ceilings, it must have jurisdiction to determine which payments constitute components of the price of natural gas.

Because ANR's action turns on the issue of whether take-or-pay payments are a component of the price of gas, FERC must have jurisdiction to hear the complaint. ANR argues that because it has already paid the statutory maximum price for gas taken from January 1984 through April 1986, the prepayments for gas not taken must be considered a component of the price paid for the gas actually received. This is so because ANR cannot make up the payments in later shipments of gas. ANR asserts that making these prepayments will raise the price of the gas above the NGPA ceilings and will render the contract illegal. ANR contends that this illegality is a complete defense to Wagner & Brown's suit.

. . . [T]he relationship between natural gas price ceilings and the cost effects of take-or-pay clauses in producer-pipeline contracts is a question best considered in the first instance by FERC.

B) FERC's Willingness to Rule on Wagner & Brown's Claim

Wagner & Brown next argues that even if FERC has jurisdiction over ANR's complaint, it will not hear the complaint because it has rebuffed all past requests that it resolve take-or-pay disputes between producers and pipelines. Wagner & Brown cites numerous cases where district courts have refused to refer take-or-pay questions to FERC because of FERC's history of inaction, and cites take-or-pay cases which courts have referred to FERC but later withdrawn because of the agency's failure to act.

Although FERC has evinced an unwillingness to act on take-or-pay cases, its reluctance does not establish that it cannot or should not hear these claims or that it will not hear them in the future. . . . [W]e believe FERC should and will act on ANR's complaint.

. . . In Order 500, [No. RM87–34–000 (August 7, 1987),] FERC recognized its need to act on take-or-pay problems, reaffirmed its jurisdiction to do so, proposed an interim response to the take-or-pay problem, solicited information from the pipelines which would be incorporated into a final rule and suggested that it might invoke its power under § 5 of the Natural Gas Act, 15 U.S.C. § 717d (1976), to set aside jurisdictional producer-pipeline contracts with take-or-pay provisions.

In light of these significant steps taken by FERC, the district court did not abuse its discretion by referring ANR's take-or-pay dispute to FERC. FERC's recent pronouncements signal a new willingness to act on producer-pipeline disputes and create a greater need to decide pending cases in conformity with anticipated rule-making proceedings.

C) Inappropriateness of Judicial Forum

Wagner & Brown next argues that its suit is more properly before a court than before FERC because FERC cannot grant Wagner & Brown damages for breach of contract.

We agree that the FERC lacks power to enforce Wagner & Brown's claim for damages under the contract. However, this does not deprive the FERC of primary jurisdiction over the take-or-pay issue. As the Supreme Court stated in *Western Pacific, supra,* primary jurisdiction may be invoked where "*enforcement* of the claim requires the resolution of issues . . . within the special competence of an administrative body." 77 S. Ct. at 165 (emphasis added). Hence, under the doctrine, a court may refer discrete issues to an administrative agency while reserving to itself the power to take final action on the litigant's claims. The district court's order as modified is in conformity with this principle. The stay does not prejudice Wagner & Brown's right to collect damages on the contract, but merely delays enforcement pending a resolution of the take-or-pay question by FERC. . . .

E) Inordinate Delay

Finally, Wagner & Brown contends that the district court improperly deferred to FERC's primary jurisdiction because the delay which will likely attend resolution of ANR's claims will needlessly tie up payments owing to Wagner & Brown under the contract and will imperil Wagner & Brown financially. Wagner & Brown cannot seek redress elsewhere while waiting for FERC to act because the dismissal order and the determination of primary jurisdiction bar Wagner & Brown from pursuing its claims in another forum.

Wagner & Brown's argument is persuasive. If the district court is allowed to decline jurisdiction, and FERC's past inaction on this issue continues, any recovery of damages from ANR could be so delayed as to be ineffective even if Wagner & Brown's rights are eventually established. Yet, the doctrine of primary jurisdiction clearly indicates that the parties should seek the expertise of FERC. These aims are not necessarily incompatible. To ensure that Wagner & Brown's rights will not be unreasonably delayed or lost, we direct that the district court modify its judgment by vacating its order of dismissal and substituting an order staying proceedings before it for a period of 180 days to afford FERC an opportunity to rule on ANR's complaint. If no such ruling is forthcoming within that time, or such extension thereof as the district court is persuaded would not irreparably harm Wagner & Brown's rights and is required for good cause shown by FERC, then the district court should proceed to adjudicate the rights of the parties without further deference to the expertise of FERC.

AFFIRMED WITH DIRECTIONS.

QUESTION SET 9.20

Review & Synthesis

1. Restate the factors courts consider when deciding whether to refer an issue to a federal agency under the primary jurisdiction doctrine.

2. "Primary jurisdiction" can refer to either of two situations. The first involves concurrent judicial and administrative authority to resolve a dispute or a discrete regulatory question within it. The second involves

an agency's exclusive authority over a dispute or issue, such that federal court jurisdiction over them is ousted. Which of these meanings applied to *Wagner & Brown*? Was the Fifth Circuit prevented from deciding the legality of pay-or-take contracts, or was it simply reluctant to do so in the first instance?

3. As *Wagner & Brown* made clear, federal courts have no authority to order a federal agency to resolve issues referred to them under the primary jurisdiction doctrine. This raises two questions. First, what should courts do when asked to adjudicate issues falling within an agency's primary jurisdiction and the agency has chosen to litigate that issue rather than resolve it? *See, e.g., United States* ex rel. *Wall v. Circle C Construction, LLC,* 697 F.3d 345, 352 (6th Cir. 2012) ("the [primary jurisdiction doctrine] does not apply when the specially competent agency is itself the plaintiff, because deference to an agency's primary jurisdiction makes little sense in the context of an enforcement proceeding initiated by the agency.") (internal quotations and citations omitted). Second, should federal courts ever *dismiss* lawsuits that raise primary jurisdiction concerns, seeing as how they have no control over whether the expert agency will ever resolve the questions referred to it?

B. SCOPE OF JUDICIAL REVIEW

Prior to passage of the Administrative Procedure Act in 1946, no uniform standard governed judicial review of agency action. This state of disuniformity persisted through the New Deal era for largely political reasons. President Roosevelt and his political allies in Congress resisted regularizing administrative procedure through a comprehensive federal statute because of perceived judicial hostility to the New Deal. Codifying procedures that would include more searching and systematic judicial review of administrative decision-making—a key feature of legislative reforms being discussed at that time—would have allowed courts to slow down or thwart policy initiatives the Roosevelt Administration considered vital to supporting the nation's economic and social well-being. The review regime in place at the time—which mostly consisted of agency-specific statutory provisions and court-created doctrines—apparently created fewer opportunities for judicial interference. The political winds shifted toward the end of World War II, and so Congress and President Truman were persuaded that the time had come to regularize federal administrative practices. *See generally*, Matthew D. McCubbins et al., *The Political Origins of the Administrative Procedure Act*, 15 J.L. Econ. & Org. 180 (1999); George B. Shepherd, *Fierce Compromise: The Administrative Procedure Act Emerges from New Deal Politics*, 90 Nw. U. L. Rev. 1557 (1996).

The APA regularized numerous aspects of administrative procedure. Among other things, it adopted default requirements for decision-making fairness and transparency, as well as uniform definitions for core administrative actions and work product (rules, rulemaking, orders, adjudications). This regularization was not meant, however, to extend to the standards courts used to review those actions and work product. Section 10 of the APA—which contained the Act's judicial review provisions and is currently codified at 5 U.S.C. § 706—granted the courts no new means by which to scrutinize (or potentially slow) administrative decision-making. As the ATTORNEY GENERAL's MANUAL explained, § 10 was intended to be "a general restatement of the principles of judicial review embodied in many statutes and judicial decisions." As such, it "not only [did] not supersede special statutory review proceedings, but also generally [left] the mechanics of judicial review to be governed by other statutes and by judicial rules." ATTORNEY GENERAL's MANUAL at 93. Put another way, § 10 was intended "to restate but not expand the right of and procedures for judicial review." *See* Allen Moore, *The Proposed Administrative Procedure Act*, in 92 CONG. REC. 2161 (1946).

Turning to the review provisions as they currently operate, and as explained earlier in this chapter, the threshold question as it relates to judicial review of agency action is whether review is available at all. Assuming the challenged action is not committed to agency discretion by law or otherwise made unreviewable by statute (5 U.S.C. § 701(a)(1) & (a)(2)), APA § 10 instructs courts to "decide all relevant questions of law, interpret constitutional and statutory provisions, and determine the meaning or applicability of the terms of an agency action." 5 U.S.C. § 706. It further instructs them to "hold unlawful and set aside agency action, findings, and conclusions found to be":

> (A) arbitrary, capricious, an abuse of discretion, or otherwise not in accordance with law;
>
> (B) contrary to constitutional right, power, privilege, or immunity;
>
> (C) in excess of statutory jurisdiction, authority, or limitations, or short of statutory right;
>
> (D) without observance of procedure required by law;
>
> (E) unsupported by substantial evidence in a case subject to sections 556 and 557 of this title or otherwise reviewed on the record of an agency hearing provided by statute; or
>
> (F) unwarranted by the facts to the extent that the facts are subject to trial *de novo* by the reviewing court.

5 U.S.C. § 706(2)(A)-(F). Perhaps because its drafters meant it as a restatement of the various review standards in operation at the time, § 10 is something of a mixed bag. At first blush, its subsections appear to overlap. For example, could not an agency's allegedly illegal taking of personal property be challenged as "not in accordance with law" and "contrary to constitutional

right"? *Cf. FCC v. Fox Television Stations, Inc.*, 556 U.S. 502, 516 (2009) (observing that judicial authority to set aside "unlawful" agency action under § 706(2)(A) "of course includes unconstitutional action"). Similarly, could not an agency's alleged failure to follow statutorily prescribed rulemaking procedures be overturned as "not in accordance with law" as well as "without observance of procedure required by law"? What's more, § 10 uses several terms—"arbitrary," "capricious," "substantial evidence," "on the record"—that are presumably defined in the case law on which it is partially based or in the APA's legislative history, but are not defined anywhere in the APA itself. In sum, § 10 is not a model of statutory precision.

The seminal explanation of the function performed by each § 10 subsection comes in a case we have previously considered, *Citizens to Preserve Overton Park, Inc. v. Volpe.*

Citizens to Preserve Overton Park, Inc. v. Volpe
401 U.S. 402 (1971)

Opinion of the Court by Mr. Justice MARSHALL, announced by Mr. Justice STEWART.

[The facts and disposition of the case are excerpted in Chapter 6 at pages 395-401.]

[Section] 706 of the Administrative Procedure Act, 5 U.S.C. § 706 (1964 ed., Supp. V) . . . provides that a "reviewing court shall . . . hold unlawful and set aside agency action, findings, and conclusions found" not to meet six separate standards. In all cases agency action must be set aside if the action was "arbitrary, capricious, an abuse of discretion, or otherwise not in accordance with law" or if the action failed to meet statutory, procedural, or constitutional requirements. 5 U.S.C. §§ 706(2) (A), (B), (C), (D) (1964 ed., Supp. V). In certain narrow, specifically limited situations, the agency action is to be set aside if the action was not supported by "substantial evidence." And in other equally narrow circumstances the reviewing court is to engage in a *de novo* review of the action and set it aside if it was "unwarranted by the facts." 5 U.S.C. §§ 706(2)(E), (F) (1964 ed., Supp. V).

Petitioners argue that the Secretary's approval of the construction of I-40 through Overton Park is subject to one or the other of these latter two standards of limited applicability. First, they contend that the "substantial evidence" standard of § 706(2)(E) must be applied. In the alternative, they claim that § 706(2)(F) applies and that there must be a *de novo* review to determine if the Secretary's action was "unwarranted by the facts." Neither of these standards is, however, applicable.

Review under the substantial-evidence test is authorized only when the agency action is taken pursuant to a rulemaking provision of the Administrative Procedure Act itself, 5 U.S.C. § 553 (1964 ed., Supp. V),* or when the agency action is based on a public adjudicatory hearing. See 5 U.S.C. §§ 556, 557 (1964 ed., Supp. V). The Secretary's decision to allow the expenditure of federal funds to build I-40 through Overton Park was plainly not an exercise of a rulemaking function. *See* 1 K. Davis, Administrative Law Treatise § 5.01 (1958). And the only hearing that is required by either the Administrative Procedure Act or the statutes regulating the distribution of federal funds for highway construction is a public hearing conducted by local officials for the purpose of informing the community about the proposed project and eliciting community views on the design and route. 23 U.S.C. § 128 (1964 ed., Supp. V). The hearing is nonadjudicatory, quasi-legislative in nature. It is not designed to produce a record that is to be the basis of agency action—the basic requirement for substantial-evidence review.

Petitioners' alternative argument also fails. *De novo* review of whether the Secretary's decision was "unwarranted by the facts" is authorized by § 706(2)(F) in only two circumstances. First, such *de novo* review is authorized when the action is adjudicatory in nature and the agency factfinding procedures are inadequate. And, there may be independent judicial factfinding when issues that were not before the agency are raised in a proceeding to enforce nonadjudicatory agency action. Neither situation exists here.

Even though there is no *de novo* review in this case and the Secretary's approval of the route of I-40 does not have ultimately to meet the substantial-evidence test, the generally applicable standards of § 706 require the reviewing court to engage in a substantial inquiry. Certainly, the Secretary's decision is entitled to a presumption of regularity. *See, e.g., Pacific States Box & Basket Co. v. White*, 296 U.S. 176, 185 (1935). But that presumption is not to shield his action from a thorough, probing, in-depth review.

The court is first required to decide whether the Secretary acted within the scope of his authority. *Schilling v. Rogers*, 363 U.S. 666, 676-677 (1960). This determination naturally begins with a delineation of the scope of the Secretary's authority and discretion. L. Jaffe, Judicial Control of Administrative Action 359 (1965). As has been shown, Congress has specified only a small range of choices that the Secretary can make. Also involved in this initial inquiry is a determination of whether on the facts the Secretary's decision can reasonably be said to be within that range. The reviewing court must consider whether the Secretary properly construed his authority to approve the use of parkland as limited to situations where there

---

* [This is incorrect. The substantial evidence test is applicable to formal (i.e., on-the-record) rulemaking under 5 U.S.C. §§ 556-557. It is *not* applicable to informal rulemaking under 5 U.S.C. § 553.—Ed.]

are no feasible alternative routes or where feasible alternative routes involve uniquely difficult problems. And the reviewing court must be able to find that the Secretary could have reasonably believed that in this case there are no feasible alternatives or that alternatives do involve unique problems.

Scrutiny of the facts does not end, however, with the determination that the Secretary has acted within the scope of his statutory authority. Section 706(2)(A) requires a finding that the actual choice made was not "arbitrary, capricious, an abuse of discretion, or otherwise not in accordance with law." 5 U.S.C. § 706(2)(A) (1964 ed., Supp. V). To make this finding the court must consider whether the decision was based on a consideration of the relevant factors and whether there has been a clear error of judgment. Jaffe, *supra*, at 182. Although this inquiry into the facts is to be searching and careful, the ultimate standard of review is a narrow one. The court is not empowered to substitute its judgment for that of the agency.

The final inquiry is whether the Secretary's action followed the necessary procedural requirements. Here the only procedural error alleged is the failure of the Secretary to make formal findings and state his reason for allowing the highway to be built through the park.

Undoubtedly, review of the Secretary's action is hampered by his failure to make such findings, but the absence of formal findings does not necessarily require that the case be remanded to the Secretary. Neither the Department of Transportation Act nor the Federal-Aid Highway Act requires such formal findings. Moreover, the Administrative Procedure Act requirements that there be formal findings in certain rulemaking and adjudicatory proceedings do not apply to the Secretary's action here. *See* 5 U.S.C. §§ 553(a)(2), 554(a) (1964 ed., Supp. V). And, although formal findings may be required in some cases in the absence of statutory directives when the nature of the agency action is ambiguous, those situations are rare. *See City of Yonkers v. United States*, 320 U.S. 685 (1944); *American Trucking Ass'ns v. United States*, 344 U.S. 298, 320 (1953). Plainly, there is no ambiguity here; the Secretary has approved the construction of I-40 through Overton Park and has approved a specific design for the project. . . .

[The whole informal adjudicative record on which the Secretary based his decision] is not . . . before us. The lower courts based their review on the litigation affidavits that were presented. These affidavits were merely "*post hoc*" rationalizations, *Burlington Truck Lines v. United States*, 371 U.S. 156, 168-169 (1962), which have traditionally been found to be an inadequate basis for review. *Burlington Truck Lines v. United States, supra*; *SEC v. Chenery Corp.*, 318 U.S. 80, 87 (1943). And they clearly do not constitute the "whole record" compiled by the agency: the basis for review required by § 706 of the Administrative Procedure Act. . . .

* * *

As *Overton Park* explains, one can read APA § 706(2)(B) through (F) as identifying discrete types of errors for which courts must reverse agency decision-making. Subsection (A) thus serves as a "final check" to catch any other errors not otherwise specified.

Whatever the distinctions Congress sought to draw here, one can reasonably question whether they make any practical difference. The reason is fairly simple: these standards seem to have only a loose relationship to those courts actually apply when reviewing agency decision-making. As one scholar has rightly observed, "the actual meaning of these [§ 706] standards has developed in a common law fashion, sometimes with little attention to the language of the governing statute." Jack M. Beermann, *Common Law and Statute Law in Administrative Law*, 63 ADMIN. L. REV. 1, 21 (2011). This is particularly true of the judicial standards for reviewing agency interpretations of ambiguous statutes and rules, and the circumstances under which those standards apply. The Supreme Court seems to have created and developed them without paying much if any attention to the APA. Accordingly, the real review standards are those developed by the Court in several seminal cases.

The following materials, which analyze those cases, can be divided into two broad categories. The first addresses agency *factual determinations and policy judgments*. Here, the focus will be on two principle standards of review: the "arbitrary and capricious" test (applicable to informal decision-making) and the "substantial evidence" test (applicable to formal decision-making). A central issue with regard to both tests is the level of evidentiary support they require. For instance, is it enough for an agency to defend its decision by pointing solely to evidence that supports its actions while ignoring evidence that does not? This approach would imply a relatively light level of judicial scrutiny which does not press agencies on whether they considered other, perhaps more compelling, courses of action. Or must reviewing courts invalidate agency actions that do not account for undermining or countervailing facts or viewpoints? This approach to judicial review would imply a much more robust level of scrutiny that requires agencies to consider the whole factual record, and to provide reasons for discounting facts or positions that do not support their decisions.

The second category of cases relates to how courts review agency *interpretations of law*, particularly how they review agency interpretations of ambiguous statutes and rules, i.e., statutes and rules that are susceptible to more than one plausible interpretation. The central issue raised by these cases involves judicial deference to how agencies resolve these ambiguities. Since courts definitively interpret ambiguous statutes outside of the administrative context, why should they not do so when agencies are involved? The materials then move to other cases addressing the propriety of courts deferring to agency interpretations. Should courts defer to how agencies interpret ambiguities in the rules the agencies themselves have promulgated? Should they defer to how agencies interpret ambiguous statutes that set the limits of the agencies' own jurisdiction?

1. Review of Agency Findings of Fact and Judgments of Policy

a. Informal Decision-Making Processes: The "Arbitrary and Capricious" Test

A substantial amount of administrative decision-making involves the exercise of discretion. Congress often instructs agency officials to consider or to disregard particular factors—economic or environmental impacts, prevailing industry practices, federalism, technological feasibility, the public's best interest, etc.—when delegating them regulatory authority. Just as often, Congress does not dictate the outcome of such consideration, but leaves ultimate resolution of the issue to agency officials. This frees the officials—gives them the discretion—to add a host of subjective factors to their decisional calculus. Accordingly, discretionary decision-making of this sort "compels the administrator to resort to a whole complex of additional concepts and attitudes, official and personal, some of which he [or she] may explicitly formulate for the decision at hand, some of which he [or she] may not express, some of which he [or she] may be unaware of." *See* 4 CHARLES H. KOCH, JR., ADMINISTRATIVE LAW & PRACTICE § 11:30 (3d ed. 2020). (quoting LOUIS JAFFE, JUDICIAL CONTROL OF ADMINISTRATIVE ACTION 555-56 (1965)). This mode of decision-making—substantially informed by factors subjectively chosen by agency officials rather than by Congress—affords the flexibility those officials often need to achieve Congress' broader policy goals. It also leaves officials with considerable freedom to deploy the government's regulatory resources in ways that are irrational, unlawful, or abusive. Balancing between the need to preserve agency discretion and the need to correct agency missteps is a difficult task, one Congress has assigned to the federal courts. The "arbitrary and capricious" standard of review—codified in 5 U.S.C. § 706(2)(A) and elaborated upon by the Supreme Court—is the mechanism by which courts strike that balance in informal agency decision-making.

The scope of review required by § 706(2)(A) has evolved considerably over the past several decades, due in part to uncertainties about its precise meaning at the time of the Administrative Procedure Act's enactment. Given the vociferous criticisms in some circles about the expansion of potentially arbitrary and abusive Executive Branch discretion during the 1930s and 1940s, the provision was given surprisingly little attention by the APA's drafters and Congress more generally. The APA's extensive legislative history presents only a handful of mentions; there was no indication of the administrative context from which the standard derived, and there was little dedicated discussion of what it required. In one of the few such instances, Senator McCarran, Chairman of the Senate Judiciary Committee, was asked during a floor debate whether judicial review was precluded whenever a statute vested discretion in an agency (a topic discussed earlier in this chapter).

McCarran replied in the negative, assuring that discretionary agency decisions would be reviewable under the Act. Moreover, he hinted at the standard to which such exercises of discretion would be held: "It must not be an arbitrary discretion. It must be a judicial [(judicious?)] discretion; it must be a discretion based on sound reasoning." *See* APA Leg. His., at 311.

Courts apparently considered the standard a highly deferential one, at least initially. This belief was informed by the Supreme Court's 1935 decision in *Pacific States Box & Basket Co. v. White*. There manufacturers of strawberry and raspberry boxes challenged uniform standards for fruit containers promulgated by the Oregon Division of Plant Industry, arguing that it was irrational and a violation of their substantive due process rights. The Court upheld the rule even though the agency made no specific factual findings to support it. Applying a standard strikingly similar to "rational basis" review of economic legislation, the Court concluded that the agency's rule must be upheld " 'if any state of facts reasonably can be conceived that would sustain it.' " *Pacific States Box & Basket Co. v. White*, 296 U.S. 176, 185 (1935) (quoting *Borden's Farm Products Co. v. Baldwin*, 293 U.S. 194, 209 (1934)). In other words, " 'there is a presumption of the existence of that state of facts.' " *Id.*

This level of judicial deference comported with the general expansion of administrative authority and faith in technical expertise that characterized the New Deal Era. As skepticism of administrative decision-making grew during the 1960s, courts grew more aggressive in asserting their supervisory powers. By the early 1970s, courts started moving away from the deference characterized by *Pacific States* and toward much more searching scrutiny of agency exercises of discretion. In particular, the D.C. Circuit transitioned to a "hard look" version of the arbitrary and capricious review standard. Under hard look review, courts examined whether *agencies* carefully considered their decisions (took a "hard look" at them) before settling on a course of action. While a court applying the standard had to ensure that the agency was sufficiently careful in making its decision, it also had to avoid unduly interfering with the policymaking authority Congress granted to that agency. The most notable early description of hard look review comes from a 1974 article authored by Judge Harold Leventhal of the D.C. Circuit:

> In the exercise of the court's supervisory function, full allowance must be given for the reality that agency matters typically involve a kind of expertise—sometimes technical in a scientific sense, sometimes more a matter of specialization in kinds of regulatory programs. Nevertheless, the court must study the record attentively, even the evidence on technical and specialist matters, to penetrate to the underlying decisions of the agency, to satisfy itself that the agency has exercised a reasoned discretion with reasons that do not deviate from or ignore the ascertainable legislative intent. It must ensure that the agency has given reasoned discretion to all the material facts and issues. The court exercises this aspect of its supervisory role

with particular vigilance if it becomes aware, especially from a combination of danger signals, that the agency has not really taken a "hard look" at the salient problems, and has not genuinely engaged in reasoned decisionmaking. Finally, if satisfied on these points, the court sustains an agency even though its findings are of less than ideal clarity, if the agency's path may reasonably be discerned. The court is not to make its own findings, or select policies.

Harold Leventhal, *Environmental Decisionmaking and the Role of the Courts,* 122 U. PENN. L. REV. 509, 511 (1974) (internal quotations omitted); *see also Greater Boston Television Corp. v. Federal Communications Commission,* 444 F.2d 841, 850-51 (D.C. Cir. 1970). The Supreme Court echoed similar sentiments when describing the arbitrary and capricious review standard in *Overton Park.* "Although this inquiry into the facts is to be searching and careful, the ultimate standard of review is a narrow one. The court is not empowered to substitute its judgment for that of the agency." *Citizens to Preserve Overton Park v. Volpe,* 401 U.S. 402, 416 (1971). These observations were only dicta, however. The Court would not make a decision to endorse or reject hard look review until the early 1980s.

The materials below explore four applications of the "arbitrary and capricious" test. The first involves the basic doctrine, considered through the seminal case of *Motor Vehicle Manufacturers Association v. State Farm Mutual Automobile Insurance Company.* The second involves two bedrock principles of administrative law: that agencies must act consistently and must explain their actions. They are addressed in the Supreme Court's recent decision in *Department of Commerce v. New York,* which scrutinizes the Commerce Department's attempt to add a citizenship question to the decennial census. Third, the materials explore the extent to which courts can review changes agencies make to preexisting policies, focusing on the Supreme Court's decision in *FCC v. Fox Television Corp.* Finally, we ask whether and how courts apply the arbitrary and capricious test to agency *inaction.* The focus of attention there is the D.C. Circuit's influential 1987 decision in *American Horse Protection Association, Inc. v. Lyng.*

i. The Basic Doctrine

Motor Vehicle Manufacturers Association v. State Farm Mutual Automobile Insurance Company
463 U.S. 29 (1983)

JUSTICE WHITE delivered the opinion of the Court.

The development of the automobile gave Americans unprecedented freedom to travel, but exacted a high price for enhanced mobility. Since 1929, motor vehicles have been the leading cause of accidental deaths and injuries in the United States. In 1982, 46,300 Americans died in motor vehicle accidents and hundreds of thousands more were maimed and injured. While a consensus exists that the current loss of life on our highways is unacceptably high, improving safety does not admit to easy solution. In 1966, Congress decided that at least part of the answer lies in improving the design and safety features of the vehicle itself. But much of the technology for building safer cars was undeveloped or untested. Before changes in automobile design could be mandated, the effectiveness of these changes had to be studied, their costs examined, and public acceptance considered. This task called for considerable expertise and Congress responded by enacting the National Traffic and Motor Vehicle Safety Act of 1966, (Act), 15 U.S.C. §§ 1381 *et seq.* (1976 and Supp. IV 1980). The Act, created for the purpose of "reduc[ing] traffic accidents and deaths and injuries to persons resulting from traffic accidents," 15 U.S.C. § 1381, directs the Secretary of Transportation or his delegate to issue motor vehicle safety standards that "shall be practicable, shall meet the need for motor vehicle safety, and shall be stated in objective terms." 15 U.S.C. § 1392(a). In issuing these standards, the Secretary is directed to consider "relevant available motor vehicle safety data," whether the proposed standard "is reasonable, practicable and appropriate" for the particular type of motor vehicle, and the "extent to which such standards will contribute to carrying out the purposes" of the Act. 15 U.S.C. § 1392(f)(1), (3), (4).

The Act also authorizes judicial review under the provisions of the Administrative Procedure Act (APA), 5 U.S.C. § 706 (1976), of all "orders establishing, amending, or revoking a Federal motor vehicle safety standard," 15 U.S.C. § 1392(b). Under this authority, we review today whether NHTSA acted arbitrarily and capriciously in revoking the requirement in Motor Vehicle Safety Standard 208 that new motor vehicles produced after September 1982 be equipped with passive restraints to protect the safety of the occupants of the vehicle in the event of a collision. Briefly summarized, we hold that the agency failed to present an adequate basis and explanation for rescinding the passive restraint requirement and that the agency must either consider the matter further or adhere to or amend Standard 208 along lines which its analysis supports.

I

The regulation whose rescission is at issue bears a complex and convoluted history. . . .

As originally issued by the Department of Transportation in 1967, Standard 208 simply required the installation of seatbelts in all automobiles. It soon became apparent that the level of seatbelt use was too low to reduce traffic injuries to an acceptable level. The Department therefore began consideration of "passive occupant restraint systems" — devices that do not depend for their effectiveness upon any action taken by the occupant except that necessary to operate the vehicle. Two types of automatic crash protection emerged: automatic seatbelts and airbags. The automatic seatbelt is a traditional safety belt, which when fastened to the interior of the door remains attached without impeding entry or exit from the vehicle, and deploys automatically without any action on the part of the passenger. The airbag is an inflatable device concealed in the dashboard and steering column. It automatically inflates when a sensor indicates that deceleration forces from an accident have exceeded a preset minimum, then rapidly deflates to dissipate those forces. The life-saving potential of these devices was immediately recognized, and in 1977, after substantial on-the-road experience with both devices, it was estimated by NHTSA that passive restraints could prevent approximately 12,000 deaths and over 100,000 serious injuries annually.

In 1969, the Department formally proposed a standard requiring the installation of passive restraints. In 1970, the agency revised Standard 208 to include passive protection requirements, and in 1972, the agency amended the standard to require full passive protection for all front seat occupants of vehicles manufactured after August 15, 1975. On review, the agency's decision to require passive restraints was found to be supported by "substantial evidence" and upheld. *Chrysler Corp. v. Dep't of Transportation,* 472 F.2d 659 (6th Cir. 1972).

In preparing for the upcoming model year, most car makers chose the "ignition interlock" option, a decision which was highly unpopular, and led Congress to amend the Act to prohibit a motor vehicle safety standard from requiring or permitting compliance by means of an ignition interlock or a continuous buzzer designed to indicate that safety belts were not in use. . . .

The effective date for mandatory passive restraint systems was extended for a year until August 31, 1976. But in June 1976, Secretary of Transportation William T. Coleman, Jr. . . . extended the optional alternatives indefinitely and suspended the passive restraint requirement. . . .

Coleman's successor as Secretary of Transportation disagreed. [Secretary Brock Adams] issued a new mandatory passive restraint regulation, known as Modified Standard 208. The Modified Standard mandated the phasing in of passive restraints beginning with large cars in model year 1982 and extending to all cars by model year 1984. The two principal systems that would satisfy the Standard were airbags and passive belts; the choice of which system to install was left to the manufacturers. . . . [T]he Court of Appeals upheld Modified Standard 208 as a rational, nonarbitrary regulation consistent with the agency's mandate under the Act. The standard also survived scrutiny by Congress, which did not exercise its authority under the legislative veto provision of the 1974 Amendments.

Over the next several years, the automobile industry geared up to comply with Modified Standard 208. As late as July, 1980, NHTSA reported: ". . . When all cars are equipped with automatic crash protection systems, each year an estimated 9,000 more lives will be saved and tens of thousands of serious injuries will be prevented." NHTSA, Automobile Occupant Crash Protection, Progress Report No. 3, p. 4.

In February 1981, however, Secretary of Transportation Andrew Lewis reopened the rulemaking due to changed economic circumstances and, in particular, the difficulties of the automobile industry. Two months later, the agency ordered a one-year delay in the application of the standard to large cars, extending the deadline to September 1982 and at the same time, proposed the possible rescission of the entire standard. After receiving written comments and holding public hearings, NHTSA issued a final rule (Notice 25) that rescinded the passive restraint requirement contained in Modified Standard 208.

II

In a statement explaining the rescission, NHTSA maintained that it was no longer able to find, as it had in 1977, that the automatic restraint requirement would produce significant safety benefits. This judgment reflected not a change of opinion on the effectiveness of the technology, but a change in plans by the automobile industry. In 1977, the agency had assumed that airbags would be installed in 60% of all new cars and automatic seatbelts in 40%. By 1981 it became apparent that automobile manufacturers planned to install the automatic seatbelts in approximately 99% of the new cars. For this reason, the life-saving potential of airbags would not be realized. Moreover, it now appeared that the overwhelming majority of passive belts planned to be installed by manufacturers could be detached easily and left that way permanently. Passive belts, once detached, then required "the same type of affirmative action that is the stumbling block to obtaining high usage levels of manual belts." 46 Fed. Reg., at 53421. For this reason, the agency concluded that there was no longer a basis for reliably predicting that the standard would lead to any significant increased usage of restraints at all.

In view of the possibly minimal safety benefits, the automatic restraint requirement no longer was reasonable or practicable in the agency's view. The requirement would require approximately $1 billion to implement and the agency did not believe it would be reasonable to impose such substantial costs on manufacturers and consumers without more adequate assurance that sufficient safety benefits would accrue. In addition, NHTSA concluded that automatic restraints might have an adverse effect on the public's attitude toward safety. Given the high expense and limited benefits of detachable belts, NHTSA feared that many consumers would regard the standard as an instance of ineffective regulation, adversely affecting the public's view of safety regulation and, in particular, "poisoning popular sentiment toward efforts to improve occupant restraint systems in the future." 46 Fed. Reg., at 53424.

State Farm Mutual Automobile Insurance Co. and the National Association of Independent Insurers filed petitions for review of NHTSA's rescission of the passive restraint Standard. . . .

III

. . . Both the Motor Vehicle Safety Act and the 1974 amendments. . . . indicate that motor vehicle safety standards are to be promulgated under the informal rulemaking procedures of § 553 of the Administrative Procedure Act. 5 U.S.C. § 553 (1976). The agency's action in promulgating such standards therefore may be set aside if found to be "arbitrary, capricious, an abuse of discretion, or otherwise not in accordance with law." 5 U.S.C. § 706(2)(A). We believe that the rescission or modification of an occupant protection standard is subject to the same test. . . .

Petitioner Motor Vehicle Manufacturers Association . . . disagrees, contending that the rescission of an agency rule should be judged by the same standard a court would use to judge an agency's refusal to promulgate a rule in the first place—a standard Petitioner believes considerably narrower than the traditional arbitrary and capricious test and "close to the borderline of nonreviewability." We reject this view. The Motor Vehicle Safety Act expressly equates orders "revoking" and "establishing" safety standards; neither that Act nor the APA suggests that revocations are to be treated as refusals to promulgate standards. Petitioner's view would render meaningless Congress' authorization for judicial review of orders revoking safety rules. Moreover, the revocation of an extant regulation is substantially different than a failure to act. Revocation constitutes a reversal of the agency's former views as to the proper course. A "settled course of behavior embodies the agency's informed judgment that, by pursuing that course, it will carry out the policies committed to it by Congress. There is, then, at least a presumption that those policies will be carried out best if the settled rule is adhered to." *Atchison, T. & S.F.R. Co. v. Wichita Bd. of Trade,* 412 U.S. 800, 807-808 (1973). Accordingly, an agency changing its course by rescinding a rule is obligated to supply a reasoned analysis for the change beyond that which may be required when an agency does not act in the first instance.

In so holding, we fully recognize that "regulatory agencies do not establish rules of conduct to last forever," *American Trucking Assoc., Inc. v. Atchison, T. & S.F.R. Co.,* 387 U.S. 397, 416 (1967), and that an agency must be given ample latitude to "adapt their rules and policies to the demands of changing circumstances." *Permian Basin Area Rate Cases,* 390 U.S. 747, 784 (1968). But the forces of change do not always or necessarily point in the direction of deregulation. In the abstract, there is no more reason to presume that changing circumstances require the rescission of prior action, instead of a revision in or even the extension of current regulation. If Congress established a presumption from which judicial review should start, that presumption—contrary to petitioners' views—is not against safety regulation, but against changes in current policy that are not justified by the rulemaking record. . . .

The Department of Transportation accepts the applicability of the "arbitrary and capricious" standard. It argues that under this standard, a reviewing court may not set aside an agency rule that is rational, based on consideration of the relevant factors and within the scope of the authority delegated to the agency by the statute. We do not disagree with this formulation. The scope of review under the "arbitrary and capricious" standard is narrow and a court is not to substitute its judgment for that of the agency. Nevertheless, the agency must examine the relevant data and articulate a satisfactory explanation for its action including a "rational connection between the facts found and the choice made." *Burlington Truck Lines v. United States,* 371 U.S. 156, 168 (1962). In reviewing that explanation, we must "consider whether the decision was based on a consideration of the relevant factors and whether there has been a clear error of judgment." *Bowman Transp. Inc. v. Arkansas-Best Freight System,* [419 U.S. 281,] 285 [(1974)]. Normally, an agency rule would be arbitrary and capricious if the agency has relied on factors which Congress has not intended it to consider, entirely failed to consider an important aspect of the problem, offered an explanation for its decision that runs counter to the evidence before the agency, or is so implausible that it could not be ascribed to a difference in view or the product of agency expertise. The reviewing court should not attempt itself to make up for such deficiencies: "We may not supply a reasoned basis for the agency's action that the agency itself has not given." *SEC v. Chenery Corp.,* 332 U.S. 194, 196 (1947). We will, however, "uphold a decision of less than ideal clarity if the agency's path may reasonably be discerned." *Bowman Transp. Inc. v. Arkansas-Best Freight System, supra,* 419 U.S., at 286. For purposes of these cases, it is also relevant that Congress required a record of the rulemaking proceedings to be compiled and submitted to a reviewing court, 15 U.S.C. § 1394, and intended that agency findings under the Act would be supported by "substantial evidence on the record considered as a whole." S. Rep. No. 1301, 89th Cong., 2d Sess. 8 (1966); H.R. Rep. No. 1776, 89th Cong., 2d Sess. 21 (1966).

IV

The Court of Appeals correctly found that the arbitrary-and-capricious test applied to rescissions of prior agency regulations, but then erred in intensifying the scope of its review based upon its reading of legislative events. . . .

V

The ultimate question before us is whether NHTSA's rescission of the passive restraint requirement of Standard 208 was arbitrary and capricious. We conclude, as did the Court of Appeals, that it was. . . .

A

The first and most obvious reason for finding the rescission arbitrary and capricious is that NHTSA apparently gave no consideration whatever to modifying the Standard to require that airbag technology be utilized. Standard 208 sought to achieve automatic crash protection by requiring automobile manufacturers to install either of two passive restraint devices: airbags or automatic seatbelts. . . .

The agency has now determined that the detachable automatic belts will not attain anticipated safety benefits because so many individuals will detach the mechanism. Even if this conclusion were acceptable in its entirety, standing alone it would not justify any more than an amendment of Standard 208 to disallow compliance by means of the one technology which will not provide effective passenger protection. It does not cast doubt on the need for a passive restraint standard or upon the efficacy of airbag technology. In its most recent rule-making, the agency again acknowledged the life-saving potential of the airbag:

> The agency has no basis at this time for changing its earlier conclusions in 1976 and 1977 that basic airbag technology is sound and has been sufficiently demonstrated to be effective in those vehicles in current use. . . ." NHTSA Final Regulatory Impact Analysis (RIA) at XI-4.

Given the effectiveness ascribed to airbag technology by the agency, the mandate of the Safety Act to achieve traffic safety would suggest that the logical response to the faults of detachable seatbelts would be to require the installation of airbags. At the very least this alternative way of achieving the objectives of the Act should have been addressed and adequate reasons given for its abandonment. But the agency not only did not require compliance through airbags, it did not even consider the possibility in its 1981 rulemaking. Not one sentence of its rulemaking statement discusses the airbags-only option. Because, as the Court of Appeals stated, "NHTSA's . . . analysis of airbags was nonexistent," 680 F.2d, at 236, what we said in *Burlington Truck Lines v. United States,* 371 U.S., at 167, is apropos here:

> There are no findings and no analysis here to justify the choice made, no indication of the basis on which the [agency] exercised its expert discretion. We are not prepared to and the Administrative Procedure Act will not permit us to accept such . . . practice. . . . Expert discretion is the lifeblood of the administrative process, but "unless we make the requirements for administrative action strict and demanding, expertise, the strength of modern government, can become a monster which rules with no practical limits on its discretion." *New York v. United States,* 342 U.S. 882, 884 (dissenting opinion) (footnote omitted).

We have frequently reiterated that an agency must cogently explain why it has exercised its discretion in a given manner, and we reaffirm this principle again today.

The automobile industry has opted for the passive belt over the airbag, but surely it is not enough that the regulated industry has eschewed a given safety device. For nearly a decade, the automobile industry waged the regulatory equivalent of war against the airbag and lost—the inflatable restraint was proven sufficiently effective. Now the automobile industry has decided to employ a seatbelt system which will not meet the safety objectives of Standard 208. This hardly constitutes cause to revoke the standard itself. Indeed, the Motor Vehicle Safety Act was necessary because the industry was not sufficiently responsive to safety concerns. The Act intended that safety standards not depend on current technology and could be "technology-forcing" in the sense of inducing the development of superior safety design. If, under the statute, the agency should not defer to the industry's failure to develop safer cars, which it surely should not do, *a fortiori* it may not revoke a safety standard which can be satisfied by current technology simply because the industry has opted for an ineffective seatbelt design.

. . . [P]etitioners recite a number of difficulties that they believe would be posed by a mandatory airbag standard. These range from questions concerning the installation of airbags in small cars to that of adverse public reaction. But these are not the agency's reasons for rejecting a mandatory airbag standard. Not having discussed the possibility, the agency submitted no reasons at all. The short—and sufficient—answer to petitioners' submission is that the courts may not accept appellate counsel's *post hoc* rationalizations for agency action. It is well-established that an agency's action must be upheld, if at all, on the basis articulated by the agency itself.

Petitioners also invoke our decision in *Vermont Yankee Nuclear Power Corp. v. NRDC,* 435 U.S. 519 (1978), as though it were a talisman under which any agency decision is by definition unimpeachable. Specifically, it is submitted that to require an agency to consider an airbags-only alternative is, in essence, to dictate to the agency the procedures it is to follow. Petitioners . . . misread *Vermont Yankee.* . . . In *Vermont Yankee,* we held that a court may not impose additional procedural requirements upon an agency. We do not require today any specific procedures which NHTSA must follow. Nor do we broadly require an agency to consider all policy alternatives in reaching decision. It is true that a rulemaking "cannot be found wanting simply because the agency failed to include every alternative device and thought conceivable by the mind of man . . . regardless of how uncommon or unknown that alternative may have been. . . ." 435 U.S., at 551. But the airbag is more than a policy alternative to the passive restraint standard; it is a technological alternative within the ambit of the existing standard. We hold only that given the judgment made in 1977 that airbags are an effective and cost-beneficial life-saving technology, the mandatory passive-restraint rule may not be abandoned without any consideration whatsoever of an airbags-only requirement.

B

Although the issue is closer, we also find that the agency was too quick to dismiss the safety benefits of automatic seatbelts. NHTSA's critical finding was that, in light of the industry's plans to install readily detachable passive belts, it could not reliably predict "even a 5 percentage point increase as the minimum level of expected usage increase." The Court of Appeals rejected this finding because there is "not one iota" of evidence that Modified Standard 208 will fail to increase nationwide seatbelt use by at least 13 percentage points, the level of increased usage necessary for the standard to justify its cost. Given the lack of probative evidence, the court held that "only a well-justified refusal to seek more evidence could render rescission non-arbitrary."

Petitioners object to this conclusion. In their view, "substantial uncertainty" that a regulation will accomplish its intended purpose is sufficient reason, without more, to rescind a regulation. We agree with petitioners that just as an agency reasonably may decline to issue a safety standard if it is uncertain about its efficacy, an agency may also revoke a standard on the basis of serious uncertainties if supported by the record and reasonably explained. Rescission of the passive restraint requirement would not be arbitrary and capricious simply because there was no evidence in direct support of the agency's conclusion. It is not infrequent that the available data does not settle a regulatory issue and the agency must then exercise its judgment in moving from the facts and probabilities on the record to a policy conclusion. Recognizing that policymaking in a complex society must account for uncertainty, however, does not imply that it is sufficient for an agency to merely recite the terms "substantial uncertainty" as a justification for its actions. The agency must explain the evidence which is available, and must offer a "rational connection between the facts found and the choice made." *Burlington Truck Lines, Inc. v. United States, supra,* 371 U.S., at 168. Generally, one aspect of that explanation would be a justification for rescinding the regulation before engaging in a search for further evidence.

In this case, the agency's explanation for rescission of the passive restraint requirement is not sufficient to enable us to conclude that the rescission was the product of reasoned decisionmaking. To reach this conclusion, we do not upset the agency's view of the facts, but we do appreciate the limitations of this record in supporting the agency's decision. We start with the accepted ground that if used, seatbelts unquestionably would save many thousands of lives and would prevent tens of thousands of crippling injuries. . . . [T]he safety benefits of wearing seatbelts are not in doubt. . . . We move next to the fact that there is no direct evidence in support of the agency's finding that detachable automatic belts cannot be predicted to yield a substantial increase in usage. The empirical evidence on the record . . . reveals more than a doubling of the usage rate experienced with manual belts. Much of the agency's rulemaking statement—and much of the controversy in this case—centers on the conclusions that should be drawn from these studies. The agency maintained that the doubling of seatbelt usage in these studies could not be extrapolated to an across-the-board mandatory standard because the passive seatbelts were guarded by ignition interlocks and purchasers of the tested cars are somewhat atypical. Respondents insist these studies demonstrate that Modified Standard 208 will substantially increase seatbelt usage. We believe that it is within the agency's discretion to pass upon the generalizability of these field studies. This is precisely the type of issue which rests within the expertise of NHTSA, and upon which a reviewing court must be most hesitant to intrude.

But accepting the agency's view of the field tests on passive restraints indicates only that there is no reliable real-world experience that usage rates will substantially increase. . . . But this and other statements that passive belts will not yield substantial increases in seatbelt usage apparently take no account of the critical difference between detachable automatic belts and current manual belts. A detached passive belt does require an affirmative act to reconnect it, but—unlike a manual seat belt—the passive belt, once reattached, will continue to function automatically unless again disconnected. Thus, inertia—a factor which the agency's own studies have found significant in explaining the current low usage rates for seatbelts—works in favor of, not against, use of the protective device. Since 20 to 50% of motorists currently wear seatbelts on some occasions, there would seem to be grounds to believe that seatbelt use by occasional users will be substantially increased by the detachable passive belts. Whether this is in fact the case is a matter for the agency to decide, but it must bring its expertise to bear on the question.

The agency is correct to look at the costs as well as the benefits of Standard 208. . . . When the agency reexamines its findings as to the likely increase in seatbelt usage, it must also reconsider its judgment of the reasonableness of the monetary and other costs associated with the Standard. In reaching its judgment, NHTSA should bear in mind that Congress intended safety to be the preeminent factor under the Act. . . .

The agency also failed to articulate a basis for not requiring nondetachable belts under Standard 208. . . . The agency did not separately consider the continuous belt option, but treated it together with the ignition interlock device. . . .

By failing to analyze the continuous seatbelts in its own right, the agency has failed to offer the rational connection between facts and judgment required to pass muster under the arbitrary and capricious standard. . . . While the agency is entitled to change its view on the acceptability of continuous passive belts, it is obligated to explain its reasons for doing so. . .

VI

"An agency's view of what is in the public interest may change, either with or without a change in circumstances. But an agency changing its course must supply a reasoned analysis . . ." *Greater Boston Television Corp. v. FCC*, 444 F.2d 841, 852 (D.C. Cir.), *cert. denied*, 403 U.S. 923 (1971). . . . [W]e . . . conclude that the agency has failed to supply the requisite "reasoned analysis" in this case. Accordingly, we vacate the judgment of the Court of Appeals and remand the case to that court with directions to remand the matter to the NHTSA for further consideration consistent with this opinion.

So ordered.

Justice REHNQUIST, with whom THE CHIEF JUSTICE, Justice POWELL, and Justice O'CONNOR join, concurring in part and dissenting in part.

I join parts I, II, III, IV, and V-A of the Court's opinion. In particular, I agree that, since the airbag and continuous spool automatic seatbelt were explicitly approved in the standard the agency was rescinding, the agency should explain why it declined to leave those requirements intact. In this case, the agency gave no explanation at all. Of course, if the agency can provide a rational explanation, it may adhere to its decision to rescind the entire standard.

I do not believe, however, that NHTSA's view of detachable automatic seatbelts was arbitrary and capricious. The agency adequately explained its decision to rescind the standard insofar as it was satisfied by detachable belts.

The statute that requires the Secretary of Transportation to issue motor vehicle safety standards also requires that "[e]ach such . . . standard shall be practicable [and] shall meet the need for motor vehicle safety." 15 U.S.C. § 1392(a). The Court rejects the agency's explanation for its conclusion that there is substantial uncertainty whether requiring installation of detachable automatic belts would substantially increase seatbelt usage. The agency chose not to rely on a study showing a substantial increase in seatbelt usage in cars equipped with automatic seatbelts and an ignition interlock to prevent the car from being operated when the belts were not in place and which were voluntarily purchased with this equipment by consumers. It is reasonable for the agency to decide that this study does not support any conclusion concerning the effect of automatic seatbelts that are installed in all cars whether the consumer wants them or not and are not linked to an ignition interlock system.

The Court rejects this explanation because "there would seem to be grounds to believe that seatbelt use by occasional users will be substantially increased by the detachable passive belts," and the agency did not adequately explain its rejection of these grounds. It seems to me that the agency's explanation, while by no means a model, is adequate. . . . The agency's obligation is to articulate a "rational connection between the facts found and the choice made." *Burlington Truck Lines v. United States,* 371 U.S. 156, 168 (1962). I believe it has met this standard. . . .

The agency's changed view of the standard seems to be related to the election of a new President of a different political party. It is readily apparent that the responsible members of one administration may consider public resistance and uncertainties to be more important than do their counterparts in a previous administration. A change in administration brought about by the people casting their votes is a perfectly reasonable basis for an executive agency's reappraisal of the costs and benefits of its programs and regulations. As long as the agency remains within the bounds established by Congress, it is entitled to assess administrative records and evaluate priorities in light of the philosophy of the administration.

QUESTION SET 9.21

Review & Synthesis

1. After reading *State Farm*, what do you think is meant by "hard look" review? What test did the Court apply to determine whether NHTSA's rescission of Standard 208 was "arbitrary and capricious"?

2. Why did the Court conclude that NHTSA's rescission of Standard 208 was arbitrary and capricious? Was it because the agency failed to support the rescission with sufficient evidence from the rulemaking record? Because the reasons it provided to support its decision were impermissible under the National Traffic and Motor Vehicle Safety Act of 1966? Some other reason?

3. In Section III of its opinion, the Court rejected the idea that an agency's decision to rescind a regulation is the same as its decision not to adopt a regulation in the first place. Do you agree? Both decisions place fewer regulations on private parties, so why not treat them the same?

4. Consider for a moment the review implications of changing from one regulatory policy to a different one, as NHTSA did in *State Farm*. A reviewing court must obviously determine whether the new policy is supported by the rulemaking record and whether it is within the agency's statutory authority to promulgate. Must it also determine whether the agency had a good reason for the change itself? In other words, should reviewing courts require agencies to explain why the old policy was no longer acceptable, in addition to requiring them to provide the legal and evidentiary basis for the new policy?

5. Does the majority's opinion encourage, or even require, agency officials to think like judges? If officials fail to anticipate what courts might consider obvious aspects of a regulatory problem, do they risk having the courts strike down their regulations for failure to provide a "reasoned analysis"? Would Justice Rehnquist's approach to arbitrary and capricious review address this concern? Reconsider the discussion of agency "ossification" and of *Vermont Yankee Nuclear Power Corp. v. Natural Resources Defense Council, Inc.* from Chapter 5.

6. If you were advising an agency that was considering rescinding or substantially amending a regulation, what advice would you offer in light of the Court's decision in *State Farm*?

7. As Justice Rehnquist alluded to in his separate opinion, NHTSA's decision to rescind the passive restraint requirement was precipitated in part by Ronald Reagan's defeat of Jimmy Carter in the 1980 presidential election. Was Rehnquist arguing that a change in political administration is a sufficient basis for a court to uphold an agency's decision to change substantive policies? If not, why did he believe the change in presidential administration was germane to the hard look inquiry?

Application & Analysis

1. Section 13 of the Transportation Recall Enhancement, Accountability and Documentation Act ("TREAD") directs the Secretary of Transportation to "complete a rulemaking . . . to require a warning system in new motor vehicles to indicate to the operator when a tire is significantly under-inflated." The Secretary delegated this responsibility to the National Highway Traffic Safety Administration ("NHTSA"). Two tire pressure monitoring systems ("TPMSs") are currently available in the market: direct systems and indirect systems. Direct TPMSs directly measure the pressure in each tire and show the results on a vehicle's dashboard display. Indirect TPMSs use a formula based on tire rotation speeds to estimate tire pressure. Direct TMPSs are expensive for automakers to install but are very accurate; they can measure and report the level of underinflation for each of a vehicle's tires. By contrast, indirect TPMSs are far less expensive and far less precise in their measurements; they accurately report underinflation 50 percent of the time and cannot specify which tire is underinflated.

   With these options in mind, NHTSA issued a notice of proposed rulemaking proposing two potential underinflation standards. The first proposed standard—called the "four-tire, 20 percent" standard—would set the maximum under-inflation level at 20 percent and would require a TPMS able to simultaneously detect four underinflated tires. The second proposed standard—called the "three-tire, 25 percent" standard—would set the maximum underinflation level at 25 percent and would require a TPMS able to simultaneously detect three under-inflated tires. NHTSA concluded that direct TPMSs could satisfy either standard, but that indirect TPMSs could satisfy neither one. However, the agency predicted that automakers would develop upgraded indirect TPMSs to satisfy the three-tire, 25 percent standard if the agency ulti-mately adopted it.

After the close of the comment period, NHTSA promulgated a final rule that divided compliance between a phase-in period and a long-term period. During the phase-in period, automakers could choose to comply with either a four-tire, 25 percent standard or with a less rigorous one-tire, 30 percent standard. After the phase-in period ended, all automakers would have to comply with the four-tire, 25 percent standard. NHTSA explained that the phase-in standard would provide additional time and flexibility for technological innovation. It adopted the four-tire, 25 per-cent (instead of 20 percent) standard so automakers could comply once they developed upgraded indirect TPMSs.

Several public advocacy groups sued NHTSA in federal district court, seeking judicial review of its tire underinflation rule. Specifically, they argued that NHTSA's adoption of the one-tire, 30 percent stan-dard was arbitrary and capricious. NHTSA countered that it was jus-tified in offering the less rigorous phase-in standard because doing so lowered costs for automakers and encouraged more development of indirect TPMSs.

You are a clerk for the district judge hearing this case. Write a mem-orandum analyzing whether NHTSA's adoption of the phase-in standard was arbitrary and capricious under *State Farm*. To inform your analysis, find NHTSA's final rule—67 Fed. Reg. 38704—on www.federalregis-ter.gov and read the following pages: 38716-18, 38724-28, 38738, and 38740-41.

---

ii. The Principles of Explanation and Consistency

Even before passage of the Administrative Procedure Act in 1946, the Supreme Court has insisted that federal agencies follow a rational decision-making process. There are two central aspects to this expectation of rationality, each of itself a fundamental principle of administrative law: agencies must act consistently, and they must explain the decisions they make. Together, these principles help to cabin the vast and largely discretionary authority Congress delegates to the administrative state. Failure to heed them invites judicial reversal on grounds that an agency's decisions are arbitrary and capricious. As one prominent scholar summarized it:

> A . . . technique which was developed to control the broad discretion granted by New Deal legislation was the requirement of reasoned consistency in agency decisionmaking. Under this doctrine, an agency might be required to articulate the reasons for reaching a choice in a given case even though the loose texture of its legislative directive allowed a range of possible choices. Courts might also impose the further requirement that choices over time be consistent, or at least that departures from established policies be persuasively justified, particularly where significant individual expectation interests were involved. Again, these requirements were not directly addressed to the substance of agency policy. Their aim was, and is, simply to ensure that the agency's action is rationally related to the achievement of some permissible societal goal, and to promote formal justice in order to protect private autonomy.

Richard B. Stewart, *The Reformation of American Administrative Law*, 88 Harv. L. Rev. 1669, 1679-80 (1975). These basic requirements of consistency and explanation appear in multiple areas of the Supreme Court's administrative law jurisprudence. For example, the Court has long required agencies to follow their own policies. *See Accardi v. Shaughnessy*, 347 U.S. 260 (1954); *Arizona Grocery Co. v. Atchison, Topeka & Santa Fe Railway*, 284 U.S. 370 (1932). When agencies do not do so, the Court has placed the burden on them to identify and explain the inconsistency. *See, e.g., FCC v. Fox Television Stations, Inc.*, 556 U.S. 502, 515 (2009) ("An agency may not . . . depart from a prior policy *sub silentio* or simply disregard rules that are still on the books."); *National Cable & Telecommunications Association v. Brand X Internet Services*, 545 U.S. 967, 981 (2005) ("*Unexplained* inconsistency is" a "reason for holding an interpretation to be an arbitrary and capricious change from agency practice") (emphasis added). For similar reasons, the Court has made clear that agencies must provide reviewing courts with the whole record that informed their decision-making, even when produced through informal proceedings that do not require the creation of a formal record. It is true that litigants are not entitled to probe an administrator's mental processes not already reflected in the administrative record without an exceptionally good reason. Nevertheless, it would be almost impossible for courts meaningfully to review agencies' decision-making—for consistency or anything else—if agencies could on their own decide what information to disclose or conceal.

Courts have also insisted that agencies be consistent in the explanations they offer to support their actions. They will consider only those justifications agencies *actually relied on* when they took the actions under judicial review. Courts will accordingly reject *post hoc* rationalizations, especially when they are concocted simply for litigation purposes and do not otherwise reflect the considered views of the agency. *See Bowen v. Georgetown University Hospital*,

488 U.S. 204, 474 (1988); *Securities and Exchange Commission v. Chenery Corp. (Chenery I)*, 318 U.S. 80 (1943).

The following case applies the *Chenery I* "actual reasons" rule to Secretary of Commerce Wilbur L. Ross' attempt to add a citizenship question to the 2020 census questionnaire. As you read it, try to suss out precisely why the government loses its case. Is it because the Secretary failed to provide *enough* of a reasonable basis for his attempt to add a citizenship question to the census? Is it because the Secretary's stated reasons for adding a citizenship question to the census were not the actual reasons he decided to do so? *Department of Commerce* also revisits an impediment to meaningful judicial review we have previously discussed: what constitutes the "whole record" when courts are tasked with reviewing informal agency decision-making? Finally, the case includes an instructive colloquy between Chief Justice Roberts and Justice Breyer on how to analyze the rationality of agency policy judgements, which often must be made under conditions of substantial uncertainty.

Department of Commerce v. New York
588 U.S. ___, 139 S. Ct. 2551 (2019)

CHIEF JUSTICE ROBERTS delivered the opinion of the Court [with respect to Parts IV-B, in which THOMAS, ALITO, GORSUCH, AND KAVANAUGH, JJ., joined; and with respect to Part V, in which GINSBURG, BREYER, SOTOMAYOR, and KAGAN, JJ., joined.]

I

A

In order to apportion Members of the House of Representatives among the States, the Constitution requires an "Enumeration" of the population every 10 years, to be made "in such Manner" as Congress "shall by Law direct." Art. I, § 2, cl. 3; Amdt. 14, § 2. In the Census Act, Congress delegated to the Secretary of Commerce the task of conducting the decennial census "in such form and content as he may determine." 13 U. S. C. § 141(a). The Secretary is aided in that task by the Census Bureau, a statistical agency housed within the Department of Commerce. *See* §§ 2, 21.

The population count derived from the census is used not only to apportion representatives but also to allocate federal funds to the States and to draw electoral districts. The census additionally serves as a means of collecting demographic information, which "is used for such varied purposes as computing federal grant-in-aid benefits, drafting of legislation, urban and regional planning, business planning, and academic and social studies." Baldrige v. Shapiro, 455 U.S. 345, 353–354, n. 9, 102 S.Ct. 1103, 71

L.Ed.2d 199 (1982). Over the years, the census has asked questions about (for example) race, sex, age, health, education, occupation, housing, and military service. It has also asked about radio ownership, age at first marriage, and native tongue. The Census Act obliges everyone to answer census questions truthfully and requires the Secretary to keep individual answers confidential, including from other Government agencies. §§ 221, 8(b), 9(a).

There have been 23 decennial censuses from the first census in 1790 to the most recent in 2010. Every census between 1820 and 2000 (with the exception of 1840) asked at least some of the population about their citizenship or place of birth. Between 1820 and 1950, the question was asked of all households. Between 1960 and 2000, it was asked of about one-fourth to one-sixth of the population. That change was part of a larger effort to simplify the census by asking most people a few basic demographic questions (such as sex, age, race, and marital status) on a short-form questionnaire, while asking a sample of the population more detailed demographic questions on a long-form questionnaire. In explaining the decision to move the citizenship question to the long-form questionnaire, the Census Bureau opined that "general census information on citizenship had become of less importance compared with other possible questions to be included in the census, particularly in view of the recent statutory requirement for annual alien registration which could provide the Immigration and Naturalization Service, the principal user of such data, with the information it needed." Dept. of Commerce, Bureau of Census, 1960 Censuses of Population and Housing 194 (1966).

In 2010, the year of the latest census, the format changed again. All households received the same questionnaire, which asked about sex, age, race, Hispanic origin, and living arrangements. The more detailed demographic questions previously asked on the long-form questionnaire, including the question about citizenship, were instead asked in the American Community Survey (or ACS), which is sent each year to a rotating sample of about 2.6% of households.

The Census Bureau and former Bureau officials have resisted occasional proposals to resume asking a citizenship question of everyone, on the ground that doing so would discourage noncitizens from responding to the census and lead to a less accurate count of the total population.

B

In March 2018, Secretary of Commerce Wilbur Ross announced in a memo that he had decided to reinstate a question about citizenship on the 2020 decennial census questionnaire. The Secretary stated that he was acting at the request of the Department of Justice (DOJ), which sought improved data about citizen voting-age population for purposes of enforcing the Voting Rights Act (or VRA)—specifically the Act's ban on diluting the influence of minority voters by depriving them of single-member districts in which they can elect their preferred candidates. DOJ explained that federal courts determine whether a minority group could constitute a majority in a particular district by looking to the citizen voting-age population of the group. According to DOJ, the existing citizenship data from the American Community Survey was not ideal: It was not reported at the level of the census block, the basic component of legislative districting plans; it had substantial margins of error; and it did not align in time with the census-based population counts used to draw legislative districts. DOJ therefore formally requested reinstatement of the citizenship question on the census questionnaire

The Secretary's memo explained that the Census Bureau initially analyzed, and the Secretary considered, three possible courses of action. The first was to continue to collect citizenship information in the American Community Survey and attempt to develop a data model that would more accurately estimate citizenship at the census block level. The Secretary rejected that option because the Bureau "did not assert and could not confirm" that such ACS-based data modeling was possible "with a sufficient degree of accuracy." [App. to Pet. for Cert.], at 551a.

The second option was to reinstate a citizenship question on the decennial census. The Bureau predicted that doing so would discourage some noncitizens from responding to the census. That would necessitate increased "nonresponse follow up" operations—procedures the Bureau uses to attempt to count people who have not responded to the census—and potentially lead to a less accurate count of the total population.

Option three was to use administrative records from other agencies, such as the Social Security Administration and Citizenship and Immigration Services, to provide DOJ with citizenship data. The Census Bureau recommended this option, and the Secretary found it a "potentially appealing solution" because the Bureau has long used administrative records to supplement and improve census data. *Id.*, at 554a. But the Secretary concluded that administrative records alone were inadequate because they were missing for more than 10% of the population.

The Secretary ultimately asked the Census Bureau to develop a fourth option that would combine options two and three: reinstate a citizenship question on the census questionnaire, and also use the time remaining until the 2020 census to "further enhance" the Bureau's "administrative record data sets, protocols, and statistical models." *Id.*, at 555a. The memo explained that, in the Secretary's judgment, the fourth option would provide DOJ with the "most complete and accurate" citizen voting-age population data in response to its request. *Id.*, at 556a.

The Secretary "carefully considered" the possibility that reinstating a citizenship question would depress the response rate. *Ibid.* But after evaluating the Bureau's "limited empirical evidence" on the question — evidence drawn from estimated non-response rates to previous American

Community Surveys and census questionnaires—the Secretary concluded that it was not possible to "determine definitively" whether inquiring about citizenship in the census would materially affect response rates. *Id.*, at 557a, 562a. He also noted the long history of the citizenship question on the census, as well as the facts that the United Nations recommends collecting census-based citizenship information, and other major democracies such as Australia, Canada, France, Indonesia, Ireland, Germany, Mexico, Spain, and the United Kingdom inquire about citizenship in their censuses. Altogether, the Secretary determined that "the need for accurate citizenship data and the limited burden that the reinstatement of the citizenship question would impose outweigh fears about a potentially lower response rate." *Id.*, at 557a.

C

[A group of plaintiffs including 18 States, the District of Columbia, various counties and cities, and the United States Conference of Mayors filed suit in Federal District Court in New York. They alleged that the Secretary's decision violated the Constitution's Enumeration Clause and the Administrative Procedure Act. A separate group of plaintiffs challenged the Secretary's decision on equal protection grounds. The Secretary moved to dismiss, arguing that his decision was unreviewable and that the plaintiffs failed to state cognizable claims under the Enumeration and Equal Protection Clauses.]

In June 2018, the Government submitted to the District Court the Commerce Department's "administrative record": the materials that Secretary Ross considered in making his decision. That record included DOJ's December 2017 letter requesting reinstatement of the citizenship question, as well as several memos from the Census Bureau analyzing the predicted effects of reinstating the question. Shortly thereafter, at DOJ's urging, the Government supplemented the record with a new memo from the Secretary, "intended to provide further background and context regarding" his March 2018 memo. App. to Pet. for Cert. 546a. The supplemental memo stated that the Secretary had begun considering whether to add the citizenship question in early 2017, and had inquired whether DOJ "would support, and if so would request, inclusion of a citizenship question as consistent with and useful for enforcement of the Voting Rights Act." *Ibid.* According to the Secretary, DOJ "formally" requested reinstatement of the citizenship question after that inquiry. *Ibid.*

Respondents argued that the supplemental memo indicated that the Government had submitted an incomplete record of the materials considered by the Secretary. They asked the District Court to compel the Government to complete the administrative record. The court granted that request, and the parties jointly stipulated to the inclusion of more than 12,000 pages of additional materials in the administrative record. Among those materials were emails and other records confirming that the Secretary and his staff began exploring the possibility of reinstating a citizenship question shortly after he was confirmed in early 2017, attempted to elicit requests for citizenship data from other agencies, and eventually persuaded DOJ to request reinstatement of the question for VRA enforcement purposes.

In addition, respondents asked the court to authorize discovery outside the administrative record. They claimed that such an unusual step was warranted because they had made a strong preliminary showing that the Secretary had acted in bad faith. *See Citizens to Preserve Overton Park, Inc. v. Volpe*, 401 U.S. 402, 420 (1971) [(discussing the presumption of regularity in agency decision-making)]. The court also granted that request, authorizing expert discovery and depositions of certain DOJ and Commerce Department officials.

In August and September 2018, the District Court issued orders compelling depositions of Secretary Ross and of the Acting Assistant Attorney General for DOJ's Civil Rights Division. We granted the Government's request to stay the Secretary's deposition pending further review, but we declined to stay the Acting AAG's deposition or the other extra-record discovery that the District Court had authorized. . . .

IV

The District Court set aside the Secretary's decision to reinstate a citizenship question on the grounds that the Secretary acted arbitrarily and violated certain provisions of the Census Act. The Government contests those rulings [on direct appeal to this Court]. . . .

B

At the heart of this suit is respondents' claim that the Secretary abused his discretion in deciding to reinstate a citizenship question. We review the Secretary's exercise of discretion under the deferential "arbitrary and capricious" standard. *See* 5 U. S. C. § 706(2)(A). Our scope of review is "narrow": we determine only whether the Secretary examined "the relevant data" and articulated "a satisfactory explanation" for his decision, "including a rational connection between the facts found and the choice made." *Motor Vehicle Mfrs. Assn. of United States, Inc. v. State Farm Mut. Automobile Ins. Co.*, 463 U. S. 29, 43 (1983) (internal quotation marks omitted). We may not substitute our judgment for that of the Secretary, *ibid.*, but instead must confine ourselves to ensuring that he remained "within the bounds of reasoned decisionmaking," *Baltimore Gas & Elec. Co. v. Natural Resources Defense Council, Inc.*, 462 U.S. 87, 105 (1983).

The District Court set aside the Secretary's decision for two independent reasons: His course of action was not supported by the evidence before him, and his stated rationale was pretextual. We focus on the first point here and take up the question of pretext later.

The Secretary examined the Bureau's analysis of various ways to collect improved citizenship data and explained why he thought the best course was to both reinstate a citizenship question and use citizenship data from administrative records to fill in the gaps. He considered but rejected the Bureau's recommendation to use administrative records alone. As he explained, records are lacking for about 10% of the population, so the Bureau would still need to estimate citizenship for millions of voting-age people. Asking a citizenship question of everyone, the Secretary reasoned, would eliminate the need to estimate citizenship for many of those people. And supplementing census responses with administrative record data would help complete the picture and allow the Bureau to better estimate citizenship for the smaller set of cases where it was still necessary to do so.

The evidence before the Secretary supported that decision. As the Bureau acknowledged, each approach — using administrative records alone, or asking about citizenship and using records to fill in the gaps — entailed tradeoffs between accuracy and completeness. Without a citizenship question, the Bureau would need to estimate the citizenship of about 35 million people; with a citizenship question, it would need to estimate the citizenship of only 13.8 million. Under either approach, there would be some errors in both the administrative records and the Bureau's estimates. With a citizenship question, there would also be some erroneous self-responses (about 500,000) and some conflicts between responses and administrative record data (about 9.5 million).

The Bureau explained that the "relative quality" of the citizenship data generated by each approach would depend on the "relative importance of the errors" in each, but it was not able to "quantify the relative magnitude of the errors across the alternatives." The Bureau nonetheless recommended using administrative records alone because it had "high confidence" that it could develop an accurate model for estimating the citizenship of the 35 million people for whom administrative records were not available, and it thought the resulting citizenship data would be of superior quality. But when the time came for the Secretary to make a decision, the model did not yet exist, and even if it had, there was no way to gauge its relative accuracy. As the Bureau put it, "we will most likely never possess a fully adequate truth deck to benchmark" the model — which appears to be bureaucratese for "maybe, maybe not." The Secretary opted instead for the approach that would yield a more complete set of data at an acceptable rate of accuracy, and would require estimating the citizenship of fewer people.

The District Court overruled that choice, agreeing with the Bureau's assessment that its recommended approach would yield higher quality citizenship data on the whole. But the choice between reasonable policy alternatives in the face of uncertainty was the Secretary's to make. He considered the relevant factors, weighed risks and benefits, and articulated a satisfactory explanation for his decision. In overriding that reasonable exercise of discretion, the court improperly substituted its judgment for that of the agency.

The Secretary then weighed the benefit of collecting more complete and accurate citizenship data against the risk that inquiring about citizenship would depress census response rates, particularly among noncitizen households. In the Secretary's view, that risk was difficult to assess. The Bureau predicted a 5.1% decline in response rates among noncitizen households if the citizenship question were reinstated.[2] It relied for that prediction primarily on studies showing that, while noncitizens had responded at lower rates than citizens to the 2000 short-form and 2010 censuses, which did not ask about citizenship, they responded at even lower rates than citizens to the 2000 long-form census and the 2010 American Community Survey, which did ask about citizenship. The Bureau thought it was reasonable to infer that the citizenship question accounted for the differential decline in noncitizen responses. But, the Secretary explained, the Bureau was unable to rule out other causes. For one thing, the evidence before the Secretary suggested that noncitizen households tend to be more distrustful of, and less likely to respond to, any government effort to collect information. For another, both the 2000 long-form census and 2010 ACS asked over 45 questions on a range of topics, including employment, income, and housing characteristics. Noncitizen households might disproportionately fail to respond to a lengthy and intrusive Government questionnaire for a number of reasons besides reluctance to answer a citizenship question — reasons relating to education level, socioeconomic status, and less exposure to Government outreach efforts.

The Secretary justifiably found the Bureau's analysis inconclusive. Weighing that uncertainty against the value of obtaining more complete and accurate citizenship data, he determined that reinstating a citizenship question was worth the risk of a potentially lower response rate. That decision was reasonable and reasonably explained, particularly in light of the long history of the citizenship question on the census.

Justice Breyer would conclude otherwise, but only by subordinating the Secretary's policymaking discretion to the Bureau's technocratic expertise. Justice Breyer's analysis treats the Bureau's (pessimistic) prediction about response rates and (optimistic) assumptions about its data modeling abilities as touchstones of substantive reasonableness rather than simply evidence for the Secretary to consider. He suggests that the Secretary should have deferred to the Bureau or at least offered some special justification for drawing his own inferences and adopting his own assumptions. But the Census Act authorizes the Secretary, not the Bureau, to make policy choices within the range of reasonable options. And the evidence before the Secretary hardly led ineluctably to just one reasonable course of action. It called for value-laden

---

[2] Several months after the Secretary made his decision, the Bureau updated its prediction to 5.8%, the figure the District Court later relied on in its standing analysis.

decisionmaking and the weighing of incommensurables under conditions of uncertainty. The Secretary was required to consider the evidence and give reasons for his chosen course of action. He did so. It is not for us to ask whether his decision was "the best one possible" or even whether it was "better than the alternatives." *FERC v. Electric Power Supply Assn.*, [136 S. Ct. 760, 782 (2016)]. By second-guessing the Secretary's weighing of risks and benefits and penalizing him for departing from the Bureau's inferences and assumptions, Justice Breyer — like the District Court — substitutes his judgment for that of the agency. . . .

V

We now consider the District Court's determination that the Secretary's decision must be set aside because it rested on a pretextual basis, which the Government conceded below would warrant a remand to the agency.

We start with settled propositions. First, in order to permit meaningful judicial review, an agency must "disclose the basis" of its action. *Burlington Truck Lines, Inc. v. United States*, 371 U. S. 156, 167-169 (1962) (internal quotation marks omitted); *see also SEC v. Chenery Corp.*, 318 U.S. 80, 94 (1943) ("[T]he orderly functioning of the process of review requires that the grounds upon which the administrative agency acted be clearly disclosed and adequately sustained.").

Second, in reviewing agency action, a court is ordinarily limited to evaluating the agency's contemporaneous explanation in light of the existing administrative record. *Vermont Yankee Nuclear Power Corp. v. Natural Resources Defense Council, Inc.*, 435 U. S. 519, 549 (1978). That principle reflects the recognition that further judicial inquiry into "executive motivation" represents "a substantial intrusion" into the workings of another branch of Government and should normally be avoided. *Arlington Heights v. Metropolitan Housing Development Corp.*, 429 U. S. 252, 268, n. 18 (1977); *see Citizens to Preserve Overton Park v. Volpe*, 401 U. S. 402, 420 (1971).

Third, a court may not reject an agency's stated reasons for acting simply because the agency might also have had other unstated reasons. Relatedly, a court may not set aside an agency's policymaking decision solely because it might have been influenced by political considerations or prompted by an Administration's priorities. Agency policymaking is not a "rarified technocratic process, unaffected by political considerations or the presence of Presidential power." *Sierra Club v. Costle*, 657 F. 2d 298, 408 (D.C. Cir. 1981). Such decisions are routinely informed by unstated considerations of politics, the legislative process, public relations, interest group relations, foreign relations, and national security concerns (among others).

Finally, we have recognized a narrow exception to the general rule against inquiring into "the mental processes of administrative decisionmakers."

Overton Park, 401 U.S., at 420. On a "strong showing of bad faith or improper behavior," such an inquiry may be warranted and may justify extra-record discovery. *Ibid.*

The District Court invoked that exception in ordering extra-record discovery here. Although that order was premature, we think it was ultimately justified in light of the expanded administrative record. Recall that shortly after this litigation began, the Secretary, prodded by DOJ, filed a supplemental memo that added new, pertinent information to the administrative record. The memo disclosed that the Secretary had been considering the citizenship question for some time and that Commerce had inquired whether DOJ would formally request reinstatement of the question. That supplemental memo prompted respondents to move for both completion of the administrative record and extra-record discovery. The District Court granted both requests at the same hearing, agreeing with respondents that the Government had submitted an incomplete administrative record and that the existing evidence supported a prima facie showing that the [Voting Rights Act] rationale was pretextual.

The Government did not challenge the court's conclusion that the administrative record was incomplete, and the parties stipulated to the inclusion of more than 12,000 pages of internal deliberative materials as part of the administrative record, materials that the court later held were sufficient on their own to demonstrate pretext. The Government did, however, challenge the District Court's order authorizing extra-record discovery, as well as the court's later orders compelling depositions of the Secretary and of the Acting Assistant Attorney General for DOJ's Civil Rights Division.

We agree with the Government that the District Court should not have ordered extra-record discovery when it did. At that time, the most that was warranted was the order to complete the administrative record. But the new material that the parties stipulated should have been part of the administrative record—which showed, among other things, that the VRA played an insignificant role in the decisionmaking process—largely justified such extra-record discovery as occurred (which did not include the deposition of the Secretary himself). We accordingly review the District Court's ruling on pretext in light of all the evidence in the record before the court, including the extra-record discovery.

That evidence showed that the Secretary was determined to reinstate a citizenship question from the time he entered office; instructed his staff to make it happen; waited while Commerce officials explored whether another agency would request census-based citizenship data; subsequently contacted the Attorney General himself to ask if DOJ would make the request; and adopted the Voting Rights Act rationale late in the process. In the District Court's view, this evidence established that the Secretary had made up his mind to reinstate a citizenship question "well before" receiving DOJ's request, and did so for reasons unknown but unrelated to the VRA.

The Government, on the other hand, contends that there was nothing objectionable or even surprising in this. And we agree—to a point. It is hardly improper for an agency head to come into office with policy preferences and ideas, discuss them with affected parties, sound out other agencies for support, and work with staff attorneys to substantiate the legal basis for a preferred policy. The record here reflects the sometimes involved nature of Executive Branch decisionmaking, but no particular step in the process stands out as inappropriate or defective.

And yet, viewing the evidence as a whole, we share the District Court's conviction that the decision to reinstate a citizenship question cannot be adequately explained in terms of DOJ's request for improved citizenship data to better enforce the VRA. Several points, considered together, reveal a significant mismatch between the decision the Secretary made and the rationale he provided.

The record shows that the Secretary began taking steps to reinstate a citizenship question about a week into his tenure, but it contains no hint that he was considering VRA enforcement in connection with that project. The Secretary's Director of Policy did not know why the Secretary wished to reinstate the question, but saw it as his task to "find the best rationale." The Director initially attempted to elicit requests for citizenship data from the Department of Homeland Security and DOJ's Executive Office for Immigration Review, neither of which is responsible for enforcing the VRA. After those attempts failed, he asked Commerce staff to look into whether the Secretary could reinstate the question without receiving a request from another agency. The possibility that DOJ's Civil Rights Division might be willing to request citizenship data for VRA enforcement purposes was proposed by Commerce staff along the way and eventually pursued.

Even so, it was not until the Secretary contacted the Attorney General directly that DOJ's Civil Rights Division expressed interest in acquiring census-based citizenship data to better enforce the VRA. And even then, the record suggests that DOJ's interest was directed more to helping the Commerce Department than to securing the data. The December 2017 letter from DOJ drew heavily on contributions from Commerce staff and advisors. Their influence may explain why the letter went beyond a simple entreaty for better citizenship data—what one might expect of a typical request from another agency—to a specific request that Commerce collect the data by means of reinstating a citizenship question on the census. Finally, after sending the letter, DOJ declined the Census Bureau's offer to discuss alternative ways to meet DOJ's stated need for improved citizenship data, further suggesting a lack of interest on DOJ's part.

Altogether, the evidence tells a story that does not match the explanation the Secretary gave for his decision. In the Secretary's telling, Commerce was simply acting on a routine data request from another agency. Yet the materials before us indicate that Commerce went to great lengths to elicit the request from DOJ (or any other willing agency). And unlike a typical case in which an agency may have both stated and unstated reasons for a decision, here the VRA enforcement rationale—the sole stated reason—seems to have been contrived.

We are presented, in other words, with an explanation for agency action that is incongruent with what the record reveals about the agency's priorities and decisionmaking process. It is rare to review a record as extensive as the one before us when evaluating informal agency action—and it should be. But having done so for the sufficient reasons we have explained, we cannot ignore the disconnect between the decision made and the explanation given. Our review is deferential, but we are "not required to exhibit a naiveté from which ordinary citizens are free." *United States v. Stanchich*, 550 F.2d 1294, 1300 (2d Cir. 1977) (Friendly, J.). The reasoned explanation requirement of administrative law, after all, is meant to ensure that agencies offer genuine justifications for important decisions, reasons that can be scrutinized by courts and the interested public. Accepting contrived reasons would defeat the purpose of the enterprise. If judicial review is to be more than an empty ritual, it must demand something better than the explanation offered for the action taken in this case.

In these unusual circumstances, the District Court was warranted in remanding to the agency, and we affirm that disposition. We do not hold that the agency decision here was substantively invalid. But agencies must pursue their goals reasonably. Reasoned decisionmaking under the Administrative Procedure Act calls for an explanation for agency action. What was provided here was more of a distraction.

* * *

The judgment of the United States District Court for the Southern District of New York is affirmed in part and reversed in part, and the case is remanded for further proceedings consistent with this opinion.

It is so ordered.

Justice Thomas, with whom Justice Gorsuch and Justice Kavanaugh join, concurring in part and dissenting in part.

In March 2018, the Secretary of Commerce exercised his broad discretion over the administration of the decennial census to resume a nearly unbroken practice of asking a question relating to citizenship. Our only role in this case is to decide whether the Secretary complied with the law and gave a reasoned explanation for his decision. The Court correctly answers these questions in the affirmative. That ought to end our inquiry.

The Court, however, goes further. For the first time ever, the Court invalidates an agency action solely because it questions the sincerity of the agency's otherwise adequate rationale. Echoing the din of suspicion and distrust that seems to typify modern discourse, the Court declares the Secretary's memorandum "pretextual" because, "viewing the evidence as a whole," his explanation that including a citizenship question on the census would help enforce the Voting Rights Act (VRA) "seems to have been contrived." The Court does not hold that the Secretary merely had additional, unstated reasons for reinstating the citizenship question. Rather, it holds that the Secretary's stated rationale did not factor *at all* into his decision. . . .

The law requires a more impartial approach. Even assuming we are authorized to engage in the review undertaken by the Court—which is far from clear—we have often stated that courts reviewing agency action owe the Executive a "presumption of regularity." *Citizens to Preserve Overton Park, Inc. v. Volpe*, 401 U. S. 402, 415 (1971). The Court pays only lipservice to this principle. But, the evidence falls far short of supporting its decision. The Court, I fear, will come to regret inventing the principles it uses to achieve today's result. I respectfully dissent from Part V of the opinion of the Court. . . .

II

. . . Respondents conceptualize pretext as a subset of "arbitrary and capricious" review. It is far from clear that they are correct. But even if they were, an agency action is not arbitrary or capricious merely because the decisionmaker has other, unstated reasons for the decision. Nor is an agency action arbitrary and capricious merely because the decisionmaker was "inclined" to accomplish it before confirming that the law and facts supported that inclination.

Accordingly, even under respondents' approach, a showing of pretext could render an agency action arbitrary and capricious only in the infinitesimally small number of cases in which the administrative record establishes that an agency's stated rationale did not factor at all into the decision, thereby depriving the action of an adequate supporting rationale.[4] This showing is extremely difficult to make because the administrative record will rarely, if ever, contain evidence sufficient to show that an agency's stated rationale did not actually factor into its decision. And we have stated that a "strong showing of bad faith or improper behavior" is necessary to venture beyond the agency's "administrative findings" and inquire into "the mental processes of administrative decisionmakers." *Overton Park*, 401 U. S., at 420.[5] We have

---

[4] We do not have before us a claim that information outside the administrative record calls into question the legality of an agency action based on an unstated, unlawful bias or motivation (e.g., a claim of religious discrimination under the Free Exercise Clause). But to the extent such a claim is viable, the analysis would have nothing to do with the arbitrary-and-capricious review pressed by respondents. *See* §§ 706(2)(A)-(C) (addressing agency actions that violate "constitutional" or "statutory" requirements, or that "otherwise [are] not in accordance with law").

[5] Insofar as *Overton Park* authorizes an exception to review on the administrative record, it has been criticized as having "no textual grounding in the APA" and as "created by the Court, without citation or explanation, to facilitate Article III review." Gavoor & Platt, *Administrative Records and the Courts*, 67 U. Kan. L. Rev. 1, 44 (2018); *see id.*, at 22 (further arguing that the exception was "neither presented by the facts of the case nor briefed by the parties"). The legitimacy and scope of the exception—which by its terms contemplates only "administrative officials who participated in the decision . . . giv[ing] testimony explaining their action," *Overton Park*, 401 U. S., at 420—is an important question that may warrant future consideration. But because the Court's holding is incorrect regardless of the validity of the *Overton Park* exception, I will apply it here.

never before found *Overton Park*'s exception satisfied, much less invalidated an agency action based on "pretext."

Undergirding our arbitrary-and-capricious analysis is our longstanding precedent affording the Executive a "presumption of regularity." *Id.*, at 415. This presumption reflects respect for a coordinate branch of government whose officers not only take an oath to support the Constitution, as we do, Art. VI, but also are charged with "faithfully execut[ing]" our laws, Art. II, § 3. *See United States v. Morgan*, 313 U. S. 409, 422 (1941) (presumption of regularity ensures that the "integrity of the administrative process" is appropriately respected). In practice, then, we give the benefit of the doubt to the agency. . . .

JUSTICE BREYER, with whom JUSTICE GINSBURG, JUSTICE SOTOMAYOR, and JUSTICE KAGAN join, concurring in part and dissenting in part.

. . . I write separately because I . . . believe that the Secretary's decision to add the citizenship question was arbitrary and capricious and therefore violated the Administrative Procedure Act (APA). . . .

II. . . .

[The Secretary's decision under review here] "reinstate[s] [a] citizenship question on the 2020 decennial census." App. to Pet. for Cert. 549a-550a. The agency's decision memorandum provided one and only one reason for making that decision — namely, that the question was "necessary to provide complete and accurate data in response to" a request from the Department of Justice (DOJ). *Id.*, at 562a. The DOJ had requested the citizenship question for "use [in] . . . determining violations of Section 2 of the Voting Rights Act." *Id.*, at 548a.

The decision memorandum adds that the agency had not been able to "determine definitively how inclusion of a citizenship question on the decennial census will impact responsiveness. However, even if there is some impact on responses, the value of more complete and accurate data derived from surveying the entire population outweighs such concerns." *Id.*, at 562a. The Secretary's decision thus rests upon a weighing of potentially adverse consequences (diminished responses and a less accurate census count) against potentially offsetting advantages (better citizenship data). In my view, however, the Secretary did not make reasonable decisions about these potential costs and benefits in light of the administrative record.

A

Consider first the Secretary's conclusion that he was "not able to determine definitively how inclusion of a citizenship question on the decennial census will impact responsiveness." Insofar as this statement implies that adding the citizenship question is unlikely to affect "responsiveness" very much (or perhaps at all), the evidence in the record indicates the contrary.

1

The administrative record includes repeated Census Bureau statements that adding the question would produce a less accurate count because non-citizens and Hispanics would be less likely to respond to the questionnaire. The Census Bureau's chief scientist said specifically that adding the question would have "an adverse impact on self-response and, as a result, on the accuracy and quality of the 2020 Census." [App. at 109.] And the chief scientist backed this statement up by pointing to "[t]hree distinct analyses." *Ibid.*

. . . [Together, the Bureau's analyses] provided additional support for the Census Bureau's determination that the citizenship question is likely to mean disproportionately fewer responses from noncitizens and Hispanics than from others. . . .

2

The Secretary's decision memorandum reached a quite different conclusion from the Census Bureau. The memorandum conceded that "a lower response rate would lead to . . . less accurate responses." But it concluded that neither the Census Bureau nor any stakeholders had provided "definitive, empirical support" for the proposition that the citizenship question would reduce response rates. The memorandum relied for that conclusion upon a number of considerations, but each is contradicted by the record. . . .

The upshot is that the Secretary received evidence of a likely drop in census accuracy by a number somewhere in the hundreds of thousands, and he received nothing significant to the contrary. The Secretary pointed out that the Census Bureau's information was uncertain, i.e., not "definitive." But that is not a satisfactory answer. Few public-policy-related statistical studies of risks (say, of many health or safety matters) are definitive. As the Court explained in *State Farm*, "[i]t is not infrequent that the available data do not settle a regulatory issue, and the agency must then exercise its judgment in moving from the facts and probabilities on the record to a policy conclusion." 463 U. S., at 52. But an agency confronted with this situation cannot "merely recite the terms 'substantial uncertainty' as a justification for its actions." *Ibid.* Instead, it "must explain the evidence which is available" and typically must offer a reasoned explanation for taking action without "engaging in a search for further evidence." *Ibid.*

The Secretary did not do so here. . . .

B

Now consider the Secretary's conclusion that, even if adding a citizenship question diminishes the accuracy of the enumeration, "the value of more complete and accurate data derived from surveying the entire population *outweighs* . . . concerns" about diminished accuracy. App. to Pet. for

Cert. 562a (emphasis added). That conclusion was also arbitrary. The administrative record indicates that adding a citizenship question to the short form would produce less "complete and accurate data," not more.

1. . . .

. . . [I] n respect to the 295 million persons for whom administrative records exist, asking the question on the short form would, at best, be no improvement over using administrative records alone. And in respect to the remaining 35 million people for whom no administrative records exist, asking the question would be no better, and in some respects would be worse, than using statistical modeling. The Census Bureau therefore told the Secretary that asking the citizenship question, even in addition to using administrative records, "would result in poorer quality citizenship data" than using administrative records alone, and would "still have all the negative cost and quality implications" of asking the citizenship question. I could find no evidence contradicting that prediction.

2

If my description of the record is correct, it raises a serious legal problem. How can an agency support the decision to add a question to the short form, thereby risking a significant undercount of the population, on the ground that it will improve the accuracy of citizenship data, when in fact the evidence indicates that adding the question will harm the accuracy of citizenship data? Of course it cannot. But, as I have just said, I have not been able to find evidence to suggest that adding the question would result in more accurate citizenship data. Neither could the District Court. After reviewing the record in detail, the District Court found that "all of the relevant evidence before Secretary Ross—*all* of it—demonstrated that using administrative records . . . would actually produce more accurate [citizenship] data than adding a citizenship question to the census."

What consideration did the Secretary give to this problem? He stated simply that "[a]sking the citizenship question of 100 percent of the population gives each respondent the opportunity to provide an answer," which "may eliminate the need for the Census Bureau to have to impute an answer for millions of people." He therefore must have assumed, *sub silentio*, exactly what the Census Bureau experts urged him not to assume—that answers to the citizenship question would be more accurate than statistical modeling. And he ignored the undisputed respects in which asking the question would make the existing data less accurate. Other than his assumption, the Secretary said nothing, absolutely nothing, to suggest a reasoned basis for disagreeing with the Bureau's expert statistical judgment. . . .

Finally, recall that the Census Act requires the Secretary to use administrative records rather than direct inquiries to "the maximum extent possible." 13 U. S. C. § 6(c). That statutory requirement highlights what should be obvious: Whether adding a citizenship question to the short form would produce more accurate citizenship data is a relevant factor—indeed, a critically important factor—that the Secretary was required to consider. Here, the Secretary did not adequately explain why he rejected the evidence that adding the question would yield less accurate data. He did not even acknowledge that the Census Act obliged him to use administrative records rather than asking a question to the extent possible. And he did not explain how obtaining citizenship data that is no better or worse than the data otherwise available could justify jeopardizing the accuracy of the census count.

In these respects, the Secretary failed to consider "important aspect[s] of the problem" and "offered an explanation for [his] decision that runs counter to the evidence before the agency." *State Farm*, 463 U. S., at 43. . . .

QUESTION SET 9.22

Review & Synthesis

1. Compare the arbitrary and capricious analyses conducted by Chief Justice Roberts, Justice Thomas, and Justice Breyer. Did any of them closely conform to the type of "hard look" review described and applied by the majority in *State Farm*? Did any of them approach the arbitrary and capricious inquiry more like Justice Rehnquist would have in *State Farm*?

2. Secretary Ross lost this case because the Court found his explanation for adding a citizenship question—that the Department of Justice had requested it—to be "pretextual" and a "distraction." Given the Court's finding that adding the question would have been supported by the administrative record, did the Secretary need the DOJ request to justify it? Stated differently, was such a request even necessary to protect his decision against judicial invalidation under APA § 706(2)(A)?

3. Consider Justice Thomas' argument that "a showing of pretext could render an agency action arbitrary and capricious only in the infinitesimally small number of cases in which the administrative record establishes that an agency's stated rationale did not factor at all into the decision, thereby depriving the action of an adequate supporting rationale." Did he mean to say that agencies can provide courts with knowingly false or misleading justifications as long as their other reasons adequately support their decisions? In other words, does his test treat false or consciously misleading rationales as tantamount to agency silence? If so, how consistent is such an understanding of arbitrary and capricious review with the principles of administrative consistency and explanation to which the Court so frequently cites?

4. As discussed throughout this chapter, both Congress and the Supreme Court have adopted a strong presumption in favor of judicial review of administrative action. How do you square that with the well-established "presumption of regularity" that limits the extent to which courts may probe administrators' thought processes under the arbitrary and capricious standard?

5. Consider Justice Breyer's conclusion that Secretary Ross did not adequately support his decision to add a citizenship question to the census. He reasoned that the record lacked a sufficient basis on which Ross could have concluded that a census question would produce more accurate citizenship information than the other methods offered by the Census Bureau. Was Justice Breyer arguing that APA § 706(2)(A) requires decision-makers like Ross to do more than just consider the conclusions of their agency experts? Must they also adopt those conclusions?

---

iii. Changes in Agency Policy

State Farm involved a change in regulatory policy. The National Highway Transportation Safety Administration ("NHTSA") adopted a deregulatory posture by rescinding Standard 208, its passive restraint rule. In essence, the Court found that NHTSA failed adequately to explain how the administrative record in front of it supported the rescission. An issue implied from *State Farm*, but not clearly addressed by it, is whether an agency must do more than simply justify its new policy when it effects change. Specifically, must an agency show that its new policy is supported by the record *and* show that its new policy *is preferable or superior to* its old policy? The question is an intuitive one. Why should an agency be permitted to adopt a new policy that is qualitatively worse than the one it seeks to abandon? Why wouldn't such a change be arbitrary and capricious if the agency is unable to show that the new policy is better than the old one? The Court tried to address these questions in the following case.

Federal Communications Commission v. Fox Television Stations, Inc.
556 U.S. 502 (2009)

Justice SCALIA delivered the opinion of the Court, except as to Part III–E.

I. STATUTORY AND REGULATORY BACKGROUND

The Communications Act of 1934, 48 Stat. 1064, 47 U.S.C. § 151 *et seq.*, established a system of limited-term broadcast licenses subject to various "conditions" designed "to maintain the control of the United States over all the channels of radio transmission," § 301 (2000 ed.). Almost 28 years ago we said that "[a] licensed broadcaster is granted the free and exclusive use of a limited and valuable part of the public domain; when he accepts that franchise it is burdened by enforceable public obligations." *CBS, Inc. v. FCC,* 453 U.S. 367, 395 (1981) (internal quotation marks omitted).

One of the burdens that licensees shoulder is the indecency ban — the statutory proscription against "utter[ing] any obscene, indecent, or profane language by means of radio communication," 18 U.S.C. § 1464 — which Congress has instructed the Commission to enforce between the hours of 6 a.m. and 10 p.m. Public Telecommunications Act of 1992, § 16(a), 106 Stat. 954, note following 47 U.S.C. § 303. Congress has given the Commission various means of enforcing the indecency ban, including civil fines, *see* § 503(b)(1), and license revocations or the denial of license renewals, *see* §§ 309(k), 312(a)(6).

The Commission first invoked the statutory ban on indecent broadcasts in 1975, declaring a daytime broadcast of George Carlin's "Filthy Words" monologue actionably indecent. At that time, the Commission announced the definition of indecent speech that it uses to this day, prohibiting "language that describes, in terms patently offensive as measured by contemporary community standards for the broadcast medium, sexual or excretory activities and organs, at times of the day when there is a reasonable risk that children may be in the audience." *Id.* at 98. . . .

In the ensuing years, the Commission took a cautious, but gradually expanding, approach to enforcing the statutory prohibition against indecent broadcasts. . . . When the full Commission next considered its indecency standard . . . it repudiated the view that its enforcement power was limited to deliberate, repetitive use of the seven words actually contained in the George Carlin monologue. The Commission determined that such a highly restricted enforcement standard was unduly narrow as a matter of law and inconsistent with the Commission's enforcement responsibilities under Section 1464. . . .

Although the Commission had expanded its enforcement beyond the "repetitive use of specific words or phrases," it preserved a distinction between literal and nonliteral (or "expletive") uses of evocative language. The Commission explained that each literal "description or depiction of sexual or excretory functions must be examined in context to determine whether it is patently offensive," but that "deliberate and repetitive use . . . is a requisite to a finding of indecency" when a complaint focuses solely on the use of nonliteral expletives. *Ibid.*

Over a decade later, the Commission emphasized that the "full context" in which particular materials appear is "critically important," but that a few "principal" factors guide the inquiry, such as the "explicitness or graphic nature" of the material, the extent to which the material "dwells on or repeats" the offensive material, and the extent to which the material was presented to "pander," to "titillate," or to "shock." *In re Industry Guidance on Commission's Case Law Interpreting 18 U.S.C. § 1464 and Enforcement Policies Regarding Broadcast Indecency*, 16 FCC Rcd. 7999, 8002, ¶ 9, 8003, ¶ 10, 2001 WL 332787 (2001) (emphasis deleted). No single factor, the Commission said, generally provides the basis for an indecency finding, but where sexual or excretory references have been made once or have been passing or fleeting in nature, this characteristic has tended to weigh against a finding of indecency.

In 2004, the Commission took one step further by declaring for the first time that a nonliteral (expletive) use of the F- and S-Words could be actionably indecent, even when the word is used only once. The first order to this effect dealt with an NBC broadcast of the Golden Globe Awards, in which the performer Bono commented, "'[T]his is really, really, f* * *ing brilliant.'" . . .

The Commission first declared that Bono's use of the F-Word fell within its indecency definition, even though the word was used as an intensifier rather than a literal descriptor. "[G]iven the core meaning of the 'F-Word,'" it said, "any use of that word . . . inherently has a sexual connotation." [*In re Complaints Against Various Broadcast Licensees Regarding Their Airing of "Golden Globe Awards" Program*, 19 FCC Rcd. 4975, 4978, ¶ 8 (2004) (*Golden Globes Order*)]. The Commission determined, moreover, that the broadcast was "patently offensive" because the F-Word "is one of the most vulgar, graphic and explicit descriptions of sexual activity in the English language," because "[i]ts use invariably invokes a coarse sexual image," and because Bono's use of the word was entirely "shocking and gratuitous." *Id.* at 4979, ¶ 9.

The Commission observed that categorically exempting such language from enforcement actions would "likely lead to more widespread use." *Ibid.* Commission action was necessary to "safeguard the well-being of the nation's children from the most objectionable, most offensive language." *Ibid.* The order noted that technological advances have made it far easier to delete ("bleep out") a "single and gratuitous use of a vulgar expletive," without adulterating the content of a broadcast. *Id.* at 4980, ¶ 11.

The order acknowledged that "prior Commission and staff action [has] indicated that isolated or fleeting broadcasts of the 'F-Word' . . . are not indecent or would not be acted upon." It explicitly ruled that "any such interpretation is no longer good law." *Ibid.*, ¶ 12. It "clarif[ied] . . . that the mere fact that specific words or phrases are not sustained or repeated does not mandate a finding that material that is otherwise patently offensive to the broadcast medium is not indecent." *Ibid.* Because, however, "existing precedent would have permitted this broadcast," the Commission determined that "NBC and its affiliates necessarily did not have the requisite notice to justify a penalty." *Id.* at 4981-4982, ¶ 15.

II. THE PRESENT CASE

This case concerns utterances in two live broadcasts aired by Fox Television Stations, Inc., and its affiliates prior to the Commission's *Golden Globes Order*. The first occurred during the 2002 Billboard Music Awards, when the singer Cher exclaimed, "I've also had critics for the last 40 years saying that I was on my way out every year. Right. So f* * * 'em." The second involved a segment of the 2003 Billboard Music Awards, during the presentation of an award by Nicole Richie and Paris Hilton, principals in a Fox television series called "The Simple Life." Ms. Hilton began their interchange by reminding Ms. Richie to "watch the bad language," but Ms. Richie proceeded to ask the audience, "Why do they even call it 'The Simple Life?' Have you ever tried to get cow s* * * out of a Prada purse? It's not so f* * *ing simple." Following each of these broadcasts, the Commission received numerous complaints from parents whose children were exposed to the language.

On March 15, 2006, the Commission released "Notices of Apparent Liability" for a number of broadcasts that the Commission deemed actionably indecent, including the two described above. Multiple parties petitioned the Court of Appeals for the Second Circuit for judicial review of the order, asserting a variety of constitutional and statutory challenges. Since the order had declined to impose sanctions, the Commission had not previously given the broadcasters an opportunity to respond to the indecency charges. It therefore requested and obtained from the Court of Appeals a voluntary remand so that the parties could air their objections. 489 F.3d 444, 453 (2007). The Commission's order on remand upheld the indecency findings for the broadcasts described above. *See* In re Complaints Regarding Various Television Broadcasts Between Feb. 2, 2002, and Mar. 8, 2005, 21 FCC Rcd. 13299 (2006) (Remand Order).

The order first explained that both broadcasts fell comfortably within the subject-matter scope of the Commission's indecency test because the 2003 broadcast involved a literal description of excrement and both broadcasts invoked the "F-Word," which inherently has a sexual connotation. The order next determined that the broadcasts were patently offensive under community standards for the medium. Both broadcasts, it noted, involved entirely gratuitous uses of "one of the most vulgar, graphic, and explicit words for sexual activity in the English language." *Id.* at 13305, ¶ 17, 13324, ¶ 59. It found Ms. Richie's use of the "F-Word" and her explicit description of the handling of excrement to be vulgar and shocking, as well as to constitute pandering, after Ms. Hilton had playfully warned her to " 'watch the bad language.' " And it found Cher's statement patently offensive in part because she metaphorically suggested a sexual act as a means of expressing hostility to her critics. The order relied upon the " 'critically important' " context of the utterances, *Id.* at 13304, ¶ 15, noting that they were aired during prime-time awards shows designed to draw a large nationwide audience that could be expected to include many children interested in seeing their favorite music stars. Indeed, approximately 2.5 million minors witnessed each of the broadcasts.

The order asserted that both broadcasts under review would have been actionably indecent under the staff rulings and Commission dicta in effect prior to the *Golden Globes Order*—the 2003 broadcast because it involved a literal description of excrement, rather than a mere expletive, because it used more than one offensive word, and because it was planned; and the 2002 broadcast because Cher used the F-Word not as a mere intensifier, but as a description of the sexual act to express hostility to her critics. [T]he order made clear [that] the *Golden Globes Order* eliminated any doubt that fleeting expletives could be actionably indecent, and the Commission disavowed [any] bureau-level decisions and its own dicta that had said otherwise. Under the new policy, a lack of repetition "weigh[s] against a finding of indecency," *Id.* at 13325, ¶ 61, but is not a safe harbor.

The order explained that the Commission's prior strict dichotomy between expletives and descriptions or depictions of sexual or excretory functions is artificial and does not make sense in light of the fact that an expletive's power to offend derives from its sexual or excretory meaning. In the Commission's view, granting an automatic exemption for isolated or fleeting expletives unfairly forces viewers (including children) to take "'the first blow'" and would allow broadcasters "to air expletives at all hours of a day so long as they did so one at a time." *Id.* at 13309, ¶ 25. Although the Commission determined that Fox encouraged the offensive language by using suggestive scripting in the 2003 broadcast, and unreasonably failed to take adequate precautions in both broadcasts, the order again declined to impose any forfeiture or other sanction for either of the broadcasts.

Fox returned to the Second Circuit for review of the Remand Order, and various intervenors including CBS, NBC, and ABC joined the action. The Court of Appeals reversed the agency's orders, finding the Commission's reasoning inadequate under the Administrative Procedure Act. The majority was "skeptical that the Commission [could] provide a reasoned explanation for its 'fleeting expletive' regime that would pass constitutional muster," but it declined to reach the constitutional question. [489 F.3d 444, 462 (2d Cir. 2007)]. . . .

III. ANALYSIS

A. Governing Principles. . . .

In overturning the Commission's judgment, the Court of Appeals here relied in part on Circuit precedent requiring a more substantial explanation for agency action that changes prior policy. The Second Circuit has interpreted the Administrative Procedure Act and our opinion in *State Farm* as requiring agencies to make clear "'why the original reasons for adopting the [displaced] rule or policy are no longer dispositive'" as well as "'why the new rule effectuates the statute as well as or better than the old rule.'" 489 F.3d, at 456-457. . . .

We find no basis in the Administrative Procedure Act or in our opinions for a requirement that all agency change be subjected to more searching review. The Act mentions no such heightened standard. And our opinion in *State Farm* neither held nor implied that every agency action representing a policy change must be justified by reasons more substantial than those required to adopt a policy in the first instance. That case, which involved the rescission of a prior regulation, said only that such action requires "a reasoned analysis for the change beyond that which may be required when an agency *does not act* in the first instance." 463 U.S., at 42 (emphasis added). Treating failures to act and rescissions of prior action differently for purposes of the standard of review makes good sense, and has basis in the text of the statute, which likewise treats the two separately. It instructs a reviewing court to "compel agency action unlawfully withheld or unreasonably delayed," 5 U.S.C. § 706(1), and to "hold unlawful and set aside agency action, findings, and conclusions found to be [among other things] . . . arbitrary [or] capricious," § 706(2)(A). The statute makes no distinction, however, between initial agency action and subsequent agency action undoing or revising that action.

To be sure, the requirement that an agency provide reasoned explanation for its action would ordinarily demand that it display awareness that it is changing position. An agency may not, for example, depart from a prior policy *sub silentio* or simply disregard rules that are still on the books. And of course the agency must show that there are good reasons for the new policy. But it need not demonstrate to a court's satisfaction that the reasons for the new policy are *better* than the reasons for the old one; it suffices that the new policy is permissible under the statute, that there are good reasons for it, and that the agency *believes* it to be better, which the conscious change of course adequately indicates. This means that the agency need not always provide a more detailed justification than what would suffice for a new policy created on a blank slate. Sometimes it must—when, for example, its new policy rests upon factual findings that contradict those which underlay its prior policy; or when its prior policy has engendered serious reliance interests that must be taken into account. *Smiley v. Citibank (South Dakota), N. A.,* 517 U.S. 735, 742 (1996). It would be arbitrary or capricious to ignore such matters. In such cases it is not that further justification is demanded by the mere fact of policy change; but that a reasoned explanation is needed for disregarding facts and circumstances that underlay or were engendered by the prior policy. . . .

B. Application to this Case

Judged under the above described standards, the Commission's new enforcement policy and its order finding the broadcasts actionably indecent were neither arbitrary nor capricious. First, the Commission forthrightly acknowledged that its recent actions have broken new ground, taking account of inconsistent "prior Commission and staff action" and explicitly disavowing them as "no longer good law." *Golden Globes Order*, 19 FCC Rcd., at 4980, ¶ 12. . . . There is no doubt that the Commission knew it was making a change. That is why it declined to assess penalties; and it relied on the *Golden Globes Order* as removing any lingering doubt.

Moreover, the agency's reasons for expanding the scope of its enforcement activity were entirely rational. It was certainly reasonable to determine that it made no sense to distinguish between literal and nonliteral uses of offensive words, requiring repetitive use to render only the latter indecent. As the Commission said with regard to expletive use of the F-Word, "the word's power to insult and offend derives from its sexual meaning." *Id.* at 13323, ¶ 58. . . . Even isolated utterances can be made in "pander[ing,] . . . vulgar and shocking" manners, Remand Order, 21 FCC Rcd., at 13305, ¶ 17, and can constitute harmful " 'first blow[s]' " to children, *Id.* at 13309, ¶ 25. It is surely rational (if not inescapable) to believe that a safe harbor for single words would "likely lead to more widespread use of the offensive language," *Golden Globes Order, supra,* at 4979, ¶ 9. . . .

The fact that technological advances have made it easier for broadcasters to bleep out offending words further supports the Commission's stepped-up enforcement policy. And the agency's decision not to impose any forfeiture or other sanction precludes any argument that it is arbitrarily punishing parties without notice of the potential consequences of their action. . . .

IV. CONSTITUTIONALITY. . . .

. . . The Commission could reasonably conclude that the pervasiveness of foul language, and the coarsening of public entertainment in other media such as cable, justify more stringent regulation of broadcast programs so as to give conscientious parents a relatively safe haven for their children. In the end, the Second Circuit and the broadcasters quibble with the Commission's policy choices and not with the explanation it has given. We decline to "substitute [our] judgment for that of the agency," *State Farm*, 463 U.S., at 43, and we find the Commission's orders neither arbitrary nor capricious.

The judgment of the United States Court of Appeals for the Second Circuit is reversed, and the case is remanded for further proceedings consistent with this opinion.

It is so ordered.

[The concurring opinion of Justice THOMAS is omitted.]

Justice KENNEDY, concurring in part and concurring in the judgment. . . .

I join Parts I, II, III-A through III-D, and IV of the opinion of the Court and agree that the judgment must be reversed. This separate writing is to underscore certain background principles for the conclusion that an agency's decision to change course may be arbitrary and capricious if the agency sets a new course that reverses an earlier determination but does not provide a reasoned explanation for doing so. In those circumstances I agree with the dissenting opinion of Justice Breyer that the agency must explain why "it now reject[s] the considerations that led it to adopt that initial policy."

The question whether a change in policy requires an agency to provide a more reasoned explanation than when the original policy was first announced is not susceptible, in my view, to an answer that applies in all cases. There may be instances when it becomes apparent to an agency that the reasons for a longstanding policy have been altered by discoveries in science, advances in technology, or by any of the other forces at work in a dynamic society. If an agency seeks to respond to new circumstances by modifying its earlier policy, the agency may have a substantial body of data and experience that can shape and inform the new rule. In other cases the altered circumstances may be so new that the agency must make predictive judgments that are as difficult now as when the agency's earlier policy was first announced. Reliance interests in the prior policy may also have weight in the analysis.

The question in each case is whether the agency's reasons for the change, when viewed in light of the data available to it, and when informed by the experience and expertise of the agency, suffice to demonstrate that the new policy rests upon principles that are rational, neutral, and in accord with the agency's proper understanding of its authority. That showing may be required if the agency is to demonstrate that its action is not "arbitrary, capricious, an abuse of discretion, or otherwise not in accordance with law." 5 U.S.C. § 706(2)(A). And, of course, the agency action must not be "in excess of statutory jurisdiction, authority, or limitations, or short of statutory right." § 706(2)(C).

These requirements stem from the administrative agency's unique constitutional position. The dynamics of the three branches of Government are well understood as a general matter. But the role and position of the agency, and the exact locus of its powers, present questions that are delicate, subtle, and complex. The Federal Government could not perform its duties in a responsible and effective way without administrative agencies. Yet the amorphous character of the administrative agency in the constitutional system escapes simple explanation.

If agencies were permitted unbridled discretion, their actions might violate important constitutional principles of separation of powers and checks and balances [such as the nondelegation doctrine]. . . .

Congress passed the Administrative Procedure Act (APA) to ensure that agencies follow constraints even as they exercise their powers. One of these constraints is the duty of agencies to find and formulate policies that can be justified by neutral principles and a reasoned explanation. To achieve that end, Congress confined agencies' discretion and subjected their decisions to judicial review. For these reasons, agencies under the APA are subject to a searching and careful review by the courts.

Where there is a policy change the record may be much more developed because the agency based its prior policy on factual findings. In that instance, an agency's decision to change course may be arbitrary and capricious if the agency ignores or countermands its earlier factual findings without reasoned explanation for doing so. An agency cannot simply disregard contrary or inconvenient factual determinations that it made in the past, any more than it can ignore inconvenient facts when it writes on a blank slate. . . .

Justice BREYER, with whom Justice STEVENS, Justice SOUTER, and Justice GINSBURG join, dissenting.

In my view, the Federal Communications Commission failed adequately to explain why it changed its indecency policy from a policy permitting a single "fleeting use" of an expletive, to a policy that made no such exception. Its explanation fails to discuss two critical factors, at least one of which directly underlay its original policy decision. Its explanation instead discussed several factors well known to it the first time around, which by themselves provide no significant justification for a change of policy. Consequently, the FCC decision is "arbitrary, capricious, an abuse of discretion." [APA § 706(2)(A)]. And I would affirm the Second Circuit's similar determination. . . .

. . . [A]gencies must follow a "logical and rational" decisionmaking "process." *Allentown Mack Sales & Service, Inc. v. NLRB*, 522 U.S. 359, 374 (1998). An agency's policy decisions must reflect the reasoned exercise of expert judgment. And, as this Court has specified, in determining whether an agency's policy choice was "arbitrary," a reviewing court "must consider whether the decision was based on a consideration of the relevant factors and whether there has been a clear error of judgment." [*Citizens to Preserve Overton Park, Inc. v. Volpe*, 401 U.S. 402, 416 (1971).]

Moreover, an agency must act consistently. The agency must follow its own rules. And when an agency seeks to change those rules, it must focus on the fact of change and explain the basis for that change. *See, e.g., National Cable & Telecommunications Assn. v. Brand X Internet Services*, 545 U.S. 967, 981 (2005) ("*Unexplained* inconsistency is" a "reason for holding an interpretation to be an arbitrary and capricious change from agency practice" (emphasis added)).

To explain a change requires more than setting forth reasons why the new policy is a good one. It also requires the agency to answer the question, "Why did you change?" And a rational answer to this question typically requires a more complete explanation than would prove satisfactory were change itself not at issue. An (imaginary) administrator explaining why he chose a policy that requires driving on the right side, rather than the left side, of the road might say, "Well, one side seemed as good as the other, so

I flipped a coin." But even assuming the rationality of that explanation for an initial choice, that explanation is not at all rational if offered to explain why the administrator changed driving practice, from right side to left side, 25 years later.

. . . [T]he law requires application of the *same standard* of review to different circumstances, namely circumstances characterized by the fact that *change* is at issue. It requires the agency to focus upon the fact of change where change is relevant, just as it must focus upon any other relevant circumstance. It requires the agency here to focus upon the reasons that led the agency to adopt the initial policy, and to explain why it now comes to a new judgment.

I recognize that sometimes the ultimate explanation for a change may have to be, "We now weigh the relevant considerations differently." But at other times, an agency can and should say more. Where, for example, the agency rested its previous policy on particular factual findings, or where an agency rested its prior policy on its view of the governing law, where an agency rested its previous policy on, say, a special need to coordinate with another agency, one would normally expect the agency to focus upon those earlier views of fact, of law, or of policy and explain why they are no longer controlling. Regardless, to say that the agency here must answer the question "why change" is not to require the agency to provide a justification that is "better than the reasons for the old [policy]." It is only to recognize the obvious fact that change is sometimes (not always) a relevant background feature that sometimes (not always) requires focus (upon prior justifications) and explanation lest the adoption of the new policy (in that circumstance) be "arbitrary, capricious, an abuse of discretion." . . . .

V. . . .

. . . [T]he FCC's answer to the question, "Why change?" is, "We like the new policy better." This kind of answer, might be perfectly satisfactory were it given by an elected official. But when given by an agency, in respect to a major change of an important policy where much more might be said, it is not sufficient. . . .

QUESTION SET 9.23

Review & Synthesis

1. According to *Fox Television*, did the FCC have to explain why its new policy was in some sense "better" than the one it replaced? Stated differently, did the majority conclude that the FCC had to justify *the decision*

to change obscenity policies *in addition to* showing adequate support for its new obscenity policy? Why or why not? Under what circumstances would Justices Kennedy and Breyer have required the FCC to provide an explanation dedicated to its decision to change policy?

2. Justice Kennedy tied the FCC's duty to explain its policy changes to separation-of-powers principles. Agencies must provide robust explanations for their decisions which, presumably, allows courts to determine whether they have exceeded the authority Congress granted them. Do you agree that requiring agencies to explain why they are changing policy advances the concerns that underlie separation-of-powers principles? If an agency fails to provide a reasonable explanation for its actions, that is a statutory violation rather than a constitutional one. If the agency acts within its statutory boundaries but wields power the Constitution denies it, then it is Congress that has exceeded its authority with an unconstitutional delegation; the agency's explanation of what it was doing would have little bearing on the matter. Is the check here on the balance of power among the three Branches, or is it just another way of ensuring that agencies follow the will of Congress?

---

iv. Agency Inaction

The Court in *State Farm* and in *Fox Television* indicated that an agency's obligation to explain changes to its policies differs from its obligation to explain its decision to take no action at all. The Court did not attempt, however, to specify the explanatory burden agencies must carry when they decline to act. As discussed earlier in this chapter, agencies have substantial discretion when deciding whether to forego enforcement proceedings. So much so, in fact, that the Court in *Heckler v. Chaney* concluded that such decisions are presumptively unreviewable by courts. That holding was narrowly focused; the Court made clear that it did not extend to rulemaking. *See Heckler v. Chaney*, 470 U.S. 821, 825 n.2 (1985) (stating that the case did not "involve the question of agency discretion not to invoke rulemaking proceedings"). Accordingly, a pressing question after *Chaney* was whether and to what extent agency decisions to engage in rulemaking benefit from the same presumption.

This issue arises when individuals petition federal agencies to initiate informal rulemaking as provided under § 553(e) of the Administrative Procedure Act. Section 553(e) "give[s] an interested person the right to petition for the issuance, amendment, or repeal of a rule." Though members of the public have a right to request agency rulemaking, the APA's drafters clearly did not intend to compel agencies to grant those requests. As the Senate Judiciary Committee report on the APA said, "[t]he mere filing of a petition does not require an agency to grant it, or to hold a hearing, or engage in any public rulemaking proceedings. The refusal of an agency to grant the petition or to hold rulemaking proceedings, therefore, would not per se be subject to judicial reversal." APA Leg. His., at 201-02. *See also* ATTORNEY GENERAL'S MANUAL at 38-39. Importantly, APA § 555(e) requires agencies promptly to explain their refusals to act on such petitions as well as other requested agency actions. Further, it provides that unless the agency is affirming a prior denial or the denial is self-explanatory, "the notice shall be accompanied by a brief statement of the grounds." While § 555(e) makes clear that agencies must explain their decisions not to initiate rulemakings upon request, it does not identify whether those decisions are subject to judicial review and, if they are, the standard of review courts must apply.

A leading case on these issues is the D.C. Circuit opinion that follows, *American Horse Protection Association, Inc. v. Lyng*, the analysis of which was later endorsed and applied by the Supreme Court. *See Massachusetts v. EPA*, 549 U.S. 497, 527 (2007) (reviewing EPA's decision not to promulgate rules regulating carbon dioxide emissions under the Clean Air Act). *American Horse* showed the D.C. Circuit walking the narrow path between meaningfully reviewing the USDA's denial of a petition to engage in rulemaking and according the agency's refusal an appropriate amount of deference. As you read through the case, take note of how the court construed the procedural requirements for submitting a rulemaking petition and the USDA's obligation to respond to it. After noting these elements of the court's analysis, ask yourself whether, on the whole, you feel that the court has shown an appropriate level of deference to the USDA. Do you think the court's approach would lead to too much judicial second-guessing of agencies' decisions not to engage in rulemaking, or too little? How well does the court's approach support public participation in the decision to initiate rulemaking?

American Horse Protection Association, Inc. v. Lyng
812 F.2d 1 (D.C. Cir. 1987)

Before: STARR and WILLIAMS, Circuit Judges, and GREEN, District Judge.

WILLIAMS, Circuit Judge:
The American Horse Protection Association (the "Association") appeals from a grant of summary judgment to the Secretary of Agriculture in its challenge to regulations under the Horse Protection Act, 15 U.S.C. §§ 1821-1831 (1982) (the "Act"). We find that summary judgment was inappropriate in view of the Secretary's failure to offer a satisfactory explanation of his refusal to institute rule making proceedings.

I. BACKGROUND

The regulations at issue concern the practice of deliberately injuring show horses to improve their performance in the ring. This practice, called soring, may involve fastening heavy chains or similar equipment, called action devices, on a horse's front limbs. As a result of wearing action devices, the horse may suffer intense pain as its forefeet touch the ground. This pain causes it to adopt a high-stepping gait that is highly prized in Tennessee walking horses and certain other breeds. . . . In the Horse Protection Act, Congress sought to end this practice by forbidding the showing or selling of sored horses. 15 U.S.C. §§ 1821-1824. Exercising broadly phrased rulemaking power under 15 U.S.C. § 1828, the Secretary issued regulations that prohibited soring devices and other soring methods in both general and specific terms. The general prohibition, 9 C.F.R. § 11.2(a) (1986), states

> Notwithstanding the provisions of paragraph (b) of this section [containing specific prohibitions], no chain, boot, roller, collar, action device, nor any other device, method, practice, or substance shall be used with respect to any horse at any horse show, horse exhibition, or horse sale or auction if such use causes or can reasonably be expected to cause such horse to be sore.

The regulations' specific prohibitions include the use of chains weighing more than eight or ten ounces (depending on the age of the horse), rollers weighing more than fourteen ounces, and certain padded shoes on young horses. *Id.* § 11.2(b). Lighter chains and rollers are not specifically prohibited.

Use of action devices in violation of either the general or specific prohibitions is unlawful under 15 U.S.C. § 1824(7) and may subject the violator to both criminal and civil penalties under 15 U.S.C. § 1825. Under the general prohibition, however, there is no penalty unless the use of the device is shown to have caused soreness or the device can "reasonably be expected to cause" soreness. . . . The regulations give no guidance as to when a device not specifically prohibited may reasonably be expected to cause soreness. There are no such definitional difficulties, of course, when a violation involves a device specifically prohibited.

The Association here contends that developments since these regulations were originally promulgated have demonstrated their inadequacy and that, accordingly, the Secretary should revise them in a new rulemaking. In fact, in its original rulemaking the agency made quite clear its recognition that the premises for not enacting broader specific prohibitions might erode. In its notice of proposed rulemaking, it stated that it relied on evidence from three test clinics which appeared to exonerate action devices weighing less than those that it proposed to forbid. 43 Fed. Reg. 18,514, 18,516-17 (1978). When the final rule was issued, the agency stated that it would consider prohibiting all action devices and padded shoes if the practice of soring continued. 44 Fed. Reg. 25,172, 25,173-74 (1979). At the same time it also mentioned that the agency had recently commissioned "a study of soring methods and techniques at a major university" that might eventually result in further changes in the regulations. *Id.* at 25,174.

This study was conducted at the Auburn University School of Veterinary Medicine between September 1978 and December 1982. The Auburn study evaluated use of eight- and ten-ounce chains and fourteen-ounce rollers—devices that the agency had declined to prohibit on the grounds that they did not cause soring when properly used under actual training conditions. 43 Fed. Reg. at 18,516-17. The study concluded that ten-ounce chains caused lesions, bleeding, edema, and inflammation. It also considered the effects of eight- and ten-ounce chains and fourteen-ounce rollers on scarred horses, and found that these devices caused raw lesions. The effects of these devices thus fell within the statutory definition of sore. In tests of two-, four-, and six-ounce chains, however, the study found no harmful effects. The Auburn study also made preliminary findings on the effects of padded shoes, suggesting they caused problems not suspected at the time of the initial rulemaking. The Association relies on these results in challenging the Agriculture Department's regulations.

Even before the Auburn study was completed, however, the agency considered revising its regulations on action devices. In a May 1981 letter to the Administrator of the Animal and Plant Health Inspection Service ("APHIS"), the Agriculture Department's Office of General Counsel recognized that soring had not been eliminated and argued that the gaps in the regulations were "undermining the Department's ability to achieve effective enforcement of the law and . . . preventing the attainment of the goal Congress ha[d] set." The letter cited administrative cases interpreting the regulations to allow soring with "legal" action devices, i.e., those not covered by the specific prohibitions.

Bureaucratic activity surged briefly, then ebbed. The Administrator of APHIS endorsed the letter from the Office of General Counsel, "OGC's comments make sense," and asked his staff for recommendations on possible changes. In early 1982, representatives of the Association met with the Administrator to propose a ban on all action devices and pads. In March, the Administrator informed the group by letter that the agency's Veterinary Services staff had already prepared a justification for such a ban and was currently drafting a proposed rulemaking to implement it. In July, he confirmed that such regulations had been drafted and that the agency had intended to publish the proposals "as soon as possible." But, he reported, these plans were now being held in abeyance in order to observe the "self-regulation efforts of the industry."

In March 1984, agency officials met with representatives of the walking horse industry, the Association, and others to discuss enforcement of the Act. The Association again requested a rulemaking. In a letter to the Association discussing this meeting, the Deputy Administrator of Veterinary Services wrote, "The apparent inconsistency of the current regulations regarding the weight of action devices with the law and research performed at Auburn University has been a matter of concern for Veterinary Services and the Office of the General Counsel for some time." Nevertheless, he reported that the agency would withhold publication of the proposed rule pending further studies by the industry. He also reported the industry representatives' remark "that the allowable weight of action devices could not be lowered and still retain the desired gait." Perhaps supposing that industry approval was required for any change in the regulations, the Deputy Administrator said, "We are . . . disappointed that no consideration has been given to restricting the weight of action devices."

II. THE STANDARD OF REVIEW

The reviewability of a refusal to institute a rulemaking has been a source of some uncertainty since the Supreme Court held refusals to take *ad hoc* enforcement steps presumptively unreviewable in *Heckler v. Chaney*, 470 U.S. 821 (1985). Although the Court expressly noted that *Chaney* did not "involve the question of agency discretion not to invoke rulemaking proceedings," 470 U.S. at 825 note 2, its reasoning applies to some extent to a refusal to institute a rulemaking. Our examination of *Chaney* persuades us, however, that it does not bar review of the agency's decision here.

The *Chaney* Court relied on three features of nonenforcement decisions in arriving at its negative presumption. First, such decisions require a high level of agency expertise and coordination in setting priorities. *See id.* at 831-32. Second, the agency in such situations will not ordinarily be exercising "its *coercive* power over an individual's liberty or property rights." *Id.* at 832 (emphasis in original). Third, such nonenforcement decisions are akin to prosecutorial decisions not to indict, which traditionally involve executive control and judicial restraint. *Id.* The first and second of these features are likely to be involved in an agency's refusal to institute a rulemaking, but the third is another matter.

Chaney says little about this third feature. To a degree, of course, it recapitulates and underscores the prior points about resource allocation and non-coercion. The analogy between prosecutorial discretion and agency nonenforcement is strengthened, however, by two other shared characteristics. First, both prosecutors and agencies constantly make decisions not to take enforcement steps; such decisions thus are numerous. Second, both types of nonenforcement are typically based mainly on close consideration of the facts of the case at hand, rather than on legal analysis. Refusals to institute rulemakings, by contrast, are likely to be relatively infrequent and more likely to turn upon issues of law. This analysis of the third *Chaney* feature finds support in the Court's distinguishing of cases where an agency "has 'consciously and expressly adopted a general policy' that is so extreme as to amount to an abdication of its statutory responsibilities." *Id.* at 833 note 4. Such abdications are likely both to be infrequent and to turn on matters remote from the specific facts of individual cases.

Furthermore, the Administrative Procedure Act ("APA") serves to distinguish between *Chaney* nonenforcement decisions and refusals to institute rulemakings. The *Chaney* Court noted that "when an agency *does* act to enforce, that action itself provides a focus for judicial review" since a court can "at least . . . determine whether the agency exceeded its statutory powers." 470 U.S. at 832 (emphasis in original). APA provisions governing agency refusals to initiate rulemakings give a similar focal point. The APA requires agencies to allow interested persons to "petition for the issuance, amendment, or repeal of a rule," 5 U.S.C. § 553(e) (1982), and, when such petitions are denied, to give "a brief statement of the grounds for denial," *id.* § 555(e). These two provisions suggest that Congress expected that agencies denying rulemaking petitions must explain their actions.

Thus, refusals to institute rulemaking proceedings are distinguishable from other sorts of nonenforcement decisions insofar as they are less frequent, more apt to involve legal as opposed to factual analysis, and subject to special formalities, including a public explanation. *Chaney* therefore does not appear to overrule our prior decisions allowing review of agency refusals to institute rulemakings.

The District Court was thus correct in finding that this case requires a determination of whether the Secretary's failure to act was "arbitrary, capricious, an abuse of discretion, or otherwise not in accordance with law" under 5 U.S.C. § 706(2)(A) (1982). Review under the "arbitrary and capricious" tag line, however, encompasses a range of levels of deference to the agency, and *Chaney* surely reinforces our frequent statements that an agency's refusal to institute rulemaking proceedings is at the high end of the range. Such a refusal is to be overturned "only in the rarest and most compelling of circumstances," [*WWHT, Inc. v. FCC*, 656 F.2d 807, 818 (D.C. Cir. 1981)], which have primarily involved "plain errors of law, suggesting that the agency has been blind to the source of its delegated power," *State Farm Mutual Automobile Insurance Co. v. Department of Transportation*, 680 F.2d 206, 221 (D.C. Cir. 1982), *vacated on other grounds*, 463 U.S. 29, 103 (1983).

In these, as in more typical reviews, however, we must consider whether the agency's decisionmaking was "reasoned." . . .

Finally, a refusal to initiate a rulemaking naturally sets off a special alert when a petition has sought modification of a rule on the basis of a radical change in its factual premises. In *Geller v. FCC*, 610 F.2d 973 (D.C. Cir. 1979), the regulations at issue had been adopted expressly to facilitate passage of certain legislation, but even after Congress adopted the legislation the agency refused to reconsider them. *Geller* was later summarized by this court as holding that "an agency may be forced by a reviewing court to institute rulemaking proceedings if a significant factual predicate of a prior decision on the subject (either to promulgate or not to promulgate specific rules) has been removed." *WWHT*, 656 F.2d at 819. The Association argues that this principle applies here.

III. THE AGENCY'S REASONING

In considering a refusal to grant a rulemaking petition, the court must examine "the petition for rulemaking, comments pro and con . . . and the agency's explanation of its decision to reject the petition." *See id.* at 817-18. The record before us contains no formal rulemaking petition, but we have no difficulty in characterizing the Association's requests for action as such. Neither the Agriculture Department's regulations, *see* 7 C.F.R. § 1.28 (1986), nor the Administrative Procedure Act, *see* 5 U.S.C. § 553(e) (1982), specifies any formalities for a rulemaking petition. Furthermore, the correspondence from agency officials to Association representatives demonstrates that the agency understood the group's requests to be petitions.

The agency's explanation for its refusal to proceed with the rulemaking is contained in its correspondence with the Association (discussed below) and in the two litigation affidavits of the Deputy Administrator of Veterinary Services of the APHIS. In response to the claim that the Auburn study presented new facts that merited a new rulemaking, the Deputy Administrator's first affidavit stated:

> 6. I have reviewed studies and other materials, relating to action devices, presented by humane groups, Walking Horse industry groups, and independent institutions, including the study referred to in the Complaint.
>
> 7. On the basis of this information, I believe that the most effective method of enforcing the Act is to continue the current regulations.

The second affidavit cites statistics indicating that the agency wrote up a generally diminishing number of alleged violations over the period beginning in 1979 and ending in 1984, although the number of horses exhibited and examined did not generally decline.

On the basis of the litigation affidavits, the District Court found that "the agency has provided a rational basis for its conclusion not to regulate. . . ." We cannot agree. The two conclusory sentences quoted above are insufficient to assure a reviewing court that the agency's refusal to act was the product of reasoned decisionmaking. *See Motor Vehicle Manufacturers*, 463 U.S. at 52. There is no articulation of "the factual and policy bases for [the] decision." [*Professional Drivers Council v. Bureau of Motor Carrier Safety*, 706 F.2d 1216, 1221 (D.C. Cir. 1983)]. We are adjured to take a critical view of an agency's "*post hoc* rationalization," *see Citizens to Preserve Overton Park, Inc. v. Volpe*, 401 U.S. 402, 420 (1971), but under even the most charitable view the agency's *post hoc* conclusory statement lacks substance. Nor do the figures on reduced findings of violations suffice. These are apparently intended to suggest that soring is being eliminated by dint of agency efforts. Litigation affidavits of Association members suggest, however, that soring continues to be widespread. Furthermore, the agency's correspondence with the Association (which was not discussed by the District Court) casts doubt on the agency's benign interpretation of this data.

In this correspondence the agency indicated that its concerns about the regulations were great enough in 1982 to cause it to draft new ones. The reason given later in 1982 for not publishing these proposed regulations—to give industry self-regulation a chance to work—was by 1984 too stale to justify continued inaction. Moreover, in 1984 the Deputy Administrator admitted the "apparent inconsistency of the current regulations regarding the weight of action devices with the law and the [Auburn] research." In the face of this "apparent inconsistency," the Deputy Administrator passively noted his disappointment that industry representatives "felt that the allowable weight of action devices could not be lowered and still retain the desired gait."

This statement suggests a belief that the Act was a sort of compromise between industry proponents of soring and persons who regarded the practice as barbarous. The agency's litigation posture in this court partially corroborates that it holds such a notion. Its brief cites an ambiguous portion of the legislative history to support the proposition that one of Congress's concerns in the Act was to allow "horse trainers and owners to compete at horse shows without unnecessary restriction. . . ." At oral argument, counsel for the Secretary did nothing to allay fears that the agency "has been blind to the source of its delegated power," *State Farm*, 680 F.2d at 221, when she appeared to resist the proposition that the Act was intended to prohibit devices reasonably likely to cause soreness. *See* 9 C.F.R. § 11.2(a) (1986).

We see nothing ambiguous in the Act's treatment of soring methods. The Act was clearly designed to end soring. . . .

We stress this simple point because the Secretary appears to have misapprehended it. It is true that the agency's regulations contain a general prohibition against devices likely to cause soreness, and under a reasonable interpretation of the present regulations no action device that caused soreness would be considered legal. *See* 9 C.F.R. § 11.2(a) (1986). Some administrative decisions, however, view the specific prohibitions of 9 C.F.R. § 11.2(b) as allowing soring with devices not listed. . . .

In sum, we conclude that the Secretary has not presented a reasonable explanation of his failure to grant the rulemaking petition of the Association, particularly in light of the apparent message of the Auburn study. Moreover, what he has said strongly suggests that he has been blind to the nature of his mandate from Congress. . . .

QUESTION SET 9.24

Review & Synthesis

1. Restate (1) the standard of review the D.C. Circuit applied to the USDA's decision to reject AHPA's rulemaking petition, and (2) the test for determining the reviewability of that decision. How do these tests relate to each other?

2. Why did the Secretary lose this case? Is it because the Deputy Secretary explained his reasons for refusing to initiate informal rulemaking but the court was not persuaded by them? If so, why did the Deputy Secretary's explanations fall short? Or is it because the reasons provided by the Deputy Secretary were deficient and thus failed to demonstrate "reasoned" decision-making? If the latter, in what way did the court find them to be deficient?

3. What must the USDA do on remand? Is it required to initiate the rulemaking requested by the AHPA? Must it provide more detailed explanations for its decision not to initiate rulemaking and resubmit them to the court? Must it simply come up with different arguments based on the same set of facts? Something else?

4. In applying the third prong of the *Heckler v. Chaney* unreviewability test, the court pointed out that decisions to enforce the law are more numerous than decisions to engage in rulemaking, and that decisions to initiate rulemaking turn on legal questions, whereas decisions to prosecute are intensely factual. How did these differences inform the court's holding? Given these differences, don't they argue *against* reviewing agency refusals to engage in rulemaking? Whereas the effect of any individual prosecutorial decision is likely to be quite narrow (limited to the circumstances of the party in that individual case), the consequences of engaging in rulemaking can be quite broad (altering the conduct of an entire industry). Shouldn't that difference alone counsel greater hesitation on the court's part?

Application & Analysis

1. A regulation promulgated by the Department of Veterans Affairs ("VA") governs the conduct of visitors at VA-controlled Medical Centers. 38 C.F.R. § 1.218(a)(14). The regulation, among other things, prohibits visitors from engaging in "demonstrations" unless authorized to do so by the head of the facility. The regulation defines "unauthorized demonstrations"

as including "partisan activities, i.e., those involving commentary or actions in support of, or in opposition to, or attempting to influence, any current policy of the Government of the United States, or any private group, association, or enterprise." § 1.218(a)(14)(ii).

Damon Jones is a Navy veteran and Chairman of the Green Party of Cook County, Illinois. In June of last year, he visited the Jesse Brown Veterans Affairs Medical Center ("VAMC") in Chicago, intending to conduct voter registration for veterans who were patients there. VAMC personnel barred Mr. Jones from engaging in his intended registration activities. Mr. Jones' attorney wrote a letter to the VA Secretary in response to the incident. Citing 5 U.S.C. § 553(e), the attorney requested that the Secretary initiate informal rulemaking to (1) rescind the "partisan activities" clause of § 1.218(a)(14), and (2) to specify how veterans who reside on VA campuses will receive assistance in registering and voting. The Secretary responded in July of last year, informing Mr. Jones that the VA would consider his "rulemaking petition."

In October, the Secretary issued a denial of Mr. Jones' rulemaking petition. Citing 38 C.F.R. § 17.33(a)(4)(iv), the Secretary asserted that "no patient in the VA medical care system may be denied the right to register and vote as provided under state law." The Secretary then described Veterans Health Administration ("VHA") Directive 2008-053, an "internal guidance" document issued in September 2008, which outlines the roles and responsibilities of facility directors and VA Voluntary Service Officers in providing voter assistance to VA patients. Finally, the Secretary supported his conclusion with data regarding the VA's recent voter assistance efforts. In the 12 months immediately preceding VA's receipt of Jones' letter, over 46,000 veterans admitted to VA facilities received voting information, more than 6,000 posters had been placed at VA facilities, and more than 165,000 flyers had been provided to new patients. The VA had partnered with nonpartisan groups to provide 80 informational voter drives, and more than 700 volunteers had been recruited to assist in voter registration. For these reasons, the Secretary concluded that initiating the informal rulemaking Mr. Jones requested would be unnecessary at this time.

Unsatisfied, Mr. Jones has filed suit in the U.S. District Court for the Northern District of Illinois. His complaint asserts that the Secretary failed to provide sufficient reasons in support of his petition denial, and as a result the denial was arbitrary and capricious. The Secretary counters that the decision to deny Mr. Jones' petition is unreviewable and, even if it is not, it was sufficiently explained.

You are a clerk for the district court judge hearing the case. Write a short memorandum analyzing the parties' arguments.

b. Formal Decision-Making Processes: The Substantial Evidence Test

As explained above, the arbitrary and capricious test, APA § 706(2)(A), applies to agency decisions produced through *informal* rulemaking and adjudication. We turn now to the "substantial evidence" test, APA § 706(2)(E), which applies to agency factual and policy determinations made through *formal* rulemakings and adjudications (e.g., those governed by APA §§ 556 and 557). The idea that agency orders must be supported by "substantial evidence" traces back well before passage of the APA and derives from the judicially developed review standard federal courts applied to orders of the Interstate Commerce Commission in the early twentieth century. *See, e.g., ICC v. Union Pacific Railroad Co.*, 222 U.S. 541 (1912). It was a deferential standard under which courts would decline to "consider [ICC orders'] expediency or wisdom . . . or whether, on like testimony, it would have made a similar ruling." *Id.* at 547. By the early 1940s, Congress had included it in numerous federal statutes. *See* E. Blythe Stason, *"Substantial Evidence" in Administrative Law*, 89 U. PENN. L. REV. 1026, 1027 (1941) (reporting that the standards was part of 19 federal statutes). It was also clear by that point that what the standard required was up for debate.

Unlike the arbitrary and capricious standard, which seemed to generate little congressional debate, the substantial evidence standard proved to be a flashpoint in the negotiations over the APA's final provisions. Critics of the standard, which included Members of Congress, were concerned that it was too deferential to agency adjudicators. Some courts had construed it as allowing affirmance of agency decisions on a fairly small quantum of evidence—far less than a preponderance. Additionally, courts had upheld agency action under the standard without reviewing the entire administrative record. They would instead rule in an agency's favor if some part of the record contained supporting evidence, even if other parts of that record contained weightier *countervailing* evidence. *See* H.R. Rep. No. 79-1980, at 279 (1946); John Dickinson, *Administrative Procedure Act: Scope and Grounds of Broadened Judicial Review*, 33 A.B.A. J. 434, 514 (1947). These concerns over the standard's rigor were more than academic quibbles. Prior to the 1960s, many agencies adopted regulatory policies through formal adjudications reviewable under the substantial evidence test. The test thus marked the border between judicial and administrative power; the more searching the inquiry it permitted, the more administrative decision-making would be subject to judicial control. The less searching the inquiry, the more federal regulatory policy would be determined by administrative judgment and expertise. For those concerned about historic expansions of the administrative state and of Executive Branch discretion, it was an important issue.

Congress attempted to resolve some of these uncertainties when it codified the substantial evidence standard in the APA. According to the Senate

Judiciary Committee's report, "substantial evidence" meant "evidence which on the whole record is clearly substantial, plainly sufficient to support a finding or conclusion under the requirements of section 7(c), and material to the issues." APA Leg. His., at 279. Apparently, Congress was concerned that agencies would issue orders based on "something less" than substantial evidence, such as "suspicion, surmise, implications, or plainly incredible evidence." *Id.* Section 10 also addressed the "whole record" concern. Now codified in the final sentence of 5 U.S.C. § 706, it provides, in relevant part, that "[i]n making the foregoing determinations, the court shall review the whole record or those parts of it cited by a party, and due account shall be taken of the rule of prejudicial error."

As Congress debated the substantial evidence test's codification in the APA, it did the same for new labor legislation to be administered by the National Labor Relations Board. The Wagner Act of 1935 empowered the Board to enforce its prohibitions on unfair labor practices through investigations, formal hearings presided over by a trial examiner, and issuance of orders against offending employers. However, these orders did not automatically bind employers; if they refused to comply voluntarily, the Board had to petition the Court of Appeals for enforcement. Such suits occasioned an interpretive difficulty. Section 10(c) of the Wagner Act provided that "[t]he findings of the Board as to the facts, if supported by evidence, shall be conclusive." The provision was thus silent on the quantum of evidence required to sustain the Board's orders, and the Supreme Court construed it as requiring "substantial" evidence. *See Washington, Virginia & Maryland Coach Co. v. National Labor Relations Board*, 301 U.S. 142, 147 (1937). Perhaps realizing that its gloss did not have the clarifying effect it hoped for, the Court returned to the issue in *Consolidated Edison Co. of New York v. National Labor Relations Board*. In an oft-quoted passage, the Court stated that "[s]ubstantial evidence is more than a mere scintilla. It means such relevant evidence as a reasonable mind might accept as adequate to support a conclusion." *Consolidated Edison Co. of New York v. National Labor Relations Board*, 305 U.S. 197, 229 (1938).

As in the debates about the growth of administrative discretion more generally, critics argued that the Courts of Appeals applied this substantial evidence test too deferentially, sustaining the Board's orders on the flimsiest of evidence. Moreover, and again echoing debates over the APA's judicial review provisions, critics were concerned that the courts were upholding the Board's orders as long as *some* evidence (rather than a preponderance of evidence) supported them. Perhaps moved in part by these arguments, Congress amended the Wagner Act by passing the Taft-Hartley Act of 1947. Although it retained the "substantial evidence" formulation, Taft-Hartley, like the APA, mandated whole-record review.

Several years later, the Supreme Court was again asked to clarify the meaning of "substantial evidence," whether used in the APA or Taft-Hartley. The *Universal Camera* saga, several opinions of which are excerpted below, addressed a question not settled in either pieces of legislation: what does the "whole record" consist of? In finding that Universal Camera had violated Taft-Hartley by engaging in unfair labor practices, the Board rejected key factual findings made by its trial examiner. Some of those findings were based on the trial examiner's first-hand assessment of witnesses testimony. Having received their live testimony, the trial examiner was in a better position to judge the witnesses' credibility than the Board, which only had access to the trial transcript. Should the Second Circuit, which the NLRB petitioned for enforcement of its order against Universal Camera, have accepted the factual record as presented by the Board without any regard for the trial examiner's findings? Should it instead have interpreted "whole record" review as including both the Board's and the trial examiner's factual findings? If the latter, should disagreements between the two have been reconciled in the Board's favor, or the trial examiner's?

The materials below begin with the NLRB's order substituting its own factual findings for those of its trial examiner. Next comes the Second Circuit's decision on whether to grant the NLRB's enforcement petition. This is followed by the Supreme Court's review of how the Second Circuit construed its responsibility to conduct "whole record" substantial evidence review. Finally, the materials turn to the Second Circuit's final opinion on the matter.

In the Matter of Universal Camera Corporation and Imre Chairman

79 N.L.R.B. No 55, Case No. 2-C-5760 (1948)

On February 18, 1947, Trial Examiner Sidney L. FEILER issued his Intermediate Report in the above-entitled proceeding, finding that the Respondent had not engaged in the unfair labor practices alleged in the complaint and recommending that the complaint be dismissed, as set forth in the copy of the Intermediate Report attached hereto. Thereafter, the complainant and counsel for the Board filed exceptions and supporting briefs. The Respondent submitted a brief in support of the Trial Examiner's Intermediate Report. . . .

The Board has reviewed the rulings made by the Trial Examiner at the hearing and finds that no prejudicial error was committed. The rulings are hereby affirmed. The Board has considered the Intermediate Report, the exceptions and briefs, and the entire record in the case, and hereby adopts the Trial Examiner's findings of fact with certain exceptions noted below, but reverses his conclusions and recommendations.

The Trial Examiner found that the evidence failed to sustain the allegation of the complaint that Chairman was discharged in violation of Section 8

(4) of the Act. We disagree. In our opinion, a preponderance of the evidence shows that Chairman's discharge was due to the Respondent's resentment against Chairman because he had testified for the Union at a representation hearing on November 30, 1943. We believe that the Trial Examiner, in finding otherwise, failed to appreciate the strength of the prima facie case against the Respondent established by the evidence, and erroneously credited certain implausible testimony adduced by the Respondent in explanation of the circumstances leading up to Chairman's discharge.

As fully detailed in the Intermediate Report, the record shows conclusively that Chairman incurred the hostility of the Respondent, and especially of Chief Engineer Kende, who ultimately discharged him, by testifying favorably to the Union's position, and unfavorably to the Respondent's at the Board hearing in a representation case on November 30, 1943. Politzer, Chairman's immediate superior, warned Chairman in advance not to testify for the Union; and a few hours after Chairman's appearance as a witness, Kende angrily upbraided him for testifying. On the following day, Kende, in conference with Politzer and Personnel Manager Weintraub, launched an investigation of Chairman's record for the purpose of finding an excuse to discharge him. Both Kende's own testimony and Politzer's contemporaneous statements to Chairman and Goldson show beyond any reasonable doubt that this search for a pretext was motivated by Kende's indignation over Chairman's testimony. The net result of this conference on December 1 was that neither of the causes for discharging Chairman then suggested by Kende proved feasible. Politzer assured Kende that Chairman was efficient and a few days later also reported, after making inquiry as he was instructed to do, that Chairman was not a Communist. Nothing, therefore, was done about Chairman at that time.

In the face of this clear evidence of the Respondent's animus against Chairman and its desire and intention to discharge him because of his testimony at the Board hearing if a pretext could be found, it was incumbent upon the Respondent to go forward to show convincingly that when Chairman was actually discharged—by Kende himself—8 weeks later, ostensibly because of an episode that was then stale, the real reason was something other than Chairman's appearance as a witness. Contrary to the Trial Examiner, we find the Respondent's explanation of the discharge implausible.

Kende ordered Chairman's discharge on January 24, 1944, ostensibly because of a complaint lodged against Chairman by Personnel Manager Weintraub, to the effect that Chairman had been guilty of "gross insubordination" in an encounter with Weintraub in the plant on the night of December 30, more than 3 weeks before. Politzer, who was Chairman's immediate superior, and was himself responsible directly to Kende, opposed Weintraub's demand for the discharge. Kende nevertheless ruled peremptorily in Weintraub's favor, without questioning Chairman himself or otherwise independently investigating the December 30 incident. That episode itself was a heated argument between Weintraub and Chairman, precipitated by

Weintraub's order that Chairman send home an employee whom Chairman had stationed on stand-by duty. The record shows that Weintraub's authority to give Chairman such an order was at least questionable. Moreover, whether or not Weintraub had this authority, the dispute ended with the two men shaking hands and agreeing to "forget" their differences. It was, at most, only a squabble between two supervisors, one of whom, Chairman, reasonably questioned the other's authority in the circumstances; it was not an instance of "gross insubordination" on Chairman's part.

During the next 3½ weeks, the Respondent neither reprimanded Chairman for his supposed impertinence to Weintraub, nor took any disciplinary action against him. Indeed, Politzer, when Chairman reported the affair to him on December 31, assured Chairman that it was Weintraub, rather than Chairman, who had been "out of order." The only testimony offered by the Respondent in explanation of the long delay between Chairman's alleged misconduct and his punishment, is that of Weintraub and Politzer to the effect that Politzer assured Weintraub, within a day or two after December 30, that Chairman intended to resign in about 10 days. The Respondent asserts that Weintraub thereupon lodged no complaint against Chairman until January 24 because he had in the meantime been expecting Chairman to leave, and only noticed, on or about January 24, that Chairman was still at work. The Trial Examiner believed this testimony, although he flatly discredited Politzer's statement, contradicted by Chairman, that Chairman had in fact agreed to resign, and although he also found both Weintraub and Politzer to be unreliable witnesses in many respects. We cannot accept the Trial Examiner's finding that Politzer, in effect, invented the story that Chairman intended to resign in order to appease Weintraub and gain time for Chairman, for this finding is irreconcilable with the other related facts, and all the other evidence bearing on Politzer's behavior and attitudes at that time. We find, then, that the record contains no credible explanation of Weintraub's failure to call for disciplinary action against Chairman, on account of their quarrel on December 30, until about a month after the event. We think that on this record, Weintraub's revival of the December 30 episode as a basis for demanding Chairman's discharge, and Kende's summary ruling on that demand, despite Politzer's opposition, are reasonably explained only by the other facts to which we previously adverted: The Respondent's extreme animus against Chairman because of his testimony at the Board hearing despite its prior warning, and its promptly conceived plan — which was initially frustrated, but not shown to have been abandoned — to find a pretext for discharging him. We find, on the entire record, that Chairman was discharged for testifying at the Board hearing, in violation of Section 8 (4) of the Act. We therefore reverse Conclusion of Law No. 3 set forth in the Intermediate Report. . . .

As it has been found that the Respondent discriminated against Chairman for having given testimony under the Act and thereby violated Section 8 (4) of the Act, we shall direct that the Respondent offer him immediate and full reinstatement to his former or a substantially equivalent position without prejudice to his seniority or other rights or privileges. We shall also order that the Respondent make Chairman whole for any loss of pay he may have suffered by reason of his discriminatory discharge by payment to him of a sum equal to the amount he would normally have earned as wages. . . .

National Labor Relations Board v. Universal Camera Corp.
179 F.2d 749 (2d Cir. 1950)

L. HAND, Chief Judge.

This case arises upon a petition to enforce an order of the Labor Board, whose only direction that we need consider was to reinstate with back pay a 'supervisory employee,' named Chairman, whom the respondent discharged on January 24, 1944, avowedly for insubordination. If the Board was right, the discharge was in fact for giving testimony hostile to the respondent at a hearing conducted by the Board to determine who should be the representative of the respondent's "maintenance employees." Chairman was an assistant engineer, whose duties were to supervise the "maintenance employees," and he testified at the hearing in favor of their being recognized as a separate bargaining unit. The respondent opposed the recognition of such a unit, and several of its officers testified to that effect, among whom were Shapiro, the vice-president, Kende, the chief engineer, and Politzer, the "plant engineer." The examiner, who heard the witnesses, was not satisfied that the respondent's motive in discharging Chairman was reprisal for his testimony; but on review of the record a majority of the Board found the opposite, and on August 31, 1948, ordered Chairman's reinstatement. The respondent argues (1) that the majority's findings are subject to a more searching review under the New Act than under the Old; (2) that in the case at bar the findings cannot be supported, because they are not supported by "substantial evidence"; and (3) that its liability to Chairman, if any, ended with the passage of the New Act. . . .

This has been the subject of so much uncertainty that we shall not try to clarify it; but we must decide what change, if any, the [Taft-Hartley Act] of 1947 has made [to the Wagner Act of 1935]. Section 10(e) now reads that the findings "shall be conclusive" "if supported by substantial evidence on the record considered as a whole"; and the original was merely that they should be conclusive, "if supported by evidence." In *National Labor Relations Board v. Pittsburgh Steamship Company* the Supreme Court refused to say whether this had made any change, and remanded the case to the court of appeals to decide the point in the first instance. Of the four decisions which have discussed it, two have held that no change, or no material change, was made; one has held that the amendment was intended "to give the courts more latitude on review," but did not decide how much; and the fourth merely held that it did not make the review a "hearing *de novo*." . . . It is true that there were efforts, especially in the House, to give to courts of appeal a wider review than before; but the Senate opposed these, and, so far as concerns the adjective, "substantial," it added nothing to the interpretation which the Supreme Court had already put upon the earlier language [in *Washington, Virginia & Maryland Coach Co. v. National Labor Relations Board*]. The most probable intent in adding the phrase, "on the record considered as a whole," was to overrule what Congress apparently supposed—perhaps rightly—had been the understanding of some courts: i.e. that, if any passage could be found in the testimony to support a finding, the review was to stop, no matter how much other parts of the testimony contradicted, or outweighed, it. That the words throughout section ten were chosen with deliberation and care is evident from the changes in Sec. 10(c), apparently intended to confine the Board to the record before it, and in Sec. 10(b), restricting it in the admission of evidence to Rule 43(a) of the Federal Rules of Civil Procedure, 28 U.S.C.A. It appears to us that, had it been intended to set up a new measure of review by the courts, the matter would not have been left so at large. We cannot agree that our review has been "broadened"; we hold that no more was done than to make definite what was already implied.

Just what that review was is another and much more difficult matter—particularly, when it comes to deciding how to treat a reversal by the Board of a finding of one of its own examiners. Obviously no printed record preserves all the evidence, on which any judicial officer bases his findings; and it is principally on that account that upon an appeal from the judgment of a district court, a court of appeals will hesitate to reverse. Its position must be: "No matter what you saw of the witnesses and what else you heard than these written words, we are satisfied from them alone that you were clearly wrong. Nothing which could have happened that is not recorded, could have justified your conclusion in the face of what is before us." That gives such findings great immunity, which the Rules extend even to the findings of masters, when reviewed by a district judge. The standing of an examiner's findings under the Labor Relations Act is not plain; but it appears to us at least clear that they were not intended to be as unassailable as a master's. The Old Act provided for "examiners"; but they did not have to make reports, and, although Sec. 10(c) of the New Act requires them to do that, it does not undertake to say how persuasive their findings are to be. On the other hand, Sec. 8(a) of the Administrative Procedure Act provides that "on appeal from or review of" the decision of an "officer" who has presided

> ### In Context
>
> A "master" (typically referred to today as a "special master") is an official appointed by a judge to hold evidentiary hearings and to issue reports with factual findings in anticipation of a trial before the court. *See* Fed. R. Civ. P. 53(c).

at a hearing, "the agency shall . . . have all the powers which it would have in making the initial decision." It is clear that these words apply to the decisions of the "agency" upon the evidence; but nothing is said as to what effect the "agency" must give to the "officer's" findings; except that, if the text be read literally, it could be argued that the "agency" was to disregard it. The reports in Congress do not help very much. The Senate Report merely said that the findings "would be of consequence, for example, to the extent that material facts in any case depend on the determination of the credibility of witnesses as shown by their demeanor or conduct at the hearing." The House Report was the same . . . although it did add that "in a broad sense the agencies reviewing powers are to be compared with that of courts under Sec. 10(a) of the bill." That would have made them as conclusive upon an "agency" as the "agency's" findings are upon a court; and it is safe to say that the words will not bear so much. When the same question came up under the Old Act, the courts left the answer equally uncertain. . . . All this leaves the question in confusion. On the one hand we are not to assume that the Board must accept the finding, unless what is preserved in the record makes it "clearly erroneous." That would assimilate examiners to masters, and, if that had been intended, we should expect a plainer statement. On the other hand, the decisions [of the lower courts addressing this issue] certainly do mean that, when the Board reverses a finding, it shall count in the court's review of the Board's substituted finding; the case does not then come up as it does, when the testimony has been taken by deposition. On the whole we find ourselves unable to apply so impalpable a standard without bringing greater perplexity into a subject already too perplexing. The weight to be given to another person's conclusion from evidence that has disappeared, depends altogether upon one's confidence in his judicial powers. The decision of a child of ten would count for nothing; that of an experienced master would count for much. Unless we are to set up some canon, universally applicable . . . each case in this statute will depend upon what competence the Board ascribes to the examiner in question. Section 4(a) provides that he shall be an employee of the Board, which will therefore have means of informing itself about his work. We hold that, although the Board would be wrong in totally disregarding his findings, it is practically impossible for a court, upon review of those findings which the Board itself substitutes, to consider the Board's reversal as a factor in the court's own decision. This we say, because we cannot find any middle ground between doing that and treating such a reversal as error, whenever it would be such, if done by a judge to a master in equity.

[After reviewing the evidence supporting the Board's order, Chief Judge Hand continued:] We should feel obliged in our turn to reverse the reversal of this finding, if we were dealing with the finding of a judge who had reversed the finding of a master, because the reasons given do not seem to us enough to overbear the evidence which the record did not preserve and which may have convinced the examiner. . . .

Nevertheless, in spite of all this we shall direct the Board's order to be enforced. If by special verdict a jury had made either the express finding of the majority that there was an agreement between Kende and Weintraub, or the alternate finding, if there be one, that Kende without Weintraub's concurrence used Weintraub's complaint as an excuse, we should not reverse the verdict; and we understand our function in cases of this kind to be the same. Such a verdict would be within the bounds of rational entertainment. When all is said, Kende had been greatly outraged at Chairman's testimony; he then did propose to get him out of the factory; he still thought at the hearings that he was unfit to remain; and he had told Weintraub to keep watch on him. We cannot say that, with all these circumstances before him, no reasonable person could have concluded that Chairman's testimony was one of the causes of his discharge, little as it would have convinced us, were we free to pass upon the evidence in the first instance. . . .

An enforcement order will issue.

[The dissenting opinion of Judge Thomas Walter Swan is omitted.]

* * *

Before proceeding to the Supreme Court's opinion in this case, it would be beneficial to ask a few clarifying questions about the Second Circuit's decision.

1. Writing for the court, Chief Judge Hand observed that "[t]he weight to be given to another person's conclusion from evidence that has disappeared, depends altogether upon one's confidence in his judicial powers." To which "disappeared" evidence did he refer? Why would its persuasiveness depend on the fact-finder's "judicial powers"?

2. Chief Judge Hand observed that "although the Board would be wrong in totally disregarding [the hearing examiner's] findings, it is practically impossible for a court, upon review of those findings which the Board itself substitutes, to consider the Board's reversal as a factor in the court's own decision." What did he mean by this? Did he mean that the substantial evidence standard required the court to scrutinize the differences between the Board's factual findings and those of its examiner? Or did he mean that the court had to disregard those differences and only look at the facts as found by the Board?

3. In trying to determine just how much deference the Board should have accorded the factual finding of its trial examiner, the court referred to two other relationships: (1) the one between an appellate court and a district court, and (2) the one between a district court and its master. According to Chief Judge Hand, how did these relationships compare to the one between the Board and its trial examiner?

Did he believe that the Board should have given comparatively more or less deference to its trial examiner?

4. Do you think the trial examiner or the Board was best positioned to determine Kende's and Weintraub's credibility as witnesses and their motives for firing Chairman? Based on this view, do you think the NLRB reached the right conclusion, or the wrong one?

Universal Camera Corporation v. National Labor Relations Board
340 U.S. 474 (1951)

Mr. Justice FRANKFURTER delivered the opinion of the Court.

The essential issue raised by this case and its companion . . . is the effect of the Administrative Procedure Act and the legislation colloquially known as the Taft-Hartley Act, 5 U.S.C.A. § 1001 *et seq.*; 29 U.S.C.A. § 141 *et seq.*, on the duty of Courts of Appeals when called upon to review orders of the National Labor Relations Board. . . .

I.

Want of certainty in judicial review of Labor Board decisions partly reflects the intractability of any formula to furnish definiteness of content for all the impalpable factors involved in judicial review. But in part doubts as to the nature of the reviewing power and uncertainties in its application derive from history, and to that extent an elucidation of this history may clear them away.

The Wagner Act provided: "The findings of the Board as to the facts, if supported by evidence, shall be conclusive." Act of July 5, 1935, § 10(e). This Court read "evidence" to mean "substantial evidence," *Washington, V. & M. Coach Co. v. Labor Board*, 301 U.S. 142, and we said that "(s)ubstantial evidence is more than a mere scintilla. It means such relevant evidence as a reasonable mind might accept as adequate to support a conclusion." *Consolidated Edison Co. v. National Labor Relations Board*, 305 U.S. 197, 229. Accordingly, it "must do more than create a suspicion of the existence of the fact to be established . . . it must be enough to justify, if the trial were to a jury, a refusal to direct a verdict when the conclusion sought to be drawn from it is one of fact for the jury." *National Labor Relations Board v. Columbian Enameling & Stamping Co.*, 306 U.S. 292, 300.

The very smoothness of the "substantial evidence" formula as the standard for reviewing the evidentiary validity of the Board's findings established its currency. But the inevitably variant applications of the standard to conflicting evidence soon brought contrariety of views and in due course bred criticism. Even though the whole record may have been canvassed in order to determine whether the evidentiary foundation of a determination by the Board was "substantial," the phrasing of this Court's process of review readily lent itself to the notion that it was enough that the evidence supporting the Board's result was "substantial" when considered by itself. It is fair to say that by imperceptible steps regard for the fact-finding function of the Board led to the assumption that the requirements of the Wagner Act were met when the reviewing court could find in the record evidence which, when viewed in isolation, substantiated the Board's findings. . . . This is not to say that every member of this Court was consciously guided by this view or that the Court ever explicitly avowed this practice as doctrine. What matters is that the belief justifiably arose that the Court had so construed the obligation to review. . . .

[After recounting the legislative history of the APA's and Taft-Hartley Act's judicial review provisions, Justice Frankfurter continued:] It is fair to say that in all this Congress expressed a mood. And it expressed its mood not merely by oratory but by legislation. As legislation that mood must be respected, even though it can only serve as a standard for judgment and not as a body of rigid rules assuring sameness of applications. Enforcement of such broad standards implies subtlety of mind and solidity of judgment. But it is not for us to question that Congress may assume such qualities in the federal judiciary.

From the legislative story we have summarized, two concrete conclusions do emerge. One is the identity of aim of the Administrative Procedure Act and the Taft-Hartley Act regarding the proof with which the Labor Board must support a decision. The other is that now Congress has left no room for doubt as to the kind of scrutiny which a court of appeals must give the record before the Board to satisfy itself that the Board's order rests on adequate proof.

It would be mischievous word playing to find that the scope of review under the Taft-Hartley Act is any different from that under the Administrative Procedure Act. The Senate Committee which reported the review clause of the Taft-Hartley Act expressly indicated that the two standards were to conform in this regard, and the wording of the two Acts is for purposes of judicial administration identical. And so we hold that the standard of proof specifically required of the Labor Board by the Taft-Hartley Act is the same as that to be exacted by courts reviewing every administrative action subject to the Administrative Procedure Act.

Whether or not it was ever permissible for courts to determine the substantiality of evidence supporting a Labor Board decision merely on the basis of evidence which in and of itself justified it, without taking into account contradictory evidence or evidence from which conflicting inferences could be drawn, the new legislation definitively precludes such a theory of review and bars its practice. The substantiality of evidence must take into account whatever in the record fairly detracts from its weight. This is clearly the significance of the requirement in both statutes that courts consider the whole record. Committee reports and the adoption in the Administrative Procedure Act of the minority views of the Attorney General's Committee demonstrate that to enjoin such a duty on the reviewing court was one of the important purposes of the movement which eventuated in that enactment.

To be sure, the requirement for canvassing "the whole record" in order to ascertain substantiality does not furnish a calculus of value by which a reviewing court can assess the evidence. Nor was it intended to negative the function of the Labor Board as one of those agencies presumably equipped or informed by experience to deal with a specialized field of knowledge, whose findings within that field carry the authority of an expertness which courts do not possess and therefore must respect. Nor does it mean that even as to matters not requiring expertise a court may displace the Board's choice between two fairly conflicting views, even though the court would justifiably have made a different choice had the matter been before it *de novo*. Congress has merely made it clear that a reviewing court is not barred from setting aside a Board decision when it cannot conscientiously find that the evidence supporting that decision is substantial, when viewed in the light that the record in its entirety furnishes, including the body of evidence opposed to the Board's view. . . .

Whatever changes were made by the Administrative Procedure and Taft-Hartley Acts are clearly within this area where precise definition is impossible. Retention of the familiar 'substantial evidence' terminology indicates that no drastic reversal of attitude was intended.

But a standard leaving an unavoidable margin for individual judgment does not leave the judicial judgment at large even though the phrasing of the standard does not wholly fence it in. The legislative history of these Acts demonstrates a purpose to impose on courts a responsibility which has not always been recognized. . . .

We conclude, therefore, that the Administrative Procedure Act and the Taft-Hartley Act direct that courts must now assume more responsibility for the reasonableness and fairness of Labor Board decisions than some courts have shown in the past. Reviewing courts must be influenced by a feeling that they are not to abdicate the conventional judicial function. Congress has imposed on them responsibility for assuring that the Board keeps within reasonable grounds. That responsibility is not less real because it is limited to enforcing the requirement that evidence appear substantial when viewed, on the record as a whole, by courts invested with the authority and enjoying the prestige of the Courts of Appeals. The Board's findings are entitled to respect; but they must nonetheless be set aside when the record before a Court of Appeals clearly precludes the Board's decision from being justified by a fair estimate of the worth of the testimony of witnesses or its informed judgment on matters within its special competence or both. . . .

II.

Our disagreement with the view of the court below that the scope of review of Labor Board decisions is unaltered by recent legislation does not of itself, as we have noted, require reversal of its decision. The court may have applied a standard of review which satisfies the present Congressional requirement.

The decision of the Court of Appeals is assailed on two grounds. It is said (1) that the court erred in holding that it was barred from taking into account the report of the examiner on questions of fact insofar as that report was rejected by the Board, and (2) that the Board's order was not supported by substantial evidence on the record considered as a whole, even apart from the validity of the court's refusal to consider the rejected portions of the examiner's report.

The latter contention is easily met. . . . [I]t is clear from the court's opinion in this case that it in fact did consider the "record as a whole," and did not deem itself merely the judicial echo of the Board's conclusion. The testimony of the company's witnesses was inconsistent, and there was clear evidence that the complaining employee had been discharged by an officer who was at one time influenced against him because of his appearance at the Board hearing. On such a record we could not say that it would be error to grant enforcement.

The first contention, however, raises serious questions to which we now turn.

III.

The Court of Appeals deemed itself bound by the Board's rejection of the examiner's findings because the court considered these findings not "as unassailable as a master's." They are not. Section 10(c) of the Labor Management Relations Act provides that "If upon the preponderance of the testimony taken the Board shall be of the opinion that any person named in the complaint has engaged in or is engaging in any such unfair labor practice, then the Board shall state its findings of fact. . . ." 61 Stat. 147, 29 U.S.C.A. § 160(c). The responsibility for decision thus placed on the Board is wholly inconsistent with the notion that it has power to reverse an examiner's findings only when they are "clearly erroneous." Such a limitation would make so drastic a departure from prior administrative practice that explicitness would be required.

The Court of Appeals concluded from this premise "that, although the Board would be wrong in totally disregarding his findings, it is practically impossible for a court, upon review of those findings which the Board itself substitutes, to consider the Board's reversal as a factor in the court's own decision. This we say, because we cannot find any middle ground between doing that and treating such a reversal as error, whenever it would be such, if done by a judge to a master in equity." Much as we respect the logical acumen of the Chief Judge of the Court of Appeals, we do not find ourselves pinioned between the horns of his dilemma.

We are aware that to give the examiner's findings less finality than a master's and yet entitle them to consideration in striking the account, is to introduce another and an unruly factor into the judgmatical process of review. But we ought not to fashion an exclusionary rule merely to reduce the number of imponderables to be considered by reviewing courts.

The Taft-Hartley Act provides that "The findings of the Board with respect to questions of fact if supported by substantial evidence on the record considered as a whole shall be conclusive." 61 Stat. 148, 29 U.S.C. (Supp. III) § 160(e), 29 U.S.C.A. § 160(e). Surely an examiner's report is as much a part of the record as the complaint or the testimony. According to the Administrative Procedure Act, "All decisions (including initial, recommended, or tentative decisions) shall become a part of the record. . . ." § 8(b), 60 Stat. 242, 5 U.S.C. § 1007(b), 5 U.S.C.A. § 1007(b). We found that this Act's provision for judicial review has the same meaning as that in the Taft-Hartley Act. The similarity of the two statutes in language and purpose also requires that the definition of "record" found in the Administrative Procedure Act be construed to be applicable as well to the term "record" as used in the Taft-Hartley Act.

It is therefore difficult to escape the conclusion that the plain language of the statutes directs a reviewing court to determine the substantiality of evidence on the record including the examiner's report. The conclusion is confirmed by the indications in the legislative history that enhancement of the status and function of the trial examiner was one of the important purposes of the movement for administrative reform.

. . . [Section] 11 of the Administrative Procedure Act contains detailed provisions designed to maintain high standards of independence and competence in examiners. Section 10(c) of the Labor Management Relations Act requires that examiners "shall issue . . . a proposed report, together with a recommended order". Both statutes thus evince a purpose to increase the importance of the role of examiners in the administrative process. High standards of public administration counsel that we attribute to the Labor Board's examiners both due regard for the responsibility which Congress imposes on them and the competence to discharge it. . . .

We do not require that the examiner's findings be given more weight than in reason and in the light of judicial experience they deserve. The "substantial evidence" standard is not modified in any way when the Board and its examiner disagree. We intend only to recognize that evidence supporting a conclusion may be less substantial when an impartial, experienced examiner who has observed the witnesses and lived with the case has drawn conclusions different from the Board's than when he has reached the same conclusion. The findings of the examiner are to be considered along with the consistency and inherent probability of testimony. The significance of his report, of course, depends largely on the importance of credibility in the particular case. To give it this significance does not seem to us materially more difficult than to heed the other factors which in sum determine whether evidence is "substantial." . . .

We therefore remand the cause to the Court of Appeals. On reconsideration of the record it should accord the findings of the trial examiner the relevance that they reasonably command in answering the comprehensive question whether the evidence supporting the Board's order is substantial. But the court need not limit its reexamination of the case to the effect of that report on its decision. We leave it free to grant or deny enforcement as it thinks the principles expressed in this opinion dictate.

Judgment vacated that cause remanded.

National Labor Relations Board v. Universal Camera Corp.

190 F.2d 429 (2d Cir. 1951)

L. HAND, Circuit Judge.

By a divided vote we decided this appeal last year upon the same record that is now before us, holding that the Board's order should be "enforced." The Supreme Court vacated our order and remanded the cause to us for reconsideration in two particulars. The first was that, although the amendment of the old act was in terms limited to adding that courts of appeal should scrutinize the whole record on reviewing findings of the Board, its implications were more extended. The second was that in considering whether the Board's findings were adequately supported by the evidence we were not altogether to disregard the findings of its examiner. As to the first, the Court . . . [concluded that the] courts of appeal [must be] less complaisant towards the Board's findings than had been proper before; not only were they to look to the record as a whole, but they were to be less ready to yield their personal judgment on the facts; at least less ready than many at times had been. Presumably that does not extend to those issues on which the Board's specialized experience equips it with major premises inaccessible to judges, but as to matters of common knowledge we are to use a somewhat stiffer standard. Just where the Board's specialized experience ends it may no doubt be hard to say; but we are to find the boundary and beyond it to deem ourselves as competent as the Board to pass upon issues of fact. We hold that all the issues at bar are beyond the boundary and for that reason we cannot accept the Board's argument that we are not in as good a position as itself to decide what witnesses were more likely to be telling the truth in this labor dispute.

Upon the second issue we had said that we could find no practicable mesne between giving the findings of an examiner the immunity which a court must give to those of a master, and saying that, although the Board should no doubt treat them as having some evidentiary value, it was impossible for us to measure what that ought to be; and that therefore we would decide the appeal, as though there had been no findings. Although this went too far, again it is plain that the weight which we should insist that the Board should give them must be left at large; except that we must count them for something, and particularly when — as indeed we said at length in our first opinion — they were based on that part of the evidence which the printed words do not preserve. Often that is the most telling part, for on the issue of veracity the bearing and delivery of a witness will usually be the dominating factors, when the words alone leave any rational choice. Perhaps as good a way as any to state the change effected by the amendment is to say that we are not to be reluctant to insist that an examiner's findings on veracity must not be overruled without a very substantial preponderance in the testimony as recorded.

In the case at bar the examiner came to the conclusion that Chairman's discharge on January 24, 1944, was not because of his testimony two months before. He believed that Politzer had told Weintraub, a day or two after Weintraub's quarrel with Chairman at the end of December, that Chairman had said he was going to resign; and, although he did not believe that Chairman had in fact said so, he found that Politzer either thought he had, or told Weintraub that he had in the hope of smoothing over their quarrel. We see nothing improbable in this story . . .

. . . It is of course true that no one can be sure what may have actuated Kende at least in part; nothing is more difficult than to disentangle the motives of another's conduct — motives frequently unknown even to the actor himself. But for that very reason those parts of the evidence which are lost in print become especially pregnant, and the Board which had no access to them should have hesitated to assume that the examiner was not right to act upon them. A story may indeed be so unreasonable on its face that no plausibility in its telling will make it tenable, but that is seldom true and certainly was not true here. . . . However limited should be the regard which the Board must give to the findings of its examiner, we cannot escape the conclusion that the record in the case at bar was such that the following finding of the examiner should have turned the scale; "the undersigned is not persuaded that Kende based his decision upon any animus against Chairman for testifying rather than on an evaluation of Weintraub's request based upon the merits." Indeed, it is at least doubtful whether the Board meant to overrule that finding except as it was involved in its own finding that Kende and Weintraub had had a joint plan to oust Chairman. . . . [U]pon a reexamination of the record as a whole, and upon giving weight to the examiner's findings—now in compliance with the Court's directions as we understand them—we think that our first disposition of the appeal was wrong, and we hold that the Board should have dismissed the complaint.

Order reversed; complaint to be dismissed.

QUESTION SET 9.25

Review & Synthesis

1. *Universal Camera* addressed three uncertainties about how the substantial evidence test applied to NLRB enforcement petitions: (1) the NLRB's freedom to reject its trial examiner's factual findings; (2) whether reviewing courts had to uphold the NLRB's orders based solely on supporting evidence in the record and without regard to countervailing evidence; and (3) whether the "whole record" the APA and the Taft-Hartley Act required courts to review included the factual findings of NLRB trial examiners. How, and on what basis, did the Court resolve each of these issues?

2. On remand, the Second Circuit reversed the NLRB's finding that Kende fired Chairman in retaliation for the latter's testimony in the Universal Camera union representation proceedings. What evidence did the court disregard in its initial consideration of the dispute that it felt compelled to consider on remand? How did that evidence factor into to the court's application of the substantial evidence test?

3. As discussed in Chapter 6, officials with a variety of titles perform adjudicative functions within agencies. Among these officials, administrative law judges enjoy the most independence; they are largely protected from intra-agency influence and removal. Other adjudicative officials, broadly called administrative judges and including trial examiners, do not enjoy the level of protection granted to ALJs. Additionally, the professional qualifications for becoming an ALJ are often more stringent than those for other administrative adjudicators. In 1972, the U.S. Civil Service Commission officially recognized that NLRB trial examiners are administrative law judges. Should the status of the agency adjudicator matter in applying the substantial evidence test? What effect would consideration of ALJ status have on how reviewing courts apply the test?

4. Also discussed in Chapter 6 was the distinction between the standard of *review* and the standard of *proof* under 5 U.S.C. § 556(d) (the quantum of evidence required to support an agency's decisions). Assume that the standard of proof in the proceedings before the trial examiner and the NLRB

was a preponderance of the evidence. Did the Second Circuit have to determine whether the NLRB's order was supported by a preponderance of the evidence? Or did it have to determine whether there was enough evidence to support the NLRB's conclusion, without also determining whether those conclusions were more likely true than not?

---

2. Review of Agency Statutory Interpretation

Statutory ambiguity is an inescapable fact of legal life. No matter how richly detailed, no matter how carefully considered, legislation will never address all of the issues that could conceivably arise under it. Congress will invariably leave gaps that other organs of government must fill. As one commentator has rightly observed, "[a]mbiguity can be intentional or unintentional; it can derive from misunderstandings about language, from simple mistakes, from a failure to plan ahead, or from the impossibility of seeing very far ahead." Saul Levmore, *Ambiguous Statutes*, U. Chi. L. Rev. 1073, 1077 (2010). It can also result from the coordination problems inherent in collective decision-making, from a lack of sufficient investigative time or resources, or from an absence of requisite subject matter expertise. Thus, Congress may try its level best to specify its intentions but fail to do so because of circumstance, simple human error, or cognitive limitation. It may also purposely build ambiguity into its statutes with the intent of allowing those with greater substantive expertise to fill in the details or to force other government actors to make policy decisions it considers too politically controversial. Whatever the cause of a statute's ambiguity, eventually someone must figure out what it means—must "interpret" it—so those to whom it applies can know what the law requires of them. Of course, when Congress unambiguously addresses an issue there is nothing for courts or for agencies to "interpret"; they simply follow the instructions Congress provided. But when ambiguities do arise they are, as a practical matter, an invitation for some other governmental authority to fill in the gaps.

All this leads to a central preoccupation of administrative law: should reviewing courts or agencies serve as the principal interpreter of federal statutes? Both have compelling functional claims to this mantle. On the one hand, the federal government's adjudicative function is assigned to the courts by Article III of the Constitution. When resolving the disputes falling within their jurisdiction, courts can only perform this function if they identify and construe the law governing the conduct of the parties appearing before them. While federal courts in diversity-of-citizenship cases have traditionally deferred to the highest state court's interpretation of its state's laws, they have not done so with Executive Branch interpretations of federal law. *See, e.g., United States v. American Trucking Associations*, 310 U.S. 534, 544

(1940) ("The interpretation of the meaning of statutes, as applied to justiciable controversies, is exclusively a judicial function. This duty requires one body of public servants, the judges, to construe the meaning of what another body, the legislators, has said."). On the other hand, Congress creates administrative agencies to implement its regulatory schemes, the details of which it frequently (sometimes purposely, sometimes unintentionally) leaves unspecified. To perform their assigned functions, agencies must use adjudication and rulemaking to resolve the ambiguities and fill policy gaps left in the regulatory statutes they administer. Stated differently, and as discussed at length in Part III of this casebook, policy formation is often an integral part of the regulatory responsibilities assigned to agencies by Congress. Additionally, agencies are likely to be more familiar with the actors and activities within their realms of regulation and may therefore be better positioned to conduct this supplemental policymaking than are generalist courts.

Answering the interpretive primacy question leads to yet another question of practical importance: what degree of interpretive independence does the mantle confer? If the Judiciary serves as Congress' primary interpreter, can a reviewing court completely ignore how an agency construes its organic statute? Alternatively, is the court obliged to consider, but not necessarily to adopt, the agency's views on that statute's meaning? If an agency is the primary interpreter of its organic statute, must a reviewing court adopt its interpretation without question? Or must that court at least check the agency's interpretation for its lawfulness? How should courts review an agency's interpretation of statutes other than its organic statute? Would deference of any sort make sense in that circumstance?

On these questions of interpretive primacy and independence, the following two Supreme Court cases are the most important decided between the end of the New Deal Era and the passage of the Administrative Procedure Act of 1946. Taken together, do they lend clarity or confusion to the subject? As you read, pay attention to how the Court chose between courts and agencies. What factors did it consider relevant to the inquiry? Also, what factors did it deem relevant in setting degrees of interpretive independence?

National Labor Relations Board v. Hearst Publications, Inc., **322 U.S. 111 (1944).** Hearst Publications, publisher of four Los Angeles daily newspapers, refused to bargain with a union representing the newsboys (who were adults rather than children) who distributed its papers within the city. The National Labor Relations Act of 1935, 29 U.S.C. § 151, *et seq.,* required companies to negotiate with the bargaining representative chosen by their employees, but it did not define who an "employee" was. The company argued that Congress intended to incorporate the common law definitions of "employee" and "independent contractor" into the Act and, pursuant to those definitions, newsboys were the latter not the former. The company accordingly insisted that it was under no obligation to engage with the newsboys' elected representative. After a hearing, the Board rejected Hearst's interpretation of the Act, finding that newsboys were in fact employees. It issued a cease and desist order against the company and ordered it to bargain with the newsboys' representative. Hearst declined to comply. The parties brought their disagreement to the Court of Appeals, Hearst petitioning for review of the order and the Board petitioning for enforcement of it. The court afforded the Board's interpretation of "employee" no deference, and ultimately rejected it. The court then conducted an independent interpretation of the Act, deciding that Congress intended to import common-law standards for defining employees into the Act. Pursuant to that interpretation, and as Hearst had initially argued, newsboys were not employees.

The Supreme Court reversed. It first rejected the court of appeals' conclusion that Congress intended to import a common law definition of "employee" into the Act. It relied on its own reading of the Act's purpose, language, and history to do this; it did not rely on any reasoning or analysis in the Board's order. The Court then addressed what the term "employee" meant, given that its meaning did not come from the common law. Here it deferred to the Board's expertise, rather than supplying a definition itself:

> It is not necessary in this case to make a completely definitive limitation around the term "employee." That task has been assigned primarily to the agency created by Congress to administer the Act. Determination of "where all the conditions of the relation require protection" involves inquiries for the Board charged with this duty. Everyday experience in the administration of the statute gives it familiarity with the circumstances and backgrounds of employment relationships in various industries, with the abilities and needs of the workers for self[-]organization and collective action, and with the adaptability of collective bargaining for the peaceful settlement of their disputes with their employers. The experience thus acquired must be brought frequently to bear on the question who is an employee under the Act. Resolving that question, like determining whether unfair labor practices have been committed, "belongs to the usual administrative routine" of the Board. *Gray v. Powell*, 314 U.S. 402, 411 (1941).
>
> In making that body's determinations as to the facts in these matters conclusive, if supported by evidence, Congress entrusted to it primarily the decision whether the evidence establishes the material facts. Hence in reviewing the Board's ultimate conclusions, it is not the court's function to substitute its own inferences of fact for the Board's, when the latter have support in the record. Undoubtedly questions of statutory interpretation, especially when arising in the first instance in judicial proceedings, are for the courts to resolve, giving appropriate weight to the judgment of those whose special duty is to administer the questioned statute. *United States v. American Trucking Associations, Inc.*, 310 U.S. 534 (1940). But where the question is one of specific application of a broad statutory term in a proceeding in which the agency administering the statute must determine it initially, the reviewing court's function is limited. . . . [T]he Board's

determination that specified persons are "employees" under this Act is to be accepted if it has "warrant in the record" and a reasonable basis in law.

. . . Stating that "the primary consideration in the determination of the applicability of the statutory definition is whether effectuation of the declared policy and purposes of the Act comprehend securing to the individual the rights guaranteed and protection afforded by the Act," the Board concluded that the newsboys are employees. The record sustains the Board's findings and there is ample basis in the law for its conclusion.

Hearst, 322 U.S. at 130-32. Writing in dissent, Justice Owen Roberts took issue with the notion that Congress could assign primary responsibility for interpreting its statutes to agencies rather than courts:

. . . Clearly . . . Congress did not delegate to the National Labor Relations Board the function of defining the relationship of employment so as to promote what the Board understood to be the underlying purpose of the statute. The question who is an employee, so as to make the statute applicable to him, is a question of the meaning of the Act and, therefore, is a judicial and not an administrative question.

Id. at 135-36 (Roberts, J. dissenting).

Skidmore v. Swift & Co., 323 U.S. 134 (1944). This case, decided about six months after *Hearst*, involved seven employees of the Swift & Co. meat packing plant in Fort Worth, Texas. They filed suit against the company under the Fair Labor Standards Act ("FLSA") for overtime, damages, and attorneys' fees. Their positions required them to stay in the company's "fire hall" several nights each week, during which time they were required to respond when fire alarms or sprinklers were set off. The need to respond was rare; the workers used most of their time in the fire hall "to sleep or [amuse themselves] as they saw fit." *Id.* at 136. As they were nevertheless on call, they claimed that these overnight stays constituted "working time" under the FLSA for which Swift & Co. should have compensated them. The Act itself provided no definitive answer to the question.

Congress delegated authority to investigate and enforce potential FLSA violations to the Department of Labor's Wage and Hour Division. The Division had previously issued an Interpretative Bulletin addressing whether the Act required compensation for on-duty but inactive employees. The Bulletin was not produced through rulemaking or formal adjudication; it was a policy guide providing general information to the public. It recommended a "flexible solution" to such wage disputes, and "suggest[ed] standards and examples to guide in particular situations." *Id.* at 138. The Administrator also filed an amicus brief applying that guidance to the facts of this case. He argued that on-call time was compensable under the FLSA, exclusive of any time Swift & Co.'s employees spent eating or sleeping. Justice Robert

H. Jackson, writing for the Court, said the following on what consideration courts should give the Administrator's interpretation:

> There is no statutory provision as to what, if any, deference courts should pay to the Administrator's conclusions. And, while we have given them notice, we have had no occasion to try to prescribe their influence. The rulings of this Administrator are not reached as a result of hearing adversary proceedings in which he finds facts from evidence and reaches conclusions of law from findings of fact. They are not, of course, conclusive, even in the cases with which they directly deal, much less in those to which they apply only by analogy. They do not constitute an interpretation of the Act or a standard for judging factual situations which binds a district court's processes, as an authoritative pronouncement of a higher court might do. But the Administrator's policies are made in pursuance of official duty, based upon more specialized experience and broader investigations and information than is likely to come to a judge in a particular case. They do determine the policy which will guide applications for enforcement by injunction on behalf of the Government. Good administration of the Act and good judicial administration alike require that the standards of public enforcement and those for determining private rights shall be at variance only where justified by very good reasons. The fact that the Administrator's policies and standards are not reached by trial in adversary form does not mean that they are not entitled to respect. This Court has long given considerable and in some cases decisive weight to Treasury Decisions and to interpretative regulations of the Treasury and of other bodies that were not of adversary origin.
>
> We consider that the rulings, interpretations and opinions of the Administrator under this Act, while not controlling upon the courts by reason of their authority, do constitute a body of experience and informed judgment to which courts and litigants may properly resort for guidance. The weight of such a judgment in a particular case will depend upon the thoroughness evident in its consideration, the validity of its reasoning, its consistency with earlier and later pronouncements, and all those factors which give it power to persuade, if lacking power to control.

Id. at 139-40.

QUESTION SET 9.26

Review & Synthesis

1. Restate the deference tests developed in *Hearst* and *Skidmore*. Would you characterize these tests as requiring strong deference (courts should defer to agency interpretations of ambiguous statutes in most cases) or weak deference (courts should independently interpret ambiguous statutes in most cases with some consideration for the implementing agency's views)?

2. Did the NLRB in *Hearst* and the Wage and Hour Administrator in *Skidmore* employ similar or different decision-making processes in developing their interpretations of the Wagner Act and the Fair Labor Standards Act, respectively? What consideration, if any, did the Court give to these processes when determining how much weight to accord the agencies' respective interpretations?

3. *Skidmore* and *Hearst* were decided in 1944. Do you think their treatment of agency interpretations of ambiguous statutory terms survived passage of the Administrative Procedure Act in 1946? Be sure to consider how APA § 10 (5 U.S.C. § 706) was intended to impact the standards of judicial review then in use by the courts.

---

3. The *Chevron* Doctrine

Try as you might, you would struggle to find a consistent analytical thread in the Supreme Court's deference case law prior to 1984. It is true that the Court applied the *Hearst* and *Skidmore* deference standards, or slight variations of them, in numerous cases after passage of the Administrative Procedure Act. *See, e.g., St. Martin Evangelical Lutheran Church v. South Dakota*, 451 U.S. 772, 783 n.13 (1981) (applying *Skidmore* deference but declining to adopt the Labor Secretary's interpretation of the term "church" in the Federal Unemployment Tax Act); *Whirlpool Corp. v. Marshall*, 445 U.S. 1, 11-13 (1980) (upholding a Department of Labor regulation under *Skidmore* and observing that it "is entitled to deference unless it can be said not to be a reasoned and supportable interpretation of the Act"); *Securities and Exchange Commission v. Sloan*, 436 U.S. 103, 118-19 (1978) (citing *Hearst* and *Skidmore* while noting that courts "are not obliged to stand aside and rubber-stamp their affirmance of administrative decisions that they deem inconsistent with a statutory mandate or that frustrate the congressional policy underlying a statute"). Nevertheless, and as described by one exasperated commentator, the Court "consistently kept the scope of review unpredictable," "substitute[d] its judgment in some cases and use[d] the reasonableness test in other cases, without providing any guide as to what actuate[d] its choices." 1 RICHARD

> ### In Context
>
> The prevailing discord in the Supreme Court's deference jurisprudence was reflected somewhat in the Justices' views following oral arguments in *Chevron*. In a 2018 interview, *Chevron*'s author, Justice John Paul Stevens, explained that the Justices initially disagreed on how it should be decided. Several, particularly Justice William Brennan, believed that it was the duty of the courts to provide independent interpretations of ambiguous statutes. Others believed that when the meaning of a statute was in doubt, deference should be given to the agency's interpretation due to its superior subject matter expertise and knowledge of particular regulatory problems. Stevens was ultimately able to draft an opinion that got unanimous (6-0) support. Asked whether he still felt the need to defend the decision in his retirement, Stevens simply responded "yes." He later added that the decision makes "a lot of sense" and that it established "a sound doctrine." *See The* Chevron *Doctrine*, C-SPAN (Oct. 5, 2018), https://www.c-span.org/video/?c4753735/chevron-doctrine.

J. Pierce Jr., Administrative Law Treatise § 3.1 (2010) (internal quotations omitted).

In 1984, the Court launched the modern era of deference jurisprudence with its landmark decision in *Chevron U.S.A., Inc. v. Natural Resources Defense Council, Inc.* In so doing, it also launched a new era of controversy and uncertainty that continues today. *Chevron* is, according to several studies, the most judicially cited administrative law decision of all time. *See, e.g.,* Thomas J. Miles & Cass R. Sunstein, *Do Judges Make Regulatory Policy?—An Empirical Investigation of* Chevron, 73 U. Chi. L. Rev. 823 (2006). Its historical, doctrinal, and philosophical underpinnings have spawned a veritable cottage industry of commentary; dozens of scholarly articles exploring its nuances are published each year. It has also become a political flashpoint in debates about the size and scope of the administrative state. Politicians at all levels of government routinely blame the *Chevron* decision for fueling a never-ending expansion of a largely unaccountable federal bureaucracy, while others just as routinely defend *Chevron* for granting agencies the policy-making power needed to protect the well-being and security of the American people.

Using *Chevron* as the focal point, the materials that follow analyze how courts currently scrutinize agency interpretations of ambiguous statutes and agency-promulgated rules. As you read, consider how *Chevron* and its follow-on cases frame the institutional competencies of, and the relationships among, Congress, the courts, and the administrative state. Who decides whether courts must defer to agency interpretations of ambiguous statutes? Do courts or agencies have greater institutional competence when it comes to interpreting ambiguous statutory provisions? Does and should it matter whether Congress created an agency to implement the regulatory statute containing the ambiguous provisions? If one assumes that interpretation of ambiguous statutes is actually an act of law-creation (creating legal obligations that did not exist previously or, at least, were not evident prior to interpretation), does judicial deference foster or inhibit political accountability? As a broad conceptual matter, what effect does the *Chevron* doctrine have on the power of the Executive Branch relative to Congress and the Judiciary?

* * *

Before reading *Chevron*, it may be helpful to preview its central interpretive issue: Whether the so-called "bubble concept" was a permissible interpretation of the term "stationary source" in the Clean Air Amendments of 1977 ("CAA"), 42 U.S.C. § 7411(a)(3), § 111(a)(3). Congress quickly realized that many states were not going to attain the ambitious air pollution reduction goals set by the Clean Air Act of 1970. It accordingly passed the CAA, which established permitting programs to reduce air pollution in so-called "nonattainment" states. The CAA barred states from issuing permits for new or modified major stationary sources unless applicants could meet stringent pollution-reduction conditions. The stringency of those conditions depended on whether the applicant wanted to modify an existing source or add an entirely new one. Expected mitigation for the latter was greater—and hence more expensive—than for the former. Critically, however, the CAA did not define the term "stationary source," and so two competing interpretations eventually emerged.

Under the first interpretation, "stationary source" referred to individual pollution-emitting *apparatuses*. Think of a powerplant with three smokestacks. Under the apparatus definition, the powerplant would need a CAA permit—and would have to comply with the CAA's pollution-control requirements—every time it replaced, modified, or added a smokestack. The second interpretation was the "bubble concept." Imagine placing the entire powerplant, with all three smokestacks, in a bubble with a hole at the top. The powerplant could replace, modify, or add smokestacks without obtaining a CAA permit as long as the *overall* level of emissions flowing out of the top stayed the same or decreased.

Consider Figure 9.1, which illustrates replacement of stationary sources under the apparatus and bubble concepts. The powerplant at the top emits a total of 300 tons of emissions per year, with each of its three individual smokestacks emitting 100 tons per year. Suppose that the powerplant's operators want to replace each of the smokestacks. Under the apparatus theory (bottom left), each smokestack would be considered a new stationary source under the CAA. Accordingly, the operators would need a new source permit from the state for each one, and they would have to install pollution-control technologies to meet the conditions of those permits. Overall emissions levels from the plant would decrease as a result. Under the bubble concept, by contrast (bottom right), the powerplant operators could replace each smokestack without triggering the CAA's permitting requirements. Overall emissions levels would stay the same, and the operators would avoid the expense of both the permitting process and the installation of any pollution-control technologies. As you might guess, the bubble concept was quite interesting to industry and quite objectionable to environmental groups.

Figure 9.1

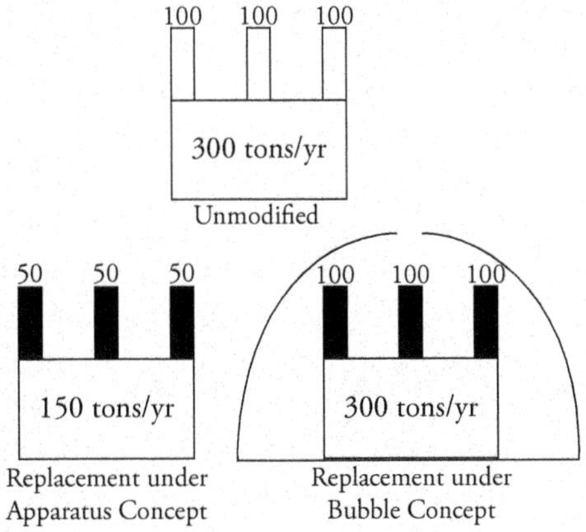

100   100   100

300 tons/yr

Unmodified

50   50   50

150 tons/yr

Replacement under
Apparatus Concept

100   100   100

300 tons/yr

Replacement under
Bubble Concept

Chevron, U.S.A., Inc. v. Natural Resources Defense Council, Inc.
467 U.S. 837 (1984)

Justice STEVENS delivered the opinion of the Court.

In the Clean Air Act Amendments of 1977, Congress enacted certain requirements applicable to States that had not achieved the national air quality standards established by the Environmental Protection Agency (EPA) pursuant to earlier legislation. The amended Clean Air Act required these "nonattainment" States to establish a permit program regulating "new or modified major stationary sources" of air pollution. Generally, a permit may not be issued for a new or modified major stationary source unless several stringent conditions are met. The EPA regulation promulgated to implement this permit requirement allows a State to adopt a plantwide definition of the term "stationary source." Under this definition, an existing plant that contains several pollution-emitting devices may install or modify one piece of equipment without meeting the permit conditions if the alteration will not increase the total emissions from the plant. The question presented by these cases is whether EPA's decision to allow States to treat all of the pollution-emitting devices within the same industrial grouping as though they were encased within a single "bubble" is based on a reasonable construction of the statutory term "stationary source."

I

The EPA regulations containing the plantwide definition of the term stationary source were promulgated on October 14, 1981. 46 Fed. Reg. 50766. The Court of Appeals set aside the regulations. *Natural Resources Defense Council, Inc. v. Gorsuch*, 685 F.2d 718 (1982).

The court observed that the relevant part of the amended Clean Air Act "does not explicitly define what Congress envisioned as a 'stationary source, to which the permit program . . . should apply,'" and further stated that the precise issue was not "squarely addressed in the legislative history." *Id.* at 723. In light of its conclusion that the legislative history bearing on the question was "at best contradictory," it reasoned that "the purposes of the nonattainment program should guide our decision here." *Id.* at 726, note 39. Based on two of its precedents concerning the applicability of the bubble concept to certain Clean Air Act programs, the court stated that the bubble concept was "mandatory" in programs designed merely to maintain existing air quality, but held that it was "inappropriate" in programs enacted to improve air quality. *Id.* at 726. Since the purpose of the permit program—its "*raison d'être*," in the court's view—was to improve air quality, the court held that the bubble concept was inapplicable in these cases under its prior precedents.

Ibid. It therefore set aside the regulations embodying the bubble concept as contrary to law. We granted certiorari to review that judgment, 461 U.S. 956 (1983), and we now reverse.

The basic legal error of the Court of Appeals was to adopt a static judicial definition of the term "stationary source" when it had decided that Congress itself had not commanded that definition.

II

When a court reviews an agency's construction of the statute which it administers, it is confronted with two questions. First, always, is the question whether Congress has directly spoken to the precise question at issue. If the intent of Congress is clear, that is the end of the matter; for the court, as well as the agency, must give effect to the unambiguously expressed intent of Congress. If, however, the court determines Congress has not directly addressed the precise question at issue, the court does not simply impose its own construction on the statute, as would be necessary in the absence of an administrative interpretation. Rather, if the statute is silent or ambiguous with respect to the specific issue, the question for the court is whether the agency's answer is based on a permissible construction of the statute.[11]

"The power of an administrative agency to administer a congressionally created . . . program necessarily requires the formulation of policy and the making of rules to fill any gap left, implicitly or explicitly, by Congress." *Morton v. Ruiz*, 415 U.S. 199, 231 (1974). If Congress has explicitly left a gap for the agency to fill, there is an express delegation of authority to the agency to elucidate a specific provision of the statute by regulation. Such legislative regulations are given controlling weight unless they are arbitrary, capricious, or manifestly contrary to the statute. Sometimes the legislative delegation to an agency on a particular question is implicit rather than explicit. In such a case, a court may not substitute its own construction of a statutory provision for a reasonable interpretation made by the administrator of an agency.

We have long recognized that considerable weight should be accorded to an executive department's construction of a statutory scheme it is entrusted to administer, and the principle of deference to administrative interpretations

> has been consistently followed by this Court whenever decision as to the meaning or reach of a statute has involved reconciling conflicting policies, and a full understanding of the force of the statutory policy in the given situation has depended upon more than ordinary knowledge respecting the matters subjected to agency regulations. See, e.g., *National Broadcasting Co.*

---

[11] The court need not conclude that the agency construction was the only one it permissibly could have adopted to uphold the construction, or even the reading the court would have reached if the question initially had arisen in a judicial proceeding. [Citing cases.]

v. United States, 319 U.S. 190 (1943); *Labor Board v. Hearst Publications, Inc.*, 322 U.S. 111 (1944); *Republic Aviation Corp. v. Labor Board*, 324 U.S. 793 (1945); *Securities & Exchange Comm'n v. Chenery Corp.*, 322 U.S. 194 (1943); *Labor Board v. Seven-Up Bottling Co.*, 344 U.S. 344 (1953).

. . . If this choice represents a reasonable accommodation of conflicting policies that were committed to the agency's care by the statute, we should not disturb it unless it appears from the statute or its legislative history that the accommodation is not one that Congress would have sanctioned. *United States v. Shimer*, 367 U.S. 374, 383 (1961).

In light of these well-settled principles it is clear that the Court of Appeals misconceived the nature of its role in reviewing the regulations at issue. Once it determined, after its own examination of the legislation, that Congress did not actually have an intent regarding the applicability of the bubble concept to the permit program, the question before it was not whether in its view the concept is "inappropriate" in the general context of a program designed to improve air quality, but whether the Administrator's view that it is appropriate in the context of this particular program is a reasonable one. Based on the examination of the legislation and its history which follows, we agree with the Court of Appeals that Congress did not have a specific intention on the applicability of the bubble concept in these cases, and conclude that the EPA's use of that concept here is a reasonable policy choice for the agency to make.

III

In the 1950's and the 1960's Congress enacted a series of statutes designed to encourage and to assist the States in curtailing air pollution. The Clean Air Amendments of 1970, Pub. L. 91-604, 84 Stat. 1676, "sharply increased federal authority and responsibility in the continuing effort to combat air pollution," 421 U.S., at 64, but continued to assign "primary responsibility for assuring air quality" to the several States, 84 Stat. 1678. Section 109 of the 1970 Amendments directed the EPA to promulgate National Ambient Air Quality Standards (NAAQS's) and § 110 directed the States to develop plans (SIP's) to implement the standards within specified deadlines. In addition, § 111 provided that major new sources of pollution would be required to conform to technology-based performance standards; the EPA was directed to publish a list of categories of sources of pollution and to establish new source performance standards (NSPS) for each. Section 111(e) prohibited the operation of any new source in violation of a performance standard.

Section 111(a) defined the terms that are to be used in setting and enforcing standards of performance for new stationary sources. It provided:

For purposes of this section:

. . . .

(3) The term "stationary source" means any building, structure, facility, or installation which emits or may emit any air pollutant. 84 Stat. 1683.

In the 1970 Amendments that definition was not only applicable to the NSPS program required by § 111, but also was made applicable to a requirement of § 110 that each state implementation plan contain a procedure for reviewing the location of any proposed new source and preventing its construction if it would preclude the attainment or maintenance of national air quality standards.

In due course, the EPA promulgated NAAQS's, approved SIP's, and adopted detailed regulations governing NSPS's for various categories of equipment. In one of its programs, the EPA used a plantwide definition of the term "stationary source." In 1974, it issued NSPS's for the nonferrous smelting industry that provided that the standards would not apply to the modification of major smelting units if their increased emissions were offset by reductions in other portions of the same plant.

Nonattainment

The 1970 legislation provided for the attainment of primary NAAQS's by 1975. In many areas of the country, particularly the most industrialized States, the statutory goals were not attained. In 1976, the 94th Congress was confronted with this fundamental problem, as well as many others respecting pollution control. As always in this area, the legislative struggle was basically between interests seeking strict schemes to reduce pollution rapidly to eliminate its social costs and interests advancing the economic concern that strict schemes would retard industrial development with attendant social costs. The 94th Congress, confronting these competing interests, was unable to agree on what response was in the public interest: legislative proposals to deal with nonattainment failed to command the necessary consensus.

In light of this situation, the EPA published an Emissions Offset Interpretative Ruling in December 1976, *see* 41 Fed. Reg. 55524, to "fill the gap," as respondents put it, until Congress acted. The Ruling stated that it was intended to address "the issue of whether and to what extent national air quality standards established under the Clean Air Act may restrict or prohibit growth of major new or expanded stationary air pollution sources." *Id.* at 55524-55525. In general, the Ruling provided that "a major new source may locate in an area with air quality worse than a national standard only if stringent conditions can be met." *Id.* at 55525. The Ruling gave primary emphasis to the rapid attainment of the statute's environmental goals. Consistent with that emphasis, the construction of every new source in nonattainment areas had to meet the "lowest achievable emission rate" under the current state of the art for that type of facility. *See Ibid.* The 1976 Ruling did not, however, explicitly adopt or reject the "bubble concept."

IV

The Clean Air Act Amendments of 1977 are a lengthy, detailed, technical, complex, and comprehensive response to a major social issue. A small portion of the statute—91 Stat. 745-751 (Part D of Title I of the amended Act, 42 U.S.C. §§ 7501-7508)—expressly deals with nonattainment areas. The focal point of this controversy is one phrase in that portion of the Amendments.

Basically, the statute required each State in a nonattainment area to prepare and obtain approval of a new SIP by July 1, 1979. In the interim those States were required to comply with the EPA's interpretative Ruling of December 21, 1976. 91 Stat. 745. The deadline for attainment of the primary NAAQS's was extended until December 31, 1982, and in some cases until December 31, 1987, but the SIP's were required to contain a number of provisions designed to achieve the goals as expeditiously as possible.

Most significantly for our purposes, the statute provided that each plan shall

> (6) require permits for the construction and operation of new or modified major stationary sources in accordance with section 173. . . . *Id.*, 747.

Before issuing a permit, § 173 requires (1) the state agency to determine that there will be sufficient emissions reductions in the region to offset the emissions from the new source and also to allow for reasonable further progress toward attainment, or that the increased emissions will not exceed an allowance for growth established pursuant to § 172(b)(5); (2) the applicant to certify that his other sources in the State are in compliance with the SIP, (3) the agency to determine that the applicable SIP is otherwise being implemented, and (4) the proposed source to comply with the lowest achievable emission rate (LAER).

The 1977 Amendments contain no specific reference to the "bubble concept." Nor do they contain a specific definition of the term "stationary source," though they did not disturb the definition of "stationary source" contained in § 111(a)(3), applicable by the terms of the Act to the NSPS program. Section 302(j), however, defines the term "major stationary source" as follows:

> (j) Except as otherwise expressly provided, the terms 'major stationary source' and 'major emitting facility' mean any stationary facility or source of air pollutants which directly emits, or has the potential to emit, one hundred tons per year or more of any air pollutant (including any major emitting facility or source of fugitive emissions of any such pollutant, as determined by rule by the Administrator). 91 Stat. 770.

V

The legislative history of the portion of the 1977 Amendments dealing with nonattainment areas does not contain any specific comment on the "bubble concept" or the question whether a plantwide definition of a stationary source is permissible under the permit program. It does, however, plainly disclose that in the permit program Congress sought to accommodate the conflict between the economic interest in permitting capital improvements to continue and the environmental interest in improving air quality. . . .

VI

As previously noted, prior to the 1977 Amendments, the EPA had adhered to a plantwide definition of the term "source" under a NSPS program. After adoption of the 1977 Amendments, proposals for a plantwide definition were considered [by the EPA]. . . .

In August 1980, however, the EPA adopted a regulation that, in essence, applied the basic reasoning of the Court of Appeals in these cases. The EPA took particular note of the two then-recent Court of Appeals decisions, which had created the bright-line rule that the "bubble concept" should be employed in a program designed to maintain air quality but not in one designed to enhance air quality. Relying heavily on those cases, EPA adopted a dual definition of "source" for nonattainment areas that required a permit whenever a change in either the entire plant, or one of its components, would result in a significant increase in emissions even if the increase was completely offset by reductions elsewhere in the plant. The EPA expressed the opinion that this interpretation was "more consistent with congressional intent" than the plantwide definition because it "would bring in more sources or modifications for review," 45 Fed. Reg. 52697 (1980), but its primary legal analysis was predicated on the two Court of Appeals decisions.

In 1981 a new administration took office and initiated a "Governmentwide reexamination of regulatory burdens and complexities." 46 Fed. Reg. 16281. In the context of that review, the EPA reevaluated the various arguments that had been advanced in connection with the proper definition of the term "source" and concluded that the term should be given the same definition in both nonattainment areas and PSD areas.

In explaining its conclusion, the EPA first noted that the definitional issue was not squarely addressed in either the statute or its legislative history and therefore that the issue involved an agency "judgment as how to best carry out the Act." *Ibid.* It then set forth several reasons for concluding that the plantwide definition was more appropriate. It pointed out that the dual definition "can act as a disincentive to new investment and modernization by discouraging modifications to existing facilities" and "can actually retard progress in air pollution control by discouraging replacement of older, dirtier processes or pieces of equipment with new, cleaner ones." *Ibid.* Moreover, the new definition "would simplify EPA's rules by using the same definition of 'source' for PSD, nonattainment new source review and the construction moratorium. This reduces confusion and inconsistency." *Ibid.* Finally, the agency explained that additional requirements that remained in place would accomplish the fundamental purposes of achieving attainment with NAAQS's as expeditiously as possible. These conclusions were expressed in a proposed rulemaking in August 1981 that was formally promulgated in October. *See id.* at 50766.

VII

In this Court respondents expressly reject the basic rationale of the Court of Appeals' decision. That court viewed the statutory definition of the term "source" as sufficiently flexible to cover either a plantwide definition, a narrower definition covering each unit within a plant, or a dual definition that could apply to both the entire "bubble" and its components. It interpreted the policies of the statute, however, to mandate the plantwide definition in programs designed to maintain clean air and to forbid it in programs designed to improve air quality. Respondents place a fundamentally different construction on the statute. They contend that the text of the Act requires the EPA to use a dual definition—if either a component of a plant, or the plant as a whole, emits over 100 tons of pollutant, it is a major stationary source. They thus contend that the EPA rules adopted in 1980, insofar as they apply to the maintenance of the quality of clean air, as well as the 1981 rules which apply to nonattainment areas, violate the statute.

Statutory Language

The definition of the term "stationary source" in § 111(a)(3) refers to "any building, structure, facility, or installation" which emits air pollution. *See supra*, at 2784. This definition is applicable only to the NSPS program by the express terms of the statute; the text of the statute does not make this definition applicable to the permit program. Petitioners therefore maintain that there is no statutory language even relevant to ascertaining the meaning of stationary source in the permit program aside from § 302(j), which defines the term "major stationary source." *See supra*, at 2786. We disagree with petitioners on this point.

The definition in § 302(j) tells us what the word "major" means—a source must emit at least 100 tons of pollution to qualify—but it sheds virtually no light on the meaning of the term "stationary source." It does equate a source with a facility—a "major emitting facility" and a "major stationary source" are synonymous under § 302(j). The ordinary meaning of the term "facility" is some collection of integrated elements which has been designed and constructed to achieve some purpose. Moreover, it is certainly no affront to common English usage to take a reference to a major facility or a major source to connote an entire plant as opposed to its constituent parts. Basically, however, the language of § 302(j) simply does not compel any given interpretation of the term "source."

Respondents recognize that, and hence point to § 111(a)(3). Although the definition in that section is not literally applicable to the permit program, it sheds as much light on the meaning of the word "source" as anything in the statute. As respondents point out, use of the words "building, structure, facility, or installation," as the definition of source, could be read to impose the permit conditions on an individual building that is a part of a plant. . . . The language may reasonably be interpreted to impose the requirement on any discrete, but integrated, operation which pollutes. This gives meaning to all of the terms — a single building, not part of a larger operation, would be covered if it emits more than 100 tons of pollution, as would any facility, structure, or installation. Indeed, the language itself implies a "bubble concept" of sorts: each enumerated item would seem to be treated as if it were encased in a bubble. While respondents insist that each of these terms must be given a discrete meaning, they also argue that § 111(a)(3) defines "source" as that term is used in § 302(j). The latter section, however, equates a source with a facility, whereas the former defines "source" as a facility, among other items.

We are not persuaded that parsing of general terms in the text of the statute will reveal an actual intent of Congress. We know full well that this language is not dispositive; the terms are overlapping and the language is not precisely directed to the question of the applicability of a given term in the context of a larger operation. To the extent any congressional "intent" can be discerned from this language, it would appear that the listing of overlapping, illustrative terms was intended to enlarge, rather than to confine, the scope of the agency's power to regulate particular sources in order to effectuate the policies of the Act.

Legislative History

In addition, respondents argue that the legislative history and policies of the Act foreclose the plantwide definition, and that the EPA's interpretation is not entitled to deference because it represents a sharp break with prior interpretations of the Act.

Based on our examination of the legislative history, we agree with the Court of Appeals that it is unilluminating. . . . We find that the legislative history as a whole is silent on the precise issue before us. It is, however, consistent with the view that the EPA should have broad discretion in implementing the policies of the 1977 Amendments.

More importantly, that history plainly identifies the policy concerns that motivated the enactment; the plantwide definition is fully consistent with one of those concerns — the allowance of reasonable economic growth — and, whether or not we believe it most effectively implements the other, we must recognize that the EPA has advanced a reasonable explanation for its conclusion that the regulations serve the environmental objectives as well. *See supra*, at 2789-2790, and note 29; *see also supra*, at 2788, note 27. Indeed, its reasoning is supported by the public record developed in the rulemaking process, as well as by certain private studies.

Our review of the EPA's varying interpretations of the word "source" — both before and after the 1977 Amendments — convinces us that the agency primarily responsible for administering this important legislation has consistently interpreted it flexibly — not in a sterile textual vacuum, but in the context of implementing policy decisions in a technical and complex arena. The fact that the agency has from time to time changed its interpretation of the term "source" does not, as respondents argue, lead us to conclude that no deference should be accorded the agency's interpretation of the statute. An initial agency interpretation is not instantly carved in stone. On the contrary, the agency, to engage in informed rulemaking, must consider varying interpretations and the wisdom of its policy on a continuing basis. Moreover, the fact that the agency has adopted different definitions in different contexts adds force to the argument that the definition itself is flexible, particularly since Congress has never indicated any disapproval of a flexible reading of the statute. . . .

Policy

The arguments over policy that are advanced in the parties' briefs create the impression that respondents are now waging in a judicial forum a specific policy battle which they ultimately lost in the agency and in the jurisdictions opting for the "bubble concept," but one which was never waged in the Congress. Such policy arguments are more properly addressed to legislators or administrators, not to judges.

In these cases, the Administrator's interpretation represents a reasonable accommodation of manifestly competing interests and is entitled to deference: the regulatory scheme is technical and complex, the agency considered the matter in a detailed and reasoned fashion, and the decision involves reconciling conflicting policies. Congress intended to accommodate both interests, but did not do so itself on the level of specificity presented by these cases. Perhaps that body consciously desired the Administrator to strike the balance at this level, thinking that those with great expertise and charged with responsibility for administering the provision would be in a better position to do so; perhaps it simply did not consider the question at this level; and perhaps Congress was unable to forge a coalition on either side of the question, and those on each side decided to take their chances with the scheme devised by the agency. For judicial purposes, it matters not which of these things occurred.

Judges are not experts in the field, and are not part of either political branch of the Government. Courts must, in some cases, reconcile competing political interests, but not on the basis of the judges' personal policy preferences. In contrast, an agency to which Congress has delegated policy-making responsibilities may, within the limits of that delegation, properly rely upon the incumbent administration's views of wise policy to inform its judgments. While agencies are not directly accountable to the people, the Chief Executive is, and it is entirely appropriate for this political branch of the Government to make such policy choices—resolving the competing interests which Congress itself either inadvertently did not resolve, or intentionally left to be resolved by the agency charged with the administration of the statute in light of everyday realities.

When a challenge to an agency construction of a statutory provision, fairly conceptualized, really centers on the wisdom of the agency's policy, rather than whether it is a reasonable choice within a gap left open by Congress, the challenge must fail. In such a case, federal judges—who have no constituency—have a duty to respect legitimate policy choices made by those who do. The responsibilities for assessing the wisdom of such policy choices and resolving the struggle between competing views of the public interest are not judicial ones: "Our Constitution vests such responsibilities in the political branches." *TVA v. Hill*, 437 U.S. 153, 195 (1978).

We hold that the EPA's definition of the term "source" is a permissible construction of the statute which seeks to accommodate progress in reducing air pollution with economic growth. "The Regulations which the Administrator has adopted provide what the agency could allowably view as . . . [an] effective reconciliation of these twofold ends. . . ." *United States v. Shimer*, 367 U.S., at 383.

The judgment of the Court of Appeals is reversed.

It is so ordered.

Justice MARSHALL and Justice REHNQUIST took no part in the consideration or decision of these cases.

Justice O'CONNOR took no part in the decision of these cases.

QUESTION SET 9.27

Review & Synthesis

1. Restate the test *Chevron* created to determine whether a reviewing court should defer to (i.e., accept as controlling) an agency's interpretation of an ambiguous statute. How many steps does the test have, and what must a reviewing court consider at each of those steps?

2. Would you characterize the *Chevron* test as adopting strong deference (courts should accept agency interpretations of ambiguous statutes in most cases) or weak deference (courts should independently interpret ambiguous statutes in most cases, with some consideration for the implementing agency's views)? In this respect, how does the deference approach adopted in *Chevron* compare with those in *NLRB v. Hearst Publications, Inc.* and *Skidmore v. Swift & Co.*?

3. By what decision-making process did the EPA Administrator conclude that the "bubble concept" was a permissible interpretation of the term "stationary source" as used in the Clean Air Act Amendments of 1977? How did this process differ from the one used by the National Labor Relations Board in *Hearst*? From the decision-making process used by the Wage and Hour Administrator in *Skidmore*? Did the Court consider the EPA's decision-making process analytically meaningful in deciding whether to defer to its interpretations of the CAA?

4. Consider that the "bubble" interpretation of "stationary source" would have lightened the overall regulatory burden placed on powerplants, consistent with then-President Ronald Reagan's deregulatory agenda. According to the Court, what role should the President's political supervision play in the decision to defer to an agency's statutory interpretation? Do you think the President can dictate how an agency interprets the statutes it is charged with enforcing? The Court implied that concerns over agencies' political accountability are answered by the fact that they ultimately answer to the President, who must stand for election. Do you agree? Does that mean courts should give less deference to statutory interpretation by independent agencies?

5. *Chevron* makes no mention of the judicial review standards enumerated in Administrative Procedure Act § 706(2) (nor of any other part of the APA for that matter). How does the *Chevron* test square with APA § 706, which instructs reviewing courts to "decide all relevant questions of law, interpret constitutional and statutory provisions, and determine the meaning or applicability of the terms of an agency action"? Doesn't this

language require reviewing courts to come to an independent judgment on the meaning of ambiguous regulatory statutes?

6. Recall from Chapter 2 that the Supreme Court has been extremely reluctant to invalidate Congress' delegations of legislative authority to federal agencies, even when those delegations are quite broad and may have been invalidated at earlier points in the Court's history. How does the deference regime established in *Chevron* relate to the Court's nondelegation jurisprudence?

7. *Chevron* frames judicial deference to agency interpretations as a function of congressional intent. Congress ultimately decides whether courts must accept administrative interpretations of ambiguous statutes. Do you think this position is constitutionally sound? In *Marbury v. Madison*, Chief Justice John Marshall famously asserted that "[i]t is emphatically the province and duty of the judicial department to say what the law is. Those who apply the rule to particular cases, must of necessity expound and interpret that rule." 5 U.S. (1 Cranch) 137, 177 (1803). Chapter 7 of the Administrative Procedure Act (5 U.S.C. §§ 701-706) can be read as echoing this idea and the interpretation of Article III underlying it. Again, § 706 instructs reviewing courts to "decide all relevant questions of law, interpret constitutional and statutory provisions, and determine the meaning or applicability of the terms of an agency action." Is the power of statutory interpretation a matter of congressional choice, or is it an inextricable part of the judicial power vested in federal courts by Article III?

Chevron distilled the judicial deference analysis into two discrete inquiries, both of which must be answered in the affirmative for courts to adopt an agency's interpretation of its organic statute. The facial simplicity of this test belies its numerous analytical complexities. Not only has each step generated substantial debate and uncertainty, the Court has in effect developed two *more* steps that generally narrow the circumstances under which courts must defer. The materials that follow address each of these steps in turn.

a. *Chevron* Step "Zero": Acting with the Force of Law

The EPA's adoption of the "bubble concept" in *Chevron* was the product of notice-and-comment rulemaking under APA § 553. Although this is routinely described as "informal" rulemaking, the process is actually quite regularized: among other things, it requires public notice and input, an explanation of a rule's purpose and identification of reasons supporting its promulgation, creation of a rulemaking record, and publication of the final rule in the Federal Register. *See* Chapter 5. By following this process, Congress permits agencies to act with the force of law: they can promulgate general rules that, like federal legislation, are legally binding on the general public.

After *Chevron*, courts struggled with whether interpretations generated in informal rulemakings or similarly formal proceedings (e.g., formal rulemaking and formal adjudication) were the only ones eligible for deference. As discussed in Chapter 4, agencies sometimes act through processes that do not feature notice to or comments from the public, wide publication, or the creation of an easily identifiable evidentiary record. Opinion letters and internal agency policy manuals are often created in this fashion. Should courts defer to interpretations generated through these processes as well?

The Supreme Court provided an initial answer to this question in *Christensen v. Harris County*, 529 U.S. 576 (2000). The Fair Labor Standards Act of 1938 allows public employers to "pay" their employees with compensatory time instead of cash. Compensatory time is essentially time off from work with full pay, and it accrues until used. Above a certain amount of accrued compensatory time, however, employers may be obligated to pay for their employees' overtime with cash. Concerned about its financial capacity to make such payments, the sheriff's department of Harris County, Texas, considered a policy that would have forced its deputy sheriffs to use their accrued compensatory time. It sought and received an opinion from the U.S. Department of Labor's Wage and Hour Division on the policy's permissibility under the FLSA and applicable regulations. In an opinion letter, the Acting Division Administrator stated "that a public employer may schedule its nonexempt employees to use their accrued FLSA compensatory time as directed if [a] prior agreement specifically provides such a provision," adding that "[a]bsent such an agreement, it is our position that neither the statute nor the regulations permit an employer to require an employee to use accrued compensatory time." Although the county had reached no prior agreement with its deputies, it adopted the policy compelling their use of accrued compensatory time anyway. The deputies sued, arguing that the Acting Administrator's opinion letter was entitled to *Chevron* deference. The Supreme Court sided with the county, making the following observations about the Acting Administrator's interpretation of the statute:

> . . . [Petitioners] argue that the agency opinion letter is entitled to deference under our decision in *Chevron U.S.A. Inc. v. Natural Resources Defense Council, Inc.*, 467 U.S. 837 (1984). In *Chevron*, we held that a court must give effect to an agency's regulation containing a reasonable interpretation of an ambiguous statute.
>
> Here, however, we confront an interpretation contained in an opinion letter, not one arrived at after, for example, a formal adjudication or notice-and-comment rulemaking. Interpretations such as those in opinion letters—like interpretations contained in policy statements, agency manuals, and enforcement guidelines, all of which lack the force of law—do not warrant *Chevron*-style deference. Instead, interpretations contained in formats such as opinion letters are "entitled to respect" under our decision

in *Skidmore v. Swift & Co.*, 323 U.S. 134, 140 (1944), but only to the extent that those interpretations have the "power to persuade," *ibid.* As explained above, we find unpersuasive the agency's interpretation of the statute at issue in this case.

529 U.S. at 586-87. Concurring in the judgment, Justice Scalia appeared somewhat surprised by the majority's reliance on *Skidmore*:

> I join the judgment of the Court and all of its opinion except Part III, which declines to give effect to the position of the Department of Labor in this case because its opinion letter is entitled only to so-called "*Skidmore* deference," *see Skidmore v. Swift & Co.*, 323 U.S. 134, 140 (1944). *Skidmore* deference to authoritative agency views is an anachronism, dating from an era in which we declined to give agency interpretations (including interpretive regulations, as opposed to "legislative rules") authoritative effect. This former judicial attitude accounts for that provision of the 1946 Administrative Procedure Act which exempted "interpretative rules" (since they would not be authoritative) from the notice-and-comment requirements applicable to rulemaking, *see* 5 U.S.C. § 553(b)(A).
>
> That era came to an end with our watershed decision in *Chevron U.S.A. Inc. v. Natural Resources Defense Council, Inc.*, 467 U.S. 837, 844 (1984), which established the principle that "a court may not substitute its own construction of a statutory provision for a reasonable interpretation made by the administrator of an agency." While *Chevron* in fact involved an interpretive regulation, the rationale of the case was not limited to that context: "'The power of an administrative agency to administer a congressionally created . . . program necessarily requires the formulation of policy and the making of rules to fill any gap left, implicitly or explicitly, by Congress.'" *Id.*, at 843, quoting *Morton v. Ruiz*, 415 U.S. 199, 231 (1974). Quite appropriately, therefore, we have accorded *Chevron* deference not only to agency regulations, but to authoritative agency positions set forth in a variety of other formats. . . .

Id. at 589-90 (Scalia, J., concurring in part and concurring in the judgment).

Drawn perhaps by unfinished business, a year later the Court again addressed whether agency interpretations outside of formal decision-making processes could receive *Chevron* deference.

United States v. Mead Corp.
533 U.S. 218 (2001)

Justice SOUTER delivered the opinion of the Court.

The question is whether a tariff classification ruling by the United States Customs Service deserves judicial deference. The Federal Circuit rejected

Customs's invocation of *Chevron U.S.A. Inc. v. Natural Resources Defense Council, Inc.,* 467 U.S. 837 (1984), in support of such a ruling, to which it gave no deference. We agree that a tariff classification has no claim to judicial deference under *Chevron,* there being no indication that Congress intended such a ruling to carry the force of law, but we hold that under *Skidmore v. Swift & Co.,* 323 U.S. 134 (1944), the ruling is eligible to claim respect according to its persuasiveness.

I

A

Imports are taxed under the Harmonized Tariff Schedule of the United States (HTSUS), 19 U.S.C. § 1202. Title 19 U.S.C. § 1500(b) provides that Customs "shall, under rules and regulations prescribed by the Secretary [of the Treasury] . . . fix the final classification and rate of duty applicable to . . . merchandise" under the HTSUS. 19 U.S.C. § 1500(b). Section 1502(a) provides that

> the Secretary of the Treasury shall establish and promulgate such rules and regulations not inconsistent with the law (including regulations establishing procedures for the issuance of binding rulings prior to the entry of the merchandise concerned), and may disseminate such information as may be necessary to secure a just, impartial, and uniform appraisement of imported merchandise and the classification and assessment of duties thereon at the various ports of entry.

See also § 1624 (general delegation to Secretary to issue rules and regulations for the admission of goods).

The Secretary provides for tariff rulings before the entry of goods by regulations authorizing "ruling letters" setting tariff classifications for particular imports. 19 CFR § 177.8 (2000). A ruling letter

> represents the official position of the Customs Service with respect to the particular transaction or issue described therein and is binding on all Customs Service personnel in accordance with the provisions of this section until modified or revoked. In the absence of a change of practice or other modification or revocation which affects the principle of the ruling set forth in the ruling letter, that principle may be cited as authority in the disposition of transactions involving the same circumstances. § 177.9(a).

After the transaction that gives it birth, a ruling letter is to "be applied only with respect to transactions involving articles identical to the sample submitted with the ruling request or to articles whose description is identical to the description set forth in the ruling letter." § 177.9(b)(2). As a general matter, such a letter is "subject to modification or revocation without notice to any person, except the person to whom the letter was addressed," § 177.9(c), and the regulations consequently provide that "no other person should rely on the ruling letter or assume that the principles of that ruling will be applied in connection with any transaction other than the one described in the letter," *ibid.* Since ruling letters respond to transactions of the moment, they are not subject to notice and comment before being issued, may be published but need only be made "available for public inspection," 19 U.S.C. § 1625(a), and, at the time this action arose, could be modified without notice and comment under most circumstances, 19 CFR § 177.10(c) (2000). A broader notice-and-comment requirement for modification of prior rulings was added by statute in 1993, Pub. L. 103-182 § 623, 107 Stat. 2186, codified at 19 U.S.C. § 1625(c), and took effect after this case arose.

Any of the 46 port-of-entry Customs offices may issue ruling letters, and so may the Customs Headquarters Office, in providing "advice or guidance as to the interpretation or proper application of the Customs and related laws with respect to a specific Customs transaction [which] may be requested by Customs Service field offices . . . at any time, whether the transaction is prospective, current, or completed," 19 CFR § 177.11(a) (2000). Most ruling letters contain little or no reasoning, but simply describe goods and state the appropriate category and tariff. A few letters, like the Headquarters ruling at issue here, set out a rationale in some detail.

B

Respondent, the Mead Corporation, imports "day planners," three-ring binders with pages having room for notes of daily schedules and phone numbers and addresses, together with a calendar and suchlike. The tariff schedule on point falls under the HTSUS heading for "registers, account books, notebooks, order books, receipt books, letter pads, memorandum pads, diaries and similar articles," HTSUS subheading 4820.10, which comprises two subcategories. Items in the first, "diaries, notebooks and address books, bound; memorandum pads, letter pads and similar articles," were subject to a tariff of 4.0% at the time in controversy. Objects in the second, covering "other" items, were free of duty.

Between 1989 and 1993, Customs repeatedly treated day planners under the "other" HTSUS subheading. In January 1993, however, Customs changed its position, and issued a Headquarters ruling letter classifying Mead's day planners as "Diaries . . . , bound" subject to tariff under subheading 4820.10.20. That letter was short on explanation, but after Mead's protest, Customs Headquarters issued a new letter, carefully reasoned but never published, reaching the same conclusion. This letter considered two definitions of "diary" from the Oxford English Dictionary, the first covering a daily journal of the past day's events, the second a book including " 'printed dates for daily memoranda and jottings; also . . . calendars. . . .' " *Id.* at 33a-34a (quoting Oxford English Dictionary 321 (Compact ed. 1982)). Customs concluded that "diary" was not confined to the first, in part because the broader definition reflects commercial usage and hence the "commercial identity of these items in the marketplace." As for the definition of "bound," Customs concluded that HTSUS was not referring to "bookbinding," but to a less exact sort of fastening described in the Harmonized Commodity Description and Coding System Explanatory Notes to Heading 4820, which spoke of binding by " 'reinforcements or fittings of metal, plastics, etc.' "

Customs rejected Mead's further protest of the second Headquarters ruling letter, and Mead filed suit in the Court of International Trade (CIT). The CIT granted the Government's motion for summary judgment, adopting Customs's reasoning without saying anything about deference. . . .

The Federal Circuit . . . reversed the CIT and held that Customs classification rulings should not get *Chevron* deference. . . . Rulings are not preceded by notice and comment as under the Administrative Procedure Act (APA), 5 U.S.C. § 553, they "do not carry the force of law and are not, like regulations, intended to clarify the rights and obligations of importers beyond the specific case under review." 185 F.3d at 1307. The appeals court thought classification rulings had a weaker *Chevron* claim even than Internal Revenue Service interpretive rulings, to which that court gives no deference; unlike rulings by the IRS, Customs rulings issue from many locations and need not be published. 185 F.3d at 1307-1308.

The Court of Appeals accordingly gave no deference at all to the ruling classifying the Mead day planners and rejected the agency's reasoning as to both "diary" and "bound." It thought that planners were not diaries because they had no space for "relatively extensive notations about events, observations, feelings, or thoughts" in the past. *Id.* at 1310. And it concluded that diaries "bound' in subheading 4810.10.20 presupposed "unbound" diaries, such that treating ring-fastened diaries as "bound" would leave the "unbound diary" an empty category. *Id.* at 1311.

We granted certiorari, in order to consider the limits of *Chevron* deference owed to administrative practice in applying a statute. We hold that administrative implementation of a particular statutory provision qualifies for *Chevron* deference when it appears that Congress delegated authority to the agency generally to make rules carrying the force of law, and that the agency interpretation claiming deference was promulgated in the exercise of that authority. Delegation of such authority may be shown in a variety of ways, as by an agency's power to engage in adjudication or notice-and-comment rulemaking, or by some other indication of a comparable congressional intent. The Customs ruling at issue here fails to qualify, although the possibility that it deserves some deference under *Skidmore* leads us to vacate and remand.

II

A

When Congress has "explicitly left a gap for an agency to fill, there is an express delegation of authority to the agency to elucidate a specific provision of the statute by regulation," *Chevron*, 467 U.S. at 843-844, and any ensuing regulation is binding in the courts unless procedurally defective, arbitrary or capricious in substance, or manifestly contrary to the statute. *See id.* at 844; *United States v. Morton*, 467 U.S. 822, 834 (1984); APA, 5 U.S.C. §§ 706(2) (A), (D). But whether or not they enjoy any express delegation of authority on a particular question, agencies charged with applying a statute necessarily make all sorts of interpretive choices, and while not all of those choices bind judges to follow them, they certainly may influence courts facing questions the agencies have already answered. "The well-reasoned views of the agencies implementing a statute 'constitute a body of experience and informed judgment to which courts and litigants may properly resort for guidance,'" *Bragdon v. Abbott*, 524 U.S. 624, 642 (1998) (quoting *Skidmore*, 323 U.S. at 139-140), and "we have long recognized that considerable weight should be accorded to an executive department's construction of a statutory scheme it is entrusted to administer. . . ." *Chevron*, *supra*, at 844 (footnote omitted). The fair measure of deference to an agency administering its own statute has been understood to vary with circumstances, and courts have looked to the degree of the agency's care, its consistency, and to the persuasiveness of the agency's position, *see Skidmore*, *supra*, at 139-140. The approach has produced a spectrum of judicial responses, from great respect at one end, *see, e.g., Aluminum Co. of America v. Central Lincoln Peoples' Util. Dist.*, 467 U.S. 380, 389-390 (1984) ("'substantial deference'" to administrative construction), to near indifference at the other, *see, e.g., Bowen v. Georgetown Univ. Hospital*, 488 U.S. 204, 212-213 (1988) (interpretation advanced for the first time in a litigation brief). Justice Jackson summed things up in *Skidmore v. Swift & Co.*:

> The weight [accorded to an administrative] judgment in a particular case will depend upon the thoroughness evident in its consideration, the validity of its reasoning, its consistency with earlier and later pronouncements, and all those factors which give it power to persuade, if lacking power to control. 323 U.S. at 140.

Since 1984, we have identified a category of interpretive choices distinguished by an additional reason for judicial deference. This Court in *Chevron* recognized that Congress not only engages in express delegation of specific interpretive authority, but that "sometimes the legislative delegation to an agency on a particular question is implicit." 467 U.S. at 844. Congress, that is, may not have expressly delegated authority or responsibility to implement a particular provision or fill a particular gap. Yet it can still be apparent from the agency's generally conferred authority and other statutory circumstances that Congress would expect the agency to be able to speak with the force of law when it addresses ambiguity in the statute or fills a space in the enacted law, even one about which "Congress did not actually have an intent" as to a particular result. *Id.* at 845. When circumstances implying such an expectation exist, a reviewing court has no business rejecting an agency's exercise of its generally conferred authority to resolve a particular statutory ambiguity simply because the agency's chosen resolution seems unwise, *see id.* at 845-846, but is obliged to accept the agency's position if Congress has not previously spoken to the point at issue and the agency's interpretation is reasonable, *see id.* at 842-845; *cf.* 5 U.S.C. § 706(2) (a reviewing court shall set aside agency action, findings, and conclusions found to be "arbitrary, capricious, an abuse of discretion, or otherwise not in accordance with law").

We have recognized a very good indicator of delegation meriting *Chevron* treatment in express congressional authorizations to engage in the process of rulemaking or adjudication that produces regulations or rulings for which deference is claimed. *See, e.g., EEOC v. Arabian American Oil Co.,* 499 U.S. 244, 257 (1991) (no *Chevron* deference to agency guideline where congressional delegation did not include the power to "'promulgate rules or regulations'" (quoting *General Elec. Co. v. Gilbert,* 429 U.S. 125, 141 (1976)); *see also Christensen v. Harris County,* 529 U.S. 576, 596-597 (2000) (Breyer, J., dissenting) (where it is in doubt that Congress actually intended to delegate particular interpretive authority to an agency, *Chevron* is "inapplicable"). It is fair to assume generally that Congress contemplates administrative action with the effect of law when it provides for a relatively formal administrative procedure tending to foster the fairness and deliberation that should underlie a pronouncement of such force. *Cf. Smiley v. Citibank (South Dakota), N. A.,* 517 U.S. 735, 74 (1996) (APA notice and comment "designed to assure due deliberation"). Thus, the overwhelming number of our cases applying *Chevron* deference have reviewed the fruits of notice-and-comment rulemaking or formal adjudication. That said, and as significant as notice-and-comment is in pointing to *Chevron* authority, the want of that procedure here does not decide the case, for we have sometimes found reasons for *Chevron* deference even when no such administrative formality was required and none was afforded, *see, e.g., NationsBank of N. C., N. A. v. Variable Annuity Life Ins. Co.,* 513 U.S. 251, 256-257 (1995). The fact that the tariff classification here was not a product of such formal process does not alone, therefore, bar the application of *Chevron.*

There are, nonetheless, ample reasons to deny *Chevron* deference here. The authorization for classification rulings, and Customs's practice in making them, present a case far removed not only from notice-and-comment process, but from any other circumstances reasonably suggesting that Congress ever thought of classification rulings as deserving the deference claimed for them here.

B

No matter which angle we choose for viewing the Customs ruling letter in this case, it fails to qualify under *Chevron*. On the face of the statute, to begin with, the terms of the congressional delegation give no indication that Congress meant to delegate authority to Customs to issue classification rulings with the force of law. We are not, of course, here making any global statement about Customs's authority, for it is true that the general rulemaking power conferred on Customs, *see* 19 U.S.C. § 1624, authorizes some regulation with the force of law. . . . It is true as well that Congress had classification rulings in mind when it explicitly authorized, in a parenthetical, the issuance of "regulations establishing procedures for the issuance of binding rulings prior to the entry of the merchandise concerned," 19 U.S.C. § 1502(a). The reference to binding classifications does not, however, bespeak the legislative type of activity that would naturally bind more than the parties to the ruling, once the goods classified are admitted into this country. And though the statute's direction to disseminate "information" necessary to "secure" uniformity, 19 U.S.C. § 1502 (a), seems to assume that a ruling may be precedent in later transactions, precedential value alone does not add up to *Chevron* entitlement; interpretive rules may sometimes function as precedents . . . and they enjoy no *Chevron* status as a class. In any event, any precedential claim of a classification ruling is counterbalanced by the provision for independent review of Customs classifications by the CIT, *see* 28 U.S.C. §§ 2638-2640; the scheme for CIT review includes a provision that treats classification rulings on par with the Secretary's rulings on "valuation, rate of duty, marking, restricted merchandise, entry requirements, drawbacks, vessel repairs, or similar matters," § 1581(h); *see* § 2639(b). It is hard to imagine a congressional understanding more at odds with the *Chevron* regime.

It is difficult, in fact, to see in the agency practice itself any indication that Customs ever set out with a lawmaking pretense in mind when it undertook to make classifications like these. Customs does not generally engage in notice-and-comment practice when issuing them, and their treatment by the agency makes it clear that a letter's binding character as a ruling stops short of third parties; Customs has regarded a classification as conclusive only as between itself and the importer to whom it was issued, 19 CFR § 177.9(c) (2000), and even then only until Customs has given advance notice of intended change, §§ 177.9(a), (c). Other importers are in fact warned against assuming any right of detrimental reliance. § 177.9(c).

Indeed, to claim that classifications have legal force is to ignore the reality that 46 different Customs offices issue 10,000 to 15,000 of them each year. Any suggestion that rulings intended to have the force of law are being churned out at a rate of 10,000 a year at an agency's 46 scattered offices is simply self-refuting. Although the circumstances are less startling here, with a Headquarters letter in issue, none of the relevant statutes recognizes this category of rulings as separate or different from others; there is thus no indication that a more potent delegation might have been understood as going to Headquarters even when Headquarters provides developed reasoning, as it did in this instance.

Nor do the amendments to the statute made effective after this case arose disturb our conclusion. The new law requires Customs to provide notice-and-comment procedures only when modifying or revoking a prior classification ruling or modifying the treatment accorded to substantially identical transactions, 19 U.S.C. § 1625(c); and under its regulations, Customs sees itself obliged to provide notice-and-comment procedures only when "changing a practice" so as to produce a tariff increase, or in the imposition of a restriction or prohibition, or when Customs Headquarters determines that "the matter is of sufficient importance to involve the interests of domestic industry," 19 CFR §§ 177.10(c)(1)(2) (2000). The statutory changes reveal no new congressional objective of treating classification decisions generally as rulemaking with force of law, nor do they suggest any intent to create a *Chevron* patchwork of classification rulings, some with force of law, some without.

In sum, classification rulings are best treated like "interpretations contained in policy statements, agency manuals, and enforcement guidelines." *Christensen*, 529 U.S. at 587. They are beyond the *Chevron* pale.

C

To agree with the Court of Appeals that Customs ruling letters do not fall within *Chevron* is not, however, to place them outside the pale of any deference whatever. *Chevron* did nothing to eliminate *Skidmore's* holding that an agency's interpretation may merit some deference whatever its form, given the "specialized experience and broader investigations and information" available to the agency, 323 U.S. at 139, and given the value of uniformity in its administrative and judicial understandings of what a national law requires, *Id.* at 140. *See generally Metropolitan Stevedore Co. v. Rambo*, 521 U.S. 121, 136, 138 (1997) (reasonable agency interpretations carry "at least some added persuasive force" where *Chevron* is inapplicable); *Reno v. Koray*, 515 U.S. 50, 61, (1995) (according "some deference" to an interpretive rule that "does not require notice and comment"); *Martin v. Occupational Safety and Health Review Comm'n*, 499 U.S. 144, 157 (1991) ("some weight" is due to informal interpretations though not "the same deference as norms that derive from the exercise of . . . delegated lawmaking powers").

There is room at least to raise a *Skidmore* claim here, where the regulatory scheme is highly detailed, and Customs can bring the benefit of specialized experience to bear on the subtle questions in this case: whether the daily planner with room for brief daily entries falls under "diaries," when diaries are grouped with "notebooks and address books, bound; memorandum pads, letter pads and similar articles," HTSUS subheading 4820.10.20; and whether a planner with a ring binding should qualify as "bound," when a binding may be typified by a book, but also may have "reinforcements or fittings of metal, plastics, etc.," Harmonized Commodity Description and Coding System Explanatory Notes to Heading 4820, p. 687 (cited in Customs Headquarters letter, App. to Pet. for Cert. 45a). A classification ruling in this situation may therefore at least seek a respect proportional to its "power to persuade," *Skidmore, supra,* at 140; *see also Christensen,* 529 U.S. at 587. Such a ruling may surely claim the merit of its writer's thoroughness, logic and expertness, its fit with prior interpretations, and any other sources of weight. . . .

* * *

Since the *Skidmore* assessment called for here ought to be made in the first instance by the Court of Appeals for the Federal Circuit or the CIT, we go no further than to vacate the judgment and remand the case for further proceedings consistent with this opinion.

It is so ordered.

Justice SCALIA, dissenting. . . .

I

Only five years ago, the Court described the *Chevron* doctrine as follows: "We accord deference to agencies under *Chevron* . . . because of a presumption that Congress, when it left ambiguity in a statute meant for implementation by an agency, understood that the ambiguity would be resolved, first and foremost, by the agency, and desired the agency (rather than the courts) to possess whatever degree of discretion the ambiguity allows," *Smiley v. Citibank (South Dakota), N. A.,* 517 U.S. 735, 740-741 (1996) (citing *Chevron U.S.A. Inc. v. Natural Resources Defense Council, Inc.,* 467 U.S. 837, 843-844 (1984)). Today the Court collapses this doctrine, announcing instead a presumption that agency discretion does not exist unless the statute, expressly or impliedly, says so. While the Court disclaims any hard-and-fast rule for determining the existence of discretion-conferring intent, it asserts that "a very good indicator [is] express congressional authorizations to engage in the process of rulemaking or adjudication that produces regulations or rulings for which deference is claimed." Only when agencies act through "adjudication[,] notice-and-comment rulemaking or . . . some other [procedure] indicating comparable congressional intent [whatever that means]" is *Chevron* deference applicable—because these "relatively formal administrative procedures [designed] to foster . . . fairness and deliberation" bespeak (according to the Court) congressional willingness to have the agency, rather than the courts, resolve statutory ambiguities. Once it is determined that *Chevron* deference is not in order, the uncertainty is not at an end—and indeed is just beginning. Litigants cannot then assume that the statutory question is one for the courts to determine, according to traditional interpretive principles and by their own judicial lights. No, the Court now resurrects, in full force, the pre-*Chevron* doctrine of *Skidmore* deference, whereby "the fair measure of deference to an agency administering its own statute . . . varies with circumstances," including "the degree of the agency's care, its consistency, formality, and relative expertness, and . . . the persuasiveness of the agency's position." The Court has largely replaced *Chevron*, in other words, with that test most beloved by a court unwilling to be held to rules (and most feared by litigants who want to know what to expect): th' ol' "totality of the circumstances" test.

The Court's new doctrine is neither sound in principle nor sustainable in practice.

A

As to principle: The doctrine of *Chevron*—that all authoritative agency interpretations of statutes they are charged with administering deserve deference—was rooted in a legal presumption of congressional intent, important to the division of powers between the Second and Third Branches. When, *Chevron* said, Congress leaves an ambiguity in a statute that is to be administered by an executive agency, it is presumed that Congress meant to give the agency discretion, within the limits of reasonable interpretation, as to how the ambiguity is to be resolved. By committing enforcement of the statute to an agency rather than the courts, Congress committed its initial and primary interpretation to that branch as well. There is some question whether *Chevron* was faithful to the text of the Administrative Procedure Act (APA), which it did not even bother to cite. But it was in accord with the origins of federal-court judicial review. Judicial control of federal executive officers was principally exercised through the prerogative writ of mandamus. That writ generally would not issue unless the executive officer was acting plainly beyond the scope of his authority. . . .

The basis in principle for today's new doctrine can be described as follows: The background rule is that ambiguity in legislative instructions to agencies is to be resolved not by the agencies but by the judges. Specific congressional intent to depart from this rule must be found—and while there is no single touchstone for such intent it can generally be found when Congress has authorized the agency to act through (what the Court says is) relatively formal procedures such as informal rulemaking and formal (and informal?) adjudication, and when the agency in fact employs such procedures. The Court's background rule is contradicted by the origins of judicial review of administrative action. But in addition, the Court's principal criterion of congressional intent to supplant its background rule seems to me quite implausible. There is no necessary connection between the formality of procedure and the power of the entity administering the procedure to resolve authoritatively questions of law. The most formal of the procedures the Court refers to — formal adjudication — is modeled after the process used in trial courts, which of course are not generally accorded deference on questions of law. The purpose of such a procedure is to produce a closed record for determination and review of the facts — which implies nothing about the power of the agency subjected to the procedure to resolve authoritatively questions of law.

As for informal rulemaking: While formal adjudication procedures are prescribed (either by statute or by the Constitution), *see* 5 U.S.C. §§ 554, 556, informal rulemaking is more typically authorized but not required. Agencies with such authority are free to give guidance through rulemaking, but they may proceed to administer their statute case-by-case, "making law" as they implement their program (not necessarily through formal adjudication). *See NLRB v. Bell Aerospace Co.,* 416 U.S. 267, 290-295 (1974); *SEC v. Chenery Corp. (Chenery II),* 332 U.S. 194, 202-203 (1947). Is it likely — or indeed even plausible — that Congress meant, when such an agency chooses rulemaking, to accord the administrators of that agency, and their successors, the flexibility of interpreting the ambiguous statute now one way, and later another; but, when such an agency chooses case-by-case administration, to eliminate all future agency discretion by having that same ambiguity resolved authoritatively (and forever) by the courts? Surely that makes no sense. It is also the case that certain significant categories of rules — those involving grant and benefit programs, for example, are exempt from the requirements of informal rulemaking. *See* 5 U.S.C. § 553(a)(2). Under the Court's novel theory, when an agency takes advantage of that exemption its rules will be deprived of *Chevron* deference, i.e., authoritative effect. Was this either the plausible intent of the APA rulemaking exemption, or the plausible intent of the Congress that established the grant or benefit program?

Some decisions that are neither informal rulemaking nor formal adjudication are required to be made personally by a Cabinet Secretary, without any prescribed procedures. *See e.g., United States v. Giordano,* 416 U.S. 505, 508 (1974) (involving application of 18 U.S.C. § 2516 (1970 ed.), requiring wiretap applications to be authorized by "the Attorney General, or any Assistant Attorney General specially designated by the Attorney General"); *D.C. Federation of Civic Assns. v. Volpe,* 459 F.2d 1231, 1248-1249 (D.C. Cir. 1971) (involving application of 23 U.S.C. § 138 (1970 ed.) requiring the Secretary of Transportation to determine that there is "no feasible and prudent alternative to the use of" publicly owned parkland for a federally funded highway), cert. denied, 405 U.S. 1030 (1972). Is it conceivable that decisions specifically committed to these high-level officers are meant to be accorded no deference, while decisions by an administrative law judge left in place without further discretionary agency review, *see* 5 U.S.C. § 557(b), are authoritative? This seems to me quite absurd, and not at all in accord with any plausible actual intent of Congress.

B

As for the practical effects of the new rule:

1

The principal effect will be protracted confusion. As noted above, the one test for *Chevron* deference that the Court enunciates is wonderfully imprecise: whether "Congress delegated authority to the agency generally to make rules carrying the force of law, . . . as by . . . adjudication[,] notice-and-comment rulemaking, or . . . some other [procedure] indicating comparable congressional intent." But even this description does not do justice to the utter flabbiness of the Court's criterion, since, in order to maintain the fiction that the new test is really just the old one, applied consistently throughout our case law, the Court must make a virtually open-ended exception to its already imprecise guidance: In the present case, it tells us, the absence of notice-and-comment rulemaking (and "[who knows?] [of] some other [procedure] indicating comparable congressional intent") is not enough to decide the question of *Chevron* deference, "for we have sometimes found reasons for *Chevron* deference even when no such administrative formality was required and none was afforded." The opinion then goes on to consider a grab bag of other factors—including the factor that used to be the sole criterion for *Chevron* deference: whether the interpretation represented the authoritative position of the agency. It is hard to know what the lower courts are to make of today's guidance.

2

Another practical effect of today's opinion will be an artificially induced increase in informal rulemaking. Buy stock in the [Government Printing Office]. Since informal rulemaking and formal adjudication are the only more-or-less safe harbors from the storm that the Court has unleashed; and since formal adjudication is not an option but must be mandated by statute or constitutional command; informal rulemaking—which the Court was once careful to make voluntary unless required by statute—will now become a virtual necessity. As I have described, the Court's safe harbor requires not merely that the agency have been given rulemaking authority, but also that the agency have employed rulemaking as the means of resolving the statutory ambiguity. (It is hard to understand why that should be so. Surely the mere conferral of rulemaking authority demonstrates—if one accepts the

Court's logic—a congressional intent to allow the agency to resolve ambiguities. And given that intent, what difference does it make that the agency chooses instead to use another perfectly permissible means for that purpose?) Moreover, the majority's approach will have a perverse effect on the rules that do emerge, given the principle (which the Court leaves untouched today) that judges must defer to reasonable agency interpretations of their own regulations. Agencies will now have high incentive to rush out barebones, ambiguous rules construing statutory ambiguities, which they can then in turn further clarify through informal rulings entitled to judicial respect.

3

Worst of all, the majority's approach will lead to the ossification of large portions of our statutory law. Where *Chevron* applies, statutory ambiguities remain ambiguities subject to the agency's ongoing clarification. They create a space, so to speak, for the exercise of continuing agency discretion. As *Chevron* itself held, the Environmental Protection Agency can interpret "stationary source" to mean a single smokestack, can later replace that interpretation with the "bubble concept" embracing an entire plant, and if that proves undesirable can return again to the original interpretation. 467 U.S. at 853-859, 865-866. For the indeterminately large number of statutes taken out of *Chevron* by today's decision, however, ambiguity (and hence flexibility) will cease with the first judicial resolution. *Skidmore* deference gives the agency's current position some vague and uncertain amount of respect, but it does not, like *Chevron*, leave the matter within the control of the Executive Branch for the future. Once the court has spoken, it becomes *unlawful* for the agency to take a contradictory position; the statute now says what the court has prescribed. It will be bad enough when this ossification occurs as a result of judicial determination (under today's new principles) that there is no affirmative indication of congressional intent to "delegate"; but it will be positively bizarre when it occurs simply because of an agency's failure to act by rulemaking (rather than informal adjudication) before the issue is presented to the courts. . . .

4

And finally, the majority's approach compounds the confusion it creates by breathing new life into the anachronism of *Skidmore*, which sets forth a sliding scale of deference owed an agency's interpretation of a statute that is dependent "upon the thoroughness evident in [the agency's] consideration, the validity of its reasoning, its consistency with earlier and later pronouncements, and all those factors which give it power to persuade, if lacking power to control"; in this way, the appropriate measure of deference will be accorded the "body of experience and informed judgment" that such interpretations often embody. Justice Jackson's eloquence notwithstanding, the rule of *Skidmore* deference is an empty truism and a trifling statement of the obvious: A judge should take into account the well-considered views of expert observers.

It was possible to live with the indeterminacy of *Skidmore* deference in earlier times. But in an era when federal statutory law administered by federal agencies is pervasive, and when the ambiguities (intended or unintended) that those statutes contain are innumerable, totality-of-the-circumstances *Skidmore* deference is a recipe for uncertainty, unpredictability, and endless litigation. To condemn a vast body of agency action to that regime (all except rulemaking, formal (and informal?) adjudication, and whatever else might now and then be included within today's intentionally vague formulation of affirmative congressional intent to "delegate") is irresponsible. . . .

III

To decide the present case, I would adhere to the original formulation of *Chevron*. "'The power of an administrative agency to administer a congressionally created . . . program necessarily requires the formulation of policy and the making of rules to fill any gap left, implicitly or explicitly, by Congress,'" 467 U.S. at 843 (quoting *Morton v. Ruiz*, 415 U.S. 199, 231, (1974)). We accordingly presume—and our precedents have made clear to Congress that we presume—that, absent some clear textual indication to the contrary, "Congress, when it left ambiguity in a statute meant for implementation by an agency, understood that the ambiguity would be resolved, first and foremost, by the agency, and desired the agency (rather than the courts) to possess whatever degree of discretion the ambiguity allows," *Smiley*, 517 U.S. at 740-741 (citing *Chevron, supra*, at 843-844). *Chevron* sets forth an across-the-board presumption, which operates as a background rule of law against which Congress legislates: Ambiguity means Congress intended agency discretion. Any resolution of the ambiguity by the administering agency that is authoritative—that represents the official position of the agency—must be accepted by the courts if it is reasonable. . . .

There is no doubt that the Customs Service's interpretation represents the authoritative view of the agency. Although the actual ruling letter was signed by only the Director of the Commercial Rulings Branch of Customs Headquarters' Office of Regulations and Rulings, the Solicitor General of the United States has filed a brief, cosigned by the General Counsel of the Department of the Treasury, that represents the position set forth in the ruling letter to be the official position of the Customs Service. No one contends that it is merely a "*post hoc* rationalization" or an "agency litigating position wholly unsupported by regulations, rulings, or administrative practice," *Bowen v. Georgetown Univ. Hospital*, 488 U.S. 204, 212 (1988).

There is also no doubt that the Customs Service's interpretation is a reasonable one, whether or not judges would consider it the best. I will not belabor this point, since the Court evidently agrees: An interpretation that was unreasonable would not merit the remand that the Court decrees for consideration of *Skidmore* deference.

IV

Finally, and least importantly, even were I to accept the Court's revised version of *Chevron* as a correct statement of the law, I would still accord deference to the tariff classification ruling at issue in this case. For the case is indistinguishable, in that regard, from *NationsBank of N.C., N.A. v. Variable Annuity Life Ins. Co.*, 513 U.S. 251 (1995), which the Court acknowledges as an instance in which *Chevron* deference is warranted notwithstanding the absence of formal adjudication, notice-and-comment rulemaking, or comparable "administrative formality." Here, as in *NationsBank*, there is a tradition of great deference to the opinions of the agency head. . . .

For the reasons stated, I respectfully dissent from the Court's judgment. I would uphold the Customs Service's construction of Subheading 4820.10.20 of the Harmonized Tariff Schedule of the United States, 19 U.S.C. § 1202, and would reverse the contrary decision of the Court of Appeals. I dissent even more vigorously from the reasoning that produces the Court's judgment, and that makes today's decision one of the most significant opinions ever rendered by the Court dealing with the judicial review of administrative action. Its consequences will be enormous, and almost uniformly bad.

QUESTION SET 9.28

Review & Synthesis

1. Restate the *Chevron* test to take account of the Court's decision in *Mead*.

2. How did Justice Souter, writing for the majority, distinguish between those agency interpretations that Congress intended to have the force of law and those for which Congress had no such intention? What governance function does this distinction perform? Does it ensure agency reasonableness and careful deliberation in policymaking? Does it support public participation in agency decision-making? Does it enforce the separation of powers by preserving the historic role of courts to "say what the law is"? Something else?

3. Characterize the process by which Customs categorized Mead's day planners as "diaries . . . , bound" subject to tariff under the Harmonized Tariff Schedule of the United States. Was it an adjudication, a rulemaking, or something else? Was it formal or informal? How do you know?

4. Clearly, courts do not have to adopt agency interpretations produced through informal decision-making processes like those at issue in *Skidmore* and *Mead*. What, then, does *Skidmore* deference actually *require* courts to do? Do they have to specifically consider the agency's interpretation in their analysis? Do they have to directly address that interpretation and provide reasons for adopting or rejecting it? What guidance can we glean from the Court's decision in *Mead*?

5. Justice Scalia attacked the Court's invocations of *Skidmore* deference in both his *Christensen* concurrence and his *Mead* dissent. Under his reading of *Chevron*, courts must defer to "authoritative" agency interpretations of ambiguous provisions in the statutes they administer as long as those interpretations are "reasonable."

   a. Given that *Chevron* itself involved the EPA's adoption of the "bubble concept" through notice-and-comment rulemaking, do you think it can support the breadth of Justice Scalia's understanding of it?

   b. Given that he joined the Court's decision in *Christensen*, does it seem that Justice Scalia favored a broad presumption in favor of *Chevron* deference, regardless of the decision-making process employed by agencies?

   c. What effects would you expect such a presumption to have on agencies' political accountability, the level of public participation in their decision-making, and the power balance among the three Branches?

   d. Recall from Chapter 4 the issue of agency policy statements being mistaken — by the public and sometimes by the agencies themselves — as legally binding pronouncements. What effect would you expect Justice Scalia's *Chevron* deference approach to have on that issue?

6. *Mead*'s deference approach provides fewer *ex ante* assurances that agency interpretations will get *Chevron* deference. Justice Scalia's approach would provide far more *ex ante* assurances, although, as evidenced by his *Christensen* concurrence, no guarantees. Which approach do you think makes the most sense, and why?

Application & Analysis

1. The Social Security Act authorizes payment of disability insurance benefits and Supplemental Security Income to individuals with disabilities. For both benefit categories, the Act defines "disability" as an "inability to engage in any substantial gainful activity by reason of any medically determinable physical or mental impairment which can be expected to

result in death or which has lasted or can be expected to last for a continuous period of not less than 12 months." 42 U.S.C. § 423(d)(1)(A). The Social Security Administration ("SSA") considers this provision ambiguous as to whether an applicant must both be impaired and unable to "engage in any substantial gainful activity" for at least 12 months. Its position is that the 12-month requirement should apply to both conditions. It has expressed this view through a series of Social Security Rulings ("SSRs"). SSRs are written by individual officials within the SSA (including, at times, the Commissioner) and are published in the Federal Register. The SSA considers them binding within the agency.

Samir Patel suffers from a serious mental illness, which caused him to lose his full-time teaching job in October 2018. He found work as a part-time grocery store cashier in June 2019, and by December he was working in that position full time. In early 2020, he applied to the SSA for both disability insurance benefits and Supplemental Security Income. The agency concluded that Patel had been disabled for only 11 months—from October 2018 when he lost his teaching job to September 2019 when he had earned enough for the SSA to consider him engaged in gainful activity. Since it evaluated Patel's application more than 12 months after he lost his teaching job, the SSA took account of the fact that he had started working again after only 11 months. As a result, it denied his benefits claims.

Patel seeks judicial review of the denial. He argues that SSA's regulations misinterpret § 423(d)(1)(A)'s clear and unambiguous language. Under his reading, the statute only requires that his inability to work be caused by his impairment; it does not also require that he be unable to work for at least 12 months. Rather, he maintains that § 423(d)(1)(A)'s 12-month condition applies only to the duration of his *impairment*. He accordingly insists that he is entitled to benefits because (1) his impairment has disabled him for more than 12 months, (2) his previous inability to work was caused by his impairment, and (3) the fact that he was out of work for only 11 months is not statutorily relevant to his benefits eligibility. In sum, he argues that the SSA's regulations are not entitled to *Chevron* deference because they conflict with the plain meaning of § 423(d)(1)(A).

You are a clerk for the district court hearing Patel's challenge. Write a brief memorandum analyzing whether the SSA's regulations are entitled to *Chevron* deference.

---

b. *Chevron* Step Minus-One? Deference for "Major Questions" and "Extraordinary" Cases

Courts and scholars have acknowledged three discrete steps (Zero, One, and Two) in the *Chevron* analysis. Step Zero was the focus of *United States v. Mead Corp.*, and Steps One and Two are discussed in greater detail below.

The materials in this subsection ask whether the Supreme Court has elevated what initially appeared to be an interpretive canon to a full *Chevron* fourth step, one we will call *Chevron* Step Minus-One.* Why Minus-One? Because this analysis can precede Step Zero. As explained in the previous subsection, Step Zero asks whether the agency acted with the force of law when it interpreted the ambiguous statute it administers. Rather than focusing on what the agency did, Step Minus-One focuses on the *importance of the regulatory subject matter*. Where the subject matter is sufficiently important—where it involves a "major question" or an "extraordinary" case—the reviewing court will be more skeptical that Congress left its resolution to agency discretion. That skepticism, in turn, may lead the reviewing court either to resolve the interpretive issue at Step One or, if the statute is ambiguous, to resolve that ambiguity itself. In either case, whether the statute is silent or ambiguous, or whether the agency is charged with its implementation, becomes irrelevant.

An early articulation of Step Minus-One can be found in a law review article by Justice Stephen Breyer (who was a First Circuit judge at the time). Justice Breyer pointed to the possibility that silence or ambiguity may not imply delegation of legislative authority to an agency, regardless of what *Chevron* says. "Congress is more likely to have focused upon, and answered, major questions, while leaving interstitial matters to answer themselves in the course of the statute's daily administration." Stephen G. Breyer, *Judicial Review of Questions of Law and Policy*, 38 ADMIN. L. REV. 363, 370 (1986). How one would identify such "major questions," he did not say. What did seem clear to Justice Breyer was that courts should not assume that Congress leaves significant policy issues to be resolved by agencies. One hears echoes of the nondelegation doctrine here, though perhaps no more than that.

The practical effect of this notion—that major questions give courts special dispensation to independently interpret ambiguous statutes—has found its way into some of the Court's notable *Chevron* decisions. Consider *MCI Telecommunications Corp. v. American Telephone & Telegraph Co.*, 512 U.S. 218 (1994). There the Court rejected the claim that the FCC's authority under Communications Act § 203(b) to "modify" long distance carriers' rate-filing requirements included the power to abandon rate-based regulation altogether. As the Court explained, "[r]ate filings are, in fact, the essential characteristic of a rate-regulated industry." *Id.* at 231. Despite holding in *Chevron* that statutory ambiguity or silence constitutes a delegation of legislative authority to the implementing agency, the *MCI* Court was unconvinced "that Congress would leave the determination of whether an industry will be entirely, or even substantially, rate-regulated to agency discretion—and even more unlikely that it would achieve that through

---

* This moniker is borrowed from Professor Daniel Farber, *Everything You Always Wanted to Know About the* Chevron *Doctrine*, 36 YALE J. ON REG.: NOTICE & COMMENT (Oct. 23, 2017), https://yalejreg.com/nc/everything-you-always-wanted-to-know-about-the-chevron-doctrine-by-dan-farber/.

such a subtle device as permission to 'modify' rate-filing requirements." *Id.* Rather than through implication, Congress must use clear statutory statements to confer legislative (which is to say policymaking) authority over such fundamental aspects of industry-wide regulation.

The Court returned to this issue in *Food and Drug Administration v. Brown & Williamson Tobacco Corp.* (which cites Justice Breyer's 1986 article). Emphasizing the importance of the issue before the Court—whether the FDA had authority to regulate tobacco products—the Court stated:

> . . . [O]ur inquiry into whether Congress has directly spoken to the precise question at issue is shaped, at least in some measure, by the nature of the question presented. Deference under *Chevron* to an agency's construction of a statute that it administers is premised on the theory that a statute's ambiguity constitutes an implicit delegation from Congress to the agency to fill in the statutory gaps. *See Chevron, supra,* at 844. In extraordinary cases, however, there may be reason to hesitate before concluding that Congress has intended such an implicit delegation. *Cf.* Breyer, *Judicial Review of Questions of Law and Policy,* 38 Admin. L. Rev. 363, 370 (1986) ("A court may also ask whether the legal question is an important one. Congress is more likely to have focused upon, and answered, major questions, while leaving interstitial matters to answer themselves in the course of the statute's daily administration").
>
> This is hardly an ordinary case. Contrary to its representations to Congress since 1914, the FDA has now asserted jurisdiction to regulate an industry constituting a significant portion of the American economy. In fact, the FDA contends that, were it to determine that tobacco products provide no "reasonable assurance of safety," it would have the authority to ban cigarettes and smokeless tobacco entirely. Owing to its unique place in American history and society, tobacco has its own unique political history. Congress, for better or for worse, has created a distinct regulatory scheme for tobacco products, squarely rejected proposals to give the FDA jurisdiction over tobacco, and repeatedly acted to preclude any agency from exercising significant policymaking authority in the area. Given this history and the breadth of the authority that the FDA has asserted, we are obliged to defer not to the agency's expansive construction of the statute, but to Congress' consistent judgment to deny the FDA this power.
>
> Our decision in *MCI Telecommunications Corp. v. American Telephone & Telegraph Co.,* 512 U.S. 218 (1994), is instructive. That case involved the proper construction of the term "modify" in § 203(b) of the Communications Act of 1934. The FCC contended that, because the Act gave it the discretion to "modify any requirement" imposed under the statute, it therefore possessed the authority to render voluntary the otherwise mandatory requirement that long-distance carriers file their rates. We rejected the FCC's construction, finding "not the slightest doubt" that Congress had directly spoken to the question. In reasoning even more apt here, we concluded that "[i]t is highly unlikely that Congress would leave the determination of whether an industry will be entirely, or even

substantially, rate-regulated to agency discretion—and even more unlikely that it would achieve that through such a subtle device as permission to 'modify' rate-filing requirements." *Id.*, at 231.

As in *MCI*, we are confident that Congress could not have intended to delegate a decision of such economic and political significance to an agency in so cryptic a fashion. . . .

529 U.S. 120, 159-60.

Compare the Court's analysis in *Brown & Williamson* with its analysis in *Massachusetts v. Environmental Protection Agency* (*Mass v. EPA*), 549 U.S. 497 (2007), decided seven years later. There, the EPA tried to use the logic underlying Step Minus-One to defend its decision not regulate greenhouse gas emissions, including carbon dioxide. A group of private organizations filed a rulemaking petition asking the EPA to regulate emissions from new motor vehicles under § 202(a)(1) of the Clean Air Act ("CAA"). Section 202(a)(1) requires the EPA Administrator to "prescribe . . . standards applicable to the emission of any air pollutant from any class or classes of new motor vehicles or new motor vehicle engines, which in his judgment cause, or contribute to, air pollution which may reasonably be anticipated to endanger public health or welfare. . . ." 42 U.S.C. § 7521(a)(1). The EPA denied the petition. It believed that Congress did not include greenhouse gases like carbon dioxide in § 202(a)(1)'s definition of "air pollutants" and, even if it had, regulating them at that time would have been unwise. The EPA claimed that it was driven to this conclusion by *Brown & Williamson*. Like the tobacco products industry, climate change had a "political history" indicating that Congress did not want the EPA to regulate it. The CAA tasked the agency with controlling *local* rather than global pollutants, and Congress had devised other ways of addressing global climate change. *Id.* at 512. The EPA further asserted that the clear-statement rule applied in *Brown & Williamson*—that Congress delegates such far-reaching policy-making authority explicitly rather implicitly—applied with even greater force to global climate change. As compared to the tobacco products industry, the political and economic consequences of climate change regulation were far more profound. *Id.* Accordingly, the EPA believed that Congress did not consider greenhouse gases "air pollutants" within the meaning of CAA § 202(a)(1). The organizations, later joined by several state intervenors, sought judicial review of the petition denial.

The Court rejected the EPA's arguments. Given critical differences in the political histories of tobacco and climate change regulation, the Court concluded that Congress intended to treat them differently. Whereas Congress had manifested no intent to ban tobacco products (which would have been required under the FDA's reading of the FDCA), its intention to regulate greenhouse gas emissions was clear. Moreover, Congress had never enacted legislation that would conflict with curtailment of new vehicle greenhouse gas emissions while it had done so with respect to tobacco regulation.

Further, the EPA had never disavowed its authority to regulate greenhouse gases prior to the petition denial under review, whereas the FDA had repeatedly done so regarding tobacco throughout its history. The Court ultimately found that Congress had clearly spoken to whether the EPA was required to regulate greenhouse gases; the CAA's definition of "air pollutants" "[o]n its face . . . embraces all airborne compounds of whatever stripe." 549 U.S. at 529.

Critically for present purposes, the "major questions" intuition underlying Step Minus-One was nowhere to be found in the Court's analysis. Since the EPA did not want to regulate greenhouse gases, characterizing their regulation as a "major question" redounded to the agency's argumentative benefit. It argued that, under *Brown & Williamson*, it was responsible for regulating greenhouse gases only if Congress had imposed that obligation explicitly. Of course, the EPA argued that § 202(a)(1) had done no such thing. The factual premise of the EPA's argument appears sound; regulating greenhouse gases *is* more politically and economically significant than regulating tobacco products. Nevertheless, the Court declined to attribute legal significance to this fact under Step Minus-One. Doing so would have implied that § 202(a)(1) contained an ambiguity that the Court would then be left to resolve. It instead concluded that § 202(a)(1) was unambiguous.

King v. Burwell, excerpted below, is one of the Supreme Court's most recent (possible) applications of the Step Minus-One. It arose from President Obama's and Congress' efforts to increase the number of Americans with adequate and affordable health insurance. Doctrinally, did the Court appear to follow either *Brown & Williamson* or *Mass v. EPA*? Conceptually, did it explain why it was necessary (or even more appropriate) for courts, rather than agencies, to decide interpretive issues of significant political or economic importance?

King v. Burwell

135 S. Ct. 2480 (2015)

Chief Justice ROBERTS delivered the opinion of the Court.

The Patient Protection and Affordable Care Act adopts a series of interlocking reforms designed to expand coverage in the individual health insurance market. First, the Act bars insurers from taking a person's health into account when deciding whether to sell health insurance or how much to charge. Second, the Act generally requires each person to maintain insurance coverage or make a payment to the Internal Revenue Service. And third, the Act gives tax credits to certain people to make insurance more affordable.

In addition to those reforms, the Act requires the creation of an "Exchange" in each State—basically, a marketplace that allows people to compare and purchase insurance plans. The Act gives each State the opportunity to establish its own Exchange, but provides that the Federal Government will establish the Exchange if the State does not.

This case is about whether the Act's interlocking reforms apply equally in each State no matter who establishes the State's Exchange. Specifically, the question presented is whether the Act's tax credits are available in States that have a Federal Exchange.

I

A

The Patient Protection and Affordable Care Act, 124 Stat. 119, grew out of a long history of failed health insurance reform. In the 1990s, several States began experimenting with ways to expand people's access to coverage. One common approach was to impose a pair of insurance market regulations—a "guaranteed issue" requirement, which barred insurers from denying coverage to any person because of his health, and a "community rating" requirement, which barred insurers from charging a person higher premiums for the same reason. Together, those requirements were designed to ensure that anyone who wanted to buy health insurance could do so.

The guaranteed issue and community rating requirements achieved that goal, but they had an unintended consequence: They encouraged people to wait until they got sick to buy insurance. Why buy insurance coverage when you are healthy, if you can buy the same coverage for the same price when you become ill? This consequence—known as "adverse selection"—led to a second: Insurers were forced to increase premiums to account for the fact that, more and more, it was the sick rather than the healthy who were buying insurance. And that consequence fed back into the first: As the cost of insurance rose, even more people waited until they became ill to buy it.

This led to an economic "death spiral." As premiums rose higher and higher, and the number of people buying insurance sank lower and lower, insurers began to leave the market entirely. As a result, the number of people without insurance increased dramatically. . . .

In 1996, Massachusetts adopted the guaranteed issue and community rating requirements and experienced similar [increases in the number of people without insurance]. But in 2006, Massachusetts added two more reforms: The Commonwealth required individuals to buy insurance or pay a penalty, and it gave tax credits to certain individuals to ensure that they could afford the insurance they were required to buy. The combination of these three reforms—insurance market regulations, a coverage mandate, and tax credits—reduced the uninsured rate in Massachusetts to 2.6 percent, by far the lowest in the Nation.

B

The Affordable Care Act adopts a version of the three key reforms that made the Massachusetts system successful. First, the Act adopts the guaranteed issue and community rating requirements. The Act provides that "each health insurance issuer that offers health insurance coverage in the individual . . . market in a State must accept every . . . individual in the State that applies for such coverage." 42 U.S.C. § 300gg-1(a). The Act also bars insurers from charging higher premiums on the basis of a person's health. § 300gg.

Second, the Act generally requires individuals to maintain health insurance coverage or make a payment to the IRS. 26 U.S.C. § 5000A. Congress recognized that, without an incentive, "many individuals would wait to purchase health insurance until they needed care." 42 U.S.C. § 18091(2)(I). So Congress adopted a coverage requirement to "minimize this adverse selection and broaden the health insurance risk pool to include healthy individuals, which will lower health insurance premiums." *Ibid.* In Congress's view, that coverage requirement was "essential to creating effective health insurance markets." *Ibid.* Congress also provided an exemption from the coverage requirement for anyone who has to spend more than eight percent of his income on health insurance. 26 U.S.C. §§ 5000A(e)(1)(A), (e)(1)(B)(ii).

Third, the Act seeks to make insurance more affordable by giving refundable tax credits to individuals with household incomes between 100 percent and 400 percent of the federal poverty line. § 36B. Individuals who meet the Act's requirements may purchase insurance with the tax credits, which are provided in advance directly to the individual's insurer. 42 U.S.C. §§ 18081, 18082.

These three reforms are closely intertwined. As noted, Congress found that the guaranteed issue and community rating requirements would not work without the coverage requirement. § 18091(2)(I). And the coverage requirement would not work without the tax credits. The reason is that, without the tax credits, the cost of buying insurance would exceed eight percent of income for a large number of individuals, which would exempt them from the coverage requirement. Given the relationship between these three reforms, the Act provided that they should take effect on the same day—January 1, 2014. *See Affordable Care Act,* § 1253, *redesignated* § 1255, 124 Stat. 162, 895; §§ 1401(e), 1501(d), *id.,* at 220, 249.

C

In addition to those three reforms, the Act requires the creation of an "Exchange" in each State where people can shop for insurance, usually online. 42 U.S.C. § 18031(b)(1). An Exchange may be created in one of two ways. First, the Act provides that "[e]ach State shall . . . establish an

American Health Benefit Exchange . . . for the State." *Ibid.* Second, if a State nonetheless chooses not to establish its own Exchange, the Act provides that the Secretary of Health and Human Services "shall . . . establish and operate such Exchange within the State." § 18041(c)(1).

The issue in this case is whether the Act's tax credits are available in States that have a Federal Exchange rather than a State Exchange. The Act initially provides that tax credits "shall be allowed" for any "applicable taxpayer." 26 U.S.C. § 36B(a). The Act then provides that the amount of the tax credit depends in part on whether the taxpayer has enrolled in an insurance plan through "an Exchange *established by the State* under section 1311 of the Patient Protection and Affordable Care Act [hereinafter 42 U.S.C. § 18031]." 26 U.S.C. §§ 36B(b)-(c) (emphasis added).

The IRS addressed the availability of tax credits by promulgating a rule that made them available on both State and Federal Exchanges. 77 Fed. Reg. 30378 (2012). As relevant here, the IRS Rule provides that a taxpayer is eligible for a tax credit if he enrolled in an insurance plan through "an Exchange," 26 CFR § 1.36B–2 (2013), which is defined as "an Exchange serving the individual market . . . regardless of whether the Exchange is established and operated by a State . . . or by HHS," 45 CFR § 155.20 (2014). At this point, 16 States and the District of Columbia have established their own Exchanges; the other 34 States have elected to have HHS do so.

D

Petitioners are four individuals who live in Virginia, which has a Federal Exchange. They do not wish to purchase health insurance. In their view, Virginia's Exchange does not qualify as "an Exchange established by the State under [42 U.S.C. § 18031]," so they should not receive any tax credits. That would make the cost of buying insurance more than eight percent of their income, which would exempt them from the Act's coverage requirement. 26 U.S.C. § 5000A(e)(1).

Under the IRS Rule, however, Virginia's Exchange would qualify as "an Exchange established by the State under [42 U.S.C. § 18031]," so petitioners would receive tax credits. That would make the cost of buying insurance less than eight percent of petitioners' income, which would subject them to the Act's coverage requirement. The IRS Rule therefore requires petitioners to either buy health insurance they do not want, or make a payment to the IRS. . . .

II

The Affordable Care Act addresses tax credits in what is now Section 36B of the Internal Revenue Code. That section provides: "In the case of an applicable taxpayer, there shall be allowed as a credit against the tax imposed by this subtitle . . . an amount equal to the premium assistance credit amount."

26 U.S.C. § 36B(a). Section 36B then defines the term "premium assistance credit amount" as "the sum of the *premium assistance amounts* determined under paragraph (2) with respect to all *coverage months* of the taxpayer occurring during the taxable year." § 36B(b)(1) (emphasis added). Section 36B goes on to define the two italicized terms—"premium assistance amount" and "coverage month"—in part by referring to an insurance plan that is enrolled in through "an Exchange established by the State under [42 U.S.C. § 18031]." 26 U.S.C. §§ 36B(b)(2)(A), (c)(2)(A)(i).

The parties dispute whether Section 36B authorizes tax credits for individuals who enroll in an insurance plan through a Federal Exchange. Petitioners argue that a Federal Exchange is not "an Exchange established by the State under [42 U.S.C. § 18031]," and that the IRS Rule therefore contradicts Section 36B. The Government responds that the IRS Rule is lawful because the phrase "an Exchange established by the State under [42 U.S.C. § 18031]" should be read to include Federal Exchanges.

When analyzing an agency's interpretation of a statute, we often apply the two-step framework announced in *Chevron*, 467 U.S. 837. Under that framework, we ask whether the statute is ambiguous and, if so, whether the agency's interpretation is reasonable. *Id.*, at 842-843. This approach "is premised on the theory that a statute's ambiguity constitutes an implicit delegation from Congress to the agency to fill in the statutory gaps." *FDA v. Brown & Williamson Tobacco Corp.*, 529 U.S. 120, 159 (2000). "In extraordinary cases, however, there may be reason to hesitate before concluding that Congress has intended such an implicit delegation." *Ibid.*

This is one of those cases. The tax credits are among the Act's key reforms, involving billions of dollars in spending each year and affecting the price of health insurance for millions of people. Whether those credits are available on Federal Exchanges is thus a question of deep "economic and political significance" that is central to this statutory scheme; had Congress wished to assign that question to an agency, it surely would have done so expressly. *Utility Air Regulatory Group v. EPA*, [573 U.S. 302], 134 S. Ct. 2427, 2444 (2014) (quoting *Brown & Williamson*, 529 U.S., at 160). It is especially unlikely that Congress would have delegated this decision to the IRS, which has no expertise in crafting health insurance policy of this sort. This is not a case for the IRS.

It is instead our task to determine the correct reading of Section 36B. If the statutory language is plain, we must enforce it according to its terms. . . .

[In the remainder of the opinion, the Court concluded that Section 36B is ambiguous as to whether tax credits are available to participants in both State and Federal Exchanges. It ultimately decided that they are. "[T]he statutory scheme compels [rejection of] petitioners' interpretation because it would destabilize the individual insurance market in any State with a Federal Exchange, and likely create the very 'death spirals' that Congress designed the Act to avoid."]

Affirmed.

Justice SCALIA, with whom Justice THOMAS and Justice ALITO join, dissenting.

[In his dissent, Justice Scalia took no issue with the majority's application of Step Minus-One. Rather, he excoriated the majority's interpretation of the phrase "Exchange established by the State" to mean "Exchange established by the state or the federal government." From his perspective, the Affordable Care Act's meaning was obvious and unambiguous; those who enrolled in health care exchanges established by the state were eligible to receive tax credits pursuant to Section 36B of the Act, and those who enrolled through exchanges established by the federal government were not. While the failure to provide tax credits to those who enrolled through federally established exchanges might have fatally undermined the Act's goal of expanding healthcare coverage, Justice Scalia concluded that that failure was Congress' alone. He insisted that correcting this flaw in the legislation could be accomplished through revision of the statute's text by Congress but not through its interpretation by the courts. As the people entrusted the making and amendment of the laws to Congress alone, he did not believe that the majority had any constitutional authority to reach the conclusion it did.]

QUESTION SET 9.29

Review & Synthesis

1. Restate the *Chevron* test to take account of *MCI, Brown & Williamson,* and *Burwell.*

2. How do *MCI, Brown & Williamson,* and *Burwell* identify the "major questions" or the "extraordinariness" that necessitates judicial rather than administrative interpretation of statutory provisions? Can you glean a pattern from the facts the Court considered in each case? Relatedly, how did the Court gauge the magnitude of the issues to determine how "major" or "extraordinary" they were?

3. In effect, *Chevron* Step Minus-One imposes a clear statement rule on Congress; if it wants to delegate policymaking authority over "major questions" to agencies, it must speak clearly. If you were advising a congressional committee drafting a statutory delegation of policymaking authority to an agency, how would you advise that they signal the importance of the regulatory subject matter? Is it feasible that Congress would designate its own legislation as addressing "minor" questions to preserve the delegations it wants to make? Would the Court even take Congress' word for it if it did? Assuming Congress unambiguously

delegated policymaking authority over a "major question" to an agency, would *Chevron* even apply?

4. *Chevron* signaled that interpretation of ambiguous statutes is a policy-making exercise. Choosing among a statute's possible meanings requires something more than legal reasoning, it requires an exercise of judgment that is typically the province of elected officials and administrators. What theory, then, underlies the idea that courts rather than agencies must interpret ambiguous statutes addressed to "major questions"? Is it that Congress implicitly delegates that authority to courts by default unless it clearly states otherwise? Is it because the Constitution requires that such questions be answered by courts unless Congress clearly makes separate arrangements? Wouldn't the importance of such questions be even more appropriately answered by agencies, who have subject matter expertise and are overseen by political appointees answerable to the President?

---

c. *Chevron* Step One: Is the Statute Clear?

Chevron Step One places reviewing federal courts in their traditional role of independently determining the meaning of statutory language. It asks "whether Congress has directly spoken to the precise question at issue." Presumably, courts are supposed to conduct the Step One analysis independently, granting no deference to the implementing agency's views on the matter. Here, and as they do under Steps Minus-One and Zero, courts serve as *Chevron* deference gatekeepers; deference is available only when they conclude that the scrutinized statutory provision does not already answer the question presented. This raises a critical question for the balance of interpretive power between courts and agencies and for the practical impact of the *Chevron* doctrine itself: how "clear" must a statutory provision be for a court to end its analysis at Step One?

The Supreme Court's answer to this question has been, somewhat ironically, less than clear. This is due at least in part to the various ways courts can frame the "question at issue." How an issue is framed can heavily influence how well it fits with an applicable statutory provision and, hence, whether it is clearly addressed by that provision. Another reason, one that has received substantial attention in the judicial and academic literature, is the difference in interpretive methods courts use to determine clarity or ambiguity. Footnote 9 of *Chevron* identified the method by which courts should answer Step One questions: "If a court, employing traditional tools of statutory construction, ascertains that Congress had an intention on the precise question at issue, that intention is the law and must be given effect." *Chevron v. Natural Resources Defense Council*, 467 U.S. 837, 843 n.9 (1984). Thus, the outcome of the Step One analysis is often driven by the "traditional tools of statutory construction" on which the reviewing court relies. There are many such interpretive tools and methods, each with their own benefits and shortcomings.

A purpose-driven interpretive approach looks for and tries to give effect to Congress' animating purposes in adopting a legislative measure. It begins with the legislative text but also considers an array of other evidentiary sources, including legislative history. This approach can lead to widely varying outcomes, as Congress often has several purposes in passing legislation from which the interpreting judge may choose. *See Holy Trinity Church v. United States*, 143 U.S. 457 (1892); John F. Manning, *The New Purposivism*, 2011 Sup. Ct. Rev. 113, 119-23.

Textualism, by contrast, eschews the search for legislative purpose and rejects reliance on legislative history when attempting to understand the meaning of statutory text. It instead focuses on finding the statute's plain meaning as aided, where necessary, by "the structure of the statute, interpretations given similar statutory provisions, and canons of statutory construction." William N. Eskridge, Jr., *The New Textualism*, 37 UCLA L. Rev. 621, 623-24 (1990). It also relies heavily on nonlegislative, extratextual sources of meaning—particularly dictionary definitions—to identify the "plain meaning" of statutory terms. For this reason, the approach has been criticized for its refusal to consider illuminating legislative context, particularly as revealed by careful resort to legislative history. *Id.* at 668-90. Moreover, "[t]he framework applied by textualist judges makes it especially difficult for them to recognize statutory ambiguity." Christine Kexel Chabot, *Selling* Chevron, 67 Admin. L. Rev. 481, 508 (2015).

The canons of statutory construction provide default rules for understanding otherwise unclear or ambiguous legislative text. There are numerous canons addressing various semantic, syntactic, contextual, and other uncertainties that may be left in statutory text. *See generally* Antonin Scalia & Bryan A. Garner, Reading Law: The Interpretation of Legal Texts (2012) (compiling an exhaustive list of interpretive canons); Eskridge, *The New Textualism*, at 663-66. One of the more frequently relied upon (particularly by textualists) is the so-called "plain meaning" rule, which advises that statutory terms should be understood in their ordinary, everyday meaning unless the statute or context indicates otherwise. Another is the common law canon of *noscitur a sociis*, under which the meaning of unclear terms should be determined by considering the words with which they are associated in statutory context.

As Justice Scalia once observed, "[b]reaking interpretive ties is one of the least controversial uses of any canon of statutory construction." *Chickasaw Nation v. United States*, 534 U.S. 84, 102 (2001). However, many of these canons have been condemned for the faulty assumptions on which they are based and for producing interpretive uncertainties of their own. *See, e.g.,* Karl N. Llewellyn, *Remarks on the Theory of Appellate Decision and the Rules or Canons About How Statutes Are To Be Construed*, 3 Vand. L. Rev. 395

(1950). *See also* 1 Richard J, Pierce, Jr., Administrative Law Treatise § 3.6 (2010) (providing an overview and critique of the "traditional tools of statutory construction" used in *Chevron* analysis).

Also consider this: whether a statute is clear or ambiguous may simply turn on how intent a judge is to find *some* meaning in it. After all, the purpose of these methods and tools of construction is to supplement meaning when the text falls short of needed specificity. In any event, the Court has never developed (and is unlikely ever to develop) a set of principles that standardizes its use of these interpretive tools and methods. To the contrary, the Justices have sharply disagreed on which are useful or even legitimate. These disagreements, in turn, have important implications for Step One analysis. Consider the following observations of Justice Scalia on this point:

> In my experience, there is a fairly close correlation between the degree to which a person is (for want of a better word) a "strict constructionist"' of statutes, and the degree to which that person favors *Chevron* and is willing to give it broad scope. The reason is obvious. One who finds more often (as I do) that the meaning of a statute is apparent from its text and from its relationship with other laws, thereby finds less often that the triggering requirement for *Chevron* deference exists. It is thus relatively rare that *Chevron* will require me to accept an interpretation which, though reasonable, I would not personally adopt. Contrariwise, one who abhors a "plain meaning"' rule, and is willing to permit the apparent meaning of a statute to be impeached by the legislative history, will more frequently find agency-liberating ambiguity, and will discern a much broader range of " 'reasonable" interpretation that the agency may adopt and to which the courts must pay deference. The frequency with which *Chevron* will require that judge to accept an interpretation he thinks wrong is infinitely greater.

Antonin S. Scalia, *Judicial Deference to Administrative Interpretations of Law*, 1989 Duke L. J. 511 (1989). Even when the Justices agree to use the same set of interpretive tools, they sometimes reach different conclusions when applying them. The wise legal analyst will learn the different tools and methods the Justices typically employ under *Chevron* Step One and will try to identify the different results those tools and methods may produce in a given case.

The following cases—also discussed in connection with Step Minus-One, above—illustrate how the Court has tested for statutory ambiguity. As you read them, consider for yourself whether the statutory language at issue was clear enough to directly answer the questions presented to the Court. While doing so, try to identify the interpretive tools and methods the Justices employed and how *reasonably* they supplemented the meaning of the statute's text. Additionally, think about possible reasons for the different results in the cases. Are the differences due to the diverging interpretive approaches, some of which seem more likely to resolve ambiguities than others? Is it because the Justices had a substantive views on the regulatory area in which the Step One analysis arose, and those views bled over into their clarity and ambiguity conclusions? Or, most innocuously, were these simply hard cases that made interpretive consistency an unreasonable expectation?

MCI Telecommunications Corp. v. American Telephone and Telegraph Co.
512 U.S. 218 (1994)

Justice SCALIA delivered the opinion of the Court.

Section 203(a) of Title 47 of the United States Code requires communications common carriers to file tariffs with the Federal Communications Commission, and § 203(b) authorizes the Commission to "modify" any requirement of § 203. These cases present the question whether the Commission's decision to make tariff filing optional for all nondominant long-distance carriers is a valid exercise of its modification authority.

I

Like most cases involving the role of the American Telephone and Telegraph Company (AT&T) in our national telecommunication system, these have a long history. An understanding of the cases requires a brief review of the Commission's efforts to regulate and then deregulate the telecommunications industry. When Congress created the Commission in 1934, AT&T, through its vertically integrated Bell system, held a virtual monopoly over the Nation's telephone service. The Communications Act of 1934, 48 Stat. 1064, as amended, authorized the Commission to regulate the rates charged for communication services to ensure that they were reasonable and nondiscriminatory. The requirements of § 203 that common carriers file their rates with the Commission and charge only the filed rate were the centerpiece of the Act's regulatory scheme.

In the 1970's, technological advances reduced the entry costs for competitors of AT&T in the market for long-distance telephone service. The Commission, recognizing the feasibility of greater competition, passed regulations to facilitate competitive entry. By 1979, competition in the provision of long-distance service was well established, and some urged that the continuation of extensive tariff filing requirements served only to impose unnecessary costs on new entrants and to facilitate collusive pricing. The Commission held hearings on the matter, following which it issued a series of rules that have produced this litigation.

The *First Report and Order*, distinguished between dominant carriers (those with market power) and nondominant carriers—in the long-distance market, this amounted to a distinction between AT&T and everyone else—and relaxed some of the filing procedures for nondominant carriers.

In the *Second Report and Order*, the Commission entirely eliminated the filing requirement for resellers of terrestrial common carrier services. This policy of optional filing, or permissive detariffing, was extended to all other resellers, and to specialized common carriers, including petitioner MCI Telecommunications Corp., by the *Fourth Report and Order*, and to virtually all remaining categories of nondominant carriers by the *Fifth Report and Order*. Then, in 1985, the Commission shifted to a mandatory detariffing policy, which prohibited nondominant carriers from filing tariffs. *See Sixth Report and Order*. The United States Court of Appeals for the District of Columbia Circuit, however, struck down the *Sixth Report*'s mandatory detariffing policy in a challenge brought—somewhat ironically as it now appears—by MCI. The Court of Appeals reasoned that § 203(a)'s command that "[e]very common carrier . . . shall . . . file" tariffs was mandatory. And although § 203(b) authorizes the Commission to "modify any requirement" in the section, the Court of Appeals concluded that that phrase "suggest[ed] circumscribed alterations—not, as the FCC now would have it, wholesale abandonment or elimination of a requirement."

In the wake of the invalidation of mandatory detariffing by the Court of Appeals, MCI continued its practice of not filing tariffs for certain services, pursuant to the permissive detariffing policy of the *Fourth Report and Order*. On August 7, 1989, AT&T filed a complaint, pursuant to the third-party complaint provision of the Communications Act, 47 U.S.C. § 208(a), which alleged that MCI's collection of unfiled rates violated §§ 203(a) and (c). MCI responded that the *Fourth Report* was a substantive rule, and so MCI had no legal obligation to file rates. AT&T rejoined that the *Fourth Report and Order* was simply a statement of the Commission's nonenforcement policy, which did not immunize MCI from private enforcement actions; and that if the *Fourth Report and Order* established a substantive rule, it was in excess of statutory authority. The Commission did not take final action on AT&T's complaint until almost 2½ years after its filing. It characterized the *Fourth Report and Order* as a substantive rule and dismissed AT&T's complaint on the ground that MCI was in compliance with that rule. It refused to address, however, AT&T's contention that the rule was *ultra vires*, announcing instead a proposed rulemaking to consider that question.

AT&T petitioned for review, arguing, *inter alia*, that the Commission lacked authority to defer to a later rulemaking consideration of an issue which was dispositive of an adjudicatory complaint. . . . The Court of Appeals characterized the Commission's failure to address its authority to promulgate the permissive detariffing policy as "a sort of administrative law shell game[.]" Addressing that question itself, the Court of Appeals concluded that the permissive detariffing policy of the *Fourth Report and Order* was rendered indefensible by the 1985 MCI decision: "Whether detariffing is made mandatory, as in the *Sixth Report*, or simply permissive, as in the *Fourth Report*, carriers are, in either event, relieved of the obligation to file tariffs under section 203(a). That step exceeds the limited authority granted the Commission in section 203(b) to 'modify' requirements of the Act." The Court of Appeals then remanded the case so that the Commission could award appropriate relief. We denied certiorari.

Moving now with admirable dispatch, less than two weeks after the decision by the Court of Appeals concerning the adjudicatory proceeding, the Commission released a Report and Order from the rulemaking proceeding commenced in response to AT&T's complaint. That is the Report and Order at issue in this case. The Commission, relying upon the § 203(b) authority to "modify" that had by then been twice rejected by the District of Columbia Circuit, determined that its permissive detariffing policy was within its authority under the Communications Act. AT&T filed a motion with the District of Columbia Circuit seeking summary reversal of the Commission's order. The motion was granted in an unpublished *per curiam* order. . . . We granted the petitions and consolidated them.

II

Section 203 of the Communications Act contains both the filed rate provisions of the Act and the Commission's disputed modification authority. It provides in relevant part:

(a) **Filing; public display.**

Every common carrier, except connecting carriers, shall, within such reasonable time as the Commission shall designate, file with the Commission and print and keep open for public inspection schedules showing all charges . . . , whether such charges are joint or separate, and showing the classifications, practices, and regulations affecting such charges. . . .

(b) **Changes in schedule; discretion of Commission to modify requirements.**

(1) **No change shall be made in the charges, classifications, regulations, or practices which have been so filed and published except after one hundred and twenty days notice to the Commission and to the public, which shall be published in such form and contain such information as the Commission may by regulations prescribe.**

(2) **The Commission may, in its discretion and for good cause shown, modify any requirement made by or under the authority of this section either in particular instances or by general order applicable to special circumstances or conditions except that the Commission may not require the notice period specified in paragraph (1) to be more than one hundred and twenty days.**

(c) Overcharges and rebates.

No carrier, unless otherwise provided by or under authority of this chapter, shall engage or participate in such communication unless schedules have been filed and published in accordance with the provisions of this chapter and with the regulations made thereunder; and no carrier shall (1) charge, demand, collect, or receive a greater or less or different compensation for such communication . . . than the charges specified in the schedule then in effect, or (2) refund or remit by any means or device any portion of the charges so specified, or (3) extend to any person any privileges or facilities in such communication, or employ or enforce any classifications, regulations, or practices affecting such charges, except as specified in such schedule. 47 U.S.C. § 203 (1988 ed. and Supp. IV).

The dispute between the parties turns on the meaning of the phrase "modify any requirement" in § 203(b)(2). Petitioners argue that it gives the Commission authority to make even basic and fundamental changes in the scheme created by that section. We disagree. The word "modify"—like a number of other English words employing the root "mod-" (deriving from the Latin word for "measure"), such as "moderate," "modulate," "modest," and "modicum"—has a connotation of increment or limitation. Virtually every dictionary we are aware of says that "to modify" means to change moderately or in minor fashion. *See, e.g.,* Random House Dictionary of the English Language 1236 (2d ed. 1987) ("to change somewhat the form or qualities of; alter partially; amend"); Webster's Third New International Dictionary 1452 (1981) ("to make minor changes in the form or structure of: alter without transforming"); 9 Oxford English Dictionary 952 (2d ed. 1989) ("[t]o make partial changes in; to change (an object) in respect of some of its qualities; to alter or vary without radical transformation"); Black's Law Dictionary 1004 (6th ed. 1990) ("[t]o alter; to change in incidental or subordinate features; enlarge; extend; amend; limit; reduce").

In support of their position, petitioners cite dictionary definitions contained in, or derived from, a single source, Webster's Third New International Dictionary 1452 (1981) (Webster's Third), which includes among the meanings of "modify," "to make a basic or important change in." Petitioners contend that this establishes sufficient ambiguity to entitle the Commission to deference in its acceptance of the broader meaning, which in turn requires approval of its permissive detariffing policy. *See Chevron U.S.A. Inc. v. Natural Resources Defense Council, Inc.,* 467 U.S. 837, 843 (1984). In short, they contend that the courts must defer to the agency's choice among available dictionary definitions, citing *National Railroad Passenger Corporation v. Boston & Maine Corp.,* 503 U.S. 407, 418 (1992).

But *Boston & Maine* does not stand for that proposition. That case involved the question whether the statutory term "required" could only mean "demanded as essential" or could also mean "demanded as appropriate." In holding that the latter was a permissible interpretation, to which *Chevron* deference was owed, the opinion did not rely exclusively upon dictionary definitions, but also upon contextual indications—which in the present cases, as we shall see, contradict petitioners' position. Moreover, when the *Boston & Maine* opinion spoke of "alternative dictionary definitions," it did not refer to what we have here: one dictionary whose suggested meaning contradicts virtually all others. It referred to alternative definitions within the dictionary cited (Webster's Third, as it happens), which was not represented to be the only dictionary giving those alternatives. To the contrary, the Court said "these alternative interpretations are as old as the jurisprudence of this Court," citing *McCulloch v. Maryland*, 4 Wheat. 316 (1819).

Most cases of verbal ambiguity in statutes involve, as *Boston & Maine* did, a selection between accepted alternative meanings shown as such by many dictionaries. One can envision (though a court case does not immediately come to mind) having to choose between accepted alternative meanings, one of which is so newly accepted that it has only been recorded by a single lexicographer. . . . But what petitioners demand that we accept as creating an ambiguity here is a rarity even rarer than that: a meaning set forth in a single dictionary (and, as we say, its progeny) which not only supplements the meaning contained in all other dictionaries, but contradicts one of the meanings contained in virtually all other dictionaries. Indeed, contradicts one of the alternative meanings contained in the out-of-step dictionary itself—for as we have observed, Webster's Third itself defines "modify" to connote both (specifically) major change and (specifically) minor change. It is hard to see how that can be. When the word "modify" has come to mean both "to change in some respects" and "to change fundamentally" it will in fact mean neither of those things. It will simply mean "to change," and some adverb will have to be called into service to indicate the great or small degree of the change.

If that is what the peculiar Webster's Third definition means to suggest has happened—and what petitioners suggest by appealing to Webster's Third—we simply disagree. "Modify," in our view, connotes moderate change. It might be good English to say that the French Revolution "modified" the status of the French nobility—but only because there is a figure of speech called understatement and a literary device known as sarcasm. . . .

Beyond the word itself, a further indication that the § 203(b)(2) authority to "modify" does not contemplate fundamental changes is the sole exception to that authority which the section provides. One of the requirements of § 203 is that changes to filed tariffs can be made only after 120 days' notice to the Commission and the public. § 203(b)(1). The only exception to the Commission's § 203(b)(2) modification authority is as follows: "except that the Commission may not require the notice period specified in paragraph (1) to be more than one hundred and twenty days." Is it conceivable that the statute is indifferent to the Commission's power to eliminate the tariff-filing requirement entirely for all except one firm in the long-distance sector, and yet strains out the gnat of extending the waiting period for tariff revision beyond 120 days? We think not. The exception is not as ridiculous as a Lilliputian in London only because it is to be found in Lilliput: in the small-scale world of "modifications," it is a big deal.

Since an agency's interpretation of a statute is not entitled to deference when it goes beyond the meaning that the statute can bear, *Chevron*, 467 U.S., at 842-843, the Commission's permissive detariffing policy can be justified only if it makes a less than radical or fundamental change in the Act's tariff-filing requirement. The Commission's attempt to establish that no more than that is involved greatly understates the extent to which its policy deviates from the filing requirement, and greatly undervalues the importance of the filing requirement itself. . . .

We do not mean to suggest that the tariff-filing requirement is so inviolate that the Commission's existing modification authority does not reach it at all. Certainly the Commission can modify the form, contents, and location of required filings, and can defer filing or perhaps even waive it altogether in limited circumstances. But what we have here goes well beyond that. It is effectively the introduction of a whole new regime of regulation (or of free-market competition), which may well be a better regime but is not the one that Congress established.

The judgment of the Court of Appeals is
Affirmed.

Justice O'CONNOR took no part in the consideration or decision of these cases.

Justice STEVENS, with whom Justice BLACKMUN and Justice SOUTER join, dissenting. . . .

. . . In my view, each of the Commission's detariffing orders was squarely within its power to "modify any requirement" of § 203. Section 203(b)(2) plainly confers at least some discretion to modify the general rule that carriers file tariffs, for it speaks of "any requirement." Section 203(c) of the Act, ignored by the Court, squarely supports the FCC's position; it prohibits carriers from providing service without a tariff "unless otherwise provided by or under authority of this Act." Section 203(b)(2) is plainly one provision that "otherwise provides," and thereby authorizes, service without a filed schedule. The FCC's authority to modify § 203's requirements in "particular instances" or by "general order applicable to special circumstances or conditions" emphasizes the expansive character of the Commission's authority: modifications may be narrow or broad, depending upon the Commission's appraisal of current conditions. From the vantage of a Congress seeking to regulate an almost completely monopolized industry, the advent of competition is surely a "special circumstance or condition" that might legitimately call for different regulatory treatment.

The only statutory exception to the Commission's modification authority provides that it may not extend the 120-day notice period set out in § 203(b)(1). *See* § 203(b)(2). The Act thus imposes a specific limit on the Commission's authority to stiffen that regulatory imposition on carriers, but does not confine the Commission's authority to relax it. It was no stretch for the FCC to draw from this single, unidirectional statutory limitation on its modification authority the inference that its authority is otherwise unlimited.

According to the Court, the term "modify," as explicated in all but the most unreliable dictionaries, rules out the Commission's claimed authority to relieve nondominant carriers of the basic obligation to file tariffs. Dictionaries can be useful aids in statutory interpretation, but they are no substitute for close analysis of what words mean as used in a particular statutory context. Even if the sole possible meaning of "modify" were to make "minor" changes, further elaboration is needed to show why the detariffing policy should fail. The Commission came to its present policy through a series of rulings that gradually relaxed the filing requirements for nondominant carriers. Whether the current policy should count as a cataclysmic or merely an incremental departure from the § 203(a) baseline depends on whether one focuses on particular carriers' obligations to file (in which case the Commission's policy arguably works a major shift) or on the statutory policies behind the tariff-filing requirement (which remain satisfied because market constraints on nondominant carriers obviate the need for rate filing). When § 203 is viewed as part of a statute whose aim is to constrain monopoly power, the Commission's decision to exempt nondominant carriers is a rational and "measured" adjustment to novel circumstances — one that remains faithful to the core purpose of the tariff-filing section. *See* Black's Law Dictionary 1198 (3d ed. 1933) (defining "modification" as "A change; an alteration which introduces new elements into the details, or cancels some of them, but leaves the general purpose and effect of the subject-matter intact").

The Court seizes upon a particular sense of the word "modify" at the expense of another, long-established meaning that fully supports the Commission's position. That word is first defined in Webster's Collegiate Dictionary 628 (4th ed. 1934) as meaning "to limit or reduce in extent or degree." The Commission's permissive detariffing policy fits comfortably within this common understanding of the term. The FCC has in effect adopted a general rule stating that "if you are dominant you must file, but if you are nondominant you need not." The Commission's partial detariffing policy — which excuses nondominant carriers from filing on condition that they remain nondominant — is simply a relaxation of a costly regulatory requirement that recent developments had rendered pointless and counterproductive in a certain class of cases.

A modification pursuant to § 203(b)(1), like any other order issued under the Act, must of course be consistent with the purposes of the statute. On this point, the Court asserts that the Act's prohibition against unreasonable and discriminatory rates "would not be susceptible of effective enforcement if rates were not publicly filed." That determination, of course, is for the Commission to make in the first instance. But the Commission has repeatedly explained that (1) a carrier that lacks market power is entirely unlikely to charge unreasonable or discriminatory rates, (2) the statutory bans on unreasonable charges and price discrimination apply with full force regardless of whether carriers have to file tariffs, (3) any suspected violations by nondominant carriers can be addressed on the Commission's own motion or on a damages complaint filed pursuant to § 206, and (4) the FCC can reimpose a tariff requirement should violations occur. The Court does not adequately respond to the FCC's explanations, and gives no reason whatsoever to doubt the Commission's considered judgment that tariff filing is altogether unnecessary in the case of competitive carriers; the majority's ineffective enforcement argument lacks any evidentiary or historical support. . . .

The filed tariff provisions of the Communications Act are not ends in themselves, but are merely one of several procedural means for the Commission to ensure that carriers do not charge unreasonable or discriminatory rates. The Commission has reasonably concluded that this particular means of enforcing the statute's substantive mandates will prove counterproductive in the case of nondominant long-distance carriers. Even if the 1934 Congress did not define the scope of the Commission's modification authority with perfect scholarly precision, this is surely a paradigm case for judicial deference to the agency's interpretation, particularly in a statutory regime so obviously meant to maximize administrative flexibility. Whatever the best reading of § 203(b)(2), the Commission's reading cannot in my view be termed unreasonable. It is informed (as ours is not) by a practical understanding of the role (or lack thereof) that filed tariffs play in the modern regulatory climate and in the telecommunications industry. Since 1979, the FCC has sought to adapt measures originally designed to control monopoly power to new market conditions. It has carefully and consistently explained that mandatory tariff-filing rules frustrate the core statutory interest in rate reasonableness. The Commission's use of the "discretion" expressly conferred by § 203(b)(2) reflects "a reasonable accommodation of manifestly competing interests and is entitled to deference: the regulatory scheme is technical and complex, the agency considered the matter in a detailed and reasoned fashion, and the decision involves reconciling conflicting policies." *Chevron U.S.A. Inc. v. Natural Resources Defense Council, Inc.*, 467 U.S. 837, 865 (1984) (footnotes omitted). The FCC has permissibly interpreted its § 203(b)(2) authority in service of the goals Congress set forth in the Act. We should sustain its eminently sound, experience-tested, and uncommonly well-explained judgment.

I respectfully dissent.

Food and Drug Administration v. Brown & Williamson Tobacco Corp.
529 U.S. 120 (2000)

Justice O'CONNOR delivered the opinion of the Court.

This case involves one of the most troubling public health problems facing our Nation today: the thousands of premature deaths that occur each year because of tobacco use. In 1996, the Food and Drug Administration (FDA), after having expressly disavowed any such authority since its inception, asserted jurisdiction to regulate tobacco products. The FDA concluded that nicotine is a "drug" within the meaning of the Food, Drug, and Cosmetic Act (FDCA or Act), 52 Stat. 1040, as amended, 21 U.S.C. § 301 *et seq.*, and that cigarettes and smokeless tobacco are "combination products" that deliver nicotine to the body. Pursuant to this authority, it promulgated regulations intended to reduce tobacco consumption among children and adolescents. The agency believed that, because most tobacco consumers begin their use before reaching the age of 18, curbing tobacco use by minors could substantially reduce the prevalence of addiction in future generations and thus the incidence of tobacco-related death and disease.

Regardless of how serious the problem an administrative agency seeks to address, however, it may not exercise its authority "in a manner that is inconsistent with the administrative structure that Congress enacted into law." *ETSI Pipeline Project v. Missouri*, 484 U.S. 495, 517 (1988). And although agencies are generally entitled to deference in the interpretation of statutes that they administer, a reviewing "court, as well as the agency, must give effect to the unambiguously expressed intent of Congress." *Chevron U.S.A. Inc. v. Natural Resources Defense Council, Inc.*, 467 U.S. 837, 842-843 (1984). In this case, we believe that Congress has clearly precluded the FDA from asserting jurisdiction to regulate tobacco products. Such authority is inconsistent with the intent that Congress has expressed in the FDCA's overall regulatory scheme and in the tobacco-specific legislation that it has enacted subsequent to the FDCA. In light of this clear intent, the FDA's assertion of jurisdiction is impermissible.

I

The FDCA grants the FDA, as the designee of the Secretary of Health and Human Services (HHS), the authority to regulate, among other items, "drugs" and "devices." See 21 U.S.C. §§ 321(g)-(h), 393 (1994 ed. and Supp. III). The Act defines "drug" to include "articles (other than food) intended to affect the structure or any function of the body." 21 U.S.C. § 321(g)(1)(C). It defines "device," in part, as "an instrument, apparatus, implement, machine, contrivance, . . . or other similar or related article, including any component, part, or accessory, which is . . . intended to affect the structure or any function of the body." § 321(h). The Act also grants the FDA the authority to regulate so-called "combination products," which "constitute a combination of a drug, device, or biological product." § 353(g)(1). The FDA has construed this provision as giving it the discretion to regulate combination products as drugs, as devices, or as both.

On August 11, 1995, the FDA published a proposed rule concerning the sale of cigarettes and smokeless tobacco to children and adolescents. The rule, which included several restrictions on the sale, distribution, and advertisement of tobacco products, was designed to reduce the availability and attractiveness of tobacco products to young people. A public comment period followed, during which the FDA received over 700,000 submissions, more than at any other time in its history on any other subject.

On August 28, 1996, the FDA issued a final rule entitled "Regulations Restricting the Sale and Distribution of Cigarettes and Smokeless Tobacco to Protect Children and Adolescents." The FDA determined that nicotine is a "drug" and that cigarettes and smokeless tobacco are "drug delivery devices," and therefore it had jurisdiction under the FDCA to regulate tobacco products as customarily marketed—that is, without manufacturer claims of therapeutic benefit. First, the FDA found that tobacco products "'affect the structure or any function of the body'" because nicotine "has significant pharmacological effects." . . . Second, the FDA determined that these effects were "intended" under the FDCA because they "are so widely known and foreseeable that [they] may be deemed to have been intended by the manufacturers[;]" consumers use tobacco products "predominantly or nearly exclusively" to obtain these effects; and the statements, research, and actions of manufacturers revealed that they "have 'designed' cigarettes to provide pharmacologically active doses of nicotine to consumers[.]" Finally, the agency concluded that cigarettes and smokeless tobacco are "combination products" because, in addition to containing nicotine, they include device components that deliver a controlled amount of nicotine to the body.

Having resolved the jurisdictional question, the FDA next explained the policy justifications for its regulations, detailing the deleterious health effects associated with tobacco use. It found that tobacco consumption was "the single leading cause of preventable death in the United States." *Id.*, at 44398. According to the FDA, "[m]ore than 400,000 people die each year from tobacco-related illnesses, such as cancer, respiratory illnesses, and heart disease." The agency also determined that the only way to reduce the amount of tobacco-related illness and mortality was to reduce the level of addiction, a goal that could be accomplished only by preventing children and adolescents from starting to use tobacco. The FDA found that 82% of adult smokers had their first cigarette before the age of 18, and more than half had already become regular smokers by that age. It also found that children were beginning to smoke at a younger age, that the prevalence of youth smoking had recently increased, and that similar problems existed with respect to smokeless tobacco. The FDA accordingly concluded that if "the number of children and adolescents who begin tobacco use can be substantially diminished, tobacco-related illness can be correspondingly reduced because data suggest that anyone who does not begin smoking in childhood or adolescence is unlikely ever to begin."

Based on these findings, the FDA promulgated regulations concerning tobacco products' promotion, labeling, and accessibility to children and adolescents. . . .

The FDA promulgated these regulations pursuant to its authority to regulate "restricted devices." See 21 U.S.C. § 360j(e). The FDA construed § 353(g)(1) as giving it the discretion to regulate "combination products" using the Act's drug authorities, device authorities, or both, depending on "how the public health goals of the act can be best accomplished." Given the greater flexibility in the FDCA for the regulation of devices, the FDA determined that "the device authorities provide the most appropriate basis for regulating cigarettes and smokeless tobacco." Under 21 U.S.C. § 360j(e), the agency may "require that a device be restricted to sale, distribution, or use . . . upon such other conditions as [the FDA] may prescribe in such regulation, if, because of its potentiality for harmful effect or the collateral measures necessary to its use, [the FDA] determines that there cannot otherwise be reasonable assurance of its safety and effectiveness." The FDA reasoned that its regulations fell within the authority granted by § 360j(e) because they related to the sale or distribution of tobacco products and were necessary for providing a reasonable assurance of safety. . . .

II. . . .

A threshold issue [in this case] is the appropriate framework for analyzing the FDA's assertion of authority to regulate tobacco products. Because this case involves an administrative agency's construction of a statute that it administers, our analysis is governed by *Chevron U.S.A. Inc. v. Natural Resources Defense Council, Inc.*, 467 U.S. 837 (1984). Under *Chevron*, a reviewing court must first ask "whether Congress has directly spoken to the precise question at issue." *Id.*, at 842. If Congress has done so, the inquiry is at an end; the court "must give effect to the unambiguously expressed intent of Congress." *Id.*, at 843. But if Congress has not specifically addressed the question, a reviewing court must respect the agency's construction of the statute so long as it is permissible. *See Auer v. Robbins*, 519 U.S. 452, 457 (1997). Such deference is justified because "[t]he responsibilities for assessing the wisdom of such policy choices and resolving the struggle between competing views of the public interest are not judicial ones," *Chevron, supra*, at 866, and because of the agency's greater familiarity with the ever-changing facts and circumstances surrounding the subjects regulated, *see Rust v. Sullivan*, 500 U.S. 173, 187 (1991).

In determining whether Congress has specifically addressed the question at issue, a reviewing court should not confine itself to examining a particular statutory provision in isolation. The meaning — or ambiguity — of certain words or phrases may only become evident when placed in context. *See Brown v. Gardner*, 513 U.S. 115, 118 (1994) ("Ambiguity is a creature not of definitional possibilities but of statutory context"). It is a "fundamental canon of statutory construction that the words of a statute must be read in their context and with a view to their place in the overall statutory scheme." *Davis v. Michigan Dept. of Treasury*, 489 U.S. 803, 809 (1989). A court must therefore interpret the statute "as a symmetrical and coherent regulatory scheme," *Gustafson v. Alloyd Co.*, 513 U.S. 561, 569 (1995), and "fit, if possible, all parts into an harmonious whole," *FTC v. Mandel Brothers, Inc.*, 359 U.S. 385, 389 (1959). Similarly, the meaning of one statute may be affected by other Acts, particularly where Congress has spoken subsequently and more specifically to the topic at hand. In addition, we must be guided to a degree by common sense as to the manner in which Congress is likely to delegate a policy decision of such economic and political magnitude to an administrative agency. *Cf. MCI Telecommunications Corp. v. American Telephone & Telegraph Co.*, 512 U.S. 218, 231.

With these principles in mind, we find that Congress has directly spoken to the issue here and precluded the FDA's jurisdiction to regulate tobacco products.

A

Viewing the FDCA as a whole, it is evident that one of the Act's core objectives is to ensure that any product regulated by the FDA is "safe" and "effective" for its intended use. *See* 21 U.S.C. § 393(b)(2) (1994 ed., Supp. III) (defining the FDA's mission). This essential purpose pervades the FDCA. . . .

In its rulemaking proceeding, the FDA quite exhaustively documented that "tobacco products are unsafe," "dangerous," and "cause great pain and suffering from illness." It found that the consumption of tobacco products presents "extraordinary health risks," and that "tobacco use is the single leading cause of preventable death in the United States." It stated that "[m]ore than 400,000 people die each year from tobacco-related illnesses, such as cancer, respiratory illnesses, and heart disease, often suffering long and painful deaths," and that "[t]obacco alone kills more people each year in the United States than acquired immunodeficiency syndrome (AIDS), car accidents, alcohol, homicides, illegal drugs, suicides, and fires, combined." Indeed, the FDA characterized smoking as "a pediatric disease," because "one out of every three young people who become regular smokers . . . will die prematurely as a result[.]"

These findings logically imply that, if tobacco products were "devices" under the FDCA, the FDA would be required to remove them from the market. . . .

Congress, however, has foreclosed the removal of tobacco products from the market. A provision of the United States Code currently in force states that "[t]he marketing of tobacco constitutes one of the greatest basic industries of the United States with ramifying activities which directly affect interstate and foreign commerce at every point, and stable conditions therein are necessary to the general welfare." 7 U.S.C. § 1311(a). More importantly, Congress has directly addressed the problem of tobacco and health through legislation on six occasions since 1965. When Congress enacted these statutes, the adverse health consequences of tobacco use were well known, as were nicotine's pharmacological effects. Nonetheless, Congress stopped well short of ordering a ban. Instead, it has generally regulated the labeling and advertisement of tobacco products, expressly providing that it is the policy of Congress that "commerce and the national economy may be . . . protected to the maximum extent consistent with" consumers "be[ing] adequately informed about any adverse health effects." 15 U.S.C. § 1331. Congress' decisions to regulate labeling and advertising and to adopt the express policy of protecting "commerce and the national economy . . . to the maximum extent" reveal its intent that tobacco products remain on the market. Indeed, the collective premise of these statutes is that cigarettes and smokeless tobacco will continue to be sold in the United States. A ban of tobacco products by the FDA would therefore plainly contradict congressional policy. . . .

B. . . .

Congress has enacted six separate pieces of legislation since 1965 addressing the problem of tobacco use and human health. Those statutes, among other things, require that health warnings appear on all packaging and in all print and outdoor advertisements; prohibit the advertisement of tobacco products through any medium of electronic communication subject to regulation by the Federal Communications Commission (FCC); require the Secretary of HHS to report every three years to Congress on research findings concerning the addictive property of tobacco; and make States' receipt of certain federal block grants contingent on their making it unlawful for any manufacturer, retailer, or distributor of tobacco products to sell or distribute any such product to any individual under the age of 18.

In adopting each statute, Congress has acted against the backdrop of the FDA's consistent and repeated statements that it lacked authority under the FDCA to regulate tobacco absent claims of therapeutic benefit by the manufacturer. In fact, on several occasions over this period, and after the health consequences of tobacco use and nicotine's pharmacological effects had become well known, Congress considered and rejected bills that would have granted the FDA such jurisdiction. Under these circumstances, it is evident that Congress' tobacco-specific statutes have effectively ratified the FDA's long-held position that it lacks jurisdiction under the FDCA to regulate tobacco products. Congress has created a distinct regulatory scheme to address the problem of tobacco and health, and that scheme, as presently constructed, precludes any role for the FDA.

. . . [O]ur conclusion does not rely on the fact that the FDA's assertion of jurisdiction represents a sharp break with its prior interpretation of the FDCA. Certainly, an agency's initial interpretation of a statute that it is charged with administering is not "carved in stone." *Chevron*, 467 U.S., at 863. As we recognized in *Motor Vehicle Mfrs. Assn. of United States, Inc. v. State Farm Mut. Automobile Ins. Co.*, 463 U.S. 29 (1983), agencies "must be given ample latitude to 'adapt their rules and policies to the demands of changing circumstances.'" *Id.*, at 42 (quoting *Permian Basin Area Rate Cases*, 390 U.S. 747, 784 (1968)). The consistency of the FDA's prior position is significant in this case for a different reason: It provides important context to Congress' enactment of its tobacco-specific legislation. When the FDA repeatedly informed Congress that the FDCA does not grant it the authority to regulate tobacco products, its statements were consistent with the agency's unwavering position since its inception, and with the position that its predecessor agency had first taken in 1914. Although not crucial, the consistency of the FDA's prior position bolsters the conclusion that when Congress created a distinct regulatory scheme addressing the subject of tobacco and health, it understood that the FDA is without jurisdiction to regulate tobacco products and ratified that position. . . .

By no means do we question the seriousness of the problem that the FDA has sought to address. The agency has amply demonstrated that tobacco use, particularly among children and adolescents, poses perhaps the single most significant threat to public health in the United States. Nonetheless, no matter how "important, conspicuous, and controversial" the issue, and regardless of how likely the public is to hold the Executive Branch politically accountable, an administrative agency's power to regulate in the public interest must always be grounded in a valid grant of authority from Congress. And "'[i]n our anxiety to effectuate the congressional purpose of protecting the public, we must take care not to extend the scope of the statute beyond the point where Congress indicated it would stop.'" *United States v. An Article of Drug . . . Bacto-Unidisk*, 394 U.S. 784, 800 (1969) (quoting *62 Cases, More or Less, Each Containing Six Jars of Jam v. United States*, 340 U.S. 593, 600 (1951)). Reading the FDCA as a whole, as well as in conjunction with Congress' subsequent tobacco-specific legislation, it is plain that Congress has not given the FDA the authority that it seeks to exercise here. For these reasons, the judgment of the Court of Appeals for the Fourth Circuit is affirmed.

It is so ordered.

Justice BREYER, with whom Justice STEVENS, Justice SOUTER, and Justice GINSBURG join, dissenting.

. . . I believe that the most important indicia of statutory meaning—language and purpose—along with the FDCA's legislative history . . . are sufficient to establish that the FDA has authority to regulate tobacco. The statute-specific arguments against jurisdiction that the tobacco companies and the majority rely upon . . . are based on erroneous assumptions and, thus, do not defeat the jurisdiction-supporting thrust of the FDCA's language and purpose. The inferences that the majority draws from later legislative history are not persuasive, since . . . one can just as easily infer from the later laws that Congress did not intend to affect the FDA's tobacco-related authority at all. And the fact that the FDA changed its mind about the scope of its own jurisdiction is legally insignificant because . . . the agency's reasons for changing course are fully justified. Finally, . . . the degree of accountability that likely will attach to the FDA's action in this case should alleviate any concern that Congress, rather than an administrative agency, ought to make this important regulatory decision. . . .

. . .[T]he statute plainly allows the FDA to consider the relative, overall "safety" of a device in light of its regulatory alternatives, and where the FDA has chosen the least dangerous path, i.e., the safest path, then it can—and does—provide a "reasonable assurance" of "safety" within the meaning of the statute. A good football helmet provides a reasonable assurance of safety for the player even if the sport itself is still dangerous. And the safest regulatory choice by definition offers a "reasonable" assurance of safety in a world where the other alternatives are yet more dangerous. . . .

In the majority's view, laws enacted since 1965 require us to deny jurisdiction, whatever the FDCA might mean in their absence. But why? Do those laws contain language barring FDA jurisdiction? The majority must concede that they do not. Do they contain provisions that are inconsistent with the FDA's exercise of jurisdiction? With one exception, the majority points to no such provision. Do they somehow repeal the principles of law . . . that otherwise would lead to the conclusion that the FDA has jurisdiction in this area? The companies themselves deny making any such claim. Perhaps the later laws "shape" and "focus" what the 1938 Congress meant a generation earlier. But this Court has warned against using the views of a later Congress to construe a statute enacted many years before. And, while the majority suggests that the subsequent history "control[s] our construction" of the FDCA, this Court expressly has held that such subsequent views are not "controlling."

Regardless, the later statutes do not support the majority's conclusion. That is because, whatever individual Members of Congress after 1964 may have assumed about the FDA's jurisdiction, the laws they enacted did not embody any such "no jurisdiction" assumption. And one cannot automatically infer an antijurisdiction intent, as the majority does, for the later statutes are both (and similarly) consistent with quite a different congressional desire, namely, the intent to proceed without interfering with whatever authority the FDA otherwise may have possessed. . . .

Until the early 1990's, the FDA expressly maintained that the 1938 statute did not give it the power that it now seeks to assert. It then changed its mind. The majority agrees with me that the FDA's change of positions does not make a significant legal difference. *See Chevron*, 467 U.S., at 863 ("An initial agency interpretation is not instantly carved in stone"). Nevertheless, it labels those denials "important context" for drawing an inference about Congress' intent. In my view, the FDA's change of policy, like the subsequent statutes themselves, does nothing to advance the majority's position. . . .

Finally, administration policy changed. Earlier administrations may have hesitated to assert jurisdiction for the reasons prior Commissioners expressed. Commissioners of the current administration simply took a different regulatory attitude. . . .

Consequently, I dissent.

QUESTION SET 9.30

Review & Synthesis

1. With respect to *MCI*:
   a. The Court concluded that the term "modify" as used in the Communications Act of 1934 has a rather specific meaning: "to change moderately or in minor fashion." Do you think this interpretation broadened or narrowed the FCC's regulatory discretion? In formulating your answer, consider two possible aspects of the question. First, what effect would pinpointing a single definition have on the FCC's regulatory powers at the time of the Court's decision? Second, what effect would a *judicial* determination of the term's meaning have on the FCC's ability to adopt a different — though arguably permissible — interpretation of that term at a later time?
   b. The Court relied almost exclusively on dictionaries to define "modify." Do you think Congress intended to adopt that particular definition when it passed the Communications Act in 1934? Do you think the textualist method of interpretation applied by the Court even required it to find Congress' intent regarding the meaning of the term? If so, was it appropriate for the Court to rely as it did on dictionaries published *after* passage of the Communications Act?
   c. In dissent, Justice Stevens argued that the majority failed to consider Congress' *purpose* in constructing the regulatory scheme established by the Communications Act. An important aspect of that scheme, in his view, was granting the FCC flexibility to adjust its regulatory approach

to match changing industry conditions. Do you agree or disagree that the goal of statutory analysis is finding Congress' legislative purpose? If so, should courts give effect to that purpose when it seems to contradict the plain meaning of specific statutory terms or provisions?

d. Even if Justice Stevens was right that Congress intended to give the FCC some regulatory flexibility, is it plausible that "modifying" the Act's tariffing requirement could include eliminating it altogether? Do you find his reliance on the Act's other provisions persuasive evidence in constructing a broader definition of "modify" than the one adopted by the majority?

e. As a general matter, do you think Justice Stevens' interpretive approach would result in more or fewer cases being resolved under *Chevron* Step One? What impact would that have on the traditional role played by courts in interpreting and applying statutory provisions?

2. With respect to *Brown & Williamson*:

a. Would you characterize the majority's interpretive approach as textualist or purposivist? In formulating your answer, consider the evidence on which Justice O'Connor relied in construing the FDA's authority to regulate tobacco products. How much did she rely on the plain meaning of the Food, Drug, and Cosmetic Act? How much did she rely on legislative or political history? Overall, is her approach more similar to the one employed by Justice Scalia or by Justice Stevens in *MCI*?

b. Based on the plain meaning of the terms, do you think nicotine is a "drug" and that chewing tobacco and cigarettes are "drug delivery systems"? If so, are you persuaded by Justice O'Connor's analysis, which found that Congress did not intend for the FDA to regulate them? Is her argument as persuasive if, contrary to her reading of the FDCA, the FDA is not *obligated* to take tobacco products off the market if they fall within its regulatory jurisdiction?

c. Why do you think Justice O'Connor disavowed the notion that her analysis relied on the FDA's about face on whether it has jurisdiction over tobacco products? Wouldn't the FDA's own previous admissions that it lacked authority over chewing tobacco and cigarettes have been powerful evidence that its subsequent assertion of jurisdiction was mistaken? Factor the point of *Chevron* analysis — to determine the dividing line between judicially and administratively driven statutory interpretation — into your response.

d. In his dissent, Justice Breyer seemed to agree with the majority's interpretive goal: determining whether Congress intended to give the FDA regulatory power over tobacco products. Where they parted ways was in choosing the evidence that would be relevant to discovering that intent. Justice Breyer rejected the majority's use of legislation passed after the FDCA as well as its use of the FDA's disavowals of jurisdiction over tobacco products. Why?

d. *Chevron* Step Two: Is the Agency's Interpretation Reasonable?

Chevron Step Two directs the reviewing court to determine whether an agency's interpretation of the ambiguous statute it administers is reasonable or, conversely, whether it falls outside the scope of that statute's silence or ambiguity. Courts have construed this as a highly deferential standard; they must accept the agency's interpretation even if they would have resolved the ambiguity differently upon independent review. Empirical analyses of how circuit courts apply *Chevron* appear to bear this out. According to one recent study, the federal appellate courts reach Step Two in 70.0 percent of the cases in which they apply *Chevron*, and they accept the agency's interpretation under Step Two in 93.8 percent of those cases. Kent Barnett & Christopher J. Walker, Chevron *in the Circuit Courts*, 116 MICH. L. REV. 1, 33 (2017).

The *Chevron* Step Two review standard is easy enough to state. Nevertheless, it raises a host of vexing practical and conceptual questions for which the Supreme Court has thus far offered little guidance. The scholarly literature on the matter is vast, but two recurring puzzles stand out: whether Step Two adds anything to the *Chevron* analysis already required by Step One and, if it does, whether its contribution is just the "arbitrary and capricious" test adopted by the Court in *Motor Vehicles Manufacturers Association v. State Farm Mutual Automobile Insurance Co.*, 463 U.S. 29 (1983).

The first puzzle presents itself in at least two forms. The first questions whether Steps One and Two are actually different: Has the agency adopted a reasonable or permissible interpretation of the statute? One scholar has described the problem this way:

> Under the structure of the *Chevron* formula, a court should not reach step two unless it has already found during step one that the statute supports the government's interpretation or at least is ambiguous with respect to it. In other words, the agency's view is not clearly contrary to the meaning of the statute. If the court has made such a finding, one would think that the government's interpretation must be at least "reasonable" in the court's eyes. Why, then is the second step not superfluous?

Ronald M. Levin, *The Anatomy of* Chevron: *Step Two Reconsidered*, 72 CHI. KENT L. REV. 1253, 1260-61 (1997). *See also* Matthew C. Stephenson & Adrian Vermeule, Chevron *Has Only One Step*, 95 VA. L. REV. 597, 599-600 (2009). The Court has at times appeared to embrace this view by collapsing Steps One and Two into a single inquiry. *See, e.g., Entergy Corp. v. Riverkeeper, Inc.*, 556 U.S. 208, 218 n.4 (2009) ("The dissent finds it puzzling that we invoke this proposition (that a reasonable agency interpretation prevails) at the outset, omitting the supposedly prior inquiry of whether Congress has directly spoken to the precise question at issue. But surely if Congress has directly spoken to an issue then any agency interpretation contradicting what Congress has said would be unreasonable."

(internal quotations omitted)) (Scalia, J. writing for the majority). *See generally* 4 CHARLES H. KOCH, JR., ADMINISTRATIVE LAW & PRACTICE § 11:36 (3d ed. 2020). Nevertheless, most courts (including the Supreme Court) continue to regard Steps One and Two as analytically distinct. *See, e.g.,* Kenneth A. Bamberger & Peter L. Strauss, Chevron's *Two Steps*, 95 VA. L. REV. 611, 624-25 (2009) (describing the differences between the two steps).

The second aspect of this Step One/Step Two relationship puzzle relates to the evidence on which courts must rely when applying them. Some have argued that the evidence used to *resolve statutory ambiguity* at Step Two should be distinct from the evidence used to *determine clarity* or ambiguity at Step One. Pursuant to this view, courts should resort to extratextual sources of statutory meaning—such as legislative history—only when they reach Step Two. This would presumably preclude their consideration at Step One, effectively limiting the Step One inquiry to whether a statute is facially silent or ambiguous. *See, e.g., Bankers Life and Cas. Co. v. United States*, 142 F.3d 973, 983 (7th Cir. 1998) (describing the Supreme Court's decision in *National P.R. Passenger Corp. v. Boston & Maine Corp.*, 503 U.S. 407, 417-18 (1992) as "reformulating the first step of *Chevron* analysis by focusing on the plain language of the statute rather than the intent of Congress"). Extratextual sources of statutory meaning—legislative history, canons of construction, dictionary definitions, prior administrative or judicial interpretations—are relied upon to add meaning when the bare language of the statute falls short. Reliance on them at Step One will at least in some cases obviate any need to reach Step Two. *Cf. I.N.S. v. Cardoza-Fonseca*, 480 U.S. 421, 454 (1987) (Scalia, J., concurring) (arguing that *Chevron* would be eviscerated if "courts may substitute their interpretation of a statute for that of an agency whenever, employing traditional tools of statutory construction, they are able to reach a conclusion as to the proper interpretation" of a statute).

The second puzzle is whether *Chevron* Step Two and *State Farm* arbitrary and capricious review are actually the same test. It stems from disagreements about the nature of the silence or ambiguity found in Step One. Courts find these silences and ambiguities when they can glean no dispositive meaning from statutory language, legislative history, or other evidence of congressional intent. This implies that "law" and legal analysis have nothing more to contribute to the interpretive problem faced by the reviewing court. Other decision-making factors—experience, expertise, judgment—must then be relied upon to give the statutory provision real-world effect. This type of decision-making is the hallmark of discretionary policymaking undertaken by elected officials and administrators, rather than by judges. Accordingly, some have argued that the proper Step Two inquiry is the one used to ensure the "reasonableness" of factual and policy judgments in informal proceedings, namely the APA § 706(2)(A) arbitrary and capricious review standard on which the Court elaborated in *State Farm*. Others disagree. They argue that Step Two and *State Farm* are distinct inquiries that address distinct problems.

The following thoughtful opinion from Judge Robert D. Sack of the U.S. Court of Appeals for the Second Circuit explores this puzzle in detail. Are you persuaded by the distinction he drew between *State Farm* and *Chevron* Step 2?

Catskill Mountains Chapter of Trout Unlimited, Inc. v. Environmental Protection Agency

846 F.3d 492 (2d Cir. 2017), cert. denied 138 S. Ct. 1164 (2018);
138 S. Ct. 1165 (2018)

Before SACK, CHIN, and CARNEY, Circuit Judges.

SACK, Circuit Judge: . . .

BACKGROUND

The Clean Water Act and the National Pollutant Discharge Elimination System ("NPDES") Permitting Program

. . . [The Clean Water Act, 33 U.S.C. § 1251 *et seq.* ("CWA" or the "Act")] "prohibits 'the discharge of any pollutant by any person' unless done in compliance with some provision of the Act." *S. Fla. Water Mgmt. Dist. v. Miccosukee Tribe*, 541 U.S. 95, 102 ("Miccosukee") (quoting 33 U.S.C. § 1311(a)). The statute defines the discharge of a pollutant as "any addition of any pollutant to navigable waters from any point source," 33 U.S.C. § 1362(12)(A), where "navigable waters" means "the waters of the United States, including the territorial seas," *id.* § 1362(7). The principal provision under which such a discharge may be allowed is Section 402, which establishes the "National Pollutant Discharge Elimination System" ("NPDES") permitting program. 33 U.S.C. § 1342. With narrow exceptions not relevant here, a party must acquire an NPDES permit in order to discharge a specified amount of a specified pollutant. *See id.*; *Miccosukee*, 541 U.S. at 102. Thus, without an NPDES permit, it is unlawful for a party to discharge a pollutant into the nation's navigable waters.

. . . Noncompliance with an NPDES permit's conditions is a violation of the Clean Water Act. 33 U.S.C. § 1342(h). Once an NPDES permit has been issued, the EPA, states, and citizens can bring suit in federal court to enforce it. See *id.* §§ 1319(a)(3), 1365(a).

The Act envisions "cooperative federalism" in the management of the nation's water resources. Reflecting that approach, states typically control the NPDES permitting programs as they apply to waters within their borders, subject to EPA approval. *See* 33 U.S.C. §§ 1314(i)(2), 1342(b)-(c). The Act also preserves states' "primary responsibilities and rights" to abate pollution, *id.* § 1251(b), including their traditional prerogatives to "plan the development and use (including restoration, preservation, and enhancement) of . . . water resources," *id.* and to "allocate quantities of water within [their] jurisdiction," *id.* § 1251(g), subject to the federal floor on environmental protection set by the Act and regulations promulgated thereunder by the EPA.

Water Transfers and the Water Transfers Rule

According to EPA regulations, a "water transfer" is "an activity that conveys or connects waters of the United States without subjecting the transferred water to intervening industrial, municipal, or commercial use." 40 C.F.R. § 122.3(i). Water transfers take a variety of forms. A transfer may be accomplished, for example, through artificial tunnels and channels, or natural streams and water bodies; and through active pumping or passive direction. There are thousands of water transfers currently in place in the United States, including at least sixteen major diversion projects west of the Mississippi River. Many of the largest U.S. cities draw on water transfers to bring drinkable water to their residents. The City of New York's water supply system relies on transfers of water among its nineteen collecting reservoirs. The City provides approximately 1.2 billion gallons of water a day to nine million people—nearly half of the population of New York State.

. . . Because much precipitation in the [Western United States] falls as snow, water authorities there must capture water when and where the snow falls and melts, typically in remote and sparsely populated areas, and then transport it to agricultural and urban sites where it is most needed. . . .

At the same time, though, water transfers, like ballast water in ships . . . can move pollutants from one body of water to another, potentially endangering ecosystems, portions of the economy, and public health near the receiving water body—and possibly beyond. Despite these risks, for many years the EPA has taken a passive approach to regulating water transfers, effectively exempting them from the NPDES permitting system. The States have also generally adopted a hands-off policy.

During the 1990s and 2000s, prior to its codification in the Water Transfers Rule, the EPA's position was challenged by, among others, environmentalist groups, which filed several successful lawsuits asserting that NPDES permits were required for some specified water transfers [citing cases]. None of these decisions classified the EPA's views on the regulation of water transfers as sufficiently formal to warrant *Chevron* deference.

In response, the EPA took steps to formalize its position. In August 2005, the EPA's Office of General Counsel and Office of Water issued a legal memorandum written by then-EPA General Counsel Ann R. Klee (the "Klee Memorandum") that argued that Congress did not intend for water transfers to be subject to the NPDES permitting program. The EPA proposed a formal rule incorporating this interpretation on June 7, 2006, 71

Fed. Reg. 32,887, and then, following notice-and-comment rulemaking proceedings, on June 13, 2008, adopted a final rule entitled "National Pollutant Discharge Elimination System (NPDES) Water Transfers Rule" (the "Water Transfers Rule"), 73 Fed. Reg. 33,697-708 (June 13, 2008) (codified at 40 C.F.R. § 122.3(i)). . . .

The Rule states that water transfers "do not require NPDES permits because they do not result in the 'addition' of a pollutant." *Id.* at 33,699. No NPDES permit is required if "the water being conveyed [is] a water of the U.S. prior to being discharged to the receiving waterbody" and the water is transferred "from one water of the U.S. to another water of the U.S." *Id.* (footnote omitted). Thus, even if a water transfer conveys waters in which pollutants are present, it does not result in an "addition" to "the waters of the United States," because the pollutant is already present in "the waters of the United States." Under the EPA's view, an "addition" of a pollutant under the Act occurs only "when pollutants are introduced from outside the waters being transferred." *Id.* at 33,701. On appeal — but not in the Water Transfers Rule itself — the EPA characterizes this interpretation of Section 402 of the Clean Water Act as embracing what is often referred to as the "unitary-waters" reading of the statutory language. . . .

In the Water Transfers Rule, the EPA justified its interpretation of the Act in an explanation spanning nearly four pages of the Federal Register, touching on the text of Section 402, the structure of the Act, and pertinent legislative history. The EPA explained that its "holistic approach to the text" of the statute was "needed here in particular because the heart of this matter is the balance Congress created between federal and State oversight of activities affecting the nation's waters." *Id.* at 33,701. The agency also responded to a wide variety of public comments on the proposed Rule.

District Court Proceedings

On June 20, 2008, a group of environmental conservation and sporting organizations[, in addition to several states and the Province of Manitoba, Canada (collectively, the "Anti-Rules States") sued] the EPA and its Administrator. . . . In their complaints, the plaintiffs requested that the district court hold unlawful and set aside the Water Transfers Rule pursuant to Section 706(2) of the Administrative Procedure Act (the "APA"), 5 U.S.C. § 706(2). . . . [T]he district court consolidated the two cases and granted a motion by the City of New York to intervene in support of the defendants.

. . . [T]he district court granted the plaintiffs' motions for summary judgment and denied the defendants' cross-motions. At the first step of the *Chevron* analysis, the district court decided that the Clean Water Act is ambiguous as to whether Congress intended the NPDES program to apply to water transfers. *Id.* at 518-32. The district court then proceeded to the second step of the *Chevron* analysis, at which it struck down the Water Transfers Rule as an unreasonable interpretation of the Act. *Id.* at 532-67. . . .

DISCUSSION

. . . We conclude that the Water Transfers Rule is a reasonable interpretation of the Clean Water Act and is therefore entitled to *Chevron* deference. Accordingly, we reverse the judgment of the district court.

We evaluate challenges to an agency's interpretation of a statute that it administers within the two-step *Chevron* deference framework. At *Chevron* Step One, we ask "whether Congress has directly spoken to the precise question at issue. If the intent of Congress is clear, that is the end of the matter; for the court, as well as the agency, must give effect to the unambiguously expressed intent of Congress." *Chevron*, 467 U.S. at 842-43. If the statutory language is "silent or ambiguous," however, we proceed to *Chevron* Step Two, where "the question for the court is whether the agency's answer is based on a permissible construction of the statute" at issue. *Id.* at 843. If it is—i.e., if it is not "arbitrary, capricious, or manifestly contrary to the statute," *id.* at 844—we will accord deference to the agency's interpretation of the statute so long as it is supported by a reasoned explanation, and "so long as the construction is 'a reasonable policy choice for the agency to make,'" *Nat'l Cable & Telecomms. Ass'n v. Brand X Internet Servs.*, 545 U.S. 967, 986 (2005) ("Brand X") (quoting *Chevron*, 467 U.S. at 845). . . .

. . . [W]e begin at *Chevron* Step One. We conclude, as did the district court, that Congress did not in the Clean Water Act clearly and unambiguously speak to the precise question of whether NPDES permits are required for water transfers. It is therefore necessary to proceed to *Chevron* Step Two, under which we conclude that the EPA's interpretation of the Act in the Water Transfers Rule represents a reasonable policy choice to which we must defer. The question is whether the Clean Water Act can support the EPA's interpretation, taking into account the full panoply of interpretive considerations advanced by the parties. Ultimately, we conclude that the Water Transfers Rule satisfies *Chevron*'s deferential standard of review because it is supported by a reasoned explanation that sets forth a reasonable interpretation of the Act.

[In Section I of its discussion, the court conducted a lengthy and highly detailed analysis of whether the CWA unambiguously spoke to whether NPDES permits are required for water transfers. It concluded that the CWA did not provide a definitive answer and thus proceeded to analyze the EPA's Water Transfers rule under *Chevron* Step Two.]

II. CHEVRON STEP TWO. . . .

A. *Legal Standard*

The question for the reviewing court at *Chevron* Step Two is "whether the agency's answer [to the interpretive question] is based on a permissible construction of the statute." *Mayo Found. for Med. Educ. & Research v. United States*, 562 U.S. 44, 54 (2011) (quoting *Chevron*, 467 U.S. at 843). We will not disturb an agency rule at *Chevron* Step Two unless it is "arbitrary or capricious in substance, or manifestly contrary to the statute." *Id.* at 53. Generally, an agency interpretation is not "arbitrary, capricious, or manifestly contrary to the statute" if it is "reasonable." *See Encino Motorcars, LLC v. Navarro*, —— U.S. ——, 136 S. Ct. 2117, 2125 (2016). The agency's view need not be "the only possible interpretation, nor even the interpretation deemed *most* reasonable by the courts." *Entergy Corp. v. Riverkeeper, Inc.*, 556 U.S. 208, 218 (2009) (emphasis in original). This approach "is premised on the theory that a statute's ambiguity constitutes an implicit delegation from Congress to the agency to fill in the statutory gaps." *FDA v. Brown & Williamson Tobacco Corp.*, 529 U.S. 120, 159 (2000). When interpreting ambiguous statutory language "involves difficult policy choices," deference is especially appropriate because "agencies are better equipped to make [these choices] than courts." *Brand X*, 545 U.S. at 980.

"Even under this deferential standard, however, agencies must operate within the bounds of reasonable interpretation," *Michigan v. EPA*, —— U.S. ——, 135 S. Ct. 2699, 2707 (2015) (internal quotation marks omitted), and we therefore will not defer to an agency interpretation if it is not supported by a reasoned explanation. An agency interpretation would surely be "arbitrary" or "capricious" if it were picked out of a hat, or arrived at with no explanation, even if it might otherwise be deemed reasonable on some unstated ground.

In the course of its *Chevron* Step Two analysis, the district court incorporated the standard for evaluating agency action under APA § 706(2)(A) set forth in *Motor Vehicle Manufacturers Association v. State Farm Mutual Automobile Insurance Company*, 463 U.S. 29 (1983), a much stricter and more exacting review of the agency's rationale and decisionmaking process than the *Chevron* Step Two standard. Under that section, a reviewing court may set aside an agency action if it is "arbitrary, capricious, an abuse of discretion, or otherwise not in accordance with law." 5 U.S.C. § 706(2)(A). . . . On appeal, the plaintiffs urge us to incorporate the *State Farm* standard into our *Chevron* Step Two analysis, and to affirm the district court's vacatur of the Rule for essentially the same reasons stated by the court. While we have great respect for the district court's careful and searching analysis of the EPA's rationale for the Water Transfers Rule, we conclude that it erred by incorporating the *State Farm* standard into its *Chevron* Step Two analysis and thereby applying too strict a standard of review. An agency's initial interpretation of a statutory provision should be evaluated only under the *Chevron* framework, which does not incorporate the *State Farm* standard. *State Farm* review may be appropriate in a case involving a non-interpretive rule or a rule setting forth a changed interpretation of a statute; but that is not so in the case before us.

As the Supreme Court, our Circuit, and other Courts of Appeals have made reasonably clear, *State Farm* and *Chevron* provide for related but distinct standards for reviewing rules promulgated by administrative agencies. *State Farm* is used to evaluate whether a rule is procedurally defective as a result of flaws in the agency's decisionmaking process. *Chevron*, by contrast, is generally used to evaluate whether the conclusion reached as a result of that process — an agency's interpretation of a statutory provision it administers — is reasonable. A litigant challenging a rule may challenge it under *State Farm*, *Chevron*, or both. As Judge Wald explained,

> there are certainly situations where a challenge to an agency's regulation will fall squarely within one rubric, rather than the other. For example, we might invalidate an agency's decision under *Chevron* as inconsistent with its statutory mandate, even though we do not believe the decision reflects an arbitrary policy choice. Such a result might occur when we believe the agency's course of action to be the most appropriate and effective means of achieving a goal, but determine that Congress has selected a different — albeit, in our eyes, less propitious — path. Conversely, we might determine that although not barred by statute, an agency's action is arbitrary and capricious because the agency has not considered certain relevant factors or articulated any rationale for its choice. Or, along similar lines, we might find a regulation arbitrary and capricious, while deciding that *Chevron* is inapplicable because Congress' delegation to the agency is so broad as to be virtually unreviewable.

Arent v. Shalala, 70 F.3d 610, 620 (D.C. Cir. 1995) (Wald, J., concurring) (citation and footnotes omitted).

Much confusion about the relationship between *State Farm* and *Chevron* seems to arise because both standards purport to provide a method by which to evaluate whether an agency action is "arbitrary" or "capricious," and *Chevron* Step Two analysis and *State Farm* analysis often, though not always, take the same factors into consideration and therefore overlap. We read the case law to stand for the proposition that where a litigant brings both a *State Farm* challenge and a *Chevron* challenge to a rule, and the *State Farm* challenge is successful, there is no need for the reviewing court to engage in *Chevron* analysis. As the Supreme Court has explained, "where a proper challenge is raised to the agency procedures, and those procedures are defective, a court should not accord *Chevron* deference to the agency interpretation." *Encino*, 136 S. Ct. at 2125. In other words, if an interpretive rule was promulgated in a procedurally defective manner, it will be set aside regardless of whether its interpretation of the statute is reasonable. If the rule is not defective under *State Farm*, though, that conclusion does not avoid the need for a *Chevron* analysis, which does not incorporate the *State Farm* standard. . . .

Several other considerations also counsel against employing the searching *State Farm* standard of review of the agency's decisionmaking and rationale at *Chevron* Step Two. The Supreme Court has decided that agencies are not obligated to conduct detailed fact-finding or cost-benefit analyses when interpreting a statute — which suggests that the full-fledged *State Farm* standard may not apply to rules that set forth for the first time an agency's interpretation of a particular statutory provision. *See, e.g., Pension Benefit Guar. Corp. v. LTV Corp.*, 496 U.S. 633, 651-52 (1990) (an agency may interpret an ambiguous statutory provision by making "judgments about the way the real world works" without making formal factual findings); *Entergy*, 556 U.S. at 223 (absent statutory language to the contrary, an agency is not required to conduct cost-benefit analysis under *Chevron*). These decisions seem to establish that while an agency may support its statutory interpretation with factual materials or cost-benefit analyses, an agency need not do so in order for its interpretation to be regarded as reasonable.

Further, the Supreme Court has cautioned that *State Farm* is "inapposite to the extent that it may be read as prescribing more searching judicial review" in a case involving an agency's "first interpretation of a new statute." *Verizon Commc'ns Inc. v. FCC*, 535 U.S. 467, 502 n.20 (2002). Dovetailing with this point, the Supreme Court held in *Brand X* and *Fox Television Stations* that when an agency changes its interpretation of a particular statutory provision, this change is reviewable under APA § 706(2)(A), and will be set aside if the agency has failed to provide a "reasoned explanation . . . for disregarding facts and circumstances that underlay or were engendered by the prior policy." *Fox Television*, 556 U.S. at 516; *Brand X*, 545 U.S. at 981 (explaining that "[u]nexplained inconsistency" is "a reason for holding an [agency] interpretation to be an arbitrary and capricious change from agency practice under the [APA]"). Of course, if all interpretive rules were reviewable under APA § 706(2)(A) and the *State Farm* standard, these pronouncements in *Brand X* and *Fox Television Stations* would have been unnecessary. We also note that applying a reasonableness standard to the agency's decisionmaking and rationale at *Chevron* Step Two instead of a heightened *State Farm*-type standard promotes respect for agencies' policymaking discretion and promotes policymaking flexibility.

For these reasons, the plaintiffs' challenge to the Water Transfers Rule is properly analyzed under the *Chevron* framework, which does not incorporate the *State Farm* standard. . . .

B. Reasoned Rationale for the EPA's Interpretation

We conclude that the EPA provided a reasoned explanation for its decision in the Water Transfers Rule to interpret the Clean Water Act as not requiring NPDES permits for water transfers. . . .

In the Water Transfers Rule, the EPA analyzed the text of the statute, explaining how its interpretation was justified by its understanding of the phrase "the waters of the United States," *id.* at 33,701, as well as by the broader statutory scheme, noting that the Clean Water Act provides for several programs and regulatory initiatives other than the NPDES permitting program that could be used to mitigate pollution caused by water transfers, *id.*

at 33,701-33,702. The EPA also justified the Rule by reference to statutory purpose, noting its view that "Congress intended to leave primary oversight of water transfers to state authorities in cooperation with Federal authorities," and that Congress intended to create a "balance . . . between federal and State oversight of activities affecting the nation's waters." *Id.* at 33,701. The EPA also stated that subjecting water transfers to NPDES permitting could affect states' ability to effectively allocate water and water rights, *id.* at 33,702, and explained how its interpretation was justified in light of the Act's legislative history, *see id.* at 33,703. The EPA concluded by addressing several public comments on the Rule, and explaining in a reasoned manner why it rejected proposed alternative readings of the Clean Water Act. *See id.* at 33,703-33,706.

This rationale, while not immune to criticism or counterargument, was sufficiently reasoned to clear *Chevron*'s rather minimal requirement that the agency give a reasoned explanation for its interpretation. We see nothing illogical in the EPA's rationale. The agency provided a sufficiently reasoned explanation for its interpretation of the Clean Water Act in the Water Transfers Rule. The Rule's interpretation of the Clean Water Act was therefore not adopted in an "arbitrary" or "capricious" manner. Accordingly, we must address whether the Rule's interpretation of the Clean Water Act was, ultimately, reasonable.

C. Reasonableness of the EPA's Interpretation

Having concluded that the EPA offered a sufficient explanation for adopting the Rule, we next examine whether the Rule reasonably interprets the Clean Water Act. We conclude that it does. The EPA's interpretation of the Clean Water Act as reflected in the Rule is supported by several valid arguments—interpretive, theoretical, and practical. The permissibility of the Rule is reinforced by longstanding practice and acquiescence by Congress, recent case law, practical concerns regarding compliance costs, and the existence of alternative means for regulating pollution resulting from water transfers. . . .

For the foregoing reasons, we defer under *Chevron* to the EPA's interpretation of the Clean Water Act in the Water Transfers Rule. Accordingly, we reverse the judgment of the district court and reinstate the challenged rule.

QUESTION SET 9.31

Review & Synthesis

1. Do you agree with Judge Sack that *State Farm*'s arbitrary and capricious review is primarily concerned with the process by which an agency makes its decisions, whereas *Chevron* Step Two is primarily concerned with

whether a by-product of that decision — the interpretation of an ambiguous statute — is reasonable?

2. The court divided its Step Two inquiry into two parts. The first focused on whether the EPA provided a "reasoned explanation" for adopting the Water Transfers Rule. The second focused on whether the interpretation of the Clean Water Act in the Water Transfers Rule was reasonable. Does this seem consistent with how the Court described the test in *Chevron* itself? Specifically, does *Chevron* require courts to accept an agency's *justifications* for choosing one plausible interpretation of an ambiguous statute over another, or does it just require that the agency's interpretation itself be permissible?

3. The court indicated that *State Farm* requires a more searching review than does *Chevron* Step Two. Why would that be the case? Was Judge Sack arguing that the persuasiveness of the justifications required by *State Farm* is greater than what is required by *Chevron* Step Two?

4. Why, as Judge Sack reasoned, would *State Farm* be applicable to agency non-interpretive rules or to agency rule changes, but not to initial interpretations of rules?

---

e. *Chevron*: Flexibility in Agency Interpretations

Courts have long acknowledged that agencies have flexibility to adapt their policies to changing conditions, so long as they stay within the statutory bounds Congress has set for them. Recall that the Supreme Court exhibited this understanding in *Chevron* itself, where the EPA changed its interpretation of the Clean Air Act term "stationary source." Based on a pair of D.C. Circuit rulings, the EPA had interpreted "stationary source" to allow use of the "bubble concept" in programs to maintain air quality but not in those to enhance air quality (i.e., in nonattainment states). The agency changed course after Ronald Reagan assumed the Presidency in 1981, reinterpreting the term to allow use of the "bubble concept" in both maintenance and non-attainment states. The Court deferred to that reinterpretation. The Court has likewise recognized this flexibility in the related context of agencies exercising policymaking authority expressly delegated by Congress. In *Federal Communications Commission v. Fox Television Stations, Inc., supra* page 935, the Court rejected a reading of APA § 706(2)(A) that would have required the FCC to demonstrate that its new obscenity policy was both reasonable and "better" than the obscenity policy it replaced. For purposes of satisfying the arbitrary and capricious review standard, demonstrating the former was sufficient.

The fact that agencies are permitted to change policy positions (within prescribed limits) raises two questions. First, must agencies demonstrate that new interpretations of the statutes they administer are "better" than old ones? In other words, does the reasoning relied upon in *Fox Television* also apply to agency interpretations of the ambiguous statutes they administer? Second, what impact does agencies' policy flexibility have on *stare decisis*? Assume that a court interprets a regulatory statute before the agency charged with administering it has a chance to do so. Is the agency subsequently bound to that interpretation because of *stare decisis*? Would allowing the agency to reject that initial judicial interpretation give it ostensible power to *reverse* a decision of an Article III court? The following case addressed these questions.

National Cable & Telecommunications Association v. Brand X Internet Services
545 U.S. 967 (2005)

Justice THOMAS delivered the opinion of the Court.

Title II of the Communications Act of 1934, 48 Stat. 1064, as amended, 47 U.S.C. § 151 *et seq.*, subjects all providers of "telecommunications servic[e]" to mandatory common-carrier regulation, § 153(44). In the order under review, the Federal Communications Commission concluded that cable companies that sell broadband Internet service do not provide "telecommunications servic[e]" as the Communications Act defines that term, and hence are exempt from mandatory common-carrier regulation under Title II. We must decide whether that conclusion is a lawful construction of the Communications Act under *Chevron U.S.A. Inc. v. Natural Resources Defense Council, Inc.*, 467 U.S. 837 (1984), and the Administrative Procedure Act, 5 U.S.C. § 551 *et seq.* We hold that it is.

I. . . .

. . . There are two principal kinds of broadband Internet service: cable modem service and Digital Subscriber Line (DSL) service. Cable modem service transmits data between the Internet and users' computers via the network of television cable lines owned by cable companies. DSL service provides high-speed access using the local telephone wires owned by local telephone companies. Cable companies and telephone companies can either provide Internet access directly to consumers, thus acting as ISPs themselves, or can lease their transmission facilities to independent ISPs that then use the facilities to provide consumers with Internet access. Other ways of transmitting high-speed Internet data into homes, including terrestrial- and satellite-based wireless networks, are also emerging.

II

At issue in these cases is the proper regulatory classification under the Communications Act of broadband cable Internet service. The Act, as amended by the Telecommunications Act of 1996, 110 Stat. 56, defines two categories of regulated entities relevant to these cases: telecommunications carriers and information-service providers. The Act regulates telecommunications carriers, but not information-service providers, as common carriers. Telecommunications carriers, for example, must charge just and reasonable, nondiscriminatory rates to their customers, 47 U.S.C. §§ 201-209, design their systems so that other carriers can interconnect with their communications networks, § 251(a)(1), and contribute to the federal "universal service" fund, § 254(d). These provisions are mandatory, but the Commission must forbear from applying them if it determines that the public interest requires it. §§ 160(a), (b). Information-service providers, by contrast, are not subject to mandatory common-carrier regulation under Title II, though the Commission has jurisdiction to impose additional regulatory obligations under its Title I ancillary jurisdiction to regulate interstate and foreign communications, *see* §§ 151-161. . . .

These two statutory classifications originated in the late 1970's, as the Commission developed rules to regulate data-processing services offered over telephone wires. That regime, the "Computer II" rules, distinguished between "basic" service (like telephone service) and "enhanced" service (computer-processing service offered over telephone lines). The Computer II rules defined both basic and enhanced services by reference to how the consumer perceives the service being offered.

In particular, the Commission defined "basic service" as "a pure transmission capability over a communications path that is virtually transparent in terms of its interaction with customer supplied information." By "pure" or "transparent" transmission, the Commission meant a communications path that enabled the consumer to transmit an ordinary-language message to another point, with no computer processing or storage of the information, other than the processing or storage needed to convert the message into electronic form and then back into ordinary language for purposes of transmitting it over the network—such as via a telephone or a facsimile. Basic service was subject to common-carrier regulation.

"[E]nhanced service," however, was service in which "computer processing applications [were] used to act on the content, code, protocol, and other aspects of the subscriber's information," such as voice and data storage services, as well as "protocol conversion" (i.e., ability to communicate between networks that employ different data-transmission formats). By contrast to basic service, the Commission decided not to subject providers of enhanced service, even enhanced service offered via transmission wires, to Title II common-carrier regulation. The Commission explained that it was unwise to subject enhanced service to common-carrier regulation given the "fast-moving, competitive market" in which they were offered.

[As used in the 1996 Act,] "[t]elecommunications service" . . . is "the offering of telecommunications for a fee directly to the public . . . regardless of the facilities used." 47 U.S.C. § 153(46). "Telecommunications" is "the transmission, between or among points specified by the user, of information of the user's choosing, without change in the form or content of the information as sent and received." § 153(43). "Telecommunications carrier[s]" — those subjected to mandatory Title II common-carrier regulation — are defined as "provider[s] of telecommunications services." § 153(44). And "information service" . . . is "the offering of a capability for generating, acquiring, storing, transforming, processing, retrieving, utilizing, or making available information via telecommunications. . . ." § 153(20).

In September 2000, the Commission initiated a rulemaking proceeding to, among other things, apply these classifications to cable companies that offer broadband Internet service directly to consumers. In March 2002, that rulemaking culminated in the Declaratory Ruling under review in these cases. In the Declaratory Ruling, the Commission concluded that broadband Internet service provided by cable companies is an "information service" but not a "telecommunications service" under the Act, and therefore not subject to mandatory Title II common-carrier regulation. In support of this conclusion, the Commission relied heavily on its Universal Service Report. The Universal Service Report classified "non-facilities-based" ISPs [("Internet Service Providers")] — those that do not own the transmission facilities they use to connect the end user to the Internet — solely as information-service providers. Unlike those ISPs, cable companies own the cable lines they use to provide Internet access. Nevertheless, in the Declaratory Ruling, the Commission found no basis in the statutory definitions for treating cable companies differently from non-facilities-based ISPs: Both offer "a single, integrated service that enables the subscriber to utilize Internet access service . . . and to realize the benefits of a comprehensive service offering." Declaratory Ruling 4823, ¶ 38. Because Internet access provides a capability for manipulating and storing information, the Commission concluded that it was an information service. *Ibid.*

The integrated nature of Internet access and the high-speed wire used to provide Internet access led the Commission to conclude that cable companies providing Internet access are not telecommunications providers. This conclusion, the Commission reasoned, followed from the logic of the Universal Service Report. The Report had concluded that, though Internet service "involves data transport elements" because "an Internet access provider must enable the movement of information between customers' own computers and distant computers with which those customers seek to interact," it also "offers end users information-service capabilities inextricably intertwined with data transport." Universal Service Report 11539–11540, ¶ 80. ISPs, therefore, were not "offering . . . telecommunications . . . directly to the public," § 153(46), and so were not properly classified as telecommunications carriers. In other words, the Commission reasoned that consumers use their cable modems not to transmit information "transparently," such as by using a telephone, but instead to obtain Internet access.

The Commission applied this same reasoning to cable companies offering broadband Internet access. Its logic was that, like non-facilities-based ISPs, cable companies do not "offe[r] telecommunications service to the end user, but rather . . . merely us[e] telecommunications to provide end users with cable modem service." Declaratory Ruling 4824, ¶ 41. Though the Commission declined to apply mandatory Title II common-carrier regulation to cable companies, it invited comment on whether under its Title I jurisdiction it should require cable companies to offer other ISPs access to their facilities on common-carrier terms. Numerous parties petitioned for judicial review, challenging the Commission's conclusion that cable modem service was not telecommunications service. By judicial lottery, the Court of Appeals for the Ninth Circuit was selected as the venue for the challenge.

The Court of Appeals granted the petitions in part, vacated the Declaratory Ruling in part, and remanded to the Commission for further proceedings. In particular, the Court of Appeals vacated the ruling to the extent it concluded that cable modem service was not "telecommunications service" under the Communications Act. It held that the Commission could not permissibly construe the Communications Act to exempt cable companies providing Internet service from Title II regulation. Rather than analyzing the permissibility of that construction under the deferential framework of *Chevron*, 467 U.S. 837, however, the Court of Appeals grounded its holding in the *stare decisis* effect of *AT & T Corp. v. Portland*, 216 F.3d 871 (9th Cir. 2000). *Portland* held that cable modem service was a "telecommunications service," though the court in that case was not reviewing an administrative proceeding and the Commission was not a party to the case. Nevertheless, *Portland*'s holding, the Court of Appeals reasoned, overrode the contrary interpretation reached by the Commission in the Declaratory Ruling.

We granted certiorari to settle the important questions of federal law that these cases present.

III

We first consider whether we should apply *Chevron*'s framework to the Commission's interpretation of the term "telecommunications service." We conclude that we should. We also conclude that the Court of Appeals should have done the same, instead of following the contrary construction it adopted in *Portland*.

A

In *Chevron*, this Court held that ambiguities in statutes within an agency's jurisdiction to administer are delegations of authority to the agency to fill the statutory gap in reasonable fashion. Filling these gaps, the Court explained, involves difficult policy choices that agencies are better equipped to make than courts. 467 U.S., at 865-866. If a statute is ambiguous, and if the implementing agency's construction is reasonable, *Chevron* requires a federal court to accept the agency's construction of the statute, even if the agency's reading differs from what the court believes is the best statutory interpretation. *Id.* at 843-844, and note 11.

The *Chevron* framework governs our review of the Commission's construction. Congress has delegated to the Commission the authority to "execute and enforce" the Communications Act, § 151, and to "prescribe such rules and regulations as may be necessary in the public interest to carry out the provisions" of the Act, § 201(b). These provisions give the Commission the authority to promulgate binding legal rules; the Commission issued the order under review in the exercise of that authority; and no one questions that the order is within the Commission's jurisdiction. *See United States v. Mead Corp.,* 533 U.S. 218, 231-234 (2001); *Christensen v. Harris County,* 529 U.S. 576, 586-588 (2000). Hence, as we have in the past, we apply the *Chevron* framework to the Commission's interpretation of the Communications Act.

Some of the respondents dispute this conclusion, on the ground that the Commission's interpretation is inconsistent with its past practice. We reject this argument. Agency inconsistency is not a basis for declining to analyze the agency's interpretation under the *Chevron* framework. Unexplained inconsistency is, at most, a reason for holding an interpretation to be an arbitrary and capricious change from agency practice under the Administrative Procedure Act. *See Motor Vehicle Mfrs. Assn. of United States, Inc. v. State Farm Mut. Automobile Ins. Co.,* 463 U.S. 29, 46–57 (1983). For if the agency adequately explains the reasons for a reversal of policy, "change is not invalidating, since the whole point of *Chevron* is to leave the discretion provided by the ambiguities of a statute with the implementing agency." *Smiley v. Citibank (South Dakota), N. A.,* 517 U.S. 735, 742 (1996). "An initial agency interpretation is not instantly carved in stone. On the contrary, the agency . . . must consider varying interpretations and the wisdom of its policy on a continuing basis," *Chevron, supra,* at 863-864, for example, in response to changed factual circumstances, or a change in administrations, *see State Farm, supra,* at 59 (Rehnquist, J., concurring in part and dissenting in part). That is no doubt why in *Chevron* itself, this Court deferred to an agency interpretation that was a recent reversal of agency policy. *See* 467 U.S., at 857-858. We therefore have no difficulty concluding that *Chevron* applies.

B

The Court of Appeals declined to apply *Chevron* because it thought the Commission's interpretation of the Communications Act foreclosed by the conflicting construction of the Act it had adopted in *Portland*. It based that holding on the assumption that *Portland*'s construction overrode the Commission's, regardless of whether *Portland* had held the statute to be unambiguous. That reasoning was incorrect.

A court's prior judicial construction of a statute trumps an agency construction otherwise entitled to *Chevron* deference only if the prior court decision holds that its construction follows from the unambiguous terms of the statute and thus leaves no room for agency discretion. This principle follows from *Chevron* itself. *Chevron* established a "presumption that Congress, when it left ambiguity in a statute meant for implementation by an agency, understood that the ambiguity would be resolved, first and foremost, by the agency, and desired the agency (rather than the courts) to possess whatever degree of discretion the ambiguity allows." *Smiley, supra*, at 740-741. Yet allowing a judicial precedent to foreclose an agency from interpreting an ambiguous statute, as the Court of Appeals assumed it could, would allow a court's interpretation to override an agency's. *Chevron*'s premise is that it is for agencies, not courts, to fill statutory gaps. *See* 467 U.S., at 843-844, and note 11. The better rule is to hold judicial interpretations contained in precedents to the same demanding *Chevron* step one standard that applies if the court is reviewing the agency's construction on a blank slate: Only a judicial precedent holding that the statute unambiguously forecloses the agency's interpretation, and therefore contains no gap for the agency to fill, displaces a conflicting agency construction.

A contrary rule would produce anomalous results. It would mean that whether an agency's interpretation of an ambiguous statute is entitled to *Chevron* deference would turn on the order in which the interpretations issue: If the court's construction came first, its construction would prevail, whereas if the agency's came first, the agency's construction would command *Chevron* deference. Yet whether Congress has delegated to an agency the authority to interpret a statute does not depend on the order in which the judicial and administrative constructions occur. The Court of Appeals' rule, moreover, would "lead to the ossification of large portions of our statutory law," *Mead*, 533 U.S., at 247 (Scalia, J., dissenting), by precluding agencies from revising unwise judicial constructions of ambiguous statutes. Neither *Chevron* nor the doctrine of *stare decisis* requires these haphazard results.

The dissent answers that allowing an agency to override what a court believes to be the best interpretation of a statute makes "judicial decisions subject to reversal by executive officers." It does not. Since *Chevron* teaches that a court's opinion as to the best reading of an ambiguous statute an agency is charged with administering is not authoritative, the agency's decision to construe that statute differently from a court does not say that the court's holding was legally wrong. Instead, the agency may, consistent with the court's holding, choose a different construction, since the agency remains the authoritative interpreter (within the limits of reason) of such statutes. In all other respects, the court's prior ruling remains binding law (for example, as to agency interpretations to which *Chevron* is inapplicable). The precedent has not been "reversed" by the agency, any more than a federal court's interpretation of a State's law can be said to have been "reversed" by a state court that adopts a conflicting (yet authoritative) interpretation of state law. . . .

. . . [T]he Court of Appeals erred in refusing to apply *Chevron* to the Commission's interpretation of the definition of "telecommunications service," 47 U.S.C. § 153(46). Its prior decision in *Portland* held only that the best reading of § 153(46) was that cable modem service was a "telecommunications service," not that it was the only permissible reading of the statute. Nothing in *Portland* held that the Communications Act unambiguously required treating cable Internet providers as telecommunications carriers. Instead, the court noted that it was "not presented with a case involving potential deference to an administrative agency's statutory construction pursuant to the *Chevron* doctrine," and the court invoked no other rule of construction (such as the rule of lenity) requiring it to conclude that the statute was unambiguous to reach its judgment. Before a judicial construction of a statute, whether contained in a precedent or not, may trump an agency's, the court must hold that the statute unambiguously requires the court's construction. *Portland* did not do so. . . .

[In Section IV of its opinion, the Court applied the *Chevron* deference analysis to the FCC's interpretation of the term "telecommunications service." It concluded that the term is ambiguous under *Chevron* Step One, and that the agency's construction of it was reasonable under *Chevron* Step Two. In Section V, the Court addressed whether the FCC acted arbitrarily and capriciously under APA § 706(2)(A) by not classifying cable modem providers as common carriers. It had assigned this classification to DSL providers who, as a result, had to make the telephone lines they used to transmit DSL service available to competing ISPs on a nondiscriminatory basis. The Court found that the FCC had provided a reasoned explanation for treating cable modem and DSL providers differently.]

* * *

The questions the Commission resolved in the order under review involve a subject matter that is technical, complex, and dynamic. The Commission is in a far better position to address these questions than we are. Nothing in the Communications Act or the Administrative Procedure Act makes unlawful the Commission's use of its expert policy judgment to resolve these difficult questions. The judgment of the Court of Appeals is reversed, and the cases are remanded for further proceedings consistent with this opinion.

It is so ordered.

[The concurring opinions of Justices STEVENS and BREYER are omitted.]

Justice SCALIA . . . dissenting. . . .

In Part III-B of its opinion, the Court continues the administrative-law improvisation project it began four years ago in *United States v. Mead*

Corp., 533 U.S. 218 (2001). To the extent it set forth a comprehensible rule, *Mead* drastically limited the categories of agency action that would qualify for deference under *Chevron U.S.A. Inc. v. Natural Resources Defense Council, Inc.,* 467 U.S. 837 (1984). For example, the position taken by an agency before the Supreme Court, with full approval of the agency head, would not qualify. Rather, some unspecified degree of formal process was required—or was at least the only safe harbor. *See Mead, supra,* at 245-246 (Scalia, J., dissenting).

This meant that many more issues appropriate for agency determination would reach the courts without benefit of an agency position entitled to *Chevron* deference, requiring the courts to rule on these issues *de novo.*[10] As I pointed out in dissent, this in turn meant (under the law as it was understood until today) that many statutory ambiguities that might be resolved in varying fashions by successive agency administrations would be resolved finally, conclusively, and forever, by federal judges—producing an "ossification of large portions of our statutory law," 533 U.S., at 247. The Court today moves to solve this problem of its own creation by inventing yet another breathtaking novelty: judicial decisions subject to reversal by executive officers.

Imagine the following sequence of events: FCC action is challenged as *ultra vires* under the governing statute; the litigation reaches all the way to the Supreme Court of the United States. The Solicitor General sets forth the FCC's official position (approved by the Commission) regarding interpretation of the statute. Applying *Mead,* however, the Court denies the agency position *Chevron* deference, finds that the best interpretation of the statute contradicts the agency's position, and holds the challenged agency action unlawful. The agency promptly conducts a rulemaking, and adopts a rule that comports with its earlier position—in effect disagreeing with the Supreme Court concerning the best interpretation of the statute. According to today's opinion, the agency is thereupon free to take the action that the Supreme Court found unlawful.

This is not only bizarre. It is probably unconstitutional. As we held in *Chicago & Southern Air Lines, Inc. v. Waterman S.S. Corp.,* 333 U.S. 103 (1948), Article III courts do not sit to render decisions that can be reversed or ignored by executive officers. . . . As I noted in my *Mead* dissent, the Court bristled at the suggestion: "Judgments within the powers vested in courts by the Judiciary Article of the Constitution may not lawfully be revised, overturned or refused faith and credit by another Department of Government."

---

[10] It is true that, even under the broad basis for deference that I propose (*viz.,* any agency position that plainly has the approval of the agency head, *see United States v. Mead Corp.,* 533 U.S. 218, 256-257 (2001) (Scalia, J., dissenting)), some interpretive matters will be decided *de novo,* without deference to agency views. This would be a rare occurrence, however, at the Supreme Court level—at least with respect to matters of any significance to the agency. Seeking to achieve 100% agency control of ambiguous provisions through the complicated method the Court proposes is not worth the incremental benefit.

Waterman, supra, at 113. That is what today's decision effectively allows. Even when the agency itself is party to the case in which the Court construes a statute, the agency will be able to disregard that construction and seek *Chevron* deference for its contrary construction the next time around.

Of course, like *Mead* itself, today's novelty in belated remediation of *Mead* creates many uncertainties to bedevil the lower courts. A court's interpretation is conclusive, the Court says, only if it holds that interpretation to be "the only permissible reading of the statute," and not if it merely holds it to be "the best reading." Does this mean that in future statutory-construction cases involving agency-administered statutes courts must specify (presumably in dictum) which of the two they are holding? And what of the many cases decided in the past, before this dictum's requirement was established? Apparently, silence on the point means that the court's decision is subject to agency reversal. . . . (I have not made, and as far as I know the Court has not made, any calculation of how many hundreds of past statutory decisions are now agency-reversible because of failure to include an "unambiguous" finding. I suspect the number is very large.) How much extra work will it entail for each court confronted with an agency-administered statute to determine whether it has reached, not only the right ("best") result, but "the only permissible" result? Is the standard for "unambiguous" under the Court's new agency-reversal rule the same as the standard for "unambiguous" under step one of *Chevron*? (If so, of course, every case that reaches step two of *Chevron* will be agency-reversible.) Does the "unambiguous" dictum produce *stare decisis* effect even when a court is affirming, rather than reversing, agency action — so that in the future the agency must adhere to that affirmed interpretation? If so, does the victorious agency have the right to appeal a Court of Appeals judgment in its favor, on the ground that the text in question is in fact not (as the Court of Appeals held) unambiguous, so the agency should be able to change its view in the future?

It is indeed a wonderful new world that the Court creates, one full of promise for administrative-law professors in need of tenure articles and, of course, for litigators. I would adhere to what has been the rule in the past: When a court interprets a statute without *Chevron* deference to agency views, its interpretation (whether or not asserted to rest upon an unambiguous text) is the law. . . .

I respectfully dissent.

QUESTION SET 9.32

Review & Synthesis

1. According to *Brand X*, must agencies that reinterpret the ambiguous statutes they administer establish the superiority of the newer interpretation? If not, do agencies have any burden in explaining such changes?

2. Under what circumstances may an agency interpretation of the statute it administers supersede the interpretation given by a federal court? Under what circumstances must an agency accept a federal court's interpretation?

3. Justice Thomas and Justice Scalia disagreed on whether the order in which agencies and courts interpret ambiguous statutes matters for definitively determining their meaning. What were their respective positions and which do you find most persuasive? For instance, do you think it is descriptively accurate to say that the Court's understanding of *Chevron* allows agencies to reverse the decisions of federal courts?

4. Justice Thomas analogized the relationship between agency and court interpretations to federal courts' interpretations of state law. How illuminating is that comparison? As part of separate, quasi-sovereign entities, state courts have authority to definitively interpret the meaning of their own laws. Can the same be said of agencies, even if they are delegated policymaking authority by Congress? Relatedly, how should courts adjust to agencies' interpretive primacy after *Brand X*? When applying state law, federal courts must interpret it as would the highest court in the state that created it. Should courts similarly anticipate and follow how an agency entitled to *Chevron* deference might interpret an ambiguous statute? Is such an assignment even feasible?

Application & Analysis

1. Pursuant to Immigration and Nationality Act ("INA") § 245(i)(2)(A), 8 U.S.C. § 1255(i)(2)(A), the Attorney General may grant lawful permanent residence to those who have entered and are residing in the country unlawfully. To be eligible for this "adjustment of status" ("AOS"), the applicant must be physically present in the United States, have a sponsor file a residence petition on his or her behalf, and pay a $1,000 fine. A different section of the INA, § 212(a)(9)(C)(i)(I), 8 U.S.C. § 1182(a)(9)(C)(i)(I), seems incompatible with the Attorney General's AOS authority. It categorically bars anyone with multiple illegal entries from gaining lawful permanent residence unless they first wait outside of the country for at least ten years. The INA's text gives no indication as to which provision supersedes the other.

   Sarah Eglund, a Canadian citizen currently residing in Denver, Colorado, entered the United States without documentation on multiple occasions but has not left the country since July 2000. Last year, Immigration and Customs Enforcement ("ICE") initiated removal proceedings against her. Eglund then petitioned for discretionary AOS under § 245(i)(2)(A). In a hearing before an Immigration Judge ("IJ"), ICE conceded that Eglund satisfies all of the AOS eligibility criteria. Nevertheless, it argued that Eglund's petition cannot be granted because

§ 212(a)(9)(C)(i)(I) trumps the Attorney General's AOS authority. The IJ agreed with the government and ordered Eglund deported. She has appealed to the Board of Immigration Appeals ("BIA").

Answer each of the following questions based on the additional facts therein, and in light of the Supreme Court's decision in *Brand X*.

a. In a 2015 decision, the Tenth Circuit addressed the conflict between § 245(i)(2)(A) and § 212(a)(9)(C)(i)(I). It concluded that the Attorney General can grant AOS relief without adhering to the ten-year waiting period. The BIA, for which you clerk, will address the conflict for the first time in Eglund's case. One of its judges has asked you whether the panel is bound by the Tenth Circuit's decision, or whether it has independent authority to resolve the conflict between the INA provisions at issue. How do you answer?

b. In a 2015 decision, the BIA concluded that the ten-year waiting period supersedes the Attorney General's AOS authority. No federal court has addressed the conflict. The BIA panel now asks you whether it can change its interpretation to prioritize the Attorney General's AOS authority over the ten-year waiting period. How do you answer?

c. In a 2015 decision, the BIA addressed the conflict between § 245(i)(2)(A) and § 212(a)(9)(C)(i)(I). It concluded that the ten-year waiting period supersedes the Attorney General's AOS authority. That decision was subsequently reviewed and upheld by the Tenth Circuit. The BIA panel now asks you whether it can change its interpretation to prioritize the Attorney General's AOS authority over the ten-year waiting period. How do you answer?

---

f. Agency Interpretations of Their Own Ambiguous Regulations

The *Chevron* cases we have considered up to this point have addressed whether courts should defer to agencies' reasonable interpretations of silent or ambiguous statutes. The following materials ask whether courts should defer to reasonable interpretations of agencies' *own regulations*. In an early case addressing this question, *Bowles v. Seminole Rock & Sand Co.*, 325 U.S. 410 (1945), the Court initially answered "yes." That case involved Seminole Rock & Sand Co.'s alleged violation of Maximum Price Regulation No. 188, promulgated by the Office of Price Administration under the Emergency Price Control Act of 1942. The regulation provided that "the maximum price for any article which was delivered or offered for delivery in March, 1942, by the manufacturer, shall be the highest price charged by the manufacturer during March, 1942 (as defined in § 1499.163) for this article." *Bowles v. Seminole Rock & Sand Co.*, 325 U.S. 410, 414 (1945). The question before the Supreme Court was whether "highest price charged during March, 1942" referred to items that had been sold but not yet delivered by that month. The Court concluded that the language of the regulation itself clearly answered that question, but before doing so it made the following observations:

> Since this involves an interpretation of an administrative regulation a court must necessarily look to the administrative construction of the regulation if the meaning of the words used is in doubt. The intention of Congress or the principles of the Constitution in some situations may be relevant in the first instance in choosing between various constructions. But the ultimate criterion is the interpretation, which becomes of controlling weight unless it is plainly erroneous or inconsistent with the regulation. The legality of the result reached by this process, of course, is quite a different matter. In this case the only problem is to discover the meaning of certain portions of Maximum Price Regulation No. 188. Our only tools, therefore, are the plain words of the regulation and any relevant interpretations of the Administrator.

Id. at 413-14. It further observed that any doubts about its interpretation were "removed by reference to the administrative construction of this method of computing the ceiling price." The Administrator had issued it in a bulletin made available to manufacturers, wholesalers, and retailers. Additionally, the agency consistently relied on it "in countless explanations and interpretations given to inquirers affected by this type of maximum price determination." *Id.* at 419.

In the post-APA era, the Court reaffirmed *Seminole Rock*'s commitment to regulation-oriented deference in *Auer v. Robbins*, 519 U.S. 452 (1997). There, St. Louis police sergeants brought suit against the city's police commissioners, claiming that they had been denied overtime pay in violation of the Fair Labor Standards Act. The commissioners argued that the Act classified the sergeants as "bona fide executive, administrative, or professional employees" exempted from overtime eligibility. 29 U.S.C. § 213(a)(1). Labor Department regulations applied the exemption to employees paid a specified minimum amount on a "salary basis" that was "regularly receive[d] each pay period on a weekly, or less frequent basis, a predetermined amount constituting all or part of his [or her] compensation," and not "subject to reduction because of variations in the quality or quantity of the work performed." 29 C.F.R. §§ 541.1(f), 541.2(e), 541.3(e), 541.118(a) (1996). The sergeants claimed that these provisions did not describe their employment situation because, under the terms of the Police Department Manual, their compensation could theoretically be reduced for a variety of disciplinary infractions related to the "quality or quantity" of their work.

The Labor Department filed an amicus brief in the case, at the Court's request. The agency interpreted its salary-basis test as denying exempt status when employers had "an actual practice of making [disciplinary or other] deductions or an employment policy that create[d] a 'significant likelihood' of such deductions." *Auer*, 519 U.S. at 461. The Department elaborated that its test "reject[ed] a wooden requirement of actual deductions, but in their absence it require[d] a clear and particularized policy—one which 'effectively communicates' that deductions will be made in specified circumstances." *Id.* The sergeants responded that this interpretation should be rejected as nothing more than a *post hoc* rationalization created for solely for litigation. Justice Scalia, writing for the Court, disagreed. He observed that "[b]ecause the salary-basis test is a creature of the Secretary's own regulations, his interpretation of it is, under our jurisprudence, controlling unless plainly erroneous or inconsistent with the regulation." *Id.* (citing *Seminole Rock*). Moreover—and anticipating arguments he would later advance in his *Mead* and *Brand X* dissents—he was unconcerned that the Department's interpretation had not been produced previously through more formal means. "There is simply no reason to suspect that the interpretation does not reflect the agency's fair and considered judgment on the matter in question." *Id.* at 462.

Auer deference, as it is now called, raises a number of puzzles. If *Chevron* assumes that Congress wanted agencies to be the primary interpreters of ambiguous statutes, does the same logic adhere when an agency promulgates an ambiguous regulation? If so, shouldn't we be concerned that agencies will *purposely* adopt ambiguous rules to grant themselves even greater policy-making latitude moving forward? *See, e.g.,* John F. Manning, *Constitutional Structure and Judicial Deference to Agency Interpretations of Agency Rules*, 96 COLUM. L. REV. 612, 618 (1996). Should courts refuse to defer to agency interpretations of ambiguous regulations in an effort to force more careful crafting of regulatory text? If so, does this place an unreasonable expectation on agencies to create all-encompassing codes, a task no law-giving body is actually capable of performing?

Consider the Court's most recent consideration of these issues and the substantial disagreement it generated among the Justices.

Kisor v. Wilkie

139 S. Ct. 2400 (2019)

Justice KAGAN announced the judgment of the Court and delivered the opinion of the Court with respect to Parts I, II-B, III-B, and IV, and an opinion with respect to Parts II-A and III-A, in which Justice GINSBURG, Justice BREYER, and Justice SOTOMAYOR join.

This Court has often deferred to agencies' reasonable readings of genuinely ambiguous regulations. We call that practice *Auer* deference, or sometimes *Seminole Rock* deference, after two cases in which we employed it. *See Auer v. Robbins*, 519 U.S. 452 (1997); *Bowles v. Seminole Rock & Sand Co.*, 325 U.S. 410 (1945). The only question presented here is whether we should overrule those decisions, discarding the deference they give to agencies. We answer that question no. . . .

I. . . .

[James] Kisor is a Vietnam War veteran seeking disability benefits from the Department of Veterans Affairs (VA). He first applied in 1982, alleging that he had developed post-traumatic stress disorder (PTSD) as a result of his participation in a military action called Operation Harvest Moon. The report of the agency's evaluating psychiatrist noted Kisor's involvement in that battle, but found that he "d[id] not suffer from PTSD." The VA thus denied Kisor benefits. There matters stood until 2006, when Kisor moved to reopen his claim. Based on a new psychiatric report, the VA this time agreed that Kisor suffered from PTSD. But it granted him benefits only from the date of his motion to reopen, rather than (as he requested) from the date of his first application.

The Board of Veterans' Appeals—a part of the VA, represented in Kisor's case by a single administrative judge—affirmed that timing decision, based on its interpretation of an agency rule. Under the VA's regulation, the agency could grant Kisor retroactive benefits if it found there were "relevant official service department records" that it had not considered in its initial denial. *See* 38 C.F.R. § 3.156(c)(1) (2013). The Board acknowledged that Kisor had come up with two new service records, both confirming his participation in Operation Harvest Moon. But according to the Board, those records were not "relevant" because they did not go to the reason for the denial—that Kisor did not have PTSD. The Court of Appeals for Veterans Claims, an independent Article I court that initially reviews the Board's decisions, affirmed for the same reason.

The Court of Appeals for the Federal Circuit also affirmed, but it did so based on deference to the Board's interpretation of the VA rule. Kisor had argued to the Federal Circuit that to count as "relevant," a service record need not (as the Board thought) counter the basis of the prior denial; instead, it could relate to some other criterion for obtaining disability benefits. The Federal Circuit found the regulation "ambiguous" as between the two readings. The rule, said the court, does not specifically address "whether 'relevant' records are those casting doubt on the agency's prior [rationale or] those relating to the veteran's claim more broadly." [*Kisor v. Shulkin*, 869 F.3d 1360, 1367 (2017)]. So how to choose between the two views? The court continued: "Both parties insist that the plain regulatory language supports their case, and neither party's position strikes us as unreasonable." *Id.* at 1368. Because that was so, the court believed *Auer* deference appropriate: The agency's construction of its own regulation would govern unless "plainly erroneous or inconsistent with the VA's regulatory framework."

Ibid. (internal quotation marks omitted). Applying that standard, the court upheld the Board's reading—and so approved the denial of retroactive benefits. . . .

II. . . .

A

[We b]egin with a familiar problem in administrative law: For various reasons, regulations may be genuinely ambiguous. They may not directly or clearly address every issue; when applied to some fact patterns, they may prove susceptible to more than one reasonable reading. Sometimes, this sort of ambiguity arises from careless drafting—the use of a dangling modifier, an awkward word, an opaque construction. But often, ambiguity reflects the well-known limits of expression or knowledge. The subject matter of a rule "may be so specialized and varying in nature as to be impossible"—or at any rate, impracticable—to capture in its every detail. *SEC v. Chenery Corp.* [*(Chenery II)*], 332 U.S. 194, 203 (1947). Or a "problem[] may arise" that the agency, when drafting the rule, "could not [have] reasonably foresee[n]." *Id.* at 202. Whichever the case, the result is to create real uncertainties about a regulation's meaning. . . .

[When that occurs,] interpreting the regulation involves a choice between (or among) more than one reasonable reading. To apply the rule to some unanticipated or unresolved situation, the court must make a judgment call. How should it do so?

In answering that question, we have often thought that a court should defer to the agency's construction of its own regulation. For the last 20 or so years, we have referred to that doctrine as *Auer* deference, and applied it often. . . .

We have explained *Auer* deference (as we now call it) as rooted in a presumption about congressional intent—a presumption that Congress would generally want the agency to play the primary role in resolving regulatory ambiguities. *See Martin v. Occupational Safety and Health Review Comm'n*, 499 U.S. 144, 151-153 (1991). Congress, we have pointed out, routinely delegates to agencies the power to implement statutes by issuing rules. *See id.* at 151. In doing so, Congress knows (how could it not?) that regulations will sometimes contain ambiguities. But Congress almost never explicitly assigns responsibility to deal with that problem, either to agencies or to courts. Hence the need to presume, one way or the other, what Congress would want. And as between those two choices, agencies have gotten the nod. We have adopted the presumption—though it is always rebuttable—that "the power authoritatively to interpret its own regulations is a component of the agency's delegated lawmaking powers." *Martin*, 499 U.S. at 151. Or otherwise said, we have thought that when granting rulemaking power to agencies, Congress usually intends to give them, too, considerable latitude to interpret the ambiguous rules they issue.

In part, that is because the agency that promulgated a rule is in the "better position [to] reconstruct" its original meaning. *Id.* at 152. Consider that if you don't know what some text (say, a memo or an e-mail) means, you would probably want to ask the person who wrote it. And for the same reasons, we have thought, Congress would too (though the person is here a collective actor). The agency that "wrote the regulation" will often have direct insight into what that rule was intended to mean. The drafters will know what it was supposed to include or exclude or how it was supposed to apply to some problem. To be sure, this justification has its limits. It does not work so well, for example, when the agency failed to anticipate an issue in crafting a rule (e.g., if the agency never thought about whether and when chest X-rays would count as a "diagnosis"). Then, the agency will not be uncovering a specific intention; at most (though this is not nothing), it will be offering insight into the analogous issues the drafters considered and the purposes they designed the regulation to serve. And the defense works yet less well when lots of time has passed between the rule's issuance and its interpretation—especially if the interpretation differs from one that has come before. All that said, the point holds good for a significant category of "contemporaneous" readings. Want to know what a rule means? Ask its author.

In still greater measure, the presumption that Congress intended *Auer* deference stems from the awareness that resolving genuine regulatory ambiguities often "entail[s] the exercise of judgment grounded in policy concerns." *Thomas Jefferson Univ. v. Shalala,* 512 U.S. 504, 512 (1994) (internal quotation marks omitted). . . .

And Congress, we have thought, knows just that: It is attuned to the comparative advantages of agencies over courts in making such policy judgments. Agencies (unlike courts) have "unique expertise," often of a scientific or technical nature, relevant to applying a regulation "to complex or changing circumstances." *Martin,* 499 U.S. at 151. Agencies (unlike courts) can conduct factual investigations, can consult with affected parties, can consider how their experts have handled similar issues over the long course of administering a regulatory program. And agencies (again unlike courts) have political accountability, because they are subject to the supervision of the President, who in turn answers to the public. *See Free Enterprise Fund v. Public Company Accounting Oversight Bd.,* 561 U.S. 477, 499 (2010). It is because of those features that Congress, when first enacting a statute, assigns rulemaking power to an agency and thus authorizes it to fill out the statutory scheme. And so too, when new issues demanding new policy calls come up within that scheme, Congress presumably wants the same agency, rather than any court, to take the laboring oar.

Finally, the presumption we use reflects the well-known benefits of uniformity in interpreting genuinely ambiguous rules. We have noted Congress's frequent "preference for resolving interpretive issues by uniform administrative decision, rather than piecemeal by litigation." *Ford Motor Credit Co. v. Milhollin,* 444 U.S. 555, 568 (1980). That preference may be strongest when the interpretive issue arises in the context of a "complex and highly technical regulatory program." *Thomas Jefferson,* 512 U.S. at 512. After all, judges are most likely to come to divergent conclusions when they are least likely to know what they are doing. . . . But the uniformity justification retains some weight even for more accessible rules, because their language too may give rise to more than one eminently reasonable reading. Consider *Auer* itself. There, four Circuits held that police captains were "subject to" pay deductions for disciplinary infractions if a police manual said they were, even if the department had never docked anyone. Two other Circuits held that captains were "subject to" pay deductions only if the department's actual practice made that punishment a realistic possibility. *See Auer,* 519 U.S. at 460. Had the agency issued an interpretation before all those rulings (rather than, as actually happened, in a brief in this Court), a deference rule would have averted most of that conflict and uncertainty. *Auer* deference thus serves to ensure consistency in federal regulatory law, for everyone who needs to know what it requires.

B

But all that said, *Auer* deference is not the answer to every question of interpreting an agency's rules. Far from it. As we explain in this section, the possibility of deference can arise only if a regulation is genuinely ambiguous. And when we use that term, we mean it—genuinely ambiguous, even after a court has resorted to all the standard tools of interpretation. Still more, not all reasonable agency constructions of those truly ambiguous rules are entitled to deference. As just explained, we presume that Congress intended for courts to defer to agencies when they interpret their own ambiguous rules. But when the reasons for that presumption do not apply, or countervailing reasons outweigh them, courts should not give deference to an agency's reading, except to the extent it has the "power to persuade." *Christopher,* 567 U.S. at 159 (quoting *Skidmore v. Swift & Co.,* 323 U.S. 134, 140 (1944)). We have thus cautioned that *Auer* deference is just a "general rule"; it "does not apply in all cases." *Christopher,* 567 U.S. at 155. And although the limits of *Auer* deference are not susceptible to any rigid test, we have noted various circumstances in which such deference is "unwarranted." *Ibid.* In particular, that will be so when a court concludes that an interpretation does not reflect an agency's authoritative, expertise-based, "fair[, or] considered judgment." *Ibid.* (quoting *Auer,* 519 U.S. at 462); *cf. United States v. Mead Corp.,* 533 U.S. 218, 229-231 (2001) (adopting a similar approach to *Chevron* deference).

We take the opportunity to restate, and somewhat expand on, those principles here to clear up some mixed messages we have sent. At times, this Court has applied *Auer* deference without significant analysis of the underlying regulation. And in a vacuum, our most classic formulation of the test—whether an agency's construction is "plainly erroneous or inconsistent with the regulation," *Seminole Rock,* 325 U.S. at 414—may suggest a caricature of the doctrine, in which deference is "reflexive." So we cannot deny that Kisor has a bit of grist for his claim that *Auer* "bestows on agencies expansive, unreviewable" authority. But in fact *Auer* does no such thing: It gives agencies their due, while also allowing—indeed, obligating—courts to perform their reviewing and restraining functions. So before we turn to Kisor's specific grievances, we think it worth reinforcing some of the limits inherent in the *Auer* doctrine.

First and foremost, a court should not afford *Auer* deference unless the regulation is genuinely ambiguous. *See Christensen v. Harris County,* 529 U.S. 576, 588 (2000); *Seminole Rock,* 325 U.S. at 414 (deferring only "if the meaning of the words used is in doubt"). If uncertainty does not exist, there is no plausible reason for deference. The regulation then just means what it means—and the court must give it effect, as the court would any law. Otherwise said, the core theory of *Auer* deference is that sometimes the law runs out, and policy-laden choice is what is left over. But if the law gives an answer—if there is only one reasonable construction of a regulation—then a court has no business deferring to any other reading, no matter how much the agency insists it would make more sense. Deference in that circumstance would "permit the agency, under the guise of interpreting a regulation, to create *de facto* a new regulation." *See Christensen,* 529 U.S. at 588. *Auer* does not, and indeed could not, go that far.

And before concluding that a rule is genuinely ambiguous, a court must exhaust all the "traditional tools" of construction. *Chevron U.S.A. Inc. v. Natural Resources Defense Council, Inc.,* 467 U.S. 837, 843, note 9 (1984) (adopting the same approach for ambiguous statutes). For again, only when that legal toolkit is empty and the interpretive question still has no single right answer can a judge conclude that it is "more [one] of policy than of law." *Pauley,* 501 U.S. at 696. That means a court cannot wave the ambiguity flag just because it found the regulation impenetrable on first read. Agency regulations can sometimes make the eyes glaze over. But hard interpretive conundrums, even relating to complex rules, can often be solved. *See id.* at 707 (Scalia, J., dissenting) (A regulation is not ambiguous merely because "discerning the only possible interpretation requires a taxing inquiry"). To make that effort, a court must "carefully consider[]" the text, structure, history, and purpose of a regulation, in all the ways it would if it had no agency to fall back on. *Ibid.* Doing so will resolve many seeming ambiguities out of the box, without resort to *Auer* deference.

If genuine ambiguity remains, moreover, the agency's reading must still be "reasonable." *Thomas Jefferson,* 512 U.S. at 515. In other words, it must come within the zone of ambiguity the court has identified after employing all its interpretive tools. (Note that serious application of those tools therefore has use even when a regulation turns out to be truly ambiguous. The text, structure, history, and so forth at least establish the outer bounds of permissible interpretation.) Some courts have thought (perhaps because of *Seminole Rock's* "plainly erroneous" formulation) that at this stage of the analysis, agency constructions of rules receive greater deference than agency constructions of statutes. But that is not so. Under *Auer,* as under *Chevron,* the agency's reading must fall "within the bounds of reasonable interpretation." *Arlington v. FCC,* 569 U.S. 290, 296 (2013). And let there be no mistake: That is a requirement an agency can fail.

Still, we are not done—for not every reasonable agency reading of a genuinely ambiguous rule should receive *Auer* deference. We have recognized in applying *Auer* that a court must make an independent inquiry into whether the character and context of the agency interpretation entitles it to controlling weight. [*See*] *Mead,* 533 U.S. at 229-231, 236-237 (requiring an analogous though not identical inquiry for *Chevron* deference). As explained above, we give *Auer* deference because we presume, for a set of reasons relating to the comparative attributes of courts and agencies, that Congress would have wanted us to. But the administrative realm is vast and varied, and we have understood that such a presumption cannot always hold. The inquiry on this dimension does not reduce to any exhaustive test. But we have laid out some especially important markers for identifying when *Auer* deference is and is not appropriate.

To begin with, the regulatory interpretation must be one actually made by the agency. In other words, it must be the agency's "authoritative" or "official position," rather than any more *ad hoc* statement not reflecting the agency's views. *Mead,* 533 U.S. at 257-259, and note 6 (SCALIA, J., dissenting). That constraint follows from the logic of *Auer* deference—because Congress has delegated rulemaking power, and all that typically goes with it, to the agency alone. Of course, the requirement of "authoritative" action must recognize a reality of bureaucratic life: Not everything the agency does comes from, or is even in the name of, the Secretary or his chief advisers. So, for example, we have deferred to "official staff memoranda" that were "published in the Federal Register," even though never approved by the agency head. *Ford Motor Credit,* 444 U.S. at 566, note 9, 567, note 10 (declining to "draw a radical distinction between" agency heads and staff for *Auer* deference). But there are limits. The interpretation must at the least emanate from those actors, using those vehicles, understood to make authoritative policy in the relevant context. *See, e.g.,* [*Paralyzed Veterans of America v. D.C. Arena L.P.,* 117 F.3d 579, 587 (D.C. Cir. 1997)] (refusing to consider a "speech of a mid-level official" as an "authoritative departmental position"). If the interpretation does not do so, a court may not defer.

Next, the agency's interpretation must in some way implicate its substantive expertise. Administrative knowledge and experience largely "account [for] the presumption that Congress delegates interpretive lawmaking power to the agency." *Martin*, 499 U.S. at 153. So the basis for deference ebbs when "[t]he subject matter of the [dispute is] distan[t] from the agency's ordinary" duties or "fall[s] within the scope of another agency's authority." *Arlington*, 569 U.S. at 309 (opinion of Breyer, J.). . . . The same idea holds good as between agencies and courts. Generally, agencies have a nuanced understanding of the regulations they administer. That point is most obvious when a rule is technical. . . . But more prosaic-seeming questions also commonly implicate policy expertise; consider the TSA assessing the security risks of pâté or a disabilities office weighing the costs and benefits of an accommodation. Once again, though, there are limits. Some interpretive issues may fall more naturally into a judge's bailiwick. Take one requiring the elucidation of a simple common-law property term . . . or one concerning the award of an attorney's fee. When the agency has no comparative expertise in resolving a regulatory ambiguity, Congress presumably would not grant it that authority.

Finally, an agency's reading of a rule must reflect "fair and considered judgment" to receive *Auer* deference. *Christopher*, 567 U.S. at 155 (quoting *Auer*, 519 U.S. at 462). That means, we have stated, that a court should decline to defer to a merely "convenient litigating position" or "*post hoc* rationalizatio[n] advanced" to "defend past agency action against attack." *Christopher*, 567 U.S. at 155 (quoting *Bowen v. Georgetown Univ. Hospital*, 488 U.S. 204, 213 (1988) and *Auer*, 519 U.S. at 462). And a court may not defer to a new interpretation, whether or not introduced in litigation, that creates "unfair surprise" to regulated parties. [*Long Island Care at Home Ltd. v. Coke*, 551 U.S. 158, 170 (2007)]. That disruption of expectations may occur when an agency substitutes one view of a rule for another. We have therefore only rarely given *Auer* deference to an agency construction "conflict[ing] with a prior" one. *Thomas Jefferson*, 512 U.S. at 515. Or the upending of reliance may happen without such an explicit interpretive change. This Court, for example, recently refused to defer to an interpretation that would have imposed retroactive liability on parties for longstanding conduct that the agency had never before addressed. *See Christopher*, 567 U.S. at 155-156. Here too the lack of "fair warning" outweighed the reasons to apply *Auer*. *Id.* at 156 (internal quotation marks omitted).

The upshot of all this goes something as follows. When it applies, *Auer* deference gives an agency significant leeway to say what its own rules mean. In so doing, the doctrine enables the agency to fill out the regulatory scheme Congress has placed under its supervision. But that phrase "when it applies" is important—because it often doesn't. As described above, this Court has cabined *Auer's* scope in varied and critical ways—and in exactly that measure, has maintained a strong judicial role in interpreting rules. What emerges is a deference doctrine not quite so tame as some might hope, but not nearly so menacing as they might fear.

III

That brings us to the lone question presented here—whether we should abandon the longstanding doctrine just described. . . .

A

Kisor first attacks *Auer* as inconsistent with the judicial review provision of the Administrative Procedure Act (APA). *See* 5 U.S.C. § 706. As Kisor notes, Congress enacted the APA in 1946—the year after *Seminole Rock*—to serve as "the fundamental charter of the administrative state." Section 706 of the Act, governing judicial review of agency action, states (among other things) that reviewing courts shall "determine the meaning or applicability of the terms of an agency action" (including a regulation). According to Kisor, *Auer* violates that edict by thwarting "meaningful judicial review" of agency rules. Courts under *Auer,* he asserts (now in the language of Section 706), "abdicate their office of determining the meaning" of a regulation. *Id.* at 27 (internal quotation marks omitted).

To begin with, that argument ignores the many ways, discussed above, that courts exercise independent review over the meaning of agency rules. . . . All of that figures as meaningful judicial review.

And even when a court defers to a regulatory reading, it acts consistently with Section 706. That provision does not specify the standard of review a court should use in "determin[ing] the meaning" of an ambiguous rule. 5 U.S.C. § 706. One possibility, as Kisor says, is to review the issue *de novo*. But another is to review the agency's reading for reasonableness. To see the point, assume that a regulatory (say, an employment) statute expressly instructed courts to apply *Auer* deference when reviewing an agency's interpretations of its ambiguous rules. Nothing in that statute would conflict with Section 706. Instead, the employment law would simply make clear how a court is to "determine the meaning" of such a rule—by deferring to an agency's reasonable reading. *Ibid.* Of course, that is not the world we know: Most substantive statutes do not say anything about *Auer* deference, one way or the other. But for all the reasons spelled out above, we have long presumed (subject always to rebuttal) that the Congress delegating regulatory authority to an agency intends as well to give that agency considerable latitude to construe its ambiguous rules. And that presumption operates just like the hypothesized statute above. . . .

To supplement his two APA arguments, Kisor turns to policy, leaning on a familiar claim about the incentives *Auer* creates. According to Kisor, *Auer* encourages agencies to issue vague and open-ended regulations, confident that they can later impose whatever interpretation of those rules they prefer. That argument received its fullest elaboration in a widely respected law review article pre-dating *Auer*. *See* Manning, 96 COLUM. L. REV., at 654-669. . . .

But the claim has notable weaknesses, empirical and theoretical alike. First, it does not survive an encounter with experience. No real evidence—indeed, scarcely an anecdote—backs up the assertion. As two noted scholars (one of whom reviewed thousands of rules during four years of government service) have written: "[W]e are unaware of, and no one has pointed to, any regulation in American history that, because of *Auer*, was designed vaguely." Cass R. Sunstein & Adrian Vermeule, *The Unbearable Rightness of* Auer, 84 U. CHI. L. REV. 297, 308 (2017). And even the argument's theoretical allure dissipates upon reflection. For strong (almost surely stronger) incentives and pressures cut in the opposite direction. "[R]egulators want their regulations to be effective, and clarity promotes compliance." Brief for Administrative Law Scholars as Amici Curiae at 18-19. Too, regulated parties often push for precision from an agency, so that they know what they can and cannot do. And ambiguities in rules pose risks to the long-run survival of agency policy. Vagueness increases the chance of adverse judicial rulings. And it enables future administrations, with different views, to reinterpret the rules to their own liking. Add all of that up and Kisor's ungrounded theory of incentives contributes nothing to the case against *Auer*.

Finally, Kisor goes big, asserting (though fleetingly) that *Auer* deference violates "separation-of-powers principles." In his view, those principles prohibit "vest[ing] in a single branch the law-making and law-interpreting functions." *Id.* at 45. If that objection is to agencies' usurping the interpretive role of courts, this opinion has already met it head-on. Properly understood and applied, *Auer* does no such thing. In all the ways we have described, courts retain a firm grip on the interpretive function. If Kisor's objection is instead to the supposed commingling of functions (that is, the legislative and judicial) within an agency, this Court has answered it often before. *See, e.g., Withrow v. Larkin,* 421 U.S. 35, 54 (1975) (permitting such a combination of functions). That sort of mixing is endemic in agencies, and has been "since the beginning of the Republic." *Arlington,* 569 U.S. at 304-305, n. 4. . . .

IV. . . .

Applying the principles outlined in this opinion, we hold that a redo is necessary for two reasons. First, the Federal Circuit jumped the gun in declaring the regulation ambiguous. We have insisted that a court bring all its interpretive tools to bear before finding that to be so. It is not enough to casually remark, as the court did here, that "[b]oth parties insist that the plain regulatory language supports their case, and neither party's position strikes us as unreasonable." 869 F.3d at 1368. Rather, the court must make a conscientious effort to determine, based on indicia like text, structure, history, and purpose, whether the regulation really has more than one reasonable meaning. The Solicitor General argued in this Court that the Board's reading is the only reasonable one. Perhaps Kisor will make the converse claim below. Before even considering deference, the court must seriously think through those positions.

And second, the Federal Circuit assumed too fast that *Auer* deference should apply in the event of genuine ambiguity. As we have explained, that is not always true. A court must assess whether the interpretation is of the sort that Congress would want to receive deference. The Solicitor General suggested at oral argument that the answer in this case might be no. He explained that all 100 or so members of the VA Board act individually (rather than in panels) and that their roughly 80,000 annual decisions have no "precedential value." He thus questioned whether a Board member's ruling "reflects the considered judgment of the agency as a whole." *Ibid.; cf. Mead,* 533 U.S. at 233 (declining to give *Chevron* deference to rulings "being churned out at a rate of 10,000 a year at an agency's 46 scattered offices"). . . . [T]he questions the Solicitor General raised are exactly the kind the court must consider in deciding whether to award *Auer* deference to the Board's interpretation.

We accordingly vacate the judgment below and remand the case for further proceedings.

It is so ordered.

[The concurring opinion of Chief Justice ROBERTS is omitted.]

Justice GORSUCH, with whom Justice THOMAS joins[, and joined in part by Justices KAVANAUGH and ALITO], concurring in the judgment. . . .

II. THE ADMINISTRATIVE PROCEDURE ACT

When this Court speaks about the rules governing judicial review of federal agency action, we are not (or shouldn't be) writing on a blank slate or exercising some common-law-making power. We are supposed to be applying the Administrative Procedure Act. The APA is a "seminal" statute that Congress wrote to define the relationship between courts and agencies. Some have even described it as a kind of constitution for our "administrative state." Yet, remarkably, until today this Court has never made any serious effort to square the *Auer* doctrine with the APA. Even now, only four Justices make the attempt. And for at least two reasons, their arguments are wholly unpersuasive.

A

The first problem lies in § 706. That provision instructs reviewing courts to "decide all relevant questions of law" and "set aside agency action . . . found to be . . . not in accordance with law." Determining the meaning of a statute or regulation, of course, presents a classic legal question. But in case these directives were not clear enough, the APA further directs courts to "determine the meaning" of any relevant "agency action," including any rule issued by the agency. The APA thus requires a reviewing court to resolve for itself any dispute over the proper interpretation of an agency regulation. A court that, in deference to an agency, adopts something other than the best reading of a regulation isn't "decid[ing]" the relevant "questio[n] of law" or "determin[ing] the meaning" of the regulation. Instead, it's allowing the agency to dictate the answer to that question. In doing so, the court is abdicating the duty Congress assigned to it in the APA.

Justice Kagan seeks to address the glaring inconsistency between our judge-made rule and the controlling statute this way. On her account, the APA tells a reviewing court to "determine the meaning" of regulations, but it does not tell the court "how" to do that. Thus, we are told, reading the regulation for itself and deferring to the agency's reading are just two equally valid ways for a court to fulfill its statutory duty to "determine the meaning" of the regulation.

But the APA isn't as anemic as that. Its unqualified command requires the court to determine legal questions—including questions about a regulation's meaning—by its own lights, not by those of political appointees or bureaucrats who may even be self-interested litigants in the case at hand. Nor can there be any doubt that, when Congress wrote the APA, it knew perfectly well how to require judicial deference to an agency when it wished—in fact, Congress repeatedly specified deferential standards for judicial review elsewhere in the statute. But when it comes to the business of interpreting regulations, no such command exists; instead, Congress told courts to "determine" those matters for themselves. Though one hardly needs to be an academic to recognize the point, "commentators in administrative law have 'generally acknowledged' that Section 706 seems to require *de novo* review on questions of law."

What the statutory language suggests, experience confirms. If *Auer* deference were really just another way for courts to "determine the meaning" of regulations under § 706, you might expect that a final judicial "determination" would at least settle, as a matter of precedent, the question of what the regulation "means." Of course, even after one court has spoken on a regulation's meaning, that court or another might properly give weight to a new agency interpretation as part of the court's own decision-making process. But in light of *National Cable & Telecommunications Assn. v. Brand X Internet Services,* courts have interpreted *Auer* as forbidding a court from ever "determin[ing] the meaning" of a regulation with the force that normally attaches to precedent, because an agency is always free to adopt a different view and insist on judicial deference to its new judgment. And if an agency can not only control the court's initial decision but also revoke that decision at any time, how can anyone honestly say the court, rather than the agency, ever really "determine[s]" what the regulation means? . . .

Nor does Justice Kagan's reading of § 706 offer any logical stopping point. If courts can "determine the meaning" of a regulation by deferring to any "reasonable" agency reading, then why not by deferring to any agency reading? If it were really true that the APA has nothing to say about how courts decide what regulations mean, then it would follow that the APA tolerates a rule that "the agency is always right." And if you find yourself in a place as absurd as that, you might want to consider whether you've taken a wrong turn along the way. . . .

C

If *Auer* cannot be squared with the text of the APA, Justice Kagan suggests it at least conforms to a reasonable "presumption about congressional intent." The theory seems to be that whenever Congress grants an agency "rulemaking power," it also implicitly gives the agency " 'the power authoritatively to interpret' " whatever rules the agency chooses to adopt. But against the clear statutory commands Congress gave us in the APA, what sense does it make to "presume" that Congress really, secretly, wanted courts to treat agency interpretations as binding? Normally, this Court does not allow hidden legislative intentions to "muddy" such plainly expressed statutory directives.

Even on its own terms, too, this argument proves pretty muddy. It goes something like this: The drafters of the APA did not intend to " 'significantly alter' " established law governing judicial review of agency action as of 1946; the *Auer* doctrine was part of that established law; therefore, the APA implicitly requires courts to afford agencies *Auer* deference. But neither of this syllogism's essential premises stands on solid ground.

Take the major premise—that those who adopted the APA intended to work no change in the established law of judicial review of agency action. Justice Kagan is right, of course, that Attorney General Clark claimed as much shortly after the APA's passage. But his view, which reflected the interests of the executive branch, was far from universally shared. Others, including many members of Congress, thought the APA would clarify, if not expand, the scope of judicial review. For example, Senator McCarran, the Chairman of the Judiciary Committee, wrote that it would be "hard . . . for anyone to argue that this Act did anything other than cut down the 'cult of discretion' so far as federal law is concerned." And both the House and Senate reports on the APA said it was intended to "provid[e] that questions of law are for courts rather than agencies to decide in the last analysis." . . .

Justice Kagan's syllogism runs into even more trouble with its minor premise—that the *Auer* doctrine was a well-established part of the common law background when Congress enacted the APA in 1946. . . . [T]his Court planted the seeds of *Auer* deference for the first time in dictum in *Seminole Rock*, just a year before Congress passed the APA. *And* that dictum did not somehow immediately become an entrenched part of the common law: For years following *Seminole Rock,* courts and "commentators largely ignored" it, and those who took notice weren't sure what to make of it. . . .

III. THE CONSTITUTION

A

. . . The founders . . . [created] an independent judiciary [to] better guard the people from the arbitrary use of governmental power. And sitting atop the judicial branch, this Court has always carried a special duty to "jealously guar[d]" the Constitution's promise of judicial independence. So we have long resisted any effort by the other branches to "'usurp a court's power to interpret and apply the law to the circumstances before it.'" The judicial power to interpret the law, this Court has held, "can no more be shared with another branch than the Chief Executive, for example, can share with the Judiciary the veto power, or the Congress share with the Judiciary the power to override a Presidential veto."

Auer represents no trivial threat to these foundational principles. Under the APA, substantive rules issued by federal agencies through notice-and-comment procedures bear "the 'force and effect of law'" and are part of the body of federal law, binding on private individuals, that the Constitution charges federal judges with interpreting. Yet *Auer* tells the judge that he must interpret these binding laws to mean not what he thinks they mean, but what an executive agency says they mean. Unlike Article III judges, executive officials are not, nor are they supposed to be, "wholly impartial." They have their own interests, their own constituencies, and their own policy goals—and when interpreting a regulation, they may choose to "press the case for the side [they] represen[t]" instead of adopting the fairest and best reading. *Auer* thus means that, far from being "kept distinct," the powers of making, enforcing, and interpreting laws are united in the same hands—and in the process a cornerstone of the rule of law is compromised. . . .

[The concurring opinion of Justice KAVANAUGH, which Justice ALITO joined, is omitted.]

QUESTION SET 9.33

Review & Synthesis

1. Writing for the majority, Justice Kagan provided a lengthy explanation of *Auer* deference. Summarize her main points by answering the following questions:

    a. What is the presumption regarding congressional intent underlying *Auer* deference, and what are the justifications supporting it?

    b. What conditions must be met before an agency's interpretation of its ambiguous regulations are eligible for *Auer* deference?

2. According to Justice Kagan, APA § 706 instructs courts to review agency interpretations of their regulations, but it does not instruct them on how to do so. Further, she argued that a statute requiring agencies to defer under *Auer* would be consistent with APA § 706's directive that courts determine the meaning of ambiguous rules.

    a. What assertions does Justice Kagan make to support the notion that *Auer* deference is consistent with APA § 706?

    b. Justice Kagan's analysis implies that Congress controls who the primary interpreter of its statutes will be, in addition to controlling the substantive content of those statutes. Why did Justice Gorsuch reject it? From his perspective, does Congress have the authority to choose whether courts or agencies definitively interpret its statutes? To choose who definitively interprets regulations?

    c. If Congress controls the substance of federal statutes, and it controls who is primarily responsible for interpreting that substance, can it also control the interpreter's methods of interpretation? For instance, could it instruct an agency not to use legislative history when construing the statute it administers? Could it lawfully issue such a directive to a federal court? In formulating your answer, consider Justice Gorsuch's argument about the effects such congressional authority would have on the Judiciary's independence.

    d. Justice Gorsuch argued that *Auer* leads courts to "adopt[] something other than the best reading of a regulation." Was that a fair reading of the Court's decision? Recall Justice Kagan's emphasis that, under either *Chevron* or *Auer*, a reviewing court is obligated to exhaust all interpretive tools at its disposal before considering whether deference to an agency's interpretation is appropriate. Once law "runs out," as Justice Kagan phrased it, there are only policy judgments left to be made. Was Justice Gorsuch arguing that these judgments should be made by courts, or was he making a different point?

3. In a portion of the opinion not excerpted above, the Court rejected Kisor's argument that *Auer* deference allows agencies to avoid the procedural strictures of APA § 553 notice-and-comment rulemaking. It reasoned that the APA was satisfied if the agency duly promulgated the rule underlying the agency's interpretation. Stated differently, "Congress, when first enacting a statute, assigns rulemaking power to an agency and thus authorizes it to fill out the statutory scheme." *Kisor*, 139 S. Ct. at 2413. Justice Gorsuch disagreed, arguing that *Auer* nullifies § 553's distinction

between interpretive rules (which do not have to go through notice-and-comment rulemaking) and substantive rules (which do). *See* Chapter 5. Which position do you find the most persuasive? In the context of ambiguous regulations, is "interpretation" the functional equivalent of amending rules or creating new ones? Does *Auer* deference function differently than *Chevron* deference in this respect?

Application & Analysis

1. In response to repeated criticisms from her constituents and colleagues about the breadth of the Supreme Court's *Chevron* and *Auer* deference doctrines, a Senator has introduced a bill to amend APA § 706. The bill provides:

   Section 706 of title 5, United States Code, is amended—
   (1) by striking "To the extent necessary" and inserting "(a) To the extent necessary";
   (2) in subsection (a), as so designated—
      (A) by striking "decide all relevant questions of law, interpret constitutional and statutory provisions, and"; and
      (B) by inserting after "of the terms of an agency action" the following: "and decide de novo all relevant questions of law, including the interpretation of constitutional and statutory provisions, and rules made by agencies. If the reviewing court determines that a statutory or regulatory provision relevant to its decision contains a gap or ambiguity, the court shall not interpret that gap or ambiguity as an implicit delegation to the agency of legislative rule making authority and shall not rely on the gap or ambiguity as a justification for interpreting agency authority expansively or for deferring to the agency's interpretation on the question of law. Notwithstanding any other provision of law, this subsection shall apply in any action for judicial review of agency action authorized under any provision of law. No law may exempt any such civil action from the application of this section except by specific reference to this section"; and
   (3) by striking "The reviewing court shall"—and inserting the following: "(b) The reviewing court shall—".

   You are legislative counsel for the Senate Judiciary Committee, which is considering this bill. The Chairperson has asked you to analyze the effects that it would have on judicial review of agency interpretations, specifically on *Chevron* and *Auer* deference. Further, the Chairperson has asked for your opinion whether these changes would be desirable or inadvisable.

g. *Chevron:* Agency Interpretation of Its Own Jurisdiction

In the seminal case of *Crowell v. Benson,* discussed in Chapter 2, Chief Justice Charles Evans Hughes flatly rejected the notion that administrative adjudicators could conclusively determine the facts establishing their own jurisdiction. He stated that allowing them to do so would "sap the judicial power as it exists under the Federal Constitution, and . . . establish a government of a bureaucratic character alien to our system." *Crowell v. Benson,* 285 U.S. 22, 57 (1932). Accordingly, courts had to review those factual findings de novo. This was a consistent feature of the otherwise limited direct review of administrative decision-making conducted by courts in the early twentieth century.

The question addressed in the following case is whether a meaningful distinction can be drawn between substantive statutory provisions and "jurisdictional" ones for *Chevron* purposes. The idea animating the inquiry is straightforward: Should courts defer to how agencies construe the scope of their own regulatory power? At first blush, the proposition seems so absurd as to be self-refuting. Such a concession would allow agencies easily to seize authority Congress never intended to give them. Many commentators have made precisely this argument. *See, e.g.,* Nathan A. Sales & Jonathan H. Adler, *The Rest Is Silence:* Chevron *Deference, Agency Jurisdiction, and Statutory Silences,* 2009 U. Ill. L. Rev. 1497 (2009). Others, however, have asserted that the line between jurisdictional and non-jurisdictional statutes when it comes to delegations of policymaking authority to agencies is largely illusory. Any time an agency interprets or fills gaps in a silent or ambiguous provision it is, in effect, granting itself authority that Congress did not specify.

The Supreme Court weighed in on this debate in the following case.

City of Arlington, Texas v. Federal Communications Commission
569 U.S. 290 (2013)

Justice Scalia delivered the opinion of the Court.

We consider whether an agency's interpretation of a statutory ambiguity that concerns the scope of its regulatory authority (that is, its jurisdiction) is entitled to deference under *Chevron U.S.A. Inc. v. Natural Resources Defense Council, Inc.,* 467 U.S. 837 (1984).

I

Wireless telecommunications networks require towers and antennas; proposed sites for those towers and antennas must be approved by local zoning authorities. In the Telecommunications Act of 1996, Congress "impose[d] specific limitations on the traditional authority of state and local governments to regulate the location, construction, and modification of such facilities," *Rancho Palos Verdes v. Abrams*, 544 U.S. 113, 115 (2005), and incorporated those limitations into the Communications Act of 1934, *see* 110 Stat. 56, 151. Section 201(b) of that Act empowers the Federal Communications Commission to "prescribe such rules and regulations as may be necessary in the public interest to carry out [its] provisions." Ch. 296, 52 Stat. 588, codified at 47 U.S.C. § 201(b). Of course, that rulemaking authority extends to the subsequently added portions of the Act.

The Act imposes five substantive limitations, which are codified in 47 U.S.C. § 332(c)(7)(B); only one of them, § 332(c)(7)(B)(ii), is at issue here. That provision requires state or local governments to act on wireless siting applications "within a reasonable period of time after the request is duly filed." Two other features of § 332(c)(7) are relevant. First, subparagraph (A), known as the "saving clause," provides that nothing in the Act, except those limitations provided in § 332(c)(7)(B), "shall limit or affect the authority of a State or local government" over siting decisions. Second, § 332(c)(7)(B)(v) authorizes a person who believes a state or local government's wireless-siting decision to be inconsistent with any of the limitations in § 332(c)(7)(B) to "commence an action in any court of competent jurisdiction."

In theory, § 332(c)(7)(B)(ii) requires state and local zoning authorities to take prompt action on siting applications for wireless facilities. But in practice, wireless providers often faced long delays. In July 2008, CTIA—The Wireless Association, which represents wireless service providers, petitioned the FCC to clarify the meaning of § 332(c)(7)(B)(ii)'s requirement that zoning authorities act on siting requests "within a reasonable period of time." In November 2009, the Commission, relying on its broad statutory authority to implement the provisions of the Communications Act, issued a declaratory ruling responding to CTIA's petition. *In re Petition for Declaratory Ruling*, 24 FCC Rcd. 13994, 14001. The Commission found that the "record evidence demonstrates that unreasonable delays in the personal wireless service facility siting process have obstructed the provision of wireless services" and that such delays "impede the promotion of advanced services and competition that Congress deemed critical in the Telecommunications Act of 1996." *Id.* at 14006, 14008. A "reasonable period of time" under § 332(c)(7)(B)(ii), the Commission determined, is presumptively (but rebuttably) 90 days to process a collocation application (that is, an application to place a new antenna on an existing tower) and 150 days to process all other applications. *Id.* at 14005.

Some state and local governments opposed adoption of the Declaratory Ruling on the ground that the Commission lacked "authority to interpret ambiguous provisions of Section 332(c)(7)." *Id.* at 14000. Specifically, they argued that the saving clause, § 332(c)(7)(A), and the judicial review provision, § 337(c)(7)(B)(v), together display a congressional intent to withhold from the Commission authority to interpret the limitations in § 332(c)(7)(B). Asserting that ground of objection, the cities of Arlington and San Antonio, Texas, petitioned for review of the Declaratory Ruling in the Court of Appeals for the Fifth Circuit.

Relying on Circuit precedent, the Court of Appeals held that the *Chevron* framework applied to the threshold question whether the FCC possessed statutory authority to adopt the 90- and 150-day timeframes. Applying *Chevron*, the Court of Appeals found "§ 332(c)(7)(A)'s effect on the FCC's authority to administer § 332(c)(7)(B)'s limitations ambiguous," and held that "the FCC's interpretation of its statutory authority" was a permissible construction of the statute. On the merits, the court upheld the presumptive 90- and 150-day deadlines as a "permissible construction of § 332(c)(7)(B)(ii) and (v) . . . entitled to *Chevron* deference." [668 F.3d 229, 265 (5th Cir. 2012).]

We granted certiorari, limited to the first question presented: "Whether . . . a court should apply *Chevron* to . . . an agency's determination of its own jurisdiction." Pet. for Cert. in No. 11-1545, p. i.

II

A

As this case turns on the scope of the doctrine enshrined in *Chevron*, we begin with a description of that case's now-canonical formulation. "When a court reviews an agency's construction of the statute which it administers, it is confronted with two questions." 467 U.S., at 842. First, applying the ordinary tools of statutory construction, the court must determine "whether Congress has directly spoken to the precise question at issue. If the intent of Congress is clear, that is the end of the matter; for the court, as well as the agency, must give effect to the unambiguously expressed intent of Congress." *Id.* at 842-843. But "if the statute is silent or ambiguous with respect to the specific issue, the question for the court is whether the agency's answer is based on a permissible construction of the statute." *Id.* at 843.

Chevron is rooted in a background presumption of congressional intent: namely, "that Congress, when it left ambiguity in a statute" administered by an agency, "understood that the ambiguity would be resolved, first and foremost, by the agency, and desired the agency (rather than the courts) to possess whatever degree of discretion the ambiguity allows." *Smiley v. Citibank (South Dakota), N. A.,* 517 U.S. 735, 740-741 (1996). *Chevron* thus provides a stable background rule against which Congress can legislate: Statutory ambiguities will be resolved, within the bounds of reasonable interpretation, not by the courts but by the administering agency. Congress knows to speak in plain terms when it wishes to circumscribe, and in capacious terms when it wishes to enlarge, agency discretion.

B

The question here is whether a court must defer under *Chevron* to an agency's interpretation of a statutory ambiguity that concerns the scope of the agency's statutory authority (that is, its jurisdiction). The argument against deference rests on the premise that there exist two distinct classes of agency interpretations: Some interpretations — the big, important ones, presumably — define the agency's "jurisdiction." Others — humdrum, run-of-the-mill stuff — are simply applications of jurisdiction the agency plainly has. That premise is false, because the distinction between "jurisdictional" and "nonjurisdictional" interpretations is a mirage. No matter how it is framed, the question a court faces when confronted with an agency's interpretation of a statute it administers is always, simply, whether the agency has stayed within the bounds of its statutory authority.

The misconception that there are, for *Chevron* purposes, separate "jurisdictional" questions on which no deference is due derives, perhaps, from a reflexive extension to agencies of the very real division between the jurisdictional and nonjurisdictional that is applicable to courts. In the judicial context, there is a meaningful line: Whether the court decided correctly is a question that has different consequences from the question whether it had the power to decide at all. Congress has the power (within limits) to tell the courts what classes of cases they may decide, but not to prescribe or superintend how they decide those cases. A court's power to decide a case is independent of whether its decision is correct, which is why even an erroneous judgment is entitled to *res judicata* effect. Put differently, a jurisdictionally proper but substantively incorrect judicial decision is not *ultra vires*.

That is not so for agencies charged with administering congressional statutes. Both their power to act and how they are to act is authoritatively prescribed by Congress, so that when they act improperly, no less than when they act beyond their jurisdiction, what they do is *ultra vires*. Because the question — whether framed as an incorrect application of agency authority or an assertion of authority not conferred — is always whether the agency has gone beyond what Congress has permitted it to do, there is no principled basis for carving out some arbitrary subset of such claims as " jurisdictional."

An example will illustrate just how illusory the proposed line between "jurisdictional" and "nonjurisdictional" agency interpretations is. Imagine the following validly-enacted statute:

Common Carrier Act
Section 1. The Agency shall have jurisdiction to prohibit any common carrier from imposing an unreasonable condition upon access to its facilities.

There is no question that this provision—including the terms "common carrier" and "unreasonable condition"—defines the Agency's jurisdiction. Surely, the argument goes, a court must determine *de novo* the scope of that jurisdiction.

Consider, however, this alternative formulation of the statute:

Common Carrier Act

Section 1. No common carrier shall impose an unreasonable condition upon access to its facilities.

Section 2. The Agency may prescribe rules and regulations necessary in the public interest to effectuate Section 1 of this Act.

Now imagine that the Agency, invoking its Section 2 authority, promulgates this Rule: "(1) The term 'common carrier' in Section 1 includes Internet Service Providers. (2) The term 'unreasonable condition' in Section 1 includes unreasonably high prices. (3) A monthly fee greater than $25 is an unreasonable condition on access to Internet service." By this Rule, the Agency has claimed for itself jurisdiction that is doubly questionable: Does its authority extend to Internet Service Providers? And does it extend to setting prices? Yet Section 2 makes clear that Congress, in petitioners' words, "conferred interpretive power on the agency" with respect to Section 1. Even under petitioners' theory, then, a court should defer to the Agency's interpretation of the terms "common carrier" and "unreasonable condition"—that is to say, its assertion that its "jurisdiction" extends to regulating Internet Service Providers and setting prices.

In the first case, by contrast, petitioners' theory would accord the agency no deference. The trouble with this is that in both cases, the underlying question is exactly the same: Does the statute give the agency authority to regulate Internet Service Providers and cap prices, or not? The reality, laid bare, is that there is no difference, insofar as the validity of agency action is concerned, between an agency's exceeding the scope of its authority (its "jurisdiction") and its exceeding authorized application of authority that it unquestionably has. "To exceed authorized application is to exceed authority. Virtually any administrative action can be characterized as either the one or the other, depending on how generally one wishes to describe the 'authority.'" *Mississippi Power & Light Co. v. Mississippi ex rel. Moore*, 487 U.S. 354, 381 (1988) (Scalia, J., concurring in judgment); *see also* Monaghan, *Marbury and the Administrative State*, 83 Colum. L. Rev. 1, 29 (1983) ("Administrative application of law is administrative formulation of law whenever it involves elaboration of the statutory norm.").

This point is nicely illustrated by our decision in *National Cable & Telecommunications Assn., Inc. v. Gulf Power Co.*, 534 U.S. 327 (2002). That case considered whether the FCC's "jurisdiction" to regulate the rents utility-pole owners charge for "pole attachments" (defined as attachments by a cable television system or provider of telecommunications service) extended to attachments that provided both cable television and high-speed Internet access (attachments for so-called "commingled services"). *Id.* at 331-336. We held, sensibly, that *Chevron* applied. 534 U.S., at 333, 339. Whether framed as going to the scope of the FCC's delegated authority or the FCC's application of its delegated authority, the underlying question was the same: Did the FCC exceed the bounds of its statutory authority to regulate rents for "pole attachments" when it sought to regulate rents for pole attachments providing commingled services?

The label is an empty distraction because every new application of a broad statutory term can be reframed as a questionable extension of the agency's jurisdiction. One of the briefs in support of petitioners explains, helpfully, that "[j]urisdictional questions concern the who, what, where, and when of regulatory power: which subject matters may an agency regulate and under what conditions." Brief for IMLA Respondents at 18-19. But an agency's application of its authority pursuant to statutory text answers the same questions. Who is an "outside salesman"? What is a "pole attachment"? Where do the "waters of the United States" end? When must a Medicare provider challenge a reimbursement determination in order to be entitled to an administrative appeal? These can all be reframed as questions about the scope of agencies' regulatory jurisdiction—and they are all questions to which the *Chevron* framework applies.

In sum, judges should not waste their time in the mental acrobatics needed to decide whether an agency's interpretation of a statutory provision is "jurisdictional" or "nonjurisdictional." Once those labels are sheared away, it becomes clear that the question in every case is, simply, whether the statutory text forecloses the agency's assertion of authority, or not. The federal judge as haruspex, sifting the entrails of vast statutory schemes to divine whether a particular agency interpretation qualifies as "jurisdictional," is not engaged in reasoned decisionmaking.

C

Fortunately, then, we have consistently held "that *Chevron* applies to cases in which an agency adopts a construction of a jurisdictional provision of a statute it administers." 1 R. Pierce, Administrative Law Treatise § 3.5, p. 187 (2010). One of our opinions explicitly says that no "exception exists to the normal [deferential] standard of review" for "'jurisdictional or legal question[s] concerning the coverage'" of an Act. *NLRB v. City Disposal Systems, Inc.,* 465 U.S. 822, 830, note 7 (1984). A prime example of deferential review for questions of jurisdiction is *Commodity Futures Trading Comm'n v. Schor,* 478 U.S. 833 (1986). That case involved a CFTC interpretation of 7 U.S.C. § 18(c), which provides that before the Commission takes action on a complaint, the complainant must file a bond to cover "any reparation award that may be issued by the Commission against the complainant *on any counterclaim* by respondent." (Emphasis added.) The CFTC, pursuant to its broad rulemaking authority, *see* § 12a(5), interpreted that oblique reference to counterclaims as granting it "the power to take jurisdiction over" not just federal-law counterclaims, but state-law counterclaims as well. *Schor, supra,* at 844. We not only deferred under *Chevron* to the Commission's "eminently reasonable . . . interpretation of the statute it is entrusted to administer," but also chided the Court of Appeals for declining to afford deference because of the putatively " 'statutory interpretation-jurisdictional' nature of the question at issue." 478 U.S., at 844-45. . . .

Our cases hold that *Chevron* applies equally to statutes designed to curtail the scope of agency discretion. For instance, in *Chemical Mfrs. Assn. v. Natural Resources Defense Council, Inc.,* 470 U.S. 116, 123 (1985), we considered a statute prohibiting the Environmental Protection Agency from "modify[ing] any requirement of this section as it applies to any specific pollutant which is on the toxic pollutant list." The EPA construed the statute as not precluding it from granting variances with respect to certain toxic pollutants. Finding no "clear congressional intent to forbid EPA's sensible variance mechanism," *Id.* at 134, we deferred to the EPA's construction of this express limitation on its own regulatory authority, *Id.* at 125.

The U.S. Reports are shot through with applications of *Chevron* to agencies' constructions of the scope of their own jurisdiction. And we have applied *Chevron* where concerns about agency self-aggrandizement are at their apogee: in cases where an agency's expansive construction of the extent of its own power would have wrought a fundamental change in the regulatory scheme. In *FDA v. Brown & Williamson Tobacco Corp.,* 529 U.S. 120 (2000), the threshold question was the "appropriate framework for analyzing" the FDA's assertion of "jurisdiction to regulate tobacco products," *Id.* at 126, 132—a question of vast "economic and political magnitude," *Id.* at 133. "Because this case involves an administrative agency's construction of a statute that it administers," we held, *Chevron* applied. 529 U.S., at 132. Similarly, in *MCI Telecommunications Corp. v. American Telephone & Telegraph Co.,* 512 U.S. 218, 224 (1994), we applied the *Chevron* framework to the FCC's assertion that the statutory phrase "modify any requirement" gave it authority to eliminate rate-filing requirements, "the essential characteristic of a rate-regulated industry," for long-distance telephone carriers.

The false dichotomy between "jurisdictional" and "nonjurisdictional" agency interpretations may be no more than a bogeyman, but it is dangerous all the same. Like the Hound of the Baskervilles, it is conjured by those with greater quarry in sight: Make no mistake—the ultimate target here is *Chevron* itself. Savvy challengers of agency action would play the "jurisdictional" card in every case. Some judges would be deceived by the specious, but scary-sounding, "jurisdictional"-"nonjurisdictional" line; others tempted by the prospect of making public policy by prescribing the meaning of ambiguous statutory commands. The effect would be to transfer any number of interpretive decisions—archetypal *Chevron* questions, about how best to construe an ambiguous term in light of competing policy interests—from the agencies that administer the statutes to federal courts. We have cautioned that "judges ought to refrain from substituting their own interstitial lawmaking" for that of an agency. *Ford Motor Credit Co. v. Milhollin*, 444 U.S. 555, 568 (1980). That is precisely what *Chevron* prevents. . . .

* * *

Those who assert that applying *Chevron* to "jurisdictional" interpretations "leaves the fox in charge of the henhouse" overlook the reality that a separate category of "jurisdictional" interpretations does not exist. The fox-in-the-henhouse syndrome is to be avoided not by establishing an arbitrary and undefinable category of agency decisionmaking that is accorded no deference, but by taking seriously, and applying rigorously, in all cases, statutory limits on agencies' authority. Where Congress has established a clear line, the agency cannot go beyond it; and where Congress has established an ambiguous line, the agency can go no further than the ambiguity will fairly allow. But in rigorously applying the latter rule, a court need not pause to puzzle over whether the interpretive question presented is "jurisdictional." If "the agency's answer is based on a permissible construction of the statute," that is the end of the matter. *Chevron*, 467 U.S., at 842.

The judgment of the Court of Appeals is affirmed.
It is so ordered.

Chief Justice ROBERTS, with whom Justice KENNEDY and Justice ALITO join, dissenting. . . .

I. . . .

The Court states that the question "is whether a court must defer under *Chevron* to an agency's interpretation of a statutory ambiguity that concerns the scope of the agency's statutory authority (that is, its jurisdiction)." That is fine—until the parenthetical. The parties, amici, and court below too often use the term "jurisdiction" imprecisely, which leads the Court to misunderstand the argument it must confront. That argument is not that "there exist two distinct classes of agency interpretations," some "big, important ones" that "define the agency's 'jurisdiction,'" and other "humdrum, run-of-the-mill" ones that "are simply applications of jurisdiction the agency plainly has." The argument is instead that a court should not defer to an agency on whether Congress has granted the agency interpretive authority over the statutory ambiguity at issue. . . .

II

. . . [B]efore a court may grant [*Chevron*] deference, it must on its own decide whether Congress—the branch vested with lawmaking authority under the Constitution—has in fact delegated to the agency lawmaking power over the ambiguity at issue. Agencies are creatures of Congress; "an agency literally has no power to act . . . unless and until Congress confers power upon it." *Louisiana Pub. Serv. Comm'n v. FCC*, 476 U.S. 355, 374 (1986). Whether Congress has conferred such power is the "relevant question[ ] of law" that must be answered before affording *Chevron* deference. 5 U.S.C. § 706. . . .

IV

. . . [T]he FCC argues that a court need only locate an agency and a grant of general rulemaking authority over a statute. *Chevron* deference then applies, it contends, to the agency's interpretation of any ambiguity in the Act, including ambiguity in a provision said to carve out specific provisions from the agency's general rulemaking authority. If Congress intends to exempt part of the statute from the agency's interpretive authority, the FCC says, Congress "can ordinarily be expected to state that intent explicitly."

If a congressional delegation of interpretive authority is to support *Chevron* deference, however, that delegation must extend to the specific statutory ambiguity at issue. The appropriate question is whether the delegation covers the "specific provision" and "particular question" before the court. *Chevron*, 467 U.S., at 844. A congressional grant of authority over some portion of a statute does not necessarily mean that Congress granted the agency interpretive authority over all its provisions.

. . . [E]ven when Congress provides interpretive authority to a single agency, a court must decide if the ambiguity the agency has purported to interpret with the force of law is one to which the congressional delegation extends. A general delegation to the agency to administer the statute will often suffice to satisfy the court that Congress has delegated interpretive authority over the ambiguity at issue. But if Congress has exempted particular provisions from that authority, that exemption must be respected, and the determination whether Congress has done so is for the courts alone.

The FCC's argument that Congress can ordinarily be expected to state that intent explicitly, goes to the merits of that determination, not to whether a court should decide the question *de novo* or defer to the agency. Indeed, that is how the Court in *American Hospital Assn. v. NLRB*, 499 U.S. 606 (1991) considered it. It was in the process of "employing the traditional tools of statutory construction" that the Court said it would have expected Congress to speak more clearly if it had intended to exclude an entire subject area—employee units for collecting bargaining—from the NLRB's general rulemaking authority. *Id.* at 613, 614. The Court concluded, after considering the language, structure, policy, and legislative history of the Act on its own — without deferring to the agency — that the meaning of the statute was "clear and contrary to the meaning advanced by petitioner." *Id.* at 609–614. To be sure, the Court also noted that "[e]ven if we *could* find any ambiguity in [the provision] after employing the traditional tools of statutory construction, we would still defer to Board's reasonable interpretation." *Id.* at 614 (emphasis added). But that single sentence of dictum cannot carry the day for the FCC here.

V

As the preceding analysis makes clear, I do not understand petitioners to ask the Court — nor do I think it necessary — to draw a "specious, but scary-sounding" line between "big, important" interpretations on the one hand and "humdrum, run-of-the-mill" ones on the other. Drawing such a line may well be difficult. Distinguishing between whether an agency's interpretation of an ambiguous term is reasonable and whether that term is for the agency to interpret is not nearly so difficult. . . .

The majority's hypothetical Common Carrier Acts do not demonstrate anything different. The majority states that in its second Common Carrier Act, Section 2 makes clear that Congress "'conferred interpretative power on the agency'" to interpret the ambiguous terms "common carrier" and "unreasonable condition." Thus, it says, under anyone's theory a court must defer to the agency's reasonable interpretations of those terms. Correct.

The majority claims, however, that "petitioners' theory would accord the agency no deference" in its interpretation of the same ambiguous terms in the first Common Carrier Act. But as I understand petitioners' argument — and certainly in my own view — a court, in both cases, need only decide for itself whether Congress has delegated to the agency authority to interpret the ambiguous terms, before affording the agency's interpretation *Chevron* deference.

For the second Common Carrier Act, the answer is easy. The majority's hypothetical Congress has spoken clearly and specifically in Section 2 of the Act about its delegation of authority to interpret Section 1. As for the first Act, it is harder to analyze the question, given only one section of a presumably much larger statute. But if the first Common Carrier Act is like most agencies' organic statutes, I have no reason to doubt that the agency would likewise have interpretive authority over the same ambiguous terms, and therefore be entitled to deference in construing them, just as with the second Common Carrier Act. There is no new "test" to worry about; courts would simply apply the normal rules of statutory construction.

That the question might be harder with respect to the first Common Carrier Act should come as no surprise. The second hypothetical Congress has more carefully defined the agency's authority than the first. Whatever standard of review applies, it is more difficult to interpret an unclear statute than a clear one. My point is simply that before a court can defer to the agency's interpretation of the ambiguous terms in either Act, it must determine for itself that Congress has delegated authority to the agency to issue those interpretations with the force of law. . . .

VI

The Court sees something nefarious behind the view that courts must decide on their own whether Congress has delegated interpretative authority to an agency, before deferring to that agency's interpretation of law. What is afoot, according to the Court, is a judicial power-grab, with nothing less than "*Chevron* itself" as "the ultimate target."

The Court touches on a legitimate concern: *Chevron* importantly guards against the Judiciary arrogating to itself policymaking properly left, under the separation of powers, to the Executive. But there is another concern at play, no less firmly rooted in our constitutional structure. That is the obligation of the Judiciary not only to confine itself to its proper role, but to ensure that the other branches do so as well.

An agency's interpretive authority, entitling the agency to judicial deference, acquires its legitimacy from a delegation of lawmaking power from Congress to the Executive. Our duty to police the boundary between the Legislature and the Executive is as critical as our duty to respect that between the Judiciary and the Executive. In the present context, that means ensuring that the Legislative Branch has in fact delegated lawmaking power to an agency within the Executive Branch, before the Judiciary defers to the Executive on what the law is. That concern is heightened, not diminished, by the fact that the administrative agencies, as a practical matter, draw upon a potent brew of executive, legislative, and judicial power. And it is heightened, not diminished, by the dramatic shift in power over the last 50 years from Congress to the Executive — a shift effected through the administrative agencies.

We reconcile our competing responsibilities in this area by ensuring judicial deference to agency interpretations under *Chevron* — but only after we have determined on our own that Congress has given interpretive authority to the agency. Our "task is to fix the boundaries of delegated authority," Henry P. Monaghan, Marbury *and the Administrative State*, 83 Colum. L. Rev. 1, 27 (1983); that is not a task we can delegate to the agency. We do not leave it to the agency to decide when it is in charge. . . .

I respectfully dissent.

QUESTION SET 9.34

Review & Synthesis

1. Writing for the Court, Justice Scalia concluded that the line between jurisdictional and non-jurisdictional statutes is illusory for *Chevron* purposes.
   a. How did Justice Scalia define "jurisdictional"? How did the contrast he drew between administrative and judicial jurisdiction inform that definition?
   b. How did Justice Scalia's definition of "jurisdictional" differ from the one apparently adopted by Chief Justice Roberts, writing in dissent? Which do you find more persuasive? What overall effect — expansion or contraction — would you expect the Chief Justice's analysis to have on deference to agency statutory interpretation?
   c. Is it clear to you that all questions of an agency's authority are "jurisdictional" questions? Suppose a statute expressly precluded an agency from regulating a category of economic or social activity otherwise covered by the enabling act it administers. Alternatively, suppose that two agencies are responsible for administering different parts of a regulatory scheme. Under *City of Arlington*, would a reviewing court have to defer to the agency's construction of those provisions, which exclude particular subjects from an agency's regulatory purview? Should we instead read *City of Arlington* as establishing a default against distinguishing between jurisdictional and non-jurisdictional provisions that can be overcome by explicit statutory language?

CHAPTER 10

The Public

Accountability through transparency is a cornerstone of American democracy. When public confidence in government has waned, Congress has passed "open government" statutes to increase public access to agency records and meetings, thereby facilitating government accountability. Through increasing administrative transparency, the public has been able to scrutinize agency practices to ensure that they faithfully perform their duties. We have seen such mechanisms of public participation and accountability in this casebook: public participation in notice-and-comment rulemaking (Chapter 5); executive orders requiring fuller disclosure of rulemaking information to the public (Chapter 5); the citizen-suit provisions of APA § 702 and in other statutes (Chapter 9). We now turn to two of the most powerful tools the public has to supervise the administrative decision-making process: The Freedom of Information Act ("FOIA") and the Government in the Sunshine Act of 1976 (the "Sunshine Act").

Part of the Administrative Procedure Act, FOIA is currently codified at 5 U.S.C. § 552. In essence, it provides the public with access to agency records. Consider the following description of the Act's importance, provided by President Barack Obama in a 2009 memorandum:

> A democracy requires accountability, and accountability requires transparency. As Justice Louis Brandeis wrote, "sunlight is said to be the best of disinfectants." In our democracy, the Freedom of Information Act (FOIA), which encourages accountability through transparency, is the most prominent expression of a profound national commitment to ensuring an open Government. At the heart of that commitment is the idea that accountability is in the interest of the Government and the citizenry alike.

Freedom of Information Act: Memorandum for the Heads of Executive Departments and Agencies, 74 Fed. Reg. 4683 (Jan. 21, 2009), https://

www.justice.gov/sites/default/files/oip/legacy/2014/07/23/presidential-foia
.pdf. The Sunshine Act, also part of the APA (5 U.S.C. § 552b) serves a
similar purpose. It opens the administrative decision-making processes to the
public by allowing access to agency meetings.

As you will see the courts have had a critical role in navigating the fine
line between facilitating public access and thereby agency accountability on
the one hand, and promoting agency efficacy, preserving personal privacy,
and protecting the administrative deliberative process, on the other. The
materials that follow study its efforts.

A. THE FREEDOM OF INFORMATION ACT

Origins and Historical Development. Concerns in America over the
spread of communism, commonly known as the "Red Scare," dominated
political and economic discourse throughout the 1940s and 1950s. In 1947,
President Harry S. Truman issued the Loyalty Order, which featured "a
loyalty investigation of every person entering civilian employment of any
department or agency of the executive branch of the Federal Government."
See Exec. Order No. 9835, 12 Fed. Reg. 1935 (Mar. 21, 1947). In 1949, the
Soviet Union conducted its first successful nuclear weapons test and Mao
Zedong led communist forces in a takeover of China. Less than a year later,
the United States entered the Korean War against the communist-supported
forces in North Korea. Fears of nuclear annihilation led some Americans to
build bomb shelters in their backyards.

Against this backdrop, California elected John E. Moss (D-CA) to the
House of Representatives in 1952. Moss feared that several Cold War initiatives were threatening American democracy by increasing government
secrecy. He believed that greater government transparency and increased
public access to government records and information would strengthen
rather than diminish national security. To that end, he introduced the
Freedom of Information Act ("FOIA") in 1955. He continued to push for
its passage for over a decade until the law was passed in 1966.

FOIA is now viewed as an essential tool of government accountability. This sentiment echoes throughout the Supreme Court's FOIA jurisprudence. *NLRB v. Robbins Tire & Rubber Co.*, for instance, declared that
"[t]he basic purpose of FOIA is to ensure an informed citizenry, vital to
the functioning of a democratic society, needed to check against corruption and to hold the governors accountable to the governed." 437 U.S.
214, 242 (1978). It requires federal agencies to "disclose any information
requested under [it] unless [that information] falls under one of nine exemptions which protect interests such as personal privacy, national security,
and law enforcement." *Frequently Asked Questions: What Is FOIA?*, Office
of Information Policy, Department of Justice, https://www.foia.gov/faq
.html (last visited Nov. 3, 2020) [hereinafter "FOIA FAQs"]. Assuming the

information an individual seeks is not already publicly available, all she need do is submit a FOIA request to the agency in possession of it.

FOIA has been amended several times in the years since it was passed, including updates that address information digitization. Of these updates, the Electronic Freedom of Information Act Amendments of 1996 are the most significant. They expanded FOIA's definition of "record" to include those maintained in any format, including those electronically stored. The federal government is now required to disclose digital records pursuant to FOIA requests, and it is encouraged to publish information in digital format as well.

Continued efforts to ensure public access and governmental account-ability are likewise evident in the most recent amendment, adopted 50 years after FOIA's passage. The day after his inauguration, President Barack Obama signaled the ongoing need for government transparency when he directed Executive Branch agencies to follow a clear presumption of openness in their FOIA request responses. Freedom of Information Act: Memorandum for the Heads of Executive Departments and Agencies, 74 Fed. Reg. 4683, 4683 (Jan. 21, 2009), https://www.justice.gov/ sites/default/files/oip/legacy/ 2014/07/23/presidential-foia.pdf. Two months later, Attorney General Eric Holder implemented this presumption of openness. He instructed federal agencies to withhold records only if they could reasonably fore-see harm resulting from disclosure. Memorandum from Eric Holder, Attorney General, U.S. Department of Justice, to Heads of Executive Departments & Agencies, The Freedom of Information Act (FOIA), (Mar. 19, 2009), https://www.justice.gov/sites/default/files/ag/legacy/2009/06/ 24/foia-memo-march2009.pdf. The policy was not new; first issued under President Bill Clinton, then rescinded by President George W. Bush, it was reestablished by President Obama.

Despite Holder's memorandum implementing the foreseeable harm stan-dard, Congress remained "concern[ed] that some agencies [were] overusing FOIA exemptions that allow[ed], but [did] not require, information to be with-held from disclosure." S. Rep. No. 114-4, at 2 (2015), as reprinted in 2016 U.S.C.C.A.N. 321, 322. Congress addressed this problem by codifying the pre-sumption of openness, making it "a permanent requirement for agencies" with the FOIA Improvement Act of 2016 ("FIA"). H.R. Rep. No. 114-391, at 9 (2016). FIA limits an agency's discretionary power to withhold documents under one of FOIA's nine enumerated exemptions. It also codified the Department of Justice's "foreseeable harm" standard. When processing a FOIA request:

> An agency shall—
>> (i) withhold information under this section only if—
>>> (I) the agency reasonably foresees that disclosure would harm an interest protected by an exemption described in subsection (b); or
>>> (II) disclosure is prohibited by law; and

(ii)(I) consider whether partial disclosure of information is possible whenever the agency determines that a full disclosure of a requested record is not possible; and

(II) take reasonable steps necessary to segregate and release nonexempt information. . . .

5 U.S.C. § 552(a)(8)(A).

Among FIA's other improvements, it provided for public inspection in electronic format instead of "inspection of documents and copying." It also required agencies to proactively disclose frequently requested information. Records requested three or more times must be made available either on the agency's or FOIA's website. *See* U.S. Dep't of Justice, Office of Info. Policy, OIP Summary of the FOIA Improvement Act of 2016, https://www.justice .gov/oip/oip-summary-foia-improvement-act-2016 (last visited July 9, 2020).

Overview of Basic Provisions. FOIA features three mechanisms under which an agency must disclose its records. *See* 5 U.S.C. § 552(a)(1)-(3). Subsections (a)(1) and (a)(2) require agencies to proactively disclose certain types of information. The first provision requires agencies to publish in the Federal Register certain types of public guidance including the "places at which, the employees . . . from whom, and the methods whereby, the public may obtain information, make submittals or requests, or obtain decisions." 5 U.S.C. § 552(a)(1)(A). Under the second proactive disclosure mechanism, each agency has an affirmative obligation to make certain records "available for public inspection in an electronic format." 5 U.S.C. § 552(a)(2). The records subject to this obligation are:

(A) final opinions, including concurring and dissenting opinions, as well as orders, made in the adjudication of cases;

(B) those statements of policy and interpretations which have been adopted by the agency and are not published in the Federal Register;

(C) administrative staff manuals and instructions to staff that affect a member of the public;

(D) copies of all records, regardless of form or format—
(i) that have been released to any person under [5 U.S.C. § 552 (a)(3)]; and
(ii) (I) that because of the nature of their subject matter, the agency determines have become or are likely to become the subject of subsequent requests for substantially the same records; or
(II) that have been requested 3 or more times; and

(E) a general index of the records referred to under subparagraph (D). . . .

5 U.S.C. § 552(a)(2)(A)-(E); *see generally* U.S. Department of Justice, Office of Information Policy, Proactive Disclosure of Non-Exempt Agency Information: Making Information Available Without the Need to File a FOIA Request (2017).

The third FOIA provision is the one most often seen in headlines. When a proper request is made for agency records, the agency "shall make the records promptly available to any person." 5 U.S.C. § 552(a)(3)(A). The agency, however, is not required to make available agency records that fall within one of FOIA's nine exemptions. *See* 5 U.S.C. § 552(b).

As one might suspect, government compliance with the third provision is far from costless. According to the Department of Justice, FOIA-related activities cost the government almost $525 million in 2019. U.S. Department of Justice, Summary of Annual FOIA Reports for Fiscal Year 2019 (2019). More than 90 percent of those costs were associated with processing requests and appeals. *Id.* Compliance is also highly concentrated; a handful of agencies receive more than 75 percent of all requests. In 2019, the Department of Homeland Security received almost half of all FOIA requests, 47 percent, while the DOJ received 11 percent. *Id.* National Archives and Records Administration, Department of Defense, and Health and Human Services, received 8 percent, 6 percent, and 4 percent, respectively. The remaining 24 percent, or 204,240 requests in 2019, fell to all remaining agencies. *Id.*

* * *

The materials that follow consider when an agency must produce records pursuant to a FOIA request. We will begin with the threshold inquiries of what an "agency record" is and when it is "improperly withheld." Afterwards, we will turn to FOIA's exemptions and the FIA's foreseeability of harm standard. Finally, we will touch on Reverse FOIA and the Sunshine Act.

1. Agency Records and Improper Withholding

To make a FOIA request, parties submit written requests to the relevant agency's FOIA office. *See* FOIA FAQs, FOIA.gov, https://www.foia.gov/faq.html (last visited Nov. 3, 2020) (providing guidance and information on making FOIA requests). The request must reasonably describe the information sought. As a general matter, FOIA requests are not limited to United States citizens; noncitizens are also able to make them. District courts have "jurisdiction to enjoin the agency from withholding agency records and to order the production of any agency records improperly withheld from the complainant." 5 U.S.C. § 552(a)(4)(B). Thus, to have a cause of action under FOIA a plaintiff must show that an agency has improperly withheld agency records. Surprisingly, FOIA does not offer a definition for "agency records" or "improperly withheld." It has been left to the courts to define the meaning of these key concepts. The Supreme Court addressed the issue in the following seminal case.

Kissinger v. Reporters Committee for Freedom of the Press
445 U.S. 136 (1980)

Mr. Justice REHNQUIST delivered the opinion of the Court:

The Freedom of Information Act (FOIA) vests jurisdiction in federal district courts to enjoin an "agency from withholding agency records and to order the production of any agency records improperly withheld from the complainant." 5 U.S.C. § 552(a)(4)(B). We hold today that even if a document requested under the FOIA is wrongfully in the possession of a party not an "agency," the agency which received the request does not "improperly withhold" those materials by its refusal to institute a retrieval action. When an agency has demonstrated that it has not "withheld" requested records in violation of the standards established by Congress, the federal courts have no authority to order the production of such records under the FOIA.

I

This litigation arises out of FOIA requests seeking access to various transcriptions of petitioner Kissinger's telephone conversations. The questions presented by the petition necessitate a thorough review of the facts.

A

Henry Kissinger served in the Nixon and Ford administrations for eight years. He assumed the position of Assistant to the President for National Security Affairs in January 1969. In September 1973, Kissinger was appointed to the office of Secretary of State but retained his National Security Affairs advisory position until November 3, 1975. After his resignation from the latter position, Kissinger continued to serve as Secretary of State until January 20, 1977. Throughout this period of Government service, Kissinger's secretaries generally monitored his telephone conversations and recorded their contents either by shorthand or on tape. The stenographic notes or tapes were used to prepare detailed summaries, and sometimes verbatim transcripts, of Kissinger's conversations. Since Kissinger's secretaries generally monitored all of his conversations, the summaries discussed official business as well as personal matters. The summaries and transcripts . . . throughout his entire tenure in Government service were stored in his office at the State Department in personal files.

On October 29, 1976, while still Secretary of State, Kissinger arranged to move the telephone notes from his office in the State Department to the New York estate of Nelson Rockefeller. . . .

After Kissinger effected this physical transfer of the notes, he entered into two agreements with the Library of Congress deeding his private papers. In the first agreement, dated November 12, 1976, Kissinger deeded . . . one collection of papers. Kissinger's telephone notes were not included in this collection. The agreement established terms obligating Kissinger to comply with certain restrictions on the inclusion of official documents in the collection and obligating the Library to respect restrictions on access. . . .

On December 24, 1976, by a second deed, Kissinger donated a second collection consisting of his telephone notes. This second agreement with the Library of Congress incorporated by reference all of the terms and conditions of the first agreement. . . .

On December 28, 1976, the transcripts were transported directly to the Library from the Rockefeller estate. . . .

B

Three separate FOIA requests form the basis of this litigation. All three requests were filed while Kissinger was Secretary of State, but only one request was filed prior to the removal of the telephone notes from the premises of the State Department. This first request was filed by William Safire, a New York Times columnist, on January 14, 1976. Safire requested the Department of State to produce any transcripts of Kissinger's telephone conversations between January 21, 1969, and February 12, 1971, in which (1) Safire's name appeared or (2) Kissinger discussed the subject of information "leaks" with certain named White House officials. The Department denied Safire's FOIA request by letter of February 11, 1976. The Department letter reasoned that the requested notes had been made while Kissinger was National Security Adviser and therefore were not agency records subject to FOIA disclosure.

The second FOIA request was filed on December 28 and 29, 1976, by the Military Audit Project (MAP) after Kissinger publicly announced the gift of his telephone notes to the United States and their placement in the Library of Congress. The MAP request, filed with the Department of State, sought records of all Kissinger's conversations made while Secretary of State and National Security Adviser. On January 18, 1977, the Legal Adviser of the Department of State denied the request on two grounds. First, he found that the notes were not agency records. Second, the deposit of the notes with the Library of Congress prior to the request terminated the Department's custody and control. The denial was affirmed on administrative appeal.

The third FOIA request was filed on January 13, 1977, by the Reporters Committee for Freedom of the Press (RCFP), the American Historical Association, the American Political Science Association, and a number of other journalists (collectively referred to as the RCFP requesters). This request also sought production of the telephone notes made by Kissinger both while he was National Security Adviser and Secretary of State. The request was denied for the same reasons given to the MAP requesters. . . .

II. . . .

B

The FOIA represents a carefully balanced scheme of public rights and agency obligations designed to foster greater access to agency records than existed prior to its enactment. That statutory scheme authorizes federal courts to ensure private access to requested materials when three requirements have been met. Under 5 U.S.C. § 552(a)(4)(B) federal jurisdiction is dependent upon a showing that an agency has (1) "improperly"; (2) "withheld"; (3) "agency records." Judicial authority to devise remedies and enjoin agencies can only be invoked, under the jurisdictional grant conferred by § 552, if the agency has contravened all three components of this obligation. We find it unnecessary to decide whether the telephone notes were "agency records" since we conclude that a covered agency—here the State Department—has not "withheld" those documents from the plaintiffs. We also need not decide the full contours of a prohibited "withholding." We do decide, however, that Congress did not mean that an agency improperly withholds a document which has been removed from the possession of the agency prior to the filing of the FOIA request. In such a case, the agency has neither the custody nor control necessary to enable it to withhold.

In looking for congressional intent, we quite naturally start with the usual meaning of the word "withhold" itself. The requesters would have us read the "hold" out of "withhold." The act described by this word presupposes the actor's possession or control of the item withheld. A refusal to resort to legal remedies to obtain possession is simply not conduct subsumed by the verb "withhold."

The Act and its legislative history do not purport to define the word. An examination of the structure and purposes of the Act, however, indicates that Congress used the word in its usual sense. An agency's failure to sue a third party to obtain possession is not a withholding under the Act. . . .

Following FOIA's enactment in 1966, the Attorney General issued guidelines for the use of all federal departments and agencies in complying with the new statute. The guidelines state that FOIA "refers, of course, only to records in being and in the possession or control of an agency. . . . [It] imposes no obligation to compile or procure a record in response to a request." Attorney General's Memorandum on the Public Information

Section of the Administrative Procedure Act 23-24 (June 1967), Source Book I, pp. 222-223. . . .

The conclusion that possession or control is a prerequisite to FOIA disclosure duties is reinforced by an examination of the purposes of the Act. The Act does not obligate agencies to create or retain documents; it only obligates them to provide access to those which it in fact has created and retained. . . .

If the agency is not required to create or to retain records under the FOIA, it is somewhat difficult to determine why the agency is nevertheless required to retrieve documents which have escaped its possession, but which it has not endeavored to recover. If the document is of so little interest to the agency that it does not believe the retrieval effort to be justified, the effect of this judgment on an FOIA request seems little different from the effect of an agency determination that a record should never be created, or should be discarded. . . .

C

This construction of "withholding" readily disposes of the RCFP and MAP requests. Both of these requests were filed after Kissinger's telephone notes had been deeded to the Library of Congress. The Government, through the Archivist, has requested return of the documents from Kissinger. The request has been refused. The facts make it apparent that Kissinger, and the Library of Congress as his donee, are holding the documents under a claim of right. Under these circumstances, the State Department cannot be said to have had possession or control of the documents at the time the requests were received. It did not, therefore, withhold any agency records, an indispensable prerequisite to liability in a suit under the FOIA.

III

The Safire request raises a separate question. At the time when Safire submitted his request for certain notes of Kissinger's telephone conversations, all the notes were still located in Kissinger's office at the State Department. For this reason, we do not rest our resolution of his claim on the grounds that there was no withholding by the State Department. As outlined above, the Act only prohibits the withholding of "agency records." We conclude that the Safire request sought disclosure of documents which were not "agency records" within the meaning of the FOIA. . . .

The FOIA does render the "Executive Office of the President" an agency subject to the Act. 5 U.S.C. § 552(e). The legislative history is unambiguous, however, in explaining that the "Executive Office" does not include the Office of the President. The Conference Report for the 1974 FOIA Amendments indicates that "the President's immediate personal staff or units in the Executive Office whose sole function is to advise and assist the

President" are not included within the term "agency" under the FOIA. H.R. Conf. Rep. No. 93-1380, p. 15 (1974), reprinted in Sourcebook II, p. 232. Safire's request was limited to a period of time in which Kissinger was serving as Assistant to the President. Thus these telephone notes were not "agency records" when they were made. . . .

The RCFP requesters nevertheless contend that if the transcripts of telephone conversations made while adviser to the President were not then "agency records," they acquired that status under the Act when they were removed from White House files and physically taken to Kissinger's office at the Department of State. We simply decline to hold that the physical location of the notes of telephone conversations renders them "agency records." The papers were not in the control of the State Department at any time. They were not generated in the State Department. They never entered the State Department's files, and they were not used by the Department for any purpose. If mere physical location of papers and materials could confer status as an "agency record" Kissinger's personal books, speeches, and all other memorabilia stored in his office would have been agency records subject to disclosure under the FOIA. It requires little discussion or analysis to conclude that the lower courts correctly resolved this question in favor of Kissinger.

Accordingly, we reverse the order of the Court of Appeals compelling production of the telephone manuscripts made by Kissinger while Secretary of State and affirm the order denying the requests for transcripts produced while Kissinger served as National Security Adviser.

It is so ordered.

[Justices MARSHALL and BLACKMUN took no part in deciding these cases.]

[The opinion of Justice BRENNAN, concurring in part and dissenting in part, is omitted.]

Mr. Justice STEVENS, concurring in part and dissenting in part.

As the Court recognizes, the requesters are entitled to prevail in this FOIA action if the State Department "has (1) 'improperly'; (2) 'withheld'; (3) 'agency records.'" . . . The Court states, and I agree, that an agency cannot "withhold" documents unless it has either custody or control of them. It then goes on, however, to equate "custody" and "control" with physical possession, holding that FOIA is simply inapplicable to any "document which has been removed from the possession of the agency prior to the filing of the FOIA request."

I cannot agree that this conclusion is compelled by the plain language of the statute; moreover, it seems to me wholly inconsistent with the congressional purpose underlying the Freedom of Information Act. The decision today exempts documents that have been wrongfully removed from the agency's files from any scrutiny whatsoever under FOIA. It thus creates an incentive for outgoing agency officials to remove potentially embarrassing documents from their files in order to frustrate future FOIA requests. It is the creation of such an incentive, which is directly contrary to the purpose of FOIA, rather than the result in this particular case, that prompts me to write in dissent.

In my judgment, a "withholding" occurs within the meaning of FOIA whenever an agency declines to produce agency records which it has a legal right to possess or control. A determination that documents have been withheld does not end the inquiry, of course, for a court must still determine whether the withholding was "improper" for purposes of the Act. Thus, in my view, correct analysis requires us to confront three separate questions in the following order: (1) are any of the requested documents "agency records"? (2) if so, have any of them been withheld because they are in the legal custody of the agency? and (3) if so, was the withholding improper?

I

I cannot accept Dr. Kissinger's argument that the summaries are private papers. As the District Court noted, they were made in the regular course of conducting the agency's business, were the work product of agency personnel and agency assets, and were maintained in the possession and control of the agency prior to their removal by Dr. Kissinger. They were also regularly circulated to Dr. Kissinger's immediate staff and presumably used by the staff in making day-to-day decisions on behalf of the agency. Finally, Dr. Kissinger himself recognized that the State Department continued to have an interest in the summaries even after they had been removed, since he had a State Department employee review them in order to extract information that was not otherwise in the agency's files. . . . [It] is clear that at least some of them [were agency records] at the time Dr. Kissinger removed them from his files at the State Department.

II

The second question to be considered is whether the State Department continued to have custody or control of the telephone summaries after they were removed from its files so that its refusal to take steps to regain them should be deemed a "withholding" within the meaning of the Freedom of Information Act. As I stated at the outset, I do not agree with the Court that the broad concepts of "custody" and "control" can be equated with the much narrower concept of physical possession. . . . [I]f an agency has a legal right to regain possession of documents wrongfully removed from its files, it continues to have custody of those documents. If it then refuses to take any steps whatsoever to demand, or even to request, that the documents be returned, then the agency is "withholding" those documents for purposes of FOIA.

In this case, I think it is rather clear that the telephone summaries were wrongfully removed from the State Department's possession. Under these circumstances, the State Department's failure even to request their return constituted a "withholding" for purposes of FOIA.

III

The third and most difficult question is whether the State Department's "withholding" was "improper." In my view, the answer to that question depends on the agency's explanation for its failure to attempt to regain the documents. If the explanation is reasonable, then the withholding is not improper. . . . The FOIA does not require federal agencies to engage in prolonged searches for documents or institute legal proceedings that will not yield any appreciable benefits to the agency.

On the other hand, if the agency is unable to advance a reasonable explanation for its failure to act, a presumption arises that the agency is motivated by a desire to shield the documents from FOIA scrutiny. Thus, if the agency believed or had reason to believe that it had a legal right to the documents and that the documents were still valuable for its own internal purposes and nevertheless did not attempt to regain them, its inaction should be deemed an improper withholding.

In this case the State Department refused the FOIA requests on the ground that the telephone summaries were not agency records and, in any event, were no longer within the agency's custody or control. By the time the FOIA actions were filed, there was substantial reason for doubting the Department's resolution of the first issue, inasmuch as the General Counsel of GSA had rendered a legal opinion that the documents were probably agency records and should be returned to the Government for proper archival screening. Because of their very nature, there was also substantial reason for believing that, if they were agency records, the summaries would have to be considered valuable documents. Finally, the fact that the documents had been removed by the head of the agency shortly before the expiration of his term of office raised an inference that the removal had been motivated by a desire to avoid FOIA disclosure. Under these circumstances, it is at least arguable that the continued inaction of the State Department, contrary to the views of the Archivist, was improper.

Accordingly, I believe the District Court had jurisdiction under FOIA to determine (a) whether the telephone summaries were in fact agency records and (b) if so, whether the State Department's failure to seek return of the documents was improper. The court's disposition of those issues seems to me to have been somewhat premature, however. . . . I would therefore remand to give the Government an opportunity to finish its examination of the documents.

* * *

On the same day the Court decided Kissinger, it decided its companion case *Forsham v. Harris*, 445 U.S. 169 (1980). In *Forsham*, the University Group Diabetes Program ("UGDP"), a private group of physicians and scientists, conducted a long-term study on the efficacy of various "diabetes treatment regimes." The study was fully funded by grants from a federal agency. Although the government had a right to access the study data and upon request could take possession of the data, it had neither accessed nor taken possession of any of it. The petitioners filed a FOIA request to obtain the study's raw data. The Court held that "written data generated, owned, and possessed by a privately controlled organization receiving federal study grants are not 'agency records' within the meaning of the Act when copies of those data have not been obtained by a federal agency subject to the FOIA." *Id.*, at 170. Furthermore, it would not compel the agency to exercise its right to access the data because in so doing the Court "effectively would be compelling the agency to 'create' an agency record since prior to that exercise the record was not a record of the agency." *Id.*, at 186. If a simple right to access made something an agency record it would "include all documents created by a private grantee to which the Government has access, and which the Government has used." *Id.*, at 169. The Court "instead [held] that an agency must first either create or obtain a record as a prerequisite to its becoming an 'agency record' within the meaning of the FOIA." *Id.*, at 169.

The following case built on the principles established by *Forsham* and *Kissinger*. In *Tax Analysts,* the Court offered further guidance on when an "agency record" is "improperly withheld."

Department of Justice v. Tax Analysts
492 U.S. 136 (1989)

Justice MARSHALL delivered the opinion of the Court.

The question presented is whether the Freedom of Information Act (FOIA or Act), 5 U.S.C. § 552 (1982 ed. and Supp. V), requires the United States Department of Justice (Department) to make available copies of district court decisions that it receives in the course of litigating tax cases on behalf of the Federal Government. We hold that it does.

I

The Department's Tax Division represents the Federal Government in nearly all civil tax cases in the district courts, the courts of appeals, and the Claims Court. Because it represents a party in litigation, the Tax Division receives copies of all opinions and orders issued by these courts in such cases.

Copies of these decisions are made for the Tax Division's staff attorneys. The original documents are sent to the official files kept by the Department. . . .

Respondent Tax Analysts publishes a weekly magazine, Tax Notes, which reports on legislative, judicial, and regulatory developments in the field of federal taxation to a readership largely composed of tax attorneys, accountants, and economists. As one of its regular features, Tax Notes provides summaries of recent federal-court decisions on tax issues.

In late July 1979, Tax Analysts filed a FOIA request in which it asked the Department to make available all district court tax opinions and final orders received by the Tax Division earlier that month. The Department denied the request on the ground that these decisions were not Tax Division records. Tax Analysts then appealed this denial administratively. While the appeal was pending, Tax Analysts agreed to withdraw its request in return for access to the Tax Division's weekly log of tax cases decided by the federal courts. . . .

. . . Tax Analysts initiated a series of new FOIA requests in 1984. . . . Tax Analysts asked the Department to make available copies of all district court tax opinions and final orders identified in the Tax Division's weekly logs. The Department denied these requests. . . .

II. . . .

The FOIA confers jurisdiction on the district courts "to enjoin the agency from withholding agency records and to order the production of any agency records improperly withheld." § 552(a)(4)(B). Under this provision, "federal jurisdiction is dependent on a showing that an agency has (1) 'improperly' (2) 'withheld' (3) 'agency records.'" *Kissinger v. Reporters Committee for Freedom of the Press*, 445 U.S. 136 (1980). Unless each of these criteria is met, a district court lacks jurisdiction to devise remedies to force an agency to comply with the FOIA's disclosure requirements.

In this case, all three jurisdictional terms are at issue. . . .

A

We consider first whether the district court decisions at issue are "agency records." . . .

Two requirements emerge from *Kissinger* and *Forsham*, each of which must be satisfied for requested materials to qualify as "agency records." First, an agency must "either create or obtain" the requested materials "as a prerequisite to its becoming an 'agency record' within the meaning of the FOIA." *Forsham*, 445 U.S., at 181. . . .

Second, the agency must be in control of the requested materials at the time the FOIA request is made. By control we mean that the materials have come into the agency's possession in the legitimate conduct of its official duties. . . . [T]he term "agency records" is not so broad as to include personal materials in an employee's possession, even though the materials may be physically located at the agency. . . .

Applying these requirements here, we conclude that the requested district court decisions constitute "agency records." First, it is undisputed that the Department has obtained these documents from the district courts. . . . The Department contends that a district court is not an "agency" under the FOIA, but this truism is beside the point. The relevant issue is whether an agency covered by the FOIA has "create[d] or obtaine[d]" the materials sought, *Forsham*, 445 U.S., at 182, not whether the organization from which the documents originated is itself covered by the FOIA.

Second, the Department clearly controls the district court decisions that Tax Analysts seeks. Each of Tax Analysts' FOIA requests referred to district court decisions in the agency's possession at the time the requests were made. . . . The Department counters that it does not control these decisions because the district courts retain authority to modify the decisions even after they are released, but this argument, too, is beside the point. The control inquiry focuses on an agency's possession of the requested materials, not on its power to alter the content of the materials it receives. . . . An authorship-control requirement thus would sharply limit "agency records" essentially to documents generated by the agencies themselves. This result is incompatible with the FOIA's goal of giving the public access to all nonexempt information received by an agency as it carries out its mandate.

The Department also urges us to limit "agency records," at least where materials originating outside the agency are concerned, "to those documents 'prepared substantially to be relied upon in agency decisionmaking.'" Brief for Petitioner 21, quoting *Berry v. Dep't of Justice*, 733 F.2d 1343, 1349 (9th Cir. 1984). . . . This argument, however, makes the determination of "agency records" turn on the intent of the creator of a document relied upon by an agency. Such a *mens rea* requirement is nowhere to be found in the Act. . . .

B

We turn next to the term "withheld," which we discussed in *Kissinger*. . . .

The construction of "withholding" adopted in *Kissinger* readily encompasses Tax Analysts' requests. There is no claim here that Tax Analysts filed its requests for copies of recent district court tax decisions received by the Tax Division after these decisions had been transferred out of the Department. On the contrary, the decisions were on the Department's premises and otherwise in the Department's control when the requests were made. . . . Thus, when the Department refused to comply with Tax Analysts' requests, it "withheld" the district court decisions for purposes of § 552(a)(4)(B).

The Department's counterargument is that, because the district court decisions sought by Tax Analysts are publicly available as soon as they are issued and thus may be inspected and copied by the public at any time, the Department cannot be said to have "withheld" them. . . . [T]o the extent the Department relies on the [term withheld], its argument is without merit. Congress used the word "withheld" only "in its usual sense." *Kissinger*, 445 U.S. 136 at 151. When the Department refused to grant Tax Analysts' requests for the district court decisions in its files, it undoubtedly "withheld" these decisions in any reasonable sense of that term. . . . We therefore reject the Department's argument that an agency has not "withheld" a document under its control when, in denying an otherwise valid request, it directs the requester to a place outside of the agency where the document may be publicly available.

C

The Department is left to argue, finally, that the district court decisions were not "improperly" withheld because of their public availability. The term "improperly," like "agency records" and "withheld," is not defined by the Act. We explained in GTE Sylvania, however, that Congress' use of the word "improperly" reflected its dissatisfaction with § 3 of the Administrative Procedure Act, 5 U.S.C. § 1002 (1964 ed.), which "had failed to provide the desired access to information relied upon in Government decisionmaking, and in fact had become 'the major statutory excuse for withholding Government records from public view.'" 445 U.S. 136 at 384, quoting H.R. Rep. No. 1497, 89th Cong., 2d Sess., 3 (1966). Under § 3, we explained, agencies had "broad discretion . . . in deciding what information to disclose, and that discretion was often abused." 445 U.S. 136 at 385.

In enacting the FOIA, Congress intended "to curb this apparently unbridled discretion" by "clos[ing] the 'loopholes which allow agencies to deny legitimate information to the public.'" *Ibid.* (citation omitted). Toward this end, Congress formulated a system of clearly defined exemptions to the FOIA's otherwise mandatory disclosure requirements. An agency must disclose agency records to any person under § 552(a), "unless they may be withheld pursuant to one of the nine enumerated exemptions listed in § 552(b)." *Dep't of Justice v. Julian*, 486 U.S. 1, 8, (1988). Consistent with the Act's goal of broad disclosure, these exemptions have been consistently given a narrow compass. . . . It follows from the exclusive nature of the § 552(b) exemption scheme that agency records which do not fall within one of the exemptions are "improperly" withheld.

The Department does not contend here that any exemption enumerated in § 552(b) protects the district court decisions sought by Tax Analysts. The Department claims nonetheless that there is nothing "improper" in directing a requester "to the principal, public source of records." Brief for Petitioner 26. The Department advances three somewhat related arguments in support of this proposition. We consider them in turn.

First, the Department contends that the structure of the Act evinces Congress' desire to avoid redundant disclosures. . . . Under subsection (a)(3), the general provision covering the disclosure of agency records, an agency need not make available those materials that have already been disclosed under subsections (a)(1) and (a)(2). . . .

The Department's argument proves too much. The disclosure requirements set out in subsections (a)(1) and (a)(2) are carefully limited to situations in which the requested materials have been previously published or made available by the agency itself. It is one thing to say that an agency need not disclose materials that it has previously released; it is quite another to say that an agency need not disclose materials that some other person or group may have previously released. Congress undoubtedly was aware of the redundancies that might exist when requested materials have been previously made available. It chose to deal with that problem by crafting only narrow categories of materials which need not be, in effect, disclosed twice by the agency. If Congress had wished to codify an exemption for all publicly available materials, it knew perfectly well how to do so. . .

. . . Even if there were some agreement over what constitutes publicly available materials, Congress surely did not envision agencies satisfying their disclosure obligations under the FOIA simply by handing requesters a map and sending them on scavenger expeditions throughout the Nation. Without some express indication in the Act's text or legislative history that Congress intended such a result, we decline to adopt this reading of the statute. . . .

III

For the reasons stated, the Department improperly withheld agency records when it refused Tax Analysts' requests for copies of the district court tax decisions in its files. Accordingly, the judgment of the Court of Appeals is
    Affirmed.

Justice WHITE concurs in the judgment.

[The dissenting opinion of Justice BLACKMUN is omitted.]

QUESTION SET 10.1

Review & Synthesis

1. What factors did the *Kissinger* Court consider when analyzing whether the requested information was a "personal record" or an "agency record"?

2. On what basis did the *Tax Analysts* Court determine that documents created by an entity other than the agency could be agency records? What if the non-agency entity created the documents in question with no agency purpose?

3. According to *Tax Analysts*, can publicly available records be withheld? If they can be withheld, can that withholding be improper? Why or why not?

4. The records in dispute in both *Kissinger* and *Tax Analysts* were not created in the agency. Using what you have learned in these two opinions, explain if and when the location where a document was created matters when determining whether the document is an agency record subject to FOIA.

5. In his *Kissinger* dissent, Justice Stevens wrote that the majority's decision to "exempt[] documents that have been wrongfully removed from the agency's files from any scrutiny whatsoever under FOIA . . . creates an incentive for outgoing agency officials to remove potentially embarrassing documents from their files in order to frustrate future FOIA requests." Do you agree? How significant a concern is this?

Application & Analysis

1. An EPA attorney still has her handwritten notes from law school. She keeps the notes in her office desk drawer at the EPA. She regularly refers to these notes during the course of her work. If included in a FOIA request, are her notes "agency records" for purposes of FOIA disclosure?

2. You spend your 2L summer working in the DOJ's antitrust division. Your supervisor invites you to sit in on an important meeting discussing the DOJ's approach to enforcement of the Foreign Corrupt Practices Act. You bring your tablet and take notes during the meeting. Later you use the notes to draft a memo summarizing the DOJ's position; however, you never send your notes to anyone else in the agency. If included in a FOIA request, are your notes agency records for purposes of FOIA disclosure? What if the request is made after you have graduated from law school and are practicing at a private law firm?

---

2. FOIA'S Exemptions

The majority of FOIA litigation grapples with whether an agency may withhold records subject to FOIA disclosure because the requested records fall within one of its nine exemptions. Litigation over the exemptions is far too voluminous to cover here. For a deeper look, the Department of Justice's Guide to the Freedom of Information Act provides detailed information on each exemption's scope, historical development, and recent litigation or changes. U.S. DEPARTMENT OF JUSTICE, DEPARTMENT OF JUSTICE'S GUIDE TO THE FREEDOM OF INFORMATION ACT, https://www.justice.gov/oip/doj -guide-freedom-information-act-0 (last visited July 6, 2020) [hereinafter DOJ FOIA GUIDE]. In general terms, if a requested record falls within one of the nine exemptions below, and "the agency reasonably foresees that disclosure would harm an interest protected by [the] exemption," the agency may withhold the requested records. 5 U.S.C. § 552(a)(8)(A)(i)(I) and (b). If "disclosure is prohibited by law" the agency also may withhold the records. 5 U.S.C. § 552(a)(8)(A)(i)(II). FOIA's general exemptions protect:

- Exemption 1: Information that is classified to protect national security.
- Exemption 2: Information related solely to the internal personnel rules and practices of an agency.
- Exemption 3: Information that is prohibited from disclosure by another federal law.
- Exemption 4: Trade secrets or commercial or financial information that is confidential or privileged.
- Exemption 5: Privileged communications within or between agencies. . . .
- Exemption 6: Information that, if disclosed, would invade another individual's personal privacy.
- Exemption 7: Information compiled for law enforcement purposes. . . .
- Exemption 8: Information that concerns the supervision of financial institutions.
- Exemption 9: Geological information on wells.

FOIA FAQs, FOIA.gov, https://www.foia.gov/faq.html (last visited Nov. 3, 2020).

Consistent with FOIA's mandate providing for broad disclosure of agency records, the nine FOIA exemptions are exclusive (courts can neither add to nor subtract from them) and the Court has repeatedly held that each of the nine exemptions "must be narrowly construed." *Department of the Air Force v. Rose*, 425 U.S. 352, 361 (1976). Even when portions of a record fall within an exemption, the Freedom of Information Improvement Act of 2016 requires that agencies produce "[a]ny reasonably segregable portion . . . of such record after deletion of the portions which are exempt under this subsection." 5 U.S.C. § 552(b).

Despite FOIA exemptions' narrow scope and requirement to produce the nonexempt portions of a record, in 2019 agencies still denied 3.9 percent of requests in full due to an exemption. U.S. DEPARTMENT OF JUSTICE, SUMMARY OF ANNUAL FOIA REPORTS FOR FISCAL YEAR 2019, at 6 (2019). Although the percentage appears small, it represents 33,866 requests. Many of FOIA's exemptions are rarely used. In 2019, FOIA's personal privacy exemptions—Exemption 6 and Exemption 7(C)—accounted for over 55 percent of exemption usage. *Id.* at 8. In contrast, Exemptions 1, 2, 8, and 9 represented less than 1 percent of the exemptions agencies cited. *Id.* Unsurprisingly, much of FOIA exemption litigation revolves around the most frequently cited exemptions.

When an agency uses an exemption to withhold a record, the agency has the burden of proving that the withholding was lawful. 5 U.S.C. § 552(a)(4)(B). To meet this burden of proof, defendant agencies commonly create a document known as a Vaughn Index. The Index can be thought of as the FOIA equivalent of a privilege log. It originated with the D.C. Circuit's decision in *Vaughn v. Rosen*, 484 F.2d 820 (D.C. Cir. 1975). When an agency withholds a document pursuant to an exemption, the holding in *Vaughn* requires the agency to prepare an itemized index specifying the claimed FOIA exemption, the records or portions of it the agency claims are subject to that exemption, and the agency's nondisclosure justification. *Id.* at 827. The Index helps the court make an informed decision as to whether the agency's withholding under the claimed exemption is proper. In the absence of a *Vaughn* Index, the only alternative would be for the court to conduct an *in camera* review as provided for in the statute. *See* 5 U.S.C. § 552(a)(4)(B) (stipulating that district courts "may examine the contents of [withheld] agency records *in camera* to determine whether such records or any part thereof shall be withheld under any of the exemptions set forth in subsection (b) of [§ 552]").

The courts' jurisprudence continuously refines the contours of FOIA's nine exemptions. This ongoing effort to establish each exemption's intended scope is apparent in the definition of "confidential" and personal privacy cases excerpted below. As you will see, courts strive to strike a balance that neither limits an exemption's scope more than FOIA's language warrants nor allows an exemption's scope to expand beyond that which the statutory language demands.

a. Exemption 4: Confidential Commercial or Financial Information

Exemption 4 protects two separate categories of agency records. First, it protects trade secrets from disclosure. Second, it protects "commercial or financial information obtained from a person [that is] privileged or confidential." 5 U.S.C. § 552(b)(4). As the D.C. Circuit explained in *Public Citizen Health Research Group v. FDA*, a trade secret for Exemption 4 purposes is "a secret, commercially valuable plan, formula, process, or device that is used for the making, preparing, compounding, or processing of trade commodities and that can be said to be the end product of either innovation or substantial effort." 704 F.2d 1280, 1288 (D.C. Cir. 1983).

Exemption 4's second category has received considerably more attention than its first. In the watershed decision excerpted below, *Food Marketing Institute v. Argus Leader Media*, the Supreme Court ruled 6-3 that the meaning of the word "confidential" in Exemption 4 must be interpreted according to the "plain and ordinary" meaning of the statute's text. 139 S. Ct. 2356, 2364 (2019). The Court held "just as we cannot properly expand Exemption 4 beyond what its terms permit, we cannot arbitrarily constrict it either by adding limitations found nowhere in its terms." *Id.*, at 2366. To this end, the Court overturned more than 45 years of precedent. Previously, courts applied the "substantial harm" test established by the highly influential D.C. Circuit decision, *National Parks and Conservation Association v. Morton's*, 498 F.2d 765 (D.C. Cir. 1974). The Court rejected this test, holding that it impermissibly narrowed the scope of the statute. In *Argus Leader*, the Court found that the plain meaning of "confidential" simply meant "'private' or 'secret.'" 139 S. Ct. at 2363.

Recall that FOIA's mandate is to provide the public with a way to be informed of "what its government is up to." *National Archives & Records Admininistration v. Favish*, 541 U.S. 157, 171 (2004) (quoting *U.S. Department of Justice v. Reporters Committee for Freedom of the Press*, 489 U.S. 749, 773 (1989)) [hereinafter *DOJ v. Reporters Committee*]. As you saw in *Tax Analyst*, FOIA does this through a "goal of broad disclosure." As you read *Argus Leader*, consider whether the majority or dissent stays true to FOIA's mandate and the manner in which they address FOIA's intended purpose.

Food Marketing Institute v. Argus Leader Media, dba Argus Leader
139 S. Ct. 2356 (2019)

Justice GORSUCH delivered the opinion of the Court.

. . . [Under Exemption 4, FOIA's disclosure requirements] do "not apply" to "confidential" private-sector "commercial or financial information" in the government's possession. But when does information provided to a federal agency qualify as "confidential"? The Food Marketing Institute says it's enough if the owner keeps the information private rather than releasing it publicly. The government suggests that an agency's promise to keep information from disclosure may also suffice to render it confidential. But the courts below imposed a different requirement yet, holding that information can never be deemed confidential unless disclosing it is likely to result in "substantial competitive harm" to the business that provided it. Finding at least this "competitive harm" requirement inconsistent with the terms of the statute, we reverse.

I

[The Court recounted the case's factual background in Section I. A South Dakota Newspaper, Argus Leader, filed a FOIA request with the United States Department of Agriculture. Argus sought five years of store-level data on annual Supplemental Nutrition Assistance Program ("SNAP") redemptions including the stores' names and addresses. The USDA denied the request claiming the requested data were protected from disclosure under FOIA Exemption 4. 5 U.S.C. § 552(b)(4). Argus sued the USDA to compel disclosure. Applying the Eighth Circuit's competitive harm test, the district court agreed that store-level SNAP data disclosure would not cause substantial competitive harm. The USDA did not appeal, but contacted the Food Marketing Institute, a trade association of grocery retailers, so it would have an opportunity to intervene. The Food Marketing Institute successfully intervened. The Eighth Circuit affirmed the district court's decision. In Section II of its opinion, the Court concluded that the Food Marketing Institute had Article III standing.]

III

A

. . . Exemption 4 shields from mandatory disclosure "commercial or financial information obtained from a person and privileged or confidential." But FOIA nowhere defines the term "confidential." So, as usual, we ask what that term's "ordinary, contemporary, common meaning" was when Congress enacted FOIA in 1966. *Perrin v. United States*, 444 U.S. 37, 42 (1979). . . .

The term "confidential" meant then, as it does now, "private" or "secret." Webster's Seventh New Collegiate Dictionary 174 (1963). Contemporary dictionaries suggest two conditions that might be required for information communicated to another to be considered confidential. In one sense, information communicated to another remains confidential whenever it is customarily kept private, or at least closely held, by the person imparting it. *See, e.g.*, Webster's Third New International Dictionary 476 (1961) ("known only to a limited few" or "not publicly disseminated"). In another sense, information might be considered confidential only if the party receiving it provides some assurance that it will remain secret. *See, e.g.*, 1 Oxford Universal Dictionary Illustrated 367 (3d ed. 1961) ("spoken or written in confidence").

Must both of these conditions be met for information to be considered confidential under Exemption 4? At least the first condition has to be; it is hard to see how information could be deemed confidential if its owner shares it freely. And there's no question that the Institute's members satisfy this condition. . . .

B

Notably lacking from dictionary definitions, early case law, or any other usual source that might shed light on the statute's ordinary meaning is any mention of the "substantial competitive harm" requirement that the courts below found unsatisfied and on which Argus Leader pins its hopes. . . .

So where did the "substantial competitive harm" requirement come from? In 1974, the D. C. Circuit declared that, in addition to the requirements actually set forth in Exemption 4, a "court must also be satisfied that non-disclosure is justified by the legislative purpose which underlies the exemption." *National Parks & Conservation Assn. v. Morton*, 498 F.2d 765, 767. Then, after a selective tour through the legislative history, the court concluded that "commercial or financial matter is 'confidential' [only] if disclosure of the information is likely . . . (1) to impair the Government's ability to obtain necessary information in the future; or (2) to cause substantial harm to the competitive position of the person from whom the information was obtained." *Id.*, at 770. Without much independent analysis, a number of courts of appeals eventually fell in line and adopted variants of the *National Parks* test. . . .

We cannot approve such a casual disregard of the rules of statutory interpretation. . . .

C

That leaves Argus Leader to try to salvage the result, if not the reasoning, of *National Parks*. . . . The company begins by rearranging the text of Exemption 4 to create a phrase that does not appear in the statute: "confidential commercial information." Then, it suggests this synthetic term mirrors a preexisting common law term of art. And finally it asserts that the common law term covers only information whose release would lead to substantial competitive harm. . . .

. . . Argus urges us to adopt a "substantial competitive harm" requirement as a matter of policy because it believes FOIA exemptions should be narrowly construed. But as we have explained in connection with another federal statute, we normally "have no license to give [statutory] exemption[s] anything but a fair reading." *Encino Motorcars, LLC v. Navarro*, 138 S. Ct. 1134, 1142 (2018). Nor do we discern a reason to depart from that rule here: FOIA expressly recognizes that "important interests [are] served by [its] exemptions," *FBI v. Abramson*, 456 U.S. 615, 630-631 (1982), and "[t]hose exemptions are as much a part of [FOIA's] purpose[s and policies] as the [statute's disclosure] requirement," *Encino Motorcars*, 138 S.Ct., at 1142. So, just as we cannot properly expand Exemption 4 beyond what its terms permit, *see, e.g.*, Milner, 562 U.S. at 570-571, 131 S.Ct. 1259, we cannot arbitrarily constrict it either by adding limitations found nowhere in its terms.

Our dissenting colleagues appear to endorse something like this final argument. They seem to agree that the law doesn't demand proof of "substantial" or "competitive" harm, but they think it would be a good idea to require a showing of some harm. Neither side, however, has advocated for such an understanding of the statute's terms. And our colleagues' brief brush with the statutory text doesn't help; they cite exclusively from specialized dictionary definitions lifted from the national security classification context that have no bearing on Exemption 4. Really, our colleagues' submission boils down to a policy argument about the benefits of broad disclosure. But as Justice Breyer has noted, when Congress enacted FOIA it sought a "workable balance" between disclosure and other governmental interests—interests that may include providing private parties with sufficient assurances about the treatment of their proprietary information so they will cooperate in federal programs and supply the government with information vital to its work. *See Milner*, 562 U.S. at 589 (dissenting opinion) (arguing for a broad exemption from FOIA disclosure obligations to honor a "workable balance" between disclosure and privacy).

* * *

At least where commercial or financial information is both customarily and actually treated as private by its owner and provided to the government under an assurance of privacy, the information is "confidential" within the meaning of Exemption 4. Because the store-level SNAP data at issue here is confidential under that construction, the judgment of the court of appeals is reversed and the case is remanded for further proceedings consistent with this opinion.

It is so ordered.

Justice Breyer, with whom Justice Ginsburg and Justice Sotomayor join, concurring in part and dissenting in part.

. . . Exemption 4 says that the Act does "not apply" to "commercial or financial information obtained from a person and . . . confidential." § 552(b)(4). The majority holds that "commercial or financial information" is "confidential" and consequently falls within the scope of this exemption "[a]t least" where it is "[1] both customarily and actually treated as private by its owner and [2] provided to the government under an assurance of privacy." The majority spells out two conditions, but in my view there is a third: Release of such information must also cause genuine harm to the owner's economic or business interests.

. . . Like the majority, I can find nothing in FOIA's language, purposes, or history that imposes so stringent a requirement [as the substantial competitive harm requirement found in *National Parks*]. Accordingly, I would clarify that a private harm need not be "substantial" so long as it is genuine.

On the other hand, I cannot agree with the majority's decision to jump to the opposite conclusion, namely, that Exemption 4 imposes no "harm" requirement whatsoever. After all, the word "confidential" sometimes refers, at least in the national security context, to information the disclosure of which would cause harm. *See, e.g.,* Webster's Third New International Dictionary 476 (1966) (defining "confidential" to mean "characterized by or relating to information considered prejudicial to a country's interests"). . . .

Reading "confidential" in this more restrictive sense is more faithful to FOIA's purpose and how we have interpreted the Act in the past. This Court has made clear that the "mandate of the FOIA" is "broad disclosure of Government records." *CIA v. Sims,* 471 U.S. 159, 166 (1985). . . . To that end, we have continuously held that FOIA's enumerated exemptions "must be narrowly construed." *Department of Air Force v. Rose,* 425 U.S. 352, 361 (1976) (citations omitted).

The majority's reading of Exemption 4 is at odds with these principles. The whole point of FOIA is to give the public access to information it cannot otherwise obtain. So the fact that private actors have "customarily and actually treated" commercial information as secret cannot be enough to justify nondisclosure. After all, where information is already publicly available, people do not submit FOIA requests—they use Google. Nor would a statute designed to take from the government the power to unilaterally decide what information the public can view, put such determinative weight on the government's preference for secrecy. . . .

For the majority, a business holding information as private and submitting it under an assurance of privacy is enough to deprive the public of access. . . .

. . . Exemption 4 can be satisfied where, in addition to the conditions set out by the majority, release of commercial or financial information will cause genuine harm to an owner's economic or business interests. . . . I would remand the case for a determination as to whether, in this instance, release of the information at issue will cause that genuine harm. To that extent, I dissent from the majority's decision.

* * *

The *Argus* Court declined to consider whether "privately held information [can] lose its confidential character for purposes of Exemption 4 if it is communicated to the government without assurances that the government will keep it private[.]" 139 S. Ct. at 2363. The DOJ issued guidance shortly after the Court addressed the issue. It also published the Step-by-Step Guide for Determining if Commercial or Financial Information Obtained from a Person is Confidential Under Exemption 4 of the FOIA, https://www.justice.gov/oip/step-step-guide-determining-if-commercial-or-financial-information-obtained-person-confidential (last visited July 6, 2020).

The guide has three sequential steps, or questions, an agency should ask to establish Exemption 4 confidentiality. Answering "yes" to a question stops the inquiry, and the agency has now determined the information is not confidential. However, if the answer is "no," the agency moves on to the next question. Answering "no" to all three questions means the information is confidential for purposes of Exemption 4. The three questions are:

1. Does the submitter customarily keep the information private or closely held?
2. Did the government provide an express or implied assurance of confidentiality when the information was shared with the government?
3. Were there express or implied indications at the time the information was submitted that the government would publicly disclose the information?

Id.

QUESTION SET 10.2

Review & Synthesis

1. Compare the tests for confidentiality offered by Justice Gorsuch and Justice Breyer. What is the key distinction between the two? In your opinion, which of the two tests is more consistent with FOIA's goals and purposes?

2. Justice Breyer argued that the majority's definition of confidential means that "a business holding information as private and submitting it under an assurance of privacy is enough to deprive the public of access." Do you agree that the majority's approach would give "the government the power to unilaterally decide what information the public can view" and "will deprive the public of information for reasons no better than convenience, skittishness, or bureaucratic inertia"? Why or why not?

---

b. Exemption 5: Deliberative Process Privilege

Exemption 5 protects from disclosure "inter-agency or intra-agency memorandums or letters that would not be available by law to a party other than an agency in litigation with the agency." 5 U.S.C. § 552(b)(5). The three privileges most often associated with Exemption 5 are the deliberative process privilege, sometimes called "executive privilege," attorney-work product privilege, and attorney-client privilege. According to the DOJ FOIA GUIDE, the deliberative process privilege is the one most commonly asserted of the three privileges. It is intended to protect agencies' decision-making processes. To wit,

> three policy purposes consistently have been held to constitute the bases for this privilege: (1) to encourage open, frank discussions on matters of policy between subordinates and superiors; (2) to protect against premature disclosure of proposed policies before they are actually adopted; and (3) to protect against public confusion that might result from disclosure of reasons and rationales that were not in fact ultimately the grounds for an agency's action.

DOJ FOIA Guide, Exemption 5, at 13 (2019).

Congress sought to preserve open and frank agency deliberation, which would be stifled if agencies were "forced to 'operate in a fishbowl.'" *EPA v. Mink*, 410 U.S. 73, 87 (1973). To ensure that agencies were able to operate efficiently, the records of their deliberations were exempt from public disclosure. The privilege protects "documents reflecting advisory opinions, recommendations and deliberations comprising part of a process by which governmental decisions and policies are formulated." *NLRB v. Sears, Roebuck & Co.*, 421 U.S. 132, 150 (1975) (internal quotations and citations omitted). To qualify for this privilege there are two requirements. The requested documents must be "'predecisional' and a part of the 'deliberative process.'" *McKinley v. Board of Governors of Federal Reserve System*, 647 F.3d 331, 339 (D.C. Cir. 2011) (internal quotations and citations omitted).

Determining Exemption 5's scope is an ongoing process meant to establish a workable balance between the privacy needed for effective governance and the transparency needed for government accountability through public access. Arguably, however, the scales have tipped too far in the direction of agency secrecy. FIA's legislative history evidences congressional concerns of general exemption overuse. The Senate Report indicated that "[t]here is a growing and troubling trend towards relying on these discretionary exemptions to withhold large swaths of Government information, even though no harm would result from disclosure." S. Rep. No. 114-4, at 3 (2015).

While there was a broad overuse worry, "Exemption five [was] singled out as a particularly problematic exemption." H.R. Rep. No. 114-391, at 10 (2016). Within Exemption 5, "[t]he deliberative process privilege is the most used privilege and the source of the most concern regarding overuse." *Id.* In fact, it is so regularly used that it has been called the "withhold it because you want to exemption." *Id.* (citation omitted). The criticism is substantiated by the frequency with which agencies utilize the exemption, along with the increases in its use year-over-year. The Senate Report worried that agencies availed themselves of the exemption "more than

79,000 times in 2012—a 41% increase from the previous year." S. Rep. No. 114-4, at 3. Congress expressed unease that Exemption 5's "deliberative process privilege [had] become the legal vehicle by which agencies continue[d] to withhold information about government operations." H.R. Rep. 114-391, at 10. The agencies' actions were the very problem FOIA was implemented to fix—"namely abuse of statutory language that was intended to [provide] public access to information about the operations of the federal government." *Id.* Congress acknowledged that it had "not yet identified language that will ensure that the Executive agencies administering FOIA will strike the appropriate balance between privacy that is absolutely necessary for candid conversations in the development of effective public policy and transparency that is necessary and expected in a government by the people and for the people." *Id.*, at 11. However, it attempted to provide some of the transparency that it deemed "necessary and expected" through placing a sunset provision on Exemption 5. *Id.*, at 11. FIA provides that "the deliberative process privilege shall not apply to records created 25 years or more before the date on which the records were requested." 5 U.S.C. § 552(b)(5). The sunset provision along with the requirement that the agency reasonably foresee harm from disclosure combined to limit the scope of Exemption 5.

The privilege is only applicable to disclosures that would reveal the agency's deliberative process. For a document to be protected under Exemption 5 it, "must be a direct part of the deliberative process in that it makes recommendations or expresses opinions on legal or policy matters. . . . [Predecisional materials] must also be a part of the agency give-and-take of the deliberative process by which the decision itself is made." *Vaughn*, 523 F.2d at 1144.

Facts are generally not considered "deliberative" because they consist of information underlying the process of debate and analysis, rather than that debate and analysis themselves. An agency cannot "withhold[] factual material otherwise available on discovery merely because it was placed in a memorandum with matters of law, policy, or opinion." *Mink*, 410 U.S. at 91, *superseded by statute on other grounds as recognized in Halpern v. FBI*, 181 F.3d 279, 291 (2nd Cir. 1999). Factual material "in a form that is severable without compromising the private remainder of the documents" is not exempt from disclosure under the deliberative process privilege. *Id.* Thus, strictly factual information is not protected under Exemption 5.

According to the Supreme Court, a final agency decision does not necessarily cause a document to lose its predecisional character, and thus it may still be protected from disclosure under Exemption 5. *Federal Open Market Committee v. Merrill*, 443 U.S. 340, 360 (1979) (holding that, because Exemption 5 is intended to protect free flow of advice, issuance of decision does not remove need for protection). Nor does the document lose its protection because the deliberations did not result in a decision. *Sears, Roebuck & Co.*, 421 U.S. at 151 n. 18 ("Agencies are, and properly should be, engaged in a continuing process of examining their policies; this process will generate memoranda containing recommendations which do not ripen into agency decisions; and the lower courts should be wary of interfering with this process.").

"Predecisional" excludes "communications made after the decision and designed to explain it" *Id.*, at 152. Thus, Exemption 5 "can never apply" to final opinions, "which not only invariably explain agency action already taken or an agency decision already made, but also constitute 'final dispositions' of matters by an agency." *Id.*, at 153-54.

QUESTION SET 10.3

Review & Synthesis

1. In response to the concerns about an overbroad application of Exemption 5's deliberative process privilege, the DOJ in *Electronic Privacy Information Center* asserted that the requested records it sought to withhold "assemble[d] relevant facts and disregard[ed] irrelevant facts, reflecting the judgment of Department employees and consultants who prepared the materials to help the Department decide what to report to the White House about evidence-based assessment tools." 320 F. Supp. 3d 110, 120 (D.D.C. 2018).

   When should facts be considered part of the deliberative process and when should they be excluded?

---

c. Exemptions 6 and 7(C): Unwarranted Invasion of Personal Privacy

FOIA primarily protects personal privacy through two exemptions. Exemption 6 applies to "personnel and medical files and similar files the disclosure of which would constitute a clearly unwarranted invasion of personal privacy," 5 U.S.C. § 552(b)(6), while Exemption 7 covers records "compiled for law enforcement purposes" where disclosure "could reasonably be expected to constitute an unwarranted invasion of personal privacy," 5 U.S.C. § 552(b)(7)(C). The word "unwarranted" found in both exemptions requires a balancing between the public interest served and the personal privacy right in question. In the seminal case on the meaning of privacy under FOIA, *DOJ v. Reporters Committee*, the Supreme Court found that "both the common law and the literal understandings of privacy encompass the individual's control of information concerning his or her person." 489 U.S. 749, 763 (1989). In *National Archives and Records Administration v. Favish*, 541 U.S. 157 (2004), the Court revisited the scope of the personal privacy right set forth in *DOJ v. Reporters Committee*.

Exemption 6. In *Favish*, the Court distinguished personal privacy rights protected under Exemption 7(C) from those protected under Exemption 6. It explained that protection under Exemption 6 has a more limited breadth—specifying that the agency may withhold records only if the disclosure "would constitute a clearly unwarranted invasion of personal privacy." The broader personal privacy interest encompassed in Exemption 7(C) is in sharp contrast to the very narrow construction found in Exemption 6.

When an agency uses Exemption 6 to withhold a document, the threshold question is whether the disclosure request includes "personnel and medical files and similar files." Identifying which records are properly classified as "personnel and medical files" has been straightforward. The same cannot be said for "similar files." The Supreme Court defined "similar files" in *U.S. Department of State v. Washington Post Co.*, holding that "similar files" included all information in Government records that "applies to a particular individual." 456 U.S. 595, 602 (1982). It reasoned that Congress had not "meant to limit Exemption 6 to a narrow class of files containing only a discrete kind of personal information." *Id.* (citing H.R. Rep. No. 89-1497, at 11 (1966)). Instead, "similar files" broadly covered "detailed Government records on an individual which can be identified as applying to that individual." *Id.* Thus only information personal in nature, connected to a particular individual, has the potential for being withheld under Exemption 6. Information that is either solely business related, or cannot be linked to a specific person, does not satisfy Exemption 6's threshold inquiry.

If an agency seeking to withhold requested records has satisfied Exemption 6's threshold inquiry, the agency must still show that disclosure "would constitute a clearly unwarranted invasion of personal privacy." Even when the individual's personal privacy rights are implicated, this right must be balanced "against the preservation of the basic purpose of the Freedom of Information Act 'to open agency action to the light of public scrutiny.'" *Rose*, 425 U.S. at 372 (citation omitted). When considering whether an invasion into privacy is unwarranted, "the only relevant 'public interest in disclosure' to be weighed in this balance is the extent to which disclosure would serve the 'core purpose of the FOIA,' which is 'contribut[ing] significantly to public understanding of the operations or activities of the government.'" *U.S. Department of Defense v. Federal Labor Relations Authority*, 510 U.S. 487, 495 (1994) (citing *DOJ v. Reporters Committee*, 489 U.S. at 775. The Supreme Court has made clear that a determination of whether the invasion of personal privacy is warranted "cannot turn on the purposes for which the request for information is made." *Id.* at 496 (quoting *DOJ v. Reporters Committee*, 489 U.S. at 771).

QUESTION SET 10.4

Review & Synthesis

1. What is the public interest protected by Exemption 6 that must be balanced against personal privacy?

2. Agencies frequently hold the information of private citizens. Moreover, there are certainly times when, in a general sense, disclosure of certain information would serve the public interest. However, not all such interests are served by FOIA. Consider the following situation, described by the Supreme Court in *DOJ v. Reporters Committee*:

   > Conceivably Medico's rap sheet would provide details to include in a news story, but, in itself, this is not the kind of public interest for which Congress enacted the FOIA. In other words, although there is undoubtedly some public interest in anyone's criminal history, especially if the history is in some way related to the subject's dealing with a public official or agency, the FOIA's central purpose is to ensure that the Government's activities be opened to the sharp eye of public scrutiny, not that information about private citizens that happens to be in the warehouse of the Government be so disclosed. Thus, it should come as no surprise that in none of our cases construing the FOIA have we found it appropriate to order a Government agency to honor a FOIA request for information about a particular private citizen.

   489 U.S. at 774-75. Did the Court give a fair indication of when the public interest is weighty enough to conclude that disclosure is not "an unwarranted invasion of personal privacy"? What test would you fashion to address this problem?

Application & Analysis

1. A civil rights organization submitted a FOIA request to Immigration and Customs Enforcement ("ICE") within the Department of Homeland Security. The request sought to obtain records with information about the factual basis for ICE stops, interrogations, and initial arrests by ICE agents as part of the agency's Criminal Alien Removal Initiative. The records requested contain identifying information of federal employees and immigration officers. The agency is concerned that if the information is produced, its employees and officers may be targeted for harassment. Assuming that the records sought are agency records properly subject to FOIA, what else must the agency show in order to withhold them under Exemption 6?

Exemption 7(C). Under FOIA Exemption 7, an agency is not required to disclose

> [R]ecords or information compiled for law enforcement purposes, but only to the extent that the production of such law enforcement records or information (A) could reasonably be expected to interfere with enforcement proceedings, (B) would deprive a person of a right to a fair trial or an impartial adjudication, (C) could reasonably be expected to constitute an unwarranted invasion of personal privacy, (D) could reasonably be expected to disclose the identity of a confidential source, including a State, local, or foreign agency or authority or any private institution which furnished information on a confidential basis, and, in the case of a record or information compiled by criminal law enforcement authority in the course of a criminal investigation or by an agency conducting a lawful national security intelligence investigation, information furnished by a confidential source, (E) would disclose techniques and procedures for law enforcement investigations or prosecutions, or would disclose guidelines for law enforcement investigations or prosecutions if such disclosure could reasonably be expected to risk circumvention of the law, or (F) could reasonably be expected to endanger the life or physical safety of any individual. . . .

5 U.S.C. § 552(b)(7).

Exemption 7(C) most directly affects personal privacy. Like all parts of Exemption 7, it only applies to "records or information compiled for law enforcement purposes." To determine whether an agency can properly withhold records under Exemption 7(C), it must show that disclosing the records "could reasonably be expected to constitute an unwarranted invasion of personal privacy." If there is a privacy interest at stake, like in Exemption 6, that privacy interest must be balanced against the public interest in disclosing the records. It is uncontroverted that Exemption 7(C) includes individuals whose privacy interests are directly affected, but is that the full scope of Exemption 7(C)? Does it also protect those whose interests are indirectly implicated by the disclosure of government records? In the two cases that follow, the Court addressed whether under Exemption 7(C) the public interest trumps individual interests.

National Archives and Records Administration v. Favish
541 U.S. 157 (2004)

Justice KENNEDY delivered the opinion of the Court.

This case requires us to interpret the Freedom of Information Act (FOIA), 5 U.S.C. § 552. FOIA does not apply if the requested data fall within one or more exemptions. Exemption 7(C) excuses from disclosure "records or information compiled for law enforcement purposes" if their production "could reasonably be expected to constitute an unwarranted invasion of personal privacy." § 552(b)(7)(C).

. . . Here, the information pertains to an official investigation into the circumstances surrounding an apparent suicide. The initial question is whether the exemption extends to the decedent's family when the family objects to the release of photographs showing the condition of the body at the scene of death. If we find the decedent's family does have a personal privacy interest recognized by the statute, we must then consider whether that privacy claim is outweighed by the public interest in disclosure.

I

Vincent Foster, Jr., deputy counsel to President Clinton, was found dead in Fort Marcy Park, located just outside Washington, D.C. The United States Park Police conducted the initial investigation and took color photographs of the death scene, including 10 pictures of Foster's body. The investigation concluded that Foster committed suicide by shooting himself with a revolver. Subsequent investigations . . . reached the same conclusion. [Petitioner Allan Favish made a FOIA request, which included the] . . . 10 [pictures] depicting various parts of Foster's body. Like the National Park Service, the Office of Independent Counsel (OIC) refused the request under Exemption 7(C).

. . . Favish sued to compel production. . . . [On the second appeal, the Ninth Circuit ordered four photographs released. These are the documents at issue in this case.] We reverse.

II

It is common ground among the parties that the death-scene photographs in OIC's possession are records or information "compiled for law enforcement purposes" as that phrase is used in Exemption 7(C). This leads to the question whether disclosure of the four photographs "could reasonably be expected to constitute an unwarranted invasion of personal privacy."

Favish contends the family has no personal privacy interest covered by Exemption 7(C). His argument rests on the proposition that the information is only about the decedent, not his family. FOIA's right to personal privacy, in his view, means only "the right to control information about oneself." . . .

We disagree. The right to personal privacy is not confined . . . to the "right to control information about oneself." Brief for Respondent Favish 4. . . . To say that the concept of personal privacy must "encompass" the individual's control of information about himself does not mean it cannot encompass other personal privacy interests as well. . . .

. . . Records or information are not to be released under FOIA if disclosure "could reasonably be expected to constitute an unwarranted invasion of personal privacy." 5 U.S.C. § 552(b)(7). This provision is in marked contrast to the language in Exemption 6, pertaining to "personnel and medical files," where withholding is required only if disclosure "would constitute a clearly unwarranted invasion of personal privacy." § 552(b)(6). The adverb "clearly," found in Exemption 6, is not used in Exemption 7(C). In addition, "whereas Exemption 6 refers to disclosures that 'would constitute' an invasion of privacy, Exemption 7(C) encompasses any disclosure that 'could reasonably be expected to constitute' such an invasion." [*DOJ v. Reporters Committee*], 489 U.S., at 756. Exemption 7(C)'s comparative breadth is no mere accident in drafting. We know Congress gave special consideration to the language in Exemption 7(C) because it was the result of specific amendments to an existing statute.

. . . The family does not invoke Exemption 7(C) on behalf of Vincent Foster in its capacity as his next friend for fear that the pictures may reveal private information about Foster to the detriment of his own posthumous reputation or some other interest personal to him. . . . Foster's relatives instead invoke their own right and interest to personal privacy. They seek to be shielded by the exemption to secure their own refuge from a sensation-seeking culture for their own peace of mind. . . .

. . . [W]e think it proper to conclude from Congress' use of the term "personal privacy" that it intended to permit family members to assert their own privacy rights against public intrusions long deemed impermissible under the common law and in our cultural traditions. This does not mean that the family is in the same position as the individual who is the subject of the disclosure. We have little difficulty, however, in finding in our case law and traditions the right of family members to direct and control disposition of the body of the deceased and to limit attempts to exploit pictures of the deceased family member's remains for public purposes.

Burial rites or their counterparts have been respected in almost all civilizations from time immemorial. They are a sign of the respect a society shows for the deceased and for the surviving family members. . . . The outrage at seeing the bodies of American soldiers mutilated and dragged through the streets is but a modern instance of the same understanding of the interests decent people have for those whom they have lost. Family members have a personal stake in honoring and mourning their dead and objecting to unwarranted public exploitation that, by intruding upon their own grief, tends to degrade the rites and respect they seek to accord to the deceased person who was once their own.

In addition this well-established cultural tradition acknowledging a family's control over the body and death images of the deceased has long been recognized at common law. Indeed, this right to privacy has much deeper roots in the common law than the rap sheets held to be protected from disclosure in [*DOJ v.*] *Reporters Committee*.

We can assume Congress legislated against this background of law, scholarship, and history when it enacted FOIA and when it amended Exemption 7(C) to extend its terms. Those enactments were also against the background of the Attorney General's consistent interpretation of the exemption to protect "members of the family of the person to whom the information pertains," U.S. Dept. of Justice, Attorney General's Memorandum on the Public Information Section of the Administrative Procedure Act 36 (June 1967), and to require consideration of the privacy of "relatives or descendants" and the "possible adverse effects [from disclosure] upon [the individual] or his family," U.S. Dept. of Justice Memorandum on the 1974 Amendments to the Freedom of Information Act 9-10 (Feb. 1975).

We have observed that the statutory privacy right protected by Exemption 7(C) goes beyond the common law and the Constitution. . . . It would be anomalous to hold in the instant case that the statute provides even less protection than does the common law.

The statutory scheme must be understood, moreover, in light of the consequences that would follow were we to adopt Favish's position. As a general rule, withholding information under FOIA cannot be predicated on the identity of the requester. . . . [C]hild molesters, rapists, murderers, and other violent criminals often make FOIA requests for autopsies, photographs, and records of their deceased victims. . . . We find it inconceivable that Congress could have intended a definition of "personal privacy" so narrow that it would allow convicted felons to obtain these materials without limitations at the expense of surviving family members' personal privacy.

. . . [W]e hold that FOIA recognizes surviving family members' right to personal privacy with respect to their close relative's death-scene images. . . .

III

. . . [Exemption 7(C)] directs nondisclosure only where the information "could reasonably be expected to constitute an unwarranted invasion" of the family's personal privacy. The term "unwarranted" requires us to balance the family's privacy interest against the public interest in disclosure. . . .

Where the privacy concerns addressed by Exemption 7(C) are present, the exemption requires the person requesting the information to establish a sufficient reason for the disclosure. First, the citizen must show that the public interest sought to be advanced is a significant one, an interest more specific than having the information for its own sake. Second, the citizen must show the information is likely to advance that interest. Otherwise, the invasion of privacy is unwarranted. . . .

. . . Only when the FOIA requester has produced evidence sufficient to satisfy this standard will there exist a counterweight on the FOIA scale for the court to balance against the cognizable privacy interests in the requested records. . . . The judgment of the Court of Appeals is reversed, and the case is remanded with instructions to grant OIC's motion for summary judgment with respect to the four photographs in dispute.

It is so ordered.

* * *

Corporations and Exemption 7(C). A few years after *Favish* clearly recognized the personal privacy rights of the deceased's surviving family under Exemption 7(C), the Court again addressed the issue of whose personal rights are protected under 7(C). In *FCC v. AT&T Inc.*, AT&T argued that as a "private corporate citizen" it was entitled to protection from "unwarranted invasion of personal privacy." 562 U.S. 397, 401 (2011). It argued that when Congress defined "the noun 'person' to include corporations, Congress necessarily defined the adjective form of that noun—'personal'—also to include corporations." *Id.* at 402. Chief Justice Roberts, writing for the Court, disagreed. The Court rejected AT&T's position that the "word 'personal' in Exemption 7(C) incorporates the statutory definition of the word 'person.'" *Id.* In the absence of a statutory definition the Court applied the term's ordinary meaning. *Id.* After providing multiple examples and statutory bases for the distinction between person and personal, the Court held that "[t]he protection in FOIA against disclosure of law enforcement information on the ground that it would constitute an unwarranted invasion of personal privacy does not extend to corporations. We trust that AT&T will not take it personally." *Id.* at 409-10.

QUESTION SET 10.5

Review & Synthesis

1. What, if any, is the difference in the personal privacy interest protected by Exemption 6 and the interest protected by Exemption 7(C)?

2. In what way, if any, are the personal privacy interest and public interests balanced differently under Exemption 6 than under Exemption 7(C)?

Application & Analysis

1. Teddy Kastansis, a self-described freelance reporter whose "interests" include "obtaining information under FOIA," submitted a FOIA request to the United States Marshals Service ("Marshals Service") requesting "copies of the mug shot photos of Gary Grimes." Grimes, the former president of Grimes Securities Corp., pled guilty to securities fraud in 2009. The Marshals Service took booking photographs ("mug shots") of Grimes after taking him into custody. Its policy is that the only law enforcement

purpose for releasing a mug shot is to address an issue involving a fugitive, which Grimes—currently in federal prison—is not. Kastansis insists that disclosing the booking photographs will help the public determine if the Marshals Service gives preferential treatment to high-profile prisoners like Bernie Madoff. The Marshals Service is concerned that releasing the booking photographs of Grimes—which show his appearance and expression while being processed—could result in his humiliation. As such, they believe they should withhold the photographs as exempt from disclosure under FOIA Exemption 7(C). They have asked for your advice.

a. Is Grimes' photograph protected under Exemption 7(C)? Why or why not?

b. Would your advice change if the Marshals Service had published Grimes' driver's license photograph through the International Criminal Police Organization ("INTERPOL") while Grimes was a fugitive from 2003 through May 2009?

c. What would be the effect on Grimes' privacy interest in the booking photographs if Grimes has appeared in open court and pleaded guilty?

---

d. The FOIA Improvement Act of 2016

As discussed earlier in this chapter, the FOIA Improvement Act ("FIA") directly amended FOIA in several ways. One of the most significant amendments was to agencies' burden of showing that requested records and information are protected under a FOIA exemption. Prior to 2016, agencies were presumably able to withhold a record once they determined the requested information fit squarely within the exemption's language. That changed when Congress enacted FIA and added another requirement that agencies now must satisfy in order to withhold information subject to a FOIA request—the "foreseeable harm" standard. FOIA Improvement Act of 2016, Pub. L. No. 114-185, 130 Stat. 538 (2016). The standard "prohibits agencies from withholding information unless (1) the agency reasonably foresees that disclosure of the record would harm an interest protected by an exemption, or (2) the disclosure is prohibited by law. 5 U.S.C. § 552(a)(8)(A)(i)." *Center for Investigative Reporting v. Department of Labor*, 424 F. Supp. 3d 771, 780 (N.D. Cal. 2019).

Unsurprisingly, plaintiffs suing to compel disclosure have argued that showing requested information met the "technical application of an exemption was not sufficient without a showing that disclosure also harmed an interest the exemption sought to protect in the first place." *Judicial Watch, Inc. v. Department of Commerce*, 375 F. Supp. 3d 93, 101 (D.D.C. 2019). After the Court's decision in *Argus Leader*, the plaintiff in *Center for Investigative Reporting* argued that even if the materials it requested had been deemed commercial and confidential, and thus exempt under Exemption 4, the Labor Department could only withhold them by meeting the foreseeable harm standard. 424 F. Supp 3d at 780. The Labor Department argued "that to impose the foreseeable harm standard would render *Argus Leader* meaningless." The court disagreed:

> The substantial competitive harm test set forth in *National Parks & Conservation Association v. Morton*, 498 F.2d 765, 768 (D.C. Cir. 1974), was fashioned from legislative history, rather than statute, which was the grounds for its abrogation. *Argus Leader*, 139 S. Ct. at 2364. Post-FIA, the foreseeable harm standard applies to all exemptions, and is not restricted to Exemption 4. As discussed at the hearing, the FOIA request in *Argus Leader* was filed before FIA was enacted, so the foreseeable harm standard was not applicable. In fact, the Supreme Court did not address the validity of the foreseeable harm standard. Today, FIA codifies the requirement that the agency articulate a foreseeable harm to an interest protected by an exemption that would result from disclosure. Here, the Government does not attempt to make such a showing, and instead relies on *Argus Leader* as the reason why it need not do so.
>
> Accordingly, the Court finds that the Government has failed to carry its burden under the FIA's foreseeable harm standard.

Id.

QUESTION SET 10.6

Review & Synthesis

1. After FIA's enactment, what must an agency show to withhold a record under each of the exemptions we have discussed in detail? Specifically, how does FIA change the burden for protecting records under Exemptions 4, 5, 6, and 7(C)?

2. *Argus Leader* overruled the decades-long test for confidentiality found in *National Parks*. However, in *Argus Leader*, the FOIA request at issue was made before FIA went into effect; thus, the Court did not apply FIA to the dispute. How does FIA affect the *Argus Leader* test for confidentiality? Does FIA render *Argus Leader* moot and reestablish the *National Parks* substantial competitive harm test? Why or why not?

---

3. "Reverse" FOIA

Undoubtedly, FOIA has provided a standardized mechanism by which the public can gain access to agency records. These records sometimes involve parties other than the requester and agency officials. What rights do these third parties have? Agencies must offer "basic procedural protections to all persons or entities who submit 'confidential commercial information' to them." FOIA Update: Executive Order on Business Data Issued, Office of Information Policy, U.S. Dep't of Justice, https://www.justice.gov/oip/blog/foia-update -executive-order-business-data-issued (last updated Aug. 13, 2014). Under Executive Order No. 12,600, when an agency is asked to disclose "records containing confidential commercial information" pursuant to a FOIA request, it must provide notice to those persons or entities who submitted them. Exec. Order No. 12600, 52 Fed. Reg. 23,781 (1987).

What happens when the person/entity who submitted the record to the agency disagrees with the agency's disclosure? As we have discussed, FOIA protects privacy rights under Exemption 6 and Exemption 7(C), as well as under Exemption 4's protection for trade secrets and confidential commercial information, but is there any other recourse for an entity to prevent agency disclosure of information subject to a proper FOIA request? In short, the answer is "yes."

When an entity institutes an action to prevent an agency from disclosing information in response to a FOIA request, it has come to be known as a "reverse-FOIA" action. In a reverse FOIA action, the party who submitted the information can challenge an agency's decision to disclose pursuant to a FOIA request if the party believes that its release will cause harm. The party seeking to prevent agency disclosure of information bears the burden of proof. In *Chrysler Corporation v. Brown*, excerpted below, the Supreme Court held that the APA provided a cause of action to enjoin an agency from disclosing information otherwise subject to FOIA.

Chrysler Corporation v. Brown
441 U.S. 281 (1979)

Mr. Justice REHNQUIST delivered the opinion of the Court.

The expanding range of federal regulatory activity and growth in the Government sector of the economy have increased federal agencies' demands for information about the activities of private individuals and corporations. These developments have paralleled a related concern about secrecy in Government and abuse of power. The Freedom of Information Act (hereinafter FOIA) was a response to this concern, but it has also had a largely unforeseen tendency to exacerbate the uneasiness of those who comply with governmental demands for information. For under the FOIA third parties have been able to obtain Government files containing information submitted by corporations and individuals who thought that the information would be held in confidence. . . .

I

[In Section I of its opinion, the Court explained that Executive Orders 11246 and 11375 require government contractors like Chrysler to "provide equal employment opportunity regardless of race or sex." Further, the Department of Labor's Office of Federal Contract Compliance Programs ("OFCCP") requires government contractors to submit reports about their compliance with the executive orders, including information about their workforce composition and affirmative-action programs. The Defense Logistics Agency ("DLA") within the Department of Defense is the designated compliance agency responsible for monitoring contractors' compliance practices, including Chrysler's.

On May 14, 1975, the DLA informed Chrysler that third parties had made a FOIA request for disclosure of records relating to the company's affirmative action plans and compliance. Chrysler objected to the records' release, relying on OFCCP's disclosure regulations and on certain FOIA exemptions. DLA determined that the requested materials were subject to FOIA disclosure and the OFCCP disclosure rules, and would therefore be released five days later.]

II

In contending that the FOIA bars disclosure of the requested equal employment opportunity information, Chrysler relies on the Act's nine exemptions and argues that they require an agency to withhold exempted material. . . .

Chrysler contends that the nine exemptions in general, and Exemption 4 in particular, reflect a sensitivity to the privacy interests of private individuals and nongovernmental entities. That contention may be conceded without inexorably requiring the conclusion that the exemptions impose affirmative duties on an agency to withhold information sought. In fact, that conclusion is not supported by the language, logic, or history of the Act. . . .

That the FOIA is exclusively a disclosure statute is, perhaps, demonstrated most convincingly by examining its provision for judicial relief. Subsection (a)(4)(B) gives federal district courts "jurisdiction to enjoin the agency from withholding agency records and to order the production of any agency records improperly withheld from the complainant." 5 U.S.C. § 552(a)(4)(B). That provision does not give the authority to bar disclosure, and thus fortifies our belief that Chrysler, and courts which have shared its view, have incorrectly interpreted the exemption provisions of the FOIA. The Act is an attempt to meet the demand for open government while preserving workable confidentiality in governmental decisionmaking. Congress appreciated that, with the expanding sphere of governmental regulation and enterprise, much of the information within Government files has been submitted by private entities seeking Government contracts or responding to unconditional reporting obligations imposed by law. . . .

Enlarged access to governmental information undoubtedly cuts against the privacy concerns of nongovernmental entities, and as a matter of policy some balancing and accommodation may well be desirable. . . .

We therefore conclude that Congress did not limit an agency's discretion to disclose information when it enacted the FOIA. It necessarily follows that the Act does not afford Chrysler any right to enjoin agency disclosure.

[In Section III of its opinion, the Court rejected Chrysler's contention that even if its suit for injunctive relief cannot be based on FOIA, it can be based on the Trade Secrets Act, 18 U.S.C. § 1905.]

IV

While Chrysler may not avail itself of any violations of the provisions of § 1905 in a separate cause of action, any such violations may have a dispositive effect on the outcome of judicial review of agency action pursuant to § 10 of the APA. Section 10(a) of the APA provides that "[a] person suffering legal wrong because of agency action, or adversely affected or aggrieved by agency action. . . , is entitled to judicial review thereof." 5 U.S.C. § 702. Two exceptions to this general rule of reviewability are set out in § 10. Review is not available where "statutes preclude judicial review" or where "agency action is committed to agency discretion by law." 5 U.S.C. §§ 701(a)(1), (2). In *Citizens to Preserve Overton Park, Inc. v. Volpe*, 401 U.S. 402, 410 (1971), the Court held that the latter exception applies "where 'statutes are drawn in such broad terms that in a given case there is no law to apply,'" quoting S. Rep. No. 752, 79th Cong., 1st Sess., 26 (1945). [W]e conclude that DLA's decision to disclose the Chrysler reports is reviewable agency action and Chrysler is a person "adversely affected or aggrieved" within the meaning of § 10(a). . . .

Vacated and remanded.

[Justice MARSHALL's concurring opinion is omitted.]

QUESTION SET 10.7

Review & Synthesis

1. What is the plaintiff's burden of proof in a reverse FOIA case?

2. What effect, if any, does FIA have on the plaintiff's burden in a reverse FOIA suit?

Application & Analysis

1. Under the Animal Welfare Act, dog breeders must annually obtain a license from the USDA. 7 U.S.C. § 2134. Breeders must file renewal applications and annual reports, Form 7003s, with the USDA's Animal and Plant Health Inspection Service ("the Service"). 9 C.F.R. § 2.5(b)(2009). Block 8 of the report includes the total number of dogs bought and sold in the previous year and the breeder's gross revenue earned from such activity. In August 2017, the Humane Society submitted a FOIA request for specified copies of Form 7003s submissions. The Service, deciding that Block 8 fell under FOIA Exemptions 4 and 6, redacted it from all of the forms it disclosed to the Humane Society. The Humane Society filed suit, seeking full disclosure.
   a. Is Block 8 exempt from disclosure under Exemption 4?
   b. Consider the public interest in disclosure and the submitters' personal privacy interest. Is Block 8 exempt from disclosure under Exemption 6?
   c. How does the FIA foreseeable harm standard affect your conclusion?
   d. What about the purpose to which the Humane Society will put the requested information?

2. While the Humane Society's suit was pending, the USDA sought information from breeders about Block 8 information. After receiving and reviewing the breeders' responses, the USDA concluded no FOIA exemption applied to requested Forms 7003s and determined the information should be disclosed, including Block 8. The Humane Society dropped the lawsuit. Per Executive Order No. 12,600, the USDA notified the licensed breeders of its decision. They immediately sued to prevent disclosure of the Block 8 information. What do the licensed breeders need to show in order for the court to enjoin Block 8 disclosure? What must the USDA demonstrate to disclose the Block 8 information?

B. THE GOVERNMENT IN THE SUNSHINE ACT

The push for increased government transparency started by Representative Moss in the 1950s only increased in intensity after Watergate. The Government in the Sunshine Act of 1976 provides that "every portion of every meeting of an agency shall be open to public observation" unless the meetings fall within one of the ten exemptions. 5 U.S.C. § 552b(b). No clearer statement of the Act's purpose can be found than the one contained in its Declaration of Policy, which states:

> It is hereby declared to be the policy of the United States that the public is entitled to the fullest practicable information regarding the decisionmaking processes of the Federal Government. It is the purpose of this Act to provide the public with such information while protecting the rights of individuals and the ability of the Government to carry out its responsibilities.

Government in the Sunshine Act, Pub. L. No. 94-409, 90 Stat 1241 (1976).

The exemptions closely mirror FOIA's exemptions, except the Act does not have a deliberative process exemption akin to FOIA Exemption 5. Like FOIA, the exemptions are narrowly interpreted. In addition, exempted portions of a meeting are considered separable from nonexempted portions, allowing the public to attend the nonexempted portion of a meeting.

Today, every state has an "open meetings" law that applies to local government, and many have laws that cover state agencies. For a guide to each state's open meetings laws see *Open Government Guide*, REPORTERS COMMITTEE FOR FREEDOM OF THE PRESS, https://www.rcfp.org/open -government-guide (last visited Nov. 3, 2020).

Under the Act, "the agency shall make public announcement, at least one week before the meeting, of the time, place, and subject matter of the meeting, whether it is to be open or closed to the public, and the name and phone number of the official designated by the agency to respond to requests for information about the meeting." 5 U.S.C. § 552b(e)(1). The public has a right to "attend and observe" but does not have a right to participate unless the meeting is a public hearing. James T. O'Reilly, *Rights Created by the Sunshine Act*, 3 FED. INFO. DISCL. § 23:4 (2020).

The Act defines "agency" more narrowly than FOIA does. In contrast to FOIA, agencies subject to the Sunshine Act are those "headed by a collegial body composed of two or more individual members, a majority of whom are appointed to such position by the President with the advice and consent of the Senate, and any subdivision thereof. . . ." 5 U.S.C. § 552b(a)(1). Further, meetings under the Sunshine Act are defined as "the deliberations of at least the number of individual agency members required to take action on behalf of the agency where such deliberations determine or result in the joint conduct or disposition of official agency business. . . ." 5 U.S.C. § 552b(a)(2).

From the time it was enacted, courts applying the Sunshine Act have grappled with ensuring the benefits of public access to agency decision-making and government transparency while protecting agency efficacy and free exchange of ideas. Courts have accordingly defined the Act's terms and narrowly construed its exemptions to strike the appropriate balance. The definition of "meeting" for purposes of the Act is one place where the Supreme Court has had to navigate the issue. Were it to define "meetings" too broadly, it would chill agency discussions. By contrast, were it to define the term too narrowly, agency officials might circumvent the "meeting" requirement by deliberating and making decisions in settings that fall outside of the Act's purview.

In *FCC v. ITT World Communications, Inc.*, excerpted below, the Court addressed what constitutes "meetings" subject to the Sunshine Act.

Federal Communications Commission v. ITT World Communications, Inc.
466 U.S. 463 (1984)

Justice POWELL delivered the opinion of the Court.

The Government in the Sunshine Act, 5 U.S.C. § 552b, mandates that federal agencies hold their meetings in public. This case requires us to consider whether the Act applies to informal international conferences attended by members of the Federal Communications Commission. . . .

I

Members of petitioner Federal Communications Commission (FCC) participate with their European and Canadian counterparts in what is referred to as the Consultative Process. This is a series of conferences intended to facilitate joint planning of telecommunications facilities through an exchange of information on regulatory policies. At the time of the conferences at issue in the present case, only three American corporations—respondents ITT World Communications, Inc. (ITT), and RCA Global Communications, Inc., and Western Union International—provided overseas record telecommunications services. Although the FCC had approved entry into the market by other competitors, European regulators had been reluctant to do so. The FCC therefore added the topic of new carriers and services to the agenda of the Consultative Process, in the hope that exchange of information might persuade the European nations to cooperate with the FCC's policy of encouraging competition in the provision of telecommunications services.

Respondents, opposing the entry of new competitors, initiated this litigation. First, respondents filed a rulemaking petition with the FCC concerning the Consultative Process meetings. . . . [T]he petition contended that the Sunshine Act required the Consultative Process sessions, as "meetings" of the FCC, to be held in public. . . . *See* 5 U.S.C. § 552b(b). . . .

. . . [T]he Court of Appeals held that the FCC had erred in concluding that the Sunshine Act did not apply to the Consultative Process sessions. We granted certiorari, to decide whether . . . the Sunshine Act applies to sessions of the Consultative Process. We reverse.

[In Section II of its opinion, the Court concluded that the district court lacked jurisdiction over respondents' claim that the FCC's actions were *ultra vires*. Exclusive jurisdiction to review the FCC's final orders, including denial of the respondents' rulemaking petition, rests with the Courts of Appeals.]

III

The Sunshine Act, 5 U.S.C. § 552b(b), requires that "meetings of an agency" be open to the public. Section 552b(a)(2) defines "meetings" as "the deliberations of at least the number of individual agency members required to take action on behalf of the agency where such deliberations determine or result in the joint conduct or disposition of official agency business." Under these provisions, the Sunshine Act does not require that Consultative Process sessions be held in public, as the participation by FCC members in these sessions constitutes neither a "meeting" as defined by § 522b(a)(2) nor a meeting "of the agency" as provided by § 552b(b).

A

Congress in drafting the Act's definition of "meeting" recognized that the administrative process cannot be conducted entirely in the public eye. "[I]nformal background discussions [that] clarify issues and expose varying views" are a necessary part of an agency's work. *See* S. Rep. No. 94-354, p. 19 (1975). The Act's procedural requirements effectively would prevent such discussions and thereby impair normal agency operations without achieving significant public benefit. Section 552b(a)(2) therefore limits the Act's application to meetings "where at least a quorum of the agency's members . . . conduct or dispose of official agency business." S. Rep. No. 94-354, at 2.

Three Commissioners, the number who attended the Consultative Process sessions, did not constitute a quorum of the seven-member Commission. The three members were, however, a quorum of the Telecommunications Committee. That Committee is a "subdivision . . . authorized to act on behalf of the agency." . . . The Sunshine Act applies to such a subdivision as well as to an entire agency. § 552b(a)(1).

It does not appear, however, that the Telecommunications Committee engaged at these sessions in "deliberations [that] determine or result in the joint conduct or disposition of official agency business." This statutory language contemplates discussions that "effectively predetermine official actions." *See* S. Rep. No. 94-354, at 19; accord, *id.*, at 18. Such discussions must be "sufficiently focused on discrete proposals or issues as to cause or be likely to cause the individual participating members to form reasonably firm positions regarding matters pending or likely to arise before the agency." R. Berg & S. Klitzman, An Interpretive Guide to the Government in the Sunshine Act 9 (1978) (hereinafter Interpretive Guide). On the cross-motions for summary judgment, however, respondents alleged neither that the Committee formally acted upon applications for certification at the Consultative Process sessions nor that those sessions resulted in firm positions on particular matters pending or likely to arise before the Committee. Rather, the sessions provided general background information to the Commissioners and permitted them to engage with their foreign counterparts in an exchange of views by which decisions already reached by the Commission could be implemented. As we have noted, Congress did not intend the Sunshine Act to encompass such discussions.

The Court of Appeals . . . inferred from the members' attendance at the sessions an undisclosed authority, not formally delegated, to engage in discussions on behalf of the Commission. The court then concluded that these discussions were deliberations that resulted in the conduct of official agency business, as the discussions "play[ed] an integral role in the Commission's policymaking process."

We view the Act differently. It applies only where a subdivision of the agency deliberates upon matters that are within that subdivision's formally delegated authority to take official action for the agency. Under the reasoning of the Court of Appeals, any group of members who exchange views or gathered information on agency business apparently could be viewed as a "subdivision . . . authorized to act on behalf of the agency." The term "subdivision" itself indicates agency members who have been authorized to exercise formally delegated authority. Moreover, the more expansive view of the term "subdivision" adopted by the Court of Appeals would require public attendance at a host of informal conversations of the type Congress understood to be necessary for the effective conduct of agency business. In any event, it is clear that the Sunshine Act does not extend to deliberations of a quorum of the subdivision upon matters not within the subdivision's formally delegated authority. Such deliberations lawfully could not "determine or result in the joint conduct or disposition of official agency business" within the meaning of the Act. As the Telecommunications Committee at the Consultative Process sessions did not consider or act upon applications for common carrier certification—its only formally delegated authority—we conclude that the sessions were not "meetings" within the meaning of the Sunshine Act.

B

The Consultative Process was not convened by the FCC, and its procedures were not subject to the FCC's unilateral control. The sessions of the Consultative Process therefore are not meetings "of an agency" within the meaning of § 552b(b). The Act prescribes procedures for the agency to follow when it holds meetings and particularly when it chooses to close a meeting. These provisions presuppose that the Act applies only to meetings that the agency has the power to conduct according to these procedures. And application of the Act to meetings not under agency control would restrict the types of meetings that agency members could attend. . . .

IV

For these reasons, we reverse the judgment of the Court of Appeals and remand the case for further proceedings consistent with this opinion.

It is so ordered.

QUESTION SET 10.8

Review & Synthesis

1. Consider the Sunshine Act's statutory definition of "meeting." If an agency wanted to avoid a session being a meeting under the Act, what can it do?

2. On what grounds did the Court decide that the sessions between the FCC subdivision members and their foreign counterparts were not meetings for purposes of the Sunshine Act?

3. Why did the Court hold that "[the Act] applies only where a subdivision of the agency deliberates upon matters that are within that subdivision's formally delegated authority to take official action for the agency"? According to the Court, what is the cost of the Court of Appeals application of the Act? What, if any, are the harmful consequences that may result from the Supreme Court's application of it? With which do you agree?

4. Some state courts have held that the definition of "meeting" for their states' sunshine laws includes both discussions and deliberations. Generally, the former is considered less formal than the latter. Does the fact that the federal Sunshine Act excludes "discussions" free agencies from disclosing their contents? If so, should the Act be amended to include both discussions and deliberations?

CHAPTER 11

Internal Agency Controls

As indicated in Chapter 1, there are four essential pillars of administrative supervision: political, judicial, public, and managerial. This chapter focuses on the last of these, the intra-agency controls on bureaucratic decision-making. As James Madison observed in *The Federalist No.* 51, "[i]n framing a government which is to be administered by men over men, the great difficulty lies in this: you must first enable the government to control the governed; and in the next place oblige it to control itself." The materials that follow accordingly focus on the administrative state's development from the patronage-based hiring and promotion system of the late nineteenth century to the (aspirational) merit-based system established in the early twentieth century that is (somewhat) in operation today. But see *Lucia v. Securities Exchange Commission* and Executive Order 13,843, discussed in Chapter 6. As you read, consider the conception of decision-making quality and accountability adopted by these managerial systems. Which do you believe is the most effective?

A. A BRIEF HISTORY OF THE U.S. CIVIL SERVICE AND ITS REFORM

The federal civil service is the overarching name given to the approximately 2.7 million civilian employees who work in the federal government's departments and agencies. *See* Cong. Rsch. Serv., R43590, Federal Workforce Statistics Sources: OPM and OMB 6 (2019). The Office of Personnel Management ("OPM") and the Merit Systems Protection Board ("MSPB") oversee that civilian workforce. Both OPM and the MSPB came into existence after the enactment of the Civil Service Reform Act of 1978 ("CSRA") and are designed to ensure that the modern civil service functions efficiently and maintains a commitment to merit-based hiring, firing, and promotions. Both civil service agencies have been key players in civil service reform, oversight, and agency control since their establishment. But at the time they came into existence, they were just the next step in what had already been a long history of civil service oversight and reform within the United States.

1. The Emergence of the Spoils System

The history of the federal civil service is one of conflict between a "spoils system" and a "merit system" for filling and overseeing government positions. The spoils system was based on patronage and allowed elected officials to fill government jobs based on who they knew or who had been politically loyal to them. The merit system uses objective testing and other forms of neutral evaluation to, in theory, ensure the best-qualified candidates fill each position.

Scholars have traced the history of the spoils system in the United States back as early as 1777, finding evidence from New York State that newly elected politicians would regularly throw members of the opposing party out of their positions upon taking office and replace them with their own loyal supporters. The system was also a central cause of the controversy behind *Marbury v. Madison*, when then-President John Adams made a number of "midnight appointments" before leaving office in an effort to cement Federalist influence in the federal government. Thomas Jefferson not only resisted those appointments but made a point of removing as many Federalists from government positions as he could to ensure his own Democratic-Republicans were in control. These early events established a foundation for spoils-driven hiring and appointments within the civil service from the country's beginnings. *See* UNITED STATES CIVIL SERVICE COMMISSION, HISTORY OF THE FEDERAL CIVIL SERVICE, 1780 TO PRESENT 3-5 (1941).

While the system was present during the first few Presidential administrations, its entrenchment began in earnest during President Andrew Jackson's Administration. Many of Jackson's advisers used their influence in government to build private political machines with public offices based on patronage. It was during this time that the country first saw many individuals seeking government jobs not for political gain but for the chance to profit from their political power. Jackson was also instrumental in backing a rotation system under which government operations were expected to improve with regular changeover of government personnel. *Id.* at 17. That line of thinking led to the enactment of the Tenure of Office Act of 1820 that set fixed terms for officeholders and proscribed removal in certain circumstances.

As the public grew accustomed to the spoils system and large-scale personnel changeovers between Presidential administrations, it became customary prior to the Civil War for waves of jobseekers to crash on the capital's shores at the start of new administrations in the hopes of lobbying or bribing their way into new positions. By the time Franklin Pierce took office in 1853, it had become standard for regular governmental activities in Washington to stop for a month so members of the incoming administration could devote all their time to sorting through the large number of jobseekers jockeying for federal work. *Id.* at 29. Congressmen during this period also recognized the ease with which they could curry political favor under the spoils system and were largely in support of continuing the system.

Despite support for the spoils system in the Executive and Legislative Branches in antebellum America, it produced a number of troubling side effects. The large-scale changeover in officeholders from the time of Jefferson until the Civil War made continuity of administrative programs difficult, and the government suffered from inefficiencies and a lack of integrity, prestige, and morale as a result. The spoils system's spread to the military also proved a hindrance during the Mexican-American War, and eventually the Civil War, as military leaders and government officials dealt with subordinates who had come into their positions because of who they knew rather than what they could do. *Id.* at 25.

Despite these problems, the spoils system continued to enjoy general support during the successive administrations of Presidents Buchanan, Lincoln, and Johnson. The practice during the Buchanan Administration extended to removing officials from the prior administration regardless of party affiliation, and Lincoln, whether directly or indirectly, oversaw a period between 1861 and 1865 when practically every Presidential office in the federal government changed hands at least once and sometimes much more frequently. *Id.* at 33. Lincoln did, however, rebuff certain spoils advocates' efforts to rotate officials out after he won a second term, marking an early strike against the rotation theory of filling government positions.

Lincoln's assassination and Andrew Johnson's assumption of the presidency at a time when a large swath of Congress distrusted him led to some debates within the federal government about the existing civil service system, particularly about the executive removal power. At the end of Lincoln's tenure and during the first few years of Johnson's, Congress had systematically passed legislation that required more Senate approval of Presidential decisions to remove executive officials. It began with consent for removals from various civilian and military offices. Then, the Tenure of Office Act of 1867 required that the Senate provide its consent before the President could remove a member of the Cabinet. President Andrew Johnson, believing the Act unconstitutional, disregarded it and removed Secretary of War Edwin Stanton, a holdover from the Lincoln Administration. The House subsequently impeached Johnson, and he survived removal by a single vote in the Senate. *See* Chapter 8, *supra*, at 608-09.

2. The Beginnings of a Merit-Based System

The first serious discussions of a departure from the spoils system came when Ulysses S. Grant, promising to introduce civil service reform, succeeded Johnson as President. Grant's Interior Secretary, followed by his Treasury Secretary, introduced merit-based systems for filling positions within their respective departments and departed from the patronage-focused spoils method. HISTORY OF THE FEDERAL CIVIL SERVICE, *supra*, at 39-40. Grant also asked Congress for a law that would have allowed him to direct civil service reforms more broadly. After several failed attempts at legislation, Congress gave Grant his wish with a rider to the 1871 appropriations bill that allowed the President "to prescribe such regulations for the admission of persons into the civil service of the United States as may best promote the efficiency thereof. . . ." *Id.* at 401-41.

Grant quickly took action and established a seven-member board first known as the Advisory Board of the Civil Service and later called the Civil Service Commission. The Board studied the existing state of civil service in 1871 and wrote up a report that included a proposed set of civil-service rules to transition parts of the civil service to a merit-based system. Grant adopted the rules in early 1872, and by April of that year competitive examinations were held for certain governmental positions in Washington and New York City. *Id.* at 42. Administrative officials, the press, and the public all praised Grant's Civil Service Commission for its work and progress, but Congress stopped allocating funds to the Commission in 1874. By 1875, Grant was forced to abandon his administration's previous efforts toward normalizing a merit system. The Commission continued in name but not function until Congress took a more concrete approach to civil service reform in the Pendleton Civil Service Act of 1883.

The period between Grant's first civil service reform efforts and the Pendleton Act was largely filled with Presidents who incrementally advanced the idea. President Rutherford B. Hayes, relying on advice from a commission he had tasked with investigating spoils-ridden hiring in New York City, made merit-based changes to some government offices and saw positive results in the form of increased fairness and efficiency. The merit system also benefited, albeit tragically, when Charles Guiteau, an unsuccessful patronage office seeker, assassinated President James Garfield in 1881. The assassination added to the public's growing aversion to the spoils system and indicated a change was on the horizon. Federal officials had also been losing interest during this period because the huge growth in government meant they could no longer oversee the filling of all the positions. Instead, federal officials largely had to delegate that power, and the political benefits that came with it, to state officials. *See* Jerry L. Mashaw, *Federal Administration and Administrative Law in the Gilded Age*, 119 YALE L.J. 1362, 1389-90 (2010).

The growing tide against a spoils-centered civil service played a role in the 1882 elections and led newly elected President Chester A. Arthur and Congress to focus on civil service reform until they enacted the Pendleton Act. The Act used Grant's previous reforms as a model to create a bipartisan Civil Service Commission led by three commissioners. The Act required that competitive examinations be held to fill certain civil service positions. It also protected classified service employees (those covered by the Act) from having to provide political contributions to maintain their jobs, and prohibited federal officials from soliciting political contributions from those employees. Altogether, the Act brought 10.5 percent or 13,900 members of the executive civil service into the "classified," merit-based system. Steven G. Calabresi & Christopher S. Yoo, *The Unitary Executive During the Second Half-Century*, 26 HARV. J.L. & PUB. POL'Y 667, 787-90 (2003). It also gave subsequent Presidents the power to expand the number of civil service jobs that were covered under the Act. *Id.*

President Arthur and his successors made ample use of that power. A common trend among them was to extend the Act to cover swathes of civil service jobs after they had lost re-election or were faced with a pending term limit. The newly classified positions were out of reach for the new administration to fill through the politically motivated spoils system and represented a way for the outgoing administration to maintain some federal government influence. President Arthur increased the classified service by 1,200 additional positions as his term was ending, and President Grover Cleveland subsequently increased the number of covered positions by 5,320 at the end of his first term in 1888 and by 32,000 during his second term. HISTORY OF THE FEDERAL CIVIL SERVICE, *supra*, at at 66, 71. Cleveland also oversaw major Civil Service Commission improvements, addressing the type and scope of written tests for positions and instituting ratings systems for appointee experience, that brought much needed uniformity to the civil service.

3. Civil Service Reform from Roosevelt to Roosevelt

The next major steps in civil service reform would come under President Theodore Roosevelt, who had served on the Civil Service Commission for six years prior to assuming the Presidency. Roosevelt had been an active member of the Commission, conducting investigations and focusing public attention on spoils system abuses. He brought similar energy to civil service reform while President. The federal government continued to expand over time, and with it came a larger number of civil service jobs. President Roosevelt ensured that many new and established positions would be filled through a merit system, including those of certain postmasters, Census Bureau employees, and War Department employees. In all, he increased the percentage of executive civil service jobs in the merit system from 41.5 percent to 63.9 percent of the civil service. *Id.* at 75.

Roosevelt also focused on stricter compliance with early prohibitions on political activity and on setting more concrete parameters for removing civil service employees, including creating a definition of "just cause" for removal. *See id.* at 81. These early efforts were later cemented in legislation enacted after Roosevelt's Administration. The Hatch Act of 1939 eventually prohibited almost all federal employees, either classified or unclassified, from engaging in certain political activities. The Lloyd-LaFollette Act of 1912 protected classified federal employees from removal, except when done to promote the efficiency of the civil service, and allowed for a proliferation of union activity. These later legislative protections were key to giving the Commission a role in reviewing and adjudicating whether employee removals had been unjust.

The United States' entrance into World War I in 1917 tested the civil service reforms of the still-young twentieth century. The number of government positions ballooned as the country moved to a war footing and the increasingly merit-based system had to both fill and oversee those positions quickly and efficiently. The civil service performed well during the war years and validated the changes the government had been making. It increased to nearly a million people by November 1918, and the number of positions subject to competitive examination rose to 82 percent in less than a year. *See id.* at 95.

The years between the end of World War I and the New Deal reforms fueled by the Great Depression saw more growth and refinement in the federal civil service. The Harding Administration saw the enactment of the Classification Act of 1923, which for the first time classified federal positions according to their responsibilities and set uniform salaries accordingly. There were also introductions of systematic retirement provisions for civil service employees, veteran preferences in government positions, and continued Presidential efforts to add civil service positions to the classified, merit-based system.

The arrival of the New Deal and its many new federal agencies once again caused the civil service to grow quickly. Congress originally conceived of the new agencies as temporary and thus created numerous agency positions outside of the classified system. *See id.* at 122. But that temporary designation changed with one act and two Roosevelt Era executive orders. The Ramspeck-O'Mahoney Post Master Act of 1938 authorized the President to extend coverage under the Pendleton Act to more than 182,000 permanent positions, including many of the jobs within the New Deal agencies. *See id.* at 137. Roosevelt used two executive orders to extend the classified federal civil service to all non-policymaking or statutorily excepted positions and, for the first time since Theodore Roosevelt's Administration, to authorize a complete revision of the civil service rules after the passage of the Ramspeck-O'Mahoney Act. *See id.* at 128, 136.

The years following FDR's Administration saw passage of a number of important civil service laws, including laws on classifying positions and their salaries, rating employees' performances, providing life insurance and other retirement benefits, ensuring proper training, and maintaining fair and proper salaries. But as the federal government oversaw and reformed the civil service, larger problems presented themselves. Among the most troublesome was the Civil Service Commission; the size and complexity of the administrative state had largely outgrown it.

Starting with a presidentially commissioned study in 1939 and continuing in studies from 1955 and 1960, recommendations were made for reforming the CSC. In addition to the problems related to its expanding adjudicative, enforcement, and policymaking responsibilities, there was a growing public distrust of federal government activities after the Watergate scandal. Reformers were thus on alert for ways to better protect against improper political influence within the federal government.

4. The Civil Service Reform Act of 1978

The rising support for a change to the oversight and management of the federal civil service led President Jimmy Carter to release Reorganization Plan No. 2 of 1978. The reorganization plan laid out the changes that were eventually codified in the Civil Service Reform Act ("CSRA"), Pub. L. No. 95-454, 92 Stat. 1111 (1978), and created a merit-based civil service system. The Act laid out nine principles to guide civil service administration, including fair and equal treatment of employees and applicants, equal pay for equal work, emphasis on efficiency and integrity, and whistleblower protections. It also laid out 12 specifically prohibited personnel practices, including unlawful discrimination based on race, sex, age, and political affiliation, as well as preferential treatment, politically motivated hiring, and nepotism. The CSRA abolished the Civil Service Commission and divided its former responsibilities between new independent agencies, including the OPM and the MSPB.

The Act designed OPM to serve as the civil service's human resources department and take over the bulk of the responsibility from the CSC for administering civil service regulations. OPM is headed by a single director who is appointed by the President with Senate consent; no more than five associate directors can be appointed by the director. The OPM director is also responsible for helping Presidents prepare changes to civil service rules to help the system function more efficiently and ensure that agencies are properly adhering to the merit system.

The MSPB took over the CSC's hearing, adjudication, and appeals functions, and the three CSC commissioners were redesignated as members of the MSPB. The three board members are appointed by the President with Senate consent to seven-year terms and can only be removed by the President for inefficiency, neglect of duty, or malfeasance in office.

The Board has the power to hear and adjudicate certain civil service matters, order federal agencies and employees to comply with its decisions, and promulgate rules to further its statutory purpose. It hears the more serious adverse federal employment claims like those on removal, a suspension of more than 14 days, a reduction in grade or pay, and a furlough of 30 days or less. *See* 5 U.S.C. § 7512; *Kloeckner v. Solis*, 568 U.S. 41, 44 (2012). It also has the power to issue subpoenas requiring attendance and testimony as well as to order depositions and responses to interrogatories. Further, if a matter before the Board concerns an interpretation or application of an OPM rule, regulation, or policy directive, the OPM director is allowed to intervene and the Board is allowed to request an advisory opinion from the director.

Much of the MSPB work is done by designated administrative law judges sitting in regional offices and empowered to hear cases within the Board's jurisdiction. If an employee or agency is dissatisfied with an ALJ's decision, the matter can be appealed to the full Board. If the employee or agency is still dissatisfied after a hearing before the Board, the matter can then be appealed to the U.S. Court of Appeals for the Federal Circuit.

The Act also created a special counsel ("Counsel") position within the MSPB, again subject to Presidential appointment with Senate consent. The Counsel is charged with investigating all potential civil service abuses, like improper personnel practices, by employees or agencies and deciding whether to pursue charges. If the special counsel determines that there is evidence of improper practices or other violations of law or regulations, the Counsel informs the MSPB, the agency involved, OPM and, depending on the circumstances, the President. If the special counsel uncovers actionable employee conduct, he or she prepares charges against the employee and presents them to the MSPB. If the employee is Presidentially appointed, the Counsel presents evidence supporting any disciplinary charges to the President.

5. The CSRA in Practice

Administrations in the years following passage of the CSRA took different approaches to civil service. President Reagan, using his powers under the Act, moved to make the administrative state more responsive to his policies, shrank the federal workforce, and reduced federal employment benefits. *See* Peter W. Schroth, *Section IV: Constitutional and Administrative Law: Corruption and Accountability of the Civil Service in the United States*, 54 Am. J. Comp. L. 553, 565 (2006). President Clinton took more of an efficiency-based approach to civil service reform, organizing a task force led by Vice President Al Gore to provide recommendations for managing the quality and efficiency of federal work within the civil service. *Id.* The Administration ultimately oversaw a period of drastic reduction in the federal civilian workforce and increased outsourcing of government work to private firms. *Id.*.

President George W. Bush's tenure included the consolidation of 22 agencies into a single Department of Homeland Security (DHS) in the aftermath of the September 11 attacks. The Bush Administration pushed to exempt 170,000 DHS employees as well as Department of Defense employees from major parts of the civil service laws, part of an effort to exert more control over their activities. *Id.* at 565-67. This proposed shift from the general civil service requirements faced heavy opposition from unions because of the proposed limits on collective bargaining and ultimately failed after they were challenged in court, keeping them from ever taking effect.

The Obama Administration focused on modernizing the civil service through emphases on diversity, recruiting young people, and technology. Some of the Administration's initiatives included closing the gender pay gap, increasing workplace flexibility for employees, focusing on creating and maintaining a diverse hiring pipeline, and using IT and data analytics to improve efficiency and work product. *See* BETH F. COBERT, OPM ACTING DIRECTOR, CABINET EXIT MEMO (2017), https://chcoc.gov/content/us-office-personnel-management-cabinet-exit-memo.

President Trump has likewise worked to reshape the civil service. He signed three executive orders in 2018 aimed at making it easier to fire poor-performing federal employees, to revamp federal employee union contracts to make them more favorable to the federal government, and to limit taxpayer-funded union work at agencies. President Trump also has pushed for cuts in federal employee retirement benefits, simplifying complex civil service rules, freezing federal pay, and focusing on skills training to incorporate modern technology. *See, e.g.,* Nicole Ogrysko, *Here's What Civil Service Modernization Looks Like in Trump's 2020 Budget Request,* FED. NEWS NETWORK (Mar. 18, 2019), https://federalnewsnetwork.com/workforce/2019/03/heres-what-civil-service-modernization-looks-like-in-trumps-2020-budget-request/; S.A. Miller, *How Trump Is Making It Easier to Say 'You're Fired!' to Bad Federal Bureaucrats,* WASH. TIMES (May 25, 2018), https://www.washingtontimes.com/news/2018/may/25/trump-makes-it-easier-fire-bad-federal-employees/.

Due to vacancies, the MSPB lacked the quorum needed to conduct official business at the start of the Trump Administration. As a consequence, its ALJs were able to issue opinions but the Board itself had no ability to review them. The MSPB subsequently operated with *no* members starting in March 2019 when the term of its sole remaining member expired. President Trump appointed three individuals to fill the completely vacant Board but as of this writing the Senate has not confirmed any nominees, leaving a backlog of about 2,500 cases for Board members to face after they are confirmed. *See TSP Nominations Return Spotlight to Longstanding Vacancies,* FEDWEEK

(May 20, 2020), https://www.fedweek.com/fedweek/tsp-nominations-return
-spotlight-to-longstanding-vacancies/.

B. LEGAL ISSUES IN THE CIVIL SERVICE REGIME: SCOPE OF MSPB AUTHORITY

Courts have been tasked with setting parameters on OPM and the MSPB's
operations since the passage of the Civil Service Reform Act of 1978. Many
of these legal issues deal with where OPM and the MSPB fit into administrative and employment regulation, with a focus on the scope of the MSPB's
authority. In discovering the parameters of that authority, the Supreme
Court has explored the CSRA's purpose and role in controlling administrative employment.

One of the first cases addressing the scope of the MSPB's authority was
United States v. Fausto, 484 U.S. 439 (1988), which asked whether a non-
preference excepted employee under the CSRA could sue for back pay in U.S.
Claims Court. The Court held that a "leading purpose of the CSRA was to
replace the haphazard arrangements for administrative and judicial review of
personnel action, part of the outdated patchwork of statutes and rules built
up over almost a century that was the civil service system." *Id.* at 444 (internal quotations omitted). The patchwork created by legislation and executive
actions from the Pendleton Act up until the CSRA had created a heavily
criticized system where the right to appeal adverse decisions, and where those
appeals were heard, was governed by the executive order, legislation, or type
of employment class in play. The Court held that the CSRA was Congress'
response to the situation and that it "replaced the patchwork system with an
integrated scheme of administrative and judicial review, designed to balance
the legitimate interests of the various categories of federal employees with the
needs of sound and efficient administration." *Id.* at 445. This interpretation
of the CSRA's purpose formed the basis for future Supreme Court decisions
about the agencies overseeing the federal civil service.

In *Elgin v. Department of the Treasury*, the Court considered whether
the CSRA provided the exclusive avenue for judicial review when a covered
employee challenged an adverse employment action by arguing a federal statute is unconstitutional.

***Elgin v. Department of the Treasury*, 567 U.S. 1 (2012).** The case involved
several male, former federal civil service employees who never registered for
the draft. Their failure to register violated the Military Selective Service Act
and meant that they were statutorily barred from being employees of any
Executive Branch agency. The employees lost their jobs after their employers
discovered they had failed to register. Only one employee, Michael Elgin,
challenged his removal to the MSPB. The others filed in federal district
court. Both Elgin and the others argued that the statutory bar to employment

because they had failed to register for the draft unconstitutionally discriminated against them on the basis of sex. The ALJ charged with adjudicating Elgin's case held that the MSPB did not have jurisdiction to consider Elgin's claim both because Elgin had been statutorily barred from federal civil service employment and because the MSPB could not determine the constitutionality of a statute. Elgin did not appeal the ALJ dismissal to the full MSPB but instead joined the others in district court. The district court held that the CSRA did not prevent the court from hearing the challenge and denied the former employees' constitutional claims on the merits. On appeal, the First Circuit held that the former employees' challenges were not exempted from the CSRA and vacated the district court's judgment. The Supreme Court granted certiorari. It outlined the CRSA's provisions as follows:

> The CSRA "established a comprehensive system for reviewing personnel action taken against federal employees." *Fausto*, 484 U.S. 439 at 455. As relevant here, Subchapter II of Chapter 75 [of the CSRA] governs review of major adverse actions taken against employees "for such cause as will promote the efficiency of the service." 5 U.S.C. §§ 7503(a), 7513(a). Employees entitled to review are those in the "competitive service" and "excepted service" who meet certain requirements regarding probationary periods and years of service. § 7511(a)(1). The reviewable agency actions are removal, suspension for more than 14 days, reduction in grade or pay, or furlough for 30 days or less. § 7512.
>
> When an employing agency proposes a covered action against a covered employee, the CSRA gives the employee the right to notice, representation by counsel, an opportunity to respond, and a written, reasoned decision from the agency. § 7513(b). If the agency takes final adverse action against the employee, the CSRA gives the employee the right to a hearing and to be represented by an attorney or other representative before the Merit Systems Protection Board (MSPB). §§ 7513(d), 7701(a)(1)-(2). The MSPB is authorized to order relief to prevailing employees, including reinstatement, backpay, and attorney's fees. §§ 1204(a)(2), 7701(g).
>
> An employee who is dissatisfied with the MSPB's decision is entitled to judicial review in the United States Court of Appeals for the Federal Circuit. That court shall review the record and hold unlawful and set aside any agency action, findings, or conclusions that are arbitrary, capricious, an abuse of discretion, or otherwise not in accordance with law, obtained without procedures required by law, rule, or regulation having been followed, or "unsupported by substantial evidence." § 7703(a)(1), (c). The Federal Circuit has exclusive jurisdiction over appeals from a final decision of the MSPB. 28 U.S.C. § 1295(a)(9); *see also* 5 U.S.C. § 7703(b)(1) (judicial review of an MSPB decision "shall be" in the Federal Circuit).

567 U.S. at 5-6.

The Court then considered the applicable standard for determining whether the CSRA provides the exclusive means of review for constitutional claims. It concluded that it must determine whether it was "fairly discernible" from the CSRA that Congress intended covered employees appealing covered agency actions to proceed exclusively through the statutory review scheme, even when the employees raise constitutional challenges to federal statutes.

> To determine whether it is "fairly discernible" that Congress precluded district court jurisdiction over petitioners' claims, we examine the CSRA's text, structure, and purpose.
>
> This is not the first time we have addressed the impact of the CSRA's text and structure on the availability of judicial review of a federal employee's challenge to an employment decision. In *Fausto*, we considered whether a so-called "nonpreference excepted service employe[e]" could challenge his suspension in the United States Claims Court, even though the CSRA did not then afford him a right to review in the MSPB or the Federal Circuit. *Id.*, at 440-441. Citing "[t]he comprehensive nature of the CSRA, the attention that it gives throughout to the rights of nonpreference excepted service employees, and the fact that it does not include them in provisions for administrative and judicial review contained in Chapter 75," the Court concluded that "the absence of provision for these employees to obtain judicial review" was a "considered congressional judgment." *Id.*, at 448. The Court thus found it "fairly discernible" that Congress intended to preclude all judicial review of Fausto's statutory claims. *Id.*, at 452 (citing [*Block v. Community Nutrition Institute*, 467 U.S. 340, 349 (1984)]).
>
> Just as the CSRA's "elaborate" framework demonstrates Congress' intent to entirely foreclose judicial review to employees to whom the CSRA denies statutory review, it similarly indicates that extrastatutory review is not available to those employees to whom the CSRA grants administrative and judicial review . . . As *Fausto* explained, the CSRA "prescribes in great detail the protections and remedies applicable to" adverse personnel actions against federal employees. *Id.*, at 443 . . . Given the painstaking detail with which the CSRA sets out the method for covered employees to obtain review of adverse employment actions, it is fairly discernible that Congress intended to deny such employees an additional avenue of review in district court. . . .
>
> The purpose of the CSRA also supports our conclusion that the statutory review scheme is exclusive, even for employees who bring constitutional challenges to federal statutes. As we have previously explained, the CSRA's "integrated scheme of administrative and judicial review" for aggrieved federal employees was designed to replace an "outdated patchwork of statutes and rules" that afforded employees the right to challenge employing agency actions in district courts across the country. [*Id.*] at 444-445. Such widespread judicial review, which included appeals in all of the Federal Courts of Appeals, produced "wide variations in the kinds of decisions . . . issued on the same or similar matters" and a double layer of judicial review that was "wasteful and irrational." *Id.*, at 445.
>
> The CSRA's objective of creating an integrated scheme of review would be seriously undermined if, as petitioners would have it, a covered employee could challenge a covered employment action first in a district

court, and then again in one of the courts of appeals, simply by alleging that the statutory authorization for such action is unconstitutional. Such suits would reintroduce the very potential for inconsistent decisionmaking and duplicative judicial review that the CSRA was designed to avoid. Moreover, petitioners' position would create the possibility of parallel litigation regarding the same agency action before the MSPB and a district court. An employee could challenge the constitutionality of the statute authorizing an agency's action in district court, but the MSPB would remain the exclusive forum for other types of challenges to the agency's decision. . . .

Finally, we note that a jurisdictional rule based on the nature of an employee's constitutional claim would deprive the aggrieved employee, the MSPB, and the district court of clear guidance about the proper forum for the employee's claims at the outset of the case . . . [T]he better interpretation of the CSRA is that its exclusivity does not turn on the constitutional nature of an employee's claim, but rather on the type of the employee and the challenged employment action.

Id. at 10-15.

The Court concluded by considering and rejecting several additional arguments the employees made that the CSRA scheme did not limit the consideration of their claims to the MSPB. The employees argued that the CSRA review scheme did not provide meaningful review of their claims because the MSPB did not have the authority to declare a federal statute unconstitutional. The Court held that the MSPB's inability to declare a statute unconstitutional did not mean that there should be district court jurisdiction because the Federal Circuit, which does have that power, can consider the constitutional question on appeal from an MSPB decision. The court also disagreed with the employees' argument that their constitutional claims were "wholly collateral" to the CSRA scheme, holding that the CSRA structures the MSPB to adjudicate removal decisions, which is what the employees were challenging. Finally, the Court rejected the former employees' argument that Congress did not mean for the constitutional claims to have to funnel through the MSPB. It held that many times, as was true in this case, the MSPB can decide employee cases on employment-related threshold questions that end the case before even reaching any alleged constitutional questions. The Court's upholding of the CSRA scheme strengthened the MSPB's power of overseeing administrative employment practices.

Kloeckner v. Solis, 568 U.S. 41 (2012), and ***Perry v. MSPB,*** 137 S. Ct. 1975 (2017). The Court in subsequent years placed more limits on the MSPB's power when confronted with employees bringing so-called "mixed cases," those in which an employee alleges both employment-related claims within the MSPB's jurisdiction and discrimination-based claims that fall outside the MSPB's jurisdiction.

In *Kloeckner v. Solis*, 568 U.S. 41 (2012), the Court confronted whether the CSRA required an MSPB dismissal of a mixed case on procedural grounds or on the merits to be appealed to the Federal Circuit, or whether it should instead be brought to federal district court. The Court held that a procedural or merit-based MSPB dismissal should be appealed to a federal district court under the CSRA, because the Act clearly indicates that discrimination challenges based on non-civil service statutes are the purview of district courts. The Court reasoned that the discrimination-based challenge triggered the district court's jurisdiction whether it was accompanied by a civil service claim or not. In coming to that decision, the Court returned again to the idea that federal employment cases, with their oftentimes intersecting federal civil rights and civil service statutory claims, "ha[ve] produced a complicated, at times, confusing, process for resolving claims of discrimination in the federal workplace." *Kloeckner*, 568 U.S. at 49. The CSRA and the Court's interpretation of its sections are attempts to straighten the complexity out.

Several years later, the Court faced a similar question in *Perry v. MSPB*, 137 S. Ct. 1975 (2017); whether the Federal Circuit or a district court should have the power to judicially review an appeal from an MSPB decision if the MSPB dismissed an employee's claim because it lacked jurisdiction. The seven-justice majority held that an appeal of an MSPB dismissal should go to a federal district court, which has jurisdiction over the discrimination claim, instead of the Federal Circuit, which does not. The two-justice dissent argued that the claims should be divided, with the discrimination claims going to a district court and the civil service claims going to the Federal Circuit. The majority, in coming to its decision, again used the CSRA's purpose of creating an orderly scheme for employee claims as a basis for its decision about MSPB and Federal Circuit jurisdiction. "[The Court's decision] best serves the CSRA's objective of creating an integrated scheme of review, which would be seriously undermined by parallel litigation regarding the same agency action."

C. LEGAL ISSUES IN THE CIVIL SERVICE REGIME: FREE SPEECH

In addition to the statutory protections federal civil service employees enjoy under the CSRA and other statutes, they also enjoy constitutional protections. One recurring area of constitutional concern for federal employees is protection of their right to procedural due process. Another is protection of their rights under the First Amendment. These cases address the difficult balance between respecting the individual right to speak freely and the government's interest in overseeing its employees.

The line of cases addressing this free speech question for public employees traces back to 1968, at least in the state context, when the Supreme

Court decided *Pickering v. Board of Education.* In that case a teacher alleged he had been fired because he sent a letter critical of his school board to the local newspaper. The Court held that any notion "teachers may constitutionally be compelled to relinquish the First Amendment rights they would otherwise enjoy as citizens to comment on matters of public interest in connection with the operation of the public schools in which they work . . . proceeds on a premise that has been unequivocally rejected in numerous prior decisions of this Court." *Pickering v. Bd. of Educ.*, 391 U.S. 563, 568 (1968). It reaffirmed that principle some 15 years later in *Connick v. Myers*, holding that the government could not "condition public employment on a basis that infringes the employee's constitutionally protected interest in freedom of expression." 461 U.S. 138, 142 (1983). It determined that a court's task was to seek a "balance between the interests of the [employee], as a citizen, in commenting upon matters of public concern and the interest of the State, as an employer, in promoting the efficiency of the public services it performs through its employees." *Id.* at 142 (quoting *Pickering*, 391 U.S. at 568). The Court held that a teacher's dismissal was impermissible because the subject of the teacher's speech was "a matter of legitimate public concern" upon which "free and open debate is vital to informed decisionmaking by the electorate." *Id.* at 145 (quoting *Pickering*, 391 U.S. at 571-72).

In the same year as the Court decided *Connick*, it also held in *Bush v. Lucas* that federal civil service employees pursuing First Amendment challenges must funnel them through the CSRA scheme of MSPB ALJs, the full MSPB, and the Federal Circuit for those challenges. The Court relied on the type of deference to the CSRA found in cases like *Elgin*, *Kloeckner*, and *Perry*, holding that the CSRA established a comprehensive system for adjudicating administrative employment claims that included First Amendment claims. 462 U.S. 367, 388 (1983).

The Supreme Court then added an extra layer to its analysis of public employee First Amendment cases in 2006 when it decided *Garcetti v. Ceballos*, 547 U.S. 410 (2006). That case involved a prosecutor who was fired after writing a memo critical of an affidavit he was reviewing, and hinged on whether a civil service employee has First Amendment protections for speech made in the course of performing official employment duties. The Court held that "when public employees make statements pursuant to their official duties, the employees are not speaking as citizens for First Amendment purposes, and the Constitution does not insulate their communications from employer discipline." *Id.* at 421. Importantly, the Court did not provide a test for what is within or outside an employee's duties. It did, however, suggest that the inquiry should be "a practical one" and that simply considering the employee's job description was not sufficient to determine the scope. *Id.* at 424-25.

The Court reasoned that restricting speech based on an employee's professional responsibilities does not infringe on the First Amendment rights to speech he or she would enjoy as a private citizen. It also determined that government employers should be given sufficient discretion to manage their operations in part because they "have heightened interests in controlling speech made by an employee in his or her professional capacity." *Id.* at 422.

Four justices dissented in the case, with three premising their disagreement on the idea that public employees can never claim First Amendment protections for speech made in the course of performing official duties. In his dissent, Justice Souter noted that public and private interests in addressing official wrongdoing and threats to health and safety can outweigh the government's interests in effective employment even when dealing with speech that results from job duties. He also based his analyses in part on the idea that it is public employees who "are often in the best position to know what ails the agencies for which they work." *Id.* at 429 (internal quotation omitted).

The *Garcetti* decision thus created a new, five-step analysis for public employee claims of First Amendment protections against adverse employment actions. First, a court must ask whether the employee is speaking pursuant to her official duties. If the employee can show that she is not speaking pursuant to official duties, the court next must determine whether the employee is speaking on a matter of public concern. If the employee was speaking on a matter of public concern, the Court engages in the *Pickering* balancing test that weighs the employee's interest in speaking against the government's interests as an employer. If the balancing test favors the employee, the employee must then show by a preponderance of the evidence that her protected speech was a substantial or motivating factor for the adverse employment action. The government then has the burden to show that it would have made the same decision in the absence of the employee's protected speech.

While there was a process in place after *Garcetti*, the Supreme Court's general lack of guidelines on the difference between official employee speech and employee speech as a private citizen left the lower courts to figure out many of the post-*Garcetti* specifics. Circuit courts in the years following the decision have split as to whether the determination about employment-related versus private-citizen speech was a question purely of law or was a mixed question of law and fact. *Compare Posey v. Lake Pend Oreille Sch. Dist. No. 84*, 546 F.3d 1121 (9th Cir. 2008) (mixed question of law and fact); *Davis v. Cook County*, 534 F.3d 650 (7th Cir. 2008); *Reilly v. City of Atl. City*, 532 F.3d 216 (3d Cir. 2008) (same), with *Charles v. Grief*, 522 F.3d 508 (5th Cir. 2008) (question of law); *Wilburn v. Robinson*, 480 F.3d 1140 (D.C. Cir. 2007) (same).

Courts have also been left to draw lines between employment speech and private speech. The circuits have relied on various considerations in deciding post-*Garcetti* cases, including the audience to which the speech is directed, the employee's formal job description, and whether the speech owes its existence to the speaker's job. *See* Thomas Keenan, Note: *Circuit*

Court Interpretations of Garcetti v. Ceballos *and the Development of Public Employee Speech*, 87 NOTRE DAME L. REV. 841, 848-56 (2011).

Scholars have debated *Garcetti* since the Court decided it, with many criticizing it for its lack of direction to lower courts, lack of recognition of the value of public employee speech, lack of protection against employers manipulating the rule with broad job descriptions, and lack of recognition that it puts publicly employed academics in a unique position. *See, e.g.*, Kermit Roosevelt III, *Not as Bad as You Think: Why* Garcetti v. Ceballos *Makes Sense*, 14 U. PA. J. CONST. L. 631, 649-56 (2012). Other scholars believe the case's critics have gone too far and that the case presents a workable system for deciding federal employees' First Amendment claims. *Id.* at 631-32.

QUESTION SET 11.1

Review & Synthesis

1. What are the relative benefits and shortcomings of the spoils system versus the merit-based system? Was the shift from the spoils system to a merit-based system an overcorrection?

2. Do you think that the requirement to exhaust administrative remedies rather than going to federal district court as required by *Elgin* sufficiently protects the constitutional interests of employees covered by the CSRA? What argumentative opportunities might a federal employee lose if he or she is unable to file their claim in federal district court?

3. After *Garcetti*, what is the five-step analysis for public employees' claims of First Amendment protections against adverse employment actions? Are public employees entitled to the same First Amendment protections as private-sector employees? Why or why not? Do you agree?

4. For all intents and purposes, Officers of the United States are still selected and appointed according to a pseudo-spoils system. Although the Appointments Clause sets the terms of their appointments, the selection of these officials is based largely on the discretion of the President (principals) or another government official of Congress' choosing (inferiors). Given that the formal power they wield is greater than even the most senior civil servant, shouldn't their selection be based primarily on merit? Is the nature of their responsibilities so different from those of civil servants to warrant an entirely separate selection system? In formulating your answer, review the materials from Chapter 9 regarding appointment and removal powers.

CONSTITUTIONAL AND STATUTORY APPENDIX

THE CONSTITUTION OF THE UNITED STATES OF AMERICA

WE THE PEOPLE of the United States, in Order to form a more perfect Union, establish Justice, insure domestic Tranquility, provide for the common defence, promote the general Welfare, and secure the Blessings of Liberty to ourselves and our Posterity, do ordain and establish this CONSTITUTION for the United States of America.

ARTICLE I

Section 1. All legislative Powers herein granted shall be vested in a Congress of the United States, which shall consist of a Senate and House of Representatives.

Section 2. [1] The House of Representatives shall be composed of Members chosen every second Year by the People of the several States, and the Electors in each State shall have the Qualifications requisite for Electors of the most numerous Branch of the State Legislature.

[2] No Person shall be a Representative who shall not have attained to the Age of twenty five Years, and been seven Years a Citizen of the United States, and who shall not, when elected, be an Inhabitant of that State in which he shall be chosen.

[3] Representatives and direct Taxes shall be apportioned among the several States which may be included within this Union, according to their respective Numbers, which shall be determined by adding to the whole Number of free Persons, including those bound to Service for a Term of Years, and excluding Indians not taxed, three fifths of all other Persons.[1] The actual Enumeration shall be made within three Years after the first Meeting of the Congress of the United States, and within every subsequent Term of ten Years, in such Manner as they shall by Law direct. The Number of Representatives shall not exceed one for every thirty Thousand, but each State shall have at Least one Representative; and until such enumeration shall be made, the State of New Hampshire shall be entitled to

---

[1] The part of this provision relating to the method for apportioning representatives among the states was amended by section 2 of the Fourteenth Amendment. The portion relating to taxes on incomes without apportionment was amended by the Sixteenth Amendment.

chuse three, Massachusetts eight, Rhode-Island and Providence Plantations one, Connecticut five, New-York six, New Jersey four, Pennsylvania eight, Delaware one, Maryland six, Virginia ten, North Carolina five, South Carolina five, and Georgia three.

[4] When vacancies happen in the Representation from any State, the Executive Authority thereof shall issue Writs of Election to fill such Vacancies.

[5] The House of Representatives shall chuse their Speaker and other Officers; and shall have the sole Power of Impeachment.

Section 3. [1] The Senate of the United States shall be composed of two Senators from each State, chosen by the Legislature thereof, for six Years; and each Senator shall have one Vote.[2]

[2] Immediately after they shall be assembled in Consequence of the first Election, they shall be divided as equally as may be into three Classes. The Seats of the Senators of the first Class shall be vacated at the Expiration of the second Year, of the second Class at the Expiration of the fourth Year, and of the third Class at the Expiration of the sixth Year, so that one third may be chosen every second Year; and if Vacancies happen by Resignation, or otherwise, during the Recess of the Legislature of any State, the Executive thereof may make temporary Appointments until the next Meeting of the Legislature, which shall then fill such Vacancies.[3]

[3] No Person shall be a Senator who shall not have attained to the Age of thirty Years, and been nine Years a Citizen of the United States, and who shall not, when elected, be an Inhabitant of that State for which he shall be chosen.

[4] The Vice President of the United States shall be President of the Senate, but shall have no Vote, unless they be equally divided.

[5] The Senate shall chuse their other Officers, and also a President pro tempore, in the Absence of the Vice President, or when he shall exercise the Office of President of the United States.

[6] The Senate shall have the sole Power to try all Impeachments. When sitting for that Purpose, they shall be on Oath or Affirmation. When the President of the United States is tried, the Chief Justice shall preside: And no Person shall be convicted without the Concurrence of two thirds of the Members present.

[7] Judgment in Cases of Impeachment shall not extend further than to removal from Office, and disqualification to hold and enjoy any Office of honor, Trust or Profit under the United States: but the Party convicted shall nevertheless be liable and subject to Indictment, Trial, Judgment and Punishment, according to Law.

---

[2] This clause was superseded by the Seventeenth Amendment.

[3] This clause was amended by the Seventeenth Amendment.

Section 4. [1] The Times, Places and Manner of holding Elections for Senators and Representatives, shall be prescribed in each State by the Legislature thereof; but the Congress may at any time by Law make or alter such Regulations, except as to the Places of chusing Senators.

[2] The Congress shall assemble at least once in every Year, and such Meeting shall be on the [first Monday in December,[4] unless they shall by Law appoint a different Day.

Section 5. [1] Each House shall be the Judge of the Elections, Returns and Qualifications of its own Members, and a Majority of each shall constitute a Quorum to do Business; but a smaller Number may adjourn from day to day, and may be authorized to compel the Attendance of absent Members, in such Manner, and under such Penalties as each House may provide.

[2] Each House may determine the Rules of its Proceedings, punish its Members for disorderly Behaviour, and, with the Concurrence of two thirds, expel a Member.

[3] Each House shall keep a Journal of its Proceedings, and from time to time publish the same, excepting such Parts as may in their Judgment require Secrecy; and the Yeas and Nays of the Members of either House on any question shall, at the Desire of one fifth of those Present, be entered on the Journal.

[4] Neither House, during the Session of Congress, shall, without the Consent of the other, adjourn for more than three days, nor to any other Place than that in which the two Houses shall be sitting.

Section 6. [1] The Senators and Representatives shall receive a Compensation for their Services, to be ascertained by Law, and paid out of the Treasury of the United States. They shall in all Cases, except Treason, Felony and Breach of the Peace, be privileged from Arrest during their Attendance at the Session of their respective Houses, and in going to and returning from the same; and for any Speech or Debate in either House, they shall not be questioned in any other Place.

[2] No Senator or Representative shall, during the Time for which he was elected, be appointed to any civil Office under the Authority of the United States, which shall have been created, or the Emoluments whereof shall have been encreased during such time; and no Person holding any Office under the United States, shall be a Member of either House during his Continuance in Office.

Section 7. [1] All Bills for raising Revenue shall originate in the House of Representatives; but the Senate may propose or concur with Amendments as on other Bills.

[2] Every Bill which shall have passed the House of Representatives and the Senate, shall, before it becomes a Law, be presented to the President of the United States; If he approve he shall sign it, but if not he shall return

---

[4] This portion of the clause was superseded by the Twentieth Amendment.

it, with his Objections to that House in which it shall have originated, who shall enter the Objections at large on their Journal, and proceed to reconsider it. If after such Reconsideration two thirds of that House shall agree to pass the Bill, it shall be sent, together with the Objections, to the other House, by which it shall likewise be reconsidered, and if approved by two thirds of that House, it shall become a Law. But in all such Cases the Votes of both Houses shall be determined by Yeas and Nays, and the Names of the Persons voting for and against the Bill shall be entered on the Journal of each House respectively. If any Bill shall not be returned by the President within ten Days (Sundays excepted) after it shall have been presented to him, the Same shall be a Law, in like Manner as if he had signed it, unless the Congress by their Adjournment prevent its Return, in which Case it shall not be a Law.

[3] Every Order, Resolution, or Vote to which the Concurrence of the Senate and House of Representatives may be necessary (except on a question of Adjournment) shall be presented to the President of the United States; and before the Same shall take Effect, shall be approved by him, or being disapproved by him, shall be repassed by two thirds of the Senate and House of Representatives, according to the Rules and Limitations prescribed in the Case of a Bill.

Section 8. [1] The Congress shall have Power To lay and collect Taxes, Duties, Imposts and Excises, to pay the Debts and provide for the common Defence and general Welfare of the United States; but all Duties, Imposts and Excises shall be uniform throughout the United States;

[2] To borrow Money on the credit of the United States;

[3] To regulate Commerce with foreign Nations, and among the several States, and with the Indian Tribes;

[4] To establish an uniform Rule of Naturalization, and uniform Laws on the subject of Bankruptcies throughout the United States;

[5] To coin Money, regulate the Value thereof, and of foreign Coin, and fix the Standard of Weights and Measures;

[6] To provide for the Punishment of counterfeiting the Securities and current Coin of the United States;

[7] To establish Post Offices and post Roads;

[8] To promote the Progress of Science and useful Arts, by securing for limited Times to Authors and Inventors the exclusive Right to their respective Writings and Discoveries;

[9] To constitute Tribunals inferior to the supreme Court;

[10] To define and punish Piracies and Felonies committed on the high Seas, and Offences against the Law of Nations;

[11] To declare War, grant Letters of Marque and Reprisal, and make Rules concerning Captures on Land and Water;

[12] To raise and support Armies, but no Appropriation of Money to that Use shall be for a longer Term than two Years;

[13] To provide and maintain a Navy;

[14] To make Rules for the Government and Regulation of the land and naval Forces;

[15] To provide for calling forth the Militia to execute the Laws of the Union, suppress Insurrections and repel Invasions;

[16] To provide for organizing, arming, and disciplining, the Militia, and for governing such Part of them as may be employed in the Service of the United States, reserving to the States respectively, the Appointment of the Officers, and the Authority of training the Militia according to the discipline prescribed by Congress;

[17] To exercise exclusive Legislation in all Cases whatsoever, over such District (not exceeding ten Miles square) as may, by Cession of particular States, and the Acceptance of Congress, become the Seat of the Government of the United States, and to exercise like Authority over all Places purchased by the Consent of the Legislature of the State in which the Same shall be, for the Erection of Forts, Magazines, Arsenals, dock-Yards, and other needful Buildings;—And

[18] To make all Laws which shall be necessary and proper for carrying into Execution the foregoing Powers, and all other Powers vested by this Constitution in the Government of the United States, or in any Department or Officer thereof.

Section 9. [1] The Migration or Importation of such Persons as any of the States now existing shall think proper to admit, shall not be prohibited by the Congress prior to the Year one thousand eight hundred and eight, but a Tax or duty may be imposed on such Importation, not exceeding ten dollars for each Person.

[2] The Privilege of the Writ of Habeas Corpus shall not be suspended, unless when in Cases of Rebellion or Invasion the public Safety may require it.

[3] No Bill of Attainder or ex post facto Law shall be passed.

[4] No Capitation, or other direct, Tax shall be laid, unless in Proportion to the Census or Enumeration herein before directed to be taken.[5]

[5] No Tax or Duty shall be laid on Articles exported from any State.

[6] No Preference shall be given by any Regulation of Commerce or Revenue to the Ports of one State over those of another; nor shall Vessels bound to, or from, one State, be obliged to enter, clear, or pay Duties in another.

[7] No Money shall be drawn from the Treasury, but in Consequence of Appropriations made by Law; and a regular Statement and Account of the Receipts and Expenditures of all public Money shall be published from time to time.

[8] No Title of Nobility shall be granted by the United States: And no Person holding any Office of Profit or Trust under them, shall, without the Consent of the Congress, accept of any present, Emolument, Office, or Title, of any kind whatever, from any King, Prince, or foreign State.

Section 10. [1] No State shall enter into any Treaty, Alliance, or Confederation; grant Letters of Marque and Reprisal; coin Money; emit Bills of Credit; make any Thing but gold and silver Coin a Tender in Payment of Debts; pass any Bill of Attainder, ex post facto Law, or Law impairing the Obligation of Contracts, or grant any Title of Nobility.

[2] No State shall, without the Consent of the Congress, lay any Imposts or Duties on Imports or Exports, except what may be absolutely necessary for executing it's inspection Laws: and the net Produce of all Duties and Imposts, laid by any State on Imports or Exports, shall be for the Use of the Treasury of the United States; and all such Laws shall be subject to the Revision and Controul of the Congress.

[3] No State shall, without the Consent of Congress, lay any Duty of Tonnage, keep Troops, or Ships of War in time of Peace, enter into any Agreement or Compact with another State, or with a foreign Power, or engage in War, unless actually invaded, or in such imminent Danger as will not admit of delay.

ARTICLE II

Section 1. [1] The executive Power shall be vested in a President of the United States of America. He shall hold his Office during the Term of four Years, and, together with the Vice President, chosen for the same Term, be elected, as follows:

[2] Each State shall appoint, in such Manner as the Legislature thereof may direct, a Number of Electors, equal to the whole Number of Senators and Representatives to which the State may be entitled in the Congress: but no Senator or Representative, or Person holding an Office of Trust or Profit under the United States, shall be appointed an Elector.

[3] The Electors shall meet in their respective States, and vote by Ballot for two Persons, of whom one at least shall not be an Inhabitant of the same State with themselves. And they shall make a List of all the Persons voted for, and of the Number of Votes for each; which List they shall sign and certify, and transmit sealed to the Seat of the Government of the United States, directed to the President of the Senate. The President of the Senate shall, in the Presence of the Senate and House of Representatives, open all the Certificates, and the Votes shall then be counted. The Person having the greatest Number of Votes shall be the President, if such Number be a Majority of the whole Number of Electors appointed; and if there be more than one who have such Majority, and have an equal Number of Votes, then the House of Representatives shall immediately chuse by Ballot one of them for President; and if no Person have a Majority, then from the five highest on the List the said House shall in like Manner chuse the President. But in chusing the President, the Votes shall be taken by States, the Representation from each State having one Vote; A quorum for this Purpose shall consist

of a Member or Members from two thirds of the States, and a Majority of all the States shall be necessary to a Choice. In every Case, after the Choice of the President, the Person having the greatest Number of Votes of the Electors shall be the Vice President. But if there should remain two or more who have equal Votes, the Senate shall chuse from them by Ballot the Vice President.[5]

[4] The Congress may determine the Time of chusing the Electors, and the Day on which they shall give their Votes; which Day shall be the same throughout the United States.

[5] No Person except a natural born Citizen, or a Citizen of the United States, at the time of the Adoption of this Constitution, shall be eligible to the Office of President; neither shall any Person be eligible to that Office who shall not have attained to the Age of thirty five Years, and been fourteen Years a Resident within the United States.

[6] In Case of the Removal of the President from Office, or of his Death, Resignation, or Inability to discharge the Powers and Duties of the said Office, the same shall devolve on the Vice President, and the Congress may by Law provide for the Case of Removal, Death, Resignation or Inability, both of the President and Vice President, declaring what Officer shall then act as President, and such Officer shall act accordingly, until the Disability be removed, or a President shall be elected.

[7] The President shall, at stated Times, receive for his Services, a Compensation, which shall neither be encreased nor diminished during the Period for which he shall have been elected, and he shall not receive within that Period any other Emolument from the United States, or any of them.

[8] Before he enter on the Execution of his Office, he shall take the following Oath or Affirmation: — "I do solemnly swear (or affirm) that I will faithfully execute the Office of President of the United States, and will to the best of my Ability, preserve, protect and defend the Constitution of the United States."

Section 2. [1] The President shall be Commander in Chief of the Army and Navy of the United States, and of the Militia of the several States, when called into the actual Service of the United States; he may require the Opinion, in writing, of the principal Officer in each of the executive Departments, upon any Subject relating to the Duties of their respective Offices, and he shall have Power to grant Reprieves and Pardons for Offences against the United States, except in Cases of Impeachment.

[2] He shall have Power, by and with the Advice and Consent of the Senate, to make Treaties, provided two thirds of the Senators present concur; and he shall nominate, and by and with the Advice and Consent of the Senate, shall appoint Ambassadors, other public Ministers and Consuls, Judges of the supreme Court, and all other Officers of the United States,

---

[5] This clause was superseded by the Twelfth Amendment.

whose Appointments are not herein otherwise provided for, and which shall be established by Law: but the Congress may by Law vest the Appointment of such inferior Officers, as they think proper, in the President alone, in the Courts of Law, or in the Heads of Departments.

[3] The President shall have Power to fill up all Vacancies that may happen during the Recess of the Senate, by granting Commissions which shall expire at the End of their next Session.

Section 3. He shall from time to time give to the Congress Information of the State of the Union, and recommend to their Consideration such Measures as he shall judge necessary and expedient; he may, on extraordinary Occasions, convene both Houses, or either of them, and in Case of Disagreement between them, with Respect to the Time of Adjournment, he may adjourn them to such Time as he shall think proper; he shall receive Ambassadors and other public Ministers; he shall take Care that the Laws be faithfully executed, and shall Commission all the Officers of the United States.

Section 4. The President, Vice President and all civil Officers of the United States, shall be removed from Office on Impeachment for, and Conviction of, Treason, Bribery, or other high Crimes and Misdemeanors.

ARTICLE III

Section 1. The judicial Power of the United States, shall be vested in one supreme Court, and in such inferior Courts as the Congress may from time to time ordain and establish. The Judges, both of the supreme and inferior Courts, shall hold their Offices during good Behaviour, and shall, at stated Times, receive for their Services, a Compensation, which shall not be diminished during their Continuance in Office.

Section 2. [1] The judicial Power shall extend to all Cases, in Law and Equity, arising under this Constitution, the Laws of the United States, and Treaties made, or which shall be made, under their Authority; — to all Cases affecting Ambassadors, other public Ministers and Consuls; — to all Cases of admiralty and maritime Jurisdiction; — to Controversies to which the United States shall be a Party; — to Controversies between two or more States; — between a State and Citizens of another State; — between Citizens of different States, — between Citizens of the same State claiming Lands under Grants of different States, and between a State, or the Citizens thereof, and foreign States, Citizens or Subjects.

[2] In all Cases affecting Ambassadors, other public Ministers and Consuls, and those in which a State shall be Party, the supreme Court shall have original Jurisdiction. In all the other Cases before mentioned, the supreme Court shall have appellate Jurisdiction, both as to Law and Fact, with such Exceptions, and under such Regulations as the Congress shall make.

[3] The Trial of all Crimes, except in Cases of Impeachment, shall be by Jury; and such Trial shall be held in the State where the said Crimes shall have been committed; but when not committed within any State, the Trial shall be at such Place or Places as the Congress may by Law have directed.

Section 3. [1] Treason against the United States, shall consist only in levying War against them, or in adhering to their Enemies, giving them Aid and Comfort. No Person shall be convicted of Treason unless on the Testimony of two Witnesses to the same overt Act, or on Confession in open Court.

[2] The Congress shall have Power to declare the Punishment of Treason, but no Attainder of Treason shall work Corruption of Blood, or Forfeiture except during the Life of the Person attainted.

Article IV

Section 1. Full Faith and Credit shall be given in each State to the public Acts, Records, and Judicial Proceedings of every other State. And the Congress may by general Laws prescribe the Manner in which such Acts, Records and Proceedings shall be proved, and the Effect thereof.

Section 2. [1] The Citizens of each State shall be entitled to all Privileges and Immunities of Citizens in the several States.

[2] A Person charged in any State with Treason, Felony, or other Crime, who shall flee from Justice, and be found in another State, shall on Demand of the executive Authority of the State from which he fled, be delivered up, to be removed to the State having Jurisdiction of the Crime.

[3] No person held to Service or Labour in one State, under the Laws thereof, escaping into another, shall, in Consequence of any Law or Regulation therein, be discharged from such Service or Labour, but shall be delivered up on Claim of the Party to whom such Service or Labour may be due.[6]

Section 3. [1] New States may be admitted by the Congress into this Union; but no new State shall be formed or erected within the Jurisdiction of any other State; nor any State be formed by the Junction of two or more States, or Parts of States, without the Consent of the Legislatures of the States concerned as well as of the Congress.

[2] The Congress shall have Power to dispose of and make all needful Rules and Regulations respecting the Territory or other Property belonging to the United States; and nothing in this Constitution shall be so construed as to Prejudice any Claims of the United States, or of any particular State.

Section 4. The United States shall guarantee to every State in this Union a Republican Form of Government, and shall protect each of

---

[6] This clause was substantially affected by the Thirteenth Amendment.

them against Invasion; and on Application of the Legislature, or of the Executive (when the Legislature cannot be convened) against domestic Violence.

ARTICLE V

The Congress, whenever two thirds of both Houses shall deem it necessary, shall propose Amendments to this Constitution, or on the Application of the Legislatures of two thirds of the several States, shall call a Convention for proposing Amendments, which, in either Case, shall be valid to all Intents and Purposes, as Part of this Constitution, when ratified by the Legislatures of three fourths of the several States, or by Conventions in three fourths thereof, as the one or the other Mode of Ratification may be proposed by the Congress; Provided that no Amendment which may be made prior to the Year One thousand eight hundred and eight shall in any Manner affect the first and fourth Clauses in the Ninth Section of the first Article; and that no State, without its Consent, shall be deprived of its equal Suffrage in the Senate.

ARTICLE VI

[1] All Debts contracted and Engagements entered into, before the Adoption of this Constitution, shall be as valid against the United States under this Constitution, as under the Confederation.

[2] This Constitution, and the Laws of the United States which shall be made in Pursuance thereof; and all Treaties made, or which shall be made, under the Authority of the United States, shall be the supreme Law of the Land; and the Judges in every State shall be bound thereby, any Thing in the Constitution or Laws of any State to the Contrary notwithstanding.

[3] The Senators and Representatives before mentioned, and the Members of the several State Legislatures, and all executive and judicial Officers, both of the United States and of the several States, shall be bound by Oath or Affirmation, to support this Constitution; but no religious Test shall ever be required as a Qualification to any Office or public Trust under the United States.

AMENDMENT I

Congress shall make no law respecting an establishment of religion, or prohibiting the free exercise thereof; or abridging the freedom of speech, or of the press; or the right of the people peaceably to assemble, and to petition the Government for a redress of grievances.

AMENDMENT V

No person shall be held to answer for a capital, or otherwise infamous crime, unless on a presentment or indictment of a Grand Jury, except in cases arising in the land or naval forces, or in the Militia, when in actual service in time of War or public danger; nor shall any person be subject for the same offence to be twice put in jeopardy of life or limb; nor shall be compelled in any criminal case to be a witness against himself, nor be deprived of life, liberty, or property, without due process of law; nor shall private property be taken for public use, without just compensation.

AMENDMENT XIV

Section 1. All persons born or naturalized in the United States, and subject to the jurisdiction thereof, are citizens of the United States and of the State wherein they reside. No State shall make or enforce any law which shall abridge the privileges or immunities of citizens of the United States; nor shall any State deprive any person of life, liberty, or property, without due process of law; nor deny to any person within its jurisdiction the equal protection of the laws. . . .

The Administrative Procedure Act and Related Provisions
5 U.S.C. § 551-559, §§ 561-568, § 570, §§ 701-706,
§§ 801-808, 5 U.S.C. § 3105

CHAPTER 5 — ADMINISTRATIVE PROCEDURE

§ 551. DEFINITIONS

For the purpose of this subchapter—
(1) "agency" means each authority of the Government of the United States, whether or not it is within or subject to review by another agency, but does not include—
(A) the Congress;
(B) the courts of the United States;
(C) the governments of the territories or possessions of the United States;
(D) the government of the District of Columbia;
or except as to the requirements of section 552 of this title—
(E) agencies composed of representatives of the parties or of representatives of organizations of the parties to the disputes determined by them;

(F) courts martial and military commissions;

(G) military authority exercised in the field in time of war or in occupied territory; or

(H) functions conferred by sections 1738, 1739, 1743, and 1744 of title 12; subchapter II of chapter 471 of title 49; or sections 1884, 1891-1902, and former section 1641(b)(2), of title 50, appendix;

(2) "person" includes an individual, partnership, corporation, association, or public or private organization other than an agency;

(3) "party" includes a person or agency named or admitted as a party, or properly seeking and entitled as of right to be admitted as a party, in an agency proceeding, and a person or agency admitted by an agency as a party for limited purposes;

(4) "rule" means the whole or a part of an agency statement of general or particular applicability and future effect designed to implement, interpret, or prescribe law or policy or describing the organization, procedure, or practice requirements of an agency and includes the approval or prescription for the future of rates, wages, corporate or financial structures or reorganizations thereof, prices, facilities, appliances, services or allowances therefor or of valuations, costs, or accounting, or practices bearing on any of the foregoing;

(5) "rule making" means agency process for formulating, amending, or repealing a rule;

(6) "order" means the whole or a part of a final disposition, whether affirmative, negative, injunctive, or declaratory in form, of an agency in a matter other than rule making but including licensing;

(7) "adjudication" means agency process for the formulation of an order;

(8) "license" includes the whole or a part of an agency permit, certificate, approval, registration, charter, membership, statutory exemption or other form of permission;

(9) "licensing" includes agency process respecting the grant, renewal, denial, revocation, suspension, annulment, withdrawal, limitation, amendment, modification, or conditioning of a license;

(10) "sanction" includes the whole or a part of an agency—

(A) prohibition, requirement, limitation, or other condition affecting the freedom of a person;

(B) withholding of relief;

(C) imposition of penalty or fine;

(D) destruction, taking, seizure, or withholding of property;

(E) assessment of damages, reimbursement, restitution, compensation, costs, charges, or fees;

(F) requirement, revocation, or suspension of a license; or

(G) taking other compulsory or restrictive action;

(11) "relief" includes the whole or a part of an agency—

(A) grant of money, assistance, license, authority, exemption, exception, privilege, or remedy;

(B) recognition of a claim, right, immunity, privilege, exemption, or exception; or

(C) taking of other action on the application or petition of, and beneficial to, a person;

(12) "agency proceeding" means an agency process as defined by paragraphs (5), (7), and (9) of this section;

(13) "agency action" includes the whole or a part of an agency rule, order, license, sanction, relief, or the equivalent or denial thereof, or failure to act; and

(14) "ex parte communication" means an oral or written communication not on the public record with respect to which reasonable prior notice to all parties is not given, but it shall not include requests for status reports on any matter or proceeding covered by this subchapter.

§ 552. Public information; Agency Rules, Opinions, Orders, Records, and Proceedings.

(a) Each agency shall make available to the public information as follows:

(1) Each agency shall separately state and currently publish in the Federal Register for the guidance of the public—

(A) descriptions of its central and field organization and the established places at which, the employees (and in the case of a uniformed service, the members) from whom, and the methods whereby, the public may obtain information, make submittals or requests, or obtain decisions;

(B) statements of the general course and method by which its functions are channeled and determined, including the nature and requirements of all formal and informal procedures available;

(C) rules of procedure, descriptions of forms available or the places at which forms may be obtained, and instructions as to the scope and contents of all papers, reports, or examinations;

(D) substantive rules of general applicability adopted as authorized by law, and statements of general policy or interpretations of general applicability formulated and adopted by the agency; and

(E) each amendment, revision, or repeal of the foregoing.

Except to the extent that a person has actual and timely notice of the terms thereof, a person may not in any manner be required to resort to, or be adversely affected by, a matter required to be published in the Federal Register and not so published. For the purpose of this paragraph, matter reasonably available to the class of persons affected thereby is deemed published in the Federal Register when incorporated by reference therein with the approval of the Director of the Federal Register.

(2) Each agency, in accordance with published rules, shall make available for public inspection in an electronic format—

(A) final opinions, including concurring and dissenting opinions, as well as orders, made in the adjudication of cases;

(B) those statements of policy and interpretations which have been adopted by the agency and are not published in the Federal Register;

(C) administrative staff manuals and instructions to staff that affect a member of the public;

(D) copies of all records, regardless of form or format—

(i) that have been released to any person under paragraph (3); and

(ii) (I) that because of the nature of their subject matter, the agency determines have become or are likely to become the subject of subsequent requests for substantially the same records; or

(II) that have been requested 3 or more times; and

(E) a general index of the records referred to under subparagraph (D); unless the materials are promptly published and copies offered for sale. For records created on or after November 1, 1996, within one year after such date, each agency shall make such records available, including by computer telecommunications or, if computer telecommunications means have not been established by the agency, by other electronic means. To the extent required to prevent a clearly unwarranted invasion of personal privacy, an agency may delete identifying details when it makes available or publishes an opinion, statement of policy, interpretation, staff manual, instruction, or copies of records referred to in subparagraph (D). However, in each case the justification for the deletion shall be explained fully in writing, and the extent of such deletion shall be indicated on the portion of the record which is made available or published, unless including that indication would harm an interest protected by the exemption in subsection (b) under which the deletion is made. If technically feasible, the extent of the deletion shall be indicated at the place in the record where the deletion was made. Each agency shall also maintain and make available for public inspection in an electronic format current indexes providing identifying information for the public as to any matter issued, adopted, or promulgated after July 4, 1967, and required by this paragraph to be made available or published. Each agency shall promptly publish, quarterly or more frequently, and distribute (by sale or otherwise) copies of each index or supplements thereto unless it determines by order published in the Federal Register that the publication would be unnecessary and impracticable, in which case the agency shall nonetheless provide copies of such index on request at a cost not to exceed the direct cost of duplication. Each agency shall make the index referred to in subparagraph (E) available by computer telecommunications by December 31, 1999. A final order, opinion, statement of policy, interpretation, or staff manual or instruction that affects a member of the public may be relied on, used, or cited as precedent by an agency against a party other than an agency only if—

(i) it has been indexed and either made available or published as provided by this paragraph; or

(ii) the party has actual and timely notice of the terms thereof.

(3) (A) Except with respect to the records made available under paragraphs (1) and (2) of this subsection, and except as provided in subparagraph (E), each agency, upon any request for records which (i) reasonably describes such records and (ii) is made in accordance with published rules stating the time, place, fees (if any), and procedures to be followed, shall make the records promptly available to any person.

(B) In making any record available to a person under this paragraph, an agency shall provide the record in any form or format requested by the person if the record is readily reproducible by the agency in that form or format. Each agency shall make reasonable efforts to maintain its records in forms or formats that are reproducible for purposes of this section.

(C) In responding under this paragraph to a request for records, an agency shall make reasonable efforts to search for the records in electronic form or format, except when such efforts would significantly interfere with the operation of the agency's automated information system.

(D) For purposes of this paragraph, the term "search" means to review, manually or by automated means, agency records for the purpose of locating those records which are responsive to a request.

(E) An agency, or part of an agency, that is an element of the intelligence community (as that term is defined in section 3(4) of the National Security Act of 1947 (50 U.S.C. § 401a(4)) shall not make any record available under this paragraph to—

(i) any government entity, other than a State, territory, commonwealth, or district of the United States, or any subdivision thereof; or

(ii) a representative of a government entity described in clause (i).

(4) (A) (i) In order to carry out the provisions of this section, each agency shall promulgate regulations, pursuant to notice and receipt of public comment, specifying the schedule of fees applicable to the processing of requests under this section and establishing procedures and guidelines for determining when such fees should be waived or reduced. . . .

(B) On complaint, the district court of the United States in the district in which the complainant resides, or has his principal place of business, or in which the agency records are situated, or in the District of Columbia, has jurisdiction to enjoin the agency from withholding agency records and to order the production of any agency records improperly withheld from the complainant. In such a case the court shall determine the matter de novo, and may examine the contents of such agency records in camera to determine whether such records or any part thereof shall be withheld under any of the exemptions set forth in subsection (b) of this section, and the burden is on the agency to sustain its action. In addition to any other matters to which a court accords substantial weight, a court shall accord substantial weight to an affidavit of an agency concerning the agency's determination as to technical feasibility under paragraph (2)(C) and subsection (b) and reproducibility under paragraph (3)(B).

(C) Notwithstanding any other provision of law, the defendant shall serve an answer or otherwise plead to any complaint made under this subsection within thirty days after service upon the defendant of the pleading in which such complaint is made, unless the court otherwise directs for good cause shown.

[(D) Repealed. Pub. L. 98-620, Title IV, § 402(2), Nov. 8, 1984, 98 Stat. 3357]

(E) (i) The court may assess against the United States reasonable attorney fees and other litigation costs reasonably incurred in any case under this section in which the complainant has substantially prevailed.

(ii) For purposes of this subparagraph, a complainant has substantially prevailed if the complainant has obtained relief through either—

(I) a judicial order, or an enforceable written agreement or consent decree; or

(II) a voluntary or unilateral change in position by the agency, if the complainant's claim is not insubstantial.

(F) . . . Whenever the court orders the production of any agency records improperly withheld from the complainant and assesses against the United States reasonable attorney fees and other litigation costs, and the court additionally issues a written finding that the circumstances surrounding the withholding raise questions whether agency personnel acted arbitrarily or capriciously with respect to the withholding, the Special Counsel shall promptly initiate a proceeding to determine whether disciplinary action is warranted against the officer or employee who was primarily responsible for the withholding. . . .

(G) In the event of noncompliance with the order of the court, the district court may punish for contempt the responsible employee, and in the case of a uniformed service, the responsible member.

(5) Each agency having more than one member shall maintain and make available for public inspection a record of the final votes of each member in every agency proceeding.

(6) [This subsection sets out time limits for agency responses to records requests. For the most part, agencies have 20 days to act on such requests. Agency heads hearing administrative appeals of denied requests likewise have 20 days to act on them. Agencies may extend these limits in "unusual circumstances." Courts hearing actions to enforce these time limits may extend them for "exceptional circumstances" if agencies use "due diligence" in attempting to comply with requests.]

(7) Each agency shall—

(A) establish a system to assign an individualized tracking number for each request received that will take longer than ten days to process and provide to each person making a request the tracking number assigned to the request; and

(B) establish a telephone line or Internet service that provides information about the status of a request to the person making the request using the assigned tracking number, including—

(i) the date on which the agency originally received the request; and

(ii) an estimated date on which the agency will complete action on the request.

(8) (A) An agency shall—

(i) withhold information under this section only if—

(I) the agency reasonably foresees that disclosure would harm an interest protected by an exemption described in subsection (b); or

(II) disclosure is prohibited by law; and

(ii) (I) consider whether partial disclosure of information is possible whenever the agency determines that a full disclosure of a requested record is not possible; and

(II) take reasonable steps necessary to segregate and release nonexempt information; and

(B) Nothing in this paragraph requires disclosure of information that is otherwise prohibited from disclosure by law, or otherwise exempted from disclosure under subsection (b)(3).

(b) This section does not apply to matters that are—

(1) (A) specifically authorized under criteria established by an Executive order to be kept secret in the interest of national defense or foreign policy and (B) are in fact properly classified pursuant to such Executive order;

(2) related solely to the internal personnel rules and practices of an agency;

(3) specifically exempted from disclosure by statute (other than section 552b of this title), if that statute—

(A) (i) requires that the matters be withheld from the public in such a manner as to leave no discretion on the issue; or

(ii) establishes particular criteria for withholding or refers to particular types of matters to be withheld; and

(B) if enacted after the date of enactment of the OPEN FOIA Act of 2009, specifically cites to this paragraph.

(4) trade secrets and commercial or financial information obtained from a person and privileged or confidential;

(5) inter-agency or intra-agency memorandums or letters that would not be available by law to a party other than an agency in litigation with the agency, provided that the deliberative process privilege shall not apply to records created 25 years or more before the date on which the records were requested;

(6) personnel and medical files and similar files the disclosure of which would constitute a clearly unwarranted invasion of personal privacy;

(7) records or information compiled for law enforcement purposes, but only to the extent that the production of such law enforcement records or information (A) could reasonably be expected to interfere with enforcement proceedings, (B) would deprive a person of a right to a fair trial or an impartial adjudication, (C) could reasonably be expected to constitute an unwarranted invasion of personal privacy, (D) could reasonably be expected to disclose the identity of a confidential source, including a State, local, or foreign agency or authority or any private institution which furnished information on a confidential basis, and, in the case of a record or information compiled by criminal law enforcement authority in the course of a criminal investigation or by an agency conducting a lawful national security intelligence investigation, information furnished by a confidential source, (E) would disclose techniques and procedures for law enforcement investigations or prosecutions, or would disclose guidelines for law enforcement investigations or prosecutions if such disclosure could reasonably be expected to risk circumvention of the law, or (F) could reasonably be expected to endanger the life or physical safety of any individual;

(8) contained in or related to examination, operating, or condition reports prepared by, on behalf of, or for the use of an agency responsible for the regulation or supervision of financial institutions; or

(9) geological and geophysical information and data, including maps, concerning wells.

Any reasonably segregable portion of a record shall be provided to any person requesting such record after deletion of the portions which are exempt under this subsection. The amount of information deleted, and the exemption under which the deletion is made, shall be indicated on the released portion of the record, unless including that indication would harm an interest protected by the exemption in this subsection under which the deletion is made. If technically feasible, the amount of the information deleted, and the exemption under which the deletion is made, shall be indicated at the place in the record where such deletion is made.

(c) (1) Whenever a request is made which involves access to records described in subsection (b)(7)(A) and—

(A) the investigation or proceeding involves a possible violation of criminal law; and

(B) there is reason to believe that (i) the subject of the investigation or proceeding is not aware of its pendency, and (ii) disclosure of the existence of the records could reasonably be expected to interfere with enforcement proceedings, the agency may, during only such time as that circumstance continues, treat the records as not subject to the requirements of this section.

(2) Whenever informant records maintained by a criminal law enforcement agency under an informant's name or personal identifier are requested by a third party according to the informant's name or personal identifier, the agency may treat the records as not subject to the requirements of this section unless the informant's status as an informant has been officially confirmed.

(3) Whenever a request is made which involves access to records maintained by the Federal Bureau of Investigation pertaining to foreign intelligence or counterintelligence, or international terrorism, and the existence of the records is classified information as provided in subsection (b)(1), the Bureau may, as long as the existence of the records remains classified information, treat the records as not subject to the requirements of this section.

(d) This section does not authorize withholding of information or limit the availability of records to the public, except as specifically stated in this section. This section is not authority to withhold information from Congress.

(e) (1) On or before February 1 of each year, each agency shall submit to the Attorney General of the United States and to the Director of the

Office of Government Information Services a report which shall cover the preceding fiscal year. . . .

(f) For purposes of this section, the term—

(1) "agency" as defined in section 551(1) of this title includes any executive department, military department, Government corporation, Government controlled corporation, or other establishment in the executive branch of the Government (including the Executive Office of the President), or any independent regulatory agency; and

(2) "record" and any other term used in this section in reference to information includes—

(A) any information that would be an agency record subject to the requirements of this section when maintained by an agency in any format, including an electronic format; and

(B) any information described under subparagraph (A) that is maintained for an agency by an entity under Government contract, for the purposes of records management.

(g) The head of each agency shall prepare and make available for public inspection in an electronic format, reference material or a guide for requesting records or information from the agency, subject to the exemptions in subsection (b), including—

(1) an index of all major information systems of the agency;

(2) a description of major information and record locator systems maintained by the agency; and

(3) a handbook for obtaining various types and categories of public information from the agency pursuant to chapter 35 of title 44, and under this section. . . .

§ 552B. OPEN MEETINGS

(a) For purposes of this section—

(1) the term "agency" means any agency, as defined in section 552(e) of this title,[7] headed by a collegial body composed of two or more individual members, a majority of whom are appointed to such position by the President with the advice and consent of the Senate, and any subdivision thereof authorized to act on behalf of the agency;

(2) the term "meeting" means the deliberations of at least the number of individual agency members required to take action on behalf of the agency where such deliberations determine or result in the joint conduct or disposition of official agency business, but does not include deliberations required or permitted by subsection (d) or (e); and

---

[7] Section 552(e) was redesignated section 552(f) by section 1802(b) of Pub. L. 99-570.

(3) the term "member" means an individual who belongs to a collegial body heading an agency.

(b) Members shall not jointly conduct or dispose of agency business other than in accordance with this section. Except as provided in subsection (c), every portion of every meeting of an agency shall be open to public observation.

(c) Except in a case where the agency finds that the public interest requires otherwise, the second sentence of subsection (b) shall not apply to any portion of an agency meeting, and the requirements of subsections (d) and (e) shall not apply to any information pertaining to such meeting otherwise required by this section to be disclosed to the public, where the agency properly determines that such portion or portions of its meeting or the disclosure of such information is likely to—

(1) disclose matters that are (A) specifically authorized under criteria established by an Executive order to be kept secret in the interests of national defense or foreign policy and (B) in fact properly classified pursuant to such Executive order;

(2) relate solely to the internal personnel rules and practices of an agency;

(3) disclose matters specifically exempted from disclosure by statute (other than section 552 of this title), provided that such statute (A) requires that the matters be withheld from the public in such a manner as to leave no discretion on the issue, or (B) establishes particular criteria for withholding or refers to particular types of matters to be withheld;

(4) disclose trade secrets and commercial or financial information obtained from a person and privileged or confidential;

(5) involve accusing any person of a crime, or formally censuring any person;

(6) disclose information of a personal nature where disclosure would constitute a clearly unwarranted invasion of personal privacy;

(7) disclose investigatory records compiled for law enforcement purposes, or information which if written would be contained in such records, but only to the extent that the production of such records or information would (A) interfere with enforcement proceedings, (B) deprive a person of a right to a fair trial or an impartial adjudication, (C) constitute an unwarranted invasion of personal privacy, (D) disclose the identity of a confidential source and, in the case of a record compiled by a criminal law enforcement authority in the course of a criminal investigation, or by an agency conducting a lawful national security intelligence investigation, confidential information furnished only by the confidential source, (E) disclose investigative techniques and procedures, or (F) endanger the life or physical safety of law enforcement personnel;

(8) disclose information contained in or related to examination, operating, or condition reports prepared by, on behalf of, or for the use of an agency responsible for the regulation or supervision of financial institutions;

(9) disclose information the premature disclosure of which would—

(A) in the case of an agency which regulates currencies, securities, commodities, or financial institutions, be likely to (i) lead to significant financial speculation in currencies, securities, or commodities, or (ii) significantly endanger the stability of any financial institution; or

(B) in the case of any agency, be likely to significantly frustrate implementation of a proposed agency action, except that subparagraph (B) shall not apply in any instance where the agency has already disclosed to the public the content or nature of its proposed action, or where the agency is required by law to make such disclosure on its own initiative prior to taking final agency action on such proposal; or

(10) specifically concern the agency's issuance of a subpoena, or the agency's participation in a civil action or proceeding, an action in a foreign court or international tribunal, or an arbitration, or the initiation, conduct, or disposition by the agency of a particular case of formal agency adjudication pursuant to the procedures in section 554 of this title or otherwise involving a determination on the record after opportunity for a hearing.

(d) (1) Action under subsection (c) shall be taken only when a majority of the entire membership of the agency (as defined in subsection (a)(1)) votes to take such action. A separate vote of the agency members shall be taken with respect to each agency meeting a portion or portions of which are proposed to be closed to the public pursuant to subsection (c), or with respect to any information which is proposed to be withheld under subsection (c). A single vote may be taken with respect to a series of meetings, a portion or portions of which are proposed to be closed to the public, or with respect to any information concerning such series of meetings, so long as each meeting in such series involves the same particular matters and is scheduled to be held no more than thirty days after the initial meeting in such series. The vote of each agency member participating in such vote shall be recorded and no proxies shall be allowed.

(2) Whenever any person whose interests may be directly affected by a portion of a meeting requests that the agency close such portion to the public for any of the reasons referred to in paragraph (5), (6), or (7) of subsection (c), the agency, upon request of any one of its members, shall vote by recorded vote whether to close such meeting.

(3) Within one day of any vote taken pursuant to paragraph (1) or (2), the agency shall make publicly available a written copy of such vote reflecting the vote of each member on the question. If a portion

of a meeting is to be closed to the public, the agency shall, within one day of the vote taken pursuant to paragraph (1) or (2) of this subsection, make publicly available a full written explanation of its action closing the portion together with a list of all persons expected to attend the meeting and their affiliation.

(4) Any agency, a majority of whose meetings may properly be closed to the public pursuant to paragraph (4), (8), (9)(A), or (10) of subsection (c), or any combination thereof, may provide by regulation for the closing of such meetings or portions thereof in the event that a majority of the members of the agency votes by recorded vote at the beginning of such meeting, or portion thereof, to close the exempt portion or portions of the meeting, and a copy of such vote, reflecting the vote of each member on the question, is made available to the public. The provisions of paragraphs (1), (2), and (3) of this subsection and subsection (e) shall not apply to any portion of a meeting to which such regulations apply: *Provided*, That the agency shall, except to the extent that such information is exempt from disclosure under the provisions of subsection (c), provide the public with public announcement of the time, place, and subject matter of the meeting and of each portion thereof at the earliest practicable time.

(e) (1) In the case of each meeting, the agency shall make public announcement, at least one week before the meeting, of the time, place, and subject matter of the meeting, whether it is to be open or closed to the public, and the name and phone number of the official designated by the agency to respond to requests for information about the meeting. Such announcement shall be made unless a majority of the members of the agency determines by a recorded vote that agency business requires that such meeting be called at an earlier date, in which case the agency shall make public announcement of the time, place, and subject matter of such meeting, and whether open or closed to the public, at the earliest practicable time.

(2) The time or place of a meeting may be changed following the public announcement required by paragraph (1) only if the agency publicly announces such change at the earliest practicable time. The subject matter of a meeting, or the determination of the agency to open or close a meeting, or portion of a meeting, to the public, may be changed following the public announcement required by this subsection only if (A) a majority of the entire membership of the agency determines by a recorded vote that agency business so requires and that no earlier announcement of the change was possible, and (B) the agency publicly announces such change and the vote of each member upon such change at the earliest practicable time.

(3) Immediately following each public announcement required by this subsection, notice of the time, place, and subject matter of a

meeting, whether the meeting is open or closed, any change in one of the preceding, and the name and phone number of the official designated by the agency to respond to requests for information about the meeting, shall also be submitted for publication in the Federal Register.

(f) (1) For every meeting closed pursuant to paragraphs (1) through (10) of subsection (c), the General Counsel or chief legal officer of the agency shall publicly certify that, in his or her opinion, the meeting may be closed to the public and shall state each relevant exemptive provision. A copy of such certification, together with a statement from the presiding officer of the meeting setting forth the time and place of the meeting, and the persons present, shall be retained by the agency. The agency shall maintain a complete transcript or electronic recording adequate to record fully the proceedings of each meeting, or portion of a meeting, closed to the public, except that in the case of a meeting, or portion of a meeting, closed to the public pursuant to paragraph (8), (9)(A), or (10) of subsection (c), the agency shall maintain either such a transcript or recording, or a set of minutes. Such minutes shall fully and clearly describe all matters discussed and shall provide a full and accurate summary of any actions taken, and the reasons therefor, including a description of each of the views expressed on any item and the record of any rollcall vote (reflecting the vote of each member on the question). All documents considered in connection with any action shall be identified in such minutes.

(2) The agency shall make promptly available to the public, in a place easily accessible to the public, the transcript, electronic recording, or minutes (as required by paragraph (1)) of the discussion of any item on the agenda, or of any item of the testimony of any witness received at the meeting, except for such item or items of such discussion or testimony as the agency determines to contain information which may be withheld under subsection (c). Copies of such transcript, or minutes, or a transcription of such recording disclosing the identity of each speaker, shall be furnished to any person at the actual cost of duplication or transcription. The agency shall maintain a complete verbatim copy of the transcript, a complete copy of the minutes, or a complete electronic recording of each meeting, or portion of a meeting, closed to the public, for a period of at least two years after such meeting, or until one year after the conclusion of any agency proceeding with respect to which the meeting or portion was held, whichever occurs later. . . .

(h) (1) The district courts of the United States shall have jurisdiction to enforce the requirements of subsections (b) through (f) of this section by declaratory judgment, injunctive relief, or other relief as may be appropriate. Such actions may be brought by any person against an agency prior to, or within sixty days after, the meeting out of which the violation of this section arises, except that if public announcement of such meeting is not initially provided by the agency in accordance with the requirements of this section, such action may be instituted pursuant to this section at any time prior to sixty days after any public announcement of such meeting. . . . In such actions a defendant shall serve his answer within thirty days after the service of the complaint. The burden is on the defendant to sustain his action. . . .

(j) [This section requires agencies to report information to Congress about open meetings, meetings exempted from the open meeting requirement, related litigation, and any legal changes that affected the agencies implementation of the Act.]

(k) Nothing herein expands or limits the present rights of any person under section 552 of this title, except that the exemptions set forth in subsection (c) of this section shall govern in the case of any request made pursuant to section 552 to copy or inspect the transcripts, recordings, or minutes described in subsection (f) of this section. The requirements of chapter 33 of title 44, United States Code, shall not apply to the transcripts, recordings, and minutes described in subsection (f) of this section.

(l) This section does not constitute authority to withhold any information from Congress, and does not authorize the closing of any agency meeting or portion thereof required by any other provision of law to be open.

(m) Nothing in this section authorizes any agency to withhold from any individual any record, including transcripts, recordings, or minutes required by this section, which is otherwise accessible to such individual under section 552a of this title.

§ 553. Rule making

(a) This section applies, according to the provisions thereof, except to the extent that there is involved—

   (1) a military or foreign affairs function of the United States; or

   (2) a matter relating to agency management or personnel or to public property, loans, grants, benefits, or contracts.

(b) General notice of proposed rule making shall be published in the Federal Register, unless persons subject thereto are named and either personally served or otherwise have actual notice thereof in accordance with law. The notice shall include—

   (1) a statement of the time, place, and nature of public rule making proceedings;

   (2) reference to the legal authority under which the rule is proposed; and

(3) either the terms or substance of the proposed rule or a description of the subjects and issues involved.

Except when notice or hearing is required by statute, this subsection does not apply—

>   (A) to interpretative rules, general statements of policy, or rules of agency organization, procedure, or practice; or

>   (B) when the agency for good cause finds (and incorporates the finding and a brief statement of reasons therefor in the rules issued) that notice and public procedure thereon are impracticable, unnecessary, or contrary to the public interest.

(c) After notice required by this section, the agency shall give interested persons an opportunity to participate in the rule making through submission of written data, views, or arguments with or without opportunity for oral presentation. After consideration of the relevant matter presented, the agency shall incorporate in the rules adopted a concise general statement of their basis and purpose. When rules are required by statute to be made on the record after opportunity for an agency hearing, sections 556 and 557 of this title apply instead of this subsection.

(d) The required publication or service of a substantive rule shall be made not less than 30 days before its effective date, except—

>   (1) a substantive rule which grants or recognizes an exemption or relieves a restriction;

>   (2) interpretative rules and statements of policy; or

>   (3) as otherwise provided by the agency for good cause found and published with the rule.

(e) Each agency shall give an interested person the right to petition for the issuance, amendment, or repeal of a rule.

§ 554. ADJUDICATIONS

(a) This section applies, according to the provisions thereof, in every case of adjudication required by statute to be determined on the record after opportunity for an agency hearing, except to the extent that there is involved—

>   (1) a matter subject to a subsequent trial of the law and the facts de novo in a court;

>   (2) the selection or tenure of an employee, except a[n] administrative law judge appointed under section 3105 of this title;

>   (3) proceedings in which decisions rest solely on inspections, tests, or elections;

>   (4) the conduct of military or foreign affairs functions;

>   (5) cases in which an agency is acting as an agent for a court; or

>   (6) the certification of worker representatives.

(b) Persons entitled to notice of an agency hearing shall be timely informed of—

(1) the time, place, and nature of the hearing;

(2) the legal authority and jurisdiction under which the hearing is to be held; and

(3) the matters of fact and law asserted.

When private persons are the moving parties, other parties to the proceeding shall give prompt notice of issues controverted in fact or law; and in other instances agencies may by rule require responsive pleading. In fixing the time and place for hearings, due regard shall be had for the convenience and necessity of the parties or their representatives.

(c) The agency shall give all interested parties opportunity for—

(1) the submission and consideration of facts, arguments, offers of settlement, or proposals of adjustment when time, the nature of the proceeding, and the public interest permit; and

(2) to the extent that the parties are unable so to determine a controversy by consent, hearing and decision on notice and in accordance with sections 556 and 557 of this title.

(d) The employee who presides at the reception of evidence pursuant to section 556 of this title shall make the recommended decision or initial decision required by section 557 of this title, unless he becomes unavailable to the agency. Except to the extent required for the disposition of ex parte matters as authorized by law, such an employee may not—

(1) consult a person or party on a fact in issue, unless on notice and opportunity for all parties to participate; or

(2) be responsible to or subject to the supervision or direction of an employee or agent engaged in the performance of investigative or prosecuting functions for an agency.

An employee or agent engaged in the performance of investigative or prosecuting functions for an agency in a case may not, in that or a factually related case, participate or advise in the decision, recommended decision, or agency review pursuant to section 557 of this title, except as witness or counsel in public proceedings. This subsection does not apply—

(A) in determining applications for initial licenses;

(B) to proceedings involving the validity or application of rates, facilities, or practices of public utilities or carriers; or

(C) to the agency or a member or members of the body comprising the agency.

(e) The agency, with like effect as in the case of other orders, and in its sound discretion, may issue a declaratory order to terminate a controversy or remove uncertainty.

§ 555. ANCILLARY MATTERS

(a) This section applies, according to the provisions thereof, except as otherwise provided by this subchapter.

(b) A person compelled to appear in person before an agency or representative thereof is entitled to be accompanied, represented, and advised by counsel or, if permitted by the agency, by other qualified representative. A party is entitled to appear in person or by or with counsel or other duly qualified representative in an agency proceeding. So far as the orderly conduct of public business permits, an interested person may appear before an agency or its responsible employees for the presentation, adjustment, or determination of an issue, request, or controversy in a proceeding, whether interlocutory, summary, or otherwise, or in connection with an agency function. With due regard for the convenience and necessity of the parties or their representatives and within a reasonable time, each agency shall proceed to conclude a matter presented to it. This subsection does not grant or deny a person who is not a lawyer the right to appear for or represent others before an agency or in an agency proceeding.

(c) Process, requirement of a report, inspection, or other investigative act or demand may not be issued, made, or enforced except as authorized by law. A person compelled to submit data or evidence is entitled to retain or, on payment of lawfully prescribed costs, procure a copy or transcript thereof, except that in a nonpublic investigatory proceeding the witness may for good cause be limited to inspection of the official transcript of his testimony.

(d) Agency subpoenas authorized by law shall be issued to a party on request and, when required by rules of procedure, on a statement or showing of general relevance and reasonable scope of the evidence sought. On contest, the court shall sustain the subpoena or similar process or demand to the extent that it is found to be in accordance with law. In a proceeding for enforcement, the court shall issue an order requiring the appearance of the witness or the production of the evidence or data within a reasonable time under penalty of punishment for contempt in case of contumacious failure to comply.

(e) Prompt notice shall be given of the denial in whole or in part of a written application, petition, or other request of an interested person made in connection with any agency proceeding. Except in affirming a prior denial or when the denial is self-explanatory, the notice shall be accompanied by a brief statement of the grounds for denial.

§ 556. Hearings; Presiding Employees; Powers and Duties; Burden of Proof; Evidence; Record as Basis of Decision

(a) This section applies, according to the provisions thereof, to hearings required by section 553 or 554 of this title to be conducted in accordance with this section.

(b) There shall preside at the taking of evidence—

(1) the agency;

(2) one or more members of the body which comprises the agency; or

(3) one or more administrative law judges appointed under section 3105 of this title.

This subchapter does not supersede the conduct of specified classes of proceedings, in whole or in part, by or before boards or other employees specially provided for by or designated under statute. The functions of presiding employees and of employees participating in decisions in accordance with section 557 of this title shall be conducted in an impartial manner. A presiding or participating employee may at any time disqualify himself. On the filing in good faith of a timely and sufficient affidavit of personal bias or other disqualification of a presiding or participating employee, the agency shall determine the matter as a part of the record and decision in the case.

(c) Subject to published rules of the agency and within its powers, employees presiding at hearings may—

(1) administer oaths and affirmations;

(2) issue subpoenas authorized by law;

(3) rule on offers of proof and receive relevant evidence;

(4) take depositions or have depositions taken when the ends of justice would be served;

(5) regulate the course of the hearing;

(6) hold conferences for the settlement or simplification of the issues by consent of the parties or by the use of alternative means of dispute resolution as provided in subchapter IV of this chapter;

(7) inform the parties as to the availability of one or more alternative means of dispute resolution, and encourage use of such methods;

(8) require the attendance at any conference held pursuant to paragraph (6) of at least one representative of each party who has authority to negotiate concerning resolution of issues in controversy;

(9) dispose of procedural requests or similar matters;

(10) make or recommend decisions in accordance with section 557 of this title; and

(11) take other action authorized by agency rule consistent with this subchapter.

(d) Except as otherwise provided by statute, the proponent of a rule or order has the burden of proof. Any oral or documentary evidence may be received, but the agency as a matter of policy shall provide for the exclusion of irrelevant, immaterial, or unduly repetitious evidence. A sanction may not be imposed or rule or order issued except on consideration of the whole record or those parts thereof cited by a party and supported by and in accordance with the reliable, probative, and substantial evidence. The agency may, to the extent consistent with the interests of justice and the policy of the underlying statutes administered by the agency, consider a violation of section 557(d) of this title sufficient grounds for a decision adverse to a party who has knowingly committed such violation or knowingly caused such violation to occur. A party is entitled to present his case or defense by oral or documentary evidence, to submit rebuttal evidence, and to conduct such cross-examination as may be required for a full and true disclosure of the facts. In rule making or determining claims for money or benefits or applications for initial licenses an agency may, when a party will not be prejudiced thereby, adopt procedures for the submission of all or part of the evidence in written form.

(e) The transcript of testimony and exhibits, together with all papers and requests filed in the proceeding, constitutes the exclusive record for decision in accordance with section 557 of this title and, on payment of lawfully prescribed costs, shall be made available to the parties. When an agency decision rests on official notice of a material fact not appearing in the evidence in the record, a party is entitled, on timely request, to an opportunity to show the contrary.

§ 557. Initial Decisions; Conclusiveness; Review By Agency; Submissions By Parties; Contents of Decisions; Record

(a) This section applies, according to the provisions thereof, when a hearing is required to be conducted in accordance with section 556 of this title.

(b) When the agency did not preside at the reception of the evidence, the presiding employee or, in cases not subject to section 554(d) of this title, an employee qualified to preside at hearings pursuant to section 556 of this title, shall initially decide the case unless the agency requires, either in specific cases or by general rule, the entire record to be certified to it for decision. When the presiding employee makes an initial decision, that decision then becomes the decision of the agency without further proceedings unless there is an appeal to, or review on motion of, the agency within time provided by rule. On appeal from or review of the initial decision, the agency has all the powers which it would have in making the initial decision except as it may limit the issues on notice or by rule. When the agency makes the decision without having presided at the reception of the evidence, the presiding employee or an employee qualified to preside at hearings pursuant to section 556 of this title shall first recommend a decision, except that in rule making or determining applications for initial licenses—

(1) instead thereof the agency may issue a tentative decision or one of its responsible employees may recommend a decision; or

(2) this procedure may be omitted in a case in which the agency finds on the record that due and timely execution of its functions imperatively and unavoidably so requires.

(c) Before a recommended, initial, or tentative decision, or a decision on agency review of the decision of subordinate employees, the parties are entitled to a reasonable opportunity to submit for the consideration of the employees participating in the decisions—

(1) proposed findings and conclusions; or

(2) exceptions to the decisions or recommended decisions of subordinate employees or to tentative agency decisions; and

(3) supporting reasons for the exceptions or proposed findings or conclusions.

The record shall show the ruling on each finding, conclusion, or exception presented. All decisions, including initial, recommended, and tentative decisions, are a part of the record and shall include a statement of—

(A) findings and conclusions, and the reasons or basis therefor, on all the material issues of fact, law, or discretion presented on the record; and

(B) the appropriate rule, order, sanction, relief, or denial thereof.

(d) (1) In any agency proceeding which is subject to subsection (a) of this section, except to the extent required for the disposition of ex parte matters as authorized by law—

(A) no interested person outside the agency shall make or knowingly cause to be made to any member of the body comprising the agency, administrative law judge, or other employee who is or may reasonably be expected to be involved in the decisional process of the proceeding, an ex parte communication relevant to the merits of the proceeding;

(B) no member of the body comprising the agency, administrative law judge, or other employee who is or may reasonably be expected to be involved in the decisional process of the proceeding, shall make or knowingly cause to be made to any interested person outside the agency an ex parte communication relevant to the merits of the proceeding;

(C) a member of the body comprising the agency, administrative law judge, or other employee who is or may reasonably be expected to be involved in the decisional process of such proceeding who receives, or who makes or knowingly causes to be made, a communication prohibited by this subsection shall place on the public record of the proceeding:

(i) all such written communications;

(ii) memoranda stating the substance of all such oral communications; and

(iii) all written responses, and memoranda stating the substance of all oral responses, to the materials described in clauses (i) and (ii) of this subparagraph;

(D) upon receipt of a communication knowingly made or knowingly caused to be made by a party in violation of this subsection, the agency, administrative law judge, or other employee presiding at the hearing may, to the extent consistent with the interests of justice and the policy of the underlying statutes, require the party to show cause why his claim or interest in the proceeding should not be dismissed, denied, disregarded, or otherwise adversely affected on account of such violation; and

(E) the prohibitions of this subsection shall apply beginning at such time as the agency may designate, but in no case shall they begin to apply later than the time at which a proceeding is noticed for hearing unless the person responsible for the communication has knowledge that it will be noticed, in which case the prohibitions shall apply beginning at the time of his acquisition of such knowledge.

(2) This subsection does not constitute authority to withhold information from Congress.

§ 558. Imposition of Sanctions; Determination of Applications for Licenses; Suspension, Revocation, and Expiration of Licenses

(a) This section applies, according to the provisions thereof, to the exercise of a power or authority.

(b) A sanction may not be imposed or a substantive rule or order issued except within jurisdiction delegated to the agency and as authorized by law.

(c) When application is made for a license required by law, the agency, with due regard for the rights and privileges of all the interested parties or adversely affected persons and within a reasonable time, shall set and complete proceedings required to be conducted in accordance with sections 556 and 557 of this title or other proceedings required by law and shall make its decision. Except in cases of willfulness or those in which public health, interest, or safety requires otherwise, the withdrawal, suspension, revocation, or annulment of a license is lawful only if, before the institution of agency proceedings therefor, the licensee has been given—

(1) notice by the agency in writing of the facts or conduct which may warrant the action; and

(2) opportunity to demonstrate or achieve compliance with all lawful requirements.

When the licensee has made timely and sufficient application for a renewal or a new license in accordance with agency rules, a license with reference to an activity of a continuing nature does not expire until the application has been finally determined by the agency.

§ 559. Effect on Other Laws; Effect of Subsequent Statute

This subchapter, chapter 7, and sections 1305, 3105, 3344, 4301(2)(E), 5372, and 7521 of this title, and the provisions of section 5335(a)(B) of this title that relate to administrative law judges, do not limit or repeal additional requirements imposed by statute or otherwise recognized by law. Except as otherwise required by law, requirements or privileges relating to evidence or procedure apply equally to agencies and persons. Each agency is granted the authority necessary to comply with the requirements of this subchapter through the issuance of rules or otherwise. Subsequent statute may not be held to supersede or modify this subchapter, chapter 7, sections 1305, 3105, 3344, 4301(2)(E), 5372, or 7521 of this title, or the provisions of section 5335(a)(B) of this title that relate to administrative law judges, except to the extent that it does so expressly.

Chapter 7 — Judicial Review

§ 701. Application; Definitions

(a) This chapter applies, according to the provisions thereof, except to the extent that—
   (1) statutes preclude judicial review; or
   (2) agency action is committed to agency discretion by law.
(b) For the purpose of this chapter—
   (1) "agency" means each authority of the Government of the United States, whether or not it is within or subject to review by another agency, but does not include—
      (A) the Congress;
      (B) the courts of the United States;
      (C) the governments of the territories or possessions of the United States;
      (D) the government of the District of Columbia;
      (E) agencies composed of representatives of the parties or of representatives of organizations of the parties to the disputes determined by them;
      (F) courts martial and military commissions;
      (G) military authority exercised in the field in time of war or in occupied territory; or
      (H) functions conferred by sections 1738, 1739, 1743, and 1744 of title 12; subchapter II of chapter 471 of title 49; or sections 1884, 1891-1902, and former section 1641(b)(2), of title 50, appendix; and
   (2) "person", "rule", "order", "license", "sanction", "relief", and "agency action" have the meanings given them by section 551 of this title.

§ 702. RIGHT OF REVIEW

A person suffering legal wrong because of agency action, or adversely affected or aggrieved by agency action within the meaning of a relevant statute, is entitled to judicial review thereof. An action in a court of the United States seeking relief other than money damages and stating a claim that an agency or an officer or employee thereof acted or failed to act in an official capacity or under color of legal authority shall not be dismissed nor relief therein be denied on the ground that it is against the United States or that the United States is an indispensable party. The United States may be named as a defendant in any such action, and a judgment or decree may be entered against the United States: *Provided*, That any mandatory or injunctive decree shall specify the Federal officer or officers (by name or by title), and their successors in office, personally responsible for compliance. Nothing herein (1) affects other limitations on judicial review or the power or duty of the court to dismiss any action or deny relief on any other appropriate legal or equitable ground; or (2) confers authority to grant relief if any other statute that grants consent to suit expressly or impliedly forbids the relief which is sought.

§ 703. FORM AND VENUE OF PROCEEDING

The form of proceeding for judicial review is the special statutory review proceeding relevant to the subject matter in a court specified by statute or, in the absence or inadequacy thereof, any applicable form of legal action, including actions for declaratory judgments or writs of prohibitory or mandatory injunction or habeas corpus, in a court of competent jurisdiction. If no special statutory review proceeding is applicable, the action for judicial review may be brought against the United States, the agency by its official title, or the appropriate officer. Except to the extent that prior, adequate, and exclusive opportunity for judicial review is provided by law, agency action is subject to judicial review in civil or criminal proceedings for judicial enforcement.

§ 704. ACTIONS REVIEWABLE

Agency action made reviewable by statute and final agency action for which there is no other adequate remedy in a court are subject to judicial review. A preliminary, procedural, or intermediate agency action or ruling not directly reviewable is subject to review on the review of the final agency action. Except as otherwise expressly required by statute, agency action otherwise final is final for the purposes of this section whether or not there has been presented or determined an application for a declaratory order, for any form of reconsideration, or, unless the agency otherwise requires by rule and provides that the action meanwhile is inoperative, for an appeal to superior agency authority.

§ 705. Relief Pending Review

When an agency finds that justice so requires, it may postpone the effective date of action taken by it, pending judicial review. On such conditions as may be required and to the extent necessary to prevent irreparable injury, the reviewing court, including the court to which a case may be taken on appeal from or on application for certiorari or other writ to a reviewing court, may issue all necessary and appropriate process to postpone the effective date of an agency action or to preserve status or rights pending conclusion of the review proceedings.

§ 706. Scope of Review

To the extent necessary to decision and when presented, the reviewing court shall decide all relevant questions of law, interpret constitutional and statutory provisions, and determine the meaning or applicability of the terms of an agency action. The reviewing court shall—

(1) compel agency action unlawfully withheld or unreasonably delayed; and

(2) hold unlawful and set aside agency action, findings, and conclusions found to be—

(A) arbitrary, capricious, an abuse of discretion, or otherwise not in accordance with law;

(B) contrary to constitutional right, power, privilege, or immunity;

(C) in excess of statutory jurisdiction, authority, or limitations, or short of statutory right;

(D) without observance of procedure required by law;

(E) unsupported by substantial evidence in a case subject to sections 556 and 557 of this title or otherwise reviewed on the record of an agency hearing provided by statute; or

(F) unwarranted by the facts to the extent that the facts are subject to trial de novo by the reviewing court.

In making the foregoing determinations, the court shall review the whole record or those parts of it cited by a party, and due account shall be taken of the rule of prejudicial error.

Chapter 8 — Congressional Review of Agency Rulemaking

§ 801. Congressional Review

(a) (1) (A) Before a rule can take effect, the Federal agency promulgating such rule shall submit to each House of the Congress and to the Comptroller General a report containing—

(i) a copy of the rule;

(ii) a concise general statement relating to the rule, including whether it is a major rule; and

(iii) the proposed effective date of the rule.

(B) On the date of the submission of the report under subparagraph (A), the Federal agency promulgating the rule shall submit to the Comptroller General and make available to each House of Congress—

(i) a complete copy of the cost-benefit analysis of the rule, if any;

(ii) the agency's actions relevant to sections 603, 604, 605, 607, and 609;

(iii) the agency's actions relevant to sections 202, 203, 204, and 205 of the Unfunded Mandates Reform Act of 1995; and

(iv) any other relevant information or requirements under any other Act and any relevant Executive orders.

(C) Upon receipt of a report submitted under subparagraph (A), each House shall provide copies of the report to the chairman and ranking member of each standing committee with jurisdiction under the rules of the House of Representatives or the Senate to report a bill to amend the provision of law under which the rule is issued.

(2) (A) The Comptroller General shall provide a report on each major rule to the committees of jurisdiction in each House of the Congress by the end of 15 calendar days after the submission or publication date as provided in section 802(b)(2). The report of the Comptroller General shall include an assessment of the agency's compliance with procedural steps required by paragraph (1)(B).

(B) Federal agencies shall cooperate with the Comptroller General by providing information relevant to the Comptroller General's report under subparagraph (A).

(3) A major rule relating to a report submitted under paragraph (1) shall take effect on the latest of—

(A) the later of the date occurring 60 days after the date on which—

(i) the Congress receives the report submitted under paragraph (1); or

(ii) the rule is published in the Federal Register, if so published;

(B) if the Congress passes a joint resolution of disapproval described in section 802 relating to the rule, and the President signs a veto of such resolution, the earlier date—

(i) on which either House of Congress votes and fails to override the veto of the President; or

(ii) occurring 30 session days after the date on which the Congress received the veto and objections of the President; or

(C) the date the rule would have otherwise taken effect, if not for this section (unless a joint resolution of disapproval under section 802 is enacted).

(4) Except for a major rule, a rule shall take effect as otherwise provided by law after submission to Congress under paragraph (1).

(5) Notwithstanding paragraph (3), the effective date of a rule shall not be delayed by operation of this chapter beyond the date on which either House of Congress votes to reject a joint resolution of disapproval under section 802.

(b) (1) A rule shall not take effect (or continue), if the Congress enacts a joint resolution of disapproval, described under section 802, of the rule.

(2) A rule that does not take effect (or does not continue) under paragraph (1) may not be reissued in substantially the same form, and a new rule that is substantially the same as such a rule may not be issued, unless the reissued or new rule is specifically authorized by a law enacted after the date of the joint resolution disapproving the original rule.

(c) (1) Notwithstanding any other provision of this section (except subject to paragraph (3)), a rule that would not take effect by reason of subsection (a)(3) may take effect, if the President makes a determination under paragraph (2) and submits written notice of such determination to the Congress.

(2) Paragraph (1) applies to a determination made by the President by Executive order that the rule should take effect because such rule is—

(A) necessary because of an imminent threat to health or safety or other emergency;

(B) necessary for the enforcement of criminal laws;

(C) necessary for national security; or

(D) issued pursuant to any statute implementing an international trade agreement.

(3) An exercise by the President of the authority under this subsection shall have no effect on the procedures under section 802 or the effect of a joint resolution of disapproval under this section.

(d) (1) In addition to the opportunity for review otherwise provided under this chapter, in the case of any rule for which a report was submitted in accordance with subsection (a)(1)(A) during the period beginning on the date occurring—

(A) in the case of the Senate, 60 session days, or

(B) in the case of the House of Representatives, 60 legislative days, before the date the Congress adjourns a session of Congress through the date on which the same or succeeding Congress first convenes its next session, section 802 shall apply to such rule in the succeeding session of Congress.

(2) (A) In applying section 802 for purposes of such additional review, a rule described under paragraph (1) shall be treated as though —

(i) such rule were published in the Federal Register (as a rule that shall take effect) on —

(I) in the case of the Senate, the 15th session day, or

(II) in the case of the House of Representatives, the 15th legislative day, after the succeeding session of Congress first convenes; and

(ii) a report on such rule were submitted to Congress under subsection (a)(1) on such date.

(B) Nothing in this paragraph shall be construed to affect the requirement under subsection (a)(1) that a report shall be submitted to Congress before a rule can take effect.

(3) A rule described under paragraph (1) shall take effect as otherwise provided by law (including other subsections of this section). . . .

§ 802. Congressional Disapproval Procedure

(a) For purposes of this sectionm, the term "joint resolution" means only a joint resolution introduced in the period beginning on the date on which the report referred to in section 801(a)(1)(A) is received by Congress and ending 60 days thereafter (excluding days either House of Congress is adjourned for more than 3 days during a session of Congress), the matter after the resolving clause of which is as follows: "That Congress disapproves the rule submitted by the _____ relating to _____, and such rule shall have no force or effect." (The blank spaces being appropriately filled in).

(b) (1) A joint resolution described in subsection (a) shall be referred to the committees in each House of Congress with jurisdiction.

(2) For purposes of this section, the term "submission or publication date" means the later of the date on which —

(A) the Congress receives the report submitted under section 801(a)(1); or

(B) the rule is published in the Federal Register, if so published.

(c) In the Senate, if the committee to which is referred a joint resolution described in subsection (a) has not reported such joint resolution (or an identical joint resolution) at the end of 20 calendar days after the submission or publication date defined under subsection (b)(2), such committee may be discharged from further consideration of such joint resolution upon a petition supported in writing by 30 Members of the Senate, and such joint resolution shall be placed on the calendar.

(d) (1) In the Senate, when the committee to which a joint resolution is referred has reported, or when a committee is discharged (under subsection (c)) from further consideration of a joint resolution described in subsection (a), it is at any time thereafter in order (even though a previous motion to the same effect has been disagreed to) for a motion to proceed to the consideration of the joint resolution, and all points of order against the joint resolution (and against consideration of the joint resolution) are waived. The motion is not subject to amendment, or to a motion to postpone, or to a motion to proceed to the consideration of other business. A motion to reconsider the vote by which the motion is agreed to or disagreed to shall not be in order. If a motion to proceed to the consideration of the joint resolution is agreed to, the joint resolution shall remain the unfinished business of the Senate until disposed of.

(2) In the Senate, debate on the joint resolution, and on all debatable motions and appeals in connection therewith, shall be limited to not more than 10 hours, which shall be divided equally between those favoring and those opposing the joint resolution. A motion further to limit debate is in order and not debatable. An amendment to, or a motion to postpone, or a motion to proceed to the consideration of other business, or a motion to recommit the joint resolution is not in order.

(3) In the Senate, immediately following the conclusion of the debate on a joint resolution described in subsection (a), and a single quorum call at the conclusion of the debate if requested in accordance with the rules of the Senate, the vote on final passage of the joint resolution shall occur.

(4) Appeals from the decisions of the Chair relating to the application of the rules of the Senate to the procedure relating to a joint resolution described in subsection (a) shall be decided without debate.

(e) In the Senate the procedure specified in subsection (c) or (d) shall not apply to the consideration of a joint resolution respecting a rule—

(1) after the expiration of the 60 session days beginning with the applicable submission or publication date, or

(2) if the report under section 801(a)(1)(A) was submitted during the period referred to in section 801(d)(1), after the expiration of the 60 session days beginning on the 15th session day after the succeeding session of Congress first convenes.

(f) If, before the passage by one House of a joint resolution of that House described in subsection (a), that House receives from the other House a joint resolution described in subsection (a), then the following procedures shall apply:

(1) The joint resolution of the other House shall not be referred to a committee.

(2) With respect to a joint resolution described in subsection (a) of the House receiving the joint resolution—

(A) the procedure in that House shall be the same as if no joint resolution had been received from the other House; but

(B) the vote on final passage shall be on the joint resolution of the other House.

(g) This section is enacted by Congress—

(1) as an exercise of the rulemaking power of the Senate and House of Representatives, respectively, and as such it is deemed a part of the rules of each House, respectively, but applicable only with respect to the procedure to be followed in that House in the case of a joint resolution described in subsection (a), and it supersedes other rules only to the extent that it is inconsistent with such rules; and

(2) with full recognition of the constitutional right of either House to change the rules (so far as relating to the procedure of that House) at any time, in the same manner, and to the same extent as in the case of any other rule of that House.

§ 803. Special Rule on Statutory, Regulatory, and Judicial Deadlines

(a) In the case of any deadline for, relating to, or involving any rule which does not take effect (or the effectiveness of which is terminated) because of enactment of a joint resolution under section 802, that deadline is extended until the date 1 year after the date of enactment of the joint resolution. Nothing in this subsection shall be construed to affect a deadline merely by reason of the postponement of a rule's effective date under section 801(a).

(b) The term "deadline" means any date certain for fulfilling any obligation or exercising any authority established by or under any Federal statute or regulation, or by or under any court order implementing any Federal statute or regulation.

§ 804. Definitions

For purposes of this chapter—

(1) The term "Federal agency" means any agency as that term is defined in section 551(1).

(2) The term "major rule" means any rule that the Administrator of the Office of Information and Regulatory Affairs of the Office of Management and Budget finds has resulted in or is likely to result in—

(A) an annual effect on the economy of $100,000,000 or more;

(B) a major increase in costs or prices for consumers, individual industries, Federal, State, or local government agencies, or geographic regions; or

(C) significant adverse effects on competition, employment, invest-ment, productivity, innovation, or on the ability of United States-based enterprises to compete with foreign-based enterprises in domestic and export markets.

The term does not include any rule promulgated under the Telecommunications Act of 1996 and the amendments made by that Act.

(3) The term "rule" has the meaning given such term in section 551, except that such term does not include—

(A) any rule of particular applicability, including a rule that approves or prescribes for the future rates, wages, prices, services, or allow-ances therefor, corporate or financial structures, reorganizations, mergers, or acquisitions thereof, or accounting practices or disclo-sures bearing on any of the foregoing;

(B) any rule relating to agency management or personnel; or

(C) any rule of agency organization, procedure, or practice that does not substantially affect the rights or obligations of non-agency parties.

§ 805. Judicial Review

No determination, finding, action, or omission under this chapter shall be subject to judicial review.

§ 806. Applicability; Severability

(a) This chapter shall apply notwithstanding any other provision of law.

(b) If any provision of this chapter or the application of any provision of this chapter to any person or circumstance, is held invalid, the appli-cation of such provision to other persons or circumstances, and the remainder of this chapter, shall not be affected thereby.

§ 807. Exemptions for Monetary Policy

Nothing in this chapter shall apply to rules that concern monetary policy proposed or implemented by the Board of Governors of the Federal Reserve System or the Federal Open Market Committee.

§ 808. Effective Date of Certain Rules

Notwithstanding section 801—

(1) any rule that establishes, modifies, opens, closes, or conducts a reg-ulatory program for a commercial, recreational, or subsistence activity related to hunting, fishing, or camping, or

(2) any rule which an agency for good cause finds (and incorporates the finding and a brief statement of reasons therefor in the rule issued) that notice and public procedure thereon are impracticable, unnecessary, or contrary to the public interest, shall take effect at such time as the Federal agency promulgating the rule determines. . . .

§ 3105. Appointment of Administrative Law Judges

Each agency shall appoint as many administrative law judges as are necessary for proceedings required to be conducted in accordance with sections 556 and 557 of this title. Administrative law judges shall be assigned to cases in rotation so far as practicable, and may not perform duties inconsistent with their duties and responsibilities as administrative law judges.

TABLE OF SOURCES

A Guide to Federal Agency Adjudication (Jeffrey Litwak, ed., 2d ed. 2012), 364, 387–388, 394

Andrews, Richard N.L., *The EPA at 40: An Historical Perspective,* 21 Duke Envtl. L. & Pol'y F. 223 (2010), 144–145

Annals of Congress (1789), 607

Asimow, Michael, *Interim-Final Rules: Making Haste Slowly,* 51 Admin. L. Rev. 703 (1999), 251

Asimow, Michael, *Nonlegislative Rulemaking and Regulatory Reform,* 1985 Duke L.J. 381, 221–222

Asimow, Michael, *The Spreading Umbrella: Extending the APA's Adjudication Provisions to All Evidentiary Hearings Required by Statute,* 56 Admin. L. Rev. 1003 (2004), 361

Bamberger, Kenneth A. & Peter L. Strauss, Chevron's *Two Steps,* 95 Va. L. Rev. 611 (2009), 1040

Barnett, Kent & Christopher J. Walker, Chevron *in the Circuit Courts,* 116 Mich. L. Rev. 1 (2017), 1039

Barnett, Kent & Russell Wheeler, *Non-ALJ Adjudicators in Federal Agencies: Status, Selection, Oversight, and Removal,* 53 Ga. L. Rev. 1 (2018), 363

Beermann, Jack M., *Common Law and Statute Law in Administrative Law,* 63 Admin. L. Rev. 1 (2011), 901

Bell, Bernard W., Marbury v. Madison *and the Madisonian Vision,* 72 Geo. Wash. L. Rev. 197 (2003), 159–160

Berg, R. & S. Klitzman, An Interpretive Guide to the Government in the Sunshine Act (1978), 1135–1136

Berger, Raoul, *Administrative Arbitrariness and Judicial Review,* 65 Colum. L. Rev. 55 (1965), 695

Berger, Raoul, *Standing to Sue in Public Actions: Is It a Constitutional Requirement?,* 78 Yale L.J. 816 (1969), 727

Black's Law Dictionary (10th ed. 2014), 665

Black's Law Dictionary (6th ed. 1990), 100, 1025

Blackstone, William, Commentaries on the Laws of England (1769), 477, 515

Bonfield, Arthur E., *Public Participation in Federal Rulemaking Relating to Public Property, Loans, Grants, Benefits, or Contracts,* 118 U. Pa. L. Rev. 577 (1970), 213

Breyer, Stephen G., et al., Administrative Law and Regulatory Policy (7th ed. 2011), 7, 34

Breyer, Stephen G., *Judicial Review of Questions of Law and Policy,* 38 Admin. L. Rev. 363 (1986), 1011

Bruff, Harold H., *Presidential Management of Agency Rulemaking,* 57 Geo. Wash. L. Rev. 533 (1989), 320

Calabresi, Guido & Saikrishna Prakash, *The President's Power to Execute the Laws,* 104 Yale L.J. 541 (1994), 636

Calabresi, Stephen G. & Christopher S. Yoo, *The Unitary Executive During the Second Half-Century,* 26 Harv. J.L. & Pub. Pol'y 667 (2003), 1143

Strauss, Peter L., *The Place of Agencies in Government: Separation of Powers and the Fourth Branch*, 84 COLUM. L. REV. 573 (1984), 308

Sunstein, Cass R., *Standing and the Privatization of Public Law*, 88 COLUM. L. REV. 1432 (1988), 730

SUNSTEIN, CASS R., THE COST-BENEFIT STATE (2002), 321

Sunstein, Cass R., *What's Standing After* Lujan? *Of Citizen Suits, "Injuries," and Article III*, 91 MICH. L. REV. 163 (1992), 727

Sunstein, Cass R. & Adrian Vermeule, *The Unbearable Rightness of* Auer, 84 U. CHI. L. REV. 297 (2017), 1071

THACH, CHARLES C., JR., THE CREATION OF THE PRESIDENCY, 1775-1789; A STUDY IN CONSTITUTIONAL HISTORY (1922), 607

THE OXFORD ENGLISH DICTIONARY (2d ed. 1989), 597

Tozzi, Jim, *OIRA's Formative Years: The Historical Record of Centralized Regulatory Review Preceding OIRA's Founding*, 63 ADMIN. L. REV. 37 (2011), 318

TRIBE, LAURENCE, AMERICAN CONSTITUTIONAL LAW (1978), 450

U.S. DEP'T OF JUSTICE, ATTORNEY GENERAL'S MANUAL ON THE ADMINISTRATIVE PROCEDURE ACT (1947), 23–24, 156, 199–200, 214–215, 248–249, 269, 308, 353, 363, 411, 660, 666, 670, 712, 738, 856, 897, 946

U.S. DEP'T OF JUSTICE, DEPARTMENT OF JUSTICE GUIDE TO THE FREEDOM OF INFORMATION ACT, EXEMPTION 5 (2019), 1117

U.S. DEP'T OF JUSTICE, SUMMARY OF ANNUAL FOIA REPORTS FOR FISCAL YEAR 2019 (2019), 1109

U.S. ENVIRONMENTAL PROTECTION AGENCY OFFICE OF ENVIRONMENTAL INFORMATION, BENCHMARK DOSE SOFTWARE USER'S MANUAL VERSION 2.0 (April 30, 2009), 90

UNITED STATES CIVIL SERVICE COMMISSION, HISTORY OF THE FEDERAL CIVIL SERVICE, 1780 TO PRESENT (1941), 1140, 1142, 1144

UNITED STATES GOVERNMENT MANUAL, 40, 41–45, 856

United States Office of Personnel, *Sizing Up the Executive Branch: Fiscal Year 2017* (Feb. 2018), 670

Van Dolsen, Stephen, *Judicial Review of Allegedly* Ultra Vires *Actions of the Veterans' Administration: Does 38 U.S.C. § 211(a) Preclude Review*, 55 FORDHAM L. REV. 579 (1987), 670–671

Verkuil, Paul R., *A Study of Informal Adjudication Procedures*, 43 U. CHI. L. REV. 729 (1976), 393–394

Vermeule, Adrian, *No*, 93 TEXAS L. REV. 1547 (2015) (reviewing PHILIP HAMBURGER, IS ADMINISTRATIVE LAW UNLAWFUL? (2014)), 48

Vile, M. J. C., CONSTITUTIONALISM AND THE SEPARATION OF POWERS (1998), 48, **49–52**

WEBSTER'S SEVENTH NEW COLLEGIATE DICTIONARY (1979), 1112

WEBSTER'S THIRD NEW INTERNATIONAL DICTIONARY (1961), 1112

WEBSTER'S THIRD NEW INTERNATIONAL DICTIONARY (1966), 1115

WEBSTER'S THIRD NEW INTERNATIONAL DICTIONARY (1971), 778

WEBSTER'S THIRD NEW INTERNATIONAL DICTIONARY (1981), 1025–1026

West, William F., *The Politics of Administrative Rulemaking*, 42 PUB. ADMIN. REV. 420 (1982), 171

WHITE, LEONARD D., THE JACKSONIANS: A STUDY IN ADMINISTRATIVE HISTORY 1829-1861 (1954), 10

WILSON, WOODROW, CONGRESSIONAL GOVERNMENT (1885), 648

Woolhandler, Ann & Caleb Nelson, *Does History Defeat Standing Doctrine?*, 102 MICH. L. REV. 689 (2004), 727

Woolhandler, Ann, *Judicial Deference to Administrative Action—A Revisionist History,* 43 ADMIN. L. REV. 197 (1991), 9, 659

Woolhandler, Ann, *Patterns of Official Immunity and Accountability,* 37 CASE W. RES. L. REV. 396 (1987), 10

YELLIN, ERIC S., RACISM IN THE NATION'S SERVICE: GOVERNMENT WORKERS AND THE COLOR LINE IN WOODROW WILSON'S AMERICA (2013), 17

Zahm, Marilyn, *Do You Have a Social Security Card? Then Take This Executive Order Personally,* WASH. POST (July 18, 2018), 374

TABLE OF CASES